THE 2000 ANNOTATED

IMMIGRATION ACT OF CANADA

Edited & annotated by

Frank N. Marrocco, Q.C.

AND

Henry M. Goslett

STATUTES OF CANADA ANNOTATED

CARSWELL
Thomson Professional Publishing

The publisher is not engaged in rendering legal, accounting or other professional advice. If legal advice or other expert assistance is required, the services of a competent professional should be sought. The analysis herein should not be construed as being either official or unofficial policy of any governmental body.

This work reproduces official English language versions of federal statutes and regulations. As this material also exists in official French language form, the reader is advised that reference to the official French language version may be warranted in appropriate circumstances.

8 The paper used in this publication meets the minimum requirements of American National Standard for Information Sciences — Permanence of Paper for Printed Library Materials, ANSI Z39.48-1984.

Canadian Cataloguing in Publication Data

The National Library of Canada has catalogued this publication as follows:

Canada

[Immigration Act, 1976]

The annotated Immigration Act of Canada

[1984] —

Annual.
Supplements accompany some issues.
ISSN 1182-1604
ISBN 0-459-27016-8 (2000: bound) ISBN 0-459-27018-4 (2000: pbk.)

1. Emmigration and immigration Law — Canada
I. Thomson Professional Publishing Canada.
II. Title III. Title: Immigration Act, 1976

KE4454.A32C65 347.71'082'02632 C90-301647-0
KF4483.15.C382

CARSWELL
Thomson Professional Publishing

One Corporate Plaza
2075 Kennedy Road
Scarborough, Ontario
M1T 3V4

Customer Relations
Toronto 1-416-609-3800
Elsewhere in Canada/U.S. 1-800-387-5164
Fax 1-416-298-5094
World Wide Web: http://www.carswell.com
E-mail: orders@carswell.com

OTHER STATUTES OF CANADA ANNOTATED

Beach, *Canada Evidence Act and Related Statutes*
Chotalia, *Canadian Human Rights Act*
David & Pelly, *Bank Act*
Gray, *Canada Evidence Act*
Houlden & Morawetz, *Bankruptcy and Insolvency Act*
Imai, *Indian Act*
Keeshan & Steeves, *Federal and Ontario Interpretation Acts*
Libman, *Contraventions Act*
MacDonald & Wilton, *Divorce Act*
Marrocco, Goslett & Désilets, *Loi sur l'immigration du Canada*
Marrocco, Goslett *Citizenship Act*
Meehan, *Canadian Charter of Rights and Freedoms*
Moscowitz & Pinsonneault, *Robic-Leger Trade-marks Act*
Northey, *Canadian Environmental Assessment and EARP Guidelines Order*
Nozick, *Competition Act*
Prabhu, *Customs Act*
Rudner, *Employment Insurance Statutes*
Sgayias, Kinnear, Rennie & Saunders, *Crown Liability and Proceedings Act*
Snyder, *Canada Labour Code*
Tamaro, *Copyright Act*
Watt, *Treameear's Related Criminal Statutes*
Watt & Fuerst, *Tremeear's Criminal Code*
Zambelli, *Refugee Convention*

To

Debbie and Mimi

And to

Alexandra, Jacqueline, Emily, Angela and Ted

PREFACE

We are indebted once again to those members of the legal profession, Citizenship and Immigration Canada and the Immigration and Refugee Board who have provided constructive criticism to us throughout the year. All of these comments were most gratefully received and many of them have been incorporated into this year's edition.

The starting point for anyone interested in immigration law is the position of the alien at common law. In this regard, Lord Denning M.R.'s concise summary of the common law in the case of *R. v. Governor of the Pentonville Prison, ex parte Azam*, [1973] 2 All E.R. 741 at 747 is most helpful:

> At common law no alien has any right to enter this country except by leave of the Crown; and the Crown can refuse leave without giving any reason: see *Schmidt v. Secretary of State for Home Affairs*, [1969] 2 Ch. 149 at 168. If he comes by leave, the Crown can impose such conditions as it thinks fit, as to his length of stay, or otherwise. He has no right whatever to remain here. He is liable to be sent home to his own country at any time if, in the opinion of the Crown, his presence here is not conducive to the public good; and for this purpose, the executive may arrest him and put him on board a ship or aircraft bound for his own country: see *R. v. Brixton Prison (Governor), ex parte Soblen*, [1963] 2 Q.B. 243 at 300, 301. The position of aliens at common law has since been covered by the various regulations; but the principles remain the same.

The annotations under section 3 of the Act provide, we hope, assistance in understanding the evolution of immigration law in Canada.

Immigration cases have traditionally been referred to as civil in nature and, consistent with that approach, the awarding of costs is now a more straight-forward matter.

We want to thank Natalie von Bergstrasesser, the librarian of the Federal Court of Canada in Toronto, and our publisher for their assistance in providing us with the unreported decisions of the court.

We wish to express our thanks to Natalie Starr and B.J. Caruso for their assistance in the preparation of the 2000 edition. We also wish to recognize the contribution of Pamela Hudson to previous editions of our text. Without the care and attention of these persons, this edition would not have been possible. This edition contains all relevant cases which have come to our attention as of June 30, 1999.

Finally, we wish to express our primary intention which is to further the understanding and thoughtful development of Canadian immigration laws and procedures.

November 1999

Frank N. Marrocco
Henry M. Goslett

SUMMARY TABLE OF CONTENTS

Table of Contents

PART III — EXCLUSION AND REMOVAL

Transitional Provisions

IMMIGRATION REGULATIONS, 1978

HUMANITARIAN DESIGNATED CLASSES REGULATIONS

REFUGEE CLAIMANTS DESIGNATED CLASS REGULATIONS

IMMIGRATION ACT FEES REGULATIONS

IMMIGRATION APPEAL DIVISION RULES

CONVENTION REFUGEE DETERMINATION DIVISION RULES

ADJUDICATION DIVISION RULES

FEDERAL COURT ACT

JURISDICTION OF TRIAL DIVISION

FEDERAL COURT RULES, 1998

FEDERAL COURT IMMIGRATION RULES, 1993

CANADA EVIDENCE ACT

PART I — APPLICATION

Disclosure of Government Information

APPENDIX I — AN ACT RESPECTING IMMIGRATION TO QUÉBEC

TABLE OF CASES

Cases are referenced to section number. Numbers without designations refer to the Immigration Act. Otherwise they refer to: Immigration Regulations *IR*; Humanitarian Designated Classes Regulations *HDCR*; Refugee Claimants Designated Class Regulations *RCDC*; Immigration Appeal Division Rules *IADR*; Convention Refugee Determination Division Class Rules *CRDD*; Adjudication Division Rules *ADR*; Federal Court Act *FCA*; Federal Court Rules *FCR*; Federal Court Immigration Rules *FCIR*.

IMMIGRATION ACT

An act respecting immigration to Canada

R.S.C. 1985, c. I-2, as am. R.S.C. 1985, c. 31 (1st Supp.), s. 99; R.S.C. 1985, c. 10, (2nd Supp.); R.S.C. 1985, c. 46 (2nd Supp.); R.S.C. 1985, c. 30 (3rd Supp.); R.S.C. 1985, c. 1 (4th Supp.), s. 27; R.S.C. 1985, c. 28 (4th Supp.); R.S.C. 1985, c. 29 (4th Supp.); R.S.C. 1985, c. 30; S.C. 1990, c. 8, ss. 51–55; c. 16, ss. 12, 13; 1990, c. 17, ss. 23, 24; 1990, c. 38; 1990, c. 44, s. 16; 1992, c. 1, ss. 73–78, 143; 1992, c. 47, ss. 77, 78; 1992, c. 49, ss. 1–107; 1992, c. 51, ss. 52–53; 1993, c. 28, s. 78 (Sched. III, items 71, 72) [Repealed 1999, c. 3, (Sched., item 15).]; 1994, c. 26, ss. 35, 36; 1994, c. 31, s. 18; 1995, c. 5, s. 25(1)(p); 1995, c. 15, ss. 1–22; 1996, c. 8, s. 32; 1996, c. 11, s. 62; 1996, c. 16, s. 60; 1996, c. 19, s. 83; 1997, c. 22, ss. 4–11; 1998, c. 30, s. 14(i); 1999, c. 3, ss. 67, 68; 1999, c. 18, s. 96; 1999, c. 31, ss. 133, 134.

Short Title

1. Short title — This Act may be cited as the Immigration Act.

Interpretation

2. (1) Definitions — In this Act,

"Adjudication Division" means that division of the Board called the Adjudication Division;

"adjudicator" means a person appointed or employed as such pursuant to section 63.3;

"admission" means entry or landing;

"Appeal Division" means that division of the Board called the Immigration Appeal Division;

"assisted relative" has the meaning assigned by the regulations;

"Board" means the Immigration and Refugee Board established by section 57;

"Canadian citizen" means a person who is a citizen within the meaning of the *Citizenship Act*;

"Chairman" [Repealed 1992, c. 49, s. 1.]

"Chairperson" means the Chairperson of the Board;

"conditional departure notice" [Repealed 1992, c. 49, s. 1.]

"conditional departure order" means a conditional departure order issued under subsection 28(1), paragraph 32.1(3)(*b*) or subsection 32.1(5) that has not become effective under subsection 28(2) or 32.1(6);

"conditional deportation order" means a conditional deportation order made under subsection 32.1(2), (3) or (4), 73(2) or 74(1) or (3) that has not become effective under subsection 32.1(6);

"conditional exclusion order" [Repealed 1992, c. 49, s. 1.]

"conditional removal order" means a conditional departure order or a conditional deportation order;

"Convention" means the United Nations Convention Relating to the Status of Refugees signed at Geneva on July 28, 1951, and includes the Protocol thereto signed at New York City on January 31, 1967;

"Convention refugee" means any person who

(a) by reason of a well-founded fear of persecution for reasons of race, religion, nationality, membership in a particular social group or political opinion,

(i) is outside the country of the person's nationality and is unable or, by reason of that fear, is unwilling to avail himself of the protection of that country, or

(ii) not having a country of nationality, is outside the country of the person's former habitual residence and is unable or, by reason of that fear, is unwilling to return to that country, and

(b) has not ceased to be a Convention refugee by virtue of subsection (2),

but does not include any person to whom the Convention does not apply pursuant to section E or F of Article 1 thereof, which sections are set out in the schedule to this Act;

"departure order" means a departure order issued under subsection 27(4) or 32(7) and includes a conditional departure order that has become effective under subsection 28(2) or 32.1(6);

"departure notice" [Repealed 1992, c. 49, s. 1.]

"dependant" has the meaning assigned by the regulations;

"deportation order" means a deportation order made under subsections 32(2), (5) or (6), 37(5) or (6), 73(2) or 74(1) or (3) and includes

(a) a deportation order made under the authority of

(i) subsection 40(10) of the *Immigration Act, 1976*, chapter 52 of the Statutes of Canada, 1976-77, as it read immediately prior to July 16, 1984, or

(ii) any immigration laws that were in force in Canada prior to April 10, 1978;

(b) a conditional deportation order that has become effective under subsection 32.1(6);

(c) a departure order that is deemed pursuant to subsection 32.02(1) to be a deportation order;

(d) a departure notice that is deemed to be a deportation order pursuant to section 113 of *An Act to amend the Immigration Act and other Acts in consequence thereof*, chapter 49 of the Statutes of Canada, 1992, and

(e) a conditional departure notice or a conditional exclusion order that becomes a deportation order pursuant to section 26 of *An Act to amend the Immigration Act*

and the Citizenship Act and to make a consequential amendment to the Customs Act, **assented to during the first session of the thirty-fifth Parliament;**

"Deputy Minister" means the deputy head of the department by which this Act is administered;

"employment" means any activity for which a person receives or might reasonably be expected to receive valuable consideration;

"entry" means lawful permission to come into Canada as a visitor;

"examination" means any procedure whereby an immigration officer determines whether a person seeking to come into Canada may be allowed to come into Canada or may be granted admission;

"exclusion order" means an exclusion order made under subsection 23(4) or (4.01), 32(5), 73(2) or 74(1) or (3);

"family" means the father and mother and any children who, by reason of age or disability, are, in the opinion of an immigration officer, mainly dependent on the father or mother for support and, for the purpose of any provision of this Act and the regulations, includes such other classes of persons as are prescribed for the purpose of that provision;

"fund" has the meaning assigned by the regulations;

"immigrant" means a person who seeks landing;

"immigrant station" means any place designated by the Minister for the examination, treatment or detention of persons for any purpose under this Act;

"immigration officer" means a person appointed or designated as an immigration officer pursuant to section 109;

"inadmissible class" means any of the classes of persons described in section 19;

"landing" means lawful permission to establish permanent residence in Canada;

"master" means the person in immediate charge or control of a vehicle;

"medical officer" means a qualified medical practitioner authorized or recognized by order of the Minister as a medical officer for the purposes of any or all provisions of this Act;

"member" [Repealed R.S.C. 1985, c. 28 (4th Supp.), s. 1.]

"member of a crew" means, except as otherwise prescribed, a person, including a master, who is employed on a vehicle to perform duties during a voyage or trip related to the operation of the vehicle or the provision of services to passengers;

"member of the family class" has the meaning assigned by the regulations;

"Minister" means such member of the Queen's Privy Council for Canada as is designated by the Governor in Council as the Minister for the purposes of this Act;

"owner", in respect of a vehicle, includes the agent of the owner of the vehicle and any other person having any interest in respect of the vehicle;

"permanent resident" means a person who

(a) has been granted landing,

(b) has not become a Canadian citizen, and

(c) has not ceased to be a permanent resident pursuant to section 24 or 25.1,

and includes a person who has become a Canadian citizen but who has subsequently ceased to be a Canadian citizen under subsection 10(1) of the *Citizenship Act*, without reference to subsection 10(2) of that Act;

"permit" means a subsisting permit issued under subsection 37(1);

"port of entry" means any place designated as a port of entry by the Minister for the examination of persons under this Act;

"prescribed" means prescribed by regulations made by the Governor in Council;

"Refugee Division" means that division of the Board called the Convention Refugee Determination Division;

"rejection order" means an order made under paragraph 13(1)(*b*);

"removal order" means a departure order, an exclusion order or a deportation order;

"senior immigration officer" means an immigration officer designated by order of the Minister to perform or carry out any or all of the duties and functions of a senior immigration officer under this Act;

"transportation company"

(a) means a person or group of persons, including any agent thereof and the government of Canada, a province or a municipality in Canada, transporting or providing for the transportation of persons or goods by vehicle or otherwise, and

(b) for the purposes of subsections 89(2) to (7), sections 92 and 93 and paragraph 114(1)(*cc*), includes any such person or group that operates a bridge or tunnel or is a designated airport authority within the meaning of the *Airport Transfer (Miscellaneous Matters) Act*;

"vehicle" means any conveyance that may be used for transportation by water, land or air;

"Vice-Chairman" [Repealed R.S.C. 1985, c. 28 (4th Supp.), s. 1.]

"visa" means a document issued or a stamp impression made on a document by a visa officer;

"visa officer" means an immigration officer stationed outside Canada and authorized by order of the Minister to issue visas;

"visitor" means a person who is lawfully in Canada, or seeks to come into Canada, for a temporary purpose, other than a person who is

(a) a Canadian citizen,

(b) a permanent resident,

(c) a person in possession of a permit, or

(d) an immigrant authorized to come into Canada pursuant to paragraph 14(2)(*b*), 23(1)(*b*) or 32(3)(*b*).

(1.1) Multiple nationalities — For the purposes of the definition "Convention refugee" in subsection (1), where a person has more than one nationality, all references to the person's nationality in that definition shall be construed as applying to each of the countries of which the person is a national.

(2) Cessation of Convention refugee status — A person ceases to be a Convention refugee when

> **(a) the person voluntarily reavails himself of the protection of the country of the person's nationality;**
>
> **(b) the person voluntarily reacquires his nationality;**
>
> **(c) the person acquires a new nationality and enjoys the protection of the country of that new nationality;**
>
> **(d) the person voluntarily re-establishes himself in the country that the person left, or outside of which the person remained, by reason of fear of persecution; or**
>
> **(e) the reasons for the person's fear of persecution in the country that the person left, or outside of which the person remained, cease to exist.**

(3) Exception — A person does not cease to be a Convention refugee by virtue of paragraph (2)(*e*) if the person establishes that there are compelling reasons arising out of any previous persecution for refusing to avail himself of the protection of the country that the person left, or outside of which the person remained, by reason of fear of persecution.

(4) Deemed notification — For the purposes of this Act, a person, including the Minister, shall, in the absence of proof to the contrary, be deemed to have been notified of a decision under this Act, other than a decision of a visa officer,

> **(a) where the decision was rendered otherwise than in the presence of the person and the person was not entitled to written reasons, on the day that is seven days after the day on which notice of the decision was sent to the person, and**
>
> **(b) where the person was entitled to written reasons, or was entitled to request, and requested within the time normally provided therefor, written reasons, on the day that is seven days after the day on which the written reasons were sent to the person,**

which notice or written reasons may be sent by mail.

R.S.C. 1985, c. 28 (4th Supp.), s. 1; 1992, c. 49, s. 1; 1994, c. 31, s. 18; 1995, c. 5, s. 1

Case Law

Section 2(1)

Adjudicator

Satiacum v. Canada (Minister of Employment & Immigration) (1985), 64 N.R. 358 (Fed. C.A.) — The circumstance that the adjudicator and the case presenting officer were both public servants employed in the same department of government, without more, did not give rise to a reasonable apprehension of bias. An informed person viewing the matter realistically and practically would not conclude that it was more likely than not that the adjudicator would decide unfairly.

Convention refugee

Editor's Note: See the Schedule to this Act for Sections E and F of Article 1 of the United Nations Convention Relating to the Status of Refugees concerning "Convention refugee" eligibility.

Ranganathan v. Canada (Minister of Citizenship & Immigration) (May 21, 1999), Doc. IMM-3326-98 (Fed. T.D.) — The applicant sought to review a decision made by a panel of the CRDD, to the effect that there was an internal flight alternative in Colombo reasonably available to the applicant. In determining undue hardship or unreasonableness, for the purpose of assessing the availability of an internal flight alternative, the Refugee Division must take into account the fact that the claimant has no relatives in Colombo when there are family members in Canada. The absence of family members available to provide emotional and material support might well consign a claimant to a quality of life that falls well below that standard of decency that is widely recognized as a human entitlement.

Serrano v. Canada (Minister of Citizenship & Immigration) (April 27, 1999), Doc. IMM-2787-98 (Fed. T.D.) — This was an application to review a decision of a panel of the CRDD. The applicants are citizens of Mexico who claim to be at risk of being killed or seriously injured if returned there. The applicant operated a small trucking business in Acapulco. In 1996, he hired a new driver who introduced him to people who wished to hire his truck for the purpose of transporting drugs. The applicant refused to deal with them, and a few days later his truck was found abandoned and damaged. Subsequently, the applicant and his family received threatening phone calls and a threatening letter. A friend of the applicant's who had agreed to work for drug traffickers was killed after he changed his mind.

The applicants' claims initially were based on a fear of persecution by reason of membership in a particular social group or political opinion. The CRDD concluded that as a matter of law the applicants were not members of a particular social group. In this case, the social group was described as "law abiding Mexican citizens". The Court agreed with the CRDD that "law abiding citizens of Mexico" were not a particular social group within the meaning of the Convention.

The Court found that to hold that everyone who fears persecution solely because of a family connection may be entitled to the protection of the Convention, would be to stretch the category of "particular social group" far beyond its proper limits. The Court did not accept that family connection was an attribute requiring Convention protection in the absence of an underlying Convention ground for the claimed protection. Accordingly, the application for judicial review was dismissed.

Elmi v. Canada (Minister of Citizenship & Immigration) (March 12, 1999), Doc. IMM-580-98 (Fed. T.D.) — The applicant, a Somalian citizen who was 16 years old at the time of the hearing, sought to review a negative decision of the CRDD. The claim was rejected because the applicant was found to have an IFA in another part of Somalia. Typically, the fact that a claimant would have no friends or relatives in the IFA does not satisfy the test of "undue hardship". The Court noted that these considerations were only deemed irrelevant by the Court of Appeal in the context of adult claimants. What is merely inconvenient for an adult may well constitute undue hardship for a child. In the case of a child whose education has already been disrupted by war and who would arrive in the IFA without any money, there arises not the question of finding suitable employment but of sustaining any livelihood at all. The Board in this case made no findings on these matters and must do so in order to answer the question posed by the second part of the IFA test.

Said v. Canada (Minister of Citizenship & Immigration), 48 Imm. L.R. (2d) 9, [1999] 2 F.C. 592 (Fed. T.D.) — The applicant sought to review two decisions. The first was an opinion of the Minister that the applicant was a danger to the public pursuant to section 53(1)(d) of the *Immigration Act*; the second was the decision of a removal officer that the applicant be removed to Afghanistan. These proceedings were in the nature of judicial review, and because the Minister whose opinion was being reviewed did not have jurisdiction to declare section 53(1)(d) unconstitutional, there was no decision of the tribunal deciding constitutionality and therefore no decision to review. Accordingly, the applicant's remedy was by way of an action to determine the constitutional validity of section 53(1)(d).

In the present case, the applicant was notified of the possible issuance of an opinion. The notice invited the applicant to make representations and provide evidence regarding the risk to him upon his return to Afghanistan. The applicant provided information on that subject, and therefore the Minister made a decision with that information in mind. This was sufficient to satisfy the requirement that there be a risk assessment before a refugee is returned to the country from which he or she has sought refuge.

Shysta-Ameer Ali et al. and The Minister of Citizenship & Immigration (1999), 235 N.R. 316, 160 F.T.R. 292 (note) (Fed. C.A.) — The appeal in this matter was dismissed. The Court of Appeal noted that the test for persecution in a civil war context was set out in *Salibian v. Canada (Minister of Employment & Immigration)*, 11 Imm. L.R. (2d) 165, [1990] 3 F.C. 250, (sub nom. *Salibian v. Canada (Ministre de l'Emploi et de l'Immigration)* (Fed. C.A.)and *Rizkallah v. Canada (Minister of Citizenship & Immigration)* (1992), 156 N.R. 1 (Fed. C.A.). The Court also approved page 6 of the Refugee Board Guidelines issued on March 7, 1996, pursuant to section 65(3) of the *Immigration Act*, dealing with refugee claims of civilian non-combatants in a civil war situation.

Canada (Minister of Citizenship & Immigration) v. Bob Smith (1998), 47 Imm. L.R. (2d) 3, [1999] 1 F.C. 31005, 154 F.T.R. 92 (Fed. T.D.); additional reasons at (December 7, 1998), Doc. IMM-3068-97 (Fed. T.D.) — The respondent, Bob Smith, 14, is a citizen of the United States and the United Kingdom. He was a victim of ongoing sexual abuse. The principal aggressor was his natural father. The Minister sought judicial review of the determination by the CRDD that the respondent, his mother and his step-father were Convention refugees. The quantum of clear and convincing evidence required to rebut the presumption of a state's ability to protect depends on its democratic processes. In a democracy such as the United States with a free and independent judicial system, it would be necessary to impeach substantially the relevant jury selection process for the independence and fair-mindedness of the judiciary.

In this case, the evidence was simply insufficient to rebut the presumption of state protection. The tribunal's finding of no state protection in the United Kingdom and the United States was made in a perverse manner and without regard to the evidence. Accordingly, the decision of the tribunal was set aside.

Sooriyakumaran v. Canada (Minister of Citizenship & Immigration) (1998), 156 F.T.R. 285 (Fed. T.D.) — A panel of the CRDD concluded that the applicant would have a safe haven in Colombo. In 1995, the applicant's only children, two boys, then aged 11 and 13, obtained refugee status in Canada. The applicant made her refugee claim shortly after her arrival in Canada in November 1996. The presence in Canada of the applicant's two children, both minors and Convention refugees is the kind of particular circumstance that the tribunal ought to have considered in assessing whether Colombo was an unduly harsh refuge for the applicant. The relevance of the children's situation is unrelated to the principle of family unity or to an application for humanitarian and compassionate consideration. The applicant's family situation is simply a human factor that ought not to be excluded in applying the second branch of the IFA test.

Elbarbari v. Canada (Minister of Citizenship & Immigration) (1998), 157 F.T.R. 111 (Fed. T.D.) — The applicants who were found by a panel of the IRB to be stateless Palestinians were also determined not to be Convention refugees.

In order to be found to be a Convention refugee a stateless person must show that on a balance of probabilities he or she would suffer persecution in any country of former habitual residence and that he or she cannot return to any of his or her other countries of former habitual residence.

Iraq, Egypt and the U.S. were countries of former habitual residence, and the applicants had no right to return to any of them. The Board found that the applicants had no well founded fear of persecution in the United States or Egypt. However, the Board did not address the issue of whether the applicants had a well founded fear of persecution in Iraq. In failing to do so, the Board erred in law. Accordingly, the decision of the Board was set aside and the matter remitted for re-determination.

Ramanathan v. Canada (Minister of Citizenship & Immigration) (1998), 44 Imm. L.R. (2d) 294, 152 F.T.R. 305 (Fed. T.D.) — This is an application to review a decision of the CRDD. The Board acknowledged that the applicant would probably not be able to attend to his daily living activities without the aid of his son, daughter-in-law and grandchildren. Notwithstanding this fact, the Board found a viable IFA in Columbo. There was no issue with respect to the fact that Colombo was a place where the applicant could live without fear of persecution. The panel refused to consider humanitarian and compassionate considerations in applying the second branch of the IFA test. A test of whether the IFA is unreasonable or unduly harsh in all the circumstances is bound to involve the consideration of some factors, at least, which will undoubtedly be the same sort of considerations that they are taken into account in humanitarian and compassionate relief.

Sandhu v. Canada (Ministre de la Citoyenneté & de l'Immigration) (1998), 149 F.T.R. 83 (Fed. T.D.) — This was an application to set aside a negative decision of the CRDD. The applicant claimed refugee status alleging a well-founded fear of persecution for reasons of political opinion. The applicant was a resident of the Punjab who supported the Akali Dal Party and had been physically abused by the police. In its decision the panel recognized that the applicant had been tortured at the time in question. It also found that as a result of changed circumstances in the Punjab, there was no longer any objective basis for his fear that he would be persecuted should he be returned.

At the hearing, the counsel for the applicant asked the panel to apply the Convention against Torture, an international agreement signed and ratified by Canada. Counsel argued that in light of the panel's finding that the applicant had been subjected to torture in the past, Canada should not return him to India, as there were substantial grounds for believing that he would be tortured again.

The panel did not have jurisdiction to apply the Convention against Torture, as there is no express provision in its enabling legislation to this effect. The panel's role is to determine whether a person is a refugee within the meaning of the Geneva Convention. Furthermore, the Convention against Torture has not been incorporated into Canadian domestic law, although Canada has signed and ratified this international agreement.

The applicant did not raise the effect of subsection 2(3) of the Act at the hearing, namely whether the torture the applicant suffered was so appalling that this experience alone is a compelling reason not to return him to his country, even if there is no longer any fear of further persecution. Because the applicant did not adduce evidence to establish that he was part of the tiny minority falling under subsection 2(3), the panel did not have to decide this issue. Accordingly the application for judicial review was dismissed.

Thabet v. Canada (Minister of Citizenship & Immigration) (1998), 48 Imm. L.R. (2d) 195, 160 D.L.R. (4th) 666 (Fed. C.A.) — The appellant was born in Kuwait and is a stateless Palestinian. He lived in Kuwait on a residency permit sponsored by his father. In 1983, the appellant left Kuwait to study in the United States where he obtained an engineering degree. In 1986, his residency status in Kuwait came to an end, and he returned to Kuwait to make an independent application to renew his residency permit, which was denied. The appellant then returned to the United States on a visitor's visa, where he lived for 11 years. After the outbreak of the Gulf War the appellant sought asylum in the United States. His application was rejected and he was ordered deported. He filed an appeal, but abandoned it and came to Canada where he applied for refugee status. Before a panel of the IRB, the appellant based his claim on the ground that Kuwait was his country of formal habitual residence and that he feared persecution if returned there. He also claimed to fear persecution in the United States, because while living in Louisiana he experienced harassment threats and violence at the hands of the Ku Klux Klan.

A panel of the IRB found that both Kuwait and the U.S. were countries of formal habitual residence and that the appellant had to demonstrate a well-founded fear of persecution against both in order to be granted refugee status. According to the Board, the appellant had not made out his fear of persecution in either country, and denied his claim.

The Trial Division judge found that the Board had erred in not asking itself whether the denial of a right to return to Kuwait was in itself an act of persecution. The Trial Division judge went on to find that a stateless person who has habitually resided in more than one country before making a refugee claim must establish his or her claim by reference to the last country of formal habitual residence. Accordingly, notwithstanding the error made by the panel in this matter the application for judicial review was dismissed.

On appeal, it was held that a stateless person must show on a balance of probabilities that he or she would suffer persecution in any country of formal habitual residence. In addition, the Court observed that so long as a claimant does not face persecution in a country of formal habitual residence that will take him or her back, he or she could not be determined to be a refugee.

Klinko v. Canada (Minister of Citizenship & Immigration) (1998), 148 F.T.R. 69 (Fed. T.D.) — Political opinion is any opinion on any matter in which the machinery of state, government, and policy may be engaged. "Engaged" in this definition means sanctioned by, condoned by, or supported by.

The panel found that the Ukraine as a State did not sanction, condone, or support the corrupt conduct of customs and police officials. As such, the panel found that the applicant's complaint against corruption was not a political opinion.

Shahpari v. Canada (Minister of Citizenship & Immigration) (1998), 44 Imm. L.R. (2d) 139, 146 F.T.R. 102 (Fed. T.D.) — The applicants sought to review the question of whether section E of Article I of the *Geneva Convention* applied to them. The applicants were citizens of Iran. In 1984 they moved to France and after seven years of temporary residence in France were issued a "Carte de Résident" which was valid for 10 years. After residing in France until 1994, the applicants came to Canada and within one month made a refugee application.

The burden of proving that section E applies rests with the party asserting it, in this case the respondent. It did not assist the applicant in this case that she allowed her visa to expire. The evidence allowed the panel to conclude that the visa could be renewed. Applicants should remember that actions they themselves take, which are intended to result in their not being able to return to a country which has already granted them refugee status, may well evidence an absence of the subjective fear of persecution in their original country. Further, if applicants are entitled to renounce the protection they receive from one country and claim protection from another, it gives them a right to emigrate to another country without complying with the usual requirements, solely by reason of their unilateral renunciation of the protection that they have been afforded by the country they are leaving.

Menaker v. Canada (Minister of Citizenship & Immigration) (October 27, 1997), Doc. IMM-3837-96 (Fed. T.D.) — The applicant sought to overturn a negative decision of the CRDD. It is entirely open to the tribunal to base its decision on documentary evidence rather than testimonial evidence. The tribunal has jurisdiction to assess the probative value of the evidence and so the Court can intervene only where the tribunal reached an unreasonable conclusion. A modern democratic state is presumed to be capable of protecting its citizens. An applicant must exhaust all available legal means before claiming that such a state cannot or will not protect him or her.

Zia v. Canada (Minister of Citizenship & Immigration) (1997), 132 F.T.R. 183 (Fed. T.D.) — The applicants applied to review a negative decision of a visa officer in Jordan rejecting applications for immigration to Canada as members of the Convention refugees seeking resettlement designated class. The applicants, who were citizens of Iraq, were applying for refugee status at the Canadian Embassy in Jordan.

A visa officer assessing a refugee claim in these circumstances has a duty to act fairly. That duty is somewhat limited by comparison with that owed Convention refugee claimants applying from within Canada by reason of the fact that persons such as the applicants are not in Canada and do not face the possibility of deportation by Canadian authorities to the country where they claim to fear persecution if their claims are disallowed. The fact that the visa officer sought the concurrence of a senior immigration officer before transmitting her decisions as she was in fact required to do, in no sense detracted from the fairness of the process. The senior immigration officer did not make the decisions under review, nor in any sense did he influence them.

Changes to Canadian immigration laws as a result of the *Singh* case, 1985 [S.C.R. 177] did not impact on the process for determination of Convention refugee claims for persons outside of Canada. The fact that the applicants briefly attended at a Canadian Embassy for an interview or other related purpose in no sense made them persons claiming refugee status from within Canada. The applications for judicial review were dismissed.

Pour-Shariati v. Canada (Minister of Employment & Immigration) (1997), 39 Imm. L.R. (2d) 103,, 215 N.R. 174 (Fed. C.A.) — Indirect persecution does not constitute persecution within the meaning of Convention refugee. The concept of indirect persecution goes directly against the decision of the Court of Appeal in *Rizkallah v. Canada (Minister of Employment & Immigration)*(1992), 156 N.R. 1 (Fed. C.A.), where it was held that there had to be a personal nexus between the claimant and the alleged persecution on one of the Convention grounds. The Convention ground of "membership in a particular social group" is a ground which allows for family concerns in an appropriate case. In addition section 46.04(1) and 46.04(3) allow for the landing of dependants of refugees.

Adar v. Canada (Minister of Citizenship & Immigration) (1997), 132 F.T.R. 35 (Fed. T.D.) — This was an application to review a decision of the CRDD which allowed the Minister's application to vacate the applicants' Convention refugee status. The applicants were accepted by the CRDD as Somalian refugees in April 1990. In November 1991, the Minister seized two Djiboutian passports with the applicants' photographs and names. In June 1992, the Minister made an application for leave to vacate the applicants' Convention refugee status. Leave was refused. There was then this subsequent application apparently on the strength of new evidence. This time leave was granted and a hearing was held, at which time it was determined that the applicants were citizens of Djibouti and not Samolia and that they had received their refugee status by concealing this fact.

Generally speaking it is difficult to apply *res judicata* to the definition of a Convention refugee, because a person's status as a refugee is fluid. This is supported by subsection 2(2) and 69.2 and 69.3 of the *Immigration Act*. The denial of leave in 1992 was not a final decision in the sense of *res judicata*, the statute gives the CRDD the powers of reconsideration.

The second ground of the application was that the CRDD made an erroneous finding of fact, viz, that the applicants were Djiboutian citizens. A passport is *prima facie* evidence of citizenship. The onus is on the applicant to prove that the applicant is of a different citizenship than that indicated in the passport. The decision that the applicants were citizens of Djibouti was properly founded on the evidence before the CRDD, accordingly, this application was dismissed.

Vidal v. Canada (Minister of Employment & Immigration) (1997), 131 F.T.R. 47 (Fed. T.D.) — The applicants sought to review a negative decision of the CRDD. The applicants were from Argentina and based their claims on a well founded fear of persecution on the grounds of political opinion and membership in a particular social group. The panel concluded that the applicant could live safely in some provinces in Argentina and accordingly found that the applicant was not a convention refugee. No notice of the consideration of an IFA was given until the issue was raised in the course of the hearing. Counsel representing the applicants gave no indication that she was taken by surprise or that she needed an adjournment to better prepare. Further, evidence on the issue of international flight alternative was presented to the panel. The Court concluded that the applicants suffered no prejudice by the failure to give notice that internal flight alternative was an issue and that therefore the failure to give notice did not constitute a reviewable error.

Hashmat v. Canada (Minister of Citizenship & Immigration) (1997), 131 F.T.R. 28 (Fed. T.D.) — The applicant sought to review a negative decision of a panel of the CRDD. A panel of the CRDD had concluded that the applicant would not suffer persecution in Northern Afghanistan. The panel failed to consider how the applicant accompanied by his wife and daughter would suffer in making the 200 kilometre journey from Kabul to the north. The documentary record revealed the wide spread rape of women and children in Afghanistan. The potential suffering of the applicant's wife and daughter was relevant to the issue of whether the applicant would undergo undo hardship in making his way north and availing himself of an IFA. This consideration was separate from the rule against the principle of indirect persecution.

Katkova v. Canada (Minister of Citizenship & Immigration) (1997), 40 Imm. L.R. (2d) 216, 130 F.T.R. 192 (Fed. T.D.) — The applicant sought to review a negative decision of the CRDD. The board ignored extensive evidence from the applicant that she did not wish to go to Israel. This evidence was important because the Law of Return in Israel provided that it only applied to "every Jew who has expressed his desire to settle in Israel". Accordingly, the applicant did not have a right to come into Israel pursuant to the provisions of the Law of Return.

In addition to the language of the legislation of a country granting citizenship the Court observed that the issue of nationality in international law is to be decided on the basis of whether there is a genuine link between the person and the state. In considering whether there is a genuine link different factors are taken into consideration: 1) the habitual residence of the individual; 2) the centre of the individual's interest; 3) the individual's family ties; 4) the individual's participation in public life; 5) the attachment shown by the individual for the country and whether the individual has inculcated in his children this attachment.

De Rojas v. Canada (Minister of Citizenship & Immigration) (January 31, 1997), Doc. IMM-1460-96 (Fed. T.D.) — The applicant sought to overturn a negative decision of the CRDD. The applicant was a citizen of Venezuela, she and her mother were both born in Columbia. The applicant moved to Venezuela at an early age and following that move and until the events giving rise to her refugee claim remained a resident of that country. The tribunal determined that the applicant had a well-founded fear of persecution if she were returned to Venezuela. The tribunal went on to determine that although the applicant lost her Columbian citizenship when she acquired Venezuelan citizenship she could reacquire Colombian citizenship upon compliance with requirements that are mere formalities.

By simply choosing not to comply with these mere formalities, the applicant could not claim that Columbia was not a country of nationality for her. The applicant was required to comply with those formalities before seeking to avail herself of refugee protection in Canada.

Kadenko v. Canada (Solicitor General) (1996), 143 D.L.R. (4th) 532, 206 N.R. 272, 124 F.T.R. 160 (note) (Fed. C.A.); leave to appeal to S.C.C. refused (sub nom. *Kadenko v. Canada (Solliciteur général))* 218 N.R. 80 (note) (S.C.C.) — Once it is assumed that the state has political and judicial institutions capable of protecting its citizens, it is clear that the refusal of certain police officers to take action cannot in itself make the state incapable of doing so. If the refusal to take action could be said to be that of the police as an institution or to be more or less a general refusal by the police force to provide the protection conferred by the country's political and judicial institutions the answer might have been different.

When the state in question is a democratic state the claimant must do more than simply show that he or she went to see some members of the police force and that his or her efforts were unsuccessful. The burden of proof that rests on the claimant is in a way directly proportional to the level of democracy in the state in question: the more democratic the state's institutions, the more the claimant must have done to exhaust all the courses of action open to him or her.

Altawil v. Canada (Minister of Citizenship & Immigration) (1996), 114 F.T.R. 241 (Fed. T.D.) — This was an application to review a negative decision of a panel of the CRDD. The applicant's family left Gaza for Saudi Arabia after the 1967 Israeli war. In 1973, the family was deported from Saudi Arabia to Egypt. The family then lived in Egypt between 1973 and 1978 when they moved to Qatar. Following completion of the applicant's high school in that country, the applicant went to university in Afghanistan, because as a stateless person he was unable to go to university in Qatar. The applicant was required by Qatar law to return every 6 months and report it to authorities. In 1986, the war in Afghanistan prevented the applicant's return within the 6 month period and when the applicant did return in September of 1986, Qatar refused him entry on the basis that his residency status had expired.

Qatar was the applicant's country of former habitual residents and he could not return there. It is clear that a denial of a right of return to a country may in its self constitute an act of persecution by a state, however, there must be something in the real circumstances which suggest persecutorial intent or persecutorial conduct. There was no such evidence in this case, and the Court was unable to conclude that the law in question which was one of general application was persecutorial in its effect.

Martinez v. Canada (Minister of Citizenship & Immigration) (1996), 114 F.T.R. 113 (Fed. T.D.) — The applicant sought to review a negative decision of the CRDD. The applicant is a citizen of El Salvador, by reason of his mother's nationality, and of Belize, by reason of his birth. The applicant's mother alleged before the CRDD a well-founded fear of persecution in El Salvador based on her membership in a particular social group.

The applicant's mother and two of her three children were found to be convention refugees as against El Salvador but the applicant as a citizen of Belize, was found not to have a well-founded fear of persecution in that country.

It is unnecessary to extend the plain meaning of the words convention refugee to include the principle of family unity. The principle of Family Unity is enshrined in the *Immigration Act* by section 46.04(1) and 46.04(3). None of the exceptions or limitations provided for in the two subsections in any way limit the applicants mother's right to apply for landing in Canada for herself and the applicant, or the obligation of an immigration officer to grant landing in the event of such an application it made. Accordingly the application for judicial review was dismissed.

Wassiq v. Canada (Minister of Citizenship & Immigration) (1996), 33 Imm. L.R. (2d) 238, 112 F.T.R. 143 (Fed. T.D.) — The applicants applied to review a negative decision of the IRB. The applicants were citizens of Afghanistan. In 1981, they successfully applied as Convention refugees in Germany. In 1991, they left Germany and came to Canada and sought refugee status here.

A panel of the IRB had decided that the applicants had a wellfounded fear of persecution in respect of Afghanistan, but that Canada had assumed responsibility for them and that Germany was obliged to allow them to return. Therefore, the Board found that the convention did not apply to the applicants by virtue of section E of Article 1.

Refugee claims were never meant to allow a claimant to seek out better protection than that from which he or she already benefitted. If by reason of their absence from Germany and sojourn in Canada, the applicants were in effect entitled to renounce the protection they received from Germany and claim protection from Canada such a result would be anomalous. In substance, it would give a person who had Convention refugee status in one country the right to emigrate to another country without complying with the usual requirements.

Whether Canada or Germany should be responsible for the applicants should ideally be determined as between the governments of Canada and Germany. A decision of a panel of IRB, that Germany should have responsibility for the applicants which is in effect the decision in this case is not binding on Germany. The real issue is whether Germany recognizes that the applicants may return.

On the evidence before it, the panel could not have arrived at such a conclusion and therefore could not have found that section E of Article 1 was applicable to the applicants. Accordingly, the application for judicial review was allowed and the matter remitted back to a differently constituted panel.

Badran v. Canada (Minister of Citizenship & Immigration) (1996), 111 F.T.R. 211 (Fed. T.D.) — The applicant sought judicial review of a negative decision of the IRB. The applicant in the instant case was a member of a particular social group-his family. He was also a member of a group which can be labelled "The Children of Police Officers Who Are Anti-terrorists Supporters". The evidence before the tribunal established that the authorities were effectively unable to protect the children of police officers and the documentary evidence supported that statement.

It is very difficult for a state to effectively protect its citizens against terrorism. In most cases, the inability to protect against random terrorist attacks will not constitute an inability of the state to protect. There is a limited exception to this however, where past, personal incidents qualify an individual as a member of the particular social group which the state is unable to protect. In the present case, there was a specifically and directly targeted applicant who was a member of a small targeted group and this distinguished the applicant's case from most cases which involved random instances of terrorism.

The negative decision of the IRB was set aside and the matter sent back to the same panel on the same record for a redetermination in the manner not inconsistent with the court's reasons.

Kanagaratnam v. Canada (Minister of Employment & Immigration) (1996), 36 Imm. L.R. (2d) 180, 194 N.R. 46 (Fed. C.A.) — The Refugee Board determined that the appellant, a native of Sri Lanka, had an internal flight alternative (IFA) within her country, and did not think it necessary to decide that the appellant otherwise had a well founded fear of persecution. A motion was brought for judicial review and the Trial Judge dismissed the motion, but certified a question for appeal, namely whether a determination of whether a claimant has a well founded fear of persecution in the area from which he or she originates, is a prerequisite to the consideration of an internal flight alternative.

In assessing whether a viable IFA exists, the Board, of course, must have regard to all the appropriate circumstances. Since an IFA existed, therefore, the claimant, by definition, could not have a well founded fear of persecution in her country of nationality. Thus, while the Board may certainly do so if it chooses, there was no need, as a matter of law, for the Board to decide whether there was persecution in the area of origin as a prerequisite to the consideration of an IFA.

Tarakhan v. Canada (Minister of Citizenship & Immigration) (1995), 32 Imm. L.R. (2d) 83, (sub nom. *Tarakhan v. Canada (Ministre de la Citoyenneté & de l'Immigration))* 105 F.T.R. 128 (Fed. T.D.) — The applicant sought to review a decision denying him convention refugee status. It was submitted that the Refugee Division erred when it determined that the applicant's last habitual residence was in Jordan. Determining habitual residence is a question of fact and not of law. The definition of Convention refugee does not preclude a person having only one habitual residence. To meet the habitual residence criterion in the *Act*, more is required than ongoing transient presence in a country. An applicant has to establish *de facto* residence for a significant period in the country in question.

In this case, notwithstanding the fact that the applicant last lived in Jordan in 1981, it was found to be his country of former habitual residence. Lebanon, Yemen and Cyprus were countries he stayed in at the request of his employer, the PLO, and in accordance with the positions or missions to which he was assigned. Accordingly, it was held not to be unreasonable for the panel to conclude that Jordan was his former country of habitual residence.

Chan v. Canada (Minister of Employment & Immigration), 128 D.L.R. (4th) 213, 187 N.R. 321, [1995] 3 S.C.R. 593 (S.C.C.) — The appellant held a managerial position at a manufacturing company, and owned a restaurant business. He fled to Hong Kong in 1990 and proceeded to Canada where he sought Convention refugee status based on his fear of persecution because of his political opinion and membership in a particular social group. The panel found that the appellant did not have good grounds for fearing persecution based on his membership in a particular social group, relying on the fact that there was no evidence adduced to suggest that the appellant was persecuted beyond the period of the cultural revolution. A panel of the CRDD also found that the appellant did not have good grounds for fearing persecution by reason of his political opinion manifested through his pro-democracy activities.

The appellant, who was a male, also claimed to fear sterilization due to the fact that he had fathered more children than the government of China's family planning policy permitted. Sterilization was found by the panel not, in itself, to be a form of persecution. Further, due to the fact that the appellant testified that he did not wish to have any more children, and due to a lack of evidence to suggest that the appellant would be physically abused during the sterilization process, the CRDD panel found that the appellant's fear of persecution was not well-founded. The appellant appealed only on the issue of forced sterilization. The appeal was dismissed with one justice dissenting.

The appellant was required to demonstrate a well-founded fear of sterilization. The majority accepted the fact that the United Nations Handbook on Procedures and Criteria for Determining Refugee Status (Geneva 1979) although not binding on the Court was highly persuasive authority in Canada. The appellant was not required to prove that persecution would be more likely than not in order to meet the objective portion of the refugee test. That test is more appropriately described as requiring the appellant to demonstrate a serious possibility of persecution.

The appellant testified, with the assistance of an interpreter; the task of an interpreter in a judicial or quasi judicial hearing is an extremely difficult one. Simultaneous translation can lead to minor infelicities of style. The Board and the Court, when reviewing the written record, are well equipped to look past grammatical errors and to grasp the general import of a claimant's testimony, particularly when that testimony is considered as a whole. This is a fundamental part of the sympathetic approach to the evidence. It is the responsibility of the presiding member of the Board to ensure that the interpretation provided to the Board and reflected in the written record, is as accurate as possible. The appellant's testimony, even with respect to his own fear of forced sterilization, was equivocal and inconsistent.

The evidence of the appellant with respect to his subjective fear of forced sterilization was equivocal, however, in the absence of an explicit finding by the Board on this point, it would not be appropriate for the Supreme Court of Canada to determine that the appellant did not have a subjective fear. Even if the appellant is given the benefit of the doubt on the question of his subjective fear it is the responsibility of the appellant to lay an evidentiary foundation upon which the Board can conclude not only that the fear existed in the mind of the appellant, but also that it was objectively well-founded.

The objective component of the refugee test requires an examination of the objective situation and the relevant factors include the conditions in the appellant's country of origin, and the laws in that country, together with the manner in which they are applied. The appellant did not meet the burden of proof on the objective aspect of the test. The appellant failed to adduce any evidence that his fear of forced sterilization was objectively well-founded. The appellant failed to adduce any evidence that forced sterilization was actually carried out and not merely threatened by the local authorities in his area. Evidence with respect to the enforcement procedures utilized in the particular region where the appellant lives, at the relevant time, should be presented to the Board. Where such evidence is not available in documentary form, the appellant may still be able to establish that the fear was objectively well founded by providing testimony with respect to similarly situated individuals. This liberal approach to establishing the facts represents a relaxation of the usual rules of evidence and is intended to grant the appellant the benefit of the doubt in cases where strict documentary evidence may be lacking.

The appellant failed to provide either documentary evidence or anecdotal evidence to substantiate his claim that the pressure from the Chinese authorities to submit to sterilization would extend beyond psychological and financial pressure to actual physical coercion. The benefit of the doubt should only be given to a refugee claimant when all available evidence has been obtained and checked and a panel is satisfied as to the claimant's general credibility. The refugee claimant's statements must be coherent and plausible, and must not run counter to generally known facts.

With respect to sterilization the available evidence shows that the Chinese authorities attempt to persuade couples with more than one child to submit to sterilization by psychological, social and financial pressure, including heavy fines. The primary agent of enforcement is the woman's work unit, but such measures can include other family members, specifically, in the case of government control licenses such as driver's licenses. The generally known facts suggest that some, but not all local authorities exceed these measures and resort to physical compulsion primarily against women.

In light of the fact that not all persons who have breached the one child policy in China face a reasonable chance of forced sterilization, the appellant is required to establish a well-founded fear of forced sterilization before he can attempt to rely on that type of persecutory treatment. On the basis of the oral testimony, and the documentary evidence presented, forced sterilization remains no more than a mere possibility. In the absence of that evidence it was open to the Board to conclude that it could not determine that the appellant had a well-founded fear of persecution in the form of a forced sterilization. Accordingly, in the opinion of the majority, the appeal should be dismissed.

Vidhani v. Canada (Minister of Citizenship & Immigration), [1995] 3 F.C. 60, 96 F.T.R. 313 (Fed. T.D.) — The applicant successfully reviewed a negative decision of the CRDD.

The applicant is a woman who has been compelled to enter into an arranged marriage without her consent. She may be, therefore, subject to persecution within the definition of Convention refugee. Women who are forced into marriages against their will have had a basic human right violated. There are United Nations Conventions, to which Canada is a party, which state that the right to enter freely into marriage is a basic human right. The restriction on the exercise of a human right, however, does not, in every case, constitute persecution. In her testimony the applicant indicated that she feared the police would sexually attack her if she made a complaint with respect to being forced into a marriage. The Board did not have any documentary evidence before it with respect to the attitude of the authorities in Kenya on complaints by women being forced into marriage without their consent. Further, there was no adverse credibility finding with respect to the applicant. Therefore, the Board should have dealt with her testimony on possible sexual attack by the police and determined whether this constituted persecution in her case. This constituted reversible error. Her matter was returned to a differently constituted panel to analyze persecution in light of the applicant's membership in a particular social group of women who were forced into marriage without their consent.

Liu v. Canada (Minister of Citizenship & Immigration) (1995), 98 F.T.R. 88 (Fed. T.D.) — The female applicant had one child while she was living in Shanghai and left China because she did not want to be sterilized. The applicant testified that there was incredible pressure on her to undergo sterilization. The work unit in which she worked would have incurred fines and a member of that unit twice accompanied her to a hospital to undergo a planned sterilization which, for medical reasons, did not take place. The panel erred in ruling that physical compulsion was the only mechanism for forcing a person to do something which they would not, of their own free choice, choose to do. The Court noted that other members of the applicant's work unit would be denied 80% of their salary if the applicant conceived a second child. Pressure of this nature is no different from physical compulsion.

The error by the panel, with respect to the characterization of the pressure upon the applicant in China, was not determinative of the application and, accordingly, did not result in the decision of the panel being overturned. The applicant had a second child born outside of China and there was no evidence to suggest that should the applicant be returned to China, her second child would be taken away from her. The assertion by the applicant in her evidence that this would be the case was unsupported by the documentary evidence. Further, the applicant and her husband, now that they had had a second child, indicated they no longer objected to the family planning policy or methods of the government of China.

Accordingly, the application was dismissed.

Al-Maisri v. Canada (Minister of Employment & Immigration) (1995), 183 N.R. 234 (Fed. C.A.) — The appellant, a citizen of Yemen, claimed a well-founded fear of persecution by reason of political opinion. Yemen had supported Iraq during the invasion of Kuwait and the appellant, when he was called up to serve in the Yemenese army, deserted rather than go to Iraq by way of Jordan, to fight in the Iraqi Army.

The Refugee Division rejected the claim on the ground that the appellant would face prosecution in Yemen for deserting his country's military rather than persecution for political opinion.

Iraq's invasion of Kuwait was condemned by the United Nations and the annexation of Kuwait by Iraq was declared by the U.N. to be null and void.

The Court was persuaded that Iraq's actions, were contrary to the basic rules of human conduct, and following the guidance afforded by paragraph 171 of the UNHCR Handbook, concluded that any punishment for desertion visited upon the appellant if he returned to Yemen would amount to persecution of which the appellant had a well-founded fear.

The appeal was allowed and the applicant was declared to be a Convention refugee.

Naguleswaran v. Canada (Minister of Citizenship & Immigration) (April 19, 1995), Doc. IMM-1116-94 (Fed. T.D.) — The applicants, a mother and son, were Tamils from Jaffna, and citizens of Sri Lanka. In domestic Canadian investigations of criminality or even terrorism, the ordinary fabric of society remains intact, permitting investigators to gather information and evidence unimpeded by terrorist intimidation of the population and the distracting first priority of seeing to the security of the civilian population. Western concepts of the administration of justice will not work in some other countries and that is why those other countries do not enjoy Canada's freedoms. Those who perpetuate rebellions, armed attacks, sabotage, and terrorism are always trying to destabilize existing governments and to make those governments harsher in their own self-defence. Some countries are more susceptible to that pressure than countries like Canada.

People are not *ipso facto* refugees because their government makes security sweeps from time to time. There may be inconvenience from security sweeps to be endured by the northern refugee settlers resident in Colombo but the Court was not able to find that there was an error when the CRDD ruled that notwithstanding the treatment the applicants received during these security sweeps, Colombo was still an internal flight alternative for them.

Atakurola v. Canada (Minister of Citizenship & Immigration) (March 23, 1995), Doc. IMM-585-94 (Fed. T.D.) — The applicant was an unsuccessful refugee claimant from Sri Lanka. On the issue of state protection the Court upheld the Board's decision and pointed out that there is a presumption that the state is capable of protecting its citizens. State protection is available when it is adequate, though not necessarily perfect, or where a state is in effective control and makes serious efforts to protect its citizens. It is not enough for a claimant to show that his government has not always been effective at protecting persons in his particular situation. Where a state is in effective control of a territory, has military, police, and civilian authority in place, and makes serious efforts to protect its citizens from terrorist activities, the fact that it is not always successful at doing so is not enough to justify a claim that there is no state protection for the particular claimant. The application for judicial review was dismissed.

Diluna v. Canada (Minister of Employment & Immigration) (1995), 29 Imm. L.R. (2d) 156, 92 F.T.R. 67 (Fed. T.D.) — The applicant, who was a citizen of Brazil, claimed refugee status on the basis that she was a member of a particular social group, specifically, the applicant chronicled in her evidence a relationship with her husband that was marked by violence. The CRDD erred in law in failing to find that the applicant had good grounds for fearing persecution on a Convention ground by reason of the continuous experience of violence against her committed by her husband and the inability or unwillingness demonstrated by state authorities to protect her from such violence in the past. Women subject to domestic violence in Brazil constitute a particular social group for purposes of the definition of Convention refugee.

Karpounin v. Canada (Minister of Employment & Immigration) (1995), 92 F.T.R. 219 (Fed. T.D.) — The applicant, a citizen of the Ukraine, had been the subject of extortion attempts as a result of his commercial success after the break-up of the Soviet Union. The Board found that the applicant had a well-founded fear of persecution but could not demonstrate a link between the persecution claimed and the grounds enumerated in the definition of a Convention refugee. It was reasonably open to the Board to find that the applicant was subject to extortion resulting from his financial success and that this was not related to political opinion or membership in a particular social group. The evidence before the Board did not allow it to arrive at the inference that the ruling government of the country considered the applicant's conduct political. Accordingly, the application for judicial review was dismissed.

Rafizade v. Canada (Minister of Citizenship & Immigration) (1995), 30 Imm. L.R. (2d) 261, 92 F.T.R. 55 (Fed. T.D.) — The applicants, 11 and 14 years of age, were citizens of Iran. The father was designated as the representative of the two minor applicants. The applicants did not testify. Only their father presented evidence. The Board found the father to be a refugee, but found that the minor applicants were not Convention refugees. The Board found there was insufficient evidence to conclude that there was a reasonable chance that the minor claimants would face persecution.

The Court found there was no justification for the development of a common-law notion of indirect persecution to account for family unity situations not covered by the *Immigration Act*. It is not the role of the Court to expand the scope of the family for immigration purposes beyond that which parliament has determined to be appropriate.

In this case the persecution directed at the father was not persecution directed at the applicants. Accordingly, the application was dismissed.

Isa v. Canada (Secretary of State) (1995), 91 F.T.R. 71 (Fed. T.D.) — The applicant comes from Somalia. The applicant fled Mogadishu and went to live in the Gedo region of Somalia. Subsequent to that the applicant and his family fled to Kenya and then eventually came to Canada. The applicant's claim was dismissed on the basis that the applicant demonstrated merely a general fear arising out of civil war and anarchy, and not persecution for a Convention reason.

A situation of civil war does not preclude an individual being found a Convention refugee. The individual must demonstrate that his or her fear arose because reprehensible acts were likely to be committed against members of a group to which he or she belonged, or against all citizens as a result of one of the reasons identified in the Convention definition of a refugee. A case will fail if it falls short of establishing that the applicants were collectively targeted differently from the general victims of a civil war. Many, if not most, civil war situations are racially or ethnically based. If racially motivated attacks in civil war circumstances alone could constitute grounds for Convention refugee status, then all individuals on either side of the conflict would qualify for refugee status.

Narvaez v. Canada (Minister of Citizenship & Immigration) (1995), 89 F.T.R. 94 (Fed. T.D.) — The applicant was a divorced female citizen of Ecuador. She feared violence at the hands of her former husband from whom she was divorced. Throughout the relationship between the applicant and her husband she was subjected to consistent physical and sexual abuse. The Court concluded that women subject to domestic violence in Equador constituted members of a particular social group. Further, there was documentary evidence showing that Ecuadorian authorities showed little, if any, interest in domestic violence, as well as further material which stated that women were generally blamed for the abuse. Thus, there was evidence that women in similar situations to the applicant did not receive state protection when it was solicited. Accordingly, the negative decision of a panel of the CRDD was set aside and the matter referred to a differently constituted panel.

Howard-Dejo v. Canada (Minister of Citizenship & Immigration) (February 2, 1995), Doc. A-1179-92 (Fed. T.D.) — The applicants were of Peruvian origin and while their subjective fears of persecution were found to be justified, their objective fear was not. The Board found that the Peruvian government was able to ensure their protection. The applicant had applied to the Peruvian police for protection against the Shining Path Guerillas. He was informed that the police had a great deal to do and that his protection was not a priority. This was fully consistent with the documentary evidence which demonstrated that the Peruvian authorities were overwhelmed by the violence and tenaciousness of the Shining Path.

This was not a case of evidence showing simply that the Peruvian government was not immediately succeeding in protecting the targets of terrorism. Rather, it was a case of evidence showing that the Peruvian authorities themselves admitted they were unable to provide protection proportionate to the threat that the CRDD took to be established. The CRDD is not entitled on the basis of such evidence, to conclude that the Peruvian government is capable of providing protection.

The application was allowed and the matter remitted back for rehearing before a differently constituted panel of the CRDD.

Paukovac v. Canada (Minister of Citizenship & Immigration) (1994), 89 F.T.R. 227 (Fed. T.D.) — The applicant, a citizen of Croatia, based her claim to Convention refugee status on fear of persecution by reason of her nationality and membership in a social group. The applicant, and members of her family, experienced much hardship and suffering arising out of the conditions of civil, or near civil, war in Croatia. Absent a situation of complete breakdown of state apparatus, it should be assumed that the State is capable of protecting a claimant. In order for the appellant to overcome the presumption that the State is capable of protecting him or her, he or she has to advance clear and convincing confirmation of the State's inability to do so. Such proof might consist of testimony that similarly situated individuals were let down by the State protection arrangement, or of past personal incidents in which State protection did not materialize. The evidence in this case fell short of establishing the inability of the State to protect.

Castellanos v. Canada (Minister of Citizenship & Immigration) (1994), 84 F.T.R. 316 (Fed. T.D.) — The applicant was a Cuban citizen as were his two daughters. His wife was a citizen of what was formerly the Soviet Union and she lived with her husband and children in Cuba on a renewable 5 year visa.

The husband was found to be a Convention refugee. His wife and two daughters were not. With respect to the wife of the principal applicant the Board erred in finding that she was a Ukrainian citizen. The decision refusing her claim was quashed and an order was made directing a new hearing.

The status of the two daughters raised the question of whether family unity was a concept recognized by Canadian refugee law. The principle of family unity requires that persons granted refugee status should not be separated from their closest family members, particularly when a situation of dependency exists. The Court found that there was no mention of family unity in the current definition of a Convention refugee, and that therefore, in order to apply the principle of family unity, it would have to extend the definition. The Court found no justification for doing so.

For a person to be considered a Convention refugee it must be shown that the person is a member of one of five enumerated classes. The class of membership in a particular social group is the basket clause of this definitional provision. The family has been accepted as a social group for purposes of a Refugee definition. One will not be deemed a Convention refugee just because one has a relative that is being persecuted. There has to be a clear nexus between the persecution that is being levelled against one of the family members and that which is taking place against the others. A family can only be considered a social group in cases where there is evidence that the persecution is taking place against the family members as a social group. Here the Board found no evidence that any persecutory activity had been levelled against the mother or the daughters, let alone any based upon their being members of the principal applicant's family. Their claims were not well founded. Finally, the Court was not prepared to accept the principle of indirect persecution as defined in *Bhatti v. Canada (Secretary of State)* (1994), 25 Imm. L.R. (2d) 275, 84 F.T.R. 145 (Fed. T.D.) as part of our refugee law. The Court held that indirect persecution did not constitute persecution within the meaning of the definition of Convention refugee.

The Court found that section 46.04 was the legislative response to the principle of family unity.

Smirnov v. Canada (Secretary of State) (1994), [1995] 1 F.C. 780, 89 F.T.R. 269 — The applicants were citizens of Ukraine. The male applicant was Jewish. The female claimant claimed to have no religious beliefs. The applicants were spouses. The male applicant's claim was based on a fear of persecution by reason of his religion.

On the issue of state protection the Court referred to the case of *Bobrik v. Canada (Minister of Citizenship & Immigration)* (1994), 85 F.T.R. 13, as a case in which too high a standard for state protection was set. The Court observed that the standard set in that case would be difficult, even for Canada to achieve. It is a reality of modern day life that state protection is sometimes ineffective. The applicants failed to discharge the burden on them to establish that the Ukraine was unable to protect them not in an absolute sense, but rather to a degree that was reasonable having regard to the circumstances of the applicants and the range of harassment inflicted on them. The application was dismissed.

Ramirez v. Canada (Solicitor General) (1994), 88 F.T.R. 208 — This was an application to review a negative decision of the CRDD. The panel declined to describe the harm suffered by the applicant in her native Nicaragua as persecution. The Court noted that discrimination will only amount to persecution where it is serious or systematic enough to be characterized as persecution and, secondly, that the dividing line between discrimination and persecution is difficult to establish with the result that the Court will not intervene unless the conclusion reached by the panel "appears to be capricious or unreasonable".

In this case the conclusion reached by the panel was neither and the application for judicial review was dismissed.

Velauthapillai v. Canada (Solicitor General) (1994), 88 F.T.R. 315 — The applicant, a Sri Lankan Tamil, based her claim on her nationality, political opinion and membership in a particular social group. The applicant testified that she had been the victim of extortion attempts by members of the Tamil Tigers. The applicant was aware of others who had refused such requests and who had been arrested and killed as a result of their refusal. It was not open to the Board to exclude extortion from the indicia of persecution without looking into the reason for extortion. The panel erred in failing to analyze whether the applicant, if she were returned to the north of Sri Lanka, would be exposed to further extortion attempts, and whether such attempts, having regard to the conditions that existed in northern Sri Lanka, would raise for the applicant, a serious possibility of persecution.

Fosu v. Canada (Minister of Employment & Immigration) (1994), 27 Imm. L.R. (2d) 95, 90 F.T.R. 182 — The applicant is a Jehovah's Witness and claimed religious persecution based on the enforcement of legislation in Ghana restricting the public activities of the applicant's religion. The claim was unsuccessful because a panel determined that the legislation prohibited religious services but did not prevent individual members from worshipping God.

The right to freedom of religion also includes the right to demonstrate one's religion or belief in public or in private by teaching, practise, worship and the performance of rites. The persecution of the practise of religion can take various forms such as prohibiting worshipping in public, or giving or receiving religious instruction or the implementation of serious discriminatory practises against persons on account of their religion. The prohibition against Jehovah's Witnesses to practice their religion could amount to persecution and the panel was obliged to consider this matter which it failed to do. Accordingly, the decision of the panel was set aside and the matter remitted for determination.

Malouf v. Canada (Minister of Citizenship & Immigration) (1994), 26 Imm. L.R. (2d) 20, 86 F.T.R. 124, [1995] 1 F.C. 537 — The applicant sought to overturn an unfavourable decision of the CRDD. The applicant, who was a citizen of Lebanon, left there in 1977 and obtained permanent resident status in the United States. The applicant pleaded guilty to possession of cocaine for the purpose of trafficking and fled to Canada before his sentencing.

The panel excluded the applicant from the refugee process by applying the exclusion in section F(b) of Article 1 of the Convention. That section excluded the applicant from the protection of the Geneva Convention on the basis that he had committed a serious, non-political crime outside of Canada and prior to his admission to Canada. Once the panel concluded that the exclusion clause might apply to the applicant, it should have, through the Refugee Hearing Officer, given notice to the Minister and provided an opportunity for the Minister to make representation. Then, whether or not the Minister intervened, it would have been open to the panel to conclude that the exclusion clause applied to the applicant.

For purposes of section F(b) the country of refuge was Canada, notwithstanding the fact that there was more than one country of refuge. There were serious reasons for considering that the applicant had committed a serious non-political crime, outside of Canada, prior to his admission to Canada as a refugee claimant.

The CRDD erred in failing to consider the applicant's Convention refugee claim as against Lebanon and in failing to balance the risk to the applicant that would flow from his return to Lebanon by reason of the exclusion clause against the seriousness of the non-political crime here at issue. Once that balancing was conducted the panel would have been in a position to determine whether the serious non-political crimes were of such a nature as to warrant the application of the exclusion clause, and the imposition on the applicant of the risk that would flow from his return to Lebanon. No balancing would be required had the panel concluded that the applicant was not, in fact, a refugee.

Risak v. Canada (Minister of Employment & Immigration) (1994), 25 Imm. L.R. (2d) 267, 86 F.T.R. 67 — Every time the male applicant complained to the police or to the army, and later on to superior officers, about the treatment he was receiving from the authorities, he was rebuffed and, on one occasion, incarcerated. These were the very people from whom a citizen could be expected to obtain the protection of the state. There is nothing in Canadian jurisprudence to the effect that in such situations the applicant has the further burden of seeking assistance from human rights organizations, or ultimately, launching an action in Court against the government.

Gil v. Canada (Minister of Employment & Immigration) (1994), 25 Imm. L.R. (2d) 209, 174 N.R. 292, 119 D.L.R. (4th) 497, [1995] 1 F.C. 508 (Fed. C.A.) — This case raises the question of what is meant by the phrase a "serious non-political crime" in section F of Article 1 of the Convention.

The appellant is an Iranian citizen, the son of a wealthy family which had been an active supporter of the Shah's regime. The family experienced considerable difficulties after the coming into power of the government that overthrew the Shah. The appellant joined an underground student group and, in due course, became associated with a larger militant group of anti-government activists. In the years 1980 and 1981 the appellant personally took part in five or six incidents of bombing and arson. Those attacks were directed against wealthy supporters of the regime. These incidents lead to the injury and death of innocent bystanders. The appellant was arrested and interrogated by the authorities but never confessed to his activities and he was ultimately released by the authorities, without being charged, and eventually fled to Canada.

A panel of the CRDD found that the appellant had a well-founded fear of persecution but that he was excluded by the provision in section 1F(b) of the Convention.

A panel of the CRDD concluded that the appellant's crimes were non-political. Accordingly, the appeal raised the question of what was meant by political crime. The characterization of crimes as political is found in both extradition and refugee law. The Court noted that there was a need for even greater caution characterizing the crime as political for the purposes of applying section 1F(b) than for the purpose of denying extradition. The Court developed an incidence test as a means of resolving whether a crime is political. The appellant met the first branch of the test because Iran, in the years in question, was a turbulent society in which a number of armed groups were in conflict with the regime and the appellant's testimony that he was a member of one such group was accepted as credible. The appellant's claim failed the second branch of the test. There was no objective rational connection between injuring the commercial interests of certain wealthy supporters of the government and any realistic goal of forcing the regime itself to fall or change. Further, the means used by the appellant excluded his crimes from any claim to be political in nature. The attacks were not carried out against armed adversaries and were bound to injure innocent bystanders. The use of deadly force against unarmed civilian commercial targets in circumstances where serious injury or death to innocent bystanders was inevitable rendered the violence used wholly disproportionate to any legitimate political objective.

Balasubramaniam v. Canada (Minister of Citizenship & Immigration) (October 4, 1994), Doc. IMM-1902-93 (Fed. T.D.) — The applicant was a citizen of Sri Lanka seeking judicial review of a negative decision of a panel of the CRDD. The applicant complained of persecution by the Sri Lankan Armed Forces. The Board found an internal flight alternative (IFA) in another part of the country also controlled by the army.

The panel's decision was set aside. There must be evidence adduced to specifically support a finding that the persecution at the hands of the army would not continue in the new area before the new area could be found to be an IFA.

Antonio v. Canada (Minister of Employment & Immigration) (1994), 85 F.T.R. 241 — The applicant was a citizen of Angola, who was born in the Cabinda region. In order to evade military service the applicant accepted a position as a telex agent with the government telecommunications facility. The applicant served as a spy for rebels against the government. Eventually, the applicant's identity was learned by the government of Angola and the applicant fled to Canada.

There was no evidence before the Board that the applicant had manifested his political opinions in any manner. Thus, there were no political opinions in respect of which it could be said that the Angolan authorities intended to punish the applicant. Accordingly, the applicant was found to fear prosecution for politically motivated acts as opposed to persecution.

After having been determined to be a spy the applicant was scheduled for summary execution. The Court was satisfied that the Board did not make a mistake in holding that the applicant was not being punished for his political opinion, and accordingly, the Court concluded that the Board was correct in not considering whether the death penalty *per se* was, irrespective of the events giving rise to that punishment, persecution.

Khatib v. Canada (Minister of Citizenship & Immigration) (1994), 83 F.T.R. 310 — The Court noted that in *Ward v. Canada (Minister of Employment & Immigration)*, [1993] 2 S.C.R. 689, the applicant was a citizen of a state which admitted that it could not provide protection. The discussion and conclusions reached in *Ward*, in the opinion of the Court, applied only to citizens of a state, and not to stateless people. A stateless person is not expected to avail himself or herself of state protection when there is no duty on the state to provide such protection.

Basic v. Canada (Minister of Citizenship & Immigration) (1994), 87 F.T.R. 214 — The applicant was formerly a citizen of Yugoslavia, and at the time of the application, a citizen of Croatia. The applicant did not want to serve in the Croatian armed forces. Documentary evidence indicated that alternative service was available in the Croatian army for those who objected to bearing arms.

The Board's decision denying refugee status was overturned. While the Board dealt with the applicant's argument concerning the non-availability of an alternative service, it did not deal with the question of whether punishment, or failing to respond to a draft notice, can be persecution if the military action which the draft notice is designed to support, is condemned by the international legal community.

Bhatti v. Canada (Secretary of State) (1994), 25 Imm. L.R. (2d) 275, 84 F.T.R. 145 — Persecution under the definition includes the principle of indirect persecution. The concept of indirect persecution is premised on the assumption that family members are likely to suffer great harm when their close relatives are persecuted. The harm may manifest itself in many ways, ranging from the loss of the victim's economic and social support to the psychological trauma associated with witnessing the suffering of loved ones.

In this case the panel erred in failing to consider the adverse effects experienced by the applicants as a result of the persecution of another person who was the father of one applicant and the husband of the other.

Bediako v. Canada (Minister of Employment & Immigration) (August 29, 1994), Doc. IMM-3059-93 (Fed. T.D.) — The applicant had a well-founded subjective and objective fear of persecution when he left Ghana. The Board concluded that the objective fear of the applicant had been removed by changes in the country conditions between December 31, 1991, when the applicant left that country, and December 30, 1992, when the Board heard evidence of the applicant's claim.

The Board, in deciding whether there has been a change in country conditions, is required to give a sufficient analysis of the conflicting documentary evidence before it. There was, in this case, a very extensive analysis of the change in country conditions and, accordingly, that aspect of the Board's decision cannot be criticized.

Country changes have to be meaningful, effective and durable. In this case there was documentary evidence that showed that democracy was not working perfectly in Ghana, however, the Board addressed in detail the changes in country conditions and found them to be fundamental and durable enough to eliminate the objective basis for the applicant's fear. Accordingly, the application was dismissed.

Hassan v. Canada (Minister of Employment & Immigration) (1994), 174 N.R. 74 (Fed. C.A.) — The appellant claimed refugee status for herself and for her four children. She was a member of the Issaq clan. She and her husband operated a small grocery store in Northern Somalia. She and her husband suffered at the hands of police in the months leading up to the outbreak of hostilities in 1988. After that time their grocery store was destroyed and her husband fled the country never to be seen again. The appellant herself fled to Canada and claimed refugee status in 1989.

The decision of the Board was set aside. The issue was not whether the difficulties the appellant had experienced in the past constituted persecution, nor was it whether the appellant had been singled out for harassment while in Somalia. The issue was whether the appellant could reasonably fear persecution in the future simply by being a member of the Issaq clan.

It is clear that the status of refugee is attached to an individual and is granted on the basis that this individual needs protection from personal harm and persecution that he or she may suffer in his or her country over and above what would come from a state of general oppression affecting all the inhabitants of the country. This principle relates to the objective fear, not to its well-foundedness or reasonability. It has nothing to do with the question of whether one may have a reasonable fear of being personally a victim of persecution for the sole reason that he or she belongs to a specific targeted group whose members are indiscriminately subject to persecution. It is this question which was at the heart of the appellant's claim. The Board missed the point and as a result its decision did not dispose of the real issue.

Valencia v. Canada (Minister of Employment & Immigration) (1994), 85 F.T.R. 218 — The applicant challenged a negative decision of the CRDD on the ground that the applicant was not given notice before the commencement of the hearing of his application that the possible existence of an internal flight alternative (IFA) would be an issue in his case. Such notice is not required. All that is required is that once the issue is raised, an adequate opportunity to respond be given to the claimant.

In the present case the applicant's hearing commenced on August 27, 1992. At the very beginning of the proceedings the Refugee Hearing Officer stated that the existence of an IFA was an issue in the proceeding. Proceedings of August 27 were subsequently adjourned and reconvened on January 12, 1993. As a result, the applicant had abundant opportunity to marshal any evidence he might wish to present on the subject of an IFA.

The second issue raised was whether the location of an IFA was reasonable in all the circumstances. Two criteria must be fulfilled in finding that a claimant has an IFA: the Board must be satisfied on the balance of probabilities that there is no serious possibility of the claimant being persecuted in the new location; and the conditions in the new location must be such that it would not be unreasonable for the claimant to seek refuge there. The Board, in doing its analysis, did not distinguish between considerations relevant to the possibility of persecution at the present time in Medellin (the place in Columbia where the claimant claimed to be at risk) and whether if such possibility of persecution existed the applicant had a viable flight alternative to somewhere outside that city. The Board's decision was upheld. An analysis of the reasonableness of an IFA outside Medellin was implicit in the Board's decision. Secondly, there was no convincing evidence as to why a location outside Medellin would not be reasonable.

Papu v. Canada (Minister of Employment & Immigration) (August 15, 1994), Doc. A-1040-92 (Fed. T.D.) — It is well established that the determination of whether an individual's treatment is sufficiently serious to constitute persecution is to be left to the members of the Board. Most states have measures which provide for the derogation of civil rights temporarily in a time of emergency. This derogation of civil rights does not necessarily amount to "persecution".

Shaat v. Canada (Minister of Employment & Immigration) (1994), 82 F.T.R. 102 — The applicant sought judicial review of a negative decision of the CRDD. The applicant is a stateless person. In allowing the application the Court concluded that an applicant was not required to prove a legal right of return to a country in order for that country to be a "former habitual residence" within the meaning of section (a)(ii) of the definition of Convention refugee in section 2(1) of the *Immigration Act*.

Silva v. Canada (Minister of Employment & Immigration) (1994), 82 F.T.R. 100 — This application to overturn a negative decision of the CRDD was successful. The Board made a fundamental error when it stated that it "is also not satisfied that the state is either unable or unwilling to offer protection should the female claimant decide to seek such protection". The question is not whether the state would be willing to protect but whether the applicant was willing to seek the protection of the state. It is the well-foundedness of the applicants' perspective regarding the state's actions which is determinative. Because the basis of the applicants' fear was the actions of individuals which, if not directly connected to the state, were identified with the ruling government, the Board erred in failing to analyze the applicants' claim from the perspective of their unwillingness to seek the protection of the state.

Hophany v. Canada (Minister of Employment & Immigration) (July 19, 1994), Doc. A-802-92 (Fed. T.D.) — The applicant refused to serve in the Afghan army because he did not wish to be involved in the killing of his fellow Afghans who were opposed to the Communist government that was then in power. The applicant argued that if he should be returned to Afghanistan he would be detained and punished severely for attempting to avoid military service.

The term "conscientious objector" applies to persons who object to *any* form of military service and does not apply to those not opposed to armed conflict as a matter of principle, but only to a *particular* armed conflict.

Zdanov v. Canada (Minister of Employment & Immigration) (1994), 81 F.T.R. 246 — The applicant sought to review a negative decision of the CRDD. The applicant was born in the Soviet Union but lived his entire life in Estonia. The applicant testified that he would be persecuted if he were returned to Estonia because he was a Russian and because he was involved with the KGB as an informer during his time in Estonia.

The evidence established that the applicant would not be granted Estonian citizenship by virtue of the protocol of February 26, 1992. The Board concluded, however, that Estonia was not the applicant's "country of former habitual residence". The definition of "country of former habitual residence" should not be unduly restrictive so as to preempt the provision of surrogate shelter to a stateless person who has demonstrated a well-founded fear of persecution.

The applicant's claim failed because he could not demonstrate good grounds for fearing persecution in Russia which was determined to be his country of nationality. The law on Citizenship of the RSFSR quite clearly indicated that the applicant was a Russian citizen. With respect to Russia there was on the evidence no more than a mere possibility that the applicant would be persecuted if returned there. Accordingly, the decision of the Board that the applicant was not a Convention refugee was upheld.

Osei v. Canada (Secretary of State) (July 14, 1994), Doc. IMM-4839-93 (Fed. T.D.) — In this decision the Court discussed the proper test be applied in a situation where there have been changes in the country which the applicants left prior to the hearing of the claim.

The Court described the unsettled state of the jurisprudence to the date of its decision and noted that there are differing views in the Court as to the proper test to be applied. One test applies the criteria set down by Professor Hathaway in his book, *The Law of Refugee Status* (1991), pages 200–203.

The Court noted that a different view also exists in the jurisprudence. That view held that the only evidence required was evidence of the change in circumstances. The tribunal's task was to reach a conclusion that a change had occurred, and by reason of that change the particular applicant's claim of persecution was no longer well founded because there was no objective basis for it.

Finally, the Court noted that with respect to the certification of decisions for appeal that there was a disturbing trend indicating that these appeals were not being pursued. The Court noted that when a trial Judge certifies a question, he or she expects that the question will be placed before the Court of Appeal. Often times a second request for certification is refused because the Judge knows that the question in issue has already been certified. Further, the Court noted that stays pending a decision on the certified question are not being sought or granted. In this case the Court refused to dispose of the case before a decision on the issue of the proper test was rendered by the Court of Appeal. The Court had previously noted that this issue was or had been already certified for consideration by the Court of Appeal.

Chun v. Canada (Minister of Employment & Immigration) (July 8, 1994), Doc. IMM-1197-93 (Fed. T.D.) — The Court construed the Federal Court of Appeal decision in *Cheung v. Canada (Minister of Employment & Immigration)* (1993), 19 Imm. L.R. (2d) 81 (Fed. C.A.), as standing for the proposition that women in China who have more than one child and are faced with forced sterilization, form a particular social group so as to come within the meaning of the definition Convention refugee. The Court also determined that the Court of Appeal found in the *Cheung* case that even if forced sterilization was accepted as a law of general application, that fact would not necessarily prevent a claim to Convention refugee status.

The Court allowed this application for judicial review because the panel that reached a negative decision in this case did not have the benefit of the decision of the Court of Appeal in *Cheung*.

Ahmad v. Canada (Minister of Employment & Immigration) (1994), 80 F.T.R. 135 — This was an application to review a negative decision of the CRDD. The primary basis of the applicant's claim was that, in Pakistan, there is systematic discrimination and persecution of Ahmadis arising from the law referred to as Ordinance No. XX of 1984.

The onus is on the applicant to show that laws of general application are either inherently or for some other reason, persecutory. The panel, in this case, indicated to counsel for the claimant that they were familiar with Pakistani cases and Ordinance No. XX, and that they would like to hear from the applicant about his personal problems. In taking this approach the panel precluded the applicant from satisfying the onus upon him.

The vast majority of refugee cases will be decided on the basis of the particular circumstances of an applicant. There may be cases, however, in which an applicant wishes to rely solely on the persecutory nature of a law of general application to a particular social group. Such an approach cannot be precluded by a panel as it was in this case. Accordingly, the application was allowed.

Chavez-Menendez v. Canada (Minister of Employment & Immigration) (1994), 81 F.T.R. 271 — This was an application to review a negative decision of the CRDD. The applicant's claim was rejected on the basis of changes in the country conditions in El Salvador. On the issue of changed country conditions the Court adopted the view that the appropriate test was propounded by James Hathaway in *The Law of Refugee Status*. The Court noted that the objective nature of the changes must be assessed against the particular circumstances of the applicant in order to determine whether the changes are so significant, effective and durable against the particular circumstances of the applicant as to effectively nullify the objective basis for the refugee claim.

The CRDD's analysis, when compared to the above test, was inadequate. The hearing took place barely 8 months after the peace accords in El Salvador came into force. Further, the documentary evidence cited by the CRDD was, at best, ambivalent as to the significance, effectiveness and durability of the changes that had taken place. In addition, documentary evidence less favourable to the position taken by the CRDD, was not analyzed, particularly the advice of the Canadian office at the United Nations High Commissioner for Refugees.

Sahota v. Canada (Minister of Employment & Immigration) (1994), 80 F.T.R. 241 — This was an application to set aside the decision of a refugee panel denying the applicant's refugee claim on the basis that the police authorities in India would not pursue the applicant as long as he remained outside the Punjab. The decision was set aside. The applicant was sixteen years of age and the Board was silent on the effect of his age in connection with the internal flight alternative (IFA) determination. The Court also noted that there was no evidence before the Board with respect to the *Convention on the Rights of the Child* adopted on November 20, 1989, signed by Canada May 28, 1990, ratified by Canada December 13, 1991, which came into force in Canada January 12, 1992.

Accordingly, the Court ordered that a new panel of the IRB consider, in relation to the IFA, the question of the age of the applicant, the *Convention on the Rights of the Child* and any other relevant evidence the parties may put before it.

Katassonov v. Canada (Secretary of State) (1994), 79 F.T.R. 302 — The applicant sought judicial review of a decision determining that he was not a Convention refugee. The decision of the Board was set aside. The Board concluded that harassment or discrimination could not be "linked to persecution". In its reasons, however, it failed to consider whether the acts were "serious or systematic enough to be characterized as persecution, or to lead to a conclusion that there was a serious possibility of persecution in the future". The failure of the Board to apply this principle in analyzing the claim constituted a reversible error.

Knarik v. Canada (Solicitor General) (1994), 79 F.T.R. 297 — This case deals with the duty on a visa officer, when considering an application for permanent residency on the ground that the person is a Convention refugee seeking resettlement. The applicant, a citizen of Iran, applied to the Canadian Embassy in Bonn for resettlement on the ground that she was a Convention refugee seeking resettlement. A visa officer determined that the applicant did not meet the requirements for immigration to Canada.

The applicant sought judicial review on the ground that she was not provided with access to an interpreter and that the officer should have recommended the appointment of legal counsel. The applicant was advised to bring an interpreter if necessary and chose to show up to the interview without one. Further, with respect to the right to counsel, the applicant did not ask for one and there is no statutory obligation to assign counsel to visa seekers or to allow them to bring their own. The application was dismissed.

Equizabal v. Canada (Minister of Employment & Immigration), 24 Imm. L.R. (2d) 277, [1994] 3 F.C. 514, 170 N.R. 329 (Fed. C.A.) — The appellant was denied refugee status on the basis that he was included in Article 1F of the Convention and therefore excluded from the definition of refugee. The specific finding of the CRDD was that the appellant had committed crimes against humanity by torturing civilians. The appellant sought and obtained leave to apply for judicial review, which application was dismissed. The Trial Division judge certified a serious question of general importance.

The Appellant was a citizen of Guatemala who was forcibly recruited by the Guatemalan military. He described in his evidence before the CRDD four military missions which involved the torture of civilians. A crime against humanity is not only a domestic offence, but is rather an offence with the additional component of barbarous cruelty. On the uncontradicted evidence of the appellant, it is obvious that he was guilty of barbarous cruelty in the four incidents he described in his evidence.

The defence of obedience to the orders of a superior based on compulsion was also considered. The first matter to be assessed was whether the orders in issue were manifestly unlawful. A manifestly unlawful order must be one that offends the conscience of every reasonable right-thinking person. It must be an order which is obviously and flagrantly wrong. The Court had no difficulty in concluding that the orders here in issue were manifestly unlawful. The appellant and two other soldiers were ordered on one occasion to beat four persons and torture them over a period of three hours. Torturing the truth out of someone is manifestly unlawful, by any standard.

On the question of compulsion, the issue was whether the appellant faced an imminent, real and inevitable threat to his life. Stern punishment or demotion would not be sufficient. The appellant's evidence summarized two reasons why, notwithstanding his understanding that the penalty for desertion was only twelve months in jail, he would be killed: firstly, he knew of three other deserters who were apprehended and never heard from again; secondly, he believed he would be killed by his lieutenant because of his knowledge of relatives of persons whom the lieutenant had tortured personally. The first reason was dismissed as it was pure speculation without any credible evidence to support it. The second reason was not supported by the record. The record established that before the third mission, the appellant advised his lieutenant that he would no longer participate in such torture. As a result he was never forced to torture anyone again. He was thereafter, on two occasions, assigned to act as a guard while others did the torturing. There was, therefore, no evidence that the appellant was facing an imminent, real and inevitable threat to his life.

Accordingly, the appeal was dismissed and the decision that the appellant had committed a crime against humanity, as that expression appears in Article 1F of the Convention relating to the status of refugees, was upheld.

Gonzalez v. Canada (Minister of Employment & Immigration), [1994] 3 F.C. 646, 24 Imm. L.R. (2d) 229, 170 N.R. 302, 115 D.L.R. (4th) 403 (Fed. C.A.) — This was an appeal from a decision of the Refugee Division, which found the appellant excluded from the definition of Convention refugee by reason of section F(a) of Article 1 of The United Nations Convention Relating to the Status of Refugees because the Board found that there was serious reason to believe that the appellant had committed a crime against humanity. The Board proceeded directly to that finding and made no finding on the merits of the refugee claim. The appellant had admitted to killing civilians on two occasions when his military unit in Nicaragua encountered armed counter-revolutionaries. The Court noted that as a practical matter it would have been better had the Refugee Division dealt with the merits of the claim as well as the applicability of the exclusion. The Court noted that if the claim was well-founded but for the application of the exclusion and if it were found on appeal that the exclusion had been wrongly applied to the appellant, then the Court could have made the necessary declaration without requiring the Refugee Division to deal with the matter again. The Court found that, on the particular facts and circumstances of this case, the appellant was a soldier engaged in an action against an armed enemy and that his actual participation in the killing of innocent civilians fell short of a crime against humanity. The Court indicated that it did not wish to be understood as saying that the killing of civilians by a soldier while engaged in an action against an armed enemy could never amount to a war crime or a crime against humanity, each case will depend on its own individual facts and circumstances.

Karthikesu v. Canada (Minister of Employment & Immigration) (1994), 81 F.T.R. 119 — The Court declined to review a negative decision of the CRDD. The onus was on the claimants, once the issue of an internal flight alternative (IFA) was raised, to demonstrate, on a balance of probabilities that there is a serious possibility of persecution in the area suggested as the IFA.

The evidence of a Toronto psychiatrist to the effect that the applicants suffered from Post Traumatic Stress Disorder was not of significant weight in determining whether there was an IFA available to the applicants. The fact that the disorder caused the applicants to be fearful of living anywhere in Sri Lanka could not be the basis for saying that it was unreasonable to expect the applicants to seek refuge in that part of their own country because, viewing the matter objectively, it did not appear that they would be in any danger in Colombo (the area suggested as an IFA).

Whether it is unreasonable for a claimant to seek the IFA is an objective test with the onus of proof resting on the claimant. It is not sufficient for a claimant simply to prefer to go to another country rather than to go to a safe part of their own country. In this case, the claimant had an unreasonable fear of living in what was, viewed objectively, a safe part of his own country. Accordingly, the application was dismissed.

Awale v. Canada (Minister of Employment & Immigration) (May 12, 1994), Doc. A-1083-92 (Fed. T.D.) — The applicant sought to review a negative determination of his refugee claim. The applicant was a citizen of Somalia and a member of a small, little-known clan. This clan was described as being neutral with respect to its position on the Barre regime. It came from a different heritage than the other clans, as evidenced, in part, by the lighter skin colour of its members. The applicant stated that the clan, including his family, were subject to harassment from all other clans in Somalia, including those loyal to and those opposed to the Barre regime. The applicant described instances of harassment and his evidence did not appear to be rejected.

It is trite law that in order to be well-founded, the applicant's fear must have both a subjective and objective component. There was nothing in the Board's decision to suggest that it doubted the applicant's credibility. If that was the case, then it must be said to have accepted the subjective element of the applicant's fear. However, there was no documentary evidence filed in the hearing to support the allegations of persecution. The Board's decision referred to only one piece of documentary evidence, which actually supported the allegation of persecution of other clans in Somalia. However, the applicant's clan was unique and therefore the evidence of the persecution of other clans cannot be said to be similar. The Board did not mention all of the documentary evidence, but it was admitted that there was nothing in that evidence concerning the applicant's clan. Without some objective evidence supporting the allegations of persecution of the applicant's clan, the Board was correct in stating that the applicant's fear was an indiscriminate fear and not a basis for Convention refugee status.

Ammery v. Canada (Secretary of State) (1994), 78 F.T.R. 73 — The applicant, a female citizen of Iran, sought to set aside a negative determination of her refugee claim. The applicant, in her evidence before the tribunal, claimed that she and other members of her family were being harassed and persecuted because of the activities of her step-father. Even though it appeared that the tribunal erred in its consideration of the meaning of the word "persecution", the Court would not have intervened if the tribunal's assessment of the evidence was made by proceeding with a careful analysis of the evidence adduced and a proper balancing of the various elements contained in that evidence. This did not happen in this case and thus the decision of the tribunal could not stand on that basis alone.

The tribunal also suggested that there was no documentary evidence to suggest that Iranian citizens were persecuted by their government because of their relatives' anti-government activities. This conclusion was not correct; there were two references in the documentary evidence on this question. Notwithstanding that fact, the Court was of the view that where there is evidence of the applicant, accepted as credible by the tribunal, even the absence of supporting documentary evidence is not a ground for finding a failure to establish good grounds for a fear of persecution.

Roble v. Canada (Minister of Employment & Immigration) (1994), 169 N.R. 125 (Fed. C.A.) — The appellant was born in Somalia and claimed a fear of persecution, if he were returned, at the hands of the National Security Service, which had been the security service used by former President Mohammed Siad Barre. The Board found as a fact that the National Security Service was no longer a factor in Somalia because the Barre government had been toppled.

The appellant submitted that when the political situation in a country is unstable and uncertain and an interim government is not yet in control, it is inappropriate for the appellant to be required to seek the protection of his state. There are situations in which the political and military circumstances in a country at a given time are such that it is impossible to speak of a government with control of the territory and able to provide effective protection. The non-existence of a government is not an obstacle to an application for refugee status. However, this statement of the law only applies to cases where a claimant has demonstrated a prospective risk of persecution based on one of the grounds enumerated in the definition. The finding that the agent of persecution — the NSS — was no longer a factor meant that the inability of the state to protect the appellant was not in itself sufficient basis for his claim.

Fathi-Rad v. Canada (Secretary of State) (1994), 77 F.T.R. 41 — The applicant sought review of a decision determining that she was not a Convention refugee. The applicant was a fifty-one year old woman whose family supported the pre-revolutionary government and the People's Democratic Front in Iran. The applicant was arrested, detained and questioned approximately once every two months between 1985 and 1988 for her failure to conform to the Islamic dress code. In overruling the Board's decision, the Court concluded that the Islamic dress code in Iran was not a law of general application. The dress code applied only to women. It dictated the manner in which women must dress to comply with the religious beliefs of the governing regime and prescribed punishments for violation of that law. A law which specifically targets the manner in which women dress may not properly be characterized, as it was in this case, as a law of general application which applies to all citizens.

For this and other reasons the decision of the Board was set aside and the matter returned to a differently constituted panel for rehearing and redetermination.

Keer v. Canada (Minister of Employment & Immigration) (March 31, 1994), Doc. IMM-2671-93 (Fed. T.D.) — The applicant sought to review a negative decision of the CRDD. The Board concluded that the applicant did not demonstrate that the state of India was unable to protect him. The Court relied on *Ward v. Canada (Minister of Employment & Immigration)*, (sub nom. *Canada (Attorney General) v. Ward)* [1993] 2 S.C.R. 689 to the effect that clear and convincing confirmation of a state's inability to protect must be provided. The burden of adducing clear and convincing confirmation of India's inability to protect was on the applicant. The Court found that the conclusion of the Board that the applicant had not met the burden of proof was reasonable on the evidence and dismissed the application for judicial review.

Kochergo v. Canada (Minister of Employment & Immigration) (1994), 76 F.T.R. 128 — The applicants were a mother and son who claimed refugee status because of political opinion and membership in a particular social group. The mother was born in Argentina, moved to the U.S.S.R. with her parents and studied and taught there until 1967. She married a Cuban national and went to Cuba in 1967, where she worked at the University of Havana. One of the issues to be determined was whether the mother was still a citizen of Argentina. The Court followed the decision in *Bouianova v. Canada (Minister of Employment & Immigration)* (1993), 67 F.T.R. 74 to the effect that a refugee claimant must establish that he is unable or unwilling to avail himself of all of his countries of nationality if his claim is to be upheld. There was no evidence that the mother had ceased to be a citizen of Argentina. Accordingly, the Board did not err in determining that the mother's claim had to be analyzed by reference to Argentina. Accordingly, the application for judicial review was dismissed.

Abadjieva v. Canada (Minister of Employment & Immigration) (February 25, 1994), Doc. IMM-1654-93 (Fed. T.D.) — The applicant based her claim to refugee status on a well-founded fear of persecution if she were required to return to her country of citizenship, Bulgaria. The applicant in 1984 became aware of a fraudulent transaction involving the government. The fraudulent transaction touched the holder of a senior office in the Communist Party. Some years later, the applicant was summoned to the offices of the Security Service and threatened in the event that she disclose knowledge of the transaction. The threats directed by the Security Service officer were very serious. Where there was state complicity in the acts of persecution, the unwillingness of the applicant to attempt to avail herself of state protection was justified.

The Court further found that the Board misinstructed itself as to the test in respect of changed country circumstances. The Court quashed the decision of the CRDD and directed the matter back for a rehearing before a differently constituted panel.

Zhu v. Canada (Minister of Employment & Immigration) (January 28, 1994), Doc. A-1017-91 (Fed. C.A.) — The appellant smuggled two students in the pro-democracy movement out of China and into Hong Kong. According to his testimony, his motivation in part was the fact that his wife was a friend of one of the smuggled young women. The panel was in error in setting up an opposition between friendship and political motivation. The appellant's motives were mixed rather than conflicting. People frequently act out of mixed motives, and it is enough for the existence of political motivation that one of the motives was political. In this respect, although the appellant was not generally politically active, he had made a financial contribution to the pro-democracy movement. Accordingly, the appeal was allowed.

Rodriguez-Hernandez v. Canada (Secretary of State) (1994), 76 F.T.R. 107 — The applicant, a citizen of Cuba, claimed persecution on the basis of religion and political opinion. The applicant left Cuba for Canada while he was in possession of a valid travel permit, which allowed him to be absent for thirty days. In determining whether the applicant faced persecution for overstaying his exit visa, the Board considered that Cuban exit laws are of general application. This finding alone did not end the matter, however, for the law must still be examined to determine whether it is persecutory. One indication that a general law is persecutory is a penalty which is disproportionate to the offence. The Board did not err in concluding that the potential punishment for violation of the Cuban exit laws by the applicant did not amount to persecution. The onus was on the applicant to bring evidence before the Board of the punishment to be faced upon return and to demonstrate that the punishment is disproportionate to the offence. This onus had not been met, and the application for judicial review was dismissed.

Maarouf v. Canada (Minister of Employment & Immigration) (1993), [1994] 1 F.C. 723, 23 Imm. L.R. (2d) 163, 72 F.T.R. 6 — The applicant lived in both Lebanon and Kuwait before going to the United States to study and then coming to Canada and claiming refugee status. The Board concluded that the applicant had neither a country of nationality nor a country of former habitual residence. The Board found that Kuwait was not a country of former habitual residence. Even though the claimant lived in that state for most of his life, on the claimant's uncontradicted evidence, there was no way that he could return there. It was the claimant's evidence that Palestinians who left Kuwait prior to the Gulf War were not allowed to return. With respect to Lebanon, the Board found that the claimant only lived there for five years during his infancy and, that while he did visit Lebanon for a short period of time, there was no significant period of *de facto* residence.

The decision of the Board was quashed. The definition of country of former habitual residence should not be unduly restrictive so as to pre-empt the provision of surrogate shelter to a stateless person who has demonstrated a well-founded fear of persecution on any of the enumerated grounds in the definition. A country of former habitual residence should not be limited to the country where the claimant initially feared persecution. The claimant does not have to be legally able to return a country of former habitual residence as a denial of a right of return may in itself constitute an act of persecution by the state. The claimant must, however, have established a significant period of *de facto* residence in the country in question.

Kulanthavelu v. Canada (Minister of Employment & Immigration) (1993), 71 F.T.R. 129 — The CRDD determined that the applicant was not a Convention refugee. The applicant was a Tamil from Sri Lanka who, for most of his life before he came to Canada, lived in the Jaffna Region. The CRDD found that there was a reasonable possibility of persecution by the LTTE if the applicant were returned to the Jaffna area today, but found an internal flight alternative (IFA) in Colombo. The CRDD acknowledged the advice of the UNHCR with regard to IFA's available to Sri Lankan Tamils from the Jaffna area. The Court construed the UNHCR letter as indicating that for Tamils from Jaffna, relatives, duration of previous residence and past employment are factors which go to the question of whether it is objectively reasonable for a claimant to live in Colombo without fear of persecution. There is no requirement for the CRDD or the Court to follow the contents of a letter from the UNHCR of the type presented in this case if there is also specific evidence before the CRDD that supports an IFA.

The question of an IFA must be expressly raised at the hearing. In this case, there was no evidence that notice was given to the applicant in advance of the hearing that the issue of an IFA would be considered. Nor was there any indication on the face of the transcript that the issue was "expressly raised at the hearing", although it was referred to in passing by counsel for the applicant. For that reason alone the Court would have allowed the application. The Court went on to further conclude that the applicant had discharged the burden on him, through the evidence of the UNHCR letter and of his personal experiences in Colombo, of proving the serious possibility of persecution throughout the country. The application was allowed and the matter referred back to the CRDD for rehearing by a differently constituted panel.

Penate v. Canada (Minister of Employment & Immigration) (1993), 71 F.T.R. 171 — The applicant sought to review the denial of his refugee claim on the basis that he was excluded pursuant to Article I(F) of the Convention. One of the issues in the appeal was the test to be applied in assessing the relevance of changed country conditions to the applicant's wife's refugee claim. There are two separate procedures respecting refugee status which exist in the *Immigration Act*: (1) the granting of Convention refugee status to someone, by the IRB, on application by that individual and with respect to which the individual has the burden of proof; and (2) the removal of that status from someone, by the Board, upon application by the Minister and with respect to which the Minister bears the burden of proof.

This latter procedure is provided for in section 69.2 of the Act. The criteria described by Professor Hathaway in his text *The Law of Refugee Status* are framed by reference to the cessation of status, that is to the revoking of status after it has been granted and with respect to which the Minister, and not the individual, has the burden of proof. When the question is whether status will be granted, CRDD panels are required to weigh the evidence of changed country conditions in the balance with all the other evidence before them in assessing the applicant's claim.

The panel did not err in its approach. It weighed the evidence of changed country conditions as one aspect of the relevant evidence. Accordingly, the application was dismissed.

Megag v. Canada (Minister of Employment & Immigration) (1993), 71 F.T.R. 64 — The applicants sought review of a decision denying them refugee status. They were citizens of Somalia who left there when the regime of Siad Barre was in power. This regime persecuted members of the applicant's tribe. The Refugee Division concluded that conditions in the north of Somalia are such that it would not have been unreasonable for the applicants to seek refuge there.

Counsel for the applicants suggested that the Refugee Division had a legal duty to do more than make an unsupported conclusion as to reasonableness. The applicant had the onus of showing that northern Somalia is not a reasonable internal flight alternative (IFA). The applicant's counsel referred to the instability in the north and the potential threats from other clans. Instability is not the only test of reasonableness. In this case, the applicant's entire family was in the north of Somalia and her uncle was a high-ranking official in that area. On that basis the conclusion that northern Somalia was not an unreasonable IFA was founded in the evidence. The Court referred to *Ahmed v. Canada (Minister of Employment & Immigration)* (1993), 23 Imm. L.R. (2d) 82 and *Akubakar v. Canada (Minister of Employment & Immigration)* (1993), 67 F.T.R. 313 as cases in which the Refugee Division panels failed to consider evidence adduced by the applicants as to why northern Somalia was not a reasonable IFA. Here, little was said by the applicant on this question. Accordingly, the application was dismissed.

Thirunavukkarasu v. Canada (Minister of Employment & Immigration) (1993), [1994] 1 F.C. 589, 22 Imm. L.R. (2d) 241, 109 D.L.R. (4th) 682, 163 N.R. 232 (Fed. C.A.) — The appellant was a citizen of Sri Lanka and a Tamil. The appellant's claim that he faced serious risk to his life in the north of Sri Lanka was accepted but his claim for refugee status was refused on the basis that there was an internal flight alternative (IFA) available to him.

The Court had occasion to review the law on the question of IFA's in this judgment.

The notion of an IFA is not a legal defence and it is not a legal doctrine. It is a convenient, short-hand way of describing a fact situation in which a person may be in danger of persecution in one part of a country, but not in another. The idea of an IFA is inherent in the definition of a Convention refugee; it is not something separate. The definition requires that claimants have a well-founded fear of persecution which renders them unwilling or unable to return to their home country. If claimants are able to seek refuge within their own country, there is no basis for finding that they are unable or unwilling to avail themselves of the protection of that country.

The burden of proof with respect to an IFA is on the claimant. The claimant must show, on a balance of probabilities, a serious possibility of persecution throughout the country, including the area which is alleged to afford an IFA.

There is an obligation on the Minister or the Board to warn a claimant that the IFA issue will be raised. If the possibility of an IFA is raised, the claimant must demonstrate that there is a serious possibility of persecution in the area alleged to constitute an IFA. A refugee claimant enjoys the benefit of the privilege of natural justice in hearings before the Refugee Division. A basic and well-established component of the right to be heard includes notice of the case to be met. The purpose of this notice is to allow a person to prepare an adequate response. The right to notice of the case against the claimant is acutely important where the claimant may be called upon to provide evidence to show that no valid IFA exists in response to an allegation by the Minister. Therefore, neither the Minister nor the Refugee Division may spring the allegation of an IFA upon a complainant without notice an IFA will be in issue at the hearing.

A claimant must seek and resort to an IFA if it is not unreasonable to do so, in the circumstances of the individual claimant. This aspect of the test is a flexible one, that takes into account the particular situation of the claimant and the particular country involved. It is an objective test and the onus of proof rests on the claimant on this issue, just as it does with all other aspects of a refugee claim. Consequently, if there is a safe haven for claimants in their own country, where they would be free of persecution, they are expected to avail themselves of it unless they can show that it is objectively unreasonable for them to do so. It is not a question of whether the IFA is more or less appealing to the claimant than a new country. The question is whether, given the persecution in the claimant's part of the country, it is objectively reasonable to expect him or her to seek safety in a different part of that country before seeking a haven in Canada or elsewhere. Stated another way, the question to be answered is, would it be unduly harsh to expect the claimant, who is being persecuted in one part of his country, to move to another less hostile part of the country before seeking refugee status abroad?

An IFA cannot be speculative or theoretical. The alternative place of safety must be realistically accessible to the claimant. Any barriers getting there should be reasonably surmountable. The claimant cannot be required to encounter great physical danger or undergo undue hardship in travelling there or staying there. For example, claimants should not be required to cross battle lines where fighting is going on at great risk to their lives in order to reach a place of safety. Similarly, claimants should not be compelled to hide out in isolated regions of their country, like a cave in the mountains, or in a desert or in a jungle, if those are the only areas of internal safety. Neither is it enough for refugee claimants to say that they do not like the weather in a safe area, or that they have no friends or relatives there, or that they may not be able to find suitable work there. If it is objectively reasonable in these latter situations to live in those places, without fear of persecution, then an IFA exists and the claimant is not a refugee.

It is not a matter of a claimant's convenience or the attractiveness of the IFA, but whether one should be expected to make do in that location, before travelling half-way around the world to seek a safe haven in another country.

The finding of an IFA, in this case, by the IRB was not sustained. The Country Profile of Sri Lanka and the Amnesty International Reports on the country did not show "quite clearly" that Tamils were safe in the south west of the country. The reports, at the time this case was argued, spoke of several violent incidents in which Tamils were persecuted by the Sri Lankan government in the southwest in retaliation for the activities of the LTTE and other Tamil groups. Accordingly, there was no IFA for this appellant and the appeal was allowed.

Pathmakanthan v. Canada (Minister of Employment & Immigration) (1993), 23 Imm. L.R. (2d) 76, 71 F.T.R. 154 — The applicants sought to review a decision that they were not Convention refugees. The Court analyzed the principles to be applied when determining that a claimant has an internal flight alternative (IFA). The first step involves a determination on the availability of the IFA. There may be an IFA if there is no evidence particular to the applicant which would lead one to conclude that there was a likelihood that the authorities would seek out the applicant. The tribunal must always examine the circumstances particular to the applicant to determine whether there is a serious possibility of this individual applicant being persecuted elsewhere in the country.

The second step in the analysis involves the determination of the reasonableness of the IFA. The reasonableness of the IFA is a question which must be determined independently from the question of availability and must take into consideration all of the circumstances of the individual applicant. In this case, the tribunal relied on the fact that the Federal Court had found in another case (*Rasaratnam v. Canada (Minister of Employment & Immigration)* (1991), [1992] 1 F.C. 706, 140 N.R. 138 that Colombo was a reasonable IFA for that applicant, therefore Colombo must be a reasonable IFA for the applicants in this case. This constituted a serious error. The tribunal must consider all of the circumstances of the applicants in its determination that an IFA is reasonable. A finding of fact based on the findings in another case is not sufficient. The decision of the CRDD panel was quashed.

Sinnathamby v. Canada (Minister of Employment & Immigration) (1993), 23 Imm. L.R. (2d) 32, 70 F.T.R. 116 — The applicant was a Jaffna Tamil from Sri Lanka. In rejecting his claim for refugee status, the Board excluded extortion from the definition of persecution. It was not open to the Board to exclude extortion from the indicia of persecution without looking into the reason for the extortion and the motivation of the applicant in paying the extortion fee. The decision of the Board was overturned and the matter was remitted back to the IRB for a hearing before a differently constituted panel.

Osoble v. Canada (Minister of Employment & Immigration) (1993), 69 F.T.R. 184 — This was an application to review a negative determination of the applicant's refugee claim. The applicant was from Somalia and based his fear of persecution on his religious convictions, political opinion and membership in a particular social group.

The test for applicants who are from a country where a civil war is going on was set out in *Salibian v. Canada (Minister of Employment & Immigration)*, [1990] 3 F.C. 250, 11 Imm. L.R. (2d) 165, 73 D.L.R. (4th) 551, 113 N.R. 123 (Fed. C.A.). A situation of civil war is not an obstacle to a claim provided the fear felt is not that felt indiscriminately by all citizens as a consequence of the civil war, but a fear felt by the applicant himself or herself, or by a group of which he or she is associated, or on account of a risk of persecution based on one of the reasons stated in the definition.

Hlavaty v. Canada (Minister of Employment & Immigration) (1993), 22 Imm. L.R. (2d) 176, 69 F.T.R. 259 — This was an application to review a decision denying refugee status. The applicant lived in Trencin. He was subjected to harassment, in his early years, for being a Slovak and not being a member of the Communist Party. He joined the Slovak National Party, whose primary goal was an independent state. The party was attacked in the media for trying to break up what was then the country of Czechoslovakia. The claimant, who was found to be generally credible, described incidents of persecution.

The applicant contended that the tribunal could not have reached the decision it did if it had genuinely considered a document entitled "Reforming the Judiciary". The tribunal, in fact, quoted from a significant number of documentary sources in its evaluation of the conditions in Slovakia. It was open to it to conclude the way it did and the fact that it did not specifically refer to the document in question did not constitute an error because it was not apparent from the decision that the tribunal had failed to consider this piece of evidence.

The Board considered that there had been a change in circumstances since the applicant fled Czechoslovakia in November 1990. Where a change in circumstances occurs prior to the determination of a claim, this change must be considered by the Board when assessing the objective basis to the claimant's fear. The nature and extent of the change in circumstances must be "significant", "material", "substantial" and "meaningful and effective".

The tribunal held that there was a valid internal flight alternative (IFA) available to the applicant. The determination of whether there is an IFA is integral to the determination of refugee status. The Court adopted the test set out in *Rasaratnam v. Canada (Minister of Employment & Immigration)* (1991), [1992] 1 F.C. 706, 140 N.R. 138 (Fed. C.A.) and added the requirement in *Ahmed v. Canada (Minister of Employment & Immigration)* (1993), 156 N.R. 221 (Fed. C.A.), which required that the claimant find a secure substitute home without undue hardship.

The material before the tribunal showed that the applicant could avoid the persecution he suffered if he moved to another area of Slovakia. There was no evidence to the effect that the state was in any way implicated in the actions of the police in Trencin, which were part of the evidence of persecution.

The application for judicial review was dismissed.

Mahmoud v. Canada (Minister of Employment & Immigration) (1993), 69 F.T.R. 100 — This was an application for judicial review of a decision of the CRDD refusing a claim for refugee status. The case dealt with what is meant by a change in circumstances. The Court held that in order to make out a change in circumstances the change must be shown to be of proven durability, and adopted the test of Professor Hathaway in *The Law of Refugee Status* (Toronto: Butterworths, 1991) at 200–203. The Court disagreed with two other Trial Division decisions on the question of proven durability, specifically *Boateng v. Canada (Minister of Employment & Immigration)* (1993), 65 F.T.R. 81 and *Tawfik v. Canada (Minister of Employment & Immigration)* (1993), 26 Imm. L.R. (2d) 148 (Fed. T.D.). In most situations some reasonable period of time must go by in order to permit the trier of facts to assess the changing conditions and their consequences, if any. In this case, a transitional government was established in Ethiopia in July of 1991 and the Board, at the applicant's hearing in August, 1991, concluded that there had been a change in circumstances in Ethiopia,which were of an enduring nature and which rendered the applicant's fear of persecution no longer well-founded. The Court also declined to follow the Trial Division decision in *Villalta v. Canada (Solicitor General)* (1993), 68 F.T.R. 304 on the degree of proof required. The decision of the Board regarding the change in circumstance in Ethiopia did not meet the requirements of the three-pronged Hathaway test and accordingly, was set aside.

Petrescu v. Canada (Solicitor General) (sub nom Petrescu v. Canada (Solliciteur général)) (1993), 73 F.T.R. 1. — The applicant was a Romanian claiming refugee status on account of his political opinion and membership in a particular social group. The Court elaborated on what was meant by a reasonable possibility of persecution and referred to *Ponniah v. Canada (Minister of Employment & Immigration)* (1991), 13 Imm. L.R. (2d) 241, 132 N.R. 32 (Fed. C.A.):

> "Good grounds" or "reasonable chance" is defined in *Adjei* as occupying the field between upper and lower limits; it is less than a 50% chance (*i.e.* a probability), but more than a minimal or mere possibility. There is no intermediate ground: what falls between the two limits is "good grounds".
>
> If the claimant, as the Board said, "... may face slightly more than a mere possibility ..." of persecution, he had crossed the lower limit and had made his case of "good grounds" or a "reasonable chance" for fearing persecution.

In this case, it was said that the claimant, when he argued that he feared a repetition of what he had suffered if he returned home and that he was in danger of losing his liberty or being the victim of a staged accident, did not persuade the panel. The Refugee Division imposed too high a standard of proof. Accordingly, the decision of the Refugee Division was quashed.

Villalta v. Canada (Solicitor General) (1993), 68 F.T.R. 304 — The applicant arrived in Canada from El Salvador and claimed refugee status on the ground that he feared forced conscription into the army and he feared harassment by the guerillas who made efforts to require him to support or join them. He strongly disagreed with the methods used by the army and would not participate in it. While originally sympathetic to the guerillas, he could not accept their methods. On December 31, 1991 a peace treaty was signed by the guerillas and the government. This treaty was the result of twenty months of UN mediated negotiations. The applicant was found not to be a Convention refugee largely based upon the changed country conditions in El Salvador.

When determining whether status has been lost, one must ascertain that the reasons for the fear have ceased to exist. When determining whether status should be granted, changed country conditions, even those stopping short of cessation, is one factor among many which can be taken into account in determining whether the individual faces a reasonable chance of persecution. If the conditions set out in section 2(2) exist, there is absolutely no doubt that the individual is not entitled to status. However, this does not mean that in order to take changed country conditions into account when determining whether to grant status, that the panel must first go through the conceptual exercise of subtracting changed conditions from their analysis and then, after making that analysis, move on to assess the significance of the changed country conditions.

The tribunal did not commit an error by taking into account changed country conditions without first determining whether the requirements of cessation under section 2(2)(e) were met. Accordingly, the application was dismissed.

Abdulle v. Canada (Minister of Employment & Immigration) (1993), 67 F.T.R. 229 — The applicant applied for judicial review pursuant to section 18.1 of the *Federal Court Act* seeking an order setting aside a decision that the applicant was not a Convention refugee. The applicant was a citizen of Somalia and a member of one of the two warring clans in that country. The Board held that the applicant's fear of persecution, based on membership in one of the warring clans, was not well-founded. There was no doubt that the applicant stood a reasonable chance of persecution upon her return to Somalia, as do all Somalians who live in Mogadishu. However, the applicant was unable to establish that she was in a different position from that of all Somalians in the capital city. The evidence did not establish that the applicant and her group would be singled out because of the conflict involving the two subclans. Accordingly, the application for judicial review was dismissed.

Kassim v. Canada (Minister of Employment & Immigration) (1993), 67 F.T.R. 126 — This application was brought to review a decision holding that the applicants were not Convention refugees. The fears of the applicants lacked an objectively valid basis, owing in part to changes in the political climate in Kenya. Changes in circumstances in the country of origin occurring prior to the hearing must be considered by the Board, since the Board must determine whether the claimant has good grounds to fear persecution in the future. The inquiry into a change in circumstances falls to be determined on a case by case, or country by country, basis. A change of circumstances is defined as a significant change occurring in the political or social situation in the country which the claimant has been forced to flee. The factor of recentness is not necessarily determinative in and of itself. The central issue to be determined by the Board is whether the change of circumstances is sufficient in terms of its effect on the social and political climate of the country of origin, given the basis of the fear on which the claimant relies. No change in government had occurred in Kenya. The lamentable human rights record of the regime in power was longstanding. The repeal of a section of the Kenyan Constitution was not sufficient to constitute a clear indication of the meaningful and effective change which is required to negate the objective basis of the applicants' claims. Accordingly, the applications were allowed.

Brar v. Canada (Minister of Employment & Immigration) (1993), 68 F.T.R. 57 — The applicant was a Sikh from the Punjab who unsuccessfully claimed refugee status on the grounds of religion, political opinion and membership in a particular social group. The Board had concluded that the applicant did not have a well-founded fear of persecution. The detention of the applicant for short periods while dignitaries were in his home village was consistent with the policy of preventive detention and represented an effort on the part of the government of the Punjab to prevent problems resulting from the potential actions of the organization of which the applicant was a member. The determination of whether or not an individual's treatment constitutes persecution is one of fact. National security and peace and order are valid social objectives for any state. Most states have measures which provide for the derogation of civil rights temporarily in time of emergency. This derogation of civil rights does not necessarily amount to persecution. Accordingly, the finding that the treatment accorded to the applicant did not amount to persecution could not be said to have been either perverse or erroneous. Accordingly, the application was dismissed.

Chen v. Canada (Solicitor General) (1993), 68 F.T.R. 9 — The CRDD found that the applicant was not a Convention refugee. At the opening of the hearing before the CRDD, counsel for the applicant introduced documentary evidence relating to a demonstration in front of the Chinese Consulate in Toronto that took place in December, 1990 or early 1991. Some of the photographic evidence apparently included pictures of the applicant, showing him to be a participant. On the final page of the CRDD decision it referred to this material, erroneously characterized the translations as uncertified, and then concluded that since there was no further reference either in the oral testimony of the claimant or in counsel's submission to this matter, the claimant had abandoned his claim to be determined as a refugee *sur place*. Notwithstanding the fact that neither the applicant nor his counsel chose to take advantage of the opportunity provided by their appearance before the CRDD to pursue this aspect of the claim, the CRDD, when it recognized the documentary evidence in question as representing a basis for a possible *sur place* claim, was obliged, either at the close of the hearing or at a later date, to invite the applicant in specific terms to either make representations on the issue or abandon that aspect of the claim.

Accordingly, the decision of the CRDD was quashed and the matter referred back for rehearing and redetermination as it relates to the *sur place* elements of the claim or a separate *sur place* claim itself. The rehearing and redetermination was to be carried out by a differently constituted panel.

Kahlon v. King (1993), 66 F.T.R. 219 — The CRDD determined that the applicant was not a Convention refugee because a viable internal flight alternative (IFA) existed. The applicant was a citizen of India who feared persecution in his native Punjab State. The CRDD accepted as a fact the assertion that it was unrealistic for the applicant to consider a return to the Punjab. The risk of persecution, if he were to return to that state, was not in question, but the CRDD found that there existed a viable IFA. The criteria relevant to an IFA were reviewed by the Federal Court of Appeal in *Rasaratnam v. Canada (Minister of Employment & Immigration)*, [1992] 1 F.C. 706, 140 N.R. 138 (Fed. C.A.). The IFA concept is inherent in the Convention refugee definition. The Board must be satisfied on a balance of probabilities that there is no serious possibility of the claimant being persecuted in that part of the country to which it finds an IFA exists. By definition a Convention refugee must be a refugee from a country, not from some subdivision or region of a country. Therefore, a claimant cannot be a Convention refugee if there is an IFA. Whether or not there is an IFA is integral to the determination of whether an applicant is or is not a refugee. The CRDD erred in failing to take into account the situations of individuals who were similarly situated to the applicant. It was not sufficient to take into account Sikhs in general living in India outside the Punjab or all Sikh men living in India outside the Punjab. The question before the tribunal was whether there was a serious possibility of the applicant being persecuted elsewhere in India. Accordingly, the decision of the CRDD was set aside and the matter referred back for rehearing before a differently constituted panel.

Chan v. Canada (Minister of Employment & Immigration), 20 Imm. L.R. (2d) 181, [1993] 3 F.C. 675, 156 N.R. 279 (Fed. C.A.), affirmed [1995] 3 S.C.C. 593, 128 D.L.R. (4th) 213, 187 N.R. 321 — This was an appeal with leave from a decision of the Convention Refugee Determination Division of the Immigration and Refugee Board deciding that the appellant was not a Convention Refugee.

The appellant was a citizen of the People's Republic of China (PRC). During the cultural revolution the appellant's family was persecuted due to his father's background as a landowner. During the students' pro-democracy demonstrations in 1989 the appellant expressed his support of the movement by giving food and drink to the students from his restaurant in Guangzhou Province. After the students' movement was crushed by the authorities and the appellant voluntarily reported his pro-democracy activities to the Public Security Bureau (PSB), officers visited his restaurant at least thirteen times, interrogating him, his staff and his customers. In November, 1989 the appellant's wife gave birth to a second child. When the PSB learned of this birth, they accused the appellant of violating the birth control policy of the PRC. Officers visited his home on a number of occasions after the birth of his child. The appellant was advised that either he or his wife would have to undergo sterilization. The appellant agreed to be sterilized but fled the PRC before the operation took place. The appellant claimed that after his departure his family continued to be harassed for violating the one child policy.

There were three decisions given by the Court, namely: the majority (Heald J.A. and Desjardins J.A.) dismissed the appeal; the minority (Mahoney J.A.) would have allowed the appeal.

Heald J.A. was not convinced on the evidence that the appellant had a well-founded fear of persecution and this determination would normally have been sufficient to dispose of the appeal. However, His Lordship went on to discuss the meaning of the phrase "particular social group" and "political opinion" in his judgment. The particular social group was defined to be parents in China with more than one child, who disagree with forced sterilization. This group was found by Heald J.A. not to be encompassed by any of the categories identified by the Supreme Court of Canada in the *Ward* decision (*Ward v. Canada (Minister of Employment & Immigration)* (1993), 20 Imm. L.R. (2d) 85, [1993] 2 S.C.R. 689). This group was found to be defined solely by the fact that its members face a particular form of persecutory treatment. Membership in the group was dictated by the finding of persecution. This logic reversed the statutory definition and voided enumerated grounds of content. The appellant's fear stemmed from what he did and not from what he was.

Disagreement with the one child policy is a political statement. There was no evidence that persons who simply voiced their opposition to this policy or to forced sterilization were not tolerated. On the question of whether the appellant who had breached the policy and failed to submit to the resulting demand for sterilization faced a well-founded fear of persecution, Heald J.A. answered in the negative. The persecutory treatment emanated not from a refusal to submit to sterilization, but from a breach of the policy. There was no indication that a breach of the one child policy and a reluctance to undergo sterilization would be perceived by the central government or the local authorities as anything more than a breach of a law and a reluctance to undergo the ensuing penalty. The one child policy is well within the jurisdiction of the Chinese government and there was a plethora of documentary evidence which articulated the rationale for this policy in China. Sanctions, in general, imposed for a breach of the policy must be accepted. A finding of persecution would have to be based uniquely on an abhorrence of the penalty. In other words the persecution alone motivates the determination of refugee status. Heald J.A. found that the definition of Convention refugee did not permit such a conclusion.

Desjardins J.A. agreed in the result and noted that with respect to the phrase "particular social group" what links the members of the group together must be so fundamental that it cannot be changed and if it were to be changed, would destroy the person as a person. The unchangeable characteristic of a particular social group must be distinguished from the basic human right which the group might decide to defend. The innate characteristic must be so strong a factor that it makes a group of individuals what they are and it must exist independently of what they are fighting for. The appellant was one of a number of persons who, individually, had resisted the one child policy and, like the others of his category, faced the general sanction, namely forced sterilization. This was not a group that was affiliated in a fundamental way so as to qualify as a particular social group. The group of which the appellant claimed to be a member was cognizable by the decision of the local Chinese authorities to use forced sterilization as a means of enforcing government policy. Thus, what linked the group together was an external factor and this was insufficient to meet the definition of the term particular social group.

With respect to the ground of "political opinion", Desjardins J.A. accepted that any opinion on any matter related to state affairs expressed or imputed to a claimant may constitute the basis for a claim under political opinion. Her Lordship, however, was unable to infer that the local authorities would impute to the appellant a political opinion in this case on account of his resistance to a general government policy. The evidence showed that there was continuing popular resistance to family planning in China and that birth rates soared the moment the pressure was eased. Her Lordship noted that the treatment, in the case at bar, related to forced sterilization. The Court assumed that this was carried out through normal procedures currently in use by those who voluntarily opt for this procedure elsewhere, including Canada. What was objected to was the absence of consent. Her Lordship concluded that, unless amended, the *Convention Relating to the Status of Refugees* would not cover violations of human rights imposed by local authorities in the pursuit of what the record showed is a legitimate state objective, namely population control.

Mahoney J.A. dissented and found this case undistinguishable from *Cheung v. Canada (Minister of Employment & Immigration)* (1993), 19 Imm. L.R. (2d) 81, [1993] 2 F.C. 314 (Fed. C.A.). He further found that none of the reasons which would justify a Court departing from its previous decisions were present in this case and that, therefore, *Cheung* had to be followed. Thus, the appellant could not be said not to belong to a particular social group. Further, he was in profound disagreement with the notion that the legitimacy of population control excluded persecution in pursuit of it from the Convention refugee definition.

Ahmed v. Canada (Minister of Employment & Immigration) (1993), 156 N.R. 221 (Fed. C.A.) — The reasons of the IRB must be read as a whole and must be sufficient to satisfy a review Court that the panel has not misdirected itself as to the essential requirements of the principles involved and the meaning of the legal concepts that come into play.

The appellant, a citizen of Bangladesh, based his claim for refugee status on his political opinion and membership in a particular social group. His evidence was accepted as clear, consistent and credible. The tribunal found that the claimant was not in danger in a village a relatively short distance away from his own and, further, that the change in government in

Bangladesh meant that the claimant could not, at the time of the hearing, have a fear of persecution which could be said to be well-founded.

Counsel for the respondent Minister maintained that these were findings of fact for which support could be found in the evidence and with which, therefore, the Court should not interfere. This was not taken to be a wholly satisfactory answer. The two grounds were not only mere findings of fact drawn directly from the evidence. In both cases the evidence had to be interpreted and inferences drawn. The mere fact that the appellant lived a certain time without significant problems in a neighbouring village did not justify the conclusion that an Internal Flight Alternative existed. Further, the mere fact that there was change in government was not sufficient to meet the requirements of a change in circumstances.

The nature and agents of persecution feared by the appellant did not suggest that the persecution would be confined to a particular area of the country. Further, the mere declarations of a four-month old government to the effect that it had favoured the establishment of law and order could hardly be seen as a clear indication of a meaningful and effective change. Accordingly, the appeal was allowed and the matter sent back for reconsideration by a differently constituted panel.

Rodionova v. Canada (Minister of Employment & Immigration) (1993), 66 F.T.R. 66 — The CRDD determined that the applicant was not a Convention refugee. The CRDD found that the applicant belonged to no definable social group for which she might fear persecution.

The Court concluded that a woman can belong to a particular social group by being in danger of domestic violence without regard to whether the state permits, condones, acquiesces in, or fails to prevent such violence. Belonging to such a social group was simply a threshold test for establishing refugee status. If a claimant belongs to such a social group, she must still show that she fears persecution approved, permitted, or not effectively combatted by the state in her country of origin. In this case, this latter question was not specifically addressed by the panel hearing the refugee claim and accordingly, the Court could not conclude that the panel had decided that there was no reasonable fear of persecution.

The matter was therefore referred back to the CRDD for reconsideration.

Ioda v. Canada (Minister of Employment & Immigration) (1993), 21 Imm. L.R. (2d) 294, 65 F.T.R. 166 — The applicant sought judicial review of a decision which found her not to be a Convention refugee.

The tribunal found that there was only a "mere risk" that the claimant might be a victim of persecution. The use of the concept "mere risk" as the appropriate basis for a finding was not correct. The claimant must establish, in order to demonstrate his or her fear of persecution as a valid basis, that he or she faces a "reasonable chance" or "good grounds" or "serious possibility" of persecution, should he or she be returned to the country of origin. A reasonable chance of persecution is anything more than a mere or minimal possibility with no intermediate ground.

Zolfagharkhani v. Canada (Minister of Employment & Immigration), 20 Imm. L.R. (2d) 1, [1993] 3 F.C. 540, 155 N.R. 311 — This was an appeal of a decision denying Convention refugee status to the appellant.

The appellant was an Iranian citizen who had served twenty-seven months in the Iranian military during the Iran/Iraq war. Subsequent to his discharge, the Revolutionary Guards requested him to report for a further six months of military service as a paramedic. The appellant reported for a one-month training course and during the last week of training discovered the apparent intention of his government to engage in chemical warfare against the Kurds. His conscience being troubled by this, he deserted and fled the country.

No issue was raised as to conscientious objection in relation to war in general. Since the appellant had no objection to serving in an active capacity in the Iranian military in the Iran/Iraq war, the issue as to conscientious objection relates solely to participation in chemical warfare.

The probable use of chemical weapons, which the Board accepted as a fact, was clearly judged by the international community to be contrary to basic rules of human conduct. Consequently, the ordinary Iranian conscription law of general application, as applied to a conflict in which Iran intended to use chemical weapons, amounted to persecution for political opinion.

The Court set forth the following general propositions relating to the status of an ordinary law of general application in determining the question of persecution:

1. The statutory definition of Convention refugee makes the intent or any principal effect of an ordinary law of general application, rather than the motivation of the claimant, relevant to the existence of persecution.

2. The neutrality of an ordinary law of general application, vis-à-vis the five grounds for refugee status, must be judged objectively by Canadian tribunals and courts when required.

3. In such consideration, an ordinary law of general application, even in non-democratic societies, should be given a presumption of validity and neutrality, and the onus should be on a claimant, as is generally the case in refugee cases, to show that the laws are either inherently or for some other reason persecutory.

4. It will not be enough for the claimant to show that a particular regime is generally oppressive, but rather that the law in question is persecutory in relation to a Convention ground.

The Court referred to *Abarca v. Canada (Minister of Employment & Immigration)*, Doc. No. W-86-4030-W, decided March 21, 1986, to the effect that a conscientious objector from El Salvador was a Convention refugee on the basis of political opinion because he probably would have been forced to participate in violent acts of persecution against non-combatant civilians, which conduct is contrary to recognized basic international principles of human rights. The Court also referred to *Cruz v. Canada (Minister of Employment & Immigration)* (1988), 10 Imm. L.R. (2d) 47 (Imm. App. Bd.), involving a deserter from the Mexican army. In the instant case there could be no doubt that the appellant's refusal to participate in the military action against the Kurds would be treated by the Iranian government as the expression of an unacceptable political opinion.

The appeal was allowed and the matter returned to a differently constituted panel for reconsideration not inconsistent with the reasons of the Court.

Bouianova v. Canada (Minister of Employment & Immigration) (1993), 67 F.T.R. 74 — The applicant was born in Komi, near Moscow in the former USSR. The applicant's place of birth is located in what is now Russia. Before coming to Canada the applicant had lived in Latvia for 14 years. The applicant claimed a well-founded fear of persecution in Latvia based on discrimination against ethnic Russians in that country. Latvia had been her country of habitual residence. The panel found that the applicant was a citizen of the Russian Federation and that there was no evidence that she had a well-founded fear of persecution in Russia. In order to become a Russian citizen, all that the applicant had to do was make an application to the Russian Embassy requesting Russian citizenship and have her USSR passport so stamped. The applicant did not do this and her counsel in this proceeding sought to claim that she was therefore stateless.

Statelessness was not an option for the applicant. The condition of not having a country of nationality must be one that is beyond the power of the applicant to control. Otherwise, a person could claim statelessness merely by renouncing his or her former citizenship.

Ward v. Canada (Minister of Employment & Immigration) (1993), 103 D.L.R. (4th) 1 (S.C.C.) — The appellant, Patrick Francis Ward, was born in Northern Ireland in 1955. He joined the Irish National Liberation Army (INLA) in 1983 as a volunteer. The INLA is a para-military organization, more violent than the Irish Republican Army (IRA) with a military-like hierarchy and strict discipline. Ward's first task as a member of the INLA was to assist in guarding two of the organization's hostages. After Ward commenced his duties the INLA ordered the hostages executed. Ward underwent what he described as "a predicament of moral conscience" and released the hostages without revealing himself to the INLA. Sometime later the police let slip to an INLA member that one of their own had assisted the hostages in their escape. Ward was court-martialled and sentenced to death, however he managed to escape. Ward was charged in the hostage incident and while he was in police custody the INLA kidnapped his wife and children to prevent him from becoming an informant.

Ward was sentenced to 3 years in prison. He did not become an informant and never publicly admitted having released the hostages. Toward the end of his prison sentence Ward obtained a Republic of Ireland passport and on his release entered Canada as a visitor in December, 1985. He claimed refugee status in 1986. Under the procedures that were in effect at that time the Minister determined that Ward was not a Convention refugee. Ward applied for redetermination of his claim to the Immigration Appeal Board, as it was then known. The Board allowed the redetermination and found Ward to be a Convention refugee.

The Attorney General brought an application in the Federal Court to set aside the Board's decision, which decision was successful. The result of the Federal Court decision was that the appellant's case was referred back to the Immigration Appeal Board for reconsideration.

The Board again found Ward to be a Convention refugee. The Minister appealed the Board's decision to the Federal Court of Appeal, which set aside the Board's decision and the appellant. Ward then appealed that decision to the Supreme Court of Canada.

International refugee law was formulated to serve as a back-up to the protection one expects from the state of which an individual is a national. It was meant to come into play only in situations when that protection is unavailable, and then only in certain situations. The international community intended that persecuted individuals be required to approach their home state for protection before the responsibility of other states became engaged.

Ward was not only a national of the Republic of Ireland, but also of Great Britain. The onus of proof in a refugee proceeding is on the claimant and it is for the claimant to show a well-founded fear of persecution in all countries of which the claimant is a national. In this case Ward was a national not only of the Republic of Ireland, but also of Great Britain and there was therefore a burden upon him to prove that he was a refugee from both countries before Canada's obligation could be engaged.

State complicity in persecution is not a prerequisite to a valid refugee claim. The claimant must establish a "well-founded fear". The claimant must be outside his or her country of nationality because of that fear and unable to avail himself or herself of its protection. Alternatively, the claimant must be both outside his or her country of nationality and unwilling to avail himself or herself of its protection by reason of that well-founded fear. If a state is able to protect a claimant, then his or her fear is not, objectively speaking, well-founded. Persecution under the Convention includes situations where the state is not an accomplice to the persecution, but is simply unable to protect its citizens.

Being unable to avail oneself of state protection implies circumstances that are beyond the will of the person concerned. There may, for example, be a state of war, civil war or other grave disturbance which prevents the country of nationality from extending protection. Protection by the country of nationality may also have been denied to the claimant. Such denial may confirm or strengthen the claimant's fear of persecution and may indeed be an element of the persecution. The term "unwilling" in the definition refers to refugees who refuse to accept the protection of the country of nationality. Where a person is willing to avail himself or herself of the protection of his or her home country, such willingness would be incompatible with a claim that he or she is outside that country owing to a well-founded fear of persecution. Whenever the protection of the country of nationality is available and there is no ground based on well-founded fear for refusing it, the person concerned is not in need of international protection and is not a refugee. Ineffective state protection is encompassed within the concept of "unable" and "unwilling". In cases of "inability", protection is denied to the claimant, whereas when the claimant is "unwilling", he or she opts not to approach the state by reason of his or her fear on one of the enumerated bases. In either case, the state's involvement in the persecution is not a necessary consideration.

Where the existence of a fear is established and where the state's inability to protect is established, it is not assuming too much to say that the fear is well-founded. The burden of showing a state's inability to protect rests on the claimant and can only be discharged by the adducing of clear and convincing confirmation of this inability to protect. In this particular case the proof was unnecessary as representatives of the state authorities conceded their inability to protect the appellant, Ward. Nations should be presumed to be capable of protecting their citizens. Security of nationals is the essence of sovereignty. Absent a situation where the state apparatus has completely broken down, such as that recognized in Lebanon in the *Zalzali* case [1991] 3 F.C. 605, it should be assumed that the state is capable of protecting its nationals.

The appellant Ward justified his claim to refugee status on the basis of a well-founded fear of persecution at the hands of the INLA by reason of his membership in a particular social group, *i.e.*, the INLA. A good working rule to determine the meaning of "particular social group" is set out in the test proposed in *Canada (Minister of Employment & Immigration) v. Mayers* (1992), 97 D.L.R. (4th) 729; *Acosta* 2986, 919850 WL 56042 (B.I.A.); and *Cheung v. Canada (Minister of Employment & Immigration)*, [1993] F.C.J. No. 309 (Q.L.), Appeal No. A-785-91. Those cases identify three possible categories:

1. groups defined by an innate or unchangeable characteristic;

2. groups whose members voluntarily associate for reasons so fundamental to their human dignity that they should not be forced to forsake the association; and

3. groups associated by a former voluntary status, unalterable due to its historical permanence.

The INLA did not meet these three tests and was therefore not a particular social group.

However, it is for the examiner to decide whether the Convention definition is met; usually there will be more than one ground for the well-founded fear of persecution. In this case the Court considered whether Ward had a well-founded fear of persecution for reasons of his political opinion. Ward believed that the killing of innocent people to achieve political change was unacceptable and thus his persecution by the INLA stemmed from that belief, which was held by the Supreme Court of Canada to be a political opinion. Any opinion on any matter in which the machinery of state, government and policy may be engaged is a political opinion. The political opinion need not have been expressed outright by the claimant and need not conform to the claimant's true beliefs. Not just any dissent to any organization will unlock the gates to Canadian asylum; the disagreement has to be rooted in political conviction.

The appeal was allowed. The decision of the Court of Appeal was set aside. The case was remitted back to the Immigration and Refugee Board so that it could determine whether Ward was also a refugee from Great Britain, his second country of nationality.

Ling v. Canada (Minister of Employment & Immigration) (1993), 64 F.T.R. 182 — The expression "a reasonable chance of persecution" has been held by the Appeal Division of the Federal Court to be an apt equivalent for a "well-founded fear of persecution".

The Court approved the following comments of MacGuigan J.A. in *Adjei v. Canada (Minister of Employment & Immigration)*, [1989] 2 F.C. 680, 7 Imm. L.R. (2d) 169, 57 D.L.R. (4th) 153, 132 N.R. 24 (Fed. C.A.):

> The fear of persecution in the definition has a two-fold aspect. On the one hand, the applicant must experience a subjective fear. A man with great fortitude may not have a subjective fear of persecution until adverse circumstances are worse for him than for his less courageous fellow countryman; nevertheless such a fear must be present in the mind of the applicant for the definition of Convention refugee to be met. The appropriate test as to whether or not a subjective fear exists is that appropriate for determining the existence of other matters of fact in a case of this kind, namely balance of probabilities.
>
> The second aspect is the object of element. The subjective fear of the applicant ... must have an objective basis.

The decision of the Board was unexceptionable, and not to be disturbed. Accordingly, the application to quash the decision of the Convention Refugee Determination Division was dismissed.

Ghazizadeh v. Canada (Minister of Employment & Immigration) (1993), 154 N.R. 236 (Fed. C.A.) — The whole concept of a refugee "sur place" requires an assessment of the situation in the applicant's country of origin after she or he has left it. The fact that the departure may have been perfectly legal is nothing to the point.

Cheung v. Canada (Minister of Employment & Immigration) (1993), 19 Imm. L.R. (2d) 81, 153 N.R. 145 (Fed. C.A.) — In 1984 Ting Ting Cheung gave birth to a baby boy in the Peoples' Republic of China. She had another child in 1987 and came to the attention of the Family Planning Bureau in her native province. Shortly after the pro-democracy demonstrations in Beijing she came to Canada and claimed to be a refugee.

The first question was whether women in China who have more than one child and are faced with forced sterilization constitute a social group within the meaning of the definition of "Convention refugee". The Court indicated that the following criteria provide a useful basis for consideration in constructing a test for being a particular social group:

> (1) a natural or non-natural group of persons with (2) similar shared background, habits, social status, political outlook, education, values, aspirations, history, economic activity or interests, often interests contrary to those of the prevailing government, and (3) sharing basic, innate, unalterable characteristics, consciousness, and solidarity or (4) sharing a temporary but voluntary status, with the purpose of their association being so fundamental to their human dignity that they should not be required to alter it.

The Court concluded that women in China who have one child and are faced with forced sterilization satisfy enough of the above criteria to be considered a particular social group. This did not mean that all women in China who have more than one child may automatically claim Convention refugee status. It is only those women who also have a well-founded fear of persecution as a result of membership in that social group who can claim such status.

The next question was whether forced or strongly coerced sterilization in the context of China's one-child policy constituted persecution. The Immigration and Refugee Board had concluded that forced sterilization in that context was not persecution. The Court disagreed.

The Court noted that forced sterilization of women was a violation of Articles 3 and 5 of the United Nations Universal Declaration of Human Rights. This declaration was adopted and proclaimed December 10, 1948 by the General Assembly of the United Nations.

Karen Lee Cheung was the second child, whose birth was contrary to the one-child policy. The Court found that the minor could also claim the benefit of Convention refugee status on the principle of family unity. Finally, there being no problems as to the credibility of the adult claimant, nor any factual questions that needed to be resolved by the Board, the Court exercised its discretion under subsection 52(c)(i) of the *Federal Court Act* and declared both appellants to be Convention refugees.

Canada (Minister of Employment & Immigration) v. Villafranca (1992), 18 Imm. L.R. (2d) 130, 99 D.L.R. (4th) 334, 150 N.R. 232 (Fed. C.A.) — The respondent was a Philippine national, who served in his home country as a policeman. He fled because he had been marked for death by a communist terrorist guerilla group and he feared for his life. The Refugee Division found him credible and held that he did have a well-founded fear of persecution by reason of his political opinion.

The Refugee Division failed to address the question of whether the respondent was unable or unwilling to avail himself of the protection of the Philippines. Where the claimant is himself an agent of the state, it makes no sense to speak of him as being unwilling to seek the state's protection. The claim can only succeed if he shows that he is unable to do so. The burden of showing that one is not able to avail oneself of the protection of one's own state is not easily satisfied. The test is an objective one and involves the claimant showing either that he is physically prevented from seeking his government's aid or that the government itself is in some way prevented from giving it. No government that makes any claim to democratic values can guarantee the protection of all its citizens at all times. Thus it is not enough for a claimant to show that his government has not always been effective at protecting persons in his particular situation. Where the state is so weak and its control over all or part of its territories so tenuous as to make it a government in name only, a refugee may justly claim to be unable to avail himself of its protection. Situations of civil war, invasion or the total collapse of internal order will normally be required. The Refugee Division having failed to address this question, its decision was quashed and the matter referred back to a differently constituted panel of the Board for a new hearing.

Urbanek v. Canada (Minister of Employment & Immigration) (1992), 17 Imm. L.R. (2d) 153, 144 N.R. 77 (Fed. C.A.) — The purpose of the refugee determination system is to provide a safe haven to those who genuinely need it and not to give a quick and convenient route to landed status for immigrants who cannot or will not obtain it in the usual way.

Orelien v. Canada (Minister of Employment & Immigration) (1991), [1992] 1 F.C. 592, 15 Imm. L.R. (2d) 1, 135 N.R. 50 (Fed. C.A.) — Canada's obligations in the area of refugees stem from the 4th Geneva Convention of August 12, 1949, and protocol due to the Geneva Convention of August 12, 1949, both approved by Acts of Parliament (*Geneva Conventions Act*, R.S.C. 1985, c. G-3, s. 2, as am. S.C. 1990, c. 14, s. 1), as well as a customary norm of temporary refuge. To return a person to Haiti in the circumstances that presently exist and have existed at relevant times in this case would have violated Canada's obligations under the Convention, the protocol and the customary norm of international law prohibiting the forceable repatriation of foreign nationals who have fled generalized violence and other threats to their lives and security arising out of internal armed conflict within their state of nationality. The Convention, the protocol and the customary norm of international law have the force of domestic law in Canada and can be enforced in the courts of Canada at the suit of a private individual. The intention to execute a deportation order which if executed would breach those laws does not colour the process under the *Immigration Act* by which a person from such a country may be ordered deported. This is not to denigrate the importance of the Convention, the protocol and the customary norms of international law. It would be a grave and justiciable matter if Canada were to execute deportation orders in circumstances which breached obligations under international law and put the life, liberty or security of persons in peril.

Rasaratnam v. Canada (Minister of Employment & Immigration) (1991), [1992] 1 F.C. 706 (Fed. C.A.) — The internal flight alternative (IFA) concept is inherent in the Convention refugee definition. In order to conclude an IFA exists the Board must be satisfied on a balance of probabilities that there is no serious possibility of a claimant being persecuted in the part of the country which is viewed upon as the internal flight alternative. Secondly, conditions in that part of the country to which the IFA applies must be such that it would not be unreasonable for the claimant to seek refuge there. Thirdly, the determination of whether there is an IFA is integral to the determination of whether the claimant is a refugee. Fourthly, the claimant is not expected to raise the question of an IFA nor is an allegation that none exists simply to be inferred from the claim itself. The question of an IFA must be expressly raised at the hearing by the refugee hearing officer or the Board and the claimant afforded the opportunity to address it with evidence and argument.

In this case, the Board did not err in concluding the appellant was not a Convention refugee because the appellant could have lived free from persecution in Colombo, Sri Lanka.

Canada (Minister of Employment & Immigration) v. Obstoj (1992), [1992] 2 F.C. 739, 93 D.L.R. (4th) 144, 142 N.R. 81 (Fed. C.A.) — The Minister applied to set aside a credible basis determination. The first-level tribunal found that given the present day change of circumstances in Poland there was no realistic possibility of the respondent suffering persecution if she would return. They found, however, that the respondent fell under the provisions of section 2(3) of the *Immigration Act* and that there were compelling reasons for her refusing to avail herself of the protection of Poland and that therefore her claim had a credible basis. The three judges of the Court of Appeal that heard the matter gave three different judgments. Hugessen J. ruled that since the Refugee Division, when conducting the hearing into the claim for refugee status, was able to hear evidence and consider questions raised by section 2(3), the credible basis tribunal, when deciding whether or not there is credible or trustworthy evidence on which the division could decide in a claimant's favour, is likewise able to consider such evidence. Subsections 2(2) and 2(3) were found to deal not only with the loss of a refugee status which had already been acquired, but also to have been incorporated into the definition of a Convention refugee by virtue of paragraph (b) of the definition.

Section 2(3) extends to anyone who has been recognized as a refugee at any time, even long after the date of the Convention, and it should also be read as requiring Canadian authorities to give recognition to refugee status on humanitarian grounds to a special and limited category of persons, that is, those persons who have suffered such appalling persecution that the experience alone is a compelling reason not to return them even though they may no longer have reason to fear further persecution.

Desjardins J.A. was of the view that paragraph (b) contained in the definition of a Convention refugee was an integral part of that definition and that a claimant must meet the requirements of both paragraphs (a) and (b) at the time that status is claimed and continuously thereafter. There is a constant relationship between the cases mentioned in paragraph (b) and the requirement of a well-founded fear mentioned in paragraph (a). Subsection 2 referred to in paragraph (b) contains 5 categories. Paragraphs (a), (b), (c) and (d) presuppose the case of an individual who does something contrary to the idea of a Convention refugee. Such an individual could then never claim that his or her fear was well founded. Such a person ceases to be a refugee first because of the requirements in paragraph (b) of the definition, and secondly because the fear of such a person is not well founded. Paragraph 2(2)(e) does not deal with an act committed by a claimant which conflicts with the idea of a well-founded fear, but rather with changes which occurred in the country of origin so that the reasons for the fear have ceased. Such a claimant does not meet paragraph (b) of the definition and further his fear is no longer well-founded as required by paragraph (a) of the definition. Subsection 2(3) creates justification which excludes the application of section 2(2)(e). While the fear of a person described in section 2(3) is not well-founded Parliament intended to recognize that such persons could claim refugee status despite this fact. Such a claim could only initially be made at a first-level tribunal, and accordingly a first-level tribunal can consider whether there is credible evidence of the justification set out in section 2(3).

Pratte J.A. dissented and would have allowed the application and ruled that a foreigner who no longer has a reason to fear persecution in his country may not be determined to be a Convention refugee for the sole reason that the persecution he suffered in the past justifies his refusal to avail himself of the protection of that country.

Editor's Note: Although decided under a different statutory framework the principles discussed may still be of interest.

Zalzali v. Canada (Minister of Employment & Immigration) (1991), 14 Imm. L.R. (2d) 81, 126 N.R. 126, [1991] 3 F.C. 605 (Fed. C.A.) — The appellant, a Lebanese national, claimed he was persecuted on account of his nationality, political opinion and membership in a particular social group. In most cases of claims for refugee status, the State while it may not itself be the agent of persecution, makes itself an accomplice by tolerance or inertia. It is then possible to speak in terms of persecution attributable to the State and to conclude that the refugee claimant had good reason to be unwilling to claim protection which the State was, in all likelihood, not going to give him. There can be persecution within the meaning of the convention and the *Immigration Act* where there is no form of guilt, complicity or participation by the State. The definition of a refugee refers to "the fear of persecution without saying that this persecution must be by the government." The natural meaning of the words "is unable" assumes an objective inability on the part of the complainant and the fact that "is unable" is not qualified by "reason of that fear" confirms that the inability in question is governed by objective criteria which can be verified independently of the fear experienced. Seeing a connection of any kind between "is unable" and "complicity by the government" would be a misreading of the definition. Persecution by someone other than the government is possible when the government is unable to offer protection. There are several reasons beyond the person's control why he or she might be unable to claim the protection of the State. One of those reasons is the non-existence of a government to which that person may resort. In this case, the decision of the Refugee Division was set aside and the matter was remitted back for a re-hearing in accordance with the reasoning of the Court.

Editor's Note: The cases which discuss the phrase "is unwilling" are Rajudeen (1984), 55 N.R. 129; Surujpal (1985), 60 N.R. 73; Satiacum (1985), 99 N.R. 171.

Hilo v. Canada (Minister of Employment & Immigration) (1991), 15 Imm. L.R. (2d) 199, 130 N.R. 236 (Fed. C.A.) — The Refugee Division was under a duty to give its reasons for casting doubt upon the appellant's credibility in clear and unmistakeable terms. The Board's credibility assessment was defective because it was couched in vague and general terms. The claimant had only attended informal meetings of a political group inside Syria. The Refugee Division viewed this group as loosely knit with apparently charitable aims, no official title or status and noted further that the claimant was only 14 years of age at the time of his attendance. The Court found that characterizing the group in this way was irrelevant. The Syrian authorities had sought to persecute the appellant because of his perceived political opinion. The proper test for evaluating political activities is not whether the division or members considered that the appellant had engaged in political activities but whether the ruling government of the country from which he claimed to be a refugee so considered his conduct.

Hoang v. Canada (Minister of Employment & Immigration) (1990), 13 Imm. L.R. (2d) 35, 120 N.R. 193 (Fed. C.A.) — The appellant was ordered deported because he was a permanent resident who had been convicted of an offence for which a term of imprisonment of more than 6 months had been imposed; he had also been convicted of an offence for which the maximum term was 5 years or greater. The appellant had come to Canada as a stateless person from Vietnam and had been determined by the Minister in 1986 to be a convention refugee. The Court noted that the Immigration Appeal Board (which had decided this matter) correctly determined that its jurisdiction is only over whether a person should be removed from Canada and not as to the country of removal. Until the issue of deportation is settled, the Minister cannot make a decision as to the country of removal. Thus a statement by the Minister's representative as to the Minister's disposition to deport the appellant to Vietnam was not taken as a formal expression of the Minister's decision since the Minister was not, at the date of that statement, empowered to make the decision.

The Court determined that in dealing with the "double jeopardy" provisions of section 11(h) of the Charter deportation was not to be seen as a punishment of the person deported but a protection of those who remained. Further, deportation for serious offences affects neither section 7 nor section 12 of the *Charter of Rights* since it is not to be conceptualized as either a deprivation of liberty or a punishment. Finally, the Court noted that with respect to Canada's international obligations the United Nations convention relating to the status of refugees contained an exception to the prohibition against refoulement where the deportee had been convicted in the country where he was making the refugee claim of a particularly serious crime. The Court noted that the phrase "particularly serious crime" and "danger to the community" were not defined in the convention and therefore presumed that Parliament responsibly fulfilled its obligation when it enacted the *Immigration Act*.

Accordingly the appellant's appeal was dismissed.

Jugpal, Re (1989), 10 Imm. L.R. (2d) 109 (Imm. & Ref. Bd. (Ref. Div.)) — This case provided an example of how the Immigration and Refugee Board analyzes a determination of a claim to refugee status. The Board reviewed the evidence and indicated that it found the evidence credible. Specifically, the Board found that the testimony was consistent, straight forward, and sufficiently detailed to provide a plausible and coherent account of the basis of the claimant's fear and, further, that the testimony was not exaggerated. Further, the claimant was able to substantiate specific facts, including his own identity, with documents that were submitted to the Board. In evaluating the well-founded fear of persecution, the Board took into consideration the fact that the persecution suffered by the claimant in the past was sufficient to substantiate his claim to a well-founded fear of persecution. The Board took into account the fact that the claimant was arrested and re-arrested and he claimed to have been tortured. Objective evidence was presented which attested to the circumstances in his country to the effect that any young Sikh could be unjustly accused, detained or killed. Of particular interest was a letter signed by three American congressmen underlining the fact that human rights are in a decline in the Punjab. The Board decided that this was not a case of prosecution but rather a case of persecution because the claimant was tortured at the time of his arrest, he was held 5 months before being released and, after being released, he was again investigated by the police and accused of harbouring terrorists and deserters in his home. Further, the claimant was able to produce a letter from the mayor of his village indicating that his father had been arrested and was being held in his place. The father was not a supporter of the same causes as the claimant.

Adjei v. Canada (Minister of Employment & Immigration), [1989] 2 F.C. 680, 7 Imm. L.R. (2d) 169, 57 D.L.R. (4th) 153, 132 N.R. 24 (Fed. C.A.) — This application focuses on the proper interpretation of the definition of Convention refugee. An accurate way of describing the requisite test is in terms of "reasonable chance": is there a reasonable chance that persecution would take place were the applicant returned to his country of origin. There need not be more than a 50 per cent chance that persecution will occur (that is, a probability). On the other hand, there must be more than a minimal possibility of persecution. This application was allowed because the Board, in describing the test set out in the definition, stated that it was whether there was a reasonable chance or "substantial grounds" for thinking that the persecution may take place. The use of the term "substantial grounds" introduced an element of ambiguity into the Board's formulation of the correct test under the refugee definition. Accordingly, the Board's decision was set aside and the matter remitted back to the Board for reconsideration.

Surujpal v. Canada (Minister of Employment & Immigration) (1985), 60 N.R. 73 (Fed. C.A.) — The applicant brought an application to quash a decision of the Immigration Appeal Board finding that the applicant was not a Convention refugee. The decision of the Immigration Appeal Board was quashed because the evidence disclosed that the police were complicit in the broader sense in the persecution and harassment of the applicant. It is not required that State participation in persecution be direct; it is sufficient that it is indirect provided that there is proof of State complicity.

Rajudeen v. Canada (Minister of Employment & Immigration) (1984), 55 N.R. 129 (Fed. C.A.) — The definition of Convention refugee does not include a definition of persecution. "Persecute" was defined by reference to a dictionary as "to harass or afflict with repeated acts of cruelty or annoyance; to afflict persistently; to afflict or punish because of particular opinions or adherence to a particular creed or mode of worship." "Persecution" was defined as "a particular course or period of systematic infliction of punishment directed against those holding a particular (religious belief); persistent injury or annoyance from any source."

There is a subjective and objective component necessary to satisfy the definition of Convention refugee. The subjective component relates to the existence of the fear of persecution in the mind of the refugee. The objective component requires that the refugee's fear be evaluated objectively to determine if there is a valid basis for that fear.

In determining whether refugee status has been extended to cover a particular case, reference should be made to the expression of underlying policy in section 3(g) of the Act. To satisfy the definition, the persecution complained of must have been committed or been condoned by the state itself and consist either of conduct directed by the state toward the individual or in the state knowingly tolerating the behaviour of private citizens or refusing or being unable to protect the individual from such behaviour.

Musial v. Canada (Minister of Employment & Immigration), [1982] 1 F.C. 290, 38 N.R. 55 (Fed. C.A.) — The applicant was a Polish seaman who left his ship in Vancouver. The Court found that his fear of punishment for refusal to serve in the military in Poland was well founded. However, army deserters and conscientious objectors were not dealt with specifically in the definition "Convention refugee". Such cases should be considered on their merits, including the applicants' motives for engaging in conduct which they fear will attract punishment. This applicant's fear of being punished for refusing to serve in Afghanistan with the Polish army, if called upon to do so, was not sufficient to differentiate his case from that of any other draft evader. Thus, the Immigration Appeal Board was quite right in ruling that there were not reasonable grounds to believe that the applicant's claim for Convention refugee status could be established.

Naredo v. Canada (Minister of Employment & Immigration) (1981), 130 D.L.R. (3d) 752, 40 N.R. 436 (Fed. C.A.) — The Federal Court held that the Immigration Appeal Board erred in imposing upon the applicant and his wife the requirement that they be subject to persecution. The statutory definition requires only that they establish a well-founded fear of persecution.

Inzunza v. Canada (Minister of Employment & Immigration) (1979), 103 D.L.R. (3d) 105 (Fed. C.A.) — Whether a person has engaged in political activity must be determined by considering the opinion of the government of the country of his nationality and not by the Immigration Appeal Board's consideration of whether the applicant has engaged in such activity.

Astudillo v. Canada (Minister of Employment & Immigration) (1979), 31 N.R. 121 (Fed. C.A.) — The Court reaffirmed that in interpreting political activities the crucial test is not whether the Immigration Appeal Board considers that the applicant engaged in political activities, but whether the ruling government of the country from which the applicant claims to be a refugee so considers his conduct.

Araya, Re (January 6, 1977), Doc. 76-1126 (Imm. App. Bd.) — The Immigration Appeal Board ruled that harassment of the wife because she knew about her husband's political activities and movements constituted persecution of a political nature.

Editor's Note: Cases interpreting Sections E & F of Article 1 are summarized under the Schedule to the Act containing those Sections.

Deportation order

Moore v. Canada (Minister of Manpower & Immigration), [1968] S.C.R. 839, 69 D.L.R. (2d) 273 (S.C.C.) — A deportation order was held to be valid in form under the *Immigration Act*, R.S.C. 1952, notwithstanding the fact that it did not name the country to which the person named was to be deported. The Court also noted that it would not be improper for the order to specify that country.

Deputy Minister

Ali v. Canada (Minister of Manpower & Immigration), [1976] 1 F.C. 185, 11 N.R. 617 (Fed. C.A.) — Where the face of a direction under the *Immigration Act*, R.S.C. 1952, was signed by someone who purported to do so for the director of the immigration branch, there was then created a presumption that such person had the authority that he purported to exercise.

Employment

Bernardez v. Canada (Minister of Citizenship & Immigration) (1995), 31 Imm. L.R. (2d) 90, 101 F.T.R. 203 (Fed. T.D.) — An adjudicator found that the applicant, a live-in caregiver, had engaged in employment in Canada contrary to her employment authorization, and instructed her to leave the country within 30 days as she had ceased to be a visitor.

The applicant's employer operated a store called the "Philippine Variety Store" and had instructed the applicant to clean the store on an occasional basis commencing in March 1993. The test for employment is not narrow, technical or restrictive, but rather the question of employment depends on the nature of the work and the circumstances in which the work is performed regardless of the relationship between the parties. The adjudicator neglected to apply that reasoning with respect to the inference that the applicant was being exploited by her domestic employer, and felt compelled to submit to her employer's reasonable demands to clean their family store. The lack of collusion with the employer, the fact that no surplus money or benefits were received by the applicant, and the fact that this domestic feared potential dismissal and was ignorant of her right to refuse the unauthorized work, all form part of the circumstances in which the work was performed. Further, the adjudicator did not consider the more serious issue of whether a domestic who is coerced or compelled to perform duties for her employer can truly be considered to be employed in that capacity. Accordingly, the decision of the adjudicator was quashed and the matter remitted for consideration by a new adjudicator in conformity with the law and the court's reasons.

Georgas v. Canada (Minister of Employment & Immigration) (1978), [1979] 1 F.C. 349, 23 N.R. 437 (Fed. C.A.) — On the facts of this case, there was evidence from which an adjudicator could conclude that the applicant had engaged in employment. However, not all work performed by a visitor for a relative with whom he or she is staying, and for which the relative would have to pay compensation if he or she chose to have it done by a stranger, falls within the definition of employment. Whether or not the work done is employment depends upon the nature of the work and the circumstances.

Examination

Peszko v. Canada (Minister of Citizenship & Immigration) (1996), 35 Imm. L.R. (2d) 148, 114 F.T.R. 52 (Fed. T.D.) — The applicant, a citizen of Poland, entered Canada as a visitor on January 28, 1990. Shortly after his arrival an undertaking of support was submitted, to sponsor the applicant as a member of the Self Exile Persons Designated Class. The sponsorship was sent to Buffalo where a visa officer on April 6, 1992 conducted an interview of the applicant. At that interview the applicant presented the visa officer with a police clearance certificate. At the conclusion of the interview, the applicant was accepted for landing pending completion of the usual medical and security requirements.

Five days after the interview, on April 11, 1992, the applicant was charged with impaired driving, an offence to which the applicant eventually, on September 30, 1992, pleaded guilty and was convicted. The Crown proceeded in respect of that offence by way of a summary conviction. The application for landing was rejected and by a letter dated June 28, 1994, immigration authorities advised the applicant that he was inadmissable under section 19(1)(c) of the *Immigration Act*. The reference to section 19(1)(c) was erroneous. In October 1994, the applicant's visitor visa expired and an inquiry was subsequently held. An adjudicator determined that based on the provisions of the *Immigration Act* in effect when the applicant filed his application for permanent residence, the applicant was not inadmissable under the criminality provisions of section 19.

The adjudicator refused to land the applicant pursuant to section 32(3)(a), because he took the view that the applicant's interviews in Buffalo and Canada did not constitute "examinations" for the purpose of an application under subsection 32(3), because they were not conducted at a port-of-entry or otherwise provided under section 12.2 of the *Immigration Regulations*. Subsection 9(1) of the Act clearly requires that the applicant apply for and obtain a visa before appearing at the port-of-entry. Pursuant to subsection 9(2) the applicant's application for an immigrant visa was to be assessed by a visa officer for the purpose of determining whether he appeared to be a person who may be granted landing. The interview was part of the process of assessing the applicant for the purposes of subsections 9(1) and 9(2) and not for the purpose of determining whether he may be granted admission as specified in the definition of the term examination in section 2 of the Act. A decision on admission could not be made until a visa had been issued as required by subsection 9(1).

It may well be that the visa officer erred in his assessment of the applicant's application for an immigrant visa, however, the visa officer's determination was only reviewable pursuant to section 18.1 of the *Federal Court Act.*

Immigrant

Reyes de Jesus v. Canada (Minister of Employment & Immigration) (1987), 1 Imm. L.R. (2d) 217 (Imm. App. Bd.) — This was an appeal from the refusal of a sponsored application for landing. The appellant was seeking to sponsor his mother. The application was refused on the basis that the mother had not satisfied the immigration officer that she complied with the definition of "immigrant" given in section 2(1) of the *Immigration Act.* This decision was based upon previous statutory declarations, which the mother had filed when she was seeking visitor's visas to come to Canada. These declarations denied an intention to reside permanently in Canada. This was found to be unfair because the declarations from the previous applications, upon which the officer relied, were not raised with the mother when she was interviewed. The Board found that it was the interviewing officer's duty to consider the mother's intention at the time of the interview and to allow her to explain the previous declarations. The Board also suggested that it would be sufficient if the mother's intention to reside permanently in Canada was formulated after the interview, which resulted in her application being rejected, but before the hearing of the sponsor's appeal.

Landing

Canada (Minister of Citizenship & Immigration) v. Nemsila (1996), 35 Imm. L.R. (2d) 56, [1997] 1 F.C. 260, 118 F.T.R. 310 (Fed. T.D.); affirmed (1997), 38 Imm. L.R. (2d) 242, 3 Admin. L.R. (3d) 83, 214 L.R. 383 (Fed. C.A.) — This was an application by the minister to review a decision of an adjudicator which provided that the applicant could not be deported pursuant to paragraph 27(2)(g) and 27(1)(e) of the *Immigration Act.* The adjudicator found that the respondent had acquired Canadian domicile under the *Immigration Act* 1952, and therefore could not be ordered deported.

The adjudicator found that the respondent had been lawfully admitted to and landed in Canada in 1950, due to the fact that he had obtained a visa and presented himself for examination at a port-of-entry and the ship's manifest had been stamped with the phrase "landed immigrant" across his name. The adjudicator further found that the respondent had made misrepresentations during interviews with visa control and immigration officers and had not fully disclosed information which would have led to the refusal of his application.

Canadian domicile under the 1952 *Immigration Act* was acquired by a person having his place of domicile for at least 5 years in Canada after having been landed in Canada. For the purposes of the 1952 Act, a person was landed in Canada when they had been lawfully admitted into Canada by an officer under that Act. The Court held that the term lawful admission in the 1952 Act, required something more than having a port-of-entry inspector rubber stamp the ship's manifest or an individual's passport with the words "landed immigrant". Lawful admission requires compliance with all of the requirements of the Act in force at the time the immigrant entered Canada.

Due to the fact that the respondent's entry into Canada in 1950 was based upon deception and misrepresentation, he was not lawfully admitted to Canada and therefore could not have gained "landing" within the meaning of that Act. Due to the fact the respondent was never landed he was held to never have acquired Canadian domicile.

Accordingly, the adjudicator's decision was set aside.

Permanent resident

Canada (Minister of Citizenship & Immigration) v. Nemsila (1996), 35 Imm. L.R. (2d) 56, [1997] 1 F.C. 260, 118 F.T.R. 310 (Fed. T.D.); affirmed (1997), 38 Imm. L.R. (2d) 242, 3 Admin. L.R. (3d) 83, 214 L.R. 383 (Fed. C.A.) — This was an application by the minister to review a decision of an adjudicator which provided that the applicant could not be deported pursuant to paragraph 27(2)(g) and 27(1)(e) of the *Immigration Act*. The adjudicator found that the respondent had acquired Canadian domicile under the *Immigration Act* 1952, and therefore could not be ordered deported.

The adjudicator found that the respondent had been lawfully admitted to and landed in Canada in 1950, due to the fact that he had obtained a visa and presented himself for examination at a port-of-entry and the ship's manifest had been stamped with the phrase "landed immigrant" across his name. The adjudicator further found that the respondent had made misrepresentations during interviews with visa control and immigration officers and had not fully disclosed information which would have led to the refusal of his application.

Canadian domicile under the 1952 *Immigration Act* was acquired by a person having his place of domicile for at least 5 years in Canada after having been landed in Canada. For the purposes of the 1952 Act, a person was landed in Canada when they had been lawfully admitted into Canada by an officer under that Act. The Court held that the term lawful admission in the 1952 Act, required something more than having a port-of-entry inspector rubber stamp the ship's manifest or an individual's passport with the words "landed immigrant". Lawful admission requires compliance with all of the requirements of the Act in force at the time the immigrant entered Canada.

Due to the fact that the respondent's entry into Canada in 1950 was based upon deception and misrepresentation, he was not lawfully admitted to Canada and therefore could not have gained "landing" within the meaning of that Act. Due to the fact the respondent was never landed he was held to never have acquired Canadian domicile.

Accordingly, the adjudicator's decision was set aside.

Canada (Minister of Employment & Immigration) v. Han (1984), 6 Admin. L.R. 25, 52 N.R. 274 (Fed. C.A.) — A person granted permanent resident status who fails to comply with the condition attached to that status, namely that he marry within 90 days, is, nevertheless, a permanent resident notwithstanding his failure to comply with this condition.

Canada (Minister of Employment & Immigration) v. Selby, [1981] 1 F.C. 273, 110 D.L.R. (3d) 126 (Fed. C.A.) — A permanent resident who has remained out of Canada for more than 183 days and who has been found by an adjudicator to have ceased to be a permanent resident has a right to appeal that question to the Immigration Appeal Board under section 72 [s. 70] of the *Immigration Act*.

Transportation Company

Flota Cubana de Pesca (Cuban Fishing Fleet) v. Canada (Minister of Citizenship & Immigration) (1997), 142 F.T.R. 47 (note), 154 D.L.R. (4th) 577, 221 N.R. 356, 41 Imm. L.R. (2d) 175, [1998] 2 F.C. 303 (Fed. C.A.) — The issues raised by these appeals depended upon the proper interpretation of the term "transportation company". For a number of years the appellant companies have conducted fishing, provisioning and fishing support operations in the waters of the Atlantic Ocean within Canada's 200 mile exclusive fishing zone. During 1993 a number of crew members deserted their ships while the ships were at Canadian ports. If the appellants were transportation companies then they are obliged to make payments to the Canadian government pursuant to the *Immigration Act*.

Due to the fact that the French and English version of the definition of transportation company are not the same, the Court had occasion to consider the principles of statutory construction which apply when construing a bilingual statute.

The English and French versions of a statute are equally authentic and authoritative. If the versions seem to conflict, the Court must attempt to reconcile them by identifying and adopting a meaning that they share. The shared meaning rule is not absolute. A Court is free to reject the shared meaning if it appears contrary to the intention to the legislature.

The overarching purpose of Part V of the *Immigration Act* is to transfer the costs associated with the entry of persons without status into Canada and their subsequent removal from the Federal government to the transportation companies which brought these persons into the country. The provisions in Part V also assist in furthering the overall objective of the Act by discouraging transportation companies from conveying persons to Canada who are not legally entitled to be or remain here. The more expansive definition of transportation company reflected in the English version of the Act best accords with this purpose and expresses the true meaning of the provision. Successive amendments to the definition over the years have revealed a clear trend toward broadening its scope.

Accordingly, where the owner or operator of a vehicle not used primarily for the purpose of transporting persons or goods, such as a vessel engaging in fishing operations, transports persons or goods into Canada aboard that vehicle the owner, operator or agent is a transportation company as defined in subsection 2(1) of the Act.

Visa

Canada (Minister of Employment & Immigration) v. De Decaro, [1993] 2 F.C. 408, 103 D.L.R. (4th) 564, 155 N.R. 129 (Fed. C.A.) — In October 1988 a visa officer issued an immigrant visa to Ignazio De Decaro. He also issued an immigrant visa to two dependants who were to accompany Mr. De Decaro, namely the respondent and her daughter. Ignazio De Decaro died before coming to Canada. The respondent did come and arrived at Dorval on July 11, 1989 accompanied by her daughter and another child, who was born in the U.S. after Ignazio De Decaro's death. This child had never obtained a visa to Canada.

The respondent then applied for landing for herself and her two children. This was denied on the ground that the respondent's admission contravened section 19(2)(d) of the *Immigration Act* because the respondent did not meet the requirements of section 9(1) of the Act.

The adjudicator found that when the respondent applied for admission to Canada, she held a valid immigrant's visa since her visa had not been revoked by the proper authorities. The adjudicator found that the respondent's husband's death did not automatically invalidate the visa. Further, the adjudicator found that there was no need to refer to section 12 of the Regulations because that provision did not enact a condition of admission, consequently its infringement did not mean the respondent could not be admitted.

The Appeal Division of the I.R.B. dismissed the Minister's appeal on the basis that the respondent, before appearing at a port-of-entry, had duly obtained an immigrant visa which had never been revoked or cancelled by the proper authorities and thus the respondent had the right to be admitted to Canada unless she was inadmissible on some other ground than the lack of a valid visa.

The Minister's appeal to the Court of Appeal was allowed. Pratte J.A. held that the definition of "accompanying dependant" illustrated that the visa issued to a person in this class was of a very special type which was issued solely to enable its holder to accompany or follow another person to Canada. The holder of such a visa who applied for admission without the other person accompanying or preceding him or her into Canada did not therefore meet the requirements of section 9(1) of the Act.

Further, after her husband's death the respondent became inadmissible by virtue of section 12 of the Regulations. Her marital status had changed since she obtained her visa and in order to be admitted to Canada she had to establish not only that she was eligible, but also that she met all the conditions for obtaining a visa. The respondent never discharged this burden of proof.

Marceau J.A. agreed that the decision of the Appeal Division should be set aside. He saw no reference in the Act or Regulations to visas which become invalid, are revoked or become ineffective. The technique in his view used to cover cases of changes in the immigrant's status between the time the visa is issued and the time he or she arrives at the Canadian border is contained in section 12 of the Regulations. In his view, issuing an immigrant visa is not the granting of landing. Such issuance simply means that the visa officer has formed the opinion that the applicant meets the requirements of the Act and Regulations for admission to Canada. The visa is evidence of a conclusion by an immigration officer whose function is to determine from outside Canada whether applicants are admissible and that conclusion will usually be accepted by his or her colleague at the port-of-entry. However, the rule is still that a foreign national arriving in Canada with a view to residing here must satisfy the immigration officer of his admissibility at the port-of-entry. Section 12 of the Regulations imposes on an immigrant a duty to disclose any change in the facts which may have influenced the issuing of the visa and if there has been such a change, it requires the immigrant to meet new requirements. The visa is not void, but the visa in itself does not confer the right of entry. It is the new requirements of section 12 of the Regulations that must be met.

In Marceau J.A.'s view the respondent could not establish that she met the requirements of section 12 since she was granted a visa in consideration of her husband's presence. The adjudicator accordingly was wrong to think that she met the conditions of admission set out by the Regulation and the Appeal Division could not confirm the adjudicator's finding on the ground that the Minister had not discharged the burden of proving that the respondent was inadmissible or that her visa had been cancelled, as the Minister was under no burden of proof and cancellation of a visa as a concept does not exist.

Given that the Court intended to allow the appeal, it then had to consider section 73(3). The majority was of the view that the respondent before her husband's death possessed a valid visa. However, after that death it was impossible for the condition attached to the visa to be performed so that the visa ceased to have any validity. Accordingly, section 73(3) conferred no right of appeal to the Appeal Division on the respondent.

Marceau J.A. was of the view that the respondent was in possession of a valid visa and that the matter should be returned to the Appeal Division as it was still under a duty to consider whether on compassionate or humanitarian grounds the respondent should not be removed from Canada.

Canada (Minister of Employment & Immigration) v. Wong (1993), 153 N.R. 237 (Fed. C.A.) — A Canadian citizen made a sponsorship application for her father and sister, the latter in the category of the father's single dependent daughter. Before the issuance of the immigration visas, the father died. Unaware of this event, Canadian immigration authorities issued visas to both sponsorees. At the point of entry to Canada, the sponsoree daughter initially lied to a Canadian immigration officer, but ultimately produced her father's death certificate. On inquiry she was ordered excluded.

The Appeal Division held that it had jurisdiction to hear the appeal since at the time of landing the sponsoree-sister was in possession of a valid immigrant visa and went on to exercise its compassionate discretion in her favour.

Where an element upon which the issuance of a visa is based subsequently ceases to exist and where the principal reason for the issuance of a visa ceased to exist before its issuance, such a visa cannot be said to be a valid immigrant visa.

The appeal was allowed and the Board's decision set aside for want of jurisdiction.

De La Cruz v. Canada (Minister of Employment & Immigration) (1988), 7 Imm. L.R. (2d) 75, 26 F.T.R. 285 — The applicants were citizens of the Philippines. They applied for permanent residence in Canada at the Canadian Consulate General in San Francisco. The applicants were scheduled to be interviewed in San Francisco; however, their applications for tourist visas to the United States were refused by the United States Embassy in Manila. They therefore decided to apply at the Consulate in Toronto for a United States visa.

However, the application for visitors' visas made at the Canadian Embassy in Manila was refused. This decision was upheld. The duty of the visa officer is to accord proper consideration to any application. The officer is not required to issue a visitor's visa unless convinced that the applicant fulfills the legislative requirements. Once the visa officer turns his mind to the issue and disposes of the application for visitors' visas, there remains no duty to be performed enforceable by *mandamus*.

To succeed on an application for *certiorari*, the applicants must do more than establish the possibility that the Court might have reached a different conclusion than the visa officer. There must be either an error of law apparent on the face of the record or a breach of the duty of fairness appropriate to this essentially administrative decision. It is not improper for the visa officer to refuse the visitors' visas on the basis of an outstanding application for permanent residence. It is the intent of the applicant that is properly the focus of the visa officer's examination. No policy dictates refusal simply because the applicants intend to apply for United States visas. Further, the officer had not based his decision solely on the refusal of United States officials to grant the applicants' request for visas to the United States. Accordingly, the decision of the visa officer was upheld.

Canada (Minister of Employment & Immigration) v. Mercier (September 16, 1980), Doc. 79-1243 (Imm. App. Bd.) — The Board held that a visa is no more than a stamp on a piece of paper issued outside of Canada which may give the holder a colour of right to come into Canada, either as a visitor or an immigrant, as the case may be, but no more.

Canada (Minister of Employment & Immigration) v. La Rose (November 28, 1979), Doc. 79-9284 (Imm. App. Bd.) — The issue in this case was whether a stamp appearing on page 9 of the respondent's passport was a valid visa. The Board held that the stamp was likely made on the passport by a visa officer. However, the Board held that section 72 [s. 70] of the *Immigration Act* when it makes reference to a "valid visa" is referring to either a non-immigrant visa authorizing entry into Canada or an immigrant visa authorizing admission as a permanent resident.

Visitor

Parediz v. Canada (Minister of Employment & Immigration) (1994), 79 F.T.R. 316 (Fed. T.D.) — The applicant and her two daughters sought to review a decision of an adjudicator determining that they were not genuine visitors to Canada. The mother had advised the officer at the port-of-entry that she was coming to Canada with her daughters to be reunited with her husband until such time as his refugee claim was determined. Her credibility was not an issue in the proceedings.

The application was dismissed. The adjudicator correctly determined that a temporary purpose can only be established if the period of the visit is not indefinite in duration. The Court noted that one can have a temporary purpose without a specific departure date as long as the length of the stay is not indefinite.

Section 2(2)

Fofanah v. Canada (Minister of Citizenship & Immigration) (1998), 46 Imm. L.R. (2d) 29, 152 F.T.R. 227 (Fed. T.D.) — This was an application to set aside a negative decision of the CRDD. The applicant was a citizen of Sierra Leone and based her claim on grounds of persecution on account of her political opinion, on account of her family status and on account of her gender. Simply because there is a change in the military government in Sierra Leone, does not mean that the CRDD can evade its responsibility to assess whether there is a reasonable possibility that the applicant will be persecuted if she is returned there. What matters is whether the political opinions which were attributed to the applicant's family by virtue of her father's ties to the previous government and the opinions which were attributed to her husband will also be perceived as being contrary to the present military government. The focus is on whether the change in government means an end to the applicant's fear of persecution. This mandates an assessment of whether the applicant's opposition to the previous military government for failing to hold democratic elections will also be perceived as a threat by the current military regime. The CRDD made no such assessment, and accordingly its decision was set aside.

Chandrakumar v. Canada (Minister of Employment & Immigration) (May 16, 1997), Doc. A-1649-92 (Fed. T.D.) — The applicants sought to review a negative decision of the CRDD. A panel of the CRDD found that the applicant's renewal of his Sri Lanka passport indicated that he had re-availed himself of the protection of Sri Lanka. A person who applies for a passport must have the intention to re-avail himself or herself of the protection of the state. Such an intention cannot simply be assumed. The panel of the CRDD in this case did not engage in an analysis of the intention of the principle applicant in renewing his passport. The panel seems to have assumed that the simple action of renewing the passport without more was sufficient to establish re-availment of the protection of Sri Lanka. Such an inference is unreasonable. Accordingly, the decision of the CRDD was set aside.

Vodopianov v. Canada (Minister of Employment & Immigration) (June 20, 1995), Doc. A-1539-92 (Fed. T.D.) — The applicant, a resident of Ukraine, applied to review a negative decision concerning his refugee claim.

The issue of so called "changed circumstances" is one of fact. The criteria of "meaningful", "effective" and "durable", or some variation on those criteria, are helpful in the analysis to determine whether a claimant at the date of the claimant's hearing has an objectively well founded fear of persecution.

In this matter there was clear indication that the dramatic changes that had taken place in the Ukraine in the months preceding the applicant's hearing, were evolving rapidly and had not stabilized. There was no basis for concluding that the changes are or would be truly effective or durable and no analysis of the meaningfulness and effectiveness of the changes was undertaken by the CRDD.

The analysis of the CRDD was simply inadequate to support its conclusion that considering the conditions prevailing in the Ukraine and all the circumstances of the applicant, the applicant no longer had a well founded fear of persecution. The decision of the CRDD was quashed.

Padilla v. Canada (Minister of Citizenship & Immigration) (March 6, 1995), Doc. IMM-2723-94 (Fed. T.D.) — The applicant, a citizen of Honduras, applied to review a negative determination of the CRDD. On the question of a change of country circumstances the Court noted that such a determination is a finding of fact and that the Court should be reluctant to intervene unless the finding is truly erroneous. A change in the political situation in the claimant's country of origin is only relevant if it may help in determining whether or not there is, at the date of the hearing, a reasonable and objectively foreseeable possibility that the claimant will be persecuted in the event of a return there. Although the Court was troubled by the fact that the decision gave very little consideration to changes in Honduras, particularly since it noted that human rights abuses were still occurring there, nevertheless the finding that there was a change of country circumstances could not be said to be erroneous and thus the application for judicial review was dismissed.

Yusuf v. Canada (Minister of Employment & Immigration) (1995), 179 N.R. 11 (Fed. C.A.) — A change in the political situation in the claimant's country of origin is only relevant if it may help in determining whether or not there is, at the date of the hearing, a reasonable and objectively foreseeable possibility that the claimant will be persecuted in the event of a return there. The use of words such as meaningful, effective or durable are only helpful if one keeps clearly in mind that the only question, and therefore the only test, is that derived from the definition of Convention refugee. The issue of so-called change in circumstances is simply one of fact. It is not a question of law.

Bediako v. Canada (Minister of Employment & Immigration) (August 29, 1994), Doc. IMM-3059-93 (Fed. T.D.) — The applicant had a well-founded subjective and objective fear of persecution when he left Ghana. The Board concluded that the objective fear of the applicant had been removed by changes in the country conditions between December 31, 1991, when the applicant left that country, and December 30, 1992, when the Board heard evidence of the applicant's claim.

The Board, in deciding whether there has been a change in country conditions, is required to give a sufficient analysis of the conflicting documentary evidence before it. There was, in this case, a very extensive analysis of the change in country conditions and, accordingly, that aspect of the Board's decision cannot be criticized.

Country changes have to be meaningful, effective and durable. In this case there was documentary evidence that showed that democracy was not working perfectly in Ghana, however, the Board addressed in detail the changes in country conditions and found them to be fundamental and durable enough to eliminate the objective basis for the applicant's fear. Accordingly, the application was dismissed.

Acevedo v. Canada (Minister of Employment & Immigration) (1994), 78 F.T.R. 316 — The applicant sought to review a negative decision of the CRDD. The Board accepted the applicant's evidence. It also found a change in the circumstances in El Salvador and for that reason dismissed the applicant's claim. Whenever the issue of a change in circumstances arises, the Board has to assess whether the changes are meaningful, effective and of such a nature as to remove the objective basis of a claimant's fears. Further, the Court noted that there was authority for the proposition that not only must these changes be meaningful and effective; they must also be durable. There was evidence before the Court that the accord in El Salvador amounted to "promises and pledges" and not effective action. The length that the accord was in effect — nine months — was not sufficient to support the conclusion that the changes were of an enduring nature. Furthermore, the Board did not refer to any of the documentary evidence indicating that notwithstanding the ceasefire, human rights abuses had continued in El Salvador. The application was allowed and the matter returned to be decided by a differently constituted panel.

Penate v. Canada (Minister of Employment & Immigration) (1993), 71 F.T.R. 171 — For digest, see section 2, subheading *Subsection (1), Convention refugee, supra.*

Hlavaty v. Canada (Minister of Employment & Immigration) (1993), 22 Imm. L.R. (2d) 176, 69 F.T.R. 259 — For digest, see section 2, subheading *Subsection (1), Convention Refugee, supra.*

Villalta v. Canada (Solicitor General) (1993), 68 F.T.R. 304 — For digest, see section 2, subheading *Subsection (1), Convention Refugee, supra.*

Canada (Minister of Employment & Immigration) v. Obstoj, [1992] 2 F.C. 739, 93 D.L.R. (4th) 144, 142 N.R. 81 (Fed. C.A.) — For digest, see section 2, subheading *Subsection (1), Convention refugee, supra.*

Section 2(3)

Jiminez v. Canada (Minister of Citizenship & Immigration) (January 25, 1999), Doc. IMM-1718-98 (Fed. T.D.) — In order to bring himself within the provisions of section 2(3) of the *Immigration Act*, the applicant is not required to show that he is suffering continual psychological after-effects from the persecution which he suffered in his country of nationality. The Board accepted as a fact that the applicant had been beaten, burned, raped, shot and left for dead. However, it did not comment on whether the nature of the applicant's persecution was sufficiently appalling and atrocious to warrant the application of section 2(3), rather it focused exclusively on whether the applicant was currently suffering from "the continued effect of past persecution". In so deciding, the Board erred in law, and the matter was remitted back for redetermination.

Sandhu v. Canada (Ministre de la Citoyenneté & de l'Immigration) (1998), 149 F.T.R. 83 (Fed. T.D.) — This was an application to set aside a negative decision of the CRDD. The applicant claimed refugee status alleging a well-founded fear of persecution for reasons of political opinion. The applicant was a resident of the Punjab who supported the Akali Dal Party and had been physically abused by the police. In its decision the panel recognized that the applicant had been tortured at the time in question. It also found that as a result of changed circumstances in the Punjab, there was no longer any objective basis for his fear that he would be persecuted should he be returned.

At the hearing, the counsel for the applicant asked the panel to apply the Convention against Torture, an international agreement signed and ratified by Canada. Counsel argued that in light of the panel's finding that the applicant had been subjected to torture in the past, Canada should not return him to India, as there were substantial grounds for believing that he would be tortured again.

The panel did not have jurisdiction to apply the Convention against Torture, as there is no express provision in its enabling legislation to this effect. The panel's role is to determine whether a person is a refugee within the meaning of the Geneva Convention. Furthermore, the Convention against Torture has not been incorporated into Canadian domestic law, although Canada has signed and ratified this international agreement.

The applicant did not raise the effect of subsection 2(3) of the Act at the hearing, namely whether the torture the applicant suffered was so appalling that this experience alone is a compelling reasons not to return him to his country, even if there is no longer any fear of further persecution. Because the applicant did not adduce evidence to establish that he was part of the tiny minority falling under subsection 2(3), the panel did not have to decide this issue. Accordingly the application for judicial review was dismissed.

Yong-Gueico v. Canada (Minister of Citizenship & Immigration) (1997), 39 Imm. L.R. (2d) 69, 134 F.T.R. 135 (Fed. T.D.) — The applicant sought to review a negative determination of his refugee claim. The tribunal accepted the principal applicant's testimony, but at the same time rejected his claim, due to a change in country conditions in Chile. The definition of convention refugee, in the Act, has two parts. Paragraph (a) contains the criteria that have to be established in order to fall within the definition. Paragraph (b) sets out one additional criteria that must be taken into account. Pursuant to the authority granted under paragraph 2(2)(e), a tribunal may determine that due to changed country conditions a person can no longer be a Convention refugee. It is possible, however for subsection 2(3) to cancel the effect of paragraph 2(2)(e). Subsection 2(3) requires the claimant to establish compelling reasons arising out of past persecution which negate the positive impact of changed country conditions in that particular claimant's circumstances.

The fact that counsel for the claimant failed to refer to or rely on subsection 2(3) did not excuse the tribunal for overlooking it. The failure of the tribunal to consider the "compelling reasons" aspect of the definition amounts to a failure by the tribunal to exercise its jurisdiction. This failure is a reviewable error in law sufficient to squash the decision.

Accordingly, the decision of the tribunal was set aside and the case was referred back to a differently constituted tribunal.

Shahid v. Canada (Minister of Citizenship & Immigration) (1995), 89 F.T.R. 106 (Fed. T.D.) — The applicant claimed that by virtue of section 2(3) of the *Immigration Act* he should not be returned to Pakistan. The Board, in refusing to apply section 2(3) determined that it required an ongoing fear of persecution. For this reason the decision was set aside. The Board, once it embarked upon the assessment of the applicant's claim under section 2(3) had the duty to consider the level of atrocity of the acts inflicted upon the applicant, the repercussions upon his physical and mental state, and determine whether this experience alone constituted a compelling reason not to return him to his country of origin. The panel failed to do this and accordingly its decision was quashed and the matter returned for a new hearing before a differently constituted tribunal.

Hassan v. Canada (Minister of Employment & Immigration) (1994), 77 F.T.R. 309 (Fed. T.D.) — The respondent conceded that the Board had erred in this case. However, counsel for the applicants was of the view that the panel had erred in its interpretation of section 2(3) of the *Immigration Act* and that if it had not been for this error the applicants would have been found to be Convention refugees.

Before the Court will refer a matter back for redetermination in accordance with a direction that the applicants be found to be Convention refugees, the following circumstances must apply:

1. the evidence must be so clearly conclusive that the only possible conclusion is that the claimant is a Convention refugee;

2. the sole issue to be decided must be a pure question of law which will be dispositive of the case;

3. the legal issue must be based on uncontroverted evidence and accepted facts; and

4. there must be no factual issues which involve conflicting evidence which are central to the claim.

To require that before section 2(3) could apply there would have to be a Convention refugee determination in respect of an applicant would make the application of section 2(3) dependent on timing alone. Section 2(3) does not require an on-going fear of persecution. It applies to only a tiny minority of present day claimants who can demonstrate that they have suffered such appalling persecution that their experience alone is a compelling reason not to return them to the country in which they suffered the persecution. Section 2(3) only applies to extraordinary cases in which the persecution is relatively so exceptional that even in the wake of changed circumstances it would be wrong to return refugee claimants. The Court did not direct that on a rehearing of the matter the Board find the applicants to be Convention refugees. The Board with its experience and expertise was best able to assess whether, having regard to the special and limited application of section 2(3), the applicants fell within its ambit.

Arguello-Garcia v. Canada (Minister of Employment & Immigration) (1993), 21 Imm. L.R. (2d) 285, 64 F.T.R. 307, 70 F.T.R. 1 — The Refugee Division found the applicant not to be a Convention refugee. The Board erred in law when it found that the facts did not amount to previous persecution. The Court noted that it had accepted a broad range of harassment and ill treatment as constituting persecution and, furthermore, that neither deprivation of physical liberty nor physical mistreatment were essential elements of persecution.

The Board, notwithstanding its findings that there was no persecution, found that there had been a change of circumstance in El Salvador. The second issue before the Court was whether the applicant fell within the special or limited category of persons to which section 2(3) of the *Immigration Act* applies. Section 2(3) is based on a general humanitarian principle which permits a person who has suffered serious past persecution to retain or obtain Convention refugee status despite fundamental changes in his or her country of origin.

The Court referred to the Concise Oxford Dictionary of Current English, Clarendon Press, Oxford, 1990 definition of atrocious and appalling. Atrocious was defined as very bad or unpleasant or alternatively extremely savage or wicked. An atrocity was defined as an extremely wicked or cruel act, especially one involving physical violence or injury. Appalling was defined as shocking, unpleasant or bad.

In this case, the torture and sexual assault experienced by the applicant qualified as atrocious and appalling acts as defined above. The right not to be subject to torture and cruel, inhuman and degrading treatment is a fundamental right which enjoys the highest international protection.

Further, there was ample evidence before the Board to show that the applicant continued to suffer severe psychological hardship as a result of the very serious persecution which he and his family members suffered in El Salvador. A psychiatric report entered in evidence stated that the applicant was suffering from post traumatic stress disorder, related to his personal and family history of violent persecution, torture and massacre. The finding by the Board that the applicant did not fit within the criteria set out in section 2(3) was on a misconstruction of the applicable test and constituted an error in law.

The application was granted and the matter returned to a differently constituted panel of the IRB to reconsider the evidence in accordance with the reasons of the Court.

Canada (Minister of Employment & Immigration) v. Obstoj, [1992] 2 F.C. 739, 93 D.L.R. (4th) 144, 142 N.R. 81 (Fed. C.A.) — For digest, see section 2, subheading *Subsection (1), Convention refugee, supra*.

Purposes of Amendments

2.1 Purposes of amendments — The purposes of the amendments set out in *An Act to amend the Immigration Act and the Criminal Code in consequence thereof*, chapter 29 of the 4th Supplement to the Revised Statutes of Canada, are the following:

> **(a) to preserve for persons in genuine need of protection access to the procedures for determining refugee claims;**

(b) to control widespread abuse of the procedures for determining refugee claims, particularly in light of organized incidents involving large-scale introduction of persons into Canada to take advantage of those procedures;

(c) to deter those who assist in the illegal entry of persons into Canada and thereby minimize the exploitation of and risks to persons seeking to come to Canada; and

(d) to respond to security concerns, including the fulfillment of Canada's obligations in respect of internationally protected persons.

R.S.C. 1985, c. 29 (4th Supp.), s. 1.

PART I — CANADIAN IMMIGRATION POLICY

Objectives

3. **Immigration objectives — It is hereby declared that Canadian immigration policy and the rules and regulations made under this Act shall be designed and administered in such a manner as to promote the domestic and international interests of Canada recognizing the need**

(a) to support the attainment of such demographic goals as may be established by the Government of Canada in respect of the size, rate of growth, structure and geographic distribution of the Canadian population;

(b) to enrich and strengthen the cultural and social fabric of Canada, taking into account the federal and bilingual character of Canada;

(c) to facilitate the reunion in Canada of Canadian citizens and permanent residents with their close relatives from abroad;

(d) to encourage and facilitate the adaptation of persons who have been granted admission as permanent residents to Canadian society by promoting cooperation between the Government of Canada and other levels of government and non-governmental agencies in Canada with respect thereto;

(e) to facilitate the entry of visitors into Canada for the purpose of fostering trade and commerce, tourism, cultural and scientific activities and international understanding;

(f) to ensure that any person who seeks admission to Canada on either a permanent or temporary basis is subject to standards of admission that do not discriminate in a manner inconsistent with the *Canadian Charter of Rights and Freedoms*;

(g) to fulfil Canada's international legal obligations with respect to refugees and to uphold its humanitarian tradition with respect to the displaced and the persecuted;

(h) to foster the development of a strong and viable economy and the prosperity of all regions in Canada;

(i) to maintain and protect the health, safety and good order of Canadian society; and

(j) to promote international order and justice by denying the use of Canadian territory to persons who are likely to engage in criminal activity.

R.S.C. 1985, c. 28 (4th Supp.), s. 2.

Case Law

Baker v. Canada (Minister of Citizenship & Immigration) (1999), 174 D.L.R. (4th) 193 (S.C.C.) — The appellant entered Canada as a visitor in 1981, and had remained ever since. She was not a permanent resident but had worked illegally for 11 years. She had 4 children all of whom were born in Canada. The appellant was ordered deported in 1992, after it was determined that she had worked illegally in Canada and had overstayed her visitor's visa.

In 1993, the appellant applied for an exemption from the requirement to apply for permanent residence outside Canada, based upon humanitarian and compassionate considerations. In April 1994, it was determined that there were insufficient humanitarian and compassionate grounds to warrant processing the appellant's application from within Canada. The letter advising her of this decision contained no reasons for the decision. The appellant's counsel was provided with the notes made by the immigration officer who interviewed Ms. Baker. These notes were used by the immigration officer who made the decision. Following the refusal of her application, the appellant was served with a direction to report to Pearson Airport for removal. Her deportation was stayed pending the result of this appeal.

At the Trial Division, the application for judicial review was dismissed. The Court held that the immigration officer who made the decision was not required to provide reasons. In the absence of evidence to the contrary, he acted in good faith and made a decision based on correct principles. The trial judge certified an appeal under the following terms: "Given that the *Immigration Act* does not expressly incorporate the language of Canada's international obligations, with respect to the international Convention on the Rights of the Child, must federal immigration authorities treat the best interests of the Canadian child as the primary consideration in assessing an application under section 114(2) of the *Immigration Act*?"

The Federal Court of Appeal held that the appeal was limited to the question that had been certified and as well, rejected a challenge to the constitutionality of section 83(1). The Court noted that a treaty cannot have legal effect in Canada unless implemented through domestic legislation and that the Convention had not been adopted in either federal or provincial legislation. The Court held that legislation should be interpreted to avoid conflicts with Canada's international obligations, but otherwise declined to apply the Convention.

The Supreme Court of Canada declined to consider the various Charter issues raised by the parties because the issues involved in the case could be resolved under principles of administrative law and statutory interpretation.

The certification of a question of general importance is the trigger by which an appeal is justified. The object of the appeal was still the judgement itself, not the certified question. Once a question has been certified, all aspects of the appeal may be considered by the Court of Appeal.

The Court reviewed the criteria that should be used in determining what procedural rights the duty of fairness requires in a given set of circumstances. The Court emphasized that underlying all of these factors was the notion that the purpose of the participatory rights contained within the duty of procedural fairness was to ensure that administrative decisions are made using a fair and open procedure appropriate to the decision being made and to its statutory, institutional and social context and to provide those affected by the decision with an opportunity to put forward their views and evidence fully and have them considered by the decision-maker.

One important consideration relevant to determining what is required by the common law duty of procedural fairness is, the more that the process provided for, the function of the tribunal, the nature of the decision-making body and the determinations that must be made to reach a decision resemble judicial decision-making, the more likely it is that procedural protections closer to the trial model will be required. A second factor is the nature of the statutory scheme and the terms of the statute pursuant to which the body operates. The third factor is the importance of the decision to the individual or individuals affected. The more important the decision the more stringent the procedural protections that will be mandated. In addition, the legitimate expectations of the person challenging the decision may also determine what procedures the duty of fairness requires. If a claimant has a legitimate expectation that a certain procedure will be followed, this procedure will be required by the duty of fairness. Similarly, if a claimant has a legitimate expectation that a certain result will be reached, fairness may require more extensive procedural rights than would otherwise be accorded. The doctrine of legitimate expectations cannot lead to substantive rights outside the procedural domain. Lastly, the analysis of what procedures the duty of fairness requires also takes into account and respects the choices of procedure made by the agency itself, particularly when the statute leaves to the decision-maker the ability to choose its own procedures or when the agency has an expertise in determining what procedures are appropriate. This list is held not to be exhaustive.

An oral hearing is not a general requirement for humanitarian and compassionate decisions. The appellant had the opportunity to put forward in written form, through her lawyer, information about her situation, her children, and their emotional dependence on her as well as documentation in support of her application provided by a social worker and a psychiatrist.

In certain circumstances, the duty of procedural fairness will require the provision of a written explanation for a decision. The circumstances in this case constituted one of the situations where reasons were necessary because of the profound importance of a humanitarian and compassionate decision to those affected. It would be unfair for a person subject to a decision such as this one, which is so critical to their future, not to be told why the result was reached. The reasons requirement was fulfilled in this case because the appellant was provided with the notes of the officer. Because there was no other record of the reasons for making the decision, the notes of the reviewing officer were taken by inference to be the reasons for the decision. Accepting documents such as these notes is part of the flexibility that is necessary when courts evaluate the requirements of the duty of fairness with a recognition of the day-to-day realities of administrative agencies.

Procedural fairness also requires that decisions be made free from a reasonable apprehension of bias. The duty to act in a manner that does not give rise to a reasonable apprehension of bias applies to all immigration officers who play a significant role in the making of any decision, whether they are subordinate reviewing officers or the ones who make the final decision. The Court concluded in this matter that a well-informed member of the community would perceive bias when reading the reviewing officer's comment. The note did not disclose the existence of an open mind or a weighing of particular circumstances free from stereotype.

The Court found that the appropriate standard of review of a humanitarian and compassionate decision was reasonableness. The Court then examined whether the decision in this case and the immigration officer's interpretation of the scope of the discretion conferred upon him was unreasonable. An unreasonable decision is one that is not supported by any reason that can stand up to a somewhat probing examination. A Court reviewing a conclusion on the reasonableness standard must determine whether any reasons support it. The defect, if there is one, could be in the evidentiary foundation itself or in the logical process by which conclusions are sought from that foundation. The Court concluded that the approach taken in regard to the children's interest indicated that this decision was unreasonable. The officer was dismissive of the interest of the children and this was an unreasonable exercise of the discretion conferred by the section, notwithstanding the important deference that should be given to the decision of the officer. Deference requires a respectful attention to the reasons offered, or which could be offered, in support of a decision.

Section 114(2) and regulation 2.1 require that a decision-maker exercise the power based upon "compassionate or humanitarian consideration". These words and their meaning must be central in determining whether an individual humanitarian and compassionate decision is a reasonable exercise of the power conferred by Parliament. Determining whether the approach taken by the officer was within the boundaries set out by the words of the statute and the values of administrative law required a contextual approach. A reasonable exercise of the power conferred by the section requires close attention to the interests and needs of children. Children's rights and attention to their interests are central humanitarian and compassionate values in Canadian society. Indication of children's interests are important considerations governing the manner in which humanitarian and compassionate powers should be exercised. One of the objectives of the Act in section 3(c) is the facilitation of the reunion in Canada of Canadian citizens and permanent residents with their close relatives from abroad. This section is consistent with a large and liberal interpretation of the values underlying the *Immigration Act* and its purposes. Parliament places a high value on keeping citizens and permanent residents together with their close relatives who are already in Canada. The obligation to take seriously and place important weight on keeping children in contact with both parents is suggested by the objective articulated in section 3(c).

The ratification by Canada of the Convention on the Rights of the Child and the recognition of the importance of children's rights and the best interests of children in other international instruments ratified by Canada, is a further indication of the importance of children's interests when making a humanitarian and compassionate decision. The Convention has not been implemented by Parliament, and, therefore, its provisions have no direct application within Canadian law. Nevertheless, the values reflected in international human rights law may help inform the contextual approach to statutory interpretation in judicial review. Finally, the guidelines issued by the Minister further emphasize that an important factor in a humanitarian and compassionate decision is the connection between family members.

The reasons for this decision did not indicate that it was made in a manner which was alive, attentive, or sensitive to the interests of the Canadian born children of the appellant and did not consider them as an important factor in making the decision. For this reason, the decision was unreasonable and must be overturned.

Hussain v. Canada (Minister of Citizenship & Immigration) (1998), 45 Imm. L.R. (2d) 13, 159 F.T.R. 203 (Fed. T.D.) — This was an application to quash the decision of a visa officer who refused the applicant's application for permanent residence. On his application form the applicant had identified executive secretary as his intended occupation. The applicant also had a letter from his superior setting out the duties he performed as an executive secretary. The visa officer attached no weight to the fact that the applicant reported to the general manager of purchasing because "based on [his] local knowledge" this was more indicative of the applicant's years of service than it was of his degree of responsibility. The visa officer's "local knowledge" constituted an extraneous factor. The applicant was unaware that the visa officer was relying in part on this local knowledge. Fairness required that the visa officer disclose this to the applicant so that he would have an opportunity to respond to it.

The principle objectives of the administration of immigration control are first, to facilitate the entry into Canada of persons who meet the requirements under the *Immigration Act* and Regulations and second, to ensure that those who do not are excluded. Both objectives are of equal importance and neither is likely to be achieved if visa officers do not adopt a procedure for determining visa applications that is calculated to produce accurate and thoughtful decisions. Officers should not be burdened by procedural duties imposed by the Court that prevent them from processing applications in an expeditious and cost effective manner.

The visa officer's practice of asking an applicant at the close of an interview whether he or she wishes to add anything is not sufficient to satisfy the duty to make reasonable inquiries imposed by the duty of fairness. This practice fails to advise an applicant of the concerns that a visa officer may have in such a way as to provide the applicant with a reasonable opportunity to disabuse the visa officer of his or her particular concerns.

Halm v. Canada (Minister of Employment & Immigration) (1995), 104 F.T.R. 81, [1996] 1 F.C. 547 (Fed. T.D.) — The applicant was convicted in New York State on a number of charges including sodomy and endangering the welfare of a child. He was released on bail pending appeal. His appeal was eventually denied by the New York Court of Appeals and the applicant was ordered to surrender himself for sentencing in New York State. Instead, the applicant entered Canada and was eventually arrested by immigration officials. The applicant was ordered deported and successfully brought an application for judicial review quashing the deportation order on the basis that the sodomy section of the *Criminal Code* of Canada was contrary to the *Charter of Rights*. This meant that the applicant was convicted of an offence outside of Canada but not one which, if committed in Canada, would constitute an offense punishable by a maximum term of 10 years or more. Subsequent to that decision the department initiated further proceedings to deport the applicant based on charges of bail jumping and misrepresentation to immigration officials.

The applicant sought to quash this second deportation order in these proceedings. The applicant alleged that in the circumstances of this case the deportation proceedings amounted to an unfair bypassing of, or disguised, extradition. The applicant argued that he could not now be extradited to the United States for his convictions for sodomy because those offences were no longer recognized in Canada as a result of the judgement striking down section 159 of the *Criminal Code*. There is no legal authority for the proposition that simply because deportation to a foreign country may result in a greater penalty to an individual than extradition to that country, the deportation is contrary to section 7 of the Charter.

The Court adopted the reasons of Austin J. in *Shepherd v. Canada (Minister of Employment & Immigration)* (1989), 70 O.R. (2d) 765 (Fed. C.A.), with respect to disguised extradition.

1. If the purpose of the exercise is to deport the person because his presence is not conducive to the public good, that is a legitimate exercise of the power of deportation.

2. If the purpose is to surrender the person as a fugitive criminal to a state because it asked for him, that is not a legitimate exercise of the power of deportation.

3. It is open to the courts to enquire whether the purpose of the government was lawful or otherwise.

4. The onus is on the party alleging an unlawful exercise of power. It is a heavy onus.

5. To succeed it would be necessary to hold that the Minister did not genuinely consider it in the public interest to expel the person in question.

6. The adoption of the Charter has not lessened the onus.

The fact that the United States wanted the applicant back, or that there were communications between U.S. and Canadian officials, is not evidence of bad faith or improper motive. Nor does the issuance of a conditional request for extradition by the United States indicate that anything improper was done by Canada in taking steps to deport the applicant.

There is a legislative basis for further inquiries being held in this type of case in section 34 of the *Immigration Act*. The Court did not infer from the evidence that the Minister was acting with improper motive in bringing the second deportation inquiry after the Court had set aside the first deportation order. Section 34 provides for what was done in this case. Section 34 is cast in broad terms.

Chan v. Canada (Minister of Employment & Immigration) (1994), 24 Imm. L.R. (2d) 305, 79 F.T.R. 263 (Fed. T.D.) — The issue in this judicial review was whether the words "that will make a significant contribution to the Canadian economy" contained in the definition of an entrepreneur are *ultra vires*.

Section 3 of the *Immigration Act* sets forth the objectives of Canada's immigration policy. Paragraph (h) recognizes the need to foster the development of a strong and viable economy and the prosperity of all regions in Canada. Therefore, the regulations made by the Governor in Council and their administration must be considered having regard to Canada's immigration policy. When Parliament authorized the Governor in Council to make regulations respecting selection standards based on personal attributes and attainments, it intended that the Governor in Council have the discretion to more fully describe the personal attributes and attainments having regard to Canada's immigration policy objectives and in particular to Canada's domestic interests, including the need to foster the development of a strong and viable economy. Therefore, the words "that will make a significant contribution to the economy" are not *ultra vires* the *Immigration Act*.

With respect to entrepreneurs, the scheme of the *Immigration Act* and regulations was that a prospective immigrant was expected to represent to a visa officer the immigrant's intention and ability to establish, purchase or invest in a business or a commercial venture in Canada. When the immigrant lands, the immigration officer at the port-of-entry attaches conditions to the immigrant's visa so that the representations made to the visa officer survive the landing and the immigrant can be required to fulfil them.

The assessment of whether an applicant has fulfilled the terms and conditions must concern itself with the two-year period following the applicant's landing. Whether a business will make a significant contribution to the Canadian economy or create or continue employment for Canadian citizens or permanent residents is not something that lends itself to a momentary assessment. The notion of a significant contribution to the economy with the continuation of employment are on-going circumstances and require more long-term assessment. The immigration officer must be permitted the scope to reasonably satisfy himself or herself that the business or commercial venture has and will make a significant contribution and that employment opportunities will be created in a meaningful way.

Finally, there may be many reasons for bankruptcy and bankruptcy alone would not preclude the applicant from having met the conditions attached to his landing, but these are circumstances for objective assessment by an immigration officer.

Orelien v. Canada (Minister of Employment & Immigration) (1991), [1992] 1 F.C. 592, 15 Imm. L.R. (2d) 1, 135 N.R. 50 (Fed. C.A.) — Canada's obligations in the area of refugees stem from the 4th Geneva Convention of August 12, 1949, and protocol due to the Geneva Convention of August 12, 1949, both approved by Acts of Parliament (*Geneva Conventions Act*, R.S.C. 1985, c. G-3, s. 2, as am. S.C. 1990, c. 14, s. 1), as well as a customary norm of temporary refuge. To return a person to Haiti in the circumstances that presently exist and have existed at relevant times in this case would have violated Canada's obligations under the Convention, the protocol and the customary norm of international law prohibiting the forceable repatriation of foreign nationals who have fled generalized violence and other threats to their lives and security arising out of internal armed conflict within their state of nationality. The Convention, the protocol and the customary norm of international law have the force of domestic law in Canada and can be enforced in the courts of Canada at the suit of a private individual. The intention to execute a deportation order which if executed would breach those laws does not colour the process under the *Immigration Act* by which a person from such a country may be ordered deported. This is not to denigrate the importance of the Convention, the protocol and the customary norms of international law. It would be a grave and justiciable matter if Canada were to execute deportation orders in circumstances which breached obligations under international law and put the life, liberty or security of persons in peril.

Kindler v. Canada (Minister of Justice), [1991] 2 S.C.R. 779, 8 C.R. (4th) 1, 67 C.C.C. (3d) 1, 6 C.R.R. (2d) 193, 84 D.L.R. (4th) 438, 45 F.T.R. 160 (note), 129 N.R. 81 (S.C.C.) — While this case dealt with whether the decision of the Minister of Justice to surrender the appellant to the United States without first seeking assurances that the death penalty would not be imposed violated the appellant's rights under the Canadian Charter of Rights and Freedoms, there are some comments in the case which are useful. The Supreme Court of Canada (per La Forest J.) noted that the Government has the right and duty to keep out and to expel aliens from Canada if it considers it advisable to do so. This right exists independently of extradition. If an alien has a serious criminal record, he can be refused admission and, by the same token, deported if he has already entered Canada. Extradition and deportation do not always have the same purposes. Cases can arise where they serve different ends, and fairness may demand that one procedure be used rather than the other. In this case, the Court would have been concerned about resorting to deportation rather than extradition because extradition has in-built protections geared to the criminal process.

Mannan v. Canada (Minister of Employment & Immigration) (1991), 16 Imm. L.R. (2d) 73, 48 F.T.R. 259 (Fed. T.D.) — This decision provides a useful statement of first principles which are to govern the Court's approach to interpreting the *Immigration Act*.

The Court stated that the purpose of the *Immigration Act* was to regulate immigration into Canada, which means that some immigration is permitted and some is rejected according to the law.

To determine the purpose of a statute the Court recommended the procedure in *Heydon's Case* (1584), 3 Co. Rep. 7a, 76 E.R. 637, to the effect that the true interpretation of a statute is to proceed according to the following principles:

1. the determination of what the common law was before the making of the *Immigration Act*;

2. the determination of the mischief and defect for which the common law did not provide;

3. the examination of the remedy that Parliament has resolved and appointed to cure the problem; and

4. it is the responsibility of judges to make such construction of the statute as required to suppress the mischief which Parliament addressed and advance the remedy which Parliament provided. The Court is to suppress subtle inventions and evasions designed to continue the mischief.

The Court noted that at Confederation section 95 of the *Constitution Act*, 1867 provided that each province can make laws in relation to immigration into the province and that the Parliament of Canada may from time to time make laws in relation to immigration into all or any of the provinces and that any provincial law in relation to immigration has effect only so long as it is not repugnant to a law of the Parliament of Canada in relation to immigration.

Further, the Court noted that section 95(25) distributed legislative power in relation to naturalization and aliens to Parliament.

The Court then went on to deal with the merits of this case and dismissed the application for judicial review.

Bhatnager v. Canada (Minister of Employment & Immigration), [1990] 2 S.C.R. 217, 44 Admin. L.R. 1, 111 N.R. 185, 71 D.L.R. (4th) 84, 43 C.P.C. (2d) 213, 12 Imm. L.R. (2d) 81 — The respondent, Bhatnager, sought a writ of *mandamus* to compel the Minister to process the application for landing of her husband, an Indian citizen living in India. There had been, to the time of her application, a delay of almost 5 years in processing the respondent's husband's application.

Prior to hearing the respondent's motion, an affidavit of an immigration officer was filed on behalf of the Minister. On July 11, 1985, in the course of cross-examination on that affidavit, counsel for the Minister agreed to produce the Ministry's New Delhi file. The hearing of the application was adjourned until September 3, 1985. Several telexes were sent to New Delhi requesting the file but over a month passed with no sign of it. The respondent brought two motions; the first adding the Secretary of State for External Affairs as a party respondent and the second ordering production of the New Delhi file. Both motions were granted on August 15, 1985 in open court and in the presence of counsel for the appellants. Part of the formal order required production of the file and sufficient time for the cross-examinations to be completed in time for the scheduled hearing on September 3, 1985. On August 20, 1985, a copy of the order was served on the appellant's solicitor by the respondent's solicitor. There is no evidence that the order was served on either of the appellants or that they were informed of its existence. On August 26, 1985, counsel for the parties agreed to continue the cross-examination of the appellant's representative on August 29 on the assumption that the file or a copy of it would be available. Counsel for the respondent received what purported to be a copy of the file on August 27, 1985 but in the course of the cross-examination it was discovered that several relevant documents were missing. In the meantime, the original file had arrived in Ottawa by diplomatic bag on August 28, 1985. For some reasons which were not explained in evidence, the file did not arrive in Toronto until August 30, 1985, the last business day before the hearing of the respondent's application for *mandamus*. The respondents were cited for contempt and the motion for *mandamus* was granted. The respondents were acquitted of contempt at the trial division. The Federal Court of Appeal overturned this decision and found the appellants guilty of contempt and remitted the matter to the trial Judge for assessment of penalty. The appellant Ministers appealed to the Supreme Court of Canada which allowed the appeal and found the appellants not guilty of contempt. The Court noted that an allegation of contempt of court is a matter of criminal dimension. A finding of guilt could have subjected the appellants to a fine of as much as $5,000 and the possibility of imprisonment to a maximum of 1 year. Common law has always required personal service or actual personal knowledge of a court order as a precondition to liability in contempt. A finding of knowledge on the part of the client may, in some circumstances, be inferred from the fact that the solicitor for the client was informed of the order. In the ordinary case in which a party is involved in isolated pieces of litigation, the inference may readily be drawn. In the case of Ministers of the Crown who administer large departments, it would be extraordinary if orders were brought routinely to their attention. In order to infer knowledge from service upon the Minister's solicitor, there must be circumstances which reveal a special reason for bringing the order to the attention of the Minister. Knowledge, in most cases, is proved circumstantially and in contempt cases, the inference of knowledge will always be available where facts capable of supporting the inference are proved. Ministers will not be able to hide behind their lawyers so as to flout orders of the Court. Any instructions to the effect that the

Minister is to be kept ignorant may attract liability on the basis of the doctrine of wilful blindness. Furthermore, a Minister of the Crown cannot be confident in any given case that the inference will not be drawn and hopefully this will serve as a sufficient incentive for the Minister to see to it that officials are impressed with the importance of complying with court orders.

Ho v. Canada (Minister of Employment & Immigration) (1989), 8 Imm. L.R. (2d) 38, 27 F.T.R. 241 (Fed. T.D.); affirmed (1990), 11 Imm. L.R. (2d) 12 (Fed. C.A.) — It is important to bear in mind that Parliament's intention in enacting the *Immigration Act* is to define Canada's immigration policy both to Canadians and to those who wish to come here from abroad. Such a policy cannot exist without complex regulations, a good many of which appear to be restrictive in nature but the policy should always be interpreted in positive terms. The purpose of the statute is to permit immigration, not prevent it, and it is the corresponding obligation of immigration officers to provide a thorough and fair assessment in compliance with the terms and spirit of the legislation.

Porter v. Canada (Minister of Employment & Immigration) (April 14, 1988), Doc. A-353-87 (Fed. C.A.) — The visa officer's refusal of an application for permanent residence which, in fact, is based on an administrative delay of the Minister's own creation is invalid in law. The Government's duty is to facilitate family class applications, not to frustrate them.

Rajudeen v. Canada (Minister of Employment & Immigration) (1984), 55 N.R. 129 (Fed. C.A.) — The definition of Convention refugee does not include a definition of persecution. "Persecute" was defined by reference to a dictionary as "to harass or afflict with repeated acts of cruelty or annoyance; to afflict persistently; to afflict or punish because of particular opinions or adherence to a particular creed or mode of worship." "Persecution" was defined as "a particular course or period of systematic infliction of punishment directed against those holding a particular (religious belief); persistent injury or annoyance from any source."

There is a subjective and objective component necessary to satisfy the definition of Convention refugee. The subjective component relates to the existence of the fear of persecution in the mind of the refugee. The objective component requires that the refugee's fear be evaluated objectively to determine if there is a valid basis for that fear.

In determining whether refugee status has been extended to cover a particular case, reference should be made to the expression of underlying policy in section 3(g) of the Act. To satisfy the definition, the persecution complained of must have been committed or been condoned by the state itself and consist either of conduct directed by the state toward the individual or in the state knowingly tolerating the behaviour of private citizens or refusing or being unable to protect the individual from such behaviour.

Gana v. Canada (Minister of Manpower & Immigration), [1970] S.C.R. 699, 13 D.L.R. (3d) 699 (S.C.C.) — This case provides an interesting historical perspective on the evolution of immigration policy. The Court, through Abbott J., points out that the scheme of the *Immigration Act*, R.S.C. 1952, was relatively simple. The only persons entitled to enter Canada as of right were Canadian citizens and persons having a Canadian domicile; all others required the permission of the Minister acting through his departmental officials. Those coming for a temporary stay were given permission to do so for a limited period as a visitor, student, or for some other purpose. Would-be immigrants were subject to examination as to their suitability on medical grounds, educational qualifications and the like. Those found satisfactory by the examining officer at the port-of-entry were granted permission to enter and remain as landed immigrants. The decision to grant or refuse such status, in accordance with the Act and Regulations, was made at the discretion of the immigration officer at the port-of-entry and was an administrative decision, not subject to review by anyone other than the Minister. Once a person was in Canada, having been granted the status of a landed immigrant, he could only be deprived of that status and ordered deported after a hearing before a special inquiry officer. If deportation was ordered, that order was subject to an appeal to the Immigration Appeal Board.

Prior to 1967, would-be immigrants who applied outside Canada or at border points and those already in Canada on a temporary basis were treated on the same basis. In 1967, however, a person who had been allowed to enter Canada as a visitor, or on some other temporary basis, was permitted to apply to an immigration officer in Canada, before the authorized period of his stay expired, for admission as a landed immigrant. A decision to refuse such an application was subject to appeal to the Immigration Appeal Board, creating the situation where persons who entered Canada ostensibly as non-immigrants were given a special consideration in relation to permanent admission as residents.

Principles

4. (1) Where right to come into Canada — A Canadian citizen and a permanent resident have a right to come into Canada except where, in the case of a permanent resident, it is established that that person is a person described in subsection 27(1).

Proposed Amendment — 4(1)

4. (1) Where right to come into Canada — A Canadian citizen and, subject to section 10.3, a permanent resident, have a right to come into Canada except where, in the case of a permanent resident, it is established that the person is a person described in subsection 27(1).

1992, c. 49, s. 2. [Not in force at date of publication.]

(2) Where right to remain in Canada — Subject to any other Act of Parliament, a Canadian citizen and a permanent resident have a right to remain in Canada except where, in the case of a permanent resident, it is established that that person is a person described in subsection 27(1).

(2.1) Right of Convention refugees — Subject to any other Act of Parliament, a person who is determined under this Act or the regulations to be a Convention refugee has, while lawfully in Canada, a right to remain in Canada except where it is established that the person is a person described in paragraph 19(1)(*c*.1), (*c*.2), (*d*), (*e*), (*f*), (*g*), (*j*), (*k*), or (*l*) or a person who has been convicted of an offence under any Act of Parliament for which a term of imprisonment of

(a) more than six months has been imposed; or

(b) five years or more may be imposed.

(3) Rights of indians — A person who is registered as an Indian pursuant to the *Indian Act* has, whether or not that person is a Canadian citizen, the same rights and obligations under this Act as a Canadian citizen.

R.S.C. 1985, c. 28 (4th Supp.) s. 3; 1992, c. 49, s. 2.

Case Law

Section 4(1)

Langner v. Canada (Minister of Employment & Immigration) (1994), 98 F.T.R. 188, affirmed (1995), 29 C.R.R. (2d) 184, 184 N.R. 230, 97 F.T.R. 118 (note) (Fed. C.A.), leave to appeal to S.C.C. refused (1995), 30 C.R.R. (2d) 188 (note), 193 N.R. 400 (note) (S.C.C.) — There are four applicants — two parents and two children. The parents sought to set aside a decision refusing an exemption under section 114(2) of the *Immigration Act*. The children sought a declaration that they were entitled to remain in Canada and that no removal order should be made against their parents. Further, there was a claim by the children to have the definition of "sponsor" in the *Immigration Regulations* declared inoperative. The plaintiff, Ewa Langner, in the action for a declaration, was appointed guardian of her children.

At the Trial Division all applications were refused.

With respect to the motion to quash the decision under section 114(2) there was no doubt that the parents, having been granted leave, had the necessary standing to challenge this decision. The parents, in their challenge, did not assert that they had personally been denied their Charter rights. Accordingly, they could not base their action on section 24(1) of the Charter. A person seeking a remedy under section 24(1) must personally have been a victim of an infringement of his or her Charter rights and such person may not base his or her application on an infringement of the rights of third parties.

The Langner children were not affected by the decision refusing to recognize the humanitarian and compassionate reasons asserted by their parents, and accordingly, they had no standing as plaintiffs in respect of the remedy of quashing the decision under section 114(2).

Both parents and children maintained a joint application to have the definition of a "sponsor" declared inoperative. It should be noted that the children are Canadian citizens. The Langner parents could not maintain an action or a declaration with respect to the definition of a "sponsor" because they were not capable of sponsoring an application for landing. Due to the fact that the parents were not given permission to make an application for landing, the children could not ever be in a position where there was anything for them to sponsor and, therefore, the children had no standing to attack the definition of "sponsor" in the Immigration Regulations.

The Court also set out the three part test for public interest standing. Those criteria are:

1. There must be a serious issue as to the Act's validity;

2. The applicants must be directly affected by the Act or have a genuine interest in its validity; and,

3. There must be no other reasonable and effective way to bring the Act's validity before the Court.

The children were found not to have met the test on the facts of this case, and therefore, could not have public interest standing for purposes of their request for a declaration.

The Court of Appeal upheld the decision of the trial judge and held that the removal of the parents would not offend the obligations contracted by Canada when it ratified the *Convention on the Rights of the Child*. The Court referred specifically to articles 9 and 10 of the Convention in that regard. It was further observed that the effect of allowing the appeal would be to create a situation in which one would need only to have a child on Canadian soil in order to avoid the effect of Canadian immigration laws — a situation which the Court was not prepared to countenance.

Finally, the Court of Appeal noted that the appellant parents' decision to take their children to Poland with them, or to leave them with family members was a private decision and one which did not involve the government of Canada. There was, therefore, no government action which could bring the Charter into play.

Alexander v. Canada (Minister of Employment & Immigration) (July 18, 1978), Doc. 78-9138 (Imm. App. Bd.) — The Board held that it had the power to determine whether a person was a permanent resident and, thus, to determine whether it had jurisdiction to hear the appellant's appeal. In this case, it found that it had jurisdiction to entertain the appeal pursuant to section 72(1) of the Act and that the appellant had, pursuant to section 4(1) of the Act, the right to come into Canada and, therefore, on his return to Canada did not have to be in possession of an immigrant visa.

Prata v. Canada (Minister of Manpower & Immigration), [1976] 1 S.C.R. 376, 52 D.L.R. (3d) 383, 3 N.R. 484 (S.C.C.) — This section alters the common law positions of Convention refugees and permanent residents. Common law was that no alien had any right to enter the country except by leave of the Crown, and that the alien was liable to be sent home to his own country at any time if, in the opinion of the Crown, his presence in the country was not conducive to the public good.

Section 4(2.1)

Boun-Leau v. Canada (Minister of Employment & Immigration), [1981] 1 F.C. 259, 133 D.L.R. (3d) 414, 36 N.R. 431 (Fed. C.A.) — An individual who is determined to be a Convention refugee by the Minister pursuant to section 45 [old Act] of the Act is not automatically "lawfully" in Canada under section 4(2). That determination only accords the right not to be returned to a place where his life or freedom would be threatened, and a right to appeal a removal or deportation order. The applicant, as a refugee, had been admitted to France and could return to that country. There was, therefore, no obligation on the Minister to permit him to remain in Canada and the applicant had no legal right to do so.

Prata v. Canada (Minister of Manpower & Immigration), [1976] 1 S.C.R. 376, 52 D.L.R. (3d) 383, 3 N.R. 484 (S.C.C.) — For digest, see section 4, subheading *subsection (1), supra.*

Section 4(3)

Watt v. Liebelt (1994), 82 F.T.R. 57, (sub nom. *Watt v. Canada (Immigration Act, Adjudicator))* [1995] 1 C.N.L.R. 230 — An aboriginal person who is an American citizen and is neither a Canadian citizen nor a status Indian under the *Indian Act*, does not have a right to come into or remain in Canada.

5. (1) Where privilege to come into or remain in Canada — No person, other than a person described in section 4, has a right to come into or remain in Canada.

(2) Where immigrant shall be granted landing — An immigrant shall be granted landing if he is not a member of an inadmissible class and otherwise meets the requirements of this Act and the regulations.

(3) Where visitors may be granted entry or allowed to remain — A visitor may be granted entry and allowed to remain in Canada during the period for which he was granted entry or for which he is otherwise authorized to remain in Canada if he meets the requirements of this Act and the regulations.

Case Law

Section 5(1)

Watt v. Liebelt (1994), 82 F.T.R. 57, (sub nom. *Watt v. Canada (Immigration Act, Adjudicator))* [1995] 1 C.N.L.R. 230 — An aboriginal person who is an American citizen and is neither a Canadian citizen nor a status Indian under the *Indian Act*, does not have a right to come into or remain in Canada.

Section 5(2)

Mahmood, Re (January 13, 1981), Doc. T-3559-80 (Fed. T.D.) — The acceptance by the Minister of an application for sponsorship, along with the representation that the application will not be dealt with until the sponsoree's husband departed from Canada, will lead to an order in the nature of *mandamus*, requiring the Minister to consider the sponsorship application, where the applicant produces some evidence that would warrant a conclusion that humanitarian and compassionate grounds exist that might justify a grant by the Minister of permanent residence. The onus is on the applicant to produce such evidence and where the applicant fails to produce such evidence, the application for an order in the nature of *mandamus* will be refused.

Section 5(3)

Kahlon v. Canada (Minister of Employment & Immigration), [1986] 3 F.C. 386, 26 C.R.R. 152, 30 D.L.R. (4th) 157 (Fed. C.A.), reversing [1985] 2 F.C. 124, 20 C.R.R. 193, 23 D.L.R. (4th) 564 (Fed. T.D.) — The applicant sponsored his relatives' family class application for permanent residence. The application was denied and the applicant appealed to the Immigration Appeal Board. The visa officer refused to issue visitors' visas to the relatives who were required as witnesses at his appeal. The visas were refused on the basis that the applicants were not *bona fide* visitors because their intention was to testify at the applicant's appeal. An order of *mandamus* was issued requiring the Minister to grant the relatives visitors' visas to allow them to testify at the appeal. This order was reversed on appeal. *Mandamus* will issue to require performance of a duty; it cannot, however, dictate the result to be reached. *Certiorari* might have been available to quash the refusal of the visitors' visas and to refer the matter back for reconsideration but the respondent had not sought this type of order.

Selection of Immigrants

6. (1) General principle of admissibility of immigrants — Subject to this Act and the regulations, any immigrant, including a Convention refugee, and all dependants, if any, may be granted landing if it is established to the satisfaction of an immigration officer that the immigrant meets the selection standards established by the regulations for the purpose of determining whether or not and the degree to which the immigrant will be able to become successfully established in Canada, as determined in accordance with the regulations.

(2) Sponsorships — Any Canadian citizen or permanent resident may, where authorized by the regulations, sponsor the application for landing of

(a) any person who, in relation to the Canadian citizen or permanent resident, is a member of the family class; and

(b) any immigrant who is a member of a class of immigrants prescribed by regulations made under paragraph 114(1)(*c*).

(3) **Displaced and persecuted** — Any Convention refugee and any person who is a member of a class designated by the Governor in Council as a class, the admission of members of which would be in accordance with Canada's humanitarian tradition with respect to the displaced and the persecuted, may be granted admission, subject to such regulations as may be established with respect thereto and to the immigration plan currently in force and notwithstanding any other regulations made under this Act.

(4) **Sponsorships** — Any body corporate incorporated by or under any Act of Parliament or the legislature of a province, and any group of Canadian citizens or permanent residents, may, where authorized by the regulations, sponsor the application for admission of

(a) any Convention refugee; and

(b) any person who is a member of a class of persons designated for the purposes of subsection (3) or of a class of immigrants prescribed by regulations made under paragraph 114(1)(*e*).

(5) **Landing on public policy or humanitarian or compassionate considerations** — Subject to subsection (8) but notwithstanding any other provision of this Act or any regulation made under paragraph 114(1)(*a*), an immigrant and all dependants, if any, may be granted landing for reasons of public policy or compassionate or humanitarian considerations if the immigrant is a member of a class of immigrants prescribed by regulations made under paragraph 114(1)(*e*) and the immigrant meets the landing requirements prescribed under that paragraph.

(6) **Selection by province** — Where an immigrant intends to reside in a province that has entered into an agreement pursuant to section 108 whereby the province has sole responsibility for the selection of certain prescribed classes of immigrants who intend to reside in the province, that immigrant and all dependants, if any, may be granted landing only if

Proposed Amendment — 6(6)(a)

(a) the immigrant is a member of a prescribed class of immigrants over which the province has, in whole or in part, responsibility for the selection thereof,

1992, c. 49, s. 3. [Not in force at date of publication.]

(b) where the immigration plan currently in force sets out, in respect of that province and in respect of the prescribed class of immigrants of which the immigrant is a member, the maximum number of visas that may be issued to immigrants of that prescribed class of immigrants in that calendar year or, as the case may be, the maximum number of immigrants of that prescribed class of immigrants who may be granted landing in that calendar year, that number has not been reached,

(c) the province has determined that the immigrant meets, or the immigrant and the dependants meet, as the case may be,

(i) where the immigrant is of a class of immigrants over which the province has sole responsibility for the selection thereof, the selection standards established by the laws of the province, and

(ii) where the immigrant is of a class of immigrants over which the province has in part responsibility for the selection thereof, either the selection standards established by the laws of the province or the selection standards established by regulations made under paragraph 114(1)(*a*),

(d) where the immigrant is of a class of immigrants prescribed by regulations made under paragraph 114(1)(*e*), the immigrant meets the landing requirements prescribed under that paragraph, and

(e) where the immigrant is of a class of immigrants other than a class of immigrants prescribed by regulations made under paragraph 114(1)(*e*), neither the immigrant nor any of the dependants, if any, is a member of an inadmissible class,

but where the requirements in paragraphs (*a*) to (*e*) are met, the immigrant, or the immigrant and all accompanying dependants, as the case may be, shall be granted landing.

(7) Idem — Where a Convention refugee seeking admission pursuant to subsection (3) or a person of a class designated for the purposes of that subsection intends to reside in a province that has entered into an agreement pursuant to section 108 whereby the province has sole responsibility for the selection of such Convention refugees or certain classes of persons designated for the purposes of subsection (3) who intend to reside in the province, that Convention refugee or person and all dependants, if any, may be granted admission only if

(a) the Convention refugee is a Convention refugee over which the province has sole responsibility for the selection thereof, or the person is of any of those designated classes over which the province has sole responsibility for the selection thereof, as the case may be;

(b) where the immigration plan currently in force sets out, in respect of that province and in respect of those Convention refugees or that designated class, the maximum number of visas that may be issued to Convention refugees or to persons of that designated class in that calendar year or, as the case may be, the maximum number of persons of that designated class who may be granted admission in that calendar year, that maximum number has not been reached,

(c) the province has determined that the Convention refugee or person meets, or the Convention refugee, or the person, and the dependants, meet, as the case may be, the selection standards established by the laws of the province, and

(d) neither the Convention refugee or the person, nor any of the dependants, if any, is a member of an inadmissible class,

but where the requirements in paragraphs (*a*) to (*d*) are met, the Convention refugee, or the person, and all accompanying dependants, as the case may be, shall be granted admission.

(8) Assessment — Where an immigrant is of a prescribed class of immigrants for which the regulations specify that the immigrant and any or all dependants are to be assessed, the immigrant and all dependants may be granted landing if it is established to the satisfaction of an immigration officer that the immigrant and the dependants who are to be assessed meet, collectively,

(a) the selection standards established by the regulations for the purpose of determining whether or not and the degree to which the immigrant and all dependants will be able to become successfully established in Canada, as determined in accordance with the regulations; or

(b) the landing requirements prescribed by regulations made under paragraph 114(1)(*e*).

1992, c. 49, s. 3.

Case Law

Section 6(1)

Gaffney v. Canada (Minister of Employment & Immigration) (1991), 12 Imm. L.R. (2d) 185, 121 N.R. 256, 40 F.T.R. 79 (note) (Fed. C.A.) — This was an appeal from a decision of the Trial Division refusing to quash the rejection of the appellant's application for landing as an independent immigrant by a visa officer in San Francisco. The visa officer considered that his duty to assess alternative occupations was limited to a category and did not extend to occupations in other categories which an immigrant was both qualified and willing to follow. The only evidence as to what transpired at the interview was set out in the appellant's affidavit. When the appellant's counsel was apprised of the refusal letter, he wrote the Consulate General pointing out that the appellant's work experience met other definitions in the *Canadian Classification and Dictionary of Occupations* (CCDO). The visa officer replied to the effect that in the interview the appellant's entire work experience had been canvassed and that these occupations had been considered. That letter was exhibited to the appellant's affidavit in support of his motion to quash. The appellant did not, of course, depose to the truth of the contents. The visa officer's notes were exhibited to the affidavit of another Immigration officer who could not depose to the truth of the notes. The visa officer has a duty to assess an applicant with reference to the occupation represented by the applicant (or his or her spouse) as the one for which he or she is qualified and prepared to pursue in Canada. That duty extends to each such occupation. The appellant in his affidavit alleged that the visa officer had failed to assess him in a number of occupations for which he was qualified and was prepared to pursue. There was no evidence to the contrary and the appeal was allowed and the Trial Division was directed to re-hear the application for *certiorari* and *mandamus*.

Uy v. Canada (Minister of Employment & Immigration) (1991), 12 Imm. L.R. (2d) 172, 121 N.R. 248, 40 F.T.R. 80 (note) (Fed. C.A.) — This is an appeal from the Trial Division which refused *certiorari* quashing the refusal by a visa officer of the appellant's independent application. The appellant had been a qualified medical doctor in the Philippines and was a resident in pediatrics in the United States when he applied for admission to Canada as a medical technologist. The visa officer refused to assess him in respect of that occupation because he did not believe that the appellant would pursue the occupation in Canada. In doing so, the visa officer erred in law. There was no suggestion in this case that the visa officer had assessed the appellant for the occupation of medical technologist. The visa officer awarded him 70 or more units and then invoked section 11(3) of the Regulations by reason of his conclusion as to the appellant's intentions. Section 6 of the Act requires a visa officer to assess any immigrant who applies for landing in the manner prescribed by the Act and Regulations. Section 8(1) of the Regulations imposes in mandatory terms a duty to assess and nothing in either the Act or Regulations permits a visa officer to refuse to assess in respect of the occupation or alternative occupations which the immigrant states he or she intends to pursue in Canada. The general discretion given a visa officer by section 9(1) of the Regulations must be subordinated to the particular discretion given by section 11(3) where, notwithstanding the award of at least 70 units, the visa officer is of the opinion that those units do not reflect the chances of the particular immigrant becoming successfully established in Canada. The reasons for that opinion must be committed to writing and submitted to and approved by a senior Immigration officer. Accordingly, the appeal was allowed.

Li v. Canada (Minister of Employment & Immigration) (1990), 9 Imm. L.R. (2d) 263 (Fed. T.D.) — The applicant requested permanent residence in Canada as an independent applicant pursuant to section 6(1) of the *Immigration Act*. Such applications involve a two-stage process during which it is the visa officer's duty to apply criteria set forth in the legislation and award points based on the ability of the applicant to become successfully established in Canada.

The first phase of the assessment is a paper-screening process in which immigration officials evaluate documents submitted by applicants and decide if the application process should be continued. If the applicant passes this phase, he is invited to an interview with a visa officer. During the interview, the officer assesses the employment experience of the applicant and awards points for other factors based on information presented at that time.

One of the most significant factors in any assessment is the applicant's possibility of employment in Canada. Points are awarded both for occupational demand in the screening step and for experience in the final assessment. This process requires reference to the *Canadian Classification and Dictionary of Occupations* (CCDO). Assessment of any one intended occupation begins with the matching of the applicant's work routine with the specific occupation from the CCDO.

There is a clear responsibility on the part of the visa officer to assess alternate occupations inherent in the applicant's work experience. Where his work experience suggests that the occupation may be appropriate, the visa officer must assess the applicant in the designated occupation regardless of which alternate occupations the officer has seen fit to consider.

The applicant's present occupation in the Philippines was that of a proprietor of two businesses. The applicant spends approximately 90 per cent of his time dealing with the wholesale distribution of office machines and considered that the best designation in the CCDO was that of "Commercial Traveller". Further, in a letter to the Canadian Consulate General, the applicant asserted that he had the necessary qualifications as a "Sales Representative, Office Machines", a subclassification of Commercial Traveller. The officer formed the impression that the applicant sold only hand calculators on a retail basis. The officer concluded that the applicant lacked product and plant experience and stated that he was "unable to assess your application in that category". The decision was set aside and the visa officer was required to evaluate the applicant's work experience in the category the applicant originally requested. The respondent Minister was directed to carry out the required assessment through a different visa officer.

Hajariwala v. Canada (Minister of Employment & Immigration) (1988), 6 Imm. L.R. (2d) 222, 34 Admin. L.R. 206, 23 F.T.R. 241, [1989] 2 F.C. 79 (Fed. T.D.) — The Court observed that those seeking landing in Canada must satisfy an immigration officer that they meet the selection standards set out in the regulations. It is the responsibility of the applicant to produce all relevant information which may assist in his application. The extent to which immigration officers may wish to offer assistance, counselling or advice may be a matter of individual preference or even a matter of departmental policy from time to time but it is not an obligation that is imposed upon the officers by the Act or the regulations.

Section 18 reviews are not appellate reviews. To succeed, the applicant must do more than establish the possibility that the Court would have reached a different conclusion than the visa officer in the assessment. There must be either an error of law apparent on the face of the record or a breach of the duty of fairness appropriate to this essentially administrative assessment. The regulations permit the applicant to be assessed in "an occupation". The factors listed in column 1 of schedule 1 require that the experience of the applicant be assessed with regard to his intended occupation. There is no reason why the actual experience and time spent in each of the various responsibilities in an occupation cannot be broken down to award units of assessment for experience in intended occupations. As a matter of fairness, the record should show that the applicant was given the opportunity to provide information in support of his current experience in each included occupation. The record must clearly indicate reasons which support the visa officer's assignment of a specific experience rating to the intended occupations or reasons which support the refusal to do so. In this case, the officer did not believe that the various responsibilities which the applicant carried out in his business in India should be broken down into separate components for the purposes of awarding units of assessment for experience in his alternative intended occupation of material purchasing or garment sales respresentative. Accordingly, the officer refused to issue a visa and in so doing erred in law. The officer's decision was set aside.

Karim v. Canada (Minister of Employment & Immigration) (1988), 6 Imm. L.R. (2d) 32, 21 F.T.R. 237 (Fed. T.D.) — The plaintiff came to Canada as a domestic helper. At the end of her second year, she was found to have failed to meet the criteria of the foreign domestic movement programme. This decision was quashed. In order for the first year of the programme to be fairly assessed, the plaintiff should have been fully advised of her rights under the programme and what was expected of her at the *beginning* of the first year. The programme was held not to have commenced for the applicant until she was appropriately counselled. The policy and guidelines surrounding this particular programme state that they are to be applied with leniency and flexibility and that the thrust of the programme is toward a gradual two-year assisted upgrading of skills. The plaintiff did not enjoy a proper initial briefing session. The counselling she was given did not provide her with any meaningful alternatives and the methods she attempted on her own initiative were discounted.

Johal v. Canada (Minister of Employment & Immigration) (1987), 4 Imm. L.R. (2d) 105, 15 F.T.R. 164 (Fed. T.D.) — The applicant had arrived in Canada in 1980 and was a valid visitor until May 14, 1981. The applicant then resided illegally in Canada until February 19, 1987, when he attended at a Canada Immigration Centre to apply for permanent resident status under the *de facto* illegal residents programme. The guidelines for this programme attempt to determine whether an illegal immigrant has economically and socially established himself in Canada. On February 16, 1987, the applicant was interviewed by an immigration officer, who then recommended to his manager that the application be favourably considered. The manager reviewed the officer's recommendation and concluded that the applicant did not meet the requirements of the programme. His decision was overturned by the Court because the guidelines for this programme were not followed nor were they applied fairly. The manager was required to do more than merely make a few telephone calls and meet with the officer in question before failing to accept the officer's recommendation. Further, the applicant was entitled to an opportunity to reply to some of the discrepancies that were affecting the manager's decision. Also, the applicant is required to establish that he has adapted himself socially to Canada. The manager had no information in this regard which would justify overturning the interviewing officer's recommendation. The Court pointed out that the shortage of personnel to handle these types of applications was no excuse for the application not being handled properly and fairly. Accordingly, the Court ordered the quashing of the decision of the respondent to refuse the applicant's application under the *de facto* illegal residents programme. Further, the Court directed the Minister to assess and determine the application under that programme in accordance with the guidelines set forth. Further, the Court ordered that the ongoing inquiry, in respect of the applicant, be prohibited from continuing.

Fulay v. Canada (Minister of Employment & Immigration) (April 19, 1984), Doc. T-152-83 (Fed. T.D.) — The applicant entered Canada in 1980 with authorization to accept employment as a domestic worker. She received various extensions of her visa, the last one being valid to August 20, 1982. In January 1982 the applicant became aware of a programme to assist foreign domestics to gain permanent residence status. In July 1982 the applicant sought an extension of her visa and, in accordance with instructions received earlier from an immigration officer, applied for consideration under the foreign domestics programme. This programme required domestics already in Canada to be treated the same as domestics who were newly entering Canada from abroad. These new entrants were given a preliminary assessment after one year and if found not suitable for landing were to be given an additional year in which to upgrade themselves. Fulay's application was not treated in a manner consistent with the procedure available to new entrants. Her application was simply rejected. The decision rejecting the application was quashed because the respondent, in discharging its administrative responsibilities, had failed to treat the applicant fairly because she was not accorded a one year extension of her visa to permit her to upgrade her skills and make herself more suitable for landing. It was referred back to the respondent for consideration of a fresh application in accordance with the foreign domestics programme.

Mahmood, Re (January 13, 1981), Doc. T-3559-80 (Fed. T.D.) — The acceptance by the Minister of an application for sponsorship, along with the representation that the application will not be dealt with until the sponsoree's husband departed from Canada, will lead to an order in the nature of *mandamus*, requiring the Minister to consider the sponsorship application, where the applicant produces some evidence that would warrant a conclusion that humanitarian and compassionate grounds exist that might justify a grant by the Minister of permanent residence. The onus is on the applicant to produce such evidence and where the applicant fails to produce such evidence, the application for an order in the nature of *mandamus* will be refused.

Section 6(2)

Jafari v. Canada (Minister of Employment & Immigration), 180 N.R. 330, 125 D.L.R. (4th) 141, [1995] 2 F.C. 595, 30 Imm. L.R. (2d) 139, 95 F.T.R. 159 (note) (Fed. C.A.) — This was an appeal from a decision of the Trial Division which declared section 3(2)(f) of the *Refugee Claimants Designated Class Regulations ultra vires* of the Governor in Council.

The respondent was a citizen of Iran who arrived in Canada on November 16, 1986 and immediately claimed refugee status. His claim had not been dealt with when the *Refugee Claimants Designated Class Regulations* were brought into effect on December 27, 1989. To be eligible for the backlog, a claimant was required to have been in Canada on January 1, 1989 and to have signified before that date an intention to make a refugee claim.

Section 3(2)(f) provided that the class did not include a person who left Canada after the coming into force of the regulations, and remained outside of Canada for more than 7 days. In July, 1990 the claimant attempted to cross into the United States surreptitiously. He was apprehended and it was necessary for him to spend 12 days in the United States before he was returned to Canada. On October 4, 1991 he was advised that he was not entitled to be dealt with under the backlog as he had absented himself from Canada for more than 7 days.

The practical effect of the backlog regulations was that those who fell within the designated class could, where found to have a credible basis for their claim, apply for landing.

It is not for a Court to determine the wisdom of delegated legislation or to assess its validity on the basis of the Court's policy preferences. The essential question is: does the statutory grant of authority permit this particular delegated legislation? In looking at the statutory source of authority, one must seek all possible indicia as to the purpose and scope of permitted delegated legislation. Any limitations, express or implied, must be taken into account. One must then look to the regulation to see whether it conforms and where it is argued that the regulation was not made for the purposes authorized by the statute, one must try to identify one or more of those purposes for which the regulation was adopted. A broad discretionary power, including a regulation making power, may not be used for a completely irrelevant purpose. The relevant powers are in sections 114(d) and (e) of the *Immigration Act*. These powers are to be exercised for the purposes of section 6(2) of the *Immigration Act*.

Section 6(2) authorizes the Governor in Council to designate classes of persons other than those already found to be Convention refugees, for purposes of admission. It requires that those classes include persons whose admission would be in accordance with Canada's humanitarian tradition with respect to the displaced and the persecuted. This does not mean that every regulation must facilitate the admission of more refugee claimants. This section combined with section 114(1)(e) authorizes regulations which classify such persons in some way and which may exempt some of those classes from some of the requirements of some of the regulations.

Section 6(2) and sections 114(d) and (e) authorize systems of classification of refugee claimants and the provision of preferential treatment for some or all of those classified. The backlog regulations might have excluded, from the backlog, anyone who had not remained in Canada constantly since making his or her claim. The regulations, whatever they may be, must, of course, be seen as in some way, related to the purpose of the Act, but this does not mean that a Court can review them to see if they are necessary, wise or effective in practice.

There was evidence on behalf of the appellant as to the purpose of the regulations. While some of the reasons were not compelling, and in some way may have been misconceived, the Court cannot say that they were completely unrelated to the purposes of the statute. Accordingly, section 3(2)(f) of the regulations is not *ultra vires* the Governor in Council.

Section 6(3)

Afkhami v. Canada (Employment & Immigration Commission) (1987), 12 F.T.R. 76 (Fed. T.D.) — The applicant was born in Iran and arrived with his wife in Canada on September 18, 1986. Upon arrival, both he and his wife requested political refugee status. The applicant was denied a Minister's permit and sought an order of *mandamus* to prevent continuation of a hearing pursuant to section 23(3) of the *Immigration Act*, and to order the Minister to issue the applicant a permit in conformity with directive B1. The application was dismissed. Unlike the provisions of the *Immigration Act* and Regulation, policies or programmes, such as this one, were held not to create legal rights enforceable by way of *mandamus*.

Young v. Canada (Minister of Employment & Immigration) (1987), 1 Imm. L.R. (2d) 77 (Fed. T.D.) — The applicant was a citizen of the People's Republic of China. He went to Guyana in 1979 because of instability in China. In 1986 he returned to China and booked the return trip to Guyana with a stop-over in Canada. The applicant sought to take advantage of the procedures for refugee claimants from the People's Republic of China; specifically, he wanted a Minister's permit with an employment authorization for 12 months. This was denied on the basis that the applicant was a permanent resident of Guyana and not eligible for the privileges available to refugee claimants from the People's Republic of China.

Unlike the provisions of the *Immigration Act* or Regulations, policies or programmes, such as this one, do not create legal rights enforceable by way of *mandamus*. The failure to accord the applicant a 12-month Minister's permit in accordance with the 12 months' special policy available to claimants from the People's Republic of China was not an infringement of the duty to act fairly. Nothing had happened to prejudice the applicant's right to claim refugee status during the course of an inquiry and thereafter to have access to the refugee determination process.

Section 6(5)

Alexander v. Canada (Minister of Citizenship & Immigration) (1996), 115 F.T.R. 258 (Fed. T.D.) — This was an application to review a decision of the acting manager at Niagara Falls not to defer removal of the applicants from Canada.

The applicants were citizens of Sri Lanka. They had made convention refugee claims and conditional exclusion orders had been issued against them pending the outcome of their refugee claims. The claims were dismissed and application for leave and for judicial review had also been dismissed. Thereafter an assessment of the applicant's circumstances was made to determine if they qualified as members of the Post Determination Refugee Claimants in Canada Class (PDRCC). The applicants were informed that they were not considered to be members of that class. Following that decision the applicants submitted an application for landing on humanitarian and compassionate grounds and that application was refused in June 1994. The applicants unsuccessfully sought to review that decision.

In March 1995, another assessment of the applicants' situation was made to determine whether they met the PDRCC requirements. The applicants were again notified that they were not eligible to be members of that class of persons.

At the time that the Niagara Falls CIC was attempting to remove them, the applicants had approximately 3 months in which they were required to remain in Canada in order to be qualified as members of the Deferred Removal Orders Class (DROC). The purpose of the DROC regulations was to permit failed refugee claimants who had been living and working in Canada for a lengthy period of time with no criminal record, without having been removed, to apply to become landed. Among the criteria for membership in that class, is that 3 years must have elapsed since the time when an applicant was determined not to be a convention refugee.

The applicants pointed to newspaper articles in which immigration officials were quoted as saying that they did not intend to remove persons at "the 11th hour". In addition, the articles said that as a matter of fairness applicants would be processed according to the LIFO policy.

Although the minister may have announced an intention to follow a LIFO (last in first out) policy of removals, she is not obliged to do so in each case. The applicants do not have a right to remain in Canada simply because they are close to qualifying under the DROC regulations. Further the applicants cannot rely on the doctrine of legitimate expectation. This doctrine does not create substantive rights. The applicants were not in fact members of the class of persons for whom deferred removal was available and accordingly there was no basis on which they could assert a substantive right not to be removed on the basis of the doctrine of legitimate expectation.

Gharib v. Canada (Minister of Citizenship & Immigration) (1995), 30 Imm. L.R. (2d) 291, 99 F.T.R. 208 (Fed. T.D.) — The applicant applied to review a decision determining that he was not a member of the Post Determination Refugee Claimant's Class (PDRCC). The applicant was found not to be a Convention refugee. Following this decision an immigration officer undertook to review the applicant's circumstances to determine whether the applicant was a member of the PDRCC. It was determined that the applicant was not a member of that class.

Section 6(5) of the *Immigration Act* permits an exemption to the visa requirement in section 9(1) by allowing an immigrant, and all dependants, to be granted landing for reasons of public policy, or compassionate and humanitarian considerations. To qualify, an immigrant must be a member of a class prescribed by regulations under subsection 114(1)(e). The Governor-in-Council has prescribed a class of immigrants defined in section 2(1) of the *Immigration Regulations* as the PDRCC class.

The decision of an immigration official not to recommend an individual as being eligible for the PDRCC class takes no right away. Being qualified as a member of the class offers an individual special and further consideration under the immigration laws and regulations. Thus, the Court will not intervene in discretionary decisions of this type unless such a discretion can be shown to have been exercised pursuant to improper purposes, irrelevant considerations, bad faith, or in a patently unreasonable way.

In this case the application was allowed because the officer relied on extrinsic evidence not disclosed to the applicant. This constituted a breach of the duty of fairness and resulted in the matter being returned to a different officer for new determination.

Dawkins v. Canada (Minister of Employment & Immigration) (1991), 45 F.T.R. 198, [1992] 1 F.C. 639 (Fed. T.D.) — The applicant sought an order quashing the decision of an immigration officer that there were insufficient humanitarian and compassionate grounds for the exercise of discretion under section 114(2). It is not appropriate for a reviewing Court to interfere with the exercise of a statutory granted discretion unless it is clear that this discretion was exercised unreasonably, in bad faith or was based on irrelevant considerations. The Court should not, in effect, substitute its own conclusion on an issue for that of the administrator vested with the discretion. The respondent Minister did not fetter the discretion of immigration officers by preventing them from considering those in the refugee backlog as eligible for the same treatment as those in the illegal *de facto* resident policy on the ground that they had previously come to the attention of the respondent. It cannot seriously be disputed that general standards are necessary for the effective exercise of discretion in section 114(2) cases. This is necessary to ensure a certain level of consistency from one decision to another and to avoid a patchwork of arbitrary and haphazard decisions. Uniformity in decision making must be balanced against a need to consider individual cases on their own merits. There is a fundamental difference between humanitarian and compassionate considerations referred to in section 114(2) and public policy also referred to in section 114(2). Public policy has no objective content and must be defined by those having the authority to define public policy. Immigration officers do not have the right and obligation to define their own public policy. With respect to the humanitarian and compassionate considerations, the guidelines are not to be regarded as exhaustive and definitive but rather the officers are expected to use their best judgment. In the context of this case, the officer was found not to have fettered her discretion or to have acted unfairly or unreasonably and accordingly the application was dismissed.

Virk v. Canada (Minister of Employment & Immigration) (1991), 46 F.T.R. 145 (Fed. T.D.) — This was an application to quash an immigration officer's refusal to find sufficient public policy grounds or humanitarian and compassionate considerations to justify relief under section 114(2) of the Act. When dealing with a matter of public policy, it is completely within the mandate of an immigration officer to seek the advice of a supervisory authority. The spousal relationship and its effect on a section 114(2) application is a public policy issue. The guidelines state that no additional hardship need be established in cases of a genuine marriage. The guidelines also say that there is no obligation to deal favourably with spouses who are inadmissible under section 19 of the *Immigration Act*. In this case, the officer's decision to refuse relief under section 114(2) was upheld.

Johal v. Canada (Minister of Employment & Immigration) (1987), 4 Imm. L.R. (2d) 105, 15 F.T.R. 164 (Fed. T.D.) — For digest, see section 6, subheading *Subsection (1), supra*.

De Gala v. Canada (Minister of Employment & Immigration) (1987), 8 F.T.R. 179 (Fed. T.D.) — The applicant was a 50-year-old single person from the Phillipines who came to Canada to work as a domestic for her niece. The applicant received negative initial and final assessments in interviews under the Foreign Domestic programme. Although the applicant was not a "new entrant" within the meaning of the Foreign Domestic guidelines, it was held that the "new entrant" portion of the guidelines applied to all domestics. The "guidelines or policy" as expressed in the Immigration Manual for the Foreign Domestic programme are significant and must be followed in order for procedural fairness to occur in a particular case. The applicant was not asked to contact a Canada Employment Centre for counselling and determination of training and skill upgrading needs. The evidence indicated that the interviewing officer was neither flexible nor lenient in either of the assessment interviews as required by the guidelines. The applicant had a grade 6 education as well as training as a seamstress, and this was held to be sufficient for someone seeking employment as a domestic.

The applicant was denied the use of her relative as an interpreter at the initial assessment and, in fact, no interpreter was provided. The Court observed that a person who is to be interviewed can and should be allowed to be accompanied during the interview. The Court observed, however, that the officer conducting the interview should have set conditions to prevent interference with the interview process. Failure to have a friend present who spoke English, as well as the failure to have an interpreter at the initial interview, and the conduct of the initial interview in English, undermined the assertion that the applicant was not sufficiently conversant in the English language to be able to establish herself in Canada. Accordingly, the applicant was found to have been treated in an unfair manner and the decision whereby she was found not to have demonstrated evidence of her ability to become self-sufficient in Canada was set aside.

Aboc v. Canada (Minister of Employment & Immigration) (1986), 7 F.T.R. 236 (Fed. T.D.) — The applicant arrived at Toronto International Airport in July 1982. She was interviewed in the usual way and ultimately was given an employment authorization, which the respondent at all times considered to be an authorization under the Foreign Domestic programme. There was no evidence of even a verbal explanation of the programme being given to the applicant at the time she entered Canada. The initial negative assessment was not communicated to the applicant. Subsequent assessments that questioned the genuineness of her degree in the Philippines were not communicated to the applicant. Due to the fact that no one had informed the applicant of what was expected of her, an order in the nature of *certiorari* setting aside the refusal to grant the applicant access to status in Canada under the Foreign Domestic programme was issued. Further, an order was made that the applicant be allowed to continue in Canada and to return to the situation the applicant was in at the port-of-entry when she first came here. This order directed that the applicant be treated as any other fresh applicant in the Foreign Domestic programme in accordance with the existing provisions of the statute and regulations.

Williams v. Canada (Minister of Employment & Immigration) (1985), [1985] 2 F.C. 153 (Fed. T.D.) — The applicant was born in Jamaica. She was unmarried and had 5 children, all of whom lived in Jamaica. The applicant arrived in Canada in September, 1979 for a 3-week visit and remained in Canada ever since. The applicant was informed by a lawyer in late 1983 that the long-term illegal migrants' programme did not apply to her because she had not been "underground" for 5 years. On May 29, 1984, the applicant was apprehended and a deportation order was made June 8, 1984. Judicial review of this order was dismissed in November 1984. The applicant's removal on December 1984 was deferred in order that the applicant's case could be reviewed to determine whether she then qualified under the long-term illegal migrants' programme. The applicant did not qualify under the programme. During the period when the applicant's case was being considered, the long-term illegal migrants' programme was modified in such a way that the applicant would have been eligible for the programme but for the fact of her apprehension. The application to restrain the applicant's removal was dismissed. Where a person has been lawfully ordered deported, and the procedure that he or she wishes to invoke is a purely discretionary one in the hope that he or she might be granted a Minister's permit to stay in Canada, any requirement of fairness in the exercise of the Minister's discretion is minimal. Such a case does not involve a benefit to which the applicant is legally entitled nor denial of any rights legally vested in the applicant. There was no denial of fairness because the applicant did not, albeit for different reasons, come within the old or new guidelines of the long-term illegal migrants' programme.

Ochnio v. Canada (Minister of Employment & Immigration) (September 23, 1985), Doc. T-1919-85 (Fed. T.D.) — The applicant sought an order quashing a refusal of an employment authorization. The applicant, Jan Ochnio, a medical research physician, was lawfully admitted to Canada as a visitor on a scholarship to undertake a year of post doctoral studies in his specialty, cancer research, at the University of British Columbia.

In January 1985, while in Canada, the applicants made inquiries about applying for permanent residence. Special assessment interviews were arranged and conducted on July 17, 1985 and August 6, 1985. The applicants were seeking an exemption from section 9(1) of the *Immigration Act* pursuant to section 115(2) of the Act, the requirement that they have an immigrant visa before appearing at a port-of-entry. The immigration officers who conducted the interviews in July and August recommended that an application for landing should be processed from within Canada and that the applicants should be exempt from section 9(1) of the Act.

After the August 6, 1985, interview, counsel for applicants was advised that he could expect a decision within two weeks. On their behalf, counsel requested an employment authorization and was advised that this could not be issued until a decision had been made to grant the exemption. Counsel was finally informed that the officers' decision to recommend positively an exemption had been forwarded to the regional office but had not been accepted at that level. The regional office indicated that it would reconsider the case should the applicants be able to obtain a letter from the British Columbia College of Physicians and Surgeons stating that there was a need for the applicants' services in British Columbia. The decision to refuse to issue an employment authorization was quashed. Operations memorandum IS 2.51 clearly indicated that the authority to make recommendations of this type was to be kept at the examining officers' level unless the officers' decision was negative, in which case the officers were to have recourse to the advice of a manager or supervisor. In this case, because the officers had decided to positively recommend an exemption from section 9(1), it was their duty to forward this recommendation to the Governor in Council and they were in error in seeking the concurrence of the regional office in their positive recommendation.

This type of decision by immigration officers was held to be an administrative function; the officers were bound to follow the policy of the government and had a duty to act fairly and conform to regulations and policy. The Court indicated that it could perceive an abuse of policy in this area if superiors, not working in the field, could override the decision of the interviewing officers, particularly in circumstances where they could reject the decision without specifying reasons or offering any explanations.

Sharma v. Canada (Minister of Employment & Immigration) (May 29, 1985), Doc. T-40-85 (Fed. T.D.). See also *Fulay v. Canada (Minister of Employment & Immigration)* (April 19, 1984), Doc. T-152-83 (Fed. T.D.) — This case asserts the proposition that the fairness of the application of the Foreign Domestic Programme to an individual is reviewable by *certiorari*.

7. (1) Immigration plan — The Minister, after consultation with the provinces and such persons, organizations and institutions as the Minister deems appropriate, shall, not later than the prescribed date in each calendar year, which prescribed date shall be

no later than November 1, cause the immigration plan for the next calendar year to be laid before each House of Parliament, or, if either House is not sitting on the prescribed date, not later than the fifteenth day next thereafter on which that House is sitting.

(2) Contents of plan — An immigration plan shall, with respect to the calendar year to which it relates, set out

(a) an estimate of the total number of immigrants, Convention refugees and persons of classes designated for the purposes of subsection 6(3) who will be admitted into Canada; and

(b) in respect of every class of immigrants prescribed by regulations made under paragraph 114(1)(*b*) and every class of persons designated for the purposes of subsection 6(3), and in respect of Convention refugees granted admission pursuant to that subsection and persons determined to be Convention refugees by the Refugee Division, the number of immigrants, persons of those designated classes and Convention refugees to whom visas may be issued or who may be granted admission, as the case may be,

(i) in respect of Canada,

(ii) in respect of each province that has entered into an agreement pursuant to section 108 whereby the province has sole responsibility for the selection of Convention refugees granted admission pursuant to subsection 6(3) or any such class of immigrants or class of persons designated for the purposes of that subsection who intend to reside in the province, and

(iii) in respect of all other provinces.

(3) Idem — An immigration plan shall, with respect to the calendar year to which it relates, set out the number of employment authorizations, not including extensions, that may be issued in respect of every class of employment for which regulations made under paragraph 114(1)(*j*.2) specify that there shall be a numerical limitation in respect thereof.

(4) Number is either estimate or maximum — The number to be established for the purposes of subparagraph (2)(*b*)(iii) in respect of Convention refugees granted admission pursuant to subsection 6(3) or a class of immigrants or persons designated for the purposes of that subsection shall be a maximum number where regulations made under subsection 114(1) specify that there shall be a numerical limitation in respect thereof and, where the regulations do not so specify, the number shall be an estimate.

(5) Idem — Subject to subsection (6), the number to be established for the purposes of subparagraph (2)(*b*)(ii) in respect of Convention refugees granted admission pursuant to subsection 6(3), in respect of each class of immigrants and in respect of persons designated for the purposes of that subsection shall be a maximum number

(a) where the province has sole responsibility pursuant to the agreement for the selection of those Convention refugees or that class or immigrants or persons and the legislation of the province specifies that there shall be a maximum number in respect thereof, and

(b) where the province does not have, pursuant to the agreement, sole responsibility for the selection of those Convention refugees or that class of immigrants or persons but regulations made under subsection 114(1) specify that there shall be a numerical limitation in respect thereof,

and, in any other case, the number shall be an estimate.

(6) **Idem** — The number to be established for the purposes of subparagraph (2)(*b*)(ii) in respect of the class of immigrants known as assisted relatives shall be a maximum number where the legislation of the province and regulations made under subsection 114(1) specify that there shall be a maximum number in respect thereof and, in any other case, the number shall be an estimate.

(7) **Idem** — Subject to subsection (8), the number to be established for the purposes of subparagraph (2)(*b*)(i) in respect of Convention refugees granted admission pursuant to subsection 6(3), in respect of a class of immigrants or in respect of persons designated for the purposes of that subsection shall be a maximum number where

(a) regulations made under subsection 114(1) specify that there shall be a numerical limitation in respect thereof, and

(b) the legislation of each province that has entered into an agreement pursuant to section 108 whereby the province has sole responsibility for the selection of Convention refugees granted admission pursuant to subsection 6(3), immigrants of that class or persons of that designated class who intend to reside in the province specifies that there shall be a numerical limitation in respect thereof,

and, in any other case, the number shall be an estimate.

(8) **Idem** — The number to be established for the purposes of subparagraph (2)(*b*)(i) in respect of the class of immigrants known as assisted relatives shall be a maximum number where

(a) regulations made under subsection 114(1), and

(b) the legislation of each province that has entered into an agreement pursuant to section 108 whereby the province has in whole or in part responsibility for the selection of assisted relatives who intend to reside in the province,

specify that there shall be a maximum number in respect thereof and, in any other case, the number shall be an estimate.

(9) **Provinces with agreement** — Where a province has entered into an agreement pursuant to section 108 whereby the province has sole responsibility for the selection of Convention refugees granted admission pursuant to subsection 6(3), certain classes of immigrants or certain classes of persons designated for the purposes of that subsection who intend to reside in the province,

(a) the proportion that the total of all numbers established for the purposes of subparagraph (2)(*b*)(ii) bears to the total of all numbers established for the purposes of paragraph (2)(*a*) may only exceed the proportion referred to in the agreement with the approval of the Minister;

(b) the numbers established for the purposes of subparagraph (2)(*b*)(ii) shall be consistent with the agreement;

(c) subject to paragraph (*e*), the numbers established for the purposes of subparagraph (2)(*b*)(ii) in respect of Convention refugees and every class of immigrants and persons designated for the purposes of subsection 6(3) in respect of which the province does not have sole responsibility for the selection thereof shall be established by the Minister in consultation with the province;

(d) the numbers established for the purposes of subparagraph (2)(*b*)(ii) in respect of Convention refugees and every class of immigrants and persons designated for the purposes of subsection 6(3) in respect of which the province has sole responsibility for the selection thereof shall be established by the province after taking into consideration advice received from the Minister; and

(e) the numbers established for the purposes of subparagraph (2)(*b*)(ii) in respect of the class of immigrants known as assisted relatives shall be established jointly by the Minister and the province.

(10) **Dependants included** — Unless the regulations provide otherwise, the numbers in an immigration plan shall include accompanying dependants.

(11) **Plan may be changed** — Where the Minister considers it necessary to do so as the result of unexpected changes in the movement of persons to Canada or as the result of a request of a province referred to in subsection (9) or for any other reason the Minister deems appropriate, the Minister may change any immigration plan that has been laid before both Houses of Parliament pursuant to subsection (1) and, where the Minister does so, the Minister shall lay the amended plan before each House of Parliament within ninety days after making the change or, if either House is not sitting on the expiration of that ninety day period, not later than fifteen days next thereafter on which that House is sitting.

(12) **Changes must be consistent with subsection (9)** — Any changes to an immigration plan must be consistent with subsection (9).

(13) **Consultations** — Where a province has entered into an agreement pursuant to section 108 whereby the province has, in part, responsibility for

(a) the selection of certain classes of immigrants who intend to reside in the province,

(b) the selection of Convention refugees granted admission pursuant to subsection 6(3) and persons of certain classes designated for the purposes of that subsection who intend to reside in the province, or

(c) the issuance of employment authorizations in respect of certain prescribed classes of employment to persons who intend to work in the province,

the Minister shall consult with that province before making any change to an immigration plan that affects that province in any of those respects.

(14) **Plan must be consistent with agreements** — An immigration plan, and any change thereto, must be consistent with all agreements entered into with provinces pursuant to section 108.

1992, c. 49, s. 3.

PART II — ADMISSION TO CANADA

General Presumption

8. (1) **Burden of proof** — Where a person seeks to come into Canada, the burden of proving that that person has a right to come into Canada or that his admission would not be contrary to this Act or the regulations rests on that person.

(2) **Presumption — Every person seeking to come into Canada shall be presumed to be an immigrant until that person satisfies the immigration officer examining him or the adjudicator presiding at his inquiry that he is not an immigrant.**

Case Law

Section 8(1)

Canada (Minister of Employment & Immigration) v. Gill (1991), 137 N.R. 373 (Fed. C.A.) — The Immigration and Refugee Board allowed the respondent Gill's appeal from a refusal to approve the application for permanent residence of the respondent's father, two sisters and one brother. The father had been convicted of a criminal offence as described in section 19(1)(c) of the *Immigration Act*. Subsection 8(1) of the *Immigration Act* imposes on a person seeking to come into Canada the burden of proving that such a person has a right to come into Canada or that such admission would not be contrary to the *Immigration Act* or Regulations. An applicant for landing like the principal applicant is inadmissible under paragraph 19(1)(c) unless he has satisfied the onus of providing evidence to the visa officer that the Governor in Council is satisfied that the principal applicant has rehabilitated himself. On this record there was no such evidence and accordingly the Minister's appeal was allowed.

Section 77(3) permits an appeal on the ground that there exist compassionate or humanitarian considerations that warrant the granting of special relief. A hearing of such nature is a hearing *de novo* in a broad sense and at such a hearing the board is entitled to consider contemporary matters which necessarily involve a consideration of a change of circumstances.

The appeal was allowed and the matter remitted to the Appeal Division to consider whether compassionate or humanitarian considerations warranted the granting of special relief.

Section 8(2)

Grewal v. Canada (Minister of Employment & Immigration) (1989), 8 Imm. L.R. (2d) 100, 99 N.R. 29, 27 F.T.R. 159 (note), [1990] 1 F.C. 192 (Fed. C.A.) — The *Immigration Act* envisages a two-stage procedure and that after compliance with both stages a visitor may be granted entry to Canada. Stage one is performed outside of Canada by visa officers. Stage two is performed inside of Canada at a port-of-entry for the most part. Acceptance of a visitor in stage one confers upon that individual a certain status including certain rights of appeal that are not otherwise available. The presumption set out in section 8(2) applies only to the examinations by an immigration officer at a port-of-entry as set out in sections 11 to 18. It does not apply to visa application proceedings pursuant to sections 9 and 10 of the Act.

Wan v. Canada (Minister of Manpower & Immigration), [1973] F.C. 578, 38 D.L.R. (3d) 733 (Fed. C.A.) — Under the *Immigration Act*, R.S.C. 1970, the onus of disproving a specific fact does not arise until the person against whom the fact is alleged is given sufficient indication of what is alleged to be in a position to disprove it.

Visas and Special Authorizations

9. (1) **Applications for visas — Except in such cases as are prescribed, and subject to subsection (1.1), every immigrant and visitor shall make an application for and obtain a visa before that person appears at a port of entry.**

(1.1) **Application on behalf of dependants** — A person who makes an application for a visa may apply on behalf of that person and every accompanying dependant.

(1.2) **Burden on visitors** — A person who makes an application for a visitor's visa shall satisfy a visa officer that the person is not an immigrant.

Proposed Addition — 9(1.3) and (1.4)

(1.3) **Information to be specified** — An immigrant who makes an application for a visa shall specify in the application

(a) the prescribed class of immigrants in respect of which the immigrant is applying;

(b) the names of the immigrant's dependants; and

(c) the province in which the immigrant intends to reside.

(1.4) **Assessment to be based on selection standards** — The assessment of an application for a visa shall be based on the selection standards that have been prescribed for the class of immigrants in respect of which the person making the application is applying.

1992, c. 49, s. 4. [Not in force at date of publication.]

(2) **Assessment by visa officer** — An application for an immigrant's visa shall be assessed by a visa officer for the purpose of determining whether the person making the application and every dependant of that person appear to be persons who may be granted landing.

(2.1) **Idem** — An application for a visitor's visa shall be assessed by a visa officer for the purpose of determining whether the person making the application and every accompanying dependant of that person appear to be persons who may be granted entry.

(3) **Duty to answer questions** — Every person shall answer truthfully all questions put to that person by a visa officer and shall produce such documentation as may be required by the visa officer for the purpose of establishing that his admission would not be contrary to this Act or the regulations.

(4) **Issuance of visa** — Subject to subsection (5), where a visa officer is satisfied that it would not be contrary to this Act or the regulations to grant landing or entry, as the case may be, to a person who has made an application pursuant to subsection (1) and to the person's dependants, the visa officer may issue a visa to that person and to each of that person's accompanying dependants for the purpose of identifying the holder thereof as an immigrant or a visitor, as the case may be, who, in the opinion of the visa officer, meets the requirements of this Act and the regulations.

(5) **Consent required** — A visa officer may refuse to issue a visa on the grounds that the person who made an application pursuant to subsection (1), or any of the person's dependants, is a member of an inadmissible class described in paragraph 19(1)(*k*) only with the written approval of the Minister and the Solicitor General of Canada.

1992, c. 49, s. 4.

Case Law

Section 9(1)

Lam v. Canada (Minister of Citizenship & Immigration) (1998), 152 F.T.R. 316 (Fed. T.D.) — A visa officer may inquire further if he or she considers that a further inquiry into an application is warranted. A visa officer cannot be wilfully blind in assessing an application and must act in good faith. However, there is no general obligation on a visa officer to make further inquiries when an application is ambiguous. The onus is on an applicant to file a clear application together with such supporting documentation as he or she considers advisable. The onus does not shift to the visa officer and there is no entitlement to a personal interview if the application is ambiguous or supporting material is not included.

Where an applicant has reason to believe that he or she may be successfully established in Canada irrespective of the units of assessment determination, he or she should apply for a determination under subsection 11(3) setting forth relevant reasons. Otherwise, while the visa officer may do so on his or her own volition, there is no obligation on the visa officer to exercise a discretion under subsection 11(3).

Dass v. Canada (Minister of Employment & Immigration) (1996), 32 Imm. L.R. (2d) 209, 193 N.R. 309, 107 F.T.R. 320 (note) (Fed. C.A.) — The respondent entered Canada as a visitor in December 1988. He married a Canadian citizen and in April 1989 requested an exemption from the requirement of subsection 9(1) which required that he apply for permanent residence from outside Canada. He completed an application for permanent residence at that time. In May 1989 he was advised that the Employment and Immigration Commission was prepared to request the Governor in Council to exempt him from subsection 9(1), but was warned not to take any irreversible steps toward his proposed migration until the Governor in Council granted the exemption and he satisfied all the immigration criteria. A request form was sent by an officer of the Canada Immigration Centre in Winnipeg, to Ottawa, specifically requesting approval of the Governor in Council of an exemption. The request form summarized the history of the respondent as follows:

> Appears to meet the requirements. Landing is recommended.

In November 1989 the respondent was charged with 4 criminal offences, two of which involved a possible sentence of 10 years imprisonment. In April 1990 the Governor in Council exempted the respondent from subsection 9(1). In March of 1991 the respondent was convicted of the four counts with which he had been charged, and in December of 1991 the Deputy Minister ordered an inquiry. One of the provisions invoked was paragraph 19(1)(c) which renders inadmissable, persons convicted of offences carrying a maximum sentence of 10 years or more. On January 2, 1992 the respondent was advised that due to the convictions the Commission was unable to continue processing his application. The respondent applied successfully for *certiorari* to quash this decision. The judge hearing the matter reached a conclusion that because of the wording of the request for the order in council the department head already determined that the respondent was entitled to landing subject only to the decision of the Governor in Council. The trial judge also ordered the Minister to grant landing without further consideration.

The Court restated the following basic propositions:

> 1. The only authority given under subsection 114(2) of the *Immigration Act* to the Governor in Council, at the time this case arose, was to exempt individuals from certain requirements or to facilitate their admission. The only action taken in this case was the granting of an exemption from the requirements of subsection 9(1).
>
> 2. The Governor in Council had no specific authority to grant landing.

3. An application for landing cannot be considered officially until an exemption has been granted by the Governor in Council from the requirements of subsection 9(1). It is a legal impossibility to say that a decision has been taken granting landing, or that final consideration has been given by the appropriate officials to the grant of landing, prior to the subsection 9(1) exemption being granted.

4. Under the scheme of the *Immigration Act* at the relevant time it was an Immigration Officer acting pursuant to subsection 14(2) or a senior Immigration Officer acting pursuant to subsection 23(2) who could grant landing to an immigrant, and they could do so only when it would not be contrary to the Act or the regulations.

When a favourable decision has been made to grant landing, a written record of landing signed by an immigration officer as authorized by subsection 14(2) of the *Act* is delivered to the applicant. A decision is taken to have been made when notice of that decision is given to the parties effected with some measure of formality.

It is of no legal consequence that immigration officers make a preliminary assessment of the merits of an application for landing, and do not normally recommend an exemption be granted until they consider that the application is likely to succeed once an exemption is granted. Patently futile applications for landing should not be the subject of a request to the Governor in Council for an order in council.

There had never been any decision communicated to the respondent other than the letter of January 2, 1992 advising him that because of his convictions, and the pending inquiry, his application for permanent residence would not proceed. No decision granting him landing was ever taken. It is not for the Court to order the Minister to grant a record of landing or even to require the Minister to continue processing the landing application when the *Immigration Act* appears to prohibit such steps in the face of the criminal convictions of the respondent.

Accordingly, the appeal was allowed.

Cumar v. Canada (Minister of Citizenship & Immigration) (1996), 106 F.T.R. 76 (Fed. T.D.) — The applicant made an application for landing from within Canada. This was based on his marriage to a landed immigrant. He sought an exemption pursuant to section 114(2) from the requirement that landing must be sought from outside the country. On February 1, 1993 the *Immigration Act* was changed. There was no longer a requirement that an order-in-council be obtained to exempt an applicant from the requirement of the *Act* that an application for landing must be made from outside the country. Authority to grant exemptions from the *Act* or the regulations was from that time on conferred upon the Minister. Under the new procedure exemptions may be made by the Minister, and therefore by his delegate, rather than the Governor in council. As a matter of practice the grant of an exemption, at least in the case of sponsorship by a spouse, was not given until the very last moment when landing was imminent. A change in the circumstances of the individual, for example, a marriage breakdown that occurs any time before the grant of landing, can now be taken into account. The applicant received a letter dated March 4, 1994, which stated that his application had been approved in principle and that he would be granted landing if he complied with all the other requirements of the *Immigration Act* and regulations. The applicant was asked to attend at an Immigration Centre to pick up his landing papers. He was instructed to bring certain documents with him. He was told that his sponsor, his wife, must accompany him. The applicant's wife did not attend because their marriage had broken down and they were separated. The wife had not withdrawn her sponsorship. The applicant was refused landing and the humanitarian and compassionate review of his circumstances resulted in a negative decision.

On the basis of the procedure employed in this case the applicant had no vested right to landing when he attended at the Immigration Centre. Accordingly, the application for judicial review was dismissed.

Nagra v. Canada (Minister of Citizenship & Immigration) (1995), 31 Imm. L.R. (2d) 165, 103 F.T.R. 261, [1996] 1 F.C. 497 — The applicant entered Canada as a visitor in February, 1985. Subsequently he was married to a Canadian citizen. His wife filed an undertaking of assistance. The applicant applied for an exemption from the requirements of subsection 9(1) of the *Immigration Act*. An immigration officer approved the application for a visa exemption and prepared the appropriate form requesting special authority from the Governor in Council for a waiver of the requirements of subsection 9(1). The Governor in Council granted the exemption.

In 1990 the applicant was convicted of two criminal offences, as a result of which he became the subject of an Immigration inquiry. The applicant asserted that he was a permanent resident because he had been granted a visa exemption. An adjudicator determined that the applicant was not a permanent resident and made a conditional removal order against the applicant. The Appeal Division concluded that the appellant was not a permanent resident and that he did not, therefore, have a right of appeal to the Appeal Division. Therefore the Appeal Division was without jurisdiction to hear and determine the appeal. Obtaining permanent residence in Canada is at least a two stage proceeding. Subsection 9(1) is the essence of the first stage requiring a visa overseas before presenting oneself at a Canadian port-of-entry. The second stage is the self presenting of the immigrant, would-be permanent resident, to an immigration officer at a port-of-entry for examination. The applicant was never exempted from complying with the provisions of the second stage such as are manifested in sections 11, 12 and 14 of the *Act*. The applicant did not comply with the requirements of the second stage and thus did not become a permanent resident of Canada. The applicant was never landed in Canada.

While the immigration proceedings were completing themselves the Supreme Court of Canada set aside the applicant's convictions and ordered a new trial. This was brought to the attention of the trial division in this judicial review application. The respondent's counsel conceded that the deportation order, which had been based on those convictions, could no longer stand. Accordingly, the order was quashed.

Ferrerya v. Canada (Minister of Employment & Immigration) (1992), 56 F.T.R. 270 (Fed. T.D.) — The applicant arrived in Canada as a visitor. He asserted a claim for Convention refugee status and that claim was found to have no credible basis. The applicant did not report to Immigration authorities and remained in Canada illegally. He finally resurfaced, making an application for landed immigrant status on the basis that he had a Canadian wife. The applicant was exempted from subsection 9(1) of the *Immigration Act*. An Order in Council exempting an individual from the visa requirements of subsection 9(1) does not confer a right to permanent residence. The exemption's effect is to allow the making of an application for landing despite the fact that the applicant is already within Canada. In this case there was no final determination of the applicant's application made on the merits prior to the subsection 9(1) waiver being given. Therefore the waiver did not accord to the applicant any right to permanent residence in Canada.

Gaffney v. Canada (Minister of Employment & Immigration) (1991), 12 Imm. L.R. (2d) 185, 121 N.R. 256, 40 F.T.R. 79 (note) (Fed. C.A.) — This was an appeal from a decision of the Trial Division refusing to quash the rejection of the appellant's application for landing as an independent immigrant by a visa officer in San Francisco. The visa officer considered that his duty to assess alternative occupations was limited to a category and did not extend to occupations in other categories which an immigrant was both qualified and willing to follow.

The only evidence as to what transpired at the interview was set out in the appellant's affidavit. When the appellant's counsel was apprised of the refusal letter, he wrote the Consulate General pointing out that the appellant's work experience met other definitions in the *Canadian Classification and Dictionary of Occupations* (CCDO). The visa officer replied to the effect that in the interview the appellant's entire work experience had been canvassed and that these occupations had been considered. That letter was exhibited to the appellant's affidavit in support of his motion to quash. The appellant did not, of course, depose to the truth of the contents. The visa officer's notes were exhibited to the affidavit of another immigration officer who could not depose to the truth of the notes. The visa officer has a duty to assess an applicant with reference to the occupation represented by the applicant (or his or her spouse) as the one for which he or she is qualified and prepared to pursue in Canada. That duty extends to each such occupation. The appellant in his affidavit alleged that the visa officer had failed to assess him in a number of occupations for which he was qualified and was prepared to pursue. There was no evidence to the contrary and the appeal was allowed and the Trial Division was directed to re-hear the application for *certiorari* and *mandamus.*

Basco v. Canada (Minister of Employment & Immigration) (1990), 14 Imm. L.R. (2d) 21, 43 F.T.R. 233 — The applicant sought to quash the refusal of her application for an employment authorization under the foreign domestic movement program. The duty of fairness requires that, wherever possible and practical, the applicant be provided with an opportunity to confront the concerns of the visa officer and to answer them. The visa officer reached a conclusion that, although the applicant had been performing domestic services as she had shown in Hong Kong for some time, she had shown disrespect for Hong Kong immigration rules and therefore would likely do the same in Canada. The failure to permit the applicant an opportunity to respond to this negative assessment resulted in the visa officer's refusal being set aside and a direction that the matter be referred to another visa officer or visa office for a fresh review of the case.

Grewal v. Canada (Minister of Employment & Immigration) (1989), 8 Imm. L.R. (2d) 100, 99 N.R. 29, 27 F.T.R. 159 (note), [1990] 1 F.C. 192 (Fed. C.A.) — The *Immigration Act* envisages a two-stage procedure and that after compliance with both stages a visitor may be granted entry to Canada. Stage one is performed outside of Canada by visa officers. Stage two is performed inside of Canada at a port-of-entry for the most part. Acceptance of a visitor in stage one confers upon that individual a certain status including certain rights of appeal that are not otherwise available. The presumption set out in section 8(2) applies only to the examinations by an immigration officer at a port-of-entry as set out in sections 11 to 18. It does not apply to visa application proceedings pursuant to sections 9 and 10 of the Act.

Dawson v. Canada (Minister of Employment & Immigration) (1988), 6 Imm. L.R. (2d) 37, 21 F.T.R. 212 (Fed. T.D.) — The applicant came to Canada with a valid visitor's visa and married a Canadian citizen sometime after his arrival. An application for permanent residence was filed in Vancouver and subsequently a Minister's Permit was issued. The Governor in Council exempted the applicant ultimately from the application of section 9(1). In addition, a child was born of the marriage. As the section 9(1) exemption was granted, the representative of the Minister indicated that the applicant had met all other necessary requirements of the Act, including the attaining of a security clearance. The wife subsequently attempted to withdraw her sponsorship. This was held to have no force or effect because the applicant had acquired the right to be granted permanent residence in Canada as a landed immigrant when the Governor in Council's exemption from section 9(1) was granted. Accordingly, the Minister was ordered to process the application for permanent residence and to grant permanent residence in Canada to the applicant.

The Court also observed that, while the mere fact of being a father of a child in Canada might be insufficient reason for there to exist humanitarian or compassionate grounds to allow an individual to remain in Canada as a permanent resident, this fact should be given careful consideration which had not occurred in this case.

Ho v. Canada (Minister of Employment & Immigration) (1986), 47 Alta. L.R. (2d) 82, 6 F.T.R. 78 (Fed. T.D.) — The applicant entered Canada on May 22, 1984 on an employment authorization, which was valid until May 2, 1985. On March 26, 1985 he married a Canadian who subsequently sponsored his application for permanent residence. On October 24, 1985, the applicant was exempted from the application of section 9(1) of the *Immigration Act.* On February 7, 1986, the sponsorship was withdrawn. On February 9, 1986, it was determined that the applicant was in violation of subsections 27(2)(b) and (e) of the Act. On February 27, 1986, the applicant's employment authorization was taken away.

On May 1, 1986, an inquiry was commenced on the basis that the applicant had violated subsections 27(2)(b) and (e) of the Act. Prohibition was granted prohibiting the Minister from proceeding with the inquiry and *mandamus* was granted directing the Minister to process the applicant's application for permanent residence from within Canada. Once the applicant had been granted exemption from the requirements of section 9(1) of the Act, he retained the right to make an application for permanent residence from within Canada, notwithstanding the fact that the sponsor purported to withdraw her sponsorship.

Jiminez-Perez v. Canada (Minister of Employment & Immigration) (1984), [1984] 2 S.C.R. 565, [1985] 1 W.W.R. 577, 9 Admin. L.R. 280, 14 D.L.R. (4th) 609, 56 N.R. 215 (S.C.C.) — The Minister of Employment and Immigration through his officers is under a duty to consider applications for exemption on compassionate or humanitarian grounds from the requirement of section 9 of the *Immigration Act* and to advise the applicants of the results of their application. An application for landing from within Canada should be considered and adjudicated upon if and when the exemption sought from section 9(1) is granted. That application would be subject to whatever rights of appeal are granted by the *Immigration Act.*

O'Grady v. Whyte, [1983] 1 F.C. 719, 138 D.L.R. (3d) 167, 42 N.R. 608 (Fed. C.A.) — The respondent, Whyte, attempted to sponsor his putative daughter who was living in Jamaica. After his daughter arrived in Canada, a sponsorship application was turned over to immigration officials in Hamilton. The respondent was advised that the application could not be dealt with because the daughter did not fall within the definition of the term as it appears in the immigration regulations, section 2(1). *Mandamus* was issued to compel the immigration official to dispose of the application. On appeal this order was set aside due to the fact that no application for permanent residence on behalf of the daughter had been made in Jamaica. An order in council had not been issued under section 115(2) of this Act exempting her from the requirement of section 9(1) (of obtaining a visa before appearing at a port-of-entry). The Court held that there was no duty upon an immigration official to make a decision on a sponsorship application because the underlying requirement of a landing application had not been met.

Reece v. Canada (Minister of Employment & Immigration), [1982] 2 F.C. 743, 130 D.L.R. (3d) 724 (Fed. T.D.) — The petitioner applied for the issue of a writ of *mandamus*, ordering the Minister to render a decision on her pending application for permanent residence, and for a writ of prohibition, preventing the holding of an inquiry. The application for *mandamus* was dismissed because there was no requirement for consideration of an application not made from abroad. Accordingly, the application for prohibition also failed.

Parcho v. Canada (Minister of Employment & Immigration) (1982), 2 F.C. 269, 39 N.R. 498 (Fed. C.A.) — The appellant's case was considered under the 1973 Immigration Amnesty Programme. His case was not finally decided. In 1981, the applicant attempted to go to the

United States to deliver an application for a Nigerian passport to a friend in New York. The applicant posed as a Canadian citizen, but was arrested by immigration authorities in the United States and paroled into the United States and ultimately ordered deported from that country. The applicant attempted to return to Canada, but was the subject of a section 20 report. At the conclusion of the inquiry, the adjudicator issued an exclusion order because the applicant was not in possession of an unexpired passport, and because he did not have a visa before appearing at a port-of-entry as is required by section 9(1). The Court upheld the adjudicator's finding and held that the fact that an application had been made under the Immigration Amnesty Programme was of no benefit to the appellant.

Lawrence v. Canada (Minister of Employment & Immigration), [1980] 1 F.C. 779 (Fed. T.D.) — The Court held that where the sponsoree had no immigrant visa but was present in Canada, the department was required to give the sponsor a decision on her application. As the sponsoree was obligated under a departure notice to leave Canada not later than April 1, 1980, the decision should be made prior to that date. The Court upheld the right of the department to refuse the application on the ground that the sponsoree did not meet the requirements of the Act or regulations in that he had not applied for or obtained a visa at a visa office outside Canada.

The Court also referred to the anomalous result that occurs where the department refuses to make a decision on the sponsorship application. Because no decision has been made, the Immigration Appeal Board lacks jurisdiction to entertain, at that stage, an appeal by the sponsor.

Section 9(1.2)

Srisuda Montatong v. Canada (Minister of Citizenship & Immigration) (1999), 48 Imm. L.R. (2d) 219 (Fed. T.D.) — This was an application to review a decision of a visa officer denying a visitor's visa to a 40-year-old Thai woman from Bangkok who applied for a visitor's visa to visit her married boyfriend. The applicant had met her boyfriend approximately 7 years earlier when she was working as a restaurant manager. The boyfriend frequented the restaurant and a relationship developed. The applicant quit her job, and her boyfriend supported her throughout the period of their relationship. Because of the boyfriend's age and health, he was no longer willing to travel frequently to Thailand and consequently had invited the applicant to come to Canada and visit him. The visitor's visa was refused and one of the reasons given was that the visa officer thought that it was logical that the applicant would want to remain closer to her boyfriend and therefore might not return home. This constituted an error. The uncontradicated evidence of the applicant was that she only wished to visit her boyfriend, and accordingly the visa officer's inference was not based on the evidence but rather was pure speculation. Secondly, the visa officer refused the visa because of her disapproval of the relationship between the applicant and her married boyfriend. This was held to be an irrelevant consideration which was reviewable in itself.

Accordingly, the decision of the visa officer was set aside.

Jie v. Canada (Minister of Citizenship & Immigration) (1998), 46 Imm. L.R. (2d) 276, 158 F.T.R. 253 (Fed. T.D.) — The applicant was refused a visitor's visa to enter Canada as a student. The applicant recorded the interview with the visa officer, and, in that interview, the visa officer indicated that the visa would not be issued because "we cannot 100% guarantee that you are going to return". Requiring a 100% guarantee is an impossible standard. The visa officer is required to consider the reasons given by the applicant concerning why he or she would return after their studies were completed. If the reasons are not strong and compelling, they need not be accepted; however, the standard must not be one that is impossible to achieve.

A visa officer may have regard to information in prior applications and interviews. Provided the visa officer decides the case on the basis of the evidence before him or her, it is not wrong for a visa officer to draw inferences from facts with respect to the applicant's intention to return. If the visa officer is looking for evidence that the applicant will return to China, it is advisable for the officer to specifically address that issue in the interview.

The application for judicial review was allowed.

Mittal (Litigation Guardian of) v. Canada (Minister of Citizenship & Immigration) (1998), 147 F.T.R. 285 (Fed. T.D.) — The applicant sought to review a visa officer's refusal to issue student authorizations to the applicants. Guidelines for the use of officers in assessing applications for student visas were in existence at the time this case arose. Guidelines serve as general policy or rough rules of thumb to structure the discretion conferred upon visa officers. Guidelines should not fetter the visa officer's exercise of discretion by crystallizing into binding and conclusive rules. The applicant and his brother were citizens of India and lived in New Delhi with their parents. In March 1997, they applied for temporary entry into Canada as students for the 1997-1998 academic year. The visa officer decided that the applicants did not have sufficient funds for their tuition fees, maintenance and transportation costs.

The applicants' material concerning the financing of their 1-year academic stay was straightforward. Letters of acceptance, courses in grades 5 and 8 from their private school in Toronto established partial payment of $7,500 tuition fee for each student. A Canadian chartered bank confirmed that it held $10,000 in mutual fund investments for each child. The applicants' uncle and aunt who reside in Scarborough, Ontario undertook to provide all material support during their stay. The same chartered bank confirmed that it employed the uncle as an accountant manager at an annual salary of $43,000. The uncle deposed that the applicants also had term deposits with the chartered bank. The visa officer received other information concerning the business and land investments of the applicants' father.

The family's net worth was not relevant to an assessment of the applicants' ability to meet the criteria of paragraph 15(1)(b) of the *Immigration Regulations*. The applicants had sufficient financial resources for the 1-year period for which the student authorizations were sought.

The visa officer also found that there were no credible reasons for the applicants to be studying in Canada. It is in the nature of student visas that they are issued for limited periods of time. The question of *bona fides* is not so much whether the applicant is a prospective immigrant but whether the applicant is a prospective illegal immigrant.

Wong (Litigation Guardian of) v. Canada (Minister of Citizenship & Immigration) (1997), 39 Imm. L.R. (2d) 78, (sub nom. *Wong v. Canada (Minister of Citizenship & Immigration)*) 134 F.T.R. 288 (Fed. T.D.); affirmed (June 23, 1999), Doc. A-533-97 (Fed. C.A.) — Through his litigation guardian the applicant sought to review a decision of a visa officer refusing him a student visa. The minor applicant was 10 years old, and had been accepted into Grade 5 at private school in Canada. During the course of the applicant's interview the applicant's mother had expressed a desire that the applicant complete the balance of his public school and his high school and university in Canada. The visa officer refused the visa on the basis that the applicant was not a genuine visitor. The officer concluded that if the applicant spent all the time in Canada that his mother intended, that he would have spent over half of his life and all of his adolescence in Canada, with the result that the applicant would have no significant ties to Hong Kong and would likely seek permanent admission to Canada at that time.

The visa officer's decision was set aside. The application for a student visa is an application for permission to come into Canada for a clearly temporary purpose. It is in the nature of student visas that they are issued for limited periods of time. If the minor applicant, together with his family, concluded in the future that he wished to continue to pursue his studies in Canada, a renewal of his visa or a new visa would be required. It would be open to the respondent at that time to examine the totality of the certain circumstances and determine whether renewal of the visa was appropriate or not. If at any stage during the course of the minor applicant's education, it became apparent that his ties to Hong Kong had so deteriorated as to demonstrate that they were insufficient to ensure his return, then the refusal of the request for renewal would be clearly justified. Accordingly, the decision of the visa officer was set aside.

Rusli v. Canada (Minister of Citizenship & Immigration) (1997), 127 F.T.R. 13 (Fed. T.D.) — The applicant sought to review the decision of a visa officer rejecting the applicant's application for a temporary employment authorization. The interview conducted by the officer did not last more than approximately 10 minutes, however, there are no time requirements for the conduct of an interview. The fact that the interview was relatively short might indicate at the very least a cursory overview of the applicant's case. Fairness is very much a question of perception. It is the content of the interview rather than its length that is a better indicator of whether the rules of fairness and natural justice were respected.

The officer's hand written notes from the interview indicate the questions he asked and the applicant's responses. The interview apparently covered a relatively wide range of topics. The notes revealed questions about the nature of the applicant's prospective employment in Canada and her previous visits, departures and sources of income.

The officer's notes indicate that he did bring to the applicant's attention his concern about the applicant's previous visits to Canada in which she had overstayed her visa. The officer thus gave the applicant an opportunity to respond to his concerns.

In considering the applicant's earlier stays in Canada the officer in his letter indicated that the applicant had overstayed contrary to paragraph 94(1)(k) of the *Immigration Act*. There was no evidence that the applicant had been charged with an offence under that section. The officer was presuming that because of her stays the applicant had acted contrary to section 94(1)(k). This was a mistake but not determinative of the officer's decision. The officer would have come to the same conclusion even if he had not cited that specific section of the *Immigration Act*. The officer did not err in considering the applicant's previous overstays, but in specifically pin pointing section 94(1)(k) as the relevant section of the *Immigration Act*.

Under section 9(1.2) in obtaining a visa the onus is on the applicant to demonstrate that she is not an immigrant. The first step in issuing an employment authorization is determining if the applicant qualifies for a visitor's visa. In determining this question the officer was permitted to look at the applicant's previous stays in Canada.

Apart from the reference to the specific section, 94(1)(k), the officer's decision was eminently reasonable. Accordingly, the application for judicial review was denied.

Section 9(2)

Patel v. Canada (Minister of Citizenship & Immigration) (1998), 155 F.T.R. (Fed. T.D.) — This was an application to review a decision of a visa officer to delete the applicant's son from an application for permanent residence. The applicant and his family were interviewed by a visa officer who determined that the son was not a genuine dependant. Later on, the applicant, through his immigration consultant, requested that the decision of this officer be reconsidered. The officer had been transferred to a different section of the Canadian High Commission in New Delhi, and a new officer took over the file. This new officer reviewed the file including the interview notes of the first officer and school documents provided by the applicant and then determined that the applicant had not been in attendance as a full-time student and was therefore not a dependant son within the meaning of the Regulations.

Although the Court recognized that a portion of the second officer's decision was based on the documentary record, it could not determine the extent to which the second officer had relied on the interview notes of the first officer. The fact of the reliance on those notes tainted the decision because it meant that the officer who heard the applicant (the first officer) did not decide the matter. Therefore the decision of the visa officer was set aside. The Court went on to indicate that it did not read the term "in attendance" in the Immigration Regulation definition of dependant son as including a qualitative aspect. The Court was of the view that if the documentary record states that the son or daughter is enrolled and is in full-time attendance then, in the Court's view, that should suffice.

Li v. Canada (Minister of Citizenship & Immigration) (1998), 46 Imm. L.R. (2d) 1, 155 F.T.R. 102 (Fed. T.D.) — The applicant sought to review the decision of a visa officer denying permanent residence on the ground that the applicant was medically inadmissible. In response to the fairness letter, the applicant forwarded further medical information concerning his condition. The official memo confirming that the medical officers had considered the additional material was not written until 13 days after the rejection letter had been sent to the applicant. The visa officer had a duty to ensure that on the face of the record the medical officers had seriously considered the additional medical reports sent to them by the applicant before issuing the final rejection letter. The fact that the rejection letter is dated 13 days prior to the memo confirming the medical officers' consideration of the additional medical information casts a serious doubt on whether or not this was done. Accordingly, the decision of the visa officer was set aside.

Fairness requires that the "fairness letter" to the applicant include the criteria actually being employed by the medical officers in forming their opinion as well as the specific nature of the services upon which the applicant can reasonably be expected to place excessive demands in order to ensure that the applicant has a meaningful opportunity to disabuse them of their opinion.

Tong v. Canada (Minister of Citizenship & Immigration) (1998), 45 Imm. L.R. (2d) 27, 153 F.T.R. 115 (Fed. T.D.) — This was an application to review a decision of a visa officer rejecting the applicant's application on medical grounds. The applicant's application for landing was filed on September 24, 1990. It was first rejected on the same grounds as the current refusal on April 25, 1994. That rejection was set aside on November 9, 1994, and the application was referred back for reconsideration. The application was again refused on October 30, 1995 on the same grounds. The second refusal was set aside on October 31, 1996 and the matter was again referred back for reconsideration on very specific terms. The decision under review represented the third rejection of the applicant's application on the same grounds.

The decision of the visa officer was again set aside. The visa officer did not ensure that there was sufficient linkage between the applicant's daughter's condition of mild mental retardation and the conclusion that such a condition on all the facts of this matter would or might reasonably be expected to cause excessive demand on Canadian social services. The medical officers took effective measures to ensure that they had an up-to-date psychological assessment of the daughter. This assessment indicated substantial progress on the daughter's part over an earlier assessment. The medical officers also had available current indications of the level of family support available to the daughter. The officers would appear to have ignored at least this latter information.

The visa officer applied an invalid medical opinion. In doing so he erred in law. The medical opinion was invalid because it was not based on the consideration of all the evidence with respect to the personal circumstances of the applicant and his family. The linkage between the daughter's condition and excessive demand on Canadian social services was not satisfactorily established in the medical notification. Accordingly, the decision of the visa officer was set aside. Costs were awarded to the applicant.

Lam v. Canada (Minister of Citizenship & Immigration) (1998), 152 F.T.R. 316 (Fed. T.D.) — A visa officer may inquire further if he or she considers that a further inquiry into an application is warranted. A visa officer cannot be wilfully blind in assessing an application and must act in good faith. However, there is no general obligation on a visa officer to make further inquiries when an application is ambiguous. The onus is on an applicant to file a clear application together with such supporting documentation as he or she considers advisable. The onus does not shift to the visa officer and there is no entitlement to a personal interview if the application is ambiguous or supporting material is not included.

Where an applicant has reason to believe that he or she may be successfully established in Canada irrespective of the units of assessment determination, he or she should apply for a determination under subsection 11(3) setting forth relevant reasons. Otherwise, while the visa officer may do so on his or her own volition, there is no obligation on the visa officer to exercise a discretion under subsection 11(3).

Yep v. Canada (Minister of Citizenship & Immigration) (1998), 152 F.T.R. 67 (Fed. T.D.) — This was an application to review a decision of a visa officer in which the applicant was denied permanent residence on the basis that she did not meet the definition of a dependant daughter.

The decision of the visa officer was set aside. The Court found that the visa officer erred in law and failed in fairness in that she extrapolated speculations from generalizations she made without qualifying herself as an expert which she was not. The Court relied upon a decision of *Zhao Guang Lun v. Canada (Minister of Citizenship & Immigration)* (December 9, 1997), involving the same visa officer in which the decision of the officer was set aside because the Court found some evidence of an impairing scepticism and an indication that the officer's frame of mind was engulfed in generalizations and speculations.

The Court directed that the applicant was not to be prejudiced by the effluxion of time from the visa officer's decision to the Court's decision setting it aside. The new visa officer was to view this matter from the point of view from which it was viewed by the first officer.

Su v. Canada (Minister of Citizenship & Immigration) (1997), 136 F.T.R. 52, 42 Imm.. L.R. (2d) 110 (Fed. T.D.); quashed (1997), 225 N.R. 34, 144 F.T.R. 320 (note) (Fed. C.A.) — This was an application to set aside the refusal by a visa officer of the applicant's application for permanent residence. A preliminary assessment of the applicant's application resulted in 73 points. An interview was required so that the applicant's level of experience could be assessed. The applicant could not attend at the interview, because the applicant could not obtain a U.S. visa. Due to the fact that the applicant failed to attend the interview his application was refused. The analyst who did the initial screening recommended that the applicant attend an interview. The record supports the conclusion that the visa officer who finally denied the application so decided because it was apparent that the applicant did not attend the interview. There is no indication that the visa officer considered the total circumstances and merits of the application. Subsection 9(2) of the *Immigration Act* requires the visa officer to assess the application on its merits. The visa officer failed to exercise any independent judgement in this matter and thereby fettered the exercise of her discretion. The application was allowed and the decision of the visa officer set aside.

Lun v. Canada (Minister of Citizenship & Immigration) (1997), 41 Imm. L.R. (2d) 300 (Fed. T.D.) — The Court set aside the visa officer's decision refusing the applicant's independent application as an entrepreneur. The application was set aside because the visa officer displayed a negative pre- disposition which unfairly affected the result. This negative pre-disposition did not give the applicant an opportunity to explain himself. The applicant was criticized for not contacting the Business Immigration Programs Unit in Alberta. The Court had not been pointed to any place in the evidence which required the applicant to do so or indeed to any evidence to suggest that the applicant knew that he would have been expected to do so.

The officer indicated in her affidavit that she had a negative opinion of applicants generally and that in her opinion some claims were inflated and that some people did not tell the truth about their intentions. She further indicated that she and others in her position placed little weight on both the alleged value of property assets and gestures of willingness to sell property for capital. These were remarkably unfair statements because they did not deal with the applicant as an individual. Rather the statements reflected an opinion which the applicant had little or no chance of deflating or reducing.

Finally the visa officer indicated that she was not satisfied that another Chinese restaurant would significantly benefit the Calgary economy. The Court could not determine what evidence there was to support that statement in any of the material before the Court. The visa officer made reference to the Alberta provincial government guidelines but there was nothing in those guidelines to substantiate such a conclusion. This finding was significant because it was a conclusion that the applicant's basic business proposition would not meet the entrepreneur requirements. The Court found that the hearing which the applicant was given was not fair and set aside the decision and referred the matter back for reconsideration. In addition the Court made an order of costs against the respondent.

Sui v. Canada (Minister of Citizenship & Immigration) (1994), 87 F.T.R. 262 — The applicant was informally adopted by a Malaysian family at a young age. The applicant's "adoptive" sister submitted an undertaking of assistance and asked for consideration under a policy dealing with last remaining family members. The visa officer's decision refusing the visa for the applicant was quashed and the applicant accorded another interview before a different officer. The Court concluded that there was a denial of procedural fairness. The visa officer was very aggressive in questioning the applicant about the number of years the applicant had lived with his "adoptive sister". In addition, the officer was concerned about the financial dependency of the applicant on the sister. This issue arose from the applicant's failure to use a significant sum of money that the sister had deposited in the applicant's bank account. No questions were posed to the applicant as to the non-use of this money.

The officer's decision was quashed because the officer was not objective in his considerations of the application. This lack of objectivity was reflected in the aggressive nature of the questioning and in the fact that it was clear that the officer had preconceived notions about the applicant's financial dependency on the sister.

Lam v. Canada (Minister of Employment & Immigration) (1991), 15 Imm. L.R. (2d) 275, 49 F.T.R. 200 (Fed. T.D.) — The applicant applied for permanent residence as a self-employed person. The visa officer rejected the application without ever affording the applicant an interview. The visa officer determined that the applicant could not have met the minimum requirement of 70 units of assessment to qualify as a self-employed person even if he had been accorded the maximum 10 units of assessment for personal suitability after an interview. Because the officer determined that the applicant did not meet the definition of a self-employed person he did not give the applicant the 30 units of assessment for self-employment described in Regulation 8(4).

Schedule 1 of the Regulations in Factor 9 describes under the criteria for personal suitability the units of assessment awarded on the basis of an interview with the person to reflect the personal suitability of the person and his dependants to become successfully established in Canada. Schedule 1, Factor 9, was taken to mean that the officer doing the assessment must award up to 10 units depending on his finding as to personal suitability. Where the maximum 10 units are awarded the interviewing officer must have been satisfied that the perspective immigrant has the personal suitability to become successfully established in Canada.

By not having granted the applicant an interview the officer was not in a position to determine whether he would have allowed the 30 units assessment in section 8(4) of the regulations. Further, section 11(3) of the regulations permits a visa officer to issue a visa even if the applicant is not awarded the necessary units of assessment. If the applicant has all the qualities mentioned in Factor 9 of Schedule 1, a visa officer cannot form a valid opinion under section 11(3) without an interview. The visa officer has no discretion not to grant the interview mentioned in Factor 9. It is incumbent upon a visa officer to follow the procedure set out in statute. The officer has no discretion in deciding whether or not to grant an interview pursuant to Factor 9 under column 1 of Schedule 1 of the regulations. The decision of the officer in this case was quashed. The Minister was directed to reconsider the applicant's application and another visa officer was to effect this reconsideration.

Editor's Note: See, however, section 11.1 of the Immigration Regulations.

Uy v. Canada (Minister of Employment & Immigration) (1991), 12 Imm. L.R. (2d) 172, 121 N.R. 248, 40 F.T.R. 80 (note) (Fed. C.A.) — This is an appeal from the Trial Division which refused *certiorari* quashing the refusal by a visa officer of the appellant's independent application. The appellant had been a qualified medical doctor in the Philippines and was a resident in pediatrics in the United States when he applied for admission to Canada as a medical technologist. The visa officer refused to assess him in respect of that occupation because he did not believe that the appellant would pursue the occupation in Canada. In doing so, the visa officer erred in law. There was no suggestion in this case that the visa officer had assessed the appellant for the occupation of medical technologist. The visa officer awarded him 70 or more units and then invoked section 11(3) of the regulations by reason of his conclusion as to the appellant's intentions. Section 6 of the Act requires a visa officer to assess any immigrant who applies for landing in the manner prescribed by the Act and regulations. Section 8(1) of the regulations imposes in mandatory terms a duty to assess and nothing in either the Act or regulations permits a visa officer to refuse to assess in respect of the occupation or alternative occupations which the immigrant states he or she intends to pursue in Canada. The general discretion given a visa officer by section 9(1) of the regulations must be subordinated to the particular discretion given by section 11(3) where, notwithstanding the award of at least 70 units, the visa officer is of the opinion that those units do not reflect the chances of the particular immigrant becoming successfully established in Canada. The reasons for that opinion must be committed to writing and submitted to and approved by a senior immigration officer. Accordingly, the appeal was allowed.

Pinto v. Canada (Minister of Employment & Immigration) (1990), 12 Imm. L.R. (2d) 194, 39 F.T.R. 273 (Fed. T.D.) — *Certiorari* was sought to quash a decision by a visa officer refusing to issue a visa with an employment authorization to Ms. Renny Quadros. Ms. Quadros, a citizen of India and a cousin of the applicant, was offered employment as a live-in domestic worker. Validation of the employment offer was secured from the CEC in Peterborough and forwarded to the Canadian High Commission in New Delhi. A visa officer interviewed Ms. Quadros and refused her application. The applicant obtained a second validation of his offer of employment and forwarded it to the High Commission in New Delhi. Ms. Quadros was interviewed again and her application refused a second time. The applicant obtained a third validation of employment offer and forwarded this to the High Commission in New Delhi. The employment officer in Peterborough sent a covering letter outlining the applicant's unique circumstances in relation to the need for a foreign domestic worker. The applicant was refused again and this application was then brought.

Policy guidelines exist for the employment of foreign domestic workers. The program is described as designed for the professional domestic or nanny able to assume management of a household and care of children or the duties specified within designated occupational qualifications and who are expected to be live-in household domestic workers. The designated occupational classifications include housekeeper, companion, servant, domestic, babysitter, child's nurse and parent's helper as defined in the CCDO. In order to qualify, a prospective temporary worker must meet the requirements set out in relation to the relevant classification. The visa officer was guided strictly by the requirements of the Immigration Manual. There was no recognition that the qualifications possessed by the applicant were to be assessed in view of the requirements of the employment offer. The preponderance of the material filed indicated that, in considering qualifications and experience, the visa officer considered the criteria contained in s. 15.61(c) of the Manual which required, in lieu of formal training, a minimum of one year's satisfactorily related full-time paid employment as a domestic. This requirement exceeded the requirements for specific vocational preparation for the designated job classifications falling within the FDM programme as set out in the CCDO. The applicant was a single parent with a teenaged daughter who had taught primary school for 16 years. To conclude that she had no training or experience in aspects of the offer of employment, including the care of an 8-year-old child, a senior couple, cooking, cleaning and regular household duties, showed reliance upon the requirement for formal training or full-time employment rather than a willingness to assess the skills possessed by the applicant as these were relevant to the employment offer.

In assessing the *bona fides* of the employment offer, the visa officer took into account the fact that the applicant had, for some 2 1/2 years, sought to employ the same person. This is a matter beyond the regulations; it has nothing to do with assessing Ms. Quadros' qualifications for the position offered for the purpose of deciding whether her employment in Canada will adversely affect employment opportunities for Canadian citizens or permanent residents in Canada. Assessing the *bona fides* of the offer of employment is not consistent with the responsibility of the visa officer under the Regulations nor is it consistent with the officer's responsibilities under the FDM policy guidelines. Accordingly, *certiorari* was allowed and the decision of the visa officer was set aside.

Ho v. Canada (Minister of Employment & Immigration) (1990), 11 Imm. L.R. (2d) 12 (Fed. C.A.) — The visa officer initially awarded the respondent eight points for experience and changed that to "nil" because the officer spoke to someone at CEIC. The discretion of a visa officer to grant an immigrant visa is to be exercised according to law, *i.e.*, the *Immigration Act* and Regulations. A visa officer cannot properly take account of general directives not having the force of law nor instructions from head office particular to the case at hand. Those improperly fetter him in the exercise of the discretion that Parliament, not the Canada Employment and Immigration Commission, has entrusted to him.

Gill v. Canada (Minister of Employment & Immigration) (1990), 12 Imm. L.R. (2d) 305 (Fed. T.D.) — The applicant was refused under the Last Surviving Family Member Program on the basis that he had been untruthful with the visa officer concerning his marital status. The applicant had denied that he was married. The decision of the visa officer was quashed. The officer received evidence that the applicant had been married. He owed it to the applicant, as a matter of fairness, to have the applicant either confirm or deny the allegation that the applicant was married. The visa officer's failure to do this constituted a fundamental breach of the duty of fairness. The visa officer was directed to resume the processing of the application and to grant the applicant an opportunity to confront the evidence that suggested that he was married and to bring any other relevant evidence to the visa officer's attention before a decision was made.

Li Yang v. Canada (Minister of Employment & Immigration) (1989), 36 Admin. L.R. 235, 8 Imm. L.R. (2d) 48, 27 F.T.R. 74 (Fed. T.D.) — This is an application for an order by way of *certiorari* quashing the decision of the respondent refusing the applicant's request for permanent residence in Canada.

Applications for permanent residence under the self-employed provisions involve a two-stage assessment process. The first phase is a paper-screening process in which immigration officials evaluate documents submitted by the applicant and decide if the application process should be continued. If the applicant passes this phase, he is invited to an interview. One of the most significant factors in any assessment is the applicant's possibility of supporting himself in Canada. Points are therefore awarded for occupational demand in the paper-screening step and for experience in the final assessment. Where an applicant is not awarded any units of assessment for experience, an immigrant visa cannot be issued unless the visa officer believes there are good reasons why the number of points do not reflect the chances of the applicant to become successfully established in Canada and those reasons have been approved by a senior immigration officer. A candidate for self-employment is also subject to the definition of a self-employed person and must be someone who intends and has the ability to establish or purchase a business in Canada that will create an employment opportunity for himself and will make a significant contribution to the economy or the artistic or cultural life of Canada. In addition, the visa officer will award 30 units of assessment to an applicant seeking to be self-employed if it is his opinion that the applicant will be able to become successfully established in his business in Canada.

The purpose of the *Immigration Act* is to permit immigration, not prevent it, and it is the corresponding obligation of immigration officers to provide a thorough and fair assessment in compliance with the terms and spirit of the legislation.

The applicant is from the People's Republic of China and had been residing in the United States since 1986. In 1987, she applied for permanent residence and stated that she was planning to pursue the profession of a self-employed music teacher. The applicant received training in China in both Oriental and Occidental music. She arrived in the United States on a student visa and was awarded a scholarship and completed a Master's degree in music. The applicant performed extensively in China and participated in one vocal competition in the United States.

The applicant was interviewed and, at the conclusion of the interview, the applicant learned that a decision could not be made until the officer consulted her colleagues and reviewed the requested documents. The applicant hand-delivered the requested documents on November 17, 1987. The applicant received a letter of refusal dated November 16, 1987.

The written refusal concentrated on the visa officer's opinion that the applicant's business would be unsuccessful and that the applicant would not make a significant contribution to the economy or cultural or artistic life of Canada. However, the visa officer's notes, taken during the interview, deal exclusively with the applicant's experience. The visa officer's notes indicate that the refusal was also based on a lack of self-employed experience in the applicant's intended occupation of self-employed music teacher. The Court noted that the applicant was an accomplished musician and had experience as a teacher and concluded that the visa officer had placed an undue emphasis on the applicant's lack of experience as a self-employed teacher and that the interpretation taken by the visa officer made it almost impossible for the applicant to succeed. This interpretation was found to be a fundamental breach of the duty of fairness.

Further, no questions were posed dealing with the possibilities of the applicant's contributions to cultural, economic or artistic life. The officer, at least partially, based her refusal on these criteria and yet did not, at the time of the interview, give any indication of a negative assessment on this basis nor provide the applicant with an opportunity to reply to these criteria.

Finally, the Court noted that the decision made by the officer pre-dated the receipt of the requested documentary information. The decision of the visa officer was set aside and the respondent was directed to carry out an assessment of the applicant in accordance with the *Immigration Act* and regulations in a manner consistent with the interpretation placed upon them in the Court's reasons.

Dubey v. Canada (Minister of Employment & Immigration) (1987), 17 F.T.R. 319 (Fed. T.D.) — The Court was asked to quash a refusal, by the respondents, of an application for a visitor's visa on the grounds that the proposed visitor was required in Canada as a witness on behalf of the applicant at an Immigration Appeal Board hearing. The applicant at the hearing was attempting to prove that his marriage to the proposed visitor was *bona fide*. The sponsor in this case had, in fact, married another woman in February 1983 and divorced her in December 1984. In February 1985, less than two months after his divorce was final, the sponsor submitted the sponsorship in question. The sponsoree, when she was questioned about the sponsor, indicated that she knew nothing about him. She did not know his level of education, what he did for a living, and did not know the names of his family members. Further, the immigration officer, who refused the visitor's visa application, noted that in India, where marriages are arranged the prospective partners are well briefed about each other and, thus, are very knowledgeable about the person with whom they have been paired. The officer was found to have been exercising his best judgment and was aware of all the facts when he opted to refuse the application. The Court was not satisfied that no other means existed whereby the evidence of the sponsoree could be reviewed. Further, the Court pointed out that the applicant was seeking an unusual benefit, namely, the admission to Canada of someone whose previous applications for admission to Canada had been refused. No denial of natural justice was found on the facts of this case. There was no evidence that the sponsoree was refused entry because she would testify on behalf of the applicant. The application was dismissed.

Toor v. Canada (Minister of Employment & Immigration) (1987), 1 Imm. L.R. (2d) 104, 9 F.T.R. 292 (Fed. T.D.) — Visitors' visas were refused to the father, mother, brother and sister of Mr. Toor. He wanted them to come to Canada to testify at his appeal before the Immigration Appeal Board, pursuant to section 79 of the Act, against the refusal to issue immigrants' visas. Two points in issue at the appeal were whether the relatives were really dependants of Mr. Toor and whether Mr. Toor was financially able to maintain them in Canada.

A decision by a visa officer that a person is not a *bona fide* visitor, simply because he wants to come to Canada and testify before the Board, would be an error in law. Here, however, the refusal of the visitors' visas was on the ground that the applicants were not answering truthfully to the questions, that they would resist returning to India once in Canada, and on the grounds that they could not afford the expenses involved. Such a decision is not open, in the absence of bad faith or bias, to review by way of *certiorari*. Accordingly, the application was denied.

Tham v. Canada (Minister of Employment & Immigration) (September 19, 1986), Doc. A-756-86 (Fed. C.A.) — A visa officer, following receipt by him of the opinion of a medical officer that the proposed immigrant was described in section 19(1)(a)(ii) of the Act, refused the father's sponsored application for landing. The refusal was communicated to the respondent in a letter dated September 12, 1983. The respondent's father was not interviewed, however, until September 19, 1983. The Court upheld the Immigration Appeal Board's decision to allow the sponsor's appeal on the basis that, at such an interview, the immigrant could have made representations with respect to the visa officer's proposed refusal that would have changed the visa officer's mind and that it was, therefore, premature and unfair for the visa officer to make his decision on September 12, 1983, seven days prior to the interview.

Kahlon v. Canada (Minister of Employment & Immigration), [1986] 3 F.C. 386, 26 C.R.R. 152, 30 D.L.R. (4th) 157 (Fed. C.A.), reversing [1985] 2 F.C. 124, 20 C.R.R. 193, 23 D.L.R. (4th) 564 (Fed. T.D.) — The applicant sponsored his relatives' family class application for permanent residence. The application was denied and the applicant appealed to the Immigration Appeal Board. The visa officer refused to issue visitors' visas to the relatives who were required as witnesses at his appeal. The visas were refused on the basis that the applicants were not *bona fide* visitors because their intention was to testify at the applicant's appeal. An order of *mandamus* was issued requiring the Minister to grant visitors' visas to the relatives to allow them to testify at the appeal. This order was reversed on appeal. *Mandamus* will issue to require performance of a duty; it cannot, however, dictate the result to be reached. *Certiorari* might have been available to quash the refusal of the visitors' visas and to refer the matter back for reconsideration but the respondent had not sought this type of order.

Section 9(3)

Hussain v. Canada (Minister of Citizenship & Immigration) (January 29, 1999), Doc. IMM-2330-98 (Fed. T.D.) — This was an application to review the decision of a visa officer to refuse a visa. The applicant applied for admission as an independent immigrant and described his intended occupation in Canada as a pharmacist.

The visa officer was entitled to require documentation from the applicant about his performance in evaluating examinations conducted by the Pharmacy Examining Board of Canada. The officer was under no obligation to make a formal assessment of the applicant, to issue a visa, or to invite him for an interview to assess his personal suitability until the required documentation was produced.

Law v. Canada (Minister of Citizenship & Immigration) (1998), 140 F.T.R. 307 (Fed. T.D.) — The applicant sought to review the rejection of his application for permanent residence. The applicant was advised by an immigration officer that his file would be "closed" if the additional medical information that had been requested was not provided. Approximately a month after this request, the immigration officer wrote a letter to the applicant's counsel which stated that no decision would be made on the application until the dependent daughter had provided the requested medical information. Approximately a year later, the immigration officer wrote to the applicant and indicated that his application had been rejected because his dependent daughter had not provided the requested medical information.

The decision of the visa officer was set aside. There was little in the official correspondence which would have warned the applicant that the failure to provide the requested medical information would result in the rejection of his application.

The Court directed that all the necessary medical information be provided by the applicant to the immigration officer within six months of the Court's decision and that a decision in this matter be made by a different immigration officer than the one whose decision was set aside.

Kaur v. Canada (Minister of Employment & Immigration) (1995), 98 F.T.R. 91 — A visa officer requested certain travel documents and tax returns from an applicant for permanent residence. This information was not provided.

Where relevant documentation is sought in connection with an application for permanent residence and is not provided, a visa officer may refuse the application by virtue of subsection 9(3) and paragraph 19(2)(d) of the *Immigration Act.*

Gill v. Canada (Minister of Employment & Immigration) (1991), 49 F.T.R. 285 (Fed. T.D.) — The plaintiff, Jhanda Gill, applied for permanent residence from India as a last remaining family member. The application was denied on the basis that he was married and that at his interview he had not been truthful concerning his marital status. The plaintiff had obtained a declaration from a court in India that he was not married, and the immigration officer in charge of his case had refused to rely on the declaration because it had been obtained *ex parte*. The statement of claim was struck out on the basis that the declaration which the plaintiff sought, namely, an order that he had never been married and an order that he had answered truthfully the questions put to him, were requests for declarations of fact. The Court struck out the statement of claim on the basis that only legal rights may be declared and that the determination of the plaintiff's marital status and whether or not he had answered truthfully questions put to him by a visa officer were questions of fact about which the Court could not make a declaration. The Court noted, however, that it was difficult to understand how an officer of the Crown could conclude that he would not accept a valid decision of an Indian court. The fact that the judgment the plaintiff obtained was *ex parte* did not in and of itself make the Indian court's judgment invalid or of no value.

Sandhu v. Canada (Minister of Employment & Immigration) (1989), 8 Imm. L.R. (2d) 312 (Imm. & Ref. Bd. (App. Div.)) — This was an appeal from a refusal to approve a sponsored application. The Board noted that it had in previous decisions held that section 9(3) of the Act will not apply as a valid ground for refusal where the false information was not relevant and material in the determination of the admissibility of the applicant and any other legally admissible dependants. The deliberate failure of the applicant to disclose information about his relationship to the appellant's first husband was a misrepresentation of a relevant material fact, however, the refusal by the visa officer on this ground was still invalid because the applicant disclosed the truth about this relationship prior to the decision on the sponsored application. The use of the present tense in section 19(2)(d) indicates that the persons therein described are those who at the time when the decision is made concerning their admissibility do not comply with the Act and Regulations. At the time of the refusal, the applicant had complied with section 9(3) and was not inadmissible under that provision.

Mundi v. Canada (Minister of Employment & Immigration) (1985), 63 N.R. 310, 24 D.L.R. (4th) 285 (Fed. C.A.) — This appeal arose from the refusal of a visa officer to approve the application of the appellant's father, Ajmer Singh Mundi, for the landing of himself, his wife, his son, Balwinder, and two daughters. The application had been sponsored by the appellant, who was at all material times a Canadian citizen. Ajmer Singh Mundi forwarded a false school-leaving certificate for the purpose of establishing the date of birth of Balwinder Singh and to prove that Balwinder was under 21 years of age at the time of the application. The failure to satisfy the visa officer, with respect to Balwinder's age, by means of this false school-leaving certificate, did not affect the admissibility of Ajmer Singh, his wife and daughters because the false certificate, respecting Balwinder's age, was not relevant to the admissibility of the other family members. Section 9(3) was not a basis for refusing Ajmer Singh and the other family members because the false certificate was relevant only to Balwinder's admissibility as a dependant and had no bearing on whether the admission of the applicant and the rest of the family was contrary to the Act or Regulations. Further, section 79(1) did not allow the visa officer to refuse the application of the entire family simply because Balwinder was not a dependant and, therefore, not entitled to a visa. The application could only be refused in total if Ajmer Singh, who made the application, did not meet the requirements of the Act or Regulations.

Kang v. Canada (Minister of Employment & Immigration), [1981] 2 F.C. 807 (Fed. C.A.) — A violation of section 9(3) may, according to the circumstances of the case, justify a decision not to grant a visa. It does not, however, have the automatic effect of making the applicant an inadmissible person.

Section 9(4)

Chan v. Canada (Minister of Citizenship & Immigration), 34 Imm. L.R. (2d) 259, [1996] 3 F.C. 349, 43 Admin. L.R. (2d) 314, 37 C.R.R. (2d) 112, 136 D.L.R. (4th) 433, 114 F.T.R. 247 (Fed. T.D.) — This was an application for judicial review of a decision of a visa officer. The decision denied the applicant's application for permanent residence on the basis that the applicant was inadmissable pursuant to paragraph 19(1)(c.2) of the *Immigration Act*.

During the course of the application the respondent advised the Court that it intended to bring an application pursuant to section 82.1(10). Section 82. 1(10) does not contravene section 7 of the *Charter of Rights and Freedoms*. The evidence withheld pursuant to section 82.1(10) is carefully reviewed by a judge of the Federal Court, who must consider whether the information could be revealed. The applicant does not get a summary of the confidential evidence as in the case of a certificate filed under section 40.1, however, the applicant is informed of the reason why he or she has been denied admission to Canada. In this case, the applicant was told that the officer had reason to believe that she was member of the Sun Yee On triad. There was nothing to prevent the applicant from seeking judicial review of the decision and of providing affidavit evidence to show that she was not a member of the triad. When disclosure of information could be injurious to national security the applicant's rights must be balanced against the state's legitimate interests.

In this case, the applicant had been issued a visa prior to the visa officer becoming concerned about her triad membership. The applicant argued that when making the decision to revoke the visa, the visa officer was *functus officio*. This doctrine applies to administrative bodies, however, the principle is more flexible and less formalistic when applied to administrative decision-making, as opposed to judicial decision-making. Administrative decision-making can be re-opened in the interest of justice where the enabling statute contemplates a reconsideration of a decision. The *Immigration Act* is silent on the question of whether a visa officer may review decisions already made. The Court noted that if an applicant was wrongly denied a visa, there would be nothing to stop a visa officer from reconsidering that decision once new information was provided. Applying the same logic the Court concluded that a visa officer, upon receiving information that the applicant was a member of the inadmissable class, had jurisdiction to reconsider the earlier decision granting in the visa.

Pinto v. Canada (Minister of Employment & Immigration) (1990), 12 Imm. L.R. (2d) 194, 39 F.T.R. 273 (Fed. T.D.) — *Certiorari* was sought to quash a decision by a visa officer refusing to issue a visa with an employment authorization to Ms. Renny Quadros. Ms. Quadros, a citizen of India and a cousin of the applicant, was offered employment as a live-in domestic worker. Validation of the employment offer was secured from the CEC in Peterborough and forwarded to the Canadian High Commission in New Delhi. A visa officer interviewed Ms. Quadros and refused her application. The applicant obtained a second validation of his offer of employment and forwarded it to the High Commission in New Delhi. Ms. Quadros was interviewed again and her application refused a second time. The applicant obtained a third validation of employment offer and forwarded this to the High Commission in New Delhi. The employment officer in Peterborough sent a covering letter outlining the applicant's unique circumstances in relation to the need for a foreign domestic worker. The applicant was refused again and this application was then brought.

Policy guidelines exist for the employment of foreign domestic workers. The program is described as designed for the professional domestic or nanny able to assume management of a household and care of children or the duties specified within designated occupational qualifications and who are expected to be live-in household domestic workers. The designated occupational classifications include housekeeper, companion, servant, domestic, babysitter, child's nurse and parent's helper as defined in the CCDO. In order to qualify, a prospective temporary worker must meet the requirements set out in relation to the relevant classification. The visa officer was guided strictly by the requirements of the Immigration Manual. There was no recognition that the qualifications possessed by the applicant were to be assessed in view of the requirements of the employment offer. The preponderance of the material filed indicated that, in considering qualifications and experience, the visa officer considered the criteria contained in section 15.61(c) of the manual which required, in lieu of formal training, a minimum of one year's satisfactorily related full-time paid employment as a domestic. This requirement exceeded the requirements for specific vocational preparation for the designated job classifications falling within the FDM programme as set out in the CCDO. The applicant was a single parent with a teenaged daughter who had taught primary school for 16 years. To conclude that she had no training or experience in aspects of the offer of employment, including the care of an 8-year-old child, a senior couple, cooking, cleaning and regular household duties, showed reliance upon the requirement for formal training or full-time employment rather than a willingness to assess the skills possessed by the applicant as these were relevant to the employment offer.

In assessing the *bona fides* of the employment offer, the visa officer took into account the fact that the applicant had, for some 2 1/2 years, sought to employ the same person. This is a matter beyond the regulations; it has nothing to do with assessing Ms. Quadros' qualifications for the position offered for the purpose of deciding whether her employment in Canada will adversely affect employment opportunities for Canadian citizens or permanent residents in Canada. Assessing the *bona fides* of the offer of employment is not consistent with the responsibility of the visa officer under the regulations nor is it consistent with the officer's responsibilities under the FDM policy guidelines. Accordingly, *certiorari* was allowed and the decision of the visa officer was set aside.

Alvero-Rautert v. Canada (Minister of Employment & Immigration), [1988] 3 F.C. 163, 4 Imm. L.R. (2d) 139, 18 F.T.R. 50 (Fed. T.D.) — The applicant wanted to sponsor her family, including a brother who was "turning twenty-one." The Canada Immigration Commission was unable to give her an interview until three days before the brother's birthday. The applicant attended at the interview and applied to sponsor her family on that date. The applicant's undertaking was dispatched to Manila by surface mail, and it took approximately one month to arrive at its destination. The Court held that, because the applicant's right to sponsor her family was abrogated, abridged, and infringed by the immigration officer's failure to transmit the applicant's sponsorship with all deliberate speed, that neither the *Immigration Act* nor the Regulations should be construed or applied in any way that might block the applicant's family sponsored application for landing. The Court also held that the applicant was subjected to unusual treatment by the immigration officials involved, and that this unusual treatment amounted to denials of equal benefit and equal protection of the law. Accordingly, the respondent's decision in this case was quashed.

Editor's Note: The age requirement that bedevilled this sponsorship case has been amended, however, the decision may have a wider import.

Sashi v. Canada (Minister of Employment & Immigration) (1987), 3 Imm. L.R. (2d) 288 (Fed. T.D.) — The applicant sought to quash a decision of a visa officer in India refusing sponsorship applications for the applicant's mother and his adopted daughter. The visa officer refused to accept the sponsorship of the daughter because, as a result of his inquiries, he concluded that the provisions of the *Hindu Adoptions and Maintenance Act* had not been complied with. It was held that a visa officer has not only a right but a duty to ensure that all immigrants meet the requirements of the Act and regulations. In this case, that included making certain that the sponsored child had been legally adopted within the meaning of section 2(1) of the regulations. The officer's decision was not reached improperly or without justification. The officer did reach a conclusion that involved an interpretation of Hindu law, and he ought to have afforded the applicant some opportunity for counter-argument. However, the relief sought in this case, *i.e.*, *certiorari* and *mandamus*, was discretionary, and in all the circumstances the motion was dismissed.

Toor v. Canada (Minister of Employment & Immigration) (1987), 1 Imm. L.R. (2d) 104, 9 F.T.R. 292 (Fed. T.D.) — For digest, see section 9, subheading *Subsection (2), supra.*

Reyes de Jesus v. Canada (Minister of Employment & Immigration) (1987), 1 Imm. L.R. (2d) 217 (Imm. App. Bd.) — This was an appeal from the refusal of a sponsored application for landing. The appellant was seeking to sponsor his mother. The application was refused on the basis that the mother had not satisfied the immigration officer that she complied with the definition of "immigrant" given in section 2(1) of the *Immigration Act*. This decision was based upon previous statutory declarations which the mother had filed when she was seeking visitor's visas to come to Canada. These declarations denied an intention to reside permanently in Canada. This was found to be unfair because the declarations from the previous applications, upon which the officer relied, were not raised with the mother when she was interviewed. The Board found that it was the interviewing officer's duty to consider the mother's intention at the time of the interview and to allow her to explain the previous declarations. The Board also suggested that it would be sufficient if the mother's intention to reside permanently in Canada was formulated after the interview, which resulted in her application being rejected, but before the hearing of the sponsor's appeal.

Kahlon v. Canada (Minister of Employment & Immigration), [1986] 3 F.C. 386, 26 C.R.R. 152, 30 D.L.R. (4th) 157 (Fed. C.A.), reversing [1985] 2 F.C. 124, 20 C.R.R. 193, 23 D.L.R. (4th) 564 (Fed. T.D.). — For digest, see section 9, subheading *Subsection (2), supra.*

10. Applications by students and workers — Except in such cases as are prescribed, every person, other than a Canadian citizen or a permanent resident, who seeks to come into Canada for the purpose of

> **(a) attending any university or college authorized by statute or charter to confer degrees,**
>
> **(b) taking any academic, professional or vocational training course at any university, college or other institution not described in paragraph (*a*), or**
>
> **(c) engaging in employment**

shall make an application to a visa officer for and obtain authorization to come into Canada for that purpose before the person appears at a port of entry.

R.S.C. 1985, c. 28 (4th Supp.), s. 4.

Case Law

Ali v. Canada (Minister of Citizenship & Immigration) (1998), 43 Imm. L.R. (2d) 264, 151 F.T.R. 1 (Fed. T.D.) — This was an application to review a decision of a visa officer denying a three-year employment authorization to the applicant. The duty of a visa officer to apprise an applicant of the visa officer's concerns is limited. Given that the applicant must establish that he has met certain criteria to enter Canada, the applicant should assume that the visa officer's concerns will arise directly from the Act or the regulations. This does not mean that the visa officer should remain silent throughout the interview while the applicant states his case. The visa officer should lead the interview and attempt to draw out relevant information about the application. An applicant for a visitor's visa who has provided weak evidence supporting his position that he has sufficient ties to his home country to ensure his return, should not expect that a visa officer will apprise him of this concern. Such a concern arises directly from the Act and Regulations. It may be preferable if the visa officer would inform the applicant of this concern, but failure to do so does not violate the duty of fairness. If the visa officer has obtained extrinsic evidence, he should give the applicant an opportunity to disabuse him of any concerns that may arise from that evidence. At an interview, the visa officer should give the applicant an opportunity to respond to those allegations or assumptions of which the applicant could not reasonably be aware.

In this case, the applicant was given a very short interview and the visa officer assumed that answers given by another applicant in another interview applied to this applicant. It was improper to attribute to this applicant statements made by someone else at their interview. Accordingly, the decision of the visa officer was set aside.

Merchant v. Canada (Minister of Citizenship & Immigration) (April 14, 1998), Doc. IMM-1607-97 (Fed. T.D.) — This applicant, along with two others, applied for temporary employment authorizations. This applicant was not in fact interviewed, but his application was refused on the basis that he had insufficient ties to Pakistan. The visa officer came to this conclusion by merely extrapolating from information received from the other two applicants whose applications were also refused. Even though all three applicants intended to come to Canada for essentially the same reasons, it did not therefore follow that they should all be treated in the same way. The decision that the applicant in this case had insufficient ties to Pakistan was made without regard to any evidence about familial, social or business ties in Pakistan that the applicant may have been able to present at an interview. While it is true that the applicant is responsible for failing to attend his interview the visa officer refused to reschedule the interview on the grounds that there was no need to inconvenience the applicant by requiring him to travel to Islamabad. The decision of the visa officer was set aside.

Rusli v. Canada (Minister of Citizenship & Immigration) (1997), 127 F.T.R. 13 (Fed. T.D.) — The applicant sought to review the decision of a visa officer rejecting the applicant's application for a temporary employment authorization. The interview conducted by the officer did not last more than approximately 10 minutes, however, there are no time requirements for the conduct of an interview. The fact that the interview was relatively short might indicate at the very least a cursory overview of the applicant's case. Fairness is very much a question of perception. It is the content of the interview rather than its length that is a better indicator of whether the rules of fairness and natural justice were respected.

The officer's hand written notes from the interview indicate the questions he asked and the applicant's responses. The interview apparently covered a relatively wide range of topics. The notes revealed questions about the nature of the applicant's prospective employment in Canada and her previous visits, departures and sources of income.

The officer's notes indicate that he did bring to the applicant's attention his concern about the applicant's previous visits to Canada in which she had overstayed her visa. The officer thus gave the applicant an opportunity to respond to his concerns.

In considering the applicant's earlier stays in Canada, the officer indicated in his letter that the applicant had overstayed contrary to paragraph 94(1)(k) of the *Immigration Act*. There was no evidence that the applicant had been charged with an offence under that section. The officer was presuming that because of her stays the applicant had acted contrary to section 94(1)(k). This was a mistake but not determinative of the officer's decision. The officer would have come to the same conclusion even if he had not cited that specific section of the *Immigration Act*. The officer did not err in considering the applicant's previous overstays, but in specifically pin pointing section 94(1)(k) as the relevant section of the *Immigration Act*.

Under section 9(1.2) in obtaining a visa the onus is on the applicant to demonstrate that she is not an immigrant. The first step in issuing an employment authorization is determining if the applicant qualifies for a visitor's visa. In determining this question the officer was permitted to look at the applicant's previous stays in Canada.

Apart from the reference to the specific section, 94(1)(k), the officer's decision was eminently reasonable. Accordingly, the application for judicial review was denied.

Pinto v. Canada (Minister of Employment & Immigration) (1990), 12 Imm. L.R. (2d) 194, 39 F.T.R. 273 (Fed. T.D.) — *Certiorari* was sought to quash a decision by a visa officer refusing to issue a visa with an employment authorization to Ms. Renny Quadros. Ms. Quadros, a citizen of India and a cousin of the applicant, was offered employment as a live-in domestic worker. Validation of the employment offer was secured from the CEC in Peterborough and forwarded to the Canadian High Commission in New Delhi. A visa officer interviewed Ms. Quadros and refused her application. The applicant obtained a second validation of his offer of employment and forwarded it to the High Commission in New Delhi. Ms. Quadros was interviewed again and her application refused a second time. The applicant obtained a third validation of employment offer and forwarded this to the High Commission in New Delhi. The employment officer in Peterborough sent a covering letter outlining the applicant's unique circumstances in relation to the need for a foreign domestic worker. The applicant was refused again and this application was then brought.

Policy guidelines exist for the employment of foreign domestic workers. The program is described as designed for the professional domestic or nanny able to assume management of a household and care of children or the duties specified within designated occupational qualifications and who are expected to be live-in household domestic workers. The designated occupational classifications include housekeeper, companion, servant, domestic, babysitter, child's nurse and parent's helper as defined in the CCDO. In order to qualify, a prospective temporary worker must meet the requirements set out in relation to the relevant classification. The visa officer was guided strictly by the requirements of the Immigration Manual. There was no recognition that the qualifications possessed by the applicant were to be assessed in view of the requirements of the employment offer. The preponderance of the material filed indicated that, in considering qualifications and experience, the visa officer considered the criteria contained in s. 15.61(c) of the manual which required, in lieu of formal training, a minimum of one year's satisfactorily related full-time paid employment as a domestic. This requirement exceeded the requirements for specific vocational preparation for the designated job classifications falling within the FDM programme as set out in the CCDO. The applicant was a single parent with a teenaged daughter who had taught primary school for 16 years. To conclude that she had no training or experience in aspects of the offer of employment, including the care of an 8-year-old child, a senior couple, cooking, cleaning and regular household duties, showed reliance upon the requirement for formal training or full-time employment rather than a willingness to assess the skills possessed by the applicant as these were relevant to the employment offer.

In assessing the *bona fides* of the employment offer, the visa officer took into account the fact that the applicant had, for some 2 1/2 years, sought to employ the same person. This is a matter beyond the regulations; it has nothing to do with assessing Ms. Quadros' qualifications for the position offered for the purpose of deciding whether her employment in Canada will adversely affect employment opportunities for Canadian citizens or permanent residents in Canada. Assessing the *bona fides* of the offer of employment is not consistent with the responsibility of the visa officer under the regulations nor is it consistent with the officer's responsibilities under the FDM policy guidelines. Accordingly, *certiorari* was allowed and the decision of the visa officer was set aside.

Grewal v. Canada (Minister of Employment & Immigration) (1989), 8 Imm. L.R. (2d) 100, 99 N.R. 29, 27 F.T.R. 159 (note), [1990] 1 F.C. 192 (Fed. C.A.) — The *Immigration Act* envisages a two-stage procedure and that after compliance with both stages a visitor may be granted entry to Canada. Stage one is performed outside of Canada by visa officers. Stage two is performed inside of Canada at a port-of-entry for the most part. Acceptance of a visitor in stage one confers upon that individual a certain status including certain rights of appeal that are not otherwise available. The presumption set out in section 8(2) applies only to the examination by an immigration officer at a port-of-entry as set out in sections 11 to 18. It does not apply to visa application proceedings pursuant to sections 9 and 10 of the Act.

Mohamed v. Canada (Minister of Employment & Immigration) (1981), 130 D.L.R. (3d) 481 (Fed. T.D.), affirmed (1982), 141 D.L.R. (3d) 384 (Fed. C.A.) — In these cases the Court held that a person who has made a claim that he is a Convention refugee may apply for an employment authorization pending the determination of his claim. Refugee status, however, can only be claimed during an inquiry pursuant to section 45(1) [old Act] of the *Immigration Act.* Therefore, individuals who have been lawfully admitted to Canada under a student or visitor's visa cannot claim refugee status until the student or visitor's status is lost or has expired, and an inquiry commences pursuant to section 27.

Swoboda and Minister of Employment & Immigration, Re (1981), 130 D.L.R. (3d) 475 (Fed. T.D.) — *Mandamus* was refused because the claimant was in status when the application for the order was launched. Thus, the Court held that the respondent Minister was justified in refusing to issue an employment authorization, because at that stage the applicant was not "a person who has made a claim that he is a Convention refugee" as set out in section 19(3)(f) of the Regulations.

Holden v. Levesque, [1979] 2 F.C. 141 (Fed. T.D.) — Where an agent of the Minister errs in his interpretation of a regulation and thereby denies without further consideration an application for the renewal of an employment authorization, *mandamus* will issue requiring the respondent Minister to consider the application for renewal in accordance with the provisions of the appropriate regulation.

Alleyne v. Canada (Minister of Manpower & Immigration), [1977] 2 F.C. 615 (Fed. C.A.) — Notwithstanding that the applicant had an approved offer of employment, the Minister was not required to admit the applicant to Canada where the applicant was inadmissible as a member of a class of prohibited persons described in the Act.

10.1 Where applications may be made — The Minister may specify the places where applications for visas, authorizations and other documents issued or made under this Act may be made and assessed.

1992, c. 49, s. 5.

Applications in Canada for Landing

10.2 (1) Application on behalf of dependants — An immigrant who makes an application in Canada for landing may apply on behalf of that person and every dependant in Canada.

1992, c. 49, s. 5.

Proposed Addition — 10.2(2)

(2) Information to be specified — An immigrant who makes an application for landing shall specify in the application

> **(a) the prescribed class of immigrants in respect of which the immigrant is applying;**
>
> **(b) the names of the immigrant's dependants, whether in Canada or outside of Canada; and**
>
> **(c) the province in which the immigrant intends to reside.**

1992, c. 49, s. 5. [Not in force at date of publication.]

Proposed Addition — 10.3

Document for Permanent Residents

10.3 (1) Document for permanent residents — Subject to the regulations, the Minister shall provide every person who is granted landing with a document that establishes, in the absence of proof to the contrary, that the person is a permanent resident.

(2) Idem — Subject to the regulations, where a visa officer is satisfied that a person outside Canada is a permanent resident, the visa officer shall provide that person with a document that establishes, in the absence of proof to the contrary, that the person is a permanent resident.

(3) Presumption — Subject to the regulations, a person who does not possess a document provided pursuant to subsection (1) or (2) is presumed, in the absence of evidence to the contrary, not to be a permanent resident.

(4) Form and contents — The Minister may, by order, prescribe the form and contents of any document to be provided for the purposes of subsections (1) and (2).

1992, c. 49, s. 5. [Not in force at date of publication.]

Examinations

11. (1) Medical examination required — Every immigrant and every visitor of a prescribed class shall undergo a medical examination by a medical officer.

(1.1) Medical examination may be required — Every person, other than a permanent resident, who claims to be a Convention refugee shall undergo a medical examination by a medical officer within such reasonable period of time as is specified by a senior immigration officer.

(2) Medical examination may be required — Every visitor and every person in possession of a permit who, in the opinion of an immigration officer or adjudicator, may be a member of the inadmissible class described in paragraph 19(1)(*a*) may be required by the immigration officer or the adjudicator to undergo a medical examination by a medical officer.

(3) Definition — For the purposes of this section, medical examination includes a mental examination, a physical examination and a medical assessment of records respecting a person.

R.S.C. 1985 (4th Supp.), c. 28, s. 5; 1992, c. 49, s. 6.

Case Law

Section 11(3)

Lee v. Canada (Minister of Employment & Immigration) (1986), 4 F.T.R. 86 (Fed. T.D.) — Early in 1984, the applicant, Sing Lee, of Hong Kong, made an application for permanent residence in Canada for himself and for four of his children, one of whom was the applicant, Hon Man Lee. Hon Man Lee was a congenital deaf mute and he was rejected on medical grounds. This decision was quashed because both medical officers had failed to consider medical reports, which had been provided by the applicant, prior to certifying that the applicant, Hon Man Lee, was medically inadmissible. This failure to consider these reports was a breach of the duty of fairness, which the respondents owed the applicant.

Podlaszecka v. Canada (Minister of Manpower & Immigration), [1972] S.C.R. 733, 23 D.L.R. (3d) 331 (S.C.C.) — Before an applicant can be denied permanent residence for failing to undergo a medical examination, there must be evidence that the applicant was asked to provide a medical certificate.

12. (1) Examination by immigration officer — Subject to the regulations, every person seeking to come into Canada shall appear before an immigration officer at a port of entry, or at such other place as may be designated by a senior immigration officer, for examination to determine whether that person is a person who shall be allowed to come into Canada or may be granted admission.

(1.1) Departure lounges — For the purposes of this Act, a person who, without leaving Canada, leaves an area at an airport that is reserved for passengers who are in transit or who are waiting to depart Canada may be interviewed by an immigration officer to determine whether the person is seeking to come into Canada.

(2) Where physically outside Canada — For the purposes of this section, a person who leaves Canada and thereafter seeks to return to Canada, whether or not that person was granted lawful permission to be in any other country, shall, unless the person is in a prescribed class of persons, be deemed to be seeking to come into Canada.

(3) Adjournment of examination — Where an immigration officer commences an examination referred to in subsection (1), the officer may, in such circumstances as the officer deems proper,

> **(a) adjourn the examination and refer the person being examined to another immigration officer for completion of the examination; and**
>
> **(b) detain or make an order to detain the person.**

(4) Duty to answer questions — Every person shall answer truthfully all questions put to that person by an immigration officer at an examination and shall produce such documentation as may be required by the immigration officer for the purpose of establishing whether the person shall be allowed to come into Canada or may be granted admission.

1990, c. 44, s. 16; 1992, c. 49, s. 7.

Case Law

Section 12(1)

R. v. Kwok (1986), 18 O.A.C. 38, 31 C.C.C. (3d) 196 (Ont. C.A.) — The appellant arrived at Pearson International Airport aboard a flight originating in London. He was examined by a senior immigration officer and detained pending an immigration inquiry. The immigration officer who interviewed the appellant had doubts as to the *bona fides* of the appellant as a genuine visitor and wrote a report pursuant to section 20 of the Act for the benefit of the acting senior immigration officer. A person is not detained within the meaning of section 10 of the *Charter of Rights and Freedoms* until the restriction on his freedom has gone beyond that required for the processing of his application for entry. The fact that some questioning preceded the advice required by section 10 did not by itself offend the section. The obligation to inform a person of his rights under section 10(b) of the Charter is an obligation to inform, without delay, but that does not mean immediately. Further, the admission into evidence of a conversation preceding the section 10 warning did not bring the administration of justice into disrepute.

Canada (Minister of Employment & Immigration) v. Mercier (September 16, 1980), Doc. 79-1243 (Imm. App. Bd.) — The Board held that a change in marital status from single to married was a material fact which must be disclosed to the Canadian immigration authorities if the marriage occurs before permanent resident status is actually granted. By failing to disclose her marriage at Dorval airport when she arrived in Canada, Mme. Mercier misrepresented a material fact and, thus, brought herself within section 27(1)(e).

Due to the fact that this was an appeal by the Minister, the provisions of section 75(3) applied giving Mme. Mercier an automatic right of appeal on equitable grounds. This appeal to the Board on equitable grounds was granted because Mme. Mercier had successfully established herself in Canada and had not committed any criminal offence or infraction of the *Immigration Act* since the granting of landing in Canada. She had stable employment, had members of her immediate family in Canada who were in a position to help her, if necessary, and, finally, the evidence established that the appellant had a child who was a minor, and a Canadian citizen by birth, and for whom the appellant was the sole provider. This child was in delicate physical health and required regular attention from a competent doctor. Having regard to this evidence, the Board allowed the appellant's appeal on equitable grounds.

Section 12(2)

Parcho v. Canada (Minister of Employment & Immigration) (1982), 2 F.C. 269, 39 N.R. 498 (Fed. C.A.) — The appellant's case was considered under the 1973 Immigration Amnesty Programme. His case was not finally decided. In 1981, the applicant attempted to go to the United States to deliver an application for a Nigerian passport to a friend in New York. The applicant posed as a Canadian citizen, but was arrested by immigration authorities in the United States and paroled into the United States and ultimately ordered deported from that country. The applicant attempted to return to Canada, but was the subject of a section 20 report. At the conclusion of the inquiry, the adjudicator issued an exclusion order because the applicant was not in possession of an unexpired passport, and because he did not have a visa before appearing at a port-of-entry as is required by section 9(1). The Court upheld the adjudicator's finding and held that the fact that an application had been made under the Immigration Amnesty Programme was of no benefit to the appellant.

Lee v. Canada (Minister of Employment & Immigration), [1980] 1 F.C. 374, 102 D.L.R. (3d) 328, 30 N.R. 575 (Fed. C.A.) — A student who leaves Canada before the expiry date in his student authorization is, nevertheless, upon his return to be treated as any other person at a port-of-entry seeking admission to Canada.

Smalenskas v. Canada (Minister of Employment & Immigration), [1979] 2 F.C. 145, 93 D.L.R. (3d) 388, 24 N.R. 581 (Fed. C.A.) — The appellant had applied for a special consideration under the 1973 Immigration Amnesty Programme; however, through no fault of his own, a hearing into his application was not held. This did not defeat the application. It was held that such a person by voluntarily leaving Canada for short visits did not automatically abandon his application for permanent residence and, unless it was determined that he did intend to abandon his application, a departure notice might not be issued against him.

Section 12(3)

Dehghani v. Canada (Minister of Employment & Immigration, [1993] 1 S.C.R. 1053, 18 Imm. L.R. (2d) 245, 10 Admin. L.R. (2d) 1, 20 C.R. (4th) 34, 101 D.L.R. (4th) 654, 150 N.R. 241, 14 C.R.R. (2d) 1 — The appellant, a citizen of Iran, arrived in Canada without valid travel or identity documents and claimed Convention refugee status. He was interviewed at the secondary examination and extensive written notes were made by an immigration officer, which notes were later entered in evidence at the credible-basis hearing. At the conclusion of that hearing the first level tribunal decided that there was no credible basis to the appellant's claim.

When the appellant was taken to a secondary examination at Canadian Immigration at Pearson Airport, he was not detained in the sense contemplated by section 10(b) of the Charter. Further, the principles of section 10(b) do not require that the appellant be provided with counsel at the pre-inquiry or pre-hearing stage of the refugee claim determination process. The secondary examination of the appellant at the port-of-entry is not analogous to a hearing. The purpose of the port-of-entry interview was to aid in the processing of the appellant's application for entry and to determine the appropriate procedures which should be invoked in order to deal with the appellant's application for Convention refugee status. The principles of fundamental justice do not include a right to counsel in these circumstances of routine information gathering.

Section 12(4)

Kang v. Canada (Minister of Employment & Immigration), [1981] 2 F.C. 807, 37 N.R. 551 (Fed. C.A.), leave to appeal to S.C.C. refused (1981), 39 N.R. 353 (S.C.C.) — The failure to respond truthfully to all questions put to him by a visa officer may justify a decision not to grant a visa, but does not have the automatic effect of making the applicant an inadmissible person described in section 19(2)(d).

13. (1) Where person cannot be properly examined — Where, in the opinion of an immigration officer, a person appearing before the officer for examination cannot for any reason be properly examined, the officer may

> **(a) cause the examination to be deferred until such time as that person may be properly examined; or**

(b) make an order for the rejection of that person from Canada.

(2) **Service of rejection order** — An order made under paragraph (1)(*b*) or a copy thereof shall be served on the person against whom it is made and on the owner or master of the vehicle by which that person was brought to Canada.

(3) **Cessation of order** — An order made under paragraph (1)(*b*) shall cease to be in force or to have effect when the person against whom it was made again appears before an immigration officer and can, in the opinion of the officer, be properly examined by the officer.

14. (1) **Where person shall be allowed to come into Canada** — Where an immigration officer is satisfied that a person whom the officer has examined

(a) has a right to come into Canada,

(b) is a person in possession of a subsisting permit,

(c) is a person against whom a removal order has been made who has been removed from or otherwise left Canada but has not been granted lawful permission to be in any other country, or

(d) is a person returning to Canada in accordance with a transfer order made under the *Mutual Legal Assistance in Criminal Matters Act* who, immediately before being transferred to a foreign state pursuant to the transfer order, was subject to an unexecuted removal order,

the officer shall allow that person to come into Canada.

(2) **Where immigrant shall be granted landing** — Where an immigration officer is satisfied that it would not be contrary to this Act or the regulations to grant landing to an immigrant whom the officer has examined, the officer shall

(a) grant landing to that immigrant; or

(b) authorize that immigrant to come into Canada on condition that the immigrant be present for further examination by an immigration officer within such time and at such place as the immigration officer who examined the immigrant may direct.

(3) **Where visitor may be granted entry** — Where an immigration officer is satisfied that it would not be contrary to this Act or the regulations to grant entry to a visitor whom the officer has examined, the officer may grant entry to that visitor and impose terms and conditions of a prescribed nature.

(4) **Further examination of immigrants** — Where an immigration officer is satisfied that it would not be contrary to this Act or the regulations to grant landing to an immigrant who has been authorized pursuant to paragraph (2)(*b*), 23(1)(*b*) or 32(3)(*b*) to come into Canada, the officer shall, after such further examination as the officer deems necessary, grant landing to the immigrant.

(5) **Terms and conditions** — An immigration officer who grants landing to an immigrant pursuant to paragraph (2)(*a*) or subsection (4)

(a) shall, if the immigrant is of a class of immigrants for which regulations made under paragraph 114(1)(*ii*.2) require the imposition of terms and conditions, impose the terms and conditions prescribed by those regulations; and

(b) subject to regulations made under paragraph 114(1)(*ii*.4), may, in the case of any immigrant, impose terms and conditions prescribed by regulations made under paragraph 114(1)(*ii*.3).

(6) Idem — Where landing is to be granted to an immigrant under subsection 6(6), an official of the province in which the immigrant intends to reside may, not later than when landing is granted, impose such terms and conditions as are authorized by the laws of the province.

(7) Effect of terms and conditions — Terms and conditions imposed under subsection (6) have the same force and effect as terms and conditions imposed pursuant to subsection (5).

R.S.C. 1985, c. 30 (4th Supp.), s. 47; 1992, c. 49, s. 8.

Case Law

Section 14(1)

Mercier v. Canada (Minister of Employment & Immigration) (April 25, 1985), Doc. T-309-85 (Fed. T.D.), affirmed (1985), 62 N.R. 73 (Fed. C.A.) — On November 17, 1982, following an inquiry, a deportation order was issued against the applicant because he had been convicted of an offence for which a maximum term of imprisonment of 10 years or more may be imposed, pursuant to section 19(1)(c) of the Act. The applicant's appeal against this deportation order was dismissed on August 14, 1984. On January 30, 1985, the applicant tried to gain admission to the United States without success and returned to Canada with the intention of provoking an inquiry where he might claim refugee status. When the applicant reappeared at the Canadian border, a senior immigration officer issued a Summons to Appear at an inquiry, pursuant to section 23 of the Act. That decision was countermanded by another senior immigration officer and the applicant's case was withdrawn on the ground that the deportation order, issued against the applicant, had never been executed. It was this decision that was attacked by the applicant, who was seeking a writ of *mandamus* requiring the adjudicator to conduct his inquiry. The decision to countermand the Summons to Inquiry was part of the administrative process. The Trial Division did not intervene because it was of the view that the applicant had not been treated unfairly and that to intervene and issue a writ of *mandamus* would create a situation in which the respondent Minister would, on the one hand, have to execute a deportation order against the applicant and, on the other hand, have to conduct an inquiry with a view to admitting the applicant to the country.

An appeal from this decision was heard on June 28, 1985 and dismissed. The appellant (applicant) sought to raise, for the first time, the assertion that the deportation order had been executed by the appellant himself when he left the country for a 6-week visit to Haiti from May 12, 1984 to June 30, 1984. No consideration was given to the submission on appeal because it was a question which was raised for the first time before the Court of Appeal. It was founded upon an allegation of fact which was never put in issue before the Trial Division. The Court noted that when sitting an appeal of the Trial Division, it sat as a Court of Appeal whose function was to decide whether the issues presented at trial were properly disposed of. It was not the Court's duty to determine other issues which, had they been raised at the Trial Division, might have resulted in a different outcome if the necessary factual basis had been established.

Section 14(5)

Gabriel v. Canada (Minister of Employment & Immigration) (1984), 60 N.R. 108 (Fed. C.A.) — The appellant was landed on condition that she marry within 90 days. This condition could not be obeyed as a result of circumstances beyond the appellant's control. Even though a condition is impossible to fulfil, so long as the person concerned knew of that condition and continued to remain in Canada in breach of that condition, such a person has knowingly contravened a condition attached to the grant of landing. Even if the word "contravene" requires a positive act, the omission to do something which a person is required to do, is the commission of a positive act. It is an act of failure to do something required to be done and, accordingly, satisfies the definition of the term "contravenes".

15. Application to vary certain terms and conditions — Where a permanent resident has been granted landing subject to terms and conditions imposed pursuant to subsection 14(5) or (6), the permanent resident may at any time make an application to an immigration officer or to an official of the province, as the case may be, to vary or cancel any of those terms and conditions.

1992, c. 49, s. 9.

Case Law

Gabriel v. Canada (Minister of Employment & Immigration) (1984), 60 N.R. 108 (Fed. C.A.) — The appellant was landed on condition that she marry within 90 days. This condition could not be obeyed as a result of circumstances beyond the appellant's control. Even though a condition is impossible to fulfil, so long as the person concerned knew of that condition and continued to remain in Canada in breach of that condition, such a person has knowingly contravened a condition attached to the grant of landing. Even if the word "contravene" requires a positive act, the omission to do something which a person is required to do is the commission of a positive act; it is an act of failure to do something required to be done and, accordingly, satisfies the definition of the term "contravenes".

16. Application by visitor in Canada — Subject to section 17.1, any visitor may make an application to an immigration officer

(a) to vary or cancel terms and conditions imposed pursuant to subsection 14(3), 17(2), 23(2) or 32(4); or

(b) to extend the period during which the visitor is authorized to remain in Canada, except where the visitor was granted entry pursuant to subsection 19(3).

R.S.C. 1985, c. 28 (4th Supp.), s. 6.

Case Law

Kouchaki v. Canada (Minister of Employment & Immigration) (November 29, 1984), T-3070-83 (Fed. T.D.) — The applicant is the plaintiff in a civil action seeking a declaration that the reason for the refusal of the extension of his student visa was unlawful and that he was entitled to remain in Canada to study, effective September 30, 1983. The plaintiff also sought the quashing of the departure notice issued at the conclusion of the inquiry herein. Where the validity of the deportation order is not in question prohibition will not lie to permit the applicant to exhaust all legal remedies. However, if the Minister wishes to refuse extensions, this must be done fairly, which implies the giving of a reason for the refusal. Because the action questions the validity of the decision to refuse to renew a student visa and raises substantial issues, justice required that the applicant be permitted to remain in Canada until trial.

Kouchaki v. Canada (Minister of Employment & Immigration); Shamsvandi v. Canada (Minister of Employment & Immigration) (April 6, 1984), Doc. T-3070-83, T-3096-83 (Fed. T.D.) — Both of these cases were applications for an interlocutory interim order prohibiting the defendant from proceeding with an inquiry. The plaintiffs entered Canada in 1981 and were authorized to study. Various extensions of this authorization were granted. On September 30, 1983 a further extension was refused and a direction for inquiry was issued and separate inquiries commenced in November 1983. In the main actions the plaintiffs are attacking the validity of the defendants' refusal to extend their authorizations to study. Pending final disposition of these actions, an interlocutory interim order was sought prohibiting the conduct of the inquiry.

An individual permitted to enter Canada to pursue a course of study should, normally, have his student authorization extended to enable him to complete those studies. Where it is alleged that the individual is conducting himself in a manner which is inconsistent with his student status, the respondent Minister is under a duty to act in accordance with the provisions of this Act. Further, the Court does not have a general power to suspend the performance of a statutory duty in cases where the performance of the statutory duty might have an adverse affect on some right which the applicant has sought to assert in another forum. Section 51 of the *Immigration Act* specifies the cases in which the execution of a removal order may be stayed. By implication this section excludes any other stay of execution, including one in the exercise of judicial discretion.

The Court should not issue an order directing the respondent not to proceed with an inquiry which he is under a statutory duty to hold solely because the applicants have not exhausted legal remedies available to them.

Brijicoomar v. Canada (Minister of Employment & Immigration) (February 7, 1984), Doc. T-16-84 (Fed. T.D.) — The respondent Minister refused to extend the applicant's visitor's visa to allow the applicant to remain in Canada pending completion of his appeal to the Immigration Appeal Board. *Mandamus* was refused. *Mandamus* will only be directed against the respondent to require it to deal with an outstanding application when it is refusing to do so.

Badhwar v. Canada (Minister of Employment & Immigration) (December 5, 1983), Doc. T-151-83 (Fed. T.D.) — The applicants sought an order of *certiorari* to quash the decision not to extend their student visas. The decision not to extend the visas was based on the fact that they had made an application to remain in Canada permanently on humanitarian and compassionate grounds and that such an application was inconsistent with their request to extend their visitor status in Canada. The refusal to extend the visitor's status on this basis was held to be wrong in principle and the application for landed immigrant status was held not in any way to be capable of influencing their status as visitors.

Parmar v. Canada (Minister of Manpower & Immigration) (1981), [1982] 1 F.C. 16 (Fed. T.D.) — The applicant came to Canada as a visitor and received several extensions of his visitor's status. Finally, he went to the immigration office on the date that his status was to expire, which date was a Saturday. The office was closed and the applicant returned on the following Monday for the purposes of obtaining a further extension. The applicant was told that his status had expired and that he was illegally in Canada. A departure notice was issued. It was held that the departure notice was properly issued and that any attempt to extend the applicant's visitor's status, after it had expired, would have been illegal.

17. (1) Power of immigration officer — Subject to the regulations, an immigration officer who receives an application made pursuant to section 15 or 16 shall approve or refuse the application.

(2) When application approved — When an application is approved under subsection (1), the immigration officer may

> **(a) vary or cancel any terms and conditions subject to which the person was granted landing or entry;**
>
> **(b) add terms and conditions of a prescribed nature; or**
>
> **(c) in the case of a visitor, extend the period of time during which the visitor is authorized to remain in Canada.**

(3) When application refused — When an application made pursuant to section 16 is refused, the person who made the application shall be allowed to remain in Canada if the period during which the person is authorized to remain in Canada has not expired unless a deportation order is made against that person.

R.S.C. 1985, c. 28 (4th Supp.), s. 7; 1992, c. 49, s. 10.

Case Law

Section 17(2)

Badhwar v. Canada (Minister of Employment & Immigration) (December 5, 1983), Doc. T-151-83 (Fed. T.D.) — The applicants sought an order of *certiorari* to quash the decision not to extend their student visas. The decision not to extend the visas was based on the fact that they had made an application to remain in Canada permanently on humanitarian and compassionate grounds and that such an application was inconsistent with their request to extend their visitor status in Canada. The refusal to extend the visitor's status on this basis was held to be wrong in principle and the application for landed immigrant status was held not in any way to be capable of influencing their status as visitors.

17.1 No application in certain circumstances — Except in such cases as are prescribed, no person in Canada may make an application to an immigration officer to obtain authorization

> **(a) to attend any university or college or take any academic, professional or vocational training course; or**
>
> **(b) to engage in employment in Canada.**

R.S.C. 1985, c. 28 (4th Supp.), s. 8.

Visitors' Security Deposits

18. (1) Security that visitors will comply — A senior immigration officer may require any visitor or group or organization of visitors arriving in Canada to deposit or arrange for the deposit with the Deputy Minister of such reasonable sum of money or other security as he deems necessary as a guarantee that the visitor or group or organization of visitors will comply with any terms and conditions that may be imposed under this Act.

(2) Where failure to comply — Where a visitor or group or organization of visitors with respect to whom a sum of money or other security has been deposited pursuant to

subsection (1) fails to comply with any term or condition that was imposed, the Deputy Minister may order that the sum of money deposited be forfeited or that proceedings be taken to realize on the other security deposited.

(3) Where security to be returned — Where a visitor or group or organization of visitors with respect to whom a sum of money or other security has been deposited pursuant to subsection (1) complies with the terms and conditions that were imposed, the sum of money or other security deposited shall be returned as soon as practicable.

Case Law

Section 18(2)

Canada (Attorney General) v. Khimani (1985), 50 O.R. (2d) 476 (Ont. Div. Ct.) — The Attorney General of Canada claimed $2,000 plus interest owing under a performance bond given by the defendant under section 18(1) of the Act. The defendant entered into the performance bond on June 10, 1982 with the result that one, Yasmin Jetha, was permitted to enter Canada as a visitor. The bond guaranteed that the visitor would leave by August 9, 1982, but the visitor left September 22, 1982. The defendant admitted to being aware on August 9, 1982 that the failure of Yasmin Jetha to leave Canada was a breach of the bond. The trial judge refused to give judgment in favour of the plaintiff, Attorney General of Canada, and purported to exercise an equitable jurisdiction set out in section 78(3) of the *Courts of Justice Act*, S.O. 1984, c. 11. This decision was overturned. It was held that, whatever sympathy the Court may have had for the defendant (respondent), the finding that the terms and conditions of the bond had been breached meant that the Court must enforce payment of the bond.

Editor's Note: On the enforcement of bonds, generally, see section 102.

Gill v. R. (1978), 88 D.L.R. (3d) 341 (Fed. T.D.) — Where an alien gives a security deposit to guarantee his departure and executes powers of attorney directing payment of the money to a third party upon his departure from Canada, a senior immigration officer may require that the alien forfeit the deposit if he remains in Canada to apply for landed immigrant status and his application is denied. The power of attorney, even though it is on a departmental form, is not an equitable assignment, it is merely a direction to pay a third party any moneys owing to the alien.

PART III — EXCLUSION AND REMOVAL

Inadmissible Classes

19. (1) Inadmissible persons — No person shall be granted admission who is a member of any of the following classes:

(a) persons who are suffering from any disease, disorder, disability or other health impairment as a result of the nature, severity or probable duration of which, in the opinion of a medical officer concurred in by at least one other medical officer,

(i) they are or are likely to be a danger to public health or to public safety, or

(ii) their admission would cause or might reasonably be expected to cause excessive demands on health or social services;

Proposed Amendment — 19(1)(a)

(a) persons who, in the opinion of a medical officer concurred in by at least one other medical officer, are persons

(i) who, for medical reasons, are or are likely to be a danger to public health or to public safety, or

(ii) whose admission would cause or might reasonably be expected to cause excessive demands, within the meaning assigned to that expression by the regulations, on health or prescribed social services;

1992, c. 49, s. 11. [Not in force at date of publication.]

(b) persons who there are reasonable grounds to believe are or will be unable or unwilling to support themselves and those persons who are dependent on them for care and support, except persons who have satisfied an immigration officer that adequate arrangements, other than those that involve social assistance, have been made for their care and support;

(c) persons who have been convicted in Canada of an offence that may be punishable under any Act of Parliament by a maximum term of imprisonment of ten years or more;

(c.1) persons who there are reasonable grounds to believe

(i) have been convicted outside Canada of an offence that, if committed in Canada, would constitute an offence that may be punishable under any Act of Parliament by a maximum term of imprisonment of ten years or more, or

(ii) have committed outside Canada an act or omission that constitutes an offence under the laws of the place where the act or omission occurred and that, if committed in Canada, would constitute an offence that may be punishable under any Act of Parliament by a maximum term of imprisonment of ten years or more,

except persons who have satisfied the Minister that they have rehabilitated themselves and that at least five years have elapsed since the expiration of any sentence imposed for the offence or since the commission of the act or omission, as the case may be;

(c.2) persons who there are reasonable grounds to believe are or were members of an organization that there are reasonable grounds to believe is or was engaged in activity that is part of a pattern of criminal activity planned and organized by a number of persons acting in concert in furtherance of the commission of any offence under the *Criminal Code* or *Controlled Drugs and Substances Act* that may be punishable by way of indictment or in the commission outside Canada of an act or omission that, if committed in Canada, would constitute such an offence, except persons who have satisfied the Minister that their admission would not be detrimental to the national interest;

(d) persons who there are reasonable grounds to believe will

(i) commit one or more offences that may be punishable under any Act of Parliament by way of indictment, other than offences designated as contraventions under the Contraventions Act, or

(ii) engage in activity that is part of a pattern of criminal activity planned and organized by a number of persons acting in concert in furtherance of the

commission of any offence that may be punishable under any Act of Parliament by way of indictment;

(e) persons who there are reasonable grounds to believe

(i) will engage in acts of espionage or subversion against democratic government, institutions or processes, as they are understood in Canada,

(ii) will, while in Canada, engage in or instigate the subversion by force of any government,

(iii) will engage in terrorism, or

(iv) are members of an organization that there are reasonable grounds to believe will

(A) engage in acts of espionage or subversion against democratic government, institutions or processes, as they are understood in Canada,

(B) engage in or instigate the subversion by force of any government, or

(C) engage in terrorism;

(f) persons who there are reasonable grounds to believe

(i) have engaged in acts of espionage or subversion against democratic government, institutions or processes, as they are understood in Canada,

(ii) have engaged in terrorism, or

(iii) are or were members of an organization that there are reasonable grounds to believe is or was engaged in

(A) acts of espionage or subversion against democratic government, institutions or processes, as they are understood in Canada, or

(B) terrorism,

except persons who have satisfied the Minister that their admission would not be detrimental to the national interest;

(g) persons who there are reasonable grounds to believe will engage in acts of violence that would or might endanger the lives or safety of persons in Canada or are members of or are likely to participate in the unlawful activities of an organization that is likely to engage in such acts of violence;

(h) persons who are not, in the opinion of an adjudicator, genuine immigrants or visitors;

(i) persons who, pursuant to section 55, are required to obtain the consent of the Minister to come into Canada but are seeking to come into Canada without having obtained such consent;

(j) persons who there are reasonable grounds to believe have committed an act or ommission outside Canada that constituted a war crime or a crime against humanity within the meaning of subsection 7(3.76) of the *Criminal Code* and that, if it had been committed in Canada, would have constituted an offence against the laws of Canada in force at the time of the act or omission.

(k) persons who constitute a danger to the security of Canada and are not members of a class described in paragraph (*e*), (*f*) or (*g*); or

(l) persons who are or were senior members of or senior officials in the service of a government that is or was, in the opinion of the Minister, engaged in terrorism, systematic or gross human rights violations or war crimes or crimes against hu-

manity within the meaning of subsection 7(3.76) of the *Criminal Code*, except persons who have satisfied the Minister that their admission would not be detrimental to the national interest.

(1.1) Meaning of "senior members of or senior officials in the service of a government" — For the purposes of paragraph (1)(*l*), "senior members of or senior officials in the service of a government" means persons who, by virtue of the position they hold or have held, are or were able to exert a significant influence on the exercise of government power and, without limiting its generality, includes

(a) heads of state or government;

(b) members of the cabinet or governing council;

(c) senior advisors to persons described in paragraph (*a*) or (*b*);

(d) senior members of the public service;

(e) senior members of the military and of the intelligence and internal security apparatus;

(f) ambassadors and senior diplomatic officials; and

(g) members of the judiciary.

(2) Inadmissible classes where entry permitted — No immigrant and, except as provided in subsection (3), no visitor shall be granted admission if the immigrant or visitor is a member of any of the following classes:

(a) persons who have been convicted in Canada of an indictable offence, or of an offence for which the offender may be prosecuted by indictment or for which the offender is punishable on summary conviction, that may be punishable under any Act of Parliament by a maximum term of imprisonment of less than ten years, other than an offence designated as a contravention under the *Contraventions Act*;

(a.1) persons who there are reasonable grounds to believe

(i) have been convicted outside Canada of an offence that, if committed in Canada, would constitute an offence that may be punishable by way of indictment under any Act of Parliament by a maximum term of imprisonment of less than ten years, or

(ii) have committed outside Canada an act or omission that constitutes an offence under the laws of the place where the act or omission occurred and that, if committed in Canada, would constitute an offence that may be punishable by way of indictment under any Act of Parliament by a maximum term of imprisonment of less than ten years,

except persons who have satisfied the Minister that they have rehabilitated themselves and that at least five years have elapsed since the expiration of any sentence imposed for the offence or since the commission of the act or omission, as the case may be;

(b) persons who

(i) have been convicted in Canada under any Act of Parliament of two or more summary conviction offences not arising out of a single occurrence, other than offences designated as contraventions under the *Contraventions Act*,

(ii) there are reasonable grounds to believe have been convicted outside Canada of two or more offences, not arising out of a single occurrence, that, if

committed in Canada, would constitute summary conviction offences under any Act of Parliament, or

(iii) have been convicted in Canada under any Act of Parliament of a summary conviction offence, other than an offence designated as a contravention under the *Contraventions Act*, and there are reasonable grounds to believe have been convicted outside Canada of an offence that, if committed in Canada, would constitute a summary conviction offence under any Act of Parliament,

where any part of the sentences imposed for the offences was served or to be served at any time during the five year period immediately preceding the day on which they seek admission to Canada;

(c) other members of a family accompanying a member of that family who may not be granted admission or who is not otherwise authorized to come into Canada; or

(d) persons who cannot or do not fulfil or comply with any of the conditions or requirements of this Act or the regulations or any orders or directions lawfully made or given under this Act or the regulations.

(3) **Discretionary grant of entry — A senior immigration officer or an adjudicator, as the case may be, may grant entry to any person who is a member of an inadmissible class described in subsection (2) subject to such terms and conditions as the officer or adjudicator deems appropriate and for a period not exceeding thirty days, where, in the opinion of the officer or adjudicator, the purpose for which entry is sought justifies admission.**

R.S.C. 1985, c. 30 (3rd Supp.), s. 3; 1992, c. 47, s. 77; 1992, c. 49, ss. 11, 122; 1995, c. 15, s. 2; 1996, c. 19, s. 83.

Case Law

Section 19(1)(a)

Tong v. Canada (Minister of Citizenship & Immigration) (1998), 45 Imm. L.R. (2d) 27, 153 F.T.R. 115 (Fed. T.D.) — This was an application to review a decision of a visa officer rejecting the applicant's application on medical grounds. The applicant's application for landing was filed on September 24, 1990. It was first rejected on the same grounds as the current refusal on April 25, 1994. That rejection was set aside on November 9, 1994, and the application was referred back for reconsideration. The application was again refused on October 30, 1995 on the same grounds.The second refusal was set aside on October 31, 1996 and the matter was again referred back for reconsideration on very specific terms. The decision under review represented the third rejection of the applicant's application on the same grounds.

The decision of the visa officer was again set aside. The visa officer did not ensure that there was sufficient linkage between the applicant's daughter's condition of mild metal retardation and the conclusion that such a condition on all the facts of this matter would or might reasonably be expected to cause excessive demand on Canadian social services. The medical officers took effective measures to ensure that they had an up-to-date psychological assessment of the daughter. This assessment indicated substantial progress on the daughter's part over an earlier assessment. The medical officers also had available current indications of the level of family support available to the daughter. The officers would appear to have ignored at least this latter information.

The visa officer applied an invalid medical opinion. In doing, so he erred in law. The medical opinion was invalid because it was not based on the consideration of all the evidence with respect to the personal circumstances of the applicant and his family. The linkage between the daughter's condition and excessive demand on Canadian social services was not satisfactorily established in the medical notification. Accordingly, the decision of the visa officer was set aside. Costs were awarded to the applicant.

Thangarajan v. Canada (Minister of Citizenship & Immigration) (1998), 152 F.T.R. 91 (Fed. T.D.); reversed (1999), 242 N.R. 183 (Fed. C.A.) — The applicant is moderately retarded. It was decided that his admission might reasonably be expected to cause excessive demands on social services in Canada. One of the factors taken into account was the cost that would be incurred in providing special education to him within the public school system. Provincial legislation, by and large, provides for children with special needs in the school system. This includes gifted as well as mentally challenged children.

Special education provided for mentally challenged children within the public school system is not a social service within the meaning of paragraph 19(1)(a)(ii) of the *Immigration Act*. Social services can be viewed in a broad sense as meaning all social type services provided to individuals by the state or in a narrower sense as meaning social services akin to welfare. If the term was being used in the broad sense in paragraph 19(1)(a)(ii), there would have been no need to identify health services as a different and distinct category from social services generally. The fact that health services are considered to be distinct from social services indicates that education, including specialized education, provided within the school system, is also distinct.

Shan v. Canada (Minister of Citizenship & Immigration) (1998), 153 F.T.R. 238 (Fed. T.D.) — This was a review of a decision by a visa officer that an applicant was medically inadmissible. The medical notification referred to the fact that the child would need extensive physiotherapy and may require various tendon releasing operative procedures on her legs, as well as speech therapy. The notification went on to say "these are expensive modalities often in short supply for other Canadians". This was a cursory statement which precisely focuses on cost and imprecisely and marginally refers to the supply of required services. As such, it was a deficient evidentiary base for the decision reached by the visa officer. There was no individual focus on the medical problems found and the individual supply of health or social services available to treat those problems. There was no analysis as to whether such treatment would cause or might reasonably be expected to cause excessive demands on those health or social services. The decision of the visa officer was set aside.

Lau v. Canada (Minister of Citizenship & Immigration) (1998), 43 Imm. L.R. (2d) 8, 146 F.T.R. 116 (Fed. T.D.) — The applicant sought to review the decision of a visa officer refusing the applicant's application for permanent residence because his daughter was medically inadmissible. The medical officers in this case failed to respect a requirement for an individualized assessment in evaluating medical inadmissibility. Medical inadmissibility cannot be premised solely on the medical condition under review, rather the individual applicant's personal circumstances must be carefully considered. The impact of family support on the demands an individual's medical condition might place on Canadian health and social services must also be considered.

In the case at bar the Court found that neither the medical officer nor the visa officer appeared to have accepted family support as a factor in determining whether the applicant's daughter's medical condition would place excessive demands on health or social services. In addition, if the family's capacity to provide supervision at home is an issue it should be raised with the applicant.

The lack of due consideration of family support represented a failure to consider all of the evidence with respect to the personal circumstances of the applicant in this matter. Accordingly, the decision of the visa officer was set aside and the matter returned to a different visa officer for rehearing and re-determination.

Sooknanan v. Canada (Minister of Citizenship & Immigration) (1998), 142 F.T.R. 155 (Fed. T.D.) — This was an application to review a decision of the Appeal Division dismissing an appeal filed pursuant to section 77 of the *Immigration Act*, from the refusal of an application for landing of the applicant's father, mother and sister. The applicant's sister was found to be medically inadmissible.

The Appeal Division indicated that it was not persuaded that unforeseen circumstances would not dictate the applicant's need to access social services for her sister. The evidence established that the applicant's parents had been providing extensive care to their daughter. There was no evidence that the parents would be able to continue to do this indefinitely, such that the applicant's sister would not outlive her parents capacity to provide such care. Further, there was no evidence before the Appeal Division that the applicant and other family members in Canada had experience in providing care for the applicant's sister in the absence of the support that had long been provided by the applicant's mother and father. In the result, the application for judicial review was dismissed.

Law v. Canada (Minister of Citizenship & Immigration) (1998), 140 F.T.R. 307 (Fed. T.D.) — The applicant sought to review the rejection of his application for permanent residence. The applicant was advised by an immigration officer that his file would be "closed" if the additional medical information that had been requested was not provided. Approximately a month after this request, the immigration officer wrote a letter to the applicant's counsel which stated that no decision would be made on the application until the dependent daughter had provided the requested medical information. Approximately a year later, the immigration officer wrote to the applicant and indicated that his application had been rejected because his dependent daughter had not provided the requested medical information.

The decision of the visa officer was set aside. There was little in the official correspondence which would have warned the applicant that the failure to provide the requested medical information would result in the rejection of his application.

The Court directed that all the necessary medical information be provided by the applicant to the immigration officer within six months of the Court's decision and that a decision in this matter be made by a different immigration officer than the one whose decision was set aside.

Cabaldon v. Canada (Minister of Citizenship & Immigration) (1998), 140 F.T.R. 296, 42 Imm. L.R. (2d) 12 (Fed. T.D.) — The applicant sought to review a decision of a visa officer denying him and his family admission to Canada. The application was denied because the applicant's dependant child suffered from a medical condition which made her inadmissible pursuant to section 19(1)(a) of the *Immigration Act*.

Neither of the medical officers, nor the visa officer committed an error in failing to consider evidence that family members resident in Canada had promised to support the applicant's family. For the purposes of forming a medical opinion considering the medical admissibility of the child, it did not matter that the applicant provided letters of support from relatives already resident in Canada. As a permanent resident, the child would have a right to the social services she requires, a right that cannot be waived through financial support promised by relatives. There was no evidence that the medical officers misconstrued that the child was a dependent applicant, rather than an independent one. Nonetheless, an applicant's potential for economic and personal physical, self-sufficiency may sometimes be a relevant factor in determining whether the applicant is medically inadmissible. It is only inappropriate for a medical officer to rely exclusively on the issue of self-sufficiency when determining whether a person's condition is likely to cause excessive demands on health or social services.

While it is for the medical officers to determine whether a particular applicant's condition is likely to cause an excessive demand, they must have some evidence before them to suggest whether the demand created by any particular medical condition is excessive. For the medical officers to form an opinion in the absence of such supporting evidence is an error of law.

Wong v. Canada (Minister of Citizenship & Immigration) (1998), 141 F.T.R. 62, 42 Imm. L.R. (2d) 17 (Fed. T.D.); additional reasons at (1998), 43 Imm. L.R. (2d) 24, 145 F.T.R. 119 (Fed. T.D.) — The applicant sought to review the refusal of his application for permanent residence because a dependant, his daughter, was mentally retarded. After receiving a copy of the medical notification, the applicant's counsel took the position that the applicant was unable to respond to concerns about the daughter's mental health. Counsel pointed out that he did not have the information he considered necessary in order to respond. Counsel requested information concerning (a) the time frame used by the medical officers in rendering their opinion; (b) whether the medical officers were assessing demand by reference to an across-Canada average or by reference to the location in which the individual intended to locate; (c) the basis on which the costs of services were estimated; (d) whether the costs were estimated by reference to the individual or by reference to some generic general average estimate and (e) whether any costs associated with home care had been included in the analysis of the applicant's daughter's situation.

No additional information was received in response to the applicant's counsel request. The non-disclosure of this information made it impossible for the applicant in an intelligent way to know what factors were considered relevant by the medical officers in reaching their opinion. The non-disclosure of the requested information constituted a breach of natural justice and a breach of the rules of fairness. Openness in general leads to better decision-making. It also leads to greater public confidence in the process and easier acceptance of negative decisions. Openness and transparency in decision-making are important in today's climate of diminishing respect for public servants and increasing cynicism towards politicians. Non-disclosure of the information left one potentially relevant matter unexplored and that is whether Canadian residence who can afford to do so are required to pay for some or all of the social services that have been identified as relevant to the applicant's situation. The extent to which individuals are expected to pay for some services, if they can do so, is relevant in the context of an opinion that assesses "excessive demand". Accordingly the application for judicial review was allowed.

Poste v. Canada (Minister of Citizenship & Immigration) (1997), 140 F.T.R. 126, 42 Imm. L.R. (2d) 84, 5 Admin. L.R. (3d) 69 (Fed. T.D.) — This was an application to review a decision of a visa officer refusing an application for permanent residence by the applicant because his son fell within section 19(1)(a). There was no evidence to show that the medical officers put their minds to the question of excessive demand as it related to the applicant's son. To the contrary, the evidence seemed to show that the medical officers only considered the demands placed on social services by the mentally disabled in general. Medical officers have a duty to assess the circumstances of each individual that comes before them. The opinion must be founded firmly on the individual's personal circumstances and all the circumstances of the case. These would include the degree of family support and commitment to the individual and the particular resources of the community. While a particular individual may cause excessive demands in one situation, in a different setting the same individual may cause minimal or no demands at all. Medical officers must address themselves to the particular circumstances of the individual, otherwise cogent evidence is ignored and opinions regarding demand become unfounded and cannot be upheld by the Court.

Tan v. Canada (Minister of Citizenship & Immigration) (1997), 40 Imm. L.R. (2d) 113 (Imm. & Ref. Bd. (App. Div.)) — The appellant appealed a decision refusing the sponsored application of his son. The application was refused on medical grounds.

The appeal was allowed. Tests of admissibility must be relevant to the purpose for which admission is sought. The evidence in this appeal disclosed that the applicant was a permanent dependant of the appellant and, therefore, the correct approach was for the medical officers to assess the applicant as a dependant son rather than an independent applicant.

The concept of mental retardation cannot be used as a stereotype. It is therefore an error for a medical officer to fail to specify the degree of mental retardation. The respondent argued that the medical officer's oversight in not specifying the degree of retardation in this matter was remedied by the issuance of a second medical opinion. The Court found that this second opinion was not an elaboration of the first, but a new medical opinion entirely. Given the fact that it had not been concurred in by another medical officer it was found to be invalid. The second opinion contained detailed information that was not previously addressed in the first. Thus, the refusal of the application was found to be invalid in law.

Tong v. Canada (Minister of Citizenship & Immigration) (October 31, 1997), Doc. IMM-2565-96 (Fed. T.D.) — The applicant sought to challenge the continued processing, by the Canadian Consulate in Buffalo, of his application for permanent residence. No final decision has been made because no final medical opinion has been rendered. Medical examinations of the applicant led to a conclusion by two medical officers that the applicant was medically inadmissible to Canada. The applicant was given 60 days to provide new medical information or new submissions in response to this medical opinion. The applicant's solicitor requested that he be provided with a copy of the applicant's medical records. A vice consul in Buffalo advised the applicant that he was unable to provide the medical file to him and suggested that the applicant direct his request to Immigration Medical Services in Ottawa who actually had the file.

The applicant commenced this application seeking among other things a declaratory order that a visa officer cannot fulfil his duties as a visa officer in cases involving a potential refusal based on a medical condition without a complete copy of a medical file.

The application was dismissed. Parliament has placed the decision-making authority for medical inadmissibility in the hands of medical officers. Once the medical officer forms an opinion the visa officer has no authority to alter that opinion which is binding upon him. It is therefore not necessary for the visa officer to review the medical file.

The vice consul's letter only identified the applicant's medical condition. This was sufficient, as the applicant was given a full opportunity to respond to that medical assessment and due to the fact that in the notification given the substance of the adverse opinion concerning the applicant's medical condition was disclosed.

Accordingly, the application for judicial review was dismissed.

Kaila v. Canada (Minister of Citizenship & Immigration) (1997), 42 Imm. L.R. (2d) 316 (Imm. & Ref. Bd. (App. Div.)) — The appellant appealed the refusal of the sponsored applications of her father, mother, brother and sister. The applications were refused because the sister was medically inadmissible. The sister was diagnosed as mentally retarded. The refusal was found to be invalid in law. The medical officers erred in focusing on the sister's probable lack of economic independence. There was no evidence that the officers assessed the probable demands that the sister would make on government services given her condition and the degree and effectiveness of the support promised by her family. There was no linkage between the evidence of the medical condition and whether the sister might reasonably be expected to cause excessive demand.

The sister had never been hospitalized, institutionalized or otherwise needed health services because of her condition, except for a period of taking medication when she was young. The evidence indicated that the sister was able to take care of herself and contribute to the household by doing chores without supervision. The sister required someone to accompany her outside the home as she is unable to read signs. There was no evidence to suggest that family support would fail. The Appeal Division noted that in Canada the sister would have even more family support than she did in India.

Accordingly, the decision that the admission of the sister might reasonably be expected to cause excessive demands on health and social services was found to be unreasonable.

Fei v. Canada (Minister of Citizenship & Immigration) (1997), 131 F.T.R. 81, 39 Imm. L.R. (2d) 266, [1998] 1 F.C. 274 (Fed. T.D.) — This was an application to review a decision of a visa officer by which decision the visa officer denied the application for permanent residence of the applicant on the ground that the applicant's dependent daughter was medically inadmissible.

At the commencement of the hearing the applicant brought a motion to strike out paragraphs of the affidavits of Dr. Gordon Hutchings and Dr. Theodore Axler. The principal basis for the motion was that the paragraphs in question were inadmissible as not having been before the visa officer at the time of her decision.

Neither party is allowed to adduce substantive evidence which was not before the visa officer except in cases where the jurisdiction of the visa officer is challenged on grounds such as for example, bias. Where an applicant challenges the medical opinion which supports the rejection of an immigration application it would be unfair and counter productive to disallow evidence which seeks to explain the reasonableness of the medical opinion. Evidence by the medical officers which explains their opinion is admissible provided that such evidence represents their views as of the time a final opinion was given, rather than at the point in time when the visa officer made the decision.

In this case, the dominant factor in the medical officer's minds as disclosed by their affidavits was that mentally retarded children require increased expenditure of public funds. Availability of services was not an issue. The ability of the family to care for the child at home was also not an issue. Inquiry was not made into these matters nor were they considered relevant by the medical officers. Neither medical officer actually examined the applicant's daughter.

The Court considered whether the visa officer was under a duty to request and obtain information necessary to confirm the reasonableness of the medical officers' opinion. The Court concluded that when a valid medical opinion is formed under subparagraph 19(1)(a)(ii), that opinion is binding on the visa officer. Where the opinion involves a patently unreasonable error of fact, is inconsistent or incoherent, or was generated in a fashion contrary to the principles of natural justice, an error of jurisdiction is involved. The opinion cannot be said to be valid. If the visa officer applies an invalid opinion then the visa officer has erred in law and his or her decision may be reviewed. Further, there is no impediment to an affected individual seeking judicial review of the medical opinion itself.

The medical narrative suggested the need for extensive social and educational support services, as well as constant supervision. The narrative indicated that these services were very expensive and often in short supply. The cross-examination of the doctors on their affidavits revealed that the doctors considered, primarily, only the cost of the extra educational services. They did not consider the supply of such services, nor did they think it relevant. They did not obtain information respecting the need for constant supervision, nor did they think it relevant. Social services required, other than educational services, were either trivial or entirely secondary in the doctors' opinion. Thus it was clear from the evidence that the medical narrative could not be sustained. Further, the applicants had no meaningful opportunity to bring to the attention of the medical officers the facts relating to excessive demand, because at no point was the applicant ever made aware of the criteria actually being employed by the medical officers in forming their opinion.

Subparagraph 19(1)(a)(ii) of the Act is open ended. It states that the medical officers must form an opinion with respect to whether admission would "cause or might reasonably be expected to cause excessive demands on health or social services." It is an error to state through the medical narrative that the reasons for exclusion were extensive social and educational support services, the need for constant supervision and the expense and supply of these services when the officers did not have information highly relevant to the determination of those factors. It was also apparent that the officers had not taken effective measures to obtain this information. The finding that constant supervision was necessary gave rise to a question of the extent of available family support. There was no evidence before the officers to support a finding of constant supervision because there was no evidence of a failure of family support.

Accordingly, the medical opinion could not be justified and could not stand. The Court concluded that the medical opinion which supported the visa officer's decision was defective, because the officer had erred in her application of the test set out in paragraph 19(1)(a)(ii) of the Act. Accordingly, the application for judicial review was allowed and the decision of the visa officer set aside.

Yogeswaran v. Canada (Minister of Citizenship & Immigration) (1997), 129 F.T.R. 151 (Fed. T.D.); affirmed (June 24, 1999), Doc. A-344-97 (Fed. C.A.) — The applicant sought to review a decision of a visa officer refusing his application for permanent residence due to the medical inadmissibility of his 11-year-old dependent son.

One of the medical doctors who provided the respondent with the opinion stated that the key social service that the boy would require was a placement in special education classes. The Court distinguished this case from an earlier decision *Fong v. Canada (Minister of Citizenship and Immigration)*(1997), 126 F.T.R. 235 (Fed. T.D.) where the applicant was 30 years of age and the Court was dealing with a demand that was not mandated by statute. In Ontario, it is compulsory that dependants with special educational requirements be accepted and, therefore, there is an additional cost automatically. There was sufficient evidence before the medical officers for them to determine that the admission of the dependant's son would cause excessive demands on social services and the Court was satisfied that education is a social service. Given that this was a medical opinion being given by the medical officers, it was not reasonable to expect a full examination of the costs of social services in such an opinion. Excessive demand means "more than normal".

The application for judicial review was dismissed.

Rudrakumar v. Canada (Minister of Citizenship & Immigration) (1996), 38 Imm. L.R. (2d) 82 (Imm. & Ref. Bd. (App. Div.)) — The appellant appealed the refusal to approve the sponsored application of her mother and her sister. The sponsored application was refused because the sister, who was a dependant of the mother, was medically inadmissable. The narrative portion of the medical notification indicated that if family ties were to breakdown, care in a long term facility for the sister would be required.

The Appeal Division may not question the correctness of a medical diagnosis, but it does have the authority to inquire into the reasonableness of the conclusion of the medical officers. Grounds for unreasonableness include; incoherence or inconsistency, absence of supporting evidence, or failure to consider cogent evidence. The finding that the sister's condition would result in excessive demands on social services was based on the potential that family ties might breakdown, in circumstances where there was no evidence to support the medical officer's speculation that that might happen. The evidence indicated that the sister had always been cared for at home, that the family had never used social services in Sri Lanka and that the appellant was prepared to continue to help support the sister in her home in Canada. Accordingly, the medical officer's opinion was unreasonable.

The Appeal Division noted that the respondent had called a witness who was a district supervisor for social services and that this witness had testified that there was a government subsidy of $771 available for handicap persons. The appeal division noted that this evidence would have been more helpful had the witness been able to adduce evidence indicating that the sister would have been eligible to receive such a benefit. The appeal was allowed.

Tam v. Canada (Minister of Citizenship & Immigration) (1995), 35 Imm. L.R. (2d) 201 (Fed. T.D.) — This was an application for judicial review of a decision denying the applicant's application for permanent residence. The applicant applied under the Assisted Relative class and included her husband and her son in her application. The officer notified the applicant that he had received the results of the medical examinations for the applicant and her family and it appeared that the applicant's husband was inadmissible. The officer's letter contained the usual statement to the effect that the applicant was free to submit further information concerning her application, within the following 30 days.

The applicant's solicitor responded to the officer's letter and asked for an extension of that 30 day period within which to make further submissions, the officer refused the applicant's solicitor's request.

Having offered the applicant an opportunity to respond, the officer had an obligation to allow a reasonable time for that purpose. Given that the medical condition was a new discovery and that the application was already four years old and that the applicant's solicitor was located near Toronto while the applicant was in Hong Kong, the request by the applicant's solicitor for an additional two weeks to submit material was reasonable in the circumstance and it was unfair of the officer to decide the case with granting the extra time.

King v. Canada (Minister of Citizenship & Immigration) (1996), 115 F.T.R. 306 (Fed. T.D.) — The visa officer refused the applicant's application for landing for medical reasons. The appeal division of the Immigration and Refugee Board allowed an appeal from that decision in law, but not in equity. The board found that the evidence did not support the conclusion of the medical notification.

When a decision of a visa officer denying an application for landing for medical reasons is overturned by the appeal division on the basis of an error in the medical assessment, the only issue that is *res judicata* is the medical decision found to be erroneous. Therefore, a visa officer can subsequently request further medical information and an applicant is required to establish that his or her admission into Canada would not be contrary to section 19.

Ludwig v. Canada (Minister of Citizenship & Immigration) (1996), 33 Imm. L.R. (2d) 213, 111 F.T.R. 271 (Fed. T.D.) — This was an application to judicially review a negative decision of a visa officer which determined that the applicant was medically inadmissible.

Medical officers must be careful not to apply the Medical Officers Handbook too rigidly. They must be flexible enough to look beyond the guidelines in the handbook and to decide the admissiablity of each applicant on the basis of that person's individual circumstances. If medical officers determine that they are bound by the handbook and cannot diverge from its guidelines, that would be a fetter on their discretion. If medical officers recognize that they may be flexible in their application of the guidelines in the handbook and determine the admissibility of each person on the basis of individual circumstances, then they will not have fettered their discretion. The handbook reflects common medical knowledge in practice, and as such, it is similar to a medical journal or textbook.

The Court concluded that the medical officer in this case did not fetter his discretion in applying the guidelines set out in the Medical Officers Handbook.

Ajanee v. Canada (Minister of Citizenship & Immigration) (1996), 33 Imm. L.R. (2d) 165, 110 F.T.R. 172 (Fed. T.D.) — This was an application to review a decision of a visa officer, determining that the applicant was medically inadmissible.

A visa officer has no authority to review the diagnostic assessment of medical officers. It is the medical officers who must reach the opinion that admission of the person concerned "would cause or might reasonably be expected to cause excessive demands on health or social services". The reasonableness of that opinion may be an issue for the visa officer. Where on the evidence before him or her a question arises whether the opinion is reasonable, the visa officer may elect to seek further medical advice. Where no serious question arises on the record before him or her, the visa officer may act on the basis of the opinion as it is presented to him or her.

In this case, the Court found that the visa officer acted on the basis of the opinion of the medical officers in circumstances where no question of the reasonableness of that opinion arose. The only medical information available to the visa officer at the time of his decision was the advice included in the form of the Medical Notification from the medical officers.

If the medical officer's determination turns out to be unreasonable, then the decision of the visa officer based on that unreasonable opinion may be set aside. A reviewing Court is competent to review the evidence to determine whether the medical officer's opinion is reasonable in the circumstances of the case. A medical opinion will be considered unreasonable because of incoherence or inconsistency, absence of supporting evidence, failure to consider cogent evidence or failure to consider the factors set out in section 22 of the regulations.

Wong v. Canada (Minister of Citizenship & Immigration) (1996), 34 Imm. L.R. (2d) 18 (Fed. T.D.) — This application succeeded on consent. The matter was sent back for reassessment by two different medical officers of health.

The Court noted that the case law indicated that a problem had arisen because a probable lack of future economic self sufficiency had been used in some cases as the sole and determining reason for reaching a negative conclusion about whether an applicant's condition would cause, or might reasonably be expected to cause, excessive demand on health and social services.

The Court directed that the medical officers of health were to assess the principal applicant's child as a dependent applicant. This assessment involved determining the probable demands that she would make on government services. The assessment of probable demands was to involve an analysis of whether on the balance of probabilities having regard to all the circumstances, including but not limited to the serverity of her condition, the degree and effectiveness of the support promised by her family, and her prospects for economic and physical self sufficiency, the dependent applicant would be cared for in her family home into the future.

Ng v. Canada (Minister of Citizenship & Immigration) (1996), 106 F.T.R. 140 (Fed. T.D.) — This application to set aside the decision of a visa officer refusing the adult applicant and his family a landed immigrant visa to Canada was allowed. Tests of admissibility must be relevant to the purpose for which admission is sought. In the present case the medical officers assessed the minor applicant without regard to the category under which his admission was sought. The minor applicant was not applying to immigrate as an independent applicant but rather was included in his father's application as a dependant. There is no requirement under the *Immigration Act* or the regulations for a dependant to establish self sufficiency.

The decision of the visa officer was set aside.

Sabater v. Canada (Minister of Citizenship & Immigration) (1995), 31 Imm. L.R. (2d) 59, 102 F.T.R. 268 (Fed. T.D.) — The applicants sought to overturn the refusal of their application for permanent residence by a visa officer. The visa officer determined that the 14-year-old female applicant was medically inadmissible.

One of the examining medical officers was of the opinion that the 14-year-old applicant was suffering from mental retardation. The opinion, however, gave no indication of the level or degree of retardation, and, as a result, it was difficult to determine the basis upon which it could be said that the applicant's admission would cause excessive demands on social services. One of the assessments relied upon by the medical officer had referred to the mental illness as "mild mental deficiency or retardation." The Court did not wish to say that a person suffering from mild mental retardation could not be found to cause excessive demands on social services. However, it would be reasonable for there to be a higher onus of proof on the medical officer to demonstrate excessive demand in such a situation.

The medical officers referred to an article prepared by the Assistant Director, Immigration, Overseas Health Services, where the effects of severe and moderate retardation were costed out. There was no costing out in the article, however, of mild mental retardation.

Accordingly, this was found to be an error making the medical officer's opinion unreasonable. The medical officers, in forming their opinion, are entitled to consider relevant factors not provided for under section 22 of the regulations. The Court further observed that services provided by schools to the handicapped may be considered as social services. The application was allowed.

Ismaili v. Canada (Minister of Citizenship & Immigration) (1995), 29 Imm. L.R. (2d) 1, 100 F.T.R. 139 (Fed. T.D.) — The applicant sought review of a decision of a visa officer denying the applicant's application for permanent residence on the ground that the applicant's minor son was inadmissible pursuant to subparagraph 19(1)(a)(ii). On judicial review applications of this type, the work of the Court would be made much simpler if the respondent would regularly make available the medical officers' record.

Section 22 of the regulations is enacted pursuant to subsection 114(1)(m). The wording of that subsection requires that section 22 of the regulations should be read as only prescribing the factors to be considered on the health and safety issue. Section 22 is not applicable to determine whether the admission of any person would cause or might reasonably be expected to cause demands on health or social services.

Choi v. Canada (Minister of Citizenship & Immigration) (1995), 29 Imm. L.R. (2d) 85, 98 F.T.R. 308 — This was an application to set aside a decision of a visa officer refusing an application for permanent residence. The applicant submitted an application in the Investor category. The application included a wife and five dependent daughters. The eldest daughter suffered from a mental disability and was found to be inadmissible on the basis that her admission would likely cause excessive demand on social services.

The Court noted that there is no precise definition of what constitutes excessive demands for medical services. The Court adopted the comments of Gibson J. in *Jim v. Canada (Solicitor General)* (1993), 22 Imm. L.R. (2d) 261, 69 F.T.R. 252, to the effect that excessive means more than normal and concluded in this case that the visa officer did not err in refusing the application for permanent residence.

Litt v. Canada (Minister of Citizenship & Immigration) (1995), 26 Imm. L.R. (2d) 253 (Fed. T.D.) — A visa officer refused admission to the applicant's father because two medical officers had formed the opinion that the father was suffering from quadriparesis, upper and lower motor neuron type. This decision was appealed to the Immigration and Refugee Board which found that the refusal was valid in law. The medical notification stated "should family support fail, he would place considerable demands on social services".

The evidence was that three family members were committed to supporting the father. There was not sufficient evidence to lead the medical officer to speculate that family support might fail. The speculation about the potential failure of family support was not based on the evidence. Further, there was an insufficient linkage between the evidence of the applicant's father's medical condition and the issue of whether the applicant's father might reasonably be expected to cause excessive demands on health or social services. The issue before the visa officer and the Appeal Division was the question of excessive demands on health or social services. It was not the father's medical condition. A medical condition itself is not necessarily evidence of a reasonable expectation of excessive demand on health or social services. This is not to say that there could not be a medical condition that, obviously, would lead to such a conclusion, but rather that such a conclusion was not obvious in this case. The decision of the visa officer was quashed.

Deol v. Canada (Minister of Employment & Immigration) (1992), 18 Imm. L.R. (2d) 1 (Fed. C.A.) — This appeal was directed against the decision of the Appeal Division of the Immigration and Refugee Board in which the Board dismissed an appeal from an immigration officer's refusal of an application for landing. The refusal was of a sponsored application of the appellant's widowed mother and her two dependent daughters on the ground that one of the daughters was suffering from mental retardation. There is now considerable authority as to the Board's role *vis-a-vis* the opinions of medical officers. It may not question the medical diagnosis, but when requested, it should enquire into the reasonableness of their conclusion as to the probable demands on government services. The Board did not enquire into the reasonableness of the medical officers' conclusion, but rather assumed from the sole fact of agreement as to the existence of mental retardation that the conclusion was reasonable. The mere invocation of mental retardation leads to no particular conclusion. Mental retardation is a condition covering a wide range of possibilities from the total inability to function to near normality. The concept cannot be used as a stereotype because it is far from a univocal notion. It is not the fact alone of mental retardation that is relevant, but the degree and the probable consequences of that degree of retardation for excessive demands on government services.

The Board had failed to make that assessment in this case and its decision was set aside. It was noted that the two medical officers had entered the sponsored dependant's intended occupation as "new worker". The tests of admissibility must be relevant to the purpose for which admission is sought. The medical officers may well have imposed a higher standard of medical admissibility because they failed to realize that the daughter in question would enter as a sponsored dependant.

Wong v. Canada (Minister of Employment & Immigration), 42 F.T.R. 209, [1991] 2 F.C. 186, affirmed (1992), 146 N.R. 319 (Fed. C.A.) — In December 1986, the applicants made an application for permanent residence in Canada. The application was refused because the son, Yiu Ting Wong, was determined to be medically inadmissible. Yiu Ting Wong suffers from Down's syndrome and the refusal was based on the assumption that persons with Down's syndrome tend to develop Alzheimer's disease. The decision was set aside on consent after considerable material was filed disputing this medical conclusion. The visa officer continued to process the application for permanent residence and again refused the applicant,

Yiu Ting Wong, on medical grounds. This application was brought alleging that the medical inadmissibility of the applicant had already been conclusively determined and that the matter was now *res judicata*. Estoppel *per rem judicatam* has two species: cause of action estoppel and issue estoppel. There are three elements of the issue estoppel species of *res judicata*: 1) the same question must have been decided in previous proceedings; 2) the previous proceedings must have been final; and 3) the parties to those proceedings must be identical to the parties to the proceeding in which the issue of *res judicata* is raised. The Court determined that the issue in the previous proceedings was not the medical inadmissibility in the generic sense of the applicant, Yiu Ting Wong, but only the issue of the connection between Down's syndrome and Alzheimer's disease. Accordingly, there was no basis for the application for the doctrine of *res judicata*. The Court also noted that immigration proceedings are matters of public law and ought to be distinguished from private adversaries disputing a private-law matter of litigation. The Court noted that there was considerable doubt whether the doctrine of *res judicata* applied in this area of public law.

Seyoum v. Canada (Minister of Employment & Immigration) (1990), 134 N.R. 233 (Fed. C.A.) — The applicant, an Eritrean, entered Canada on a student visa. While that visa was in effect, the applicant was found unfit, by reason of insanity, to stand trial for murder. The inquiry was convened, alleging that the applicant overstayed as a visitor. The applicant claimed refugee status and a conditional deportation order was made in part on the basis that the applicant was inadmissible under section 19(1)(a) because of the health impairment.

It appeared on the face of the medical notification that the opinion of the medical officers was based entirely on the judicial decision as to the applicant's sanity and not on an independent assessment of medical evidence. The applicant's detention, under a Lieutenant Governor's warrant following the finding of unfitness to stand trial, cannot automatically support the conclusion that he might be reasonably expected to cause excessive demands on health and social services. An independent medical examination must take place before the medical officers give their opinion. The finding that the applicant was described in section 19(1)(a) was accordingly not sustainable. The conditional deportation order was sustained on other grounds.

Bola v. Canada (Minister of Employment & Immigration) (1990), 11 Imm. L.R. (2d) 14, 107 N.R. 311 (Fed. C.A.) — The majority agreed that the Court of Appeal should refrain from intervening to contradict an honest assessment by the Immigration and Refugee Board of the sufficiency of a medical certificate on the basis of which the visa officer abroad had formed an opinion so long as the assessment was not tainted by any misconception of the law or any patently erroneous understanding of the medical officer's expressed statement of opinion.

The Court of Appeal is sitting in appeal and its role is not to re-do what the Board did as if it was, itself, a second Immigration and Refugee Board. In this particular case, the majority thought that the Board's reasons were clear and accurate as to the law and that the analysis of the medical certificate was carefully made and, accordingly, the appeal was dismissed.

Jiwanpuri v. Canada (Minister of Employment & Immigration) (1990), 10 Imm. L.R. (2d) 241, 109 N.R. 293 (Fed. C.A.) — The visa officer refused to grant the applications for landing which the respondent had sponsored on behalf of her father and her sister. The respondent disputed the refusal. The Immigration and Refugee Board allowed the appeal, a decision from which the Minister appealed to the Court.

Members of the Board do not have the expertise required to question the correctness of the medical diagnosis reached by the medical officers. Even with the help of medical witnesses, it is not a function of the Board to do so. The Board is not expected to make a choice between the written opinion of the medical officers and that of other doctors as to the diagnosis of a medical condition of an applicant for landing. The Act has made membership in the inadmissible class in section 19(1)(a) the immediate consequence of the expressed opinion of two medical officers, without providing for a different result, if other doctors could be found who would be of a different opinion.

In this case, the Board was, therefore, wrong in finding that, in the case of the father, the diagnosis of mental retardation was erroneous and incorrect. However, it is within the province of the Board to inquire into the reasonableness of the opinion, although that reasonableness is to be assessed at the time when the visa officer made his decision since it is that decision which is being appealed. The reasonableness of the opinion is not to be assessed strictly on the basis of the facts as they appear to the visa officers or the medical officers, and is open to the appellant to show that those facts were wrongly seen or interpreted or that they were insufficient to lead to the conclusion drawn. The decision of the Board, taken as a whole in this case, was to the effect that the opinion of the medical officers was unreasonable. The factors which medical officers must take into account are set out in section 22 of the regulations. The medical officers, in arriving at their opinion, applied only one relevant factor as set out in section 22. They also applied a number of factors which are not set out in the regulations. Accordingly, the Board was justified in concluding that their opinion was not reasonable.

Sall v. Canada (Minister of Employment & Immigration) (1989), 9 Imm. L.R. (2d) 179, 29 F.T.R. 176 (Fed. T.D.) — The applicants were refused permanent residence status on medical grounds. In upholding this decision, the Court relied on *Mohamed v. Canada (Minister of Employment & Immigration)*, [1986] 3 F.C. 90 (Fed. C.A.) which observed that it was open to the applicant to show that the medical officer's opinion was unreasonable. The Court further observed that evidence which simply tended to show that the person was no longer suffering from the medical condition which formed the basis of the medical officer's opinion was not sufficient. The decision of *Stefanska v. Canada (Minister of Employment & Immigration)* (1988), 6 Imm. L.R. (2d) 66 (Fed. T.D.) observed that the decision must be made by a duly constituted authority acting without abuse of power, in good faith and with objectivity. The Court observed that the diagnosis stated in the medical notification was accurate and fully supported the opinion of the physicians who signed it that these were questions of fact and not of law. Where the entries in the medical notification were so inconsistent with each other that they made the document as a whole incoherent, then, of course, such a medical notification would not constitute the opinion of a medical officer.

Badwal v. Canada (Minister of Employment & Immigration) (1989), 9 Imm. L.R. (2d) 85, 64 D.L.R. (4th) 561 (Fed. C.A.) — The appellant's father was refused a visa for admission to Canada for health reasons. The Immigration Appeal Board upheld the visa officer's decision and dismissed the appeal. The Federal Court of Appeal allowed the appeal because of the wording of the medical narrative. Certainty in prognosis is not required. The Act requires an expression of probabilities. The use of the word "may" does not automatically mean that the narrative is insufficient where the medical narrative makes excessive demands on the health or social system contingent upon deterioration of the appellant's current state. The corollary must be that, in the absence of deterioration, there will be no excessive demands. Parliament requires a judgment of probability based upon an appreciation of the applicant's present condition. Where the narrative does not address the probability of deterioration, the opinion that the sponsored father's presence in Canada will make excessive demands on the health or social system is self-contradictory.

Canada (Minister of Employment & Immigration) v. Sihota (1989), 8 Imm. L.R. (2d) 1 (Fed. C.A.) — This was an appeal by the Minister of Employment and Immigration from a decision of the Immigration Appeal Board that allowed the respondent's appeal against the refusal of the sponsored application of her father for landing in Canada. The Board erred by finding confusion in the medical notification where none existed. Fairly read, the medical notification clearly supported the visa officer's conclusion and no other. The other ailments disclosed in the notification were not susceptible to the description expressed in the narrative of the medical notification as a "condition which is likely to endanger public health." "Pulmonary tuberculosis possibly active" is amenable to that description. Section 22 of the *Immigration Regulations* only requires that the medical notification address specifically and clearly those diseases which alone or in combination are relevant to the opinion under section 19(1)(a) of the Act.

Anvari v. Canada (Employment & Immigration Commission) (1988), 10 C.H.R.R. D/5816, (sub nom. *Canada (Attorney General) v. Anvari))* 152 N.R. 241 (Human Rights Trib.), varied (1993), 14 C.H.R.R. D/292 (Human Rights Review Trib.), reversed (1993), 19 Imm. L.R. (2d) 192 (Fed. C.A.) — The complaint brought by Mr. Anvari was that the respondent Commission had breached the *Canadian Human Rights Act.* Mr. Anvari was denied admission to Canada pursuant to section 19(1)(a) of the *Immigration Act.* The *Immigration Act* has general scope to provide a service to the public. Under this Act and its regulations, the officials involved in the processing of individuals toward landed immigrant status carry out an official duty as agents of the Crown. Therefore, the tribunal has jurisdiction to make a decision under the *Canadian Human Rights Act.* In the case of Mr. Anvari, the medical evidence did not meet the tests set out in section 19(1)(a). That section requires evidence of a reasonable expectation to be the least possible evidence needed to satisfy the Act. The Tribunal accepted the statement of a doctor that surgery for scoliosis is purely elective surgery. Accordingly, the evidence from the medical officials of the Immigration Department, whose investigation of this particular case was cursory at best, would not justify the discrimination which Mr. Anvari suffered because of his medical disability. Thus, the Canadian Human Rights Commission ordered the Canada Employment and Immigration Commission to process Mr. Anvari to landed immigrant status forthwith and, in addition, awarded costs against the Commission in the amount of $3,000.

On appeal, the decision of the Human Rights Review Tribunal was upheld with some slight modifications to the award of compensation to Mr. Anvari.

Pattar v. Canada (Minister of Employment & Immigration) (1988), 8 Imm. L.R. (2d) 79, 98 N.R. 98 (Fed. C.A.) — The Immigration Appeal Board must determine, when confronted by medical certificates, whether the certificate contains on its face the clear expression of the medical opinion required to give effect to the inadmissibility enacted by section 19(1)(a) of the *Immigration Act.* In doing so, the Board must look to the document as a whole. Furthermore, the Court strongly disagreed with the suggestion that a difficulty, or even an impossibility, in determining the exact cause of an observed health disorder or illness were decisive impediments to giving the contemplated certificate. The minority decision sought to distinguish the *Hiramen* case on the basis that the medical officer had failed to fill in the part of the form containing the certificate and had given a narrative and medical profile that were completely incoherent.

The majority concluded, however, that the Board in fact had done nothing more than give an honest assessment of the sufficiency of the certificate and, therefore, that the appeal by the Minister should be dismissed.

Uppal v. Canada (Minister of Employment & Immigration) (1987), 2 Imm. L.R. (2d) 143, 78 N.R. 152 (Fed. C.A.) — The appellant, a Canadian citizen, sponsored applications for landing of members of the family class, namely his father, mother, one brother and two sisters. The applications were refused by the visa officer. The visa officer relied upon the opinion of two medical officers, as defined in section 2 of the Act. The appellant appealed to the Immigration Appeal Board and sought to adduce medical evidence to contradict the medical officer's diagnosis. The Immigration Appeal Board declined to receive this evidence and dismissed the appeal. The appellant then, pursuant to section 84, appealed to the Court of Appeal. The majority of the Court of Appeal held that the Board was required to receive the additional evidence in considering the correctness of the visa officer's opinion. The minority judgment was of the view that the Board was correct in refusing to receive evidence tendered to contradict the opinion given by the two medical officers. The minority view was that the visa officer was required to base his rejection on the opinion of these two officers and, so long as he properly did that, his opinion was entitled to be sustained. The opinions of other medical experts on the subject presented to the Board were, in the minority view, not pertinent to the issue of the correctness of the formation of the visa officer's opinion. The Court was unanimous in concluding that the relevant time to be considered by the Board on the appeal was the time of the visa officer's decision and not the time of the Board's hearing of the appellant's appeal.

The Court of Appeal was unanimous in pointing out that a consent judgment has no precedential value. The Court granting a consent judgment is concerned with only two things: the capacity of the parties to agree; and the Court's jurisdiction to make the order that the parties have agreed to ask it to make. Consent judgment reflects neither findings of fact nor a considered application of the law to the facts by the Court.

Finally, the Court unanimously agreed that evidence of the current medical condition of the appellant's father and sister was relevant to the question of whether humanitarian or compassionate considerations existed that would warrant the Board granting special relief.

Shanker v. Canada (Minister of Employment & Immigration) (June 25, 1987), Doc. A-535-86 (Fed. C.A.) — This was an appeal by a Canadian citizen from a decision of the Immigration Appeal Board dismissing an appeal against refusals of the sponsored applications of the citizen's father, mother and two brothers. The basis for the refusal was the opinion of a medical officer, concurred in by a second medical officer, that the mother was suffering from pulmonary tuberculosis, "possibly active." A visa officer found her inadmissible under section 19(1)(a)(i) of the *Immigration Act*. At the Immigration Appeal Board hearing, new evidence as to the mother's condition, subsequent to the rejection, was provided. This Court adopted the view that evidence as to the mother's condition, subsequent to the visa officer's refusal, was not relevant to the question of whether that refusal was lawful. It was argued that the medical notification, upon which the refusal was based, had not taken into account the results of subsequent medical inquiries. This argument failed because neither the transcript of the hearing before the Board, nor any document on the record, suggested that there was any response to the request for further medical information. Nor was there any suggestion that the appellant's mother had complied with the request to contact the doctor who examined her so that he might reply to the visa officer.

Mohamed v. Canada (Minister of Employment & Immigration), [1986] 3 F.C. 90, 68 N.R. 220 (Fed. C.A.) — This was an appeal from a decision of the Immigration Appeal Board dismissing an appeal from a refusal to approve a sponsored application for landing made by the appellant's father, mother, brother and sister. The ground for that refusal was that the appellant's mother was medically inadmissible. By the time of the appeal before the Immigration Appeal Board, the mother was no longer suffering from the medical condition that made her inadmissible. The first issue was whether her condition, at the time of the hearing of the appeal, was relevant. Mr. Justice Hugessen and Mr. Justice McQuaid concluded that the medical condition at the time the visa officer refused the application was relevant. The Chief Justice concluded that the relevant medical condition was that which the mother was in at the time of her appeal before the Immigration Appeal Board. The majority were of the view that the fact of the improvement in the mother's medical condition was relevant to whether special relief should be granted on the appeal pursuant to section 79(2)(b). The Court was unanimous, however, in quashing the Immigration Appeal Board's decision on other grounds.

Fung v. Canada (Minister of Employment & Immigration) (1986), 18 Admin. L.R. 260, 4 F.T.R. 118 (Fed. T.D.) — The applicant, Lap Szeto, a Canadian citizen, filed an undertaking of assistance sponsoring his co-applicants for permanent residence. Gun Sui Fung was notified that he appeared to have tuberculosis in June 1982 and he was directed to undergo a one-year course of treatment. In July 1982, Fung attended the Canton City Pulmonary Clinic for the required treatment and testing. In March 1983, Fung was advised to provide a further X-ray. He did so and was immediately rejected. This decision was attacked by a notice of motion seeking a writ of *certiorari* to quash the decision and a writ of *mandamus* directing the respondents to consider and process the applications in accordance with the *Immigration Act* and regulations. The application succeeded because the rejection of the applicants occurred before the treatment had run its full course, and because the rejection decision was based on consideration of only three tests results from the Canton clinic, whereas the evidence disclosed that at least 24 such tests had been carried out.

Hiramen v. Canada (Minister of Employment & Immigration) (1986), 65 N.R. 67 (Fed. C.A.) — This appeal was with leave under section 84 of the *Immigration Act*. The visa officer refused the applicant because his admission would cause, or might reasonably be expected to cause, excessive demands on health or social services. The visa officer's opinion was upheld by the Immigration Appeal Board and both decisions were based on a medical report by Health and Welfare, Canada. The entries on the medical certification were inconsistent with each other to the point of incoherence and, hence, the report could not constitute the opinion of a medical officer concurred in by at least one other medical officer. First, the boxes on the document corresponding to the appropriate subparagraph of section 19 had not been checked. Second, the medical categorizations, as completed in the document, were inconsistent with each other. One categorization suggested that the applicant would respond to treatment and the other suggested that no effective treatment was available. Finally, the statement on the form, to the effect that the applicant's condition "could" deteriorate and her medical condition "may affect her physical as well as mental health," were couched in the language of possibility rather than that of probability, while section 19(1)(a)(ii) of the Act requires an expression of probability. Thus, the appeal was allowed and the decision of the Board and the visa officer was set aside.

Mangat v. Canada (Secretary of State) (February 25, 1985), Doc. T-153-85 (Fed. T.D.) — The applicant gave a undertaking of assistance to the application for permanent residence of certain of his relatives. The relatives were refused for medical reasons. The Immigration Appeal Board allowed the applicant's appeal because the medical reports, upon which rejection of the family application had been based, had expired. Subsequent to the successful appeal, a new decision was taken that again rejected the applications for permanent residence of the applicant's family. Counsel for the applicant contended that the Board's decision on the first appeal meant that the medical problem, identified in the expired certificates, could no longer be taken into account by the visa officer even if confirmed by new unexpired certificates. This argument was rejected. The Board was held to have taken no "decision" that the medical problem was to be ignored but, rather, it was concluded that the Board had decided that the condition of rejection had not, as a matter of law, been properly proved and, thus, consideration of new and proper medical evidence was not precluded.

Mandamus was granted directing a visa officer to reconsider issuing a visitor's visa. The previous application for a visitor's visa had been rejected on the basis that the applicant had not satisfied relevant health requirements. The Court noted that the circumstances, relevant to medical opinions given under section 19(1)(a) of the Act, are different depending on the purpose and duration for which admission is sought. Here, the only medical opinions that the visa officer could have had available were those prepared in relation to the family's application for admission for permanent residence. Thus, the visa officer's decision to refuse to issue a visa was quashed and *mandamus* was ordered against the respondents requiring that they direct a visa officer to reconsider the question of issuing a visitor's visa to the applicant's family.

Ahir v. Canada (Minister of Employment & Immigration) (1983), 49 N.R. 185, 2 D.L.R. (4th) 163 (Fed. C.A.) — The appellant, a citizen of India, sought to enter Canada to visit her father. She was required to undergo a medical examination after her arrival at a Canadian port-of-entry. Thereafter, a report was prepared stating, in the opinion of two medical officers, that the appellant's admission to Canada might cause excessive demands on health or social services. An adjudicator ignored this opinion and granted the appellant admission to Canada as a visitor for a period of two months on condition that she not attend any school in Canada and that she not engage in employment. The Minister appealed to the Immigration Appeal Board which set aside the adjudicator's decision. The Court of Appeal quashed the Immigration Appeal Board's ruling and restored the decision of the adjudicator. The relevant test is that the applicant's admission would cause or "might reasonably be expected to cause" excessive demand on health or social services. The medical examinations were done without regard to the prospective status of the appellant. Accordingly, the adjudicator was correct in ruling that the medical opinions were not reasonable because they were formulated on an improper basis using improper criteria.

Tsang v. Canada (Minister of Employment & Immigration) (April 1, 1981), Doc. T80-9437 (Imm. App. Bd.) — The appellant sponsored the application for permanent residence of her father. The father's application was refused on the grounds that he did not satisfy the medical requirements for immigrants and that his admission would cause excessive demands on health or social services. The appellant sought an order from the Immigration Appeal Board directing the Minister to produce the medical information upon which the decision was based. The Board found that the sponsoree, having signed a medical release in his application for permanent residence, authorized the release of medical information by Health and Welfare Canada to the Minister of Employment and Immigration and, thus, found that the Minister was entitled to the medical information, which was in fact in the possession of Health and Welfare Canada. The Board concluded that it had jurisdiction to order production prior to the hearing of the appeal of the medical information sought by the appellant. The order for production was not made in this case because it was premature as no application for an order to produce had been given to the doctors from Health and Welfare Canada from whom production was sought.

Section 19(1)(b)

Khakoo v. Canada (Minister of Citizenship & Immigration) (1995), 103 F.T.R. 284 (Fed. T.D.) — The applicants arrived in Canada on November 6, 1990 and entered as "visitors." In March 1991 they made a claim for refugee status which was ultimately rejected. Their application for admission was sponsored in 1994 by a daughter of the female applicant who is a Canadian citizen. The visa office in Detroit denied the application on the basis that the applicant had been receiving welfare benefits for four years and that there was a long-term and continuing lack of support from the sponsor.

It was not disputed that the applicant's sponsor had a right of appeal to the Appeal Division of the IRB. However, the applicants had no such right and therefore the Court held that the applicants could bring an application for judicial review to quash the visa officer's decision.

The visa officer was acting under subsection 6(1) of the Regulations. Within the terms of paragraph 6(1)(b), the applicants were sponsored, the sponsor had given an undertaking and there was no evidence that the sponsor was in default under any other undertakings given by her, and there was the express opinion of another immigration officer that the sponsor would be able to fulfil this undertaking. In these circumstances, the applicants fell within the exception contained within section 19(1)(b) of the *Immigration Act*, and, accordingly, the refusal of the application was an error in law. The refusal was quashed.

Nicolau v. Canada (Minister of Employment & Immigration) (1994), 74 F.T.R. 38 — The applicant sought to review a decision by an adjudicator which decided that the applicant was described in section 19(1)(b). The adjudicator was satisfied that the applicant would be able to support herself if she were permitted to work. The applicant could not work in Canada. The witnesses, who testified on behalf of the applicant and indicated a willingness to offer emotional and, to a limited extent, financial support, did not establish that they had made adequate arrangements such that the applicant would not require social assistance.

There was no doubt that the applicant was willing to support herself but the evidence was clear that she was unable to do so because she could not legally work.

The adjudicator's decision in finding the applicant described in section 19(1)(b) was upheld.

Orantes v. Canada (Minister of Employment & Immigration) (1990), 34 F.T.R. 184 — The Court criticized very strongly the fact that the application for leave was not filed by the Student Legal Aid Clinic because of the onset of Christmas holidays but nevertheless extended the time for filing a notice seeking leave to appeal. The applicant sought orders in the nature of *certiorari* and *mandamus* in regard to the respondent's having invoked section 19(1)(b) of the Act and their not having invoked section 114(1) of the Act in his favour. The denial of permanent residence was based on the fact that the applicant and his dependants had been in receipt of social assistance since 1986 and that neither his Canadian citizen son nor permanent resident son were in a financial position to sponsor him or his dependants. Section 114(2), it was noted, provides that the Cabinet may, by regulation, exempt any person from any regulation made under section 114(1). Cabinet cannot repeal, suspend or override or exempt anyone from any provision of the *Immigration Act* itself, just the regulations. Without parliamentary authority, the Governor in Council has no authority to exempt anyone from the law. If parliamentary democracy is to survive in Canada, Parliament must make choices about which foreigners, if any, may be legally admitted for permanent residence and not become helpless in the face of asserted entries by aliens no matter how sympathetic their cases. It takes a certain degree of intellectual toughness to support the principles of democracy in the face of various individuals who seek migration into Canada against the will of the democratically elected representatives of the people. If the Charter is interpreted in such a manner as to obviate the will of Parliament in a matter such as this, it is the sort of frustration which would ultimately destroy national government by amputating the lawful means of governance. Whether it is even appropriate to require genuine refugees to be able to support themselves in this applicant's circumstances is a question of policy which cannot be resolved by a Court since the requirement does not violate the Constitution. Accordingly, the application for leave to appeal was dismissed.

Canada (Attorney General) v. Jolly, [1975] F.C. 216, 54 D.L.R. (3d) 277, 7 N.R. 271 (Fed. C.A.) — For a discussion of the phrase "reasonable grounds to believe" although in a different context, see *Jolly v. Canada (Minister of Manpower & Immigration), infra, Paragraph (f)* of *Subsection (1)* (s. 19).

Section 19(1)(c)

Smith v. Canada (Minister of Citizenship & Immigration), 44 Imm. L.R. (2d) 154, [1998] 3 F.C. 144 (Fed. T.D.) — The applicant had two applications before the Court, one in respect of the deportation order and the other in respect of an exclusion order. In July 1995, the applicant was found to be described in section 19(1)(c) of the *Immigration Act* on the basis of two convictions for drug trafficking. The applicant was ordered deported. In October 1995, before the deportation order was executed the applicant left Canada for personal reasons, believing he would be able to return. Upon his return in November 1995, the applicant was examined at the airport and an exclusion order was made against him on the basis that the applicant was a person described in paragraph 19(1)(i) because he requires Ministerial consent before he could return to Canada which he failed to obtain. A few days before the exclusion order, the applicant was pardoned in respect of the drug trafficking conviction.

The *Criminal Records Act* does not erase the conviction in the sense that the conviction is deemed not to have existed. The purpose of the Act is to bar any further disadvantage that arises from the pardoned conviction by cleansing the individual of the stain caused by the conviction and limiting the uses to which the fact of the conviction can be put.

The Court found that the deportation order was issued while the conviction was outstanding and that, therefore, the deportation order was valid. After the grant of the pardon the disqualification of the applicant under paragraph 19(1)(c) was removed. Enforcement of the deportation order after the granting of the pardon would have the effect of enforcing a disqualification which had been removed and would be in violation of the *Criminal Records Act.*

With respect to the exclusion order, it was sufficiently linked to the convictions that it too cannot be enforced without violating section 5 of the *Criminal Records Act.* The Court ruled, therefore, that the deportation order was valid. The Court declared that enforcement of the order and enforcement of the exclusion order would be illegal and contrary to section 5 of the *Criminal Records Act.*

Taei v. Canada (Minister of Employment & Immigration) (1993), 19 Imm. L.R. (2d) 187, 64 F.T.R. 311 (Fed. T.D.) — The applicant sought leave for a judicial review to obtain an order compelling the respondent to process his application for landing. The applicant arrived in Canada in 1989 and made a claim for refugee status. His claim was determined affirmatively but before landed immigrant status was granted, the applicant was charged with aggravated assault, attempted murder and extortion and these charges were pending at the time of this application. The respondent had refused to process the application until the criminal charges were disposed of by the courts. Leave to institute judicial review was denied. The presumption of innocence requires the respondent to do nothing but stay the applicant's request for admission until the criminal charges are disposed of. It would be against public policy for the respondent to heedlessly grant permanent resident status until the criminal charges were completed. If the applicant is acquitted, then the respondent should proceed with granting admission. If the applicant is convicted, then he will have disqualified himself from landing.

Canada (Minister of Employment & Immigration) v. Burgon, 13 Imm. L.R. (2d) 102, 78 D.L.R. (4th) 103, [1991] 3 F.C. 44, (sub nom. *Burgon v. Canada (Minister of Employment & Immigration))* 122 N.R. 228 (Fed. C.A.) — This was an appeal from a decision of the Appeal Division allowing the respondent to remain in Canada.

Susan Mary Burgon, the respondent, was arrested on drug charges in the United Kingdom in 1987. While awaiting trial in prison she learned that her elder son had also become involved in drug trafficking. This caused her to give a statement to the police which led to the imprisonment of her son, her father and a well known drug dealer. The respondent had pleaded guilty in England to conspiracy to supply a controlled drug and was given a suspended sentence. In March 1987 the respondent, who had married a Canadian citizen, was subject of a sponsorship application by her husband. On December 7, 1987, with the help of her probation officer, she received an English discharge order which had the effect of clearing her completely.

Ms. Burgon's application for permanent residence was rejected. It was refused on two basis. Initially, because of her "conviction" it was the opinion of Immigration that she was caught by section 19(1)(c) of the *Immigration Act*. Secondly, because of her previous addiction she was thought to be inadmissable by virtue of section 19(1)(a).

The more complex question was whether Ms. Burgon was excluded pursuant to section 19(1)(c). It is clear that the word "convicted" does not have a universal immutable meaning. This word, like so many other words, may have different meanings depending on the context in which it is used.

What must be decided is whether the policy of the *Immigration Act* predominates in arriving at the meaning of the word "convicted", whether the policy of the criminal law should be controlling, or whether the Court should seek to harmonize the legislation in these two areas. Also, in this case, there was a foreign element which required the Court to consider what recognition, if any, should be given to the laws of the foreign country in this interpretation exercise.

The policy of the criminal law in Canada in relation to criminal records has been changed in recent years to reflect altering social attitudes towards those who violated the criminal law. The first legislative response was the *Criminal Records Act*, S.C. 1969–70, c. 40, which permitted a pardon by the Governor in Council after the lapse of a certain period of time upon the recommendation of the National Parole Board. The effect of such a pardon was that the conviction was vacated. Not long after the *Criminal Code* was amended to allow Judges to impose absolute and conditional discharges in appropriate cases. This amendment had the effect of the accused being deemed not to have been convicted of the offence in question.

Similar provisions aimed at helping those convicted of crimes to make a new beginning were enacted in the United Kingdom as well as other countries. The British went further than Canada. In addition to allowing absolute and conditional discharges it enacted the *Powers of Criminal Courts Act*, 1973, to the effect that when an offender was placed on probation his conviction would be deemed not to be a conviction. It was this provision which enabled Ms. Burgon to have her conviction expunged in the U.K.

When parliament reenacted the *Immigration Act* in 1976 it must be taken to have known about its own earlier penal legislation which allowed for the elimination of criminal convictions from records of deserving individuals. In using the word convicted in 19(1)(c) parliament meant a conviction that had not been expunged. If a conviction had been erased by the provisions of another law of parliament, it was not meant to be treated in the same way as a conviction that had not been removed. In this way the policy of the criminal law is incorporated within the *Immigration Act*. The further question to consider was whether the U.K. legislation, which was similar in purpose, but not identical to the Canadian law, should be treated in the same way. In both countries certain offenders are granted the advantage of avoiding the stigma of a criminal record to facilitate their rehabilitation. There is no good reason for immigration law to thwart the goal of this British legislation which is consistent with the Canadian law. The two legal systems are based on similar foundations and share similar values. Unless there is a valid basis for deciding otherwise, the legislation of countries, similar to our own, especially when their aims are identical, ought to be accorded respect. While a Court is not required to go so far as to "attorn" to the law of all foreign jurisdiction, it is appropriate to do so in this case because the laws and the legal system of the other country are similar to ours.

Accordingly, the Court ruled that there being no conviction in the United Kingdom, and there being no reason to refuse to grant recognition to the law of the United Kingdom, Ms. Burgon was not "convicted" for the purpose of section 19(1)(c).

Singleton v. Canada (Minister of Employment & Immigration) (November 7, 1983), Doc. A-813-83 (Fed. T.D.) — The Court noted that a certificate of the applicant's conviction would be the best evidence of such conviction and that the lack of such a certificate leaves something to be desired in the particularity of the evidence. Where, however, the evidence as a whole is sufficient to support the finding of the adjudicator that the applicant was a person described in section 27(2)(d) of the *Immigration Act*, an application to set aside such decision will fail.

Section 19(1)(c.1)

Tei v. Canada (Minister of Citizenship & Immigration) (1998), 48 Imm. L.R. (2d) 120, 161 F.T.R. 51 (Fed. T.D.) — The applicant submitted an application for permanent residence under the investor category and included his wife. The applicant's wife had a conviction for making a false statement for the purpose of obtaining a certificate of identity and had been sentenced to a fine of $1,500 Hong Kong dollars. The applicant submitted an application for rehabilitation, and the applicant and his wife were interviewed in June 1997 for the purpose of determining whether the visa officer would recommend to the program manager that the wife was rehabilitated. The result of the interview was a negative recommendation and on July 16, 1997, the program manager concurred with this recommendation.

The applicant's Notice of Motion challenged the visa officer's decision refusing the applicant's application for permanent residence, when in fact, the applicant was really challenging the Minister's decision refusing to grant rehabilitation. The Minister is the decision-maker. The visa officer's role is that of advisor in that he made a recommendation and submitted the application along with supporting documents. If the visa officer drew unreasonable conclusions or relied on erroneous facts or indeed failed to take into account relevant facts, then these defects or errors would be germane in a review of the decision itself which was made by the Minister's delegate. By challenging the visa officer's recommendation, the applicant is also putting into play the validity of the Minister's decision. The applicant should have sought judicial review of the Minister's determination. The Court noted that leave of the Court would have been required to review this decision and that leave had not been obtained.

Accordingly, the application for judicial review was dismissed.

Masasi v. Canada (Minister of Citizenship & Immigration) (1997), 40 Imm. L.R. (2d) 133, 138 F.T.R. 121 (Fed. T.D.) — This was an application to review a decision of an adjudicator determining that the applicant was inadmissible pursuant to subparagraph 19(1)(c.1)(i). The applicant was a citizen of Tanzania. In 1993, he was in the United States and was involved in a bar-room fight which resulted in his being convicted of assault in the second degree. At the inquiry in Canada, the adjudicator found that that offence was equivalent to section 267(b) of the *Criminal Code*. The essential elements of the U.S. offence where assault on another person with a dangerous weapon and the infliction of substantial bodily harm

The adjudicator made no specific finding with respect to the definition of bodily harm as set out in the *Criminal Code* and the way it was treated in the U.S. statute at the material time. Due to the fact that the adjudicator had determined that bodily harm was an essential element of both offences, it was incumbent upon her to address the definition in terms of Canadian and U.S. law in order to establish equivalency. Having identified the essential elements of the Canadian and U.S. offences, it was necessary to actually examine them in order to determine whether they were equivalent or not.

Accordingly, the decision of the adjudicator was set aside.

Legault v. Canada (Secretary of State) (1997), 42 Imm. L.R. (2d) 192, 133 F.T.R. 320 (note), 219 N.R. 376 (Fed. C.A.); leave to appeal to S.C.C. refused (1998), 227 N.R. (note) (S.C.C.) — An adjudicator issued a conditional deportation order against the respondent, on the basis that he had reasonable grounds to believe that the respondent came within 19(1)(c.1)(ii) of the *Immigration Act*. A motions judge quashed the adjudicator's decision.

The appeal was allowed. The adjudicator was entitled to view the indictment and the warrant for the arrest of the respondent as sufficient evidence to allow him to arrive, reasonably, at the conclusion that the respondent was described in 19(1)(c.1)(ii).

Lui v. Canada (Minister of Citizenship & Immigration) (1997), 39 Imm. L.R. (2d) 60, 134 F.T.R. 308 (Fed. T.D.) — The applicant sought to review a deportation order based on a 1976 conviction for assault occasioning bodily harm in Hong Kong. The adjudicator was of the opinion that the applicant was described in 19(1)(c.1)(i).

Before the adjudicator, the applicant produced a "Certificate of No Criminal Conviction" from the Commissioner of Police in Hong Kong. That document stated that the 1976 conviction was regarded as spent in Hong Kong by virtue of section 2(1) of the *Rehabilitation of Offenders Ordinance*. The applicant argued that the operation of the ordinance was similar to the *Criminal Records Act of Canada*, under which persons who have been convicted of a criminal offence in Canada may seek pardons. The applicant argued that the adjudicator should have treated the 1976 Hong Kong conviction as if it had been vacated under the *Criminal Records Act*, in which case the applicant would not have been inadmissible.

The Court enunciated the following test:

1. The laws and legal system of the foreign jurisdiction must be similar to Canada's.
2. The foreign law in question must be similar in (a) aim or purpose; (b) content; and (c) effect, but not necessarily identical to the Canadian law.

The Court found that the laws and legal system of Hong Kong were similar to Canada's. Hong Kong had been a British colony for over 150 years at the time of this application, and its legal system had as its basis, English law.

The Court found that the purpose or aim of the Hong Kong Ordinance was similar to that of the *Criminal Records Act*, namely to give convicted persons a second chance by "wiping their slate clean". The content and effect of the ordinance was found not to be similar to the *Criminal Records Act*. The effect of the *Criminal Records Act* was to vacate a conviction if the National Parole Board granted a pardon and to remove any disqualifications flowing from the conviction. The effect of the Hong Kong Ordinance while being similar was subject to numerous exceptions.

Accordingly, the Court concluded that the Hong Kong Ordinance was not similar in content and effect to the Canadian law. In respect of disqualifications, the Hong Kong and Canadian laws were inconsistent. Therefore, the vacating of the conviction by the Hong Kong Ordinance could not be recognized by Canada.

Accordingly, the application for judicial review was dismissed.

Barnett v. Canada (Minister of Citizenship & Immigration) (1996), 33 Imm. L.R. (2d) 1, 109 F.T.R. 154 (Fed. T.D.) — This was an application to set aside the decision of an adjudicator which held that the applicant was the member of an inadmissable class pursuant to paragraph 19(1)(c.1)(i). The applicant, a U.K. citizen, entered Canada in September 1993. In May 1994 he was reported for working without an employment authorization. An inquiry opened in May 1994 and was adjourned. The applicant was subsequently served with a report alleging that he had been convicted in the United Kingdom with impaired driving. Later, a further section 27 report was served alleging that the applicant, in 1977, had been convicted of burglary. The applicant's position was that pursuant to the *U.K. Rehabilitation of Offenders Act*, 1974, his conviction for burglary was spent on October 7, 1982 and he was no longer deemed to be convicted of the offence. The adjudicator decided that although the conviction for burglary was spent under United Kingdom law, it was not spent for purposes of the Canadian *Immigration Act.*

Where another country, whose legal system is based on similar foundation and values as our own, has enacted legislation which reflects goals and objectives analogous to those encompassed within our own system, then that law should be accorded respect and recognized for purposes of Canadian immigration law. The question is not whether Canada has identical legislation in place but whether the underlying rationale of the foreign legislation is consistent with some fundamental principle of justice esteemed within our society.

The applicant has been treated in the United Kingdom as not having been convicted of the offence of burglary and there is no solid rationale for refusing to recognize the rehabilitation of the *Offenders Act* of the U.K. Accordingly, the applicant has not been convicted as that term is used in paragraph 19(1)(c.1)(i) of the *Immigration Act*, and is not excluded on that basis.

Kiani v. Canada (Minister of Citizenship & Immigration) (1995), 96 F.T.R. 241, 31 Imm. L.R. (2d) 269 — An adjudicator determined the applicant to be a person described in paragraph 19(1)(c.1). The adjudicator had before him a police report prepared very shortly after the incident in which the applicant acknowledged that he had participated. The applicant had lost a leg by reason of a gun shot wound inflicted by police while the applicant was participating in a demonstration in 1986. Finally, the adjudicator had evidence upon which he could reasonably conclude that the applicant's denial of guilt with respect to the charges pending in Pakistan was neither credible nor trustworthy. These items of evidence constituted a sufficient basis for the adjudicator to conclude that the "reasonable grounds to believe" required by section 19(1)(c.1) existed.

Halm v. Canada (Minister of Employment & Immigration) (1995), 27 C.R.R. (2d) 23, 91 F.T.R. 106 — This application successfully set aside a conditional deportation order.

The applicant had been ordered deported on the ground that there were reasonable grounds to believe that he had been convicted of an offence outside of Canada which, if committed in Canada, would constitute an offence punishable by a maximum term of imprisonment of 10 years or more. The applicant was convicted in New York State of 5 counts of sodomy, and 3 counts of endangering the welfare of a child.

The applicant successfully argued that section 159 of the *Criminal Code* was unconstitutional and that, therefore, there was no comparable offence in Canada to the sodomy offence of which he had been convicted in the United States. It was common ground between the parties that there was no comparable offence in Canada to the offence of endangering the welfare of a child.

The right to counsel includes being given a reasonable amount of time to retain and instruct counsel and this includes sufficient time to make financial arrangements. The adjudicator was correct when he indicated that if he were to continue to adjourn the applicant's inquiry to await the processing of the legal aid application that he would be relinquishing control over the timing of the proceedings to the applicant, his counsel, and the legal aid authorities. In this case the adjudicator had adjourned the inquiry 5 times to allow the applicant to obtain some firm commitment that counsel would be representing him.

Counsel for the applicant had argued that it was unfair for the deportation process to be used instead of extradition. The Court noted that extradition and deportation served different purposes. Extradition is initiated by a request from a foreign state. In the absence of any such request a proceeding never begins. Deportation is initiated by the expelling state which does not wish the illegal alien to remain within its borders. There is nothing inherently unfair in a foreign state delaying extradition proceedings when it is known that the individual in question is likely to be deported.

Finally, the Court noted that for purposes of section 19(1)(c.1) equivalency is not required to be proven beyond a reasonable doubt. All that is required is that the adjudicator determine that the applicant is a person with respect to whom there are "reasonable grounds to believe" that he has been convicted outside of Canada of an equivalent offence.

Legault v. Canada (Secretary of State) (1995), 26 Imm. L.R. (2d) 255, 90 F.T.R. 145 — The applicant, an American citizen, was the subject of an indictment by a grand jury in Louisiana. The adjudicator erred in finding, on the basis of the warrant for arrest and indictment from the United States of America, that he had reasonable grounds to believe that the applicant had committed, outside Canada, certain acts or omissions which constituted offences under the laws of the United States. The contents of the warrant for arrest and the indictment did not constitute evidence of the commission of alleged criminal offences by the applicant. An indictment performs the same function in the United States as it does in Canada in that it is the formal legal document containing the alleged indictable criminal offences upon which the accused will be tried. The indictment does not constitute evidence and may not be used as evidence by the trier of fact in the criminal proceedings.

Lei v. Canada (Solicitor General) (1994), 74 F.T.R. 67 — The adjudicator held that the applicant was a member of an inadmissible class of persons described in section 19(2)(a.1)(i). The applicant was convicted of reckless driving pursuant to the Rules of the Road of State of Washington. A comparison of the wording of the Washington Statute and the Canadian *Criminal Code* revealed that the Canadian statute is narrower than its American counterpart. When this occurred it was necessary for the adjudicator to go beyond the wording of the statute in order to determine whether the essential ingredients of the offence in Canada had been proven in the foreign proceedings. This could only be accomplished by obtaining evidence of the circumstances which resulted in the charge in the State of Washington. There was no such evidence before the adjudicator and accordingly, his decision was set aside.

Taei v. Canada (Minister of Employment & Immigration) (1993), 19 Imm. L.R. (2d) 187, 64 F.T.R. 311 — For digest, see section 19, subheading *subsection (1), Paragraph (c), supra.*

See *R. v. McInnis* (1973) 1 O.R. (2d) 1, 23 C.R.N.S. 152, 13 C.C.C. (2d) 471 (Ont. C.A.) for various meanings that are attached to the word "conviction" and hence "convicted".

Mohammad v. Canada (Minister of Employment & Immigration), [1989] 2 F.C. 363, 55 D.L.R. (4th) 321, 21 F.T.R. 240 (note) (Fed. C.A.) — It is not a pre-condition to the operation of section 19(1)(c) that the Governor in Council shall have considered the question of rehabilitation and be dissatisfied that the person concerned has brought himself within the exception. The report mandated by section 27(1) requires the authorizing immigration officer to possess information that the person concerned has been convicted of the kind of criminal act specified in section 19(1)(c) and to have knowledge that the person concerned has not satisfied the Governor in Council as to his rehabilitation.

Policy directives, whether made pursuant to regulatory authority or general administrative capacity, are no more than directions and are unenforceable by members of the public. The procedural formalities which are required in respect to an immigration officer when initiating a section 27(1) report are minimal, firstly, because this is a purely administrative decision and, secondly, because the officer when issuing the section 27(1) report is merely the initiator of the inquiry process. An immigration officer before issuing a section 27(1) report is, therefore, not required to give the person concerned an opportunity to answer allegations contained in that report. On the facts, the immigration officer who issued the section 27(1) report had sufficient knowledge and information upon which to base the report, and further, the applicant was given full particulars on the allegations against him.

The Court of Appeal adopted the motion's judge's findings, that there was nothing irregular in the fact that the high-profile nature of the case placed pressure on the respondent's representatives to proceed with dispatch.

The requirement of institutional independence is included in the rules of natural justice as well as enshrined in the Charter. The test for institutional independence is whether a reasonable and right-minded individual, having informed himself of the scheme whereby adjudicators are appointed under the *Immigration Act* and of the basis upon which they perform their duties, would be likely to conclude that an adjudicator appointed under and acting pursuant to that scheme, more likely than not, would decide fairly the inquiries under the *Immigration Act* over which he presided. While the case-presenting officers and adjudicators are both civil servants under the direction of the same Minister, they operate in separate and distinct divisions of the Commission. Case-presenting officers have no supervisory role, *vis-à-vis* adjudicators. They do not report to a common superior and it is only at the apex of the organization chart that their respective hierarchies merge. As far as legal direction is concerned, adjudicators can and do seek advice on difficult legal issues from lawyers on the staff of the Adjudication Directorate, who have no connection or association with the Enforcement Branch. On the subject of monitoring, there is evidence that the monitoring practice focuses primarily on how hearings are conducted; with respect to security of tenure, adjudicators, like other civil servants, have the protection afforded pursuant to section 31 of the *Public Service Employment Act*. Additionally, they have the protection of a three-stage grievance procedure. The fact that adjudicators are members of the same bargaining unit as case-presenting officers, is a neutral circumstance that does not give rise to any apprehension one way or the other. The practice of appointing adjudicators to other positions on an acting basis does not give rise to reasonable apprehension of a lack of independence. The Court relied on the uncontradicted evidence of an adjudicator to the effect that the decisions made by him were made independently and without direction from anyone else.

Finally, it was pointed out that the assignment of cases is rationally based; complex cases are usually assigned to the more experienced adjudicators. There was nothing to suggest that particular cases were assigned to particular adjudicators, let alone any evidence to suggest that the adjudicator chosen to conduct this inquiry was chosen on any basis other than the rational basis referred to previously. The Court concluded, for these reasons, that reasonable persons, reasonably informed, would view adjudicators appointed under the *Immigration Act* as being independent, keeping in mind the fact that they are for the most part laypersons in the hierarchy of quasi-judicial tribunals; and bearing in mind that their decisions are subject to judicial review by the Court; and that they have all taken an oath of office to "faithfully and honestly fulfill their duties" devolving upon them. Accordingly, the appellant's appeal was dismissed.

Steward v. Canada (Minister of Employment & Immigration) (1988), 84 N.R. 236 (Fed. C.A.) — The Court articulated the procedure to be followed when deciding the question of equivalency. It stated and adopted as correct the statement that, whatever the names given the offences or the words used in defining them, one must determine the essential elements of each and be satisfied that the essential elements correspond. One must, of course, expect differences in the wording of statutory offences in different countries.

"Equivalency" can be determined in three ways:

1. by comparison of the precise wording in each statute both through documents and, if available, through the evidence of an expert or experts in the foreign law with a view to determining the essential ingredients of the respective offences;

2. by examining the evidence adduced before the adjudicator, both oral and documentary, to ascertain whether or not that evidence was sufficient to establish that the essential ingredients of the offence in Canada had been proven in the foreign proceedings, whether precisely described in the initiating documents or in the statutory provisions in the same words or not; and

3. by a combination of the two.

The Court, using this approach, determined that equivalency had not been established between an Oklahoma offence of arson and a Canadian offence of arson.

Dayan v. Canada (Minister of Employment & Immigration) (1987), 78 N.R. 134 (Fed. C.A.) — The applicant, a citizen of Israel, was convicted of an offence involving the theft of money and the use of weapons in Israel. No evidence of any kind was adduced of Criminal Statutes of Israel, so that a comparison of any provision of Israel's Criminal Statutes with the appropriate provisions of the Canadian *Criminal Code* was impossible.

"Equivalency" can be determined in three ways:

1. by a comparison of the precise wording in each statute, both through documents and through the evidence of an expert or experts in the foreign law, and determining, therefrom, the essential ingredients of the respective offences;

2. by examining the evidence adduced before the adjudicator, both oral and documentary, to ascertain whether the evidence was sufficient to establish that the essential ingredients of the offence in Canada had been proven in the foreign proceedings; and

3. by a combination of paragraphs 1 and 2.

Because no comparison was possible, the question here was whether the findings of fact established that the essential ingredients of the offence in Canada must have been proven in order to have secured the conviction of the applicant in a court of Israel.

Transcripts of evidence in the record established, beyond doubt, that the applicant was a party to a theft of money to which none of the participants had any colour of right and the stealing of which was unlawful as the list of criminal convictions disclosed. Having accepted all of the evidence, including the fact that the applicant had been convicted of robbery in Israel and that a weapon had been used in the commission of that offence, the adjudicator was entitled to conclude that the applicant had been convicted of an offence punishable under section 302 of the Canadian *Criminal Code*.

By virtue of section 303 of the *Criminal Code*, a sentence of more than ten years might have been imposed, and, therefore, the adjudicator had evidence before him in supporting the finding that the applicant was a member of the inadmissible class described in section 19(1)(c) of the Act.

The Court noted that proof of the statutory provisions of the law of Israel ought to have been made in this case. Alternatively, the absence of such provisions in the statute law, if that is the fact, ought to have been established. Reliance on the concept of offences as *malum in se* to prove equivalency with the provisions of the Canadian *Criminal Code* is a device that should be resorted to only when, for a very good reason, proof of foreign law has been difficult to make, and then only when the foreign law is that of a non-common law country.

Hill v. Canada (Minister of Employment & Immigration) (1987), 1 Imm. L.R. (2d) 1, 73 N.R. 315 (Fed. C.A.) — The issue here was whether the applicant was inadmissible by virtue of section 19(1)(c) of the *Immigration Act*. The applicant had been convicted in Texas of an offence of burglary. The only evidence of Texas law before the adjudicator was the production of a copy of two sections of the *Texas Penal Code*. One of them was a definition of burglary, which stated that a person committed that offence if he entered a habitation or building with the intent to commit a theft. Because the definition of theft as it pertains in the Texas statute was not produced before the adjudicator, the Court could not conclude that Texas law included the important additional requirement that the taking be "without colour of right" which is an essential ingredient of the offence of theft in Canada. Accordingly, the deportation order was set aside.

Lavi v. Canada (Minister of Employment & Immigration) (April 24, 1985), Doc. T-83-9929 (Imm. App. Bd.) — The Minister contended that the conviction rendered against the husband of the appellant made the husband inadmissible by reason of section 19(2)(a)(i) of the *Immigration Act*. The refusal letter referred to the equivalent Canadian offences as being either section 233(1) or 233(4) of the *Criminal Code*. The Board asserted in its decision that the reference in the refusal to those subsections did not restrict the Board to make a determination of whether either of those two provisions was the correct equivalent Canadian offence. The Board, asserted that in making its determination it may, if necessary, explore various other provisions of the Canadian law.

Editor's Note: Section 19(2)(a) has been amended, but this principle may still be valid.

Singleton v. Canada (Minister of Employment & Immigration) (November 7, 1983), Doc. A-813-83 (Fed. T.D.) — For digest, see section 19, subheading *Subsection (1), Paragraph (c), supra*.

Taubler v. Canada (Minister of Employment & Immigration), [1981] 1 F.C. 620 (Fed. C.A.) — In the absence of evidence to the contrary it was presumed that the Austrian law of misappropriation involved the element of *mens rea* and that a conviction under that law indicates that a finding of guilty intent was made.

Canada (Minister of Employment & Immigration) v. Fenner (December 11, 1981), Doc. V81-6126 (Imm. App. Bd.) — The respondent, Fenner, was convicted in the State of Washington following a guilty plea to the offence of "negligent homicide by means of a motor vehicle". This offence is equivalent to that set out under section 203 of the *Criminal Code*. The respondent was given a deferred sentence which meant that at the end of a period of probation he could request the opportunity to withdraw his guilty plea and have the charge dismissed. This, in fact, occurred in this case. The Board decided that this procedure, unknown to Canadian law, was not equivalent to an absolute or conditional discharge and that the conviction in the first instance remained part of Fenner's record. Therefore, Fenner fell within the provisions of section 19(1)(c). The Board allowed the Minister's appeal and directed the deportation of Mr. Fenner.

Lee v. Canada (Minister of Employment & Immigration) (July 21, 1981), Doc. V80-6432 (Imm. App. Bd.) — Robbery is basically theft with violence and so falls within the *malum in se* exception and the presumption results that the law of the foreign country coincides with that in Canada.

See *Brannson v. Canada (Minister of Employment & Immigration)* (1980), 34 N.R. 411 (Fed. C.A.) for an analysis of the method of equivalencing.

Anderson v. Canada (Minister of Employment & Immigration), [1981] 2 F.C. 30, 113 D.L.R. (3d) 243, 36 N.R. 423 (Fed. C.A.) — In attempting to determine which Canadian offence is equivalent to the offence for which the applicant was convicted in the United States, the adjudicator should determine the precise definition of the offence in the United States, so that he can evaluate the essential ingredients of that offence and thus be in a position to find the equivalent Canadian offence. An order, based on an absence of such evidence, will be set aside.

Robertson v. Canada (Minister of Employment & Immigration), [1979] 1 F.C. 197, 43 C.C.C. (2d) 354, 91 D.L.R. (3d) 93 (Fed. C.A.) — Section 19(1)(c) of the Act can only be used to deport a person when that person has been convicted of an offence for which the maximum punishment is 10 years' imprisonment at the date of the deportation order. Thus, where at the date of the order the maximum period is under 10 years the applicant may not be deported pursuant to section 19(1)(c) even if the offence carried a maximum term of imprisonment of 10 years at the time the applicant was convicted.

R. v. Wardley (1978), 43 C.C.C. (2d) 345 (Ont. C.A.) — Where an accused charged with the indictable offence of possession of marijuana for the purpose of trafficking pleads guilty to the included offence of possession of marijuana, the plea constitutes a plea of guilty to the indictable offence of possession. The maximum sentence for the conviction of the indictable offence of simple possession governs with respect to penalty.

Button v. Canada (Minister of Manpower & Immigration), [1975] F.C. 277, 55 D.L.R. (3d) 559, 8 N.R. 545 (Fed. C.A.) — One cannot assume that the law of a foreign country coincides with Canadian statute law except where the offence falls within one of the traditional offences commonly referred to as *malum in se*.

See *R. v. McInnis* (1973), 1 O.R. (2d) 1, 23 C.R.N.S. 152, 13 C.C.C. (2d) 471 (Ont. C.A.) for various meanings that are attached to the word "conviction" and hence "convicted".

Section 19(1)(c.2)

Yuen v. Canada (Minister of Citizenship & Immigration) (1999), 48 Imm. L.R. (2d) 24, 63 C.R.R. (2d) 333 (Fed. T.D.) — The applicant sought to review the decision of an adjudicator that determined the applicant was inadmissible pursuant to the provisions of section 19(1)(c.2). The applicant was a member of the 14K Triad gang, which he had joined in Hong Kong as a teenager. While a member of that gang the applicant was convicted of theft in Hong Kong. In September 1988, the applicant was arrested in Toronto and charged with several drug offences which were later stayed at the request of the Crown. Section 19(1)(c.2) of the *Immigration Act* does not offend section 2(d) of the *Charter of Rights*. The right conferred by that section does not extend beyond the boundaries of Canada to protect the right of a foreign national to be a member of a foreign criminal organization.

The Court also found that the adjudicator did not err in determining that the essential elements of the offence of theft in the Canadian *Criminal Code* correspond to those in the Hong Kong statute.

Chiau v. Canada (Minister of Citizenship & Immigration), 141 F.T.R. 81, [1998] 2 F.C. 642 (Fed. T.D.) — The applicant sought to judicially review the decision of a visa officer denying him permanent residence in Canada on the basis of paragraph 19(1)(c.2). The visa officer wrote to the applicant requesting him to attend at an interview. The letter indicated that the aim of the interview was to ascertain if the applicant had maintained links with organized criminal elements in Hong Kong.

The visa officer fulfilled all the requirements of procedural fairness. The applicant was informed in advance by letter of the case he had to meet. The information provided by the visa officer was sufficient to enable the applicant to prepare himself for the interview and to disabuse the visa officer of any of his concerns. In the course of the interview, questions were put to the applicant with reference to his relationship with triad members and with respect to a gun shot incident involving the applicant and the press reports on it. There was no obligation upon the visa officer to provide the applicant with a summary of any confidential information relied upon by the visa officer.

With respect to the phrase "reasonable grounds" in paragraph 19(1)(c.2), the phrase requires more than a flimsy suspicion but less than the civil test of balance of probabilities. It is a *bona fide* belief in a serious possibility based on credible evidence.

The visa officer in this case had extensive experience and specialized knowledge with reference to triad activities in Hong Kong. It was well within his competence to define the meaning of membership in a triad and the officer was clearly well aware of his role to protect and maintain the interests of Canadian security and his crucial obligation to ensure that members of criminal organizations were not admitted to Canada. The Court therefore must view with considerable deference the officer's view of reasonable grounds and the meaning of the term member.

The purpose of paragraph 19(1)(c.2) was to prevent the expansion of organized criminal activities in Canada through the prohibition of the entry of those who are believed on reasonable grounds to be members of those criminal organizations.

Section 19(1)(c.2) must be read in conjunction with the enforcement objectives of the Act, which are set out in subsections 3(i) and 3(j). The term "member" cannot be limited to a card carrying member whose name appears on a membership list. Being a member of a criminal organization means simply belonging to a criminal organization.

Section 19(1)(d)

Taei v. Canada (Minister of Employment & Immigration) (1993), 19 Imm. L.R. (2d) 187, 64 F.T.R. 311 — For digest, see section 19, subheading *Subsection (1), Paragraph (c), supra.*

See *Jolly v. Canada (Minister of Manpower & Immigration), infra, Paragraph (f) of Subsection (1)* (s. 19) for a discussion of the phrase "reasonable grounds to believe" although in a different context.

Section 19(1)(e)

See *Jolly v. Canada (Minister of Manpower & Immigration), infra, Paragraph (f) of Subsection (1)* (s. 19) for a discussion of the phrase "reasonable grounds to believe" although in a different context.

Section 19(1)(f)

Suresh v. Canada (Minister of Citizenship & Immigration (1998), 40 Imm. L.R. (2d) 247, 141 F.T.R. 152 (Fed. T.D.); reversed in part 47 Imm. L.R. (2d) 1, [1998] 4 F.C. 192, 229 N.R. 240, 55 C.R.R. (2d) 157 (Fed. C.A.) — These were the reasons of the Court determining that reasonable grounds existed for the Solicitor General and the Minister of Employment and Immigration to have issued a certificate pursuant to section 40.1 of the *Immigration Act.* It was not necessary to define the content of the term "terrorist" or "terrorist act" as it is referred to in section 19. The Act "must be seen through the eyes of a Canadian for the purposes of a section 40.1 application." The term "terrorism or terrorist act" must receive a wide and unrestricted interpretation for the purposes of a section 40.1 application.

Membership in an organization cannot and should not be narrowly interpreted when it involves the issue of Canada's national security. Membership does not only refer to persons who have engaged in or who might engage in terrorist activities. The Court looked at the nature of Mr. Suresh's activities in support of the organization that he was supposed to be a member of and his own admission of his close association with that organization.

Kashmiri v. Canada (Minister of Citizenship & Immigration) (1996), 37 C.R.R. (2d) 264, 116 F.T.R. 316 (Fed. T.D.) — The applicant sought to review a decision of an adjudicator determining that he was a person who there were reasonable grounds to believe was a member of an organization engaged in terrorism. The applicant, a citizen of Pakistan, resided in the portion of Kashmir within Pakistan. He joined the Jammu Kashmir Liberation Front, which was an organization directed to securing an independent Kashmir. The organization was linked to acts of terrorism against civilians in documentary evidence that was before the adjudicator.

On arriving in Canada, the applicant claimed refugee status. Before his claim was heard, the decision of the adjudicator which is a subject to this matter was made. Subsequent to the adjudicator's decision the applicant was determined to be a Convention refugee and was invited to apply for permanent residence in Canada. His application by reason of the earlier decision was refused.

The closing words of paragraph 19(1)(f) place an onus on a person such as the applicant who acknowledges membership in an organization allegedly responsible for terrorist acts to satisfy the Minister that his or her admission would not be detrimental to the national interest.

The decision of the adjudicator to the effect that the applicant had not satisfied him that his admission would not be detrimental to the national interest was not reviewable. The onus to so satisfy the adjudicator on behalf of the Minister remained on the applicant.

McAllister v. Canada (Minister of Citizenship & Immigration) (1996), 108 F.T.R. 1 (Fed. T.D.) — The applicant sought to review a decision of the Minister declaring that it was the Minister's opinion that it would be contrary to the public interest to have the applicant's refugee claim determined under the Act. The applicant was born in Northern Ireland and came to Canada in December 1988 with his wife and four children. Soon after his arrival the applicant and his wife made separate refugee claims. From July 1981 until February 1982 the applicant was a member of the Irish National Liberation Army (INLA). In July 1981, the applicant was charged with a number of serious offenses for which he was later convicted, including conspiracy to commit murder, wounding with intent, possession of a fire arm, and belonging to a proscribed organization. On conviction he was sentenced to 7 years in jail. In 1987, he was convicted of assaulting police and of resisting police, and in 1988 he was convicted of driving while under the influence of alcohol. These later convictions resulted in fines without further incarceration. In March 1993, Mr. McAllister was interviewed by immigration officials about his refugee claim. In July 1993, an immigration officer made a report pursuant to section 27 reporting that the applicant fell within subsection 19(1)(c.1)(i). A further direction in November 1993 was issued for an inquiry to determine if the applicant was described in paragraphs 27(2)(a) and 19(1)(f)(iii)(B). At the conclusion of the inquiry pursuant to these directions a conditional deportation order was made.

In March 1994, the applicant received a letter from the Minister indicating that the Minister would be considering "whether or not it is in the public interest to have your refugee claim determined under the *Act*". The applicant, through his counsel, made submissions to the Minister in March 1994 and in May 1994 the Minister informed the applicant that having reviewed the submission it was the Minister's opinion that it would be contrary to the public interest to have the applicant's refugee claim determined under the Act.

There was no issue of credibility in this case. The letter from the Minister indicated that the Minister's opinion would be based upon evidence submitted at the inquiry and any representations the applicant might make. The Minister's letter conveying his decision specifically stated that the submissions and the available information concerning the applicant had been reviewed. There was no evidence that any other information had been available to the Minister than that indicated. There was no oral hearing and no interview provided to the applicant. The process here followed ensured that the applicant was apprised of the case he had to meet and was given an adequate opportunity to make written submissions in relation to the issue the Minister had served notice he would consider and decide. The fair hearing requirements under the *Charter of Rights*, and the common law duty of fairness, were met. The Court found that the word "terrorism" in subparagraph 19(1)(f)(iii)(B) and "public interest" in subparagraph 46.01(1)(e)(ii) were not so imprecise and vague that its application by the Minister could not be subject to review in a proper case on an application for judicial review.

The concept of vagueness could be summed up as follows:

> A law will be found unconstitutionally vague if it so lacks in precision as to not give sufficient guidance for legal debate. The threshold for finding a law vague is relatively high.

The applicant argued that he had a right to have his claim to be a Convention refugee determined in accord with the law prevailing at the time his claim was made, i.e. December 1988. Subparagraphs 19(1)(f)(iii)(B) or 46.01(1)(e)(ii) were not applied retrospectively in the circumstances of this case. The legislation in force at the time the decisions were made was given effect. It is not retrospective legislation to adopt a rule that henceforth excludes persons from Canada on the basis of their conduct in the past. The applicant having made a claim to be a Convention refugee had no vested or entrenched rights to have that claim considered under the rules prevailing at the time of this application. Rather, he only had a right to have his claim considered under the rules prevailing when it was considered. The applicant was a person with no right to enter or remain in Canada except as provided by the *Immigration Act* and any claim that he might make to enter or remain in Canada is subject to the law prevailing when that claim is determined, not when the claim is made.

Baroud, Re (1995), 98 F.T.R. 99 (Fed. T.D.) — The purpose of subparagraphs 19(1)(f)(ii) and 19(1)(f)(iii) of the *Immigration Act*, in very general terms, is to prevent the arrival of persons considered to be a danger to Canadian society. The term terrorism must, therefore, receive an unrestrictive interpretation and will unavoidably include the political connotations which it entails. In the light of the evidence submitted to the Court there existed reasonable grounds to believe that the applicant was described in section 19(1)(f)(iii).

Canada (Attorney General) v. Jolly, [1975] F.C. 216, 54 D.L.R. (3d) 277, 7 N.R. 271 (Fed. C.A.) — The question under this section is not whether the persons subject to the proceeding will engage in or instigate the subversion by force of any government, but whether there are reasonable grounds for believing that the persons will so behave. Even if evidence is given negating this fact, it is only necessary for the Minister to show the existence of reasonable grounds for believing the fact. It is not necessary for the Minister to go further in establishing the subversive character of the persons subject to the proceeding.

Section 19(1)(g)

See *Jolly v. Canada (Minister of Manpower & Immigration), supra*, for discussion of the phrase "reasonable grounds to believe" although in a different context.

Yamani v. Canada (Solicitor General) (1995), 31 Imm. L.R. (2d) 191, 129 D.L.R. (4th) 226, 32 C.R.R. (2d) 295, (sub nom. *Al Yamani v. Canada (Solicitor General))* 103 F.T.R. 105, [1996] 1 F.C. 174 — These were two applications for judicial review in relation to a decision of the Security Intelligence Review Committee (SIRC) made August 3, 1994 and a decision of the Governor General in Council made August 25, 1994, based upon the decision and report of SIRC.

The applicant is a stateless person, a male of Palestinian origin. His father was said to be one of the founders of the Popular Front for the Liberation of Palestines (PFLP). Though he was born in Beirut, the applicant is not a citizen of Lebanon, but has carried and has travelled on a Lebanese travel document.

The applicant is a landed immigrant who arrived in Canada in 1985. He resided in Canada since that time, made an application for citizenship in 1988 and as a result of that application became the subject of security screening by the Canadian Security Intelligence Service (CSIS). He was interviewed by a CSIS officer and subsequently received a letter signed by the Minister of Employment and Immigration and the Solicitor General stating that they had made a report to SIRC because they were of the opinion that the applicant was a person described in paragraphs 19(1)(e), 19(1)(g) and 27(1)(c). SIRC's finding related only to paragraph 19(1)(g).

Subsequent to the Minister's report, the applicant was the subject of a hearing before a single member of SIRC. This hearing resulted in the applicant being found to be a person described in 19(1)(g). SIRC reported that fact to the Governor in Council and recommended that a certificate be issued against the applicant under section 40(1) of the Act. That report was the subject of the first judicial review application.

Upon receipt of the report the Governor in Council issued an order-in-council reciting that after considering the report of SIRC it was satisfied that the applicant was a person described in paragraph 19(1)(g) of the Act. That decision also directed the Solicitor General to issue a security certificate pursuant to section 40 so designating the applicant.

The Court found that pursuant to sections 18 and 18.1 of the *Federal Court Act*, it does have jurisdiction to review the decision of SIRC. SIRC is a federal board, commission, or tribunal as defined in section 2 of the *Federal Court Act* since it is a body exercising jurisdiction or powers conferred by an act of parliament. Relief against a decision of SIRC is available under section 18 of the *Federal Court Act* upon an application for judicial review pursuant to section 18.1.

The Court granted intervenor status to the Canadian Arab Federation (CAF). The CAF sought to argue that paragraph 19(1)(g) violated section 15 of the Charter. The Court declined to hear such an argument. It would be an exceptional case in which the Court would determine an issue that was not raised in argument by the parties in judicial review, but rather was raised by an intervenor in the proceedings. The CAF standing as an intervenor does not support recognition of any right or standing to raise issues that are not raised by the parties to the proceeding.

The ordinary standard of proof in civil as opposed to criminal matters is the basis for findings of fact by SIRC. That is, those findings must be based on a balance of probabilities. Further, there is no basis for construing the words in paragraph 19(1)(g) as implying any standard of proof other than the traditional standard, that is a balance of probabilities, for findings required under that provision. Thus, the SIRC report did not err by reliance on that traditional standard and not insisting on some higher standard of probability. Paragraph 19(1)(g) is to be interpreted so that "likely" ("susceptible") with reference to the organizations referred to means "capable of" and not simply probable. The conclusion of SIRC in this case would be acceptable if the organization were merely judged capable of, and not necessarily that it would probably be engaging in acts of violence as described in the paragraph. There is no necessity in construing the words in 19(1)(g) to establish the obligations of membership in such an organization, or that the individual member has a record of, or an obligation to participate in, acts of violence under the aegis and on the direction of the organization.

Sections 39 and 40(1) provide for an investigation by SIRC. Parliament intended that the process of a hearing in regard to security considerations should be undertaken at the stage of the investigation by SIRC. Upon conclusion of its investigation and submission of its report to the Governor General in Council, the Governor General in Council would be expected to accept and act upon the SIRC's conclusion, at least where the Governor General in Council is satisfied that the person investigated is a person included in the *Act's* descriptions of those considered as presenting sufficient risk to warrant deportation. The duty of fairness does not require a further opportunity for submissions to the Governor in Council by the person concerned before action is taken. The case to be answered by the person concerned has already been brought to his attention through the provision of a statement of circumstances at the beginning of the SIRC process, and full opportunity to respond and to make submissions has been provided through that process. The only circumstance where the duty of fairness might clearly require a further opportunity for submissions after delivery of the SIRC report would be where SIRC's report is favourable to the permanent resident and does not recommend the issue of a certificate but the Governor in Council not satisfied with that report, determines, in the exercise of its discretion, that the person concerned is indeed one against whom a certificate should be issued under section 40(1).

Section 19(1)(g) does directly restrict freedom of association, providing for persons who are not citizens ultimately to be excluded or deported from Canada because there are reasonable grounds to believe they are members of an organization likely to engage in acts of violence of the sort described. It is the association of persons as members of the organizations described that leads to their classification for exclusion or deportation. It is not their individual records of participating in violent activities, nor a determination that they are likely to participate in such activities. Rather it is simply the fact of membership that is the reason for the application for paragraph 19(1)(g). By providing ultimately for deportation of permanent residents who are members of an organization loosely defined, the statute does infringe on the freedom of permanent residents to associate together in organization. Often such persons, at least those comparatively new to this country, may maintain association or membership with organizations associated with their home land, many of which may have had some historic record of violence, but which serve a variety of purposes as the PFLP was found to do in this case. To expose all permanent residents to the possibility of deportation because of their membership in such organizations, in my view, clearly infringes on their freedom of association. This infringement was found not to be saved by section 1 of the Charter, thus paragraph 19(1)(g) was declared to be of no force and affect. Thus, the determination and conclusion of SIRC, which was based on paragraph 19(1)(g) could not stand and an order was issued setting aside the report and its conclusion. Further, the determination of the Governor in Council, because it was based on the grounds set out in the report by SIRC, including the direction to the Solicitor General to issue a certificate, was declared to be invalid.

Section 19(1)(h)

Kahlon v. Canada (Minister of Employment & Immigration), [1986] 3 F.C. 386, 26 C.R.R. 152, 30 D.L.R. (4th) 157 (Fed. C.A.), reversing [1985] 2 F.C. 124, 20 C.R.R. 193, 23 D.L.R. (4th) 564 (Fed. T.D.) — The applicant sponsored his relatives' family class application for permanent residence. The application was denied and the applicant appealed to the Immigration Appeal Board. The visa officer refused to issue visitors' visas to the relatives who were required as witnesses at his appeal. The visas were refused on the basis that the applicants were not *bona fide* visitors because their intention was to testify at the applicant's appeal. An order of *mandamus* was issued requiring the Minister to grant the relatives visitors' visas to allow them to testify at the appeal. This order was reversed on appeal. *Mandamus* will issue to require performance of a duty; it cannot, however, dictate the result to be reached. *Certiorari* might have been available to quash the refusal of the visitors' visas and to refer the matter back for reconsideration but the respondent had not sought this type of order.

Canada (Minister of Employment & Immigration) v. Bechan (May 18, 1983), Doc. A-812-82 (Fed. C.A.) — Bechan sponsored an application for landing by a member of the family class. The application was refused on the basis that the applicant for landing was a person described in section 19(1)(h). The Federal Court of Appeal upheld the Immigration Appeal Board's decision allowing the appeal on the basis that section 19(1)(h) referred only to immigrants at a point of entry. The applicant had made her application for landing at Port of Spain, Trinidad and, accordingly, the basis for the rejection of her application was invalid. Therefore, the Minister's appeal from the Immigration Appeal Board's decision was dismissed. The Court noted that the sponsor is entitled to be accurately informed of the grounds for the rejection of the application for permanent residence so that proper preparation of the appeal permitted by this Act could be effected.

Rai v. Canada (Minister of Employment & Immigration), [1981] 1 F.C. 112 (Fed. C.A.) — An adjudication made without regard to the totality of the material before the adjudicator may be overturned on a section 28 application (*e.g.*, the failure of the adjudicator to have regard to the fact that the ticket in possession of the prospective visitor was non-refundable).

Gill v. Canada (Minister of Employment & Immigration), [1981] 1 F.C. 615 (Fed. C.A.) — An applicant's purpose in being in Canada may be temporary within the meaning of the statute if his intention is to stay as long as the Minister will allow. The Court did say, however, that this conclusion was peculiar to the circumstances of this case.

Gill v. Canada (Minister of Employment & Immigration) (September 17, 1980), Doc. 449-80 (Fed. C.A.) — Evidence that the applicant sought to evade telling the immigration officer at the port-of-entry of his application for a student visa and of the reason for its refusal could, in all circumstances of the case, support a conclusion that the applicant was not a genuine visitor to Canada.

Dhesi v. Canada (Minister of Manpower & Immigration) (December 8, 1978), Doc. A-503-78 (Fed. C.A.) — Where there is sufficient evidence to support a finding by the adjudicator that the applicant is not a person seeking to come into Canada for a temporary purpose, the Court of Appeal will not disturb the exclusion order made by the adjudicator.

Chan v. Canada (Minister of Manpower & Immigration) (1977), [1978] 1 F.C. 217, 16 N.R. 301 (Fed. C.A.) — The Court of Appeal felt that it was difficult to see how the purpose of a person seeking entry to Canada can be temporary when the duration of the stay is indefinite.

Section 19(1)(i)

Canada (Solicitor General) v. Kainth (1994), 26 Imm. L.R. (2d) 226, 81 F.T.R. 318n, 170 N.R. 367 (Fed. C.A.) — The Appeal Division allowed the appeal of the respondent and overturned a refusal by an immigration officer of the sponsored application for landing of the respondent's spouse. The Board decided that, although the refusal was legal and, moreover, that the spouse had been deported a few years previously, there were sufficient humanitarian or compassionate grounds to grant the spouse permanent residence. This decision was upheld by the Trial Division on a judicial review application. However, the Trial Division judge certified a serious question of general importance. The Solicitor General then appealed to the Court of Appeal.

Section 69.4(2) is broad enough to permit the Appeal Division to decide that it has jurisdiction to permit the respondent's spouse to be landed, notwithstanding the fact that the spouse did not have the Minister's consent as required by section 55(1) and notwithstanding the provisions of section 19(1)(i).

Accordingly, the appeal was dismissed.

Bhawan v. Canada (Minister of Employment & Immigration) (1987), 41 D.L.R. (4th) 382, 14 F.T.R. 230 (Fed. T.D.) — The applicant sought prohibition to prevent his removal from Canada pursuant to a deportation order dated January 5, 1984. The applicant came to Canada from Fiji as a landed immigrant. He became subject to a deportation order on January 5, 1984 and filed an appeal to the Immigration Appeal Board. While the appeal was pending, the applicant voluntarily returned to Fiji, and, in April 1986, the applicant came back to Canada. Prior to his return to Canada, the applicant's solicitor withdrew the appeal to the Immigration Appeal Board. The applicant's contention that the deportation was carried out by his leaving Canada for Fiji was rejected. The applicant could only leave Canada and select the country for destination with authorization from the Minister, and this was lacking in this case. Accordingly, the applicant had not complied with section 54 [s. 52] and the deportation order, dated January 5, 1984, could be executed to cause the applicant's removal from Canada.

Mercier v. Canada (Minister of Employment & Immigration) (1986), 3 Imm. L.R. (2d) 316, 14 F.T.R. 28 (Fed. T.D.) — The applicant was admitted to Canada in 1974. Between 1978 and 1984 he was convicted of a number of criminal offences. During this period, on November 17, 1982, he was ordered deported. The applicant returned to his country of origin between May 12 and June 30, 1984. The applicant sought a declaration that the deportation order made against him had ceased to be valid by virtue of section 54 of the *Immigration Act*. It was held that the voluntary departure of someone who is the subject of a deportation order could only be made under section 54 with leave of the Minister. In the absence of such leave, the applicant could not be said to have carried out the removal order himself.

Grewal v. Canada (Minister of Employment & Immigration) (1980), [1981] 1 F.C. 12, 112 D.L.R. (3d) 30, 37 N.R. 535 (Fed. C.A.) — Where an applicant attempts to re-enter Canada prior to the 12-month period described in section 57(2), such person cannot be excluded by order of an adjudicator made more than twelve months after the time described in section 57(2).

Vargas-Cataldo v. Canada (Minister of Manpower & Immigration), [1973] F.C. 313, 35 D.L.R. (3d) 748 (Fed. C.A.) — The circumstances surrounding the making of an earlier order of deportation may not be reviewed by an adjudicator conducting an inquiry based on the return of the applicant subsequent to this earlier order.

Section 19(1)(j)

Rudolph v. Canada (Minister of Employment & Immigration) (1992), 73 C.C.C. (3d) 442, 91 D.L.R. (4th) 686 (Fed. C.A.) — Paragraph 19(1)(j) is not retrospective. Canada adopted legislation which hence forward excluded persons from Canada on the basis of their conduct in the past. The double criminality requirement of paragraph 19(1)(j) mandates the notional transfer to Canadian soil of the *actus reus* only and not of the entire surrounding circumstances so as to permit a plea of obedience to *de facto* foreign state authority. In concrete terms, in deciding if the applicant's conduct would have constituted an offence against the laws of Canada, his acts and omissions, but not the entire state apparatus of the foreign country, are transferred to Canada. The fact that the German government ordered or condoned the applicant's conduct during World War II is no defence to a charge of doing the same thing in Canada.

Section 19(1)(j) makes reference to section 7(3.76) of the *Criminal Code*. That subsection incorporates by reference into Canadian law both customary and conventional international law. Therefore, in determining whether the conduct in question was prohibited by custom or conventional international law, one first looks at international conventions in effect at the time that the conduct occurred. In this particular case the Court considered the *Convention on the Laws and Customs of War on Land* concluded at the Hague on October 18, 1907. Secondly, the Court looked to customary international law. Such a body of law existed in the period 1943–45 with regard to war crimes and crimes against humanity. Further, the Charter of the International Military Tribunal which following the end of the war in Europe in 1945 created a tribunal to try war crimes was, in Article 6, declaratory of existing customary international law. Further, the Charter of the International Military Tribunal was expressly recognized and affirmed by Regulation 95(1) of the General Assembly of the United Nations adopted December 11, 1946. These instruments are very strong evidence of the content of existing customary international law during the relevant period.

Editor's Note: See also case annotations under the Schedule — Sections E and F of Article 1 of the United National Convention Relating to the Status of Refugees.

Section 19(1)(l)

Esse v. Canada (Minister of Citizenship & Immigration) (January 16, 1998), Doc. IMM-4523-96 (Fed. T.D.) — This was a judicial review of a decision of the Minister under paragraph 19(1)(l). The applicant was a citizen of Somalia. From January 1990 to August 1991, he was the Somalia Ambassador to the United Arab Emirates. On October 12, 1993, the Barre regime was declared by the then Minister of Citizenship and Immigration to have engaged in gross human rights violations.

The applicant was found to be a Convention refugee. He then applied for permanent resident status and while his application was pending an inquiry was convoked to determine whether he was the person described in paragraph 19(1)(l). Before a decision was issued by the adjudicator, the applicant sought to obtain a determination that the Minister was satisfied that his admission to Canada would not be detrimental to the national interest. On October 25, 1996, the Minister determined that it would be contrary to the national interest to allow the applicant to be landed in Canada.

The focus of section 19(1)(l) and section 19(1.1), is to ensure as far as possible that Canada does not become a haven for persons who have engaged in terrorism, systematic or gross human rights violations, war crimes or crimes against humanity. The scheme of the legislation is to consider senior members or officials of a government as persons who are able to exert a significant influence on the exercise of the government's power such that they must take responsibility for the objectionable acts of their government. Persons holding specific positions within a government are deemed to be senior members of or senior officials in the service of a government for that purpose. To obtain a Minister's acceptance, one would have to demonstrate that notwithstanding his/her position there was no complicity in the objectionable acts of that government.

On the face of this record the Court found nothing to indicate that the Minister's decision was perverse and accordingly the application was dismissed.

Waizi v. Canada (Minister of Citizenship & Immigration) (1997), 41 Imm. L.R. (2d) 220 (Imm. & Ref. Bd. (App. Div.)) — The appellant appealed the refusal of the application of her father, her mother, her two brothers and her sister. The appellant's father was refused because he was inadmissible pursuant to paragraph 19(1)(l) of the *Immigration Act.*

The legislation does not allow the Appeal Division in the circumstances of this type of refusal to grant discretionary relief. Such an exercise would be wholly incompatible with the non-delegatable discretion granted solely to the Minister with respect to "persons who have satisfied the Minister that their admission would not be made detrimental to the national interest".

The legislation has not erased all of the appellant's rights to appeal. The wording of subsection 19(1.1) allows for an examination by the tribunals to whether any particular individual fits the description of a "person who by virtue of the position they hold or have held are or were able to exert significant influence". The language of subsection 1.1 puts the onus on someone such as the appellant's father (a member of the judiciary), to rebut the presumption that by virtue of his position he was able to exert significant influence on government power.

It is the Minister who determines that a particular government is or was engaged in the prescribed activities set out in section 19(1)(l). After the Minister has made this determination, there then begins the task of factually determining who are or were senior members or senior officials in the service of such a government. Persons enumerated in subparagraphs (a) to (g), section 19(1.1) are presumed to have held positions of influence unless they can show by credible or trustworthy evidence that they did not.

Hussein v. Canada (Minister of Citizenship & Immigration) (1997), 41 Imm. L.R. (2d) 42 (Can. Imm. & Ref. Bd. (App. Div.)) — The appellant sponsored the application of her husband. This application was refused because the visa officer concluded there were reasonable grounds to believe that the husband was a senior official in the Somalia government of President Barre. The applicant was the personal secretary to his uncle, who was the Minister of Higher Education and Culture in Somalia, between 1984 and 1987. The applicant enrolled in a training institute for diplomatic personnel in January 1988, and remained there until March 1989. From April 1989 to January 1991, he worked at the headquarters at the Ministry of Foreign Affairs as a first secretary in the education sector. The applicant stated that his working career was involved exclusively with educational matters and he never participated in political activities and was never part of the regime. The applicant testified he was a civil servant carrying out his duties.

The applicant was not a senior member or official when he served his uncle in a secretarial capacity, a position that was limited to preparing his uncle's mail and handling his appointments. The position of first secretary in the Ministry of Foreign Affairs education sector was more important in terms of influence or power, but that in itself did not indicate seniority. No guide was produced to establish a dividing line between senior and non-senior staff in the Somalia Ministry of Foreign Affairs. The applicant's involvement with the Somalia government is not tantamount to having been a senior official in that government. There is no evidence to counter the applicant's assertion that the positions he held were not senior, accordingly, the appeal was allowed.

Adam v. Canada (Minister of Citizenship & Immigration) (1997), (sub nom. *Canada (Minister of Citizenship & Immigration) v. Adam)* 137 F.T.R. 68 (Fed. T.D.); reconsideration granted (December 3, 1997), Doc. IMM-3380-96 (Fed. T.D.) — The applicant sought to review a decision of the Immigration Appeal Division which determined that a rebuttable presumption existed in paragraph 19(1)(l) and that the respondent's husband satisfied the exemption contained therein.

In its decision, the panel for the IAD concluded that the respondent's husband had satisfied the rebuttable presumption in paragraph 19(1)(l), and that the refusal of landing was not valid in law and allowed the appeal. The decision was based primarily on a letter from the former United States Ambassador to Somalia. In the letter, the Ambassador stated that the respondent's husband, although a member of the Cabinet in Somalia had limited or no influence on human rights policies and was in fact a vocal advocate for peaceful change.

There is no rebuttable presumption in section 19(1)(l). It was clear from the evidence that the respondent's husband was a member of the Somalia cabinet and therefore fell within the provisions of paragraph 19(1)(l). Notwithstanding this, the Court declined to set aside the Appeal Divisions decision.

Section 19(1)(l) contains a discretionary statutory exception. Only the Minister has the discretion to make the exception and it appeared in this case that the Minister declined to do so.

In matters where ministerial discretion may be exercised, reasons may be required where the decision on its face seems perverse. The letter from the former United States Ambassador on behalf of the respondent's husband was compelling and perhaps determinative. In light of the fact that the sole determining factor for excluding the husband was the cabinet position he held, the letter on his behalf should have been addressed in the Minister's decision. This silence by the Minister in the face of such compelling evidence clearly makes this decision, without reasons, perverse.

The application for judicial review was dismissed in part. Pursuant to subsection 77(5) of the *Immigration Act*, the matter was sent back for re-determination in accordance with the court's reasons.

Section 19(1.1)

Esse v. Canada (Minister of Citizenship & Immigration) (January 16, 1998), Doc. IMM-4523-96 (Fed. T.D.) — This was a judicial review of a decision of the Minister under paragraph 19(1)(l). The applicant was a citizen of Somalia. From January 1990 to August 1991, he was the Somalia Ambassador to the United Arab Emirates. On October 12, 1993, the Barre regime was declared by the then Minister of Citizenship and Immigration to have engaged in gross human rights violations.

The applicant was found to be a Convention refugee. He then applied for permanent resident status and while his application was pending an inquiry was convoked to determine whether he was the person described in paragraph 19(1)(l). Before a decision was issued by the adjudicator, the applicant sought to obtain a determination that the Minister was satisfied that his admission to Canada would not be detrimental to the national interest. On October 25, 1996, the Minister determined that it would be contrary to the national interest to allow the applicant to be landed in Canada.

The focus of section 19(1)(l) and section 19(1.1), is to ensure as far as possible that Canada does not become a haven for persons who have engaged in terrorism, systematic or gross human rights violations, war crimes or crimes against humanity. The scheme of the legislation is to consider senior members or officials of a government as persons who are able to exert a significant influence on the exercise of the government's power such that they must take responsibility for the objectionable acts of their government. Persons holding specific positions within a government are deemed to be senior members of or senior officials in the service of a government for that purpose. To obtain a Minister's acceptance, one would have to demonstrate that notwithstanding his/her position there was no complicity in the objectionable acts of that government.

On the face of this record the Court found nothing to indicate that the Minister's decision was perverse and accordingly the application was dismissed.

Waizi v. Canada (Minister of Citizenship & Immigration) (1997), 41 Imm. L.R. (2d) 220 (Imm. & Ref. Bd. (App. Div.)) — The appellant appealed the refusal of the application of her father, her mother, her two brothers and her sister. The appellant's father was refused because he was inadmissible pursuant to paragraph 19(1)(l) of the *Immigration Act*.

The legislation does not allow the Appeal Division in the circumstances of this type of refusal to grant discretionary relief. Such an exercise would be wholly incompatible with the non-delegatable discretion granted solely to the Minister with respect to "persons who have satisfied the Minister that their admission would not be made detrimental to the national interest".

The legislation has not erased all of the appellant's rights to appeal. The wording of subsection 19(1.1) allows for an examination by the tribunals to whether any particular individual fits the description of a "person who by virtue of the position they hold or have held are or were able to exert significant influence". The language of subsection 1.1 puts the onus on someone such as the appellant's father (a member of the judiciary), to rebut the presumption that by virtue of his position he was able to exert significant influence on government power.

It is the Minister who determines that a particular government is or was engaged in the prescribed activities set out in section 19(1)(l). After the Minister has made this determination, there then begins the task of factually determining who are or were senior members or senior officials in the service of such a government. Persons enumerated in subparagraphs (a) to (g), section 19(1.1) are presumed to have held positions of influence unless they can show by credible or trustworthy evidence that they did not.

Hussein v. Canada (Minister of Citizenship & Immigration) (1997), 41 Imm. L.R. (2d) 42 (Can. Imm. & Ref. Bd. (App. Div.)) — The appellant sponsored the application of her husband. This application was refused because the visa officer concluded there were reasonable grounds to believe that the husband was a senior official in the Somalia government of President Barre. The applicant was the personal secretary to his uncle who was the Minister of Higher Education and Culture in Somalia, between 1984 and 1987. The applicant enrolled in a training institute for diplomatic personnel in January 1988, and remained there until March 1989. From April 1989 to January 1991, he worked at the headquarters at the Ministry of Foreign Affairs as a first secretary in the education sector. The applicant stated that his working career was involved exclusively with educational matters and he never participated in political activities and was never part of the regime. The applicant testified he was a civil servant carrying out his duties.

The applicant was not a senior member or official when he served his uncle in a secretarial capacity, a position that was limited to preparing his uncle's mail and handling his appointments. The position of first secretary in the Ministry of Foreign Affairs education sector was more important in terms of influence or power, but that in itself did not indicate seniority. No guide was produced to establish a dividing line between senior and non-senior staff in the Somalia Ministry of Foreign Affairs. The applicant's involvement with the Somalia government is not tantamount to having been a senior official in that government. There is no evidence to counter the applicant's assertion that the positions he held were not senior, accordingly, the appeal was allowed.

Section 19(2)(a)

Kanes v. Canada (Minister of Employment & Immigration) (1993), 22 Imm. L.R. (2d) 223, 72 F.T.R. 226 (Fed. T.D.) — This was an application for judicial review of a decision of the Toronto Refugee Backlog Office refusing the applicant's application for permanent residence because he was considered criminally inadmissible.

The applicant came to Canada in 1986 and made a refugee claim. He heard nothing further with respect to his claim until 1992 when he was asked to fill in a personal information form. The applicant was advised that there was a credible basis for his claim and that pursuant to the backlog procedures his application for permanent residence would be processed from within Canada. While this processing was taking place, the applicant was convicted of the summary offence of failing to remain at the scene of an accident.

In January 1993 the applicant was contacted by Immigration and asked to provide documentation confirming that the conviction in question was for a summary conviction offence. This confirmation was delivered prior to February 1, 1993, the date on which the current section 19(2)(a) came into force. The transitional provisions dictated that if the application was still pending on February 1, 1993, then the new section 19(2)(a) would apply and the summary conviction offence would prevent the applicant from receiving permanent residence.

The Court found on the evidence that the application had been accepted prior to February 1, 1993 and that receipt of the confirmation of the applicant's summary conviction was just the last step required to formalize his status as a landed immigrant. Given that the document demonstrating the applicant's criminal admissibility to Canada was delivered prior to the change in legislation, there was no reason to conclude that the applicant ought not to be admitted to Canada. A final decision had been made to grant the application for residence. The application was not still pending at the time the legislation changed.

Accordingly, the matter was referred back to the Immigration department for reconsideration.

Singleton v. Canada (Minister of Employment & Immigration) (November 7, 1983), Doc. A-813-83 (Fed. T.D.) — For digest, see section 19, subheading *Subsection (1), Paragraph (c), supra.*

R. v. Wardley (1978), 43 C.C.C. (2d) 345 (Ont. C.A.) — For digest, see section 19, subsection, *Subheading (1), Paragraph (c.1), supra.*

Section 19(2)(a.1)

Tei v. Canada (Minister of Citizenship & Immigration) (1998), 48 Imm. L.R. (2d) 120, 161 F.T.R. 51 (Fed. T.D.) — The applicant submitted an application for permanent residence under the investor category and included his wife. The applicant's wife had a conviction for making a false statement for the purpose of obtaining a certificate of identity and had been sentenced to a fine of $1,500 Hong Kong dollars. The applicant submitted an application for rehabilitation, and the applicant and his wife were interviewed in June 1997 for the purpose of determining whether the visa officer would recommend to the program manager that the wife was rehabilitated. The result of the interview was a negative recommendation and on July 16, 1997, the program manager concurred with this recommendation.

The applicant's Notice of Motion challenged the visa officer's decision refusing the applicant's application for permanent residence, when in fact, the applicant was really challenging the Minister's decision refusing to grant rehabilitation. The Minister is the decision-maker. The visa officer's role is that of advisor in that he made a recommendation and submitted the application along with supporting documents. If the visa officer drew unreasonable conclusions or relied on erroneous facts or indeed failed to take into account relevant facts, then these defects or errors would be germane in a review of the decision itself which was made by the Minister's delegate. By challenging the visa officer's recommendation, the applicant is also putting into play the validity of the Minister's decision. The applicant should have sought judicial review of the Minister's determination. The Court noted that leave of the Court would have been required to review this decision and that leave had not been obtained.

Accordingly, the application for judicial review was dismissed.

Lui v. Canada (Minister of Citizenship & Immigration) (1997), 39 Imm. L.R. (2d) 60, 134 F.T.R. 308 (Fed. T.D.) — The applicant sought to review a deportation order based on a 1976 conviction for assault occasioning bodily harm in Hong Kong. The adjudicator was of the opinion that the applicant was described in 19(1)(c.1)(i).

Before the adjudicator, the applicant produced a "Certificate of No Criminal Conviction" from the Commissioner of Police in Hong Kong. That document stated that the 1976 conviction was regarded as spent in Hong Kong by virtue of section 2(1) of the *Rehabilitation of Offenders Ordinance*. The applicant argued that the operation of the ordinance was similar to the *Criminal Records Act of Canada*, under which persons who have been convicted of a criminal offence in Canada may seek pardons. The applicant argued that the adjudicator should have treated the 1976 Hong Kong conviction as if it had been vacated under the *Criminal Records Act*, in which case the applicant would not have been inadmissible.

The Court enunciated the following test:

1. The laws and legal system of the foreign jurisdiction must be similar to Canada's.
2. The foreign law in question must be similar in (a) aim or purpose; (b) content; and (c) effect, but not necessarily identical to the Canadian law.

The Court found that the laws and legal system of Hong Kong were similar to Canada's. Hong Kong had been a British colony for over 150 years at the time of this application, and its legal system had as its basis, English law.

The Court found that the purpose or aim of the Hong Kong Ordinance was similar to that of the *Criminal Records Act*, namely to give convicted persons a second chance by "wiping their slate clean". The content and effect of the ordinance was found not to be similar to the *Criminal Records Act*. The effect of the *Criminal Records Act* was to vacate a conviction if the National Parole Board granted a pardon and to remove any disqualifications flowing from the conviction. The effect of the Hong Kong Ordinance while being similar was subject to numerous exceptions.

Accordingly, the Court concluded that the Hong Kong Ordinance was not similar in content and effect to the Canadian law. In respect of disqualifications, the Hong Kong and Canadian laws were inconsistent. Therefore, the vacating of the conviction by the Hong Kong Ordinance could not be recognized by Canada.

Accordingly, the application for judicial review was dismissed.

Li v. Canada (Minister of Citizenship & Immigration) (1996), 34 Imm. L.R. (2d) 109, [1997] 1 F.C. 235, 37 C.R.R. (2d) 360, 138 D.L.R. (4th) 275, 200 N.R. 307, 119 F.T.R. 130 (note) (Fed. C.A.) — This was an appeal from an order of the Trial Division, which refused to quash a decision of the Adjudication Division determining that the appellants were inadmissable pursuant to paragraph 19(2)(a.1)(i) of the *Immigration Act*.

The appellant, a former chairman of the Hong Kong Stock Exchange, was convicted in October 1990, on two offences under section 9 of the Hong Kong Prevention of Bribery Ordinance and sentenced to 4 years in prison. The appellants sought to enter Canada in April 1994. A report under section 20 was issued and an inquiry was convened before an adjudicator commencing in August 1994. It was agreed by the parties that the appellant's wife would be included in any order made against him.

It would be consistent with the purposes of the statute and not inconsistent with the jurisprudence of the Court to conclude that what equivalency of offences requires is essentially the similarity of definitions of the offences. A definition is similar if it involves similar criteria for establishing that an offence has occurred, whether those criteria are manifested in elements, or defences, in the two sets of laws. The definition of an offence involves the elements and defences particular to that offence and perhaps to that class of offence. For the purpose of subparagraph 19(2)(a.1)(i), it is not necessary to compare all the general principles of criminal responsibilities in the two systems. What is being examined is the comparability of offences not the comparability of possible convictions in the two countries.

The motions judge took the position the defences need not be taken into account. The Court concluded the appeal must be allowed. The word corruptly in paragraph 426(1)(a) of the *Criminal Code* means without disclosure. Such disclosure must have been effected in an adequate and timely manner to be a defence under Canadian law. Once made, however, the taking of the reward by an agent cannot be found to have been done corruptly. This makes the Canadian offence much narrower than the Hong Kong offence. According to the *Prevention of Bribery Ordinance* the mere disclosure of the taking of the advantage would not render the taking innocent. The Hong Kong ordinance creates an offence where the advantage is taken without lawful authority or reasonable excuse. It is easy to conceive that an agent in Hong Kong might disclose that he had received a benefit, but if the principle did not give "lawful authority" for the agent to do so, the offence would have still been committed.

It might have been possible to demonstrate through particulars of the Hong Kong charges or from the evidence from the trials there that in fact, what the appellant did would have constituted an offence within a somewhat narrower Canadian *Criminal Code* provision. There was nothing however, to indicate that such evidence was before the adjudicator and therefore the appeal must be allowed.

The Court further noted that the purpose of subparagraph 19(2)(a.1)(i) is to render inadmissable persons who have been convicted of acts abroad which if committed in Canada would be denounced, by giving rise to liability for prosecution by way of indictment. While proceedings in Canada under the *Immigration Act* must no doubt be conducted in accordance with the Charter, it is not inappropriate for Canadian tribunals to recognize and accept the validity of foreign legal systems without measuring them against the Charter. Therefore, in determining the equivalence of offences an adjudicator should not compare the procedural or evidentiary rules of the two jurisdictions, even if the Canadian rules are mandated by the Charter.

Lei v. Canada (Solicitor General) (1994), 74 F.T.R. 67 — For digest, see section 19, subheading *Subsection (1), Paragraph (c.1), supra.*

Steward v. Canada (Minister of Employment & Immigration) (1988), 84 N.R. 236 (Fed. C.A.) — For digest, see section 19, subheading *Subsection (1), Paragraph (c.1), supra.*

Lavi v. Canada (Minister of Employment & Immigration) (April 24, 1985), Doc. T-83-9929 (Imm. App. Bd.) — For digest, see section 19, subheading *Subsection (1), Paragraph (c.1), supra.*

Taubler v. Canada (Minister of Employment & Immigration) (1980), [1981] 1 F.C. 620 (Fed. C.A.) — For digest, see section 19, subheading *Subsection (1), Paragraph (c.1), supra.*

See: *Brannson v. Canada (Minister of Employment & Immigration)*, [1981] 2 F.C. 141, 34 N.R. 410 (Fed. C.A.) for an analysis of the method of equivalencing .

Anderson v. Canada (Minister of Employment & Immigration), [1981] 2 F.C. 30, 113 D.L.R. (3d) 243, 36 N.R. 423 (Fed. C.A.) — For digest, see section 19, subheading *Subsection (1), Paragraph (c.1), supra.*

Potter v. Canada (Minister of Employment & Immigration) (1979), [1980] 1 F.C. 609, 108 D.L.R. (3d) 92, 31 N.R. 158 (Fed. C.A.) — This case is an example of the operation of section 19(2)(a). Potter was convicted of receiving stolen goods valued at approximately $30

(Canadian) in England. The Court held that given the provisions of section 313 of the *Criminal Code* it was clear that Potter was a person who had committed, outside of Canada, an offence that might be punishable by way of indictment and for which a maximum term of less than ten years might be imposed had the offence been committed in Canada.

Note: See also cases referred to under section 19(1)(c) and 19(1)(c.1).

Section 19(2)(b)

Lui v. Canada (Minister of Citizenship & Immigration) (1997), 39 Imm. L.R. (2d) 60, 134 F.T.R. 308 (Fed. T.D.) — The applicant sought to review a deportation order based on a 1976 conviction for assault occasioning bodily harm in Hong Kong. The adjudicator was of the opinion that the applicant was described in 19(1)(c.1)(i).

Before the adjudicator, the applicant produced a "Certificate of No Criminal Conviction" from the Commissioner of Police in Hong Kong. That document stated that the 1976 conviction was regarded as spent in Hong Kong by virtue of section 2(1) of the *Rehabilitation of Offenders Ordinance*. The applicant argued that the operation of the ordinance was similar to the *Criminal Records Act of Canada*, under which persons who have been convicted of a criminal offence in Canada may seek pardons. The applicant argued that the adjudicator should have treated the 1976 Hong Kong conviction as if it had been vacated under the *Criminal Records Act*, in which case the applicant would not have been inadmissible.

The Court enunciated the following test:

1. The laws and legal system of the foreign jurisdiction must be similar to Canada's.
2. The foreign law in question must be similar in (a) aim or purpose; (b) content; and (c) effect, but not necessarily identical to the Canadian law.

The Court found that the laws and legal system of Hong Kong were similar to Canada's. Hong Kong had been a British colony for over 150 years at the time of this application, and its legal system had as its basis, English law.

The Court found that the purpose or aim of the Hong Kong Ordinance was similar to that of the *Criminal Records Act*, namely to give convicted persons a second chance by "wiping their slate clean". The content and effect of the ordinance was found not to be similar to the *Criminal Records Act*. The effect of the *Criminal Records Act* was to vacate a conviction if the National Parole Board granted a pardon and to remove any disqualifications flowing from the conviction. The effect of the Hong Kong Ordinance while being similar was subject to numerous exceptions.

Accordingly, the Court concluded that the Hong Kong Ordinance was not similar in content and effect to the Canadian law. In respect of disqualifications, the Hong Kong and Canadian laws were inconsistent. Therefore, the vacating of the conviction by the Hong Kong Ordinance could not be recognized by Canada.

Accordingly, the application for judicial review was dismissed.

Alouache v. Canada (Minister of Citizenship & Immigration) (1995), 31 Imm. L.R. (2d) 68, 102 F.T.R. 1 (Fed. T.D.); affirmed (1996), 197 N.R. 305 (Fed. C.A.); reconsideration refused (June 26, 1996), Doc. A-681-95 (Fed. C.A.) — The applicant came to Canada in 1989 and married a Canadian citizen. The couple had two children. While the applicant's wife sponsored him for landing, she withdrew her sponsorship on three occasions and reinstated it on two. The final withdrawal remained in effect as at the date of this application.

The applicant was convicted of three summary conviction offences: failing to comply with a condition of his recognizance; theft under $1,000; and threatening to use a weapon in the commission of an assault. All three offenses related to the applicant's difficult relationship with his spouse. Counsel for the applicant argued that the three convictions arose out of a single occurrence, namely the applicant's difficult relationship with his former spouse and that the applicant was therefore not described in subparagraph 19(2)(b)(i).

The three summary conviction offences were committed on different dates and arose out of different occurrences rather than a single occurrence. The term "occurrence" was regarded as synonymous with the terms "event" and "incident" and not as synonymous with "a course of events" which was an apt description for the course of the breakdown of the applicant's marriage.

Lei v. Canada (Solicitor General) (1994), 74 F.T.R. 67 — For digest, see section 19, subheading *Subsection (1), Paragraph (c.1), supra.*

Steward v. Canada (Minister of Employment & Immigration) (1988), 84 N.R. 236 (Fed. C.A.) — For digest, see section 19, subheading *Subsection (1), Paragraph (c.1), supra.*

Libby v. Canada (Minister of Employment & Immigration) (1988), 50 D.L.R. (4th) 573 (Fed. C.A.) — The appellant sought to review and set aside a decision of the adjudicator issuing a departure notice to the appellant. The appellant was a United States citizen who married a Canadian. The marriage broke down and the Canadian husband withdrew his sponsorship. The appellant was convicted of theft under $1,000. Pursuant to that charge, she was required to present herself for fingerprinting, which she failed to do, and she was subsequently convicted of a summary offence for failing to report for fingerprinting. The adjudicator erred in determining that the appellant was a person who had been convicted of two or more offences not arising out of a single occurrence. Both offences had their source in the same event.

Singleton v. Canada (Minister of Employment & Immigration) (November 7, 1983), Doc. A-813-83 (Fed. T.D.) — For digest, see section 19, subheading *Subsection (1), Paragraph (a), supra.*

Taubler v. Canada (Minister of Employment & Immigration) (1980), [1981] 1 F.C. 620 (Fed. C.A.) — For digest, see section 19, subheading *Subsection (1), Paragraph (c.1), supra.*

Anderson v. Canada (Minister of Employment & Immigration) (1980), [1981] 2 F.C. 30, 113 D.L.R. (3d) 243, 36 N.R. 423 (Fed. C.A.) — For digest, see section 19, subheading *Subsection (1), Paragraph (c.1), supra.*

Section 19(2)(c)

Saini v. Canada (Minister of Manpower & Immigration) (1978), 22 N.R. 22, 86 D.L.R. (3d) 492 (Fed. C.A.) — Although this case dealt with the *Immigration Act*, R.S.C. 1970, the Court, with the consent of counsel for the Crown, set aside a deportation order against the wife of the applicant because she was not herself the subject of a section 22 report.

Section 19(2)(d)

Kaur v. Canada (Minister of Employment & Immigration) (1995), 98 F.T.R. 91 — A visa officer requested certain travel documents and tax returns from an applicant for permanent residence. This information was not provided.

Where relevant documentation is sought in connection for an application for permanent residence and is not provided, a visa officer may refuse the application by virtue of subsection 9(3) and paragraph 19(2)(d) of the *Immigration Act.*

Canada (Minister of Employment & Immigration) v. De Decaro, [1993] 2 F.C. 408, 103 D.L.R. (4th) 564, 155 N.R. 129 (Fed. C.A.) — In October 1988 a visa officer issued an immigrant visa to Ignazio De Decaro. He also issued an immigrant visa to two dependants who were to accompany Mr. De Decaro, namely the respondent and her daughter. Ignazio

De Decaro died before coming to Canada. The respondent did come and arrived at Dorval on July 11, 1989 accompanied by her daughter and another child, who was born in the U.S. after Ignazio De Decaro's death. This child had never obtained a visa to Canada.

The respondent then applied for landing for herself and her two children. This was denied on the ground that the respondent's admission contravened section 19(2)(d) of the *Immigration Act* because the respondent did not meet the requirements of section 9(1) of the Act.

The adjudicator found that when the respondent applied for admission to Canada, she held a valid immigrant's visa since her visa had not been revoked by the proper authorities. The adjudicator found that the respondent's husband's death did not automatically invalidate the visa. Further, the adjudicator found that there was no need to refer to section 12 of the regulations because that provision did not enact a condition of admission, consequently its infringement did not mean the respondent could not be admitted.

The Appeal Division of the I.R.B. dismissed the Minister's appeal on the basis that the respondent, before appearing at a port-of-entry, had duly obtained an immigrant visa which had never been revoked or cancelled by the proper authorities and thus the respondent had the right to be admitted to Canada unless she was inadmissible on some other ground than the lack of a valid visa.

The Minister's appeal to the Court of Appeal was allowed. Pratte J.A. held that the definition of "accompanying dependant" illustrated that the visa issued to a person in this class was of a very special type which was issued solely to enable its holder to accompany or follow another person to Canada. The holder of such a visa who applied for admission without the other person accompanying or preceding him or her into Canada did not therefore meet the requirements of section 9(1) of the Act.

Further, after her husband's death the respondent became inadmissible by virtue of section 12 of the regulations. Her marital status had changed since she obtained her visa and in order to be admitted to Canada she had to establish not only that she was eligible, but also that she met all the conditions for obtaining a visa. The respondent never discharged this burden of proof.

Marceau J.A. agreed that the decision of the Appeal Division should be set aside. He saw no reference in the Act or regulations to visas which become invalid, are revoked or become ineffective. The technique in his view used to cover cases of changes in the immigrant's status between the time the visa is issued and the time he or she arrives at the Canadian border is contained in section 12 of the regulations. In his view, issuing an immigrant visa is not the granting of landing. Such issuance simply means that the visa officer has formed the opinion that the applicant meets the requirements of the Act and regulations for admission to Canada. The visa is evidence of a conclusion by an immigration officer whose function is to determine from outside Canada whether applicants are admissible and that conclusion will usually be accepted by his or her colleague at the port-of-entry. However, the rule is still that a foreign national arriving in Canada with a view to residing here must satisfy the immigration officer of his admissibility at the port-of-entry. Section 12 of the regulations imposes on an immigrant a duty to disclose any change in the facts which may have influenced the issuing of the visa and, if there has been such a change, it requires the immigrant to meet new requirements. The visa is not void, but the visa, in itself, does not confer the right of entry. It is the new requirements of section 12 of the regulations that must be met.

In Marceau J.A.'s view the respondent could not establish that she met the requirements of section 12 since she was granted a visa in consideration of her husband's presence. The adjudicator accordingly was wrong to think that she met the conditions of admission set out by the regulation, and the Appeal Division could not confirm the adjudicator's finding on the ground that the Minister had not discharged the burden of proving that the respondent was inadmissible or that her visa had been cancelled, as the Minister was under no burden of proof and cancellation of a visa as a concept does not exist.

Given that the Court intended to allow the appeal, it then had to consider section 73(3). The majority was of the view that the respondent, before her husband's death, possessed a valid visa. However, after that death it was impossible for the condition attached to the visa to be performed so that the visa ceased to have any validity. Accordingly, section 73(3) conferred no right of appeal to the Appeal Division on the respondent.

Marceau J.A was of the view that the respondent was in possession of a valid visa and that the matter should be returned to the Appeal Division as it was still under a duty to consider whether on compassionate or humanitarian grounds the respondent should not be removed from Canada.

Sandhu v. Canada (Minister of Employment & Immigration) (1989), 8 Imm. L.R. (2d) 312 (Imm. & Ref. Bd. (App. Div.)) — This was an appeal from a refusal to approve a sponsored application. The Board noted that it had in previous decisions held that section 9(3) of the Act will not apply as a valid ground for refusal where the false information was not relevant and material in the determination of the admissibility of the applicant and any other legally admissible dependants. The deliberate failure of the applicant to disclose information about his relationship to the appellant's first husband was a misrepresentation of a relevant material fact. However, the refusal by the visa officer on this ground was still invalid because the applicant disclosed the truth about this relationship prior to the decision on the sponsored application. The use of the present tense in section 19(2)(d) indicates that the persons therein described are those who at the time when the decision is made as to their admissibility do not comply with the Act and regulations. At the time of the refusal, the applicant had complied with section 9(3) and was not inadmissible under that provision.

Klassen-Funk v. Canada (Minister of Employment & Immigration) (October 18, 1984), Doc. A-578-84 (Fed. C.A.) — The applicant sought admission to Canada while accompanied by her fiancé, a Canadian citizen, whom she subsequently married while in Canada. The applicant was excluded because she was a person described in section 19(2)(d) of the *Immigration Act* in that she was a person seeking admission to Canada but had not applied for and obtained a visa before appearing at a port-of-entry. The adjudicator determined that the applicant was not seeking entry as a visitor but, rather, was seeking admission as an immigrant and refused to apply section 19(3) of the Act to such a person. The adjudicator's decision was upheld by the Court which ruled that section 19(3) was intended to permit the adjudicator, in his discretion, to grant limited entry only to those persons who have been determined by the adjudicator to be seeking entry to Canada as visitors.

Grewal v. Canada (Minister of Employment & Immigration) (January 18, 1984), Doc. V82-6005 (Imm. App. Bd.) — This was a sponsorship appeal from the refusal to accept the application for permanent residence of the father of the sponsor and his accompanying dependants. It was possible to establish the relationship of the father, the mother and one brother of the sponsor. It was not possible to establish the relationship of another young man and woman who were alleged to be a brother and a sister of this sponsor. A majority was of the opinion that entry should be denied to only those not proven eligible and that the father, the mother and brother whose relationship to the sponsor was established should be permitted to come to Canada. The minority would have disallowed the application of all the parties because other alleged dependants were inadmissible under the Regulations.

Kang v. Canada (Minister of Employment & Immigration), [1981] 2 F.C. 807, 37 N.R. 55 (Fed. C.A.); leave to appeal to S.C.C. refused 39 N.R. 353n (S.C.C.) — A violation of section 9(3) may, according to the circumstances of the case, justify a decision not to grant a visa. It does not, however, have the automatic effect of making the applicant an inadmissible person described in this paragraph.

Sidhu v. Canada (Minister of Employment & Immigration) (June 19, 1980), Doc. A-259-80 (Fed. C.A.) — When a person who appears at a port-of-entry without an immigrant visa is proceeded against under this paragraph, and testifies that she was not seeking admission as an immigrant, the adjudicator must first determine whether the applicant, at the time of her examination by an immigration officer, had in fact sought admission as a visitor or as an immigrant. Failure to do so will result in the quashing of any order made.

Section 19(3)

Stuart v. Canada (Minister of Employment & Immigration) (April 16, 1987), Doc. T-2591-86 (Fed. T.D.) — This application was made to obtain *certiorari* to quash the respondent's decision not to grant a visitor's visa to the applicant's spouse to enter Canada for the purpose of testifying as a witness at the applicant's appeal hearing before the Immigration Appeal Board. The applicant had sought to sponsor his spouse for entry as a member of the family class, but the respondent claimed that the marriage was entered into only for the purposes of gaining admission to Canada. It was determined that the applicant would be denied a fair hearing if he was prevented from calling his wife as a witness. Her son, who was five years old, was not granted permission to enter Canada. *Certiorari* was granted on condition that the applicant's spouse remain in custody for the purpose of ensuring her immediate return to Guyana after any attendance before the Immigration Appeal Board. The basis for admission was section 19(3) of the Act.

Manlangit v. Canada (Minister of Employment & Immigration) (1987), 2 Imm. L.R. (2d) 33, 78 N.R. 1 (Fed. C.A.) — This section 28 application was brought to set aside an exclusion order on the basis that the adjudicator who made it "refused to exercise" his jurisdiction under section 19(3) of the *Immigration Act*.

The applicant arrived in the United States approximately five years prior to this incident. He was engaged to be married to a United States citizen. She went on a day's outing to Bob-Lo Island, an amusement park in the Detroit River. This amusement park is, in fact, in Canada and the applicant was refused readmission to the United States. She was then excluded from Canada on the basis that she was not a genuine visitor. During the course of the inquiry, relief under section 19(3) of the Act was discussed. The adjudicator did not finally determine this matter and made no reference to section 19 in the Reasons for Judgment.

In dealing with the request under section 19(3), an adjudicator is only to have regard to the following factors:

1. that the applicant be a member of an inadmissible class described in section 19(2);
2. that the purpose of the entry justifies admission;
3. if entry is to be granted, the appropriate terms and conditions thereof and for the duration of the stay in Canada.

While the decision in this case did not contain express words of refusal, such words were not required to give the Court jurisdiction under section 28 of the *Federal Court Act*. The adjudicator's conduct was seen as constituting a refusal. The matter was, accordingly, referred back to the adjudicator for reconsideration and redetermination.

Klassen-Funk v. Canada (Minister of Employment & Immigration) (October 18, 1984), Doc. A-578-84 (Fed. C.A.) — For digest, see section 19, subheading *Subsection (2), Paragraph (d), supra*.

Brenner v. Canada (Minister of Employment & Immigration), [1983] 1 F.C. 172 (Fed. T.D.) — The adjudicator determined that the applicant was a person described in section 27(2)(a), because the applicant was inadmissible as a member of a class described in section 19(2)(a)(ii). The applicant applied to the adjudicator for a grant of entry under section 19(3). The adjudicator decided that she had no jurisdiction to entertain the application. A writ of *mandamus* compelling the adjudicator to consider the application under section 19(3) was refused on the ground that her decision brought the person within section 32(6) and, therefore, the adjudicator had no discretion to grant entry to such a person under section 19(3).

Editor's Note: See section 16(1)(b) of the Act.

Removal at Ports of Entry

20. (1) Reports at port of entry — Where an immigration officer is of the opinion that it would or may be contrary to this Act or the regulations to grant admission to a person examined by the officer or otherwise let that person come into Canada, the officer may detain or make an order to detain that person and shall

> **(a) subject to subsection (2), report that person in writing to a senior immigration officer; or**
>
> **(b) allow that person to leave Canada forthwith.**

(2) Temporary exclusion of persons arriving from U.S. — Where an immigration officer at a port of entry is of the opinion that it would or may be contrary to this Act or the regulations to grant admission to or otherwise let come into Canada a person who is arriving from the United States, the officer may, where a senior immigration officer to whom the officer would otherwise make a report pursuant to paragraph (1)(*a*) is not reasonably available, direct that person to return to the United States until such time as a senior immigration officer is available.

1992, c. 49, s. 12.

Case Law

Section 20(1)

Chan v. Canada (Minister of Employment & Immigration) (1987), 2 Imm. L.R. (2d) 99 (Fed. T.D.) — The applicant was sponsored by his wife, and, upon the applicant's arrival at Vancouver Airport, the immigration officer who interviewed him signed his record of landing, assisted him in an application for a Social Insurance Card and then advised him that his wife had withdrawn her sponsorship. The applicant knew, prior to leaving Hong Kong, that his wife was seeking a divorce, but he had not been informed that she was withdrawing her sponsorship of his application for permanent residence. A section 20 report was prepared, and, ultimately, an exclusion order was issued. The applicant appealed unsuccessfully to the Immigration Appeal Board. Similarly, an application for leave to appeal to the Federal Court under section 84 was also refused.

At this point, the applicant brought these proceedings in the Trial Division attacking the validity of the section 20 report on the basis that, having been granted landing, any attempt to deal with him as an immigrant seeking landing was unauthorized. The Court determined that section 59 [old Act] precluded attacks by way of *certiorari* on matters confined exclusively to the Immigration Appeal Board. Further, in reaching a conclusion as to whether it had the capacity to hear this appeal, the Immigration Appeal Board was taken to have determined whether the removal order, upon which the appeal was based, was valid.

Finally, reference was made to the rule of administrative law that holds that once a final decision has been reached by a statutory body, the myriad of decisions necessarily made on route to that decision must be taken to have merged in it, and it is no longer subject to judicial review under section 18 of the *Federal Court Act*. Thus, the Trial Division concluded that it was without jurisdiction to grant relief under section 18, and the application was dismissed.

R. v. Kwok (1986), 18 O.A.C. 38, 31 C.C.C. (3d) 196 (Ont. C.A.) — The appellant arrived at Pearson International Airport aboard a flight originating in London. He was examined by a senior immigration officer and detained pending an immigration inquiry. The immigration officer who interviewed the appellant had doubts as to the *bona fides* of the appellant as a genuine visitor and wrote a report pursuant to section 20 of the Act for the benefit of the acting senior immigration officer. A person is not detained within the meaning of section 10 of the *Charter of Rights and Freedoms* until the restriction on his freedom has gone beyond that required for the processing of his application for entry. The fact that some questioning preceded the advice required by section 10 did not by itself offend the section. The obligation to inform a person of his rights under section 10(b) of the Charter is an obligation to inform, without delay, but that does not mean immediately. Further, the admission into evidence of a conversation preceding the section 10 warning did not bring the administration of justice into disrepute.

Mercier v. Canada (Minister of Employment & Immigration) (April 25, 1985), Doc. T-309-85 (Fed. T.D.), affirmed (1985), 62 N.R. 73 (Fed. C.A.) — On November 17, 1982, following an inquiry, a deportation order was issued against the applicant because he had been convicted of an offence for which a maximum term of imprisonment of ten years or more may be imposed, pursuant to section 19(1)(c) of the Act. The applicant's appeal against this deportation order was dismissed on August 14, 1984. On January 30, 1985, the applicant tried to gain admission to the United States without success and returned to Canada with the intention of provoking an inquiry where he might claim refugee status. When the applicant reappeared at the Canadian border, a senior immigration officer issued a Summons to Appear at an inquiry, pursuant to section 23 of the Act. That decision was countermanded by another senior immigration officer and the applicant's case was withdrawn on the ground that the deportation order, issued against the applicant, had never been executed. It was this decision that was attacked by the applicant who was seeking a writ of *mandamus* requiring the adjudicator to conduct his inquiry. The decision to countermand the Summons to Inquiry was part of the administrative process. The Court did not intervene because it was of the view that the applicant had not been treated unfairly and that to intervene and issue a writ of *mandamus* would create a situation in which the respondent Minister would, on the one hand, have to execute a deportation order against the applicant and, on the other hand, have to conduct an inquiry with a view to admitting the applicant to the country.

An appeal from this decision was heard on June 28, 1985 and dismissed. The appellant (applicant) sought to raise, for the first time, the assertion that the deportation order had been executed by the appellant himself when he left the country for a 6-week visit to Haiti from May 12, 1984 to June 30, 1984. No consideration was given to the submission on appeal because it was a question which was raised for the first time before the Court of Appeal. It was founded upon an allegation of fact which was never put in issue before the Trial Division. The Court noted that when sitting an appeal of the Trial Division, it sat as a Court of Appeal whose function was to decide whether the issues presented at trial were properly disposed of. It was not the Court's duty to determine other issues which, had they been raised at the Trial Division, might have resulted in a different outcome if the necessary factual basis had been established.

Singh v. Canada (Minister of Employment & Immigration) (September 21, 1984), Doc. A-258-84 (Fed. C.A.) — The section 20 report convoking the inquiry alleged that the applicant was described in section 19(1)(h) of the *Immigration Act*. In the course of the inquiry, the applicant testified that he intended to remain permanently in Canada. He was, therefore, a person described in section 19(2)(d) because of his failure to obtain an immigrant visa before appearing at a port-of-entry contrary to section 9(1) of the Act. The exclusion order was based on sections 19(2)(d) and 9(1). The exclusion order was set aside because the subject of the inquiry must be advised of the allegations against him at the outset of the inquiry and if those allegations are changed, altered or substituted during the course of the inquiry, he must then be advised of the revised allegations and given an opportunity to meet them. This finding was supported by the provisions of sections 29 and 31 of the Regulations and the requirement of procedural fairness.

Kaur v. Canada (Minister of Employment & Immigration) (1984), 58 N.R. 221 (Fed. C.A.) — The applicant sought admission to Canada as an immigrant. Following a report made pursuant to section 20(1) of the *Immigration Act*, she was made the subject of an inquiry. That inquiry was adjourned after the applicant claimed to be a Convention refugee. During the adjournment the applicant left the country for the United States, was refused permission to enter that country and immediately came back to Canada where she reapplied to be admitted as an immigrant. The inquiry which had been adjourned culminated in an exclusion order. The adjudicator who presided over the inquiry did not lose jurisdiction when the applicant left Canada for the United States. Once a person seeking admission to Canada has been made the subject of an inquiry in order to determine her admissibility, the mere fact that she, after the start of the inquiry either left Canada or manifested an intention no longer to seek admission, does not deprive the adjudicator of his jurisdiction to continue the inquiry.

21. Grounds for removal order — Where a removal order is made against any person with respect to whom an inquiry is held as a result of a report made pursuant to paragraph 20(1)(*a*), the removal order against that person may be made on the basis that that person is a member of any inadmissible class.

Case Law

Frias v. Canada (Minister of Manpower & Immigration), [1974] 2 F.C. 306, 5 N.R. 179 (Fed. C.A.) — It still may be necessary to give a person seeking admission at a port-of-entry notice of the fact that the removal order is going to be made on a basis other than the basis set out in the report under section 20(1).

22. Where person shall be allowed to come into Canada — Where a senior immigration officer receives a report made pursuant to paragraph 20(1)(*a*) concerning a person who seeks to come into Canada, the officer shall let the person come into Canada if the officer is satisfied that the person is a person described in subsection 14(1).

23. (1) Where immigrant shall be granted landing — Where a senior immigration officer receives a report made pursuant to paragraph 20(1)(*a*) concerning an immigrant, the officer shall

(a) grant landing to that immigrant, or

(b) authorize that immigrant to come into Canada on condition that the immigrant be present for further examination by an immigration officer within such time and at such place as the senior immigration officer may direct,

if the officer is satisfied that it would not be contrary to this Act or the regulations to grant landing to or otherwise authorize that immigrant to come into Canada.

(1.1) **Terms and conditions** — A senior immigration officer who grants landing to an immigrant pursuant to paragraph (1)(*a*)

(a) shall, if the immigrant is of a class of immigrants for which regulations made under paragraph 114(1)(*ii*.2) require the imposition of terms and conditions, impose the terms and conditions prescribed by those regulations; and

(b) subject to regulations made under paragraph 114(1)(*ii*.4), may, in the case of any immigrant, impose terms and conditions prescribed by regulations made under paragraph 114(1)(*ii*.3).

(2) **Where visitor may be granted entry** — Where a senior immigration officer receives a report made pursuant to paragraph 20(1)(*a*) concerning a visitor, the officer may grant entry to that visitor and, except in the case of a person who may be granted entry pursuant to paragraph 19(3), impose terms and conditions of a prescribed nature if the officer is satisfied that it would not be contrary to this Act or the regulations to grant entry to that visitor.

(3) **Where person not allowed into Canada or granted admission** — Where a senior immigration officer adjourns the examination of a person who is the subject of a report made pursuant to paragraph 20(1)(*a*) or does not let a person come into Canada pursuant to section 22 and does not grant admission to or otherwise authorize the person to come into Canada pursuant to subsection (1) or (2), the officer may, subject to subsections (4), (4.01), (4.2) and (6),

(a) detain or make an order to detain the person;

(b) release the person from detention subject to such terms and conditions as the officer deems appropriate in the circumstances, including the payment of a security deposit or the posting of a performance bond; or

(c) impose on the person such terms and conditions as the officer deems appropriate in the circumstances, including the payment of a security deposit or the posting of a performance bond.

(4) **Exclusion order** — Subject to section 28, a senior immigration officer shall allow a person to leave Canada forthwith or make an exclusion order against the person where the senior immigration officer receives a report made pursuant to paragraph 20(1)(*a*) in respect of the person and the senior immigration officer is satisfied that

(a) the person is a member of

(i) the class of persons referred to in paragraph 19(1)(*i*), or

(ii) the class of persons referred to in paragraph 19(2)(*d*) by reason of the fact that the person does not possess a valid and subsisting passport, visa or student or employment authorization and was not granted landing or was granted landing but later became subject to a removal order; and

Conditional Amendment — 23(4)(a)(ii)

On the day on which section 10.3 of the Immigration Act, as enacted by section 5 of An Act to amend the Immigration Act and other Acts in consequence thereof, S.C. 1992, c. 49 comes into force, subparagraph 23(4)(a)(ii) will be replaced with the following:

> **(ii) the class of persons referred to in paragraph 19(2)(*d*) by reason of the fact that the person does not possess a valid and subsisting passport, visa or student or employment authorization and is not a person to whom a document was provided pursuant to section 10.3; and**

1995, c. 15, s. 25(1). [Not in force at date of publication.]

(b) the person is not a member of an inadmissible class other than an inadmissible class referred to in paragraph (*a*).

(4.01) **Other powers of senior immigration officer** — **Subject to section 28, a senior immigration officer may allow a person to leave Canada forthwith, make an exclusion order against the person on the basis that the person is a member of either or both of the inadmissible classes described in paragraph (*a*) or, subject to subsections (4.3) and (5), cause an inquiry to be held as soon as is reasonably practicable concerning whether the person is a member of any or all of the inadmissible classes described in paragraph (*a*) or (*b*) where the senior immigration officer receives a report made pursuant to paragraph 20(1)(*a*) in respect of the person and is satisfied that**

(a) the person is a member of

(i) the inadmissible class described in paragraph 19(1)(*i*), or

(ii) the inadmissible class described in paragraph 19(2)(*d*) by reason of the fact that the person does not possess a valid and subsisting passport, visa or student or employment authorization and was not granted landing or was granted landing but later became subject to a removal order; and

Conditional Amendment — 23(4.01)(a)(ii)

On the day on which section 10.3 of the Immigration Act, as enacted by section 5 of An Act to amend the Immigration Act and other Acts in consequence thereof, S.C. 1992, c. 49, comes into force, subparagraph 23(4.01)(a)(ii) will be replaced with the following:

> **(ii) the inadmissible class described in paragraph 19(2)(*d*) by reason of the fact that the person does not possess a valid and subsisting passport, visa or student or employment authorization and is not a person to whom a document was provided pursuant to section 10.3; and**

1995, c. 15, s. 25(2). [Not in force at date of publication.]

(b) the person is a member of an inadmissible class other than an inadmissible class referred to in paragraph (*a*).

(4.1) **Duty to provide information** — **Every person referred to in subsection (4) or (4.01) shall truthfully provide such information as may be required by the senior immigration officer for the purpose of establishing whether the person is to be allowed to come into Canada or may be granted admission.**

(4.2) **Inquiry or permission to leave Canada** — **Subject to subsections (4.3) and (5), where a senior immigration officer does not make an exclusion order under subsec-**

tion (4) or (4.01), or a conditional departure order under subsection 28(1), the senior immigration officer shall

> **(a) cause an inquiry to be held concerning the person as soon as is reasonably practicable; or**
>
> **(b) allow the person to leave Canada forthwith.**

Transitional Provision

Note: S.C. 1995, c. 15, s. 27(1) provides: where a senior immigration officer has caused an inquiry to be held under subsection 23(4.2) of the Immigration Act as that provision read on July 9, 1995 with respect to a person described in paragraph 23(4)(b) of the Immigration Act as that provision read on July 9, 1995 and the adjudicator has not commenced the hearing on or before July 10, 1995, the case shall be referred to a senior immigration officer who shall take the appropriate action under subsection 23(4) or (4.01) of the Immigration Act.

(4.3) **Reports relating to persons who constitute a danger to the security of Canada — Where a senior immigration officer receives a report that a person is a member of an inadmissible class described in paragraph 19(1)(*k*), the senior immigration officer shall cause an inquiry to be held only if**

> **(a) in the case of a permanent resident, a certificate has been issued under subsection 40(1) in respect of the person; and**
>
> **(b) in the case of a person other than a permanent resident, a certificate has been signed and filed in respect of the person by the Minister and the Solicitor General of Canada in accordance with subsection 40.1(1) and the Federal Court has not quashed the certificate pursuant to paragraph 40.1(4)(*d*).**

(5) **Temporary exclusion by senior immigration officer — Where, pursuant to subsection (4.2), a senior immigration officer is required to cause an inquiry to be held with respect to a person who is arriving from the United States, the officer may, where an adjudicator is not reasonably available to preside at the inquiry, direct that person to return to the United States until such time as an adjudicator is available.**

(6) **Where person not to be detained, etc. — No person shall be detained or ordered detained by a senior immigration officer pursuant to paragraph (3)(*a*) and any person who has been detained pursuant to subsection 20(1) shall be released from detention by a senior immigration officer pursuant to paragraph (3)(*b*), unless the senior immigration officer is satisfied that there are reasonable grounds to believe that the person poses a danger to the public or would not appear for an examination or inquiry.**

(7) **Copy of report to be made available — Where a senior immigration officer causes an inquiry to be held concerning a person with respect to whom a report has been made pursuant to subsection 20(1)(*a*), the officer shall make a copy of the report available to that person.**

1992, c. 49, s. 13; 1995, c. 15, s. 3.

Case Law

Section 23(3)

R. v. Kwok (1986), 18 O.A.C. 38, 31 C.C.C. (3d) 196 (Ont. C.A.) — The appellant arrived at Pearson International Airport aboard a flight originating in London. He was examined by a senior immigration officer and detained pending an Immigration inquiry. The immigration officer who interviewed the appellant had doubts as to the *bona fides* of the appellant as a genuine visitor and wrote a report pursuant to section 20 of the Act for the benefit of the acting senior immigration officer. A person is not detained within the meaning of section 10 of the *Charter of Rights and Freedoms* until the restriction on his freedom has gone beyond that required for the processing of his application for entry. The fact that some questioning preceded the advice required by section 10 did not by itself offend the section. The obligation to inform a person of his rights under section 10(b) of the *Charter* is an obligation to inform, without delay, but that does not mean immediately. Further, the admission into evidence of a conversation preceding the section 10 warning did not bring the administration of justice into disrepute.

Monfort v. Canada (Minister of Employment & Immigration), [1980] 1 F.C. 478, 105 D.L.R. (3d) 463, 30 N.R. 174 (Fed. C.A.) — The applicant has no right to be advised of his right to counsel before a senior immigration officer has made a decision to convene an inquiry. Procedural fairness requires that a person seeking admission be advised of his right to counsel at the subsequent inquiry.

Section 23(4)

Daher v. Canada (Minister of Citizenship & Immigration) (1998), 46 Imm. L.R. (2d) 309, 153 F.T.R. 131 (Fed. T.D.) — The applicant sought a judicial review of, and an order setting aside, a decision of a senior immigration officer refusing to reconsider an exclusion order made against the applicant. Section 44(1) of the *Immigration Act* precludes a senior immigration officer from re-opening a decision to exclude a person from Canada. No authority to do so arises by virtue of section 7 of the *Charter* or the principles of fairness at common law.

Accordingly the senior immigration officer was held not to have erred in denying the applicant's request, and the application for judicial review was dismissed.

Chen v. Canada (Minister of Citizenship & Immigration) (1998), 44 Imm. L.R. (2d) 129, 151 F.T.R. 8 (Fed. T.D.) — The applicant sought to review an exclusion order made against her by a senior immigration officer. The applicant was detained by immigration officials for secondary examination because she lacked the necessary travel documents. At the time the applicant indicated that she had no problems in China and did not fear returning there. She failed to make any reference to wishing to make a refugee claim and signed a statutory declaration to the effect that she did not wish to make such a claim.

The Court was of the view that fairness did not require the applicant in these circumstances to be advised of the nature and effect of the secondary examination. Furthermore, the Court reaffirmed that fundamental justice as provided for under the *Charter of Rights* did not impart the right to counsel at a secondary examination interview such as the one conducted in this case.

Loss of Status

24. (1) Where person ceases to be permanent resident — A person ceases to be a permanent resident when

> **(a) that person leaves or remains outside Canada with the intention of abandoning Canada as that person's place of permanent residence; or**
>
> **(b) a removal order has been made against that person and the order is not quashed or its execution is not stayed pursuant to subsection 73(1).**

(2) Where residence deemed abandoned — Where a permanent resident is outside Canada for more than one hundred and eighty-three days in any one twelve month period, that person shall be deemed to have abandoned Canada as his place of permanent residence unless that person satisfies an immigration officer or an adjudicator, as the case may be, that he did not intend to abandon Canada as his place of permanent residence.

1995, c. 15, s. 4.

Case Law

Section 24(1)

Duckworth v. Canada (Minister of Citizenship & Immigration) (1997), 41 Imm. L.R. (2d) 26 (Imm. & Ref. Bd. (App. Div.)) — The appellant was born in the United States and along with her siblings, she was raised by her mother. During her childhood she was subjected to verbal, emotional, physical and sexual abuse. Her home life was chaotic. The appellant obtained landing in Canada in July 1972, and was the subject of continuing abuse in Canada. Eventually the appellant ran away and returned to the United States and lived with her maternal grandparents. She lived and travelled with them for a year and again was subjected to abuse until she ran away once more, this time successfully. She remained in California for nine years avoiding contact with all members of her family. She worked to support herself and also married. In 1983, she was again reunited with her family and her husband divorced her. Finally, in 1995, she made contact with a sister who had remained in Canada and travelled to Canada to visit her sister. The appellant's reunion with her sister was a warm one. Her sister had undergone extensive counselling and, as a result, had turned her life around. The appellant resolved to remain in Canada and eventually came to the attention of immigration officials who conducted an immigration inquiry and made an exclusion order against her.

The adjudicator who conducted the inquiry accepted the fact that the appellant was essentially forced to leave Canada in 1973 having barely obtained the age of majority. The adjudicator found, however, that when the circumstances which led to her original departure resolved themselves, the appellant should have taken the first available opportunity to return to Canada. Having not done that the adjudicator concluded the appellant had abandoned Canada as a place of permanent residence and thereby ceased to be a permanent resident.

The appellant testified that after she left Canada in 1973, she was complety unaware of the possibility that she could come into and remain in Canada as a permanent resident. She testified that she made no conscious choice to remain outside Canada, stating that she simply lived where she found herself, aware of her citizenship in the United States, and assuming she had no option but to live there. It was in that frame of mind that she came to Canada in 1995 characterizing herself as a visitor.

A permanent resident intention is central to the operation of section 24 of the *Immigration Act*. Common sense understanding provides that a person intends or forms an intention about something only after adverting to it and considering it in a particular context. The intention which is central to the operation of section 24 is an intention to abandoned Canada as a place of permanent residence. Evidence of settlement elsewhere might demonstrate that a person has formed the intention to abandon Canada. However, evidence that a person has an explanation for living elsewhere for a lengthy period of time, has maintained personal and professional connections with Canada, manifested a desire to return and actually returned here as quickly as circumstances allow might demonstrate the opposite. In this case, the Court found that the appellant could only advert to and consider and form the intention to abandon Canada once she became aware that Canada was a place of permanent residence for her. When the appellant became aware of this for the first time in 1996, she moved quickly to claim the benefits of having obtained landing here in 1972.

The Appeal Division found that the appellant did not at any time intend to abandon Canada as her place of permanent residence.

Canada (A.G.) v. Chanoine (1987), 4 Imm. L.R. (2d) 136, 15 F.T.R. 143 (Fed. T.D.) — The Attorney General applied for a writ of *certiorari* and a writ of *mandamus* setting aside the decision of an adjudicator not to hold an inquiry concerning the respondent and ordering the adjudicator to proceed with the inquiry.

The respondent was given the status of a permanent resident and subsequently left Canada for a period of 3 years. Just before returning to Canada, the respondent unsuccessfully applied for a visitor's visa. The respondent entered Canada and made no disclosures of any kind to the officer at the port-of-entry. A report was prepared indicating that the respondent was a person described in section 27(2)(b) and 27(2)(g) of the *Immigration Act*. The adjudicator declined jurisdiction, adopting the argument that the respondent should have been proceeded with under section 27(1), which applied to permanent residents.

This decision of the adjudicator was set aside and the adjudicator was directed to continue the inquiry.

A permanent resident has been defined as a person who has been granted landing and who has not ceased to be a permanent resident pursuant to section 24(1). Accordingly, the respondent automatically lost his permanent resident status, pursuant to section 24(1), by reason of his having been outside Canada for more than 183 days, unless he satisfied the adjudicator that he had not done so.

Editor's Note: This case should be read with Canada (Minister of Employment & Immigration) v. Selby, [1981] 1 F.C. 273 (Fed. C.A.).

Canada (Minister of Employment & Immigration) v. Han (1984), 6 Admin. L.R. 25, 52 N.R. 274 (Fed. C.A.) — A person granted permanent resident status who fails to comply with the condition attached to that status, namely that he marry within 90 days, is, nevertheless, a permanent resident notwithstanding his failure to comply with this condition.

Eyzaguirre v. Canada (Minister of Employment & Immigration) (December 11, 1980), Doc. T79-9268 (Imm. App. Bd.) — The appellant was compelled into a series of actions by her husband who made the ultimate decisions on everything which affected the lives of the family members. These actions resulted in the appellant abandoning Canada and returning to Chile to live permanently. The appellant then separated from her husband in Chile and, upon obtaining custody of her children and an exit permit from that country, immediately returned to Canada. The Court held that where there is a lengthy absence from Canada that absence must be reasonably explained and that the Board must be satisfied that the absence and delay in returning to Canada were not motivated by any intention to abandon Canada permanently. In this case the appellant was absent from Canada from 1974 until 1978. Having regard to the finding of the Board (that the husband had foisted his intentions upon his wife), the appellant's appeal was allowed and a deportation order against her quashed.

Daniels v. Canada (Minister of Employment & Immigration) (November 27, 1980), Doc. T80-925 (Imm. App. Bd.) — The Board determined on all the evidence that the appellant was not a permanent resident and, therefore, did not have a right of appeal pursuant to section 72 [s. 70] of the *Immigration Act* and, thus, dismissed his appeal. The appellant had returned to Scotland to live with his wife and family who had adamantly refused to live in Canada. The appellant was faced with a difficult choice between abandoning Canada as his place of permanent residence or abandoning his family. The Board held that the appellant exercised the difficult choice and established his permanent residence in Scotland. They sought to make a distinction between cases where the individual left Canada for a temporary purpose or a limited duration and returned as soon as the temporary condition was resolved, and cases where the person was not voluntarily residing outside of Canada but was forced to do so due to circumstances beyond the individual's control. In cases such as this one the decision to leave was voluntary and neither element of residence, neither bodily residence nor intent, was met, with the result that permanent resident status in Canada was lost.

Canada (Minister of Employment & Immigration) v. White (October 22, 1980), Doc. M80-1005 (Imm. App. Bd.) — The Board held that there were two elements of this section: the departure from and the remaining outside Canada, and the intent to abandon Canada as a place of permanent residence. In this case the Board agreed with the adjudicator's decision and dismissed the Minister's appeal. Michelle White left Canada because she was forced to follow her father, and, therefore, her absence from Canada was fully explained. Second, her absences and delays in returning to Canada were not motivated by any intention on her part to abandon permanent residence in Canada. The appellant had returned to Canada temporarily on more than one occasion while completing her studies in Jamaica.

The Board also approved of the notion that the word "residence" or "residing in Canada" should be given a liberal interpretation in order to further the stated objectives of the *Immigration Act*. Two fundamental elements essential to create a residence are bodily residence in a place and the intention of remaining in that place. It added that neither bodily presence alone, nor intention alone will suffice. Thus, residence can only be changed by the union of fact and intent.

Editor's Note: This case contains a very helpful review of many authorities dealing with the elements of section 24.

D'Souza v. Canada (Minister of Employment & Immigration) (October 8, 1980), Doc. 79-9012 (Imm. App. Bd.) — When the appellant was 11 years of age he was granted landing with his parents and sisters. His family remained in Canada for four months and then left. Three years later when the appellant was 14 years of age, he returned to Canada and announced his intention to remain in Canada as a permanent resident. The Board held that the appellant could not, at the age of 11, have formed the decision to abandon Canada as his place of permanent residence. The appellant, upon his return to Canada, was 14 years of age and was held to be capable at that time of forming an intent to return to Canada and establish his permanent residence in Canada. It was held that the appellant could not be deemed to have abandoned Canada as his place of permanent residence and, therefore, was not a person described under this section.

Canada (Minister of Employment & Immigration) v. Hass (February 6, 1980), Doc. 79-6130 (Imm. App. Bd.) — The Board ruled that the adjudicator was right in finding that the respondent was a permanent resident notwithstanding the fact that Hass was a citizen of West Germany who, at the age of 29, was admitted to Canada as a landed immigrant and remained in Canada for a period of only 3 months before leaving the country for 12 years to look after his sick mother. The Board upheld the adjudicator, notwithstanding that on his return to Canada in 1979, Hass's passport was stamped with a "visitor's visa" for 7 days.

Roberts, Re (1978), 92 D.L.R. (3d) 76 (Fed. T.D.) — The effect of these provisions is that where a person has been admitted to Canada as a permanent resident, but leaves Canada for extended periods of time in the course of his employment, he does not lose his status if he can show that he did not intend to lose it. The possession of a returning resident permit is *prima facie* proof thereof.

Adams v. Canada (Minister of Employment & Immigration) (October 3, 1978), Doc. 78-9455 (Imm. App. Bd.) — There were two fundamental elements essential to the creation of a residence:

1. bodily residence in that place; and

2. the intention of remaining in that place.

Neither bodily presence alone nor intention alone is sufficient to create a residence. Residence can only be changed by the union of fact and intent and in order to accomplish change of residence, there must be intent accompanied by the fact of abode.

Alexander v. Canada (Minister of Employment & Immigration) (July 18, 1978), Doc. 78-9138 (Imm. App. Bd.) — The appellant, a citizen of Egypt, was landed in Canada in 1968. His mother, in Egypt, became ill in 1972 and he left Canada to look after her, leaving some personal effects here at his brother's home. Due to the sickness of his mother and then his sister, the appellant remained in Egypt until 1978. When the appellant returned to Canada he was admitted as a visitor and on one occasion had his visitor's visa renewed.

The Board held that Alexander had not lost his permanent residence status. The Board further held that it had the power to determine whether a person was a permanent resident and, thus, to determine whether it had jurisdiction to hear the appellant's appeal. In this case, it found that it had jurisdiction to entertain the appeal pursuant to section 72(1) of the Act and that the appellant had, pursuant to section 4(1) of the Act, the right to come into Canada and, therefore, on his return to Canada did not have to be in possession of an immigrant visa.

Webber v. Canada (Minister of Employment & Immigration) (June 14, 1978), Doc. T78-9125 (Imm. App. Bd.) — The appellant was landed in Canada in 1971, he left in 1975 to return to South Africa to care for his children and to arrange for them to join him in Canada. Due to lack of funds he left with a one way ticket only. The Board found that the appellant family's circumstances and finances were such that he was obliged to remain in South Africa until 1978 and, therefore, ruled that the appellant had retained his permanent resident status in Canada.

Section 24(2)

Canada (A.G.) v. Chanoine (1987), 4 Imm. L.R. (2d) 136, 15 F.T.R. 143 (Fed. T.D.) — For digest, see section 24(1), *supra*.

Editor's Note: This case should be read with Canada (Minister of Employment & Immigration) v. Selby, [1981] 1 F.C. 273 (Fed. C.A.).

Papadopoulos v. Canada (Minister of Employment & Immigration) (June 7, 1983), Doc. T-83-9231 (Imm. App. Bd.) — The appellant became a landed immigrant in Canada at such a young age that he was unaware of this fact. The appellant left Canada shortly after becoming a landed immigrant and returned to Greece with his parents. Fourteen years later, when the appellant applied for and obtained a visitor's visa to Canada with permission to study, the appellant overstayed his visa and in the course of his inquiry produced evidence of his previously having been granted landed immigrant status. The appellant could *not* be said to have not intended to abandon Canada as his place of permanent residence when he left with his parents because the appellant at that time did not know that he had the status of a landed immigrant. Accordingly, the appellant's appeal was dismissed and a deportation order against him was held to be valid.

Khairulla v. Canada (Minister of Employment & Immigration) (April 24, 1979), Doc. 79-9123 (Imm. App. Bd.) — Due to the fact that the appellant had been out of Canada in excess of 183 days in a 12-month period, there was a rebuttable presumption that the appellant had abandoned his permanent residence in Canada. The Board held that the onus is on the appellant to satisfy, firstly, the immigration officer, then the Immigration Appeal Board, that he had not abandoned Canada as his place of permanent residence.

25. (1) Applications for returning resident permits — Where a permanent resident intends to leave Canada for any period of time or is outside Canada, that person may in prescribed manner make an application to an immigration officer for a returning resident permit.

(2) Proof of intention — Possession by a person of a valid returning resident permit issued to that person pursuant to the regulations is, in the absence of evidence to the contrary, proof that the person did not leave or remain outside Canada with the intention of abandoning Canada as his place of permanent residence.

Proposed Amendment — 25

25. (1) Application of section 24 — Section 24 applies only in respect of persons who left Canada before the day on which this section comes into force and who do not possess a valid returning resident permit described in section 25 of this Act as that section read immediately before that day.

(2) Exception — Possession by a person of a valid returning resident permit referred to in subsection (1) is, in the absence of evidence to the contrary, proof that the person did not leave or remain outside Canada with the intention of abandoning Canada as the person's place of permanent residence.

1992, c. 49, s. 14. [Not in force at date of publication.]

Case Law

Section 25(1)

El-Amin v. Canada (Minister of Citizenship & Immigration) (1997), 38 Imm. L.R. (2d) 45, 127 F.T.R. 283 (Fed. T.D.) — This was an application to review a decision of an immigration officer refusing to issue a returning resident permit (RRP) to the applicant.

The applicant, a citizen of Lebanon but born in Kuwait, arrived in Canada in 1990, and obtained permanent residency in 1992. The applicant subsequently travelled to Lebanon, married and upon returning to Canada took training in AutoCAD design. The applicant immediately obtained employment after this training but was laid off after 7 months. Subsequent to losing his job, the applicant was unable to find permanent employment in Canada. In 1993, the applicant travelled to Kuwait where he had previously worked and in January 1994, secured employment in that country. In May 1994, the applicant returned to Canada in order to accompany his wife whom he sponsored. At the end of May, both the applicant and his wife returned to Kuwait. The applicant returned to Canada in September 1994 leaving again in October. The applicant returned to Canada in November 1995 and upon his return was admitted as a permanent resident. The applicant's intention at this point was to keep his employment in Kuwait for 2 additional years, after which time he would come to Canada since he had no permanent status in Kuwait and was not permitted to own property there. On his last visit to Canada the applicant purchased a condominium.

The visa officer refused the applicant's application because the reason for his absence was to be employed by a non-Canadian company. The immigration officer did not exercise her discretion properly when determining whether to grant the RRP, because she required the applicant to meet the sole criterion set out in section 26(2)(c)(i). In doing so the visa officer fettered her discretion and accordingly her decision was set aside.

Section 25(2)

Roberts, Re (1978), 92 D.L.R. (3d) 76 (Fed. T.D.) — The effect of these provisions is that where a person has been admitted to Canada as a permanent resident but leaves Canada for extended periods of time in the course of his employment, he does not lose his status if he can show that he did not intend to lose it. The possession of a returning resident permit is *prima facie* proof thereof.

Proposed Addition — 25.1

25.1 Where person ceases to be permanent resident — A person ceases to be a permanent resident when

(a) subject to the regulations, the person ceases to ordinarily reside in Canada; or

(b) a removal order has been made against that person and the order is not quashed or the execution thereof is not stayed pursuant to subsection 73(1).

1992, c. 49, s. 14. [Not in force at date of publication.]

26. (1) Where person ceases to be visitor — A person ceases to be a visitor in Canada when

(a) that person fails to comply with any term or condition subject to which he is authorized to remain in Canada;

(b) without authorization, that person attends any university or college, takes any academic, professional or vocational training course or engages in employment in Canada;

(c) that person remains in Canada for a period of time greater than that for which he is authorized to remain in Canada;

(c.1) that person enters Canada as or to become a member of a crew of a vehicle and ceases to be a member of the crew or fails to become a member of the crew within the time specified in any terms and conditions subject to which the person was granted entry or, if no time is specified, within forty-eight hours after being granted entry; or

(d) a departure order or deportation order has been made against that person that is not quashed or the execution of which is not stayed pursuant to subsection 73(1).

(e) [Repealed 1992, c. 49, s. 15.]

(2) Idem — Unless otherwise specified in writing by an immigration officer or adjudicator, a visitor is not authorized to remain in Canada for a period in excess of three months from the day on which the visitor is granted entry, except where a longer period of time is prescribed by the regulations.

1992, c. 49, s. 15.

Case Law

Section 26(1)(b)

Miles v. Canada (Minister of Employment & Immigration) (February 13, 1984), Doc. A-1121-83 (Fed. C.A.) — The Court upheld the decision of an adjudicator finding that the applicant had engaged in employment without authorization and that thereafter the applicant was in breach of one of the conditions of her entry to Canada as a visitor. The Court upheld the adjudicator's finding that the applicant was, therefore, a person described in section 27(2)(e) of the *Immigration Act* and subject to an inquiry.

R. v. Malhotra (1980), [1981] 2 W.W.R. 563, 57 C.C.C. (2d) 539 (Man. Prov. Ct.) — Where there is some evidence that the accused is engaged in employment, section 26(1)(b) of the Act operates so as to strip the accused of his status as a visitor. Therefore, there is a *prima facie* case against the accused under section 95(k).

Removal After Admission

27. (1) Reports on permanent residents — An immigration officer or a peace officer shall forward a written report to the Deputy Minister setting out the details of any information in the possession of the immigration officer or peace officer indicating that a permanent resident is a person who

(a) is a member of an inadmissible class described in paragraph 19(1)(*c*.2), (*d*), (*e*), (*f*), (*g*), (*k*) or (*l*);

(a.1) outside Canada,

(i) has been convicted of an offence that, if committed in Canada, constitutes an offence that may be punishable under any Act of Parliament by a maximum term of imprisonment of ten years or more, or

(ii) has committed, in the opinion of the immigration officer or peace officer, based on a balance of probabilities, an act or omission that would constitute an offence under the laws of the place where the act or omission occurred and that, if committed in Canada, would constitute an offence that may be punishable under any Act of Parliament by a maximum term of imprisonment of ten years or more,

except a person who has satisfied the Minister that the person has been rehabilitated and that at least five years have elapsed since the expiration of any sentence imposed for the offence or since the commission of the act or omission, as the case may be;

(a.2) before being granted landing, was convicted in Canada of

(i) an indictable offence, or

(ii) an offence for which the offender may be prosecuted by indictment or for which the offender is punishable on summary conviction,

that may be punishable by way of indictment under any Act of Parliament by a maximum term of imprisonment of less than ten years;

(a.3) before being granted landing,

(i) was convicted outside Canada of an offence that, if committed in Canada, would constitute an offence referred to in paragraph (*a*.2), or

(ii) committed outside Canada, in the opinion of the immigration officer or peace officer, based on a balance of probabilities, an act or omission that constitutes an offence under the laws of the place where the act or omission occurred and that, if committed in Canada, would constitute an offence referred to in paragraph (*a*.2),

except a person who has satisfied the Minister that the person has been rehabilitated and that at least five years have elapsed since the expiration of any sentence imposed for the offence or since the commission of the act or omission, as the case may be;

(b) if that person was granted landing subject to terms and conditions, has knowingly contravened any of those terms or conditions;

(c) [Repealed 1992, c. 49, s. 16.]

(d) has been convicted of an offence under any Act of Parliament, other than an offence designated as a contravention under the Contraventions Act, for which a term of imprisonment of more than six months has been, or five years or more may be, imposed;

(e) was granted landing by reason of possession of a false or improperly obtained passport, visa or other document pertaining to his admission or by reason of any fraudulent or improper means or misrepresentation of any material fact, whether exercised or made by himself or by any other person;

(f) wilfully fails to support himself or any dependant member of his family in Canada;

(g) is a member of the inadmissible class described in paragraph 19(1)(*j*) who was granted landing subsequent to the coming into force of that paragraph; or

(h) became a member of the inadmissible class described in paragraph 19(1)(*j*) subsequent to the coming into force of that paragraph.

(2) **Reports on visitors and other persons — An immigration officer or a peace officer shall, unless the person has been arrested pursuant to subsection 103(2), forward a written report to the Deputy Minister setting out the details of any information in the possession of the immigration officer or peace officer indicating that a person in Canada, other than a Canadian citizen or permanent resident, is a person who**

(a) is a member of an inadmissible class, other than an inadmissible class described in paragraph 19(1)(*h*) or 19(2)(*c*);

(b) has engaged or continued in employment in Canada contrary to this Act or the regulations;

(c) [Repealed 1992, c. 49, s. 16.]

(d) has been convicted of

(i) an offence under the *Criminal Code*,

(ii) an indictable offence under any Act of Parliament other than the *Criminal Code* or this Act, or

(iii) an offence, other than an offence designated as a contravention under the *Contraventions Act*, for which the offender may be prosecuted by indictment or for which the offender is punishable on summary conviction under any Act of Parliament other than the *Criminal Code* or this Act;

(e) entered Canada as a visitor and remains in Canada after that person has ceased to be a visitor;

(f) came into Canada at any place other than a port of entry and failed to report forthwith to an immigration officer or eluded examination or inquiry under this Act or escaped from lawful custody or detention under this Act;

(g) came into Canada or remains in Canada with a false or improperly obtained passport, visa or other document pertaining to that person's admission or by reason of any fraudulent or improper means or misrepresentation of any material fact, whether exercised or made by himself or by any other person;

(h) came into Canada contrary to section 55;

(i) ceased to be a Canadian citizen pursuant to subsection 10(1) of the *Citizenship Act* in the circumstances described in subsection 10(2) of that Act;

(j) [Repealed 1992, c. 49, s. 16.]

(k) was authorized pursuant to paragraph 14(2)(*b*), 23(1)(*b*) or 32(3)(*b*) to come into Canada and failed to be present for further examination within such time and at such place as was directed; or

(l) wilfully fails to support any dependant member of that person's family in Canada.

(2.01) For greater certainty — For greater certainty.

(a) a person described in paragraph (1)(*a*) includes a person who, if applying for landing, would not or might not be granted landing by reason of being a member of an inadmissible class referred to in that paragraph;

(b) a person described in paragraph (2)(*a*) includes a person who, if applying for entry, would not or might not be granted entry by reason of being a member of an inadmissible class, other than an inadmissible class described in paragraph 19(1)(*h*) or 19(2)(*c*); and

(c) for the purposes of this Act, a person is deemed to be a member of the inadmissible class by reason of which the person is described in paragraph (1)(*a*) or (2)(*a*), as the case may be.

(2.1) New authorization — Subject to any order or direction of the Minister, the Deputy Minister may, on receiving a report pursuant to subsection (2) indicating that a person who was granted entry as a visitor has ceased to be a visitor by reason of any of paragraphs 26(1)(*a*) to (*c*) and remains in Canada, authorize the person to remain in Canada as a visitor, on such terms and conditions, and for such period, as the Deputy Minister considers appropriate.

(3) Referral of report — Subject to subsection (3.1) and any order or direction of the Minister, the Deputy Minister, on receiving a report pursuant to subsection (1) or (2), shall, if the Deputy Minister considers it appropriate to do so in the circumstances, forward a copy of that report to a senior immigration officer and may

(a) direct that a determination be made with respect to any or all of the allegations mentioned in the report where the person is a person described in

(i) paragraph (2)(*a*) by reason of paragraph 19(2)(*d*),

(ii) paragraph (2)(*e*) by reason of paragraph 26(1)(*c*), or

(iii) paragraph (2)(*h*) or (*k*); or

(b) in any case, direct that an inquiry be held.

(3.1) Reports relating to persons who constitute a danger to the security of Canada — Where the Deputy Minister receives a report that a person is a person described in paragraph (1)(*a*) or (2)(*a*) by reason of being a member of an inadmissible class described in paragraph 19(1)(*k*), the Deputy Minister shall forward a copy of the report and the direction only if

(a) in the case of a permanent resident, a certificate has been issued under subsection 40(1) in respect of the person; and

(b) in the case of a person other than a permanent resident, a certificate has been signed and filed in respect of the person by the Minister and the Solicitor General of Canada in accordance with subsection 40.1(1) and the Federal Court has not quashed the certificate pursuant to paragraph 40.1(4)(*d*).

(4) Departure order — Subject to section 28, where a senior immigration officer receives a report and a direction made pursuant to paragraph (3)(*a*) in respect of a person, or where a person has been arrested pursuant to subsection 103(2), the senior immigration officer shall

(a) allow the person to remain in Canada if it would not be contrary to this Act or the regulations to allow the person to remain in Canada; or

(b) make a departure order against the person if the senior immigration officer is satisfied that the person is a person described in

(i) paragraph (2)(*a*) by reason of paragraph 19(2)(*d*),

(ii) paragraph (2)(*e*) by reason of paragraph 26(1)(*c*), or

(iii) paragraph (2)(*h*) or (*k*).

(5) Duty to provide information — Every person referred to in subsection (4) shall truthfully provide such information as may be required by the senior immigration officer for the purpose of establishing whether the person is to be allowed to remain in Canada.

(6) Inquiry — A senior immigration officer shall cause an inquiry to be held concerning a person as soon as is reasonably practicable where the senior immigration officer receives a direction made pursuant to paragraph (3)(*b*).

Transitional Provision

[Note: S.C. 1995, c. 15, s. 27(1) provides: where a senior immigration officer has caused an inquiry to be held under subsection 27(6) of the Immigration Act as that provision read on July 9, 1995 with respect to a person described in paragraph 27(4)(b) and the adjudicator has not commenced the hearing on or before July 10, 1995, the case shall be referred to a senior immigration officer who shall take the appropriate action under subsection 27(4) of the Immigration Act.]

R.S.C. 1985, c. 30 (3rd Supp.), s. 4; 1992, c. 47, s. 78; 1992, c. 49, ss. 16, 123; 1995, c. 15, s. 5.

Case Law

Section 27(1)(a.1)

Mohammad v. Canada (Minister of Employment & Immigration), [1989] 2 F.C. 363, 55 D.L.R. (4th) 321, 21 F.T.R. 240n (Fed. C.A.) — It is not a pre-condition to the operation of section 19(1)(c) that the Governor in Council shall have considered the question of rehabilitation and be dissatisfied that the person concerned has brought himself within the exception. The report mandated by section 27(1) requires the authorizing immigration officer to possess information that the person concerned has been convicted of the kind of criminal act specified in section 19(1)(c) and to have knowledge that the person concerned has not satisfied the Governor in Council as to his rehabilitation.

The policy directives, whether made pursuant to regulatory authority or general administrative capacity, are no more than directions and are unenforceable by members of the public. The procedural formalities which are required in respect of an immigration officer when initiating a section 27(1) report are minimal. First, because this is a purely administrative decision, and second, because the officer when issuing the section 27(1) report is merely the initiator of the inquiry process. An immigration officer before issuing a section 27(1) report is, therefore, not required to give the person concerned an opportunity to answer allegations contained in that report. On the facts, the immigration officer who issued the section 27(1) report had sufficient knowledge and information upon which to base the report; further, the applicant was given full particulars of the allegations against him.

The Court of Appeal adopted the motion's judge's findings, that there was nothing irregular in the fact that the high profile nature of the case, placed pressure on the respondent's representatives to proceed with dispatch.

The requirement of institutional independence is included in the rules of natural justice as well as enshrined in the *Charter*. The test for institutional independence is whether a reasonable and right-minded individual, having informed himself of the scheme whereby adjudicators are appointed under the *Immigration Act* and of the basis upon which they perform their duties, would be likely to conclude that an adjudicator appointed under and acting pursuant to that scheme, more likely than not, would decide fairly the inquiries under the *Immigration Act* over which he presided. While the case-presenting officers and adjudicators are both civil servants under the direction of the same Minister, they operate in separate and distinct divisions of the Commission. Case-presenting officers have no supervisory role, *vis-à-vis* adjudicators. They do not report to a common superior and it is only at the apex of the organization chart that their respective hierarchies merge. As far as legal direction is concerned, adjudicators can and do seek advice on difficult legal issues from lawyers on the staff of the Adjudication Directorate, who have no connection or association with the Enforcement Branch. On the subject of monitoring, there is evidence that monitoring practice focuses primarily on how hearings are conducted; with respect to security of tenure, adjudicators, like other civil servants, have the protection afforded pursuant to section 31 of the *Public Service Employment Act*. Additionally, they have the protection of a three stage grievance procedure. The fact that adjudicators are members of the same bargaining unit as case-presenting officers is a neutral circumstance which does not give rise to any apprehension one way or the other. The practice of appointing adjudicators to other positions on an acting basis does not give rise to reasonable apprehension of a lack of independence. The Court relied on the uncontradicted evidence of an adjudicator to the effect that the decisions made by him were made independently and without direction from anyone else.

Finally, it was pointed out that the assignment of cases is rationally based; complex cases are usually assigned to the more experienced adjudicators. There was nothing to suggest that particular cases were assigned to particular adjudicators, let alone any evidence to suggest that the adjudicator chosen to conduct this inquiry was chosen on any basis other than the rational basis referred to previously. The Court concluded for these reasons that reasonable persons, reasonably informed, would view adjudicators appointed under the *Immigration Act* as being independent, keeping in mind the fact that they are for the most part laypersons in the hierarchy of *quasi*-judicial tribunals; and bearing in mind that their decisions are subject to judicial review by the Court; and that they have all taken an oath of office to "faithfully and honestly fulfill their duties" evolving upon them. Accordingly, the appellant's appeal was dismissed.

Editor's Note: Section 19(1)(c) has been amended, but the remarks dealing with rehabilitation may be important under subsections 27(1)(a.1) and (a.3).

Singleton v. Canada (Minister of Employment & Immigration) (November 7, 1983), Doc. A-813-83 (Fed. T.D.) — The Court noted that a certificate of the applicant's conviction would be the best evidence of such conviction and that the lack of such a certificate leaves something to be desired in the particularity of the evidence. Where, however, the evidence as a whole is sufficient to support the finding of the adjudicator that the applicant was a person described in section 27(2)(d) of the *Immigration Act*, an application to set aside such decision will fail.

Canada (Minister of Employment & Immigration) v. Fenner (December 11, 1981), Doc. V81-6126 (Imm. App. Bd.) — The respondent, Fenner, was convicted in the State of Washington following a guilty plea to the offence of "negligent homicide by means of a motor vehicle". This offence is equivalent to that set out under section 203 of the *Criminal Code.* The respondent, Fenner, was given a deferred sentence which meant that at the end of a period of probation he could request the opportunity to withdraw his guilty plea and have the charge dismissed. This, in fact, occurred in this case. The Board decided that this procedure, unknown to Canadian law, was not equivalent to an absolute or conditional discharge and that the conviction in the first instance remained part of Fenner's record and, therefore, he fell within the provisions of section 19(1)(c). The Board allowed the Minister's appeal and directed the deportation of Mr. Fenner.

Section 27(1)(a.2)

Jares v. Canada (Minister of Employment & Immigration) (June 1, 1981), Doc.79-6098 (Imm. App. Bd.) — The warrant of committal which was filed at the inquiry proceedings was on a preprinted form and headed "*Summary Convictions Act — Criminal Code.*" The charge for which the appellant had been convicted was trafficking in narcotics, which, pursuant to the *Narcotic Control Act*, R.S.C. 1970, c. N-1, was an indictable offence carrying life imprisonment as a maximum penalty. The Board stated that the issue was whether the substance of the charges or the heading on the form should govern. It held that the adjudicator was correct in determining that although the warrant of committal upon conviction did not specifically state that the conviction was by way of indictment, that the adjudicator was entitled to consider the provisions of the *Narcotic Control Act* and come to the conclusion that the appellant was convicted of an indictable offence for which a penalty of 5 years or more may be imposed.

R. v. Wardley (1978), 43 C.C.C. (2d) 345 (Ont. C.A.) — Where an accused charged with the indictable offence of possession of marijuana for the purpose of trafficking pleads guilty to the included offence of possession of marijuana, the plea constitutes a plea of guilty to the indictable offence of possession. The maximum sentence for the conviction of the indictable offence of simple possession governs with respect to penalty.

McMahon, Re, [1978] 2 F.C. 624, 40 C.C.C. (2d) 250, 21 N.R. 170 (Fed. C.A.) — A plea of guilty accepted by a court constitutes a conviction where the person has absconded prior to sentencing.

Kalicharan v. Canada (Minister of Manpower & Immigration), [1976] 2 F.C. 123, 67 D.L.R. (3d) 555 (Fed. T.D.) — The granting of a conditional discharge by the Court of Appeal means that a conviction is deemed never to have been registered. Therefore, the basis for making a deportation under this subsection is deemed not to have existed at all. Accordingly, prohibition will be granted against the execution of a deportation order.

Douglas v. Canada (Minister of Manpower & Immigration), [1972] F.C. 1050 (Fed. C.A.) — Where the Minister is proceeding in respect of a conviction for an offence that is under appeal, prohibition will not issue to stop the inquiry. The proper procedure is to put the accused before the officer conducting the inquiry and, if necessary, proceed by way of appeal from his decision.

Section 27(1)(a.3)

Mohammad v. Canada (Minister of Employment & Immigration), [1989] 2 F.C. 363, 55 D.L.R. (4th) 321, 21 F.T.R. 240n (Fed. C.A.) — For digest, see section 27(1)(a.1), (a.2), *supra*.

Singleton v. Canada (Minister of Employment & Immigration) (November 7, 1983), Doc. A-813-83 (Fed. T.D.) — For digest, see section 27, subheading *Subsection (1), Paragraph (a.1), supra.*

Canada (Minister of Employment & Immigration) v. Fenner (December 11, 1981), Doc. V81-6126 (Imm. App. Bd.) — For digest, see section 27, subheading *Subsection (1), Paragraph (a.1), supra.*

Section 27(1)(b)

Gabriel v. Canada (Minister of Employment & Immigration) (1984), 60 N.R. 108 (Fed. C.A.) — The appellant was landed on condition that she marry within 90 days. This condition could not be obeyed as a result of circumstances beyond the appellant's control. Even though a condition is impossible to fulfil, so long as the person concerned knew of that condition and continued to remain in Canada in breach of that condition, such a person has knowingly contravened a condition attached to the grant of landing. Even if the word "contravene" requires a positive act, the omission to do something which a person is required to do, is the commission of a positive act. It is an act of failure to do something required to be done and, accordingly, satisfies the definition of the term "contravenes".

Buguing v. Canada (Minister of Employment & Immigration) (January 11, 1982), Doc. T81-9601 (Imm. App. Bd.) — The Board in this case declined to accept the common law relationship as compliance with a term and condition of the granting of landed immigrant status that required the landed immigrant to marry within 90 days of her arrival in Canada.

Dela Cruz v. Canada (Minister of Employment & Immigration) (August 12, 1980), Doc. T-79-9373 (Imm. App. Bd.) — Section 27(1)(b) requires that the permanent resident have simply knowledge of the contravention of the terms and conditions imposed upon him as a condition of landing. It does not require *mens rea* or wilful non-compliance with the conditions by the permanent resident.

Section 27(1)(d)

Galati v. Canada (Minister of Citizenship & Immigration) (1996), 35 Imm. L.R. (2d) 1, 120 F.T.R. 41 (Fed. T.D.) — The applicant acquired domicile in Canada on December 18, 1961. He committed 25 criminal offences between 1961 and April 9, 1978 when a new *Immigration Act* came into force and since that time accumulated 37 additional convictions. Based on the convictions subsequent to April 9, 1978, a report was made against the applicant, an inquiry held and a deportation order issued. The applicant appealed the deportation ordered to the Board which appeal was denied and it was of that decision which the applicant sought judicial review. The *Immigration Act* 1952, contained the concept of domicile. The applicant argued, as a domicile holder under the former act, he could not be deported for the crimes of which he was convicted.

The concept of domicile under the former Act conveyed to its holder those rights which had accrued under the former Act while it was in force. Because such rights had accrued the applicant could claim them despite the repeal of the statute under which they arose. However, once the legislation ceased to attach rights to a given status as occurred in 1978 with respect to domicile holders under the former Act, the status took on decreasing significance. Under the new Act the applicant was no longer shielded from deportation with respect to specified criminal acts committed after its enactment.

Accordingly, the applicant could be ordered deported on the basis of the criminal convictions which occurred after the *Immigration Act* 1978 came into effect.

Nguyen v. Canada (Minister of Employment & Immigration) (1993), 18 Imm. L.R. (2d) 165, 100 D.L.R. (4th) 151, 151 N.R. 69, 14 C.R.R. (2d) 146 (Fed. C.A.) — The applicant, who was a permanent resident, was seeking to quash a deportation order. The applicant had been found described in subparagraphs 27(1)(d)(i) and 27(1)(d)(ii). Further, when the applicant attempted to obtain refugee status, a representative of the Minister tendered into evidence a certificate signed by the Minister stating that the applicant constituted a danger to the public of Canada with the result that, under the legislation then in effect, the applicant was not able to claim refugee status. Legislation which purports to define conditions for eligibility to claim refugee status may violate the Charter only if those conditions have the effect of subjecting a group of claimants to discriminatory treatment within the meaning of section 15. To deny dangerous criminals the right, generally conceded to immigrants who flee persecution, is not a form of illegitimate discrimination.

The Minister does not need to be compelled to follow formal guidelines stating the factors that should be taken into account in forming his opinion. The Minister's opinion in respect of public danger is as reliable as that of a court.

Counsel challenged the scheme set up by the Minister for the issuance of a certificate and complained that it did not provide for an oral hearing nor did it contain any provision for judicial review. Those submissions did not have to be addressed. The Court was sitting in judicial review of the decision of a tribunal which did not have jurisdiction to examine whether the public danger certificate has been issued in accordance with the rules of natural justice. The mandate of the tribunal did not entitle it to look behind the certificate, fully valid on its face. The decision to issue a certificate is subject to judicial review by the Court only and not by immigration officers. The Court observed that the procedure set up and followed, in this case, accorded the applicant a full opportunity to make his case.

The scheme of the Act, established by subparagraph 27(1)(d)(i), subsection 32(2) and subparagraph 46.01(1)(e)(ii), is constitutionally sound and the decisions made against the applicant did not infringe his rights guaranteed under the Charter.

Chiarelli v. Canada (Minister of Employment & Immigration), 16 Imm. L.R. (2d) 1, [1992] 1 S.C.R. 711 (S.C.C.) — This appeal calls into question the constitutionality of the statutory scheme pursuant to which a permanent resident can be deported from Canada if he is found to have been convicted of an offence for which a term of imprisonment of 5 years or more may be imposed. A further attack was brought against the interaction of that scheme with the investigations conducted by the Security Intelligence Review Committee (SIRC) into the activities of persons reasonably believed to be involved in certain types of criminal or subversive activity.

The respondent was convicted of a number of criminal offences and in January 1986 a report was written pursuant to section 27 of the *Immigration Act* identifying the respondent as a permanent resident described in section 27(1)(d)(ii). As a result of this report an inquiry was directed pursuant to section 27(3). A deportation order was made against the respondent pursuant to section 32(2). The respondent appealed to the Immigration Appeal Board. That appeal was adjourned after the Solicitor General and the Minister of Employment and Immigration made a joint report to SIRC. The report indicated that in the opinion of the Ministers the respondent was a person described in section 19(1)(d)(ii). The SIRC conducted the required investigation and reported to the Governor in Council pursuant to section 81(7). The Governor in Council adopted the conclusion of SIRC and directed the appellant Minister to issue a certificate under section 82(1) with respect to the respondent's appeal. This certificate was issued, with the result that the respondent could not assert compassionate grounds as a reason for allowing the appeal.

SIRC conducted its investigation and hearing first by reading a document entitled "Statement of Circumstances" as well as two summaries of information. The first day's hearing was held *in camera* and the respondent was excluded from the hearing and provided only with a summary of the evidence. The respondent was permitted to attend the second day of the hearing. The respondent declined, objected to the fairness and constitutionality of the proceeding before the SIRC, submitted no evidence at the hearing, and chose not to cross-examine two RCMP witnesses who had testified on the first day. Counsel did make submissions to the SIRC.

Section 27(1) requires an immigration officer in possession of information that a permanent resident falls into one of its enumerated classes to forward a report to the Deputy Minister. An inquiry is then held by an adjudicator in cases where the Deputy Minister considers one is warranted. Section 32(2) provides that where an adjudicator decides that a person who is the subject of an inquiry does fall within one of the classes in section 27(1), the adjudicator shall, except in the case of a Convention refugee, make a deportation order. All persons who fall within section 27(1)(d)(ii) have deliberately violated an essential condition under which they were permitted to remain in Canada. In such a situation there is no breach of fundamental justice in giving practical effect to the termination of their right to remain in Canada. In the case of a permanent resident deportation is the only way in which to accomplish this. There is nothing inherently unjust about a mandatory order. The fact of the deliberate violation of the condition imposed by sections 27(1)(d)(ii) is sufficient to justify a deportation order. Accordingly, sections 27(1)(d)(ii) and 32(2) are not contrary to section 7 of the *Charter of Rights*.

The deportation authorized by sections 27(1)(d)(ii) and 32(2) is not cruel and unusual punishment as described in section 12 of the *Charter of Rights*.

Section 6 of the *Charter* specifically provides for differential treatment of citizens and permanent residents. Accordingly, sections 27(1)(d)(ii) and 32(2) do not violate section 15 of the *Charter*. Permanent residents are given mobility rights in section 6(2). Only citizens are accorded the right to enter, remain in and leave Canada in section 6(1). There is no discrimination contrary to section 15 in a deportation scheme that applies to permanent residents but not citizens.

The effect of the security certificate in this case is to direct the Immigration Appeal Board to dismiss any appeal based on the existence of compassionate or humanitarian considerations. The permanent resident's right of appeal after a certificate has been issued is restricted to questions of law, fact or mixed law and fact.

The *Immigration Act*, S.C. 1910, c. 27, did not provide any specific grounds of appeal. A person ordered deported could only resort to the Minister, who had authority to overturn a deportation order on unspecified grounds. The *Immigration Act*, R.S.C. 1952, c. 325, provided for an immigration appeal board, however, appeals against deportation orders remained under the control of the Minister. The Board heard only those appeals directed to it by the Minister, and the Minister retained the power to confirm or quash the Appeal Board's decision or substitute his decision as he deemed just and proper. The 1966 *White Paper on Immigration* recommended that a reconstituted Immigration Appeal Board have authority to deal conclusively with appeals against deportation orders except in security cases. The *Immigration Appeal Board Act*, 1967 for the first time conferred upon the Board the power to stay or quash a deportation order made against a permanent resident on the basis of all the circumstances of the case. This new power was subject to the discretion of the Minister and the Solicitor General, who could certify their opinion based on security or criminal intelligence reports that it would be contrary to the national interest to permit such relief. This reserves to the Crown the right similar to the prerogative right which existed at common law, to determine that the continued presence in Canada of an alien, subject to a deportation order, was not conducive to the public good. The *Immigration Appeal Board Act* was repealed by the *Immigration Act*, 1976. However, this new Act did not change the nature of the decision that could be made by the Board having regard to all the circumstances of the case. That decision remained as it had been under the 1967 Act, an exercise of discretion based on compassionate grounds. Section 83 of the *Immigration Act*, 1976 limited the availability of relief based on all the circumstances of the case. Such an appeal had to be dismissed if the Minister and Solicitor General certified their opinion that it would be contrary to the national interest to permit such an appeal. In 1984 the SIRC was established by the *Canadian Security Intelligence Service Act*, S.C. 1984, c. 21. The Review Committee was assigned various functions under several Acts, including the *Immigration Act*, 1976. Sections 83 and 82.1 of the *Immigration Act*, 1976 were repealed and amended versions were substituted. The decision as to whether to direct the issuance of a security certificate, however, remained with the Governor in Council. Thus, there has never been a universally available right of appeal from a deportation order on humanitarian or compassionate grounds or "having regard to all the circumstances of the case." Such an appeal has historically been a purely discretionary matter. The right of appeal required to comply with the principles of fundamental justice is a true appeal which enables the decision of first instance to be questioned on factual and legal grounds. The absence of an appeal on wider grounds does not violate section 7.

The procedure followed by the Security Intelligence Review Committee in this case recognized competing individual and state interests and attempted to find a reasonable balance between them. It was not necessary that the respondent be given details of the criminal intelligence investigation techniques or police sources used to acquire the information upon which the two Ministers relied in issuing the certificate. The respondent was given an opportunity to respond by calling his own witnesses or by requesting that he be allowed to cross-examine the RCMP officers who testified *in camera*. Such a procedure was sufficient to meet the requirements of the principles of fundamental justice.

Canepa v. Canada (Minister of Employment & Immigration), [1992] 3 F.C. 270, 93 D.L.R. (4th) 589, 10 C.R.R. (2d) 348 (Fed. C.A.) — The appellant was born in Italy in 1962 and came to Canada as a permanent resident with his family at the age of 5. He became a drug addict and to support his addiction turned to a life of crime. Between 1978 and 1987 he was convicted of 37 offences. Eventually a report was issued pursuant to section 27(1)(d) and the adjudicator at the ensuing inquiry made a deportation order. This deportation order is in effect reversible on equitable grounds pursuant to section 70. When the scheme of the Act is looked at in total, on appeal, the tribunal must take into account all of the circumstances of the case which include the person in his total context and the good of society as well as that of the individual.

Section 70(1)(b) requires that every extenuating circumstance that can be adduced in favour of the deportee be considered by the Board on appeal.

This treatment of the appellant as mandated by sections 27 and 70 is not cruel and unusual treatment so as to contravene section 12 of the *Charter.*

Hurd v. Canada (Minister of Employment & Immigration) (1988), 90 N.R. 31 (Fed. C.A.) — The appellant was a permanent resident of Canada who was granted landing in November 1968, when he was 19 years of age. The appellant had a number of criminal convictions between 1971 and 1983 and, ultimately, an inquiry was held pursuant to a report issued under section 27(1)(d)(i). The appellant argued that section 11(h) of the Charter was infringed because deportation was, in effect, a double punishment, being imposed upon him for the crimes that he had committed and for which he had been sentenced. It was held that a deportation proceeding is not within section 11(h) of the Charter. The necessary redressing of the wrong done to society by criminal conduct and the goal of deterrence of others had been accomplished through the criminal convictions. The purpose of deportation is not a larger social purpose; it is merely to remove from Canada an undesirable person. Deportation to a deportee's country of birth is not a true penal consequence. It is analogous to the loss of a licence or to dismissal from a police force or to the forfeiture of a right to practise a profession. Accordingly, the appellant's appeal was dismissed.

Jares v. Canada (Minister of Employment & Immigration) (June 1, 1981), Doc. 79-6098 (Imm. App. Bd.) — For digest, see section 27(1)(a.2), *supra.*

Anderson v. Canada (Minister of Employment & Immigration) (1980), [1981] 2 F.C. 30, 113 D.L.R. (3d) 243, 36 N.R. 423 (Fed. C.A.) — An immigration officer forwarded a written report to the Deputy Minister setting out information which suggested that the applicant was a person described in section 19(1)(c) of the *Immigration Act.* The adjudicator issued a departure notice after an inquiry in which he determined on the evidence that the applicant was not a person described in section 19(1)(c) of the *Immigration Act*, but was a person described in section 19(2)(a) of the Act. The departure notice was set aside. The Court held that the adjudicator could only make the appropriate order where he found the actual grounds set out in the report to be established.

McMahon, Re, [1978] 2 F.C. 624, 40 C.C.C. (2d) 250, 21 N.R. 170 (Fed. C.A.) — For digest, see section 27(1)(a.2), *supra.*

R. v. Wardley (1978), 43 C.C.C. (2d) 345 (Ont. C.A.) — For digest, see section 27(1)(a.2), *supra.*

Kalicharan v. Canada (Minister of Manpower & Immigration), [1976] 2 F.C. 123, 67 D.L.R. (3d) 555 (Fed. T.D.) — For digest, see section 27(1)(a.2), *supra.*

Douglas v. Canada (Minister of Manpower & Immigration), [1972] F.C. 1050 (Fed. C.A.) — For digest, see section 27, subheading *Subsection (1), Paragraph (a.2), supra.*

Section 27(1)(e)

Mohammed v. Canada (Minister of Citizenship & Immigration), [1997] 3 F.C. 299, 130 F.T.R. 294 (Fed. T.D.) — This was an application to review the decision of the Appeal Division of the IRB which had affirmed an earlier decision of a judicator to the effect that the applicant had gained entry to Canada by reason of fraudulent or improper means or misrepresentation of a material fact. The applicant, a citizen of Bangladesh, applied with his family for permanent residence in Canada. The applicant was put forward as a dependant of his father. The applicant arrived in Canada with his parents and 5 siblings in 1992. Upon arrival in Canada the applicant and his family met with immigration officials following which they were granted permanent residence. In November 1992, shortly before leaving for Canada the applicant was married, however, upon arriving in Canada the applicant had not indicated on his immigration visa and his landing document did not indicate that he had married, but rather his marital status was reported as being single. Further, upon his arrival the applicant did not notify the immigration officer that he had married. When immigration officials subsequently learned of the applicant's true marital status an inquiry was held and the applicant was ordered deported. This decision was appealed to the Appeal Division of the IRB unsuccessfully.

Section 27(1)(e) contemplates 3 instances in which an immigration officer would be required to forward a written report to the deputy minister. These are where a permanent resident has been granted landing: 1) by reason of possession of a false or improperly obtained passport, visa or other document pertaining to his admission; 2) by reason of any fraudulent or improper means; or 3) by reason of misrepresentation of a material fact whether exercised or made by himself or any other person. The phrase "whether exercised or made by himself or any other person" clearly refers to both "means" and "misrepresentation". The words "fraudulent and improper" should not be read so as to modify both "means" and "representation".

The Court rejected the argument that in order for there to be "misrepresentation" there must be an act of concealment. One can misrepresent as easily and effectively by silence as one can by actively stating a lie. The Court rejected the argument that a misrepresentation must be knowingly or wilfully made. The absence of such language in the section gives rise to the implication that such a requirement deliberately excluded by parliament. The information which the applicant failed to disclose, namely the change in his marital status, was clearly material information in that it potentially would have had a direct or inducing influence on whether or not he was granted landing in Canada. The applicant's situation was to be distinguished from that in which the information not disclosed was information of which the applicant was truly subjectively unaware.

Canada (Minister of Citizenship & Immigration) v. Nemsila (1996), 35 Imm. L.R. (2d) 56, [1997] 1 F.C. 260, 118 F.T.R. 310 (Fed. T.D.); affirmed (1997), 38 Imm. L.R. (2d) 242, 3 Admin. L.R. (3d) 83, 214 N.R. 383 (Fed. C.A.) — This was an application by the minister to review a decision of an adjudicator which provided that the applicant could not be deported pursuant to paragraph 27(2)(g) and 27(1)(e) of the *Immigration Act*. The adjudicator found that the respondent had acquired Canadian domicile under the *Immigration Act* 1952, and therefore could not be ordered deported.

The adjudicator found that the respondent had been lawfully admitted to and landed in Canada in 1950, due to the fact that he had obtained a visa and presented himself for examination at a port-of-entry and the ship's manifest had been stamped with the phrase "landed immigrant" across his name. The adjudicator further found that the respondent had made misrepresentations during interviews with visa control and immigration officers and had not fully disclosed information which would have led to the refusal of his application.

Canadian domicile under the 1952 *Immigration Act* was acquired by a person having his place of domicile for at least 5 years in Canada after having been landed in Canada. For the purposes of the 1952 Act, a person was landed in Canada when they had been lawfully admitted into Canada by an officer under that Act. The Court held that the term lawful admission in the 1952 Act required something more than having a port-of-entry inspector rubber stamp the ship's manifest or an individual's passport with the words "landed immigrant". Lawful admission requires compliance with all of the requirements of the Act in force at the time the immigrant entered Canada.

Due to the fact that the respondents entry into Canada in 1950 was based upon deception and misrepresentation, he was not lawfully admitted to Canada and therefore could not have gained "landing" within the meaning of that Act. Due to the fact the respondent was never landed he was held to never have acquired Canadian domicile.

Accordingly, the adjudicator's decision was set aside.

Medel v. Canada (Minister of Employment & Immigration), 10 Imm. L.R. (2d) 274, [1990] 2 F.C. 345, 113 N.R. 1 (Fed. C.A.) — The appellant entered Canada as a visitor and, while in Canada, met and married a Canadian citizen. The appellant returned to Honduras and her husband sponsored her as his wife. After a visa was issued to the appellant, the husband then withdrew his sponsorship and began living with another woman. The Canadian Embassy in Guatemala attempted to retrieve the permanent visa which had been issued to the appellant suggesting to her that there was an error in the visa and that it should be returned to the Embassy. The appellant, through an English speaking uncle, reviewed the visa and could not find any error. The appellant entered Canada as a permanent resident, discovered the fact that her husband had withdrawn his sponsorship and was now, in fact, living with another woman and was later the subject of an inquiry under section 27(1)(e).

An adjudicator determined that the appellant was not described in section 27(1)(e). The Minister appealed and the Board allowed the appeal and issued something called a "Suspended Deportation Order". The nondisclosure was the fact that the appellant did not volunteer to the admitting officer the information that the Embassy in Guatemala had requested the return of her visa and that she did not produce for scrutiny the Embassy's telegram to her requesting the return of the visa. It was found as a fact that the appellant was subjectively unaware that she was holding anything back as she had no knowledge of her husband's withdrawal of the sponsorship and her impression was that the Embassy was being excessively bureaucratic. The Court distinguished *Brooks* on the basis that in that case the claimant concealed information about a conviction for bigamy and about criminal charges and deportation proceedings, and *Gudino* where the claimant had been telephoned by the Embassy and told that his visa was no longer valid and that he should not attempt to enter Canada. Accordingly, the appeal was allowed, the decision of the Immigration Appeal Board was set aside, and the matter was returned to the Board for reconsideration on the basis that the appellant was not granted landing by reason of any fraudulent or improper means.

Anthony v. Canada (Minister of Employment & Immigration) (December 16, 1985), Doc. T-84-9706 (Imm. App. Bd.) — The appellant, a citizen of Jamaica, was granted landing at Toronto International Airport on August 8, 1981, in order to marry her sponsor, Frank Anthony. The application for permanent residence, completed on January 27, 1981, was false in that the appellant listed only 2 of her 4 children and wrote, in her own handwriting, "I have no other children". The appellant's misrepresentations diverted the visa officer from carrying out his duties under the Act and Regulations, which required that he determine whether *all* the appellant's dependants met the requirements of the Act and Regulations before he could issue an immigrant visa to her. The Board dismissed the appellant's appeal, ruling that a deportation order, made under section 27(1)(e) of the Act, was valid.

D'Souza v. Canada (Minister of Employment & Immigration), [1983] 1 F.C. 343 (Fed. C.A.) — This was an appeal under section 84 of the *Immigration Act* from a decision of the Immigration Appeal Board dismissing the appellant's appeal from a deportation order. The ground for deportation was that the appellant was a person who had been granted landing by reason of a misrepresentation of a material fact made by another person, his mother. The appellant made an application of his own on which there were no misrepresentations. The appellant was, however, granted entry as a dependant of his mother. The Court held that the person concerned, to be described in section 27(1)(e), need not have knowledge of the material misrepresentation made on his behalf. The Court also noted that the Board, in determining whether to grant special relief, cannot be required to state every feature given consideration by it, and it was not to be presumed from the failure to mention a feature of the situation that the feature had not been considered and taken into account.

Canada (Minister of Employment & Immigration) v. Gudino (1981), [1982] 2 F.C. 40, 124 D.L.R. (3d) 748, 38 N.R. 361 (Fed. C.A.) — The applicant obtained a visa permitting him to enter Canada as a permanent resident. This visa was based in part on an offer of employment with Aero Mexico, an airline with offices in Toronto. The applicant lost his employment with Aero Mexico. He was then advised by telephone by a visa officer in Mexico that his visa was no longer valid and that he should not proceed to Canada. The applicant, however, flew to Toronto from Mexico in spite of being so informed. The Court held that a permanent resident visa issued under the *Immigration Act*, R.S.C. 1970, could be revoked by reason of a change in circumstances and found that a change in circumstances had occurred in this case. The change in circumstances was material and should have been disclosed to the immigration officer at the port-of-entry. The Court held that the method of communicating the revocation of the visa (*i.e.*, by telephone) was the most appropriate and effective method in the circumstances.

Khamsei v. Canada (Minister of Employment & Immigration), [1981] 1 F.C. 222 (Fed. C.A.) — Whether a misrepresentation was of a material fact is a question of fact. There does not need to be direct evidence that a visa would not have been granted had there been no misrepresentation. Where the failure to disclose all previous visa applications averts further inquiries, it is open to the adjudicator to find that there was a misrepresentation of a material fact.

Canada (Minister of Employment & Immigration) v. Mercier (September 16, 1980), Doc. 79-1243 (Imm. App. Bd.) — A visa is no more than a stamp on a piece of paper issued outside Canada which may give the holder a colour of right to come into Canada, either as a visitor or an immigrant, as the case may be, but no more. Immigration status is acquired at the port-of-entry. The Board held that a change in marital status from single to married was a material fact which must be disclosed to the Canadian immigration authorities if it occurs before permanent resident status is actually granted. By failing to disclose her marriage at Dorval airport when she arrived in Canada, Mme. Mercier misrepresented a material fact and thus brought herself within section 27(1)(e).

Devrim v. Canada (Minister of Employment & Immigration) (April 24, 1979), Doc. 78-6192 (Imm. App. Bd.) — The appellant acted in good faith in dealing with the immigration authorities. During her initial interview at Ankara, she stated that she was engaged, which the Board found she honestly believed herself to be. At her second visit to the Canadian Embassy, she disclosed the fact of her marriage and received some misleading information. At the airport in Toronto she was not examined in her native language and had no idea what was shown on her immigrant record card.

The Board held that section 27(1)(e) of the Act imposed an obligation of absolute liability and, thus, the defence of due diligence was not available. Under section 72(1)(b) of the Act the Board allowed the appeal, finding as it did that the appellant acted in good faith and finding that she was seriously misled by information given to her at her second attendance at the embassy in Ankara and that she was disadvantaged by the absence of a Turkish interpreter at the airport on her arrival.

Moore v. Canada (Minister of Employment & Immigration) (December 6, 1978), Doc. 78-3016 (Imm. App. Bd.) — Mrs. Moore misrepresented herself as single in her application for permanent residence and on her immigrant record card. She signed her maiden name to both these documents. The Board held that this was a misrepresentation of a material fact within the meaning of this subsection and accepted the proposition that *mens rea* would not be an element of this subsection, at least insofar as the disclosure of the existence of dependants was concerned and, thus, held that it was no excuse for the appellant to say that the question as to the existence of dependants was never directly asked by an immigration officer.

Canada (Minister of Manpower & Immigration) v. Brooks, [1974] S.C.R. 850, 36 D.L.R. (3d) 522 (S.C.C.) — The determination of whether a document pertains to a person's admission into Canada is not a question of fact; it follows automatically from and depends upon a prior construction of the scope of the relevant words of the section under consideration.

Canada (Minister of Manpower & Immigration v. Brooks), supra — The phrase "by reason of" imports something beyond merely giving false or misleading information. It connotes an inducing influence of the information and thus brings into question the notion of materiality. Inadvertence or carelessness in an answer must be weighed as to its consequences in this context.

Canada (Minister of Manpower & Immigration) v. Brooks, supra — The phrase, "fraudulent or improper means", is broad enough to embrace non-disclosure of facts which, if known, would be material to admission or non-admission.

Section 27(1)(g)

Canada (Minister of Citizenship & Immigration) v. Nemsila (1996), 35 Imm. L.R. (2d) 56, [1997] 1 F.C. 260, 118 F.T.R. 310 (Fed. T.D.); affirmed (1997), 38 Imm. L.R. (2d) 242, 3 Admin. L.R. (3d) 83, 214 N.R. 383 (Fed. C.A.) — This was an application by the minister to review a decision of an adjudicator which provided that the applicant could not be deported pursuant to paragraph 27(2)(g) and 27(1)(e) of the *Immigration Act*. The adjudicator found that the respondent had acquired Canadian domicile under the *Immigration Act* 1952, and therefore could not be ordered deported.

The adjudicator found that the respondent had been lawfully admitted to and landed in Canada in 1950, due to the fact that he had obtained a visa and presented himself for examination at a port-of-entry and the ship's manifest had been stamped with the phrase "landed immigrant" across his name. The adjudicator further found that the respondent had made misrepresentations during interviews with visa control and immigration officers and had not fully disclosed information which would have led to the refusal of his application.

Canadian domicile under the 1952 *Immigration Act* was acquired by a person having his place of domicile for at least 5 years in Canada after having been landed in Canada. For the purposes of the 1952 Act a person was landed in Canada when they had been lawfully admitted into Canada by an officer under that Act. The Court held that the term lawful admission in the 1952 Act, required something more than having a port-of-entry inspector rubber stamp the ship's manifest or an individual's passport with the words "landed immigrant". Lawful admission requires compliance with all of the requirements of the Act in force at the time the immigrant entered Canada.

Due to the fact that the respondents entry into Canada in 1950 was based upon deception and misrepresentation, he was not lawfully admitted to Canada and therefore could not have gained "landing" within the meaning of that Act. Due to the fact the respondent was never landed he was held to never have acquired Canadian domicile.

Accordingly, the adjudicator's decision was set aside.

Section 27(2)(a)

Cortez v. Canada (Secretary of State) (1994), 74 F.T.R. 9 — The applicant came to Canada in 1987. The record does not indicate his status, but he was not a Canadian citizen or a permanent resident at the time of this case. The applicant was convicted of impaired driving on September 19, 1989. Two other convictions followed on October 23, 1989 and March 16, 1990. The latter convictions related to having a blood alcohol level higher than .08. A report was made on November 5, 1990. This report provided that the applicant was described in section 27(2)(a) in that he was inadmissible by virtue of section 19(2)(b)(i). On December 1, 1992 an inquiry was held and the adjudicator, relying on *Ruparel v. Canada (Minister of Employment & Immigration)*, [1990], 3 F.C. 615, 11 Imm. L.R. (2d) 190, 36 F.T.R. 140, concluded that the allegation that the applicant was inadmissible was not valid.

On February 1, 1993 section 19(2) was amended. On March 2, 1993 a new report was issued in respect of the applicant relying on the same convictions. An inquiry was held in May 1993 and a deportation order issued.

There was no question of retrospectivity. A determination had to be made at the time of the second inquiry of the applicant's admissibility and that determination had to be made on the facts and the provisions of the Act, namely sections 27(2)(a) and 19(2)(a), as they read after the 1993 amendments.

Section 34 excludes *res judicata* in the specific context of section 27 and, therefore, the adjudicator had jurisdiction to examine the applicant's admissibility to Canada.

There was no unreasonable delay. The report in question (March 19, 1993) was written approximately one month after the amendments to the Act and the inquiry was held two months later. There was, therefore, no unreasonable delay.

R. v. Parker (July 12, 1985), Doc. 85-01-00584 (Man. Q.B.) — An inquiry concerning Mr. Parker was held upon two reports under section 27. At the conclusion of the inquiry, the adjudicator found in Mr. Parker's favour with respect to the allegation under section 27(2)(a) and in favour of the Commission with respect to the allegation under section 27(2)(b). A departure notice was issued to Mr. Parker. The Commission was unhappy with the result, as it had been seeking a deportation order. No appeal of the adjudicator's decision was made; instead, fresh proceedings under section 27(2)(a) were commenced. Mr. Parker was arrested and detained in connection with these new proceedings. The warrant for arrest and the order of detention were quashed and it was determined that the applicant was not properly detained. The Commission, at the time of the first inquiry, was aware of the fact that the applicant had an extensive criminal record. The Commission made a calculated decision to proceed with the information that it could prove and did not seek an adjournment to obtain the information that was the subject of the second inquiry. Thus, the issue to be dealt with on the second inquiry was held to have been already decided as a result of the first inquiry and there was, therefore, no jurisdictional basis for the second inquiry.

Brenner v. Canada (Minister of Employment & Immigration), [1983] 1 F.C. 172 (Fed. T.D.) — The adjudicator determined that the applicant was a person described in section 27(2)(a), because the applicant was inadmissible as a member of a class described in section 19(2)(a)(ii). The applicant applied to the adjudicator for a grant of entry under section 19(3). The adjudicator decided that she had no jurisdiction to entertain the application. A writ of *mandamus* compelling the adjudicator to consider the application under section 19(3) was refused on the ground that her decision brought the person within section 32(6) and, therefore, the adjudicator had no discretion to grant entry to such a person under section 19(3).

Editor's Note: Section 19(2)(a) has been amended, but the principle may still be valid.

Section 27(2)(b)

Grewal v. Canada (Minister of Employment & Immigration) (October 1, 1984), Doc. A-836-84 (Fed. C.A.) — An inquiry was held to determine whether the applicant was a person who had entered Canada as a visitor and remained in Canada after ceasing to be a visitor. The

Court concluded that once a person has been made the subject of an inquiry to determine his right to stay in Canada, the mere fact that after the start of the inquiry he leaves the country for a time does not deprive the adjudicator of his jurisdiction to continue and complete the inquiry.

Kaur v. Canada (Minister of Employment & Immigration) (September 6, 1984), Doc. A-295-84 (Fed. C.A.) — The applicant sought admission to Canada as an immigrant. Following a report made pursuant to section 20(1) of the *Immigration Act*, she was made the subject of an inquiry. That inquiry was adjourned after the applicant claimed to be a Convention refugee. During the adjournment the applicant left the country for the United States, was refused permission to enter that country and immediately came back to Canada where she reapplied to be admitted as an immigrant. The inquiry, which had been adjourned, culminated in an exclusion order. The adjudicator who presided over the inquiry did not lose jurisdiction when the applicant left Canada for the United States. Once a person seeking admission to Canada has been made the subject of an inquiry in order to determine her admissibility, the mere fact that she, after the start of the inquiry, either left Canada or manifested an intention no longer to seek admission, does not deprive the adjudicator of his jurisdiction to continue the inquiry.

Miles v. Canada (Minister of Employment & Immigration) (February 13, 1984), Doc. A-1121-83 (Fed. C.A.) — The Court upheld the decision of an adjudicator finding that the applicant had engaged in employment without authorization and that thereafter the applicant was in breach of one of the conditions of her entry to Canada as a visitor. The Court upheld the adjudicator's finding that the applicant was, therefore, a person described in section 27(2)(e) of the *Immigration Act* and subject to an inquiry.

R. v. Malhotra (1980), [1981] 2 W.W.R. 563, 57 C.C.C. (2d) 539 (Man. Prov. Ct.) — Where there is some evidence that the accused is engaged in employment, section 26(1)(b) of the Act operates so as to strip the accused of his status as a visitor. Therefore, there is a *prima facie* case against the accused under section 95(k).

Georgas v. Canada (Minister of Employment & Immigration) (1978), [1979] 1 F.C. 349, 23 N.R. 437 (Fed. C.A.) — On the facts of this case, there was evidence from which an adjudicator could conclude that the applicant had engaged in employment. However, not all work performed by a visitor for a relative with whom he or she is staying, and for which the relative would have to pay compensation if he or she chose to have it done by a stranger, falls within the definition of employment. Whether the work done is employment depends upon the nature of the work and the circumstances.

Section 27(2)(d)

Estrada v. R. (1987), 1 Imm. L.R. (2d) 24, 8 F.T.R. 317 (Fed. T.D.) — The applicant was the subject of an immigration inquiry. The inquiry was based on a defective report because the report alleged that the applicant had been convicted of an offence under section 3(1) of the *Narcotic Control Act* without making it clear that the allegation related to the conviction for an indictable offence under another Act of Parliament and not the *Criminal Code*. The report was amended. However, during the course of argument, the adjudicator and the case presenting officer became concerned about the validity of the proceedings. The case presenting officer received instructions from her superiors to withdraw the direction. The adjudicator indicated that the procedure being followed was correct and that no withdrawal of the direction was necessary. The case presenting officer requested an adjournment to consider her position. Her request was denied, whereupon she withdrew the direction. A new direction for inquiry was forthcoming. The report alleged that the applicant was convicted of one count of possession of a narcotic contrary to the *Narcotic Control Act*. This was held not to be an abuse of process. The Court characterized the Minister as having acted in a very cautious way in order to avoid any error of law. The Court found nothing so oppressive or vexatious as to constitute an abuse of process. The fact of the withdrawal of the direction in order to terminate the inquiry, coupled with the allowing of another direction for inquiry to be made and based upon the same facts, although under a different paragraph of section 27, did not, in the circumstances, constitute an abuse of process.

Singleton v. Canada (Minister of Employment & Immigration) (November 7, 1983), Doc. A-813-83 (Fed. T.D.) — For digest, see section 27(1)(a.1), *supra.*

McMahon, Re, [1978] 2 F.C. 624, 40 C.C.C. (2d) 250, 21 N.R. 170 (Fed. C.A.) — For digest, see section 27(1)(a. 2), *supra.*

Kalicharan v. Canada (Minister of Manpower & Immigration), [1976] 2 F.C. 123, 67 D.L.R. (3d) 555 (Fed. T.D.) — For digest, see section 27(1)(a.2), *supra.*

Section 27(2)(e)

Grewal v. Canada (Minister of Employment & Immigration) (October 1, 1984), Doc. A-836-84 (Fed. C.A.) — For digest, see section 27(2)(b), *supra.*

Canada (Minister of Employment & Immigration) v. Tighe (February 17, 1984), Doc. M83-1128E (Imm. App. Bd.) — The Minister appealed under section 73 of the *Immigration Act.* The adjudicator had decided that the respondent was not a person described in section 27(2)(e) of the Act. As a result of this finding the adjudicator did not make a removal order against the respondent or issue a departure notice to him. The respondent had claimed to be a Canadian citizen at the inquiry. This claim was not disposed of due to the adjudicator's decision that the respondent was not described in section 27(2)(e) of the Act. The Board ruled that it did not have the power to allow the Minister's appeal pursuant to section 75(2) of the Act because it could not make a removal order against the respondent. The removal order could not be made because the respondent's claim to Canadian citizenship had never been resolved in accordance with the provisions of the Act. Accordingly, the Minister's appeal was dismissed.

Miles v. Canada (Minister of Employment & Immigration) (February 13, 1984), Doc. A-1121-83 (Fed. C.A.) — For digest, see section 27(2)(b), *supra.*

Canada (Minister of Employment & Immigration) v. Swapp (December 16, 1983), Doc. T83-9093 (Imm. App. Bd.) — The adjudicator refused to find the respondent a person described in section 27(2)(e) of the *Immigration Act* because the respondent was unable to extend his visa or leave the country by virtue of the fact that he was in jail from the time of his arrival until several days after the expiry of his visa. The Minister's appeal was allowed. The Board ruled that it was not reasonable that the respondent should benefit from his criminal activity by receiving more favourable treatment from immigration laws than he was otherwise entitled to.

Canada (Minister of Employment & Immigration) v. Cembranos-Alvarez (December 11, 1981), Doc. V81-6106 (Imm. App. Bd.); affirmed (June 6, 1983), Doc. 267-82 (Fed. T.D.) — The respondent entered Canada as a visitor and overstayed, failing to leave Canada by September 25, 1978. A Minister's permit was issued on February 20, 1979. This permit was cancelled. The Board held that the issuance of the Minister's permit did not take away the very essence of the violation alleged against the respondent (*i.e.*, that he overstayed). The issuance of the permit temporarily suspended the opportunity to make the section 27 report until the permit had either run its course or been cancelled. The Board held that the adjudicator erred in failing to direct the deportation of the respondent and allowed the Minister's appeal and directed the respondent's deportation.

R. v. Malhotra (1980), [1981] 2 W.W.R. 563, 57 C.C.C. (2d) 539 (Man. Prov. Ct.) — For digest, see section 27(2)(b), *supra*.

Heras v. Canada (Minister of Employment & Immigration), [1981] 2 F.C. 605 (Fed. T.D.), affirmed [1983] 1 F.C. 347 (Fed. C.A.). — When a Minister's permit is issued to a person who has overstayed his visit in Canada, such person may, upon the expiration or cancellation of the permit, be dealt with under this paragraph as a visitor who remained in Canada after he ceased to be a visitor.

Section 27(2)(f)

Rios v. Canada (Minister of Employment & Immigration), 11 Imm. L.R. (2d) 122, 115 N.R. 394, [1990] 3 F.C. 632 — This case raises the question of what is meant by the word "elude" in section 27(2)(f) of the *Immigration Act*. The majority concluded that the word "elude" has the connotation either of artifice or surreptitiousness or of the intention to repudiate the obligation or escape the effect of the law in a general way. In the context of this case it would mean, not only not being present at a particular inquiry, but also of not complying with the obligation of the law. Failure to attend at an examination raises a *prima facie* case under section 27(2)(f) such that an immigration officer could believe that the person in question eluded examination or inquiry and take appropriate enforcement action. The person concerned would be able, however, to have his or her case subsequently adjudicated upon in relation to his or her real intentions and this did not happen in this case. This will not render administration of the Act difficult. Accordingly the majority ruled that the section 28 application to set aside the deportation order issued against the applicant should succeed. The minority agreed that a person does not elude an inquiry within the meaning of section 27(2)(f) if that person has reasonable grounds for believing that he has good cause for not appearing at the inquiry.

Section 27(2)(g)

Canada (A.G.) v. Chanoine (1987), 4 Imm. L.R. (2d) 136, 15 F.T.R. 143 (Fed. T.D.) — The Attorney General applied for a writ of *certiorari* and a writ of *mandamus* setting aside the decision of an adjudicator not to hold an inquiry concerning the respondent and ordering the adjudicator to proceed with the inquiry.

The respondent was given the status of a permanent resident and subsequently left Canada for a period of three years. Just before returning to Canada, the respondent unsuccessfully applied for a visitor's visa. The respondent entered Canada and made no disclosures of any kind to the officer at the port-of-entry. A report was prepared indicating that the respondent was a person described in section 27(2)(b) and 27(2)(g) of the *Immigration Act*. The adjudicator declined jurisdiction adopting the argument that the respondent should have been proceeded with under section 27(1), which applied to permanent residents.

This decision of the adjudicator was set aside and the adjudicator was directed to continue the inquiry.

A permanent resident has been defined as a person who has been granted landing and who has not ceased to be a permanent resident pursuant to section 24(1). Accordingly, the respondent automatically lost his permanent resident status, pursuant to section 24(1), by reason of his having been outside of Canada for more than 183 days, unless he satisfied the adjudicator that he had not done so.

Editor's Note: This case should be read with Canada (Minister of Employment & Immigration) v. Selby, [1981] 1 F.C. 273, 110 D.L.R. (3d) 126 (Fed. C.A.).

Coombs v. Canada (Minister of Employment & Immigration) (1981), [1982] 1 F.C. 113 (Fed. C.A.) — The Court held that the question, "are you a 'resident' of Canada?," did not necessarily mean, "permanent resident" of Canada. There was, therefore, no basis for the adjudicator to assume that the expression "permanent resident of Canada" was the same as "resident of Canada".

Canada (Minister of Employment & Immigration) v. Gudino (1981), [1982] 2 F.C. 40, 124 D.L.R. (3d) 748, 38 N.R. 361 (Fed. C.A.) — For digest, see section 27(1)(e), *supra*.

Khamsei v. Canada (Minister of Employment & Immigration), [1981] 1 F.C. 222 (Fed. C.A.) — Whether a misrepresentation was of a material fact is a question of fact. There does not need to be direct evidence that a visa would not have been granted had there been no misrepresentation. Where the failure to disclose all previous visa applications prevents further inquiries, it is open to the adjudicator to find that there was a misrepresentation of a material fact.

Canada (Minister of Manpower & Immigration) v. Brooks, [1974] S.C.R. 850, 36 D.L.R. (3d) 522 (S.C.C.) — "With" in the context of a similar paragraph in the *Immigration Act*, R.S.C. 1970 (section 18(1)(e)(viii)), is not limited in meaning to possessed of, but contextually extends to "agreeably to" or "because of" or "by use of".

Canada (Minister of Manpower & Immigration) v. Brooks, supra — The determination of whether a document was one pertaining to a person's admission to Canada was held not to be a question of fact, as it followed automatically from, and depended upon, a prior construction of the scope of the relevant words of a similar paragraph under the *Immigration Act*, R.S.C. 1970.

Canada (Minister of Manpower & Immigration) v. Brooks, supra — The phrase "fraudulent or improper means" is broad enough to embrace non-disclosure of facts which would be material to admission or non-admission if known.

Canada (Minister of Manpower & Immigration) v. Brooks, supra — Under section 18(1)(e)(viii) of the old Act, which bears some similarity to this subsection, intentional or wilful deception is not implied by the word "false", and thus an honest belief that a document was valid is not relevant.

Section 27(2)(h)

Vega v. Canada (Minister of Employment & Immigration) (February 15, 1983), Doc. A-261-82 (Fed. C.A.) — The applicant had left and re-entered Canada after having been ordered deported. The adjudicator erred in ruling that it was the applicant's responsibility to prove that he had obtained the Minister's consent before coming back into the country. That burden clearly lay upon the Commission. This error did not vitiate the adjudicator's decision since he did not rely upon the onus of proof to reach the conclusion that the applicant did not have the Minister's consent. The Court held, as well, that the consent of the Minister must be expressed and could not be implied.

Vargas-Cataldo v. Canada (Minister of Manpower & Immigration), [1973] F.C. 313 (Fed. C.A.) — The adjudicator has no power to question the validity of a previous deportation order in proceedings under this paragraph.

Section 27(2.1)

Qi v. Canada (Minister of Citizenship & Immigration) (January 16, 1996), Doc. IMM-469-95 (Fed. T.D.) — The applicants arrived in Canada on May 10, 1994. They came as visitors.They were retirees and came to visit their son, a research assistant at the University of

Calgary and a Canadian citizen. The son sent an application on October 28, 1994 to the Canadian Consulate in Buffalo to sponsor his parents for permanent residence. His parents' visitors' visas expired on December 10, 1994. Through inadvertence they did not seek an extension. An application was subsequently prepared to seek reinstatement pursuant to subsection 27(2.1). An application to this effect was forwarded to the respondent on January 3, 1995. While this request was pending the applicants were notified that an interview had been scheduled for them with a senior immigration officer to determine whether they had overstayed their visitors' visas and were unlawfully in Canada. The paralegal tried to persuade the officer to adjourn that proceeding until after a reply had been received with respect to the subsection 27(2.1) application. The senior immigration officer refused. The officer also denied the paralegal an opportunity to take part in the interview.

The decision of the senior immigration officer was set aside. It cannot be presumed that individuals are being invited to engage counsel with the expense that entails merely for the purpose of being present as an observer. After issuing the invitation to have counsel present to deny the applicants' representative the right to take part in the interview was a breach of natural justice. The Court also held that the senior immigration officer ought to have adjourned the interview until after the respondent had made a decision on the request pursuant to section 27(2.1).

Section 27(3)

Moreno v. Canada (Minister of Citizenship & Immigration) (1998), 157 F.T.R. 85 (Fed. T.D.) — This application arises out of the respondent's refusal to cause an inquiry to be held pursuant to subsection 27(6). The applicant sought an order in the nature of *mandamus* to compel the respondent to cause an inquiry to be held. The applicant, a Peruvian citizen, entered Canada with his wife on January 31, 1987. At an immigration inquiry on March 2, 1987, the applicant claimed refugee status. That claim was processed under the Refugee Backlog Program then in effect. As part of that process, a report alleging that the applicant was a person described in section 19(1)(j) of the Act was prepared. That report formed the basis for the refusal of permanent resident status to both the applicant and his wife. On October 5, 1993, a direction for inquiry was issued. Before the inquiry could be held, however, the following events transpired. First, the applicant was informed by the IRB on March 1, 1995, that his refugee claim could not be adjudicated because persons who have committed war crimes are excluded from the definition of refugee. The applicant never attempted to have that finding set aside. Secondly, on February 26, 1997, the applicant and his wife filed a second application for permanent resident status on humanitarian and compassionate grounds that was denied on April 7, 1997. Thirdly, a new section 27(2) report was written on April 18, 1997 alleging that the applicant was inadmissible on the ground that he had not presented a valid immigrant visa or travel document at a port of entry in 1987. This report resulted in the issuance of a removal order against the applicant on April 30, 1997. The applicant sought to have this removal order set aside, but that application was discontinued. On May 15, 1997, the October 5, 1993 direction for inquiry was cancelled, and the applicant and his wife voluntarily left Canada on May 29, 1997.

The issuance of a direction for inquiry flows directly from the Deputy Minister's discretionary power. It follows that the Deputy Minister may, likewise, choose not to direct such an inquiry. The two possibilities enjoy a rationale and complimentary co-existence within the realm of the Deputy Minister's discretionary power. Finally, there is no absolute prohibition against the modification or withdrawal of a direction for inquiry following its issuance. Accordingly, the application for *mandamus* was denied.

Asante v. Canada (Minister of Employment & Immigration) (1993), 64 F.T.R. 10 — The applicant was a citizen of Ghana. She came to Canada on October 12, 1989, having obtained a visitor's visa to Canada. Her visitor's visa was valid for one month and this visa was later extended to January 11, 1990. When the applicant could not go to the United States to study she claimed refugee status, but subsequently had her visitor's visa extended to July 11, 1990. On May 29, 1990 an immigration officer made a report pursuant to paragraph 27(2)(e) of the *Immigration Act*. A direction for inquiry was issued on July 4, 1990. At the conclusion of the inquiry the adjudicator issued a departure notice to the applicant. Later, a first-level panel concluded that there was no credible basis for the applicant's claim for Convention refugee status.

At the time the section 27 report was made and at the time the direction for inquiry was issued, the applicant was in Canada on a validly subsisting visitor's visa. There was no authority under the Act to make a report or to issue a direction for inquiry. Therefore, the adjudicator had no jurisdiction to proceed with the inquiry and issue a departure notice. Accordingly, the departure notice issued in this case was set aside.

Blanusa v. Canada (Minister of Employment & Immigration) (1989), 27 F.T.R. 107 (Fed. T.D.) — The applicant argued that, because there were grounds under the *Extradition Act* and the Extradition Treaty with the United States upon which he might resist extradition under those instruments, proceedings under the *Immigration Act* to deport him ought to be prohibited. It was contended that to proceed with the deportation hearing would automatically violate section 7 of the *Charter* because the applicant would not be able to raise in the deportation proceedings objections to his removal which were, by their nature, only available in the extradition proceedings. Extradition and immigration proceedings are separate processes. The applicant was being proceeded against under the *Immigration Act* because he violated the laws of Canada by staying in this country for over 2 years. He was being proceeded against under the *Extradition Act* and Treaty because he had allegedly committed kidnappings and murders in the United States. There was no basis for thinking that the deportation hearing was illegal or unconstitutional and accordingly the application was dismissed.

Kindler v. Canada (Minister of Employment & Immigration), [1987] 3 F.C. 34, 26 Admin. L.R. 186, 3 Imm. L.R. (2d) 38, 32 C.R.R. 346, 80 N.R. 388, 41 D.L.R. (4th) 78 (Fed. C.A.) — The respondent, Kindler, is an American citizen who was convicted of first degree murder, kidnapping and criminal conspiracy in Pennsylvania, U.S.A. The jury recommended the death sentence, but Kindler escaped before the sentence was formally pronounced. He was discovered by the R.C.M.P. in St. Adele, Quebec and was arrested and charged with offences under the *Immigration Act* and *Criminal Code*. Before the date set for his inquiry under the *Immigration Act*, the Trial Division issued a writ of *certiorari* quashing the direction of the Deputy Minister under section 27(3) of the Act. A writ of prohibition forbidding an inquiry was also issued. The respondent escaped custody in October 1986 and has not been heard from since that time.

Nevertheless, his counsel appeared for him on this appeal. It was noted that while there is a general duty of fairness resting on all public decision-makers, there is a flexible gradation of procedural fairness through the administrative spectrum.The decision of the Deputy Minister under section 27(3) to issue a direction for inquiry, the decision of a senior immigration officer under section 27(4) to cause that inquiry to be held, and the parallel decision of an officer under section 28 to cause that inquiry to be held are purely administrative decisions. A senior immigration officer is merely a conduit through whom the inquiry is caused by operation of the Act. The Deputy Minister has only to decide that an inquiry is warranted, and this he would do on the existence of a *prima facie* case. His decision is analogous to that of any prosecutor who decides to proceed with a charge before the Court. These types of decisions are ones with respect to the respondent, but they cannot be described as decisions against him. These decisions do not deprive the respondent of his life, liberty, or security of the person, or even of his property. Accordingly, the respondent is not entitled to a "paper hearing" in the circumstances with respect to the decision to grant the hearing. Further, the hearing prescribed by the *Immigration Act* meets the procedural requirements of fundamental justice. The respondent has a full opportunity to present his case on the facts and to challenge those of the other side, all with the aid of counsel. The fact that the penalty is prescribed in no way lessens the fairness of the hearing.

Finally, it was held that the Court should not, in a case such as this, take into account other possible consequences of deportation, such as the possibility of capital punishment for the respondent.

Editor's Note: The sections of the Act referred to have been substantially altered, but the principles may still be useful.

Russell v. Canada (Minister of Employment & Immigration) (1986), 21 Admin. L.R. 99, 4 F.T.R. 11 (Fed. T.D.) — This was an application for *certiorari* to quash an inquiry and the order to conduct an inquiry under section 27(4). The acting Director General, Enforcement Branch, on behalf of the Deputy Minister, directed, pursuant to section 27(3), that an inquiry be held to determine if the applicant fell within section 27(1)(d). The inquiry was held and the applicant was ordered deported. The applicant, a landed immigrant, appealed to the Immigration Appeal Board and 2 years later, while his appeal was pending, brought the present application, which was dismissed. The applicant contended that it was unfair that the Deputy Minister or his representatives, should direct an inquiry pursuant to section 27(3) without first affording the applicant at least a hearing in writing on the question of whether an inquiry was warranted. This argument was rejected. Although it was agreed that a duty of fairness was attached to the administrative decision authorized in section 27(3), relief by way of *certiorari* was discretionary and the Court declined to exercise its discretion because the appeal route, open to the applicant under section 72 [s. 70], provided a fully adequate recourse. There was, therefore, no justification for the Court intervening.

Editor's Note: The sections of the Act referred to have been substantially altered, but the principles may still be useful.

Canada (Minister of Manpower & Immigration) v. Brooks, [1974] S.C.R. 850, 36 D.L.R. (3d) 522 (S.C.C.) — Duplicity in a direction for inquiry is not a ground for annulling the deportation order made at such inquiry. All that is required is that the subject of the inquiry be made aware of the allegations made against him under the relevant provisions of the *Immigration Act* and that he is given an opportunity to meet them.

Section 27(4)

Qi v. Canada (Minister of Citizenship & Immigration) (January 16, 1996), Doc. IMM-469-95 (Fed. T.D.) — The applicants arrived in Canada on May 10, 1994. They came as visitors. They were retirees and came to visit their son, a research assistant at the University of Calgary and a Canadian citizen. The son sent an application on October 28, 1994 to the Canadian Consulate in Buffalo to sponsor his parents for permanent residence. His parents' visitors' visas expired on December 10, 1994. Through inadvertence they did not seek an extension. An application was subsequently prepared to seek reinstatement pursuant to subsection 27(2.1). An application to this effect was forwarded to the respondent on January 3, 1995. While this request was pending, the applicants were notified that an interview had been scheduled for them with a senior immigration officer to determine whether they had overstayed their visitors' visas and were unlawfully in Canada. The paralegal tried to persuade the officer to adjourn that proceeding until after a reply had been received with respect to the subsection 27(2.1) application. The senior immigration officer refused. The officer also denied the paralegal an opportunity to take part in the interview.

The decision of the senior immigration officer was set aside. It cannot be presumed that individuals are being invited to engage counsel with the expense that entails merely for the purpose of being present as an observer. After issuing the invitation to have counsel present to deny the applicants' representative the right to take part in the interview was a breach of natural justice. The Court also held that the senior immigration officer ought to have adjourned the interview until after the respondent had made a decision on the request pursuant to section 27(2.1).

Conditional Departure Order

28. (1) Conditional departure order — Where a senior immigration officer is of the opinion that a person who claims to be a Convention refugee is eligible to have their claim referred to the Refugee Division and is a person in respect of whom the senior immigration officer would, but for this section, have made an exclusion order under subsection 23(4) or (4.01) or a departure order under subsection 27(4), the senior immigration officer shall make a conditional departure order against the person.

(2) When conditional order becomes effective — No conditional departure order made pursuant to subsection (1) against a person who claims to be a Convention refugee is effective unless and until

(a) the person withdraws the claim to be a Convention refugee;

(a.1) the person is determined by a senior immigration officer not to be eligible to make a claim to be a Convention refugee and has been so notified;

(b) the person is declared by the Refugee Division to have abandoned the claim to be a Convention refugee and has been so notified;

(c) the person is determined by the Refugee Division not to be a Convention refugee and has been so notified; or

(d) the person is determined pursuant to subsection 46.07(1.1) or (2) not to have a right under subsection 4(2.1) to remain in Canada and has been so notified.

1992, c. 49, s. 17; 1995, c. 15, s. 6.

Conduct of Inquiries

29. (1) Inquiry is public — Subject to subsections (2) and (3), an inquiry by an adjudicator shall be conducted in public, and shall be held in the presence of the person with respect to whom the inquiry is to be held wherever practicable, unless the person consents in writing to the inquiry being conducted without a hearing and in the person's absence.

(2) Confidentiality — Where an adjudicator is satisfied that there is a serious possibility that the life, liberty or security of any person would be endangered by reason of an inquiry being conducted in public, the adjudicator may, on application therefor, take such measures and make such order as the adjudicator considers necessary to ensure the confidentiality of the inquiry.

(3) Idem — Where an adjudicator considers it appropriate to do so, the adjudicator may take such measures and make such order as the adjudicator considers necessary to ensure the confidentiality of any hearing held in respect of any application referred to in subsection (2).

(4) Minors and incompetents — Where an inquiry is held with respect to any person under the age of eighteen years or any person who, in the opinion of the adjudicator presiding at the inquiry, is unable to appreciate the nature of the proceedings, the person may, subject to subsection (5), be represented by a parent or guardian.

(5) Where representative designated by adjudicator — Where at an inquiry a person described in subsection (4) is not represented by a parent or guardian or where, in the opinion of the adjudicator presiding at the inquiry, the person is not properly represented by a parent or guardian, the inquiry shall be adjourned and the adjudicator shall designate some other person to represent that person at the expense of the Minister.

(6) Resumption — Where an inquiry has been adjourned pursuant to this Act or the regulations, the inquiry may be resumed by an adjudicator other than the adjudicator who presided at the adjourned inquiry where

> **(a) the person who is the subject of the inquiry consents to the inquiry being resumed by another adjudicator;**
>
> **(b) no substantive evidence was presented at the adjourned inquiry; or**
>
> **(c) the adjudicator, before adjourning the inquiry, had found that the person who is the subject of the inquiry was a person described in subsection 27(2), and that all that remains to be presented is the substantive evidence that will determine whether a deportation order should be made against the person.**

R.S.C. 1985, c. 31 (1st Supp.), s. 99; 1992, c. 49, s. 18.

Case Law

Section 29(1)

Gervasoni v. Canada (Minister of Citizenship & Immigration), 30 Imm. L.R. (2d) 219, 97 F.T.R. 307, [1995] 3 F.C. 189 — The applicant sought an order setting aside a decision of an adjudicator finding the applicant to be a person described in paragraph 27(2)(a). During the inquiry it was made apparent to the adjudicator that certain members of the public interested in attending the hearing of the inquiry were not admitted to the Correctional Centre where the inquiry was taking place. Counsel for the applicant noted that certain people who wanted to attend were not permitted to do so. Counsel indicated that he did not know who these people were, but noted that the press had called him earlier and that he had indicated to them that the hearing was to be opened to the public. The adjudicator indicated that the prison authorities, concerned with the security of the institution, did not have sufficient time to carry out security checks on those who sought to be admitted and they therefore refused to admit those persons. Counsel suggested to the adjudicator that he should hear from those persons who wanted to attend and then decide whether or not to admit them. The adjudicator declined to agree to this suggestion and declined to adjourn the inquiry to a more public place.

The *Immigration Act*, in specifying that an inquiry be conducted in public, provides a mandatory requirement. The adjudicator exceeded his jurisdiction when he proceeded with the inquiry when it was clear to him that it would not be conducted in public, when it was known that some members of the public had indicated an interest in attending but were not permitted to do so. Aside from the exemption specified by Parliament, or conceivably circumstances similar to those exceptions, the provisions of s. 29(1) are mandatory.

The application was allowed and the decision of the adjudicator set aside.

Altamirano v. Canada (Minister of Employment & Immigration) (1991), 15 Imm. L.R. (2d) 86, 48 F.T.R. 88 — This application for leave was dismissed. The applicant objected to being limited to 45 minutes in oral submissions after the filing of written arguments. This was held to raise no arguable violation of the *Immigration Act* or a denial of fairness or natural justice. The applicant's counsel had already filed 1400 pages of evidence and the applicant's sole complaint was that his counsel was not permitted to summarize this evidence orally and make oral submissions based on it and on the law. Requiring written submissions and limiting the time for oral submissions was held to be consistent with the practice followed in many Canadian courts, including the Supreme Court of Canada.

Ragunauth v. Canada (Minister of Employment & Immigration) (June 28, 1985), Doc. T-1295-85 (Fed. T.D.) — The applicant was the subject of a deportation order and made this application for an interlocutory injunction to restrain the Minister from carrying out the order. The applicant was ordered deported under an assumed name. Eventually, her true identity was discovered and while in transit out of the country she committed an aggravated assault and was sentenced to 2 years in prison for that offence. On November 30, 1983, the applicant refused to attend at the commencement of her hearing at the Kingston Prison for Women because she wanted to hire a lawyer and was frightened to proceed with the case on her own. The applicant was advised, in writing, by the adjudicator that her voluntary absence from the inquiry would not prevent a decision from being reached and she was advised to attend at the next sitting of her inquiry whether or not counsel was present. On December 22, 1983, the applicant again refused to attend at her inquiry at the Kingston Prison for Women. A few days later the applicant was advised that a deportation order had been made against her. Early in 1984, the applicant was visited by duty counsel and an application was made to the Ontario Legal Aid Plan, and this was refused. In February 1985, the applicant wrote to the adjudicator and requested that the inquiry be re-opened in order to permit her to adduce evidence of her claim for refugee status. The adjudicator decided that a claim to being a refugee was neither additional evidence nor testimony in the meaning of section 35(1) of the Act and refused to re-open the inquiry. The Court concluded that the adjudicator was probably wrong in ruling that a claim to being a Convention refugee was neither additional evidence nor testimony. The Court held that the refusal to re-open the inquiry was not unfair because the applicant had spurned three opportunities to make such a claim. The first opportunity occurred when she was initially arrested and gave a false name. The second occurred when she refused to attend her own inquiry on November 30, 1983, and the third occasion occurred when she refused to attend at her own inquiry in December 1983. Those three refusals, plus the adjudicator's letter to the applicant urging her to attend her inquiry, suggested to the Court that the refusal to re-open the inquiry was not unfair. Further, the Court concluded that there was no deprivation of the right to life, liberty and security under section 7 of the *Charter* because any deprivation of such rights was the applicant's own doing and was self-inflicted. It could not, therefore, be imputed to the State or its officers or employees.

Cheung v. Canada (Minister of Employment & Immigration), [1981] 2 F.C. 764, 122 D.L.R. (3d) 41, 36 N.R. 563 (Fed. C.A.) — An inquiry is not a criminal or civil trial.

Ali v. Canada (Minister of Manpower & Immigration) (1975), [1976] 1 F.C. 185, 11 N.R. 617 (Fed. C.A.) — Whether a person signing on behalf of the Deputy Minister had the authority to do so is a question of fact which in an appropriate case can be proved in the Federal Court. In such a case the burden will be on the applicant. This burden had to be distinguished from the onus of establishing facts sufficient to support the deportation order or departure notice.

Section 29(4)

Quinteros v. Canada (Minister of Citizenship & Immigration) (1995), 102 F.T.R. 314 — The applicant argued that the adjudicator presiding at the credible basis inquiry erred in law by failing to determine whether the applicant was unable to appreciate the nature of the proceedings before he appointed her mother to be her representative at the inquiry.

Subsection 29(4) of the Act creates two separate and distinct categories of persons who may be represented by a parent or guardian at an inquiry:

> Any person under the age of 18 years or any person who, in the opinion of the adjudicator presiding at the inquiry, is unable to appreciate the nature of the proceedings.

Nothing in this subsection requires the adjudicator to determine whether a person under the age of 18 is unable to appreciate the nature of the proceedings. The application for judicial review is dismissed.

Azdo v. Canada (Minister of Employment & Immigration), [1980] 2 F.C. 645, 36 N.R. 361 (Fed. C.A.) — The word guardian is used in this subsection in its narrow legal sense: one who legally has the care and management of the person, or the estate, or both, during the minority of the child. The determination that a person is a guardian must be made on evidence considered trustworthy by the adjudicator upon a balance of probabilities.

Kissoon v. Canada (Minister of Employment & Immigration), [1979] 1 F.C. 301, 90 D.L.R. (3d) 766, 23 N.R. 82 (Fed. C.A.) — This subsection gives minors the right to be represented by a parent or guardian. This right is distinct from and additional to the right to counsel guaranteed by section 30. Failure to comply with this provision will result in the setting aside of the exclusion order. The Court also held that the applicant may not be excused from testifying because he is a minor.

Section 29(5)

Quinteros v. Canada (Minister of Citizenship & Immigration) (1995), 102 F.T.R. 314 — For digest, see section 29(4), *supra*.

Azdo v. Canada (Minister of Employment & Immigration), [1980] 2 F.C. 645, 36 N.R. 361 (Fed. C.A.) — For digest, see section 29(4), *supra*.

Karim v. Canada (Minister of Employment & Immigration), [1980] 2 F.C. 109 (Fed. C.A.) — The exclusion order in this case was set aside because the adjudicator, without foundation, assumed that the applicant's older sister was in fact her guardian for the purposes of this subsection of the *Immigration Act*.

Kissoon v. Canada (Minister of Employment & Immigration) (1978), [1979] 1 F.C. 301, 90 D.L.R. (3d) 766, 23 N.R. 82 (Fed. C.A.) — For digest, see section 29(4), *supra*.

Section 29(6)

Hall v. Canada (Minister of Citizenship & Immigration) (1996), 32 Imm. L.R. (2d) 260, 108 F.T.R. 116 (Fed. T.D.) — The applicant was born in England in 1949 and came to Canada with his mother and his grandmother 3 months later. His mother was a British citizen and came to Canada to marry a Canadian citizen who may very well have been the applicant's natural father. The applicant's parents were married in 1950 and the applicant was adopted by his father in March 1953 in British Columbia. In February 1969 the applicant was convicted of trafficking marijuana and was sentenced to 14 months in prison. During the course of a parole hearing the applicant was released on his promises to return to England, which he did. In 1985 in England the applicant was convicted of possession of marijuana and in 1987 the applicant returned to Canada and began living here. In January 1989 a deportation order was issued against the applicant on the ground that he was described in paragraph 19(1)(c) in that he had been convicted of an offence under an act of parliament for which a defined maximum term of imprisonment might be imposed and also, under paragraph 19(2)(d) in that he had not made an application for, and obtained a visa before appearing at a port-of-entry. The application appealed the deportation order on the ground that he had received a pardon for his 1969 conviction. The deportation order was quashed, however, an exclusion order was issued against the applicant on the basis that he was described in paragraph 19(2)(d). The applicant was given a departure notice and left Canada for the United Kingdom in November 1989. In September 1991 the applicant returned to Canada as a visitor and in March 1992 a report was made with respect to the applicant's conviction for possession of narcotics in England. In March 1992 a direction for inquiry was made to determine if the applicant was described in paragraph 19(2)(a). The inquiry was scheduled for March 23, 1992. The applicant appeared before the inquiry at which time the inquiry was adjourned to November so that the applicant could clarify his status in relation to his citizenship. The applicant did not apply for an extension of his visitor status which terminated in March 1992, and a further report was issued on the ground that he had overstayed his visitor status. When the applicant's inquiry resumed on December 1, 1992 the allegation in relation to the applicant's conviction in England was withdrawn, however, the inquiry continued into the allegation that the applicant had overstayed his visitor's authorized term. When that inquiry resumed in May 1993 a new adjudicator presided, and that adjudicator ultimately made a departure order against the applicant which later became a deportation order because the applicant did not leave Canada by the stipulated date.

Paragraphs (a), (b) and (c) in section 29(6) are to be read disjunctively. They set out three separate circumstances in which it is appropriate for a new adjudicator to resume an inquiry that has been previously adjourned. The allegations considered in an inquiry can be changed, altered or substituted for, during the course of the inquiry. The report of the applicant overstaying his visitor status had not been the subject of any substantive evidence when the new adjudicator took over. Accordingly, the new adjudicator had jurisdiction to decide the matter.

The Court further found that the adjudicator had not made an error in concluding that the applicant was not a Canadian citizen. Despite the opportunity provided through the adjournments for the applicant to seek a determination of his status by the citizenship authorities, no record of a finding by them was produced. Accordingly, there was no evidence before the adjudicator that the applicant was a Canadian citizen and her decision that the applicant was not a Canadian citizen was correct.

30. Right to counsel — Every person with respect to whom an inquiry is to be held shall be informed of the person's right to obtain the services of a barrister or solicitor or other counsel and to be represented by any such counsel at the inquiry and shall be given a reasonable opportunity, if the person so desires, to obtain such counsel at the person's own expense.

R.S.C. 1985, c. 28 (4th Supp.), s. 9; 1990, c. 8, s. 51; 1992, c. 49, s. 19.

Case Law

B. (A.) v. Canada (Minister of Citizenship & Immigration) (1997), 142 F.T.R. 161 (Fed. T.D.) — The plaintiff instituted three proceedings. In all proceedings he sought the same confidentiality order and raised the same basic issue as a ground for declaratory relief or for quashing a negative decision on behalf of the Minister.

The applicant was found to be a Convention refugee. He then made application for landing as a permanent resident. Processing of that application was delayed because of an allegation on behalf of the Minister that the applicant was a person described in paragraph 19(1)(j). If so found, the applicant would not be admissible as a permanent resident and would be subject to deportation. For more than a year from August 1996 counsel acting for the applicant sought appropriate disclosure of the facts alleged and the evidence to be adduced. Except for apparently inadvertent disclosure of two documents in December 1996, virtually nothing else was disclosed until mid-July 1997 when the Crown produced 10 volumes of documentary evidence.

In the fall of 1996, the applicant applied for legal aid. His application was approved, but support was limited to only 16 hours of preparation time. The Ontario plan allows for discretionary increases but any such increase would only be considered once the inquiry was completed.

The applicant wrote to the Minister in October 1996 requesting funding for counsel to assist him. That request was not answered. In April 1997, the applicant wrote again renewing his request. In May 1997, the Minister refused the applicant's request.

Section 30 of the Act recognizes that the persons involved in the proceedings under the Act are entitled to be represented by counsel if they desire, but that shall be at the person's own expense. In light of that clear expression of legislative intent there is no statutory jurisdiction in the Court to direct that representation by counsel be funded, even if there were a duty implied under the common law which would obviously be affected by the statute's clear direction. Further, section 7 of the *Charter of Rights* does not imply a general right to counsel funded by public funds for an impecunious person who is the subject of an immigration inquiry, even where the inquiry concerns very serious allegations.

Accordingly, the statement of claim was struck out and the other two applications for judicial review commenced by the plaintiff were also dismissed.

Montiel v. Canada (Minister of Citizenship & Immigration) (1995), 29 Imm. L.R. (2d) 211, 93 F.T.R. 303 — An adjudicator ordered the applicant deported on the basis that the applicant worked in Canada without the appropriate authorization. The applicant was represented throughout by a well-intentioned woman who was a neighbour. The record established that the applicant suffered actual prejudice as the result of the virtually total incompetence exhibited by her representative in the conduct of the hearing. In those circumstances the applicant was denied a fair hearing by virtue of the incompetence of her representative and a breach of natural justice occurred.

The transcript revealed that the representative had no understanding of the procedure to be followed or the criteria which had to be met in order for the adjudicator to make a departure order rather than a deportation order. The representative adduced no evidence from the applicant to support her position that a departure order should be issued. At the conclusion of the evidence the representative made completely irrelevant submissions concerning the humanitarian and compassionate nature of the case and failed to address any matters pertinent to the question of the issuance of a departure notice.

The application for judicial review was allowed and the deportation order quashed.

Halm v. Canada (Minister of Employment & Immigration) (1995), 27 C.R.R. (2d) 23, 91 F.T.R. 106 — This application successfully set aside a conditional deportation order.

The applicant had been ordered deported on the ground that there were reasonable grounds to believe that he had been convicted of an offence outside of Canada which, if committed in Canada, would constitute an offence punishable by a maximum term of imprisonment of 10 years or more. The applicant was convicted in New York State of 5 counts of sodomy, and 3 counts of endangering the welfare of a child.

The applicant successfully argued that section 159 of the *Criminal Code* was unconstitutional and that, therefore, there was no comparable offence in Canada to the sodomy offence of which he had been convicted in the United States. It was common ground between the parties that there was no comparable offence in Canada to the offence of endangering the welfare of a child.

The right to counsel includes being given a reasonable amount of time to retain and instruct counsel and this includes sufficient time to make financial arrangements.

The adjudicator was correct when he indicated that if he were to continue to adjourn the applicant's inquiry to await the processing of the legal aid application that he would be relinquishing control over the timing of the proceedings to the applicant, his counsel, and the legal aid authorities. In this case the adjudicator had adjourned the inquiry 5 times to allow the applicant to obtain some firm commitment that counsel would be representing him.

Counsel for the applicant had argued that it was unfair for the deportation process to be used instead of extradition. The Court noted that extradition and deportation served different purposes. Extradition is initiated by a request from a foreign state. In the absence of any such request a proceeding never begins. Deportation is initiated by the expelling state which does not wish the illegal alien to remain within its borders. There is nothing inherently unfair in a foreign state delaying extradition proceedings when it is known that the individual in question is likely to be deported.

Finally, the Court noted that for purposes of section 19(1)(c.1) equivalency is not required to be proven beyond a reasonable doubt. All that is required is that the adjudicator determine that the applicant is a person with respect to whom there are "reasonable grounds to believe" that he has been convicted outside of Canada of an equivalent offence.

Jouzichin v. Canada (Minister of Citizenship & Immigration) (December 6, 1994), Doc. IMM-1686-94 (Fed. T.D.) — In dealing with the refusal of a request for an adjournment the Court noted that the general rule is that Counsel's conduct is not separate from the client's. Counsel is acting as agent for the client and the client must bear the consequences of having hired poor counsel. The fact that counsel came and said that he was not prepared was not a good reason for seeking an adjournment.

Vargas v. Canada (Minister of Employment & Immigration) (1994), 79 F.T.R. 290 — The applicant was determined, under the old Convention refugee rules, not to have a credible basis for her refugee claim. The applicant was unrepresented by counsel at the inquiry. The record indicated that the applicant was informed of her right to counsel, but not of the availability of legal aid.

The Court concluded that the tribunal provided the applicant a reasonable opportunity to retain counsel and those subject to inquiry are not required to be informed of the availability of legal aid. It would be beneficial for the tribunal to advise claimants of the possibility of obtaining legal aid, but the failure to do so must be examined in each case. In this case the applicant was directed for advice to community organizations or law schools at her second appearance. She had been in Canada about 15 months prior to her inquiry and had married a Canadian citizen. The Court was of the opinion that the applicant had sufficient opportunity to obtain information respecting the availability of legal aid. Accordingly, the application was dismissed.

Afrane v. Canada (Minister of Employment & Immigration) (1993), 14 Admin. L.R. (2d) 201, 20 Imm. L.R. (2d) 312, 64 F.T.R. 1 — This was an application for judicial review to quash an exclusion order. The issue was whether the applicant had been denied the right to counsel by reason of the adjudicator refusing an adjournment.

The applicant and his counsel had agreed to proceed on December 16, 1992 with a resumption of the applicant's inquiry. Subsequent to agreeing to this date, the applicant retained new counsel and on December 16 the applicant attended with a letter from his new counsel, which letter indicated that the applicant's new counsel was unable to attend on December 16 and suggested dates in January to resume the inquiry. The adjudicator refused the adjournment.

This decision reviewed a number of cases dealing with the right to counsel. The Court noted that the refusal to adjourn so that counsel might attend has been upheld on appeal where there were enumerable adjournments and attempts to agree on dates to proceed and where the hearing to proceed was scheduled peremptorily.

The Court noted that there was no suggestion that the applicant or his counsel had deliberately attempted to delay the process and further that the resumption of the inquiry had not been scheduled peremptorily. Further, counsel's request to adjourn the December 16 proceeding was the first adjournment requested.

Accordingly, the exclusion order was quashed and the matter was returned to a new adjudicator for resumption of the applicant's inquiry.

The Court observed that normally the material in a case of this type should contain a candid and full explanation of the circumstances. On this record there was no indication when the applicant's present counsel was retained and no cogent reason given why counsel did not communicate with the respondent in advance of December 16, 1992 to indicate his unavailability and to discuss alternative dates. Further, the Court noted that it was preferable for some description of the prejudice suffered by the applicant to be described in the materials in support of the application. The Court observed that the right to be represented by counsel is not an absolute right. It is predicated on the parties and counsel acting reasonably in all the circumstances.

Kamtapersaud v. Canada (Minister of Employment & Immigration) (1993), 70 F.T.R. 61 — The applicant's mother was the subject of immigration proceedings on the basis that she had overstayed her visitor's permit and accepted employment without being authorized to do so. The first day of the hearing the adjudicator appointed the mother the representative of her three infant children, one of whom was the applicant. The applicant was seventeen years of age at the time and seven weeks short of her eighteenth birthday.

At the inquiry the applicant's mother was found to have overstayed her visitor's permit but not to have engaged in unauthorized employment. The mother's refugee claim was found to have no credible basis.

The credible basis panel then issued a deportation order against the mother and the infant children, including the applicant.

The legislation does not permit an adjudicator to assume all minors are unable to appreciate the nature of the proceedings. The language used in section 29(4) requires the adjudicator to enter into an inquiry on that very question in order to make a determination and form an opinion. The age of the minor in question will play a significant role. Where infants of tender years are involved there may be little doubt with respect to their ability to understand the nature of the proceedings. However, if the minor is of an age which enables her to understand the nature of the proceedings and would permit her to make constructive representations concerning her own interests, her guarantee to representation by counsel, as provided for in section 30(1), and her right to make submissions at the inquiry pursuant to section 33(2) is not satisfied merely by the appointment of a parent or guardian. Such an appointment may, in some cases, satisfy those requirements but the duty of fairness which rests on an adjudicator requires him or her to make such inquiries as are necessary to ensure that this is so.

The deportation order against the applicant was set aside.

Dehghani v. Canada (Minister of Employment & Immigration), [1993] 1 S.C.R. 1053, 18 Imm. L.R. (2d) 245, 10 Admin. L.R. (2d) 1, 20 C.R. (4th) 34, 101 D.L.R. (4th) 654, 150 N.R. 241, 14 C.R.R. (2d) 1 — The appellant, a citizen of Iran, arrived in Canada without valid travel or identity documents and claimed Convention refugee status. He was interviewed at the secondary examination and extensive written notes were made by an immigration officer, which notes were later entered in evidence at the credible-basis hearing. At the conclusion of that hearing the first level tribunal decided that there was no credible basis to the appellant's claim. When the appellant was taken to a secondary examination at Canadian Immigration at Pearson Airport, he was not detained in the sense contemplated by section 10(b) of the Charter.

Further, the principles of section 10(b) do not require that the appellant be provided with counsel at the pre-inquiry or pre-hearing stage of the refugee claim determination process. The secondary examination of the appellant at the port-of-entry is not analogous to a hearing. The purpose of the port-of-entry interview was to aid in the processing of the appellant's application for entry and to determine the appropriate procedures which should be invoked in order to deal with the appellant's application for Convention refugee status. The principles of fundamental justice do not include a right to counsel in these circumstances of routine information gathering.

Edumadze v. Canada (Minister of Employment & Immigration) (1993), 59 F.T.R. 269 (Fed. T.D.) — This is an example of a case where an adjudicator's decision to proceed in the absence of counsel was not quashed. The Court noted that if every refugee claimant was entitled to judicial review because of the non-availability of counsel, the system would be in chaos. In this case five adjournments were granted, two of which were peremptory, before the decision was made to proceed in the absence of counsel.

Ha v. Canada (Minister of Employment & Immigration) (1992), 8 Admin. L.R. 59, 56 F.T.R. 74 (Fed. T.D.) — An immigration officer rejected the applicant's request for landing on humanitarian and compassionate grounds. An order was also sought prohibiting the commencement of the credible basis hearing until such time as a new humanitarian and compassionate interview was conducted. The applicant was a refugee claimant from Hong Kong. He was in the refugee backlog and received a notice to attend an interview to determine whether sufficient humanitarian and compassionate grounds existed to grant landing. Counsel for the applicant was unable to attend this interview due to short notice. He did write a four-page letter in which he requested that the interview be rescheduled. The immigration officer who conducted the interview declined to reschedule and concluded that no sufficient humanitarian and compassionate grounds existed to justify landing the applicant.

There is no obligation under subsection 114(2) to conduct an interview or hearing. There is no authority for the submission that the claimant is entitled to be represented by counsel once an interview is offered. The right to counsel is dealt with in section 30 of the Act and in sections 27 to 39 of the regulations. These provisions refer to the right to counsel at an inquiry. There is no corresponding statutory right to counsel during a subsection 114(2) interview.

Given that an interview is offered there is a duty to act fairly. The concept of what constitutes procedural fairness in purely administrative proceedings varies depending on the type and nature of the proceedings, the nature of the rights involved, possible burdens of the process and the possibility of harm if an adverse decision is reached. The applicant has no legal right to remain in Canada until such time as he is found to be a Convention refugee. The determination of whether humanitarian and compassionate grounds exist is discretionary and can be made without personal appearance. It is a decision that involves no complex legal issues. A negative determination does not lead to removal, but rather the claim then proceeds to the next stage in the process, an oral hearing into the merits, at which time there is a right to legal representation. The duty of fairness dictates that the *audi alteram partem* principle be adhered to and in many instances this will require the services of a qualified interpreter.

The Court concluded that there was no procedural unfairness and dismissed the application.

Editor's Note: The Act and the Regulations have been amended, but the principle may still be important.

Basdeo v. Canada (Minister of Employment & Immigration) (June 4, 1984), Doc. A-87-84 (Fed. C.A.) — Counsel for the applicant wanted to adjourn this section 28 application until judgments of the Supreme Court of Canada had been rendered in a series of appeals attacking the procedure set out in section 71(1) [old Act] of the *Immigration Act*. No section 28 application was ever brought from the decision of the Immigration Appeal Board in this case and the time for so doing has long since expired. Therefore, that decision of the Immigration Appeal Board was not open to collateral attack in this review application which sought to set aside an exclusion order made after the resumption of the applicant's inquiry following the disposition of his refugee claim. The motion for adjournment was dismissed.

The sole ground for attacking the exclusion order was the incompetence of the applicant's counsel. Counsel was chosen by the applicant after having been properly advised of his right to be represented by legally trained counsel. The applicant understood his counsel's degree of competence in the English language and the quality of representation in no way affected the outcome of the inquiry, therefore, the section 28 application was dismissed.

Tam v. Canada (Minister of Employment & Immigration) (1982), [1983] 2 F.C. 31, 46 N.R. 1 (Fed. C.A.) — An inquiry was adjourned for the applicant to seek consideration from the Minister under section 115(2) of the Act. On June 15, 1982, when the inquiry resumed, the applicant had received no final decision, although the Minister had undertaken to give one after consulting his local officials. The adjudicator refused a further adjournment and ordered the applicant deported. The deportation order was quashed because fairness required that the inquiry not proceed until the applicant had received the Minister's answer. The deportation order was also set aside, per Heald J., because the adjudicator erred in refusing to allow the applicant's counsel to make submissions with respect to the section 115(2) application.

Cheung v. Canada (Minister of Employment & Immigration) (1981), 122 D.L.R. (3d) 41, 36 N.R. 563 (Fed. C.A.) — The applicant has the right to cross-examine any witness presented by the case presenting officer. An adjudicator can only refuse to allow the person concerned to present evidence and cross-examine when there are proper grounds for so doing. Where this right to cross-examine is interfered with improperly, a deportation order will be set aside.

Man Yee So v. Canada (Minister of Employment & Immigration), [1980] 1 F.C. 453 (Fed. C.A.) — Where the applicant has retained qualified counsel, and where that counsel sends a less qualified associate who is not a member of the bar, the applicant cannot claim that the failure of her counsel to make submissions that ought to have been made, amounts to a denial of natural justice.

Monfort v. Canada (Minister of Employment & Immigration) (1979), [1980] 1 F.C. 478, 105 D.L.R. (3d) 463, 30 N.R. 174 (Fed. C.A.) — It was held that the immigration officer who first interviewed the applicant upon his arrival at the Toronto International Airport and who informed the applicant of the possibility of withdrawing the application to enter Canada and of the consequences of withdrawing or not withdrawing that application was not obliged to further inform the applicant at that stage of the matter of his right to counsel. A distinction was drawn between the requirements of the Act and Regulation that a person be informed of his right to counsel at an inquiry. It was also noted that there was no provision, under section 23(3), for the right to counsel at a pre-inquiry stage such as the proceedings before the senior immigration officer.

Sewjattan v. Canada (Minister of Employment & Immigration), [1979] 2 F.C. 256 (Fed. C.A.) — The applicant expressed a desire to retain counsel and, initially, was given a 30-minute adjournment to do so. The deportation order was set aside because the adjudicator had informed the applicant of his right to counsel in a manner which left the impression that that 30-minute period was the only period which would be allowed to the applicant to arrange for the presence of counsel.

Pierre v. Canada (Minister of Manpower & Immigration), [1978] 2 F.C. 849, 21 N.R. 91 (Fed. C.A.) — This section 28 application to set aside a deportation order was refused because the Court concluded that the applicant was well aware of his right to counsel and his obligation with respect to producing counsel, and had ample opportunity to produce competent counsel to represent him. The applicant had more than one counsel and many adjournments were granted. Finally, after retaining new counsel, the applicant again sought an adjournment which was refused, at which point counsel withdrew. The Court held that the special inquiry officer did not lose his jurisdiction by proceeding in the absence of counsel.

Molina v. Canada (Minister of Manpower & Immigration) (1975), 12 N.R. 317 (Fed. C.A.) — A deportation order was quashed because of the cumulative effect of a number of inadequacies in the conduct of the special inquiry, none of which, taken alone, would have provided a sufficient basis for quashing the order. There was a failure to explain to the applicant his right to counsel in terms he would understand. There was a short adjournment to a pre-emptory date, when no further assistance was given in eliciting information from the applicant as to his success or lack thereof in obtaining counsel. There was a failure to inform the applicant fully and properly of the purpose of the inquiry and the possible results flowing therefrom.

31. (1) Decision after inquiry — An adjudicator shall give a decision as soon as possible after an inquiry has been completed.

(2) Person informed of basis for order — Where the decision of an adjudicator results in the making of a removal order or conditional removal order against a person, the adjudicator shall inform the person of the basis on which the order was made.

R.S.C. 1985, c. 28 (4th Supp.), s. 10; 1992, c. 49, s. 20.

32. (1) Where person shall be allowed to come into or remain in Canada — Where an adjudicator decides that a person who is the subject of an inquiry is a person described in subsection 14(1) or a person who has a right to remain in Can-

ada, the adjudicator shall let that person come into Canada or remain therein, as the case may be.

(2) **Where person is a permanent resident** — Where an adjudicator decides that a person who is the subject of inquiry is a permanent resident described in subsection 27(1), the adjudicator shall, subject to subsections (2.1) and 32.1(2), make a deportation order against that person.

(2.1) **Departure order** — Where a person referred to in subsection (2) is a person described in paragraph 27(1)(*b*), the adjudicator may, subject to subsection 32.1(2.1), make a departure order against the person if the adjudicator is satisfied that the person should be allowed to return to Canada without the written consent of the Minister and that the person will leave Canada within the applicable period specified in the regulations for the purposes of subsection 32.02(1).

(3) **Where immigrant shall be granted landing** — Where an adjudicator decides that a person who is the subject of an inquiry is a person who, at the time of his examination, was seeking landing and that it would not be contrary to any provision of this Act or the regulations to grant landing to that person, the adjudicator shall

(a) grant landing to that person; or

(b) authorize that immigrant to come into Canada on condition that the immigrant present himself for further examination by an immigration officer within such time and at such place as the adjudicator may direct.

(3.1) **Terms and conditions** — An adjudicator who grants landing to a person pursuant to paragraph (3)(*a*)

(a) shall, if the person is of a class of immigrants for which regulations made under paragraph 114(1)(*ii*.2) require the imposition of terms and conditions, impose the terms and conditions prescribed by those regulations; and

(b) subject to regulations made under paragraph 114(1)(*ii*.4), may, in the case of any person, impose terms and conditions prescribed by regulations made under paragraph 114(1)(*ii*.3).

(4) **Where visitor may be granted entry** — Where an adjudicator decides that a person who is the subject of an inquiry is a person who, at the time of his examination, was seeking entry and that it would not be contrary to any provision of this Act or the regulations to grant entry to that person, the adjudicator may grant entry to that person and, except in the case of a person who may be granted entry pursuant to subsection 19(3), impose terms and conditions of a prescribed nature.

(5) **Removal where seeking admission** — Where an adjudicator decides that a person who is the subject of an inquiry is a person who, at the time of the person's examination, was seeking admission and is a member of an inadmissible class, the adjudicator shall, subject to subsection 32.1(3),

(a) make a deportation order against that person, if that person is a member of an inadmissible class described in paragraph 19(1)(*c*), (*c*.1), (*c*.2), (*d*), (*e*), (*f*), (*g*), (*j*), (*k*) or (*l*) or 19(2)(*a*), (*a*.1) or (*b*); or

(b) make an exclusion order against that person, if that person is a member of an inadmissible class other than an inadmissible class referred to in paragraph (*a*).

(6) Deportation or departure of other than permanent residents — Where an adjudicator decides that a person who is the subject of an inquiry is a person described in subsection 27(2), the adjudicator shall, subject to subsections (7) and 32.1(5), make a deportation order against that person.

(7) Departure of other than permanent residents — Where the person referred to in subsection (6) is a person other than a person described in paragraph 19(1)(*c*), (*c*.1), (*c*.2), (*d*), (*e*), (*f*), (*g*), (*j*), (*k*) or (*l*) or 27(2)(*h*) or (*i*), the adjudicator may, subject to subsection 32.1(5), make a departure order against the person if the adjudicator is satisfied that the person should be allowed to return to Canada without the written consent of the Minister and that the person will leave Canada within the applicable period specified in the regulations for the purposes of subsection 32.02(1).

R.S.C. 1985, c. 30 (3rd Supp.), s. 5; R.S.C. 1985, c. 28 (4th Supp.), ss. 11, 36; 1992, c. 49, s. 21.

Case Law

Section 32(2)

Chiarelli v. Canada (Minister of Employment & Immigration), [1992] 1 S.C.R. 711, 16 Imm. L.R. (2d) 1 (S.C.C.) — This appeal calls into question the constitutionality of the statutory scheme pursuant to which a permanent resident can be deported from Canada if he is found to have been convicted of an offence for which a term of imprisonment of 5 years or more may be imposed. A further attack was brought against the interaction of that scheme with the investigations conducted by the Security Intelligence Review Committee (SIRC) into the activities of persons reasonably believed to be involved in certain types of criminal or subversive activity.

The respondent was convicted of a number of criminal offences and in January 1986 a report was written pursuant to section 27 of the *Immigration Act* identifying the respondent as a permanent resident described in 27(1)(d)(ii). As a result of this report an inquiry was directed pursuant to section 27(3). A deportation order was made against the respondent pursuant to section 32(2). The respondent appealed to the Immigration Appeal Board. That appeal was adjourned after the Solicitor General and the Minister of Employment and Immigration made a joint report to the SIRC. The report indicated that in the opinion of the Ministers the respondent was a person described in section 19(1)(d)(ii). The SIRC conducted the required investigation and reported to the Governor in Council pursuant to section 81(7). The Governor in Council adopted the conclusion of the SIRC and directed the appellant Minister to issue a certificate under section 82(1) with respect to the respondent's appeal. This certificate was issued, with the result that the respondent could not assert compassionate grounds as a reason for allowing the appeal.

The SIRC conducted its investigation and hearing first by reading a document entitled "Statement of Circumstances" as well as two summaries of information. The first day's hearing was held *in camera* and the respondent was excluded from the hearing and provided only with a summary of the evidence. The respondent was permitted to attend the second day of the hearing. The respondent declined, objected to the fairness and constitutionality of the proceeding before the SIRC, submitted no evidence at the hearing, and chose not to cross-examine two RCMP witnesses who had testified on the first day. Counsel did make submissions to the SIRC.

Section 27(1) requires an immigration officer in possession of information that a permanent resident falls into one of its enumerated classes to forward a report to the Deputy Minister. An inquiry is then held by an adjudicator in cases where the Deputy Minister considers one is warranted. Section 32(2) provides that where an adjudicator decides that a person who is the subject of an inquiry does fall within one of the classes in section 27(1), the adjudicator shall, except in the case of a Convention refugee, make a deportation order. All persons who fall within section 27(1)(d)(ii) have deliberately violated an essential condition under which they were permitted to remain in Canada. In such a situation there is no breach of fundamental justice in giving practical effect to the termination of their right to remain in Canada. In the case of a permanent resident deportation is the only way in which to accomplish this. There is nothing inherently unjust about a mandatory order. The fact of the deliberate violation of the condition imposed by section 27(1)(d)(ii) is sufficient to justify a deportation order. Accordingly, sections 27(1)(d)(ii) and 32(2) are not contrary to section 7 of the *Charter of Rights*.

The deportation authorized by sections 27(1)(d)(ii) and 32(2) is not cruel and unusual punishment as described in section 12 of the *Charter of Rights*.

Section 6 of the *Charter* specifically provides for differential treatment of citizens and permanent residents. Accordingly, sections 27(1)(d)(ii) and 32(2) do not violate section 15 of the *Charter*. Permanent residents are given mobility rights in section 6(2). Only citizens are accorded the right to enter, remain in and leave Canada in section 6(1). There is no discrimination contrary to section 15 in a deportation scheme that applies to permanent residents but not citizens.

The effect of the security certificate in this case is to direct the Immigration Appeal Board to dismiss any appeal based on the existence of compassionate or humanitarian considerations. The permanent resident's right of appeal after a certificate has been issued is restricted to questions of law, fact or mixed law and fact.

The *Immigration Act*, S.C. 1910, c. 27, did not provide any specific grounds of appeal. A person ordered deported could only resort to the Minister, who had authority to overturn a deportation order on unspecified grounds. The *Immigration Act*, R.S.C. 1952, c. 325, provided for an immigration appeal board; however, appeals against deportation orders remained under the control of the Minister. The Board heard only those appeals directed to it by the Minister, and the Minister retained the power to confirm or quash the Appeal Board's decision or substitute his decision as he deemed just and proper. The 1966 *White Paper on Immigration* recommended that a reconstituted Immigration Appeal Board have authority to deal conclusively with appeals against deportation orders except in security cases. The *Immigration Appeal Board Act*, 1967 for the first time conferred upon the Board the power to stay or quash a deportation order made against a permanent resident on the basis of all the circumstances of the case. This new power was subject to the discretion of the Minister and the Solicitor General, who could certify their opinion based on security or criminal intelligence reports that it would be contrary to the national interest to permit such relief. This reserves to the Crown the right similar to the prerogative right which existed at common law, to determine that the continued presence in Canada of an alien, subject to a deportation order, was not conducive to the public good. The *Immigration Appeal Board Act* was repealed by the *Immigration Act*, 1976. However, this new Act did not change the nature of the decision that could be made by the Board having regard to all the circumstances of the case. That decision remained as it had been under the 1967 Act, an exercise of discretion based on compassionate grounds. Section 83 of the *Immigration Act*, 1976 limited the availability of relief based on all the circumstances of the case. Such an appeal had to be dismissed if the Minister and Solicitor General certified their opinion that it would be contrary to the national interest to permit such an appeal. In 1984 the SIRC was established by the *Canadian Security Intelligence Service Act*, S.C. 1984, c. 21. The Review Committee was assigned various functions under several Acts, including the *Immigration Act*, 1976. Sections 83 and 82.1 of the *Immi-*

gration Act, 1976 were repealed and amended versions were substituted. The decision as to whether to direct the issuance of a security certificate, however, remained with the Governor in Council. Thus, there has never been a universally available right of appeal from a deportation order on humanitarian or compassionate grounds or "having regard to all the circumstances of the case." Such an appeal has historically been a purely discretionary matter. The right of appeal required to comply with the principles of fundamental justice is a true appeal which enables the decision of first instance to be questioned on factual and legal grounds. The absence of an appeal on wider grounds does not violate section 7.

The procedure followed by the Security Intelligence Review Committee in this case recognized competing individual and state interests and attempted to find a reasonable balance between them. It was not necessary that the respondent be given details of the criminal intelligence investigation techniques or police sources used to acquire the information upon which the two Ministers relied in issuing the certificate. The respondent was given an opportunity to respond by calling his own witnesses or by requesting that he be allowed to cross-examine the RCMP officers who testified *in camera*. Such a procedure was sufficient to meet the requirements of the principles of fundamental justice.

Gressman v. Canada (Minister of Manpower & Immigration) (1980), [1981] 1 F.C. 667 (Fed. C.A.) — The adjudicator was correct in deciding that he had no jurisdiction to review a previous decision denying landing status to the applicant. The adjudicator correctly concluded that his jurisdiction was to determine whether or not landing status had been in fact previously granted.

Morrison, Re, [1974] 2 F.C. 115, 47 D.L.R. (3d) 255 (Fed. C.A.) — Under the *Immigration Act*, R.S.C. 1970, a deportation order was valid if any one of the grounds upon which it was based was sufficient. In this case, however, the applicant's attack on the deportation order failed on all grounds.

R. v. Samejima, [1932] S.C.R. 640, 58 C.C.C. 300, [1932] 4 D.L.R. 246 (S.C.C.) — An order made by a board of inquiry held under the *Immigration Act*, R.S.C. 1927, for the deportation of an alien was quashed by a court of competent jurisdiction for not being in accordance with the Act; the order could not be amended to comply with the Act since it was held there was nothing to amend.

Section 32(3)

Peszko v. Canada (Minister of Citizenship & Immigration) (1996), 35 Imm. L.R. (2d) 148, 114 F.T.R. 52 (Fed. T.D.) — The applicant, a citizen of Poland, entered Canada as a visitor on January 28, 1990. Shortly after his arrival an undertaking of support was submitted to sponsor the applicant as a member of the Self Exile Persons Designated Class. The sponsorship was sent to Buffalo where a visa officer on April 6, 1992 conducted an interview of the applicant. At that interview the applicant presented the visa officer with a police clearance certificate. At the conclusion of the interview the applicant was accepted for landing pending completion of the usual medical and security requirements.

Five days after the interview, on April 11, 1992, the applicant was charged with impaired driving, an offence to which the applicant eventually, on September 30, 1992, pleaded guilty and was convicted of the offence. The Crown proceeded in respect of that offence by way of a summary conviction. The application for landing was rejected and by a letter dated June 28, 1994, immigration authorities advised the applicant that he was inadmissable under section 19(1)(c) of the *Immigration Act*. The reference to section 19(1)(c) was erroneous. In October 1994, the applicant's visitor visa expired and an inquiry was subsequently held. An adjudicator determined that based on the provisions of the *Immigration Act* in effect when the applicant filed his application for permanent residence, the applicant was not inadmissable under the criminality provisions of section 19.

The adjudicator refused to land the applicant pursuant to section 32(3)(a), because he took the view that the applicant's interviews in Buffalo and Canada did not constitute "examinations" for the purpose of an application under subsection 32(3), because they were not conducted at a port-of-entry or otherwise provided under section 12.2 of the *Immigration Regulations*. Subsection 9(1) of the Act clearly requires that the applicant apply for and obtain a visa before appearing at the port-of-entry. Pursuant to subsection 9(2) the applicant's application for an immigrant visa was to be assessed by a visa officer for the purpose of determining whether he appeared to be a person who may be granted landing. The interview was part of the process of assessing the applicant for the purposes of subsections 9(1) and 9(2) and not for the purpose of determining whether he may be granted admission as specified in the definition of the term examination in section 2 of the Act. A decision on admission could not be made until a visa had been issued as required by subsection 9(1).

It may well be that the visa officer erred in his assessment of the applicant's application for an immigrant visa, however, the visa officer's determination was only reviewable pursuant to section 18.1 of the *Federal Court Act.*

Sidhu v. Canada (Minister of Employment & Immigration) (June 19, 1980), Doc. A-259-80 (Fed. C.A.) — The exclusion order was set aside because the adjudicator failed first to determine whether the applicant at the time of her examination by an immigration officer had in fact sought admission as a visitor or as an immigrant. The Court also pointed out that whether or not the applicant sought admission as a visitor was a question entirely distinct from the question of whether or not she was a genuine or *bona fide* visitor within the meaning of section 19(1)(h).

Section 32(4)

Sidhu v. Canada (Minister of Employment & Immigration) (June 19, 1980), Doc. A-259-80 (Fed. C.A.) — For digest, see section 32, subheading *Subsection (3), supra.*

Section 32(5)

Smart v. Canada (Minister of Employment and Immigration) (1991), 13 Imm. L.R. (2d) 266, 134 N.R. 76 (Fed. C.A.) — The applicant came from Costa Rica and was admitted as a visitor. While in Canada, she married a Canadian who took steps to sponsor her application for landing. An Order in Council had not yet been adopted to relieve the applicant from the obligation to obtain an immigrant visa outside of Canada when her husband withdrew his application for sponsorship. The applicant's marriage had broken down and the husband had instituted divorce proceedings. The applicant went to an Immigration Centre and asked permission to be allowed to remain in Canada for humanitarian reasons while her application for permanent residence was being processed. While that application was pending, a section 27 report was made alleging that the applicant had remained in Canada after ceasing to be a visitor. While that inquiry was proceeding, the request to remain in Canada was disposed of negatively by the Minister. The inquiry proceeded to a conclusion and a deportation order was made against the applicant. The deportation order was attacked on the ground that the policy which led to the refusal of the request to remain in Canada offended section 15 of the Charter. The Court declined to give effect to this argument. The adjudicator committed no error of law. His role was merely to determine whether the allegation made against the appellant was well founded and whether a deportation order or departure notice should be made. The adjudicator had no power to pass judgment on the legality of the direction enjoining him to hold the inquiry or on the validity of a policy that he, himself, did not have to apply.

Section 32(7)

Rahal v. Canada (Secretary of State) (1995), 91 F.T.R. 103 — The applicant, while in Canada, was convicted of a crime where the penalty was less than 10 years imprisonment. The applicant had also claimed refugee status but his claim had been rejected by a panel of the CRDD.

Failed refugee claimants are not "claimants" within the meaning of section 32.1. When the words of a section are clear, a statute may not be extended to meet a case for which provision has not been made. The legislature did not include in the definition of a claimant provision for failed refugee claimants with pending applications for judicial review. Accordingly, before a departure order could be issued to the applicant, both of the requirements set out in section 32(7) must be met. The applicant is not entitled to the less restrictive test set out in section 32.1(5).

Jeffery v. Canada (Minister of Employment & Immigration) (1993), 151 N.R. 190 (Fed. C.A.) — The adjudicator decided not to issue a departure notice because he relied on circumstances which were conclusions based on pure speculation without supporting evidence, including the speculative possibility of the applicant returning to Canada and again abusing the refugee determination system. A breach of the *Immigration Act* cannot, alone, be a circumstance supporting the exercise of discretion to refuse a departure notice because everyone liable to be deported has breached the Act in some way and Parliament must have had something more in mind in giving adjudicators the discretion it did. The unsuccessful pursuit of a refugee claim is a circumstance from which a present unwillingness to leave Canada can be inferred.

Khan v. Canada (Minister of Employment & Immigration) (1992), 54 F.T.R. 150 — The applicant sought an order staying a departure notice issued by the respondent. The Court concluded that it had no jurisdiction to stay the departure notice. The Court noted that section 50 of the *Immigration Act* provides that removal orders can be stayed in certain circumstances but is silent with respect to departure notices. Once a departure notice is issued the Minister has no authority to force the applicant to leave by the specified date. If the applicant chooses to remain beyond the specified date then the Minister can convene another inquiry and a deportation order may be issued. At that point the Court will have jurisdiction over the matter.

Ali v. Canada (Minister of Employment & Immigration) (1989), 9 Imm. L.R. (2d) 27, 103 N.R. 393 (Fed. C.A.) — The applicant was a citizen of Bangladesh. He entered Canada as a visitor and ultimately claimed to be a Convention refugee. This claim was rejected and the applicant was finally ordered deported. The adjudicator was not satisfied that the applicant would return to Bangladesh. In that respect, her decision to make a deportation order was not open to challenge. However, the applicant had arranged for temporary admission to the United States for the purpose of applying for a visa admitting him to Canada. He had been unable to leave Canada and seek lawful admission during the inquiry because the Minister had his passport. Section 32(6)(b) speaks of a willingness to leave Canada, not of a willingness to return or go to a particular country. Certainly, the avowed willingness to leave Canada must be assessed realistically. It must be supported by evidence establishing, on a balance of probabilities, that the country to which the person concerned is willing to go is willing to admit him. In this case, arrangements had been made to have the applicant admitted to the United States for 48 hours. While there was no guarantee that the U.S. would admit him, it was sheer speculation to consider the possibility that they might not. The deportation was quashed and the matter remitted to the adjudicator.

Medeiros v. Canada (Minister of Employment & Immigration) (1988), 5 Imm. L.R. (2d) 92 (Fed. C.A.) — This section 28 application was made to set aside a deportation order. In deciding to deport the applicant rather than issue a departure notice, the adjudicator placed much reliance on the circumstance that the applicant worked illegally in Canada and, "thereby, abused the refugee determination system." Parliament did not intend that breaches of various provisions of the Act should be the only matters considered in the exercise of the adjudicator's discretion.

With respect to the decision that the applicant would not leave Canada on a date specified in a departure notice, this finding was set aside as being made without regard to the evidence. The adjudicator described the applicant's testimony as candid and straightforward. The applicant had testified that he was willing to leave Canada by airplane on a date specified and that he had sufficient money to purchase his ticket. Accordingly, the finding by the adjudicator to the contrary was unsupported by the evidence.

Yan v. Canada (Minister of Employment and Immigration) (1987), 4 Imm. L.R. (2d) 90, 84 N.R. 210 (Fed. C.A.) — In this case, the applicant was ordered deported on the basis of his having overstayed and engaged in unauthorized employment. The decision to deport him was set aside. The fact that the applicant deliberately overstayed in itself cannot be a determining factor in the deport/depart decision.

Stephens v. Canada (Minister of Employment & Immigration) (September 4, 1986), Doc. A-854-85 (Fed. C.A.) — The Court qualified its decision in *Frankie Hak Wo Lau.* That case was held to stand for the proposition that it was in error for the adjudicator to conclude that by reason of the simple fact of a breach of the *Immigration Act* any possibility of issuing a departure notice was, therefore, foreclosed.

Hopkins v. Canada (Minister of Employment & Immigration) (December 6, 1985), Doc. A-183-85 (Fed. C.A.) — The deportation order was set aside because the adjudicator ordered the applicant deported and one of her infant children but not the other. Ignoring the existence in Canada of the latter child, the adjudicator had failed entirely to consider the evidence adduced by the applicant in relation to that child. Accordingly, the Court could not be certain that the adjudicator had regard to certain evidence that might well have influenced him not to order deportation but, rather, to issue a departure notice.

Bredwood v. Canada (Minister of Employment & Immigration) (1984), 59 N.R. 316 (Fed. C.A.) — The applicant's attack was limited to the adjudicator's decision making a deportation order rather than issuing a departure notice. There was no evidence whatever to the applicant's credit to be weighed in the balance against her wilfull and deliberate violation of Canadian immigration laws. Thus, the decision to make a deportation order was not subject to attack.

The courts distinguished this case from *Lau v. Canada (Minister of Employment & Immigration)*, [1984] 1 F.C. 434 (Fed. C.A.), on the ground that in that case there was a good deal of evidence before the adjudicator reflecting on the credit of Mr. Lau which was ignored by the adjudicator in making a deportation order.

Lau v. Canada (Minister of Employment & Immigration), [1984] 1 F.C. 434, 6 D.L.R. (4th) 676, 52 N.R. 63 (Fed. C.A.) — The applicant was ordered deported because he was a person described in section 27(2)(b) and (e) of the *Immigration Act*. In practically every case of this nature, the actions of the applicant are deliberate and wilful in that the applicant consciously overstays and consciously accepts employment without authorization. These circumstances by themselves are not always sufficient to entitle an adjudicator to decline to issue a departure notice. The adjudicator must have regard to *all* of the circumstances of the case in making his deport/depart decision.

Wander v. Canada (Minister of Employment & Immigration) (1983), 52 N.R. 384 (Fed. C.A.) — Dilatory tactics by the person concerned or his counsel may very well serve as an indication of an unwillingness to leave Canada and, thus, may be properly considered by an adjudicator in deciding whether a departure notice ought to issue.

Beeston v. Canada (Minister of Employment & Immigration) (1982), 132 D.L.R. (3d) 766, 41 N.R. 260 (Fed. C.A.) — The decision of the adjudicator to issue a deportation order rather than a departure notice was upheld. The Court held that the adjudicator was justified in viewing, as a very important circumstance, the fact that the applicant had remained in Canada illegally and without status since September 1976. However, the adjudicator did specifically consider the other circumstances of the case prior to exercising his discretion.

Stalony v. Canada (Minister of Employment & Immigration) (1980), 36 N.R. 609 (Fed. C.A.) — The appellant's intention to appeal an adjudicator's decision to the Federal Court is not of itself sufficient reason for an adjudicator to refuse to exercise his discretion under this section. However, where this intention to appeal was only one of the considerations which the adjudicator took into account and where other factors existed which suggested that the applicant would not, or could not, leave by a specified date, the decision to make a deportation order was not set aside. The other factors were the inability of the applicant to say how long it would take him to wind up his affairs and the uncertainty as to where he would go due to his stated preference to remain in Canada and not return to his home country.

32.01 Examination of person subject to departure order — A person against whom a departure order has been made shall appear or be brought before an immigration officer so that the immigration officer can verify the person's departure from Canada and issue a certificate of departure in the prescribed form to the person.

1992, c. 49, s. 22.

32.02 (1) Where no certificate issued — Where no certificate of departure is issued within the applicable period specified in the regulations to a person against whom a departure order has been made, the departure order is deemed to be a deportation order made against the person.

(2) Deemed deportation — Where by the operation of subsection (1) a departure order made against a person is deemed to be a deportation order and the person is at that time no longer in Canada, the person is deemed to have been deported from Canada.

(3) Exception — Subsection (1) does not apply to any person who is detained under this Act at any time after

> **(a) where a conditional departure order was made against the person, the day on which the conditional departure order became effective, or**
>
> **(b) where a departure order was made against the person, the day on which the departure order was made,**

and who is still in detention under this Act at the expiration of the applicable period specified in the regulations for the purposes of subsection (1).

1992, c. 49, s. 22.

32.1 (1) Definition of "claimant" — In this section, "claimant" means a person who claims to be a Convention refugee and whose claim has been referred

(a) to a senior immigration officer for a determination of whether the person is eligible to make such a claim; or

(b) to the Refugee Division for a determination of the claim.

(2) Where claimant is a permanent resident — Where an adjudicator decides that a claimant who is the subject of an inquiry is a permanent resident described in subsection 27(1), the adjudicator shall, subject to subsection (2.1), make a conditional deportation order against the claimant.

(2.1) Conditional departure order — Where a claimant referred to in subsection (2) is a person described in paragraph 27(1)(*b*), the adjudicator may make a conditional departure order against the claimant if the adjudicator is satisfied the the claimant should be allowed to return to Canada without the written consent of the Minister and that the claimant will leave Canada within the applicable period specified in the regulations for the purposes of subsection 32.02(1).

(3) Where claimant seeking admission — Where an adjudicator decides that a claimant who is the subject of an inquiry is a person who, at the time of the claimant's examination, was seeking admission and is a member of an inadmissible class, the adjudicator shall

(a) make a conditional deportation order against the claimant if the claimant is a member of an inadmissible class described in paragraph 19(1)(*c*), (*c*.1), (*c*.2), (*d*), (*e*), (*f*), (*g*), (*j*), (*k*) or (*l*) or 19(2)(*a*), (*a*.1) or (*b*); or

(b) make a conditional departure order against the claimant if the claimant is a member of an inadmissible class other than an inadmissible class referred to in paragraph (*a*).

(4) Where claimant not a permanent resident — Where an adjudicator decides that a claimant who is the subject of an inquiry is a person described in subsection 27(2), the adjudicator shall, subject to subsection (5), make a conditional deportation order against the claimant.

(5) Conditional departure order — Where the claimant referred to in subsection (4) is a person other than a person described in paragraph 19(1)(*c*), (*c*.1), (*c*.2), (*d*), (*e*), (*f*), (*g*), (*j*), (*k*) or (*l*) or 27(2)(*h*) or (*i*), the adjudicator may make a conditional departure order against the claimant if the adjudicator is satisfied that the person should be allowed to return to Canada without the written consent of the Minister.

(6) When conditional order becomes effective — No conditional removal order made against a claimant is effective unless and until

(a) the claimant withdraws the claim to be a Convention refugee;

(a.1) the claimant is determined by a senior immigration officer not to be eligible to make a claim to be a Convention refugee and has been so notified;

(b) the claimant is declared by the Refugee Division to have abandoned the claim to be a Convention refugee and has been so notified;

(c) the claimant is determined by the Refugee Division not to be a Convention refugee and has been so notified; or

(d) the claimant is determined pursuant to subsection 46.07(2) not to have a right under subsection 4(2.1) to remain in Canada and has been so notified.

R.S.C. 1985, c. 28 (4th Supp.), s. 12; 1992, c. 49, s. 23.

Case Law

Section 32.1(5)

Rahal v. Canada (Secretary of State) (1995), 91 F.T.R. 103 — The applicant, while in Canada, was convicted of a crime where the penalty was less than 10 years imprisonment. The applicant had also claimed refugee status but his claim had been rejected by a panel of the CRDD.

Failed refugee claimants are not "claimants" within the meaning of section 32.1. When the words of a section are clear a statute may not be extended to meet a case for which provision has not been made. The legislature did not include in the definition of a claimant provision for failed refugee claimants with pending applications for judicial review. Accordingly, before a departure order could be issued to the applicant, both of the requirements set out in section 32(7) must be met. The applicant is not entitled to the less restrictive test set out in section 32.1(5).

33. (1) Where dependants — Where a removal order or conditional removal order is made by an adjudicator against a member of a family on whom other members of the family in Canada are dependent for support, any member of the family dependent on that member may be included in that order and be removed from or required to leave Canada unless the dependant is a Canadian citizen or a permanent resident nineteen or more years of age.

(2) Hearing required — No person may be included in an order under subsection (1) unless the person has been given an opportunity to be heard at an inquiry.

(3) Deeming provision — A person who is included in a deportation order or conditional deportation order pursuant to subsection (1) shall, except for the purposes of subsection 55(1), be deemed to be a person against whom a deportation order or conditional deportation order, as the case may be, has been made.

R.S.C. 1985, c. 28 (4th Supp.), s. 12; 1992, c. 49, s. 24.

Case Law

Section 33(1)

Hopkins v. Canada (Minister of Employment & Immigration) (December 6, 1985), Doc. A-183-85 (Fed. C.A.) — The deportation order was set aside because the adjudicator ordered the applicant deported and one of her infant children, but not the other. Ignoring the existence in Canada of the latter child, the adjudicator had failed entirely to consider the evidence adduced by the applicant in relation to that child. Accordingly, the Court could not be certain that the adjudicator had regard to certain evidence that might well have influenced him not to order deportation but, rather, to issue a departure notice.

Morataya v. Canada (Minister of Manpower & Immigration), [1977] 1 F.C. 571, 15 N.R. 421 (Fed. C.A.) — This case provides an example of a situation where members of a family ordinarily dependent on persons subject to inquiry were found not to be financially dependent on such persons during their stay in Canada.

Denis v. R., [1976] 1 F.C. 499 (Fed. C.A.) — The appellant, a child and a Canadian citizen, contended that to deport her mother would violate the *Canadian Bill of Rights* since it would oblige her mother to take her with her thus exiling the appellant. The Court stated that proper relief for the appellant lies in the discretion of the Immigration Appeal Board to grant compassionate or humanitarian relief. However, it was doubtful whether it could be said that deporting the mother resulted in arbitrary exile or cruel and unusual punishment for the child.

Moshos v. Canada (Minister of Manpower & Immigration), [1969] S.C.R. 886, 7 D.L.R. (3d) 180 (S.C.C.) — Under the *Immigration Act*, R.S.C. 1952, proper notice to a dependent family member required that the dependant be told that he or she had the right to an opportunity to establish that he or she should not be included in the deportation order. A mere reading of the section allowing dependent family members to be included when the family member was on the stand as a witness was held to be insufficient compliance.

Section 33(2)

Kamtapersaud v. Canada (Minister of Employment & Immigration) (1993), 70 F.T.R. 61 — The applicant's mother was the subject of immigration proceedings on the basis that she had overstayed her visitor's permit and accepted employment without being authorized to do so. The first day of the hearing the adjudicator appointed the mother the representative of her three infant children, one of whom was the applicant. The applicant was seventeen years of age at the time and seven weeks short of her eighteenth birthday.

At the inquiry the applicant's mother was found to have overstayed her visitor's permit but not to have engaged in unauthorized employment. The mother's refugee claim was found to have no credible basis.

The credible basis panel then issued a deportation order against the mother and the infant children, including the applicant.

The legislation does not permit an adjudicator to assume all minors are unable to appreciate the nature of the proceedings. The language used in section 29(4) requires the adjudicator to enter into an inquiry on that very question in order to make a determination and form an opinion. The age of the minor in question will play a significant role. Where infants of tender years are involved there may be little doubt with respect to their ability to understand the nature of the proceedings. However, if the minor is of an age which enables her to understand the nature of the proceedings and would permit her to make constructive representations concerning her own interests, her guarantee to representation by counsel, as provided for in section 30(1), and her right to make submissions at the inquiry pursuant to section 33(2) is not satisfied merely by the appointment of a parent or guardian. Such an appointment may, in some cases, satisfy those requirements but the duty of fairness which rests on an adjudicator requires him or her to make such inquiries as are necessary to ensure that this is so.

The deportation order against the applicant was set aside.

Rodney v. Canada (Minister of Manpower & Immigration), [1972] F.C. 663, 27 D.L.R. (3d) 756 (Fed. C.A.) — A dependent family member, the wife, was sworn as a witness at an inquiry against her husband. She was then warned that she could be included in her husband's deportation order and advised that she had the right to be represented by counsel. The wife was then asked to establish why she should not be included in the order. The Court held that such conduct by the inquiry officer gave her insufficient time to prepare an answer.

Moshos v. Canada (Minister of Manpower & Immigration), [1969] S.C.R. 886, 7 D.L.R. (3d) 180 (S.C.C.) — For digest, see section 33, subheading *Subsection (1), supra*.

34. Further inquiries may be held — No decision given under this Act prevents the holding of a further inquiry by reason of the making of another report under paragraph 20(1)(*a*) or subsection 27(1) or (2) or by reason of arrest and detention for an inquiry pursuant to section 103.

Case Law

Halm v. Canada (Minister of Employment & Immigration), 104 F.T.R. 81, [1996] 1 F.C. 547 — The applicant was convicted in New York State on a number of charges including sodomy and endangering the welfare of a child. He was released on bail pending appeal. His appeal was eventually denied by the New York Court of Appeals and the applicant was ordered to surrender himself for sentencing in New York State. Instead, the applicant entered Canada and was eventually arrested by immigration officials. The applicant was ordered deported and successfully brought an application for judicial review quashing the deportation order on the basis that the sodomy section of the *Criminal Code* of Canada was contrary to the *Charter of Rights*. This meant that the applicant was convicted of an offence outside of Canada but not one which, if committed in Canada, would constitute an offense punishable by a maximum term of 10 years or more. Subsequent to that decision the department initiated further proceedings to deport the applicant based on charges of bail jumping and misrepresentation to immigration officials.

The applicant sought to quash this second deportation order in these proceedings. The applicant alleged that in the circumstances of this case the deportation proceedings amounted to an unfair bypassing of, or disguised, extradition. The applicant argued that he could not now be extradited to the United States for his convictions for sodomy because those offenses were no longer recognized in Canada as a result of the judgement striking down section 159 of the *Criminal Code*. There is no legal authority for the proposition that simply because deportation to a foreign country may result in a greater penalty to an individual than extradition to that country, the deportation is contrary to section 7 of the *Charter*.

The Court adopted the reasons of Austin J. in *Shepherd v. Canada (Minister of Employment & Immigration)* (1989), 70 O.R. (2d) 765 (Ont. C.A.), with respect to disguised extradition.

1. If the purpose of the exercise is to deport the person because his presence is not conducive to the public good, that is a legitimate exercise of the power of deportation.

2. If the purpose is to surrender the person as a fugitive criminal to a state because it asked for him, that is not a legitimate exercise of the power of deportation.

3. It is open to the courts to enquire whether the purpose of the government was lawful or otherwise.

4. The onus is on the party alleging an unlawful exercise of power. It is a heavy onus.

5. To succeed it would be necessary to hold that the Minister did not genuinely consider it in the public interest to expel the person in question.

6. The adoption of the *Charter* has not lessened the onus.

The fact that the United States wanted the applicant back, or that there were communications between U.S. and Canadian officials, is not evidence of bad faith or improper motive. Nor does the issuance of a conditional request for extradition by the United States indicate that anything improper was done by Canada in taking steps to deport the applicant.

There is a legislative basis for further inquiries being held in this type of case in section 34 of the *Immigration Act*. The Court did not infer from the evidence that the Minister was acting with improper motive in bringing the second deportation inquiry after the Court had set aside the first deportation order. Section 34 provides for what was done in this case. Section 34 is cast in broad terms.

Cortez v. Canada (Secretary of State) (1994), 74 F.T.R. 9 — The applicant came to Canada in 1987. The record does not indicate his status, but he was not a Canadian citizen or a permanent resident at the time of this case. The applicant was convicted of impaired driving on September 19, 1989. Two other convictions followed on October 23, 1989 and March 16, 1990. The latter convictions related to having a blood alcohol level higher than .08. A report was made on November 5, 1990. This report provided that the applicant was described in section 27(2)(a) in that he was inadmissible by virtue of section 19(2)(b)(i). On December 1, 1992 an inquiry was held and the adjudicator, relying on *Ruparel v. Canada (Minister of Employment & Immigration)*, [1990] 3 F.C. 615, 11 Imm. L.R. (2d) 190, 36 F.T.R. 140, concluded that the allegation that the applicant was inadmissible was not valid.

On February 1, 1993 section 19(2) was amended. On March 2, 1993 a new report was issued in respect of the applicant relying on the same convictions. An inquiry was held in May 1993 and a deportation order issued.

There was no question of retrospectivity. A determination had to be made at the time of the second inquiry of the applicant's admissibility and that determination had to be made on the facts and the provisions of the Act, namely sections 27(2)(a) and 19(2)(a), as they read after the 1993 amendments.

Section 34 excludes *res judicata* in the specific context of section 27 and therefore the adjudicator had jurisdiction to examine the applicant's admissibility to Canada.

There was no unreasonable delay. The report in question (March 19, 1993) was written approximately one month after the amendments to the Act and the inquiry was held two months later. There was, therefore, no unreasonable delay.

Canada (Minister of Employment & Immigration) v. Steward (1991), 132 N.R. 159 (Fed. C.A.) — In an earlier proceeding, the adjudicator was concerned exclusively with the question of whether the respondent's admitted conviction in Oklahoma met the equivalency test of section 19(1)(c). The Court concluded that the adjudicator was correct in deciding that there was absolutely no evidence from which he could properly decide that there was equivalency in that previous proceeding. That finding did not preclude the Minister from considering the previous conviction together with proper evidence of equivalency in determining whether or not the respondent, Steward, should be granted landing. The finding also did not bar the holding of a further inquiry pursuant to section 34 of the Act.

Estrada v. R. (1987), 1 Imm. L.R. (2d) 24, 8 F.T.R. 317 (Fed. T.D.) — The applicant was the subject of an immigration inquiry. The inquiry was based on a defective report because the report alleged that the applicant had been convicted of an offence under section 3(1) of the *Narcotic Control Act* without making it clear that the allegation related to the conviction for an indictable offence under another Act of Parliament and not the *Criminal Code*. The report was amended. However, during the course of argument, the adjudicator and the case presenting officer became concerned about the validity of the proceedings. The case presenting officer received instructions from her superiors to withdraw the direction. The adjudicator indicated that the procedure being followed was correct and that no withdrawal of the direction was necessary. The case presenting officer requested an adjournment to consider her position, and her request was denied, whereupon she withdrew the direction. A new direction for inquiry was forthcoming. The report alleged that the applicant was convicted of one count of possession of a narcotic contrary to the *Narcotic Control Act*. This was held not to be an abuse of process. The Court characterized the Minister as having acted in a very cautious way in order to avoid any error of law. The Court found nothing so oppressive or vexatious as to constitute an abuse of process. The fact of the withdrawal of the direction in order to terminate the inquiry, coupled with the allowing of another direction for inquiry to be made and based upon the same facts, although under a different paragraph of section 27, did not, in the circumstances, constitute an abuse of process.

Rabbat v. Canada (Minister of Employment & Immigration), [1986] 2 F.C. 46 (Fed. T.D.); affirmed (January 21, 1987), Doc. A-100-85 (Fed. C.A.); leave to appeal to S.C.C. refused (1987), 80 N.R. 319n (S.C.C.) — The applicant held the status of permanent resident since 1972. In December 1981, he was arrested. Shortly afterwards, an immigration officer filed a report pursuant to section 27(2) reporting that the applicant was described in section 19(1)(c). The adjudicator concluded that the applicant was a permanent resident and, therefore, a person not described in the report. Two years after this decision, a senior immigration officer signed a new report based on the same facts but under section 27(1). Section 34 of the Act was held to exclude the principle of *res judicata* for all practical purposes in the specific context of the sections to which it referred. The delay was not so unreasonable as to constitute an injustice of the type described in section 7 of the *Charter*.

R. v. Parker (July 12, 1985), Doc. 85-01-00584 (Man. Q.B.) — An inquiry concerning Mr. Parker was held upon two reports under section 27. At the conclusion of the inquiry, the adjudicator found in Mr. Parker's favour with respect to the allegation under section 27(2)(a) and in favour of the Commission with respect to the allegation under section 27(2)(b). A departure notice was issued to Mr. Parker. The Commission was unhappy with the result, as it had been seeking a deportation order. No appeal of the adjudicator's decision was made; instead, fresh proceedings under section 27(2)(a) were commenced. Mr. Parker was arrested and detained in connection with these new proceedings. The warrant for arrest and the order of detention were quashed and it was determined that the applicant was not properly detained. The Commission, at the time of the first inquiry, was aware of the fact that the applicant had an extensive criminal record. The Commission made a calculated decision to proceed with the information that it could prove and did not seek an adjournment to obtain the information that was the subject of the second inquiry. Thus, the issue to be dealt with on the second inquiry was held to have been already decided as a result of the first inquiry and there was, therefore, no jurisdictional basis for the second inquiry.

Au v. Canada (Attorney General), [1977] 2 F.C. 254 (Fed. T.D.) — The Court emphasized that *res judicata* only applied when the first tribunal was competent and had jurisdiction to hear and determine the matter before it. Accordingly, where the first deportation order was set aside because the special inquiry officer lacked jurisdiction to conduct the inquiry, *res judicata* could not apply. Prohibition has to be sought against a specific individual and the Attorney General of Canada was not in that category.

Okolakpa v. Lanthier (1976), [1977] 1 F.C. 437 (Fed. T.D.) — This case was decided under the *Immigration Act*, R.S.C. 1970, the relevant provisions of which have been worded slightly differently in the present Act. Prohibition was granted where the Minister sought to proceed on a "subsequent report" which was not based on new information but in which the recommendation was based on a different subparagraph of the *Immigration Act*. The Court of Appeal previously had held that the subparagraph on which the Court originally based its decision was not applicable. Therefore, the petitioner or applicant had a right to a determination of his original application (for an extension of his student visa) which the Court directed should be made forthwith. The decision on the extension of a student visa had not been given pending a summons for further inquiry.

35. [Repealed 1992, c. 49, s. 25.]

36. Notice of right of appeal — **Where a removal order or conditional removal order is made against any person who has a right of appeal to the Appeal Division pursuant to section 70, the adjudicator shall forthwith inform that person of the right of appeal.**

R.S.C. 1985, c. 28 (4th Supp.), s. 13.

Minister's Permits

37. (1) Issue of permits — **The Minister may issue a written permit authorizing any person to come into or remain in Canada if that person is**

(a) in the case of a person seeking to come into Canada, a member of an inadmissible class; or

(b) in the case of a person in Canada, a person with respect to whom a report has been or may be made under subsection 27(2).

(2) When permit may not be issued — **Notwithstanding subsection (1), no permit may be issued to**

(a) a person against whom a removal order has been made who has not been removed from Canada pursuant to such an order or has not otherwise left Canada, unless an appeal from that order has been allowed; or

(b) [Repealed 1992, c. 49, s. 26.]

(c) a person in Canada with respect to whom an appeal made pursuant to section 77 has been dismissed.

(3) Conditions of permit — **A permit shall be in force for such period not exceeding three years as is specified in the permit.**

(4) Extension and cancellation — **The Minister may at any time, in writing, extend or cancel a permit.**

(4.1) Leaving Canada cancels permit — **Unless a permit specifies that a person may leave and re-enter Canada, the permit is cancelled if the person to whom the permit was issued leaves Canada.**

(5) Deportation order following cancellation of permit — **The Minister may, on the cancellation or expiration of a permit, make a deportation order against the person to whom the permit was issued or direct that person to leave Canada within a specified period.**

(6) Deportation — **Where a person who has been directed by the Minister to leave Canada within a specified period of time fails to do so, the Minister may make a deportation order against that person.**

(7) Annual report to Parliament — **The Minister shall, within thirty days following the commencement of each fiscal year or, if Parliament is not then sitting, within the first thirty days next thereafter that either House of Parliament is sitting, cause to be laid before Parliament a report specifying the number of permits issued during the preceding calendar year and in respect of each permit issued**

(a) to a person seeking to come into Canada, the inadmissible class of which that person is a member; or

(b) to a person in Canada, the applicable paragraph of subsection 27(2) pursuant to which a report has been or may be made.

1992, c. 49, s. 26.

Case Law

Section 37(1)

Dee v. Canada (Minister of Employment & Immigration) (1991), 14 Imm. L.R. (2d) 5, 135 N.R. 241, 53 F.T.R. 85 (note) (Fed. C.A.) — This was an appeal from an order of the Trial Division dismissing an application for an order quashing the Minister's decision not to issue the applicant a Minister's permit and for an order requiring the Minister to give the applicant a fair hearing before deciding whether to issue a permit. The argument in support of the appeal was based on the Minister's policy to issue permits to those who had been found to be Convention refugees. The appellant knew of that policy and, as a consequence, had a legitimate expectation that the policy would be applied in his case and that he would obtain a permit as a matter of course. The Court determined that the Minister was not under a duty as a result of the policy, and the appellant's expectation, to issue a permit to the appellant. Further, due to the fact that a removal order had been made against the appellant subsequent to the Minister's refusal to issue a permit and, due to the fact that this removal order was still in effect, no useful purpose was served by this appeal. The Minister could not issue a permit to the applicant at this point in time. Accordingly, the appeal was dismissed.

Donoso v. Canada (Minister of Employment & Immigration) (1989), 9 Imm. L.R. (2d) 32, 38 Admin. L.R. 219, 30 F.T.R. 241 (Fed. T.D.) — The applicant is a citizen of Chile who arrived in Canada and made a claim for convention refugee status. He was granted convention refugee status. Prior to being granted permanent resident, he was convicted of several serious criminal offences. The second inquiry was convened to determine whether Mr. Donoso could remain in Canada. During the inquiry, convention refugee status was again sought. Mr. Donoso was informed that his second claim had been accepted. Prior to the resumption of the second inquiry, Mr. Donoso sought an interview for the purpose of establishing the circumstances which favoured a Minister's permit. The request for an interview was refused as was the Minister's permit. The resumption of the second inquiry was stayed pending disposition of this case.

In making decisions regarding Minister's permits, immigration officials are obliged to fulfil the requirements of the duty of fairness. Whether the fairness standard will involve submissions of written materials, oral interviews, formal hearings or legal representations necessarily varies according to the facts of each case. The *Charter* applies to administrative decisions but, before relief can be provided pursuant to the *Charter*, the applicant has to demonstrate that the security of his person is threatened as a result of the decision to refuse him a permit. The decision relating to a permit will not cause the applicant to be removed to Chile. It is the adjudicator, upon the resumption of the inquiry, who will issue a departure notice or a deportation order and the decision relating to removal can be appealed. If these appeals are unsuccessful, it will then become necessary to decide to which country the applicant should be removed and the applicant will have opportunities at that time to make representations to the Minister outlining why he should not be returned to Chile. The existence of these numerous steps prior to actual removal determine that the applicant's life, liberty or security of the person were not threatened by the decision to refuse a Minister's permit and accordingly the application was dismissed.

Prassad v. Canada (Minister of Employment & Immigration), [1989] 1 S.C.R. 560, [1989] 3 W.W.R. 289, 36 Admin. L.R. 72, 7 Imm. L.R. (2d) 253, 93 N.R. 81, 57 D.L.R. (4th) 663

(S.C.C.) — The issue was whether the adjudicator of an immigration inquiry must adjourn to enable the person concerned to pursue an application to the Minister under s. 37(1) of the *Immigration Act*. In a four to two decision, the majority of the Court held that the adjudicator is neither bound to accede to a request for an adjournment to enable an application under s. 37 to be brought, nor is the adjudicator required to refuse it. The adjudicator must consider such factors as the number of adjournments already granted and the length of time for which an adjournment is sought in exercising discretion to adjourn. The adjudicator also must consider the opportunity available to the subject of the inquiry to apply to the Minister prior to the request for an adjournment. The majority of the Court distinguished the case at bar with *Ramawad v. Canada (Minister of Manpower & Immigration)*, [1978] 2 S.C.R. 375, 81 D.L.R. (3d) 687, 18 N.R. 69 (S.C.C.), and held that *Ramawad* must be read in the context of its facts and the particular employment visa provisions in effect at the time of that decision.

Canada (Minister of Employment & Immigration) v. Widmont, [1984] 2 F.C. 274, 56 N.R. 198 (Fed. C.A.) — The respondent legally entered Canada from Poland. She spoke neither French nor English. The immigration officer spoke no Polish and there was no interpreter. The respondent was admitted for four days. Unaware of this limitation she stayed for a much longer period and married her husband, a Canadian citizen. The respondent sought to clarify her status with the result that a direction for inquiry was issued in her case. She applied for a Minister's permit during the course of the inquiry. Prohibition was granted by the trial division to prevent the inquiry from concluding before the Minister gave his decision on whether to issue a permit. On appeal it was held that the refusal of the adjudicator to adjourn was consistent with earlier decisions of the Federal Court on this question. There is a particularly strong dissent on this question by Mr. Justice MacGuigan and the law of *stare decisis* is described in the judgment of Mr. Justice Urie who concurred in the majority decision. This was important because the majority judgment ruled that previous courts considered the issue raised by this case and, accordingly, the Court in this case was obliged to follow its previous decisions. Mr. Justice Urie noted that the Federal Court of Appeal should refuse to follow its previous decisions only if it was convinced that the earlier decisions were incorrect.

Dolack v. Canada (Minister of Manpower & Immigration), [1983] 1 F.C. 194, 140 D.L.R. (3d) 767, 45 N.R. 146 (Fed. C.A.), affirming in part [1982] 1 F.C. 396 (Fed. C.A.) — The fact that a non-resident has an interest or claim to an interest in property of whatever nature in Canada does not affect the Minister's right to refuse an entry permit if the applicant is a member of an inadmissible class.

Beeston v. Canada (Minister of Employment & Immigration) (1982), 132 D.L.R. (3d) 766, 41 N.R. 260 (Fed. C.A.) — The applicant applied for adjournment so that his request for a Minister's permit could be dealt with directly by the Minister of Employment and Immigration. The adjournment was refused because the manager of the immigration centre in Vancouver had already refused, on behalf of the Minister, the request for issuance of a Minister's Permit. Because this authority had been delegated pursuant to the provisions of section 123 of the Act, it was held that the adjudicator was correct in refusing the request for an adjournment.

Stalony v. Canada (Minister of Employment & Immigration) (1980), 36 N.R. 609 (Fed. C.A.) — Section 37 does not create a right to a ministerial permit; it simply gives to the Minister the power to grant one. The issuance of the deportation order would have deprived the Minister of that power regardless of when the order was made. Therefore, the attack on the validity of the deportation order failed.

Hardayal v. Canada (Minister of Manpower & Immigration) (1977), [1978] 1 S.C.R. 470, 75 D.L.R. (3d) 465, 15 N.R. 396 (S.C.C.) — Granting a Ministerial permit under the *Immigration Act*, R.S.C. 1970, c. I-2, was an administrative matter requiring no notice to, or hearing of, the recipient. Such an act was not required to be taken on a judicial or *quasi*-judicial basis. In the opinion of Parliament, power to issue permits was necessary to give flexibility to the administration of immigration policy. The exercise of this power is not subject to any right of a fair hearing. The Minister is required to act fairly and for a proper motive and his failure to do so may well give the person effected the right to take proceedings under section 18(a) of the *Federal Court Act*, R.S.C. 1970 (2nd Supp.), c. 10. The decision to cancel or not issue a permit is not subject to review under section 28 of the *Federal Court Act.*

Section 37(4)

Singh (P.N.) v. Canada (1986), 3 F.T.R. 196 (Fed. T.D.) — The Minister's permit, which the applicant held, and which was dated June 4, 1985, was cancelled. This was done after the Minister's representative, through extensive interviews, had heard very relevant evidence from the applicant and had given the applicant every opportunity to explain his position. Because there are no statutory criteria for the exercise of the discretion to extend or cancel a permit, the discretion is unlimited. Nothing further was required by the Minister to validly exercise his power to cancel the permit. The applicant was not claiming refugee status and had not alleged that any danger to his life, liberty or the security of his person would flow from the cancellation of the Minister's permit. Thus, there was no interest protected by section 7 of the Canadian *Charter of Rights and Freedoms* at stake in these proceedings. The content of the "principles of fundamental justice" prescribed in section 7 varies with the nature of the interests involved. Any entitlement the applicant had to remain in Canada pursuant to the Minister's permit was, in the absence of being admitted for permanent residence, subject to the purely discretionary power of the Minister to cancel his permit.

Ally v. Canada (Minister of Employment & Immigration) (May 15, 1984), Doc. T-1080-83 (Fed. T.D.) — The applicant was issued a Minister's permit in accordance with the "last remaining family member" policy. Subsequent information established that the applicant was not the last remaining family member. Even though there was no evidence to suggest that the respondent Minister was ever deliberately misled by anyone, there was also no justification for ordering that the applicant be given the benefit of a policy which did not apply to her. The Minister, in refusing to extend the permit, was discharging an administrative responsibility and had not failed in his duty to treat the applicant fairly and, accordingly, the application to quash the deportation order issued against the applicant was dismissed.

Mauger v. Canada (Minister of Employment & Immigration) (1980), 109 D.L.R. (3d) 246 (Fed. T.D.), affirmed (1980), 119 D.L.R. (3d) 54, 36 N.R. 91 (Fed. C.A.) — The cancellation of a permit to remain in Canada is an administrative act and in exercising this power the Minister must act fairly and from a proper motive. The Court concluded that the Minister clearly did so. The applicant entered as a visitor and remained after he ceased to be a visitor. Due to the sponsorship of his wife, he was issued a Minister's permit. When the sponsorship was withdrawn, the permit was cancelled. The Court noted that the requirements of fairness must be balanced by the dictates of the administrative process under examination. The appellant appraised the immigration commission of his side of the marital story. The Court also held that a person in the position of the appellant is not entitled to counsel during the administrative process.

Manhas, Re (1976), [1977] 1 F.C. 156 (Fed. T.D.) — When a ministerial permit has expired, the holder ceases to have any legal right to remain in Canada.

Section 37(5)

Canada (Minister of Employment & Immigration) v. Cembranos-Alvarez (June 6, 1983), Doc. A-267-82 (Fed. C.A.) — The appellant had remained in Canada without interruption since he had ceased to be a visitor on September 25, 1978. He was during that time a person described in section 27(2)(e), however, as long as he had a Minister's permit he was entitled to be here. Once the permit expired that entitlement came to an end and he could be the subject of a section 27 inquiry.

Section 37(6)

R. v. Gittens (1982), 68 C.C.C. (2d) 438 (Fed. T.D.) — The applicant came to Canada in 1965 at the age of five. He became a permanent resident but not a Canadian citizen. A deportation order was made based on section 27(1)(d)(i) and (ii) of the *Immigration Act*. An appeal against the deportation order was dismissed by the Immigration Appeal Board and the Federal Court of Appeal refused leave to appeal the Immigration Appeal Board's decision. The applicant, at the time of the giving of judgment, had completed serving all of the sentences for his criminal offences and was being kept in custody pending the execution of the deportation order. The application for an order quashing the deportation order against the applicant was dismissed because the *Charter* is not retrospective in its operation. The application for an order seeking the release of the applicant was denied on the basis that section 10 of the *Charter* stipulated that the validity of the detention was to be determined by way of *habeas corpus* and the Court noted that it had no jurisdiction to grant *habeas corpus*. The Court did not express an opinion on whether it had jurisdiction to grant *habeas corpus* with *certiorari* in aid, pursuant to the *Charter*. If execution *per se* of a valid deportation order would constitute an infringement or denial of an applicant's fundamental rights and freedoms, the Court had jurisdiction in the first instance to entertain an application for an appropriate remedy. Freedom of association as envisaged by section 2(d) of the *Charter* will not be violated by the execution of a deportation order. Execution of the order will sever immediate links with family, friends and others. To the extent that these are licit associations, they are social and familial. Assuming that they are the type of associations contemplated by section 2(d) of the *Charter*, they are subject to such reasonable limits prescribed by law as can demonstrably be justified in a free society. The reasonableness of the right of a free and democratic state to deport alien criminals was held to be self-evident and, therefore, demonstrably justified. Section 11(h) of the *Charter* was not violated because deportation was held not to be punishment for the offences, his conviction of which had rendered him liable to deportation in the first place. In this case, the probative value of the evidence of the conditions in Guyana was minimal. The Court accepted that economic conditions and prospects were not nearly as favourable to the individual there as in Canada and that the human rights of persons politically opposed to those in power were not, generally, respected by the Government of Guyana. The Court noted that neither the applicant nor his family had in any way been politically active so as to attract the attention of those in power in Guyana and that, therefore, the treatment the applicant could expect in Guyana would depend entirely upon his conduct there. Thus, the Court concluded that the evidence did not support the claim that execution of the deportation order would deprive the applicant of the right to life, liberty and security of the person afforded by section 7 and, therefore, the Court declined to grant relief.

Finally, the Court noted that the incidents of deportation, whatever their degree, do not render deportation a cruel and unusual treatment of an adult. As a norm, execution of a deportation order is not in the abstract rule an unusual treatment. The Court was not persuaded by the evidence that deportation of the applicant to Guyana would be cruel and unusual treatment in the context of this case. Accordingly, the application was dismissed.

38. (1) Landing authorized by Governor in Council — Notwithstanding any other provision of this Act or the regulations, but subject to subsection (2), the Gover-

nor in Council may authorize the landing of any person who at the time of landing has resided continuously in Canada for at least five years under the authority of a written permit issued by the Minister under this Act.

(2) Consent of province required — Where the Minister has entered into an agreement with a province pursuant to section 108 whereby the province has sole responsibility for the selection of certain classes of immigrants who intend to reside in that province, an immigrant of any of those classes of immigrants who intends to reside in that province may be granted landing under subsection (1) only if the province has given its consent.

1992, c. 49, s. 27.

Safety and Security of Canada

38.1 Purpose of provisions — Recognizing that persons who are not Canadian citizens or permanent residents have no right to come into or remain in Canada and that permanent residents have only a qualified right to do so, and recognizing the necessity of cooperation with foreign governments and agencies in maintaining national security, the purposes of sections 39 to 40.2 are

(a) to enable the Government of Canada to fulfil its duty to remove persons who constitute a threat to the security or interests of Canada or whose presence endangers the lives or safety of persons in Canada;

(b) to ensure the protection of sensitive security and criminal intelligence information; and

(c) to provide a process for the expeditious removal of persons found to be members of an inadmissible class referred to in section 39 or 40.1.

1992, c. 49, s. 28.

39. (1) Definition of "Review Committee" — In this section and sections 39.1, 39.2 and 40 "Review Committee" has the same meaning as in the *Canadian Security Intelligence Service Act*.

(2) Report, notice and referral — Where the Minister and the Solicitor General of Canada are of the opinion, based on security or criminal intelligence reports received and considered by them, that a permanent resident is a person described in paragraph 19(1)(*c*.2), subparagraph 19(1)(*d*)(ii), paragraph 19(1)(*e*), (*f*), (*g*), (*k*) or (*l*) or 27(1)(*a*.1), subparagraph 27(1)(*a*.3)(ii) or paragraph 27(1)(*g*) or (*h*), they may make a report to the Review Committee.

(3) Notice — The Minister and the Solicitor General of Canada shall, within ten days after a report referred to in subsection (2) is made, cause a notice to be sent informing the person who is the subject of the report that following an investigation in relation thereto, a deportation order may be made against that person.

(4) Filing of a document — Where a report is made to the Review Committee under subsection (2), the Minister may cause to be filed with an immigration officer, a senior immigration officer or an adjudicator, as required for the purposes of this Act, a document stating that, in the opinion of the Minister and the Solicitor General of Canada, the person named in the document is a person described in paragraph 19(1)(*c*.2),

subparagraph 19(1)(*d*)(ii), paragraph 19(1)(*e*) (*f*), (*g*), (*k*) or (*l*) or 27(1)(*a*.1), subparagraph 27(1)(*a*.3)(ii) or paragraph 27(1)(*g*) or (*h*) as the case may be.

(5) Application of the Canadian Security Intelligence Service Act — Where a report is made to the Review Committee pursuant to subsection (2), the Review Committee shall investigate the grounds on which it is based and for that purpose subsections 39(2) and (3) and sections 43, 44 and 48 to 51 of the *Canadian Security Intelligence Service Act* apply, with such modifications as the circumstances require, to the investigation as if the investigation were conducted in relation to a complaint made pursuant to section 42 of that Act, except that

(a) a reference in any of those provisions to "deputy head" shall be read as a reference to the Minister and the Solicitor General of Canada; and

(b) paragraph 50(*a*) of that Act does not apply with respect to the person concerning whom the report is made.

(5.1) Investigation to cease — If the Review Committee is of the opinion that it cannot perform its duties described in subsections (5) and (6) to (10), it must cease its investigation and give notice to the Minister and the person referred to in subsection (2).

(6) Statement to be sent to person affected — The Review Committee shall, as soon as practicable after a report is made to it pursuant to subsection (2), send to the person with respect to whom the report is made a statement summarizing such information available to it as will enable the person to be as fully informed as possible of circumstances giving rise to the report.

(7) [Repealed 1992, c. 49, s. 29.]

(8) Idem — Notwithstanding anything in this Act, where a report is made to the Review Committee pursuant to subsection (2), an inquiry under this Act concerning the person in respect of whom the report is made shall not be commenced or, if commenced, shall be adjourned until the Review Committee has, pursuant to subsection (9), made a report to the Governor in Council with respect to that person and the Governor in Council has made a decision in relation thereto.

(9) Report to Governor in Council — The Review Committee shall, on completion of an investigation in relation to a report made to it pursuant to subsection (2), make a report to the Governor in Council containing its conclusion whether or not a certificate should be issued under subsection 40(1) and the grounds on which that conclusion is based.

(10) Report to person concerned — The Review Committee shall, at the same time as or after a report is made pursuant to subsection (9), provide the person with respect to whom the report is made with a report containing the conclusion referred to in that subsection.

R.S.C. 1985, c. 30 (3rd Supp.), s. 6; R.S.C. 1985, c. 29 (4th Supp.), s. 2; 1992, c. 49, s. 29; 1997, c. 22, s. 4.

Case Law

Editor's Note: If, before section 7 of 1997, c. 22 comes into force, a legal proceeding has been commenced with respect to an investigation under subsection 81(4) of the Immigration Act, a final decision in that proceeding that the Review Committee must cease its investiga-

tion is deemed to be the decision of the Review Committee under subsection 81(4.1) of that Act, as enacted by subsection 7(2) of this Act. 1997, c. 22, s. 11(2).

Moumdjian v. Canada (Security Intelligence Review Committee) (1997), 6 Admin. L.R. (3d) 239, (sub nom. *Moumdjian v. Security Intelligence Review Committee)* 221 N.R. 188, (sub nom. *Moumdjian v. Security Intelligence Review Committee)* 141 F.T.R. 80 (note) (Fed. C.A.) — This was an appeal from an order of a Judge of the Trial Division, sitting as a judge designated by the Chief Justice pursuant to section 38(1) of the *Canada Evidence Act.* The issue was whether the designated judge erred in sustaining an objection to the disclosure of information that had been placed before the Security Intelligence Review Committee (SIRC) during the course of an investigation by SIRC pursuant to section 39 of the *Immigration Act.*

In the course of its investigation and in the absence of the appellant and his counsel, SIRC received evidence in the form of oral testimony and documents. The disclosure of this evidence was objected to in the certificate filed pursuant to section 37(1) of the *Canada Evidence Act.* The disclosure of correspondence between SIRC and CSIS containing information supplied to SIRC and miscellaneous documents containing other information supplied to SIRC by CSIS was also objected to. All of this evidence was listed in a schedule attached to the section 37(1) certificate. The appellant was provided with a summary of the evidence that was submitted to SIRC in his absence and also with a summary of the argument that was presented to SIRC.

The Court referred to *Henrie v. Canada,* [1989] 2 F.C. 229 (T.D.) for a description of the competing interests at stake and the proper balancing of these interests where an application for judicial review of a SIRC decision is brought. This decision described the balancing that must occur between the principles of openness in the judicial process and the public interest in not disclosing evidence in certain types of cases.

In order to succeed on the appeal, the appellant must satisfy the Court that the Trial Division judge erred in law in refusing to order disclosure. The function of the Court of Appeal in this instance is limited to reviewing the decision of the designated judge so as to be satisfied that it does not disclose an error of the sort enumerated in subsection 18.1(4) of the *Federal Court Act.* If the decision does not reveal such an error, the matter ends and the Court is not entitled to examine any of the information which the judge found ought not to be disclosed.

Yamani v. Canada (Solicitor General) (1995), 31 Imm. L.R. (2d) 191, 129 D.L.R. (4th) 226, 32 C.R.R. (2d) 295, (sub nom. *Al Yamani v. Canada (Solicitor General))* 103 F.T.R. 105, [1996] 1 F.C. 174 (Fed. T.D.) — These were two applications for judicial review in relation to a decision of the Security Intelligence Review Committee (SIRC) made August 3, 1994 and a decision of the Governor General in Council made August 25, 1994, based upon the decision and report of SIRC.

The applicant is a stateless person, a male of Palestinian origin. His father was said to be one of the founders of the Popular Front for the Liberation of Palestines (PFLP). Though he was born in Beirut the applicant is not a citizen of Lebanon, but has carried and has travelled on a Lebanese travel document.

The applicant is a landed immigrant who arrived in Canada in 1985. He resided in Canada since that time, made an application for citizenship in 1988 and as a result of that application became the subject of security screening by the Canadian Security Intelligence Service (CSIS). He was interviewed by a CSIS officer and subsequently received a letter signed by the Minister of Employment and Immigration, and the Solicitor General stating that they had made a report to SIRC because they were of the opinion that the applicant was a person described in paragraphs 19(1)(e), 19(1)(g) and 27(1)(c). SIRC's finding related only to paragraph 19(1)(g).

Subsequent to the Minister's report the applicant was the subject of a hearing before a single member of SIRC. This hearing resulted in the applicant being found to be a person described in 19(1)(g). SIRC reported that fact to the Governor in Council and recommended that a certificate be issued against the applicant under section 40(1) of the Act. That report was the subject of the first judicial review application.

Upon receipt of the report the Governor in Council issued an order-in-council reciting that after considering the report of SIRC it was satisfied that the applicant was a person described in paragraph 19(1)(g) of the Act. That decision also directed the Solicitor General to issue a security certificate pursuant to section 40 so designating the applicant.

The Court found that pursuant to sections 18 and 18.1 of the *Federal Court Act* it does have jurisdiction to review the decision of SIRC. SIRC is a federal board, commission, or tribunal as defined in section 2 of the *Federal Court Act* since it is a body exercising jurisdiction or powers conferred by an act of parliament. Relief against a decision of SIRC is available under section 18 of the *Federal Court Act* upon an application for judicial review pursuant to section 18.1.

The Court granted intervenor status to the Canadian Arab Federation (CAF). The CAF sought to argue that paragraph 19(1)(g) violated section 15 of the *Charter*. The Court declined to hear such an argument. It would be an exceptional case in which the Court would determine an issue that was not raised in argument by the parties in judicial review, but rather was raised by an intervenor in the proceedings. The CAF standing as an intervenor does not support recognition of any right or standing to raise issues that are not raised by the parties to the proceeding.

The ordinary standard of proof in civil as opposed to criminal matters is the basis for findings of fact by SIRC. That is, those findings must be based on a balance of probabilities. Further, there is no basis for construing the words in paragraph 19(1)(g) as implying any standard of proof other than the traditional standard, that is a balance of probabilities, for findings required under that provision. Thus, the SIRC report did not err by reliance on that traditional standard and not insisting on some higher standard of probability. Paragraph 19(1)(g) is to be interpreted so that "likely" ("susceptible") with reference to the organizations referred to means "capable of" and not simply probable. The conclusion of SIRC in this case would be acceptable if the organization were merely judged capable of, and not necessarily that it would probably be engaging in acts of violence as described in the paragraph. There is no necessity in construing the words in 19(1)(g) to establish the obligations of membership in such an organization, or that the individual member has a record of, or an obligation to participate in, acts of violence under the aegis and on the direction of the organization.

Sections 39 and 40(1) provide for an investigation by SIRC. Parliament intended that the process of a hearing in regard to security considerations should be undertaken at the stage of the investigation by SIRC. Upon conclusion of its investigation and submission of its report to the Governor General in Council, the Governor General in Council would be expected to accept and act upon the SIRC's conclusion, at least where the Governor General in Council is satisfied that the person investigated is a person included in the Act's descriptions of those considered as presenting sufficient risk to warrant deportation. The duty of fairness does not require a further opportunity for submissions to the Governor in Council by the person concerned before action is taken. The case to be answered by the person concerned has already been brought to his attention through the provision of a statement of circumstances at the beginning of the SIRC process, and full opportunity to respond and to make submissions has been provided through that process. The only circumstance where the duty of fairness might clearly require a further opportunity for submissions after delivery of the SIRC report would be where SIRC's report is favourable to the permanent resident and does not recommend the issue of a certificate but the Governor in Council not satisfied with that report, determines, in the exercise of its discretion, that the person concerned is indeed one against whom a certificate should be issued under section 40(1).

Section 19(1)(g) does directly restrict freedom of association, providing for persons who are not citizens ultimately to be excluded or deported from Canada because there are reasonable grounds to believe they are members of an organization likely to engage in acts of violence of the sort described. It is the association of persons as members of the organizations described that leads to their classification for exclusion or deportation. It is not their individual records of participating in violent activities, nor a determination that they are likely to participate in such activities. Rather it is simply the fact of membership that is the reason for the application for paragraph 19(1)(g). By providing ultimately for deportation of permanent residents who are members of an organization loosely defined, the statute does infringe on the freedom of permanent residents to associate together in organization. Often such persons, at least those comparatively new to this country, may maintain association or membership with organizations associated with their home land, many of which may have had some historic record of violence, but which serve a variety of purposes as the PFLP was found to do in this case. To expose all permanent residents to the possibility of deportation because of their membership in such organizations, in my view, clearly infringes on their freedom of association. This infringement was found not to be saved by section 1 of the *Charter*, thus paragraph 19(1)(g) was declared to be of no force and affect. Thus, the determination and conclusion of SIRC, which was based on paragraph 19(1)(g) could not stand and an order was issued setting aside the report and its conclusion. Further, the determination of the Governor in Council, because it was based on the grounds set out in the report by SIRC, including the direction to the Solicitor General to issue a certificate, was declared to be invalid.

Chiarelli v. Canada (Minister of Employment & Immigration), 16 Imm. L.R. (2d) 1, [1992] 1 S.C.R. 711 (S.C.C.) — This appeal calls into question the constitutionality of the statutory scheme pursuant to which a permanent resident can be deported from Canada if he is found to have been convicted of an offence for which a term of imprisonment of 5 years or more may be imposed. A further attack was brought against the interaction of that scheme with the investigations conducted by the Security Intelligence Review Committee (SIRC) into the activities of persons reasonably believed to be involved in certain types of criminal or subversive activity.

The respondent was convicted of a number of criminal offences and in January 1986 a report was written pursuant to section 27 of the *Immigration Act* identifying the respondent as a permanent resident described in section 27(1)(d)(ii). As a result of this report an inquiry was directed pursuant to section 27(3). A deportation order was made against the respondent pursuant to section 32(2). The respondent appealed to the Immigration Appeal Board. That appeal was adjourned after the Solicitor General and the Minister of Employment and Immigration made a joint report to SIRC. The report indicated that in the opinion of the Ministers the respondent was a person described in section 19(1)(d)(ii). The SIRC conducted the required investigation and reported to the Governor in Council pursuant to section 81(7). The Governor in Council adopted the conclusion of SIRC and directed the appellant Minister to issue a certificate under section 82(1) with respect to the respondent's appeal. This certificate was issued, with the result that the respondent could not assert compassionate grounds as a reason for allowing the appeal.

The SIRC conducted its investigation and hearing first by reading a document entitled "Statement of Circumstances" as well as two summaries of information. The first day's hearing was held *in camera* and the respondent was excluded from the hearing and provided only with a summary of the evidence. The respondent was permitted to attend the second day of the hearing. The respondent declined, objected to the fairness and constitutionality of the proceeding before the SIRC, submitted no evidence at the hearing, and chose not to cross-examine two RCMP witnesses who had testified on the first day. Counsel did make submissions to the SIRC.

Section 27(1) requires an immigration officer in possession of information that a permanent resident falls into one of its enumerated classes to forward a report to the Deputy Minister. An inquiry is then held by an adjudicator in cases where the Deputy Minister considers one is warranted. Section 32(2) provides that where an adjudicator decides that a person who is the subject of an inquiry does fall within one of the classes in section 27(1), the adjudicator shall, except in the case of a Convention refugee, make a deportation order. All persons who fall within section 27(1)(d)(ii) have deliberately violated an essential condition under which they were permitted to remain in Canada. In such a situation there is no breach of fundamental justice in giving practical effect to the termination of their right to remain in Canada. In the case of a permanent resident deportation is the only way in which to accomplish this. There is nothing inherently unjust about a mandatory order. The fact of the deliberate violation of the condition imposed by sections 27(1)(d)(ii) is sufficient to justify a deportation order. Accordingly, sections 27(1)(d)(ii) and 32(2) are not contrary to section 7 of the *Charter of Rights*.

The deportation authorized by sections 27(1)(d)(ii) and 32(2) is not cruel and unusual punishment as described in section 12 of the *Charter of Rights*.

Section 6 of the *Charter* specifically provides for differential treatment of citizens and permanent residents. Accordingly, sections 27(1)(d)(ii) and 32(2) do not violate section 15 of the *Charter*. Permanent residents are given mobility rights in section 6(2). Only citizens are accorded the right to enter, remain in and leave Canada in section 6(1). There is no discrimination contrary to section 15 in a deportation scheme that applies to permanent residents but not citizens.

The effect of the security certificate in this case is to direct the Immigration Appeal Board to dismiss any appeal based on the existence of compassionate or humanitarian considerations. The permanent resident's right of appeal after a certificate has been issued is restricted to questions of law, fact or mixed law and fact.

The *Immigration Act*, S.C. 1910, c. 27, did not provide any specific grounds of appeal. A person ordered deported could only resort to the Minister, who had authority to overturn a deportation order on unspecified grounds. The *Immigration Act*, R.S.C. 1952, c. 325, provided for an immigration appeal board; however, appeals against deportation orders remained under the control of the Minister. The Board heard only those appeals directed to it by the Minister, and the Minister retained the power to confirm or quash the Appeal Board's decision or substitute his decision as he deemed just and proper. The 1966 *White Paper on Immigration* recommended that a reconstituted Immigration Appeal Board have authority to deal conclusively with appeals against deportation orders except in security cases. The *Immigration Appeal Board Act*, 1967 for the first time conferred upon the Board the power to stay or quash a deportation order made against a permanent resident on the basis of all the circumstances of the case. This new power was subject to the discretion of the Minister and the Solicitor General, who could certify their opinion based on security or criminal intelligence reports that it would be contrary to the national interest to permit such relief. This reserves to the Crown the right similar to the prerogative right which existed at common law, to determine that the continued presence in Canada of an alien, subject to a deportation order, was not conducive to the public good. The *Immigration Appeal Board Act* was repealed by the *Immigration Act*, 1976. However, this new Act did not change the nature of the decision that could be made by the Board having regard to all the circumstances of the case. That decision remained as it had been under the 1967 Act, an exercise of discretion based on compassionate grounds. Section 83 of the *Immigration Act*, 1976 limited the availability of relief based on all the circumstances of the case. Such an appeal had to be dismissed if the Minister and Solicitor General certified their opinion that it would be contrary to the national interest to permit such an appeal. In 1984 the SIRC was established by the *Canadian Security Intelligence Service Act*, S.C. 1984, c. 21. The Review Committee was assigned various functions under several Acts, including the *Immigration Act*, 1976. Sections 83 and 82.1 of the *Immigration Act*, 1976 were repealed and amended versions were substituted. The decision as to whether to direct the issuance of a security certificate, however, remained with the Governor in Council. Thus, there has never been a universally available right of appeal from a deportation order on humanitarian or compassionate grounds or "having regard to all the circumstances of the case." Such an appeal has historically been a purely discretionary matter. The right of appeal required to comply with the principles of fundamental justice is a true appeal which enables the decision of first instance to be questioned on factual and legal grounds. The absence of an appeal on wider grounds does not violate section 7.

The procedure followed by the Security Intelligence Review Committee in this case recognized competing individual and state interests and attempted to find a reasonable balance between them. It was not necessary that the respondent be given details of the criminal intelligence investigation techniques or police sources used to acquire the information upon which the two Ministers relied in issuing the certificate. The respondent was given an opportunity to respond by calling his own witnesses or by requesting that he be allowed to cross-examine the RCMP officers who testified *in camera*. Such a procedure was sufficient to meet the requirements of the principles of fundamental justice.

39.1 (1) Appointment of a judge — After consultation by the Prime Minister of Canada with the Leader of the Opposition in the House of Commons and the leader in the House of Commons of each party having at least twelve members in that House, the Governor in Council may appoint a retired judge of a superior court for a term of three to five years to perform the duties of the Review Committee described in subsections 39(5) and (6) to (10).

(2) Tenure and reappointment — The appointed person holds office during good behaviour and may be removed by the Governor in Council at any time for cause. The person is eligible to be re-appointed.

(3) Remuneration and expenses — The appointed person shall be paid, for each day that the person performs duties under this Act, such remuneration as is fixed by the Governor in Council, and is entitled to be paid reasonable travel and living expenses incurred in the course of their duties under this Act while absent from their ordinary place of residence.

1997, c. 22, s. 5.

39.2 (1) Referral — The Minister may refer to the person appointed under subsection 39.1(1) any case that the Review Committee has ceased to investigate under subsection 39(5.1) and, in that case, the Minister must make a report described in subsection 39(2) to the appointed person and send the notice described in subsection 39(3).

(2) Application of subsections 39(5) and (6) to (10) — Subsections 39(5) and (6) to (10) apply to the appointed person as if that person were the Review Committee.

1997, c. 22, s. 5.

39.3 Annual reports — The person appointed under subsection 39.1(1) must, not later than September 30 in each fiscal year, submit to the Solicitor General of Canada a report of the activities of the person during the preceding fiscal year and the Solicitor General of Canada must cause the report to be laid before each House of Parliament on any of the first fifteen days on which that House is sitting after the day the Solicitor General of Canada receives it.

1997, c. 22, s. 5.

40. (1) Security certificates — Where, after considering a report made under subsection 39(9) by the Review Committee or the person appointed under subsection 39.1(1), the Governor in Council is satisfied that the person with respect to whom the report was made is a person described in paragraph 19(1)(*c*.2), subparagraph 19(1)(*d*)(ii), paragraph 19(1)(*e*), (*f*), (*g*), (*k*) or (*l*) or 27(1)(*a*.1), subparagraph 27(1)(*a*.3)(ii) or paragraph 27(1)(*g*) or (*h*), the Governor in Council may direct the Minister to issue a certificate to that effect.

(2) Effect of certificate — A certificate issued under subsection (1) is, in any prosecution or other proceeding under or arising out of this Act, conclusive proof of the matters stated therein without proof of the signature or official character of the person appearing to have signed the certificate unless called into question by the Minister.

R.S.C. 1985, c. 30 (3rd Supp.), s. 7; R.S.C. 1985, c. 29 (4th Supp.), s. 3; 1992, c. 49, s. 30; 1997, c. 22, s. 6.

Case Law

Section 40(1)

Yamani v. Canada (Solicitor General) (1995), 31 Imm. L.R. (2d) 191, 129 D.L.R. (4th) 226, 32 C.R.R. (2d) 295, (sub nom. *Al Yamani v. Canada (Solicitor General)*) 103 F.T.R. 105, [1996] 1 F.C. 174 (Fed. T.D.) — These were two applications for judicial review in relation to a decision of the Security Intelligence Review Committee (SIRC) made August 3, 1994 and a decision of the Governor General in Council made August 25, 1994, based upon the decision and report of SIRC.

The applicant is a stateless person, a male of Palestinian origin. His father was said to be one of the founders of the Popular Front for the Liberation of Palestines (PFLP). Though he was born in Beirut the applicant is not a citizen of Lebanon, but has carried and has travelled on a Lebanese travel document.

The applicant is a landed immigrant who arrived in Canada in 1985. He resided in Canada since that time, made an application for citizenship in 1988 and as a result of that application became the subject of security screening by the Canadian Security Intelligence Service (CSIS). He was interviewed by a CSIS officer and subsequently received a letter signed by the Minister of Employment and Immigration, and the Solicitor General stating that they had made a report to SIRC because they were of the opinion that the applicant was a person described in paragraphs 19(1)(e), 19(1)(g) and 27(1)(c). SIRC's finding related only to paragraph 19(1)(g).

Subsequent to the Minister's report the applicant was the subject of a hearing before a single member of SIRC. This hearing resulted in the applicant being found to be a person described in 19(1)(g). SIRC reported that fact to the Governor in Council and recommended that a certificate be issued against the applicant under section 40(1) of the Act. That report was the subject of the first judicial review application.

Upon receipt of the report the Governor in Council issued an order-in-council reciting that after considering the report of SIRC it was satisfied that the applicant was a person described in paragraph 19(1)(g) of the Act. That decision also directed the Solicitor General to issue a security certificate pursuant to section 40 so designating the applicant.

The Court found that, pursuant to sections 18 and 18.1 of the *Federal Court Act*, it does have jurisdiction to review the decision of SIRC. SIRC is a federal board, commission, or tribunal as defined in section 2 of the *Federal Court Act* since it is a body exercising jurisdiction or powers conferred by an act of parliament. Relief against a decision of SIRC is available under section 18 of the *Federal Court Act* upon an application for judicial review pursuant to section 18.1.

The Court granted intervenor status to the Canadian Arab Federation (CAF). The CAF sought to argue that paragraph 19(1)(g) violated section 15 of the Charter. The Court declined to hear such an argument. It would be an exceptional case in which the Court would determine an issue that was not raised in argument by the parties in judicial review, but rather was raised by an intervenor in the proceedings. The CAF standing as an intervenor does not support recognition of any right or standing to raise issues that are not raised by the parties to the proceeding.

The ordinary standard of proof in civil, as opposed to criminal, matters is the basis for findings of fact by SIRC. That is, those findings must be based on a balance of probabilities. Further, there is no basis for construing the words in paragraph 19(1)(g) as implying any standard of proof other than the traditional standard, that is a balance of probabilities, for findings required under that provision. Thus, the SIRC report did not err by reliance on that traditional standard and by not insisting on some higher standard of probability. Paragraph 19(1)(g) is to be interpreted so that "likely" ("susceptible") with reference to the organizations referred to means "capable of" and not simply probable. The conclusion of SIRC in this case would be acceptable if the organization were merely judged capable of, and not necessarily that it would probably be engaging in acts of violence as described in the paragraph. There is no necessity, in construing the words in 19(1)(g), to establish the obligations of membership in such an organization, or that the individual member has a record of, or an obligation to participate in, acts of violence under the aegis and on the direction of the organization.

Sections 39 and 40(1) provide for an investigation by SIRC. Parliament intended that the process of a hearing in regard to security considerations should be undertaken at the stage of the investigation by SIRC. Upon conclusion of its investigation and submission of its report to the Governor General in Council, the Governor General in Council would be expected to accept and act upon the SIRC's conclusion, at least where the Governor General in Council is satisfied that the person investigated is a person included in the Act's descriptions of those considered as presenting sufficient risk to warrant deportation. The duty of fairness does not require a further opportunity for submissions to the Governor in Council by the person concerned before action is taken. The case to be answered by the person concerned has already been brought to his attention through the provision of a statement of circumstances at the beginning of the SIRC process, and full opportunity to respond and to make submissions has been provided through that process. The only circumstance where the duty of fairness might clearly require a further opportunity for submissions after delivery of the SIRC report would be where SIRC's report is favourable to the permanent resident and does not recommend the issue of a certificate but the Governor in Council not satisfied with that report, determines, in the exercise of its discretion, that the person concerned is indeed one against whom a certificate should be issued under section 40(1).

Section 19(1)(g) does directly restrict freedom of association, providing for persons who are not citizens ultimately to be excluded or deported from Canada because there are reasonable grounds to believe they are members of an organization likely to engage in acts of violence of the sort described. It is the association of persons as members of the organizations described that leads to their classification for exclusion or deportation. It is not their individual records of participating in violent activities, nor a determination that they are likely to participate in such activities. Rather it is simply the fact of membership that is the reason for the application for paragraph 19(1)(g). By providing ultimately for deportation of permanent residents who are members of an organization loosely defined, the statute does infringe on the freedom of permanent residents to associate together in organization. Often such persons, at least those comparatively new to this country, may maintain association or membership with organizations associated with their home land, many of which may have had some historic record of violence, but which serve a variety of purposes as the PFLP was found to do in this case. To expose all permanent residents to the possibility of deportation because of their membership in such organizations, in my view, clearly infringes on their freedom of association. This infringement was found not to be saved by section 1 of the Charter, thus paragraph 19(1)(g) was declared to be of no force and affect. Thus, the determination and conclusion of SIRC, which was based on paragraph 19(1)(g) could not stand and an order was issued setting aside the report and its conclusion. Further, the determination of the Governor in Council, because it was based on the grounds set out in the report by SIRC, including the direction to the Solicitor General to issue a certificate, was declared to be invalid.

Chiarelli v. Canada (Minister of Employment & Immigration), 16 Imm. L.R. (2d) 1, [1992] 1 S.C.R. 711 (S.C.C.) — This appeal calls into question the constitutionality of the statutory scheme pursuant to which a permanent resident can be deported from Canada if he is found to have been convicted of an offence for which a term of imprisonment of 5 years or more may be imposed. A further attack was brought against the interaction of that scheme with the investigations conducted by the Security Intelligence Review Committee (SIRC) into the activities of persons reasonably believed to be involved in certain types of criminal or subversive activity.

The respondent was convicted of a number of criminal offences and in January 1986 a report was written pursuant to section 27 of the *Immigration Act* identifying the respondent as a permanent resident described in 27(1)(d)(ii). As a result of this report an inquiry was directed pursuant to section 27(3). A deportation order was made against the respondent pursuant to section 32(2). The respondent appealed to the Immigration Appeal Board. That appeal was adjourned after the Solicitor General and the Minister of Employment and Immigration made a joint report to the SIRC. The report indicated that, in the opinion of the Ministers, the respondent was a person described in section 19(1)(d)(ii). The SIRC conducted the required investigation and reported to the Governor in Council pursuant to section 81(7). The Governor in Council adopted the conclusion of the SIRC and directed the appellant Minister to issue a certificate under section 82(1) with respect to the respondent's appeal. This certificate was issued, with the result that the respondent could not assert compassionate grounds as a reason for allowing the appeal.

The SIRC conducted its investigation and hearing first by reading a document entitled "Statement of Circumstances" as well as two summaries of information. The first day's hearing was held *in camera* and the respondent was excluded from the hearing and provided only with a summary of the evidence. The respondent was permitted to attend the second day of the hearing. The respondent declined, objected to the fairness and constitutionality of the proceeding before the SIRC, submitted no evidence at the hearing, and chose not to cross-examine two RCMP witnesses who had testified on the first day. Counsel did make submissions to the SIRC.

Section 27(1) requires an immigration officer in possession of information that a permanent resident falls into one of its enumerated classes to forward a report to the Deputy Minister. An inquiry is then held by an adjudicator in cases where the Deputy Minister considers one is warranted. Section 32(2) provides that where an adjudicator decides that a person who is the subject of an inquiry does fall within one of the classes in section 27(1), the adjudicator shall, except in the case of a Convention refugee, make a deportation order. All persons who fall within section 27(1)(d)(ii) have deliberately violated an essential condition under which they were permitted to remain in Canada. In such a situation there is no breach of fundamental justice in giving practical effect to the termination of their right to remain in Canada. In the case of a permanent resident, deportation is the only way in which to accomplish this. There is nothing inherently unjust about a mandatory order. The fact of the deliberate violation of the condition imposed by section 27(1)(d)(ii) is sufficient to justify a deportation order. Accordingly, sections 27(1)(d)(ii) and 32(2) are not contrary to section 7 of the *Charter of Rights.*

The deportation authorized by sections 27(1)(d)(ii) and 32(2) is not cruel and unusual punishment as described in section 12 of the *Charter of Rights.*

Section 6 of the *Charter* specifically provides for differential treatment of citizens and permanent residents. Accordingly, sections 27(1)(d)(ii) and 32(2) do not violate section 15 of the Charter. Permanent residents are given mobility rights in section 6(2). Only citizens are accorded the right to enter, remain in and leave Canada in section 6(1). There is no discrimination contrary to section 15 in a deportation scheme that applies to permanent residents but not citizens.

The effect of the security certificate in this case is to direct the Immigration Appeal Board to dismiss any appeal based on the existence of compassionate or humanitarian considerations. The permanent resident's right of appeal after a certificate has been issued is restricted to questions of law, fact or mixed law and fact.

The *Immigration Act*, S.C. 1910, c. 27, did not provide any specific grounds of appeal. A person ordered deported could only resort to the Minister, who had authority to overturn a deportation order on unspecified grounds. The *Immigration Act*, R.S.C. 1952, c. 325, provided for an immigration appeal board; however, appeals against deportation orders remained under the control of the Minister. The Board heard only those appeals directed to it by the Minister, and the Minister retained the power to confirm or quash the Appeal Board's decision or substitute his decision as he deemed just and proper. The 1966 *White Paper on Immigration* recommended that a reconstituted Immigration Appeal Board have authority to deal conclusively with appeals against deportation orders except in security cases. The *Immigration Appeal Board Act*, 1967 for the first time conferred upon the Board the power to stay or quash a deportation order made against a permanent resident on the basis of all the circumstances of the case. This new power was subject to the discretion of the Minister and the Solicitor General, who could certify their opinion based on security or criminal intelligence reports that it would be contrary to the national interest to permit such relief. This reserves to the Crown the right similar to the prerogative right which existed at common law, to determine that the continued presence in Canada of an alien, subject to a deportation order, was not conducive to the public good. The *Immigration Appeal Board Act* was repealed by the *Immigration Act*, 1976. However, this new Act did not change the nature of the decision that could be made by the Board having regard to all the circumstances of the case. That decision remained as it had been under the 1967 Act, an exercise of discretion based on compassionate grounds. Section 83 of the *Immigration Act*, 1976 limited the availability of relief based on all the circumstances of the case. Such an appeal had to be dismissed if the Minister and Solicitor General certified their opinion that it would be contrary to the national interest to permit such an appeal. In 1984 the SIRC was established by the *Canadian Security Intelligence Service Act*, S.C. 1984, c. 21. The Review Committee was assigned various functions under several Acts, including the *Immigration Act*, 1976. Sections 83 and 82.1 of the *Immigration Act*, 1976 were repealed and amended versions were substituted. The decision as to whether to direct the issuance of a security certificate, however, remained with the Governor in Council. Thus, there has never been a universally available right of appeal from a deportation order on humanitarian or compassionate grounds or "having regard to all the circumstances of the case." Such an appeal has historically been a purely discretionary matter. The right of appeal required to comply with the principles of fundamental justice is a true appeal which enables the decision of first instance to be questioned on factual and legal grounds. The absence of an appeal on wider grounds does not violate section 7.

The procedure followed by the Security Intelligence Review Committee in this case recognized competing individual and state interests and attempted to find a reasonable balance between them. It was not necessary that the respondent be given details of the criminal intelligence investigation techniques or police sources used to acquire the information upon which the two Ministers relied in issuing the certificate. The respondent was given an opportunity to respond by calling his own witnesses or by requesting that he be allowed to cross-examine the RCMP officers who testified *in camera*. Such a procedure was sufficient to meet the requirements of the principles of fundamental justice.

40.1 (1) Certificate — Notwithstanding anything in this Act, where the Minister and the Solicitor General of Canada are of the opinion, based on security or criminal intelligence reports received and considered by them, that a person, other than a Canadian citizen or permanent resident, is a person described in subparagraph 19(1)(*c*.1)(ii), paragraph 19(1)(*c*.2), (*d*), (*e*), (*f*), (*g*), (*j*), (*k*) or (*l*) or subparagraph 19(2)(*a*.1)(ii), they may sign and file a certificate to that effect with an immigration officer, a senior immigration officer or an adjudicator.

(2) Delay of inquiry — Where a certificate is signed and filed in accordance with subsection (1),

> **(a) an inquiry under this Act concerning the person in respect of whom the certificate is filed shall not be commenced, or if commenced shall be adjourned, until the determination referred to in paragraph (4)(*d*) has been made; and**
>
> **(b) a senior immigration officer or an adjudicator shall, notwithstanding section 23 or 103 but subject to subsection (7.1), detain or make an order to detain the person named in the certificate until the making of the determination.**

(3) Reference to Federal Court — Where a certificate referred to in subsection (1) is filed in accordance with that subsection, the Minister shall

> **(a) forthwith cause a copy of the certificate to be referred to the Federal Court for a determination as to whether the certificate should be quashed; and**
>
> **(b) within three days after the certificate has been filed, cause a notice to be sent to the person named in the certificate informing the person that a certificate under this section has been filed and that following a reference to the Federal Court a deportation order may be made against the person.**

(4) **Judicial consideration of certificate** — Where a certificate is referred to the Federal Court pursuant to subsection (3), the Chief Justice of that Court or a judge of that Court designated by the Chief Justice for the purposes of this section shall

(a) examine within seven days, *in camera*, the security or criminal intelligence reports considered by the Minister and the Solicitor General and hear any other evidence or information that may be presented by or on behalf of those Ministers and may, on the request of the Minister or the Solicitor General, hear all or part of such evidence or information in the absence of the person named in the certificate and any counsel representing the person where, in the opinion of the Chief Justice or the designated judge, as the case may be, the evidence or information should not be disclosed on the grounds that the disclosure would be injurious to national security or to the safety of persons;

(b) provide the person named in the certificate with a statement summarizing such information available to the Chief Justice or the designated judge, as the case may be, as will enable the person to be reasonably informed of the circumstances giving rise to the issue of the certificate, having regard to whether, in the opinion of the Chief Justice or the designated judge, as the case may be, the information should not be disclosed on the grounds that the disclosure would be injurious to national security or to the safety of persons;

(c) provide the person named in the certificate with a reasonable opportunity to be heard;

(d) determine whether the certificate filed by the Minister and the Solicitor General is reasonable on the basis of the evidence and information available to the Chief Justice or the designated judge, as the case may be, and, if found not to be reasonable, quash the certificate; and

(e) notify the Minister, the Solicitor General and the person named in the certificate of the determination made pursuant to paragraph (*d*).

(5) **Evidence** — For the purposes of subsection (4), the Chief Justice or the designated judge may, subject to subsection (5.1), receive, accept and base the determination referred to in paragraph (4)(*d*) on such evidence or information as the Chief Justice or the designated judge sees fit, whether or not the evidence or information is or would be admissible in a court of law.

(5.1) **Information obtained in confidence from foreign governments** — For the purposes of subsection (4),

(a) the Minister or the Solicitor General of Canada may make an application, *in camera* and in the absence of the person named in the certificate and any counsel representing the person, to the Chief Justice or the designated judge for the admission of information obtained in confidence from the government or an institution of a foreign state or from an international organization of states or an institution thereof;

(b) the Chief Justice or the designated judge shall, *in camera* and in the absence of the person named in the certificate and any counsel representing the person,

(i) examine that information, and

(ii) provide counsel representing the Minister or the Solicitor General of Canada with a reasonable opportunity to be heard as to whether the information is relevant but should not be disclosed to the person named in the certificate on the grounds that the disclosure would be injurious to national security or to the safety of persons;

(c) that information shall be returned to counsel representing the Minister or the Solicitor General of Canada and shall not be considered by the Chief Justice or the designated judge in making the determination referred to in paragraph (4)(*d*), if

(i) the Chief Justice or the designated judge determines

(A) that the information is not relevant, or

(B) that the information is relevant and should be summarized in the statement to be provided pursuant to paragraph (4)(*b*) to the person named in the certificate, or

(ii) the Minister or the Solicitor General of Canada withdraws the application; and

(d) if the Chief Justice or the designated judge determines that the information is relevant but should not be disclosed to the person named in the certificate on the grounds that the disclosure would be injurious to national security or to the safety of persons, the information shall not be summarized in the statement provided pursuant to paragraph (4)(*d*) to the person named in the certificate but may be considered by the Chief Justice or the designated judge in making the determination referred to in paragraph (4)(*d*).

(6) **No appeal** — A determination under paragraph (4)(*d*) is not subject to appeal or review by any court.

(7) **Certificate is conclusive proof** — Where a certificate has been reviewed by the Federal Court pursuant to subsection (4) and has not been quashed pursuant to paragraph (4)(*d*),

(a) the certificate is conclusive proof that the person named in the certificate is a person described in subparagraph 19(1)(*c*.1)(ii), paragraph 19(1)(*c*.2), (*d*), (*e*), (*f*), (*g*), (*j*), (*k*) or (*l*) or subparagraph 19(2)(*a*.1)(ii); and

(b) the person named in the certificate shall, notwithstanding section 23 or 103 but subject to subsection (7.1), continue to be detained until the person is removed from Canada.

(7.1) **Release of person named in certificate** — The Minister may order the release of a person who is named in a certificate that is signed and filed in accordance with subsection (1) in order to permit the departure from Canada of the person, regardless of whether the Chief Justice or the designated judge has yet made the determination referred to in paragraph (4)(*d*).

(8) **Right to apply** — Where a person is detained under subsection (7) and is not removed from Canada within 120 days after the making of the removal order relating to that person, the person may apply to the Chief Justice of the Federal Court or to a judge of the Federal Court designated by the Chief Justice for the purposes of this section for an order under subsection (9).

(9) **Order for release** — On an application referred to in subsection (8) the Chief Justice or the designated judge may, subject to such terms and conditions as the Chief

Justice or designated judge deems appropriate, order that the person be released from detention if the Chief Justice or designated judge is satisfied that

(a) the person will not be removed from Canada within a reasonable time; and

(b) the person's release would not be injurious to national security or to the safety of persons.

(10) Hearing of application — On the hearing of an application referred to in subsection (8), the Chief Justice or the designated judge shall

(a) examine, *in camera*, and in absence of the person making the application and any counsel representing that person, any evidence or information presented to the Minister in relation to national security or the safety of persons;

(b) provide the person making the application with a statement summarizing the evidence or information available to the Chief Justice or designated judge in relation to national security or the safety of persons having regard to whether, in the opinion of the Chief Justice or the designated judge, as the case may be, the evidence or information should not be disclosed on the grounds that the disclosure would be injurious to national security or to the safety of persons; and

(c) provide the person making the application with a reasonable opportunity to be heard.

(11) Evidence — For the purposes of subsection (10), the Chief Justice or the designated judge may receive and accept such evidence or information as the Chief Justice or the designated judge sees fit, whether or not such evidence or information is or would be admissible in a court of law.

R.S.C. 1985, c. 29 (4th Supp.), s. 4; 1992, c. 49, s. 31.

Case Law

Section 40.1(1)

Canada (Minister of Citizenship & Immigration) v. Singh (I.) (1998), 44 Imm. L.R. (2d) 309, 151 F.T.R. 101 (Fed. T.D.) — This was a decision on the merits under paragraph 40.1(4)(d) dealing with whether a certificate filed by the applicants in relation to the respondent was reasonable. In section 40.1 proceedings, where there are reasonable grounds to believe that a person is a member of an organization, there must also be reasonable grounds to believe that the organization is engaged in subversion or terrorism. Standard of proof is on a balance of probabilities.

In his testimony, a supervisor with the counter-terrorist branch of CSIS expressed the opinion that terrorism included politically motivated violence often with an indiscriminate target. A politically motivated organization which sets off bombs killing innocent people or which engages in assassinations is an organization engaged in terrorism.

The Court concluded that the term "member" incorporated into section 40.1 by reference to section 19 was to be interpreted broadly. The context of this provision in immigration legislation is public safety and national security, the most serious concerns of government. Terrorist organizations do not issue membership cards, there is no formal test for membership and members are therefore not easily identifiable. In this context, it is obvious that Parliament intended that the term "member" be given an unrestricted and broad interpretation.

Ahani v. R. (1996), 37 C.R.R. (2d) 181, 201 N.R. 233, 119 F.T.R. 80 (note) (Fed. C.A.); leave to appeal to S.C.C. refused [1997] 2 S.C.R. v, 44 C.R.R. (2d) 376 (note), 223 N.R. 72

(note) (S.C.C.) — The Court adopted the reasons of the trial judge in this matter and affirmed her decision.

Between a determination by the designated judge that the section 40.1 certificate is reasonable and a possible removal of the person concerned to the country where he or she fears persecution, there must be a second opinion formed by the Minister of Immigration, based on a determination that the person constitutes "a danger to the public in Canada", or "a danger to the security of Canada". Such a determination will have to be made in accordance with the principles of fundamental justice and will be subject to judicial review.

Section 40.1 is in no way akin to a criminal proceeding. In a section 40.1 proceeding there exists an alien who may lose the qualified right to stay in Canada that he or she gained by being given refugee status, but whose liberty will not then be otherwise impeded. While it is true that the filing of the certificate has the immediate unfortunate effect of leading to the arrest and detention of the person concerned, it must not be forgotten that this detention is not imposed as a punishment, but rather as a means of providing preventative protection to the Canadian public. This detention is not arbitrary or excessive. The test for the issuance of the certificate is the reasoned opinion of two Ministers based on security information. The scheme provides for the obligatory judicial scrutiny of the reasonableness of those opinions within an acceptably short period of time; further, at any time, the person can agree to leave the country and thereby end his or her detention. Finally, this procedure deals with a type or class of individual who is believed to be associated with terrorism.

Baroud, Re (1995), 98 F.T.R. 99 (Fed. T.D.) — The purpose of subparagraphs 19(1)(f)(ii) and 19(1)(f)(iii) of the *Immigration Act*, in very general terms, is to prevent the arrival of persons considered to be a danger to Canadian society. The term terrorism must therefore receive an unrestrictive interpretation and will unavoidably include the political connotations which it entails. In the light of the evidence submitted to the Court there existed reasonable grounds to believe that the applicant was described in section 19(1)(f)(iii).

Section 40.1(4)

Canada (Minister of Citizenship & Immigration) v. Singh (I.) (1998), 46 Imm. L.R. (2d) 103, 153 F.T.R. 183 (Fed. T.D.) — In the course of proceedings under section 40.1, the respondent made a motion for the production of the transcripts and/or translations of wiretapped telephone communications, involving calls made by the respondent from his own telephone. Without conceding that the respondent's telephone line was tapped, the applicants objected to the respondent's motion on national security grounds.

Section 40.1(4)(a) refers to the following categories of evidence: 1) the security or criminal intelligence reports considered by the Ministers; 2) other evidence or information presented by or on behalf of the Ministers heard in the absence of the person named in the certificate; and 3) other evidence or information presented by or on behalf of the Ministers heard in the presence of the person named in the certificate. Evidence or information not disclosed to the person named in the certificate is to be provided in accordance with the procedures set out in section 40.1(4)(b). The person named in the certificate is to be provided with a statement summarizing such information available to the designated judge as will enable that person to be reasonably informed of the circumstances giving rise to the issuance of the certificate.

Disclosure of information in the security intelligence report is effected only by way of summary statement under paragraph 40.1(4)(b). Under paragraph 40.1(4)(a), the security intelligence report is to be examined *in camera*. This is to be contrasted with the treatment of "other evidence or information" which the Ministers may request that the designated judge hear in the absence of the person named in the certificate. In the case of such evidence there will be a hearing regarding whether the "other evidence or information" is heard in the presence or in the absence of the person named in the certificate, and this will be determined by the designated judge.

The Court took the view that the documentation underlying the security and intelligence report was incorporated by reference into it. Without disclosing the existence or non-existence of wiretaps of telephone calls, the Court concluded that the respondent need not be provided with the disclosure requested in order that he be reasonably informed of the circumstances giving rise to the certificate.

Singh (I.) v. Canada (Minister of Citizenship & Immigration), 47 Imm. L.R. (2d) 68, [1998] 3 F.C. 616, 149 F.T.R. 49 (Fed. T.D.) — The Ministers' certificate issued under section 40.1 is a final decision. The reasonableness hearing is a court review of the Ministers' certificate. The certificate is a decision of a Federal tribunal, i.e. the Ministers', that it is by law referred to the Federal Court for a determination as to whether it is reasonable and if not, whether it should be quashed, by necessary implication means that it is a final decision.

The abuse of process issue which the applicant sought to raise in this case could be considered at the reasonableness inquiry. The applicant's assertions raised the question of the *bona fides* of the Ministers' certificate and if the Court were to find that the evidence on which the Ministers' certificate was based was not reliable, that would go directly to reasonableness of the certificate.

Finally, the applicant sought interim relief and the Court turned its attention to the tripartite test.

The Court noted that the *Immigration Act* charges the Ministers with protecting the public interest. Signing, filing and referring of the certificate respecting the applicant was pursuant to the duty imposed on the Ministers by the Act. No evidence was tended that would rebut the presumption that the objectives of paragraphs 19(1)(e) and (f) as incorporated in section 40.1 and as applied by the Ministers are in the public interest. Accordingly, the Court should assume that irreparable harm to the public interest would result from the restraint of government action. The Court should not as a general rule enquire into whether actual harm would result from the restraints sought by the applicant. The Court concluded that there would be irreparable harm to the public interest from the restraint of government action sought by the applicant.

Suresh, Re (1997), 40 Imm. L.R. (2d) 247, 140 F.T.R. 88 (Fed. T.D.) — These were the reasons of the court determining that reasonable grounds existed for the Solicitor General and the Minister of Employment and Immigration to have issued a certificate pursuant to section 40.1 of the *Immigration Act*. It was not necessary to define the content of the term "terrorist" or "terrorist act" as it is referred to in section 19. The Act "must be seen through the eyes of a Canadian for the purposes of a section 40.1 application." The term "terrorism or terrorist act" must receive a wide and unrestricted interpretation for the purposes of a section 40.1 application.

Membership in an organization cannot and should not be narrowly interpreted when it involves the issue of Canada's national security. Membership does not only refer to persons who have engaged in or who might engage in terrorist activities. The Court looked at the nature of Mr. Suresh's activities in support of the organization that he was supposed to be a member of and his own admission of his close association with that organization.

Suresh v. R. (1996), (sub nom. *Suresh v. Canada)* 105 F.T.R. 299, (sub nom. *Suresh v. Canada)* 34 C.R.R. (2d) 337 (Fed. T.D.) — The clear language of section 40.1 of the *Immigration Act* is incompatible with extensive *Charter* review. The designated judge in the review of a certificate does not have jurisdiction to consider arguments and grant remedies pursuant to subsection 24(1) of the Canadian Charter of Rights and Freedoms and subsection 52(1) of the *Constitution Act*, 1982.

Singh (H.), Re (1994), 83 F.T.R. 219 (Fed. T.D.) — This case dealt with a certificate signed pursuant to section 40.1. The Court's role in this type of case is difficult, for it is not to concede or find that the Ministers were correct in their assessment of the evidence presented to them, but rather to find whether or not, based on the facts and evidence presented to them, their opinion was a reasonable one.

Farahi-Mahdavieh, Re (1993), 19 Imm. L.R. (2d) 222, 63 F.T.R. 120 (Fed. T.D.) — Robab Farahi-Mahdavieh illegally entered Canada from the United States at the border near Vancouver. While preparing to fly to Toronto she was stopped and detained by immigration officials acting under a certificate issued under section 40.1(1) and (2) of the *Immigration Act*. The certificate stated that Ms. Mahdavieh was a member of an inadmissible class described in section 19(1)(g).

The Court must determine whether on the basis of the evidence and information available, the certificate is reasonable when it identifies Ms. Mahdavieh as a person who, there is reasonable grounds to believe, will engage in acts of violence that would or might endanger the lives or safety of persons in Canada, or is a member of, or likely to participate in the unlawful activities of, an organization that is likely to engage in such acts of violence (section 19(1)(g)).

As the person named in such a certificate is subject to mandatory detention, a higher standard of reasonableness should be applied in reviewing this type of administrative action. Actual membership in an organization described in section 19(1)(g) is not required. It is sufficient to meet the statutory requirement that the evidence show that there are reasonable grounds to believe that the person is a member of such an organization. The test is the one understood in *Canada (Attorney General) v. Jolly*, [1975] F.C. 216, 54 D.L.R. (3d) 277, 7 N.R. 271 (Fed. C.A.). In this case the Court found the certificate to be reasonable.

Editor's Note: Although the sections in question have been amended, the principles in this case may still be applicable.

Smith v. R., 14 Imm. L.R. (2d) 57, 4 Admin. L.R. (2d) 97, 42 F.T.R. 81, [1991] 3 F.C. 3 (Fed. T.D.) — The applicants applied to be admitted to Canada as refugees. They were detained as possible security risks and then brought before an adjudicator who reviewed the circumstances of their detention and ordered that they were to be released. The Minister then issued a certificate pursuant to section 40.1 stating the opinion that the applicants were members of classes described in section 19(1)(f) and 19(1)(g) of the *Immigration Act*. The issuance of this certificate caused the adjudicator to order the applicants' detention. Once the certificate is issued, the Court is to determine whether the certificate is reasonable on the evidence and information provided to the judge. Until this determination is made, an inquiry into the refugee status of the applicant may not be commenced or, if already commenced, must be adjourned. The applicants were referred to in the proceedings as Joseph Smith and Sarah Smith which were pseudonyms. The Court concluded that the word "shall" in section 40.1(3)(b) was directory and not mandatory. Further, the Court ruled that compliance with the notice provision was not a pre-condition to the exercise by the Court of its review function under section 40.1(4) having concluded that the Court had jurisdiction to consider the reasonableness of the certificate. The Court concluded that section 40.1(4)(a) provided it with jurisdiction to proceed *ex parte* to extend the time to serve the applicants with notice of the proceedings. The Court ruled as well that section 40.1(4)(a) authorizes the Court to hear oral evidence *in camera*. The Court also determined that the word "forthwith" as required by section 40.1(3)(a) meant "as soon as was reasonably possible in the circumstances". The

Court found that in this particular case the reference to the Court was made forthwith in all circumstances.

Section 40.1(4) gives the Court sitting on review of the certificate discretion to determine whether any part of the information or evidence put before the Court should not be disclosed on the grounds that the disclosure would be injurious to national security or the safety of persons. The Court concluded that disclosure of the sealed file material would be injurious to national security. The Court noted that an "informed reader", that is, a person who is both knowledgeable regarding security matters and is a member or associate of a group which constitutes a threat or potential threat to the security of Canada, may, at times, by fitting pieces of apparently innocuous information into a general picture, be in a position to arrive at damaging deductions regarding the investigation conducted by our security services. This damage could be an understanding of the duration, scope, intensity and degree of success of an investigation, the investigative techniques of CSIS, the typographic and teleprinter systems employed by CSIS, the internal security procedures, the nature and content of classified documents and the identity of personnel involved in the investigation. Applying this consideration to the case at bar, the Court concluded that certain information should not be made public.

On the ultimate issue, the Court determined that the word "reasonable" in section 40.1(4)(d) adopted a standard of reasonableness set out in *R. v. Secretary of State for Home Department*, [1984] 1 A.C. 74 (U.K. H.L.). There the Court said that in cases of restraint put by the executive upon the liberty of an individual the civil standard should be flexibly applied. It was not necessary to import the formula devised by judges for the guidance of juries in criminal cases. Liberty is at stake and that is a grave matter. The reviewing Court must be satisfied that the facts which are required for the justification of the restraint do exist. The Court will require a high degree of probability which is appropriate to what is at stake. Applying that standard in this case, the Court concluded that it was not reasonable to issue a certificate. The certificate was quashed and the applicants were set free.

Section 40.1(8)

Ahani v. Canada (Minister of Citizenship & Immigration) (1998), 48 Imm. L.R. (2d) 308, 159 F.T.R. 252 (Fed. T.D.) — The Court had previously determined in this matter that a certificate issued by the two Ministers involved was reasonable. The applicant was not removed from Canada within the 120 days set out in section 40.1(8) with the result that he filed a motion for release from detention.

The judge hearing this matter was the same judge who determined that the certificate was reasonable. In the course of that determination, the judge made a general finding that the applicant lacked credibility. Accordingly, counsel for the applicant asked the judge to recuse himself.

The Court dismissed the motion concluding that a fully informed person well aware of the requirements of the Act and of the certificate previously issued against the applicant would appreciate the narrow parameters to be observed by the designated judge under this section and therefore not have a reasonable apprehension of bias relative to this application.

Suresh v. Canada (Minister of Citizenship & Immigration), 47 Imm. L.R. (2d) 1, [1998] 4 F.C. 192, 229 N.R. 240, 55 C.R.R. (2d) 157 (Fed. C.A.) — The appellant was not removed from Canada within 120 days after the making of the removal order, as provided for in section 40.1 of the *Immigration Act*. Accordingly, the appellant applied pursuant to subsections 40.1(8) and (9) for release from custody.

There is nothing in the Act limiting a designated judge on jurisdictional grounds from considering constitutional issues on a subsection 40.1(8) application.

Section 40.1(9)

Ahani v. Canada (Minister of Citizenship & Immigration) (1999), 49 Imm. L.R. (2d) 86 (Fed. T.D.) — This was an application for release from detention pursuant to subsections 40.1(8) and (9) of the *Immigration Act*. Under these sections, the onus is on the applicant to show that his or her removal will not occur within a reasonable time and that his or her release would not be injurious to national security or to the safety of persons. Had parliament intended to put the onus on the Minister it would have put the obligation in a positive form instead of a negative one.

The judge should not order the release of an applicant if he or she is satisfied that there are reasonable grounds to believe that the applicant does not meet the statutory criteria. Pursuant to paragraph 40.1(7)(a), the certificate previously reviewed conclusive proof that the applicant is a person that there are reasonable grounds to believe is a person who has engaged or will engage in terrorism or is or was a member of an organization that there are reasonable grounds to believe is or was engaged in terrorism. On a motion for release, the designated judge does not have to retry the merits of the case. The application for release is not a hearing *de novo* on the merit of the status of the applicant, rather it is a hearing on the question of whether he or she should be released on terms and conditions as long as he or she meets the two criteria of subsections 40.1(9)(a) and (b). The judge hearing the release application is bound by the previous determination of reasonableness which is conclusive proof that the person is a threat to Canada.

Baroud v. Canada (Minister of Citizenship & Immigration) (1995), 121 D.L.R. (4th) 308, 22 O.R. (3d) 255, 77 O.A.C. 26, 26 C.R.R. (2d) 318 (Ont. C.A.) — The appellant, a stateless refugee claimant who had been detained pursuant to a certificate issued under section 40.1, applied for release from detention by means of a writ of *habeas corpus* with *certiorari* in aid. The appellant was a Palestinian who entered Canada and claimed refugee status in 1991. About 3 years later the Minister of Employment and Immigration, and the Solicitor General of Canada certified their belief that the appellant was not admissible to Canada under section 19(1)(f) of the *Immigration Act*. The appellant was detained in June, 1994 and remained in detention when this application was heard.

The Federal Court trial division has no jurisdiction to grant *habeas corpus*. The hearing, available under section 40.1, would take place approximately the same time as the argument on the return of *habeas corpus* and, accordingly, the Federal Court trial procedure was an adequate and effective alternative remedy which provided relief to the appellant in a forum where proceedings relating to the appellant's detention were in progress. The mandatory language of section 10 of the Charter was subject to section 1 of the Charter. Once there is a finding that an alternative remedy is equally effective it is axiomatic that the denial of the right to the issuance of a writ of *habeas corpus* is a justifiable limit. Accordingly, the *habeas corpus* application was dismissed.

40.2 Effect of certificate — An adjudicator does not have jurisdiction to determine the constitutionality of sections 39 to 40.1.

1992, c. 49, s. 32.

Claims to Canadian Citizenship

41. (1) Where claim to Canadian citizenship at inquiry — Where, at any time during an inquiry, the person who is the subject of the inquiry claims to be a Canadian citizen and the adjudicator presiding at the inquiry is not satisfied that the person is a Canadian citizen, the inquiry shall be continued and, if it is determined that, but for the person's claim that the person is a Canadian citizen, a removal order would be made against that person, the inquiry shall be adjourned.

(2) Application for certificate of citizenship — Where an inquiry in respect of a person is adjourned pursuant to subsection (1), that person's claim that he is a Canadian citizen shall be referred to such member of the Queen's Privy Council for Canada as is designated by the Governor in Council as the Minister for the purposes of the *Citizenship Act* and that person shall forthwith make an application for a certificate of citizenship pursuant to subsection 12(1) of that Act.

1992, c. 49, s. 33.

Case Law

Section 41(1)

Canada (Minister of Employment & Immigration) v. Tighe (February 17, 1984), Doc. M83-1128E (Imm. App. Bd.) — The Minister appealed under section 73 of the *Immigration Act.* The adjudicator had decided that the respondent was not a person described in section 27(2)(e) of the Act. As a result of this finding the adjudicator did not make a removal order against the respondent or issue a departure notice to him. The respondent had claimed to be a Canadian citizen at the inquiry. This claim was not disposed of due to the adjudicator's decision that the respondent was not described in section 27(2)(e) of the Act. The Board ruled that it did not have the power to allow the Minister's appeal pursuant to section 75(2) of the Act because it could not make a removal order against the respondent. The removal order could not be made because the respondent's claim to Canadian citizenship had never been resolved in accordance with the provisions of the Act. Accordingly, the Minister's appeal was dismissed.

42. (1) Where certificate of citizenship issued — Where a certificate of citizenship is issued under section 12 of the *Citizenship Act* to a person who is the subject of an inquiry, the adjudicator who was presiding at the inquiry or any other adjudicator shall terminate the inquiry and let that person come into or remain in Canada, as the case may be.

(2) Where inquiry resumed — An inquiry that was adjourned pursuant to subsection 41(1) shall be resumed as soon as reasonably practicable, by the adjudicator who was presiding at the inquiry or by any other adjudicator, where

(a) the person who was the subject of the inquiry does not forthwith make an application for a certificate of citizenship pursuant to subsection 12(1) of the *Citizenship Act*;

(b) a certificate of citizenship is not issued under section 12 of the *Citizenship Act* to that person within six months from the day on which the inquiry was adjourned or within such greater period of time as the adjudicator considers appropriate in the circumstances; or

(c) the adjudicator who was presiding at the inquiry or any other adjudicator is notified by the Minister that it has been determined that a certificate of citizenship will not be issued to that person.

(3) Idem — Where an inquiry is resumed pursuant to subsection (2), the adjudicator shall make the removal order that would have been made but for the claim of the person who was the subject of the inquiry that the person was a Canadian citizen.

1992, c. 49, s. 34.

Convention Refugee Claims

43. [Repealed 1992, c. 49, s. 35.]

44. (1) Refugee claim — Any person who is in Canada, other than a person against whom a removal order has been made but not executed, unless an appeal from that order has been allowed, and who claims to be a Convention refugee may seek a determination of the claim by notifying an immigration officer.

(2) Reference to senior immigration officer — An immigration officer who is notified pursuant to subsection (1) shall forthwith refer the claim to a senior immigration officer.

(3) Determination by adjudicator — Where a person who is the subject of an inquiry claims in accordance with subsection (1) to be a Convention refugee, the adjudicator shall determine whether the person may be permitted to come into or remain in Canada, as the case may be, and shall take the appropriate action under subsection 32(1), (3) or (4) or section 32.1, as the case may be, in respect of the person.

(4) Idem — Where a claim to be a Convention refugee by a person who is the subject of an inquiry is referred to a senior immigration officer and the senior immigration officer determines, before the conclusion of the inquiry, that the person is not eligible to have the claim determined by the Refugee Division, the adjudicator shall take the appropriate action under section 32 in respect of the person.

(5) Deemed single claim — Subject to sections 46.3 and 46.4, where a person makes more than one claim to be a Convention refugee, those claims are, for the purposes of this Act, deemed to be a single claim.

R.S.C. 1985, c. 28 (4th Supp.), s. 14; 1992, c. 49, s. 35; 1995, c. 15, s. 7.

Case Law

Section 44(1)

Mustazar Raza v. Canada (Minister of Citizenship & Immigration) (1998), 47 Imm. L.R. (2d) 257, [1999] 2 F.C. 185, 157 F.T.R. 161 (Fed. T.D.) — The applicant came from Pakistan in 1988 and made a claim for refugee status. In 1992, the applicant was found not to be a Convention refugee and an exclusion order was issued against the applicant. In the summer of that year, the applicant learned that his wife, who continued to reside in Pakistan, was ill, and he went home to be with her. The applicant did not confirm his departure with immigration authorities. A removal order was delivered to the applicant's last known address in May of 1993, but did not come to his attention as he had already left the country. While he was back in Pakistan, the applicant claimed that he was persecuted. The applicant returned to

Canada in 1996 and made a claim for refugee status at that time. The applicant was informed in April 1997, by a senior immigration officer, that his claim could not be referred to the CRDD on the basis that he was a person against whom a removal order had been made, but not executed under section 44 of the *Immigration Act*.

The applicant argued that subsection 44(1) of the *Immigration Act* contravenes section 7 of the *Charter*. As a preliminary matter counsel for the respondent raised the question of whether the Court had jurisdiction to hear the constitutional argument. The respondent asserted that the constitutionality of subsection 44(1) must be raised by way of an action and not by way of an application for judicial review, as the SIO did not have the authority to make a constitutional determination.

Pursuant to section 18.1 of the *Federal Court Act*, declarations of invalidity may be granted by the Trial Division even in regard to constitutional matters where the acts of a decision maker have the effect of infringing a person's rights as guaranteed by the Charter.

The Court concluded that section 7 of the *Charter* was not engaged by subsection 44(1) of the *Immigration Act*. The Court concluded that as the applicant did not seek the Minister's consent before leaving Canada, it could not be said that the SIO erred in holding that the applicant had not executed his removal order. The application for judicial review was dismissed.

Daher v. Canada (Minister of Citizenship & Immigration) (1998), 46 Imm. L.R. (2d) 309, 153 F.T.R. 131 (Fed. T.D.) — The applicant sought a judicial review of, and an order setting aside, a decision of a senior immigration officer refusing to reconsider an exclusion order made against the applicant. Section 44(1) of the *Immigration Act* precludes a senior immigration officer from re-opening a decision to exclude a person from Canada. No authority to do so arises by virtue of section 7 of the *Charter* or the principles of fairness at common law.

Accordingly the senior immigration officer was held not to have erred in denying the applicant's request, and the application for judicial review was dismissed.

Nguyen v. Canada (Minister of Citizenship & Immigration) (1996), 34 Imm. L.R. (2d) 129 (Imm. & Ref. Bd. (App. Div.)) — The appellant was ordered removed from Canada because of his criminal record. The appellant's appeal in part was a challenge to the legal validity of the removal order.

The appellant's 1993 conviction for aggravated assault led to an enquiry at the Joyceville institution where the appellant was incarcerated. The inquiry commenced on April 19, 1994 and was adjourned to allow the appellant to retain counsel. In June 1994, the appellant signified that he wish to proceed and the inquiry proceeded to a conclusion at which time an adjudicator issued the deportation order now under appeal.

The principles of natural justice, in particular those associated with the *audi alteram partem* rule, do not oblige an adjudicator to inquire about a fear of persecution or to indicate that a deportation order forecloses access to the convention refugee determination process in Canada, even in circumstances where the person before the adjudicator is unrepresented.

The panel noted that the appellant did not at any time during his inquiry suggest that he feared persecution should he be returned to Vietnam. Had he done so, in the opinion of the panel, the adjudicator's duty as an immigration officer would have been quite different. Section 44 of the *Immigration Act* appears to require that a possible claim to convention refugee status be canvassed in such circumstances.

Raman v. Canada (Minister of Citizenship & Immigration) (1996), 37 Imm. L.R. (2d) 294, 125 F.T.R. 50 (Fed. T.D.); affirmed (June 8, 1999), Doc. A-30-97 (Fed. C.A.) — The applicant sought to review a decision of a senior immigration officer wherein she determined that she did not have jurisdiction to re-open the inquiry conducted by a senior officer which lead to an exclusion order against the applicant.

A senior immigration officer does not have jurisdiction either at common law or pursuant to section 7 of the Charter and section 52(1) of the *Constitution Act*, 1982 to consider re-opening a hearing. Subsection 44(1) of the Act clearly precludes the senior immigration officer from re-opening a decision to exclude. Once that decision is made a refugee may not seek determination of a refugee claim, unless an appeal from that order has been allowed.

45. (1) Determination by senior immigration officer — Where a person's claim to be a Convention refugee is referred to a senior immigration officer, the senior immigration officer shall

> **(a) subject to subsection (2), determine whether the person is eligible to have the claim determined by the Refugee Division; and**
>
> **(b) if the person is the subject of a report under subsection 20(1) or 27(1) or (2) or has been arrested pursuant to subsection 103(2), take the appropriate action referred to in any of subsections 23(4), (4.01) or (4.2) or 27(4) or (6) or section 28.**

(2) Exception — Where a person referred to in subsection (1) is alleged to be a person described in paragraph 19(1)(*c*), subparagraph 19(1)(*c*.1)(i) or paragraph 19(1)(*e*), (*f*), (*g*), (*j*), (*k*) or (*l*), the senior immigration officer shall not make the determination referred to in paragraph (1)(*a*) until an adjudicator determines that the person is, or is not, a person described in any of those paragraphs.

(3) Determination to be in writing — On making a determination under paragraph (1)(*a*), the senior immigration officer shall notify the person in writing of the determination and, where the person is determined not to be eligible to have a claim to be a Convention refugee referred to the Refugee Division, shall include in the notification the basis for the determination.

(4) Burden of proof — The burden of proving that a person is eligible to have a claim to be a Convention refugee determined by the Refugee Division rests on the person.

(5) Duty to provide information — Every person who claims to be a Convention refugee shall truthfully provide such information as may be required by the senior immigration officer to whom the person's claim is referred for the purposes of determining whether the person is eligible to have the claim determined by the Refugee Division.

R.S.C. 1985, c. 28 (4th Supp.), s. 14; 1992, c. 49, s. 35; 1995, c. 15, s. 8.

46. [Repealed 1992, c. 49, s. 35.]

46.01 (1) Access criteria — A person who claims to be a Convention refugee is not eligible to have the claim determined by the Refugee Division if the person

> **(a) has been recognized as a Convention refugee by a country, other than Canada, that is a country to which the person can be returned;**
>
> **(b) came to Canada, directly or indirectly, from a country, other than a country of the person's nationality or, where the person has no country of nationality, the country of the person's habitual residence, that is a prescribed country under paragraph 114(1)(*s*);**

(c) has, since last coming into Canada, been determined

(i) by the Refugee Division not to be a Convention refugee or to have abandoned the claim, or

(ii) by a senior immigration officer not to be eligible to have the claim determined by the Refugee Division;

(d) has been determined under this Act or the regulations, to be a Convention refugee; or

(e) has been determined by an adjudicator to be

(i) a person described in paragraph 19(1)(*c*) or subparagraph 19(1)(*c*.1)(i) and the Minister is of the opinion that the person constitutes a danger to the public in Canada,

(ii) a person described in paragraph 19(1)(*e*), (*f*), (*g*), (*j*), (*k*) or (*l*) and the Minister is of the opinion that it would be contrary to the public interest to have the claim determined under this Act,

(iii) a person described in subparagraph 27(1)(*a*.1)(i) and the Minister is of the opinion that the person constitutes a danger to the public in Canada, or

(iv) a person described in paragraph 27(1)(*d*) who has been convicted of an offence under any Act of Parliament for which a term of imprisonment of ten years or more may be imposed and the Minister is of the opinion that the person constitutes a danger to the public in Canada.

(1.1) Idem — A person who claims to be a Convention Refugee on or after the day on which this subsection comes into force is not eligible to have the claim determined by the Refugee Division if

(a) the person had, before that day, claimed to be a Convention Refugee and the person was determined not to have a credible basis for the claim;

(b) the person was, before that day, issued a departure notice; and

(c) the person has not left Canada since the departure notice was issued.

(2) Application may be suspended — The Minister may, by order, suspend the application of paragraph (1)(*b*) for such period, or in respect of such classes of persons, as may be specified in the order.

(3) Coming to Canada — For the purposes of paragraph (1)(*b*),

(a) subject to any agreement entered into pursuant to section 108.1, a person who is in a country solely for the purpose of joining a connecting flight to Canada shall not be considered as coming to Canada from that country; and

(b) a person who comes to Canada from a country shall be considered as coming to Canada from that country whether or not the person was lawfully in that country.

(4) Burden of proof — For the purposes of paragraph (1)(*b*), where a person who has come to Canada in a vehicle seeks to come into Canada without a valid and subsisting passport or travel document issued to that person and claims to be a Convention refugee, the burden of proving that the person has not come to Canada from the country in which the vehicle last embarked passengers rests on that person.

(5) Last coming to Canada — A person who goes to another country and returns to Canada within ninety days shall not, for the purposes of paragraph (1)(*c*), be considered as coming into Canada on that return.

(6) [Repealed 1992, c. 49, s. 36.]

(7) [Repealed 1992, c. 49, s. 36.]

R.S.C. 1985, c. 28 (4th Supp.), s. 14; 1992, c. 1, s. 73; 1992, c. 49, s. 36; 1995, c. 15, s. 9.

Case Law

Section 46.01(1)

Jekula v. Canada (Minister of Citizenship & Immigration) (1998), 47 Imm. L.R. (2d) 218, [1999] 1 F.C. 266, 154 F.T.R. 268 (Fed. T.D.) — The applicant sought to review two closely related decisions. The first found the applicant to be ineligible to have her refugee claim reviewed by a panel of the CRDD, and the second, which was consequential on the first, was the issuance of an exclusion order. These two applications were heard together because they shared similar facts. The applicant, a citizen of Liberia, was recognized as a refugee in Sierra Leone. Eventually the applicant and one of her daughters and other family members made their way to Canada in August 1997. When she arrived at Pearson Airport, the applicant told an immigration officer that she was fleeing from civil war and claimed refugee status. In October 1997, the applicant met with a senior immigration officer who advised her that she was not admissible to Canada. Before she went for the appointment, her social worker asked the immigration officer if the applicant needed to have a lawyer with her. The immigration officer indicated this would not be necessary. The immigration officer found the applicant to be ineligible to have a refugee determination in Canada on the ground that she had already been recognized as a Convention refugee in Sierra Leone. The immigration officer then issued an exclusion order against the applicant on the ground that she did not have any travel documents normally required for those seeking entry into Canada.

The duty of fairness is breached when a decision-maker improperly refuses to permit a person to be represented at a hearing. It does not normally impose a positive obligation on an administrative decision maker to advise the person concerned that they may be represented by counsel, much less to give their opinion that it is in the person's best interest to avail themselves of that opportunity. The applicant had the assistance of a social worker whose responsibilities included referring families to appropriate agencies and who could be expected to have some familiarity with immigration matters. This person accepted the immigration officer's opinion without thinking it necessary to inform and seek the advice of a lawyer. Fairness does not require procedural perfection, and there was nothing in the immigration officer's advice that could be characterized as a refusal of representation or as misleading or otherwise unfair or erroneous in law.

A decision under paragraph 46.01(1)(a) does not deprive the applicant of the right to life, liberty or security of the person. A finding of ineligibility deprives the claimant of access to the right to have a claim determined by the refugee division, but this right is not included in the right to life, liberty and security of the person. It may well be a breach of section 7 to return a non-citizen to a country where she fears that she is likely to be subjected to physical violence or imprisonment, however, a determination that a refugee claimant is not eligible to have access to the refugee division is merely one step in the administrative process that may eventually lead to removal from Canada. The procedure followed at the risk assessment to which the applicant will be entitled under section 53 before she is removed can be subject to constitutional scrutiny to ensure that it complies with the principles of fundamental justice, even though the procedure is not prescribed in the Act or Regulation.

The words "can be returned" in paragraph 46.01(1)(a) do not require the senior immigration officer to determine whether the claimant has a well founded fear of persecution in the country that has already granted asylum. Subsection 53(1) specifically prohibits the removal of persons who have been found ineligible to have their refugee claims referred to the refugee division where the person's life or freedom would be threatened on Convention grounds in the country to which it is proposed to remove the person.

Vasquez v. Canada (Minister of Citizenship & Immigration) (September 16, 1998), Doc. IMM-1979-97; additional reasons at (1998), 160 F.T.R. 142 (Fed. T.D.) — Paragraph 46.01(1)(c) is a statutory formulation of the principle of *res judicata*. Subsection 46.01(5) creates an exception to the bar to future applications. This exception covers the situation of changed country conditions.

Nguyen v. Canada (Minister of Citizenship & Immigration) (1997), 133 F.T.R. 210 (Fed. T.D.) — The applicant sought to review two decisions of the Minister. The first is the opinion of the Minister dated May 27, 1996 pursuant to subparagraph 46.01(1)(e)(iv) of the *Immigration Act*, that the applicant constitutes a danger to the public in Canada. The second, was the opinion of the Minister dated May 27, 1996, pursuant to subsection 70(5) of the *Immigration Act* that the applicant constituted a danger to the public in Canada.

The applicant was born in Vietnam. After spending four years in a refugee camp in the Philippines, he was granted an immigrant visa in January 1991. In February 1994, the applicant was found guilty of eight counts in an indictment which arose from a single transaction — a robbery in which the applicant was the driver of the getaway car.

The applicant was released from prison in February 1996, and at the same time received a letter indicating that the Minister was considering whether to issue a danger to the public opinion. The applicant's counsel made written submissions to the Minister in April 1996.

On May 27, 1996, the Minister's delegate issued an opinion that the applicant constituted a danger to the public under both subsection 70(5) in subparagraph 46.01(1)(e)(iv).

In June 1996, the applicant was arrested, however, he was released by an adjudicator who came to the conclusion that the applicant was not a danger to the public. At the detention review hearing, one of the documents submitted was a report entitled "Danger to the Public Ministerial Report". This document was not part of the material disclosed for the applicant in February 1996, as the document had not yet been created. In that document, the officer who prepared it commented on the fact that he or she had spoken to the applicant's parole officer and had been advised that since his release the applicant had not been employed, was collecting welfare, his relationship with his former common law wife had broken down, and that his relationship with his daughter was continuing.

There was information in the applicant's file, which disclosed the applicant was unemployed and collecting welfare. The applicant's counsel in his submissions to the Minister at the time the danger opinion was being formed, had raised the question of the applicant's relation with his common law wife and had indicated in those submissions that it was unclear whether the relationship would continue or not.

The Court concluded that there was nothing in the document which constituted evidence to which the applicant did not have an opportunity to respond. If counsel submits certain matters in a letter to the Minister, the Minister's representatives are entitled to make contrary statements as long as the statements are either in the applicant's file or based on information which is available to the applicant. In this case, the applicant knew his common law relationship had terminated.

The Court also observed that there was no difference in the level of fairness owed under subsection 70(5) and section 46.01.

The application for judicial review was dismissed.

Gervasoni v. Canada (Minister of Citizenship & Immigration) (1996), 34 Imm. L.R. (2d) 80, 110 F.T.R. 297 (Fed. T.D.); affirmed (June 8, 1999), Doc. A-440-96 (Fed. C.A.) — The applicant sought to review a decision of the Minister, wherein the Minister rendered an opinion pursuant to subparagraph 46.01(1)(e)(i) of the *Immigration Act*, that the applicant constituted a danger to the public of Canada.

The decision under review is a discretionary administrative decision and therefore there is a minimal duty of fairness. There is no duty incumbent on the Minister to provide reasons for his opinion. The only way that the applicant can succeed on this argument would be to show that the Minister acted in bad faith or erred in law.

It was also argued that the subparagraph was inconsistent with sections 7 of the Charter because it failed to provide for the application of the principles of fairness and there was no provision for court review. The Court rejected this argument and found the decision in *Nguyen v. Canada*, [1993] 1 F.C. 696 (Fed. C.A.) dispositive of this question.

Finally, the Court found that the Minister can validly form the opinion on cogent facts any time before or after the adjudicator's finding. The Minister's opinion would only become dysfunctional if the adjudicator's finding was quashed and if the new adjudicator appointed to hear the matter a second time, declined to come to the same decision as the first adjudicator. The Ministers opinion however, would remain alive until such second determination was announced.

McAllister v. Canada (Minister of Citizenship & Immigration), [1996] 2 F.C. 190, 108 F.T.R. 1 (Fed. T.D.) — The applicant sought to review a decision of the Minister declaring that it was the Minister's opinion that it would be contrary to the public interest to have the applicant's refugee claim determined under the Act. The applicant was born in Northern Ireland and came to Canada in December 1988 with his wife and four children. Soon after his arrival the applicant and his wife made separate refugee claims. From July 1981 until February 1982 the applicant was a member of the Irish National Liberation Army (INLA). In July 1981 the applicant was charged with a number of serious offences for which he was later convicted, including conspiracy to commit murder, wounding with intent, possession of a fire arm, and belonging to a proscribed organization. On conviction he was sentenced to 7 years in jail. In 1987 he was convicted of assaulting police and of resisting police, and in 1988 he was convicted of driving while under the influence of alcohol. These later convictions resulted in fines without further incarceration. In March 1993 Mr. McAllister was interviewed by immigration officials about his refugee claim. In July 1993 an immigration officer made a report pursuant to section 27 reporting that the applicant fell within subsection 19(1)(c.1)(i). A further direction in November 1993 was issued for an inquiry to determine if the applicant was described in paragraphs 27(2)(a) and 19(1)(f)(iii)(B). At the conclusion of the inquiry pursuant to these directions a conditional deportation order was made.

In March 1994 the applicant received a letter from the Minister indicating that the Minister would be considering "whether or not it is in the public interest to have your refugee claim determined under the *Act*". The applicant, through his counsel, made submissions to the Minister in March 1994 and in May 1994 the Minister informed the applicant that having reviewed the submission it was the Minister's opinion that it would be contrary to the public interest to have the applicant's refugee claim determined under the Act.

There was no issue of credibility in this case. The letter from the Minister indicated that the Minister's opinion would be based upon evidence submitted at the inquiry and any representations the applicant might make. The Minister's letter conveying his decision specifically stated that the submissions and the available information concerning the applicant had been reviewed. There was no evidence that any other information had been available to the Minister than that indicated. There was no oral hearing and no interview provided to the applicant. The process here followed ensured that the applicant was apprised of the case he had to meet and was given an adequate opportunity to make written submissions in relation to the issue the Minister had served notice he would consider and decide. The fair hearing requirements under the *Charter of Rights*, and the Common Law Duty of Fairness, were met. The Court found that the word "terrorism" in subparagraph 19(1)(f)(iii)(B) and "public interest" in subparagraph 46.01(1)(e)(ii) were not so imprecise and vague that its application by the Minister could not be subject to review in a proper case on an application for judicial review.

The concept of vagueness could be summed up as follows:

> A law will be found unconstitutionally vague if it so lacks in precision as to not give sufficient guidance for legal debate. The threshold for finding a law vague is relatively high.

The applicant argued that he had a right to have his claim to be a Convention refugee determined according to the law prevailing at the time his claim was made, *i.e.* December 1988. Subparagraphs 19(1)(f)(iii)(B) or 46.01(1)(e)(ii) were not applied retrospectively in the circumstances of this case. The legislation in force at the time the decisions were made was given effect. It is not retrospective legislation to adopt a rule that henceforth excludes persons from Canada on the basis of their conduct in the past. The applicant, having made a claim to be a Convention refugee, only had a right to have his claim considered under the rules prevailing when it was considered. The applicant was a person with no right to enter or remain in Canada except as provided by the *Immigration Act* and any claim that he might make to enter or remain in Canada is subject to the law prevailing when that claim is determined, not when the claim is made.

Seyhoon v. Canada (Minister of Citizenship & Immigration) (1995), 28 Imm. L.R. (2d) 87 (Fed. T.D.) — The Court dismissed a motion for a stay of a deportation order. The applicant was convicted of possession of a narcotic for the purpose of trafficking. He was released on parole and failed to appear for his immigration inquiry. He also failed to report to his parole supervisor and a provincial parole warrant and an immigration warrant were issued for his arrest. After the applicant was apprehended on the warrant the Minister certified that the applicant constituted a danger to the public which had the effect of excluding the applicant from the Convention refugee determination system. The Minister is not required to follow formal guidelines as to the factors he should take into account in forming his opinion. Further, the Minister's opinion in respect of public danger is as reliable as the Court's.

In this case the Court was satisfied that the applicant had not demonstrated a serious issue to be tried and declined to stay the deportation order.

Nguyen v. Canada (Minister of Employment & Immigration) (1993), 18 Imm. L.R. (2d) 165, 100 D.L.R. (4th) 151, 151 N.R. 69, 14 C.R.R. (2d) 146 (Fed. C.A.) — The applicant, who was a permanent resident, was seeking to quash a deportation order. The applicant had been found described in subparagraphs 27(1)(d)(i) and 27(1)(d)(ii). Further, when the applicant attempted to obtain refugee status, a representative of the Minister tendered into evidence a certificate signed by the Minister stating that the applicant constituted a danger to the public of Canada with the result that, under the legislation then in effect, the applicant was not able to claim refugee status. Legislation which purports to define conditions for eligibility to claim refugee status may violate the Charter only if those conditions have the effect of subjecting a group of claimants to discriminatory treatment within the meaning of section 15. To deny dangerous criminals the right, generally conceded to immigrants who flee persecution, is not a form of illegitimate discrimination.

The Minister does not need to be compelled to follow formal guidelines stating the factors that should be taken into account in forming his opinion. The Minister's opinion in respect of public danger is as reliable as that of a court.

Counsel challenged the scheme set up by the Minister for the issuance of a certificate and complained that it did not provide for an oral hearing nor did it contain any provision for judicial review. Those submissions did not have to be addressed. The Court was sitting in judicial review of the decision of a tribunal which did not have jurisdiction to examine whether the public danger certificate had been issued in accordance with the rules of natural justice. The mandate of the tribunal did not entitle it to look behind the certificate which was fully valid on its face. The decision to issue a certificate is subject to judicial review by the Court only and not by immigration officers. The Court observed that the procedure set up and followed, in this case, accorded the applicant a full opportunity to make his case.

The scheme of the Act, established by subparagraph 27(1)(d)(i), subsection 32(2) and subparagraph 46.01(1)(e)(ii), is constitutionally sound and the decisions made against the applicant did not infringe his rights guaranteed under the Charter.

Bembenek v. Canada (Minister of Employment & Immigration) (February 17, 1984), DeCarlo (Adjudicator), Lazo (Member) (Imm. & Ref. Bd. (Adjud. Div.)) — Section 46.01(1)(e)(ii) in itself fails to meet the requirements of section 7 of the Charter. It does not provide for an application of the principles of fundamental justice where an individual is denied the right to life, liberty or security of the person. It makes no provision for a review, judicial or otherwise, of a decision by the Ministry to issue a certificate. The various irregularities in the issuance of the certificate in this case demonstrate the need for procedures to be prescribed by law before section 46.01(1)(e)(ii) can be said to be constitutional. Furthermore, this section cannot be saved by section 1. No lawful justification of the violation of section 7 described in this subparagraph was demonstrated at the inquiry. Accordingly, the impugned provision was not saved by section 1 of the *Charter of Rights and Freedoms*. Pursuant to the provisions of section 52, the adjudicator and Refugee Board member declined to give effect to the subparagraph in question and permitted the applicant to call evidence to demonstrate a credible basis for her claim to refugee status.

Editor's Note: The eligibility criteria have been amended, but the application of section 7 of the Charter of Rights and Freedoms to the Ministerial determination in paragraph (e) may still be important.

Section 46.01(1.1)

Canada (Minister of Employment & Immigration) v. Agbasi (1993), 10 Admin. L.R. (2d) 94, 61 F.T.R. 254 (Fed. T.D.) — The respondent left Nigeria in 1986 and entered Canada with authorizations to study and work. His family joined him shortly after his arrival in Canada. The student and employment authorizations were extended from time to time. In January 1989 while the authorizations to study and work were in force, Agbasi secured employment and was the subject of a section 27 report as a person who had engaged in employment contrary to the Act. In September 1989 his application for a visa extension pending completion of his inquiry was denied. At the conclusion of the proceedings the original paragraph of the allegation dealing with the unauthorized employment was held to be unfounded. The respondent was found, however, because his visa had expired, to be a person in paragraph 27(2)(e) (an overstay) and a departure notice was issued against him.

The respondent attempted to enter the United States but was unable to obtain a visa. Consequently, he did not leave Canada and was reported under paragraph 27(2)(i). At the second inquiry the respondent claimed refugee status. At the credible-basis hearing it was decided that to deny the respondent access to the Refugee Division pursuant to section 46.01(1)(f) would be contrary to section 7 of the Charter. This decision was upheld. The respondent was found to have overstayed because of Immigration's refusal to extend his visa. Had the visa been extended pending the outcome of the first inquiry, no ground for issuing a removal order would have existed once the respondent was cleared of the original allegation. Under those circumstances it was found to be unfair to apply paragraph 46.01(1)(f). Accordingly that section was found to be of no force and effect so far as the respondent was concerned.

Editor's Note: While the legislative scheme has changed since this decision, the principles may have a more general application.

46.02 Right to make a claim — Where a senior immigation officer determines that a person is eligible to have a claim determined by the Refugee Division, the senior immigration officer shall forthwith refer the claim to the Refugee Division in the manner and form prescribed by rules made under subsection 65(1).

R.S.C. 1985, c. 28 (4th Supp.), s. 14; 1992, c. 49, s. 37.

46.03 (1) Reference of claim to Refugee Division — Where a removal order is made against a person who has been determined not to be eligible to have a claim to be a Convention refugee determined by the Refugee Division on the basis that the person is a person described in paragraph 46.01(1)(*b*), but the person

> **(a) cannot be removed from Canada to a country prescribed pursuant to paragraph 114(1)(*s*),**
>
> **(b) having been removed from Canada, is allowed to come into Canada pursuant to paragraph 14(1)(*c*), or**
>
> **(c) having been allowed to leave Canada voluntarily, has not been permitted entry to the country from which the person had come to Canada and is allowed to come to Canada pursuant to paragraph 14(1)(*c*),**

a senior immigration officer shall forthwith refer the claim to the Refugee Division in the manner and form prescribed by rules made under subsection 65(1).

(2) Obligation to provide information — A person whose claim is referred to the Refugee Division pursuant to section 46.02 or subsection (1) shall, in the manner and within the period prescribed by rules made under subsection 65(1), provide the Refugee Division with such information as is required by the rules.

R.S.C. 1985, c. 28 (4th Supp.), s. 14; 1992, c. 49, s. 37.

Case Law

Section 46.03(1)

Orelien v. Canada (Minister of Employment & Immigration) (1991), [1992] 1 F.C. 592, 15 Imm. L.R. (2d) 1, 135 N.R. 50 (Fed. C.A.) — Canada's obligations in the area of refugees stem from the 4th *Geneva Convention* of August 12, 1949, and protocol due to the *Geneva Convention* of August 12, 1949, both approved by Acts of Parliament (*Geneva Conventions Act*, R.S.C. 1985, c. G-3, s. 2, as am. S.C. 1990, c. 14, s. 1), as well as a customary norm of temporary refuge. To return a person to Haiti in the circumstances that presently exist and have existed at relevant times in this case would have violated Canada's obligations under the Convention, the protocol and the customary norm of international law prohibiting the forceable repatriation of foreign nationals who have fled generalized violence and other threats to their lives and security arising out of internal armed conflict within their state of nationality. The Convention, the protocol and the customary norm of international law have the force of domestic law in Canada and can be enforced in the courts of Canada at the suit of a private individual. The intention to execute a deportation order which, if executed, would breach those laws does not colour the process under the *Immigration Act* by which a person from such a country may be ordered deported. This is not to denigrate the importance of the Convention, the protocol and the customary norms of international law. It would be a grave and justiciable matter if Canada were to execute deportation orders in circumstances which breached obligations under international law and put the life, liberty or security of persons in peril.

46.04 (1) Application for landing — Any person who is determined by the Refugee Division to be a Convention refugee may, within the prescribed period, apply to an immigration officer for landing of that person and any dependant of that person, unless the Convention refugee is

> **(a) a permanent resident;**
>
> **(b) a person who has been recognized by any country, other than Canada, as a Convention refugee and who, if removed from Canada, would be allowed to return to that country;**
>
> **(c) a national or citizen of a country, other than the country that the person left, or outside of which the person remains, by reason of fear of persecution; or**
>
> **(d) a person who has permanently resided in a country, other than the country that the person left, or outside of which the person remains, by reason of fear of persecution, and who, if removed from Canada, would be allowed to return to that country.**

(2) [Repealed 1992, c. 49, s. 38.]

(3) Grant of landing — Notwithstanding any other provision of this Act, but subject to subsections (3.1) and (8), an immigration officer to whom an application is made under subsection (1) shall grant landing to the applicant, and to any dependant for whom landing is sought if the immigration officer is satisfied that neither the applicant nor any of those dependants is a person described in paragraph 19(1)(*c*.1), (*c*.2), (*d*), (*e*), (*f*), (*g*), (*j*), (*k*) or (*l*) or a person who has been convicted of an offence under any Act of Parliament for which a term of imprisonment of

> **(a) more than six months has been imposed; or**
>
> **(b) five years or more may be imposed.**

(3.1) Exception — An immigration officer may grant landing under subsection (3) only if

> **(a) the time normally limited for filing an application for leave to commence an application for judicial review under the *Federal Court Act* in respect of the Refugee Division's determination that the person is a Convention Refugee has elapsed without such an application having been filed; or**
>
> **(b) where the Minister has filed an application for leave to commence an application for judicial review under the *Federal Court Act* within the time normally limited for doing so, a judgment is made in respect of the Refugee Division's determi-**

nation by the Federal Court — Trial Division, Federal Court of Appeal or Supreme Court of Canada that finally disposes of the matter.

(4) **Terms and conditions — An immigration officer who grants landing to an applicant pursuant to this section may impose terms and conditions of a prescribed nature in connection therewith.**

(5) **Abandonment of application — If an applicant under subsection (1) is, in the opinion of the immigration officer, in default in the prosecution of the application, the immigration officer may, after giving the applicant a reasonable opportunity to be heard, declare the application to have been abandoned.**

(6) **Notice of decision — An immigration officer to whom an application is made under subsection (1) shall render the decision on the application as soon as possible and shall send a written notice of the decision to the applicant.**

(7) **Deeming provision — Where a person who is determined to be a Convention refugee is a person against whom a removal order or conditional removal order is made is granted landing under this section, the order shall be deemed never to have been made.**

(8) **No grant of landing — An immigration officer shall not grant landing either to an applicant under subsection (1) or to any dependant of the applicant until the applicant is in possession of a valid and subsisting passport or travel document or a satisfactory identity document.**

R.S.C. 1985, c. 28 (4th Supp.), s. 14; 1992, c. 1, s. 143 (Sched. VI, item 12); 1992, c. 49, s. 38.

Case Law

Section 46.04(1)

Abdirahman v. Canada (Minister of Citizenship & Immigration) (1997), 40 Imm. L.R. (2d) 291, 125 F.T.R. 191 (Fed. T.D.) — This was an application to review the decision of an immigration officer who determined that the applicants could not be landed pursuant to section 46.04(3) of the *Immigration Act.*

The applicants are a mother, and her four children all of whom are citizens of Somalia. In 1991, the applicant and her husband entered Canada and made separate refugee claims, the children were included in the mother's claim. In April 1992, both the applicant and her husband were granted convention refugee status. Following that determination, both applied for landing. In August 1992, the family was informed that their applications had been provisionally accepted. The applicant's husband had served as the Somali Ambassador to Canada from 1984 to 1987 and the Ambassador to Nigeria from 1987 to 1991. On the basis of his employment, the applicant's husband was found to be described in section 19(1)(l) of the Act. As a result of this finding the applicant's husband was ordered deported. The applicants in this application were not included in that order. The applicant was denied permanent resident status on the basis that she was a dependant of her husband who had been refused landing.

Section 46.04(1) of the Act allows convention refugees and any dependants to apply to an immigration officer for landing. This provision gives the right to each convention refugee to apply for landing. It also allows convention refugees to apply on behalf of a dependant. Due to the fact that the applicant was found to be a convention refugee she had the right to apply for landing independent of her husband. Accordingly, the decision refusing her the right to apply for landing was quashed.

Martinez v. Canada (Minister of Citizenship & Immigration) (1996), 114 F.T.R. 113 (Fed. T.D.) — The applicant sought to review a negative decision of the CRDD. The applicant is a citizen of El Salvador, by reason of his mother's nationality, and of Belize, by reason of his birth. The applicant's mother, alleged before the CRDD a well-founded fear of persecution in El Salvador based on her membership in a particular social group.

The applicant's mother and two of her three children were found to be convention refugees as against El Salvador but the applicant as a citizen of Belize, was found not to have a well-founded fear of persecution in that country.

It is unnecessary to extend the plain meaning of the words convention refugee to include the principle of family unity. The principle of Family Unity is enshrined in the *Immigration Act* by section 46.04(1) and 46.04(3). None of the exceptions or limitations provided for in the two subsections in any way limit the applicant's mother's right to apply for landing in Canada for herself and the applicant, or the obligation of an immigration officer to grant landing in the event of such an application. Accordingly the application for judicial review was dismissed.

Rafizade v. Canada (Minister of Citizenship & Immigration) (1995), 92 F.T.R. 55, 30 Imm. L.R. (2d) 261 (Fed. T.D.) — The applicants, 11 and 14 years of age, were citizens of Iran. The father was designated as the representative of the two minor applicants. The applicants did not testify. Only their father presented evidence. The Board found the father to be a refugee, but found that the minor applicants were not Convention refugees. The Board found there was insufficient evidence to conclude that there was a reasonable chance that the minor claimants would face persecution.

The Court found there was no justification for the development of a common-law notion of indirect persecution to account for family unity situations not covered by the *Immigration Act*. It is not the role of the Court to expand the scope of the family for immigration purposes beyond that which parliament has determined to be appropriate.

In this case the persecution directed at the father was not persecution directed at the applicants. Accordingly, the application was dismissed.

Castellanos v. Canada (Minister of Citizenship & Immigration) (1994), 84 F.T.R. 316 (Fed. T.D.) — The applicant was a Cuban citizen as were his two daughters. His wife was a citizen of what was formerly the Soviet Union and she lived with her husband and children in Cuba on a renewable 5 year visa.

The husband was found to be a Convention refugee. His wife and two daughters were not. With respect to the wife of the principal applicant, the Board erred in finding that she was a Ukraine citizen. The decision refusing her claim was quashed and an order was made directing a new hearing.

The status of the two daughters raised the question of whether family unity was a concept recognized by Canadian refugee law. The principle of family unity requires that persons granted refugee status should not be separated from their closest family members, particularly when a situation of dependency exists. The Court found that there was no mention of family unity in the current definition of a Convention refugee, and that therefore, in order to apply the principle to family unity, it would have to extend the definition. The Court found no justification for doing so.

For a person to be considered a Convention refugee it must be shown that the person is a member of one of five enumerated classes. The class of membership in a particular social group is the basket clause of this definitional provision. The family had been accepted as a social group for purposes of a Refugee definition. One will not be deemed a Convention refugee just because one has a relative that is being persecuted. There has to be a clear nexus between the persecution that is being levelled against one of the family members and that which is taking place against the others. A family can only be considered a social group in cases where there is evidence that the persecution is taking place against the family members as a social group. Here the Board found no evidence that any persecutory activity had been levelled against the mother or the daughters, let alone any based upon their being members of the principal applicant's family. Their claims were not well founded on the basis that they were being persecuted as members of a social group. Finally, the Court was not prepared to accept the principal of indirect persecution as defined in *Bhatti v. Canada (Secretary of State)* (1994), 25 Imm. L.R. (2d) 275, 84 F.T.R. 145 (Fed. T.D.) as part of our refugee law. The Court held that indirect persecution did not constitute persecution within the meaning of the definition of Convention refugee.

The Court found that section 46.04 was the legislative response to the principle of family unity.

Yarmohammadi v. Canada (Minister of Employment & Immigration) (1994), 26 Imm. L.R. (2d) 76, 85 F.T.R. 297 (Fed. T.D.) — The male applicant unsuccessfully claimed refugee status. The female applicant successfully claimed refugee status and applied for landing pursuant to section 46.04 of the *Immigration Act*. The female applicant determined that she was entitled to include the male applicant in her application for landing, and purported to do so on May 15 and June 4, 1992. Her application for permanent residence was pending on February 1, 1993 when section 46.04 was amended by Bill C-86. Those amendments only permitted the inclusion of the male applicant if he was dependent upon the female. Since this was not the case only the female applicant became a permanent resident in April 1993. The Court found that the amendments to section 46.04 applied to the application and the male applicant was properly refused permanent resident status. This case was to be distinguished from one where a final decision had been made to grant the application before the coming into force of the amendment.

Chahoud v. Canada (Minister of Employment & Immigration) (1992), 16 Imm. L.R. (2d) 108 (Fed. C.A.) — In order to obtain Convention refugee status claimants must establish that they are unable or unwilling to avail themselves of the protection of all their countries of nationality. Subsection 46.04(1)(c) has as a focal point the landing of refugee claimants rather than their status as Convention refugees and has no application in considering the refugee status of a person who is a national or citizen of a second non-persecuting country. The Court affirmed its decision in *Ward v. Canada (Minister of Employment & Immigration)* (1990), 108 N.R. 60 and (Fed. C.A.) and *Canada (Minister of Employment & Immigration) v. Akl* (1990), 140 N.R. 323 (Fed. C.A.).

Section 46.04(3)

Taei v. Canada (Minister of Employment & Immigration) (1993), 19 Imm. L.R. (2d) 187, 64 F.T.R. 311 (Fed. T.D.) — The applicant sought leave for a judicial review to obtain an order compelling the respondent to process his application for landing. The applicant arrived in Canada in 1989 and made a claim for refugee status. His claim was determined affirmatively but before landed-immigrant status was granted, the applicant was charged with aggravated assault, attempted murder and extortion and these charges were pending at the time of this application. The respondent had refused to process the application until the criminal charges were disposed of by the courts. Leave to institute judicial review was denied. The presumption of innocence requires the respondent to do nothing but stay the applicant's request for admission until the criminal charges are disposed of. It would be against public policy for the respondent to heedlessly grant permanent resident status until the criminal charges were completed. If the applicant is acquitted, then the respondent should proceed with granting admission. If the applicant is convicted, then he will have disqualified himself from landing.

Section 46.04(6)

Singh (S.) v. Canada (Minister of Citizenship & Immigration) (1998), 47 Imm. L.R. (2d) 83 (Fed. T.D.) — This was an application for an order of *mandamus*. The applicant came to Canada in 1992 and was granted refugee status in April 1995. The applicant then applied for landing pursuant to s. 46.04(1) in June 1995. The applicant had one CSIS interview in May 1996 and a second one in April 1997. As at the date of the hearing of the application, no decision had been made.

The applicant's last CSIS meeting was in April 1997, and according to the affidavit evidence filed, the applicant's file now formed part of a backlog of cases at security review and it was estimated that security review would be in a position to make a recommendation to the local CIC in eight to ten months. The Court found that in the circumstances of this case, the delay was not unreasonable. Accordingly, s. 46.04(1) had not been breached. The Court declined to attribute systemic delays to the respondent and accordingly dismissed the application.

46.05 [Repealed 1992, c. 49, s. 39.]

46.06 [Repealed 1992, c. 49, s. 39.]

46.07 (1) Direction to reopen inquiry — Where any person against whom a removal order or conditional removal order is made by an adjudicator is determined by the Refugee Division to be a Convention refugee and

(a) is a person described in paragraph 46.04(1)(*a*), (*b*), (*c*) or (*d*),

(b) fails to apply for landing under section 46.04 within the time limited therefor,

(c) is declared to have abandoned an application under section 46.04,

(d) withdraws an application for landing under section 46.04, or

(e) is refused landing on an application under section 46.04,

a senior immigration officer shall cause the inquiry with respect to the person to be reopened by the adjudicator who presided at the inquiry or by any other adjudicator as soon as practicable.

(1.1) Determination of right to remain in Canada — Subject to subsection (6), where any person against whom a removal order or conditional removal order is made by a senior immigration officer is determined by the Refugee Division to be a Convention refugee and the person is a person described in any of paragraphs (1)(*a*) to (*e*), a senior immigration officer shall determine whether or not the person has a right under subsection 4(2.1) to remain in Canada.

(2) Determination of right to remain in Canada — Where an inquiry is reopened pursuant to this section, the adjudicator shall determine whether or not the person who is the subject of the inquiry has a right under subsection 4(2.1) to remain in Canada.

(3) Where no right to remain in Canada — Where a senior immigration officer or an adjudicator determines that a person does not have a right under subsection 4(2.1) to remain in Canada, the senior immigration officer or adjudicator shall

(a) confirm the order made against that person; or

(b) quash the order made with respect to that person and take the appropriate action under subsection 23(4), (4.01) or (4.2) or 27(4) or (6) or section 32.

(4) Where right to remain in Canada — Where a senior immigration officer or an adjudicator determines that a person has a right under subsection 4(2.1) to remain in Canada, the senior immigration officer or the adjudicator shall quash the removal order or conditional removal order and, notwithstanding any other provision of this Act or the regulations, shall allow the person to remain in Canada.

(5) Additional allegations — In making the determination referred to in subsection (1.1) or (2) and in taking the appropriate action with respect to a person under subsection 23(4), (4.01) or (4.2) or 27(4) or (6) or section 32, the senior immigration officer or adjudicator may take into consideration

(a) any allegation respecting the person not previously made if that person is the subject of a report under paragraph 20(1)(*a*); or

(b) where that person is not the subject of a report under paragraph 20(1)(*a*), any allegation that is set out in a report under subsection 27(1) or (2) if the Deputy Minister has issued a direction pursuant to subsection 27(3) that a determination be made with respect to the allegation.

(6) Inquiry — Where any additional allegation referred to in subsection (5) in respect of a person is not an allegation with respect to which a senior immigration officer may made a removal order, the senior immigration officer shall, as soon as is practicable, cause an inquiry to be held with respect to that person.

R.S.C. 1985, c. 28 (4th Supp.), s. 14; 1992, c. 49, s. 40; 1995, c. 15, s. 10.

46.1 (1) Notification to Refugee Division by senior immigration officer — A senior immigration officer shall forthwith notify the Refugee Division and, in the circumstances described in subsection 23(4.01) or (4.2) or 27(6), shall cause an inquiry to be held concerning the person as soon as is reasonably practicable where, after a person's claim has been referred to the Refugee Division, the senior immigration officer believes on reasonable grounds that

(a) the person is a member of an inadmissible class described in paragraph 19(1)(*c*) or subparagraph 19(1)(*c*.1)(i);

(b) the person is a person described in subparagraph 27(1)(*a*.1)(i); or

(c) the person is a person described in paragraph 27(1)(*d*) who has been convicted of an offence under any Act of Parliament for which a term of imprisonment of ten years or more may be imposed.

(2) Suspension of consideration of case — On being notified pursuant to subsection (1), the Refugee Division shall suspend its consideration of the case and shall

(a) continue its consideration of the case, where it receives notice that a senior immigration officer has made a determination under paragraph 45(1)(*a*) that the person is eligible to have their claim determined by the Refugee Division; or

(b) terminate its consideration of the case, where it receives notice that a senior immigration officer has made a determination under paragraph 45(1)(*a*) that the person is not eligible to have their claim determined by the Refugee Division.

R.S.C. 1985, c. 29 (4th Supp.), s. 5; c. 28 (4th Supp.), s. 35; 1995, c. 15, s. 11.

[Note: S.C. 1995, c. 15, s. 11(2) provides that section 46.1 applies to any claim that has been referred to a Refugee Division on or before July 10, 1995 but in respect of which the Refugee Division has not made a determination.]

46.2 (1) Resumption of consideration of case — A senior immigration officer shall request that the Refugee Division forthwith resume its consideration of a person's claim where the senior immigration officer believes on reasonable grounds that, because a final decision has been made in the matter, the person to whom section 46.1 applies is no longer a member of an inadmissible class referred to in paragraph 19(1)(*c*) or subparagraph 19(1)(*c*.1)(i) or a person described in subparagraph 27(1)(*a*.1)(i) or paragraph 27(1)(*d*).

(2) Effect — Where subsection (1) applies and, immediately before the decision referred to in paragraph 46.1(2)(*b*) was made, the person was subject to a removal order on a basis other than that the person is a person referred to in subsection 46.1(1), the person is deemed to be subject to a conditional departure order or a conditional deportation order, as the case may be, from the day on which the person ceases to belong to an inadmissible class referred to, or to be a person described, in that subsection.

(3) Application of certain provisions — Subsections 28(2) and 32.1(6) apply in respect of a conditional order referred to in subsection (2).

1995, c. 15, s. 11.

46.3 (1) Multiple claims — Where a person's claim has been referred to the Refugee Division, a senior immigration officer shall forthwith notify the Refugee Division where

(a) the senior immigration officer is satisfied that the person has made more than one claim to be a Convention Refugee; and

(b) the claim that was referred to the Refugee Division is not the first claim to have been referred to a senior immigration officer with respect to that person.

(2) Effect — On being notified pursuant to subsection (1), the Refugee Division shall terminate its consideration of the claim and any decision made by the Refugee Division in respect of the claim is null and void.

1995, c. 15, s. 11.

[Note: S.C. 1995, c. 15, s. 11(3) provides that section 46.3 applies to any claim that has been referred to the Refugee Division on or before July 10, 1995.]

46.4 (1) Fraudulent claims — Where a person's claim has been referred to the Refugee Division and a senior immigration officer is satisfied that the decision with respect to the eligibility of the person to have their claim referred was based on fraud or a misrepresentation of a material fact and the person would not otherwise be eligible to have their claim referred, the senior immigration officer shall forthwith

(a) make a determination that the person is ineligible to have their claim referred to the Refugee Division; and

(b) notify the Refugee Division of that determination.

(2) effect — On being notified pursuant to subsection (1), the Refugee Division shall terminate its consideration of the claim and any decision made by the Refugee Division in respect of the claim is null and void.

1995, c. 15, s. 11.

[Note: S.C. 1995, c. 15, s. 11(3) provides that section 46.3 applies to any claim that has been referred to the Refugee Division on or before July 10, 1995.]

Case Law

Gwala v. Canada (Minister of Citizenship & Immigration) (1999), 242 N.R. 173 (Fed. C.A.) — Senior immigration officers do not have the implied jurisdiction to decide questions of law. The Trial Division of the Federal Court has jurisdiction in judicial review proceedings to decide constitutional questions which a senior immigration officer could not entertain.

Gwala v. Canada (Minister of Citizenship & Immigration), 44 Imm. L.R. (2d) 1, [1998] 4 F.C. 43, 147 F.T.R. 246 (Fed. T.D.); affirmed (1999), 242 N.R. 173 (Fed. C.A.) — This was an application to review a decision of a senior immigration officer declaring that the applicant was ineligible to have his refugee claim determined by a panel of the CRDD. The applicant challenged the constitutionality of section 46.4 of the *Immigration Act*, due to the fact that it required the making of an order, which the applicant maintained violated his constitutional rights.

The Court concluded that a senior immigration officer acting under section 36.4 does not have jurisdiction to decide questions of law, and accordingly that the Federal Court Trial Division lacked jurisdiction on an application for judicial review to consider the constitutional validity of section 46.4 of the Act.

The Court went on to find that if it was wrong on the constitutional question, that section 46.4 was nevertheless constitutional.

Service of Orders

47. Service of orders — A removal order or conditional removal order or a copy thereof shall, in such manner as is prescribed, be served on the person against whom it is made and on such other persons as are prescribed.

R.S.C. 1985, c. 28 (4th Supp.), s. 15.

Execution of Orders

48. Time of execution — Subject to sections 49 and 50, a removal order shall be executed as soon as reasonably practicable.

Case Law

Umukoro v. Canada (Minister of Citizenship & Immigration) (March 31, 1999), Doc. IMM-1430-99 (Fed. T.D.) — The applicant sought to stay the execution of a removal order. A removal officer has some discretion concerning removal once the officer has become involved in making deportation arrangements. In appropriate circumstances a legitimate consideration in the exercise of that discretion might include the fact that it would be reasonable to await a pending decision on a humanitarian and compassionate application. The fact that such an application is outstanding is not, in and of itself, a bar to the execution of an order.

Whether it is appropriate for a removal officer to take into account the fact that there is an outstanding humanitarian and compassionate application will depend on the circumstances of each case. In the present case, the Court found that the evidence on irreparable harm was speculative and hypothetical and refused to grant a stay.

Mahadeo v. Canada (Minister of Citizenship & Immigration) (March 5, 1999), Doc. IMM-889-99 (Fed. T.D.) — The applicants sought to stay a removal order made against them. On the question of irreparable harm, the applicants who were 17 and 18 years of age respectively argued that the disruption of their education due to the execution of the removal order before the end of the school year would constitute irreparable harm. Personal difficulties of this nature although inconvenient do not constitute irreparable harm, as serious as they may be to the applicant.

San Vicente Freitas v. Canada (Minister of Citizenship & Immigration), 49 Imm. L.R. (2d) 33, (sub nom. *Freitas v. Canada (Minister of Citizenship & Immigration))* [1999] 2 F.C. 432 (Fed. T.D.) — These reasons arose out of an application for judicial review of a decision of a panel of the CRDD that they determine the applicant not to be a Convention refugee. The applicant was born in Trinidad, but moved to Venezuela at a very young age. In Venezuela he was a political activist. The applicant came to Canada in 1967 and became a landed immigrant. The applicant was steadily employed in Canada for a period of 10 years and then returned to Venezuela as a visitor in 1981. The applicant found conditions had changed and decided to remain there. After the presidential election in 1983, the applicant ceased any political activities in Venezuela and ultimately in 1986, obtained a false passport and returned to Canada. After being back in Canada, the applicant was convicted of a serious criminal offence and sentenced to 9 years imprisonment. The applicant claimed refugee status against Venezuela.

The applicant's claim was refused, and he applied for leave to review that decision. Leave was granted. However, an application to stay execution of the removal order was refused. The decision of the Supreme Court of Canada in the *Pushpanathan v. Canada (Minister of Citizenship & Immigration)*, [1998] 1 S.C.R. 982, mandated that in this case the interpretation of the panel of Article 1F(c) of the Convention was wrong. Accordingly the decision of the panel was set aside. The execution of the removal order did not render the judicial review proceedings moot.

The Court refused to provide a meaningless remedy in the form of a reference back to the CRDD for redetermination that could only be a determination that the applicant is not a Convention refugee because he is not outside the country of his nationality. Similarly, the Court was not prepared to order the respondent to return the applicant to Canada if the return of the applicant should prove to be unnecessary to an effective redetermination by the CRDD. The Court ordered that if the panel of the CRDD determined that it was necessary for the applicant to appear again to allow it to comply with the order of the Court directing a rehearing, the respondent was ordered forthwith to make best efforts to return the applicant to Canada at the respondent's expense. If the panel, without requiring the return of the applicant, working on the assumption that the applicant was in Canada was able to determine that the applicant was a Convention refugee, then the respondent was ordered forthwith to make best efforts to return the applicant to Canada at the respondent's expense.

Torres-Samuels (Guardian ad litem of) v. Canada (Minister of Citizenship & Immigration) (1998), 47 Imm. L.R. (2d) 9, 57 B.C.L.R. (3d) 357, [1999] 6 W.W.R. 207, (sub nom. *Torres-Samuels v. Canada (Minister of Citizenship & Immigration))* 113 B.C.A.C. 214, (sub nom. *Torres-Samuels v. Canada (Minister of Citizenship & Immigration))* 184 W.A.C. 214, 166 D.L.R. (4th) 611 (B.C. C.A.) — This petition was brought on behalf of the children of Jose Lino Torres Hurtado who were aged 7 and 2 at the time the petition was launched. They were seeking to enjoin or prohibit the deportation of their father, under a valid order of deportation, on the ground that it would not be in their best interests to be deprived of his attention and care. The petition invoked the *parens patriae* jurisdiction of the Supreme Court of British Columbia. The petitioners appealed from the dismissal of their petition by Mr. Justice Paris.

One of the underlying principles by which the discretion must be exercised is that it is not to be used to override a statutory provision, although it may be used to fill a gap in a legislative scheme.

There is no indication in the *Immigration Act* or elsewhere of a legislative intent to leave with the provincial superior courts, a power to review the validity of a deportation order under the *parens patriae* jurisdiction. Accordingly, the appeal was dismissed.

Ukponmwan v. Canada (Minister of Citizenship & Immigration) (1998), 151 F.T.R. 317 (Fed. T.D.) — On August 10, 1998, the applicant applied for leave to review a decision of an immigration enforcement officer directing the applicant to report for removal on August 13, 1998. This decision gave effect to a deportation order dated January 29, 1996, that became executory when the applicant's claim for refugee status was denied and leave to review that decision was refused.

The applicant's grounds for his application were that he would likely be subject to detention and torture by the Nigerian authorities on return, both because he is a member of a particular tribe and a member of a resistance group. Since it would undermine the jurisdiction of the Court over this application if the applicant were removed to Nigeria prior to its disposition, the Court held that it had jurisdiction to stay a removal until the application had been determined.

Secondly, the Court found that it had jurisdiction to review the validity of the directions for the applicant's removal to Nigeria.

Saini v. Canada (Minister of Citizenship & Immigration), 45 Imm. L.R. (2d) 279, [1998] 4 F.C. 325, 150 F.T.R. 148 (Fed. T.D.) — The applicant sought to review a decision which was in the form of a communication from a removal officer to the applicant, to the effect that the applicant would be removed from Canada on May 5, 1997.

Removal officers do not have jurisdiction to conduct risk assessments and make risk determinations in the course of making destination decisions. The options open to removal officers in making destination decisions are circumscribed by section 52 of the Act.

Pursuant to section 48 of the *Immigration Act* removal officers have a discretion to delay the execution of a deportation order. In principle, a removal officer can delay a removal to await the determination of a humanitarian and compassionate application. A removal officer may have regard to cogent evidence of risk in removal to a particular destination and as to whether or not an appropriate risk assessment has been conducted and evaluated for the purpose of informing his or her exercise of discretion regarding deferral.

In this case, the applicant's materials in respective risk filed before the removals officer were properly before that officer but only for the limited purpose of determining whether or not an appropriate assessment had been conducted and evaluated and whether or not a delay in making removal arrangements was warranted. The representations in respective risk properly constitute part of a certified record in this application.

The material indicates that no appropriate risk assessment was done or determination made. The material disclosed is not evidence that exercise of discretion to delay was considered. The removal officer's failure to consider whether or not to exercise his or her discretion under section 48 pending an appropriate risk assessment and risk determination constituted a reviewable error in the nature of a failure or refusal to exercise jurisdiction.

Francis (Litigation Guardian of) v. Canada (Minister of Citizenship & Immigration) (1998), 160 D.L.R. (4th) 557 (Ont. Gen. Div.) — The applicants are two sisters aged six and eight, and their brother who is 15. The two sisters are Canadian citizens born and living in Canada. The brother was born in Grenada and came to Canada at the age of seven and has lived here ever since. All of the children live with their mother, one of the respondents, Maria Joyce Francis, a single mother born in Grenada who came to Canada 10 years ago.

The applicants applied to the Court for permission to stay with their mother. They are seeking a declaration that any and all orders of deportation be declared a nullity, a declaration that it is in the best interest of the applicants, that their permanent residence in Canada not be disturbed and an interim order enjoining the Minister from taking steps to interfere with the continued permanent residence in Canada, of the applicants or their mother.

The basis of the Court's jurisdiction is the dependence of children and the need for the state through its courts to protect their interests, particularly in cases where parents or guardians are unable to do so. The issues to be decided in this application arise in an immigration context, but they are not so much immigration issues as children's and human rights issues. The rights of the children are in no way dependent on the status of their mother.

The Court was not satisfied that the Federal Court, whose jurisprudence and procedures in immigration matters are informed by the principle underlying the *Immigration Act*, was a better forum to the determination of the constitutional rights of Canadian citizens than was the Ontario Court General Division.

Fundamental justice, like natural justice, is not the creation of any particular national judicial system. Accordingly, the *United Nations Convention on the Rights of the Child* may be looked at. This Convention does not purport to create rights but to declare them. Its ratification by so many countries including Canada suggests that the rights declared therein are consistent with the views of justice in the adopting countries.

The *Immigration Act* and its procedures have no provisions designed to protect the rights and interests of Canadian children whose parent is the subject of deportation proceedings. The existence and rights of Canadian-born children, are only considered during immigration proceedings, if and so far as a parent subject to immigration proceedings may raise the issue. The immigration authorities and tribunals do not recognize any duty to enquire as to the existence or interests of Canadian-born children to give them notice of the proceedings concerning their parent, to take any steps to see that they are afforded representation. The mere possibility that an immigration officer may choose to enquire about children does not meet the requirements of fundamental justice. At a minimum those requirements encompass the identification of such children, some notice to them of the proceedings and some method of seeing that their rights and interests are considered.

The Canadian-born children who are applicants in this matter were deprived of their rights under section 7 of the Charter, without any compliance with the requirements of fundamental justice.

The Court quashed all deportation orders outstanding against the mother, and the Court quashed all directions outstanding against the mother and against the Canadian-born children. Finally, no orders or directions were to issue subsequent to these proceedings, except after the Canadian-born children were given notice and except after their best interests were considered in accordance with the rules of fundamental justice.

With respect to Cleavon Francis, the 15-year-old applicant, he was found to be an alien with no right to remain in Canada. The state of the record in this case did not permit any determination of his claims. Eventual determination of his mother's claim to remain in Canada will be an important if not controlling factor in any possible consideration of Cleavon Francis's claim. Under the circumstances, the Court continued the present restraining order preventing the deportation of Cleavon Francis until 30 days after the final determination of the status of his mother. Finally, the Court declared, based on all of the material before it, that it was in the best interests of the applicants that they remain in Canada with their mother and in her care.

Muncan v. Canada (Minister of Citizenship & Immigration) (1998), 141 F.T.R. 241 (Fed. T.D.) — The applicant applied for a stay of a pending removal order. The applicant was convicted of a number of criminal offences and was ordered deported. The applicant appealed to the Appeal Division of the IRB against the deportation order. The Minister declared the applicant to be a danger to the public and the applicant sought to set aside the danger opinion and to stay the execution of the deportation order pending review of the opinion.

There is no jurisdictional limit to the discretion that the Court is empowered to apply under section 18.2. The whole question of whether the discretion should be exercised relates to the merits of each individual case. Regarding an application for a stay of a removal order, the issue is whether it is fair and just to grant it. In considering the entire context in deciding whether to exercise the discretion provided under section 18.2, the Court found that it was far too technical of a perspective to require the deportation order to be challenged on judicial review or to limit the application of the appropriate injunctive test to the circumstances of the deportation order itself.

Suresh v. R. (1998), 44 Imm. L.R. (2d) 181, (sub nom. *Suresh v. Canada)* 49 C.R.R. (2d) 131, 38 O.R. (3d) 267 (Ont. Gen. Div.) — This was an application to stay the execution of a removal order. On the issue of the balance of convenience, counsel for the Crown contended that even if there was a serious issue to be tried and irreparable harm to the applicant that, nevertheless, the balance of convenience favoured Canada. Canada was not to be allowed to become a haven for terrorists and their supporters. The Court noted that the Federal Court had determined that the decision to regard the applicant as a danger to Canada was not unreasonable. The Court noted, however, that the applicant had not personally committed any acts of violence either in Canada or in Sri Lanka and that his activity in this country was heading an organization which raises significant funds for the LTTE, who are said to have prolonged the civil war. While it is the duty of the executive to make these sorts of judgments, the Court noted that it was its duty to weigh the balance of convenience among the public interest generally: the interest of the Crown as litigant and the interest of the applicant. The harm to the applicant if the order was refused was self evident, deportation would *de facto* finally decide the case against him since the applicant would be unable to return to Canada should he obtain any relief from the courts in this country. [Affirmed (January 8, 1999), Doc. 46/98 (Ont. Div. Ct.)]

The Court concluded that the harm to the public interest occasioned by deporting the applicant without allowing him to challenge the lawfulness of his deportation greatly outweighed the interest of the Crown and that the balance of convenience favoured the applicant.

Editor's Note: Affirmed on appeal by the Ontario Divisional Court, January 8, 1999, court file number 46/98.

Paszkowski v. R. (1998), (sub nom. *Paszkowski v. Canada (Minister of Citizenship and Immigration))* 141 F.T.R. 149 (Fed. T.D.) — This was an application for an interlocutory injunction pending the resolution of an action brought by the applicant by way of a statement of claim seeking a declaration that the applicant was granted landed immigrant status in 1984 and therefore had the right to enter and remain in Canada.

Counsel for the Crown argued that the Court did not have jurisdiction to grant the relief claimed due to the fact that this was an immigration matter and accordingly the proper procedure was by way of judicial review. This position was rejected. The cases relied upon by the Crown involved matters where decisions had been rendered by an administrative tribunal and were therefore subject to the immigration rules, which required that the parties proceed by way of judicial review after having obtained leave. In this case, there was no decision being challenged that had already been dealt with in previous proceedings. The issue in this action was the applicant's permanent status, a question which had never been debated, nor had any decision ever been rendered, from which one could seek judicial review. The only remedy available to the plaintiff in this case was by way of statement of claim.

On the question of the balance of convenience, even though the Court accepted there would be no threat to the applicant's security or freedom if he were returned to Poland, the Court considered the applicant had been in Canada for 12 years, had been employed, had not been involved in any wrong doing, had a wife and two children residing in Canada and concluded that the balance of convenience was in favour of the applicant.

Suresh v. Canada (Minister of Citizenship & Immigration) (1998), 141 F.T.R. 152 (Fed. T.D.); reversed in part 47 Imm. L.R. (2d) 1, [1998] 4 F.C. 192, 229 N.R. 240, 55 C.R.R. (2d) 157 (Fed. C.A.) — This is an application to stay the execution of a removal order. The Court was unable to find irreparable harm due to the assurance given by the High Commissioner of Sri Lanka that the applicant would not be tortured or killed if returned to Sri Lanka. The high profile media attention given to the Sri Lankan government's commitment puts its international reputation at stake and as such it was reasonable to conclude that the authorities would take the necessary measures to ensure that their commitment would be respected.

Fok (Guardian ad litem of) v. Canada (Minister of Citizenship & Immigration) (1997), 41 Imm. L.R. (2d) 304 (B.C. S.C.) — The infant petitioner was five years of age and was born in Canada and therefore a Canadian citizen. The infant petitioner's mother was a permanent resident of Canada and the infant petitioner's father was a citizen of the People's Republic of China as well as the subject of a deportation order. The father had entered Canada and made an unsuccessful claim for Convention refugee status, and in addition, during the time that the father was the subject of a removal order, he was convicted of theft over $1,000, possession for the purposes of trafficking and welfare fraud and sentenced to 20 months and 18 months for the latter two convictions.

The applicant sought to rely upon the Court's *parens patriae*. The applicant asked the Court to protect its best interests by preventing the Minister from removing his father from Canada. Pending a determination of the petition the Court issued an interim injunction preventing deportation of the applicant's father on condition that the petition be set down for a hearing on an expedited basis.

The Court found pursuant to the law in British Columbia that there was a fair question to be tried. The Court stated that the question was whether a Supreme Court judge in reliance on his or her *parens patriae* jurisdiction, would in the circumstances grant a permanent injunction restraining the Minister from deporting the petitioner's father.

Parasidis v. Canada (Minister of Citizenship & Immigration) (1997), 38 Imm. L.R. (2d) 288, 133 F.T.R. 73 (Fed. T.D.) — The applicant sought to stay the execution of a removal order on the basis that there was a statutory stay by virtue of section 49(1)(b) of the *Immigration Act*. The applicant was a citizen of Greece who had been ordered deported by reason of his having been convicted of a criminal offence. The applicant appealed to the Appeal Division of the IRB and while his appeal was pending the applicant was certified as a danger to the public under section 70(5) of the *Immigration Act*.

The applicant was not seriously asking the Court for judicial stay but rather a declaration that a statutory stay operated to preclude his removal. This was a final determination which should properly be left to the judge hearing the judicial review application.

If the Court had been required to render a decision it would have concluded that there was no statutory stay. Assuming for the moment that all requirements of section 70(5) have been met the danger opinion has the effect of discharging the statutory stay.

The applicant's counsel also argued that there was no evidence that the adjudicator had determined that the applicant had been convicted of an offence for which a term of imprisonment of 10 years or more may be imposed. It is preferable that the adjudicator state expressly in the words of that provision, that an individual has been convicted of an offence for which a term of imprisonment of 10 years or more may be imposed. That is not however, a statutory requirement, it may be obvious from the material that such a determination has been made. In the present case, the material submitted by the applicant led the Court to infer that the evidence before the adjudicator caused him to issue the deportation order because the applicant was convicted under subsection 4(2) of the *Narcotic Control Act* — an indictable offence punishable by a maximum punishment of life imprisonment. Accordingly, the application for stay was dismissed.

Darboe v. Canada (Minister of Citizenship & Immigration) (1996), 37 Imm. L.R. (2d) 72, 123 F.T.R. 1 (Fed. T.D.) — The applicant had been ordered deported and was also facing outstanding criminal charges in the Ontario Court General Division. A representative from the Ministry of the Attorney General of Ontario indicated that immediately upon the applicants removal from Canada, a criminal charge outstanding against the applicant would be withdrawn. In addition it was also indicated that bail could be varied to provide for the accused's release provided that immigration would continue to detain the accused under the *Immigration Act*. Pursuant to the outstanding criminal charge the accused was required to report for court subsequent to the date on which the immigration officials proposed to remove him from Canada.

Section 50(1)(a) of the *Immigration Act* operated to stay the removal order so long as the criminal charge remained outstanding. The Court directed, however, that the respondent could immediately execute the removal order upon the withdrawal of the Ontario court charges.

Kandasamy v. Canada (Minister of Citizenship & Immigration) (1996), 36 Imm. L.R. (2d) 237, 119 F.T.R. 262 (Fed. T.D.) — The applicant is 16 years of age, a male, and a citizen of Sri Lanka. In 1983, he moved with his mother to the Federal Republic of Germany to join his father who fled Sri Lanka in 1981. In June 1995, the applicant left Germany and arrived in Canada by himself. Upon arriving at Fort Erie the applicant was questioned by an immigration officer who concluded that the applicant was a convention refugee in Germany. Subsequently, the applicant claimed refugee status in Canada. In August 1995, the applicant was determined to be ineligible to have his claim considered on a basis that he was a convention refugee in Germany. The applicant was ordered to be removed from Canada. Subsequently, the applicant learned that he had not been accepted as a convention refugee in Germany and the applicant sought to have his eligibility reconsidered in 1996. The request to reconsider was refused and the applicant applied for judicial review of that determination and a stay of the execution of the removal order.

The Court found irreparable harm. The applicant was 16 years of age. It was the respondents intention to remove the applicant to the United States. The evidence before the Court indicated that throughout his entire life and since his arrival in Canada the applicant had continued to live under the care and supervision of adults: his parents in Germany and an uncle in this country. There was no evidence that the applicant was experienced in looking after himself or an individual who had demonstrated himself to be capable of surviving on his own. Should the applicant be removed to the United States, there was no evidence before the Court to suggest that arrangements existed there, so that the applicant could receive the support and care to which he was accustomed. Thus, removal to the United States in those circumstances would create irreparable harm pending determination of the application for judicial review.

Rizzo v. Canada (Minister of Citizenship & Immigration) (August 21, 1996), Doc. IMM-2268-96 (Fed. T.D.) — The issue on this stay application was the question of irreparable harm. The applicant had over 20 criminal convictions and was addicted to drugs. His irreparable harm submission was based on his need for continuing medical attention in Canada. The need for such medical attention and support has been caused by the applicant's criminal activities and his drug addiction. Criminal activities and drug addiction cannot be the foundation upon which a claim of irreparable harm can be based for purposes of staying the execution of a deportation order.

Calabrese v. Canada (Minister of Citizenship & Immigration) (1996), 115 F.T.R. 213 (Fed. T.D.) — The applicant sought to quash a decision of the respondent that the applicant constituted a danger to the public in Canada.

The applicant was born in Italy in 1961, he came to Canada with his family at the age of three and became a permanent resident, but never acquired Canadian citizenship. The applicant's family members live in Canada, the applicant does not speak Italian, the applicant has lived in a common law relationship for the past 14 years and has an 11-year-old son who is a Canadian citizen. The applicant's companion is expecting their second child.

The applicant had a long criminal record that included a number of convictions for serious offences. The applicant acknowledged a substance abuse problem.

The basis for the claim of irreparable harm was that the applicant, if deported, would be separated from the professional and community base support, upon which he was relying to remain drug free and as a consequence crime-free. In addition, it was submitted that there was a lack of equivalent support in the country to which the applicant would be deported and that because of the applicant's inability to speak Italian, the applicant would be faced with significant difficulties in attempting to establish himself again in that country.

The loss of family, professional and community support are capable of constituting irreparable harm. The Court found the elements in this case parallel to those in *Toth v. Canada (M.E.I.)*, (1988) 6 Imm L.R. (2d) 123 (Fed. C.A.). The Court disagreed with the decision of Simpson J. in *Calderon v. Canada (Minister of Citizenship & Immigration)* (1995), 92 F.T.R. 107 (Fed. T.D.) which decision concluded that irreparable harm implied the serious likelihood of jeopardy to the applicants life or safety.

Shayesteh v. Canada (Minister of Citizenship & Immigration) (1996), 34 Imm. L.R. (2d) 101, 112 F.T.R. 161 (Fed. T.D.) — This was an application to stay the execution of a deportation order pending determination of an application for leave and for judicial review of a decision made pursuant to subsection 70(5) of the *Immigration Act*. In dealing with the balance of convenience test, the Court noted that there was inconvenience to the respondent if the stay was granted and acknowledged that there was a public interest in having the respondent's duties under the *Immigration Act* fulfilled in a timely manner. The Court found the balance to lie in the applicant's favour, noting that the deportation order was issued in November 1984 and the process which lead to the issuing of the Ministers opinion was not implemented until September 1995, and the opinion not communicated to the applicant until March 28, 1996. On those facts the balance of convenience was held to lie in favour of granting the stay.

Duve v. Canada (Minister of Citizenship &Immigration) (March 26, 1996), Doc. IMM-3416-95 (Fed. T.D.) — The Court accepted the reasoning of Simpson J. in *Calderon v. Canada (Minister of Citizenship & Immigration)* (1995), 92 F.T.R. 107 (Fed. T.D.), on the question of irreparable harm. For purposes of a stay, irreparable harm implies the serious likelihood of jeopardy to the applicant's life or safety. This is a very strict test and it is premised upon the fact that the irreparable harm must be more than the unfortunate hardship associated with the breakup or relocation of a family.

Hogan v. Canada (Minister of Citizenship & Immigration) (1996), 32 Imm. L.R. (2d) 97, 108 F.T.R. 143 (Fed. T.D.) — This was an application to stay the execution of a Deportation Order pending the determination of an application for leave and for judicial review of a decision of the respondent pursuant to subsection 70(5) of the *Immigration Act*. The Court allowed the application. The Court concluded that the balance of convenience test had been met, after noting that the deportation order was outstanding in July 1995 when section 70(5)came into effect. Since that time there was no evidence to indicate that the applicant was evading implementation of the order. The evidence was to the contrary. It was only on the eve of the hearing of the applicant's appeal that the respondent turned to subsection 70(5) and it then took the respondent from mid-November 1995 to mid-February 1996 to execute the order. This led the Court to conclude that the applicant did not rank high on the respondent's list of individuals constituting a danger to the public.

The Court also referred to, with approval, *Yhap v. Canada (Minister of Employment & Immigration)* (1989), 29 F.T.R. 231 (Fed. T.D.), to the effect that the amendments which brought about section 70(5) had not yet been tested as to constitutionality, legality or fairness which had the effect of leaving the federal law in the area in a state of imprecision and flux.

Singh (R.) v. Canada (Minister of Citizenship & Immigration) (1995), 31 Imm. L.R. (2d) 281, 104 F.T.R. 35 (Fed. T.D.) — This was a successful application to stay a removal order. There were three applicants. The first applicant was a citizen of Sri Lanka, the second applicant was his 5 year old son, and the third applicant was the wife of the first applicant who was a citizen of India. All three made refugee claims. The refugee claim of the father and son was denied and their judicial review application was dismissed. They were, thus, eligible for removal from Canada. For reasons undisclosed by the evidence, the wife's claim had not been concluded at the time of the judicial review application. The Court found irreparable harm in the fact that, if the Minister was allowed to execute the removal order, the 5 year old child would be separated from his mother. This would occur not a result of any actions taken by the child, but rather because the processes controlled by the respondent Minister had not dealt with all of the applications at the same time. Removal of an infant child in such circumstances should be avoided. It is a primary goal of the *Immigration Act* to foster family relationships and family unity. The fact that these persons had been treated differently under the administration of the Act raised a serious dilemma for the family. That dilemma results from the department's choice to process the mother's claim at a different time than the other 2 applicants.

The balance of convenience favours the applicants. This order for a stay is temporary pending disposition of the application for leave and judicial review now filed in this court which simply postpones, but does not permanently preclude, the Minister undertaking removal proceedings.

Muñoz v. Canada (Minister of Citizenship & Immigration) (1995), 30 Imm. L.R. (2d) 166, 100 F.T.R. 201 (Fed. T.D.) — The applicant and his family arrived in Canada from Peru. The applicants were seeking to have their humanitarian and compassionate application determined before their removal. The Court noted that there is a duty cast upon the respondent through its officers to consider H&C applications. The respondent is not entitled to discharge that mandate unjustly, or in a way that neutralizes the legislation. It would be absurd and deleterious to the laws due administration if the Minister was accorded such latitude as would defeat parliament's intent in enacting section 114(2). In the extreme circumstances of this case a stay for a deportation order was granted.

Owusu v. Canada (Minister of Citizenship & Immigration) (August 28, 1995), Doc. IMM-2247-95 (Fed. T.D.) — The applicants requested a stay of a deportation order in circumstances where they had not directly attacked the validity of the order.

The Court concluded that it had jurisdiction to stay the order but declined to grant relief in this case. The Court commented on the decision in *Shchelkanov v. Canada (Minister of Employment & Immigration)* (1994), 76 F.T.R. 151 (Fed. T.D.) and pointed out that the judge in that case did not suggest any lack of jurisdiction, but rather determined that the applicants had no right to a stay of the order in that case.

Raman v. Canada (Minister of Citizenship and Immigration) (1995), 30 Imm. L.R. (2d) 300, 100 F.T.R. 67 — The applicant arrived in Canada from Nigeria in June, 1995. On his arrival, using a Zimbabwean passport, the applicant advised Immigration officials that he had come to Canada to visit a friend in Montreal and would only be staying for a week. The applicant, in response to a specific question, denied that he wished to make a refugee claim. The applicant was, however, excluded from entry. The applicant then advised Immigration officials that the passport he was using was fraudulent, that he was a citizen of Nigeria and that he wished to make a refugee claim. The applicant was advised that, an exclusion order having been made against him, it was too late for him to claim refugee status. The applicant retained counsel and sought to re-open the section 23(4) inquiry. A senior Immigration officer refused to re-open the inquiry on the basis that she did not have jurisdiction to do so. The applicant sought to judicially review this decision. This application was dismissed on the basis that the applicant would not suffer irreparable harm if the exclusion order were executed. The only evidence that the applicant might suffer irreparable harm was the applicant's own affidavit.

The applicant brought a second application for stay of execution of the exclusion order and this time filed more extensive evidence of irreparable harm. With respect to this second application for a stay the parties to it were the same as those on the first application. The question was the same as that decided on the first application. The Court indicated that it was satisfied that *res judicata* or issue estoppel applied in respect of the second application. It is an abuse of the process of the court to bring forward the same application a second time with what might prove to be better evidence. Accordingly, this second application for a stay was dismissed.

Sannes v. Canada (Minister of Citizenship & Immigration) (June 26, 1995), Doc. IMM-1008-95 (Fed. T.D.) — The applicant/plaintiff commenced an action against the respondent/defendant, then applied for a stay of the execution of a deportation order. The plaintiff had maintained in an immigration inquiry that he was a Canadian citizen but had been unable to provide proper proof of that fact. Accordingly, his deportation order was issued and the adjudicator's decision was appealed to the Appeal Division which appeal was dismissed.

The applicant/plaintiff then filed a statement of claim in the Federal Court wherein he claims status as a Canadian citizen by virtue of the provisions Section 3(1)(e) of the *Citizenship Act*. The applicant/plaintiff maintained that his situation was similar to the case of *Benner v. Canada (Secretary of State)* (1993) 155 N.R. 321 (Fed. C.A.) which case was before the Supreme Court of Canada at the time of the commencement of the action.

In the evaluation of irreparable harm, there are three basic elements that must be considered: a) the kind of harm, b) the level of risk, and c) whether the harm is irreparable and not compensable in damages.

Personal inconvenience, even if serious, is not equivalent to irreparable harm. Irreparable harm implies the serious likelihood of jeopardy to the applicant's life and safety if he/she were to be returned to his/her country of origin.

The Court found no irreparable harm. There was no doubt that the applicant would be deprived of an extensive support network of friends in groups which he established in Canada in order to help him deal with his rehabilitation from alcoholic, drug and sexual abuse. This did not constitute irreparable harm. Similarly, being returned to Norway and thrust into a foreign environment also did not constitute irreparable harm. If the applicant requires further treatment for his alcohol and sexual problems, it is admitted that Norway is capable of providing such services.

Merely because the issue raised in the proceedings was a Charter issue did not mean that it was necessary for the Court to assume that the harm in question was irreparable. The Court distinguished *RJR-MacDonald Inc. v. Canada (Attorney General)*, [1994] 1 S.C.R. 311 (S.C.C.) on the basis that it dealt with an issue whereby the applicants would incur major expense in altering their packaging and that even though this may be quantifiable, it was determined that because of the *Charter* argument, there were special reasons to conclude there that the harm would be irreparable. Accordingly, the Court found no relation between the facts in *RJR-McDonald* and the case at bar. The application for a stay was denied.

Calderon v. Canada (Minister of Citizenship & Immigration) (March 17, 1995), Doc. IMM-5067-94 (Fed. T.D.) — In an earlier case the Court dismissed an application for a stay of a departure order on the basis that it could find no irreparable harm. That case concerned a decision made by an adjudicator. At the time of that first application this present application, based on a negative humanitarian and compassionate decision, was outstanding. In this application the issue of irreparable harm could not be relitigated. The doctrine of issue estoppel operated as a bar to the reargument of the issue. Irreparable harm was fundamental to the earlier decision and identical to the issue raised in this application. This conclusion was not dispositive of this application. The tests for injunctive relief are significant guideposts in the decision-making process when a stay is sought. They are not iron shackles. A court must assess all the circumstances and do what is just.

The Court decided to hear submissions about why, quite apart from the question of irreparable harm, it should, or should not, grant a stay of the deportation order.

Kronenfeld v. Canada (Secretary of State) (1995), 29 Imm. L.R. (2d) 231 (Fed. T.D.) — The Court declined to grant a stay in this case due to the delay occasioned by counsel for the applicant. The application for a stay was scheduled to be heard on April 10, 1995 at 9:30 in the morning. At approximately 10:00 a.m. on April 10, 1995 the Court received a 37 page affidavit from the applicant which had been prepared on April 9, 1995.

The Court noted that in urgent matters it will hear an application for a stay on weekends if counsel requests. There was no adequate explanation for counsel's delay in bringing this application and his failure to perfect it in a timely fashion. The lengthy affidavit was sworn the day before the hearing but was only provided to the Court at the very last moment. The Court concluded that this application for a stay was, in fact, an abuse of its processes and refused to hear the application.

Langner v. Canada (Minister of Employment & Immigration) (1995), 29 C.R.R. (2d) 184, (sub nom. *Langner v. Ministre de l'Emploi & de l'Immigration)* 184 N.R. 230, 97 F.T.R. 118 (note) (Fed. C.A.) — The appellants arrived in Canada with valid visitors visas in 1988.

They did not travel to the United States but rather remained in Canada eventually claiming refugee status. While they were waiting for their refugee applications to be disposed of, the parents had 2 children, both of whom had, by virtue of their birth on Canadian soil, Canadian citizenship and Polish citizenship.

The appellant parents' refugee claims had been rejected. They requested a waiver under section 114(2), of the requirement that they leave Canada in order to make an application for permanent residence. This request was refused and requests for a review of that decision were also refused. Deportation orders were issued against the parents in October 1992.

The parents proceeded by way of an action for a declaratory judgment seeking a declaration that by virtue of the fact that they had 2 children who were Canadian citizens the Canadian government was prevented from executing the deportation orders made against them.

The Canadian Charter of Rights and Freedoms has no application in this case. The appellant parents' decision to take their children to Poland with them, or to leave them with family members in Canada, is a decision which is their own to make. The Canadian government has nothing to do with this decision. There is no government action which could bring the Charter into play. The appellant children's rights and freedoms, which attach to their Canadian citizenship are not an issue. Regardless of the decision made by their parents, the children will retain their Canadian citizenship and will be subject to no constraints in the exercise of the rights and liberties associated with their citizenship other than the constraints the parents impose in the exercise of their parental authority.

Calderon v. Canada (Minister of Citizenship & Immigration) (1995), 92 F.T.R. 107, 30 Imm. L.R. (2d) 256 (Fed. T.D.) — In this application for a stay the Court concluded that it had jurisdiction to stay a departure order in appropriate circumstances. Further, on the question of irreparable harm, the Court observed that for purposes of a stay application irreparable harm implies the serious likelihood of jeopardy to an applicant's life or safety. The Court declined to find irreparable harm in the separation of the applicant from her husband and the separation of her son from his father. The Court observed that there was no medical evidence on this issue before the Court and, further, that no one in the applicant's family depended upon her for support. The application for a stay was refused on the basis that irreparable harm was not demonstrated.

Gomes v. Canada (Minister of Citizenship & Immigration) (1995), 26 Imm. L.R. (2d) 308 (Fed. T.D.) — The applicant requested a stay of a deportation order so that he could commence judicial review proceedings of a decision of an Immigration officer who determined that there were insufficient humanitarian and compassionate grounds to allow the applicant to remain in Canada. The applicant overstayed his visitor's authorization and was convicted of assault causing bodily harm. The applicant received a deportation order and married his common-law spouse and attempted to regularize his status.

In denying the request for a stay the Court noted that with respect to the balance of convenience test the fact that the applicant had been convicted of a criminal offence weighed heavily in favour of the respondent.

Rajan v. Canada (Minister of Employment & Immigration) (1994), 86 F.T.R. 70 — The applicant applied for a stay in circumstances where the applicant had been issued a departure order and intended to remain in Canada, with the result that the departure order, would become a deportation order.

The Court does not have jurisdiction pursuant to section 18(2) to prevent the departure order from becoming a deportation order.

Kilonzo v. Canada (Secretary of State) (September 30, 1994), Doc. IMM-4089-94 (Fed. T.D.) — The Court dismissed an application to stay the execution of a removal order. At the time the application was heard the applicant had already been removed from Canada and thus the application was moot. The Court went on to note that when an application is presented at the last minute the applicant must bring forward all relevant facts in order for the Court to have a full and clear picture of the circumstances which have brought about the removal order. It is not sufficient for the applicants to simply offer a partial story showing only those facts which are favourable to their case.

Rambharose (Litigation Guardian of) v. R. (1994), 28 Imm. L.R. (2d) 109 (Fed. T.D.) — This was a motion for an order to stay the execution of a removal order issued against the plaintiff's litigation guardian (mother). The plaintiff was a Canadian born child whose parents came to Canada from Trinidad in 1988. The plaintiff's mother was the subject of a section 20 report for not having obtained an immigrant visa prior to appearing at a port-of-entry as required by section 9 of the Act. A subsequent humanitarian and compassionate grounds review was rejected. The mother then applied for Convention refugee status but was found not to have a credible basis for her claim and an exclusion order was issued against her. A second humanitarian and compassionate review was rejected. The plaintiff's father is still awaiting a decision on his humanitarian and compassionate review.

This action was commenced to prevent the Minister from removing the plaintiff's parents. The plaintiff, through a litigation guardian, argued that his rights under the Canadian *Charter of Rights and Freedoms* would be violated if his mother was removed from Canada and he was forced to either depart from Canada or be separated from his mother.

The Court found that the plaintiff would suffer irreparable harm as a result of being separated from his mother at such a tender age. Given the serious prejudice which the plaintiff would likely suffer if the removal order was executed, the balance of convenience favoured granting a stay.

Bajwa v. Canada (Secretary of State) (February 24, 1994), Doc. IMM-838-94 (Fed. T.D.) — The applicant applied for a stay of a deportation order, which was refused.

The granting of a stay of a deportation order is a discretionary matter. In that regard, the conduct of the applicant is a relevant consideration. The applicant's conduct in its total context is relevant. It is not merely a question of whether there has been an excessive delay.

The applicant voluntarily undertook expanded family responsibilities knowing there was an outstanding deportation order issued him. He had not even met his wife prior to the issuance of that order. He was married in February 1993, but did not seek an H & C review until November 1993 and, at the time he sought a stay of a deportation order, his wife was pregnant.

It was not appropriate for the Court to exercise its discretion to grant a stay because the applicant was now trying to rely on a situation in which he purposely placed himself.

De Medeiros v. Canada (Minister of Employment & Immigration) (January 11, 1994), Doc. IMM-7508-93 (Fed. T.D.) — The Court granted the stay of the execution of a deportation order until such time as it had rendered its decision in respect of an application for leave and for judicial review of a decision of the Appeal Division. On the issue of irreparable harm, the Court found that the Appeal Division had an ongoing and continuing equitable jurisdiction with respect to the applicant, which jurisdiction would cease to exist upon the applicant's departure from Canada. This cessation of the Appeal Division's equitable jurisdiction was held to constitute irreparable harm.

Boquoi v. Canada (Minister of Employment & Immigration) (1993), 67 F.T.R. 232 — The applicant and his wife sought to stay departure notices requiring them to leave Canada for Germany before the end of September 1993. The application failed because the applicants were unable to establish irreparable harm. The application for a stay contained affidavits swearing to the fact that the applicants had become very attached to the persons in their community and wished to prevent the separation of their two sons from the community which the sons knew as home. The youngest son was a Canadian citizen born in Prince Edward Island and, further, the applicants alleged that they had no home in Germany to go to and were fearful for their children's safety and security if they were required to return there. This was not a fear of persecution, but rather a fear of the stress and uncertainty of removal to Germany at this time. The applicants stated that prior to their arrival in Canada, there was no work available for them in Germany and that since their arrival they had managed to establish a home here and had been accepted and strongly supported by the community in Prince Edward Island, where they were living. Such factors did not establish irreparable harm. Mere economic dislocation or difficulties or inconvenience do not establish irreparable harm in circumstances where neither applicant has a right to remain in Canada.

Da Costa v. Canada (Minister of Employment & Immigration) (1993), 19 Imm. L.R. (2d) 295, 64 F.T.R. 233 — This was an application for a stay of execution of a removal order. The application was filed on Friday, June 4, 1993 and removal was scheduled for 7:30 a.m. Monday, June 7, 1993. The request for a stay of the removal order was denied on the ground of delay by the applicant in bringing the application.

The removal order was issued on January 23, 1992. Before the end of that month the applicant married a Canadian citizen and assumed parental responsibility for a young child. The applicant received a "call in notice" from Immigration dated February 2, 1992 to attend an interview April 2, 1992. This interview, however, did not take place. Thus, the applicant was aware before his marriage of his precarious situation in Canada and did nothing to attempt to resolve his problem, except to continue to expand his family responsibilities. It was only when he was confronted with a specific date for his removal that he began to examine options open to him to prolong his stay or regularize his status.

The applicant had from January 23, 1992 more than an adequate opportunity to seek legal advice.

No risk to the applicant's life or safety was alleged if he were deported to Jamaica. It was acknowledged, however, that his wife and children would be substantially prejudiced. His wife was expecting a third child and had been hospitalized from time to time because of the pregnancy and thus was disabled from working within or outside the home.

The Court concluded that the magnitude of the harm faced here derived in large part from the failure of the applicant to do anything in the interval since January 23, 1992 to mitigate the problem. It therefore did not rest easily with him to plead now for an extraordinary remedy. Accordingly, the request for a stay was dismissed.

Grar v. Canada (Minister of Employment & Immigration) (1993), 20 Imm. L.R. (2d) 301, 64 F.T.R. 6 — The fact that the applicant's removal from Canada before May 28, 1993 would mean that the applicant was not able to complete a three-year program of studies and receive a diploma, constituted irreparable harm. Deportation would mean that those studies would never be completed; if they were to be completed, it would only be after several years.

There would be no irreparable harm caused to the applicant if he were removed from Canada after the date that the studies were expected to be concluded (May 28) and for that reason the stay of execution of the deportation order was not to extend beyond May 28, when the applicant's studies were expected to be completed.

Bal v. Canada (Minister of Employment & Immigration), [1993] 2 F.C. 199, 63 F.T.R. 226 — The applicant sought a stay of a removal order pending an application for leave to seek judicial review of a decision refusing special treatment on humanitarian and compassionate grounds. Sukhjinder Bal brought his two nephews to Canada because their natural father had received demands for money from members of the All Sikh Student Federation coupled with threats against the children's lives. Upon their entry into Canada the children's citizenship was not disclosed and the immigration officer wrongly assumed them to be their uncle's children. When the true citizenship of the two young children was discovered by Immigration, a conditional deportation order was obtained. The claim for refugee status on the children's behalf was dismissed. The uncle then petitioned for an order of adoption in the Supreme Court of British Columbia. When this was completed the uncle sponsored an application for permanent residence on behalf of the children and requested that the applications be processed from within Canada. This latter request was denied and it was that decision which the applicant sought to question.

Mr. Justice Noel had previously held that the Court did not have jurisdiction to issue a stay in the circumstances of this case. Other judges of the Court had expressed the opposite view. His Lordship was of the view that if he had jurisdiction to grant a stay he would have done so on the facts of this case. The Court determined that it was imperative that there be consistency in the manner in which fundamental issues of jurisdiction are dealt with by the Court. There was an open question as to the jurisdiction to grant relief. Accordingly, the Court determined that the uncertainty about the Court's jurisdiction should be resolved in favour of the party seeking the relief. To do otherwise would deprive a party of a remedy on the assumption that those members of the Court who have assumed the jurisdiction to grant the remedy were wrong. The Court was of the view that the contrary assumption should be made unless and until the Court of Appeal decides otherwise.

Accordingly, a stay in the execution of the removal orders was granted.

Agyakwa v. Canada (Minister of Employment & Immigration) (1993), 62 F.T.R. 118 — This was an application to stay the execution of a removal order. The applicant arrived in Canada from Ghana and made a claim for refugee status. While the applicant was in Canada he met and married a Canadian citizen. The marriage occurred before his refugee claim was dismissed. After getting married the applicant applied for landing from within Canada. The refugee claim was dismissed and the applicant was advised that there would be no recommendation that he be landed from within Canada because the immigration officer had serious reservations about whether the marriage was for immigration purposes.

The request for a stay was granted. Irreparable harm was found to be established, not only to the applicant, but to his family. Uncontradicted affidavit evidence established that the applicant's spouse had three children by a previous marriage and that the applicant had in effect become a father to those children. Further, the whole family was heavily dependent upon the applicant for support. The Court found more than personal inconvenience to the applicant at stake.

Harper v. Canada (Minister of Employment & Immigration) (1993), 19 Imm. L.R. (2d) 233, 62 F.T.R. 96 — This was an application to stay a deportation order. The applicant claimed refugee status, which claim was found to have no credible basis. The applicant had applied for leave to review a decision finding sufficient humanitarian and compassionate grounds in the applicant's case to warrant a positive recommendation under section 114(2). In support of the application for a stay, the applicant's counsel filed an affidavit from his personal assistant. In the affidavit the personal assistant reiterated facts about the case that had been told to her by counsel for the applicant. There was no direct evidence from the applicant and no explanation as to why such direct evidence could not be provided. A stay application is in the nature of an interlocutory motion and an affidavit based on belief is acceptable. However, it will have little weight when it consists of hearsay upon hearsay. The courts can only make decisions on the basis of evidence. The affidavit of an employee in which the employee purports to truly believe certain facts of which she has no personal knowledge, in circumstances where she has not even spoken to the person who would have such personal knowledge, is evidence of little probative value.

Information comes to the Court by way of evidence and counsel should ensure that they present evidence that the Court may rely upon with confidence. This is of heightened importance when motions are brought on short notice and the respondent has no practical opportunity to cross-examine on the affidavit or to present an affidavit in response.

One of the attachments to the legal assistant's affidavits was a nine-page letter from counsel to the manager of the Central Removals Unit in Mississauga, Ontario. She also referred to this letter during argument to establish some of the facts relating to the applicant. This raises the difficulty of counsel who was appearing before the Court relying on a letter that counsel has written to establish the truth about facts relating to the client. Evidence and submissions of counsel are not one and the same. Merely because counsel has written a letter containing information about the client and attached it to an affidavit, does not make it evidence of the truth of what is contained in it.

The application for a stay was refused.

Petit v. Canada (Minister of Employment & Immigration) (1993), 19 Imm. L.R. (2d) 133 (Fed. T.D.) — The applicant arrived in Canada with her two children and claimed refugee status. She married her present husband while she was in Canada. A number of requests were made by the applicant after the date of her marriage for a determination of whether there were sufficient humanitarian and compassionate grounds to allow her to apply for landing from within Canada, on the ground that she was married to a Canadian citizen. On February 5, 1993 the applicant and her husband were asked to attend a marriage interview. On February 9, 1993 the applicant was notified that she would be required to leave Canada by February 26, 1993 and that there were insufficient humanitarian and compassionate grounds to justify allowing her to apply for landing from within Canada. It is in respect of that decision that leave to commence an application for judicial review was being sought. In those circumstances, section 18.2 of the *Federal Court Act* gave the Court jurisdiction to grant a stay.

On the question of whether the applicant would suffer irreparable harm, the Court noted that generally when a person is being returned to a country where there is no threat of physical danger or persecution, it would be hard to argue that irreparable harm exists. However, the Court noted that the applicant and her children found themselves in an "eleventh hour" situation created by the respondent. The applicant had written to the respondent on two or perhaps three occasions requesting a marriage interview. Had the interview been conducted in a timely manner, the applicant would have had an opportunity to test the validity of any decision made before being required to leave Canada. On the facts, the applicant had been called in for a marriage interview on the eve of deportation. She was told by the interviewer that "everything looked good". That decision was reversed by a supervisor with no explanation. The Court found that the execution of the removal order in those circumstances, before the applicant had an opportunity to obtain leave to challenge the decision, was unfair.

The Court does not look favourably upon applicants who appear at the last minute, before a removal order is to be executed, with a new spouse or with new requests for humanitarian and compassionate reviews. The position in which they put themselves in those circumstances is largely of their own making. In this case, the position in which the applicant and her children found themselves was largely of the respondent's making and thus, it was appropriate to grant a stay of the removal order.

Seegobin v. Canada (Minister of Employment & Immigration) (1993), 59 F.T.R. 310 (Fed. T.D.) — The Court lacks jurisdiction to grant the stay of a deportation order in circumstances where its validity is not in dispute.

Mahadeo v. Canada (Minister of Employment & Immigration) (November 27, 1992), Doc. 92-T-757 (Fed. T.D.) — This was an application for a stay of execution of a deportation order. The applicant, a native of Trinidad, arrived in Canada as a visitor and made a claim for refugee status. While the claim was pending, the applicant divorced her husband in Trinidad and married a man in Canada and gave birth to twin daughters who were approximately two years old at the time this application was heard.

In granting the stay the Court noted that the application for leave to seek judicial review was ready for consideration but had not been brought forward for the attention of a judge for some three months. The delay of the Court in dealing with the matter ought not to work to the disadvantage of the applicant. Irreparable harm to the applicant and her family, sufficient to warrant a stay, arose from the inevitable disruption of the family, if the stay were not granted. Finally, the granting of the stay did not seriously prejudice the respondent Minister in carrying out his obligations. If the application for leave was denied, any delay in the removal of the applicant would be of some short duration. If leave was granted, then the disruption of the applicant's family would have been avoided.

Membreno-Garcia v. Canada (Minister of Employment & Immigration), 7 Admin. L.R. (2d) 38, 17 Imm. L.R. (2d) 291, 55 F.T.R. 104, [1992] 3 F.C. 306 (Fed. C.A.) — The applicant had applied for refugee status but a first-level tribunal found that there was no credible basis to the applicant's claim. The applicant applied for leave to commence an application for judicial review, which leave was granted. The applicant then sought a stay of the deportation order pending the outcome of the appeal.

In the present case, the deportation order flowed from and was underpinned by the decision finding no credible basis to the applicant's claim. If that decision was invalid then the deportation order was invalid. In such circumstances, a challenge has in fact been made to the validity of the deportation order.

In *Lodge v. Canada (Minister of Employment & Immigration)*, [1979] 1 F.C. 775 (Fed. C.A.), the Court stated the principle to be applied in deciding whether a permanent injunction should be granted to restrain a Minister of the Crown from performing his statutory duty. In *Toth v. Canada (Minister of Employment & Immigration)* (1988), 6 Imm. L.R. (2d) 123 (Fed. C.A.), the Court held that it had jurisdiction to grant a stay in cases such as this one. Since that time the Trial Division's jurisdiction has been made clear by the addition of section 18.2 of the *Federal Court Act*.

The only requirement under section 18.2 is that the judge consider the interim order "appropriate". It may be that in the absence of at least an indirect attack on the deportation order the Court would not consider a stay appropriate.

In determining when a stay order is "appropriate" the Court referred to the criteria set out in *Toth*. Given that leave had been granted, the applicant clearly had an arguable case. On the basis of the applicant's affidavit evidence it would be hard to reach any other conclusion than that the applicant would suffer irreparable harm if he was returned to El Salvador. Insofar as the balance of convenience is concerned, the test set out in *Metropolitan Stores (MTS) Ltd. v. Manitoba Food & Commercial Workers, Local 832*, [1987] 1 S.C.R. 110 (S.C.C.), is not relevant. In that case, the validity of one section of the statute was under attack and thus an interlocutory injunction order in favour of one litigant would by implication lead to similar orders respecting all individuals covered by the allegedly unconstitutional section in question. The section itself would in fact be rendered inoperative pending the determination of its validity. In the present case the legislative provisions of the statute were not challenged. One decision by an adjudicative body operating under the statute with respect to one specific individual was being challenged. Rendering an injunction or a stay order in such a case will not suspend the operation of any part of the legislation. Thus, the public interest considerations expressed in *Metropolitan Stores Ltd.* are not in issue.

When considering the balance of convenience in these types of cases the extent to which the granting of the stay might become a practice which thwarts the efficient operation of the immigration legislation is a valid consideration. The present procedures were put in place because a practice had grown up in which cases totally devoid of merit were initiated in court for the sole purpose of buying the applicants further time in Canada. There is a public interest in having a system which operates in an efficient, expeditious and fair manner and which, to the greatest extent possible, does not lend itself to abusive practices. This is the public interest which must be weighed against the potential harm to the applicant if a stay is not granted.

The situation in this case is quite different from that which exists, for example, when applicants seek humanitarian and compassionate reviews on the eve of the execution of a deportation order and then argue that a stay should be granted because of the uncompleted nature of that review. Such a case is the type of situation in which there is a potential for creating a practice which undermines the orderly operation of the legislation.

Another significant factor in considering the balance of convenience test is the degree of delay which is incurred, if any, in prosecuting the applicant's appeal. Similarly, when the applicant knows of the decision which underlies the challenge to the deportation order and does not seek leave to commence a section 18 proceeding until the very last moment, there is reason to assume that the seeking of leave and the subsequent request for the staying of the deportation order are primarily time-buying manoeuvres.

In the present case, the balance of convenience was said to lie with the applicant and the stay was granted.

Editor's Note: Although the refugee procedures have changed, the principle stated herein may still be useful.

Vaccarino v. Canada (Minister of Employment & Immigration) (June 9, 1992), Doc. 92-T-778 (Fed. T.D.) — The Court is entitled, on an application for a stay, to take into consideration delay on the part of the applicant in seeking the injunction. The material filed in this case did not justify the applicant taking no steps to challenge or delay the execution of the departure notice until six days prior to her scheduled departure. The fact that the adjudicator, prior to issuing the departure notice, did not comply with paragraph 36(1)(b) of the regulation and advise the applicant of her right to seek judicial review is a factor for consideration on her application for leave, but it is no justification for the applicant taking no steps whatever until the last moment to obtain legal advice on any possible ways to delay the execution of the departure notice.

Khan v. Canada (Minister of Employment & Immigration) (1992), 53 F.T.R. 158 (Fed. T.D.) — An earlier inquiry concerning the applicant's continuing presence in Canada was quashed by decision of the Court (*Khan v. Canada (Minister of Employment & Immigration)* (1989), 9 Imm. L.R. (2d) 107 (Fed. T.D.)). The preliminary question was whether the application for a stay was properly before the Court in light of the decision in *Ontario Khalsa Darbar Inc. v. Canada (Minister of Employment & Immigration)* (1991), 15 Imm. L.R. (2d) 179 (Fed. T.D.), which held that leave is required to bring an application for a stay in immigration proceedings pursuant to 82.1 of the *Immigration Act.* Previously, *Toth v. Canada (Minister of Employment & Immigration)* (1988), 6 Imm. L.R. (2d) 123, 86 N.R. 302 (Fed.

C.A.) acknowledged the inherent jurisdiction of the court to deal with an application for a stay in appropriate circumstances without the necessity of leave being applied for. Section 18.2 of the *Federal Court Act*, enforced since February 1, 1992, provided authority for the issuance of interim orders in relation to the matters before the Court and was sufficient to give jurisdiction to consider an application for a stay which in this case was interrelated with an application for leave to seek judicial review.

In this case there was no evidence of irreparable harm and the application for a stay was dismissed. The inquiry in question might result in a departure notice and, further, even if a deportation order were issued, removal would only occur after a pre-removal review. This review could result in a decision that there were humanitarian or compassionate considerations which justified permanent residence. Accordingly, the concerns of the applicant about the outcome of the inquiry were speculative and as such not evidence of irreparable harm.

Hosein v. Canada (Minister of Employment & Immigration) (1992), 17 Imm. L.R. (2d) 125, 4 Admin. L.R. (2d) 162, 53 F.T.R. 86 (Fed. T.D.) — This was an application for an order staying an inquiry until the applicant's application for leave to commence judicial review proceedings was determined, and, if leave be granted, until those proceedings were finally disposed of by the Court. This application was accompanied by an application for leave pursuant to 82.1. The orders in question were sought in respect of a decision by a first-level tribunal to the effect that it would not hear evidence and argument in relation to section 7 of the Charter. The tribunal then proceeded to find the applicant did not have a credible basis for his claim to being a Convention refugee. The tribunal adjourned and then scheduled a resumption of its hearing. The application for leave to seek judicial review was not considered when this application for a stay was heard.

The Court's jurisdiction to order a stay of proceedings was not limited by section 18.2 of the *Federal Court Act* by the necessity to apply for leave to seek judicial review. In an appropriate case, particularly one where the issue raised in an application for leave is arguable but would be moot or the jurisdiction of the Court would be rendered nugatory by failure to grant a stay, a stay may be ordered within the discretion of the Court.

The Court was not persuaded that a stay of proceedings was required at the time the application was heard. Further steps in the process of consideration of the applicant's situation were required before he would be excluded from Canada. The leave for judicial review now sought by the application could proceed in the ordinary course. If the leave application was not completed before steps were taken to remove the applicant, the applicant could apply for leave to stay implementation of those procedures at that time. The test for intervention is set out in the *Toth* case (*Toth v. Canada (Minister of Employment & Immigration)* (1988), 6 Imm. L.R. (2d) 123, 86 N.R. 302 (Fed. C.A.)).

It was determined that it was inappropriate at this stage to stay proceedings of the tribunal and the application was dismissed.

Pavlov v. Canada (Minister of Employment & Immigration), 16 Imm. L.R. (2d) 105, [1992] 2 F.C. 289, 53 F.T.R. 253 — The requirements for issuing stays of deportation orders in the context of applications filed pursuant to section 82.1 seeking leave to commence a proceeding under section 18 of the *Federal Court Act* are as follows:

1. the applicant must demonstrate that there is a serious question to be determined;
2. that the applicant would suffer irreparable harm if the stay were not granted; and
3. that as between the applicant and the respondent Minister the harm to the applicant would be greater if a stay were not granted than to the respondent if one were granted.

In the context of this particular case the application for stay was granted.

The Court in arriving at these requirements applied the decision of *Toth v. Canada (Minister of Employment & Immigration)* (1988), 6 Imm. L.R. (2d) 123 (Fed. C.A.).

Mathura (Litigation Guardian of) v. Canada (Minister of Employment & Immigration) (January 13, 1992), Doc. T-2571-91 (Fed. T.D.) — This application to stay the adjudication proceedings was refused. The stay which was sought hinged on a constitutional challenge to certain provisions of the *Immigration Act* and regulations. Leave had not yet been granted to commence a proceeding based on those challenges. No challenge was made by the motion to the validity of the proceedings. Granting a stay in such circumstances would have set a precedent that could have had significant detrimental effects on the integrity of immigration proceedings. The Court ordered disposition of the application for leave within seven days so that the request for a stay might be determined after the decision to grant leave had been made.

Bada v. Canada (Minister of Employment & Immigration) (1992), 17 Imm. L.R. (2d) 233, 56 F.T.R. 106 (Fed. T.D.) — The applicant sought to stay a deportation order. The deportation order itself is not an issue in the proceedings. The applicant was seeking to quash a decision that there were no humanitarian or compassionate grounds to allow the applicant to apply for landing from within Canada. The Court observed that whether the Trial Division had jurisdiction to grant a stay of deportation orders in circumstances where the orders themselves were not subject to attack, was an issue that should be taken to the Federal Court of Appeal. In this particular case the Court did not resolve the issue because it determined that there were not sufficient grounds to grant a stay in the event that the Court had jurisdiction to do so.

The Court observed that one factor which gave concern was that the applicant had effectively been denied a determination of his leave application before the date for the execution of his deportation order because the respondent did not file the documentation respecting his case within the required time limits. These time limits had been extended because an Immigration officer was on vacation and the Court observed that this might not have been a proper basis for extending the time limits if the effect of the extension meant that the applicant would be removed from Canada before his application for leave was decided.

Mashni v. Canada (Minister of Employment & Immigration) (1992), 56 F.T.R. 103 (Fed. T.D.) — The Court re-affirmed that *Cegarra v. Canada (Minister of Employment & Immigration)* (1992), 56 F.T.R. 241 (Fed. T.D.) decided that a stay would inevitably be issued if the file was incomplete or otherwise not ready for adjudication in terms of the leave application. The Court noted that stay proceedings can always be avoided by a timely undertaking on the Minister's part in regard to the timing of removals. The Court noted that the Minister was not being asked to avoid his duty to remove an illegal immigrant, but only to see that those who wished to question the legality of removal have a proper opportunity to do so. Once the matter of leave is determined, further action may be possible. Those without leave will, of course, be forced to depart Canada. Those with leave may be compelled to leave Canada if they are destined for a country where and from which they can still instruct their solicitors.

Cegarra v. Canada (Minister of Employment & Immigration) (1992), 56 F.T.R. 241 — Judges who decide immigration leave applications inevitably need the whole file, including the tribunal's records, so that the judge can determine whether the tribunal apparently went as badly off the rails as the applicant alleges. If the file raises an arguable case for judicial review, leave will be granted.

The applicant applied on July 30, 1992 for an eleventh-hour stay. The Court convoked a telephone hearing so that the respondent could be heard on July 30, before the applicant would have been removed from Canada. The removal order was made on June 9, 1992. The applicant's motion for leave was filed on June 16, 1992. The applicant was notified on July 14, 1992 that he was to be removed from Canada on Sunday August 2, 1992. The Court observed that it could have been determined on July 14, 1992 or shortly thereafter that the tribunal's record would not become available before the August 2 removal date.

The execution of a removal order will inevitably be stayed if the file is not complete and, in the absence of the tribunal's record, it is not complete and the Court cannot properly determine the leave application. When the removal is scheduled for a time before that at which the Court and the respondent are prepared to address an already launched application for leave to commence proceedings, then, pursuant to section 18.1 of the *Federal Court Act*, the execution order will almost always be stayed.

Eleventh-hour emergency applications for a stay will result in a dilatory solicitor being personally ordered to pay the costs of the application. Whenever a client comes to consult a solicitor at the last moment the client's affidavit should make clear reference to that fact, lest the emergency be seen to be an unnecessary ploy or negligence on the solicitor's part. A solicitor who has acted for an applicant at the tribunal hearing can hardly ever assert tardy consultation by the client.

The Court noted in this case that counsel requesting the stay had only been retained at the last minute and was not responsible for the last-minute application.

Duggal v. Canada (Minister of Employment & Immigration) (1992), 18 Imm. L.R. (2d) 20 (Fed. C.A.) — The Court of Appeal has no power to stay the execution of a removal order where it is deprived of jurisdiction by section 82.2(1) of the *Immigration Act* to entertain an appeal from a decision of the Trial Division. The power to stay can only be implied from the Court's power to hear an appeal. If such jurisdiction is denied, then the power to stay is absent. Not even the allegation that its Charter right is being violated can give the Court of Appeal a statutory jurisdiction to hear an appeal where Parliament has seen fit to withhold it.

Thompson v. Canada (Minister of Employment & Immigration) (1992), 18 Imm. L.R. (2d) 67 (Fed. T.D.) — The applicant sought a stay of an exclusion order pending final disposition of the applicant's application for leave to seek judicial review. A credible-basis panel constituted under the previous legislation had determined that there was no credible-basis to the applicant's refugee claim. On the question of irreparable harm, the findings of the credible-basis tribunal are not conclusive because those findings are, at least in substantial part, matters raised by the applicant in his application for leave to seek judicial review. To accept those findings of credibility, the question of irreparable harm, as it is posed in the stay application, would amount to pre-judging the matter raised by the application for leave. The Court is therefore left with the applicant's claim as stated in his affidavits and therefore, for purposes of the stay application, the Court was prepared to find that the applicant would suffer irreparable harm if he were removed to Ghana before his application to seek judicial review had been considered and determined by the Court.

Editor's Note: Although decided under previous legislation, the principle enunciated in this case may have a broader implication.

Nananso v. Canada (Minister of Employment & Immigration) (1992), 56 F.T.R. 234 (Fed. T.D.) — The applicant sought an interim order for prohibition pursuant to section 18 of the *Federal Court Act*, to prohibit his removal from Canada. The failure of the applicant to perfect his application for a stay in a timely manner did not deprive the Court of jurisdiction. There was no legitimate reason for the application being brought a mere two hours before the applicant's removal from Canada. The Court disapproved of the practice of bringing applications to stay deportation orders on an emergency basis and agreed with the proposition that the bringing of an application for a stay of a deportation order at the very last minute may constitute a sufficient basis for rejecting the application. No adequate explanation for the failure to perfect this application was forthcoming in the affidavit material and, therefore, the application was dismissed.

Berhan v. Canada (Minister of Employment & Immigration) (1992), 56 F.T.R. 183 (Fed. T.D.) — The applicant sought a stay of a deportation order pending a decision by the Immigration and Refugee Board on an application to re-open the claim to refugee status. Leave to review the decision denying refugee status had been sought and denied.

No decision on the application to re-open had been given prior to the date of this application, which was immediately before the date of the applicant's deportation.

No stay was granted because the Court did not have the authority to do so. Stays can be granted when the validity of a deportation order is itself being challenged. It is also arguable that stays can be given when there is a proceeding before the Court to which section 18.2 of the *Federal Court Act* applies. Neither situation pertained in this case and, accordingly, the Court did not have the authority to grant a stay.

Osei v. Canada (Minister of Employment & Immigration) (1988), 8 Imm. L.R. (2d) 69, 25 F.T.R. 270 — In this case, the Court reviewed a variety of judicial pronouncements dealing with the Court's jurisdiction to stay an executive order in general or a deportation order in particular:

1. The Court noted that the Minister cannot be enjoined from executing a deportation order when the validity of the order has not been challenged;

2. The Federal Court of Appeal cannot, in the absence of statutory authorization to do so, stay the execution of an order that it has not pronounced, which it has no power to vary, and the validity of which is not challenged;

3. The Immigration Appeal Board has no jurisdiction to reconsider its decision confirming the deportation of a person and the only grounds for so doing would be evidence of new facts; and

4. The Court distinguished the *Toth* case because the issue arose in that case, not out of a refugee status determination but, with respect to a removal order made against a permanent resident of Canada where a statutory right of appeal was provided. Further, the Court noted that, in the *Toth* case, the order itself was being challenged.

Espinelli v. Canada (Minister of Employment & Immigration) (1988), 6 Imm. L.R. (2d) 21 (Fed. T.D.) — The applicant had been ordered deported. She then complained to the Human Rights Commission that the deportation proceedings violated the prohibition under the *Canadian Human Rights Act* against discrimination on the basis of marital status. The applicant sought a stay of the deportation order so that she could remain in Canada until her complaint was adjudicated upon. Her application was dismissed. While the *Canadian Human Rights Act* is a fundamental law, it does not clothe the Federal Court Trial Division with the power to stay a deportation order confirmed by the Immigration Appeal Board and maintained by the Federal Court of Appeal. Where the validity of the deportation is not itself an issue, the Trial Division has no jurisdiction under the Charter to paralyze an otherwise valid executory order.

Wood v. Canada (Minister of Employment & Immigration) (1986), 2 F.T.R. 58 (Fed. T.D.) — The Minister can only defer the execution of a deportation order if the person who is to be deported is subject to a judicial order containing specific provisions that would be violated if the deportation order were to be executed. Accordingly, where the applicant was subject to a probation order, which contained no conditions compelling the presence of the applicant in Canada or his attendance in court at a specified time and place, there was no obligation on the part of the Minister to defer his responsibility to execute the valid deportation order.

Williams v. Canada (Minister of Employment & Immigration), [1985] 2 F.C. 153 (Fed. T.D.) — The applicant was born in Jamaica. She was unmarried and had five children, all of whom lived in Jamaica. The applicant arrived in Canada in September 1979 for a 3-week visit and had remained in Canada ever since. The applicant was informed by a lawyer in late 1983 that the long-term illegal migrants' programme did not apply to her because she had not been "underground" for 5 years. On May 29, 1984, the applicant was apprehended and a deportation order was made June 8, 1984. Judicial review of this order was dismissed in November 1984. The applicant's removal in December 1984 was deferred in order that the applicant's case could be reviewed to determine whether she then qualified under the long-term illegal migrants' programme. The applicant did not qualify under the programme. During the period when the applicant's case was being considered, the long-term illegal migrants' programme was modified in such a way that the applicant would have been eligible for the programme but for the fact of her apprehension. The application to restrain the applicant's removal was dismissed. Where a person has been lawfully ordered deported, and the procedure that he or she wishes to invoke is a purely discretionary one in the hope that he or she might be granted a Minister's permit to stay in Canada, any requirement of fairness in the exercise of the Minister's discretion is minimal. Such a case does not involve a benefit to which the applicant is legally entitled nor denial of any rights legally vested in the applicant. There was no denial of fairness because the applicant did not, albeit for different reasons, come within the old or new guidelines of the long-term illegal programme.

Mercier v. Canada (Minister of Employment & Immigration) (April 25, 1985), Doc. T-309-85 (Fed. T.D.); affirmed (1985), 62 N.R. 73 (Fed. C.A.) — On November 17, 1982, following an inquiry, a deportation order was issued against the applicant because he had been convicted of an offence for which a maximum term of imprisonment of 10 years or more may be imposed, pursuant to section 19(1)(c) of the Act. The applicant's appeal against this deportation order was dismissed on August 14, 1984. On January 30, 1985, the applicant tried to gain admission to the United States without success and returned to Canada with the intention of provoking an inquiry where he might claim refugee status. When the applicant reappeared at the Canadian border, a senior immigration officer issued a Summons to Appear at an inquiry, pursuant to section 23 of the Act. That decision was countermanded by another senior immigration officer and the applicant's case was withdrawn on the ground that the deportation order, issued against the applicant, had never been executed. It was this decision that was attacked by the applicant, who was seeking a writ of *mandamus* requiring the adjudicator to conduct his inquiry. The decision to countermand the Summons to Inquiry was part of the administrative process. The Court did not intervene because it was of the view that the applicant had not been treated unfairly and that to intervene and issue a writ of *mandamus* would create a situation in which the respondent Minister would, on the one hand, have to execute a deportation order against the applicant and, on the other hand, have to conduct an inquiry with a view to admitting the applicant to the country.

An appeal from this decision was heard on June 28, 1985, and dismissed. The appellant (applicant) sought to raise, for the first time, the assertion that the deportation order had been executed by the appellant himself when he left the country for a 6-week visit to Haiti from May 12, 1984, to June 30, 1984. No consideration was given to the submission on appeal because it was a question which was raised for the first time before the Court of Appeal. It was founded upon an allegation of fact which was never put in issue before the Trial Division. The Court noted that when sitting an appeal of the Trial Division, it sat as a Court of Appeal whose function was to decide whether the issues presented at trial were properly disposed of. It was not the Court's duty to determine other issues which, had they been raised at the Trial Division, might have resulted in a different outcome if the necessary factual basis had been established.

Farhan v. Canada (Minister of Employment & Immigration) (August 14, 1984), Doc. T-1313-84 (Fed. T.D.) — The applicant sought an injunction restraining the respondent from effecting her removal to her native Iraq. A deportation order had been made against the applicant. While the order was not attacked, the grounds for the injunction were that returning the applicant to her native land subjected her to cruel and unusual treatment contrary to the Canadian Charter of Rights. The applicant had, in Canada, what would be in Iraq an illicit or adulterous relationship and feared members of her family would physically harm her, even to the point of killing her, should she be returned. The Court assumed that it was proper to take into account the particular circumstances of the applicant in deciding the application and held that the evidence fell far short of establishing the applicant's position and, accordingly, the application was dismissed.

Kee v. Canada (Minister of Employment & Immigration) (March 9, 1984), Doc. T-2776-83 (Fed. T.D.) — The applicant sought an order prohibiting the respondent from proceeding with the execution of a deportation order, pending the determination of the applicant's criminal conviction appeal and the application pursuant to section 115(2) of the *Immigration Act* for special consideration. Prohibition will not issue directing the Minister of Employment and Immigration to disobey a valid deportation order which he is under a statutory duty to carry out solely on the grounds that the applicant had not exhausted every legal remedy available to him.

Persad v. Canada (Minister of Employment & Immigration) (October 18, 1983), Doc. A-140-83 (Fed. C.A.) — In view of the provisions of sections 50, 51 and 52 of the *Immigration Act*, the Court was not prepared to import into the provisions of section 115(2) a power to suspend a deportation order pending a decision by the Governor in Council on the appellant's application under section 115(2).

R. v. Gittens (1982), 68 C.C.C. (2d) 438 (Fed. T.D.) — The applicant came to Canada in 1965 at the age of five. He became a permanent resident but not a Canadian citizen. A deportation order was made based on section 27(1)(d)(i) and (ii) of the *Immigration Act.* An appeal against the deportation order was dismissed by the Immigration Appeal Board and the Federal Court of Appeal refused leave to appeal the Immigration Appeal Board's decision. The applicant, at the time of the giving of judgment, had completed serving all of the sentences for his criminal offences and was being kept in custody pending the execution of the deportation order. The application for an order quashing the deportation order against the applicant was dismissed because the Charter is not retrospective in its operation. The application for an order seeking the release of the applicant was denied on the basis that section 10 of the Charter stipulated that the validity of the detention was to be determined by the way of *habeas corpus* and the Court noted that it had no jurisdiction to grant *habeas corpus.* The Court did not express an opinion whether or not it had jurisdiction to grant *habeas corpus* with *certiorari* in aid, pursuant to the Charter. If execution *per se* of a valid deportation order would constitute an infringement or denial of an applicant's fundamental rights and freedoms, the Court had jurisdiction in the first instance to entertain an application for an appropriate remedy. Freedom of association as envisaged by section 2(d) of the Charter will not be violated by the execution of a deportation order. Execution of the order will sever immediate links with family, friends and others. To the extent that these are licit associations, they are social and familial. Assuming that they are the type of associations contemplated by section 2(d) of the Charter, they are subject to such reasonable limits prescribed by law as can demonstrably be justified in a free society. The reasonableness of the right of a free and democratic state to deport alien criminals was held to be self-evident and, therefore, demonstrably justified. Section 11(h) of the Charter was not violated because deportation was held not to be punishment for the offences, his conviction for which had rendered him liable to deportation in the first place. In this case, the probative value of the evidence of the conditions in Guyana was minimal. The Court accepted that economic conditions and prospects were not nearly as favourable to the individual there as in Canada and that the human rights of persons politically opposed to those in power were not, generally, respected by the Government of Guyana. The Court noted that neither the applicant nor his family had in any way been politically active so as to attract the attention of those in power in Guyana and that, therefore, the treatment the applicant could expect in Guyana would depend entirely upon his conduct there. Thus, the Court concluded that the evidence did not support the claim that execution of the deportation order would deprive the applicant of the right to life, liberty and security of the person afforded by section 7 and, therefore, the Court declined to grant relief.

Finally, the Court noted that the incidents of deportation, whatever their degree, do not render deportation a cruel and unusual treatment of an adult. As a norm, execution of a deportation order is not in the abstract rule an unusual treatment. The Court was not persuaded by the evidence that deportation of the applicant to Guyana would be cruel and unusual treatment in the context of this case. Accordingly, the application was dismissed.

Canada (Minister of Employment & Immigration) v. Hudnik (1979), [1980] 1 F.C. 180, 103 D.L.R. (3d) 308 (Fed. C.A.) — The Minister was not relieved of his duty under section 50 [s. 48] merely because, after being ordered deported, the respondent claimed Convention refugee status.

Lodge v. Canada (Minister of Employment & Immigration), [1979] 1 F.C. 775, 94 D.L.R. (3d) 326, 25 N.R. 437 (Fed. C.A.) — An application for an order enjoining the Minister from executing the removal order was denied since enforcement of the provisions of the *Immigration Act* was not a denial of access to goods, services, facilities or accommodation customarily available to the general public. Further, the enforcement of the order was not in itself a discriminatory practice within the meaning of the *Canadian Human Rights Act*, S.C. 1976-77, c. 33.

Pereira v. Canada (Minister of Manpower & Immigration) (1978), 21 O.R. (2d) 828 (Ont. C.A.) — The respondent Minister and various immigration officials were not found to be in contempt of court in attempting to execute the deportation order while an appeal of a dismissal of a *habeas corpus* application and an application for an injunction staying the deportation order were both pending. However, no attempt should have been made at that stage to execute the deportation order which was the subject matter of the *habeas corpus* and injunction applications. The reserved judgment ultimately went against the applicant and his appeal of that judgment was dismissed. The Court held that attempts to execute the deportation order at that stage could not constitute contempt of the Court of Appeal, which had pronounced judgment without ordering a stay of the effect thereof pending any further appeals by the applicant. Service of a Notice of Motion for leave to appeal to the Supreme Court of Canada and a Notice of Motion to the Supreme Court of Ontario for an injunction did not have the effect of staying the deportation order. In addition, the Court held that once the Notice of Motion for leave to appeal to the Supreme Court of Canada was abandoned, the applicant lacked the status to pursue his application to have the respondent Minister and various officials committed for contempt. Such a motion was a motion in the cause, and the cause was ended.

Denis v. R., [1976] 1 F.C. 499 (Fed. C.A.) — The appellant appealed from an order dismissing an application for an interlocutory injunction to restrain the execution of a deportation order pending trial of her actions for a permanent injunction and damages. The Court did not decide whether, in a proper case, an injunction could be granted against the Minister of Manpower and Immigration, assuming that the necessary steps were taken to make him a party to the proceedings. The Court refused the injunction because the removal of the appellant would not be a direct and unavoidable result of the application of the law of Canada; rather it would be the result of the decision of the appellant's mother as to whether to take her with her or leave her in Canada.

Sun v. Canada (Attorney General) (1960), [1961] S.C.R. 70, 26 D.L.R. (2d) 63 (S.C.C.) — A removal order will not be quashed because the applicant is the mother of a child who is a natural born Canadian citizen and has a right to live in Canada.

49. (1) Stay of execution — Subject to subsection (1.1), the execution of a removal order made against a person is stayed

(a) in any case where the person against whom the order was made has a right of appeal to the Appeal Division, at the request of that person until the time provided for the filing of the appeal has elapsed;

(b) in any case where an appeal from the order has been filed with the Appeal Division, until the appeal has been heard and disposed of or has been declared by the Appeal Division to be abandoned;

(c) subject to paragraphs *(d)* and *(f)*, in any case where a person has been determined by the Refugee Division not to be a Convention refugee or a person's appeal from the order has been dismissed by the Appeal Division,

(i) where the person against whom the order was made files an application for leave to commence a judicial review proceeding under the *Federal Court Act* or signifies in writing to an immigration officer an intention to file such an application, until the application for leave has been heard and disposed of or the time normally limited for filing an application for leave has elapsed and, where leave is granted, until the judicial review proceeding has been heard and disposed of,

(ii) in any case where the person has filed with the Federal Court of Appeal an appeal of a decision of the Federal Court — Trial Division where a judge of that Court has at the time of rendering judgment certified in accordance with subsection 83(1) that a serious question of general importance was involved and has stated that question, or signifies in writing to an immigration officer an intention to file a notice of appeal to commence such an appeal, until the appeal has been heard and disposed of or the time normally limited for filing the appeal has elapsed, as the case may be, and

(iii) in any case where the person files an application for leave to appeal or signifies in writing to an immigration officer an intention to file an application for leave to appeal a decision of the Federal Court of Appeal on an appeal referred to in subparagraph (ii) to the Supreme Court of Canada, until the application for leave to appeal has been heard and disposed of or the time normally limited for filing an application for leave to appeal has elapsed and, where leave to appeal is granted, until the appeal has been heard and disposed of or the time normally limited for filing the appeal has elapsed, as the case may be;

(d) in any case where a person who has claimed to be a Convention refugee or whose appeal has been dismissed by the Appeal Division has been determined by an adjudicator to be a person described in paragraph 19(1)*(c)*, *(c.1)*, *(c.2)*, *(d)*, *(e)*,

(*f*), (*g*), (*j*), (*k*) or (*l*), 19(2)(*a*), (*a*.1) or (*b*), 27(1)(*a*), (*a*.1), (*a*.2), (*a*.3), (*d*), (*g*) or (*h*) or 27(2)(*d*), until seven days have elapsed from the time the order was made or became effective, whichever is later, unless the person agrees that the removal order may be executed before the expiration of that seven day period;

(e) in any case where a person has been determined to be not eligible to have a claim to be a Convention refugee referred to the Refugee Division, until seven days have elapsed from the time the order was made or became effective, whichever is later, unless the person agrees that the removal order may be executed before the expiration of that seven day period; and

(f) in any case where a person has been determined pursuant to subsection 69.1(9.1) not to have a credible basis for the claim to be a Convention refugee, until seven days have elapsed from the time the order became effective, unless the person agrees that the removal order may be executed before the expiration of that seven day period.

(1.1) **Exception — Subsection (1) does not apply to**

(a) a person residing or sojourning in the United States or St. Pierre and Miquelon who is the subject of a report made pursuant to paragraph 20(1)(*a*); or

(b) a person who has been determined to be not eligible to make a claim to be a Convention refugee by reason of paragraph 46.01(1)(*b*) and who is to be removed to a country with which the Minister has entered into an agreement under section 108.1 for sharing the responsibility for examining refugee claims.

(2) [Repealed 1999, c. 31, s. 133.]

R.S.C. 1985, c. 28 (4th Supp.), s. 16; 1990, c. 8, s. 52; 1992, c. 49, s. 41; 1999, c. 31, s. 133.

Case Law

Section 49(1)

Pratt v. Canada (Minister of Citizenship & Immigration) (1997), 130 F.T.R. 137 (Fed. T.D.) — There were actually 2 applications for judicial review referred to in this decision. The first application sought to review a decision that, in the opinion of the Minister's delegate, the applicant constituted a danger to the public and the second decision was one to execute an outstanding deportation order.

The applicant was a permanent resident of Canada, who remained here all of his life until he was removed in December 1995. In 1992 and 1993, he was convicted of a number of offences under the *Criminal Code* and as a result of those offences was ordered deported. The applicant filed an appeal and while the appeal was pending the Minister issued an opinion to the effect that the applicant was a danger to the public in Canada.

The applicant's appeal to the appeal division was effectively rendered nugatory or was effectively extinguished by Parliament's determination that the applicant could not, after having been found to be a danger to the public exercise the right of appeal granted by section 70(1). While it was true in this case that the Appeal Division had not heard and disposed of the appeal, it could provide no possible disposition other than to recognize that under the Act, by virtue of the Minister's opinion, it had no jurisdiction to deal with the appeal. Thus, the statutory stay under paragraph 49(1)(b) was effectively removed by the rendering of the Minister's opinion and this statutory stay was therefore not a bar to the applicant's removal from Canada.

Solis v. Canada (Minister of Citizenship & Immigration), [1997] 2 F.C. 693, 127 F.T.R. 218 (Fed. T.D.) — The applicant sought to stay the execution of a removal order. The applicant came to Canada as a refugee. In 1990, he and his family were granted landed immigrant status. Since 1992, the applicant has been convicted of a number of criminal offences. On the basis of some of the convictions an inquiry was held and a conditional deportation order issued against the applicant. The applicant filed an appeal to the Appeal Division which was still outstanding at the time of this application. While the appeal was pending the Minister determined that the applicant constituted a danger to the public in Canada. The applicant sought leave to review this opinion and that application was pending when this application for a stay was heard. The Appeal Division, notwithstanding the issuance of the Minister's opinion, had not decided that it had no jurisdiction to entertain the applicant's appeal with the result that the appeal before the Appeal Division was still outstanding at the time this application was heard.

The application for a stay pursuant to section 18.2 of the *Federal Court Act* was dismissed on the basis that there already existed a statutory stay pursuant to paragraph 49(1)(b). In reaching this decision the Court declined to follow the decision of the Court of Appeal and *Tsang v. Canada (Minister of Citizenship & Immigration* (1997), 37 Imm. L.R. (2d) 1 (Fed. C.A.) on the basis that the application of section 49(1)(b) was not before the Court of Appeal in that case.

Silva v. Canada (Minister of Citizenship & Immigration) (August 15, 1996), Doc. IMM-2450-96 (Fed. T.D.) — This decision arose out of an application for an order staying the execution of a deportation order. An adjudicator had ordered the applicant, who was a permanent resident of Canada, deported. The applicant appealed, which had the effect of staying the execution of the deportation order. The respondent issued an opinion pursuant to section 70(5) stating that the applicant constituted a danger to the public in Canada. When the appeal division was notified of the opinion it treated the notification as a motion to dismiss the appeal and invited submissions.

When the injunction application was heard the respondent had not yet made submissions on the motion to dismiss.

The Court found that for the purposes of the application for a stay, the question of whether or not the opinion of the minister under section 70(5) lifted the statutory stay arising out of paragraph 49(1)(b) was a serious issue to be tried.

Pierristil v. Canada (Minister of Citizenship & Immigration) (1995), 93 F.T.R. 207, (sub nom. *Pierristil v. Canada (Ministre de la Citoyenneté & de l'Immigration))* — The applicant sought to stay execution of a removal order pending this application for leave to appeal from a decision of the Appeal Division, dismissing his application to re-open his hearing. The applicant cannot rely on section 49(1)(c) and thus enjoy an automatic stay of the execution of the removal order.

Section 49(1)(c) is applicable only to a person who has been denied Convention refugee status which is not the applicant's case. The applicant is a permanent resident against whom a removal order has been made following an inquiry at which an adjudicator found that the applicant was described in section 27(1)(d)(ii) of the Act.

Sholev v. Canada (Minister of Employment & Immigration) (1994), 78 F.T.R. 188 (Fed. T.D.) — The applicant was a refused refugee claimant who learned of the refusal of his claim on April 11, 1994. The applicant, on May 10, filed an application for leave and for judicial review, including an application for an extension of time to commence the proceedings. The applicant applied for a stay of the removal order on the basis that the removal order was automatically stayed by virtue of section 49(1)(c)(i). A stay of execution of a removal order becomes effective by operation of section 49(1)(c)(i) once the applicant files in the Federal Court an application for leave and for judicial review, even if the application is filed beyond the 15-day period ordinarily provided by section 82.1(2), whenever the application includes or is accompanied by an application for an extension of time to commence proceedings. The stay was effective from May 10, 1994. From that day the matter was before the Court, subject to the applicant meeting all further requirements to perfect the application. If those further steps are not taken the application will be dismissed and thus disposed of by the Court.

Parliament, by enacting section 82.1(5), recognized that there may be special cases which warrant proceedings for leave and judicial review to commence, even though the applicant had not met the time ordinarily limited for filing. It would be inconsistent to construe section 49(1)(c)(i) as not providing for a stay of execution of a removal order pending determination of whether special reasons for an extension exist. Otherwise, the most deserving cases initiated by late filing would not have the benefit of the statutory stay.

Hamilton v. Canada (Minister of Employment & Immigration) (1990), 11 Imm. L.R. (2d) 255, 36 F.T.R. 167, [1991] 1 F.C. 3 (Fed. T.D.) — The applicant sought a stay of the execution of a deportation order which had been issued against her. The stay was sought pending resolution of proceedings which the applicant initiated under section 18 of the *Federal Court Act*. The applicant was challenging the validity of the Minister's refusal to recommend that she be granted an exemption, on compassionate and humanitarian grounds, from certain requirements of the *Immigration Act*. The applicant filed an application for leave coincident with filing the application for a stay.

The respondent Minister had consented to delay execution of the deportation order until a decision was rendered by the Court on the applicant's present application. The Court assumed jurisdiction to issue a stay even though the validity of the deportation order was not directly an issue.

The Court distinguished the case of *Lodge v. Canada (Minister of Employment & Immigration)*, [1979] 1 F.C. 775 because, in that case, the injunction, if granted, would have been final in nature and was not an interlocutory order. Where a permanent injunction is sought, the validity of the deportation order itself must be questioned in the proceedings before the Court can have jurisdiction to issue a stay. Where the application for a stay is connected to a proceeding pending before the Court, different considerations apply. Granting a stay is always a discretionary remedy. If special and compelling circumstances can be shown to exist, a stay can be granted in the absence of leave having been given to commence the proceeding. One of the main issues to be decided in considering whether to grant a stay is whether a serious question to be tried exists and where such an issue is not resolved in favour of the applicant a stay will not be granted.

Marwin v. Canada (Minister of Employment & Immigration) (1989), 38 Admin. L.R. 298, 9 Imm. L.R. (2d) 122, 93 N.S.R. (2d) 120, 242 A.P.R. 120 (N.S. T.D.) — This was an application in the Supreme Court of Nova Scotia for an injunction to stay the implementation of a deportation order until the final disposition of the applicant's intended section 28 application. The applicant moved in the Provincial Supreme Court because the *Federal Court Act* contained, in the applicant's view, no provision for a stay of proceedings while an appeal was pending.

The saving provision of section 54 of the *Immigration Act* did not assist the applicant on the facts of this case. The applicant satisfied the Court that sufficient grounds existed for the review of the decision of the adjudicator. On the question of jurisdiction, the Court accepted the proposition that provincial superior courts have jurisdiction to hear a matter concerning a federal tribunal and the actions of federal officials when a constitutional violation or unconstitutional behaviour is being alleged.

The suggested constitutional violation, in this case, was a conflict between the appeal provisions and the equality provisions in section 15 of the Charter. Specifically, the inequality was found in the fact that certain classes of persons (to none of which the applicant belongs) have a right of appeal and a related right to have the deportations order stayed pending the appeal. Persons, like the applicant, who must resort to the *Federal Court Act* (section 18 or 28) have no right to such a stay. The requested injunction was granted.

Toth v. Canada (Minister of Employment & Immigration) (1988), 6 Imm. L.R. (2d) 123, 86 N.R. 302 (Fed. C.A.) — This was an application for an order staying the execution of a deportation order. The application failed to apply in a timely way for leave to appeal from the Immigration Appeal Board's decision. Therefore, section 51(1)(c) did not operate to stay the deportation order. An application for an extension of time within which to apply for leave to appeal is not encompassed by the words employed in section 51(1)(c).

The Court has an implied jurisdiction to grant a stay. Such an order will only be granted where the applicant demonstrates that:

1. He has raised a serious issue to be tried;
2. He would suffer irreparable harm if no order was granted; and
3. The balance of convenience considering the total situation of both parties favours the order. The balance of convenience test requires that the Court give equal consideration to the fact that the injunction is being sought against a public authority exercising a statutory power.

Espinelli v. Canada (Minister of Employment & Immigration) (1988), 6 Imm. L.R. (2d) 21 (Fed. T.D.) — The applicant had been ordered deported. She then complained to the Human Rights Commission that the deportation proceedings violated the prohibition under the *Canadian Human Rights Act* against discrimination on the basis of marital status. The applicant sought a stay of the deportation order so that she could remain in Canada until her complaint had been adjudicated upon. Her application was dismissed. While the *Canadian Human Rights Act* is a fundamental law, it does not clothe the Federal Court Trial Division with the power to stay a deportation order confirmed by the Immigration Appeal Board and maintained by the Federal Court or Appeal. Where the validity of the deportation is not itself an issue, the Trial Division had no jurisdiction under the Charter to paralyze an otherwise valid executory order.

50. (1) Execution stayed where other proceedings — A removal order shall not be executed where

(a) the execution of the order would directly result in a contravention of any other order made by any judicial body or officer in Canada; or

(b) the presence in Canada of the person against whom the order was made is required in any criminal proceedings and the Minister stays the execution of the order pending the completion of those proceedings.

(2) Not to be executed until after sentence completed — A removal order that has been made against a person who was, at the time it was made, an inmate of a penitentiary, jail, reformatory or prison or becomes an inmate of such an institution before the order is executed shall not be executed until the person has completed the

sentence or term of imprisonment imposed, in whole or as reduced by a statute or other law or by an act of clemency.

Case Law

Section 50(1)

Cuskic v. Canada (Minister of Citizenship & Immigration) (1997), 39 Imm. L.R. (2d) 316, 130 F.T.R. 232 (Fed. T.D.) — The applicant became a landed immigrant in 1975. In 1994, he was convicted of an unlawful confinement and sexual assault and sentenced to 2 years less one day in a reformatory. At the expiration of the sentence he was placed on probation for a period of 2 years to expire in March 1998.

In December 1994, he was ordered deported. In November 1996, the applicant was directed to report to a CIC Centre at Pearson Airport for removal to Bosnia. In January 1997, the applicant was removed to that country.

The applicant sought to set aside the direction to report. The applicant was required to report to a probation officer once per month. Execution of the deportation order prevented the applicant from complying with the probation order. Execution of the removal order directly resulted in a contravention of the probation order and therefore was in violation of section 50(1)(a) of the *Immigration Act.*

If the Minister wishes to deport an individual who is the subject of a probation order the Minister may take steps under section 732.2 of the *Criminal Code* to have the order changed in such a way as to permit the deportation of the person under probation. Section 50 of the *Immigration Act* requires the Minister even in carrying out the public interest as perceived by her to respect the orders of a court.

The direction to report was quashed, the Court declined to direct the minister to arrange for the return of the applicant. The Court concluded that Parliament did not enact section 50 to benefit offenders. Section 50 was enacted to provide direction in the case of conflict between orders made by the Minister and orders of other judicial bodies or officers in Canada. The Court did not condone the Minister acting in contravention of section 50, but concluded that it would not be sensible to require the Minister to arrange for the return of the applicant, so that the Minister could then commence proceedings to deport the applicant again.

Darboe v. Canada (Minister of Citizenship & Immigration) (1996), 37 Imm. L.R. (2d) 72, 123 F.T.R. 1 (Fed. T.D.) — The applicant had been ordered deported and was also facing outstanding criminal charges in the Ontario Court General Division. A representative from the Ministry of the Attorney General of Ontario indicated that immediately upon the applicants removal from Canada, a criminal charge outstanding against the applicant would be withdrawn. In addition it was also indicated that bail could be varied to provide for the accused's release provided that immigration would continue to detain the accused under the *Immigration Act.* Pursuant to the outstanding criminal charge the accused was required to report for court subsequent to the date on which the immigration officials proposed to remove him from Canada.

Section 50(1)(a) of the *Immigration Act* operated to stay the removal order so long as the criminal charge remained outstanding. The Court, directed, however that the respondent could immediately execute the removal order upon the withdrawal of the Ontario court charges.

Mobtagha v. Canada (Minister of Employment & Immigration) (1992), 53 F.T.R. 249 — The applicant applied to stay the execution of a deportation order. The applicant was found not guilty of all criminal charges on account of insanity and placed in custody in Douglas Hospital in Quebec pursuant to an order of the Lieutenant Governor. The deportation order was not in contravention of an order made by a judicial body. An order made by a Lieutenant Governor of the province of Quebec is not an order made by a judicial body or officer in Canada as provided in section 50. Accordingly, the execution of the deportation order was not prohibited by the Court.

Sharoni v. Canada (Minister of Employment & Immigration) (November 30, 1988), Doc. T-1002-88 (Fed. T.D.) — This application for an order of *mandamus* directing the respondent Minister to issue a work authorization pursuant to sections 20(5)(a) and 19(4)(k)(v) of the regulation was dismissed. Mr. Sharoni arrived at a Toronto immigration office on May 17, 1988. He indicated that he had been in Canada illegally since 1985 and intended to pursue a claim for refugee status. On May 20, 1988, the applicant returned to the immigration office and asked for a work permit. He indicated that he had been charged with a criminal offence and was released on a recognizance. It was his submission that he had thereby become a person whose presence was required in a criminal proceeding. Section 19(4)(k)(v) of the regulation did not benefit the applicant because it was confined to those whose presence was required as a witness in criminal proceedings.

Wood v. Canada (Minister of Employment & Immigration) (1986), 2 F.T.R. 58 (Fed. T.D.) — The Minister can defer the execution of a deportation order only if the person who is to be deported is subject to a judical order containing specific provisions that would be violated if the deportation order were to be executed. Accordingly, where the applicant was subject to a probation order which contained no conditions compelling the presence of the applicant in Canada or his attendance in court at a specified time and place, there was no obligation on the part of the Minister to defer his responsibility to execute the valid deportation order.

Kee v. Canada (Minister of Employment & Immigration) (March 9, 1984), Doc. T-2776-83 (Fed. T.D.) — The applicant sought an order prohibiting the respondent from proceeding with the execution of a deportation order, pending the determination of the applicant's criminal conviction appeal and the application pursuant to section 115(2) of the *Immigration Act* for special consideration. Prohibition will not issue directing the Minister of Employment and Immigration to disobey a valid deportation order which he is under a statutory duty to carry out solely on the grounds that the applicant has not exhausted every legal remedy available to him.

Williams v. Canada (Minister of Employment & Immigration) (1983), [1984] 2 F.C. 269 (Fed. T.D.) — An interim release order executed by a duly constituted provincial court judge requiring the applicant to appear in court on a specified date is an order within section 52(1)(a) and prohibition will issue to prevent the deportation of the applicant.

Section 50(2)

Kee v. Canada (Minister of Employment & Immigration) (March 9, 1984), Doc. T-2776-83 (Fed. T.D.) — For digest, see section 50, subheading *Subsection (1), supra.*

51. Validity not affected by lapse of time — No removal order becomes invalid by reason of any lapse of time between its making and execution.

52. (1) Voluntary departure — Unless otherwise directed by the Minister, a person against whom an exclusion order or a deportation order is made may be allowed to

leave Canada voluntarily and to select the country for which that person wishes to depart.

(2) **Place to which removed — Where a person is not allowed to leave Canada voluntarily and to select the country for which he wishes to depart pursuant to subsection (1), that person shall, subject to subsection (3), be removed from Canada to**

(a) the country from which that person came to Canada;

(b) the country in which that person last permanently resided before he came to Canada;

(c) the country of which that person is a national or citizen; or

(d) the country of that person's birth.

(3) **Idem — Where a person is to be removed from Canada and no country referred to in subsection (2) is willing to receive him, the person, with the approval of the Minister, or the Minister, may select any other country that is willing to receive that person within a reasonable time as the country to which that person shall be removed.**

(4) **Idem — Notwithstanding subsections (1) and (2), where a removal order is made against a person described in paragraph 19(1)(*j*), the person shall be removed from Canada to a country selected by the Minister that is willing to receive the person.**

R.S.C. 1985, c. 30 (3rd Supp.), s. 7; 1992, c. 49, s. 42.

Case Law

Section 52(1)

Bhawan v. Canada (Minister of Employment & Immigration) (1987), 41 D.L.R. (4th) 382, 14 F.T.R. 230 (Fed. T.D.) — The applicant sought prohibition to prevent his removal from Canada pursuant to a deportation order dated January 5, 1984. The applicant came to Canada from Fiji as a landed immigrant. He became subject to a deportation order on January 5, 1984 and filed an appeal to the Immigration Appeal Board. While the appeal was pending, the applicant voluntarily returned to Fiji, and, in April 1986, the applicant came back to Canada. Prior to his return to Canada, the applicant's solicitor withdrew the appeal to the Immigration Appeal Board. The applicant's contention that the deportation was carried out by his leaving Canada for Fiji was rejected. The applicant could only leave Canada and select the country of destination with authorization from the Minister, and this was lacking in this case. Accordingly, the applicant had not complied with section 54 and the deportation order, dated January 5, 1984, could be executed to cause the applicant's removal from Canada.

Mensinger v. Canada (Minister of Employment & Immigration) (1986), [1987] 1 F.C. 59, 24 C.R.R. 360, 5 F.T.R. 64 (Fed. T.D.) — A motion was made by the applicant for an order in the nature of *certiorari* quashing the decision of the Minister and his delegate directing the deportation of the applicant to the United States. Further, the applicant sought an order for a *mandamus* directing the Minister to provide the applicant with an opportunity to make submissions, prior to exercising his discretion, pursuant to section 54(1) and (2), and to provide reasons for the exercise of such discretion. In addition, an order was requested directing the respondents to permit the applicant to leave Canada voluntarily for Great Britain, and, finally, a writ of prohibition was requested to prevent the respondents from removing the applicant to the United States.

The applicant, a citizen of both the United States and Great Britain, entered Canada at Port Francis on April 10, 1986. He was arrested by the Port Francis police when they discovered that the applicant had outstanding warrants for his arrest in the United States. The applicant had failed to appear for sentencing in Pecos, Texas on a narcotics charge and failed to appear for trial in Berlin County, Michigan. The applicant had an airplane ticket to England and a British passport, but the Acting Director General for Ontario, as the Minister's delegate, refused, under section 54, to allow the applicant to leave Canada voluntarily and return to Great Britain and directed that the applicant be deported to the United States. *Mandamus* did not lie compelling the respondents to permit the applicant to depart for Great Britain.

There are four requirements for the issue of a writ of *mandamus*:

1. There must be a legal right to performance of the duty by the statutory authority;

2. There must be proof that performance of the duty is due because the Court will not enforce a future obligation;

3. The function must be such that there is no discretion in the decision-maker to perform the duty; and

4. There must be a prior demand that the duty be performed and a refusal to do so.

Pursuant to section 54, the only obligation imposed on the Minister is to make a decision whether the applicant should be allowed to leave Canada voluntarily and depart for Great Britain. *Mandamus* cannot then be used to order the Minister, having performed his duty, to exercise the discretion afforded to him by this section in a certain way. Prohibition was refused because there is no stay or removal guaranteed, either in law or by operation of the *Immigration Act*, where there are applications under section 18 or 28 of the Federal Court pending. Relief was further denied because the applicant was unable to show that the deportation proceedings were a form of disguised extradition. The onus of such proof was on the applicant. There were reasonable grounds for the Port Francis police to arrest the applicant. The United States authorities were not involved at any stage in the decision to arrest. There was no evidence that the Minister's decision was influenced by or based upon any form of agreement between Canada and the United States. There were no arrangements with the United States police for the return of the applicant and no request was ever made by the United States police or immigration authorities for the return of the applicant. With respect to the failure to give reasons, there is no general rule of law that reasons must be given for administrative decisions, and, in particular, there was no duty incumbent on the Minister in this case to provide reasons for his decision. It is the facts, the circumstances and the nature of the decision being made that will determine whether a decision-maker is required to give reasons in order to comply with the principles of fairness.

Mercier v. Canada (Minister of Employment & Immigration) (1986), 3 Imm. L.R. (2d) 316, 14 F.T.R. 28 (Fed. T.D.) — The applicant was admitted to Canada in 1974. Between 1978 and 1984 he was convicted of a number of criminal offences. During this period, on November 17, 1982, he was ordered deported. The applicant returned to his country of origin between May 12 and June 30, 1984. The applicant sought a declaration that the deportation order made against him had ceased to be valid by virtue of section 54 of the *Immigration Act*. It was held that the voluntary departure of someone who is the subject of a deportation order could only be made under section 54 with leave of the Minister. In the absence of such leave, the applicant could not be said to have carried out the removal order himself.

Cole v. Canada (Minister of Employment & Immigration) (October 9, 1980), T-1994-80 (Fed. T.D.) — The right under section 54(1) is available only to those permitted to leave Canada voluntarily; it was held not to extend to the plaintiff, who had been ordered deported and lacked permission to leave voluntarily.

Ramkissoon v. Canada (Minister of Manpower & Immigration), [1978] 2 F.C. 290, 82 D.L.R. (3d) 406, 20 N.R. 361 (Fed. C.A.), leave to appeal to S.C.C. refused 20 N.R. 445n (S.C.C.) — Under the *Immigration Act*, R.S.C. 1970, a deportation order was considered executed when the person ordered deported was removed from Canada either voluntarily or involuntarily.

Section 52(2)

Farhadi v. Canada (Minister of Citizenship & Immigration) (1998), 144 F.T.R. 76, 52 C.R.R. (2d) 51 (Fed. T.D.) — The applicant sought to review, in two applications, a determination that the applicant constituted a danger to the public and a decision that the applicant report for removal. The applicant was a citizen of Iran. His refugee claim under the procedures in effect when it was made was determined to have a credible basis and the applicant was landed from within Canada. In 1995, the applicant was convicted on conspiracy to traffic in a narcotic.

The applicant was entitled to a risk assessment and determination as part of the decision to remove the applicant to Iran. The risk assessment process does not necessarily involve an oral hearing unless the credibility of an applicant is put at issue.

In the result, the judicial review application with respect to the danger opinion was dismissed. The application in respect of the removal decision was allowed, the decision quashed and the matter referred back to the respondent for re-determination following a risk assessment and determination.

Hoang v. Canada (Minister of Employment & Immigration) (1990), 13 Imm. L.R. (2d) 35, 120 N.R. 193 (Fed. C.A.) — The appellant was ordered deported because he was a permanent resident who had been convicted of an offence for which a term of imprisonment of more than 6 months had been imposed; he had also been convicted of an offence for which the maximum term was 5 years or greater. The appellant had come to Canada as a stateless person from Vietnam and had been determined by the Minister in 1986 to be a convention refugee. The Court noted that the Immigration Appeal Board (which had decided this matter) correctly determined that its jurisdiction is only over whether a person should be removed from Canada and not as to the country of removal. Until the issue of deportation is settled, the Minister cannot make a decision as to the country of removal. Thus, a statement by the Minister's representative as to the Minister's disposition to deport the appellant to Vietnam was not taken as a formal expression of the Minister's decision since the Minister was not, at the date of that statement, empowered to make the decision.

The Court determined that in dealing with the "double jeopardy" provisions of section 11(h) of the Charter, deportation was not to be seen as a punishment of the person deported but a protection of those who remained. Further, deportation for serious offences affects neither section 7 nor section 12 of the *Charter of Rights* since it is not to be conceptualized as either a deprivation of liberty or a punishment. Finally, the Court noted that, with respect to Canada's international obligations, the United Nations convention relating to the status of refugees contained an exception to the prohibition against refoulement where the deportee had been convicted, in the country where he was making the refugee claim, of a particularly serious crime. The Court noted that the phrase "particularly serious crime" and "danger to the community" were not defined in the convention and therefore presumed that Parliament responsibly fulfilled its obligation when it enacted the *Immigration Act*.

Accordingly the appellant's appeal was dismissed.

Mensinger v. Canada (Minister of Employment & Immigration), [1987] 1 F.C. 59, 24 C.R.R. 360, 5 F.T.R. 64 (Fed. T.D.) — For digest, see section 52, subheading *Subsection (1), supra*.

Moore v. Canada (Minister of Manpower & Immigration), [1968] S.C.R 839, 69 D.L.R. (2d) 273 (S.C.C.) — Under the *Immigration Act*, R.S.C. 1952, the power to specify a destination and the mode of exercise of the power did not give rise to a question of law reviewable by the Supreme Court of Canada. In this case the Supreme Court held, *inter alia*, that it was not necessary for the deportation order made under that Act to specify the destination to which the appellant was to be deported.

Section 52(3)

Sivaraj v. Canada (Minister of Citizenship & Immigration) (1996), 107 F.T.R. 64 (Fed. T.D.); affirmed (May 23, 1996), Doc. A-42-96, A-72-96, A-74-96 (Fed. C.A.) — The respondent was attempting to remove the applicants to Sri Lanka. The applicants applied for a stay of the execution of the removal orders and the respondent took the position that the statements of claim which the applicants had used to commence these proceedings did not disclose a reasonable cause of action.

The applicants came to Canada from Sri Lanka. They unsuccessfully claimed refugee status with the result that removal orders were issued. The applicants then filed a statement of claim in order to obtain declaratory relief that the removal orders violated sections 7 and 12 of the *Canadian Charter of Rights and Freedoms*, and that they contravened the *Geneva Conventions Act*.

The Minister's decision in determining the country of removal was, in fact, a decision made by a federal board, commission, or other tribunal within the meaning of section 18, and is therefore subject to review under section 18.1.

The applicants should not have proceeded by way of action to obtain declaratory relief under the Charter. The proper procedure was by way of applications for judicial review. The Court has often, under the rules of judicial review, examined the constitutionality under the Charter of decisions made by federal boards.

The Court did, however, stay the execution of the removal orders and to avoid a vacuum being created whereby the applicants would have no proceedings before the Court, the Court exercised its jurisdiction under rules 2 and 303 of the Federal Court Rules and presumed the proceedings to have been commenced as applications for judicial review.

52.1 Return to Canada — Where a removal order, other than a removal order that may be appealed to the Appeal Division, has been made against a person and the person is removed from or otherwise leaves Canada, the person may, at the expense of the Minister, return to Canada, if the person is subsequently successful in having the removal order set aside.

R.S.C. 1985, c. 28 (4th Supp.), s. 17.

53. (1) Prohibited removal — Notwithstanding subsections 52(2) and (3), no person who is determined under this Act or the regulations to be a Convention refugee, nor any person who has been determined to be not eligible to have a claim to be a Convention refugee determined by the Refugee Division on the basis that the person is a person described in paragraph 46.01(1)(*a*), shall be removed from Canada to a country where the person's life or freedom would be threatened for reasons of race, religion, nationality, membership in a particular social group or political opinion unless

> **(a) the person is a member of an inadmissible class described in paragraph 19(1)(*c*) or subparagraph 19(1)(*c*.1)(i) and the Minister is of the opinion that the person constitutes a danger to the public in Canada;**

(b) the person is a member of an inadmissible class described in paragraph 19(1)(*e*), (*f*), (*g*), (*j*), (*k*) or (*l*) and the Minister is of the opinion that the person constitutes a danger to the security of Canada; or

(c) the person is a person described in subparagraph 27(1)(*a*.1)(i) and the Minister is of the opinion that the person constitutes a danger to the public in Canada; or

(d) the person is a person described in paragraph 27(1)(*d*) who has been convicted of an offence under any Act of Parliament for which a term of imprisonment of ten years or more may be imposed and the Minister is of the opinion that the person constitutes a danger to the public in Canada.

(2) Idem — Notwithstanding subsections 52(2) and (3), no person who has been determined not to be eligible to have a claim to be a Convention refugee determined by the Refugee Division on the basis that the person is a person described in paragraph 46.01(1)(*b*) shall be removed from Canada to any country other than the country from which the person came to Canada as determined for the purposes of that paragraph unless

(a) the country to which the person is to be removed is a prescribed country under paragraph 114(1)(*s*); or

(b) the person, following a reference of the claim to the Refugee Division pursuant to subsection 46.03, is determined by the Refugee Division not to be a Convention refugee.

R.S.C. 1985, c. 28 (4th Supp.), s. 17; 1992, c. 49, s. 43; 1995, c. 15, s. 12.

Transitional Provision

S.C. 1995, c. 15, s. 26 provides: A conditional departure notice or a conditional exclusion order issued before February 1, 1993 becomes a deportation order on the latest of:

(a) July 10, 1995,

(b) the expiration of the period normally allowed for making an application for judicial review, in accordance with the Immigration Act, of a decision of the Refugee Division,

(c) the day on which a decision is made under the Immigration Act: (i) refusing to grant leave for judicial review of a decision of the Refugee Division, or (ii) refusing to grant leave to appeal a decision of the Refugee Division in accordance with the Immigration Act, as it read immediately before February 1, 1993,

(d) the expiration of the period normally allowed for taking an appeal, in accordance with the Immigration Act, from a decision of the Federal Court-Trial Division in relation to a decision of the Refugee Division, and

(e) the expiration of the period normally allowed for taking an appeal from a decision of the Federal Court of Appeal in relation to a decision of the Refugee Division, the day on which application for leave to appeal from a decision of the Federal Court of Appeal is dismissed by the Supreme Court of Canada or, where leave to appeal is granted, the day on which the Supreme Court reaches a decision in the matter.

Case Law

Section 53(1)

Said v. Canada (Minister of Citizenship & Immigration), 48 Imm. L.R. (2d) 9, [1999] 2 F.C. 592 (Fed. T.D.) — The applicant sought to review two decisions. The first was an opinion of the Minister that the applicant was a danger to the public pursuant to section 53(1)(d) of the Immigration Act; the second was the decision of a removal officer that the applicant be removed to Afghanistan. These proceedings were in the nature of judicial review, and because the Minister whose opinion was being reviewed did not have jurisdiction to declare section 53(1)(d) unconstitutional, there was no decision of a tribunal deciding constitutionality and therefore no decision to review. Accordingly, the applicant's remedy was by way of an action to determine the constitutional validity of section 53(1)(d).

In the present case, the applicant was notified of the possible issuance of an opinion. The notice invited the applicant to make representations and provide evidence regarding the risk to him upon his return to Afghanistan. The applicant provided information on that subject, and therefore the Minister made a decision with that information in mind. This was sufficient to satisfy the requirement that there be a risk assessment before a refugee is returned to the country from which he or she has sought refuge.

Moghaddam v. Canada (Minister of Citizenship & Immigration) (1997), 42 Imm. L.R. (2d) 101 (Fed. T.D.) — This is an application to review a decision pursuant to paragraph 53(1)(d) of the *Immigration Act*, that the applicant is a person who constitutes a danger to the public in Canada and therefore should be deported to Iran. Case Management Branch forwarded a memorandum to the delegate. The six-page memorandum provided the background of the applicant; a brief resume of the applicant's counsel's 200 page submission; a risk assessment; the conclusion and a recommendation. Clearly the applicant's submission was not on the list of documents forwarded to the delegate. Counsel for the respondent at the hearing asserted that the procedure followed by the Case Management Branch was to forward the applicant's submissions along with all other relevant documents to the delegate. This answer was not sufficient. In view of the fact that the applicant had raised the issue in his memorandum of argument, the respondent ought to have filed an affidavit either from Case Management Branch or from the delegate to the effect that the applicant's submissions were provided to the delegate.

The decision of the delegate was set aside and an order made that the matter was to be reconsidered with a specific direction that the applicant's submissions were to be placed before the Minister's delegate.

Kaberuka v. Canada (Minister of Employment & Immigration), [1995] 3 F.C. 252, 32 Imm. L.R. (2d) 38, 98 F.T.R. 241 — The applicant, a citizen of Rwanda, was accepted as a Convention refugee in Kenya. Accordingly, when the applicant attempted to claim refugee status at a port-of-entry in Canada, he was declared ineligible pursuant to paragraph 46.01(1)(a). The purpose served by this subsection is consistent with the practice in many jurisdictions of preventing asylum shopping, that is, preventing a multiplicity of claims by those seeking the most favourable conditions of asylum. A person ineligible to claim Convention refugee status is granted the right not to be removed from Canada notwithstanding a valid removal order where removal would threaten his or her life or freedom for any ground specified in the definition of Convention refugee.

Section 53(1) does not offend section 7 or section 15 of the *Charter of Rights*. Further, the ineligibility provision and the review of the applicant's removal do not involve the question of cruel and unusual punishment, and accordingly, section 53 does not infringe on section 12 of the *Charter*.

Barrera v. Canada (Minister of Employment & Immigration) (1992), 18 Imm. L.R. (2d) 81, 99 D.L.R. (4th) 264, 151 N.R. 28 (Fed. C.A.) — The applicant was a permanent resident of Canada and also a person determined to be a Convention refugee. The applicant was convicted in Canada in 1983 of beating a 16-year-old boy unconscious, sodomizing him, and raping his 13-year-old girlfriend. Upon his release from jail the applicant was ordered deported notwithstanding the fact that he had previously been found to be a Convention refugee. The Court declined to consider the *Charter* issues raised by a ministerial decision to deport the refugee to his home country until the Minister had in fact exercised his discretion in that regard. The application was dismissed notwithstanding the Court's considerable reasons outlining the Charter issues involved in such a decision by the Minister.

Hoang v. Canada (Minister of Employment & Immigration) (1990), 13 Imm. L.R. (2d) 35, 120 N.R. 193 (Fed. C.A.) — The appellant was ordered deported because he was a permanent resident who had been convicted of an offence for which a term of imprisonment of more than 6 months had been imposed; he had also been convicted of an offence for which the maximum term was 5 years or greater. The appellant had come to Canada as a stateless person from Vietnam and had been determined by the Minister in 1986 to be a Convention refugee. The Court noted that the Immigration Appeal Board (which had decided this matter) correctly determined that its jurisdiction is only over whether a person should be removed from Canada and not as to the country of removal. Until the issue of deportation is settled, the Minister cannot make a decision as to the country of removal. Thus a statement by the Minister's representative as to the Minister's disposition to deport the appellant to Vietnam was not taken as a formal expression of the Minister's decision since the Minister was not, at the date of that statement, empowered to make the decision.

The Court determined that in dealing with the "double jeopardy" provisions of section 11(h) of the Charter deportation was not to be seen as a punishment of the person deported but a protection of those who remained. Further, deportation for serious offences affects neither section 7 nor section 12 of the *Charter of Rights* since it is not to be conceptualized as either a deprivation of liberty or a punishment. Finally, the Court noted that with respect to Canada's international obligations the United Nations convention relating to the status of refugees contained an exception to the prohibition against refoulement where the deportee had been convicted, in the country where he was making the refugee claim, of a particularly serious crime. The Court noted that the phrase "particularly serious crime" and "danger to the community" were not defined in the convention and therefore presumed that Parliament responsibly fulfilled its obligation when it enacted the *Immigration Act*.

Accordingly the appellant's appeal was dismissed.

54. (1) Where no execution of removal order — Where a person against whom a removal order is made is removed from or otherwise leaves Canada, the order shall be deemed not to have been executed if the person is not granted lawful permission to be in any other country, and that person may, notwithstanding section 55(1), come into Canada without the consent of the Minister.

(2) Idem — Where a person against whom a removal order is made is transferred to a foreign state in accordance with a transfer order made under the *Mutual Legal Assistance in Criminal Matters Act*, the removal order shall be deemed not to have been executed by reason only of the transfer of the person to the foreign state, and that person may, notwithstanding subsection 55(1), come into Canada without the consent of the Minister.

(3) Idem — Where a person against whom a conditional removal order is made is transferred to a foreign state in accordance with a transfer order made under the *Mutual Legal Assistance in Criminal Matters Act* and the conditional removal order subsequently becomes effective under subsection 32.1(6), the removal order shall be deemed not to have been executed by reason only of the transfer of the person to the foreign

state, and that person may, notwithstanding subsection 55(1), come into Canada without the consent of the Minister.

R.S.C. 1985, c. 30 (4th Supp.), s. 48; 1992, c. 1, s. 76; 1992, c. 49, s. 44.

Case Law

Section 54(2)

Saprai v. Canada (Minister of Employment & Immigration) (1986), 3 F.T.R. 215 (Fed. T.D.) — The plaintiff was ordered deported on December 9, 1977 and contended that he had executed his own deportation order, lawfully entering the United States on January 12, 1986. The plaintiff contended that he had complied with section 56. Section 56 was held to be a provision that accorded a person, whom other countries refused to receive, the right to return to Canada until other arrangements could be made for deportation. It accords a temporary haven in Canada but does not operate to dissolve the deportation order against the person who, for example, passes through U.S. customs and immigration posts. There was no evidence that permission to be in the United States had been obtained from the American customs and immigration authorities if their permission was that described in section 56. Further, if the permission contemplated by section 56 was one that must be granted according to Canadian law, then it was obvious on the facts that the Minister had never granted the applicant permission to be in any other country except India. Had the plaintiff removed himself voluntarily to India, then it might have been arguable that the plaintiff, himself, had executed his own deportation order. The Court refused to enjoin the Minister from detaining the plaintiff and deporting him to India. The plaintiff had not been allowed, pursuant to section 54, to leave Canada voluntarily and select the country for which he wished to depart, and, therefore, pursuant to section 54(2), the Minister, in attempting to detain the plaintiff for the purpose of deporting him to India, was performing the duties imposed by law.

Mercier v. Canada (Minister of Employment & Immigration) (April 25, 1985), Doc. T-309-85 (Fed. T.D.); affirmed (1985), 62 N.R. 73 (Fed. C.A.) — On November 17, 1982, following an inquiry, a deportation order was issued against the applicant because he had been convicted of an offence for which a maximum term of imprisonment of 10 years or more may be imposed, pursuant to section 19(1)(c) of the Act. The applicant's appeal against this deportation order was dismissed on August 14, 1984. On January 30, 1985, the applicant tried to gain admission to the United States without success and returned to Canada with the intention of provoking an inquiry where he might claim refugee status. When the applicant reappeared at the Canadian border, a senior immigration officer issued a Summons to Appear at an inquiry, pursuant to section 23 of the Act. That decision was countermanded by another senior immigration officer and the applicant's case was withdrawn on the ground that the deportation order, issued against the applicant, had never been executed. It was this decision that was attacked by the applicant, who was seeking a writ of *mandamus* requiring the adjudicator to conduct his inquiry. The decision to countermand the Summons to Inquiry was part of the administrative process. The Court did not intervene because it was of the view that the applicant had not been treated unfairly and that to intervene and issue a writ of *mandamus* would create a situation in which the respondent Minister would, on the one hand, have to execute a deportation order against the applicant and, on the other hand, have to conduct an inquiry with a view to admitting the applicant to the country.

An appeal from this decision was heard on June 28, 1985, and was dismissed. The appellant (applicant) sought to raise, for the first time, the assertion that the deportation order had been executed by the appellant himself when he left the country for a 6-week visit to Haiti from May 12, 1984, to June 30, 1984. No consideration was given to the submission on appeal because it was a question which was raised for the first time before the Court of Appeal. It was founded upon an allegation of fact which was never put in issue before the Trial Division. The Court noted that when sitting on appeal from the Trial Division, it sat as a Court of Appeal whose function was to decide whether the issue presented at trial was properly disposed of. It was not the Court's duty to determine other issues which, had they been raised at the Trial Division, might have resulted in a different outcome if the necessary factual basis had been established.

Effect of Removal Orders

55. (1) Effect of deportation order — Subject to section 56, where a deportation order is made against a person, the person shall not, after he is removed from or otherwise leaves Canada, come into Canada without the written consent of the Minister unless an appeal from the order has been allowed.

(2) Effect of exclusion order — Subject to section 56, where an exclusion order is made against a person, other than a person who has claimed to be a Convention Refugee, the person shall not, after the person is removed from or otherwise leaves Canada, come into Canada without the written consent of the Minister during the twelve month period immediately following the day on which that person is removed from or otherwise leaves Canada unless an appeal from the order has been allowed.

(3) Person may return to Canada — A person against whom a departure order has been made

> **(a) who**
>
> > **(i) complies with section 32.01, is issued a certificate of departure under that section and leaves Canada voluntarily before the expiration of the applicable period specified for the purposes of subsection 32.02(1), or**
> >
> > **(ii) is removed from Canada before the expiration of that period and has been issued a certificate of departure under section 32.01, or**
>
> **(b) who is detained before the expiration of the applicable period specified for the purposes of subsection 32.02(1), who is still in detention under this Act at the expiration of that period and who is subsequently removed from Canada,**

may, if the person otherwise meets the requirements of this Act and the regulations, return to Canada without the written consent of the Minister.

1992, c. 49, s. 45.

Case Law

Section 55(1)

R. v. Jones (February 19, 1997), Doc. CA C25992 (Ont. C.A.) — This was a crown appeal against sentence. The respondent, an American citizen, was convicted under section 55(1) and 95 of the *Immigration Act*, for entering Canada without a Minister's permit after having been deported.

The trial judge erred in principle in imposing a sentence at the lower range of available sentences. The respondent had an extensive criminal record including 8 immigration offences over a period of 8 years for the same or similar offences as the one before the Court. The sentence was varied and increased to 15 months.

Bridgemohan v. Canada (Minister of Citizenship & Immigration) (1996), 36 Imm. L.R. (2d) 91, 109 F.T.R. 32 (Fed. T.D.) — The applicant sought an order quashing a decision of a visa officer not to grant him a permanent visa. The applicant's counsel wrote to the relevant visa officer in support of the applicant's application and requested the Minister's consent to overcome a deportation order which had previously been issued to the applicant's wife. In such circumstances it was unfair to reject the application on the ground of the wife's inadmissibility. It is a practice in many visa offices not to process a subsection 55(1) request for Ministerial consent until the visa application has been assessed. If the application would not, in any event, be successful, little is to be gained by processing the subsection 55(1) request. The applicant's educational background was crucial to the application and a review of the file and the visa officer's affidavit led the Court to the conclusion that the assessment in this respect was not properly done. It is a failure of natural justice to reject an application because a subsection 55(1) consent had not been obtained when a request for such a consent had been made at the time the application was filed. The decision of the visa officer was quashed.

The Court distinguishes an earlier decision in respect of the applicant's brother in which a request for Ministerial consent had not been made.

Bridgemohan v. Canada (Minister of Citizenship & Immigration) (1995), 31 Imm. L.R. (2d) 110, 103 F.T.R. 62 (Fed. T.D.) — A visa officer refused the applicant permission to come to Canada as a permanent resident. The applicant was a citizen of Trinidad and Tobago who had entered Canada in 1988 and made an unsuccessful refugee claim. The applicant was deported in December 1992. One of the bases for refusing the applicant's application for a permanent visa was that the applicant, having been deported, required the Minister's consent under section 55 of the Act, and that failing such consent the applicant was inadmissible as described in paragraph 19(1)(i) of the *Immigration Act*.

There is no basis for the proposition that an applicant should not have to pursue the Minister's consent until the applicant is aware of whether or not, but for the lack of consent, his application for landing would otherwise be approved. There is no basis in law for an assumption that the visa officer would, in the course of his or her consideration of the application, seek the Minister's consent on the applicant's behalf.

Accordingly, the visa officer's refusal of the application on this basis was upheld.

Canada (Solicitor General) v. Kainth (1994), 26 Imm. L.R. (2d) 226, 81 F.T.R. 318 (note), 170 N.R. 367 (Fed. C.A.) — The Appeal Division allowed the appeal of the respondent and overturned a refusal by an immigration officer of the sponsored application for landing of the respondent's spouse. The Board decided that, although the refusal was legal and moreover that the spouse had been deported a few years previously, there were sufficient humanitarian and compassionate grounds to grant the spouse permanent residence. This decision was upheld by the Trial Division on a judicial review application. However, the Trial Division judge certified a serious question of general importance. The Solicitor General then appealed to the Court of Appeal.

Section 69.4(2) is broad enough to permit the Appeal Division to decide that it has jurisdiction to permit the respondent's spouse to be landed, notwithstanding the fact that the spouse did not have the Minister's consent as required by section 55(1) and notwithstanding the provisions of section 19(1)(i).

Accordingly, the appeal was dismissed.

Kaur v. Canada (Minister of Employment & Immigration) (1990), 12 Imm. L.R. (2d) 1 (Fed. C.A.) — Satnam Singh made an application for permanent residence which was sponsored by the appellant, a landed immigrant, who had married him in India. The application was refused and the sponsor's appeal was dismissed by the Immigration Appeal Board. Satnam Singh had been deported from Canada and the consent of the Minister required for his admission into the country had been refused. Requirement of the Minister's written consent set out in section 57(1) of the *Immigration Act* cannot be overcome and replaced by a favourable decision of the Immigration Appeal Board based on its so-called "equitable jurisdiction". The Court further noted that in the context of this case no evidence had been adduced which would have warranted the granting of equitable relief in any event. The Court distinguished *Canada (Minister of Employment & Immigration) v. Narwal* (1990), 10 Imm. L.R. (2d) 183 (Fed. C.A.), on the basis that in that case the good faith of the spouses had never been in doubt.

Bhawan v. Canada (Minister of Employment & Immigration) (1987), 41 D.L.R. (4th) 382, 14 F.T.R. 230 (Fed. T.D.) — The applicant sought prohibition to prevent his removal from Canada pursuant to a deportation order dated January 5, 1984. The applicant came to Canada from Fiji as a landed immigrant. He became subject to a deportation order on January 5, 1984, and filed an appeal to the Immigration Appeal Board. While the appeal was pending, the applicant voluntarily returned to Fiji, and, in April 1986, the applicant came back to Canada. Prior to his return to Canada, the applicant's solicitor withdrew the appeal to the Immigration Appeal Board. The applicant's contention that the deportation was carried out by his leaving Canada for Fiji was rejected. The applicant could only leave Canada and select the country of destination with authorization from the Minister, and this was lacking in this case. Accordingly, the applicant had not complied with section 54 [s. 52], and the deportation order, dated January 5, 1984, could be executed to cause the applicant's removal from Canada.

Mercier v. Canada (Minister of Employment & Immigration) (1986), 3 Imm. L.R. (2d) 316 (Fed. T.D.) — The applicant was admitted to Canada in 1974. Between 1978 and 1984 he was convicted of a number of criminal offences. During this period, on November 17, 1982, he was ordered deported. The applicant returned to his country of origin between May 12 and June 30, 1984. The applicant sought a declaration that the deportation order made against him had ceased to be valid by virtue of section 54 of the *Immigration Act*. It was held that the voluntary departure of someone who is the subject of a deportation order could only be made under section 54 with leave of the Minister. In the absence of such leave, the applicant could not be said to have carried out the removal order himself.

Singh (C.K.) v. Canada (Minister of Employment & Immigration) (1986), 6 F.T.R. 15 (Fed. T.D.) — This application for *certiorari* quashing the decision of the respondent Minister not to grant the Minister's consent to Saudagar Gill to enter Canada for the purpose of testifying as a witness before the Immigration Appeal Board was dismissed.

The applicant was the wife of Saudagar Gill. Her sponsorship of her husband had been refused and she had appealed to the Immigration Appeal Board. The Board issued a summons to the husband who was in India. The Minister's consent was required for the attendance of the witness because Gill had been previously deported. The original sponsorship had been refused for a variety of reasons, one of which was that the marriage offended section 4(3) of the Regulations. The Minister declined to give his consent to Gill returning to Canada, and, thus, Gill was unable to appear as a witness at the Immigration Appeal Board. It was held that the Minister's decision under section 57 was administrative. The Minister was not, in refusing consent, exercising a *quasi*-judicial function; therefore, he was not required to give reasons for his decision. Consequently, the failure to give reasons, in this case, could not give rise to relief by way of *certiorari*. Further, the relief sought was discretionary, and no basis for exercising that discretion in favour of the applicant was to be found on the facts of this case.

Cambouras v. Canada (Minister of Employment & Immigration) (1984), 68 N.R. 158 (Fed. C.A.) — The applicant had been ordered deported at an earlier proceeding and entered Canada without a Minister's permit. At his inquiry, after the latter entry, he sought to establish that he was a permanent resident of Canada. The Federal Court approved the adjudicator's refusal to hear this evidence concluding that the applicant was in fact asking the adjudicator to revise the previous deportation order which was beyond the adjudicator's jurisdiction.

R. v. Maunder (1983), 46 Nfld. & P.E.I.R. 361, 135 A.P.R. 361 (Nfld. C.A.) — The appellant appealed a sentence of one year imposed under section 96. The appeal was dismissed because the appellant had disregarded other deportation orders, and following his removal from Canada pursuant to such orders, had returned to Canada without the consent of the Minister and engaged in criminal activity.

Vega v. Canada (Minister of Employment & Immigration) (February 15, 1983), Doc. A-261-82 (Fed. C.A.) — The applicant had left and re-entered Canada after having been ordered deported. The adjudicator erred in ruling that it was the applicant's responsibility to prove that he had obtained the Minister's consent before coming back into the country. That burden clearly lay upon the Commission. This error did not vitiate the adjudicator's decision since he did not rely upon the onus of proof to reach the conclusion that the applicant did not have the Minister's consent. The Court held, as well, that the consent of the Minister must be expressed and could not be implied.

Ali v. Canada (Minister of Manpower & Immigration), [1978] 2 F.C. 277, 82 D.L.R. (3d) 401, 20 N.R. 337 (Fed. C.A.) — The applicant was granted landed immigrant status in Canada on February 15, 1973. A deportation order was made against her on March 12, 1975. The applicant appealed the deportation order to the Immigration Appeal Board, that Board dismissed the appeal, and the deportation order was executed on February 24, 1976. The applicant returned to Canada without the permission of the Minister on June 26, 1976. A second deportation order was made on July 15, 1976 on the ground that the applicant had returned to Canada without the consent of the Minister. The applicant was informed that she had no right of appeal in respect of the second order. The applicant appealed in any event and the Board dismissed the application "for want of jurisdiction". The applicant asserted that she was a permanent resident according to the definition of that term under the old *Immigration Appeal Board Act.* The Court concluded that the term "permanent resident" under the old Act did not include persons who were previously permanent residents and who had been validly deported.

Section 55(2)

Vega v. Canada (Minister of Employment & Immigration) (February 15, 1983), Doc. A-261-82 (Fed. C.A.) — For digest, see section 55, subheading *Subsection (1), supra.*

Grewal v. Canada (Minister of Employment & Immigration) (1980), [1981] 1 F.C. 12, 112 D.L.R. (3d) 30, 37 N.R. 535 (Fed. C.A.) — The applicant sought to enter Canada on January 2, 1980. An inquiry followed, at the conclusion of which an adjudicator excluded the applicant on the ground that he was described in section 19(1)(i). It was common ground that the applicant was a person described under section 19(1)(i) on January 2, 1980. However, when the adjudicator made the order, more than twelve months had elapsed since the applicant left Canada and the Court ruled that the applicant was, at that time, not a member of the inadmissible class described in section 19(1)(i). The relevant time was when the adjudicator made his order rather than when the immigration officer dated his report.

55.1 Repayment of costs of deportation — A person to whom a departure order is issued that is deemed under section 32.02 to be a deportation order and who is subsequently removed from Canada shall not come into Canada unless the person has paid to Her Majesty the removal costs prescribed under regulations made pursuant to paragraph 114(*1*)(*r*) or, in the absence of any such regulations, has reimbursed Her Majesty for any costs incurred by Her Majesty in deporting the person.

1992, c. 49, s. 46.

56. (1) Where person allowed to return by appeal division — Where, pursuant to section 75, the Appeal Division allows a person to return to Canada for the hearing of his appeal against a removal order, the person may come into Canada for that purpose without the consent of the Minister.

(2) Where execution of removal order stayed — Where, pursuant to subsection 73(1), the Appeal Division directs that the execution of a removal order be stayed, the person against whom the order was made does not require the consent of the Minister to come into Canada at any time during the period for which that execution is stayed.

R.S.C. 1985, c. 28 (4th Supp.), s. 33.

Transitional Provision

S.C. 1995, c. 15, s. 26 provides: A conditional departure notice or a conditional exclusion order issued before February 1, 1993 becomes a deportation order on the latest of:

(a) July 10, 1995,

(b) the expiration of the period normally allowed for making an application for judicial review, in accordance with the Immigration Act, of a decision of the Refugee Division,

(c) the day on which a decision is made under the Immigration Act: (i) refusing to grant leave for judicial review of a decision of the Refugee Division, or (ii) refusing to grant leave to appeal a decision of the Refugee Division in accordance with the Immigration Act, as it read immediately before February 1, 1993,

(d) the expiration of the period normally allowed for taking an appeal, in accordance with the Immigration Act, from a decision of the Federal Court-Trial Division in relation to a decision of the Refugee Division, and

(e) the expiration of the period normally allowed for taking an appeal from a decision of the Federal Court of Appeal in relation to a decision of the Refugee Division, the day on which application for leave to appeal from a decision of the Federal Court of Appeal is dismissed by the Supreme Court of Canada or, where leave to appeal is granted, the day on which the Supreme Court reaches a decision in the matter.

PART IV — CLAIMS AND APPEALS

Establishment of Board

57. (1) Board continued — The Immigration and Refugee Board, comprising three divisions, to be called the Convention Refugee Determination Division, the Immigration Appeal Division and the Adjudication Division, is hereby continued.

(2) **Constitution of board** — The Board shall consist of the Chairperson of the Immigration and Refugee Board and the members of the Refugee Division, the Appeal Division and the Adjudication Division.

R.S.C. 1985, c. 10 (2nd Supp.), s. 1; R.S.C. 1985, c. 28 (4th Supp.), s. 18; 1992, c. 49, s. 47.

58. (1) **Chairperson** — The Chairperson shall be appointed by the Governor in Council to hold office during good behaviour for a term not exceeding seven years, but may be removed by the Governor in Council at any time for cause.

(2) **Chairperson is member of all divisions** — The Chairperson is by virtue of holding that office a member of the Refugee Division, the Appeal Division and the Adjudication Division.

(3) **Chief executive officer** — The Chairperson is the chief executive officer of the Board and has supervision over and direction of the work and staff of the Board.

(4) **Delegation** — The Chairperson may authorize any Deputy Chairperson or Assistant Deputy Chairperson of the Refugee Division or Appeal Division and any coordinating member of the Refugee Division to exercise any power or perform any duty or function of the Chairperson under this Act, other than

(a) the power to make rules under subsection 65(1),

(b) any power, duty or function in relation to the Adjudication Division, or

(c) the power to delegate under this subsection,

and, if so exercised or performed, the power, duty or function shall be deemed to have been exercised or performed by the Chairperson.

(4.1) **Idem** — The Chairperson may authorize the Director General of the Adjudication Division or any director of the Adjudication Division to exercise any power or perform any duty or function of the Chairperson under this Act in relation to the Adjudication Division, other than

(a) the power to make rules under subsection 65(1), or

(b) the power to delegate under this subsection,

and, if so exercised or performed, the power, duty or function shall be deemed to have been exercised or performed by the Chairperson.

(5) **Absence, incapacity or vacancy** — In the event of the absence or incapacity of the Chairperson, or if the office of Chairperson is vacant, the Minister may authorize the Deputy Chairperson (Convention Refugee Determination Division) or the Deputy Chairperson (Immigration Appeal Division) to act as Chairperson for the time being, and a Deputy Chairperson so acting has and may exercise all the powers and perform all the duties and functions of the Chairperson.

R.S.C. 1985, c. 28 (4th Supp.), s. 18; 1992, c. 49, s. 48.

59. (1) **Constitution of Refugee Division** — The Refugee Division shall consist of such full-time members and part-time members as are appointed by the Governor in Council.

(2) **Designations** — The Governor in Council shall designate from among the full-time members of the Refugee Division

(a) one member to be Deputy Chairperson (Convention Refugee Determination Division); and

(b) not more than ten members to be Assistant Deputy Chairpersons (Convention Refugee Determination Division).

(3) **Coordinating members** — The Governor in Council shall designate from among the full-time members of the Refugee Division members to be coordinating members at the ratio of one coordinating member to every fifteen members of the Refugee Division.

(4) **Membership in other division** — The members of the Refugee Division are by virtue of holding that office members of the Appeal Division, and the members of the Appeal Division are by virtue of holding that office members of the Refugee Division, but members of the Refugee Division shall not be counted in determining the membership of the Appeal Division under subsection 60(1).

R.S.C. 1985, c. 10 (2nd Supp.), s. 2; R.S.C. 1985, c. 28 (4th Supp.), s. 18; 1992, c. 49, s. 49.

60. (1) **Constitution of appeal division** — The Appeal Division shall consist of not more than thirty members.

(2) **Designations** — The Governor in Council shall designate from among the members of the Appeal Division one member to be Deputy Chairperson (Immigration Appeal Division) and not more than five members to be Assistant Deputy Chairpersons (Immigration Appeal Division).

R.S.C. 1985, c. 28 (4th Supp.), s. 18; 1992, c. 49, s. 49.

61. (1) **Appointment and tenure of members** — Each member of the Refugee Division and the Appeal Division shall be appointed by the Governor in Council to hold office during good behaviour for a term not exceeding seven years.

(2) **Qualification** — The Deputy Chairperson (Immigration Appeal Division), a majority of the Assistant Deputy Chairpersons (Immigration Appeal Division) and not less than ten per cent of the members of the Refugee Division and the Appeal Division shall be barristers or advocates of at least five years standing at the bar of a province or notaries of at least five years standing at the *Chambre des notaires du Québec*.

(3) **Re-appointment** — The Chairperson, each member of the Refugee Division and each member of the Appeal Division are eligible for re-appointment in the same or another capacity.

(4) [Repealed 1992, c. 49, s. 50.]

(5) **Full-time members** — The Chairperson, each full-time member of the Refugee Division and each member of the Appeal Division shall devote the whole of their time to the performance of their duties under this Act.

R.S.C. 1985, c. 10 (2nd Supp.), s. 3; R.S.C. 1985, c. 28 (4th Supp.), s. 18; 1992, c. 49, s. 50.

62. (1) Remuneration — The Chairperson, each full-time member of the Refugee Division and each member of the Appeal Division shall be paid such remuneration as is fixed by the Governor in Council.

(2) Fees — Each part-time member of the Refugee Division shall be paid such fees for services rendered under this Act as are fixed by the Governor in Council.

(3) Expenses — The Chairperson, each member of the Refugee Division and each member of the Appeal Division are entitled to be paid reasonable travel and living expenses incurred by them while absent from their ordinary place of residence in the course of the performance of their duties under this Act.

(4) Application of public service superannuation act — For the purposes of the *Public Service Superannuation Act*, the Chairperson and the members of the Refugee Division and the Appeal Division shall be deemed to be employed in the Public Service.

R.S.C. 1985, c. 10 (2nd Supp.), s. 4; R.S.C. 1985, c. 28 (4th Supp.), s. 18; 1992, c. 49, s. 51.

63. (1) Disposition after member ceases to hold office — Any person who has resigned or otherwise ceased to hold office as a member of the Refugee Division, Adjudication Division or Appeal Division may, at the request of the Chairperson, at any time within eight weeks after that event, make, or take part in, the disposition of any matter previously heard by that person and, for that purpose, the person shall be deemed to be such a member.

(2) Disposition where member unable to take part — Where a person to whom subsection (1) applies or any other member by whom a matter has been heard is unable to take part in the disposition thereof or has died, the remaining members, if any, who heard the matter may make the disposition and, for that purpose, shall be deemed to constitute the Refugee Division or the Appeal Division, as the case may be.

R.S.C. 1985, c. 28 (4th Supp.), s. 18; 1992, c. 49, s. 52.

Case Law

Section 63(2)

Singh (R.N.H.) v. Canada (Minister of Citizenship & Immigration), 224 N.R. 227, [1998] 3 F.C. 127, 146 F.T.R. 160 (note), 10 Admin L.R. (3d) 167 (Fed. C.A.) — This was an appeal from an order of the Trial Division by which a decision signed by one member only of the two-member panel was set aside. The objective of section 63 is to permit the Board to retain jurisdiction over a claim in cases where one of the Board's members who participated in the hearing is unable to take part in the decision. The provision is intended to free the Board from having to re-open the claim and conduct a new hearing.

Subsection 63(1) bestows upon the chairperson the power of requesting that a Board member participate in the disposition of a matter previously heard within eight weeks of that member resigning. Absent such a request, the departed member would possess no authority to take part in the decision. Subsection 63(1) does not require such a person to participate in the disposition of a matter, it merely permits that person to do so. Subsection 63(2) describes the circumstances in which one Board member alone may dispose of a matter previously heard by a panel of two members. It addresses four situations: (1) where a person is unable to take part in the disposition of a matter; (2) where any other member by whom a matter has been heard is unable to take part in the disposition; (3) where a person to whom subsection (1) applies has died; and (4) where any other member by whom a matter has been previously heard has died.

In this case, after Board member Guthrie ceased to hold office, he was requested to take part in the disposition of a matter previously heard for up to eight weeks after the end of his term of office. When the decision was rendered the eight-week extension had expired. This called into play section 63(2). The invocation of subsection 63(2) is a serious matter which denies claimants the statutory right to a decision by a two-member panel. The remaining Board members' bald statement that the departed member "participated in the disposition of the claim and in accordance with section 63(1) of the Act", is not satisfactory. The statement shed no light whatsoever on the circumstances that prevented the two-member panel from rendering a decision before the expiry of the eight-week period of extension. When subsection 63(2) is engaged, where a Board member receives an extension pursuant to subsection 63(1), a more detailed explanation of the material circumstances giving rise to the departed member's inability to participate in the disposition of the matter within the extension period is required.

The expiration of the Board member's term is a sufficient ground to invoke section 63(2). The appeal was dismissed, however, on the ground that the member who signed the decision failed to provide a complete statement of the material circumstances as required by the decision in *Weerasinge v. The Minister of Employment and Immigration*, [1994] 1 F.C. 330.

Hamad v. Canada (Minister of Citizenship & Immigration) (1997), 135 F.T.R. 280 (Fed. T.D.) — This was an application to review a negative decision of the CRDD. The applicant arrived in Canada in 1995 and claimed refugee status. A refugee determination hearing was held in March and April of 1996. The panel was made up of two persons, one of whom resigned on June 28 and was permitted to take part in decisions up to July 4, 1996. On October 4, 1996, the CRDD released its decision. The reasons were signed by one member alone and those reasons explained that the decision was arrived at by both panelists on June 18, 1996.

The Court followed *Garrison v. Canada* (1995), 28 Imm. L.R. (2d) 113, and accepted the statement in the reasons to the effect that both members had participated in the disposition of the claim, although only one member wrote and signed the decision. There was no reason to doubt this statement and accordingly the Court found that the CRDD had satisfied the requirements of section 63(2) of the *Immigration Act*.

Eryilmazli v. Canada (Minister of Citizenship & Immigration) (1997), 131 F.T.R. 22 (Fed. T.D.) — The applicant sought to review a negative determination of his refugee claim. The hearing of the applicant's claim occurred on August 4, 1995 and September 7, 1995 before a two-member panel. One of the panel members ceased to hold office on February 23, 1996. The chairperson requested that the member participate in the disposition of matters previously heard by him for an eight-week period pursuant to subsection 63(1). That period ended on April 19, 1996. The reasons for decision in this matter are dated July 11, 1996 and they were signed on July 19, 1996 by only one member. The retiring member had signed a document entitled a "Final Disposition Sheet" on April 3, 1996.

There was no decision until July 19, 1996 when the order and reasons were communicated to the applicant. Section 69.1(11)(a) mandates the giving of reasons in a case where the decision is against the person making the refugee claim.

In this case, the panel did not deal with why the matter was not decided within the eight-week period other than to state that the member had retired as required under section 63.1. There was no statement of the material circumstances which prevented the matter from being disposed of within eight weeks of the retiring member having ceased to hold office as required under section 63.1.

Accordingly, the application for judicial review was allowed.

Sereguine v. Canada (Minister of Citizenship & Immigration) (1996), 108 F.T.R. 133 (Fed. T.D.) — At the conclusion of the applicant's refugee claim a decision was rendered which was signed by only one of the two members who heard the claim. The second member had ceased to hold office prior to the rendering of a decision. The applicant did not consent to have the decision in this case rendered by only one member. The only other situation allowing for a one member decision is that described in section 63(2) of the Act.

Board members are appointed by Order-in-Council for a fixed term not exceeding 7 years, after which they cease to hold office. The chairperson of the Board has a discretion to request the departed member to participate at any time within 8 weeks of ceasing to hold office in the disposition of any matter previously heard by that person. In such a situation the person shall be deemed to be a member of the Board. In the absence of such a request the person is no longer a member of the Board and is unable to perform the functions of that office. The word "unable" in section 63(2) means lacking the ability to perform the functions of the office, including participating in decisions.

The hearing of this refugee claim was heard on December 22, 1994, February 10, 1995, and April 7, 1995. The decision of the Board was dated August 3, 1995. The departed member ceased to hold his office on June 9, 1995. Accordingly, on August 3rd the departed member was unable to take part in the disposition of the claim, and the remaining member had jurisdiction by virtue of section 63(2) to make the disposition.

Singh (R.N.H.) v. Canada (Minister of Citizenship & Immigration) (1995), 104 F.T.R. 312 (Fed. T.D.) — This was an application to set aside a negative decision of a panel of the IRB in part because the decision was signed by one Board member only.

The remaining two Board members, Messrs. Berman and Guthrie, heard this refugee claim. The decision was given on April 7, 1995 by Mr. Berman who explained that Mr. Guthrie ceased to hold office on December 27, 1994. Mr. Berman explained that Mr. Guthrie participated in the disposition of the claim in accordance with section 63(1) of the *Immigration Act*. He further explained that the present reasons written and signed by himself reflected the thinking of the panel when the decision was made.

There was no written documentation recording Mr. Guthrie's decision. There was no indication that he saw or reviewed a draft of the reasons and agreed to them. There was no evidence that Mr. Guthrie was "unable" to take part in the decision. The normal expiration of a Board member's term of office is not a circumstance to which subsection 63(2) was intended to apply.

De Arce v. Canada (Minister of Citizenship & Immigration) (1995), 32 Imm. L.R. (2d) 74, 103 F.T.R. 72 — The applicant, a citizen of Argentina, claimed refugee status on the basis of a well-founded fear of persecution by reason of membership in a particular social group and political opinion. The hearing was held before the Refugee Division on October 26, 1994. At the time of the hearing, the Board was comprised of two members, Mr. Davis and Mr. Bal. On November 6, 1994, Mr. Bal ceased to act as a member of the CRDD. The panel's decision was rendered on November 17, 1994 by Mr. Davis.

Section 63 does not oblige the Refugee Division to make its decision within eight weeks from the time a panel member ceases to hold office nor does it oblige a member who has ceased to hold office to participate in a decision which is made within eight weeks of that event. The use of the word "may" indicates the participation in the disposition of a previously heard matter within eight weeks of a member having ceased to hold office as purely discretionary. Section 63(2) specifically contemplates one-member panel decisions where one of the individuals who heard the claim is unable to participate in its disposition.

Mirzaei v. Canada (Minister of Citizenship & Immigration) (1995), 32 Imm. L.R. (2d) 69 (Fed. T.D.) — The applicant sought to overturn a decision of the IRB on the basis that the statement of the circumstances which prevented one member of the panel from participating in the decision was incomplete. According to the decision, B.C. Vickers' term as a member of the IRB expired, and accordingly, the refugee claim would fail to be decided by the other member of the panel who heard the claim. An affidavit exhibit filed by the applicant contained a letter from the IRB which indicated that the chairperson had authorized Mr. Vickers to take part in the disposition of the claim within eight weeks of his departure.

No explanation appeared on the record as to why Mr. Vickers had not participated in the decision within eight weeks of his departure. Accordingly, the explanation given was incomplete and the decision of the Board set aside.

Brailko v. Canada (Minister of Citizenship & Immigration) (1995), 97 F.T.R. 129 — The applicants' claim for refugee status was heard on two days and the panel's decision was rendered 9 months later. By that time one of the panel members had ceased to hold office. Her term had expired on August 8, 1994. In September 1994 the applicants submitted further evidence in support of their claim and the panel's decision was rendered in November 1994.

Two lines of authority appear to have developed in this area. The first holds that as long as an explanation is placed on the record stating that the members inability arose because that member ceased to hold office, this is sufficient for the purposes of s. 63(2). The other line of authority indicates that in circumstances where Board members know, at the time they participate in hearings, that they will not be available to take part in the decisions there will be a breach of natural justice. Further, when it is clear from the record that Board members anticipate taking part in decisions before the expiration of their term, and then do not do so, a fuller explanation respecting the reasons for that inability is required. A mere statement that the individuals' term of office expired will not suffice.

The word "unable" must be read in association with the companion circumstance "or has died". Being unable to take part in the decision refers to a situation in which something unexpected and beyond the control of the Board member occurs to render the person unable to take part in the decision. It is not sufficient if a Board member simply declines to make a decision. This is particularly so in the face of legislative provisions which require a hearing by two Board members and which give the benefit of a split decision to the applicant. There was no reason why the Board member in this case could not simply have taken a piece of paper at sometime during the 9 month period after the conclusion of the hearing and written a few paragraphs documenting her decision. She did not have to wait for the other member to make up his mind.

There was an added factor in this application. The hearing of a matter is not completed until all evidence has been filed and submissions made thereon. Accordingly, this matter had not concluded until September of 1994 by which time the Board member in question had ceased to hold office. The applicant had not consented under s. 69.1(8) to having the claim determined by one member. Accordingly, the Board lacked jurisdiction to reach a decision in this case and its decision must be quashed.

Odameh v. Canada (Minister of Employment & Immigration) (1995), 185 N.R. 9 (Fed. C.A.) — The decision of the CRDD had been made by one member, the other member having ceased to hold office. The decision was upheld. If section 63(2) is invoked with the explanation that the other member has ceased to hold office as a member, that invocation carries with it the clear implication that the departed member was not requested by the Chair to participate in the decision of the matter within 8 weeks of departure, and did not, in fact, participate in the decision either then or earlier.

Kutovsky-Kovaliov v. Canada (Secretary of State) (1995), 93 F.T.R. 293 — The applicant appealed a negative decision of a panel of the CRDD and raised a preliminary question of jurisdiction. Only one Board member decided this case. The requirement imposed by the Federal Court of Appeal in such a situation is that when subsection 63(2) is engaged a complete statement of the material circumstances should be put on the record.

The reasons disclosed that the term of one of the Board members expired and that she was therefore unable to take part in the disposition of the claim. This was not sufficient because it appeared from the transcript that the member who did not take part in the disposition intended to participate notwithstanding her imminent departure from the Board. In such a situation the record must contain a statement about why the presiding member was later unable to participate as planned.

Accordingly, the matter was sent back for redetermination.

Zivkovic v. Canada (Minister of Employment & Immigration) (1994), 25 C.R.R. (2d) 264, 88 F.T.R. 192 — The hearing of the applicant's refugee claim took place on August 11 and 30, 1993. On September 6 one of the Board member's term expired. This Board member was not reappointed, and took no further part in the decision. The decision was rendered by a single Board member on January 17, 1994. The expiry of the Board member's term of office was known well in advance. It did not occur as a sudden or unexpected event. The Board member in question was assigned to, and sat on a case in circumstances in which it was known that the Board member would not be available for more than a few days after the conclusion of the hearing. Given the lengthy periods which habitually exist between hearings and the issuance of decisions it must have been known and anticipated by both members at the time the applicant's claim was being heard that only one of them would be rendering a decision. A decision by one member in these circumstances constitutes a breach of fundamental justice.

The Convention refugee hearing engages section 7 of the Charter and a claimant is entitled to a two-member panel and the benefit of any disagreement between them. The purposeful action by a panel member which has the effect of denying an individual that right renders the decision invalid.

Soukhaniouk v. Canada (Minister of Employment & Immigration) (1994), 85 F.T.R. 55 — The applicants sought to review a negative decision of the CRDD. The claim was heard by two members, however, before a decision was given, one panel member was unable to take part in the decision. The applicant had not consented to a single member determining the claim. Section 63(2) permits a single member to negatively determine a Convention refugee claim.

Weerasinge v. Canada (Minister of Employment & Immigration) (1993), 22 Imm. L.R. (2d) 1, [1994] 1 F.C. 330, 17 Admin. L.R. (2d) 214, 161 N.R. 200 (Fed. C.A.) — Absent consent, a claimant is entitled to a hearing by a two-member panel and is entitled to the benefit of any disagreement between them. Recourse to section 63(2) is a serious matter. As a matter of law and to ensure that justice is seen to have been done, when section 63(2) is properly engaged a complete statement of the material circumstances should be put on the record. Such a statement may, of course, be included in the reasons for decision. This appeal was allowed because there was nothing properly on the record which supported a recourse to section 63(2).

63.1 (1) Inquiries — Where the Chairperson considers it appropriate to do so, the Chairperson may recommend to the Minister that an inquiry be held as to whether any

member of the Refugee Division or Appeal Division should be subject to any disciplinary measures for any reason set out in any of paragraphs 63.2(2)(*a*) to (*d*).

(2) Appointment — Where the Minister considers that it is appropriate that an inquiry under this section be held, a judge, supernumerary judge or former judge of the Federal Court, in this section and section 63.2 referred to as the "judge", shall conduct the inquiry.

(3) Powers — A judge conducting an inquiry under this section has all the powers, rights and privileges that are vested in a superior court and, without restricting the generality of the foregoing, has the power

(a) to issue a summons to any person requiring that person to appear at the time and place mentioned therein to testify with respect to all matters within that person's knowledge relative to the inquiry and to bring and produce any document, book or paper that the person has or controls relative to the inquiry; and

(b) to administer oaths and examine any person on oath.

(4) Inquiry public — Subject to subsections (5) and (6), an inquiry under this section shall be conducted in public.

(5) Confidentiality — Where a judge conducting an inquiry under this section is satisfied, during the inquiry, or as a result of the inquiry being conducted in public, as the case may be,

(a) that matters involving public security may be disclosed,

(b) that financial or personal or other matters may be disclosed of such a nature that the desirability of avoiding public disclosure of those matters in the interest of any person affected or in the public interest outweighs the desirability of adhering to the principle that the inquiry be conducted in public, or

(c) that there is a serious possibility that the life, liberty or security of a person would be endangered,

the judge may, on application therefor, take such measures and make such order as the judge considers necessary to ensure the confidentiality of the inquiry.

(6) Idem — Where a judge conducting an inquiry under this section considers it appropriate to do so, the judge may take such measures and make such order as the judge considers necessary to ensure the confidentiality of any hearing held in respect of any application referred to in subsection (5).

(7) Rules of evidence — A judge conducting an inquiry under this section is not bound by any legal or technical rules of evidence and, in any proceedings of the inquiry, the judge may receive and base a decision on evidence adduced in the proceedings and considered credible or trustworthy in the circumstances of the case.

(8) Right to be heard — Every person in respect of whom an inquiry under this section is conducted shall be given reasonable notice of the subject-matter of the inquiry and of the time and place of any hearing thereof and shall be given an opportunity, in person or by counsel, to be heard at the hearing, to cross-examine witnesses and to adduce evidence.

1992, c. 49, s. 53.

Case Law

Section 63.1(8)

Balachandran v. Canada (Minister of Employment & Immigration) (April 21, 1993), Doc. A-773-91 (Fed. C.A.) — The appellant's claim for refugee status was dismissed on the basis that he had no reasonable fear of persecution and that he had an internal flight alternative in his own country.

The question of an internal flight alternative was expressly raised by the refugee hearing officer in the questions he put to the appellant during the course of the hearing. Further, the question was debated in the submissions made to the Board by the refugee hearing officer and counsel for the claimant (appellant). This constituted sufficient notice of that issue being raised and made alive before the Board. There was no need for a more formalistic kind of notice or procedure.

63.2 (1) Report of inquiry — After an inquiry under section 63.1 has been completed, the judge who conducted the inquiry shall report the conclusions of the inquiry to the Minister and submit the report of the inquiry to the Minister.

(2) Recommendations — Where an inquiry under section 63.1 has been held and, in the opinion of the judge who conducted the inquiry, the member of the Refugee Division or Appeal Division in respect of whom the inquiry was held

> **(a) has become incapacitated from the due execution of that office by reason of infirmity,**
>
> **(b) has been guilty of misconduct,**
>
> **(c) has failed in the due execution of that office, or**
>
> **(d) has been placed, by conduct or otherwise, in a position that is incompatible with the due execution of that office,**

the judge may, in the report of the inquiry, recommend that the member be suspended without pay or be removed from office or may recommend that such other disciplinary measure as the judge may specify be taken.

(3) Governor in council may suspend or remove — Forthwith on receiving a report under subsection (1) the Minister shall forward the report to the Governor in Council, who may suspend without pay, remove from office or take any other disciplinary measure against the member to whom the report relates.

1992, c. 49, s. 53.

63.3 (1) Composition of adjudication division — The Adjudication Division shall consist of the Director General of the Adjudication Division and such directors and adjudicators as are necessary to carry out the duties and functions of adjudicators under this Act.

(2) Appointment — The Director General, the directors of the Adjudication Division and the adjudicators shall be appointed or employed in accordance with the *Public Service Employment Act*.

(3) Powers, duties and functions — The Chairperson, the Director General and the directors of the Adjudication Division have all the powers and may carry out the duties and functions of adjudicators.

1992, c. 49, s. 53.

Case Law

Section 63.3

Mohammad v. Canada (Minister of Employment & Immigration), [1989] 2 F.C. 363, 55 D.L.R. (4th) 321, 21 F.T.R. 240 (note) (Fed. C.A.) — It is not a pre-condition to the operation of section 19(1)(c) that the Governor in Council shall have considered the question of rehabilitation and be dissatisfied that the person concerned has brought himself within the exception. The report mandated by section 27(1) requires the authorizing immigration officer to possess information that the person concerned has been convicted of the kind of criminal act specified in section 19(1)(c) and to have knowledge that the person concerned has not satisfied the Governor in Council as to his rehabilitation.

Policy directives, whether made pursuant to regulatory authority or general administrative capacity, are no more than directions and are unenforceable by members of the public. The procedural formalities which are required in respect to an immigration officer when initiating a section 27(1) report are minimal, firstly, because this is a purely administrative decision and, second, because the officer when issuing the section 27(1) report is merely the initiator of the inquiry process. An immigration officer before issuing a section 27(1) report is, therefore, not required to give the person concerned an opportunity to answer allegations contained in that report. On the facts, the immigration officer who issued the section 27(1) report had sufficient knowledge and information upon which to base the report; further, the applicant was given full particulars on the allegations against him.

The Court of Appeal adopted the motion's judge's findings, that there was nothing irregular in the fact that the high-profile nature of the case placed pressure on the respondent's representatives to proceed with dispatch.

The requirement of institutional independence is included in the rules of natural justice as well as enshrined in the Charter.

The test for institutional independence is whether a reasonable and right-minded individual, having informed himself of the scheme whereby adjudicators are appointed under the *Immigration Act* and of the basis upon which they perform their duties, would be likely to conclude that an adjudicator appointed under and acting pursuant to that scheme, more likely than not, would decide fairly the inquiries under the *Immigration Act* over which he presided. While the case-presenting officers and adjudicators are both civil servants under the direction of the same Minister, they operate in separate and distinct divisions of the Commission. Case-presenting officers have no supervisory role, vis-à-vis adjudicators. They do not report to a common superior and it is only at the apex of the organization chart that their respective hierarchies merge. As far as legal direction is concerned, adjudicators can and do seek advice on difficult legal issues from lawyers on the staff of the Adjudication Directorate, who have no connection or association with the Enforcement Branch. On the subject of monitoring, there is evidence that the monitoring practice focuses primarily on how hearings are conducted; with respect to security of tenure, adjudicators, like other civil servants, have the protection afforded pursuant to section 31 of the *Public Service Employment Act*. Additionally, they have the protection of a three-stage grievance procedure. The fact that adjudicators are members of the same bargaining unit as case-presenting officers, is a neutral circumstance that does not give rise to any apprehension one way or the other. The practice of appointing adjudicators to other positions on an acting basis does not give rise to reasonable apprehension of a lack of independence. The Court relied on the uncontradicted evidence of an adjudicator to the effect that the decisions made by him were made independently and without direction from anyone else.

Finally, it was pointed out that the assignment of cases is rationally based; complex cases are usually assigned to the moree experienced adjudicators. There was nothing to suggest that particular cases were assigned to particular adjudicators, let alone any evidence to suggest that the adjudicator chosen to conduct this inquiry was chosen on any basis other than the rational basis referred to previously. The Court concluded for these reasons that reasonable persons, reasonably informed, would view adjudicators appointed under the *Immigration Act* as being independent, keeping in mind the fact that they are for the most part laypersons in the hierarchy of quasi-judicial tribunals; and bearing in mind that their decisions are subject to judicial review by the Court; and that they have all taken an oath of office to "faithfully and honestly fulfill their duties" devolving upon them. Accordingly, the appellant's appeal was dismissed.

64. (1) Head office — The head office of the Board shall be in the National Capital Region as described in the schedule to the *National Capital Act* and the Chairperson and such members of the Refugee Division and members of the Appeal Division as may be designated by the Governor in Council shall live in that Region or within reasonable commuting distance thereof.

(2) Executive director — There shall be an Executive Director of the Board, who shall be appointed by the Governor in Council to hold office during pleasure for a term fixed by the Governor in Council and shall be paid such remuneration as the Governor in Council may fix and who shall exercise or perform such administrative powers, duties or functions as may be prescribed by rules made under subsection 65(1) or assigned by the Chairperson.

(3) Other staff — Such officers, employees and counsel and refugee hearing officers as are necessary for the proper conduct of the business of the Board shall be appointed in accordance with the *Public Service Employment Act*.

(4) Application of public service superannuation act — For the purposes of the *Public Service Superannuation Act*, the Executive Director of the Board and the officers, employees and counsel of the Board shall be deemed to be employed in the Public Service.

(5) Experts — The Chairperson may engage and, subject to the approval of the Treasury Board, fix the remuneration of experts or persons who have special knowledge to assist the Refugee Division, Appeal Division or Adjudication Division in any matter.

R.S.C. 1985, c. 28 (4th Supp.), s. 18; 1992, c. 49, s. 54.

65. (1) Rules — Subject to the approval of the Governor in Council, the Chairperson, in consultation with the Deputy Chairperson (Convention Refugee Determination Division), the Deputy Chairperson (Immigration Appeal Division) and the Director General (Adjudication Division) may make rules

(a) governing the activities of, and the practice and procedure in, the Refugee Division, the Appeal Division and the Adjudication Division, including the functions of counsel employed by the Board;

(b) prescribing a system of priorities for dealing with matters before the Refugee Division, Appeal Division or Adjudication Division;

(c) prescribing the information that may be required under subsection 46.03(2) and the manner and the time within which it must be provided;

(d) governing the determination under subsection 69.1(7.1) of claims of persons who claim to be Convention refugees; and

(e) prescribing any matter that is authorized by this Act to be prescribed by the rules.

(2) **Tabling in Parliament — The Minister shall cause a copy of all rules made pursuant to subsection (1) to be laid before each House of Parliament on any of the first fifteen days on which that House is sitting after the approval of the rules by the Governor in Council.**

(3) **Guidelines — The Chairperson may, after consulting with the Deputy Chairperson and the Assistant Deputy Chairpersons of the Refugee Division and the Appeal Division and the coordinating members of the Refugee Division, issue guidelines to assist the members of the Refugee Division and Appeal Division in carrying out their duties under this Act.**

(4) **Idem — The Chairperson may, after consulting with the Director General and the directors of the Adjudication Division, issue guidelines to assist the members of the Adjudication Division in carrying out their duties under this Act.**

R.S.C. 1985, c. 28 (4th Supp.), s. 18; 1992, c. 49, s. 55.

66. Annual report — The Chairperson shall, before the commencement of each fiscal year, submit to the Minister a report on the activities of the Board in the preceding calendar year, and the Minister shall cause a copy of the report to be laid before each House of Parliament on any of the first fifteen days on which that House is sitting after the Minister receives the report.

R.S.C. 1985, c. 28 (4th Supp.), s. 18; 1992, c. 49, s. 56.

Convention Refugee Determination Division

67. (1) Sole and exclusive jurisdiction — The Refugee Division has, in respect of proceedings under section 69.1 and 69.2, sole and exclusive jurisdiction to hear and determine all questions of law and fact, including questions of jurisdiction.

(2) **Powers — The Refugee Division, and each member thereof, has all the powers and authority of a commissioner appointed under Part I of the *Inquiries Act* and, without restricting the generality of the foregoing, may, for the purposes of a hearing,**

(a) issue a summons to any person requiring that person to appear at the time and place mentioned therein to testify with respect to all matters within that person's knowledge relative to the subject-matter of the hearing and to bring and produce any document, book or paper that the person has or controls relative to that subject-matter;

(b) administer oaths and examine any person on oath;

(c) issue commissions or requests to take evidence in Canada; and

(d) do any other thing necessary to provide a full and proper hearing.

R.S.C. 1985, c. 28 (4th Supp.), s. 18.

Case Law

Section 67(1)

Pushpanathan v. Canada (Minister of Employment & Immigration) (1998), 43 Imm. L.R. (2d) 117, 226 N.R. 201, (sub nom. *Pushpanathan v. Canada (Minister of Citizenship & Immigration))* 160 D.L.R. (4th) 193, (sub nom. *Pushpanathan v. Canada (Ministre of Citizenship & Immigration))* [1998] 1 S.C.R. 982, 11 Admin. L.R. (3d) 1 (S.C.C.); amended (sub nom. *Pushpanathan v. Canada (Minister of Citizenship & Immigration))* [1998] 1 S.C.R. 1222, 11 Admin. L.R. (3d) 130 (S.C.C.) — This appeal raised two questions, firstly, the standard of judicial review over decisions of the IRB and secondly, the meaning of the exclusion from refugee status set out in Article 1F(c) of the United Nations *Convention Relating to the Status of Refugees*. The appellant left Sri Lanka in 1983 and spent time in India and France before arriving in Canada via Italy in March 1985. He claimed Convention refugee status. The claim was never adjudicated because the appellant was granted permanent resident status in May 1987 under an administrative program. In December 1987, the appellant was arrested and charged with conspiracy to traffic in heroin. The appellant was convicted and sentenced to eight years in prison.

In September 1991, the appellant, then on parole, renewed his claim to Convention refugee status. In June 1992, a conditional deportation order was issued against the appellant. Deportation was conditional upon a determination that the claimant was not a Convention refugee and accordingly the appellant's claim was referred to the CRDD. The Board decided that the appellant was not a Convention refugee. The Federal Court Trial Division and the Federal Court of Appeal refused to reverse that decision on an application for judicial review.

A correctness standard applies to the determinations of law by the IRB.

Conspiracy to traffic in a narcotic is not a violation of Article 1F(c) of the United Nations *Convention Relating to the Status of Refugees*.

Even though international trafficking in drugs is an extremely serious problem that the United Nations has taken extraordinary measures to eradicate, in the absence of clear indications that the international community recognizes drug trafficking as a sufficiently serious and sustained violation of fundamental human rights as to amount to persecution, either through a specific designation as an act contrary to the purposes and principles of the United Nations, or through international instruments which otherwise indicate that trafficking is a serious violation of fundamental human rights, individuals should not be deprived of the essential protections contained in the Convention for having committed those acts.

Osei v. Canada (Minister of Citizenship & Immigration) (1998), 146 F.T.R. 48 (Fed. T.D.) — This is an application to review a decision of a panel of the CRDD which granted the Minister's application to vacate a determination that the applicant was a Convention refugee. Counsel argued that a substantial part of the evidence used to argue that the applicant had obtained her refugee status by fraudulent means was available prior to the determination that the applicant was a refugee. The withholding of this evidence and the delay in using it, in the applicant's submission, raised an issue of abuse of process which should have been considered by the CRDD panel. Section 67 of the *Immigration Act* gives the panel jurisdiction to deal with this type of objection and its failure to deal with it in this case was reviewable error.

Zelzle v. Canada (Minister of Citizenship & Immigration), [1996] 3 F.C. 20, 34 Imm. L.R. (2d) 24, 110 F.T.R. 161 (Fed. T.D.) — This was an application to review an interlocutory decision of a panel of the CRDD, wherein it was determined that a previous CRDD panel had failed to render a decision, leaving the CRDD open to hear the applicant's refugee claim *de novo*.

The applicant made a claim for refugee status on November 26, 1992. The applicant, appeared for a hearing on the 15th of November 1993. At the commencement of the hearing, a positive Notice of Decision was found in the CRDD file. This Notice of Decision was dated May 10, 1993. The decision had apparently been made pursuant to the expedited hearing process. The November 15, 1993 panel adjourned the matter pending an inquiry to the Registrar. On May 4, 1994, the applicant received a letter stating that the May 10th decision had been signed and left in the file as a result of an administrative error and, as such, that the case would proceed *de novo*. At the *de novo* hearing on January 9, 1995, the applicant made a motion that the panel did not have jurisdiction. On May 29, 1995, this motion was dismissed.

Once the tribunal has rendered a final decision that tribunal's jurisdiction ceases and the tribunal becomes *functus officio*. In the case of the administrative tribunals, however, justice may require the re-opening of administrative proceedings in order to provide relief which would otherwise be available on appeal. This exception was established to allow an administrative tribunal to re-open proceedings where, if the hearing of an application had not been held according to the rules of natural justice, the administrative tribunal may treat its decision as a nullity and reconsider the matter. This exception has usually been invoked by unsuccessful refugee claimants where, for example, the CRDD failed to consider evidence of changed country conditions. While the principal of *functus officio* favours the finality of proceedings, its application is flexible in the case of administrative tribunals.

In the instant case, the CRDD discharged the function committed to it by its enabling legislation by issuing the May 10, 1993 decision, which decision was valid on its face.

The decision on May 29, 1995 resulted in the panel exceeding its jurisdiction in looking beyond the decision and determining that it was an "administrative error". The panel had no jurisdiction to question a decision validly made in conformity with the Act. Once such a decision was made, the November 15 and May 29 panels were *functus officio*, since the decision in respect of the applicant's refugee status had been made. If the Minister had concerns regarding the legitimacy of the May 10, 1993 decision, the proper method by which to address those concerns would have been by way of an application for judicial review.

Connor v. Canada (Minister of Citizenship & Immigration) (1995), 95 F.T.R. 66 — The applicant's case was based on the allegation that a panel of the IRB made three unsupported findings of implausibility. The Court found that the findings of implausibility were supported by the evidence. The Court noted, however, that it did not accord a high degree of deference to decisions of the IRB. The Court did not consider the Board to be an expert tribunal in the same way that a Securities Commission is expert in a technical area. The Board did have an extensive expertise as a result of dealing with a large number of cases, although the Court noted that this can have a deadening and fatiguing affect rather than sharpening an expertise.

Khakh v. Canada (Minister of Employment & Immigration) (1993), [1994] 1 F.C. 548, 23 Imm. L.R. (2d) 38, 70 F.T.R. 26 — The applicant sought to overturn a decision of a credible basis panel holding a hearing under refugee provisions no longer in effect. The applicant alleged a reasonable apprehension of bias. The respondent argued that in failing to raise an objection on this basis before the credible basis panel, the applicant waived his rights to subsequently raise the issue. A reasonable apprehension of bias should be raised at the first opportunity. There is no waiver unless the party entitled to make the objection is fully aware of the nature of the disqualification and has adequate opportunity to make the objection. The Court will imply waiver where a party or its representative knows of the facts that give rise to an apprehension of bias and, notwithstanding, does not object. The party or its representative must be fully cognisant of the right to take objection. In this case, the adjudicator had, after the applicant requested an interpreter, refused the interpreter after testing the applicant in English. As the hearings progressed the adjudicator noticed that the applicant's English was deteriorating and this was taken to mean that the adjudicator had formed the view that the applicant was not doing his best in English. The failure of the unrepresented applicant to object to the adjudicator's jurisdiction on the basis of reasonable apprehension of bias, after this comment was made, was not taken to be a waiver of his rights to object before the Federal Court.

Urbanek v. Canada (Minister of Employment & Immigration) (1992), 17 Imm. L.R. (2d) 153, 144 N.R. 77 (Fed. C.A.) — The purpose of the refugee determination system is to provide a safe haven to those who genuinely need it and not to give a quick and convenient route to landed status for immigrants who cannot or will not obtain it in the usual way.

Section 67(2)

Kuslitsky v. Canada (Ministre de la Citoyenneté & de l'Immigration) (1998), 148 F.T.R. 136 (Fed. T.D.) — The applicants who are citizens of Israel, claimed Convention refugee status alleging fear by reason of their nationality. The applicants based their allegation of persecution on the fact that the wife is recognized in Israel as being of Russian nationality. The tribunal wanted to see the wife's Israeli identity card, and the wife replied that she had lost that document when there was a fire at their home. The tribunal sought confirmation of the wife's nationality from the Israeli Consulate in Montreal and received a reply from the consulate shortly after the hearing indicating that the wife was of Jewish nationality. Based on that document, a copy of which was sent to the applicants, the tribunal decided in their absence that they were not Convention refugees.

The procedure followed was not acceptable. The information requested from the Israeli consulate and obtained in the absence of the parties should not have been considered to be final and conclusive. The tribunal ought to have reopened the hearing to enable the applicants to consider and refute the new evidence or even to cross-examine the author of the document in question.

Canada (Minister of Citizenship & Immigration) v. Haji-Dodi (1996), 111 F.T.R. 109 (Fed. T.D.) — This was an application on behalf of the Minister for review of a decision dismissing an application by the Minister to a three member panel of the CRDD to vacate an earlier decision.

On January 9, 1992, a panel of the CRDD determined the respondent to be a Convention Refugee. On February 17, 1993, the chairperson of the IRB granted the Minister leave to make an application pursuant to section 69.2(3) for reconsideration. In support, a declaration made by Mr. William MacIntyre with attachments was filed.

On May 25, 1995, the panel appointed to consider the Minister's application convened. The panel indicated that the Minister would be invited to establish whether there had been a misrepresentation and that if such a basis were laid the respondent would be given an opportunity to address the issues raised by the evidence aduced by the Minister. At the hearing without having led any evidence, counsel for the Minister sought to call the respondent as a witness. Counsel for the respondent objected and the tribunal agreed with the representations made on behalf of the respondent who then did not testify at the hearing. No other witnesses were called. With respect to the declaration of Mr. MacIntyre and the attachments, the tribunal gave the declarations little or weight.

The tribunal did not err in law by declining to compel the respondent to testify when counsel for the Minister sought to examine him as a witness. The tribunal determined as a matter of its own proceedings in accord with section 67(2) that the respondent should not be compelled to testify and circumstances where no evidence had been presented at the hearing by the Minister and documentary evidence presented in support of the application in advance of the hearing was not entirely satisfactory from the prospective of the tribunal.

Further, the respondent was free to deal with the application by the Minister as he saw fit. The respondent was under no obligation to provide documentary evidence or to provide *viva voce* evidence unless compelled by the tribunal. The respondent was free to seek to cross-examine the declarant in advance of the hearing, just as he would have been as a party to other proceedings before the Court in dealing with affidavits produced by the other side, but he was not bound to do so. The Minister having put forward the declaration should have been prepared to produce the declarant for cross-examination. Where there is no request by the respondent the tribunal is under no obligation to direct that there be cross-examination in relation to the documentary evidence it found questionable and before it determined what of the evidence aduced by the Minister would be admitted and what weight it would have.

Zverev v. Canada (Secretary of State) (June 13, 1994), Doc. A-1512-92 (Fed. C.A.) — A panel of the Refugee Division is not *functus officio* until it has made a determination of the claim and the panel therefore has the right to re-open the claim in order to consider a new document while allowing the respondent a right to reply.

Szylar v. Canada (Minister of Employment & Immigration) (1994), 79 F.T.R. 47 — This application raised the narrow issue of the right of the Refugee Division to ask the Documentation Centre for additional information after it had concluded the refugee hearing and its decision was reserved.

When the hearing of the refugee claim had concluded the CRDD members found, based on an Amnesty International report, that a revision of the Polish penal code had been carried out through 1990 and that it was necessary to verify the status of the Polish penal code at the time the applicant was sentenced. The tribunal asked its Documentation Centre for additional information. The Documentation Centre sent three documents in reply to this request. After obtaining those documents the tribunal gave notice to the applicant and his counsel and a new hearing was held.

The tribunal acted within its jurisdiction. While its decision was reserved and on the basis of evidence before it, it had the authority to "do anything necessary to provide a full and proper hearing". Since it had not yet ruled on the claim, the division was not *functus officio* and had the authority to do what it did provided that it did so properly by giving the claimant an opportunity to be heard at the reconvened hearing.

Accordingly, the application for judicial review was dismissed.

Kusi v. Canada (Minister of Employment & Immigration) (1993), 19 Imm. L.R. (2d) 281, 65 F.T.R. 58 (Fed. T.D.) — An adjudicator and member of the Immigration and Refugee Board were conducting a credible basis hearing into the claim of a Convention refugee claimant, pursuant to provisions of the *Immigration Act* in effect on August 19, 1992.

The tribunal accepted as evidence notes taken by an immigration officer, which recorded answers given to him at the port-of-entry by the applicant. The applicant contested the accuracy of the notes and asked that the officer be produced for cross-examination, a request which was denied by the tribunal.

The decision by the tribunal that there was no credible basis to the applicant's claim was set aside and the matter was remitted back for determination in accordance with the law. Specifically, the Court found that given the importance of the interest, namely the applicant's claim to be a Convention refugee, and given the fact that the applicant contested the accuracy of the notes which were relied upon by the tribunal, the rules of natural justice and of fundamental justice required that the cross-examination, which was sought, be allowed. The Court relied on the jurisprudence in *Canada (Minister of Employment & Immigration) v. Leal* (1991), 129 N.R. 383 (Fed. C.A.) and *Cheung v. Canada (Minister of Employment & Immigration)* (1981), 122 D.L.R. (3d) 41 (Fed. C.A.).

Editor's Note: Although occurring in the context of a repealed refugee hearing procedure, the principle in this case may have a broader application.

Sivaguru v. Canada (Minister of Employment & Immigration) (1992), 16 Imm. L.R. (2d) 85 (Fed. C.A.) — The appellant testified that he was a supporter or member of a Tamil organization known as LTTE. He said that he was unaware of any violence engaged in by the LTTE between 1979 and 1983. A Board member hearing the evidence initiated on his own a request for information from the Board's documentation centre on the violent activities of the LTTE. After obtaining the information and without disclosing it to the Refugee Hearing Officer or counsel, the Board member then questioned the appellant and contradicted him with the information.

The appellant testified that he had been warned about the particular member in question and had been warned not to tell him the truth about any violent activities of the LTTE or risk being classified as a terrorist and not allowed to remain in Canada.

The Immigration and Refugee Board does not possess the powers of the Court. Its members are not judges. They are not bound by any legal or technical rules of evidence. They are required to deal with all proceedings as informally and expeditiously as the circumstances and the considerations of fairness permit.

An essential requirement for such a hearing is that the Board act with impartiality. Impartiality refers to a state of mind or attitude. It connotes an absence of bias, actual or perceived. For a "hearing" to be worthy of the description the Board must be willing to give the evidence the dispassionate and impartial consideration it requires in order to arrive at the truth. The difficulty in getting at the full story is recognized by the nature of powers which are conferred by subsections 67(2) and 68(4). The flexible provisions of the latter subsection permit the Board to take judicial notice of facts and to take notice of other facts, information and opinion within its specialized knowledge provided it does so in the manner authorized by the statute. The Act does not permit a member of the Board to embark upon a quest for evidence in the manner which was adopted in this case. That method of proceeding subverts its function as an impartial tribunal regardless of the legitimate concern which motivated the request. The search for evidence was secretly initiated and the tenor of the questions put after the information was acquired suggested that the information was going to be used to devastating effect. The Board member might have openly revealed his misgivings about the evidence at the hearing where a course of action known to all concerned could have been decided upon and initiated. Accordingly, the appeal was allowed, the decision of the Board set aside, and the matter referred back for rehearing and redetermination by a differently constituted panel of the Refugee Division.

Salinas v. Canada (Minister of Employment & Immigration), 17 Imm. L.R. (2d) 118, 6 Admin. L.R. (2d) 154, 142 N.R. 211, [1992] 3 F.C. 247, 57 F.T.R. 159n (Fed. C.A.) — This was an appeal from an order of the Trial Division whereby a decision of the Refugee Division to reconvene a hearing into the respondent's claim for refugee status was quashed and the Refugee Division ordered to render a decision on the basis of the evidence before it. The basis of the respondent's claim was her fear of persecution by agents of the state of Panama, which was headed by General Noriega. Some time after the conclusion of the respondent's hearing, but before a decision was rendered, the political situation in Panama changed. The presiding member of the panel notified the respondent that the hearing would be reconvened for the purpose of hearing evidence on these recent changes.

The appeal was allowed. The Refugee Division did not exceed its jurisdiction in reconvening the hearing. Section 68 endows the Refugee Division with powers and duties in relation to any proceedings before it. The distinction has been drawn by Parliament between "proceedings" and a "hearing" before the Refugee Division. The hearing is to be conducted in a manner required by section 69.1. The "hearing" is a step in any proceedings. "Proceedings" is a wider term encompassing the entire matter before the Refugee Division including the hearing itself. The Minister, pursuant to section 69.2(1), is able to initiate proceedings for a determination whether any person who was determined to be a Convention refugee has ceased to be so. The Court found force in the argument that evidence as to the change of conditions is better addressed in the same proceedings to the Refugee Division's determination.

The Refugee Division was not *functus officio*. It had yet to make a determination of the claim. Until it did, the proceedings were pending and finality had not been reached. In order to arrive at its decision, the Refugee Division could exercise the power conferred by the statute, provided it did so properly by giving the respondent an opportunity to be heard at the reconvened hearing. An inquiry into any change of conditions in the appellant's homeland comes within the general mandate of the Refugee Division in determining the claim.

In *Lawal v. Canada (Minister of Employment & Immigration)*, [1991] 2 F.C. 404 (Fed. C.A.), the Court ruled that the only way for the Refugee Division, after the end of a hearing but before decision, to consider new evidence beyond that of which it might take judicial notice was by re-opening the hearing. The Court's decision in *Longia v. Canada (Minister of Employment & Immigration)*, [1990] 3 F.C. 288 (Fed. C.A.), applies only where the Refugee Division has already reached a decision.

The appeal was allowed. The order of the Trial Division was set aside and the respondent's claim for refugee status was referred back to the Refugee Division for a continuation of the reconvened hearing.

Mahendran v. Canada (Minister of Employment & Immigration) (1991), 14 Imm. L.R. (2d) 30, 134 N.R. 316 (Fed. C.A.) — Members of the Refugee Division of the Immigration and Refugee Board are enabled to examine any person on oath. If a board member has problems with testimony, he or she is entitled to conduct questioning of the appellant in the proper discharge of his or her duties. The nature of the questioning, however, can be examined to determine whether there is merit to the submission that a member of the tribunal assumed the role of prosecutor and crossed the line between acceptable conduct and unacceptable conduct for members of the quasi-judicial body. The Court expressed concern at the lengthy nature of the cross examination in this case and noted that it would have been preferable for the board member to have left the main burden of questioning the appellant to the refugee hearing officer. There was, however, no basis for allowing an appeal from the Refugee Division decision that the appellant was not a convention refugee. A further objection was made about the admissibility of a photocopy of a telex. The Court noted that the scheme of the Act and Regulations leaves it to the tribunal to decide the weight which it will ascribe to any of the evidence before it. Here there was other cogent evidence which supported the Board's negative findings on credibility and this ground of appeal was for that reason also unsuccessful.

Lawal v. Canada (Minister of Employment & Immigration) (1991), 78 D.L.R. (4th) 522 (Fed. C.A.) — The applicant made a refugee claim and, after the credible basis hearing had adjourned, the applicant's counsel sent a letter requesting a re-opening of the hearing for the purpose of introducing into evidence an article from a newspaper in Nigeria. The Board, upon receipt of the letter, instituted its own inquiries, requested information from its own document centre and then forwarded those documents to counsel for the applicant informing counsel that it proposed to take "judicial notice" of all this material. The Board, in addition, seems to have initiated further inquiries with respect to the authenticity of the material provided by the applicant's counsel. Section 67(2) only gives the Board power to institute inquiries on its own "for the purpose of a hearing" and these powers may only be invoked "if necessary to provide a full and proper hearing." Finally, the Court noted that section 69.1(4) specifically requires the Refugee Division to hold its hearings in the presence of the claimant. Accordingly, the section 28 application was allowed, the decision of the Board was set aside and the matter was remitted for a new hearing to be held in the presence of the claimant.

68. (1) Sittings — The Refugee Division shall sit at such times and at such places in Canada as are considered necessary by the Chairperson for the proper conduct of its business.

(2) Informal proceedings — The Refugee Division shall deal with all proceedings before it as informally and expeditiously as the circumstances and the considerations of fairness permit.

(3) Rules of evidence — The Refugee Division is not bound by any legal or technical rules of evidence and, in any proceedings before it, it may receive and base a decision on evidence adduced in the proceedings and considered credible or trustworthy in the circumstances of the case.

(4) Notice of facts — The Refugee Division may, in any proceedings before it, take notice of any facts that may be judicially noticed and, subject to subsection (5), of any other generally recognized facts and any information or opinion that is within its specialized knowledge.

(5) Notification of intention — Before the Refugee Division takes notice of any facts, information or opinion, other than facts that may be judicially noticed, in any proceedings, the Division shall notify the Minister, if present at the proceedings, and the person who is the subject of the proceedings of its intention and afford them a reasonable opportunity to make representations with respect thereto.

R.S.C. 1985, c. 28 (4th Supp.), s. 18; 1992, c. 49, s. 57.

Case Law

Section 68(2)

Sivaguru v. Canada (Minister of Employment & Immigration) (1992), 16 Imm. L.R. (2d) 85 (Fed. C.A.) — The appellant testified that he was a supporter or member of a Tamil organization known as LTTE. He said that he was unaware of any violence engaged in by the LTTE between 1979 an 1983. A Board member hearing the evidence initiated on his own a request for information from the Board's documentation centre on the violent activities of the LTTE. After obtaining the information and without disclosing it to the Refugee Hearing Officer or counsel, the Board member then questioned the appellant and contradicted him with the information.

The appellant testified that he had been warned about the particular member in question and had been warned not to tell him the truth about any violent activities of the LTTE or risk being classified as a terrorist and not allowed to remain in Canada.

The Immigration and Refugee Board does not possess the powers of the Court. Its members are not judges. They are not bound by any legal or technical rules of evidence. They are required to deal with all proceedings as informally and expeditiously as the circumstances and the considerations of fairness permit.

An essential requirement for such a hearing is that the Board act with impartiality. Impartiality refers to a state of mind or attitude. It connotes an absence of bias, actual or perceived. For a "hearing" to be worthy of the description the Board must be willing to give the evidence the dispassionate and impartial consideration it requires in order to arrive at the truth. The difficulty in getting at the full story is recognized by the nature of powers which are conferred by subsections 67(2) and 68(4). The flexible provisions of the latter subsection permit the Board to take judicial notice of facts and to take notice of other facts, information and opinion within its specialized knowledge provided it does so in the manner authorized by the statute. The Act does not permit a member of the Board to embark upon a quest for evidence in the manner which was adopted in this case. That method of proceeding subverts its function as an impartial tribunal regardless of the legitimate concern which motivated the request. The search for evidence was secretly initiated and the tenor of the questions put after the information was acquired suggested that the information was going to be used to devastating effect. The Board member might have openly revealed his misgivings about the evidence at the hearing where a course of action known to all concerned could have been decided upon and initiated. Accordingly, the appeal was allowed, the decision of the Board set aside, and the matter referred back for rehearing and redetermination by a differently constituted panel of the Refugee Division.

Section 68(3)

Siad v. Canada (Secretary of State) (1996), 36 Imm. L.R. (2d) 1, [1997] 1 F.C. 608, 206 N.R. 127, 123 F.T.R. 79 (note) (Fed. C.A.); leave to appeal to S.C.C. refused (1997), 223 N.R. 70 (note) (S.C.C.) — The respondent was found to have a well-founded fear of persecution if returned to Somalia. He was also excluded from refugee protection because there were serious reasons for considering that he had committed crimes against humanity, and that he was guilty of acts contrary to the purposes and principles of the United Nations. The finding of exclusion depended upon the tribunal's finding of fact that during the 1980's the respondent had served as governor of a prison in Somalia which was used to torture, abuse and kill political prisoners. The respondent denied that he had ever served in a position of authority at the prison, although he admitted that his father had had him imprisoned there for 18 months during the 1970s.

The factual determination that the respondent had served as governor was based upon the evidence of three persons. Two lay witnesses, who provided affidavits swearing that they had worked near the prison and had seen the respondent in a position of authority there and knew that he was a governor and a report of a professor who was an expert in Somali history and who taught at Rutgers University.

Five days before the respondent's hearing was scheduled to commence, the Minister's representative informed the respondent's counsel that he would be calling two witnesses who would testify as to the respondent's role as governor of the prison. The next day the respondent's counsel requested the names of the witnesses and the evidence that they were expected to give. That same day the Minister's representative telephoned the respondent's counsel and advised him of the names of the witnesses, the period to be covered by their evidence, places of work in Somalia, the fact that they would testify that the respondent had been governor of the prison, that one of them had had official dealings at the prison, and that both had personal knowledge of the respondent's position at the prison. Respondent's counsel made no further disclosure requests until the hearing. The hearing did not proceed as scheduled but was adjourned due to the respondent's ill health.

At the hearing, counsel learned that the lay witnesses had been accepted as convention refugees and demanded disclosure of their personal information forms. This request was denied. On the second day, counsel requested disclosure of all of the information that had been obtained in the investigation of the respondent's claim and based his request on *Stinchcombe v. The Queen*, [1991] 3 S.C.R. 326 (S.C.C.).

With respect to the report of the professor at Rutgers University the Minister's representative provided copies to the respondent and invited counsel to contact him if he had any questions. The only response of the respondent's counsel was to request a copy of the letter by which the Minister had requested the report. Counsel made no request and raised no objections regarding the report until the commencement of the hearing when he objected to the admission of the report unless he could cross-examine the author. Cross-examination was denied by the tribunal.

A high standard of natural justice applies in cases such as this one where the Minister takes an adversarial position in relation to refugee claimants. Section 69.1(5) of the *Immigration Act*, requires that the tribunal afford the claimant a reasonable opportunity to present evidence, cross examine witnesses and make representations, although Stinchcombe, a criminal case does not apply directly in the immigration context it is instructive.

In the context of this case, the Minister's disclosure obligation was satisfied. More than a month before the hearing the Minister's representative provided to the respondent's counsel a summary of the anticipated evidence of his witnesses over the telephone; the testimony of the witnesses ultimately conformed to this summary. If counsel considered the disclosure inadequate he should have objected to it before the hearing began as he had ample opportunity to do. In criminal, as well as civil proceedings the obligation to disclose arises only upon the request of opposing counsel. The tribunal does not owe an independent duty to require disclosure where counsel neglects to request it. If the Minister fails to comply with his disclosure obligation it is reasonable to expect the claimant's counsel to object in a timely manner and to draw this failure to the attention of the tribunal at the earliest opportunity. Counsel's failure to do so is an important factor in determining whether a new hearing should be ordered. Counsel for the respondent was dilatory in seeking disclosure and then sought to delay the proceedings with an 11th hour disclosure request. While the last minute disclosure request was denied, counsel was afforded ample opportunity to cross examine the witnesses with regard to their work in Somalia and their knowledge of the claimant and he did so. The opportunity afforded to question the witnesses was reasonable.

A tribunal is required by subsection 68(2) to conduct hearings fairly and expeditiously. The presiding judge in the trial division erred when he held that the professor's report was inadmissable. This decision was contrary to section 68(3) of the *Immigration Act*, which relieves the tribunal of the legal and technical rules of evidence which would bind the courts. The professor's report was relevant to the allegations against the respondent and the tribunal was entitled to admit the report if it considered it to be credible and trustworthy in the circumstances. The report was to be distinguished from situations where immigration officials had alleged in written statements that they had heard the claimant make damaging statements or admissions which the claimant denied having made. The professor's report does not allege any prior statements by the claimant, rather it describes the claimant's role in Somalia on the basis of this professor's expert knowledge of the Somalia political situation and his interview with informants. Further, the admission of the evidence was not unfair in the circumstances, because counsel was afforded every opportunity to raise objections to its submission before the hearing, to request cross-examination before the hearing, to call rebuttal evidence and to make submissions as to the weight the tribunal should attach to it.

Accordingly, the appeal was allowed and the decision of the trial division set aside.

Merino v. Canada (Secretary of State) (1994), 87 F.T.R. 225 — The applicant met with an immigration consultant for the purpose of completing a personal information form (PIF). During the meeting the applicant provided information relating to his claim and signed a blank PIF. The information was later transcribed onto the signed PIF and eventually transmitted to the CRDD. The applicant also provided a written statement summarizing the basis of his claim. The applicant later retained a lawyer who prepared a new PIF and sought to withdraw the old one. The Board agreed not to receive the first PIF but did receive into evidence the statement which the applicant had given to the immigration consultant.

The statement was not protected by privilege. In order to determine whether the statement is protected by privilege, four principles must be met:

1. The communications must originate in a *confidence* that they will not be disclosed.

2. This element of *confidentiality must be essential* to the full and satisfactory maintenance of the relation between the parties.

3. The *relation* must be one which in the opinion of the community ought to be sedulously *fostered.*

4. The *injury* that would inure to the relation by the disclosure of the communications must be *greater than the benefit* thereby gained for the correct disposal of litigation.

The statement failed this test because it was prepared in the expectation that it would be provided to immigration officials.

Section 68(3) does not suspend the application of the principle of solicitor-client privilege in the context of refugee hearings. The solicitor-client privilege is a fundamental civil and legal right and cannot be considered a legal or technical rule of evidence.

Sidortseva v. Canada (Secretary of State) (1994), 89 F.T.R. 314 — At the hearing of the applicant's claim for refugee status the personal information from (PIF) of her husband was filed as an exhibit. She was confronted with several contradictions and discrepancies between her testimony and the events related by her husband.

The panel made no error in allowing the PIF of the husband to be entered in evidence at the hearing of the claim. The PIF formed part of the record of the Federal Court of Appeal in 1991 in support of the husband's application for leave to appeal. The document was available to the public. The PIF of the husband was relevant to the question of credibility and the panel made no error in its assessment or its use of this evidence.

Arumuganathan v. Canada (Minister of Employment & Immigration) (1994), 75 F.T.R. 161 — The applicant was a citizen of Sri Lanka and with her three infant children claimed refugee status on the basis of their race, religion, political opinion and membership in a particular social group. The rejection of the applicant's claims was based on the negative finding of credibility. The tribunal admitted into evidence the Minister's factum from the husband's leave application for judicial review. The husband's claim to Convention refugee status had been advanced separately from the wife's and had been rejected because it had no credible basis. The refugee hearing officer suggested to the Board that, to the extent that the applicant's claim depended on her husband's experiences, it would not be unreasonable to conclude that if the husband's claim was unsuccessful, her claim was likewise "hollow".

The Board was correct in determining that the Minister's factum could be admitted into evidence and that it was the duty of the Board to assess that evidence and decide what weight to ascribe to it. However, given the inflammatory nature of the evidence it was also incumbent on the Board to indicate in its decision what weight, if any, it had in fact ascribed to the factum. Having failed to refer to the evidence in its decision, the Board erred and its decision was set aside.

Barrera v. Canada (Minister of Employment & Immigration) (November 10, 1993), Doc. A-1552-92 (Fed. T.D.) — The applicant sought to challenge a negative decision of the CRDD on the basis that the Board did not have the right to refer to the personal information form (PIF) in its decision, as that document had not been entered in evidence. Although the PIF was not entered in evidence as an exhibit, the members of the Board, the hearing officer, and counsel for the applicant referred to it during the hearing. Several contradictions between the testimony and the PIF were noted by the Board and the hearing officer, and were pointed out to the applicant during the hearing. The applicant was often unable to explain the contradictions. Counsel for the claimant made no objection to the fact that the PIF was not entered as an exhibit. The failure of the Board to enter the PIF as an exhibit was merely an omission that goes only to form. It does not constitute an error of law requiring the intervention of the Court. In its decision the Court sought to distinguish *Aquino v. Canada (Minister of Employment & Immigration)* (1992), 144 N.R. 315 (Fed. C.A.).

Fajardo v. Canada (Minister of Employment & Immigration) (1993), 21 Imm. L.R. (2d) 113, 157 N.R. 392 (Fed. C.A.) — The applicant's claim for refugee status was denied. The applicants, a mother and her daughter, had put forward a fear of persecution based on perceived political opinion and as a result of a son's alleged membership in a guerilla group and the mother's being a teacher and a member of the teachers' union and her having given involuntary support to the guerrilla group when it occupied the area where they were living. The son had been previously determined to have a credible basis for his claim under the *Refugee Claimant Designated Class Regulations*. The mother's story was not accepted. Her evidence was corroborated in part by the affidavit of a nun, the principal at the school where she had taught prior to fleeing El Salvador. There was no suggestion that the nun's credibility was in question. The nun's affidavit attested to incidents of which the mother had testified. The nun was not available for cross-examination and therefore the tribunal gave very little weight to her evidence. The Court noted that by section 68(3) of the *Immigration Act*, the Refugee Division is not bound by legal or technical rules of evidence and may base a decision on evidence considered credible and trustworthy. The suggestion that the affidavit of a patently respectable deponent as to facts within her knowledge should be discounted because, in the very nature of the process, the deponent was not available to be cross-examined, was wrong. The Refugee Division must not impose on itself or claimants evidentiary fetters of which Parliament has freed them.

The appeal was allowed, in part for this reason, and the decision of the Refugee Division set aside.

Aquino v. Canada (Minister of Employment & Immigration) (1992), 144 N.R. 315 (Fed. C.A.) — The appellant claimed to be a Convention refugee. The Convention Refugee Determination Division (CRDD) dismissed the appellant's claim and made adverse findings as to the appellant's credibility.

The appellant objected to the quality of the interpretation the interpreter provided during the hearing. The transcript indicated that the appellant had appeared to answer some questions without waiting for translation and the panel member interrupted the interpreter on several occasions to correct the translation. Further, the appellant's counsel did not object to the interpretation during the hearing. Accordingly, this objection to the quality of the interpretation was not a ground upon which the appeal could succeed.

The PIF form was not identified on the record nor entered as an exhibit, although it was clearly on the table at the hearing and referred to in some of the questions. It was the perceived inconsistencies between the PIF and the appellant's testimony which formed a basis for the finding that the appellant was not credible. These inconsistencies were not put to the appellant at the hearing.

The PIF is a document required to be filed by every Convention refugee claimant. It is among the material an adjudicator is required to file with the registry of the CRDD when a claim is referred there. It is not a document which may be judicially noticed or which any legislative provision deems to be evidence in a proceeding before the Division. Accordingly, the PIF cannot in the present circumstances be found to be "evidence adduced in the proceedings" within section 68(3). Thus, the CRDD erred in law in basing findings of credibility on perceived discrepancies between the PIF, which was not in evidence, and the appellant's *viva voce* evidence. The decision of the CRDD was set aside and the matter remitted for rehearing by a differently constituted panel.

Mahendran v. Canada (Minister of Employment & Immigration) (1991), 14 Imm. L.R. (2d) 30, 134 N.R. 316 (Fed. C.A.) — Members of the Refugee Division of the Immigration and Refugee Board are enabled to examine any person under oath. If a board member has problems with testimony, he or she is entitled to conduct questioning of the appellant in the proper discharge of his or her duties. The nature of the questioning, however, can be examined to determine whether there is merit to the submission that a member of the tribunal assumed the role of prosecutor and crossed the line between acceptable conduct and unacceptable conduct for members of the quasi-judicial body. The Court expressed concern at the lengthy nature of the cross examination in this case and noted that it would have been preferable for the board member to have left the main burden of questioning the appellant to the refugee hearing officer. There was, however, no basis for allowing an appeal from the Refugee Division decision that the appellant was not a convention refugee. A further objection was made about the admissibility of a photocopy of a telex. The Court noted that the scheme of the Act and Regulations leaves it to the tribunal to decide the weight which it will ascribe to any of the evidence before it. Here there was other cogent evidence which supported the Board's negative findings on credibility and this ground of appeal was for that reason also unsuccessful.

Section 68(4)

Bula v. Canada (Secretary of State) (June 19, 1996), Doc. A-329-94 (Fed. C.A.) — This appeal from a decision of the trial division dismissing an application for judicial review failed.

In the course of brief reasons, the Court approved of the trial judge's comment to the effect that it was of the very essence of the role of the tribunal that it hear witnesses to rule on their credibility. The Court thought it was not only normal but inevitable that in doing so members would be influenced by the experience that they may have acquired in the exercise of their duty. As long as the members were relying only on their experience and not on specific information, subsections (4) and (5) of section 68 were not engaged.

Appau v. Canada (Minister of Employment & Immigration) (1995), 91 F.T.R. 225 — The applicant, a citizen of Ghana, sought to review a negative decision of the CRDD. In the course of its decision the CRDD panel stated that it was aware of the meticulous scrutiny given travel documents by Swiss security and noted that it did not believe that the applicant would be successful in clearing this screening when travelling to and from Switzerland as the applicant had testified he did.

The CRDD was not entitled to rely on its alleged knowledge of procedures at Swiss border points or procedures on Swiss Air. The Court doubted that such knowledge could be described as "generally recognized facts" or "information or opinion that is within its specialized knowledge".

Barrera v. Canada (Minister of Employment & Immigration) (November 10, 1993), Doc. A-1552-92 (Fed. T.D.) — For digest, see section 68 *Subsection (3), supra.*

Aquino v. Canada (Minister of Employment & Immigration) (1992), 144 N.R. 315 (Fed. C.A.) — For digest, see section 68, subheading *Subsection (3), supra.*

Tung v. Canada (Minister of Employment & Immigration) (1991), 124 N.R. 388 (Fed. C.A.) — This was an appeal from the Refugee Division of the Immigration and Refugee Board. While there is no statutory requirement for keeping a complete record of the proceedings before the Refugee Division, the Board has a policy of recording those proceedings on tape and making a full transcript available for possible use on an appeal. The Board's policy was not implemented in this case and disadvantage accrued to the appellant. It is no answer to say that the recording equipment broke down through no fault of the Board's. The quality of interpretation was found wanting. The appellant was entitled, through the interpreter, to tell the story of his fear in his own language, as well as he might have done had he been able to communicate to the Board in the English language (the language of this hearing). The failure to provide an adequate interpreter prejudiced the appellant in the proceedings before the Refugee Division and before the Court of Appeal, who were required to review important aspects of the Board's decision on a deficient record.

The Refugee Division found that the appellant's failure to claim "asylum" in any of the countries he visited en route to Canada was inconsistent with the conduct of a person who fears for his life. There was no evidence that any of the countries the appellant visited had ratified the 1951 U.N. convention and the 1967 protocol or that they had adopted laws implementing those instruments. The Board is authorized under section 68(2) to take notice of any facts that may be judicially noticed. It is wrong for the Board to speculate that refugee protection was available in the countries that the appellant stopped in (Hong Kong, Thailand, Bolivia and Peru). The Court noted that the appellant was at all times in transit to Canada and had already decided to claim refugee status after he arrived here. The Court noted that the Board is normally required to give detailed reasons for disbelieving a claimant. The absence of such reasons may suggest that the Board had no overriding concern with the appellant's credibility. There was no expressed or implied rejection of the appellant's credibility as a witness on his own behalf. The Refugee Division decision betrayed a possible confusion as to the proper test. The Refugee Division members said that they were not convinced that the motivation behind the client fleeing China was fear. The Court noted that the issue at this point was the well-foundedness of the appellant's fear and that the words used introduced the subjective element into a test, which at that stage was entirely objective.

Section 68(5)

Bula v. Canada (Secretary of State) (June 19, 1996), Doc. A-329-94 (Fed. C.A.) — This appeal from a decision of the trial division dismissing an application for judicial review failed.

In the course of brief reasons, the Court approved of the trial judge's comment to the effect that it was of the very essence of the role of the tribunal that it hear witnesses to rule on their credibility. The Court thought it was not only normal but inevitable that in doing so members would be influenced by the experience that they may have acquired in the exercise of their duty. As long as the members were relying only on their experience and not on specific information, subsections (4) and (5) of section 68 were not engaged.

Zas Garcia v. Canada (Minister of Employment & Immigration) (1994), 75 F.T.R. 220 — The applicant sought judicial review of a negative decision of the Refugee Division. The applicant based his claim to status on a reasonable fear of persecution because of his political opinion and membership in a particular social group. During the applicant's testimony, the question of a change of circumstances in El Salvador was raised, and several documents were introduced which referred to the peace accords between the guerrilla forces and the government authorities. Counsel for the applicant stated her intention to make submissions on this point during argument, which she did. When the evidence had been completed and argument heard, the members of the Refugee Division withdrew for about thirty minutes, planning to render a decision the same day. Subsequent to the adjournment, the tribunal returned and entered a document, which it had obtained, as an exhibit. By seeking out documents when the hearing was over and argument had been heard and entering this exhibit in evidence without giving the applicant an opportunity to make submissions, the Refugee Division acted contrary to the mandatory provisions of sections 68(5) and 69.1(5).

Salinas v. Canada (Minister of Employment & Immigration), 17 Imm. L.R. (2d) 118, 6 Admin. L.R. (2d) 154, 93 D.L.R. (4th) 631, 142 N.R. 211, [1992] 3 F.C. 247, 57 F.T.R. 159n (Fed. C.A.) — This was an appeal from an order of the Trial Division whereby a decision of the Refugee Division to reconvene a hearing into the respondent's claim for refugee status was quashed and the Refugee Division ordered to render a decision on the basis of the evidence before it. The basis of the respondent's claim was her fear of persecution by agents of the state of Panama, which was headed by General Noriega. Some time after the conclusion of the respondent's hearing, but before a decision was rendered, the political situation in Panama changed. The presiding member of the panel notified the respondent that the hearing would be reconvened for the purpose of hearing evidence on these recent changes.

The appeal was allowed. The Refugee Division did not exceed its jurisdiction in reconvening the hearing. Section 68 endows the Refugee Division with powers and duties in relation to any proceedings before it. The distinction has been drawn by Parliament between "proceedings" and a "hearing" before the Refugee Division. The hearing is to be conducted in a manner required by section 69.1. The "hearing" is a step in any proceedings. "Proceedings" is a wider term encompassing the entire matter before the Refugee Division including the hearing itself. The Minister, pursuant to section 69.2(1), is able to initiate proceedings for a determination whether any person who was determined to be a Convention refugee has ceased to be so. The Court found force in the argument that evidence as to the change of conditions is better addressed in the same proceedings rather than in new proceedings initiated by the Minister subsequent to the Refugee Division's determination.

The Refugee Division was not *functus officio*. It had yet to make a determination of the claim. Until it did, the proceedings were pending and finality had not been reached. In order to arrive at its decision, the Refugee Division could exercise the power conferred by the statute, provided it did so properly by giving the respondent an opportunity to be heard at the reconvened hearing. An inquiry into any change of conditions in the appellant's homeland comes within the general mandate of the Refugee Division in determining the claim.

In *Lawal v. Canada (Minister of Employment & Immigration)*, [1991] 2 F.C. 404, the Court ruled that the only way for the Refugee Division, after the end of a hearing but before decision, to consider new evidence beyond that of which it might take judicial notice was by reopening the hearing. The Court's decision in *Longia v. Canada (Minister of Employment & Immigration)*, [1990] 3 F.C. 288, applies only where the Refugee Division has already reached a decision.

The appeal was allowed. The order of the Trial Division was set aside and the respondent's claim for refugee status was referred back to the Refugee Division for a continuation of the reconvened hearing.

68.1 Power of refugee hearing officer — A refugee hearing officer who is appointed under subsection 64(3) may, in accordance with rules made under subsection 65(1) governing the activities of the Refugee Division, call and question any person who claims to be a Convention refugee and any other witnesses, present documents and make representations.

1992, c. 49, s. 58.

69. (1) Right to counsel — In any proceedings before the Refugee Division, the Minister may be represented at the proceedings by counsel or an agent and the person who is the subject of the proceedings may, at that person's own expense, be represented by a barrister or solicitor or other counsel.

(2) Confidentiality — Subject to subsections (3) and (3.1), proceedings before the Refugee Division shall be held in the presence of the person who is the subject of the proceedings, wherever practicable, and be conducted *in camera* or, if an application therefor is made, in public.

(3) Idem — Where the Refugee Division is satisfied that there is a serious possibility that the life, liberty or security of any person would be endangered by reason of any of its proceedings being held in public, it may, on application therefor, take such measures and make such order as it considers necessary to ensure the confidentiality of the proceedings.

(3.1) Idem — Where the Refugee Division considers it appropriate to do so, it may take such measures and make such order as it considers necessary to ensure the confidentiality of any hearing held in respect of any application referred to in subsection (3).

(3.2) United nations high commissioner for refugees — Notwithstanding subsection (2) or any measure taken or order made pursuant to subsection (3) or (3.1), the Refugee Division shall allow any representative or agent of the United Nations High Commissioner for Refugees to attend any proceedings before it as an observer.

(4) Representation — Where a person who is the subject of proceedings before the Refugee Division is under eighteen years of age or is unable, in the opinion of the Division, to appreciate the nature of the proceedings, the Division shall designate another person to represent that person in the proceedings.

(5) Honorarium and expenses — A person who is designated pursuant to subsection (4) to represent a person in proceedings before the Refugee Division shall be paid such honorarium as is fixed by the Chairperson and such reasonable expenses as are incurred by the designated person in connection with the representation, unless the designated person is the parent or guardian of the person represented.

(6) Adjournments — The Refugee Division shall not adjourn any proceedings before it, unless it is satisfied that an adjournment would not unreasonably impede the proceedings.

(7) Presiding member where proceedings adjourned — Proceedings before the Refugee Division that are adjourned may be resumed before any member or mem-

bers of the Refugee Division other than the member or members who presided at the adjourned proceedings if the person who is the subject of the proceedings and the Minister, if taking part in the proceedings, consent thereto or if no substantive evidence was adduced before the adjournment.

R.S.C. 1985, c. 10 (2nd Supp.), s. 5; R.S.C. 1985, c. 28 (4th Supp.), s. 18; 1992, c. 49, s. 59.

Case Law

Section 69(1)

Adam v. Canada (Minister of Citizenship & Immigration) (1998), 60 C.C.R. (2d) 354, 16 F.T.R. 42 (Fed. T.D.) — A Post Claim Determination Officer has no discretion inherent or otherwise to extend the time limits for a PDRCC application.

The applicant had also suggested in this case that sections 11.4(2)(b) and 11.4(3)(b) were in violation of section 7 of the Charter of Rights. The applicant was found not to have exhausted his legislative avenues of recourse by making an H&C application prior to making this argument and therefore was found not to be able to establish a Charter breach.

Finally, the applicant complained about the inadequacy of her counsel. The age of the applicant, her particular vulnerability without parents to guide her and her reliance on friends, relatives and her lawyer for advice made the applicant an unusual and particularly sympathetic case. However, this was not that type of "extraordinary case that would necessitate overturning the decision to the inadequacy of counsel."

Adade v. Canada (Minister of Employment & Immigration) (1994), 27 Imm. L.R. (2d) 79 (Fed. T.D.) — A panel of the CRDD reached a negative decision with respect to the applicant's refugee claim by relying on a forensic report that was filed months after the hearing. The applicant did not receive a copy of the report until his appeal was filed, however, his previous counsel had received it and had filed a brief submission with the Board thereafter. While the applicant's counsel may have been negligent in not discussing the report with his client, the law requires that it must be apparent to the Board that there is a failure on the part of the applicant's counsel to adequately represent the applicant. The Board had no way of knowing that the applicant may have had an explanation for one matter in the forensic report.

Jouzichin v. Canada (Minister of Citizenship & Immigration) (December 6, 1994), Doc. IMM-1686-94 (Fed. T.D.) — In dealing with the refusal of a request for an adjournment the Court noted that the general rule is that counsel's conduct is not separate from the client's. Counsel is acting as agent for the client and the client must bear the consequences of having hired poor counsel. The fact that counsel came and said that he was not prepared was not a good reason for seeking an adjournment.

Castroman v. Canada (Secretary of State) (1994), 81 F.T.R. 227, 27 Imm. L.R. (2d) 129 — The applicant sought judicial review of a negative decision of the CRDD. During the hearing the applicant was represented by counsel. After counsel had finished examining the applicant, the Refugee Hearing Officer (RHO) commenced her examination. The RHO questioned why the evidence indicating that a particular person was persecuting the applicant was not contained in the personal information form (PIF). Counsel for the applicant objected to that on the basis that the line of questioning was getting into an area of solicitor-client privilege. The Board allowed the questions and then counsel withdrew from the case. The PIF is a form the Immigration and Refugee Board requires. The object of the form is to provide the claimant with an opportunity to tell his or her story early in the process. One of the primary ways that the Board tests a claimant's credibility is by comparing the PIF with the claimant's oral testimony. It is not proper for a lawyer to interfere with the RHO or a member's questioning of the claimant with respect to his or her PIF. The lawyer cannot attempt to shield the client from questioning about why certain matters were omitted from the PIF.

Counsel is not at liberty to leave a client in the middle of a case simply because he or she does not agree with the ruling of the administrative tribunal. Counsel is entitled to make objections to rulings and to take whatever procedings are required at the conclusion of the case to have the matter reviewed.

The Board in this case completed the hearing without new counsel being appointed. Not all decisions to proceed without providing the applicant the benefit of counsel will result in reviewable error. In this case though, the Board denied the applicant the right of re-examination after completion of cross-examination, thus the applicant had no opportunity to explain any of his answers given in cross-examination. Further, the Board misled the applicant into thinking he had no right of re-examination by stating that the next stage of the hearing was to receive documentary evidence.

The criteria for determining whether the Board has properly exercised its discretion to disallow counsel was set out in *Howard v. Stony Mountain Institution, Presiding Officer of Inmate Disciplinary Ct.* (1984), 19 D.L.R. (4th) 502 (Fed. C.A.). Those criteria are:

1. The seriousness of the charge and of the potential penalty;
2. whether any points of law are likely to arise;
3. the capacity of a particular person to present his own case;
4. procedural difficulties;
5. the need for reasonable speed in making the adjudication;
6. the need for fairness as between prisoners and as between prisoners and prison officers.

Obviously, the latter category has no relevance in immigration proceedings. On the facts of this case there was a denial of natural justice and the application for judicial review was allowed.

Section 69(2)

Phillip v. Canada (Minister of Citizenship & Immigration) (1998), 47 Imm. L.R. (2d) 252, 159 F.T.R. 49 (Fed. T.D.) — At the commencement of the hearing, a panel of the CRDD ordered the applicant to leave the hearing room with her youngest child so that questions could be asked of her other children, 5 and 8 years of age, in her absence. After the questions were asked, the applicant was invited back into the hearing room and provided with a very brief summary of the questions asked of the children.

The conduct of the panel contravened subsection 69(2) of the *Immigration Act*. This was not a situation in which the panel was saved because there was no objection. The requirement of presence of the parties under subsection 69(2) was mandatory.

The applicant was not designated as the representative of the infant children until after she had been excluded, the children examined in her absence, and she had been invited back into the hearing. A late designation pursuant to subsection 69(4) may not invalidate all proceedings in all circumstances; however, it is proper practice that the designation take place at the outset in order to avoid the risk of spoiling the proceedings.

The usual formalities when young children are asked to give evidence were not adhered to in this case. If the evidence is to have any prohibitive value, a tribunal must establish that the children understand right from wrong, the importance of telling the truth, and the consequences of not telling the truth. The application was allowed and the matter remitted to a differently constituted panel.

Section 69(4)

Espinoza v. Canada (Minister of Citizenship & Immigration), [1999] 3 F.C. 73 (Fed. T.D.) — The applicant sought to review a negative decision of the CRDD. The applicant was a citizen of El Salvador who married a citizen of Mexico. They had three children who were the minor applicants in this application. The applicant claimed a fear of persecution in El Salvador and Mexico. His wife and children feared persecution in Mexico only. On the review, the applicant argued that he did not understand the meaning or the legal consequences of being the children's designated representative and that the Board should have ensured that he did before designating him as such.

Subsection 69(4) requires that the refugee division designate a representative where a person, whether under 18 or not, is unable to appreciate the nature of the proceedings. This subsection imposes upon the Board a duty to assess whether the person to be designated appreciates the nature of the proceedings. This is particularly so in the case of a designated representative for children. The role of a parent acting as a designated representative is not that of a legal representative. The Board was or should have been aware that the particular facts of this case could have given rise to the possibility that one of the parent's claims would be rejected which would affect the outcome of the children's claim. The children, through their designated representative, should have been informed that their claim could be affected by the outcome of their designated representative's claims. Thus there was a denial of natural justice with respect to the children.

Phillip v. Canada (Minister of Citizenship & Immigration) (1998), 47 Imm. L.R. (2d) 252, 159 F.T.R. 49 (Fed. T.D.) — For digest, see section 69(2), *supra*.

Section 69(5)

Uppal v. Canada (Secretary of State) (1994), 72 F.T.R. 207 — The applicant was a Sikh from the Punjab and a citizen of India who had made a claim for refugee status. The applicant sought to quash the decision, in part on the basis that he was not told by the Refugee Division that his counsel was not a barrister or solicitor. There is no absolute right to legal representation in matters before the Board. The applicant was represented throughout by an immigration consultant. No significant issue was taken with the nature of the representation provided. The applicant filed an affidavit expressing displeasure with the fact that his consultant was not a lawyer who could represent him on his appeal. Nevertheless, the applicant was clearly represented by counsel within the meaning of the *Immigration Act*.

The application for judicial review was dismissed.

Section 69(7)

Hernandez v. Canada (Minister of Employment & Immigration) (1993), 162 N.R. 391 (Fed. C.A.) — The appellant's hearing began in October, 1989. The Refugee Division received the pertinent documentary evidence, including the appellant's personal information form (PIF). The appellant was sworn and attested to corrections to the PIF. A question arose as to why this claim was not being processed under the *Refugee Claimants Designated Class Regulations* and the hearing was adjourned. A differently constituted panel was present when the hearing reconvened. The appellant refused to consent and objected to the matter proceeding. The panel decided to proceed *de novo*. The documentary evidence was introduced afresh. Section 69(7) governs the resumption or continuation of a hearing. It does not preclude the constitution of a hearing *de novo*. Had the panel, in the face of the appellant's objection, simply carried on from the point of the adjournment, it would have run afoul of section 69(7). It did not and accordingly there was no merit in the appeal.

69.1 (1) Hearing into refugee claims — Subject to subsection (2), where a person's claim to be a Convention refugee is referred to the Refugee Division pursuant to section 46.02 or 46.03, the Division shall, as soon as practicable, commence a hearing into the claim.

(2) Idem — Where a person's claim to be a Convention refugee is referred to the Refugee Division pursuant to section 46.02 or 46.03, the Division shall, if the Minister so requests in writing at the time of the referral, provide the Minister with the information referred to in subsection 46.03(2) and, as soon as is practicable after the expiration of the period referred to in subsection (7.1), commence a hearing into the claim.

(3) Notice of hearing — The Refugee Division shall notify the person who claims to be a Convention refugee and the Minister in writing of the time and place set for the hearing into the claim.

(4) [Repealed 1992, c. 49, s. 60.]

(5) Opportunity to be heard — At the hearing into a person's claim to be a Convention refugee, the Refugee Division

(a) shall give

(i) the person a reasonable opportunity to present evidence, question witnesses and make representations, and

(ii) the Minister a reasonable opportunity to present evidence and, if the Minister notifies the Refugee Division that the Minister is of the opinion that matters involving section E or F of Article 1 of the Convention or subsection 2(2) of this Act are raised by the claim, to question the person making the claim and other witnesses and make representations; and

(b) may, if it considers it appropriate to do so, give the Minister a reasonable opportunity to question the person making the claim and any other witnesses and to make representations concerning the claim.

(6) Abandonment of claim — Where a person who claims to be a Convention refugee

(a) fails to appear at the time and place set by the Refugee Division for the hearing into the claim,

(b) fails to provide the Refugee Division with the information referred to in subsection 46.03(2), or

(c) in the opinion of the Division, is otherwise in default in the prosecution of the claim,

the Refugee Division may, after giving the person a reasonable opportunity to be heard, declare the claim to have been abandoned and, where it does so, the Refugee Division shall send a written notice of its decision to the person and to the Minister.

(7) Quorum — Subject to subsection (8), two members constitute a quorum of the Refugee Division for the purposes of a hearing under this section.

(7.1) **Acceptance of claim without hearing** — Notwithstanding subsections (1) and (2), where the Minister does not, at any time within the period prescribed by rules made under subsection 65(1), notify the Refugee Division that the Minister intends to participate in accordance with subsection (5) at any hearing into a person's claim to be a Convention refugee, a member of the Refugee Division may, in accordance with any rules made under paragraph 65(1)(*d*), determine that the person is a Convention refugee without a hearing into the matter.

(8) **Exception** — One member of the Refugee Division may hear and determine a claim under this section if the person making the claim consents thereto, and the provisions of this Part apply in respect of a member so acting as they apply in respect of the Refugee Division, and the disposition of the claim by the member shall be deemed to be the disposition of the Refugee Division.

(9) **Decision** — The Refugee Division shall determine whether or not the person referred to in subsection (1) is a Convention refugee and shall render its decision as soon as possible after completion of the hearing and send a written notice of the decision to the person and to the Minister.

(9.1) **Where no credible basis for claim** — If each member of the Refugee Division hearing a claim is of the opinion that the person making the claim is not a Convention refugee and is of the opinion that there was no credible or trustworthy evidence on which that member could have determined that the person was a Convention refugee, the decision on the claim shall state that there was no credible basis for the claim.

(10) **Split decision** — Subject to subsection (10.1), in the event of a split decision, the decision favourable to the person who claims to be a Convention refugee shall be deemed to be the decision of the Refugee Division.

(10.1) **Idem** — Where, with respect to any person who claims to be a Convention refugee, both members of the Refugee Division hearing the claim are satisfied

(a) that there are reasonable grounds to believe that the person, without valid reason, has destroyed or disposed of identity documents that were in the person's possession,

(b) that the person has, since making the claim, visited the country that the person claims to have left, or outside of which the person claims to have remained, by reason of fear of persecution, or

(c) that the country that the person claims to have left, or outside of which the person claims to have remained, by reason of fear of persecution is a country that is prescribed under paragraph 114(1)(s.1) to be a country that respects human rights,

then, in the event of a split decision on the claim, the decision not favourable to the person shall be deemed to be the decision of the Refugee Division.

(11) **Written reasons** — The Refugee Division may give written reasons for its decision on a claim, except that

(a) if the decision is against the person making the claim, the Division shall, with the written notice of the decision referred to in subsection (9), give written reasons with the decision; and

(b) if the Minister or the person making the claim requests written reasons within ten days after the day on which the Minister or the person is notified of the decision, the Division shall forthwith give written reasons.

(12) If authority to proceed under Extradition Act — If an authority to proceed has been issued under section 15 of the *Extradition Act* with respect to a person for an offence under Canadian law that is punishable under an Act of Parliament by a maximum term of imprisonment of 10 years or more, a hearing under subsection (1) or (2) shall not be commenced with respect to the person, or if commenced, shall be adjourned, until the final decision under that Act with respect to the discharge or surrender of the person has been made.

(13) When person discharged under Extradition Act — If the person is finally discharged under the *Extradition Act*, the hearing may be commenced or continued, or the Refugee Division may proceed, as though there had not been any proceedings under the *Extradition Act*.

(14) When person ordered surrendered under Extradition Act — If the person is ordered surrendered by the Minister of Justice under the *Extradition Act* and the offence for which the person was committed by the judge under section 29 of that Act is punishable under an Act of Parliament by a maximum term of imprisonment of 10 years or more, the order of surrender is deemed to be a decision by the Refugee Division that the person is not a Convention refugee because of paragraph (b) of Section F of its Article 1, except that no appeal or judicial review of the decision shall be permitted except to the extent that a judicial review of the order of surrender is provided for under the *Extradition Act*.

(15) If no claim made before Extradition Act order — For greater certainty, if the person has not made a claim under section 44 before the order of surrender referred to in subsection (14), the person may not do so before the surrender.

R.S.C. 1985, c. 28 (4th Supp.), s. 18; 1992, c. 49, s. 60; 1999, c. 18, s. 96

Case Law

Section 69.1(2)

Canada (Secretary of State) v. Mostameh (1994), 84 F.T.R. 13, (sub nom. *Canada (Secrétaire d'Etat) v. Mostameh)* (Fed. T.D.) — The Minister brought this application. The respondent's case was referred to the Refugee Division on February 17, 1993, and the request for information by the Minister was not made until March 18, 1993.

The Refugee Division may determine that a person is a Convention refugee without holding a hearing if the Minister does not notify the Division within the period specified by the rules that he intends to participate in the hearing. Section 8(2)(b) provides that a member may determine that a person is a Convention refugee without a hearing where the Minister has not requested information under section 69.1(2) during the 28 day period immediately after the day on which the claim is referred to the Refugee Division. In this case the Refugee Division was entitled to confer refugee status on the claimant on April 21, 1993, a date compatible with the 28 day deadline specified in section 8(2)(b). The deadlines in this case are specified by law and it must be assumed that the Minister was aware of them.

There is a significant difference between the nature of the Minister's rights and those of the claimant. The claimant has an established right to participate pursuant to the guarantees made by section 7 of the *Charter of Rights*. The Minister, on the other hand, cannot argue that the right to life, liberty or security of the person has been infringed if the deadlines are strictly enforced. If the Minister intends to intervene it has a duty to notify the Division within the specified deadline, and if through negligence it fails to do so, its right to participate is lost.

Section 69.1(5)

Tambwe-Lubemba v. Canada (Minister of Citizenship & Immigration) (April 15, 1999), Doc. IMM-1979-98 (Fed. T.D.) — The applicants sought to review a negative decision of a panel of the CRDD which took place on January 19, 1998. The panel's decision is dated March 13, 1998. The applicant's counsel shortly after that date, was told erroneously by an employee of the Board that the decision had not yet been given. The applicant's counsel then delivered to the Board by hand, on March 25, 1998, a document which contained information with respect to the risk that the applicant maintained he was exposed to if returned home to the Congo. The applicant received a notice of decision dated April 3, 1998. The Board had no obligation to consider the additional evidence after it had signed its reasons dated March 13, 1998. The Board was *functus*; there was no request to re-open the hearing. Accordingly, the application for judicial review was set aside.

Kouama v. Canada (Ministre de la Citoyenneté & de l'Immigration) (1998), 160 F.T.R. 122 (Fed. T.D.) — This is an application to review a negative decision of the CRDD. The applicant was from the Congo. He testified that he had experienced acts of persecution at the hands of one of the military militias functioning in the Congo in 1993 and 1994. In the case at bar, the hearing lasted only 20 minutes. This alone was not a sufficient reason to conclude that justice had been denied. The Refugee Board controls its own process and the time allocated for each hearing. The Board has the necessary discretion and expertise to estimate the time required for dealing with cases. The facts were relatively straightforward, and the record showed that the applicant and his counsel did not object to the length of the hearing. The application for judicial review was dismissed.

Del Moral v. Canada (Minister of Citizenship & Immigration) (1998), 46 Imm. L.R. (2d) 98 (Fed. T.D.) — The applicants sought to review a negative decision of the CRDD. Counsel who represented the applicants before the trial division challenged the panel's decision on the ground that it showed bias against the applicants, in particular, and all applicants from Mexico in general. The courts have clearly established that a party reasonably apprehensive of bias on the part of a tribunal must allege a violation of natural justice at the earliest practicable opportunity. The application for judicial review was dismissed.

Kuslitsky v. Canada (Ministre de la Citoyenneté & de l'Immigration) (1998), 148 F.T.R. 136 (Fed. T.D.) — The applicants who are citizens of Israel, claimed Convention refugee status alleging fear by reason of their nationality. The applicants based their allegation of persecution on the fact that the wife is recognized in Israel as being of Russian nationality. The tribunal wanted to see the wife's Israeli identity card, and the wife replied that she had lost that document when there was a fire at their home. The tribunal sought confirmation of the wife's nationality from the Israeli Consulate in Montreal and received a reply from the consulate shortly after the hearing indicating that the wife was of Jewish nationality. Based on that document, a copy of which was sent to the applicants, the tribunal decided in their absence that they were not Convention refugees.

The procedure followed was not acceptable. The information requested from the Israeli consulate and obtained in the absence of the parties should not have been considered to be final and conclusive. The tribunal ought to have reopened the hearing to enable the applicants to consider and refute the new evidence or even to cross-examine the author of the document in question.

Ganji v. Canada (Minister of Citizenship & Immigration) (1997), 40 Imm. L.R. (2d) 95, 135 F.T.R. 283 (Fed. T.D.) — The applicants sought to review a negative decision of the CRDD. In this case, the CRDD seized control of the applicants' case, ordered that one of the children who was unrepresented testify, and itself conducted her examination. All of the foregoing was done to the clear distress of the principal applicant and without providing her an opportunity to first testify. Counsel for the principal applicant, however, did not object to what was taking place.

On the facts of this case, it must have been apparent to members of the CRDD that the course of proceeding they adopted took the applicants' case completely out of their hands without any notice and without any support to them from their counsel. The CRDD had an obligation in the circumstances in accordance with its responsibility to act fairly to ensure that the applicants had an opportunity to meet with their counsel and to reassume control of their case. In the absence of any evidence that the CRDD endeavoured to provide such an opportunity the decision of the CRDD was set aside.

Xhelilaj v. Canada (Minister of Citizenship & Immigration) (1997), 39 Imm. L.R. (2d) 47, 132 F.T.R. 161 (Fed. T.D.) — This was an application to review a negative decision of the CRDD. Throughout the hearing there were complaints by the applicants and their counsel about the quality of interpretation. The first two interpreters were not speaking the same dialect as the applicants. The third interpreter on the third day appeared to have a better comprehension of the evidence of the applicants.

Section 14 of the *Charter of Rights* stipulates that a party to, or a witness in any proceeding who does not understand or speak the language has the right to the assistance of an interpreter. The quality of the interpretation must meet at least these five criteria: continuity, precision, impartiality, competency and contemporaneousness. The interpretation of testimony should be as good as — no better and no worse than — the testimony that the applicant would give if the source language were the language of the Court.

A perusal of the transcript at the hearing coupled with the fact that three different interpreters had to be called in and the fact that the board had to carry out audits of the work of two of the interpreters, indicate that the quality of the translation did not meet the standards required. Accordingly, the application for judicial review was allowed.

Siad v. Canada (Secretary of State) (1996), 36 Imm. L.R. (2d) 1, [1997] 1 F.C. 608, 206 N.R. 127, 123 F.T.R. 79 (note) (Fed. C.A.); leave to appeal to S.C.C. refused (1997), 223 N.R. 70 (note) (S.C.C.) — The respondent was found to have a well-founded fear of persecution if returned to Somalia. He was also excluded from refugee protection because there were serious reasons for considering that he had committed crimes against humanity, and that he was guilty of acts contrary to the purposes and principles of the United Nations. The finding of exclusion depended upon the tribunal's finding of fact that during the 1980's the respondent had served as governor of a prison in Somalia which was used to torture, abuse and kill political prisoners. The respondent denied that he had ever served in a position of authority at the prison, although he admitted that his father had had him imprisoned there for 18 months during the 1970s.

The factual determination that the respondent had served as governor was based upon the evidence of three persons. Two lay witnesses, who provided affidavits swearing that they had worked near the prison and had seen the respondent in a position of authority there and knew that he was a governor and a report of a professor who was an expert in Somali history and who taught at Rutgers University.

Five days before the respondent's hearing was scheduled to commence, the Minister's representative informed the respondent's counsel that he would be calling two witnesses who would testify as to the respondent's role as governor of the prison. The next day the respondent's counsel requested the names of the witnesses and the evidence that they were expected to give. That same day the Ministers representative telephoned the respondent's counsel and advised him of the names of the witnesses, the period to be covered by their evidence, places of work in Somalia, the fact that they would testify that the respondent had been governor of the prison, that one of them had had official dealings at the prison, and that both had personal knowledge of the respondent's position at the prison. Respondent's counsel made no further disclosure requests until the hearing. The hearing did not proceed as scheduled but was adjourned due to the respondent's ill health.

At the hearing, counsel learned that the lay witnesses had been accepted as convention refugees and demanded disclosure of their personal information forms. This request was denied. On the second day, counsel requested disclosure of all of the information that had been obtained in the investigation of the respondent's claim and based his request on *R. v. Stinchcombe*, [1991] 3 S.C.R. 326 (S.C.C.).

With respect to the report of the professor at Rutgers University the Minister's representative provided copies to the respondent and invited counsel to contact him if he had any questions. The only response of the respondent's counsel was to request a copy of the letter by which the Minister had requested the report. Counsel made no request and raised no objections regarding the report until the commencement of the hearing when he objected to the admission of the report unless he could cross-examine the author. Cross-examination was denied by the tribunal.

A high standard of natural justice applies in cases such as this one where the Minister takes an adversarial position in relation to refugee claimants. Section 69.1(5) of the *Immigration Act*, requires that the tribunal afford the claimant a reasonable opportunity to present evidence, cross examine witnesses and make representations, although Stinchcombe, a criminal case does not apply directly in the immigration context it is instructive.

In the context of this case, the Minister's disclosure obligation was satisfied. More than a month before the hearing the Minister's representative provided to the respondent's counsel a summary of the anticipated evidence of his witnesses over the telephone; the testimony of the witnesses ultimately conformed to this summary. If counsel considered the disclosure inadequate he should have objected to it before the hearing began as he had ample opportunity to do. In criminal, as well as civil proceedings the obligation to disclose arises only upon the request of opposing counsel. The tribunal does not owe an independent duty to require disclosure where counsel neglects to request it. If the Minister fails to comply with his disclosure obligation it is reasonable to expect the claimant's counsel to object in a timely manner and to draw this failure to the attention of the tribunal at the earliest opportunity. Counsel's failure to do so is an important factor in determining whether a new hearing should be ordered. Counsel for the respondent was dilatory in seeking disclosure and then sought to delay the proceedings with an 11th hour disclosure request. While the last minute disclosure request was denied, counsel was afforded ample opportunity to cross examine the witnesses with regard to their work in Somalia and their knowledge of the claimant and he did so. The opportunity afforded to question the witnesses was reasonable.

A tribunal is required by subsection 68(2) to conduct hearings fairly and expeditiously. The presiding judge in the trial division erred when he held that the professor's report was inadmissable. This decision was contrary to section 68(3) of the *Immigration Act*, which relieves the tribunal of the legal and technical rules of evidence which would bind the courts. The professor's report was relevant to the allegations against the respondent and the tribunal was entitled to admit the report if it considered it to be credible and trustworthy in the circumstances. The report was to be distinguished from situations where immigration officials had alleged in written statements that they had heard the claimant make damaging statements or admissions which the claimant denied having made. The professor's report does not allege any prior statements by the claimant, rather it describes the claimant's role in Somalia on the basis of this professor's expert knowledge of the Somalia political situation and his interview with informants. Further, the admission of the evidence was not unfair in the circumstances, because counsel was afforded every opportunity to raise objections to its submission before the hearing, to request cross-examination before the hearing, to call rebuttal evidence and to make submissions as to the weight the tribunal should attach to it.

Accordingly, the appeal was allowed and the decision of the trial division set aside.

Zaroud v. Canada (Secretary of State) (1996), 45 Admin. L.R. (2d) 318 (Fed. T.D.) — This was an application to review of negative decision of the CRDD.

The applicant, a citizen of Algeria, came to Canada in 1989 and made a claim for refugee status. The panel which heard that claim concluded that the applicant was not credible. After the decision was rendered the applicant returned to Algeria, where according to the applicant, he was again a subject of threats, which resulted in the applicant and his wife and children leaving Algeria and coming to Canada and making claim for refugee status a second time. At the second hearing one of the members of the panel, was the same person who had been a member of the panel which had dismissed the earlier claim. This fact was the basis for the application for judicial review on a ground that there was a reasonable fear of bias. This argument was rejected. At the time, the second hearing took place counsel for the applicant did not ask the board member to withdraw, rather counsel asked the board member if the board member would be able to hear and decide the claim impartially. The board member indicated in response to this question that he would be able to decide the matter impartially.

Counsel for the applicant should have clearly indicated to the panel that the applicant had a fear of bias, and should have asked the member to withdraw. The applicant having made no such objection could not raise the matter on an application for judicial review.

Lezcano v. Canada (Minister of Citizenship & Immigration) (January 5, 1996), Doc. A-633-92 (Fed. T.D.) — The applicant sought to review a negative decision of a panel of the IRB. At the conclusion of the hearing the applicant's counsel and the Refugee Hearing Officer (RHO) agreed to make their submissions in writing. It was agreed that the officer would file her submissions first so that counsel could exercise his right of reply. Sometime later the Assistant Deputy Chairman of the Board wrote to counsel advising him that the submissions of the officer had not been received and that consequently the officer had waived her right to make submissions. Counsel was instructed to proceed with his own written submissions. Counsel wrote back pointing out that the applicant would be prejudiced by the absence of submissions by the officer and requested a reconvening of the hearing to allow him to appear and make his oral submissions before the panel. This request was refused. This matter should have been handled by the panel before whom it was agreed to file written submissions. Secondly, since the officer had reneged on the agreement, counsel for the applicant was no longer bound by it.

A requirement to submit written arguments after the hearing by itself does not constitute a denial of fairness, especially where both parties have agreed to it. But a change of the procedure agreed to by both parties, and imposed by an official who is not a member of the panel which heard the matter, does constitute denial of fairness.

Lin v. Canada (Minister of Citizenship & Immigration) (1995), 101 F.T.R. 192 — The applicant sought to overturn a negative decision of the CRDD. The applicant was interviewed at a port-of-entry on his arrival in Canada. The interview was conducted with the aid of an interpreter. The interviewing officer made notes of the interview which were read back to the applicant through the interview. The applicant was not invited to sign or initial the notes. A copy of the notes was made available to the applicant's counsel some 5 days before his hearing. The notes contain a story that differed in significant aspects from the events recounted in the applicant's PIF and in his oral testimony. The applicant sought to quash the decision on the basis of a denial of the opportunity to cross examine the author of the notes. Due to the fact that the applicant was given 5 days notice of the CRDD's intention to consider the notes, the applicant's failure to subpoena the author of the notes, and the interpreter, was fatal to the applicant's position. The onus was not on the CRDD to make those persons available for examination at the hearing.

Ousman v. Canada (Minister of Citizenship & Immigration) (1995), 95 F.T.R. 230 — The applicant unsuccessfully claimed refugee status. His first counsel was sent a package of documentary materials relating to Guyana. The applicant's first counsel withdrew his services when the applicant was unable to obtain legal aid and the applicant's new refugee hearing was scheduled on a peremptory basis. At this new hearing the applicant was given a copy of the package after the applicant stated at the hearing that he had not received it previously. The applicant, in the circumstances, did not have timely disclosure of the documentary package. It was unreasonable to expect that the applicant could have comprehended the volume of the material that was presented to him in a short time during the course of the second hearing. It would not have imposed a great hardship for the Board to adjourn the hearing once again and permit the applicant adequate time to consider the documentary evidence, or alternatively, the Board could have permitted the applicant to make written submissions concerning the documentary evidence after the conclusion of the hearing.

Notwithstanding the fact that the Court was of the view that the applicant had a weak claim, a new hearing was ordered with the Court relying on the decision of *Cardinal v. Kent Institution*, [1985] 2 S.C.R. 643 (S.C.C.) to the effect that the denial of a fair hearing must always render a decision invalid.

Nakhuda v. Canada (Minister of Citizenship & Immigration) (1995), 95 F.T.R. 225 — The applicant sought to overturn a negative decision of the CRDD on the basis that there was a failure to make clear to the applicant in a timely fashion before the hearing, the documentary evidence upon which the panel was going to rely, in particular the Standardized Country File and the Index to that file. The applicant was not represented at his hearing and maintained in an affidavit in support of his application for judicial review that he was therefore not given disclosure of the documentary evidence.

Where an applicant seeking refugee status appears without counsel, that is a factor that will affect the way in which the tribunal seeks to fairly discharge its responsibilities. The Refugee Division's practise of maintaining a Standard File of public documents about each of various countries at or through documentation centres, and entering an Index of those documents as evidence at the hearing, is consistent with principles of natural justice and fairness provided there is no indication of a refusal by the panel to disclose the documents included in the Standard File. Here, all the documentary evidence entered and considered by the tribunal was in the Standard Country File in the form of documents available from the public domain and collected by the Refugee Division. There was no documentary evidence prepared with particular reference to the applicant. Accordingly,the tribunal did not breach its obligation to follow a process of procedural fairness or violate the principles of natural justice. The transcript demonstrated that the tribunal was conscious of the fact that the applicant was representing himself and sought to ensure he understood the process and had a full opportunity to ask questions or make submissions. The applicant made no request for disclosure of the documentary evidence in advance of or at the hearing and presented no testimony or documentary evidence which did more than establish an expressed fear of persecution. Accordingly, the applicant could not object to the panel's reference to the Standard Country File in its decision. The application for judicial review was dismissed.

Arica v. Canada (Minister of Employment & Immigration) (1995), 182 N.R. 392 (Fed. C.A.), leave to appeal to S.C.C. refused (1995), 198 N.R. 239 (note) (S.C.C.) — The appellant was denied refugee status because there were serious reasons for considering that he had been involved in acts constituting crimes against humanity.

Under section 69.1(5) there is no obligation on the Minister to give notice to claimants of the former's intention to participate in the hearing. The purpose of the notice, which is directed solely at the Board, is to empower the Minister to question a claimant and other witnesses and to make representations, otherwise the Minister's participation is limited to the presentation of evidence.

Further the Board was not required to balance the nature of the crimes committed by the appellant against the fate that awaits him should he be returned to Peru. This was the finding of the Court in *Gonzalez v. Canada (Minister of Employment & Immigration)* (1994), 24 Imm. L.R. (2d) 229 (Fed. C.A.). Section 7 of the Charter, which was not argued in the Gonzalez case, does not alter the extant law. A decision in which it was found that the appellant was not entitled to claim refugee status. The exclusion of an individual from claiming such status does not, by itself, imply or lead to any positive act which may affect the life, liberty or security of the person.

Dong v. Canada (Minister of Employment & Immigration) (March 30, 1995), Doc. A-911-91 (Fed. T.D.) — The applicant is a citizen of the People's Republic of China who unsuccessfully claimed refugee status by reason of his political opinion and membership in a particular social group. The hearing of this matter was scheduled for a morning half day. Counsel, in accordance with what he understood to be the normal practise, scheduled some other matter for the afternoon. When the allotted half day had expired the CRDD offered counsel the opportunity to make oral representations. Counsel explained that he could not do so and requested an adjournment. The CRDD denied this request and offered counsel, in the alternative, an opportunity to make written submissions.

The CRDD did not fail to observe a principle of natural justice or procedural fairness. It offered the applicant, and his counsel, a reasonable opportunity to make representations at the applicant's hearing and in the presence of the applicant. The fact that counsel had so organized his schedule that he was unable to avail himself of the opportunity provided was not a problem of the CRDD's making. The CRDD is under the obligation to deal with all proceedings before it as informally and expeditiously as the circumstances permit. When counsel found himself unable to avail of that reasonable opportunity the CRDD offered the alternative of written submissions. There was no denial of natural justice or procedural fairness in the way the CRDD proceeded.

If the applicant had been successful in respect of an allegation of a failure to observe a principle of natural justice of procedural fairness or other procedure that the CRDD was required, by law, to observe, the application would have succeeded regardless of the merits of the substance of the CRDD's decision. It is not for the Court to deny a right to a fair hearing on the basis of speculation as to what the result might have been had there been a fair hearing.

Khan c. Canada (Solliciteur général) (1994), 110 F.T.R. 139 (C.F. (1re inst.)) — The applicant sought to review a negative decision of the CRDD. The applicant was a Pakistani national and claimed refugee status on account of a fear of persecution for his political opinion. The applicant's testimony was found to lack credibility. The panel noted as a premise in its reasons that there have been a number of claims by Pakistani nationals coming primarily from the province of Punjab who claim to have been persecuted because of their membership in the Pakistan People's Party. The panel noted that all of these claims were fabricated and that it had not yet found a single credible claimant.

The panel concluded its observation by saying that all of these claimants appear to have been exploited by agents.

Such comments, not being based on any documents in the record, and not discussed with the applicant during his examination, reflected a prejudice against Pakistani applicants and thus created a reasonable apprehension of bias with respect to the tribunal.

Canada (Secretary of State) v. Ilbeigi-Asli (1995), 92 F.T.R. 22 — The Secretary of State sought judicial review of a decision that the respondents were Convention refugees. Pursuant to section 69.1(5) the Minister sought an opportunity to be heard on the question of whether "the claimants are excluded from the Convention pursuant to section E of Article 1 of the U.N. Convention".

If a party wishes to have a matter considered by the Board it is essential that the party give some indication of the issue that they want the Board to consider. The Board had no inkling from the Minister's representative that he was interested in anything other than the question of exclusion. The Board, therefore, did not deny the Minister a reasonable opportunity to present evidence, to question persons making the claim and any other witnesses, or to make submissions. It is up to the parties who appear before the Board to ensure that all issues in which the parties have an interest, are raised. Accordingly, the application by the Minister was dismissed.

Begum v. Canada (Minister of Citizenship & Immigration) (1995), 92 F.T.R. 222 — The applicant is a 57 year old female Ahmadi from Pakistan who claimed refugee status on the basis of a well-founded fear of persecution by reason of her religion. A panel of the CRDD found that she was not a Convention refugee.

A law associate of the applicant's counsel discovered in the summer of 1991 that panel members in a case she was arguing had been exchanging derogatory notes about her during the course of the hearing. This exchange of notes had become public and the Board members in question had been asked to apologize. Counsel for the applicant had written a letter to *The Globe and Mail* criticizing the government's failure to have the Board members in question removed from their positions.

On the date of this hearing, counsel, who had written a letter to *The Globe and Mail*, learned that the presiding member was one of the persons about whom he had written a letter. Counsel made inquiries and determined that another panel was free to hear the matter and asked on the record, at the hearing, that the presiding member remove himself. This application was denied.

The Board's decision was set aside. Although a tribunal's decision will rarely be set aside on grounds of bias, in this type of situation in light of the past history between the Board member and counsel the Board's persistent refusal to provide an alternative panel might have been viewed by an ordinary person as creating a situation of impartiality and bias. The decision of the CRDD was set aside and the matter returned to a newly constituted panel.

Yao v. Canada (Minister of Employment & Immigration) (1995), 91 F.T.R. 212 — At the applicant's refugee determination hearing the Refugee Hearing Officer presented two sets of documents as exhibits. Notice that the first set of documents would be presented was provided to an earlier counsel but not to counsel representing the applicant at the hearing. No notice whatsoever had been given with respect to the second set of documents.

Counsel for the applicant had not inquired in advance of the hearing whether documentary evidence would be presented. At the opening counsel neither objected to the presentation of the documents as exhibits, nor requested an adjournment to allow him to effectively prepare in light of the documentary evidence. At the close of the hearing counsel requested time to prepare written argument, but did not cite as a reason that he needed time to consider and respond to the documentary evidence that he had not had an opportunity to review. In the absence of any expression of concern by the applicant's counsel throughout the hearing the Court was not prepared to conclude that there had been a denial of fairness in the production of the documents.

Tekyi v. Canada (Minister of Citizenship & Immigration) (1995), 28 Imm. L.R. (2d) 60, 90 F.T.R. 300 — The applicant sought to overturn a negative decision of the CRDD by alleging bias on the part of one of the panel members. The allegation of bias was not raised until after a negative decision was rendered. Generally, counsel has an obligation to raise an allegation of bias during the hearing. There was, however, no evidence that the applicant was aware of the grounds upon which the bias was alleged at the time of her hearing before the CRDD. Counsel before the Federal Court was not the same as counsel at the refugee hearing. Accordingly, there was no waiver by the applicant of her rights to raise the allegation of bias.

Johnpillai v. Canada (Secretary of State) (1995), 93 F.T.R. 288 — The applicant complained about the pre-filing with panel members of highly prejudicial notes before the commencement of the applicant's refugee hearing. The filing of these notes was expressly brought to the attention of counsel for the applicant by the Refugee Hearing Officer. It appeared that the notes had been filed in error because the hearing officer had given explicit instructions that the material not be pre-filed.

It is not a breach of natural justice for a decision-maker to be provided with information, including prejudicial information, personal to the applicant before an oral hearing, provided the applicant has an adequate opportunity to respond to that information. The provision of such information when an applicant does not consent, might lead to an aborted hearing if the panel subsequently concluded that the material was inadmissable and the panel decided it would prefer another panel to hear the claim.

Accordingly, the pre-filing of this prejudicial material was not a ground for complaint in this case and the application was dismissed.

Canada (Minister of Citizenship & Immigration) v. Patel (1995), 27 Imm. L.R. (2d) 4, 90 F.T.R. 234 — The Appeal Division determined that the adoption ceremony, by which the respondent adopted a female child, had not been proven. The Appeal Division stated that the issue to be decided was whether there had been an actual giving and taking with intent to transfer in compliance with the *Hindu Adoption and Maintenance Act*. Affidavit evidence filed on the judicial review application indicated that the Appeal Division had stated at the time of the arguing of the appeal that intent to transfer was not a relevant consideration and directed that no further cross-examination of the respondent take place in that matter. The transcript was not clear whether questioning had been cut off or whether counsel had simply halted this line of questioning since the Appeal Division indicated which authorities it would follow. The Court concluded that the curtailing of cross-examination had resulted in a breach of the rules of natural justice and following the case of *Cardinal v. Kent Institution,* [1985] 2 S.C.R. 643 (S.C.C.) held that the denial of a fair hearing must always render a decision invalid, whether or not it may appear to a reviewing Court that the hearing would have resulted in a different decision.

Li v. Canada (Minister of Citizenship & Immigration) (1995), 90 F.T.R. 151 — The applicant sought judicial review of a negative decision of the CRDD. The Board sent a package of documentary evidence to the applicant. The applicant submitted that the documents upon which the Board intended to rely should have been translated. The failure to translate documentary evidence does not constitute a breach of a principle of fundamental justice. The application for judicial review was dismissed.

Zaribaf v. Canada (Minister of Citizenship & Immigration) (1994), 85 F.T.R. 83 — The applicant sought to set aside a negative decision of the CRDD in part on the basis that there was a reasonable apprehension of bias. This apprehension was based on media coverage that had been given to a report prepared for the chairperson of the IRB. The apprehension of bias must be a reasonable one, held by a reasonable and right-minded person, applying himself or herself to the question and obtaining thereon the required information. The reasonable or right-minded person must have thought the matter through, and concluded more likely than not that the decision maker would, consciously or unconsciously, not decide fairly.

Yushchuk v. Canada (Minister of Employment & Immigration) (1994), 25 Imm. L.R. (2d) 241, 83 F.T.R. 146 — The applicant claimed refugee status. After the applicant's hearing concluded, but before the Board made a decision, the applicant's counsel forwarded a report from a research fellow at the Centre for Refugee Studies at York University. This paper was not considered by the Board in reaching a negative decision with respect to the applicant's refugee claim.

The Board, on receipt of the report from the research fellow, ought to have re-opened the hearing to consider its admissibility.

The Court referred to the decision of the Supreme Court of Canada in *Cardinal v. Kent Institution*, [1985] 2 S.C.R. 643 (S.C.C.), to the effect that the denial of the right to a fair hearing must always render a decision invalid, whether or not it may appear to a reviewing Court that the hearing would likely have resulted in a different decision. The right to fair hearing must be regarded as an independent, unqualified right which finds its essential justification in the sense of procedural justice, which any person, affected by an administrative decision, is entitled to have.

The Court noted that there are some decisions where prerogative relief has been denied on a substantive matter. No case exists where such relief has been denied in the light of the finding of an error based on the failure to consider the admissibility of evidence. Accordingly, the application was allowed and the decision of the Board set aside.

Li v. Canada (Minister of Citizenship & Immigration) (July 20, 1994), Doc. A-1657-92 (Fed. T.D.) — The applicant was discouraged by a comment from a Board Member from elaborating on what took place during a Swedish T.V. interview. The failure to so elaborate was relied by the Board in reaching its decision. When the Board acts in a manner so as to discourage an applicant from adducing evidence on a particular point, it cannot rely on the failure of the applicant to offer such evidence in reaching its decision, unless it subsequently puts questions to the applicant concerning those matters.

The Court also commented negatively, on a trend in a number of Board decisions in that they relied on the fact that the applicant cannot demonstrate or prove that the persecuting state authorities have specific knowledge of the applicant's conduct.

Tetteh-Louis v. Canada (Secretary of State) (July 8, 1994), Doc. IMM-4218-93 (Fed. T.D.) — The applicant sought judicial review of a negative decision of the CRDD. The applicant was cross-examined on the document entitled "Case Highlights" in circumstances where the applicant had not been given disclosure of the document until cross-examination. The Board clearly based its decision on the document in question. To adequately meet the test of fairness, disclosure, in matters of this kind, must be timely and meaningful. The fact that the disclosure occurred after in-chief testimony and during cross-examination, coupled with the fact that the document, and its impact on the applicant's credibility, were critical to the Board's decision required that the application be allowed and the decision of the CRDD set aside.

Castroman v. Canada (Secretary of State) (1994), 81 F.T.R. 227, 27 Imm. L.R. (2d) 129 — The applicant sought judicial review of a negative decision of the CRDD. During the hearing the applicant was represented by counsel. After counsel had finished examining the applicant, the Refugee Hearing Officer (RHO) commenced her examination. The RHO questioned why the evidence indicating that a particular person was persecuting the applicant was not contained in the personal information form (PIF). Counsel for the applicant objected to that on the basis that the line of questioning was getting into an area of solicitor-client privilege. The Board allowed the questions and then counsel withdrew from the case. The PIF is a form the Immigration and Refugee Board requires. The object of the form is to provide the claimant with an opportunity to tell his or her story early in the process. One of the primary ways that the Board tests a claimant's credibility is by comparing the PIF with the claimant's oral testimony. It is not proper for a lawyer to interfere with the RHO or a member's questioning of the claimant with respect to his or her PIF. The lawyer cannot attempt to shield the client from questioning about why certain matters were omitted from the PIF.

Counsel is not at liberty to leave a client in the middle of a case simply because he or she does not agree with the ruling of the administrative tribunal. Counsel is entitled to make objections to rulings and to take whatever proceedings are required at the conclusion of the case to have the matter reviewed.

The Board in this case completed the hearing without new counsel being appointed. Not all decisions to proceed without providing the applicant the benefit of counsel will result in reviewable error. In this case though, the Board denied the applicant the right of re-examination after completion of cross-examination, thus the applicant had no opportunity to explain any of his answers given in cross-examination. Further, the Board misled the applicant into thinking he had no right of re-examination by stating that the next stage of the hearing was to receive documentary evidence.

The criteria for determining whether the Board has properly exercised its discretion to disallow counsel was set out in *Howard v. Stony Mountain Institution, Presiding Officer of Inmate Disciplinary Ct.* (1984), 19 D.L.R. (4th) 502 (Fed. C.A.). Those criteria are:

1. The seriousness of the charge and of the potential penalty;
2. whether any points of law are likely to arise;
3. the capacity of a particular person to present his own case;
4. procedural difficulties;
5. the need for reasonable speed in making the adjudication;
6. the need for fairness as between prisoners and as between prisoners and prison officers.

Obviously, the latter category has no relevance in immigration proceedings. On the facts of this case there was a denial of natural justice and the application for judicial review was allowed.

Ahmad v. Canada (Minister of Employment & Immigration) (1994), 80 F.T.R. 135 — This was an application to review a negative decision of the CRDD. The primary basis of the applicant's claim was that, in Pakistan, there is systematic discrimination and persecution of Ahmadis arising from the law referred to as Ordinance No. XX of 1984. The onus is on the applicant to show that laws of general application are either inherently or for some other reason, persecutory. The panel, in this case, indicated to counsel for the claimant that they were familiar with Pakistani cases and Ordinance No. XX, and that they would like to hear from the applicant about his personal problems. In taking this approach the panel precluded the applicant from satisfying the onus upon him.

The vast majority of refugee cases will be decided on the basis of the particular circumstances of an applicant. There may be cases, however, in which an applicant wishes to rely solely on the persecutory nature of a law of general application to a particular social group. Such an approach cannot be precluded by a panel as it was in this case. Accordingly, the application was allowed.

Yassine v. Canada (Minister of Employment & Immigration) (1994), 27 Imm. L.R. (2d) 135, 172 N.R. 308 (Fed. C.A.) — At the hearing into the claim for refugee status, the appellant testified that he feared persecution from the Amal Shi'ite militia in Lebanon because he had been a victim of its forced recruitment policy. Subsequent to the applicant's hearing but before a decision was rendered, new information concerning the withdrawal of the Amal militia away from Beirut came to the attention of the Board. The presiding member directed that the refugee hearing officer make copies of the material available to counsel and invite counsel to submit a reply within two weeks. The appellant did not raise an objection to this way of proceeding and did not file a reply. The appellant only objected to the procedure after a negative decision was reached with respect to the refugee claim. The Court viewed the appellant's conduct as an implied waiver of any breach of natural justice that might have occurred. A breach of natural justice normally requires a new hearing because the right to a fair hearing is an independent right. An exception to this rule occurs in circumstances where the demerits of the claim are such that a rehearing of the matter would be hopeless. The limits of this distinction or exception have yet to be established. In this appeal, the adverse finding of credibility, having been properly made, the claim could only be rejected if the matter were reheard. Accordingly, the appeal was dismissed.

Keita v. Canada (Minister of Employment & Immigration) (April 29, 1994), Doc. IMM-343-93 (Fed. T.D.) — The negative decision of the CRDD, from which the applicants sought relief, was dated December 1, 1992. Notice of the decision was signed on February 2, 1993 and the applicant was informed of the decision later in the month of February. On December 28, 1992 and January 19, 1993, counsel for the applicant wrote to the CRDD asking it to consider additional documentary evidence which he attached in his letters.

The applicant sought to overturn the decision made by the CRDD on the basis that it failed to take into account this evidence. The application was dismissed.

Once the CRDD had made its decision on December 1, 1992, it could not consider the additional evidence that counsel submitted to it.

Wu v. Canada (Minister of Employment & Immigration) (1994), 81 F.T.R. 33 — The applicant sought judicial review of a negative decision of the CRDD. The applicant raised the issue of whether certain comments made by one panel member gave rise to a reasonable apprehension of bias. The Court concluded that the comments of the panel member did not give rise to a reasonable apprehension of bias. The Court also noted that the issue of bias should have been raised by the applicant when the matter arose before the Board. Bias was not raised at that time nor was it was raised by the applicant in her written submissions to the Board at the conclusion of the refugee hearing. Failure to raise the issue would have led the Court to conclude that the applicant had waived her right to raise an objection on this ground in the event that the comments of the panel member had been sufficient to give rise to a reasonable apprehension of bias.

Kanagasekarampillai v. Canada (Secretary of State) (1994), 169 N.R. 119 (Fed. C.A.) — The appellant, a Tamil and citizen of Sri Lanka, claimed refugee status on the basis of persecution on account of race. When counsel attempted to elicit testimony on re-examination, he encountered difficulty from the presiding member. The interference with counsel's attempt to re-examine was a denial of natural justice. In the course of cross-examination new events and circumstances may have been brought out to explain, contradict or amplify matters that were raised in-chief. The re-examination can legitimately explore these events and circumstances to explain or qualify them. While the appellant's response under cross-examination may have appeared on the surface to have been exhaustive, that was no reason to deny him an opportunity of testifying on the point in question by way of re-examination. In addition to the common law, the "reasonable opportunity" of presenting evidence which the statute grants to a refugee claimant at a hearing is denied, where a re-examination is improperly restricted.

Bangoura v. Canada (Minister of Employment & Immigration) (April 18, 1994), Doc. IMM-784-93 (Fed. T.D.) — The applicant sought to review a negative decision of the CRDD. At the conclusion of the hearing the applicant was asked to produce originals of certain documents that he had tendered as photocopies. When these documents were forwarded to the Board the question of their authenticity arose as a result of an RCMP laboratory report. Accordingly, a second hearing was scheduled at which time the RCMP report was considered. The hearing adjourned again so that the author of the report could be located and, when that was impossible, the RCMP report was withdrawn. On the judicial review application counsel for the applicant submitted that having recognized the relevance of the RCMP report the refugee division could not remove the exhibit from the record.

In dismissing the application the Court found that the applicant waived his procedural fairness argument by not objecting to the removal of the exhibit at the time it was contemplated by the tribunal. Accordingly, the application was dismissed.

Rahmatizadeh v. Canada (Minister of Employment & Immigration) (April 6, 1994), Doc. IMM-2696-93 (Fed. T.D.) — The applicant sought judicial review of a negative decision of the CRDD. An issue was raised as to the applicant's real nationality. Counsel for the plaintiff at the hearing stated that if there was any doubt that his client was Kurdish he would call expert evidence to seek to establish that fact.

Applicants must not rely on the members of the division or the hearing officer to prove their case. It is up to the applicants alone to introduce into evidence all material that they consider to be essential to establish that their claim is well founded. In this case counsel was asking the division to tell him what its judgment would be as to whether the applicant was of the Kurdish nationality, and if the division had any doubts or was inclined to render a negative decision then the applicant was prepared to present additional witnesses. This procedure is not recommended, nor is it acceptable.

The Court concluded that the division's decision on the question of nationality was drawn in an arbitrary manner and that the division had exaggerated the importance of insignificant details and accordingly allowed the application notwithstanding the above comments.

Kone v. Canada (Minister of Employment & Immigration) (1994), 79 F.T.R. 63 — The applicant sought to review a negative decision with respect to his refugee claim. The applicant was a public servant employed by the Department of Agriculture in Mali. He was in charge of marketing fruits and vegetables from a large agricultural farm belonging to the wife of the president. There was no refugee hearing officer present at the hearing; however, at the conclusion of the hearing, the tribunal raised the question of the applicability of sections E and F of Article 1 of the Convention. While the applicant was testifying, the tribunal seemed to believe that the applicant was personally responsible for the unfair competition in which the agricultural farm engaged. In addition, the tribunal seemed to believe that the applicant was possibly responsible for other crimes, given his close association to the regime of the former president.

The purpose of the examination by the Board members was not solely to clarify answers given by the applicant in response to questions put to the applicant by his counsel. A great many of the questions asked by the members of the tribunal were for the purpose of determining whether there was anything that would bring the exclusion clause into play. The tribunal usurped the function that would have belonged to the Minister or his representative. An informed person viewing the matter realistically and practically would conclude that the members of the tribunal, whether consciously or unconsciously, would not decide fairly.

The Court quoted again from Lord Denning in *Jones v. National Coal Board*, [1957] 2 Q.B. 55 (Eng. C.A.). The Court noted that Lord Denning's comments should be tempered in view of section 67(2).

The application was allowed and the matter referred back to a differently constituted panel for rehearing.

Del Castillo v. Canada (Minister of Employment & Immigration) (1994), 79 F.T.R. 207 — The applicant sought to review a negative decision of the refugee division. From the outset the presiding member interrupted the examination of the applicant and intervened with his own questions. This conduct continued until the end of the applicant's examination. Counsel did agree at the outset of the hearing that the division could intervene to clarify facts "as necessary as we go along". The conduct of the presiding member went well beyond what had been agreed to. Throughout the examination counsel never had the opportunity to examine the applicant in order to bring out the evidence that she believed to be essential and necessary. Counsel, therefore, for all practical purposes, never examined the applicant. Rather it was the presiding member who examined the applicant, occasionally permitting counsel to ask questions.

Notwithstanding the fact that the Court was unable to find an error in the merits of the decision, the decision was set aside. The Court quoted Lord Wright in *General Council of Medical Education & Registration of United Kingdom v. Spackman*, [1943] A.C. 627 (U.K. H.L.), at page 644:

> If the principles of natural justice are violated in respect of any decision it is, indeed, immaterial whether the same decision would have been arrived at in the absence of the departure from the essential principles of justice. The decision must be declared to be no decision.

The application was allowed and the matter remitted to a new panel for re-hearing.

Joseph v. Canada (Minister of Employment & Immigration) (March 9, 1994), Doc. IMM-2623-93 (Fed. T.D.) — The Board held that the applicant's fear of persecution was not objectively based. It held that it was difficult to believe that the rapes, which it accepted as true from the applicant's PIF without oral testimony, were connected to the applicant's involvement in, what the Board characterized as a peaceful, religious march. At the outset of the hearing, the Board informed the applicant that she need not testify about the rapes because the Board was accepting them as fact from the applicant's PIF. However, the Board then found that the rapes were not connected to the applicant's involvement in the march and hence her political opinion. Since this was clearly the basis for the negative decision, the applicant should have been given the opportunity to testify as to the rapes and the circumstances. The application for judicial review was allowed and the matter referred back to a differently constituted Board.

De Yanex v. Canada (Secretary of State) (1994), 75 F.T.R. 141 — Prior to the date scheduled for the credible basis hearing, counsel for the applicant requested in writing that the respondent Minister provide disclosure of any and all information in the file of the applicant in accordance with the requirement of pre-hearing disclosure and natural justice. No response was received to this request. At the outset of the credible basis hearing, counsel requested an adjournment of the proceedings on the basis that he had not received the disclosure. The adjudicator denied the request indicating that the only information required by counsel to conduct the hearing could be obtained from the applicant and therefore the principle of disclosure was academic.

Jurisprudence has established that failure to provide disclosure of relevant information within a reasonable period of time prior to a hearing of a refugee claim on its merits constitutes a breach of the principles of natural justice by denying the claimant the right to a fair hearing. This principle is also extended to the procedures governing credible basis hearings. Accordingly, the decision of the credible basis tribunal was set aside.

Editor's Note: Although the provision for the adjudication of refugee claims has changed, the principle in this case may be of more general application.

Zas Garcia v. Canada (Minister of Employment & Immigration) (1994), 75 F.T.R. 220 — The applicant sought judicial review of a negative decision of the Refugee Division. The applicant based his claim to status on a reasonable fear of persecution because of his political opinion and membership in a particular social group. During the applicant's testimony, the question of a change of circumstances in El Salvador was raised, and several documents were introduced which referred to the peace accords between the guerrilla forces and the government authorities. Counsel for the applicant stated her intention to make submissions on this point during argument, which she did. When the evidence had been completed and argument heard, the members of the Refugee Division withdrew for about thirty minutes, planning to render a decision the same day. Subsequent to the adjournment, the tribunal returned and entered a document, which it had obtained, as an exhibit. By seeking out documents when the hearing was over and argument had been heard and entering this exhibit in evidence without giving the applicant an opportunity to make submissions, the Refugee Division acted contrary to the mandatory provisions of sections 68(5) and 69.1(5).

Puerto v. Canada (Minister of Employment & Immigration) (February 16, 1994), Doc. IMM-1753-93 (Fed. T.D.) — The applicant sought to review a negative decision of the CRDD. The Court found that presiding members of the CRDD intervened extensively in the presentation of the applicant's case. Section 69.1(5) requires the CRDD to give the applicant a reasonable opportunity to present evidence. The Court did not find the interferences to be of such a "gross" nature so as to constitute a denial of natural justice. The Court remarked, however, that an opportunity for CRDD members to question applicants arises in the ordinary course of proceedings and therefore, except in circumstances where it is manifestly evident that intervention in the orderly presentation of an applicant's case is necessary for the effective and efficient management of the hearing, interventions should be reserved by CRDD members to a more appropriate stage of the hearing.

The decision of the CRDD was set aside on the basis of errors in law conceded to by the respondent, involving a misstating and misunderstanding and misconstruing of evidence. The decision was quashed and the matter referred for redetermination before a differently constituted panel.

Kaler v. Canada (Minister of Employment & Immigration) (1994), 73 F.T.R. 217 — This application sought to review a negative determination of the applicant's claim to refugee status. The Court commented on the type of notice necessary to an applicant where the issue of an internal flight alternative (IFA) was going to be canvassed. The question should still remain whether the applicant had an ample opportunity to speak to the IFA issue. The Court in *Thirunavukkarasu v. Canada (Minister of Employment & Immigration)*, [1994] 1 F.C. 589, 22 Imm. L.R. (2d) 241, 109 D.L.R. (4th) 682, 163 N.R. 232 (Fed. C.A.) did not intend that an applicant, whose counsel was fully capable of addressing and did in fact fully address the issue of an IFA at the hearing, could be able to rely on lack of prior notice. Such a conclusion is too strict a reading of the Court of Appeal's decision in *Thirunavukkarasu v. Canada (Minister of Employment & Immigration).*

Shirwa v. Canada (Minister of Employment & Immigration) (1993), 23 Imm. L.R. (2d) 123, 71 F.T.R. 136 — This was an application for judicial review of a decision denying the applicant Convention refugee status. The applicant was a Somali who originally had a lawyer, but on the eve of his hearing the lawyer indicated that he would not be appearing and that a Mr. Gerald Flynn would be representing the applicant at the refugee hearing. The word "counsel" was interpreted to the applicant as "lawyer" even though it transpired later that Mr. Flynn not a member of the Law Society of Upper Canada. The claim for refugee status was denied, despite the fact that the applicant was found to be a credible witness. In *Mathon v. Canada (Minister of Employment & Immigration)* (1988), 28 F.T.R. 217 at 235, 38 Admin. L.R. 193, 9 Imm. L.R. (2d) 132 (Fed. T.D.), the Court found that section 7 of the *Charter of Rights and Freedoms* included the right to be represented by competent and careful counsel. The standard of care is described in *Central & Eastern Trust Company v. Rafuse*, [1986] 2 S.C.R. 147 at 208, 31 D.L.R. (4th) 481, 69 N.R. 321 (S.C.C.), varied [1988] 1 S.C.R. 1206 (S.C.C.) which decision indicates that a solicitor is required to bring reasonable care, skill and knowledge to the performance of the professional service he has undertaken. The incompetence of counsel in the context of a refugee hearing provides grounds for review on the basis of a breach of natural justice. In circumstances where a hearing occurs, the decision of the tribunal can only be reviewed in extraordinary circumstances, where there is sufficient evidence to establish the exact dimensions of the problem and where the review is based on a precise factual foundation. Where the incompetence or negligence of the applicant's representation is sufficiently specific and clearly supported by the evidence, such negligence or incompetence is inherently prejudicial and will warrant overturning the decision, notwithstanding the lack of bad faith or absence of a failure to do anything on the part of the tribunal.

The circumstances here warranted overturning the decision. The fact that Mr. Flynn was not a lawyer did not provide a basis for review. However, there was sufficient evidence in the record to support the applicant's allegation that:

1. Mr. Flynn led the applicant to believe that he was a lawyer and that this misrepresentation was not corrected at the hearing.

2. Mr. Flynn was negligent in his representation of the applicant.

3. No proper explanation for failing to fulfil the responsibility to provide written submissions on the issues of credibility or change of circumstances was provided. This was particularly important in light of the tribunal's finding that the applicant was a credible witness.

Accordingly, the decision was overturned.

Liyanagamage v. Canada (Secretary of State) (1993), 71 F.T.R. 67 — In this application to review a decision denying refugee status, the issue was whether the Board failed to observe a principle of natural justice or procedural fairness by not giving the applicant an opportunity to reply to new case law. The failure to provide the parties an opportunity to deal with new case law is a matter which, in the circumstances of this case, was contrary to procedural fairness. There may be cases where there would not be denial of procedural fairness when a Board relied on a case decided after the hearing and submissions were completed, but before the Board rendered its decision. In the context of this case the decision denying refugee status was set aside.

Iossifov v. Canada (Minister of Employment & Immigration) (1993), 71 F.T.R. 28 — On this application to review a decision of the CRDD refusing refugee status the Court found that the Board members were not interested in evidence of past persecution, constantly interrupted the applicant in the presentation of his case and prevented counsel from proceeding in an orderly fashion. This conduct was found to be a breach of natural justice. It was no answer to say that the Board allowed the applicant ultimately to put into evidence all evidence relating to past persecution when it was clear from the transcript that the Board members were not interested. The well-foundedness of the fear of future persecution could not be decided without determining if there was past persecution.

Gonzales v. Canada (Secretary of State) (1993), 71 F.T.R. 26 — The applicant sought judicial review of a decision refusing refugee status. Counsel complained that there was an apprehension of bias because one of the two members of the tribunal presided at the hearing of the applicant's daughter. The daughter's claim was found not to be credible. The Court found no evidence indicating a predisposition by any members of the tribunal as to the issue to be decided at this refugee hearing. In and of itself, the fact that a member happened to preside over the claim of the applicant's daughter was insufficient to raise a reasonable apprehension of bias. Furthermore, the Court noted that counsel for the applicant, at the hearing, was given a copy of the decision in the daughter's case before the hearing began and did not raise the question of bias until the second day of the hearing. The application was dismissed.

Nrecaj v. Canada (Minister of Employment & Immigration), 65 F.T.R. 171, [1993] 3 F.C. 630, 14 Admin. L.R. (2d) 161, 20 Imm. L.R. (2d) 252 — This was an application for judicial review of a decision of the CRDD determining that the applicant was not a Convention refugee. The applicant was a citizen of Yugoslavia. He was convicted in Canada of assault with a weapon, uttering a threat and aggravated assault and received a sentence of three years in custody in July 1991. These convictions followed upon earlier convictions in both Yugoslavia and Italy. The CRDD concluded that the applicant's evidence was not credible or trustworthy.

Following his arrival in Canada, the applicant had an extensive interview with the manager of a Canadian Immigration Commission office in British Columbia. The manager made notes of the interview. The manager testified at the refugee hearing and the contradiction between the applicant's *viva voce* testimony before the CRDD and his interview with the manager formed the basis for the adverse finding of credibility. The hearing commenced in May of 1991 and was not concluded until April 13, 1992. On February 17, 1992 counsel for the applicant contacted the refugee hearing officer (RHO) requesting disclosure of any documents, witness statements and evidence in her possession. Disclosure was refused. The Court held that the principles set out in *R. v. Stinchcombe*, [1991] 3 S.C.R. 326 (S.C.C.) applied to proceedings before a tribunal such as the CRDD. To adequately meet the test of fairness it was decided that the disclosure must be sufficiently timely to allow counsel to fully and effectively fulfil his or her role and to allow the party requesting disclosure to prepare.

It should be noted that the interview notes in question were shared with counsel on April 13, 1992, the last day of the refugee determination proceedings. This disclosure was found to be insufficient to meet the obligation to disclose contemplated by the Court.

Seth v. Canada (Minister of Employment & Immigration), 20 Imm. L.R. (2d) 271, [1993] 3 F.C. 348, 155 N.R. 67, 105 D.L.R. (4th) 365 (Fed. C.A.) — This application for judicial review raised the issue of the right of a Convention refugee claimant to seek an adjournment of his claim pending the determination of outstanding criminal charges laid after his arrival in Canada.

Accordingly, the Court ruled that the adjudicator did not commit any reviewable error in the exercise of his discretion when he decided not to adjourn the credible basis hearing until the criminal charges were concluded. The credible basis hearing was not so devoid of any legitimate public purpose that to allow it to take place would constitute an injustice and might offend the basic sense of fairness which underlies the principles of fundamental justice. Further, the credible basis inquiry was not designed to assist in the prosecution of the witness. It would require exceptional circumstances to stay the proceedings of an administrative tribunal, whose functions, powers and decisions have absolutely nothing to do with the criminal liability of the person compelled to testify and offer evidence before it, for the reason that that person, because he was criminally charged, had claimed the right to silence. The state, in this case, was merely engaging itself in a most legitimate process, which is by law to be expeditious, of determining the status of a person who seeks the right to remain in Canada as a refugee.

Editor's Note: Although the provisions for adjudicating refugee claims have changed, the principle in this case may be of more general application.

Kusi v. Canada (Minister of Employment & Immigration) (1993), 19 Imm. L.R. (2d) 281, 65 F.T.R. 58 (Fed. T.D.) — An adjudicator and member of the Immigration and Refugee Board were conducting a credible basis hearing into the claim of a Convention refugee claimant, pursuant to provisions of the *Immigration Act* in effect on August 19, 1992.

The tribunal accepted as evidence notes taken by an immigration officer, which recorded answers given to him at the port-of-entry by the applicant. The applicant contested the accuracy of the notes and asked that the officer be produced for cross-examination, a request which was denied by the tribunal.

The decision by the tribunal that there was no credible basis to the applicant's claim was set aside and the matter was remitted back for determination in accordance with the law. Specifically, the Court found that given the importance of the interest, namely the applicant's claim to be a Convention refugee, and given the fact that the applicant contested the accuracy of the notes which were relied upon by the tribunal, the rules of natural justice and of fundamental justice required that the cross-examination, which was sought, be allowed. The Court relied on the jurisprudence in *Canada (Minister of Employment & Immigration) v. Leal* (1991), 129 N.R. 383 (Fed. C.A.) and *Cheung v. Canada (Minister of Employment & Immigration)* (1981), 122 D.L.R. (3d) 41 (Fed. C.A.).

Editor's Note: Although occurring in the context of a repealed refugee hearing procedure, the principle in this case may have a broader application.

Pal v. Canada (Minister of Employment & Immigration) (1993), 70 F.T.R. 289 — The applicant sought review of a decision denying him Convention refugee status.

The applicant was not granted a recess, when he requested one, in order to review documents which were introduced into evidence and which he had not seen previously. The documents were introduced to contradict evidence which he had given. They were written in English. The applicant was testifying through an interpreter. The Court found that in refusing to allow the applicant and his counsel an opportunity to review the evidence, the applicant was denied the opportunity to answer the case against him and a breach of natural justice occurred.

The Court pointed out that relief under section 18.1(4) of the *Federal Court Act* is discretionary and thus, if no prejudice is caused by an erroneous procedure or decision, an order quashing that decision will not normally be given. If no real purpose will be served by requiring another hearing, one will not be ordered.

The Court was unable to conclude that the breach of natural justice which occurred in the context of this case was minor and could not appreciably affect the final decision. The breach was not cured by subsequent actions and accordingly, the decision of the tribunal was quashed.

Velauthar v. Canada (Minister of Employment & Immigration) (1992), 141 N.R. 239 (Fed. C.A.) — Following receipt of the evidence, the panel indicated that it was concerned with whether the persecution feared by the appellants was caused by a "Convention reason" and invited written submissions from the appellant's counsel and the refugee hearing officer. An invitation which was accepted. The decision denied the claim on the basis of the appellant's credibility.

There was a gross denial of natural justice. The panel had stipulated that the appellants had feared persecution and that the only issue was whether that persecution was encompassed in the Convention refugee definition. It proceeded on grounds of credibility to negate its stipulation, thus denying the appellants the opportunity to know and answer the case against them by a deliberate decision. The decision of the Convention Refugee Determination Division was quashed and the matter was referred back for rehearing by a differently constituted panel.

Sivaguru v. Canada (Minister of Employment & Immigration) (1992), 16 Imm. L.R. (2d) 85 (Fed. C.A.) — The appellant testified that he was a supporter or member of a Tamil organization known as LTTE. He said he was unaware of any violence engaged in by the LTTE between 1979 and 1983. A Board member hearing the evidence initiated on his own a request for information from the Board's documentation centre on the violent activities of the LTTE. After obtaining the information and without disclosing it to the Refugee Hearing Officer or counsel, the Board member then questioned the appellant and contradicted him with the information.

The appellant testified that he had been warned about the particular member in question and had been warned not to tell him the truth about any violent activities of the LTTE or risk being classified as a terrorist and not allowed to remain in Canada.

The Immigration and Refugee Board does not possess the powers of the Court. Its members are not judges. They are not bound by any legal or technical rules of evidence. They are required to deal with all proceedings as informally and expeditiously as the circumstances and the considerations of fairness permit.

An essential requirement for such a hearing is that the Board act with impartiality. Impartiality refers to a state of mind or attitude. It connotes an absence of bias, actual or perceived. For a "hearing" to be worthy of the description the Board must be willing to give the evidence the dispassionate and impartial consideration it requires in order to arrive at the truth. The difficulty in getting at the full story is recognized by the nature of powers which are conferred by subsections 67(2) and 68(4). The flexible provisions of the latter subsection permit the Board to take judicial notice of facts and to take notice of other facts, information and opinion within its specialized knowledge provided it does so in the manner authorized by the statute. The Act does not permit a member of the Board to embark upon a quest for evidence in the manner which was adopted in this case. That method of proceeding subverts its function as an impartial tribunal regardless of the legitimate concern which motivated the request. The search for evidence was secretly initiated and the tenor of the questions put after the information was acquired suggested that the information was going to be used to devastating effect. The Board member might have openly revealed his misgivings about the evidence at the hearing where a course of action known to all concerned could have been decided upon and initiated. Accordingly, the appeal was allowed, the decision of the Board set aside, and the matter referred back for rehearing and redetermination by a differently constituted panel of the Refugee Division.

Yusuf v. Canada (Minister of Employment & Immigration) (1991), [1992] 1 F.C. 629, (sub nom. *Yusuf v. Ministre de l'emploi et de l'immigration))* 133 N.R. 391 (Fed. C.A.) — There is no doubt that members of the Refugee Division have the right to cross-examination witnesses they hear. In determining whether the limits had been exceeded the Court of Appeal examined the length of the cross-examination and the tone and content of the questions. In this case the Court found that the comments made by the members of the Board were harassing and unfair. Further, the Court found that the observations by one member of the Refugee Division were sexist, unwarranted, and highly irrelevant. The Court noted that a judge who indulges in that loses his cloak of impartialty and his decision cannot stand. The appeal was allowed, the decision denying refugee status was set aside, and the matter was referred back to another quorum of the Refugee Division.

Section 69.1(6)

Ibacache v. Canada (Ministre de la Citoyenneté & de l'Immigration) (1997), 146 F.T.R. 175 (Fed. T.D.) — This was an application to review a decision of a panel of the CRDD dismissing the applicant's motion to re-open the refugee claim. The applicants were citizens of Chile, and their refugee claims were dismissed as abandoned. The applicants were not served with notice because the Refugee Division did not have their addresses or the name of their legal representative.

Although the obligation to serve is expressly set out in the Rules, that obligation is not absolute. Applicants can waive service implicitly by being negligent. The applicants were responsible for providing the Division with the information it needed to contact them, especially since service by publication cannot be effected without violating the tribunal's duty of confidentiality.

No one is bound to do the impossible and as a result the application was dismissed.

Ressam v. Canada (Minister of Citizenship & Immigration) (1996), 36 Imm. L.R. (2d) 99, (sub nom. *Ressam v. Canada (Ministre de la Citoyenneté de l'Immigration))* 110 F.T.R. 50 (Fed. T.D.) — This was an application to quash a decision of the CRDD declaring a refugee claim abandoned. When a claimant appears before the Board under subsection 69.1(6) he is appearing not for the hearing of his claim but rather to make argument relating to the finding that he has abandoned his claim. When pursuant to section 69.1(6)(b) the refugee division gives the person concerned an opportunity to be heard, it is the very purpose of that abandonment hearing to allow the person concerned to explain the reasons why he believes he did not abandon the claim. It is only when the Refugee Division has allowed the claimant to explain his reasons and concluded that they were valid, that it may proceed to hear the claim.

Section 69.1(9)

Gengeswaran v. Canada (Minister of Citizenship & Immigration) (May 19, 1999), Doc. IMM-4318-98 (Fed. T.D.) — Although there is no obligation on the Board to discuss every piece of evidence, it is required to address those pieces which contradict the Board's finding on key issues. The absence of any analysis of documentary evidence which directly contradicts the Board's finding, permits the Court to infer, from the silence, that the tribunal made an erroneous finding of fact without regard to evidence.

Vijayarajah v. Canada (Minister of Citizenship & Immigration) (May 12, 1999), Doc. IMM-4538-98 (Fed. T.D.) — This was an application to review a negative decision of a panel of the CRDD. The applicant alleged that the panel ignored relevant documentary evidence including a medical report and photographs which supported his story.

The applicant submitted an original document from the Colombo Magistrate's Court which indicated that the applicant was detained and subsequently released. The panel totally disregarded the significance of the document in providing convincing evidence of the applicant's detention. The applicant also submitted photographs of scars on his body along with a medical report which confirmed that he bore both physical and psychological scars consistent with the torture he described.

The panel concluded in its decision that it did not believe that the applicant's fear of persecution was genuine. The magistrate's document, the medical evidence, and the photographs, were highly pertinent and should have been considered by the Board. Where there is documentary evidence which could influence the Board's assessment of a file that evidence must be dealt with in its reasons. The Board's burden of explanation increases with the relevance of the evidence in question to the disputed facts.

Razm v. Canada (Minister of Citizenship & Immigration) (March 17, 1999), Doc. IMM-3796-98 (Fed. T.D.) — The applicant, an Iranian national, maintained that he had converted from Islam to Zoroastrianism, an offence punishable by death in Iran. His claim was denied, and the applicant challenged this determination. The second of two tapes used to record the tribunal hearing had been misplaced.

In the absence of a statutory right to a recording, the Court must determine whether the record before it allows it to properly dispose of the application for appeal or review. If so, the absence of a transcript will not violate the rules of natural justice. Where the statute does mandate a recording however, natural justice may require a transcript. In the absence of a statutory right to a recorded hearing, a party's rights to natural justice will only be infringed where the Court has an inadequate record upon which to base its decision.

Neither the *Immigration Act*, nor the CRDD rules requires the recording of the hearing. It appears to be the common practice, that the tribunal chose to record its proceedings. The partial transcript alone disclosed three apparently unsubstantiated findings by the tribunal. The applicant's failure to provide a more fulsome affidavit concerning his testimony on the missing tape was saved by the important discrepancies in comparing the reasons for decision with that part of the transcript that was available.

The application for judicial review was allowed.

Grigorenko v. (Ministre de la Citoyenneté & de l'Immigration) (1998), 152 F.T.R. 285 (Fed. T.D.) — A panel of the CRDD had before it a claim by an Israel citizen of Ukrainian nationality and the claim was dismissed. The panel stating that it did not believe the claimant's testimony and that there was no credible basis for his case. The claimant asked a member of the panel to recuse himself because the panel member has stayed in a kibbutz in Israel and was director of information for the Canada Israel Committee at different times in the 1970's and 1980's. The member refused to recuse himself and eventually the claimant's claim was rejected. An application for judicial review was commenced.

A judge or a panel member who is asked to recuse himself or herself by reason of appearance of bias must place himself or herself in the shoes of an informed or reasonable observer and determine whether there is any merit in the application. It is common place for a person to excuse himself or herself not only because of their a real or apprehended conflict with a party but also because of the appearance of an apprehension of bias.

The panel member examined the question of apprehension of bias from the standpoint of an informed and reasonable observer as he was required to do. Accordingly, the application for judicial review was dismissed.

Abubakar v. Canada (Minister of Citizenship & Immigration) (1998), Imm. L.R. (2d) 186, 152 F.T.R. 87 (Fed. T.D.) — The applicant sought to review a negative decision of the CRDD in which the central question focused upon whether the claimant was who she claimed to be. During the course of the hearing the CRDD panel members gave no direct signals of any concern that the evidence they were hearing from the claimant was not the truth. Apart from one piece of independent evidence, the only evidence respecting the claimant's identity came from her own testimony. The error in judgement by the counsel in not calling further confirmatory evidence was facilitated by the panel not being direct and specifically raising the veracity concern which formed the heart of its decision. In doing so, the panel did not allow the matter to be adequately and fully addressed. The panel is not obliged to take over the presentation of the applicant's case. It is only fair however, for the panel to give notice of the importance of an issue which does not seem important to counsel at the time. The decision of the CRDD was set aside and the matter remitted to a differently constituted panel for redetermination.

Cicek v. Canada (Minister of Citizenship & Immigration) (October 24, 1997), Doc. IMM-4477-96 (Fed. T.D.) — The applicant sought to review a negative decision of the CRDD.

The applicant complained that in spite of her request to the tribunal she was not provided with the tapes of her hearing. Transcripts of the hearing, however, were made available. In the absence of any express statutory requirement, the traditional common law requirement for a record of an administrative tribunal's proceedings include the document which initiated the proceedings and the document containing the tribunal's adjudication. Neither the reasons for the ruling nor evidence presented at the hearing have been considered necessary elements of the record to be presented to the superior tribunal upon appeal or review.

In the absence of a statutory right to a recording, courts must determine whether the record before it allows it to properly dispose of the application for appeal or review. If so, the absence for a transcript will not violate the rules of natural justice.

The Court concluded that the available transcripts and documentary evidence before it made it possible for the Court in this particular situation to properly dispose of the judicial review application. Accordingly, the application was dismissed.

Yong-Gueico v. Canada (Minister of Citizenship & Immigration) (1997), 39 Imm. L.R. (2d) 69, 134 F.T.R. 135 (Fed. T.D.) — The applicants sought to review a negative determination of his refugee claim. The tribunal accepted the principal applicant's testimony, but at the same time rejected his claim, due to a change in country conditions in Chile. The definition of Convention refugee, in the Act, has two parts. Paragraph (a) contains the criteria that have to be established in order to fall within the definition. Paragraph (b) sets out one additional criteria that must be taken into account. Pursuant to the authority granted under paragraph 2(2)(e), a tribunal may determine that due to changed country conditions a person can no longer be a Convention refugee. It is possible, however, for subsection 2(3) to cancel the effect of paragraph 2(2)(e). Subsection 2(3) requires the claimant to establish compelling reasons arising out of past persecution which negate the positive impact of changed country conditions in that particular claimant's circumstances.

The fact that counsel for the claimant failed to refer to or rely on subsection 2(3) did not excuse the tribunal for overlooking it. The failure of the tribunal to consider the "compelling reasons" aspect of the definition amounts to a failure by the tribunal to exercise its jurisdiction. This failure is a reviewable error in law sufficient to squash the decision.

Accordingly, the decision of the tribunal was set aside and the case was referred back to a differently constituted tribunal.

Suliman v. Canada (Minister of Citizenship & Immigration) (1997), 133 F.T.R. 178 (Fed. T.D.) — The applicants sought to review a negative decision of a panel of the CRDD. The Board found that the male applicant was excluded under Article 1(F)(a) of the Convention, on the basis that he committed crimes against humanity. The decision of the panel was set aside. The Board did not expressly consider whether the crimes committed by the police constituted crimes against humanity. Crimes against humanity must generally be committed in a wide spread systematic fashion. This requirement does not mean that a crime against humanity cannot be committed against one person, but in order to elevate a domestic crime such as murder or assault to the realm of international law an additional element will have to be found. This element is that the person who has been victimized is a member of a group which has been targeted systematically and in a widespread manner for one of the crimes of murder, extermination, enslavement, deportation or other inhuman acts. The Board should have considered whether the victims of police abuse in this case were "...members of a group which have been targeted systematically and in a widespread manner for one of the crimes mentioned..."

Canada (Minister of Citizenship & Immigration) v. Pinnock (1996), 122 F.T.R. 68 (Fed. T.D.) — The Minister sought judicial review of a decision of the appeal division staying a removal order against the respondent. The tribunal was unable to provide reasons for its decision due to the fact that the board member who heard the case was medically incapacitated at the time the request for reasons was received. The principles of natural justice require that a decision of the tribunal be subject to judicial review. Without reasons for a decision there is no alternative means by which an applicant can establish what was in the mind of the member or members of the tribunal that led to their decision.

The incapacity of the tribunal to fulfil its statutory obligation prejudices the applicant in prosecuting this application. In the result the decision of the tribunal will be set aside and the matter remitted back for reconsideration.

Vairavanathan v. Canada (Minister of Citizenship & Immigration) (1996), 34 Imm. L.R. (2d) 307, 43 Admin. L.R. (2d) 121 (Fed. T.D.) — This is an application to review a negative decision of a panel of the CRDD. The applicant's refugee claim was heard on February 17, 1995 and at its conclusion the applicant's counsel was asked to provide written submissions. This she did on March 17, 1995.

The problem arose because in April of 1995, the truce in Sri Lanka ended and fighting resumed. The applicant's counsel faxed to the Board a covering note and three newspaper articles describing the changes in circumstances. The second submission was relevant. The 7 pages of material were sent to the board in a sensible time frame, and to the Board's correct fax number. The problem is there is no evidence that the second submission reached the relevant panel member. They do not mention it in their decision and it does not appear in the tribunal record.

The second submission was unexpected and in situations where counsel decide to forward post hearing submissions which the board has not requested, there is a duty on counsel to obtain a confirmation from the relevant panel members that the submission was actually received. In future cases, counsel would be expected to obtain such confirmation. In this case, the application was allowed and the matter remitted back for re-hearing.

Magana v. Canada (Minister of Citizenship & Immigration) (May 8, 1996), Doc. IMM-1608-95 (Fed. T.D.) — In dismissing an application to overturn a negative decision of a panel of the IRB, the Court summarized the function of the Board as follows:

The primary function of the Refugee Board is to weigh and assess the evidence before it. It is not necessary for the tribunal to list every conceivable factor which may have influenced its decision or summarize all of the evidence which was before it. What is required is that the Board's reasons demonstrate an understanding of the pertinent issues and of the relevant evidence.

After reviewing the decision the Court concluded that the claim should be dismissed. There was no perverse or capricious finding of fact nor any reviewable error of law.

Otoo v. Canada (Minister of Citizenship & Immigration) (February 9, 1996), Doc. IMM-5056-94 (Fed. T.D.) — This was an application to review a negative decision of a panel of the IRB. The claimant worked for the Ashanti Goldfields Corporation in Ghana and was active with the union there. He was arrested, held without charge and beaten. He claimed refugee status upon his arrival in Canada.

The Board determined that there was no objective basis for the claimant's fear of persecution should he return to Ghana. No mention was made by the Board in its decision of a wanted poster of the claimant distributed by the police and dated February 20, 1987, two days after the applicant fled the country.

The Board is not required to refer to each piece of evidence that was before it. When there is evidence which directly contradicts its findings the Board must, at least, acknowledge it. The wanted poster indicated that the applicant could be arrested in Ghana. Given the treatment that he suffered at the hands of the police in the past, it was not unreasonable to suspect that persecution might await him upon his return. The panel committed an error in law by not making any reference to the wanted poster in its decision. Accordingly, the application was allowed and the matter remitted to a differently constituted panel.

Kanagaratnam v. Canada (Minister of Employment & Immigration) (1996), 26 Imm. L.R. (2d) 180, 112 F.T.R. 240 (note), 194 N.R. 46 (Fed. C.A.) — The Refugee Board determined that the appellant, a native of Sri Lanka, had an internal flight alternative (IFA) within her country, and did not think it necessary to decide that the appellant otherwise had a well founded fear of persecution. A motion was brought for judicial review and the trial judge dismissed the motion, but certified a question for appeal, namely whether a determination of whether a claimant has a well founded fear of persecution in the area from which he or she originates, is a prerequisite to the consideration of an internal flight alternative.

In assessing whether a viable IFA exists, the Board, of course, must have regard to all the appropriate circumstances. Since an IFA existed, therefore, the claimant, by definition, could not have a well founded fear of persecution in her country of nationality. Thus, while the Board may certainly do so if it chooses, there was no need, as a matter of law, for the Board to decide whether there was persecution in the area of origin as a prerequisite to the consideration of an IFA.

Ahmedi v. Canada (Secretary of State) (December 15, 1994), Doc. IMM-2068-94 (Fed. T.D.) — The applicant had been a teacher under the communist regime in Afghanistan. His claim of persecution was based on the fact that he would be perceived by the present government as having been a member of the communist party and, therefore, at special risk from fundamentalist Muslim groups. The panel did not accurately describe the applicant's claim and, therefore, failed to properly address in its reasons, evidence which was central to that claim. Accordingly, the application was allowed and the matter remitted to a differently constituted panel of the IRB.

Gourenko v. Canada (Solicitor General) (1994), 93 F.T.R. 264 — The issue raised by the applicant in this application for judicial review of a negative decision of a panel of the IRB was whether the Board ought to have commented on certain documents in addition to those mentioned in its reasons. The applicant, a Jewish citizen of Moldova, was found to have been a victim of discrimination. In addition, the Board did not find that the applicant had an objectively well-founded fear of persecution. The Board cannot comment on all documents in its record and the fact that no mention is made of a document does not necessarily mean that the document has been ignored.

In order for a document to be so important that the failure to mention it would be considered a reviewable error, the following must be true:

1. The document must be timely in the sense that it bears on the relevant time period described by the applicant in his or her claim;

2. The document must be prepared by a reputable independent author who is in a position to be the most reliable source of information; and,

3. The topic addressed in the document must be directly relevant to the applicant's claim.

The Court gave two examples. Documents sent to or received by an applicant, or prepared for an applicant or about an applicant, which bear on relevant issues, would, in the ordinary course, be mentioned in the reasons. In addition, documents directly relevant to the facts alleged by the applicant would normally be expected to be mentioned in the Board's reasons. Finally, the Court noted that numerous other documents may only be marginally relevant and it is not a reviewable error for the Board to fail to deal with such documents. In the context of this case there was no reviewable error in the manner in which the Board dealt with the documents in the case, and the application for judicial review was dismissed.

Ke v. Canada (Minister of Citizenship & Immigration) (1995), 100 F.T.R. 46, 31 Imm. L.R. (2d) 309 — The applicant sought to review a negative decision of CRDD. The panel, it was conceded, had committed a breach of natural justice by issuing reasons prior to hearing submissions. The issue that arose was whether the Board remedied this breach by considering the applicant's submissions after it had reached its decision and then issuing an addendum to the decision.

A final disposition cannot be re-opened. This rule applies only after the formal judgment has been drawn up, issued and entered, and is subject to two exceptions: (1) where there is a slip in drawing up the final judgment, and (2) where there is an error in expressing the manifest intention of the Court.

The error that the panel made in making its decision without the submissions of counsel tainted the whole proceeding so as to require that the matter be heard again.

Chen v. Canada (Minister of Citizenship & Immigration) (July 19, 1995), IMM-4381-94 (Fed. T.D.) — The applicant applied to review a negative decision of the CRDD. The applicant, a citizen of China, claimed to have a well-founded fear of persecution based on the fact that her parents and grandparents were members of the landlord class, thus the applicant feared persecution based upon membership in that social group.

The applicant submitted a number of letters from physicians and psychiatrists which indicated that the applicant was suffering from a mental disability and post-traumatic stress disorder arising from a beating by a police officer.

The panel concluded that some of the applicant's statements were not credible. Credibility, even when it is based primarily upon implausibilities, implicitly takes into account general demeanour or the Board's gut reaction to the applicant's testimony. When the applicant's demeanour is affected by a mental condition, it could have an impact on his credibility. The Board should at least acknowledge this on the record. Although it is the Board's prerogative to find that the injury does not affect its decision, the Board cannot skirt the issue by simply making no mention of it. In failing to address the applicant's mental medical condition on the record, the Board ignored relevant evidence and erred in law. This was a material error, and as a result, the decision of the Board was set aside.

Singh (G.) v. Canada (Minister of Citizenship & Immigration) (1995), 30 Imm. L.R. (2d) 226, 97 F.T.R. 139 — This was an application to review a negative decision of the CRDD. In the course of the applicant's refugee hearing, he argued that the tribunal should consider the application of subsection 2(3) of the *Immigration Act* in this case. In its reasons for the decision, the Tribunal neither considered the applicability of the subsection, nor did it consider a medical report tendered in furtherance of that aspect of the case. Counsel for the respondent submitted that there was no obligation upon the Tribunal to consider subsection 2(3) because of its finding that the applicant was not, in fact, a refugee.

Counsel for the applicant explicitly raised the issue of subsection 2(3) at the beginning of the hearing and filed a medical report in support of its claim. It is not for the Court to speculate on the reasons why the Tribunal believed subsection 2(3) did not apply. The failure of the Tribunal to consider the issue in its reasons amounted to reviewable error.

Memarpour v. Canada (Minister of Citizenship & Immigration) (1995), 104 F.T.R. 55 — At the opening of the hearing of the applicant's refugee claim the presiding Board member made a statement which indicated that certain evidence about events in Iran was accepted for purposes of the hearing. The Board then, in rendering its decision, made an adverse credibility finding in respect of those events. This was held to be a failure of natural justice. There is no general duty to confront a witness with issues of credibility. Such a requirement exists if credibility becomes an issue for the Board when it has previously been deleted by the Board as a relevant issue.

Having decided that there was a denial of a fair hearing the Court then must ask itself whether it is nonsensical and contrary to notions of finality and the affective use of public funds and the Board's resources to require a re-hearing. The Court relied upon *Mobile Oil Canada Ltd. v. Canada-Newfoundland (Offshore Petroleum Board)*, [1994] 1 S.C.R. 202 (S.C.C.) at p. 205. In this case the Court concluded that even if the applicant were to be believed about the events in Iran which were the subject matter of the application, a panel of the IRB would certainly conclude that the applicant did not have a subjective fear of persecution. In those circumstances the application was dismissed.

Liu v. Canada (Minister of Citizenship & Immigration) (1995), 98 F.T.R. 88 (Fed. T.D.) — The female applicant had one child while she was living in Shanghai and left China because she did not want to be sterilized. The applicant testified that there was incredible pressure on her to undergo sterilization. The work unit in which she worked would have incurred fines and a member of that unit twice accompanied her to a hospital to undergo a planned sterilization which, for medical reasons, did not take place. The panel erred in ruling that physical compulsion was the only mechanism for forcing a person to do something which they would not, of their own free choice, choose to do. The Court noted that other members of the applicant's work unit would be denied 80% of their salary if the applicant conceived a second child. Pressure of this nature is no different from physical compulsion.

The error by the panel, with respect to the characterization of the pressure upon the applicant in China, was not determinative of the application and, accordingly, did not result in the decision of the panel being overturned. The applicant had a second child born outside of China and there was no evidence to suggest that should the applicant be returned to China, her second child would be taken away from her. The assertion by the applicant in her evidence that this would be the case was unsupported by the documentary evidence. Further, the applicant and her husband, now that they had had a second child, indicated they no longer objected to the family planning policy or methods of the government of China.

Accordingly, the application was dismissed.

Singh (R.) v. Canada (Minister of Citizenship & Immigration) (May 8, 1995), Doc. IMM-2382-94 (Fed. T.D.) — A panel of the IRB concluded that the applicant's testimony was not credible. Counsel argued that the Board's failure to address a psychiatric report dealing with post-traumatic stress disorder, was a reviewable error. The report was timely, dated approximately 1 month before the hearing. Furthermore, the credentials of the psychiatrist were not in dispute and it was a reviewable error for the Board to fail to refer to the report. However, the Board's finding of credibility made it clear that it did not believe the underlying facts upon which the report was based. Clearly the Board would not have accepted the doctor's perception over its own on the issue of demeanour.

The Court distinguished the situation in this case from those where the tribunal's findings on the question of credibility were tentative, or otherwise not firm. The application for judicial review was dismissed.

Ameyaw v. Canada (Minister of Citizenship & Immigration) (May 1, 1995), Doc. A-999-92 (Fed. T.D.) — The applicant, a citizen of Ghana, sought to review a negative decision by a panel of the IRB respecting his refugee claim. The applicant testified that he had spoken against the concept of a one-party state at a community meeting and at a meeting of the Sunday School class.

In rejecting the applicant's claim the Board cited considerable documentary evidence which indicated that free speech was being tolerated in Ghana and that the country was moving towards a system of democratic rule. The Board found that the applicant's experiences in Ghana were not consistent with reports from credible sources in the documentary evidence submitted at the hearing.

The applicant submitted that the main reason for the Board's negative determination was that the applicant's narrative was inconsistent with the submitted documentary evidence. The applicant submitted that the reasons of the Board were very sparse in this regard. The Board is not required to refer to each piece of evidence that was before it, however, where there is documentary evidence which directly contradicts the Board's findings, the Board must at least acknowledge that evidence. In the case at bar there was clearly evidence which indicated that a person who opposed the government faced persecution despite increased liberalization and democratization in Ghana. By failing to acknowledge the directly contradictory evidence in the record the Board erred in law. Accordingly, the decision was set aside and the matter referred back to a differently constituted Board.

Benavente v. Canada (Minister of Citizenship & Immigration) (1995), 95 F.T.R. 125 — The applicants successfully reviewed a negative decision of a panel of the CRDD. The applicants asserted fear as a result of the older applicant's outspoken opposition to the government of Guatemala. An affidavit was filed by counsel for the applicants which contradicted the recitation of facts in the Board's reasons. No transcript was available.

The absence of a transcript alone is not a breach of natural justice or fairness. In a dispute as to what was said during any unrecorded portion of the hearing the Court will give the benefit of the doubt to the applicant because the applicant had no administrative responsibility for, or control over, the recording and transcription process.

Rivas v. Canada (Minister of Citizenship & Immigration) (April 24, 1995), Doc. IMM-4289-94 (Fed. T.D.) — The applicant sought judicial review of a negative decision of the CRDD. The applicant testified that his father, a union activist and an FMLN mayoralty candidate, was shot in his home in El Salvador. The applicant believed that his father was killed by a right wing death squad because of his FMLN connection. The Board viewed the evidence of the applicant as being too speculative.

Documentary evidence supported the fact that the killing of individuals, like the applicant's father, did take place in El Salvador during the relevant period. The Board stated in its reasons "we could certainly speculate, as does the claimant, that his father was murdered by a right wing death squad because of his FMLN connection, however, we could equally well speculate that his father was the victim of common crime". The Board has a responsibility to make clear findings on the evidence that is before them. A finding of fact has been described as a determination that a phenomenon has happened, is or will happen, independent of any determination as to its legal effect. Speculation is not a substitute for that responsibility. The Board fell into error when instead of making clear findings of fact, they engaged in their own speculation as to the reason for the death of the father.

The application for judicial review was allowed and the matter returned to a differently constituted panel.

Ali v. Canada (Minister of Employment & Immigration) (February 24, 1995), Doc. A-1114-92 (Fed. T.D.) — The applicant, a citizen of Ghana, sought to review a negative decision of the CRDD. The application was allowed.

The Court described a number of errors in the decision of the panel of the CRDD. It then concluded that when read as a whole the decision of the CRDD was so replete with errors and misstatements of the evidence as to be not sustainable. The Court relied upon *Singh (G.) v. Canada (Minister of Employment & Immigration)* (1993), 69 F.T.R. 142 (Fed. T.D.) as authority for the proposition that the question to be determined was whether this was the kind of a decision which should be sent back for rehearing or whether there remained enough of the decision that was not challengeable to support the Board's decision.

Shahid v. Canada (Minister of Citizenship & Immigration) (1995), 28 Imm. L.R. (2d) 130, 89 F.T.R. 106 (Fed. T.D.) — The applicant claimed that by virtue of section 2(3) of the *Immigration Act* he should not be returned to Pakistan. The Board, in refusing to apply section 2(3) determined that it required an on-going fear of persecution. For this reason the decision was set aside. The Board, once it embarked upon the assessment of the applicant's claim under section 2(3) had the duty to consider the level of atrocity of the acts inflicted upon the applicant, the repercussions upon his physical and mental state, and determine whether this experience alone constituted a compelling reason not to return him to his country of origin. The panel failed to do this and accordingly its decision was quashed and the matter returned for a new hearing before a differently constituted tribunal.

Torres v. Canada (Solicitor General) (February 1, 1995), Doc. IMM-503-94 (Fed. T.D.) — The applicant had been active in the labour movement in Mexico and as a result of his involvement had been mistreated by Mexican authorities. The applicant testified that if he were to return to Mexico he would not re-join the labour movement because he feared persecution as a party member and also because he would not be welcome. The Board relied on this portion of the applicant's testimony in coming to a negative conclusion about the possibility of future persecution. Counsel for the applicant suggested that the question should only be whether there is reason to believe that the claimants decision to exercise his right to form an opinion would place him in jeopardy.

The applicant was dismissed. Refugee claims are not to be connsidered on a theoretical level which ignores the practical realities of the evidence. When the Board received evidence to the effect that this applicant had no intention of re-joining the labour movement, and indeed could not do so, it was entitled to make a practical assessment of the possibility of future persecution.

Zheng v. Canada (Minister of Citizenship & Immigration) (1995), 27 Imm. L.R. (2d) 101 (Fed. T.D.) — The applicant testified at her refugee hearing that she was arrested for speaking with a foreign reporter. The Board found this evidence to be implausible. There was documentary evidence before the Board which indicated that Chinese citizens were detained and arrested for talking to foreign reporters. The respondent argued that the persons referred to in the articles were not similarly situated to the applicant. The Court found that the evidence was sufficiently compelling and should have been considered. The Board does not require to refer to each piece of evidence that was before it. However, when there is evidence which directly contradicts its findings, the Board must at least acknowledge this evidence.

As a result of this error, the decision of a panel of the Refugee Division was quashed and the matter remitted back to a differently constituted panel.

Njoko v. Canada (Minister of Employment & Immigration) (January 25, 1995), Doc. A-1698-92 (Fed. T.D.) — The applicant had testified that she was sexually assaulted while in prison in Zaire. The Board found that any fear that the claimant might have arising out of this experience could be characterized as a fear of private violence, albeit, by persons employed by a State. In order to support the panel's assertion that the sexual assault of a political detainee by agents of the government is an act of private violence there must be evidence before the Board to illustrate that the government in question does not tolerate such abuse and diligently prosecutes those who commit it. Here the documentary evidence before the Board revealed there was no mechanism in place to discourage such acts of abuse. Further, the conclusion that the applicants would not be apprehended upon their return to Zaire, notwithstanding the fact that they escaped prison, was pure speculation. Accordingly, the decision of the panel was set aside.

Gyimah v. Canada (Minister of Citizenship & Immigration) (1994), 25 Imm. L.R. (2d) 132, 83 F.T.R. 34 — The applicant, a citizen of Ghana, sought to overturn a negative decision of the CRDD. During her hearing the applicant produced a summons which she said was given to her and which required her to appear before a public tribunal in Ghana on a charge of conspiring against the government and of having acted contrary to the spirit of the revolution. The CRDD found that it was implausible that someone could be charged under the laws under which the summons purported to charge. The CRDD had commented on the fact that the summons was not addressed to the applicant at her home but rather at another address and found it to be implausible that a formal notice to appear before a public tribunal would be addressed in such an informal manner.

The conclusions of the CRDD regarding the form and precision of a summons requiring an individual to appear before a public tribunal in Ghana were simply not supported by the documentary evidence or indeed any evidence. The implausibility findings with respect to the applicant's testimony and the lack of authenticity of the summons were inextricably linked. In the result, the decision of the CRDD was set aside.

Navarro v. Canada (Minister of Citizenship & Immigration) (December 20, 1994), Doc. A-1699-92 (Fed. T.D.) — The applicant made an unsuccessful claim for refugee status. The applicant testified that he did not hold a political opinion, although he indicated in his personal information form (PIF) that this was the ground upon which he was claiming refugee status. The applicant argued in the Federal Court that his fear of persecution was, and continued to be, related to the ground of membership in a particular social group. The applicant contended that the group was composed of El Salvadorean males of military age. This ground was not argued before the panel that considered the refugee claim and was not dealt with anywhere in the reasons for decision.

The negative decision was set aside. The evidence submitted by the applicant pointed to a ground of membership in a particular social group as founding a possible fear of persecution. The Board should have considered this ground as part of the claim to refugee status, notwithstanding the fact that the claim was not expressly relied upon in the PIF.

Parizi v. Canada (Minister of Citizenship & Immigration) (1994), 90 F.T.R. 189 — The applicant was a 26 year old from Iran who claimed refugee status and who was found not to be a credible witness. A panel of the IRB has considerable discretion in assessing credibility. The standard of judicial review for credibility findings was summarized in *Boye v. Canada (Minister of Employment & Immigration)* (1994), 83 F.T.R. 1 (Fed. T.D.). Despite the degree of discretion granted to the Board in assessing credibility, the Board has an obligation to express any negative findings of credibility in clear and unmistakeable terms. This generally includes the obligation to give examples or illustrations of the basis for not accepting the applicant's testimony.

The standard of judicial deference that applies to finding of implausibility is set out in *Aguebor v. Canada (Minister of Employment & Immigration)* (1993), 160 N.R. 315 (Fed. C.A.). The reviewing the Court should refuse to interfere with decisions which assess credibility or plausibility provided that the decisions are properly founded on evidence, do not ignore evidence, or are supported by evidence.

In this case the Court did not defer to the Board's finding on credibility because it was not satisfied that the Board had considered and weighed all of the evidence adduced by the applicant.

Rathor v. Canada (Minister of Employment & Immigration) (1994), 27 Imm. L.R. (2d) 192 (Fed. T.D.) — This was an application setting aside a negative decision of a panel of the CRDD. The applicant, a citizen of Pakistan, claimed Convention refugee status due to his religion and membership in a particular social group.

The Board's reasons contain many passages including findings of fact which are virtually identical to passages contained in decisions rendered by differently constituted panels in other Pakistani Ahmadi refugee cases. This raises the fear that the Board took a predetermined stance with respect to all claimants from this area, or alternatively, that the panel has been influenced by extraneous factors. Accordingly the decision was set aside and the matter remitted to a differently constituted panel.

Theiventhiran v. Canada (Minister of Citizenship & Immigration) (1994), 88 F.T.R. 94 — There is no general duty on a Court or tribunal to invite submissions by the parties on a new decision rendered by a higher Court before relying on that decision. A decision to invite such representations is purely discretionary in nature.

If the new decision of the higher Court results in a fundamental change in the law, as a matter of fairness one would expect that counsel for the parties would be allowed to make representations on their clients' behalf. When the new decision does not constitute a fundamental change in the law, but is merely an elaboration or clarification of existing law, there is no such practical imperative.

If the decision of the higher Court represents a fundamental change in the law and if the parties or their counsel know about the decision and ask to make representations to the inferior tribunal, it would be a breach of natural justice for the tribunal to refuse to hear them.

Finally, whether a change is fundamental or not must be viewed from the particular circumstances of the decision under review and how the alteration, or clarification of the law found in the new decision, impacted on those particular circumstances.

Sivayoganathan v. Canada (Minister of Citizenship & Immigration) (1994), 86 F.T.R. 152 — The applicant was an unsuccessful refugee claimant from Sri Lanka who presented documentary evidence in the form of a letter from a Canadian doctor indicating that the applicant suffered psychologically from her difficult years in her country of origin.

The Board commented negatively on the applicant's demeanour, remarking on her emotional response to her counsel's questioning and determined that she was evasive, incoherent and disjointed in her testimony.

The medical report was evidence explaining the applicant's demeanour. It was not open to the Board to disregard that evidence without indicating its reasons for so doing. The error was most significant in that it was the applicant's demeanour which led to a finding of lack of credibility.

Gaoukman v. Canada (Minister of Employment & Immigration) (November 3, 1994), Doc. A-1311-92 (Fed. T.D.) — The applicants unsuccessfully claimed refugee status and claimed persecution on the basis of their religion and nationality.

It is within the tribunal's expertise to determine that the incidents experienced by the applicants amount only to discrimination and harassment, and not persecution. Intervention by the Court is not warranted unless the conclusion reached by the panel appears to be capricious or unreasonable.

Markovskaia v. Canada (Minister of Citizenship & Immigration) (1994), 86 F.T.R. 74 — The applicant sought to overturn a negative decision of a panel of the CRDD. The panel decided that the applicant was not of either the Jewish nationality or faith. The panel found the applicant not to be a credible witness on this question. The applicant had submitted at the hearing a birth certificate and internal passport, both of which stated that both of the applicant's parents were Jewish and that the applicant's nationality was Jewish.

A panel in its decision made no reference to these documents. The authenticity of these documents was not questioned or challenged at the hearing. A failure to recite all the evidence does not necessarily result in a reviewable error. However, the tribunal should address material evidence which specifically relates to the applicant's claim. The application was allowed and the decision of the panel set aside.

Andemariam v. Canada (Minister of Employment & Immigration) (1994), 83 F.T.R. 313 — This decision of the Board was overturned because the Board relied on evidence to the effect that none of the Human Rights monitors in Ethiopia expressed concern that there was any intention on the part of a new government to persecute those they had detained for investigation. It is wrong to require a presence of a persecutory intent when a persecutory effect will be sufficient to meet the definition.

Kathiravel v. Canada (Minister of Employment & Immigration) (1994), 83 F.T.R. 3 — The applicant was the only person to testify at her refugee hearing. Her testimony, as well as the information disclosed in her personal information form (PIF), revealed a long history of hardship and suffering at the hands of the Sri Lankan Armed Forces, the Indian Peace Keeping Forces and the Liberation Tigers of Tamil Eelam. The Board did not challenge the claimant's credibility but concluded that the events described by her did not give rise to an objectively well-founded fear of persecution.

The onus proving that the claimant falls within the confines of the Convention refugee definition, falls on the applicant. The panel responsible for determining a case must properly consider the evidence before it. If the panel disregards or misconstrues relevant evidence, and what is overlooked is *prima facie* material to the decision reached, the decision cannot be reasonable. While it is open to a panel to determine the weight of the evidence given by an applicant, it is not open to the panel to completely ignore documentary or testimonial evidence, material to its decision without some justification. A conclusion that flows from a failure on the part of the panel to satisfactorily address key evidence that is directly related to its decision, is that such a decision is patently unreasonable.

The panel's failure to properly consider the facts before it in respect of a well-founded fear of persecution was a reviewable error.

Farouji v. Canada (Minister of Employment & Immigration) (1994), 84 F.T.R. 97, (sub nom. *Farouji v. Ministre de l'Emploi & de l'Immigration)* (Fed. T.D.) — The applicants' claim for refugee status was dismissed on the basis that the father, whose claim served as a basis for the claims of the other members of the family, was not considered credible. Nor was his wife considered credible. Counsel for the applicants requisitioned the transcript of the hearing. The transcript was not available because the cassettes used to record the testimony could not be transcribed. The failure to file part of the transcript of the testimony given before a panel of the Refugee Division does not invalidate the panel's decision. An incomplete transcript can be supplemented by the adjudicator's notes and the applicants' own affidavit. The applicant's father and wife filed lengthy affidavits in support of their application and refuted point by point the conclusions and inferences drawn by the panel. The absence of a transcript in this case, left the Court unable to verify the contradictions and improbabilities noted by the Refugee Division panel and to rule on the reasonableness of the panel's conclusion. Accordingly, the decision of the panel was set aside.

The lack of a transcript is not *per se* a breach of the rules of fundamental justice. In some circumstances, however, the absence of a transcript may amount to a denial of natural justice, for example, when a case revolves around an assessment of credibility and lengthy testimony was given at the hearing. The application was allowed and the decision of the panel set aside.

Khan v. Canada (Minister of Employment & Immigration) (August 23, 1994), Doc. IMM-415-93 (Fed. T.D.) — The tribunal concluded that the applicant had fabricated a key element of his claim. However, the applicant's account of the events, which the tribunal found to be fabricated, was supported by documentary evidence which made specific reference to the applicant and corroborated his testimony. The Board failed to deal explicitly with this evidence which, if authentic, substantiated the applicant's claim. Accordingly, the application was allowed and the Board's decision set aside.

Mahanandan v. Canada (Minister of Employment & Immigration) (August 23, 1994), Doc. A-608-91 (Fed. C.A.) — The applicant's claim for refugee status was rejected on the basis it was not objectively well-founded. The objective basis for the appellant's fear was supported by documentary evidence which had been received in evidence. The Board, in its decision, acknowledged having received the evidence but did not indicate, in its reasons, the impact, if any, that such evidence had upon the applicant's claim. This was a fatal omission and the decision of the Board was set aside.

Tharmalingam v. Canada (Minister of Employment & Immigration) (1994), 76 F.T.R. 190 — The tribunal found that the applicant's testimony was not credible in six areas. This finding of lack of credibility was not a general one such that it had determined that the applicant was not a credible witness and that there was no credible evidence supporting his fear of persecution. Therefore, even though the finding of lack of credibility in the six areas of testimony was not unreasonable, there was still an obligation on the Board to determine from the remaining credible evidence whether or not there was an objective basis for the applicant's fear of persecution. The Board failed to do this, and its decision was set aside.

Li v. Canada (Minister of Citizenship & Immigration) (July 20, 1994), Doc. A-1657-92 (Fed. T.D.) — The applicant was discouraged by a comment from a Board Member from elaborating on what took place during a Swedish T.V. interview. The failure to so elaborate was relied on by the Board in reaching its decision. When the Board acts in a manner so as to discourage an applicant from adducing evidence on a particular point, it cannot rely on the failure of the applicant to offer such evidence in reaching its decision, unless it subsequently puts questions to the applicant concerning those matters.

The Court also commented negatively, on a trend in a number of Board decisions in that they relied on the fact that the applicant cannot demonstrate or prove that the persecuting state authorities have specific knowledge of the applicant's conduct.

Khandokar v. Canada (Minister of Employment & Immigration) (1994), 82 F.T.R. 76 — The central issue in this case involved the manner in which the Board cast doubt upon the authenticity of an arrest warrant. A copy of the warrant was provided but the panel found that the document was not authentic. The document was stamped on the reverse side without any date or signature.

There was no evidence before the panel with respect to the procedures regarding the issuance of warrants or the form of those warrants thus there was insufficient evidence to support a finding that the warrant was not genuine. This resulted in the application being allowed and the matter remitted to a differently constituted panel.

Chaudhry v. Canada (Minister of Employment & Immigration) (1994), 25 Imm. L.R. (2d) 139, 83 F.T.R. 81, [1995] 1 F.C. 104 — The applicants applied to quash a decision of the CRDD whereby the applicants' motion for a rehearing of their Convention refugee claim was dismissed.

The applicants were citizens of Pakistan who sought to be recognized as Convention refugees by reason of a well-founded fear of persecution based on their religion and membership in a particular social group. They were determined not to be Convention refugees and sought to re-open their claims to present evidence not available at the time of the CRDD decision to the effect that a change in country conditions had occurred since the decision in their case. Specifically, they sought to adduce evidence showing an increase in incidents of persecution against members of their religion.

The CRDD found that it had the jurisdiction to address the issue of whether or not it had the jurisdiction to re-open a claim. It then concluded that it could not re-open a matter where the sole purpose of the re-opening would be the hearing of new facts.

The Court found that the CRDD did not err in law in finding that, notwithstanding the Charter, it could not re-open the hearing solely for the purpose of hearing new evidence of changed country conditions.

The mechanism for dealing with post-proceeding evidence is section 114(2) of the *Immigration Act.* That section, and the Minister's practise in connection with that section, ensures that claimants have a meaningful opportunity to have new evidence of changed country conditions heard by an authoritative body. In this regard the Court noted that the discretionary decisions of post-claim determination officers are subject to judicial review by the Federal Court if such discretion is exercised pursuant to improper purposes, or based on irrelevant considerations, or made with bad faith, or otherwise, patently unreasonable. Accordingly, the application for judicial review in this case was dismissed.

Vasudevan v. Canada (Secretary of State) (1994), 83 F.T.R. 126 — This application sought to overturn a negative decision of the CRDD. In the course of the hearing there was before the Board, a paper dated December 19, 1992 prepared by the Research Director, Documentation, Information and Research Branch of the IRB. During the course of the proceeding counsel for the applicant and the Refugee Hearing Officer both referred to the document. Counsel for the applicant indicated that the document was fairly central to the applicant's argument.

The existence of the document was not acknowledged anywhere in the decision of the CRDD. The Court was satisfied that the CRDD had ignored the evidence. The ignoring of this evidence constituted an error of law. Accordingly, the decision of the CRDD was set aside.

Vettivelu v. Canada (Minister of Employment & Immigration) (July 6, 1994), Doc. IMM-2091-93 (Fed. T.D.) — The applicant sought judicial review of a negative decision of the CRDD. The applicant's oldest daughter and son-in-law, two other sons, and two other daughters had been found to be Convention refugees. The reasons her older children were found to be Convention refugees apparently had to do with the family's political activity.

The panel deciding the applicant's claim did not attempt to distinguish the applicant's situation from those of her children. The onus is on the applicant to show that she is similarly situated to her own children. Where the applicant leads evidence as to the Convention refugee status of her children, presumably to convince the panel that she should be granted the same status, the panel ought to address the issue in its analysis. If the panel concluded that the applicant was not similarly situated, it should have either said that there was no evidence by the applicant that she was similarly situated or otherwise distinguished the applicant's situation. Its failure to do so suggests that the panel ignored an important part of the applicant's case and thereby erred in law.

Accordingly, the applicantion was allowed and the matter remitted to the Board for consideration by a differently constituted panel.

Zapata v. Canada (Solicitor General) (1994), 82 F.T.R. 34, (sub nom. *Zapata v. Canada (Minister of Employment & Immigration))* (Fed. T.D.) — This was an application for judicial review of a negative decision with respect to the applicant's refugee claim. The applicant called, as an expert witness, a psychiatrist who testified that the applicant was suffering from Post Traumatic Stress Disorder consistent with his history of detention, torture and fear for his life. This opinion was rejected on the ground that it was based on what the psychiatrist was told by the applicant. This finding ignored the fact that the psychiatrist based his diagnosis also on his trained, professional observation of the applicant. Specifically the psychiatrist concluded that the applicant's "manner of reporting his history and his emotional reactions while reporting it were consistent with the history which he provided". Thus, the Board erred in its dismissal of the professional opinion. Accordingly, the decision was set aside and the matter returned for a new hearing.

Lameen v. Canada (Secretary of State) (June 7, 1994), Doc. A-1626-92 (Fed. T.D.) — This was an application for judicial review of a negative decision of the CRDD. The applicant was a citizen of Libya who had come to Canada in 1988 and failed to claim refugee status until February 10, 1992. Delay is an important factor to consider in assessing the subjective basis for the applicant's fear. Each case must be decided on its own merits for the purpose of determining how much delay is too much. Delay is a factor to be considered although not decisive on its own.

In this case the delay was taken into account and relied upon in assessing the applicant's subjective basis for his fear. The Board's conclusion on this point is not one which should be interfered with in the context of this case. Where an applicant states that he did not claim refugee status because he wanted to know what was needed to claim that status, it is open to the Board to interpret his actions of renewing his visa twice without inquiring about claiming refugee status as evidence that there was no subjective basis for his fear. Accordingly, the application for judicial review was dismissed.

Munkoh v. Canada (Minister of Employment & Immigration) (June 3, 1994), Doc. IMM-4056-93 (Fed. T.D.) — This was an application for judicial review of a decision refusing refugee status. The applicant, a citizen of Ghana, based his claim on persecution by reason of political opinion and membership in a particular social group. The CRDD made no adverse finding in respect of the credibility of the applicant. Without a clear finding of want of credibility with respect to the applicant's sworn testimony, there was, in the context of this case, no justification for the preference of documentary evidence over that of the applicant. An adequate analysis of the totality of the evidence before the CRDD, on the issue of country conditions, including the documentary evidence and sworn testimony, might have given rise to a conclusion that the total weight of evidence was against an objective basis to the claimant's subjective fear of persecution. However, such an analysis was not before the Court. The application was allowed and the matter remitted back for redetermination.

Leung v. Canada (Minister of Employment & Immigration) (1994), 81 F.T.R. 303 — The applicants applied for judicial review of a decision of the CRDD which determined that their fear of persecution was not objectively well-founded.

Inferences based on the degree of the claimant's political involvement are rarely reasonable, particularly where it is acknowledged that the claimant has indeed been persecuted. It was unreasonable for the Board to conclude that the applicant's fear of persecution was not objectively well-founded given the fact that the Public Security Bureau in China had attempted to arrest one of the applicants because of her involvement in the pro-democracy movement. The Court has held in the past that the Board's decisions must be based on the totality of the evidence contained in the record and this duty becomes particularly important where the finding of non-credibility is based on perceived implausibility in the claimant's story rather than on internal inconsistencies and contradictions or upon demeanour. Findings of implausibility are inherently subjective assessments which are largely dependant on the individual Board member's perceptions of what constitutes rational behaviour. The appropriateness of a particular finding can therefore only be assessed if the Board's decision clearly identifies all of the facts which form the basis for its conclusions.

The clear obligation on the Board to base its decisions on the totality of the evidence, combined with the duty to justify credibility findings, leads one to assume that the Board's reasons contain a reasonably complete account of the facts which form the basis of the Board's decision. The Board will therefore err when it fails to refer to relevant evidence which could potentially refute its conclusions of implausibility.

In this case, in concluding that the applicants' narrative was implausible, the Board ignored numerous references in the record which corroborated the applicants' assertions that the Public Security Bureau began its crackdown by first targeting the participants in pro-democracy demonstrations and then moving on to the organizers. Further, in concluding that it was implausible that the Security Bureau would not have realized that both applicants were wanted, and then have taken more aggressive steps to arrest them, the Board failed to deal with the copies of two summonses which were tendered in evidence and which had been issued by the Security Bureau against the second applicant. These summonses confirmed that the Security Bureau attended at the applicants' home on at least two occasions in an attempt to arrest the second applicant and therefore served to corroborate the applicants' testimony and should have at least been considered by the Board.

The application was allowed and the matter returned to a newly constituted panel.

Gonzalez v. Canada (Minister of Employment & Immigration), [1994] 3 F.C. 646, 24 Imm. L.R. (2d) 229, 170 N.R. 302, 115 D.L.R. (4th) 403 (Fed. C.A.) — This was an appeal from a decision of the Refugee Division, which found the appellant excluded from the definition of Convention refugee by reason of section F(a) of Article 1 of the *United Nations Convention Relating to the Status of Refugees* because the Board found that there was serious reason to believe that the appellant had committed a crime against humanity. The Board proceeded directly to that finding and made no finding on the merits of the refugee claim. The appellant had admitted to killing civilians on two occasions when his military unit in Nicaragua encountered armed counter-revolutionaries. The Court noted that as a practical matter it would have been better had the Refugee Division dealt with the merits of the claim as well as the applicability of the exclusion. The Court noted that if the claim was well-founded but for the application of the exclusion and if it were found on appeal that the exclusion had been wrongly applied to the appellant, then the Court could have made the necessary declaration without requiring the Refugee Division to deal with the matter again. The Court found that, on the particular facts and circumstances of this case, the appellant was a soldier engaged in an action against an armed enemy and that his actual participation in the killing of innocent civilians fell short of a crime against humanity. The Court indicated that it did not wish to be understood as saying that the killing of civilians by a soldier while engaged in an action against an armed enemy could never amount to a war crime or a crime against humanity. Each case will depend on its own individual facts and circumstances.

Costa v. Canada (Minister of Employment & Immigration) (1994), 80 F.T.R. 12 — The applicants were from Uruguay and appealed a negative determination of their refugee claim. The tribunal's finding that the claim was not objectively based was the subject matter of the judicial review application. The decision of the tribunal was set aside. The analysis of the documentary evidence by the tribunal was deficient. The tribunal referred to only two sources: the U.S. Country Reports and the "Response to Information Request" made by the CRDD. It is not the Court's task to substitute its opinion of the weight to be accorded the documentary evidence that was before the tribunal. The tribunal simply cited documentary evidence in favour of its conclusion that the circumstances in Uruguay were such as to reduce or eliminate the risk of persecution to the applicants. This left the Court in doubt as to whether the tribunal had taken into account the totality of the documentary evidence before it. Accordingly, the decision of the tribunal was set aside.

Ammery v. Canada (Secretary of State) (1994), 78 F.T.R. 73 — The applicant, a female citizen of Iran, sought to set aside a negative determination of her refugee claim. The applicant, in her evidence before the tribunal, claimed that she and other members of her family were being harassed and persecuted because of the activities of her step-father. Even though it appeared that the tribunal erred in its consideration of the meaning of the word "persecution", the Court would not have intervened if the tribunal's assessment of the evidence was made by proceeding with a careful analysis of the evidence adduced and a proper balancing of the various elements contained in that evidence. This did not happen in this case and thus the decision of the tribunal could not stand on that basis alone.

The tribunal also suggested that there was no documentary evidence to suggest that Iranian citizens were persecuted by their government because of their relatives' anti-government activities. This conclusion was not correct; there were two references in the documentary evidence on this question. However, notwithstanding that fact, the Court was of the view that where there is evidence of the applicant accepted as credible by the tribunal, even the absence of documentary evidence that would support it is not a ground for concluding that the applicant failed to establish good grounds for a fear of persecution.

Kone v. Canada (Minister of Employment & Immigration) (1994), 79 F.T.R. 63 — For digest, see section 69.1, subheading *Subsection (5), supra.*

Villacorta v. Canada (Secretary of State) (1994), 77 F.T.R. 304 — The applicant from El Salvador sought to quash a negative decision of the CRDD.

The first kind of relief sought was an order directing a particular determination by the CRDD, namely that the applicant was a Convention refugee. If, as a result of judicial review proceedings, the Court finds an error of the sort set out in section 18.1(4) of the *Federal*

Court Act, it may set aside the impugned decision, but it has no authority to make a determination or to order that a particular determination be made on the refugee status of a claimant.

The fact that the tribunal did not refer to all documentary evidence that would raise questions about or would support its conclusion was not fatal to its decision. The decision made reference to documentary evidence not supportive of its conclusion that conditions in El Salvador had changed sufficiently to remove the basis for a well-founded fear and thus the decision could not be said to be perverse or capricious or without regard to the evidence.

Singh v. Canada (Minister of Employment & Immigration) (1994), 77 F.T.R. 234 — The applicant, a Sikh and a citizen of India, sought to review a negative determination of his refugee claim. The question was whether the panel correctly determined that the applicant had an internal flight alternative. In a contentious case, in which there is seriously conflicting evidence, the tribunal should not rely on one piece of general documentary evidence to arrive at its conclusion on this question to the exclusion of other evidence about the particular circumstances of the applicant. Where there is no conflicting evidence and no evidence at all about the applicant's personal circumstances, the Board does not err when it refers to evidence in support of its conclusion in a summary manner.

Pouranfar v. Canada (Minister of Employment & Immigration) (May 3, 1994), Doc. IMM-914-93 (Fed. T.D.) — The applicant, a citizen of Iran, sought judicial review of a negative decision of the CRDD. The application was unsuccessful.

The applicant's counsel sought to persuade the Court that if a decision about a lack of credibility was based on implausibilities, the Court should be more inclined to substitute its judgment for that of the Board than if the decision was based on internal inconsistencies or the demeanour of the witness. Two different tests do not exist. It may be easier to have a finding of implausibility reviewed where it results from inferences than to have a finding of non-credibility reviewed where it results from the conduct of the witness and from inconsistencies in the testimony. In saying this, the Court did not exclude the issue of the plausibility of an account from the Board's field of expertise, nor did it lay down a different test for intervention, depending on whether the issue is plausibility or credibility. The Refugee Division is a specialized tribunal and has complete jurisdiction to determine the plausibility of testimony and, as long as the inferences drawn are not so unreasonable as to warrant intervention, the findings are not open to judicial review.

Flores v. Canada (Minister of Employment & Immigration) (1994), 77 F.T.R. 137 — The applicant claimed refugee status alleging a well-founded fear of persecution by reason of her political opinion. The principal applicant's father was a sergeant in the Presidential Guard under the Somoza regime in Nicaragua. When the Sandinistas assumed power in 1979, the principal applicant's father was arrested, detained and mistreated. The principal applicant's family was identified as espousing policies and a philosophy not in accord with those of the Sandinistas. The family were harassed in a variety of ways between 1983 and 1991.

On the question of changed country circumstances, the CRDD erred in not conducting an adequate analysis of the conflicting documentary evidence and then in not turning, in any significant way, to an evaluation of the changes with respect to the particular circumstances of the applicant.

Having reached a conclusion on the issue of changed country conditions, the CRDD went on to state that it was "not satisfied that the principal applicant would be persecuted by reason of her perceived political opinion or the overlapping ground of membership in a particular social group, namely an anti-Sandinista family, were she to return to Nicaragua." In addition, the panel indicated that it was not persuaded that the applicant, who did not participate in any political or military activities against the Sandinistas, would be at risk of persecution by the Sandinistas now. Neither of these two restatements of the test for Convention refugee status conformed to the *Adjei* test. For both of these reasons the decision of the panel was set aside.

Alfred v. Canada (Minister of Employment & Immigration) (1994), 76 F.T.R. 231 — In this application to review a negative decision of the CRDD, the applicant argued that the tribunal erred in misconstruing "persecution" and that the tribunal erred in law by ignoring or misconstruing the evidence before it. The respondent made reference to portions of the transcript of the hearing and to the documentary evidence before the tribunal, which it argued would warrant the conclusion that the findings of the tribunal were reasonable. The Court must review the decision as rendered by the tribunal and not the evidence to which the decision itself makes no reference but which would have warranted the conclusions reached by the tribunal if the tribunal had expressed reasons relying upon such evidence. The simple statement that the tribunal had reached its decision "after careful consideration of all the evidence adduced at the hearing" was not sufficient when the decision made little or no reference to the principal bases of the applicant's claim. The application was allowed in this case and the matter sent back for rehearing before a differently constituted panel of the CRDD.

Arumuganathan v. Canada (Minister of Employment & Immigration) (1994), 75 F.T.R. 161 — The applicant was a citizen of Sri Lanka and with her three infant children claimed refugee status on the basis of their race, religion, political opinion and membership in a particular social group. The rejection of the applicant's claims was based on the negative finding of credibility. The tribunal admitted into evidence the Minister's factum from the husband's leave application for judicial review. The husband's claim to Convention refugee status had been advanced separately from the wife's and had been rejected because it had no credible basis. The refugee hearing officer suggested to the Board that, to the extent that the applicant's claim depended on her husband's experiences, it would not be unreasonable to conclude that if the husband's claim was unsuccessful, her claim was likewise "hollow".

The Board was correct in determining that the Minister's factum could be admitted into evidence and that it was the duty of the Board to assess that evidence and decide what weight to ascribe to it. However, given the inflammatory nature of the evidence it was also incumbent on the Board to indicate in its decision what weight, if any, it had in fact ascribed to the factum. Having failed to refer to the evidence in its decision, the Board erred and its decision was set aside.

Thurairajah v. Canada (Minister of Employment & Immigration) (March 11, 1994), Doc. IMM-2339-93 (Fed. T.D.) — The applicant, a Tamil from Sri Lanka, sought judicial review of a negative decision of the CRDD. The question of the assessment of a claimant's demeanour during testimony by a tribunal is unassailable on judicial review in the absence of perverseness on the part of the tribunal. The fact that the tribunal does not elaborate on its conclusions is not sufficient to allow the Court to review its finding. Inferences with respect to credibility must be based on the evidence presented; the tribunal cannot make a negative finding while ignoring explanations given by the claimant for apparent inconsistencies.

With respect to the destruction of a passport, the Court relied on the decision in *Attakora v. Canada (Minister of Employment & Immigration)* (1989), 99 N.R. 168 (Fed. C.A.) to the effect that there was nothing inherently incredible in a refugee saying that he had destroyed false travel documents in order to avoid detection and arrest once they had served their purpose. The Court found that the tribunal had made a number of errors that tainted its negative assessment on the issue of credibility and quashed the decision and remitted the matter back to a differently constituted panel.

Mannan v. Canada (Minister of Employment & Immigration) (March 8, 1994), Doc. IMM-2892-93 (Fed. T.D.) — The applicants were a family of Ahmadi Muslims from Pakistan who claimed refugee status based on the harassment and discrimination that they suffered as a result of being Ahmadi. The Board found that the situation for Ahmadis in Pakistan was improving. It appeared to the Court that the Board did not properly consider all the material before it. It was not necessary for the Board to mention all the documentary evidence. Where, however, there was a large amount of material which contradicted a finding by the Board, that material deserved some comment. Where, as in this case, there was no comment, it was then difficult for the Court to determine if the material had been considered by the Board. Accordingly, the application was allowed and the matter referred back to a differently constituted Board.

Que v. Canada (Minister of Employment & Immigration) (1994), 75 F.T.R. 154 — The tribunal failed to make reference to the documentary evidence specific to the applicant's claim and to indicate why that evidence was rejected. The Court commented that the Refugee Division is obligated, at the very least, to comment on the information. If the documentation is accepted or rejected, the applicant should be advised of the reasons why, especially as the documentation supports the applicant's position. The decision of the CRDD was set aside.

Kandiah v. Canada (Minister of Employment & Immigration) (1994), 75 F.T.R. 166 — The tribunal concluded that the evidence did not establish that there was "a good possibility" that all female Tamils of the claimant's age in Colombo, Sri Lanka would be persecuted and therefore rejected her claim to refugee status. Such a statement implied that the tribunal had imposed a higher standard of proof than was required by law. The tribunal's statement may be an error in form, and not intended by the tribunal. Nevertheless it was an error in law which warranted allowing the application and accordingly, the decision of the tribunal was set aside.

Ezi-Ashi v. Canada (Secretary of State) (February 28, 1994), Doc. IMM-1257-93 (Fed. T.D.) — The applicant was a citizen of Nigeria and applied for judicial review of a negative determination of his claim for refugee status. The Board drew an adverse inference against the applicant's credibility from the facts surrounding the applicant's plans to leave the country.

Credibility findings can be made in a number of ways. In assessing the reliability of testimony, the Board may consider vagueness, hesitation, inconsistencies, contradictions and demeanour. With respect to these types of credibility findings, the Court normally defers to the Board. Credibility findings may also be based on inferences. When such inferences are made they must be reasonable and based upon the evidence before the Board. When the Court draws a different inference than the Board, this in and of itself is not normally a reason to set aside a decision.

The inferences drawn by the Board were not reasonable. The Board failed to adequately explain why the applicant's plans to leave Nigeria and his delay in claiming refugee status should cast "the ring of untruth" upon his accounts of his arrest and the attacks against him and his property.

The decision of the Board was set aside.

Dumitru v. Canada (Minister of Employment & Immigration) (1994), 76 F.T.R. 116 — The applicant based his claim on a fear of persecution because of his political opinion. He became a member of the Peasant Party and, as a member of that party, took part in demonstrations against the National Salvation Front in Victory Square in Bucharest. The tribunal did not believe that the applicant was recognized by a police officer at one of the demonstrations and that an order was given to a miner to beat up the applicant. Based on that conclusion the tribunal constructed its own hypotheses as to how the events had transpired and used those hypotheses to reject certain essential portions of the applicant's testimony. The tribunal concluded that the applicant had voluntarily decided to confront the miners and that the injuries he suffered resulted from that confrontation and not from an act deliberately committed by a representative of the police.

In setting aside the Board's decision, the Court drew a distinction between reasonable inferences drawn from evidence and pure conjecture. A conjecture may be plausible but it is of no legal value, for its essence is that it is a mere guess. An inference in the legal sense is a deduction from the evidence and if it is a reasonable deduction it may have the validity of legal proof.

The tribunal drew its conclusions from pure conjecture and this error went to the very essence of its decision. Accordingly, the matter was remitted back to a differently constituted panel for hearing.

Bovbel v. Canada (Minister of Employment & Immigration) (1994), 18 Admin. L.R. (2d) 169, 167 N.R. 10, 113 D.L.R. (4th) 415 (Fed. C.A.) — This was an appeal from an order of the Trial Division allowing the respondent's application for judicial review of an Immigration and Refugee Board decision determining that the respondent was not a Convention refugee. The motion judge allowed the application on the grounds that members of the Board were governed by a policy — Reasons Review Policy — the existence of which was sufficient to taint all the decisions rendered by the Board while the policy was in force because it created a reasonable apprehension of lack of independence. If the Reasons Review Policy proscribed a procedure that offended the principles of natural justice, that defect could only affect the validity of decisions rendered in accordance with that procedure. There was no evidence showing that the two members of the Board who disposed of the respondent's claim to refugee status actually followed the policy in the case under review.

The Court went on to conclude that there was nothing wrong with the Reasons Review Policy followed by the Board. The participation of "outsiders" in the decision-making process of an administrative tribunal may sometimes cause a problem. The decisions of the tribunal must indeed be rendered by those on whom Parliament has conferred power to decide and their decisions must, unless the relevant legislation impliedly or expressly provides otherwise, meet the requirements of natural justice. When the procedure followed by members of an administrative tribunal does not violate natural justice and does not infringe on their ability to decide according to their opinion even though it may influence that opinion, it cannot be criticized. That is why the Federal Court of Appeal in *Weerasinge v. Canada (Minister of Employment & Immigration)* (1993), [1994] 1 F.C. 330, 22 Imm. L.R. (2d) 1, 161 N.R. 200, 17 Admin. L.R. (2d) 214 (C.A.) approved of the practice of the IRB having the reasons of its members reviewed by legal advisors before their release.

The fact that the Reasons Review Policy was to be generally applied was not in and of itself objectionable. There is nothing wrong with a legal advisor making his or her comments known to the other member of the Board who is asked to concur in the reasons being reviewed.

The fact that legal advisors had access to the entire file is not objectionable in the context of the Reasons Review Policy because the legal advisors were not expected to discuss the findings of fact made by the members, but merely, if there was a factual inconsistency in the reasons, to look at the file in order to determine how the inconsistency could be resolved. There is always a possibility that legal advisors, since they were in possession of a file, exceed their mandate and try to influence the factual findings of the Board. However, any policy is susceptible of abuse. Accordingly, the appeal was allowed.

Sanchez v. Canada (Minister of Employment & Immigration) (1994), 75 F.T.R. 135 — In dismissing the applicant's claim for Convention refugee status, the Board applied the concept of "a reasonable chance of persecution". This concept was found to fall within the parameters of the test as set out in *Adjei v. Canada (Minister of Employment & Immigration),* [1989] 2 F.C. 680, 7 Imm. L.R. (2d) 169, 57 D.L.R. (4th) 153, 132 N.R. 24 (Fed. C.A.) and *Ponniah v. Canada (Minister of Employment & Immigration)* (1991), 13 Imm. L.R. (2d) 241, 132 N.R. 32 (Fed. C.A.).

The CRDD does not have to recite or refer to all of the documentary evidence before it in reaching its decision. The fact that it recites some of that documentary evidence makes it clear that it had regard to the documentary evidence. The fact that it recites certain of the documentary evidence and not all of it is not evidence that it has ignored or disregarded the totality of the evidence before it.

This application to set aside a negative determination by the CRDD was dismissed.

Ponce-Yon v. Canada (Minister of Employment & Immigration) (1994), 73 F.T.R. 317 — The applicant was a student in Guatemala and participated on a number of occasions in anti-government demonstrations. The applicant described incidents that he maintained amounted to persecution. The Board ruled that the applicant's fear was not objectively well-founded.

The common thread running through the jurisprudence is that inferences based on the degree of a claimant's political involvement are rarely reasonable, particularly in situations where it is acknowledged that the claimant has indeed been persecuted or where the agent of persecution is known to target all members of a particular group, regardless of the extent of their political involvement. The Board accepted that the applicant had been the victim of persecution at the hands of the Guatemalan military. The fact that the applicant's political involvement was only relatively minor cannot therefore be considered relevant in determining if his fear of persecution was reasonable.

The Board accepted that the applicant abandoned his studies and went into hiding because of numerous threats. Given this finding, it was unreasonable for the Board to conclude that the fear of persecution was not well-founded because the applicant did not experience any difficulties during his time in hiding.

The evidence confirmed that the Guatemalan military, and not the civilian government, was the prime agent of persecution. There was uncontradicted evidence that the government did not restrict the foreign travel of its citizens, including its critics. The board therefore erred in relying on the applicant's lack of difficulty in obtaining a passport as a basis for denying his claim.

The negative decision of the Refugee panel was overturned.

Litvinskii v. Canada (Minister of Employment & Immigration) (February 16, 1994), Doc. IMM-2403-93 (Fed. T.D.) — The applicant, from the Ukraine, claimed refugee status on the ground of a fear of persecution by reason of his origin, his religion, his political opinions and his membership in a particular social group. The Court commented on the difference between discrimination and persecution; the issue being whether the discrimination is serious or systematic enough to be characterized as persecution, or to lead to a conclusion that there was a possibility of persecution in the future. The dividing line is difficult to establish. The identification of persecution behind incidents of discrimination is a question of mixed fact and law. It is for the Board to draw the conclusions in a particular factual context by proceeding with a careful analysis of the evidence adduced and a proper balancing of the various elements contained in that evidence. There was nothing to justify setting aside the decision of the tribunal that the incidents to which the applicant referred were more in the nature of discrimination than persecution, and the application was dismissed.

Mohamed v. Canada (Secretary of State) (1994), 73 F.T.R. 159 — The applicant and her minor daughter sought to review a decision of the Board determining that they were not refugees. The applicant was a citizen of Kenya. The case was heard before the chairperson of the Board issued guidelines on gender-related persecution. Since the Board had not yet rendered its decision on this matter, counsel for the applicant wrote and requested it to consider the issue of gender-related persecution in light of the evidence adduced at the hearing. Counsel for the respondent submitted that a review of the reasons of the Board indicated that it implicity addressed the question. Even if the reasons may properly be interpreted in this fashion, this was not a sufficient discharge of the Board's obligation to provide clear reasons on all material issues raised by the applicant. The Board failed to deliver reasons in the case which squarely addressed the issue of gender-related persecution. In addition, the Board either misunderstood or misapprehended a portion of the evidence on a crucial aspect of the claim. The Board's decision was set aside.

Cardenas v. Canada (Minister of Employment & Immigration) (1994), 74 F.T.R. 214 — The applicant was unsuccessful in his claim for refugee status because he was found to have been an accomplice to crimes against humanity. The applicant was from Chile and had an association with the political faction, the Manuel Rodriguez Patriotic Front. In quashing the Board's decision, the Court noted that the Board had made little effort to link the applicant to specific criminal activities. Rather, it chose to refer only in general terms to shootings and bombings. The Board should have endeavoured to carefully detail the criminal acts which it considered the applicant to have committed.

The Board's decision was quashed on this and other grounds.

Mladenov v. Canada (Minister of Employment & Immigration) (1994), 74 F.T.R. 161 — The applicant, a native of Bulgaria, concluded his hearing for refugee status in January 1991. Before a decision was rendered, the applicant received a letter from his parents which contained information regarding a State Security Investigation of the applicant. Counsel forwarded this letter to the Board requesting that it be considered in relation to the decision which was then on reserve. When the decision was rendered, no reference was made by the Board members to the letters received from counsel. One of the letters had relevance to at least two of the three principal reasons relied on by the Board. It was not consistent with the principles of fairness that a decision should stand when it made no reference to relevant evidence proffered in letters submitted before the decision, leaving the applicant and the Court uncertain whether or not the evidence was considered at all. The decision of the Board was set aside.

Ghassemzadeh v. Canada (Secretary of State) (1994), 72 F.T.R. 145 — The applicant, who was a citizen of Iran, claimed refugee status. The applicant had unknowingly assisted a member of an anti-government organization. He was arrested, held for five days and released on bail. A short time later he was summoned to appear before the revolutionary court but he left Iran prior to personally receiving the summons and prior to his court date.

The applicant did not receive a summons directly from the prosecutor's office, but had received it from his family after his departure. The Board had a duty to assess the direct implications of the summons of the revolutionary court on the applicant's objective fear. If the summons was prospective and did not cease to operate, then the Board should have considered the effect of the summons on the applicant's prospective fear of persecution. If the summons was ongoing and affected the objective fear of persecution, then the Board should also have considered the documentary evidence regarding human rights abuses of the revolutionary court in Iran. The tribunal did not consider the impact of the summons in conjunction with the documentary evidence on the objective fear and accordingly, its decision was set aside.

Rosales v. Canada (Minister of Employment & Immigration) (1993), 23 Imm. L.R. (2d) 100, 72 F.T.R. 1 — The applicant was a citizen of Guatemala. He was politically active in that country and had unsuccessfully run for political office. The applicant detailed evidence of persecution but his claim was rejected on the basis that political dissent was tolerated in Guatemala and reliance was placed on the United States Department of State Country Report for 1990. The decision of the panel was set aside. The panel justified its rejection of the applicant's assertion that political dissent was not tolerated by a selective and minimal reference to the documentary evidence. The question of whether a panel accepts or does not accept an applicant's assertion is normally left to the panel. But when it arrives at its conclusion by ignoring relevant and apparently overwhelming evidence to the contrary, its decision will not be allowed to stand.

Iazlovitskaia v. Canada (Minister of Employment & Immigration) (November 25, 1993), Doc. A-70-93 (Fed. T.D.) — The applicant was an ethnic Russian and a citizen of the Ukraine. She based her claim to Convention refugee status on a fear of persecution by reason of her nationality and political opinion. In her Personal Information Form she elaborated on a long series of events, beginning in 1982 and culminating in the termination of her employment as a teacher in 1990.

The test for Convention refugee status is forward looking. The finding that the harassments which the applicant suffered do not amount to persecution is in no way determinative of the issue of whether the applicant has a reasonable fear of persecution if she is required to return to the Ukraine. The fact that the applicant was able to maintain a livelihood and the speculation that she might in the future be able to maintain a livelihood are equally not determinative. Counsel for the respondent sought to support the decision by urging upon the Court inferences that should be drawn from the Board's analysis. However, the Court concluded that a claimant or his counsel and the Court should not have to rely on inferences to support a far-reaching conclusion that a claimant is not a refugee.

Rosales v. Canada (Minister of Employment & Immigration) (October 29, 1993), Doc. A-1492-92 (Fed. T.D.) — The applicant sought to review a negative determination of her claim to refugee status. The applicant claimed that her brother had been kidnapped by guerrillas and that she had been able to escape. She indicated that strangers had been looking for her since the time of her brother's kidnapping and that she had had to flee the country. The Refugee Division found that her fear of persecution if she returned home was not reasonable.

Counsel for the applicant argued that the Refugee Division had imposed too heavy a burden on the applicant and referred to a sentence in the panel's reasons for decision. The Court dismissed the application and adopted the words of Marceau J.A. in *Lesanu v. Canada (Minister of Employment & Immigration)* (September 17, 1993), Doc. A-481-92 (Fed. C.A.):

> Clumsiness of language or expression is often understandable, and no consequence must be given to it, provided that on reading the decision as a whole it can be seen that the members of the Board did not go astray in terms of their role or the manner in which it should be carried out.

Derbas v. Canada (Minister of Employment & Immigration) (August 18, 1993), Doc. A-1128-92 (Fed. T.D.) — The applicant sought to appeal the decision of the IRB that he was not a Convention refugee. The Board indicated to the applicant during the course of the proceeding that he was a credible witness and need not call further evidence. The Board then rejected the applicant's claim on the basis that there was no objective foundation for the expressed fear. The application was dismissed. By accepting the applicant's version of events as fact, the Board was not bound to accept the interpretation he put on those events. The Board still had to look at whether the events, viewed objectively, provided sufficient basis for a well-founded fear of persecution. There was no violation of the requirements of natural justice in this case and the appeal was dismissed.

Racek v. Canada (Minister of Employment & Immigration) (1993), 67 F.T.R. 155 — This was an application for judicial review of the decision that the applicant was not a Convention refugee. The reasons for the Board's decision were signed by the two members of the Board who were in attendance at the hearing. The notice of decision signed by the Registrar erroneously identified one member of the Board. The obligation to notify is a formal requirement. The improper designation of a decision maker on the notice of a decision could affect its formal validity if, as a result, the identity of the decision which is the subject of the notice cannot readily be determined. Here, however, a reading of the notice of decision and the reasons for decision indicates that the two members who heard the applicant's claim signed the written reasons, that the conclusions set forth in the written reasons correspond with that of the notice of decision, and that the applicants were provided with a copy of the Board's written reasons. The error in the notice of decision, therefore, does not affect its formal validity.

Guajardo-Espinoza v. Canada (Minister of Employment & Immigration) (1993), 161 N.R. 132 (Fed. C.A.) — At the time of the hearing of the appeal, counsel for the appellants relied on the Supreme Court of Canada decision in *Ward v. Canada (Minister of Emplyment & Immigration)* (1993), 20 Imm. L.R. (2d) 85 (S.C.C.) and argued that the Refugee Division made an error in not ruling on the appellant's political views or examining the political basis of their claim. The appellant was a police officer and alleged Chilean military authorities assigned him to investigate a theft of equipment on a military base. His investigation, he testified, attributed the theft to lax security measures and this resulted in disciplinary action against the person responsible for security. The security officer was also implicated in the explosion of an electric transformer. The security officer and certain of his friends, including a military judge, were upset with the report and with the appellant for writing it. In the appellant's personal information form was a four-line reference, which the appellant argued in the Court of Appeal constituted a claim for fear of persecution based on political opinion.

The appellants, once the Refugee Division decision has been rendered, cannot change the nature of the argument they made to the tribunal. The Refugee Division cannot be faulted for not deciding an issue that had not been argued and did not emerge perceptibly from the evidence presented as a whole. Saying the contrary would lead to a guessing game and oblige the Refugee Division to undertake interminable investigations to eliminate reasons that did not apply in any case, that no one had raised and that the evidence did not support, to say nothing of frivolous and pointless appeals that would certainly follow.

Aguebor v. Canada (Minister of Employment & Immigration) (1993), 160 N.R. 315 (Fed. C.A.) — The Refugee Division did not find the claimant's participation in the coup d'etat nor the manner in which he fled the country to be plausible. In dismissing his appeal, the Court sought to put its own decision, *Giron v. Canada (Minister of Employment and Immigration)* (1992), 143 N.R. 238 (Fed. C.A.), in perspective. It may be easier to have a finding of implausibility reviewed where it results from inferences than to have a finding of non-credibility reviewed where it results from the conduct of the witness and from inconsistencies in the testimony. The Refugee Division is a specialized tribunal which has complete jurisdiction to determine the plausibility of testimony and, as long as the inferences drawn by the tribunal are not so unreasonable as to warrant the Court's intervention, its findings are not open to judicial review. In the area of plausibility the unreasonableness of a decision may be more palpable, and so more easily identifiable, since the account appears on the face of the record. The *Giron* case in no way reduces the burden that rests on an appellant of showing that the inferences drawn by the Refugee Division could not reasonably have been drawn.

Ahortor v. Canada (Minister of Employment & Immigration) (1993), 21 Imm. L.R. (2d) 39, 65 F.T.R. 137 — This was an application to review the decision of the CRDD, which denied the applicant Convention refugee status. The CRDD found that crucial aspects of the applicant's evidence were not credible and trustworthy.

The Court reviewed a number of its own previous decisions, which all dealt with when decisions of the CRDD would be overturned notwithstanding that they were based on findings of credibility.

The Court affirmed that the Board is under a duty to state in clear, unambiguous terms the reason for casting doubt upon a claimant's credibility. Further, the Board acts arbitrarily in choosing to disbelieve an applicant's testimony where there exists no valid reason to doubt the truthfulness of it. Further, the Court affirmed that a finding of lack of credibility must be based on internal contradictions and inconsistencies and not extrinsic criteria upon which the Board draws inferences which are unsupported by the evidence.

Finally, the Court affirmed that it is open to the CRDD as a trier of fact to evaluate the evidence and accord due weight to it.

The inconsistencies upon which the Board relied were reasonably explained by the applicant's evidence and it was therefore not open to the CRDD to draw adverse inferences and conclude that the applicant was not believable.

Finally, the Board erred in finding the applicant not credible because he was unable to provide documentary evidence supporting his claim. The failure to offer documentary evidence, while a correct finding of fact, in this case cannot be related to the applicant's credibility in the absence of evidence to contradict the allegations made by the applicant in his testimony before the CRDD.

Accordingly, the Court held that the CRDD erred in law when it concluded that the applicant was not credible and set aside the decision and referred the matter to a differently constituted panel to reconsider the evidence in accordance with the Court's reasons.

Handal v. Canada (Minister of Employment & Immigration) (June 10, 1993), Doc. 92-A-6875 (Fed. T.D.) — This was a judicial review application against the decision of the Refugee Board holding that the applicants were not Convention refugees. At the opening of the hearing the Board made reference to findings by a differently constituted panel hearing the case of the claimant's husband. The Board ruled that it had no jurisdiction to review that decision in the context of hearing the applicant's refugee claim. The Board simply accepted the findings of a different board with respect to a different applicant as being determinative of the current matter. The decision of the Board was set aside. Each applicant must have his claim determined individually and must have the opportunity to present his case. The applicant had not agreed to be bound by the findings made by the Board in her husband's case. Accordingly, the conduct of the Board in being bound by those findings was not justified. The decision of the Board was quashed and the matter remitted back to a differently constituted Board.

Mosa v. Canada (Minister of Employment & Immigration) (1993), 154 N.R. 200 (Fed. C.A.) — The appellant's claim for refugee status was rejected. Not every inaccuracy of interpretation, no matter how trivial, will furnish a good ground for interfering with the decision of the Refugee Division. The Court will only interfere where it is apparent that an error causes some prejudice to a claimant.

In this case, the Court found that an accurate translation of a portion of the evidence might well have enabled the Refugee Division to put further questions to the appellant as to the nature of her fear, to determine whether such fear was well-founded. The inaccurate interpretation prevented that line of questioning. This demonstrated potential prejudice to the appellant in establishing her claim. Accordingly, the decision of the Refugee Division was set aside.

Villalta v. Canada (Solicitor General) (1993), 68 F.T.R. 304 — The applicant arrived in Canada from El Salvador and claimed refugee status on the ground that he feared forced conscription into the army and he feared harassment by the guerillas who made efforts to require him to support or join them. He strongly disagreed with the methods used by the army and would not participate in it. While originally sympathetic to the guerillas, he could not accept their methods. On December 31, 1991 a peace treaty was signed by the guerillas and the government. This treaty was the result of 20 months of UN mediated negotiations. The applicant was found not to be a Convention refugee largely based upon the changed country conditions in El Salvador.

When determining whether status has been lost, one must ascertain that the reasons for the fear have ceased to exist. When determining whether status should be granted, changed country conditions, even those stopping short of cessation, is one factor among many which can be taken into account in determining whether the individual faces a reasonable chance of persecution. If the conditions set out in section 2(2) exist, there is absolutely no doubt that the individual is not entitled to status but this does not mean that in order to take changed country conditions into account when determining whether to grant status, that the panel must first go through the conceptual exercise of subtracting changed conditions from their analysis and then, after making that analysis, move on to assess the significance of the changed country conditions.

The tribunal did not commit an error by taking into account changed country conditions without first determining whether the requirements of cessation under section 2(2)(e) were met. Accordingly, the application was dismissed.

Miranda v. Canada (Minister of Employment & Immigration) (1993), 63 F.T.R. 81 — This was an application for judicial review of a decision of the Refugee Board determining that the applicant was not a Convention refugee. A Refugee Board decision must be interpreted as a whole. It should not be subject to microscopic examination nor should particular statements in the decision be subject to a semantic autopsy. The decision must be analyzed in the context of the evidence to determine if the conclusions reached were reasonable or patently unreasonable. Where one finds error in the Board's decision, one must also find the error to be material to the decision reached. Artful readers can find any number of errors when dealing with decisions of administrative tribunals. Whereas here the conclusions of the Board are well-founded on the evidence, the decision will be upheld.

Ye v. Canada (Minister of Employment & Immigration) (1992), 17 Imm. L.R. (2d) 77 (Fed. C.A.) — The appellant appealed a negative decision of the Convention Refugee Determination Division. In overturning the Board's decision the Court noted that a finding of lack of credibility based on problems internal to the claimant's testimony is more insulated from appellate review than a finding of implausibility based only on extrinsic criteria. The Board drew inferences which were subject to challenge.

The appellant feared persecution not only because of his presence in certain demonstrations but also because he donated to the demonstrators' cause; because he videotaped and distributed television broadcasts from Hong Kong; because six of his similarly situated friends were arrested and not seen again; because the authorities actually came for him and because after he went into hiding they continued to pursue him through his family; and finally because they closed his business. Little of the appellant's real case was explicitly faced by the Board.

The decision of the Board was set aside and the matter returned to a differently constituted Board for rehearing and redetermination.

Shanmugarajah v. Canada (Minister of Employment & Immigration) (June 22, 1992), Doc. A-609-91 (Fed. C.A.) — The appellants appealed a negative decision of the Convention Refugee Determination Division. The Board concluded that the appellants' fears were purely speculative. In allowing the appeal the Board noted that it is almost always foolhardy for a Board in a refugee case where there is no general issue as to credibility to make the assertion that the claimants had no subjective element in their fear.

Velauthar v. Canada (Minister of Employment & Immigration) (1992), 141 N.R. 239 (Fed. C.A.) — Following receipt of the evidence, the panel indicated that it was concerned with whether the persecution feared by the appellants was caused by a "Convention reason" and invited written submissions from the appellant's counsel and the refugee hearing officer. It was an invitation which was accepted. The decision denied the claim on the basis of the appellant's credibility.

There was a gross denial of natural justice. The panel had stipulated that the appellants had feared persecution and that the only issue was whether that persecution was encompassed in the Convention refugee definition. It proceeded on grounds of credibility to negate its stipulation, thus denying the appellants the opportunity to know and answer the case against them by a deliberate decision. The decision of the Convention Refugee Determination Division was quashed and the matter was referred back for rehearing by a differently constituted panel.

Komanov v. Canada (Minister of Employment & Immigration) (1992), 17 Imm. L.R. (2d) 15, 7 Admin. L.R. (2d) 135, 143 N.R. 233 (Fed. C.A.) — This application to re-open the applicant's request for leave to appeal a negative decision of the Refugee Division of the Immigration and Refugee Board was refused. Counsel for the applicant alleged the discovery of the existence of "standardized pattern negative decisions for refugee claimants from Bulgaria" and submitted them to the Court as a basis for an allegation of bias. The "pattern negative decisions for Bulgarian claimants" represented a course of conduct not to be recommended for an administrative tribunal like the Immigration and Refugee Board, but nevertheless those decisions that were presented to the Court did not appear to prejudge any issue and made it quite clear that such "pattern decisions" should only be used once members who had heard a particular case had made up their minds to reject the claim. These decisions went to form and not to substance.

Abarajithan v. Canada (Minister of Employment & Immigration) (January 28, 1992), Doc. A-805-90 (Fed. C.A.) — The Refugee Division decided that the appellant was not a Convention refugee. As the law stood at the time of this decision, the failed claimant had a right of appeal to the Federal Court of Appeal. The Court noted that not every misunderstanding of evidence by a tribunal is fatal to its decision. In cases such as this one, however, where the tribunal has made the erroneous view of the evidence the centrepiece of its reasoning, the decision cannot stand. In this particular appeal the tribunal had misunderstood the appellant's testimony about his ability to obtain employment in Sri Lanka. Accordingly, the decision of the Refugee Division was set aside and the matter referred back to a differently constituted panel for rehearing and redetermination in a manner not inconsistent with the Court's reasoning.

Sivaguru v. Canada (Minister of Employment & Immigration) (1992), 16 Imm. L.R. (2d) 85 (Fed. C.A.) — For digest, see section 69.1, subheading *Subsection (5), supra.*

Ponniah v. Canada (Minister of Employment & Immigration) (1991), 13 Imm. L.R. (2d) 241, 132 N.R. 32 (Fed. C.A.) — This was an appeal from a decision of the Refugee Division denying the applicant's refugee claim. An applicant does not have to prove that persecution would be more likely than not. He has to establish good grounds or a reasonable chance for fearing persecution. Good grounds or reasonable chance is defined as occupying the field between upper and lower limits. It is less than a 50% chance but more than a minimal or mere possibility. There is no intermediate ground; what falls between the two limits is "good grounds". If the claimant may face slightly more than a mere possibility of persecution, he has crossed over the lower limit and made his case of "good grounds" for fearing persecution.

Retnem v. Canada (Minister of Employment & Immigration) (1991), 13 Imm. L.R. (2d) 317, 132 N.R. 53 (Fed. C.A.) — The Board's failure to deal with the cumulative nature of the persecution the claimant alleged led to a reversal of its decision. Even though the claimant did not leave Sri Lanka for some years after his detention and torture, that incident was still current as a basis for fear when linked with all of the smaller previous and subsequent harassment he endured the same month the couple were married.

Tung v. Canada (Minister of Employment & Immigration) (1991), 124 N.R. 388 (Fed. C.A.) — This was an appeal from the Refugee Division of the Immigration and Refugee Board. While there is no statutory requirement for keeping a complete record of the proceedings before the Refugee Division, the Board has a policy of recording those proceedings on tape and making a full transcript available for possible use on an appeal. The Board's policy was not implemented in this case and disadvantage accrued to the appellant. It is no answer to say that the recording equipment broke down through no fault of the Board's. The quality of interpretation was found wanting. The appellant was entitled, through the interpreter, to tell the story of his fear in his own language, as well as he might have done had he been able to communicate to the Board in the English language (the language of this hearing). The failure to provide an adequate interpreter prejudiced the appellant in the proceedings before the Refugee Division and before the Court of Appeal, who were required to review important aspects of the Board's decision on a deficient record.

The Refugee Division found that the appellant's failure to claim "asylum" in any of the countries he visited en route to Canada was inconsistent with the conduct of a person who fears for his life. There was no evidence that any of the countries the appellant visited had ratified the 1951 U.N. convention and the 1967 protocol or that they had adopted laws implementing those instruments. The Board is authorized under section 68(2) to take notice of any facts that may be judicially noticed. It is wrong for the Board to speculate that refugee protection was available in the countries that the appellant stopped in (Hong Kong, Thailand, Bolivia and Peru). The Court noted that the appellant was at all times in transit to Canada and had already decided to claim refugee status after he arrived here. The Court noted that the Board is normally required to give detailed reasons for disbelieving a claimant. The absence of such reasons may suggest that the Board had no overriding concern with the appellant's credibility. There was no expressed or implied rejection of the appellant's credibility as a witness on his own behalf. The Refugee Division decision betrayed a possible confusion as to the proper test. The Refugee Division members said that they were not convinced that the motivation behind the client's fleeing China was fear. The Court noted that the issue at this point was the well-foundedness of the appellant's fear and that the words used introduced the subjective element into a test, which at that stage was entirely objective.

Hilo v. Canada (Minister of Employment & Immigration) (1991), 15 Imm. L.R. (2d) 199, 130 N.R. 236 (Fed. C.A.) — The Refugee Division was under a duty to give its reasons for casting doubt upon the appellant's credibility in clear and unmistakable terms. The Board's credibility assessment was defective because it was couched in vague and general terms. The claimant had only attended informal meetings of a political group inside Syria. The Refugee

Division viewed this group as loosely knit with apparently charitable aims, no official title or status and noted further that the claimant was only 14 years of age at the time of his attendance. The Court found that characterizing the group in this way was irrelevant. The Syrian authorities had sought to persecute the appellant because of his perceived political opinion. The proper test for evaluating political activities is not whether the division or members considered that the appellant had engaged in political activities but whether the ruling government of the country from which he claimed to be a refugee so considered his conduct.

Padilla v. Canada (Minister of Employment & Immigration) (1991), 13 Imm. L.R. (2d) 1 (Fed. C.A.) — The appellant appealed a decision of the Convention Refugee Determination Division that the appellant was not a refugee. The Board found that the appellant's fear of returning to El Salvador was fear of prosecution not persecution. The Board appeared to have accepted the appellant's evidence that he was a conscientious objector. The appellant also testified that he thought he would be executed extra-judicially upon his return to El Salvador. This belief was supported in the documentary evidence presented. It was not reasonable for the Board to conclude that an army deserter might not be subjected extra-judicially to treatment of the type the appellant feared. By confining its consideration of the consequences of the appellant's desertion to what might occur through due legal process, the Board ignored the basis upon which the appellant asserted his fear of persecution as well as the appellant's evidence whose credibility the Board did not question. The appeal was allowed and the matter referred back to the Board for full rehearing by a differently constituted panel.

Rajaratnam v. Canada (Minister of Employment & Immigration) (1991), 135 N.R. 300 (Fed. C.A.) — This was an appeal from a decision of the Immigration and Refugee Board refusing the appellant's claim for refugee status. A properly arrived at decision of the Board based purely and simply on the claimant's credibility affords no basis in law for interference by the Court of Appeal. Contradictions or discrepancies in the evidence of a refugee claimant are a well-accepted basis for a finding of the lack of credibility. Refugee claimants, however, are in a peculiar position because their mother tongue is neither of the official languages. The personal information form is prepared and the testimony is given almost always with the assistance of an interpreter. This does not mean that a refugee claimant is absolved of the duty of telling the truth, but it does mean that the tribunal hearing the evidence is required to give reasons for a finding of a lack of credibility in clear and unmistakable terms. Internal inconsistencies between the evidence and the personal information form can sometimes be innocent misunderstandings due to the fact the claimants are assisted on separate occasions by different interpreters.

A Board member during the course of this hearing intervened in the questioning of the applicant on a fairly extensive basis and explored areas which the appellant's counsel and the Refugee Hearing Officer had already explored. The Board member by his or her questioning removed her judicial hat and put on the hat of an advocate.

There are very sound reasons why a judge must stay within proper bounds in questioning a witness. A judge who observes the demeanour of witnesses while they are being examined has a much more favourable opportunity of forming a just appreciation of the witnesses' credibility. If the judge descends into the arena his or her vision may become clouded by the dust of conflict. Unconsciously a judge, in such a situation, deprives him or herself of the advantage of calm and dispassionate observations. Further, the demeanour of a witness is apt to be very different when the questioner is a judge as opposed to counsel, particularly when the judge's examination is prolonged and covers practically the whole of the crucial matters in issue. When this happens it is open to an appellate court to find that the view of the trial judge as to the demeanour of the witness was ill-founded.

The Court of Appeal adopted the observations of Lord Denning in *Jones v. National Coal Board*, [1957] 2 Q.B. 55 at 64 (Eng. C.A.):

> The judge's part in all this is to hearken to the evidence, only himself asking questions of witnesses when it is necessary to clear up any point that has been overlooked or left obscure; to see that the advocates behave themselves seemly and keep to the rules laid down by law; to exclude irrelevancies and discourage repetition; to make sure by wise intervention that he follows the points that the advocates are making and can assess their worth; and at the end to make up his mind where the truth lies. If he goes beyond this, he drops the mantle of a judge and assumes the robe of an advocate; and the change does not become him well.

In the result, the appeal was allowed, the decision of the Refugee Division set aside and the matter referred back to a differently constituted panel for redetermination.

Mensah v. Canada (Minister of Employment & Immigration) (November 23, 1989), Doc. A-1173-88 (Fed. C.A.) — The decision of the Immigration Appeal Board determining the applicant not to be a convention refugee was overturned primarily because the facts which the Board itself said were not contested satisfied, at least on a *prima facie* basis, both the subjective and the objective elements of the test for refugee status. The Board could not, in those circumstances, simply disregard those facts.

Gracielome v. Canada (Minister of Employment & Immigration) (1989), 9 Imm. L.R. (2d) 237 (Fed. C.A.) — The Federal Court of Appeal overturned a decision of the Immigration Appeal Board on a question of credibility based on three alleged contradictions in the evidence of the applicant. In none of the three cases were the contradictions put to the witness. The Court concluded that each example was found by the majority of the Board after the fact from a painstaking analysis of the transcript. In those circumstances, the Board was held to be in no better position to weigh the contradictions than the Federal Court itself and the application was allowed and the decision of the Board set aside.

Owusu-Ansah v. Canada (Minister of Employment & Immigration) (1989), 8 Imm. L.R. (2d) 106, 98 N.R. 312 (Fed. C.A.) — Adverse findings of credibility based on inconsistencies in the record which often go unnoted during the hearing and unremarked by counsel in argument will result in decisions which can be attacked on appeal. The Court noted that reasons for a decision are composed by the Board some considerable time after the decision and not, as in the usual judicial proceeding, as a critical part of the decision-making process. Where the Court feels that the Board has overreached itself in its search for inconsistencies, the Board's decision will be set aside.

Yaliniz v. Canada (Minister of Employment & Immigration) (1988), 7 Imm. L.R. (2d) 163 (Fed. C.A.) — The applicant's claim for refugee status was denied by the Immigration Appeal Board on the basis that, in the Board's opinion, the evidence of the applicant was not credible. This opinion was not based on discrepancies or contradictions in the applicant's testimony, but merely on the feeling that there were obvious exaggerations in what he was recounting. The decision of the Board was set aside. The Board's apparent complete rejection of the applicant's statements was not justified. The Board should have asked itself whether, even assuming some exaggerations, the applicant had not shown that he had been undoubtedly the victim of harassment of a variety of forms amounting to persecution, making his fear to go back to his former home not only genuine but objectively founded.

Saddo v. Canada (Immigration Appeal Board) (1981), 126 D.L.R. (3d) 764 (Fed. C.A.) — The decision of the Board that the applicant was not a Convention refugee was set aside because the Board decided, incorrectly, that extracts from newspapers had no evidentiary value. It was incorrect for the Board to say that a claimant must establish, other than by the production of newspaper articles, that he has a well-founded fear of persecution. The Court held that newspaper articles have evidentiary value and that they must be weighed by the Board with all the other elements of proof submitted in support of the applicant's claim.

Woolaston v. Canada (Minister of Manpower & Immigration) (1972), [1973] S.C.R. 102 (S.C.C.) — The Supreme Court of Canada declined to conclude that, because certain evidence was not mentioned in the Board's reasons, the Board had failed to consider it.

Section 69.1(9.1)

Mathiyabaranam v. Canada (Minister of Employment & Immigration) (1997), (sub nom. *Mathiyabaranam v. Minister of Employment & Immigration)* 221 N.R. 351, (sub nom. *Canada (Minister of Employment & Immigration) v. Mathiyabaranam))* 156 D.L.R. (4th) 301, 41 Imm. L.R. (2d) 197, (sub nom. *Mathiyabaranam v. Minister of Employment & Immigration)* 140 F.T.R. 263 (note) (Fed. C.A.) — The respondent was a Tamil male of the Hindu faith and a citizen of Sri Lanka. He was found not to be a Convention refugee and at the same time the Board also found that there was no credible basis to his claim. At the Trial Division the decision was set aside on the ground that there was a denial of natural justice, because the claimant was never specifically informed that the Board was considering the matter of a no credible basis finding at the hearing.

There is no right to receive any extra notice about the possibility of a finding of no credible basis. Such a requirement would establish a *de facto*, two-stage, hearing process, something Parliament sought to stop by enacting the present provisions to the *Immigration Act*.

Manimaran v. Canada (Minister of Citizenship & Immigration) (1995), 102 F.T.R. 199 — A panel of the CRDD dismissed the applicant's refugee claim. The Board also decided, pursuant to section 69.1(9.1) that there was no credible basis for her claim. The consequences of such a finding are severe. Under section 49(1)(f) an applicant may be removed 7 days after receiving notice of a decision under the section and such applicants are not entitled to a consideration under the PDRCC process.

As a matter of fundamental justice, notice ought to be given at the conclusion of evidence or during submissions once the Board realizes that section 69.1(9.1) might apply. Notice is to be given so that counsel may, if so advised, make submissions on the circumstances in which the section should or should not be applicable.

Judicial review of the Board's decision pursuant to the section 69.1(9.1) was allowed. With respect to the merits of the refugee claim, however, the panel's decision was upheld and that application for judicial review was dismissed.

Mathiyabaranam v. Canada (Minister of Employment & Immigration) (1995), 29 Imm. L.R. (2d) 218, 94 F.T.R. 262 — The panel determined, after considering the applicant's testimony, that there was no credible basis for the applicant's claim to Convention refugee status. The applicant was never informed that the Board was considering the issue of credible basis at the hearing. Given the serious consequences of a finding of no credible basis the Board should give an indication to the applicant at any time before or during the hearing, or even after submissions, that it is considering issuing an order under section 69.1(9.1). At that stage the applicant could make further submissions with respect to the credible basis finding. In this case no notice was given and the finding of no credible basis was set aside.

Section 69.1(10.1)

Gebremariam v. Canada (Minister of Citizenship & Immigration) (1995), 92 F.T.R. 41 — This case involved a split decision of a panel of the CRDD. Both panel members agreed that the claimant had disposed of her travel documents without a valid reason. The claimant had disposed of her travel document, which was a false document, by turning it over to a person with whom she stayed in Washington, D.C. The claimant was 15 years old and had been instructed by her mother that the man to whom she surrendered the passport would take care of her.

The Court found that the word "dispose" in this section connotes intention or an act of will and that it is not a word that connotes victimization by theft, robbery, trickery or intimidation.

The claimant was a 15 year old girl in a bewildering strange country who had been instructed to put trust in the person who would take care of her and, accordingly, this demanded a much lower standard of "valid reason" than for a more worldly, wise, or self-assured adult.

The decision of the CRDD was quashed and the Court declared the applicant to be a refugee.

Sebastiampillai v. Canada (Minister of Citizenship & Immigration) (1994), 87 F.T.R. 259 — The panel members reached diametrically opposite conclusions with respect to whether the applicant was a Convention refugee. Both members agreed that the case fell within section 69.1(10.1)(a) and therefore agreed that the applicant's claim would not succeed.

The applicant was questioned concerning the facts surrounding her disposition of the fraudulent travel documents. There was no suggestion by either panel member that they might assess this evidence for the purpose of applying section 69.1(10.1)(a). Counsel was not alerted to this possibility. No representations were made by either the applicant's counsel or the Refugee Hearing Officer on the possible applicability of the section. For that reason the panel's decision was quashed.

Section 69.1(11)

Asfaw v. Canada (Minister of Citizenship & Immigration) (March 25, 1999), Doc. IMM-2786-98 (Fed. T.D.) — The applicant sought to review a negative decision of a panel of the CRDD. In its reasons, the panel based its negative assessment of the applicant's credibility on the fact that he had stated in his personal information form and in his oral evidence that he had participated in a 1994 protest in his home country and had not mentioned this fact in his eligibility interview.

The eligibility interview relates to the "access criteria" in section 46.01 and is intended only to determine whether the applicant must be excluded from the process for one of a number of listed reasons. The eligibility interview is not intended to assess the merits of the applicant's refugee claim. The information provided in the course of that interview is not, and is not intended to be, the basis of the refugee claim.

The CRDD did not act fairly in reaching a negative conclusion on the applicant's credibility in this fashion. Accordingly, the decision of the panel was set aside.

Badurdeen v. Canada (Minister of Citizenship & Immigration) (March 17, 1999), Doc. IMM-1312-98 (Fed. T.D.) — This was an application to review a negative decision of a panel of the CRDD. The hearing of the claim was conducted by a two-member panel. The applicant had neither requested nor consented to the hearing and determination of his claim by a single member. The two members retired at the conclusion of the oral submissions and no more than 30 minutes later one of the members returned and informed those present that her colleague had left for the day because he was feeling unwell. The member then proceeded to deliver orally their reasons for refusing the claim. Approximately one month later the applicant received a written notification of the decision together with the reasons which both members who had heard the claim had signed.

The manner in which the decision was given was unobjectionable. There was no evidence that the member who was unwell simply left the responsibility for making the decision and fashioning the reasons to his colleague.

With respect to the internal flight alternative, evidence was lead by the applicant to the effect that the police in Colombo have not permitted non-resident Tamils to remain in that city for more than a few days. If accepted, this evidence would render Colombo a destination that was not realistically accessible to the applicant. The panel made no reference in its reasons to this apparently significant piece of evidence about police practice. It is therefore possible only to speculate on how the refugee division treated it, or if they had regard to it at all. It is not imposing too high a standard to expect the panel to have addressed this evidence in the reasons and to have indicated what weight it attached to it. In failing to do so, the panel erred in law and its decision was set aside.

Numbi v. Canada (Minister of Citizenship & Immigration) (February 17, 1999), Doc. IMM-1378-98 (Fed. T.D.) — The failure of the Board to address the specific and relevant documentary evidence which appeared to corroborate important aspects of the applicant's claim in its analysis constituted a reviewable error.

Miral v. Canada (Minister of Citizenship & Immigration) (February 12, 1999), Doc. IMM-3392-97 (Fed. T.D.) — The applicant challenged a negative decision of the CRDD. The applicant who was from Sri Lanka was found not to be a credible witness by the panel.

Considerable deference is given on judicial review to credibility findings made by the CRDD. It is perfectly acceptable for a tribunal to find an applicant lacking in credibility according to implausibilities in the applicant's testimony. Where the tribunal finds a lack of credibility based on inferences, there must be a basis in the evidence to support the inferences. Such inferences must be reasonably open to this tribunal based on the evidence on the applicant. Where the tribunal's inferences are based on what seem to be "common sense or rational perceptions about how a government regime in another country might be expected to act", there is an obligation to provide an opportunity for the applicant to address those inferences on which the tribunal relies. In the case at bar, the tribunal found that the applicant's evidence was perfunctory and lacked the kind of detail that could be expected of someone as articulate and well educated as the claimant.

The Court found that the panel had engaged in speculation as to regular or normal police procedures in Sri Lanka and had no evidence before it on which to base such conclusions. The applicant offered a plausible explanation for the police's repeated acceptance of bribes. The panel, in making its finding regarding probable police procedure, made no references to any documentary evidence to support such a finding. While there may have been a basis in the evidence for such a finding, the panel neglected to point to it. In addition, the panel referred to a lack of corroborating evidence regarding the applicant's detention as significant in the negative determination of her claim. A failure to offer documentation cannot be linked to an applicant's credibility in the absence of evidence to contradict the applicant's testimony. It is not open to the CRDD to require documentary evidence to support an applicant's uncontradicted testimony regarding her arrest and detention.

The decision of the tribunal was set aside.

Cepeda-Gutierrez v. Canada (Minister of Citizenship & Immigration) (1998), 157 F.T.R. 35 (Fed. T.D.) — This was an application to set aside a decision of a panel of the CRDD. The applicant relied on section 18.1(4)(d) of the *Federal Court Act*. The applicant was a citizen of Mexico who arrived in Canada and claimed refugee status. The Refugee Division found that while he was a taxi driver in Mexico City he had been the subject of beatings and threats of violence by the federal police. The panel found that the claimant's evidence was credible and held that the claimant had a well-founded fear of persecution in Mexico City; however, they rejected his claim on the basis that he had an internal flight alternative.

Section 18.1(4)(d) of the *Federal Court Act* does not authorize the Court to substitute its view of the facts for that of the Board which has the benefit of not only seeing and hearing the witnesses, but also of the expertise of its members in assessing evidence relating to facts that are within their area of specialized expertise. The efficient allocation of decision-making resources between administrative agencies and the courts strongly indicates that the role to be played in fact-finding by the Court on an application for judicial review should be nearly residual. Thus, in order to attract judicial intervention, the applicant must satisfy the Court not only that the Board made a palpably erroneous finding of material fact, but also that the finding was made without regard to the evidence. The Court may infer that the administrative agency made the erroneous finding of fact without regard to the evidence from the agency's failure to mention in its reasons some evidence before it that was relevant to the finding and pointed to a different conclusion from that reached by the agency. Just as a Court will only defer to an agency's interpretation of its constituent statute if it provides reasons for its conclusion, so a Court will be reluctant to defer to an agency's factual determinations in the absence of express findings and an analysis of the evidence that shows how the agency reached its results. Reasons given by an administrative agency are not to be read hypercritically, nor are agencies to be required to refer to every piece of evidence that they received that is contrary to their finding and to explain how they dealt with it. A statement by the agency in its reasons for decision that in making its findings it considered all of the evidence before it will often suffice to assure a reviewing Court that the agency directed itself to the totality of the evidence. The more important the evidence that is not mentioned specifically, the more willing a Court will be to infer from the silence that the agency made an erroneous finding of fact without regard to the evidence. When the agency refers in some detail to evidence supporting its finding, but is silent on evidence pointing to the opposite conclusion, it will be easier to infer that the agency overlooked the contradictory evidence when making its finding of fact. The Court was not persuaded that the Board erred when it found that the applicant faced no serious possibility of persecution outside Mexico City and therefore it was unnecessary to consider whether the Board's finding was made without regard to the evidence.

The applicant called a psychologist as a witness to explain why it was not reasonable to require the applicant to return to Mexico. In making its decision the panel did not refer to the psychologist's evidence. This evidence was so important to the applicant's case that it can be inferred from the refugee division's failure to mention it that the finding made by the panel was made without regard to this evidence. This inference was made easier by the fact that the Board's reasons dealt with other items of evidence indicating that return would not be unduly harsh. The inclusion of the "boilerplate" assertion that the Board considered all the evidence was not sufficient to prevent this inference from being drawn. Accordingly, the decision of the panel was set aside and the matter remitted to a differently constituted panel.

Nebea v. Canada (Minister of Citizenship & Immigration) (1998), 45 Imm. L.R. (2d) 61, 152 F.T.R. 106 (Fed. T.D.) — The applicant successfully reviewed a decision by a panel of the IRB to the effect that the applicant was not a convention refugee. After hearing the evidence but at the beginning of submissions by counsel for the applicant on the subject of the applicant's identity and nationality, the Board advised counsel that it accepted the applicant's identification and that she was a national of Kenya. As a result, the counsel made no more oral submissions on these issues and in subsequent written submissions confined herself to the arguments made before the Board prior to being advised that the Board was already satisfied on these points. In its decision the Board found the evidence insufficient to prove identity and nationality. The misleading of counsel to the effect that an issue need not be argued and then a finding against counsel's client on that issue was a denial of natural justice.

The Board also concluded that the applicant's claim, to having been persecuted in 1996 for providing information to newspapers was implausible. It based its conclusion on what the documentary evidence contained and on what it did not contain. This finding of fact based on inferences drawn from documentary evidence, also available for review by the Court, is open to scrutiny by the Court which is in as good a position to draw its own inferences. The Court concluded that the inferences drawn in this case were illogical and, for this reason, was prepared to set aside the decision.

Khan v. Canada (Minister of Citizenship and Immigration) (August 21, 1998), Doc. IMM-3428-97 (Fed. T.D.) — Reasons under section 69.1(11) must be sufficiently clear, precise and intelligible so that the claimant knows why his or her claim has failed.

Gill v. Canada (Minister of Citizenship & Immigration) (August 4, 1998), Doc. IMM-5243-97 (Fed. T.D.) — The applicant sought to review a negative decision of the IRB. The panel found that the applicant was persecuted by the Punjabi police in the past. The sole issue framed by the panel was whether the applicant had an internal flight alternative. The panel's analysis however, did not proceed. The actual analysis dealt with whether conditions had changed sufficiently in India and in particular in the Punjab such that the applicant was no longer at risk of persecution. In making its assessment of the profiles of people currently at risk, the panel relied on documentary evidence. A panel is entitled to accept, reject and weigh documentary evidence. If a panel states that it is relying on specific documentary evidence however, it cannot arbitrarily disregard integral portions of that evidence.

Yu v. Canada (Minister of Citizenship & Immigration) (1998), 150 F.T.R. 240 (Fed. T.D.) — This was an application to review a negative decision of the CRDD. The applicant, a citizen of China, stated that he became a Roman Catholic in 1992. The applicant has 3 children and had to pay a fine for having the third child. The applicant alleged that he became actively involved in a house church and that this eventually lead to the authorities attempting to arrest him. The applicant fled China and arrived in Canada in December 1995. The applicant submitted a summons which he had received, stating that he must appear at trial because he was charged with being involved in illegal religious activity. The panel failed to discuss this summons in its decision.

The decision of the panel was set aside. The summons was a timely document. There was no contention that it was not reliable. The summons was directly relevant to the applicant's claim and directly relevant to the facts he alleged. It should have had some bearing upon the decision of the panel and it is unclear whether they considered it and it is unclear how much weight they gave it. Even if the panel believed the applicant lacked credibility, they should have considered the summons and then set it aside because of the applicant's lack of credibility.

Sarker v. Canada (Minister of Citizenship & Immigration) (1998), 45 Imm. L.R. (2d) 209, 150 F.T.R. 284 (Fed. T.D.) — The applicant sought to set aside a negative determination of the CRDD. There is no obligation on the panel to signal its conclusions on implausibility or on the general credibility of evidence in advance of a decision. The onus remains on the applicant to establish his claim to be considered a convention refugee by credible evidence. The panel did not err or fail to ensure procedural fairness in concluding that there were implausibilities in the applicant's evidence without first bringing those to the attention of the applicant and providing an opportunity for him to respond.

Adibi v. Canada (Minister of Citizenship & Immigration) (June 25, 1998), Doc. IMM-4906-97 (Fed. T.D.) — The applicant sought to review a negative decision of the CRDD. While it is not necessary for the Board to mention all the evidence that was before it, it should have acknowledged a document which corroborated the applicant's story and directly contradicted its findings. Failure to do this constituted a reviewable error. Application for judicial review was granted, and the matter was referred back for a rehearing by a differently constituted panel.

Isiaku v. Canada (Minister of Citizenship & Immigration) (1998), 46 Imm. L.R. (2d) 79, 150 F.T.R. 143 (Fed. T.D.) — The Board heard the applicant's refugee claim on November 13, 1996. At the conclusion of the hearing, the Board delivered oral reasons for its decision indicating that written reasons would follow. There was no breach of procedural fairness as a result of the Board proceeding in this manner. The rules of procedural fairness do not require the Board to reserve all of its decisions.

Abramov v. Canada (Minister of Citizenship & Immigration) (1998), 150 F.T.R. 119 (Fed. T.D.) — This was an application to review a negative decision of the CRDD. The applicant, a citizen of Russia, fled his home country to evade military service because he opposed Russian intervention in Chechnya. The applicant was forcibly taken from his home by military officials, declared fit for service and ordered to report for duty which the applicant failed to do. The applicant alleged that if he returned to Russia, he would be persecuted for having avoided military service.

The Board was not convinced that this would be the case and relied on a Tass article whose source was a General of the Russian army. The panel found that the documentary evidence did not support the contention that the applicant would be forced to serve in the military. The applicant argued that the Board did not take into consideration relevant documentary evidence, in particular a letter from a journalist, who had researched army conditions and whose opinion it was that recruitment officers were especially brutal toward draft dodgers.

The Board committed a reviewable error in ignoring material evidence which contradicted its finding. The Board should have explained why it gave more weight to the evidence of a General of the Russian army than they did to evidence from objective sources. The journalist's letter and other documentary evidence were relevant to the issue before the panel and should have been addressed in its decision.

Iordanov v. Canada (Minister of Citizenship & Immigration) (1998), 145 F.T.R. 289 (Fed. T.D.) — The applicant sought to review a negative decision of the panel of the CRDD. The applicant submitted a videotape which included an interview with a Bulgarian evangelical pastor. The applicant included this tape as support for his claim that he had a well-founded fear of persecution based on his religious beliefs. The panel did not review the video during the hearing. In its written reasons the panel made no reference to the video. The video was not just a obscure paragraph in an plethora of documents. It was the principal evidence offered by the applicant to prove his claim.

By not mentioning whether it did in fact view the video or say what it made of the video, the tribunal fell short of its duty to be fair and evince natural justice. Accordingly, the decision of the panel was set aside.

Randhawa v. Canada (Minister of Citizenship & Immigration) (February 2, 1998), Doc. IMM-2474-97 (Fed. T.D.) — The applicants sought to review a negative decision of the panel of the CRDD. The issue of whether the applicant was part of a social group was not argued before the panel, with the result that the panel had to decide on its own whether the evidence supported such a conclusion. The panel concluded that the applicant was persecuted, not because he was a Sikh, but rather because he was a wealthy farmer and therefore denied his claim.

Given the extensive evidence of persecution of Sikhs in India, the panel erred in compartmentalizing the applicant as a Sikh, from the fact that he was a prominent wealthy person. The Board should have considered the applicant to be a member of a social group, namely "prominent wealthy Sikhs". The decision of the panel was set aside.

D'Mello v. Canada (Minister of Citizenship & Immigration) (January 22, 1998), Doc. IMM-1236-97 (Fed. T.D.) — The applicant sought to overturn a negative decision of a panel of the CRDD. The applicant was born in India and was a citizen of that country. The applicant claimed Convention refugee status on the basis of membership in a particular social group, that of abused women, and in the case of the minor applicant, that of members of the families of abused women.

The panel relied upon an expert from Human Rights Briefs, Women in India as authority for the proposition that there is, in India, a legislative and a procedural framework to which women subject to domestic violence can have recourse. The panel failed to make reference to paragraphs in that brief which reflected the difficulties encountered by women in relying on that framework and thus its ineffectiveness. The principal applicant's fear did not rest on the lack of a legislative and procedural framework in India to protect abused women, but rather on the lack of police support to such women and the difficulty, given the lack of such support, in effectively taking advantage of that legislative and procedural frame work. Thus the panel had inadequately analyzed the totality of the documentary evidence and its decision was set aside.

Yada v. Canada (Minister of Citizenship & Immigration) (1998), 140 F.T.R. 264 (Fed. T.D.) — This was an application to review a negative decision of the CRDD. The applicant submitted that the tribunal erred by ignoring recent and relevant documentary evidence which contradicted the panel's finding that country conditions in El Salvador had changed. Much of the contradictory evidence relied upon by the applicant originated from sources that were ordinarily accepted in refugee hearings. In addition, the material relied upon by the applicant was published later than the documents relied on by the panel. The absence of reference to this material lead the Court to the conclusion that the panel assessment of country conditions was unreasonable.

Abdi v. Canada (Minister of Citizenship & Immigration) (1998), 46 Imm. L.R. (2d) 146 (Fed. T.D.) — This was an application to review a negative decision of the CRDD. At issue was the question whether the applicant had an IFA inside Somalia. The Board had before it, a letter from the Somalia Immigrant Aid Organization, which stated that the Canadian government could give no assurances that a person being returned to Somalia would be directed to a specific area without travelling through hostile territory.

The decision of the Board was set aside on the basis that it failed to consider this item of documentary evidence. The document in question was evidence with respect to whether the IFA was "a realistic obtainable option". Accordingly, the decision of the panel was set aside and a re-hearing directed.

Ramalingam v. Canada (Minister of Citizenship & Immigration) (January 8, 1998), Doc. IMM-1298-97 (Fed. T.D.) — The applicant sought to review a negative decision of the CRDD. The applicant alleges to be a citizen of Sri Lanka and a Sri Lankan Tamil. The applicant presented a passport, a birth certificate, and a statement of a Justice of the Peace of Sri Lanka. The Board rejected the applicant's birth certificate, because the document bore the official stamp of "Ceylon". That allegation was not raised in the course of the hearing but appeared in written submissions filed by the Refugee Claim officer after the hearing. To meet that concern, counsel for the applicant obtained an e-mail message from the Sri Lankan High Commission in Ottawa confirming that birth certificates of Sri Lankans born after 1972 which have seals or stamps with the words "Ceylon" instead of "Sri Lanka" are valid. Counsel for the respondent objected unsuccessfully to the admissibility of such a document on the ground that it was not produced at the hearing. This objection was unsuccessful because the issue regarding the validity of the birth certificate was only raised by the refugee claims officer after the close of the proceedings. Identity documents issued by a foreign government are presumed to be valid unless evidence adduce to prove otherwise.

The Board challenged the validity of the birth certificate without adducing any evidence in support of its contention. This constituted the reviewable error. Accordingly, the judicial review application was allowed.

Sasan v. Canada (Minister of Citizenship & Immigration) (1998), 141 F.T.R. 158 (Fed. T.D.) — The applicants sought to review a negative decision of the panel of a CRDD. The hearing commenced on October 15, 1995 when the bulk of the evidence was given. It was then adjourned to January 10, 1996, but at that time the presiding member of the panel was ill. The hearing did not resume until August 1996 when it was completed. Credibility was the only issue in the panel's 3 1/2-page decision, which was rendered on March 5, 1997. Thus a period of some 18 months elapsed between the hearing of the majority of the evidence and the credibility determination.

The decision itself revealed a misinterpretation of the evidence and the combination of this fact with the unexplained delay lead to a setting aside of the decision. A panel must adjust its own schedule and require counsel to make an adjustment in their schedules so that a case can be concluded in a timely manner.

Selvarajah v. Canada (Minister of Citizenship & Immigration) (1997), 138 F.T.R. 237 (Fed. T.D.) — The CRDD determined that this Sri Lankan family, a mother, her 10-year-old son and two younger daughters were not Convention refugees. The CRDD failed to disclose its reasons concerning the claimants' fear of a boys recruitment by Liberation Tigers.

Unless a tribunal orders otherwise the claims of the principal applicant and the dependants are heard jointly pursuant to Rule 10 of the CRDD rules. Each decision is separate, however, and one may be set aside without disturbing the others. The tribunal made a negative finding concerning the mother's testimony, it did not focus, however, in its decision, specifically on the son's fear of persecution arising from his forced recruitment by the Tamil Tigers. The Court concluded that the outcome of the son's claim may have affected the decision concerning the family's internal flight alternative. Accordingly, the tribunal's decision with respect to the four claimants was set aside.

Menaker v. Canada (Minister of Citizenship & Immigration) (October 27, 1997), Doc. IMM-3837-96 (Fed. T.D.) — The applicant sought to overturn a negative decision of the CRDD. It is entirely open to the tribunal to base its decision on documentary evidence rather than testimonial evidence. The tribunal has jurisdiction to assess the probative value of the evidence and so the Court can intervene only where the tribunal reached an unreasonable conclusion. A modern democratic state is presumed to be capable of protecting its citizens. An applicant must exhaust all available legal meanings before claiming that such a state cannot or will not protect him or her.

Kabongo v. Canada (Minister of Citizenship & Immigration) (October 24, 1997), Doc. IMM-3050-96 (Fed. T.D.) — The applicant sought to review a negative decision of a panel of the CRDD. The panel found that while the applicant might be persecuted in some regions in Zaire that she could seek refuge elsewhere and avoid being persecuted because of her ethnicity. The applicant in her testimony indicated that there were problems faced by deportees when they arrived at the international airport in Zaire. Accordingly, the panel erred in failing to make a finding as to this potential problem when considering the question of internal refuge. If it was true that deportees who are returned to Zaire are persecuted because of the shame they bring on the country, the applicant could then encounter a serious barrier that might prevent her from travelling to a part of the country where she would be safe. Accordingly, the decision of the panel was set aside.

Syed v. Canada (Minister of Employment & Immigration) (1994), 83 F.T.R. 283 — The function of written reasons is to allow an individual, adversely affected by an administrative tribunal's decision, to know the underlying rationale for the decision. To that end, the reasons must be proper, adequate and intelligible, and must give consideration to the substantial points of argument raised by the party. Although it is within the tribunal's jurisdiction to accept or reject evidence, it cannot simply ignore it. The Refugee Division is obligated, at the very least, to comment on the evidence adduced by the applicant at the hearing. If that evidence is accepted or rejected, the applicant should be advised of the reasons why.

Hussain v. Canada (Minister of Employment & Immigration) (1994), 174 N.R. 76 (Fed. C.A.) — At the conclusion of the appellant's refugee hearing the presiding member announced that the panel had reached a decision and that the decision would be delivered orally from the bench. The presiding member announced that the oral reasons would constitute the written reasons subject to the Board's ability to correct errors in grammar and content if necessary. The presiding member delivered the oral reasons. These events occurred on July 17, 1991. On August 21, 1991 the appellant received an edited version of the oral reasons together with the formal decision of the Refugee Division which was signed that same day, August 21, 1991. The two sets of reasons were practically identical. The decision of the Refugee Division was adverse to the claimant.

The appeal was allowed. The statute is silent concerning the legislative policy which underlies the requirement that written reasons be given with any decision that is adverse to a claimant. This requirement is intended to allow a claimant to know in good time the precise reasons that a claim is rejected and thereby enable the claimant to assess his or her chances before incurring the trouble and expense of further proceedings.

The reservation as to content contained in the presiding member's announcement on July 17, 1991, was particularly important. Parliament did not intend that an unsuccessful claimant should be left in the position of not knowing, with certainty, the content of the adverse decision. The Refugee Division did send out a set of written reasons with the signed decision on August 21, 1991, but these written reasons were not given with the decision of July 17, 1991, as the statute requires.

Mehterian v. Canada (Minister of Employment & Immigration) (June 17, 1992), Doc. A-717-90 (Fed. C.A.) — The requirement that the Refugee Division give written reasons for any decision against a claimant mandates that the reasons must be sufficiently clear, precise and intelligible so that the claimant may know why his claim has failed and decide whether to seek leave to appeal.

Sebaratnam v. Canada (Minister of Employment & Immigration) (1991), 13 Imm. L.R. (2d) 264, 131 N.R. 158 (Fed. C.A.) — This was an appeal from a decision of the Refugee Division rejecting the appellant's claim to be a convention refugee. The Refugee Division referred to the evidence in considerable detail but said next to nothing by way of a comment upon it. A finding of lack of credibility must be drawn in clear and unmistakeable terms.

69.2 (1) Application for determination of cessation of refugee status — The Minister may make an application to the Refugee Division for a determination

whether any person who was determined under this Act or the regulations to be a Convention refugee has ceased to be a Convention refugee.

(2) Application to vacate — The Minister may, with leave of the Chairperson, make an application to the Refugee Division to reconsider and vacate any determination made under this Act or the regulations that a person is a Convention refugee on the ground that the determination was obtained by fraudulent means or misrepresentation, suppression or concealment of any material fact, whether exercised or made by that person or any other person.

(3) Leave to apply — An application to the Chairperson for leave to apply to the Refugee Division under subsection (2) shall be made *ex parte* and in writing and the Chairperson may grant that leave if the Chairperson is satisfied that evidence exists that, if it had been known to the Refugee Division, could have resulted in a different determination.

(4) Notice — An application to the Refugee Division under this section shall be instituted by filing, in the manner and form prescribed by the rules of the Board, a notice of application with the Refugee Division.

(5) Copy — Where a notice of application is filed with the Refugee Division pursuant to subsection (4), the Minister shall forthwith send a copy of the notice to the person who is the subject of the application.

R.S.C. 1985, c. 28 (4th Supp.), s. 18; 1992, c. 49, s. 61.

Case Law

Section 69.2(1)

Youssef v. Canada (Minister of Citizenship & Immigration) (March 29, 1999), Doc. IMM-990-98 (Fed. T.D.) — This was an application to review a decision of a panel of the IRB allowing an application by the Minister under subsection 69.2(1). The applicant is a stateless Palestinian who was born in Lebanon. The applicant and her children were granted refugee status without a hearing. The applicant made an application for permanent residence for herself and her children. In it she listed her husband as a dependent outside of Canada. The basis of the applicant's refugee claim had been that her husband had become a fundamentalist and was violent and aggressive toward her and her children. The test dealing with a change of circumstances in a refugee case does not apply in this type of situation. The applicant did not base her refugee claim on the political or social circumstances in Lebanon and on how these political or social circumstances affected her. The initial claim and the Minister's application for cessation referred to personal circumstances related to the behaviour and religious convictions of the applicant's husband. The applicant feared violence and torture after her husband embraced fundamentalist religious convictions. She said that she was afraid her husband would force their eldest daughter to marry a fundamentalist and go through the Islamic religious court to force the applicant to return to the matrimonial home.

When an application is made pursuant to section 69.2(1) for a determination of cessation of refugee status, the burden to show that there is a cessation rests on the Minister. The evidence that must be brought before the Board depends on the particular circumstances. In this case, the decision of the Board that a cessation has occurred was open to it on the evidence, and the application was dismissed.

Emina v. Canada (Minister of Citizenship & Immigration) (1998), 167 D.L.R. (4th) 764, 160 F.T.R. 317 (Fed. T.D.) — This is an application to review a decision to grant the Minister's application to reconsider and vacate a refugee determination. At the hearing of the motion to reconsider and vacate, the applicant attempted to call the Chair of the panel that granted the applicant refugee status. The panel was informed that the Chair was willing to testify. The panel refused the applicant permission to call the Chair as a witness based on the doctrine of judicial immunity.

To permit a panel member to voluntarily testify would defeat the whole concept of judicial immunity. The doctrine of judicial immunity applies both to the compellability and the competency of members of administrative tribunals.

Penate v. Canada (Minister of Employment & Immigration) (1993), 71 F.T.R. 171 — The applicant sought to review the denial of his refugee claim on the basis that he was excluded pursuant to Article I(F) of the Convention. One of the issues in the appeal was the test to be applied in assessing the relevance of changed country conditions to the applicant's wife's refugee claim. There are two separate procedures respecting refugee status which exist in the *Immigration Act*: (1) the granting of Convention refugee status to someone, by the IRB, on application by that individual and with respect to which the individual has the burden of proof; and (2) the removal of that status from someone, by the Board, upon application by the Minister and with respect to which the Minister bears the burden of proof.

This latter procedure is provided for in section 69.2 of the Act. The criteria described by Professor Hathaway in his text *The Law of Refugee Status* are framed by reference to the cessation of status, that is to the revoking of status after it has been granted and with respect to which the Minister, and not the individual, has the burden of proof. When the question is whether status will be granted, CRDD panels are required to weigh the evidence of changed country conditions in the balance with all the other evidence before them in assessing the applicant's claim.

The panel did not err in its approach. It weighed the evidence of changed country conditions as one aspect of the relevant evidence. Accordingly, the application was dismissed.

Salinas v. Canada (Minister of Employment & Immigration), 17 Imm. L.R. (2d) 118, 6 Admin. L.R. (2d) 154, 93 D.L.R. (4th) 631, 142 N.R. 211, [1992] 3 F.C. 247, 57 F.T.R. 159 (note) (Fed. C.A.) — This was an appeal from an order of the Trial Division whereby a decision of the Refugee Division to reconvene a hearing into the respondent's claim for refugee status was quashed and the Refugee Division ordered to render a decision on the basis of the evidence before it. The basis of the respondent's claim was her fear of persecution by agents of the state of Panama, which was headed by General Noriega. Some time after the conclusion of the respondent's hearing, but before a decision was rendered, the political situation in Panama changed. The presiding member of the panel notified the respondent that the hearing would be reconvened for the purpose of hearing evidence on these recent changes.

The appeal was allowed. The Refugee Division did not exceed its jurisdiction in reconvening the hearing. Section 68 endows the Refugee Division with powers and duties in relation to any proceedings before it. The distinction has been drawn by Parliament between "proceedings" and a "hearing" before the Refugee Division. The hearing is to be conducted in a manner required by section 69.1. The "hearing" is a step in any proceedings. "Proceedings" is a wider term encompassing the entire matter before the Refugee Division including the hearing itself. The Minister, pursuant to section 69.2(1), is able to initiate proceedings for a determination whether any person who was determined to be a Convention refugee has ceased to be so. The Court found force in the argument that evidence as to the change of conditions is better addressed in the same proceedings rather than in new proceedings initiated by the Minister subsequent to the Refugee Division's determination.

The Refugee Division was not *functus officio*. It had yet to make a determination of the claim. Until it did, the proceedings were pending and finality had not been reached. In order to arrive at its decision, the Refugee Division could exercise the power conferred by the statute, provided it did so properly by giving the respondent an opportunity to be heard at the reconvened hearing. An inquiry into any change of conditions in the appellant's homeland comes within the general mandate of the Refugee Division in determining the claim.

In *Lawal v. Canada (Minister of Employment & Immigration)*, [1991] 2 F.C. 404, the Court ruled that the only way for the Refugee Division, after the end of a hearing but before a decision, to consider new evidence beyond that of which it might take judicial notice was by re-opening the hearing. The Court's decision in *Longia v. Canada (Minister of Employment & Immigration)*, [1990] 3 F.C. 288, applies only where the Refugee Division has already reached a decision.

The appeal was allowed. The order of the Trial Division was set aside and the respondent's claim for refugee status was referred back to the Refugee Division for a continuation of the reconvened hearing.

Section 69.2(2)

Mahdi v. Canada (Minister of Citizenship & Immigration) (1995), 32 Imm. L.R. (2d) 1, 191 N.R. 170, 103 F.T.R. 240 (note) (Fed. C.A.) — The respondent left Somalia in 1985 for the United States where she lived until 1990. While there, she married and had two children. In 1990, shortly after obtaining permanent resident status in the United States she separated from her husband and returned to Somalia with her two children. In May 1991 she came to Canada with her children and sought admission as a Convention refugee. The respondent made a false statement to a panel of the CRDD concealing the fact that she lived in the United States and had become a permanent resident of that country. On the basis of her false statements the respondent was found to be a Convention refugee. The Minister learned of the misrepresentation and applied under section 69.2(2) to vacate the decision that the respondent was a refugee.

The respondent applied to the Trial Division to set aside that determination. That application was successful and it was from that decision of the Trial Division that the respondent Minister appealed in this case.

The Trial Division was correct in concluding that the Refugee Division did not engage in the analysis contemplated by subsection 69.3(5). The Trial Division judge concluded that the evidence before the Refugee Division showed first, that the respondent had given up her residence in the United States, and secondly that permanent residents of the United States may lose their status if they abandon their residence there. Thus, the Trial Division was not satisfied that Article 1E of the Convention applied to the respondent.

The decision of the Trial Division was upheld. The fact that the respondent voluntarily renounced the protection of the United States to return to Somalia did not preclude her from later claiming Convention refugee status in Canada if she realized that she still had good reason to fear persecution in Somalia. Secondly, the fact that the respondent had conducted herself in such a way as to create a serious possibility, if not a probability, that the American authorities would no longer recognize her as a permanent resident, had to be taken into account in deciding whether it was established on a balance of probabilities that the American authorities still recognized her as a permanent resident. Finally, the Court of Appeal pointed out that this was not a case where a person had voluntarily renounced the protection of one country in order to seek refuge elsewhere. Accordingly, the Minister's appeal was dismissed.

Bayat v. Canada (Minister of Citizenship & Immigration) (1995), 96 F.T.R. 76 — The applicants, a husband and wife, were citizens of Afghanistan. They applied for permanent residence to a visa officer who determined them to be Convention refugees and permitted them to come to Canada on immigrant visas. It was later determined that the applicants had provided false statutory declarations and false identity documents to the visa officer and the Minister made an application to vacate the visa officers decision. At such a hearing the Refugee Division may reject the Minister's application on the basis that, notwithstanding the false information, there was other sufficient information upon which the officer could have based his or her decision.

The Court determined that the other sufficient evidence referred to in subsection 69.3(5) relates only to evidence that was actually before the visa officer. The Refugee Division ought not to speculate as to what documentary evidence might have been available, thus the majority was correct in refusing to permit the filing of other evidence that could have been made available at the time the decision in question was made.

A panel of the IRB hearing such an application by the Minister does not have the authority to declare the person concerned not to be a refugee. On an application pursuant to sections 69.2(2) the Refugee Division has two alternatives. It can either approve or reject the application to vacate the earlier decision. It cannot go further and determine that there is no merit in the claim for refugee status.

Section 69.2(5)

Canada (Minister of Citizenship & Immigration) v. Haji-Dodi (1996), 111 F.T.R. 109 (Fed. T.D.) — This was an application on behalf of the Minister for review of a decision dismissing an application by the Minister to a three member panel of the CRDD to vacate an earlier decision.

On January 9, 1992, a panel of the CRDD determined the respondent to be a Convention Refugee. On February 17, 1993, the chairperson of the IRB granted the Minister leave to make an application pursuant to section 69.2(3) for reconsideration. In support, a declaration made by Mr. William MacIntyre with attachments was filed.

On May 25, 1995, the panel appointed to consider the Minister's application convened. The panel indicated that the Minister would be invited to establish whether there had been a misrepresentation and that if such a basis were laid the respondent would be given an opportunity to address the issues raised by the evidence aduced by the Minister. At the hearing without having led any evidence, counsel for the Minister sought to call the respondent as a witness. Counsel for the respondent objected and the tribunal agreed with the representations made on behalf of the respondent who then did not testify at the hearing. No other witnesses were called. With respect to the declaration of Mr. MacIntyre and the attachments, the tribunal gave the declarations little or no weight.

The tribunal did not err in law by declining to compel the respondent to testify when counsel for the Minister sought to examine him as a witness. The tribunal determined as a matter of its own proceedings in accordance with section 67(2) that the respondent should not be compelled to testify in circumstances where no evidence had been presented at the hearing by the Minister and documentary evidence presented in support of the application in advance of the hearing was not entirely satisfactory from the perspective of the tribunal.

Further, the respondent was free to deal with the application by the Minister as he saw fit. The respondent was under no obligation to provide documentary evidence or to provide *viva voce* evidence unless compelled by the tribunal. The respondent was free to seek to cross-examine the declarant in advance of the hearing, just as he would have been as a party to other proceedings before the Court in dealing with affidavits produced by the other side, but he was not bound to do so. The Minister having put forward the declaration should have been prepared to produce the declarant for cross-examination. Where there is no request by the respondent the tribunal is under no obligation to direct that there be cross-examination in relation to the documentary evidence it found questionable and before it determined what part of the evidence adduced by the Minister would be admitted and what weight it would have.

69.3 (1) Hearing — Where an application to the Refugee Division is made under section 69.2, the Refugee Division shall conduct a hearing into the application, after having notified the Minister and the person who is the subject of the application of the time and place set for the hearing, and shall afford the Minister and that person a reasonable opportunity to present evidence, cross-examine witnesses and make representations.

(2) Abandonment of application — If the Minister's counsel or agent fails to appear at the time and place set by the Refugee Division for the hearing into the application or, in the opinion of the Division, is otherwise in default in the prosecution of the application, the Division may, after giving the Minister a reasonable opportunity to be heard, declare the application to have been abandoned.

(3) Quorum — Three members constitute a quorum of the Refugee Division for the purposes of a hearing under this section.

(4) Decision — The Refugee Division shall approve or reject the application and shall render its decision as soon as possible after completion of the hearing and send a written notice of the decision to the Minister and the person who is the subject of the application.

(5) Rejection of otherwise established application — The Refugee Division may reject an application under subsection 69.2(2) that is otherwise established if it is of the opinion that, notwithstanding that the determination was obtained by fraudulent means or misrepresentation, suppression or concealment of any material fact, there was other sufficient evidence on which the determination was or could have been based.

(6) Split decision — In the event of a split decision, the decision of the majority of the members hearing the application shall be deemed to be the decision of the Refugee Division.

(7) Written reasons — The Refugee Division may give written reasons for its decision on an application, except that

> **(a) if the decision is against the person who is the subject of the application, the Division shall, with the written notice of the decision referred to in subsection (4), give written reasons with the decision; and**
>
> **(b) if the Minister or the person who is the subject of the application requests written reasons within ten days after the day on which the Minister or person is notified of the decision, the Division shall forthwith give written reasons.**

R.S.C. 1985, c. 28 (4th Supp.), s. 18; 1992, c. 49, s. 62.

Case Law

Section 69.3(5)

Bayat v. Canada (Minister of Citizenship & Immigration) (1995), 96 F.T.R. 76 — The applicants, a husband and wife, were citizens of Afghanistan. They applied for permanent residence to a visa officer who determined them to be Convention refugees and permitted them to come to Canada on immigrant visas. It was later determined that the applicants had provided false statutory declarations and false identity documents to the visa officer and the Minister made an application to vacate the visa officers decision. At such a hearing the Refugee Division may reject the Minister's application on the basis that, notwithstanding the false information, there was other sufficient information upon which the officer could have based his or her decision.

The Court determined that the other sufficient evidence referred to in subsection 69.3(5) relates only to evidence that was actually before the visaofficer. The Refugee Division ought not to speculate as to what documentary evidence might have been available, thus the majority was correct in refusing to permit the filing of other evidence that could have been made available at the time the decision in question was made.

A panel of the IRB hearing such an application by the Minister does not have the authority to declare the person concerned not to be a refugee. On an application pursuant to sections 69.2(2) the Refugee Division has two alternatives. It can either approve or reject the application to vacate the earlier decision. It cannot go further and determine that there is no merit in the claim for refugee status.

Section 69.3(7)

Armson v. Canada (Minister of Employment & Immigration) (1989), 9 Imm. L.R. (2d) 150 (Fed. C.A.) — This section 28 application sought to set aside the unanimous decision of the Immigration Appeal Board that the applicant was not a convention refugee.

The applicant asserted a fear of persecution because of his political opinion and his membership in a particular social group. The Board disbelieved the applicant. The reasons for disbelieving the applicant were sparse. The Board owed a duty to the applicant to give reasons for rejecting his claim on the ground of credibility in clear and unmistakable terms. The Board's reasons did not contain a single word as to why the applicant's evidence was not credible. This formed an additional basis for setting aside the Board's decision. The application was allowed and the decision of the Board set aside and the matter remitted for a full hearing by a differently constituted panel.

Immigration Appeal Division

69.4 (1) Court of record — The Appeal Division is a court of record and shall have an official seal, which shall be judicially noticed.

(2) Sole and exclusive jurisdiction — The Appeal Division has, in respect of appeals made pursuant to sections 70, 71 and 77, sole and exclusive jurisdiction to hear and determine all questions of law and fact, including questions of jurisdiction, that may arise in relation to the making of a removal order or the refusal to approve an application for landing made by a member of the family class.

(3) Powers — The Appeal Division has, as regards the attendance, swearing and examination of witnesses, the production and inspection of documents, the enforcement of

its orders and other matters necessary or proper for the due exercise of its jurisdiction, all such powers, rights and privileges as are vested in a superior court of record and, without limiting the generality of the foregoing, may

> **(a) issue a summons to any person requiring that person to appear at the time and place mentioned therein to testify with respect to all matters within that person's knowledge relative to a subject-matter before the Division and to bring and produce any document, book or paper that the person has or controls relative to that subject-matter;**
>
> **(b) administer oaths and examine any person on oath; and**
>
> **(c) during a hearing, receive such additional evidence as it may consider credible or trustworthy and necessary for dealing with the subject-matter before it.**

(4) Notification of disposition — The Appeal Division shall, in accordance with rules made under subsection 65(1), notify the parties to an appeal made pursuant to section 70 or 71 of its disposition of the appeal.

(5) Written reasons — The Appeal Division shall forthwith give written reasons for its disposition of any appeal made pursuant to section 70 or 71 where either of the parties to the appeal has so requested within ten days after having been notified of the disposition of the appeal.

R.S.C. 1985, c. 28 (4th Supp.), s. 18; 1992, c. 49, s. 63.

Case Law

Section 69.4(1)

Srivastava v. Canada (Minister of Employment & Immigration), [1973] F.C. 138 (Fed. C.A.) — Under section 23 of the *Immigration Appeal Board Act*, R.S.C. 1970, the appellant had a right to produce evidence before the Immigration Appeal Board and was not limited in his appeal to the record of the special inquiry. The Immigration Appeal Board constituted a Court of Record with the power to summon witnesses *etc.* and, accordingly, the Board erred in limiting the scope of an appeal to a consideration of the record of the special inquiry.

Section 69.4(2)

Canada (Minister of Citizenship & Immigration) v. Christopher Michael Harrison, 47 Imm. L.R. (2d) 173, [1998] 4 F.C. 557, 155 F.T.R. 251 — This is an appeal by the Minister from a decision of the Appeal Division of the Immigration and Refugee Board re-opening an earlier decision dismissing an appeal to it by the respondent. The decision was dated February 17, 1998, and at that time the respondent was no longer in Canada because he had been deported. The respondent was born in 1966 in England and was landed in Canada as an accompanying dependent of his parents in 1978. On July 11, 1991, he was ordered deported because he had been convicted of a criminal offence. The respondent appealed that decision, but his appeal was dismissed on February 13, 1992, for want of prosecution. On March 23, 1992, the respondent was arrested and on March 24, 1992, he sought leave to have the IAD re-open his appeal. The respondent also filed a motion for a stay of the removal order. That motion was dismissed on April 2, 1992, and the respondent was deported to the United Kingdom on April 6, 1992. On August 3, 1993, the IAD granted the March 24, 1992 motion and re-opened the respondent's appeal. The Minister successfully appealed that order and obtained an order remitting the motion to re-open back to the IAD for re-determination. The motion to re-open was dealt with on its merits in January 1998, and a decision to re-open was rendered in February 1998.

The minister's execution of a deportation order does not terminate a motion to re-open an appeal, where a motion to re-open was brought prior to deportation.

Shergill v. Canada (Minister of Citizenship & Immigration) (1998), 149 F.T.R. 157 (Fed. T.D.) — The applicant sought to review a decision of the Immigration Appeal Division which upheld a decision of a visa officer not approving the sponsorship application of the applicant's "adopted" daughter. In the proceedings before the Appeal Division, there was conflicting evidence relating to Indian law. While the evidence was as to the interpretation of Indian law, the weighing of such evidence is no different than the weighing of any other evidence by a tribunal. It is the function of the IAD and, barring legal error, the Court will not reweigh the evidence. In this case, the matter was not beyond doubt and indeed the applicant's evidence was relatively persuasive. However, it was still open to the IAD to prefer the respondent's evidence.

It was submitted that as a result of a declaratory judgement obtained from a court in India that it must be presumed that the adoption was in compliance with Indian law. The Court concluded that the IAD was not bound by the declaratory judgement.

Nguyen v. Canada (Minister of Citizenship & Immigration) (1998), 42 Imm. L.R. (2d) 148, (sub nom. *Canada (Minister of Citizenship & Immigration) v. Nguyen)* 141 F.T.R. 139 (Fed. T.D.) — The Appeal Division quashed a removal order made against the respondent. The removal order was based on a determination that the respondent was a permanent resident, who was granted landing by reason of a fraudulent misrepresentation of a material fact. The IAD determined that it had jurisdiction under subsection 70(1) of the *Immigration Act* to consider the appeal against the removal order.

Section 69.4(2) is not privative clause in relation to this application. There is no ground to conclude that special deference is owed to the IAD. Determination or jurisdiction in the context here at issue was essentially a matter of statutory interpretation.

The principal reasons for the issuance of the respondent's visas cease to exist before its issuance. The visa was therefore void on issuance and the Appeal Division had no jurisdiction to entertain the respondent's appeal.

Canada (Minister of Citizenship & Immigration) v. Reynolds (1997), 42 Imm. L.R. (2d) 175, 139 F.T.R. 315 (Fed. T.D.) — This was a judicial review of a decision of the Appeal Division of the IRB. The applicant, a permanent resident of Canada, was ordered deported for reasons of criminality and while his appeal to the Appeal Division was pending the Minister issued a danger opinion pursuant to section 70(5). The Appeal Division decided to treat the Minister's opinion and related correspondence as a motion to dismiss for lack of jurisdiction. The Appeal Division concluded that it had jurisdiction to determine its own jurisdiction under subsection 70(5) and to conduct the limited inquiry into the constitutional validity to subsection 70(5). Specifically, the tribunal concluded that it had no jurisdiction to inquire into the procedural aspects of the subsection but could consider its substantive validity.

Section 69.4(2) empowers the tribunal to consider questions of law and determine its own jurisdiction. This power undoubtedly includes the power to address constitutional questions in certain situations. Nevertheless, logic demands that the Appeal Division's general power to consider questions or law and jurisdiction does not empower it to treat subsection 70(5) as unconstitutional and thereby ignore an express limitation that Parliament had placed on its own jurisdiction.

Accordingly, the Minister's application for judicial review was allowed.

Drummond v. Canada (Minister of Citizenship & Immigration) (1996), 33 Imm. L.R. (2d) 258, 112 F.T.R. 33 (Fed. T.D.) — A majority of a panel of the Immigration Appeal Division dismissed the applicant's appeal of her deportation order. The dissenting member would have stayed the order for four years.

The applicant sought a re-opening of the decision of the IAD on the grounds that her counsel at the Appeal Division hearing (who was not her counsel on the judicial review application) had been incompetent and that this incompetence may have effected the outcome of the appeal.

By the time the applicant's present counsel was retained the 15 day time limit for seeking judicial review of the Appeal Division decision had past. The applicant's new counsel was of the view that seeking a re-opening of the appeal by the IAD was the appropriate remedy for the applicant to pursue.

The IAD dismissed the re-opening application. It found that it did not have the authority to rule on the competency of counsel.

The IAD has jurisdiction to deal with matters of natural justice. Where counsel is freely chosen it is the professional accreditation body and not the courts which have the mandate to deal with incompetence, however, in extraordinary cases the competency of counsel may gave rise to a natural justice issue. In such cases, the facts must be specific and clearly proven. The evidence must be so clear and unequivocal and the circumstances so egregious that the unfairness to an applicant is virtually obvious.

While the standard to be met to obtain a re-opening on these grounds presents an onerous burden to an applicant it is a matter that the IAD cannot decline to address if it is raised. Accordingly, the judicial review application was allowed.

Sheriff v. Canada (Minister of Employment & Immigration) (1995), 31 Imm. L.R. (2d) 246 (Fed. C.A.) — The Appeal Division, when considering an appeal under subsection 77, has the initial jurisdiction and an obligation to determine whether the appeal comes within that section and thus within its authority to hear and to so decide it may be necessary for it to determine certain jurisdictional facts. In this case, it had to determine whether there was in fact a valid declaration by a parent within subparagraph 6(5)(a)(iii) of the *Immigration Regulations* which would exclude the appellant's son from the Family Class. Such a determination can involve the Board in the examination of the circumstances in which the declaration was signed to determine its validity.

Canada (Solicitor General) v. Kainth (1994), 26 Imm. L.R. (2d) 226, 81 F.T.R. 318 (note), 170 N.R. 367 (Fed. C.A.) — The Appeal Division allowed the appeal of the respondent and overturned a refusal by an immigration officer of the sponsored application for landing of the respondent's spouse. The Board decided that, although the refusal was legal and moreover that the spouse had been deported a few years previously, there were sufficient humanitarian or compassionate grounds to grant the spouse permanent residence. This decision was upheld by the Trial Division on a judicial review application. However, the Trial Division judge certified a serious question of general importance. The Solicitor General then appealed to the Court of Appeal.

Section 69.4(2) is broad enough to permit the Appeal Division to decide that it has jurisdiction to permit the respondent's spouse to be landed, notwithstanding the fact that the spouse did not have the Minister's consent as required by section 55(1) and notwithstanding the provisions of section 19(1)(i).

Accordingly, the appeal was dismissed.

Khakh v. Canada (Minister of Employment & Immigration) (1993), [1994] 1 F.C. 548, 23 Imm. L.R. (2d) 38, 70 F.T.R. 26 — The applicant sought to overturn a decision of a credible basis panel holding a hearing under refugee provisions no longer in effect. The applicant alleged a reasonable apprehension of bias. The respondent argued that in failing to raise an objection on this basis before the credible basis panel, the applicant waived his rights to subsequently raise the issue. A reasonable apprehension of bias should be raised at the first opportunity. There is no waiver unless the party entitled to make the objection is fully aware of the nature of the disqualification and has adequate opportunity to make the objection. The Court will imply waiver where a party or its representative knows of the facts that give rise to an apprehension of bias and, notwithstanding, does not object. The party or its representative must be fully cognisant of the right to take objection. In this case, the adjudicator had, after the applicant requested an interpreter, refused the interpreter after testing the applicant in English. As the hearings progressed the adjudicator noticed that the applicant's English was deteriorating and this was taken to mean that the adjudicator had formed the view that the applicant was not doing his best in English. The failure of the unrepresented applicant to object to the adjudicator's jurisdiction on the basis of reasonable apprehension of bias, after this comment was made, was not taken to be a waiver of his rights to object before the Federal Court.

Gagliardi v. Canada (Minister of Employment & Immigration) (January 9, 1990), Doc. A-1142-87 (Fed. C.A.) — The appellant argued that the execution of the deportation order, having regard to all the circumstances, contravened his right not to be subjected to cruel and unusual treatment or punishment within the meaning of section 12 of the Charter. The Immigration Appeal Board was required to determine objectively the issue of cruel and unusual treatment. Was it also necessary for the Board to study the personal characteristics of the appellant as well as the particular circumstances of the case? Section 12 governs the quality of the punishment and is concerned with the effect that the punishment may have on the persons on whom it is imposed. Though the state may impose punishment, the effect of that punishment must not be grossly disproportionate to what would have been appropriate.

Section 69.4(3)

Lê Dang v. Canada (Minister of Citizenship & Immigration) (1997), 38 Imm. L.R. (2d) 273, 132 F.T.R. 189 (Fed. T.D.) — This was an application to review a decision of the registrar of the Appeal Division of the IRB, wherein she advised the applicant that the applicant's claim for Convention refugee status would be scheduled prior to her appeal to the Appeal Division. There is nothing in the *Immigration Act* to prevent the IAD from scheduling it's hearing as it sees fit, provided that hearings are held within a reasonable period of time. Consequently it cannot be said that the IRD acted without jurisdiction or erred in law in deciding to schedule the applicant's hearings as it did.

Canada (Minister of Citizenship and Immigration) v. Jhatu (1996), 35 Imm. L.R. (2d) 66, 117 F.T.R. 236 (Fed. T.D.); affirmed (1998), 226 N.R. 127 (Fed. C.A.) — This was an application by the Minister to set aside a decision of the Appeal Division of the IRB. The Appeal Division had stayed the execution of a removal order for a period of 6 years. The respondent had an extensive criminal record in Canada and the Appeal Division had refused to hear the evidence of children of one of the victims of the applicant's criminal offenses.

The application was refused. Section 69.4(3)(c) of the *Immigration Act* gives the Appeal Division the discretion to receive any evidence which it considers credible or trustworthy and necessary for dealing with the subject matter before it. The panel clearly recognized that the respondent had committed a very serious crime and noted that the victim had 6 children. The Appeal Division was of the view that the victim's impact evidence had no probative value to the issue before it. That is, whether in all of the circumstances the respondent should be deported. That conclusion was within the panel's jurisdiction and was not so unreasonable as to warrant court intervention.

Editor's Note: Appeal dismissed, (1998), 226 N.R. 127 (Fed. C.A.).

Kusi v. Canada (Minister of Employment & Immigration) (1993), 19 Imm. L.R. (2d) 281, 65 F.T.R. 58 (Fed. T.D.) — An adjudicator and member of the Immigration and Refugee Board were conducting a credible basis hearing into the claim of a Convention refugee claimant, pursuant to provisions of the *Immigration Act* in effect on August 19, 1992.

The tribunal accepted as evidence notes taken by an immigration officer, which recorded answers given to him at the port-of-entry by the applicant. The applicant contested the accuracy of the notes and asked that the officer be produced for cross-examination, a request which was denied by the tribunal.

The decision by the tribunal that there was no credible basis to the applicant's claim was set aside and the matter was remitted back for determination in accordance with the law. Specifically, the Court found that given the importance of the interest, namely the applicant's claim to be a Convention refugee, and given the fact that the applicant contested the accuracy of the notes which were relied upon by the tribunal, the rules of natural justice and of fundamental justice required that the cross-examination, which was sought, be allowed. The Court relied on the jurisprudence in *Canada (Minister of Employment & Immigration) v. Leal* (1991), 129 N.R. 383 (Fed. C.A.) and *Cheung v. Canada (Minister of Employment & Immigration)* (1981), 122 D.L.R. (3d) 41.

Editor's Note: Although occurring in the context of a repealed refugee hearing procedure, the principle in this case may have a broader application.

Singh (R.) v. Canada (Minister of Employment & Immigration) (September 22, 1992), Doc. A-859-88 (Fed. C.A.) — The appellant was a Canadian citizen who, in 1982, sponsored his adopted daughter. The visa officer was not satisfied that the adoption was legal according to the laws of India and had refused the application. The appellant had appealed to the Appeal Division and his appeal had been dismissed. The appeal to the Appeal Division was a proceeding *de novo*. The appellant had the burden of establishing that the adoption was not void under the *Hindu Adoptions and Maintenance Act*. The Appeal Division had accepted as trustworthy evidence an antedated version of the *Hindu Adoptions and Maintenance Act*, without proof that it was in force at the time of the adoption. The discretion as to the evidence that will be accepted as trustworthy is very broadly defined. In this case it was for the appellant to challenge the version of the Act being used by the Appeal Division and to lead evidence in support of that challenge. The appellant failed to do this and the discretion conferred upon the Board by this section was broad enough to permit it to act upon the version of the *Hindu Adoptions and Maintenance Act* that was before it.

Filipe v. Canada (Minister of Employment & Immigration) (1988), 6 Imm. L.R. (2d) 119 (Fed. C.A.) — This was a section 28 application seeking review of an Immigration Appeal Board decision determining that the applicant was not a Convention refugee. At the hearing, documentary evidence was filed which was not supported by an affidavit or a statutory declaration. The Board ruled that such a deficiency merely affected credibility and trustworthiness rather than admissibility. Accordingly, the Board did not err in concluding that the documents in question were admissible. Further, because the applicant's counsel was given an opportunity to make significant submissions as to the evidentiary value of the documents, there was no denial of natural justice or procedural unfairness in the proceedings before the Board. Accordingly, this section 28 application was dismissed.

Canada (Minister of Employment & Immigration) v. Dan-Ash (1988), 5 Imm. L.R. (2d) 78 (Fed. C.A.) — Section 65(2)(c) has the purpose and effect of freeing the Board's hearings from all the technical rules of evidence and, particularly, the "best evidence" and "hearsay" rules. Accordingly, the certificate of a fingerprint examiner was admissible. The actual examiner himself was not required to testify.

Fleming v. Canada (Minister of Employment & Immigration) (1987), 4 Imm. L.R. (2d) 207 (Fed. C.A.) — This case was a section 28 application to review and set aside a decision of the Immigration Appeal Board. The Board had dismissed the applicant's motion requesting the Board to set aside its decision dismissing the applicant's appeal from a deportation order and re-open the appeal in order to permit the applicant to adduce further evidence in support of a plea that the Board exercise its equitable jurisdiction in the applicant's favour.

The case illustrates the difference between additional evidence and new evidence. The party seeking to adduce additional evidence must satisfy the Board that:

1. He could not have obtained such evidence by reasonable diligence before the original hearing of the appeal; and

2. The evidence sought to be introduced is of such a nature that, if satisfactorily proved, it would furnish a sufficient reason for the reconsideration of the Court's original disposition of the appeal. New evidence is evidence which was not in existence at the time of the hearing of the appeal. It must be examined by the Board to determine whether or not it was of sufficient weight in relation to the other evidence in the case that the Board should exercise its discretion and re-open the case.

The application was granted. The Immigration Appeal Board had failed to recognize that some of the applicant's material was new evidence as opposed to additional evidence and, accordingly, had not applied the relevant test in dismissing the applicant's application.

Shanker v. Canada (Minister of Employment & Immigration) (June 25, 1987), Doc. A-535-86 (Fed. C.A.) — This was an appeal by a Canadian citizen from a decision of the Immigration Appeal Board dismissing an appeal against refusals of the sponsored applications of the citizen's father, mother and two brothers. The basis for the refusal was the opinion of a medical officer, concurred in by a second medical officer, that the mother was suffering from pulmonary tuberculosis, "possibly active". A visa officer found her inadmissible under section 19(1)(a)(i) of the *Immigration Act*. At the Immigration Appeal Board hearing, new evidence as to the mother's condition, subsequent to the rejection, was provided. This Court adopted the view that evidence as to the mother's condition, subsequent to the visa officer's refusal, was not relevant to the question of whether that refusal was lawful. It was argued that the medical notification, upon which the refusal was based, had not taken into account the results of subsequent medical inquiries. This argument failed because neither the transcript of the hearing before the Board, nor any document on the record, suggested that there was any response to the request for further medical information. Nor was there any suggestion that the appellant's mother had complied with the request to contact the doctor who examined her so that he might reply to the visa officer.

Rajpaul v. Canada (Minister of Employment & Immigration) (1987), 24 Admin. L.R. 153 (Fed. T.D.); varied 31 Admin. L.R. 191, 96 N.R. 32, 5 Imm. L.R. (2d) 97, [1988] 3 F.C. 157 (Fed. C.A.) — This application was made to obtain *certiorari* to quash the respondent's decision not to grant a visitor's visa to the applicant's spouse to enter Canada for the purpose of testifying as a witness at the applicant's appeal hearing before the Immigration Appeal Board. The applicant had sought to sponsor his spouse for entry as a member of the family class, but the respondent claimed that the marriage was entered into only for the purposes of gaining admission to Canada. It was determined that the applicant would be denied a fair hearing if he was prevented from calling his wife as a witness. Her son, who was 5 years old, was not granted permission to enter Canada. *Certiorari* was granted on condition that the applicant's spouse remain in custody for the purpose of ensuring her immediate return to

Guyana after any attendance before the Immigration Appeal Board. The basis for admission was section 19(3) of the Act.

Uppal v. Canada (Minister of Employment & Immigration) (1987), 2 Imm. L.R. (2d) 143 (Fed. C.A.) — The appellant, a Canadian citizen, sponsored applications for landing of members of the family class, his father, mother, one brother and two sisters. The applications were refused by the visa officer. The visa officer relied upon the opinion of two medical officers, as defined in section 2 of the Act. The appellant appealed to the Immigration Appeal Board and sought to adduce, before the Board, medical evidence to contradict the medical officer's diagnosis. The Immigration Appeal Board declined to receive this evidence and dismissed the appeal. The appellant then, pursuant to section 84, appealed to the Court of Appeal. A majority of the Court of Appeal held that the Board was required to receive the additional evidence in considering the correctness of the visa officer's opinion. The minority judgment was of the view that the Board was correct in refusing to receive evidence tendered to contradict the opinion given by the two medical officers. The minority view was that the visa officer was required to base his rejection on the opinion of these two officers and, so long as he properly did that, his opinion was entitled to be sustained. The opinions of other medical experts on the subject presented to the Board were, in the minority view, not pertinent to the issue of the correctness of the formation of the visa officer's opinion. The Court was unanimous in concluding that the relevant time to be considered by the Board on the appeal was the time of the visa officer's decision and not the time of the Board's hearing of the appellant's appeal.

The Court of Appeal was unanimous in pointing out that a consent judgment has no precedential value. The Court granting a consent judgment is concerned with only two things: the capacity of the parties to agree; and the Court's jurisdiction to make the order that the parties have agreed to ask it to make. Consent judgment reflects neither findings of fact nor a considered application of the law to the facts by the Court.

Finally, the Court unanimously agreed that evidence of the current medical condition of the appellant's father and sister was relevant to the question of whether humanitarian or compassionate consideration existed that would warrant the Board granting special relief.

Rajpaul v. Canada (Minister of Employment & Immigration) (1987), 24 Admin. L.R. 153 (Fed. T.D.); varied 31 Admin. L.R. 191, 96 N.R. 32, 5 Imm. L.R. (2d) 97, [1988] 3 F.C. 157 (Fed. C.A.) — The applicant sought *certiorari* quashing the respondent's decision not to grant a visitor's visa to Sumintra Ramdas to enter Canada for the purpose of testifying as a witness. The applicant had applied to sponsor Ramdas, whom he alleged to be his wife. The application was refused on the basis that the marriage had been entered into primarily for the purpose of gaining admission into Canada as a family class immigrant and not with the intention of residing permanently with the other spouse. *Certiorari* was granted.

The outcome of the applicant's appeal to the Immigration Appeal Board, obviously, would depend upon the Board's assessment of the spouse's credibility on the issue of her primary purpose in entering into the marriage. The applicant had a substantive right to a fair hearing and could not be denied the opportunity to present this crucial evidence and testimony to the Board. It was a condition of the discretionary remedy that the spouse remain in detention pending the giving of evidence at the respondent's option. This latter condition was agreed to during the argument by counsel for the applicant.

The Court noted that in this case there was no previous conduct in Canada by the sponsoree that would justify the Court withholding *certiorari.*

Toor v. Canada (Minister of Employment & Immigration) (1987), 1 Imm. L.R. (2d) 104 (Fed. T.D.) — Visitor's visas were refused to the father, mother, brother and sister of Mr.

Toor. He wanted them to come to Canada to testify at his appeal before the Immigration Appeal Board, pursuant to section 79 of the Act, against the refusal to issue immigrants' visas. Two points in issue in the appeal were whether the relatives were really dependants of Mr. Toor and whether Mr. Toor was financially able to maintain them in Canada.

A decision by a visa officer that a person was not a *bona fide* visitor, simply because he wants to come to Canada and testify before the Board, would be an error in law. Here, however, the refusal of the visitors' visas was on the grounds that the applicants were not answering truthfully to the questions, that they would resist returning to India once in Canada, and on the grounds that they could not afford the expenses involved. Such a decision is not open, in the absence of bad faith or bias, to review by way of *ceritorari*. Accordingly, the application was denied.

Singh (C.K.) v. Canada (Minister of Employment & Immigration) (1986), 6 F.T.R. 15 (Fed. T.D.) — This application for *certiorari* quashing the decision of the respondent Minister not to grant the Minister's consent to Saudagar Gill to enter Canada for the purpose of testifying as a witness before the Immigration Appeal Board was dismissed.

The applicant was the wife of Saudagar Gill. Her sponsorship of her husband had been refused and she had appealed to the Immigration Appeal Board. The Board issued a summons to the husband who was in India. The Minister's consent was required for the attendance of the witness because Gill had been previously deported. The original sponsorship had been refused for a variety of reasons, one of which was that the marriage offended section 4(3) of the Regulations. The Minister declined to give his consent to Gill returning to Canada, and, thus, Gill was unable to appear as a witness at the Immigration Appeal Board. It was held that the Minister's decision under section 57 was administrative. The Minister was not, in refusing consent, exercising a *quasi*-judicial function; therefore, he was not required to give reasons for his decision. Consequently, the failure to give reasons, in this case, could not give rise to relief by way of *certiorari*. Further, the relief sought was discretionary, and no basis for exercising that discretion in favour of the applicant was to be found on the facts of this case.

Kahlon v. Canada (Minister of Employment & Immigration), [1986] 3 F.C. 386 (Fed. C.A.), reversing [1985] 2 F.C. 124 (Fed. T.D.) — The applicant sponsored his relatives' family class application for permanent residence. The application was denied and the applicant appealed to the Immigration Appeal Board. The visa officer refused to issue visitors' visas to the relatives who were required as witnesses at his appeal. The visas were refused on the basis that the applicants were not *bona fide* visitors because their intention was to testify at the applicant's appeal. An order of *mandamus* was issued requiring the Minister to grant the relatives visitors' visas to allow them to testify at the appeal. This order was reversed on appeal. *Mandamus* will issue to require performance of a duty; it cannot, however, dictate the result to be reached. *Certiorari* might have been available to quash the refusal of the visitors' visas and to refer the matter back for reconsideration but the respondent had not sought this type of order.

Canada (Attorney General) v. Jolly, [1975] F.C. 216, 54 D.L.R. (3d) 277, 7 N.R. 271 (Fed. C.A.) — Once the board admits evidence, it does not err in giving it little or no weight.

Section 69.4(5)

Nguyen v. Canada (Minister of Citizenship & Immigration) (1997), 129 F.T.R. 73 (Fed. T.D.) — This was an application to review a decision of the Appeal Division dismissing the applicant's appeal against a removal order. The applicant is legally married and his wife resides in Vietnam. In 1990, when he came to Canada, the applicant, in order to qualify as a dependant of his mother, stated that he was single and never married, when in fact this was not the case. In 1991, when the applicant attempted to sponsor his wife an inquiry resulted and the applicant was ordered deported on the basis that he had been landed as a result of a misrepresentation of a material fact. The Appeal Division dismissed the applicant's appeal and found the applicant not to be a credible and trustworthy witness.

Decision makers must listen to the testimony in its entirety and with an objective and open mind. Testimony given under oath is presumed to be true, unless there are valid reasons to doubt its truthfulness. All witnesses are entitled to start from a position where they are respected and their evidence is believed. In this case, no reasons were given for the credibility findings that were made and this was found to be an error. In addition however, the court considered the evidence upon which the findings were made and could not see how on a fair interpretation of that evidence the Appeal Division arrived at its conclusions. The Court found the applicant was very forthright about his actions in misrepresenting his marriage upon landing. The credibility finding had an unfair impact upon the Appeal Division's consideration of whether "having regard to all the circumstances of the case" the applicant should not be removed. The only way that the Appeal Division could have dispelled the court's concern was to have stated precisely why it did not believe the applicant which the Appeal Division did not do. Accordingly, the decision of the Appeal Division was set aside.

Canada (Minister of Citizenship & Immigration) v. Pinnock (1996), 122 F.T.R. 68 (Fed. T.D.) — The Minister sought judicial review of a decision of the Appeal Division staying a removal order against the respondent. The tribunal was unable to provide reasons for its decision due to the fact that the board member who heard the case was medically incapacitated at the time the request for reasons was received. The principles of natural justice require that a decision of the tribunal be subject to judicial review. Without reasons for a decision there is no alternative means by which an applicant can establish what was in the mind of the member or members of the tribunal that led to their decision.

The incapacity of the tribunal to fulfil its statutory obligation prejudices the applicant in prosecuting this application. In the result the decision of the tribunal will be set aside and the matter remitted back for reconsideration.

Liu v. Canada (Minister of Citizenship & Immigration) (July 24, 1996), Doc. IMM-3480-95 (Fed. T. D.) — There is no requirement under either the *Immigration Act* or the Immigration Appeal Division Rules that reasons be given, by an Immigration Appeal Division (IAD) member, for dismissing a motion requesting an extension of time for an appellant to obtain written reasons from the IAD for a decision rendered on a section 70 or 71 appeal.

Section 69.4(5) requires the IAD to give written reasons only when a request is made within the 10 day period as set out therein.

Paul v. Canada (Minister of Employment & Immigration) (1994), 81 F.T.R. 14 (Fed. T.D.) — This was a motion on behalf of the applicant for an order compelling the Appeal Division to provide written reasons for its denial of the applicant's appeal of a deportation order. Section 69.4(5) requires reasons to be given, where they are requested, within ten days of the disposition of the appeal. The applicant did not request written reasons within that period of time, but nevertheless argued that Rule 9 of the *Federal Court Rules* must take precedence over the *Immigration Act*. The application was dismissed.

The true purpose of Rule 9 is to ensure that all parties are provided with reasons when they are available, and notified when they are not available. Neither the *Immigration Act* nor the Rules compel the Board to produce written reasons, unless requested to do so by one of the parties within ten days following the communication of the decision. Absent an attack on the vires of section 69.4(5), the Board's refusal to provide written reasons, where none were requested, must be upheld.

Restrepo v. Canada (Minister of Employment & Immigration) (1989), 8 Imm. L.R. (2d) 161 (Fed. C.A.) — The respondent obtained permanent residence status in 1974. He returned to Colombia in 1978 and did not return to Canada until 1986. Following an inquiry, an adjudicator held that the respondent had lost his permanent residence status. The respondent appealed to the Immigration Appeal Board. The Board purported to allow the appeal notwithstanding the fact that the adjudicator's decision was in accordance with the law in "view of the circumstances of the instant case." The Minister filed an appeal and requested written reasons from the Board. The Board issued a set of written reasons which did not justify their original decision but which put forward a new basis for their decision.

When requested to provide reasons, the Board has no further jurisdiction. The only thing the Board can do in its written reasons is correct the material errors in the original decision.

The second decision was substantially different from the first and there was no indication that the Board was merely correcting a material error. Accordingly, an appeal from both decisions was allowed and the matter was referred back to the Board.

69.5 (1) Sittings — The Appeal Division shall sit at such times and at such places in Canada as are considered necessary by the Chairperson for the proper conduct of its business.

(2) Quorum — Three members constitute a quorum of the Appeal Division.

(3) Exception — Notwithstanding subsection (2), the Chairperson may designate a member of the Appeal Division to hear and determine

(a) an appeal made under section 70, 71 or 77,

(b) an application made under section 75, or

(c) a motion made pursuant to rules made under section 65(1),

and the provisions of this Part apply in respect of a member so designated as they apply in respect of the Appeal Division and the disposition of the appeal, application or motion by the member shall be deemed to be the disposition of the Appeal Division.

R.S.C. 1985, c. 28 (4th Supp.), s. 18; 1992, c. 49, s. 64.

70. (1) Appeals by permanent residents and persons in possession of returning resident permits — Subject to subsections (4) and (5), where a removal order or conditional removal order is made against a permanent resident or against a person lawfully in possession of a valid returning resident permit issued to that person pursuant to the regulations, that person may appeal to the Appeal Division on either or both of the following grounds, namely,

Proposed Amendment — 70(1)

70. (1) Appeals by permanent residents — Subject to subsection (4), where a removal order or conditional removal order is made against a permanent resident or against a person lawfully in possession of a document provided to that person pursuant to section 10.3 and in accordance with the regulations, that person may appeal to the Appeal Division on either or both of the following grounds.

1992, c. 49, s. 65. [Not in force at date of publication.]

(a) on any ground of appeal that involves a question of law or fact, or mixed law and fact; and

(b) on the ground that, having regard to all the circumstances of the case, the person should not be removed from Canada.

Proposed Addition — 70(1.1)

(1.1) **Appeal or refusal under s. 10.3(2)** — A person to whom a visa officer refused to provide a document under subsection 10.3(2) may appeal that refusal to the Appeal Division on any ground of appeal that involves a question of law or fact, or mixed law and fact.

1992, c. 49, s. 65. [Not in force at date of publication.]

(2) **Appeals by Convention refugees and persons with visas** — Subject to subsections (3) to (5), an appeal lies to the Appeal Division from a removal order or conditional removal order made against a person who

(a) has been determined under this Act or the regulations to be a Convention refugee but is not a permanent resident; or

(b) seeks landing or entry and, at the time that a report with respect to the person was made by an immigration officer pursuant to paragraph 20(1)(*a*), was in possession of a valid immigrant visa, in the case of a person seeking landing, or a valid visitor's visa, in the case of a person seeking entry.

(3) **Grounds for appeal** — An appeal to the Appeal Division under subsection (2) may be based on either or both of the following grounds:

(a) on any ground of appeal that involves a question of law or fact, or mixed law and fact; and

(b) on the ground that, having regard to the existence of compassionate or humanitarian considerations, the person should not be removed from Canada.

(3.1) **Limitation** — No appeal may be made to the Appeal Division by a person with respect to whom a certificate has been filed under subsection 40.1(1) where it has been determined, pursuant to paragraph 40.1(4)(*d*), that the certificate is reasonable.

(4) **Where limited right of appeal** — A person described in subsection (1) or paragraph (2)(*a*) against whom a deportation order or conditional deportation order is made may appeal to the Appeal Division on any ground of appeal that involves a question of law or fact, or mixed law and fact, where the person is

(a) a person, other than a person described in subsection (5), with respect to whom a certificate referred to in subsection 40(1) has been issued; or

(b) a person, other than a person described in subsection (3.1), who has been determined by an adjudicator to be a member of an inadmissible class described in paragraph 19(1)(*e*), (*f*), (*g*), (*j*), or (*l*).

(5) **Where limited right of appeal** — No appeal may be made to the Appeal Division by a person described in subsection (1) or paragraph (2)(*a*) or (*b*) against whom a deportation order or conditional deportation order is made where the Minister is of the

opinion that the person constitutes a danger to the public in Canada and the person has been determined by an adjudicator to be

(a) a member of an inadmissible class described in paragraph 19(1)(*c*), (*c*.1), (*c*.2) or (*d*);

(b) a person described in paragraph 27(1)(*a*.1); or

(c) a person described in paragraph 27(1)(*d*) who has been convicted of an offence under any Act of Parliament for which a term of imprisonment of ten years or more may be imposed.

[Note: 1995, c. 15, s. 13(4) provides that subsection 70(5) of the Act, as enacted by subsection (3), applies to an appeal that has been made on or before the coming into force of that subsection and in respect of which the hearing has not been commenced, but a person who has made such an appeal may, within fifteen days after the person has been notified that, in the opinion of the Minister, the person constitutes a danger to the public in Canada, make an application for judicial review under section 82.1 of the Act with respect to the deportation order or conditional deportation order referred to in subsection 70(5). This provision was contained in Bill C-44 which was proclaimed into law on July 10, 1995. We have included it here for ease of reference.]

(6) Exception — Where the Appeal Division directs that the execution of a deportation order or conditional deportation order be stayed, the direction is of no effect and, notwithstanding subsection 74(2), the Appeal Division may not review the case, where the Minister is of the opinion that the person has breached the terms and conditions set by the Appeal Division and that the person constitutes a danger to the public in Canada and the person has been determined by an adjudicator to be

(a) a member of an inadmissible class described in paragraph 19(1)(*c*), (*c*.1), (*c*.2) or (*d*);

(b) a person described in paragraph 27(1)(*a*.1); or

(c) a person described in paragraph 27(1)(*d*) who has been convicted of an offence under any Act of Parliament for which a term of imprisonment of ten years or more may be imposed.

R.S.C. 1985, c. 30 (3rd Supp.), s. 8; R.S.C. 1985, c. 28 (4th Supp.), ss. 18, 35; R.S.C. 1985, c. 29 (4th Supp.), s. 6; 1992, c. 49, s. 65; 1995, c. 15, s. 13.

Case Law

Section 70(1)

Chieu v. Canada (Minister of Citizenship & Immigration) (1998), 46 Imm. L.R. (2d) 163, [1999] 1 F.C. 605, 234 N.R. 112, 169 D.L.R. (4th) 173 (Fed. C.A.) — The issue on this appeal was whether the Appeal Division may consider, while "having regard to all the circumstances of the case", the country conditions at a potential destination to which a non-refugee may be removed.

The Board cannot, in exercising its equitable jurisdiction pursuant to paragraph 70(1)(b), consider as a circumstance country conditions in potential destinations of deportees. Evidence relating to these countries is irrelevant and inadmissible. The Board's jurisdiction under paragraph 70(1)(b) is only to determine whether a person should be removed from Canada.

Sagban v. Canada (Minister of Citizenship & Immigration) (1998), 48 Imm. L.R. (2d) 1, 234 N.R. 173 (Fed. C.A.) — This decision was released on the same day as *Chieu v. Canada*

(Minister of Citizenship & Immigration) (1998), 46 Imm. L.R. (2d) 163, [1999] 1 F.C. 605, 234 N.R. 112, 169 D.L.R. (4th) 173 (Fed. C.A.), and reaches a similar conclusion.

Canada (Minister of Citizenship & Immigration) v. Chico (1998), 48 Imm. L.R. (2d) 64, 153 F.T.R. 25 (Fed. T.D.) — The respondent submitted an application for permanent residence. She was sponsored by her mother, a Canadian citizen. At that time, the respondent indicated that her marital status was "unmarried (never married)" and that she had no children. Subsequent to signing her application, and leaving it with Canadian immigration authorities the applicant married and later had a child. These events were not reported to Canadian immigration authorities either before a visa was issued or on the arrival and landing of the respondent. Immigration authorities eventually proceeded against the respondent under paragraph 27(1)(e) of the Immigration Act and a deportation order was issued. The respondent appealed to the Appeal Division, the Appeal Division assumed jurisdiction to hear and decide the appeal, and it is from this decision that the Minister sought relief.

The application was dismissed. If the visa was void *ab initio* then by definition the outstanding removal order against the respondent was not issued in accordance with the law, issuing as it did under section 27(1) rather than 27(2). The applicant cannot accept the validity of the determination approving the removal order while challenging its validity in the context of proceedings before the IAD to appeal the removal order.

Archibald v. Canada (Minister of Citizenship & Immigration) (1995), 29 Imm. L.R. (2d) 259, 95 F.T.R. 308 (Fed. T.D.) — The applicant sought to review a decision of the Appeal Division dismissing his appeal from a deportation order. The applicant had been in Canada since 1969, he was 11 years old when he immigrated here with his parents. He has been out of Canada only once for a 3-week holiday in 1980.

The applicant was an alcoholic; he came from a family which had a problem with alcoholism and grew up and lived in a community which had alcohol problems. The event which gave rise to the deportation order against the applicant was a conviction for manslaughter. The applicant killed his then common law wife of 8 years.

In dismissing his appeal, the IAD concluded that the applicant was not established in Canada. The IAD focused on whether the applicant had accumulated property in Canada. It described the applicant as having no assets and concluded that although the applicant had spent over 25 years in Canada it could not be said that he had successfully established himself here.

The existence of property may be a factor to consider, particularly in assessing hardship which might arise from being deported. Its accumulation or lack thereof cannot out-weigh all the other factors which are relevant in determining establishment. These factors include length of residence in Canada; the age at which one comes to Canada; the length of residence elsewhere; frequency of trips abroad; and the quality of contacts with people there; where one is educated, particularly during the teens and later years; the location of one's immediate family; the location of one's nuclear family; and the ties which the members thereof have with the local community; where the individual is located; where his friends are located; the existence of professional or employment qualifications which tie one to a place; the existence of employment contacts.

The Court concluded that the decision of the Appeal Division should be aside and returned the matter for reconsideration by a differently constituted panel.

Canada (Minister of Citizenship & Immigration) v. Seneca, 43 Imm. L.R. (2d) 13, [1998] 3 F.C. 494, 146 F.T.R. 193 (Fed. T.D.) — This was an application to review a decision of the Appeal Division which dismissed the Minister's preliminary motion to dismiss the appeal of the respondent for lack of jurisdiction.

The respondent was married on July 3, 1976 and had two children born in 1977 and 1983. In November 1986, the respondent applied for permanent residence as a member of the family class. Based on inaccurate information provided by the respondent, the visa officer concluded that the marriage the respondent did admit to, was not legally binding. In June 1987, the respondent was issued an immigrant visa. The respondent arrived in Canada in August 1987, and 10 days later the respondent was married in Red Deer, Alberta. In 1989, an RCMP investigation revealed the fact that the respondent had been married in 1976 and that his marriage had never been dissolved. In January 1994, a conditional removal order was made against the respondent. The respondent appealed, pursuant to section 70(1), and, in response to the notice of appeal, the applicant filed the preliminary motion with the Appeal Division which is the subject of these proceedings.

Where an adjudicator has found that a person was granted landing by means of an improperly obtained visa pursuant to paragraph 27(1)(e) and a removal order has been issued against that person, such a person is entitled to appeal the removal order pursuant to subsection 70(1) of the Act. The suggestion that the person concerned has no status because he or she was not lawfully admitted in the first place cannot take away the right of appeal on that very question.

Accordingly, the Minister's application was dismissed.

Sikilaa v. Canada (Minister of Citizenship & Immigration) (January 23, 1998), Doc. IMM-1025-97 (Fed. T.D.) — This was an application to review a decision of the Appeal Division wherein the applicant's appeal from a removal order was dismissed. In making a determination whether a person should or should not be removed from Canada pursuant to paragraph 70(1)(b), the Appeal Division must take into account "all the circumstances of the case", which necessarily includes, "the good of society as well as that of the individual person". In this case, the Appeal Division speculated that the Minister might consent to the applicant's return to Canada and took this into account when assessing "all the circumstances of the case". A future determination by the Minister is an irrelevant consideration for the purposes of section 70(1)(b) of the *Immigration Act.*

Nguyen v. Canada (Minister of Citizenship & Immigration) (1998), 42 Imm. L.R. (2d) 148, (sub nom. *Canada (Minister of Citizenship & Immigration) v. Nguyen)* 141 F.T.R. 139 (Fed. T.D.) — The Appeal Division quashed a removal order made against the respondent. The removal order was based on a determination that the respondent was a permanent resident who was granted landing by reason of a fraudulent misrepresentation of a material fact. The IAD determined that it had jurisdiction under subsection 70(1) of the *Immigration Act* to consider the appeal against the removal order.

Section 69.4(2) is not a privative clause in relation to this application. There is no ground to conclude that special deference is owed to the IAD. Determination or jurisdiction in the context here at issue was essentially a matter of statutory interpretation.

The principal reasons for the issuance of the respondent's visas cease to exist before its issuance. The visa was therefore void on issuance and the Appeal Division had no jurisdiction to entertain the respondent's appeal.

Sagban v. Canada (Minister of Citizenship & Immigration) (1997), (sub nom. *Al Sagban v. Canada (Minister of Citizenship and Immigration))* [1998] 1 F.C. 501, (sub nom. *Al Sagban v. Canada (Minister of Citizenship and Immigration))* 137 F.T.R. 283 (Fed. T.D.); reversed (1998), 48 Imm. L.R. (2d) 1, 234 N.R. 173 (Fed. C.A.) — The applicant, an Iraq national, came to Canada from Egypt with his parents when he was still a dependent child. His father had been granted asylum at that time in Egypt. Counsel for the respondent had argued before the Appeal Division of the Immigration and Refugee Board that it was premature to consider potential harm to the applicant if he were returned to Iraq, because the country to which he would be deported was unknown. Counsel had argued the applicant might be returned to Egypt. The Court noted that previously a judge of the Trial Division had granted a stay of the execution of the deportation order in this case and that the evidence disclosed on that stay application indicated that the travel plans were that the applicant would be deported to Iraq.

The Court concluded that the Appeal Division, when hearing an appeal pursuant to section 70(1) of the Act, when considering whether to invoke its equitable jurisdiction, take into account the potential physical harm to an applicant that could occur as a result of persecution should the applicant be returned to his country of origin.

The Court observed that the factors that the Board should consider in deciding whether or not to exercise its equitable jurisdiction were set out in *Ribic v. Canada* 1985, [I.A.B.D. 4] August 20, 1985, No. T84-9623 (IAB). These factors were: a) all the circumstances of the case, including the seriousness of the offence or offences leading to deportation; b) the possibility of rehabilitation; c) the length of time spent in Canada; d) the degree to which the appellant is established in Canada; e) family in Canada; f) the support available for the applicant not only within the family but also within the community; and g) the degree of hardship that would be caused to the appellant by his return to his country of nationality.

Yu v. Canada (Minister of Citizenship & Immigration) (1997), 39 Imm. L.R. (2d) 97, 132 F.T.R. 226 (Fed. T.D.) — This was an application by the Minister to review a decision of the Appeal Division of the IRB allowing the respondent's appeal under section 70 of the *Immigration Act* and quashing the deportation order issued against her.

The respondent was ordered deported after it was discovered that she had been married and therefore was not eligible to be a dependant of her father when he immigrated to Canada. The respondent, while still single, had been sponsored by her brother in 1988. She married her fiance in January 1989 before receiving her immigration visa. She did not disclose this fact to the Canadian immigration authorities nor to her own family. In July 1992, she filed an undertaking of assistance for her husband listing him as her fiance. In October 1992, she returned to the Philippines and married her husband a second time before his application was processed as her fiance.

There was a misrepresentation *ab initio* on the part of the respondent with the result that the foundation on which rested the issuance of her visa never existed. She was not a dependent daughter at the time of the application for the visa. Accordingly, the Appeal Division had no jurisdiction to entertain her appeal. The principle reason for the issuance of her visa had ceased to exist before the issuance of the visa.

Accordingly the application for judicial review was granted and the decision of the Appeal Division quashed.

Tran v. Canada (Minister of Citizenship & Immigration) (1996), 36 Imm. L.R. (2d) 275, 124 F.T.R. 186 (Fed. T.D.) — This was an application to review a decision of the Appeal Division dismissing the applicant's appeal brought pursuant to section 70 of the *Immigration Act*.

The applicant's original application for permanent residence was correctly completed, however, five years later the applicant married and did not disclose personally or through her father when he was interviewed by a visa officer, that the material fact of her marital status had changed. Her immigration visa arrived 15 months after her marriage and approximately 6 years after her application for landed status was made. There was no evidence that the applicant made any other misleading statements or applied in bad faith. There was also no evidence that she was a member of an inadmissable class. The applicant herself brought the change in her marital status to the attention of immigration officers when she commenced an application to sponsor her husband 7 months after being granted landed immigrant status in Canada.

An adjudicator issued a deportation order in November 1994, on the basis that the applicant was a person described in paragraph 27(1)(e). The adjudicator advised the applicant during her hearing that she would have a right to explain all the circumstances of her case in an appeal under section 70 of the Act to the Appeal Division. The applicant filed a notice of appeal in November 1994, and her appeal hearing commenced in September 1995, at this point for the first time an appeal officer questioned the Appeal Division's jurisdiction to hear the appeal. The appeal officer's motion was eventually granted and the board determined that it had no jurisdiction to hear the appeal.

Under the *Immigration Act*, as it exists now, parliament has provided a complete statutory scheme to address issues involving admission of persons to Canada or removal of persons from Canada and within that complete statutory scheme parliament has also provided for specific appeal rights in certain cases. The rights of permanent residents appealing a deportation order issued against them are different and broader than the appeal rights available to persons in possession of valid visas or the sponsors seeking to appeal the refusal of an immigration visa to a sponsoree. In the case of a permanent resident, who has been deported, the equitable jurisdiction of the Appeal Division directs the tribunal to have regard to "all the circumstances of the case", where as in the more limited rights of appeal by persons with valid visas or by sponsors, the equitable jurisdiction of the Appeal Division is limited to having regard to the "existence of compassionate or humanitarian considerations".

The applicant should have been dealt with as a permanent resident under paragraph 27(1)(e) and subsection 70(1). The Appeal Division therefore had jurisdiction and the matter is returned to the appeal division for a determination on the merits of the case.

Peralta v. Canada (Minister of Citizenship & Immigration) (1996), 123 F.T.R. 153 (Fed. T.D.) — This is an application to review a decision of the Appeal Division dismissing the applicants appeal for lack of jurisdiction. The applicant became a permanent resident of Canada on March 20, 1993 as a member of the family class (an accompanying dependant son of his father). The applicant's completed application for permanent residence indicated that he was unmarried, which was true when the application was prepared but untrue when the applicant arrived at the port-of-entry and entered as a permanent resident. It became known only after he was landed and granted permanent resident status that the applicant had misrepresented his marital status. As a result an inquiry was convened and the applicant was ordered deported in April 1995. The applicant appealed to the Appeal Division which found that the applicant's visa became void on the date of his marriage and prior to his entry into Canada.

The *Hundal* case recognized four exceptions to the general principle that once a visa is issued it remains valid. The first exception occurs when a supervening act makes the satisfaction of the condition of the visa impossible. The applicant's marriage prior to his entry into Canada was a supervening act that made satisfaction of the condition of the visa impossible. Accordingly, the applicant was not a permanent resident and the Appeal Division was correct in declining jurisdiction.

Nguyen v. Canada (Minister of Citizenship & Immigration) (1996), 38 Imm. L.R. (2d) 108 (Imm. & Ref. Bd. (App. Div.)); reversed (1998), 42 Imm. L.R. (2d) 148, (sub nom. *Canada (Minister of Citizenship & Immigration) v. Nguyen)* 141 F.T.R. 139 (Fed. T.D.) — The appellant was a permanent resident against whom a removal order had been made on the basis that he had misrepresented a material fact and as a consequence thereof was granted landing.

The respondent Minister raised initially a jurisdictional argument submitting that the Appeal Division did not have jurisdiction to hear this appeal because the appellant was not a permanent resident.

Section 69.4(2) of the *Immigration Act* grants the Appeal Division sole and exclusive jurisdiction with respect to section 70 appeals from removal orders by permanent residents, to determine all questions and fact and law including questions of jurisdiction. Previous decisions of the Appeal Division have held that in similar circumstances the Appeal Division does have jurisdiction to hear this type of appeal. The panel was not disposed to decline jurisdiction and to truncate rights of appellants which have been exercised over many years in the absence of binding authority to the contrary. The panel declined to follow *Canada (Minister of Citizenship & Immigration) v. Nemsila* (1996), 35 Imm. L.R. (2d) 56, [1997] 1 F.C. 260, 118 F.T.R. 310 (Fed. T.D.), affirmed (1997), 38 Imm. L.R. (2d) 242, 3 Admin. L.R. (3d) 83, 214 N.R. 383 (Fed. C.A.), due to the fact that it was a case dealing primarily with the 1952 *Immigration Act*. The panel found that the line of cases culminating in *Hundal v. Canada* (1995), 96 F.T.R. 306, 30 Imm. L.R. (2d) 52 (*sub nom. Canada (Minister of Citizenship & Immigration) v. Hundal)* [1995] 3 F.C. 32 (Fed. T.D.), affirmed (1996), 36 Imm. L.R. (2d) 153, *(sub nom. Canada (Minister of Citizenship & Immigration) v. Hundal)* 206 N.R. 184 (Fed. C.A.) dealt with port-of-entry issues and the validity of visas.

After taking jurisdiction in the matter, the panel decided that the appeal brought pursuant to section 70(1)(b) ought to be allowed.

Nguyen v. Canada (Minister of Citizenship & Immigration) (1996), 34 Imm. L.R. (2d) 129 (Imm. & Ref. Bd. (App. Div.)) — The appellant was ordered removed from Canada because of his criminal record. The appellant's appeal in part was a challenge to the legal validity of the removal order.

The appellant's 1993 conviction for aggravated assault led to an inquiry at the Joyceville institution where the appellant was incarcerated. The inquiry commenced on April 19, 1994, and was adjourned to allow the appellant to retain counsel. In June 1994, the appellant signified that he wish to proceed and the inquiry proceeded to a conclusion at which time an adjudicator issued the deportation order now under appeal.

The principles of natural justice, in particular those associated with the *audi alteram partem* rule, do not oblige an adjudicator to inquire about a fear of persecution or to indicate that a deportation order forecloses access to the Convention refugee determination process in Canada, even in circumstances where the person before the adjudicator is unrepresented.

The panel noted that the appellant did not at any time during his inquiry suggest that he feared persecution should he be returned to Vietnam. Had he done so, in the opinion of the panel, the adjudicator's duty as an immigration officer would have been quite different. Section 44 of the *Immigration Act* appears to require that a possible claim to convention refugee status be canvassed in such circumstances.

Drummond v. Canada (Minister of Citizenship & Immigration) (1996), 33 Imm. L.R. (2d) 258, 112 F.T.R. 33 (Fed. T.D.) — A majority of a panel of the Immigration Appeal Division dismissed the applicant's appeal of her deportation order. The dissenting member would have stayed the order for four years.

The applicant sought a re-opening of the decision of the IAD on the grounds that her counsel at the Appeal Division hearing (who was not her counsel on the judicial review application) had been incompetent and that this incompetence may have effected the outcome of the appeal.

By the time the applicant's present counsel was retained the 15 day time limit for seeking judicial review of the appeal division decision had past. The applicant's new counsel was of the view that seeking a re-opening of the appeal by the IAD was the appropriate remedy for the applicant to pursue.

The IAD dismissed the re-opening application. It found that it did not have the authority to rule on the competency of counsel.

The IAD has jurisdiction to deal with matters of natural justice. Where counsel is freely chosen it is the professional accreditation body and not the courts which have the mandate to deal with incompetence, however, in extraordinary cases the competency of counsel may gave rise to a natural justice issue. In such cases, the facts must be specific and clearly proven. The evidence must be so clear and unequivocal and the circumstances so egregious that the unfairness to an applicant is virtually obvious.

While the standard to be met to obtain a re-opening on these grounds presents an onerous burden to an applicant it is a matter that the IAD cannot decline to address if it is raised. Accordingly, the judicial review application was allowed.

Bubla v. Canada (Solicitor General) (1995), 179 N.R. 375 (Fed. C.A.) — The appellant became a permanent resident of Canada on February 24, 1986. On November 24, 1987, the appellant was convicted in Austria for importing heroin and was sentenced to 5 years in prison. On March 3, 1992, an adjudicator ordered the appellant deported because he had been convicted of an offence outside of Canada that constituted an offence that may be punishable under an Act of Parliament and for which a maximum term was 10 years of imprisonment or more. On that same day, March 3, 1992, the appellant filed an appeal of the adjudicator's decision to the Appeal Division of the IRB. Before the appeal was heard several amendments to the *Immigration Act* came into force on February 1, 1993, and section 19(1)(c) was amended. The appellant's appeal was heard on February 2, 1993, one day after the amendments to section 19(1)(c) came into force. The substantive law as amended should apply to determine the validity of the deportation order.

The Appeal Division concluded that section 110 did not apply because "the hearing" before the Appeal Division did not commence until after the law was amended. Therefore, the Appeal Division concluded that the Appeal was not excepted from the general provisions of section 109.

When the application for judicial review was heard by the Trial Division that Judge concluded that the law existing prior to the amendments should have been applied. The Trial Division Judge concluded that the "inquiry" commenced before the adjudicator and had not yet been determined because the decision flowing from it was under appeal and the appeal thus fell within section 110. The Trial Division Judge quashed the decision of the Appeal Division on the basis that it wrongly had resorted to section 109.

The Court of Appeal found that the Trial Judge wrongly concluded that section 110 applied to the appeal. The reference to "hearing" in section 110 must be taken to refer to the actual sitting of the Appeal Division at which oral evidence and argument were presented to the Board. This hearing commenced on February 2, 1993, the day after the amendments came into effect. Therefore, the situation before the Court did not fall within the special provisions of section 110. The appeal was launched on March 3, 1992, and was heard commencing February 2, 1993. It was thus a proceeding which was pending on February 1, 1993, when the amendments came into effect. Therefore, section 109 made those amendments applicable to that proceeding.

It is a fundamental principle of law that an appeal body, unless clearly empowered otherwise, is obliged to determine whether the decision of the body appealed from was correct at the time it was made and in the circumstances under which it was made. The authority of the Appeal Division, both before and after the amendments in question, is set out in section

70(1). The Appeal Division may consider the correctness in law of the decision to issue a deportation order, but clearly such a decision involves examining the law as it stood at the time the deportation order was made. The Appeal Division can, pursuant to section 70(1)(b) consider "all the circumstances of the case" to see if the person should be removed from Canada. This obviously may include factors not before the adjudicator on the inquiry. The Appeal Division in the present case never directed its mind to its jurisdiction under section 70(1)(b) because it treated the deportation order as being wrong in law. This latter finding was based not on the correctness of the deportation order at the time it was made but on the law as it existed after February 1, 1993. The jurisdiction of the Appeal Division remains exactly as it was before and that jurisdiction is to determine the correctness in law of a decision already taken by the adjudicator. Such correctness must be measured by the law in force at the time the adjudicator decided unless Parliament has clearly indicated otherwise.

Accordingly, the Court of Appeal agreed with the principle result reached by the Trial Judge, namely that the matter should be referred back to the Appeal Division.

Canada (Attorney General) v. Chanoine (1987), 4 Imm. L.R. (2d) 136, 15 F.T.R. 143 (Fed. T.D.) — Attorney General applied for a writ of *certiorari* and a writ of *mandamus* setting aside the decision of an adjudicator not to hold an inquiry concerning the respondent and ordering the adjudicator to proceed with the inquiry.

The respondent was given the status of a permanent resident and subsequently left Canada for a period of three years. Just before returning to Canada, the respondent unsuccessfully applied for a visitor's visa. The respondent entered Canada and made no disclosures of any kind to the officer at the port-of-entry. A report was prepared indicating that the respondent was a person described in section 27(2)(b) and 27(2)(g) of the *Immigration Act*. The adjudicator declined jurisdiction adopting the argument that the respondent should have been proceeded with under section 27(1), which applied to permanent residents.

This decision of the adjudicator was set aside and the adjudicator was directed to continue the inquiry.

A permanent resident has been defined as a person who has been granted landing and who has not ceased to be a permanent resident pursuant to section 24(1). Accordingly, the respondent automatically lost his permanent resident status, pursuant to section 24(1), by reason of his having been outside of Canada for more than 183 days, unless he satisfied the adjudicator that he had not done so.

Editor's Note: This case should be read with Canada (Minister of Employment & Immigration) v. Selby (1980), [1981] 1 F.C. 273, 110 D.L.R. (3d) 126 (Fed. C.A.).

Lardizabal v. Canada (Minister of Employment & Immigration) (November 30, 1981), Doc. 80-6248, 80-6267 (Imm. App. Bd.) — The Board reaffirmed that it will allow motions to reopen where the party seeking to introduce evidence proves that he could not have obtained it through reasonable diligence before the original hearing, and that the evidence would constitute sufficient grounds for reconsideration of the Board's original disposition. In this case the Board held that the Minister, if responding favourably to a family's appeal for special consideration, would consider the family as a unit; it was reasonable to expect the Minister's decision before execution of a deportation order.

Canada (Minister of Employment & Immigration) v. Selby (1980), [1981] 1 F.C. 273 (Fed. C.A.) — The Immigration Appeal Board has jurisdiction to decide whether the applicant or appellant before it is a permanent resident; it, thus, has power to review a decision by the adjudicator that the applicant ceased to be a permanent resident of Canada when he left with the intention of abandoning Canada as his place of permanent residence.

Eyzaguirre v. Canada (Minister of Employment & Immigration) (December 11, 1980), Doc. T79-9268 (Imm. App. Bd.) — The appellant was compelled into a series of actions by her husband, who made the ultimate decisions on all matters affecting the lives of family members. These actions resulted in the appellant's abandoning Canada and returning to Chile to live permanently. The appellant separated from her husband in Chile and, upon obtaining custody of her children and an exit permit immediately returned to Canada. The Court held that any lengthy absence from Canada must be reasonably explained and the Board must be satisfied that the absence and delay in returning to Canada were not motivated by an intention to abandon Canada permanently. In this case the appellant was absent from Canada from 1974 until 1978. Having regard to the Board's finding that the husband had foisted his intentions upon his wife, the appeal was allowed and a deportation order against the appellant quashed.

Lew v. Canada (Minister of Manpower & Immigration), [1974] 2 F.C. 700 (Fed. C.A.) — The appellant was convicted of an offence under the Criminal Code and was ordered deported. He appealed the conviction, was granted an absolute discharge, and subsequently appealed the deportation order to the Immigration Appeal Board. The Court held that the Immigration Appeal Board ought to have considered the appeal to it in light of the absolute discharge. The Board erred in considering circumstances existing at the time the deportation order was made to the exclusion of circumstances existing at the time the appeal was heard.

O'Connor v. Canada (Minister of Employment & Immigration) (1992), 21 Imm. L.R. (2d) 64 (Imm. & Ref. Bd. (App. Div.)) — The appellant, who was a permanent resident of Canada, was ordered deported on May 16, 1991. The appellant was convicted of second degree murder and obstructing justice. On February 20, 1985, he was sentenced to imprisonment with no possibility of parole for a term of 12 years. The Appeal Division referred to its decision in *Ribic v. Canada (Minister of Employment & Immigration)* (August 20, 1985), Doc. I.A.B. T84-9623 (Imm. App. Bd.), as a useful yardstick as to the circumstances relevant to the exercise of the Board's discretion. Factors include:

1. the seriousness of the offence leading to the deportation order;
2. the possibility of rehabilitation;
3. the length of time spent in Canada and the degree to which the appellant is established here;
4. the family in Canada and the dislocation to the family that deportation would cause;
5. the support available to the appellant, not only within the family but also within the community; and
6. the degree of hardship that would be caused to the appellant by his return to his country of nationality.

These factors are not exhaustive and the weight attached to each of them will vary according to the circumstances of the case. Further, the Appeal Division is required to exercise its discretion in a manner consistent with the objectives of the *Immigration Act*.

The murder was a situational and isolated act. The appellant at the time was a drug and alcohol addict. During his time in prison the appellant came to terms with his drinking and with the abuse which he had suffered as a child at the hands of his parents. The appellant was genuinely remorseful, not only for the life he took but also for the time he spent under the influence of drugs and alcohol. The deportation order was stayed with condition. The appellant was required to report to a Canada Immigration Centre and advise on employment and marital status each fifth month; report all changes of address to the Canada Immigration

Centre and to the Appeal Division within 48 hours; and abstain from alcohol and all drugs excluding prescription or over-the-counter medication.

Canepa v. Canada (Minister of Employment & Immigration), [1992] 3 F.C. 270, 10 C.R.R. (2d) 348, 93 D.L.R. (4th) 589 (C.A.) — The appellant was born in Italy in 1962 and came to Canada as a permanent resident with his family at the age of five. He became a drug addict and to support his addiction turned to a life of crime. Between 1978 and 1987 he was convicted of 37 offences. Eventually a report was issued pursuant to section 27(1)(d) and the adjudicator at the ensuing inquiry made a deportation order. This deportation order is in effect reversible on equitable grounds pursuant to section 70. When the scheme of the Act is looked at in total, on appeal, the tribunal must take into account all of the circumstances of the case which include the person in his total context and the good of society as well as that of the individual.

Section 70(1)(b) requires that every extenuating circumstance that can be adduced in favour of the deportee be considered by the Board on appeal.

This treatment of the appellant as mandated by sections 27 and 70 is not cruel and unusual treatment so as to contravene section 12 of the Charter.

Aujla v. Canada (Minister of Employment & Immigration) (1991), 13 Imm. L.R. (2d) 81 (Fed. C.A.) — The appellant was admitted to Canada on condition that she marry a particular person. That person refused to marry her and she married someone else. She was not informed that she could apply to vary the terms and conditions of her visa. She was subject to an inquiry and ordered deported. The Appeal Division dismissed her appeal. In considering whether compassionate or humanitarian considerations warranted granting special relief, the Board failed to remark on the failure of the authorities to consider the possibility of varying the conditions of the appellant's admission and to take into account the marriage that she had entered into. Further, the Appeal Division failed to deal with the appellant's evidence as to the social stigma that would attach to her should she return to her native India. Accordingly, the Appeal Division had failed to take into account all of the relevant circumstances in declining to find humanitarian and compassionate conditions that might have warranted special relief. The decision of the Appeal Division was set aside and the matter remitted to a differently constituted panel.

Willis v. Canada (Minister of Employment & Immigration) (1988), 6 Imm. L.R. (2d) 57, 87 N.R. 216 (Fed. C.A.) — This was an application to review and set aside a decision of the Immigration Appeal Board refusing to re-open proceedings before that Board which led to a determination that the applicant should be deported. When the Board is assessing the application to re-open proceedings, in light of its continuing equitable jurisdiction to reconsider whether or not a deportation order should be issued, the Board should apply the requirement that the "new evidence" should be evidence that had not been before the Board at the earlier date.

Castro v. Canada (Minister of Employment & Immigration) (1988), 5 Imm. L.R. (2d) 87, 86 N.R. 356 (Fed. C.A.) — The applicant apealed a decision of the Immigration Appeal Board refusing to re-open his appeal before the Board. The Immigration Appeal Board is not *functus* once it has rendered its decision. It has a continuing equitable jurisdiction with respect to an individual until that individual is deported from Canada. In the present case, the additional evidence came into existence after the original Board hearing. This type of *ex post facto* evidence can be entertained by the Board if it is relevant to the application to re-open. In order to justify re-opening, the proffered evidence need only be such as to support a conclusion that there is a reasonable possibility, as opposed to probability, that the evidence could lead the Board to change its original decision. If the Board reaches the decision that the application to re-open is not *bona fide* and that it is merely a delaying tactic, it can rightly refuse an application to re-open on the ground of lack of *bona fides*.

Parra v. Canada (Minister of Employment & Immigration) (March 25, 1988), Doc. A-507-87 (Fed. C.A.) — This was an appeal from a refusal by a member of the Immigration Appeal Board to re-open an appeal from a deportation order which had been dismissed against the applicant. The re-opening should not be granted unless the Board is satisfied that the evidence sought to be introduced, could not have been obtained by reasonable diligence for the original hearing, or unless the Board recognizes that it has failed in some way to observe the rules of natural justice. The applicant argued that he had demonstrated reasonable diligence by obtaining the services of a lawyer to ensure proper presentation of his case and, therefore, he should not be fixed with the failure of his chosen counsel to use diligence in carrying out his obligation to put forward all relevant evidence to support the applicant's appeal. Counsel in this case had advised the applicant to bring his witnesses to the hearing. The fact that the applicant's common-law wife refused or neglected to come was, therefore, the responsibility of the applicant. Further, there was nothing to indicate the proposed evidence could have influenced the Board in such a way as to change the exercise of its discretion under section 72(2)(d).

Sandhu v. Canada (Minister of Employment & Immigration) (1987), 1 Imm. L.R. (2d) 159 (Fed. C.A.) — This application was brought to review an order of the Immigration Appeal Board, which refused to re-open a hearing to consider evidence that arose subsequent to the Board's decision. The Court relied on *Grillas v. Canada (Minister of Manpower & Immigration)* (1971), [1972] S.C.R. 577 (S.C.C.), for the proposition that the Board's equitable jurisdiction is a continuing one. The fact that the evidence sought to be adduced in this case related to developments subsequent to the Board's decision did not limit the Board's power to re-open a hearing. The only limit on the Board's power to re-open was held to be the Board's own good judgment.

Sandhu v. Canada (Minister of Employment & Immigration) (1987), 1 Imm. L.R. (2d) 159 (Fed. C.A.) — The Board has the power to re-open an appeal after dismissing it because its equitable jurisdiction is a continuing one. *Ex post facto* evidence can, in the Board's discretion, justify the re-opening of an appeal.

Cheema v. Canada (Minister of Employment & Immigration) (December 20, 1982), Doc. V80-6404 (Imm. App. Bd.) — In this case the appellant had been ordered deported because he failed to disclose to the Minister, when he obtained landed immigrant status, that he had been previously deported from Canada. The appellant had been previously deported from Canada because he was not a "*bona fide* visitor". He had been in Canada 6 years as a landed immigrant. He was married, had been steadily employed, had paid taxes for the 6 years that he had been in the country and the appellant produced letters of good character from prominent members of the East Indian community. The Board concluded that the appellant's financial achievements, good work record and character references indicated that he was an asset to the community in which he lived and, accordingly, concluded that the appellant should not be removed from Canada.

Canada (Minister of Employment & Immigration) v. Mercier (September 16, 1980), Doc. 79-1243 (Imm. App. Bd.) — The Board held that a visa is no more than a stamp on a piece of paper, issued outside Canada, which may give the holder a colour of right to enter Canada, either as a visitor or immigrant. A change in marital status is a material fact which must be disclosed to the Canadian immigration authorities if it occurs before permanent residence is actually granted. By failing to disclose her marriage upon arrival in Canada, the appellant misrepresented a material fact and thus brought herself within section 27(1)(e). Because the Minister had appealed, the provisions of section 75(3) gave the appellant an automatic right of appeal on equitable grounds. The appellant had gradually established herself in Canada, had a stable job and had not committed any criminal offence or infraction of the *Immigration Act* since the granting of landing. Members of the appellant's immediate family in Canada were in a position to help her, if necessary, and the appellant had a minor child for whom she was the sole provider and who was a Canadian citizen by birth. This child was in delicate physical health and required regular attention from a competent doctor. Having regard to all the evidence, the Board allowed the appellant's appeal on equitable grounds.

De la Cruz v. Canada (Minister of Employment & Immigration) (August 12, 1980), Doc. T-79-9373 (Imm. App. Bd., Toronto) — The appellant had no family in Canada, no major assets and held no position of responsibility in connection with her employment. She had been considerably more successful in her home in the Philippines and the Board concluded in all the circumstances that her roots were there and not in Canada. Accordingly, they found there were no considerations that would merit the granting of special relief.

Simpson v. Canada (Minister of Employment & Immigration) (April 17, 1980), Doc. 79-9467 (Imm. App. Bd., Toronto) — The appellant was convicted of robbery involving a shotgun and sentenced to 3 years' imprisonment; he sought a stay of the deportation order. The appellant's mother testified that she was willing to have the 22-year-old appellant live with her and support him. The Board noted that the appellant had no close relatives living in Jamaica and that his conviction was an isolated one, although the offence was serious. The deportation order was stayed for a period of 2 years from the date of the appellant's release on parole.

Baky v. Canada (Minister of Employment & Immigration) (1979), [1980] 2 F.C. 35 (Fed. C.A.) — A decision of the Immigration Appeal Board dismissing the applicant's motion to re-open his appeal was set aside because the Board stated it had never and would not exercise its jurisdiction to grant special relief owing to consequences arising from the applicant's failure to meet his military obligations in his homeland. The Court held that the statement reflected a failure to exercise jurisdiction which amounted to a complete denial of jurisdiction.

Devrim v. Canada (Minister of Employment & Immigration) (April 24, 1979), Doc. 78-6192 (Imm. App. Bd.) — The Board found that the appellant acted in good faith by stating she was engaged at her initial interview and disclosing her marriage at her second interview in Ankara, Turkey. At her second interview the appellant received some misleading information and, at the airport in Toronto, she was not examined in her native language and did not understand the contents of her immigrant record card. The Board held that section 27(1)(e) of the Act imposed an obligation of absolute liability and, thus, the defence of due diligence was not available. Under section 72(1)(b) of the Act the Board allowed the appeal, finding that the appellant acted in good faith but was seriously misled by information given to her at the embassy in Ankara and seriously disadvantaged by the absence of a Turkish interpreter at the airport on her arrival.

Reid v. Canada (Minister of Employment & Immigration) (February 15, 1979), Doc. 78-9170 (Imm. App. Bd.) — Notwithstanding evidence that the appellant had established himself satisfactorily in Canada and had adapted to the country, the Board did not grant special relief. The Board could not condone or overlook the calculated deceit by means of which the appellant entered Canada and gained acceptance for permanent residence. In bringing his wife and four children to Canada without proper authorization the appellant was, in effect, gambling that he would ultimately be permitted to remain in Canada permanently. The Board noted that in accepting immigrants for permanent residence, the department must accept any sworn statements of the applicant and, therefore, the honesty of the applicant was essential to the proper implementation of immigration policies. In this case the appellant's brother had falsely represented that the appellant was single on the nomination application and the appellant made this representation on his application for admission to Canada as a permanent resident.

Hilario v. Canada (Minister of Manpower & Immigration) (1977), [1978] 1 F.C. 697 (Fed. C.A.) — The test by which the exercise of a statutory discretion must be judged was that it was exercised *bona fide*, uninfluenced by irrelevant considerations, and not in an arbitrary or illegal manner. A Court is not entitled to interfere merely because it would have exercised the discretion differently.

Vu v. Canada (Minister of Manpower & Immigration), [1973] F.C. 529 (Fed. C.A.) — In rendering its decision, the Board posed a number of questions without answering them. The relevance of the answers was not apparent and, thus, the decision was open to the objection that it had been based on irrelevant considerations. The Court held that the Board should have determined, first, whether there existed any compassionate or humanitarian considerations and, second, whether those considerations warranted the granting of special relief. In failing to so consider the matter, the Board had failed to exercise its statutory jurisdiction.

Grillas v. Canada (Minister of Manpower & Immigration) (1971), [1972] S.C.R. 577 (S.C.C.) — Until a deportation order has actually been executed, the Board is entitled to re-open an appeal, hear new evidence, revise its former decision, and exercise its discretion to allow an appellant to remain in Canada because of compassionate or humanitarian considerations. The Board did not err in law in accepting an argument of counsel for the respondent in its judgment. The Court distinguished between acceptance of statements from counsel as argument and acceptance of statements from counsel as evidence, the latter being unacceptable. When a decision is made to re-open an appeal, it is not necessary that the new hearing be held before the same panel that made the original decision.

Section 70(2)

McLeod v. Canada (Minister of Employment & Immigration) (1998), 46 Imm. L.R. (2d) 295, (sub nom. *McLeod v. Canada (Minister of Citizenship & Immigration))* [1999] 1 F.C. 257, 234 N.R. 89 (Fed. C.A.) — The two appellants and their mother obtained immigrant visas in 1992 while in Jamaica. The mother was the principal applicant and the appellants applied as accompanying dependants. These visas were to expire on December 21, 1992. On November 23, 1992, the mother died. On December 3, 1992, they proceeded to Canada and informed immigration officers of their mother's death. They were denied admission and an inquiry was held on April 8, 1993. They were issued exclusion orders based on paragraph 19(2)(d) of the Act and section 12 of the Regulations. They appealed to the Appeal Division. The Appeal Division held that the appellants were in possession of valid visas and that the Appeal Division therefore had jurisdiction to entertain the appeal. The exclusion orders were quashed on the basis of compassion or humanitarian consideration. The Minister launched an application for judicial review and Noel J., on the consent of both parties, allowed the application and set the Appeal Division decision aside. By agreement he certified this question: "when does a validly issued immigrant visa cease to be valid?"

The Court concluded that there was no adequate basis for deducing from the language of the Act a sanction of invalidity based on a change of circumstances after the issue of a visa. Such a change of circumstances may be a ground for refusal of admission under section 12 of the Regulations, but not on the basis of the invalidity of the visa.

Canada (Minister of Citizenship & Immigration) v. Mansoobi (March 27, 1997), Doc. IMM-2991-95 (Fed. T.D.) — The respondent was born and raised in Iran. In 1985, he successfully claimed refugee status from that country. The respondent was convicted of several offences in Canada between the date of his arrival in 1985 and 1993. In March 1994, the respondent appeared before an adjudicator who found the respondent described in paragraph 19(1)(c) and made a removal order against him. The respondent appealed to the Appeal Division of the IRB which allowed the appeal.

The tribunal exceeded its jurisdiction in considering the persecution the respondent could face if returned to Iran. In an appeal under section 70, it is beyond the tribunal's jurisdiction to consider the possible implication of the person's return to his or her country of nationality. The tribunal was bound to consider humanitarian and compassionate considerations only.

Tran v. Canada (Minister of Citizenship & Immigration) (1996), 36 Imm. L.R. (2d) 275, 124 F.T.R.186 (Fed. T.D.) — This was an application to review a decision of the Appeal Division dismissing the applicant's appeal brought pursuant to section 70 of the *Immigration Act.*

The applicant's original application for permanent residence was correctly completed, however, five years later the applicant married and did not disclose personally or through her father when he was interviewed by a visa officer, that the material fact of her marital status had changed. Her immigration visa arrived 15 months after her marriage and approximately 6 years after her application for landed status was made. There was no evidence that the applicant made any other misleading statements or applied in bad faith. There is also no evidence that she was a member of an inadmissable class. The applicant herself brought the change in her marital status to the attention of immigration officers when she commenced an application to sponsor her husband 7 months after being granted landed immigrant status in Canada.

An adjudicator issued a deportation order in November 1994, on the basis that the applicant was a person described in paragraph 27(1)(e). The adjudicator advised the applicant during her hearing that she would have a right to explain all the circumstances of her case in an appeal under section 70 of the Act to the Appeal Division. The applicant filed a notice of appeal in November 1994, and her appeal hearing commenced in September 1995. At this point, for the first time an appeal officer questioned the Appeal Division's jurisdiction to hear the appeal. The appeal officer's motion was eventually granted and the Board determined that it had no jurisdiction to hear the appeal.

Under the *Immigration Act*, as it exists now, Parliament has provided a complete statutory scheme to address issues involving the admission of persons to Canada or the removal of persons from Canada and within that complete statutory scheme Parliament has also provided for specific appeal rights in certain cases. The rights of permanent residents appealing a deportation order issued against them are different and broader than the appeal rights available to persons in possession of valid visas or the sponsors seeking to appeal the refusal of an immigration visa to a sponsoree. In the case of a permanent resident, who has been deported the equitable jurisdiction of the Appeal Division directs the tribunal to have regard to "all the circumstances of the case", where as in the more limited rights of appeal by persons with valid visas or by sponsors the equitable jurisdiction of the Appeal Division is limited to having regard to the "existence of compassionate or humanitarian considerations".

The applicant should have been dealt with as a permanent resident under paragraph 27(1)(e) and subsection 70(1). The Appeal Division therefore had jurisdiction and the matter is returned to the Appeal Division for a determination on the merits of the case.

Peralta v. Canada (Minister of Citizenship & Immigration) (1996), 123 F.T.R. 153 (Fed. T.D.) — This is an application to review a decision of the Appeal Division dismissing the applicants appeal for lack of jurisdiction. The applicant became a permanent resident of Canada on March 20, 1993 as a member of the family class (an accompanying dependent son of his father). The applicant's completed application for permanent residence indicated that he was unmarried, which was true when the application was prepared but untrue when the applicant arrived at the port-of-entry and entered as a permanent resident. It became known only after he was landed and granted permanent resident status that the applicant had misrepresented his marital status. As a result, an inquiry was convened and the applicant was ordered deported in April 1995. The applicant appealed to the Appeal Division which found that the applicant's visa became void on the date of his marriage and prior to his entry into Canada.

The *Hundal* case recognized four exceptions to the general principle that once a visa is issued it remains valid. The first exception occurs when a supervening act makes the satisfaction of the condition of the visa impossible. The applicant's marriage prior to his entry into Canada was a supervening act that made satisfaction of the condition of the visa impossible. Accordingly, the applicant was not a permanent resident and the Appeal Division was correct in declining jurisdiction.

Bruan v. Canada (Secretary of State) (1995), 97 F.T.R. 10 — The Minister sought to review a decision of the Appeal Division of the IRB quashing an exclusion order directed against the respondent. The respondent, a citizen of the Philippines, was sponsored by his mother. The respondent's mother died in July, 1991. In September, 1991, the Canadian Embassy in Manila provided the respondent with a permanent visa to Canada. The respondent was never asked whether his mother was still living and did not inform the Embassy that his mother had died. When the respondent appeared at Vancouver International Airport in response to a question from an immigration officer the respondent disclosed the fact that his mother had died. A report under subsection 20(1)(a) was prepared and an inquiry was held, and at the conclusion of the inquiry the respondent was excluded. The applicant Minister successfully argued that the Appeal Division did not have jurisdiction to hear the appeal. The Court agreed that even though the applicant was in possession of a "valid immigration visa" when he sought landing, where the principal reason for the issuance of a visa ceases to exist prior to the issuance thereof, the visa cannot be said to be a valid immigrant visa. Therefore, the Appeal Division was held not to have jurisdiction to hear the respondent's appeal. The application for judicial review was allowed and the matter referred back to the Appeal Division for reconsideration in light of the court's reasons. The Court declined to certify a question for appeal.

Hundal v. Canada (Minister of Employment & Immigration) (1995), 96 F.T.R. 306 (Fed. T.D.), affirmed (1996), 36 Imm. L.R. (2d) 153 (sub nom. *Canada (Minister of Citizenship & Immigration v. Hundal*) 206 N.R. 184, 122 F.T.R. 319 (note) (Fed. C.A.) — The respondent was married to a permanent resident on January 9, 1989. On August 30, 1989, the permanent resident signed an undertaking of assistance wherein she undertook to sponsor the respondent's immigration to Canada. On April 29, 1991 the respondent was issued an immigrant visa by the Canadian High Commission in New Delhi. On December 16, 1991 the respondent's spouse signed a statutory declaration withdrawing her sponsorship. The respondent presented himself at Immigration on January 3, 1992, where he was examined by an immigration officer who made a report under paragraph 20(1) of the *Immigration Act* which resulted in the exclusion order on February 27,1992.

The respondent appealed the exclusion order to the Appeal Division of the IRB. The Appeal Division allowed the respondent's appeal on humanitarian and compassionate grounds.

The issue was whether the visa was valid when the report of January 3,1992 was made. If it was, the Appeal Division had jurisdiction to make the decision it did.

There are four exceptions to the general principle that once a visa is issued it remains valid.

1. This may be characterized as a situation where there is a frustration or impossibility of performance of a condition on which the visa was issued. It applies when a supervening act makes the satisfaction of the condition impossible. The Court referred to *Canada (Minister of Employment & Immigration) v. De Decaro*, [1993] 2 F.C. 408 (Fed. C.A.) as an example of this type of exception. In this case the person upon whose continued existence dependants' visas were issued died, in which case the visa of the dependant becomes invalid.

2. The second exception occurs where there is a failure to meet a condition of the granting of the visa before the visa is issued. An example of this occurred in *Canada (Minister of Employment & Immigration) v. Wong* (1993), 153 N.R. 237 (Fed. C.A.).

3. The third exception to a visa remaining valid will be where it expires, thus if there is an expiry date on a visa and the time expires, the visa will clearly not be valid after the expiry date.

4. The fourth exception to a visa remaining valid will be where it is revoked by a visa officer. The cancellation or invalidation of a visa requires a decision to that effect by the visa officer. As long as a decision to cancel has been made the visa is no longer valid.

Subject to the four exceptions described above the Court concluded that once a visa is issued it is and remains valid for the purposes of paragraph 70(2)(b) of the *Immigration Act.*

In the case at bar none of the four exceptions applied and therefore the visa was still valid for purposes of giving the Appeal Division jurisdiction to hear the respondent's appeal. Accordingly, the Minister's application for judicial review was dismissed.

Canada (Minister of Employment & Immigration) v. Wong (1993), 153 N.R. 237 (Fed. C.A.) — A Canadian citizen made a sponsorship application for her father and sister, the latter in the category of the father's single dependant daughter. Before the issuance of the immigration visas, the father died. Unaware of this event, Canadian immigration authorities issued visas to both sponsorees. At the point of entry to Canada, the sponsoree daughter initially lied to a Canadian immigration officer, but ultimately produced her father's death certificate. On inquiry she was ordered excluded.

The Appeal Division held that it had jurisdiction to hear the appeal since at the time of landing the sponsoree-sister was in possession of a valid immigrant visa and went on to exercise its compassionate discretion in her favour.

Where an element upon which the issuance of a visa is based subsequently ceases to exist and where the principal reason for the issuance of a visa ceased to exist before its issuance, such a visa cannot be said to be a valid immigrant visa.

The appeal was allowed and the Board's decision set aside for want of jurisdiction.

Section 70(3)

Canada (Attorney General) v. Canada (Immigration Appeal Board) (July 5, 1985), Doc. T-1240-85 (Fed. T.D.) — The words "valid visa" in this section cover both someone holding an immigrant visa and someone holding a visitor's visa. Accordingly, this section confers a right of appeal on both groups where a removal order has been made.

Canada (Minister of Employment & Immigration) v. Dmitrovic (February 8, 1983), Doc. A-45-81 (Fed. C.A.) — The facts of this case are contained in the Immigration Appeal Board decision of September 17, 1980. Dmitrovic entered Canada as a visitor. He attempted to claim refugee status in the Yukon Territories and in Vancouver while in status. On each occasion he was told that he must either leave the country to make that claim or overstay his visitor's visa and make the claim at the resulting inquiry. Dmitrovic overstayed his visitor's visa and made a claim for refugee status which was accepted by the Minister. No Minister's permit was issued upon the determination that Dmitrovic was a Convention refugee with the result that the inquiry continued to a conclusion notwithstanding the determination and Dmitrovic was ordered deported. The Immigration Appeal Board allowed his appeal and quashed the deportation order. This decision was overruled upon the appeal of the Minister and the matter was sent back to the Immigration Appeal Board for consideration under section 72(2)(d) of the *Immigration Act*. The determination by the Minister that a person is a Convention refugee does not confer on that person a status of some undefined nature. It gives him rights such as not to be returned to a country where his life or freedom would be threatened, a right granted by virtue of section 55 of the Act and the right to appeal a removal order pursuant to section 72(2)(a) and (3) of the Act.

Canada (Minister of Employment & Immigration) v. La Rose (November 28, 1979), Doc. 79-9284 (Imm. App. Bd.) — The issue was whether a stamp appearing on the respondent's passport was a valid visa. The Board held that the stamp was likely made on the passport by a visa officer. However, the Court held that when section 72 of the Act makes reference to a "valid visa," it is referring to either a non-immigrant visa authorizing entry into Canada or an immigrant visa authorizing admission as a permanent resident.

McConnel v. Canada (Minister of Employment & Immigration) (March 20, 1979), Doc. 78-9201 (Imm. App. Bd.) — The Board, being a creature of statute, must derive its jurisdiction from the statute creating it. Section 72(2) did not provide for an appeal from the issuance of a departure notice and, accordingly, the Board was without jurisdiction to entertain the appeal.

Hilario v. Canada (Minister of Manpower & Immigration) (1977), [1978] 1 F.C. 697 (Fed. C.A.) — The test by which the exercise of a statutory discretion must be judged was that it was exercised *bona fide*, uninfluenced by irrelevant considerations, and not in an arbitrary or illegal manner. A Court is not entitled to interfere merely because it would have exercised the discretion differently.

Section 70(4)

Chiarelli v. Canada (Minister of Employment & Immigration), 16 Imm. L.R. (2d) 1, [1992] 1 S.C.R. 711 (S.C.C.) — This appeal calls into question the constitutionality of the statutory scheme pursuant to which a permanent resident can be deported from Canada if he is found to have been convicted of an offence for which a term of imprisonment of five years or more may be imposed. A further attack was brought against the interaction of that scheme with the investigations conducted by the Security Intelligence Review Committee (SIRC) into the activities of persons reasonably believed to be involved in certain types of criminal or subversive activity.

The respondent was convicted of a number of criminal offences and in January 1986, a report was written pursuant to section 27 of the *Immigration Act* identifying the respondent as a permanent resident described in 27(1)(d)(ii). As a result of this report an inquiry was directed pursuant to section 27(3). A deportation order was made against the respondent pursuant to section 32(2). The respondent appealed to the Immigration Appeal Board. That appeal was adjourned after the Solicitor General and the Minister of Employment and Immigration made a joint report to the SIRC. The report indicated that in the opinion of the Ministers the respondent was a person described in section 19(1)(d)(ii). The SIRC conducted the required investigation and reported to the Governor in Council pursuant to section 81(7). The Governor in Council adopted the conclusion of the SIRC and directed the appellant Minister to issue a certificate under section 82(1) with respect to the respondent's appeal. This certificate was issued, with the result that the respondent could not assert compassionate grounds as a reason for allowing the appeal.

The SIRC conducted its investigation and hearing first by reading a document entitled "Statement of Circumstances" as well as two summaries of information. The first day's hearing was held *in camera* and the respondent was excluded from the hearing and provided only with a summary of the evidence. The respondent was permitted to attend the second day of the hearing. The respondent declined, objected to the fairness and constitutionality of the proceeding before the SIRC, submitted no evidence at the hearing, and chose not to cross-examine two RCMP witnesses who had testified on the first day. Counsel did make submissions to the SIRC.

Section 27(1) requires an immigration officer in possession of information that a permanent resident falls into one of its enumerated classes to forward a report to the Deputy Minister. An inquiry is then held by an adjudicator in cases where the Deputy Minister considers one is warranted. Section 32(2) provides that where an adjudicator decides that a person who is the subject of an inquiry does fall within one of the classes in section 27(1), the adjudicator shall, except in the case of a Convention refugee, make a deportation order. All persons who fall within section 27(1)(d)(ii) have deliberately violated an essential condition under which they were permitted to remain in Canada. In such a situation there is no breach of fundamental justice in giving practical effect to the termination of their right to remain in Canada. In the case of a permanent resident deportation is the only way in which to accomplish this. There is nothing inherently unjust about a mandatory order. The fact of the deliberate violation of the condition imposed by section 27(1)(d)(ii) is sufficient to justify a deportation order. Accordingly, sections 27(1)(d)(ii) and 32(2) are not contrary to section 7 of the *Charter of Rights.*

The deportation authorized by sections 27(1)(d)(ii) and 32(2) is not cruel and unusual punishment as described in section 12 of the *Charter of Rights.*

Section 6 of the *Charter* specifically provides for differential treatment of citizens and permanent residents. Accordingly, sections 27(1)(d)(ii) and 32(2) do not violate section 15 of the Charter. Permanent residents are given mobility rights in section 6(2). Only citizens are accorded the right to enter, remain in and leave Canada in section 6(1). There is no discrimination contrary to section 15 in a deportation scheme that applies to permanent residents but not citizens.

The effect of the security certificate in this case is to direct the Immigration Appeal Board to dismiss any appeal based on the existence of compassionate or humanitarian considerations. The permanent resident's right of appeal after a certificate has been issued is restricted to questions of law, fact or mixed law and fact.

The *Immigration Act*, S.C. 1910, c. 27, did not provide any specific grounds of appeal. A person ordered deported could only resort to the Minister, who had authority to overturn a deportation order on unspecified grounds. The *Immigration Act*, R.S.C. 1952, c. 325, provided for an Immigration Appeal Board; however, appeals against deportation orders remained under the control of the Minister. The Board heard only those appeals directed to it by the Minister, and the Minister retained the power to confirm or quash the Appeal Board's decision or substitute his decision as he deemed just and proper. The 1966 *White Paper on Immigration* recommended that a reconstituted Immigration Appeal Board have authority to deal conclusively with appeals against deportation orders except in security cases. The *Immigration Appeal Board Act*, 1967 for the first time conferred upon the Board the power to stay or quash a deportation order made against a permanent resident on the basis of all the circumstances of the case. This new power was subject to the discretion of the Minister and the Solicitor General, who could certify their opinion based on security or criminal intelligence reports that it would be contrary to the national interest to permit such relief. This reserves to the Crown the right similar to the prerogative right which existed at common law, to determine that the continued presence in Canada of an alien, subject to a deportation order, was not conducive to the public good. The *Immigration Appeal Board Act* was repealed by the *Immigration Act*, 1976. However, this new Act did not change the nature of the decision that could be made by the Board having regard to all the circumstances of the case. That decision remained as it had been under the 1967 Act, an exercise of discretion based on compassionate grounds. Section 83 of the *Immigration Act*, 1976 limited the availability of relief based on all the circumstances of the case. Such an appeal had to be dismissed if the Minister and Solicitor General certified their opinion that it would be contrary to the national interest to permit such an appeal. In 1984 the SIRC was established by the *Canadian Security Intelligence Service Act*, S.C. 1984, c. 21. The Review Committee was assigned various functions under several Acts, including the *Immigration Act*, 1976. Sections 83 and 82.1 of the *Immigration Act*, 1976 were repealed and amended versions were substituted. The decision as to whether to direct the issuance of a security certificate, however, remained with the Governor in Council. Thus, there has never been a universally available right of appeal from a deportation order on humanitarian or compassionate grounds or "having regard to all the circumstances of the case." Such an appeal has historically been a purely discretionary matter. The right of appeal required to comply with the principles of fundamental justice is a true appeal which enables the decision of first instance to be questioned on factual and legal grounds. The absence of an appeal on wider grounds does not violate section 7.

The procedure followed by the Security Intelligence Review Committee in this case recognized competing individual and state interests and attempted to find a reasonable balance between them. It was not necessary that the respondent be given details of the criminal intelligence investigation techniques or police sources used to acquire the information upon which the two Ministers relied in issuing the certificate. The respondent was given an opportunity to respond by calling his own witnesses or by requesting that he be allowed to cross-examine the RCMP officers who testified *in camera*. Such a procedure was sufficient to meet the requirements of the principles of fundamental justice.

Section 70(5)

Baker v. Canada (Minister of Citizenship & Immigration) (1999), 174 D.L.R. (4th) 193 (S.C.C.) — The appellant entered Canada as a visitor in 1981, and had remained ever since. She was not a permanent resident but had worked illegally for 11 years. She had four children all of whom were born in Canada. The appellant was ordered deported in 1992, after it was determined that she had worked illegally in Canada and had overstayed her visitor's visa.

In 1993, the appellant applied for an exemption from the requirement to apply for permanent residence outside Canada, based upon humanitarian and compassionate considerations. In April 1994, it was determined that there were insufficient humanitarian and compassionate grounds to warrant processing the appellant's application from within Canada. The letter advising her of this decision contained no reasons for the decision. The appellant's counsel was provided with the notes made by the immigration officer who interviewed Ms. Baker, which notes were used by the immigration officer who made the decision. Following the refusal of her application, the appellant was served with a direction to report to Pearson Airport for removal. Her deportation was stayed pending the result of this appeal.

In certain circumstances, the duty of procedural fairness will require the provision of a written explanation for a decision. The circumstances in this case constituted one of the situations where reasons were necessary. The profound importance of a humanitarian and compassionate decision to those affected militated in favour of the requirement that reasons be provided. It would be unfair for a person subject to a decision such as this one, which is so critical to their future, not to be told why the result was reached. The reasons requirement was fulfilled in this case because the appellant was provided with the notes of the officer. Because there was no other record of the reasons for making the decision, the notes of the reviewing officer were taken by inference to be the reasons for the decision. Accepting documents such as these notes, was part of the flexibility that was necessary when courts evaluate the requirements of the duty of fairness with a recognition of the day-to-day realities of administrative agencies.

Chu v. Canada (Minister of Citizenship & Immigration) (1998), 45 Imm. L.R. (2d) 1, 161 D.L.R. (4th) 499, 225 N.R. 378 (Fed. C.A.); leave to appeal to S.C.C. refused (1998), 236 N.R. 387 (note) (S.C.C.) — This appeal dealt with the question of whether consideration by a decision-maker of documentary evidence regarding country information could be relied upon by a section 70(5) decision-maker without being identified or copied to a Convention refugee who is the subject of the opinion.

The Court referred to the fact that each case will have to be decided according to its own circumstances. In reaching a conclusion in this case the Court had regard to a) the nature of the proceedings, and the rules under which the decision-maker was acting; b) the context of the proceeding; and c) the nature of the documents at issue in the proceeding.

The impugned document had been prepared by the High Commissioner for Refugees at the request of the Immigration Department. It was received by the Department some six months before the notice to the applicant that a danger opinion was being sought. There was no evidence that the document was not available and accessible at the documentation centres maintained by the Department.

The Court answered the question in the context of this case in the negative, and dismissed the appeal.

Rampersaud v. Canada (Minister of Citizenship & Immigration) (1998), 44 Imm. L.R. (2d) 32, 146 F.T.R. 201 (Fed. T.D.) — This was an application to review a danger opinion. The Minister's delegate had no evidence explaining the circumstances of the applicant's drug convictions, such as the police officer's arrest reports or the applicant's explanation. The delegate did not have the decision of the Parole Board which presumably would express the Board's belief that the applicant could leave prison because the risk of recidivism was low. Evidence concerning an applicant's risk to the public should be placed before the Minister. This is especially true in a case where the applicant lacks sophistication and does not have a lawyer prior to the decision of the delegate.

The danger opinion was set aside. The Minister's delegate was required to re-determine the matter with the addition of the Parole Board decisions, the arrest reports and any statement the applicant wished to make concerning the drug convictions.

Ashton v. Canada (Minister of Citizenship & Immigration) (1998), 142 F.T.R. 97 (Fed. T.D.) — The Court noted that the evidence taken as a whole strongly supported the applicant's submission, that at the time the danger opinion was rendered he was not a danger to the public and would not be in the future. The Minister's decision was so profoundly unresponsive to the evidence that it was on its face perverse. The evidence manifestly required a different result. Further, there were no reasons to explain the Minister's opinion or how it was reached.

The Court also noted the reviewing officer's recommendations and while observing that these were not reasons for the opinion felt that the recommendation required comment by the Court. The Court found the recommendation to be a remarkably unfair interpretation of the evidence and further that the recommendation was given without regard to the evidence that was submitted by the applicant. In the result, the danger opinion was set aside.

Farshid-Ghazi v. Canada (Minister of Citizenship & Immigration) (1998), 44 Imm. L.R. (2d) 63, 142 F.T.R. 117 (Fed. T.D.) — The applicant sought to review a danger opinion issued under section 70(5) of the *Immigration Act*. There are 3 sections of the *Immigration Act* which deal with a danger opinion, each having different consequences.

A person found to be a danger pursuant to section 46.01 loses his or her right to have his or her refugee claim heard. A person found to be a danger under subsection 53(1) may, inspite of being recognized as a Convention refugee and a permanent resident, be deported back to the country of his or her nationality. Finally a person found to be a danger pursuant to subsection 70(5) loses his or her opportunity to pursue an appeal before the Appeal Division.

The criminal backlog review prepared for the Minister's delegate contained a "danger to public assessment" and "other considerations", the latter dealing with humanitarian and compassionate grounds and removal risk consideration. The risk assessment was not disclosed to the applicant and for this reason the decision of the Minister's delegate was set aside. The report should have been disclosed and accordingly the applicant was entitled to an opportunity to make further representations in support and submit further documentary material on the issue of risk assessment. The matter was remitted back to the Minister for proper exercise of the Minister's discretion in accordance with these reasons.

Thai v. Canada (Minister of Citizenship & Immigration) (1998), 42 Imm. L.R. (2d) 28 (Fed. T.D.) — The applicant sought to set aside a danger opinion issued by the Minister's delegate pursuant to subsection 70(5). A danger to the public opinion involves an assessment of present or future danger. That is, is there reason to think that the individual will repeat the particular activities which gave rise to his incarceration or engage in other activities that would make him a danger to the public. The commission of one offence is not evidence of recidivism, although some offences, by their nature, may be of a type that invites such a conclusion.

There was virtually nothing in this record except for the speculative and unsupported opinions of one case management officer who interviewed the applicant on one occasion. While all that is required in these cases is some evidence to support a decision of the delegate, that evidence must have a substantial basis and be supported by facts. Accordingly, the decision of the delegate was set aside.

Correira v. Canada (Minister of Citizenship & Immigration) (December 16, 1997), Doc. IMM-1057-96 (Fed. T.D.) — At issue was a danger opinion pursuant to section 70(5) of the *Immigration Act*. The applicant had been convicted of murder and was not eligible for parole until the year 2011. Nothing in subsection 70(5) precluded the issuance of the danger opinion while the applicant was still in jail. Accordingly, the opinion was not invalid for prematurity.

Astudillo v. Canada (Minister of Citizenship & Immigration) (1997), 139 F.T.R. 47, 41 Imm. L.R. (2d) 213 (Fed. T.D.) — The applicant sought to set aside a danger opinion issued pursuant to subsection 70(5). The Minister relied upon the CPIC printout, police occurrence reports, and a Correctional Service report, which the Court found to be "extrinsic evidence". These documents were not provided by the applicant nor were they available to the applicant. There was no evidence that these reports were considered by the Minister's delegate. They were, however, considered by a reviewing officer who prepared a memorandum for use by the Minister's delegate. Information from those reports found its way into the memorandum in a way that was prejudicial to the applicant.

The application for judicial review was allowed and the danger opinion set aside.

Holmes v. Canada (Minister of Citizenship & Immigration) (1997), 41 Imm. L.R. (2d) 241 (Fed. T.D.) — In this case, the decision being reviewed was that of a Minister's delegate made under section 70(5) of the Act. The opinion was set aside because the evidence manifestly required a different result. In the absence of reason the Court could not determine how the opinion of the decision-maker was rational and therefore, set aside the decision on the basis that the decision-maker had failed to consider relevant facts.

Meikle v. Canada (Minister of Citizenship & Immigration) (1997), 137 F.T.R. 304, 41 Imm. L.R. (2d) 293 (Fed. T.D.); reconsideration refused (June 11, 1998), Doc. IMM-1031-96 (Fed. T.D.) — The applicant sought to set aside a danger opinion issued pursuant to section 70(5) of the *Immigration Act.* The applicant is a citizen of the United Kingdom who came to Canada at the age of seven. He has been convicted of a large number of offences since 1973. While most of the offences are minor, one was a conviction for possession of a narcotic for the purpose of trafficking. A deportation order was made against the applicant in January 1993. On the same day the applicant commenced an appeal to the Appeal Division. The notice of appeal pursuant to the rules was served on the adjudicator. Inexplicably the notice was not forwarded to the registry of the IAD until October 1994. The applicant did not receive a hearing from the Appeal Division because of the danger opinion which was the subject of this application.

The applicant did all that he was required to do pursuant to the IAD rules. The Court can grant a remedy where negligent delay has caused undue prejudice. Ultimately Parliament is assumed to have intended its laws to be administrated in an equitable manner and in conforming with the principles of natural justice. There is a nexus between the breach of the principles of natural justice and the opinion. The causal nexus and the prejudice to the applicant is that the opinion had the effect of removing the right of appeal, a right that vested before subsection 70(5) came into effect.

The unexplained and lengthy delay in depositing the applicant's notice of appeal with the Appeal Division constituted a failure to observe a principle of natural justice and procedural fairness and resulted in the quashing of the opinion.

Ip v. Canada (Minister of Citizenship & Immigration) (1997), 136 F.T.R. 34 (Fed. T.D.) — The applicant sought to set aside a danger opinion issued by the Minister's delegate pursuant to section 70(5) of the *Immigration Act.* The applicant's counsel sought an extension of the 15-day time period, which had been allotted to him for the purpose of explaining why a danger opinion should not be issued. The Court observed that the 15 day period is very short especially having regard to the fact that the respondent had a virtually unlimited time within which to prepare its case. This creates an unfair imbalance with respect to the individual's ability to put material before the Minister's delegate, before the delegate makes a decision that has enormous consequences for the individual. In this case, counsel requested an extension and received no answer. Counsel for the respondent argued that despite the failure to respond to the request for an extension of time, the applicant and his counsel were able to file extensive submissions. The Court noted, however, that the applicant's counsel wrote in the letter that he sent with the submissions that he had been compelled to make those submissions without the benefit of full disclosure and the requested extension.

The failure to respond was a breach of procedural fairness and the opinion was set aside.

Da Costa v. Canada (Minister of Citizenship & Immigration) (1997), 41 Imm. L.R. (2d) 12, 137 F.T.R. 268, [1998] 2 F.C. 182 (Fed. T.D.) — The applicant sought to quash a danger opinion made by the Minister's delegate pursuant to section 70(5) of the *Immigration Act*. The applicant, at the relevant time, was held by order of the Ontario Criminal Code Review Board. He was detained involuntarily at the St. Thomas Psychiatric Hospital. The order of that Board provided that the applicant be detained at the hospital in a program of treatment pending his possible rehabilitation. Under the *Criminal Code*, while detained, the applicant was to be assessed at least annually to determine whether he continued to be a dangerous person from whom the public should be protected. So long as he was adjudged so to be, he was to remain in detention.

The applicant is a person under a disability by reason of his mental illness. There was no evidence that service of the notice of the Minister's possible opinion was made in accordance with the law of Ontario. Without appropriate notice as required by Ontario law, applicable in the case of administrative processes in regard to persons under a disability, provincial officials responsible for the applicant's interest may not have notice of the proceedings that may affect him or their responsibilities for him. Absent an appropriate notice, the proceedings were faulty and the opinion cannot stand.

Athwal v. Canada (Minister of Citizenship & Immigration) (1997), 220 N.R. 355, 133 F.T.R. 320 (note), 40 Imm. L.R. (2d) 160, [1998] 1 F.C. 489 (Fed. C.A.); leave to appeal refused (1998), 227 N.R. 91 (note) (S.C.C.) — The Immigration Appeal Division of the IRB declined to hear the respondent's appeal. The IAD found it lacked jurisdiction due to paragraph 70(5)(c) of the *Immigration Act*. The respondent successfully reviewed the IAD's decision on the basis that the adjudicator failed to make the specific finding required by section 70(5)(c) — namely that the respondent was a person convicted of an offence for which a term of imprisonment of 10 years or more may be imposed.

The appeal was allowed. Parliament intended to vest the IAD with the responsibility of determining whether a person had been convicted of an offence for which a prison term of 10 years or more could have been imposed.

Nguyen v. Canada (Minister of Citizenship & Immigration) (1997), 40 Imm. L.R. (2d) 103, 135 F.T.R. 230 (Fed. T.D.) — The applicant sought to set aside a danger opinion formed pursuant to section 70(5) of the *Immigration Act*. The applicant, a stateless person from Vietnam, had three convictions: mischief, possession of a weapon and trafficking in cocaine. A removal order was made and the respondent undertook an investigation to determine whether or not an opinion should be formed. The immigration officer who prepared the ministerial opinion report did not believe that the subject was a danger to the public. The officer's manager did not concur. Without further documentation and without reasons to explain the choice between the conflicting recommendations, the danger opinion issued.

The Court noted that in forming an opinion, the possibility or likelihood of re-offending is only relevant to the extent that the re-offending may or is likely to represent a danger to the public.

The discretionary decision here under review on its face was perverse. In the absence of reasons the Court could find not rational explanation for the opinion formed by respondent's delegate.

Seivewright v. Canada (Minister of Citizenship & Immigration) (July 28, 1997), Doc. IMM-2496-96 (Fed. T.D.) — The applicant sought to review a decision of the Appeal Division dismissing his appeal for lack of jurisdiction.

The Minister formed the opinion that the applicant was a danger to the public and thereby removed the applicant's statutory right of appeal. The applicant sought to review the danger opinion, but was unsuccessful due to the fact that the applicant did not file an application record. Subsequent to the dismissal of the applicant's application to review the Minister's opinion, the Appeal Division of the Immigration and Refugee Board dismissed the applicant's appeal, for want of jurisdiction based on section 70(5)(c) of the *Immigration Act*. The applicant then sought to judicially review that decision.

The Board's only jurisdiction is that granted by Parliament pursuant to section 70(5). The Board in dismissing the applicant's appeal was doing what it was statutorily mandated to do. The applicant could not, in this proceeding, challenge the danger opinion formed by the Minister.

Accordingly, the application for judicial review was dismissed.

Frances v. Canada (Minister of Citizenship & Immigration) (1997), 44 Imm. L.R. (2d) 202 (Fed. T.D.) — The applicant sought to set aside a ministerial opinion that he constituted a danger to the public in Canada. It is fundamental to the proper to exercise of ministerial discretion that the conclusions, opinions or inferences expressed be made on the basis of true and substantial facts. The brief to the Minister did not make reference to the fact that charges which had been laid against the applicant and referred to in the briefing notes, had been either dismissed or withdrawn. The briefing spoke in broad, negative and unqualified terms of the applicant being a danger to the public with no reference to the seven-year period during which he had been free of any criminal convictions. The application for judicial review was allowed.

Nguyen v. Canada (Minister of Citizenship & Immigration) (1997), 133 F.T.R. 210 (Fed. T.D.) — The applicant sought to review two decisions of the Minister. The first is the opinion of the Minister dated May 27, 1996, pursuant to subparagraph 46.01(1)(e)(iv) of the *Immigration Act*, that the applicant constitutes a danger to the public in Canada. The second was the opinion of the Minister dated May 27, 1996, pursuant to subsection 70(5) of the *Immigration Act* that the applicant constituted a danger to the public in Canada.

The applicant was born in Vietnam. After spending four years in a refugee camp in the Philippines, he was granted an immigrant visa in January 1991. In February 1994, the applicant was found guilty of eight counts in an indictment which arose from a single transaction — a robbery in which the applicant was the driver of the getaway car.

The applicant was released from prison in February 1996, and at the same time received a letter indicating that the Minister was considering whether to issue a danger to the public opinion. The applicant's counsel made written submissions to the Minister in April 1996.

On May 27, 1996, the Minister's delegate issued an opinion that the applicant constituted a danger to the public under both subsection 70(5) and subparagraph 46.01(1)(e)(iv).

In June 1996, the applicant was arrested. However, he was released by an adjudicator who came to the conclusion that the applicant was not a danger to the public. At the detention review hearing, one of the documents submitted was a report entitled "Danger to the Public Ministerial Report". This document was not part of the material disclosed for the applicant in February 1996, as the document had not yet been created. In that document, the officer who prepared it commented on the fact that he or she had spoken to the applicant's parole officer and had been advised that since his release, the applicant had not been employed, was collecting welfare, his relationship with his former common law wife had broken down, and that his relationship with his daughter was continuing.

There was information in the applicant's file, which disclosed the applicant was unemployed and collecting welfare. The applicant's counsel in his submissions to the Minister at the time the danger opinion was being formed, had raised the question of the applicant's relation with his common law wife and had indicated in those submissions that it was unclear whether the relationship would continue or not.

The Court concluded that there was nothing in the document which constituted evidence to which the applicant did not have an opportunity to respond. If counsel submits certain matters in a letter to the Minister, the Minister's representatives are entitled to make contrary statements as long as the statements are either in the applicant's file or based on information which is available to the applicant. In this case, the applicant knew his common law relationship had terminated.

The Court also observed that there was no difference in the level of fairness owed under subsection 70(5) and section 46.01.

The application for judicial review was dismissed.

Parasidis v. Canada (Minister of Citizenship & Immigration) (1997), 38 Imm. L.R. (2d) 288, 133 F.T.R. 73 (Fed. T.D.) — The applicant sought to stay the execution of a removal order on the basis that there was a statutory stay by virtue of section 49(1)(b) of the *Immigration Act.* The applicant was a citizen of Greece who had been ordered deported by reason of his having been convicted of a criminal offence. The applicant appealed to the Appeal Division of the IRB and while his appeal was pending the applicant was certified as a danger to the public under section 70(5) of the *Immigration Act.*

The applicant was not seriously asking the Court for judicial stay but rather a declaration that a statutory stay operated to preclude his removal. This was a final determination which should properly be left to the judge hearing the judicial review application.

If the Court had been required to render a decision it would have concluded that there was no statutory stay. Assuming for the moment that all requirements of section 70(5) have been met, the danger opinion has the effect of discharging the statutory stay.

The applicant's counsel also argued that there was no evidence that the adjudicator had determined that the applicant had been convicted of an offence for which a term of imprisonment of 10 years or more may be imposed. It is preferable that the adjudicator state expressly in the words of that provision, that an individual has been convicted of an offence for which a term of imprisonment of 10 years or more may be imposed. That is not, however, a statutory requirement, it may be obvious from the material that such a determination has been made. In the present case, the material submitted by the applicant led the Court to infer that the evidence before the adjudicator caused him to issue the deportation order because the applicant was convicted under subsection 4(2) of the *Narcotic Control Act* — an indictable offence punishable by a maximum punishment of life imprisonment. Accordingly, the application for stay was dismissed.

Nguyen v. Canada (Minister of Citizenship & Immigration) (1997), 132 F.T.R. 51 (Fed. T.D.) — The applicant sought to set aside an opinion of the Minister's delegate to the effect that the applicant was a danger to the public in Canada. The applicant was born in South Vietnam and escaped by boat in June 1982. The applicants were resettled in Canada in November 1983. In December 1986, the applicant became mentally ill and began committing a series of criminal offences. A conditional removal order was made against the applicant and the applicant appealed to the Appeal Division of the IRB. While the appeal was pending, the Minister formed the opinion that the applicant was a danger to the public.

In the Criminal Backlog Review Ministerial Report, there appears almost a full page quotation from a report dated May 4, 1995 from the United Nations High Commissioner for Refugees. There was no evidence that this report was made available to the applicant nor was there evidence that the report was "publicly available documentary material". The Court concluded that the Minister's delegate erred in a reviewable manner by taking into account extrinsic evidence not provided to the applicant which evidence was not otherwise publicly available. Accordingly, the opinion was set aside.

Shankaran v. Canada (Minister of Citizenship & Immigration) (1997), 40 Imm. L.R. (2d) 268, 130 F.T.R. 201 (Fed. T.D.) — This was an application to review a decision of a delegate of the Minister to the effect that the applicant constituted a danger to the public.

The applicant argued that written representations made to his counsel by an immigration officer created a "legitimate expectation" that he would be given an opportunity to review and respond to any submissions or reports made to the Minister by local immigration officers.

When a public authority has promised to follow a certain procedure, it is in the interest of good administration that it should act fairly and should implement its promise, so long as implementation does not interfere with its statutory duty. When the promise was made the authority must have considered that it would be assisted in discharging its duty fairly by allowing any representations from interested parties and as a general rule that is correct.

The Court found that giving effect to the immigration officer's promise would not conflict or interfere with the statutory duty of the Minister. Further the immigration officer was not disentitled to make the representation that he did. Thus, it was a breach of procedural fairness for the Minister not to have honoured the undertaking.

Accordingly, the opinion of the Minister's delegate was quashed and the matter returned for reconsideration.

Williams v. Canada (Minister of Citizenship & Immigration), 147 D.L.R. (4th) 93, 212 N.R. 63, [1997] 2 F.C. 646, 4 Admin. L.R. (3d) 200 (Fed. C.A.); leave to appeal to S.C.C. refused (1997), 150 D.L.R. (4th) viii (note), 224 N.R. 320 (note) (S.C.C.) — This was an appeal from an order of the Trial Division which set aside a decision made on behalf of the Minister under subsection 70(5). The decision was set aside on the basis that the Minister was obliged by principles of fundamental justice and of the common law to provide reasons for her decision.

The respondent was born in Jamaica and entered Canada in 1976 at the age of 10 years old and has had the status of a permanent resident since that time. The respondent never acquired Canadian citizenship. Between 1984 and 1989 he was convicted of 5 offences including assault and 4 involving trafficking in narcotics. For one of these offences he was sentenced to 4 years imprisonment.

The Court found that the Trial Division judge had exaggerated the effect of the Minister's opinion and that this exaggeration had distorted the analysis of the requirements of fundamental justice in the circumstances.

The Court noted that section 70(5) was adopted after the respondent had filed his appeal with the Appeal Division, but before his appeal had been heard. The effect of the Minister's opinion was to prevent the appeal being heard. However, a transitional provision provided the respondent with an opportunity to seek judicial review of the deportation order. The Court noted that the respondent had not done so in this case.

As a result of the Minister forming the opinion that he was a danger to the public, the respondent lost the right to pursue an appeal under paragraph 70(1)(a) on any question of law or fact or mixed law and fact. In place of this, he was given the right to seek a judicial review which would be fully as effective in respect of any questions of law but not as complete a review of findings of fact. As previously noted by the Court in this case, the applicant had not sought to review the decision issuing the deportation order. Substitution of judicial review for a right of appeal by virtue of the Minister forming an opinion did not appear to the Court to have a serious effect on the respondent's right.

The Court noted that the respondent also lost the opportunity to have the Appeal Division consider under paragraph 70(1)(b) whether having "regard to all the circumstances" he should not be removed from Canada. There was no consideration that the Board could make under paragraph (b) which would not be equally available through the exercise of the Minister's discretion under subsection 114(2). The Court noted that such a review was always available before deportation and that the process employed in this case specifically requested the respondent to make such submissions to the Minister at the same time as making submissions on the question of whether he represented a danger to the public. The Court noted that the respondent's counsel had made such submissions at some considerable length.

The respondent also lost the statutory stay of the deportation order to which he was entitled under paragraph 49(1)(b) of the Act. In place of this, the Court noted that the respondent was put in the position, once the Minister's opinion issued, of having to launch judicial review proceedings against the deportation order and then having to convince a judge that the deportation order should be stayed pending determination of the judicial review. The Court did not see this transformation as an invasion of the respondent's fundamental rights.

The Minister's opinion was not the cause of the respondent's deportation. The respondent faced deportation because as a non-citizen he had committed serious crimes in Canada. It was not suggested that the respondent had received other than fair trials leading up to his convictions and that his deportation order was wrong in law or in fact or that he lacked the opportunity to express his views on all the material submitted to the Minister when she was forming her danger to the public opinion.

The Court noted that the test is not whether the permanent resident is a danger to the public but whether the Minister is "of the opinion" that he is such a danger. Such opinions can only be reviewed on grounds that the decision maker acted in bad faith, erred in law or acted upon the basis of the irrelevant considerations. The Court is not being asked to affirm the correctness of the Minister's opinion but only to determine whether there is any lawful basis for its review.

The Court concluded that the Minister's opinion did not engage a liberty or security of the person interest under section 7 of the Charter.

The Court found that section 70(5) was not constitutionally vague. The subsection required the Minister to form an opinion in good faith that the respondent was a possible re-offender whose presence in Canada created an unacceptable risk to the public. The Court noted that it is impossible to prove future conduct. There is always a risk and the extent to which society should be prepared to accept that risk can involve political considerations not inappropriate for a Minister. The danger must be a present or future danger. The Court found it hard to understand why it would not be open to the Minister to forecast future misconduct on the basis of past misconduct, particularly having regard to the circumstances of the offences and comments by the sentencing judges.

The Court declined to treat the Minister's decision as a kind of *letter de cachet*, an arbitrary order issued by a despotic official ordering a random imprisonment or exile of otherwise innocent citizens.

The Court confirmed that it is usually preferable that both courts and tribunals give reasons for their decisions. The Court noted many advantages in issuing reasons: they enable the parties to know why they have won or lost; the articulation of reasons imposes a discipline upon a court or tribunal; reasons assist a court later in disposing of an appeal or exercising powers of judicial review. The basic tenets of our legal system however, have never imposed a duty on tribunals to give reasons where a statute has not specifically so provided. Where a discretionary decision is either on its face perverse or where there is evidence of facts being before the tribunal which manifestly required a different result or which were irrelevant yet apparently determinative of the result, then a court may be obliged to conclude that in the absence of reasons that the decision has to be set aside for one of the established grounds for judicial review (error of law, bad faith, consideration of irrelevant factors, failure to consider relevant factors...). In such cases the decision is set aside not because of a lack of reasons but because, in the absence of reasons, it is not possible to overcome the inference of perversity or error derived from the result or the surrounding circumstances of the decision.

The separation of powers and ordinary principles of judicial deference require that it is for the person attacking a discretionary decision to demonstrate that it is unlawful.

The Court concluded that section 70(5) was not invalid for not requiring the giving of reasons. In the result the appeal was allowed.

Chedid v. Canada (Minister of Citizenship & Immigration) (1997), 127 F.T.R. 81 (Fed. T.D.) — This was an application to quash an opinion of the Minister under section 70(5) of the *Immigration Act* that the applicant was a danger to the public. The applicant became a landed immigrant in October 1991. In March 1993 the applicant was arrested and charged with 5 counts of trafficking in narcotics. The applicant was released on bail following his arrest and remained out on bail for approximately 2 years until the time of his sentencing. The applicant pleaded guilty to 3 counts of trafficking and was sentenced to one year in prison on each count to be served concurrently. After serving 4 months of his sentence the applicant was released. The applicant had no criminal record prior to above offences and has incurred no further criminal record since.

Section 70(5) refers to a present or future threat posed by the person. The mere fact of conviction on one or more criminal offences does not in itself support a determination that a person is, may be or is likely to pose a danger to the public.

The Court concluded that the minister based her determination on the mere fact of the applicant's convictions and without regard to other circumstances of the case. While it is not impossible to found a danger opinion on a single serious conviction, this cannot be done when there is no evidence that a person poses a present or future danger. Absent evidence of a likelihood to commit further offences as may be established through a pattern of violent or criminal behaviour or an individual's criminal lifestyle or values, deciding that a person is likely to pose a danger to the public by reason of a previous criminal conviction is perverse.

The decision of the parole board, releasing the applicant on parole was not included in the record before the Minister. This document was crucial to the question of whether the applicant was a danger to the public or not as it provided evidence as to the unlikelihood of recidivism. It is essential that such relevant, crucial information be before the Minister for subsection 70(5) determinations and that it be taken into account in such determinations.

The opinion of the Minister was set aside.

Fairhurst v. Canada (Minister of Citizenship & Immigration) (1996), 37 Imm. L.R. (2d) 122, 124 F.T.R. 142 (Fed. T.D.) — This was an application to set aside the Minister's determination that the applicant constituted a danger to the public. The applicant was a permanent resident of Canada and had established a successful business in British Columbia. In May 1994, the applicant pleaded guilty to three counts of trafficking in cocaine for which he received a sentence of four years, on one count and six months on each of the others. The director of case management recommended the designation of danger to the public solely on the basis of the clients criminal conviction. The Minister's delegate accepted the director's recommendation.

In forming a danger to the public opinion, natural justice and procedural fairness require the Minister to take into account all of the relevant and particular circumstances of each case.

The fact that an individual has a criminal conviction is not necessarily in and of itself a sufficient reason to conclude that he or she posses a danger to the public.

The Court noted a number of factual errors and unsubstantiated allegations and commented on the fact that the Minister chose not give reasons for his decision which fact only served to reinforce the perception that the errors and unsubstantiated information affected the forming of the opinion.

Smith v. Canada (Minister of Citizenship & Immigration) (1996), 36 Imm. L.R. (2d) 95 (Fed. T.D.) — The applicant was in the process of appealing a deportation order based on section 27(1)(d)(ii) of the *Immigration Act* to the Appeal Division. His hearing in that division was postponed because the Minister who had the applicant in custody, claimed to be unable to bring the applicant to his hearing. During the delay the Minister formed the opinion that the applicant was a danger to the public within the meaning of section 70(5). The Appeal Division then found itself without jurisdiction. The decision as to the jurisdiction of the Appeal Division will depend on the validity of the Minister's decision. The only part of that decision which could be challenged on this motion, and that indirectly, would be the constitutionality of section 70(5). The attack here, is not on the constitutionality of section 70(5) but on the constitutionality of the formation of the opinion by the Minister. That question was not before the Court on this file. Accordingly, the applicant had not shown an arguable case for leave to have judicial review of the Appeal Division's decision that it no longer had jurisdiction. Accordingly, the application for an extension of time to file a record was dismissed.

Adamson v. Canada (Minister of Citizenship & Immigration) (1996), 35 Imm. L.R. (2d) 101 (Fed. T.D.) — This was an application to review a decision of a delegate of the Minister determining that the applicant was a danger to the public in Canada.

Commission of a single infraction does not necessarily give rise to a likelihood that its author will repeat. However, it does establish that the person in question was capable of committing the infraction at the time when it was committed, and it invites the person concerned to demonstrate why this is no longer the case. The applicant had failed to offer such evidence in this case.

The application to quash the finding was dismissed.

Thompson v. Canada (Minister of Citizenship & Immigration) (1996), 37 Imm. L.R. (2d) 9, 41 Admin. L.R. (2d) 10, 118 F.T.R. 269 (Fed. T.D.) — The applicant sought leave to review a decision by a delegate of the Minister pursuant to subsection 70(5) of the *Immigration Act*. The applicant was granted landed immigrant status in 1980. In 1985, the applicant incurred 2 convictions for theft under $200. In March 1992, the applicant was convicted of sexual interference under section 151 of the *Criminal Code* and sentenced to 2 years less one day in jail to be followed by a 2 year probation period. The offence involved sexual intercourse with a 13 year old neighbour of the applicant who had sought assistance of the applicant and his wife when she was having difficulty with her home situation. The applicant was released on parole supervision in June 1994.

In October 1995, the applicant was informed of the possibility of the issuance of a ministerial opinion pursuant to subsection 70(5). Submissions were invited and were made by counsel for the applicant. In December 1995, the Minister gave an opinion that the applicant constituted a danger to the public. The applicant was arrested in January 1996, and ordered deported in that same month after an inquiry in which it was determined that the applicant was a person described in 27(1)(d) of the *Immigration Act*. The applicant unsuccessfully sought to stay execution of that deportation order.

The nature of the respondent's decision making power in subsection 70(5) is broadly discretionary. The language of "opinion" clearly denotes a legislative intent to provide the respondent Minister with a wide discretion. To succeed in his attack, the applicant must show that the decision maker erred in law, proceeded on some wrong or improper principle or acted in bad faith. It is a heavy burden.

Although there may be no need to impose formal guidelines on the respondent regarding what constitutes a danger to the public, the phrase must have some meaning in itself; it must constitute more than mere duplication of the conviction for a serious offence. Parliament did not intend for danger opinions to have no meaning. In order for the respondent to form an opinion the fact of a conviction alone is an insufficient basis. The circumstances of each case must over and above the conviction indicate a danger to the public. There may be an instance where a danger opinion could be properly issued where a person had only one conviction, there must however, be circumstances in the case additional to a single conviction that indicate a danger to the public.

In subsection 70(5) Parliament chose not to narrow the scope of the respondent's discretion by a "reasonable grounds" standard or by specific factors to be considered. It would be inappropriate and wrong in law to judicially impose criteria for consideration where Parliament has not. The phrase "danger to the public" has a plain meaning and that meaning is to be a "present or future danger to the public". For the respondent to reach the opinion, there must be some evidence of the person being a present or future danger to other persons in Canada. In this case, the respondent erred in law in making a determination that the applicant constituted a danger to the public. On the material that was before the respondent there was no evidence that the applicant posed a present or future danger. The evidence disclosed that the applicant was not a paedophile; testing indicated that the applicant demonstrated low sexual arousal in all areas based on testing conducted well after the events that lead to his conviction. The appellant's conviction occurred nearly 4 years before the danger opinion and there was no evidence of criminal activity in the interim. Throughout his dealings with police and probation officers and with immigration officials the applicant was co-operative. There was no basis for the issuance of the opinion beyond the fact of the single serious conviction and the relatively singular series of events leading to that conviction.

The application was allowed, the opinion of the respondent was set aside and the matter was referred back to the respondent for redetermination which was to be made taking into account these reasons.

Silva v. Canada (Minister of Citizenship & Immigration) (August 15, 1996), Doc. IMM-2450-96 (Fed. T.D.) — This decision arose out of an application for an order staying the execution of a deportation order. An adjudicator had ordered the applicant, who was a permanent resident of Canada, deported. The applicant appealed which had the effect of staying the execution of the deportation order. The respondent issued an opinion pursuant to section 70(5) stating that the applicant constituted a danger to the public in Canada. When the Appeal Division was notified of the opinion it treated the notification as a motion to dismiss the appeal and invited submissions.

When the injunction application was heard the respondent had not yet made submissions on the motion to dismiss.

The Court found that through the process of the application for a stay, the question of whether or not the opinion of the Minister under section 70(5) lifted the statutory stay arising out of paragraph 49(1)(b) was a serious issue to be tried.

Proposed Addition — 70.1

70.1 (1) Permanent resident document to be issued — Subject to subsection (2), where a person appeals a refusal under subsection 70(1.1) and the appeal is

allowed, the Minister shall provide the person with a document that establishes, in the absence of proof to the contrary, that the person is a permanent resident.

(2) Stay — Where the Minister has been notified by the Appeal Division that an appeal under subsection 70(1.1) has been allowed and the Minister makes an application for leave to commence an application for judicial review, the application of subsection (1) shall be stayed until the application is disposed of and, where leave is granted, until the judicial review proceeding has been heard and disposed of and all appeals therefrom have been heard and disposed of or the time normally limited for filing such appeals has elapsed.

1992, c. 49, s. 66. [Not in force at date of publication.]

71. Appeal by minister — The Minister may appeal to the Appeal Division from a decision by an adjudicator in the course of an inquiry on any ground of appeal that involves a question of law or fact or mixed law and fact.

R.S.C. 1985, c. 28 (4th Supp.), s. 18; 1995, c. 15, s. 14.

72. (1) Reopening of inquiry — The Appeal Division may order that an inquiry that has given rise to an appeal be reopened before the adjudicator who presided at the inquiry or any other adjudicator for the receiving of any additional evidence or testimony.

(2) Minutes and adjudicator's assessment — The adjudicator who presides at an inquiry reopened under subsection (1) shall file a copy of the minutes of the reopened inquiry, together with the adjudicator's assessment of the additional evidence or testimony, with the Appeal Division for its consideration in disposing of the appeal.

R.S.C. 1985, c. 28 (4th Supp.), s. 18.

Case Law

Section 72(2)

Fleming v. Canada (Minister of Employment & Immigration) (1987), 4 Imm. L.R. (2d) 207 (Fed. C.A.) — This case was a section 28 application to review and set aside a decision of the Immigration Appeal Board. The Board had dismissed the applicant's motion requesting the Board to set aside its decision dismissing the applicant's appeal from a deportation order and re-open the appeal in order to permit the applicant to adduce further evidence in support of a plea that the Board exercise its equitable jurisdiction in the applicant's favour.

The case illustrates the difference between additional evidence and new evidence.

The party seeking to adduce additional evidence must satisfy the Board that:

1. He could not have obtained such evidence by reasonable diligence before the original hearing of the appeal; and

2. The evidence sought to be introduced is of such a nature that, if satisfactorily proved, it would furnish a sufficient reason for the reconsideration of the Court's original disposition of the appeal.

New evidence is evidence which was not in existence at the time of the hearing of the appeal. It must be examined by the Board to determine whether or not it was of sufficient weight in relation to the other evidence in the case that the Board should exercise its discretion and re-open the case.

The application was granted. The Immigration Appeal Board had failed to recognize that some of the applicant's material was new evidence as opposed to additional evidence and, accordingly, had not applied the relevant test in dismissing the applicant's application.

Fogel v. Canada (Minister of Manpower & Immigration), [1975] F.C. 121 (Fed. C.A.) — The applicant was not denied natural justice when a member of the Board that dismissed the applicant's appeal from a deportation order sat on the Board that refused to re-open the inquiry that resulted in the deportation order.

73. (1) Disposition of appeal — The Appeal Division may dispose of an appeal made pursuant to section 70

(a) by allowing it;

(b) by dismissing it;

(c) in the case of an appeal pursuant to paragraph 70(1)(*b*) or 70(3)(*b*), respecting a removal order, by directing that execution of the order be stayed; or

(d) in the case of an appeal made pursuant to paragraph 70(1)(*b*) or 70(3)(*b*) respecting a conditional removal order, by directing that execution of the order on its becoming effective be stayed.

(2) Idem — The Appeal Division may dispose of an appeal made pursuant to section 71

(a) by allowing it and making the removal order or conditional removal order that the adjudicator who was presiding at the inquiry should have made; or

(b) by dismissing it.

(3) Deemed appeal in a certain cases where appeal allowed — Where the Appeal Division disposes of an appeal made pursuant to section 71 by allowing it and making a removal order or conditional removal order against the person concerned, that person shall, where the person would have had an appeal pursuant to this Act if the order had been made by an adjudicator after an inquiry, be deemed to have made an appeal to the Appeal Division pursuant to paragraph 70(1)(*b*) or 70(3)(*b*), as the case may be.

R.S.C. 1985, c. 28 (4th Supp.), s. 18.

Case Law

Section 73(1)

Toth v. Canada (Minister of Employment & Immigration) (1988), 6 Imm. L.R. (2d) 249, 95 N.R. 60, [1989] 1 F.C. 535 (Fed. C.A.) — The appellant was ordered deported under the old *Immigration Act* (R.S.C. 1952, c. 325). Various stays of the execution of that order were in effect until June 25, 1980, when the Board cancelled the stay of the deportation order and directed that it be executed as soon as possible. On September 1, 1987, a Vice-Chairman of the Board allowed the appellant's application to review the deportation order. The appellant at the review hearing expressly declined to challenge the validity of the deportation order. The only issue was whether the Board should exercise its so-called "equitable jurisdiction" to stay once again the execution of the order. On March 29, 1988, the Board declined to order a further stay of execution of the deportation order and an appeal was taken from that decision. In the absence of a statutory power to reconsider a final order, a tribunal has no such power except:

1. Where there has been an error in drawing up the order;

2. Where there has been an error in expressing its manifest intention; or

3. Where there has been a manifest denial of natural justice in the proceeding that resulted in the order.

None of those exceptions was held to apply in the present case. Because the stay was not subsisting in 1988, the previous legislation was not held to permit the Board to reconsider the validity of the deportation order. The power to quash a deportation order must be exercised in conjunction with the cancellation of the stay and not by way of an independent reconsideration of the validity of the deportation order. There was, accordingly, no subsisting stay which would have provided a basis for jurisdiction to review the validity of the deportation order.

Baky v. Canada (Minister of Employment & Immigration) (1979), [1980] 2 F.C. 35 (Fed. C.A.) — A decision of the Immigration Appeal Board dismissing the applicant's motion to re-open his appeal was set aside because the Board stated it had never and would not exercise its jurisdiction to grant special relief owing to consequences arising from the applicant's failure to meet military obligations in his homeland. The Court held that the statement reflected a failure to exercise jurisdiction which amounted to a complete denial of jurisdiction.

Hilario v. Canada (Minister of Manpower & Immigration) (1977), [1978] 1 F.C. 697 (Fed. C.A.) — The test by which the exercise of a statutory discretion must be judged was that it was exercised *bona fide*, uninfluenced by irrelevant considerations, and not in an arbitrary or illegal manner. A Court is not entitled to interfere merely because it would have exercised the discretion differently.

Wilby v. Canada (Minister of Manpower & Immigration), [1975] F.C. 636 (Fed. C.A.) — A decision that is subject to attack as having been made without procedural fairness has continuing legal effect until, at the instance of the aggrieved party, it is found by a competent Court to be defective; in this case it may be nullified *ab initio* by judgment of the Court. Where the Board exercised power under this paragraph, there is no retroactive effect in terms of the validity of the order.

Lal v. Canada (Minister of Manpower & Immigration), [1972] F.C. 1017 (Fed. C.A.) — The Immigration Appeal Board may re-open a hearing only for the purpose of giving further consideration to granting equitable relief. Where there is an objection to the fairness of the hearing, the proper remedy is by way of an appeal from the order dismissing the appeal.

Section 73(2)

Canada (Minister of Employment & Immigration) v. Tighe (February 17, 1984), Doc. M83-1128E (Imm. App. Bd.) — The Minister appealed under section 73 of the *Immigration Act.* The adjudicator had decided that the respondent was not a person described in section 27(2)(e) of the *Immigration Act.* As a result of this finding the adjudicator did not make a removal order against the respondent or issue a departure notice to him. The respondent had claimed to be a Canadian citizen at the inquiry. This claim was not disposed of due to the adjudicator's decision that the respondent was not described in section 27(2)(e) of the Act. The Board ruled that it did not have the power to allow the Minister's appeal pursuant to section 75(2) of the Act because it could not make a removal order against the respondent. The removal order could not be made because the respondent's claim to Canadian citizenship had never been resolved in accordance with the provisions of the Act. Accordingly, the Minister's appeal was dismissed.

Cembranos-Alvarez v. Canada (Minister of Employment & Immigration) (June 6, 1983), Doc. A-267-82 (Fed. C.A.) — The Immigration Appeal Board may not allow an appeal by the Minister and issue a removal order under this subsection unless it is satisfied on the basis of the evidence before it that the adjudicator should have made such a removal order rather than issue a departure notice.

Gyali v. Canada (Minister of Employment & Immigration) (July 10, 1979), Doc. 79-9030 (Imm. App. Bd.) — The Board quashed a deportation order made January 10, 1979, and ordered the applicant deported on grounds that the Board felt had been disclosed at the inquiry. The deportation order was dated July 10, 1979. The Board felt there was evidence before the adjudicator which would have justified a removal order under section 27(1)(e) and that grounds for removal should have been included in the order made by the adjudicator. It is interesting to note that the Board exercised its jurisdiction under section 72(1)(b) and the removal order made by the Board was then quashed by the Board.

Section 73(3)

Canada (Minister of Employment & Immigration) v. De Decaro, [1993] 2 F.C. 408, 155 N.R. 129, 103 D.L.R. (4th) 564 (Fed. C.A.) — In October 1988, a visa officer issued an immigrant visa to Ignazio De Decaro. He also issued an immigrant visa to two dependants who were to accompany Mr. De Decaro, namely the respondent and her daughter. Ignazio De Decaro died before coming to Canada. The respondent did come and arrived at Dorval on July 11, 1989, accompanied by her daughter and another child, who was born in the U.S. after Ignazio De Decaro's death. This child had never obtained a visa to Canada.

The respondent then applied for landing for herself and her two children. This was denied on the ground that the respondent's admission contravened section 19(2)(d) of the *Immigration Act* because the respondent did not meet the requirements of section 9(1) of the Act.

The adjudicator found that when the respondent applied for admission to Canada, she held a valid immigrant's visa since her visa had not been revoked by the proper authorities. The adjudicator found that the respondent's husband's death did not automatically invalidate the visa. Further, the adjudicator found that there was no need to refer to section 12 of the regulations because that provision did not enact a condition of admission, consequently its infringement did not mean the respondent could not be admitted.

The Appeal Division of the IRB dismissed the Minister's appeal on the basis that the respondent, before appearing at a port-of-entry, had duly obtained an immigrant visa which had never been revoked or cancelled by the proper authorities and thus the respondent had the right to be admitted to Canada unless she was inadmissible on some other ground than the lack of a valid visa.

The Minister's appeal to the Court of Appeal was allowed. Pratte J.A. held that the definition of "accompanying dependant" illustrated that the visa issued to a person in this class was of a very special type which was issued soley to enable its holder to accompany or follow another person to Canada. The holder of such a visa who applied for admission without the other person accompanying or preceding him or her into Canada did not therefore meet the requirements of section 9(1) of the Act.

Further, after her husband's death the respondent became inadmissible by virtue of section 12 of the regulations. Her marital status had changed since she obtained her visa and in order to be admitted to Canada she had to establish not only that she was eligible, but also that she met all the conditions for obtaining a visa. The respondent never discharged this burden of proof.

Marceau J.A. agreed that the decision of the Appeal Division should be set aside. He saw no reference in the Act or regulations to visas which become invalid, are revoked or become ineffective. The technique in his view used to cover cases of changes in the immigrant's status between the time the visa is issued and the time he or she arrives at the Canadian border is contained in section 12 of the regulations. In his view, issuing an immigrant visa is not the granting of landing. Such issuance simply means that the visa officer has formed the opinion that the applicant meets the requirements of the Act and regulations for admission to Canada. The visa is evidence of a conclusion by an immigration officer whose function is to determine from outside Canada whether applicants are admissible and that conclusion will usually be accepted by his or her colleague at the port-of-entry. However, the rule is still that a foreign national arriving in Canada with a view to residing here must satisfy the immigration officer of his admissibility at the port-of-entry. Section 12 of the regulations imposes on an immigrant a duty to disclose any change in the facts which may have influenced the issuing of the visa and if there has been such a change, it requires the immigrant to meet new requirements. The visa is not void, but the visa in itself does not confer the right of entry. It is the new requirements of section 12 of the regulations that must be met.

In Marceau J.A.'s view the respondent could not establish that she met the requirements of section 12 since she was granted a visa in consideration of her husband's presence. The adjudicator accordingly was wrong to think that she met the conditions of admission set out by the regulation and the Appeal Division could not confirm the adjudicator's finding on the ground that the Minister had not discharged the burden of proving that the respondent was inadmissible or that her visa had been cancelled, as the Minister was under no burden of proof and cancellation of a visa as a concept does not exist.

Given that the Court intended to allow the appeal, it then had to consider section 73(3). The majority was of the view that the respondent before her husband's death possessed a valid visa. However, after that death it was impossible for the condition attached to the visa to be performed so that the visa ceased to have any validity. Accordingly, section 73(3) conferred no right of appeal to the Appeal Division on the respondent.

Marceau J.A. was of the view that the respondent was in possession of a valid visa and that the matter should be returned to the Appeal Division as it was still under a duty to consider whether on compassionate or humanitarian grounds the respondent should not be removed from Canada.

74. (1) Where appeal allowed — Where the Appeal Division allows an appeal made pursuant to section 70, it shall quash the removal order or conditional removal order that was made against the appellant and may

> **(a) make any other removal order or conditional removal order that should have been made; or**
>
> **(b) in the case of an appellant other than a permanent resident, direct that the appellant be examined as a person seeking admission at a port of entry.**

(2) Terms of stay of execution — Where the Appeal Division disposes of an appeal by directing that execution of a removal order or conditional removal order be stayed, the person concerned shall be allowed to come into or remain in Canada under such terms and conditions as the Appeal Division may determine and the Appeal Division shall review the case from time to time as it considers necessary or advisable.

(3) Appeal division may amend terms or cancel direction — Where the Appeal Division has disposed of an appeal by directing that execution of a removal order or conditional removal order be stayed, the Appeal Division may, at any time,

(a) amend any terms and conditions imposed under subsection (2) or impose new terms and conditions; or

(b) cancel its direction staying the execution of the order and

(i) dismiss the appeal and direct that the order be executed as soon as reasonably practicable, or

(ii) allow the appeal and take any other action that it might have taken pursuant to subsection (1).

R.S.C. 1985, c. 28 (4th Supp.), s. 18; 1992, c. 49, s. 67.

Case Law

Section 73(2)

Theobalds v. Canada (Minister of Citizenship & Immigration) (January 29, 1998), Doc. IMM-588-97 (Fed. T.D.) — The applicant sought to set aside a decision of the Appeal Division which dismissed the applicant's appeal. The applicant was ordered deported in 1984. The applicant appealed to the Board which stayed the execution of the order on October 21, 1987. The order staying the execution of deportation was extended on numerous occasions. The most recent order is dated December 17, 1993, and was signed on January 6, 1994. It indicates that the stay is extended for a period of one year and that the Board will review the matter on or about December 1994. On October 19, 1994, the Board gave notice that it proposed to review the case. On December 13, 1994, the Minister filed an application pursuant to Rule 33 for an order cancelling the stay.

The applicant submitted that the Board had no jurisdiction to consider the Rule 33 application because the stay had expired and the applicant was a permanent resident entitled to enter and remain unconditionally in Canada. The applicant's position was that the Board was *functus*.

Only the action of allowing or dismissing an appeal is a final disposition. The action of granting a stay is a temporary measure. It is for the Board to decide whether to allow or dismiss the appeal. The appellant cannot acquire an unconditional right to remain in Canada in the context of this case, absent an order of the Board.

Eltassi v. Canada (Minister of Employment & Immigration), 9 Imm. L.R. (2d) 96, [1989] 3 F.C. 444, 30 F.T.R. 91 (Fed. T.D.) — In January 1987, the Immigration Appeal Board stayed the execution of a removal order against the applicant. The Minister ultimately applied to the Board for an order dismissing the applicant's appeal and directing that the removal order against him be executed. At the hearing of that motion, counsel for the applicant objected to the fact that the Board, in considering that application, was different than the panel which directed that the removal order be stayed. The applicant argued that he was entitled, on a review of his case, to the same Board panel that originally heard his appeal. This argument was rejected. The appropriate body to consider any review of the 1987 order is the Immigration Appeal Division. The original panel does not remain seized of the matter after ordering that the removal order be stayed.

Canada (Minister of Employment & Immigration) v. Lewis (1988), 4 Imm. L.R. (2d) 31, 87 N.R. 192 (Fed. C.A.) — The respondent Lewis, a United States citizen, was admitted to Canada as a permanent resident in 1981, and ordered deported in 1983. On his appeal, the Immigration Appeal Board stayed the execution of the removal order until February 20, 1989. By an application, dated February 26, 1986, the Minister sought an order dismissing the appeal and directing that the removal be executed as soon as reasonably practicable.

The Board correctly appreciated that the process requires that successive decisions must be made. Firstly, the Board must decide whether a review under section 76(2) of the Act is advisable. If it decides a review is not advisable, that is the end of the process. If a review is advisable, the Board must decide which, if any, of the actions authorized by section 76(3) are appropriate.

The decision to initiate the process was entirely within the Board's discretion. There was no error for the Board to limit the evidence it would accept from an application for review to that submitted in a timely fashion. It is obvious that a myriad of circumstances, not contemplated in a stay order, could arise that would impel the Board in a proper exercise of its discretion to review a case and vacate a stay. Further, the Board did not err in refusing to consider a circumstance that was in existence at the time the stay was originally imposed. The finding by the Board was that the warrant, in this case, could, with reasonable diligence, have been brought into evidence at the original hearing. Further, the Board found that the existence of the warrant had been the subject of extensive press comment, and yet the Minister had made no effort to obtain evidence of the warrant prior to the initial hearing. Thus, the Board was within its jurisdiction in refusing to consider it.

Kumar v. Canada (Minister of Employment & Immigration) (November 29, 1984), Doc. A-1533-83 (Fed. C.A.) — The Board is entitled to exercise its discretion by refusing the adjournment of the hearing sought by the appellant pending disposition of outstanding criminal charges, and to proceed with the review. If it does so, the existence of the charges ought not to play any part in the decision to grant, or not grant, the extension of the stay being asked for. Where it is doubtful that the existence of the criminal charges was ignored, the decision of the Board will be set aside and the matter referred back to the Board for a rehearing.

Section 73(3)

Eltassi v. Canada (Minister of Employment & Immigration), 9 Imm. L.R. (2d) 96, [1989] 3 F.C. 444, 30 F.T.R. 91 (Fed. T.D.) — For digest, see section 74, subheading *Subsection (2), supra.*

Canada (Minister of Employment & Immigration) v. Lewis (1988), 4 Imm. L.R. (2d) 31, 87 N.R. 192 (Fed. C.A.) — For digest, see section 74, subheading *Subsection (2), supra.*

75. Return to Canada for hearing of appeal — Where a person against whom a removal order or conditional removal order has been made is removed from or otherwise leaves Canada and informs the Appeal Division in writing of his desire to appear in person before the Appeal Division on the hearing of the appeal against the order, the Appeal Division may, if an appeal has been made, allow the person to return to Canada for that purpose under such terms and conditions as it may determine.

R.S.C. 1985, c. 28 (4th Supp.), s. 18.

76. Appeal declared abandoned — Where a person against whom a removal order or conditional removal order has been made files an appeal against that order with the Appeal Division but fails to communicate with the Appeal Division upon being requested to do so or fails to inform the Appeal Division of the person's most recent address, the Appeal Division may declare the appeal to be abandoned.

R.S.C. 1985, c. 28 (4th Supp.), s. 18.

Appeals by Sponsors

77. (1) **Where sponsored applications for landing may be refused — Where a person has sponsored an application for landing made by a member of the family class, an immigration officer or a visa officer, as the case may be, may refuse to approve the application on the grounds that**

> **(a) the person who sponsored the application does not meet the requirements of the regulations respecting persons who sponsor applications for landing, or**
>
> **(b) the member of the family class does not meet the requirements of this Act or the regulations,**

and the person who sponsored the application shall be informed of the reasons for the refusal.

(2) **Sponsor to be informed — Notwithstanding subsection (1), where an application for landing made by a member of the family class is refused on the grounds that the member of the family class is a person described in any of paragraphs 19(1)(*c*.1) to (*g*), (*k*) and (*l*), the person who sponsored the application shall be informed of those grounds but not of the reasons on which those grounds are based.**

(3) **Appeals by sponsors — Subject to subsections (3.01) and (3.1), a Canadian citizen or permanent resident who has sponsored an application for landing that is refused pursuant to subsection (1) may appeal to the Appeal Division on either or both of the following grounds:**

> **(a) on any ground of appeal that involves a question of law or fact, or mixed law and fact; and**
>
> **(b) on the ground that there exist compassionate or humanitarian considerations that warrant the granting of special relief.**

(3.01) **Limitation — No appeal lies to the Appeal Division under subsection (3) in respect of a person**

> **(a) with respect to whom a certificate has been filed under subsection 40.1(1) where it has been determined, pursuant to paragraph 40.1(4)(*d*), that the certificate is reasonable; or**
>
> **(b) who is a member of an inadmissible class described in paragraph 19(1)(*c*), (*c*.1), (*c*.2) or (*d*) where the Minister is of the opinion that the person constitutes a danger to the public in Canada.**

[Note: 1995, c. 15, s. 15(3) provides that subsection 77(3.01) of the Act, as enacted by subsection (2), applied to an appeal that has been made on or before the coming into force of that subsection and in respect of which the hearing has not been commenced, but a person who has made such an appeal may, within fifteen days after the person has been notified that, in the opinion of the Minister, the person constitutes a danger to the public in Canada, make an application for judicial review under section 82.1 of the Act with respect to the matter that was the subject of the decision made under subsection 77(1). This provision was contained in Bill C-44 which was proclaimed into law on July 10, 1995. We have it here for ease of reference.]

(3.1) **Exception — No appeal lies to the Appeal Division under subsection (3) on any grounds referred to in paragraph (3)(*a*) where the Canadian citizen or permanent resident who has sponsored the application for landing that is refused pursuant to subsec-**

tion (1) resides in a province that has entered into an agreement pursuant to section 108 whereby the province has sole responsibility for establishing and applying financial criteria in relation to sponsors if

(a) the refusal is based on the rejection of the person's application for sponsorship by an official of that province on the grounds that the person failed to meet those criteria or failed to comply with any prior undertaking concerning the sponsorship of any application for landing; and

(b) the laws of that province provide the person with a right to appeal the rejection of the person's application for sponsorship.

(3.2) **Information obtained in confidence** — With respect to any appeal referred to in subsection (3),

(a) the Minister may make an application to the Federal Court — Trial Division, *in camera*, and in the absence of the appellant and any counsel representing the appellant, for the non-disclosure to the appellant of information obtained in confidence from the government or an institution of a foreign state or from an international organization of states or an institution thereof;

(b) the Court shall, *in camera*, and in the absence of the appellant and any counsel representing the appellant,

(i) examine the information, and

(ii) provide counsel representing the Minister with a reasonable opportunity to be heard as to whether the information should not be disclosed to the appellant on the grounds that the disclosure would be injurious to national security or to the safety of persons;

(c) the information shall be returned to counsel representing the Minister and shall not be considered by the Appeal Division in making its determination on the appeal if, in the opinion of the Court, the disclosure of the information to the appellant would not be injurious to national security or to the safety of persons; and

(d) if the Court determines that the information should not be disclosed to the appellant on the grounds that the disclosure would be injurious to national security or to the safety of persons, the information shall not be disclosed but may be considered by the Appeal Division in making its determination.

(3.3) **Delay of appeal** — Where an application referred to in paragraph (3.2)(*a*) is made, the appeal to which the application relates shall not be commenced or, if commenced, shall be adjourned, until the Federal Court — Trial Division has made a determination of the application.

(4) **Disposition by appeal division** — The Appeal Division may dispose of an appeal made pursuant to subsection (3) by allowing it or by dismissing it, and shall notify the Minister and the person who made the appeal of its decision and the reasons therefor.

(5) **Where appeal allowed** — Subject to subsection (6), where the Minister has been notified by the Appeal Division that an appeal has been allowed pursuant to subsection (4), the Minister shall cause the review of the application to be resumed by an immigration officer or a visa officer, as the case may be, and the application shall be approved where it is determined that the person who sponsored the application and the

member of the family class meet the requirements of this Act and the regulations, other than those requirements on which the decision of the Appeal Division has been given.

(6) Stay — Where the Minister has been notified by the Appeal Division that an appeal has been allowed pursuant to subsection (4) and the Minister makes an application for leave to commence an application for judicial review in respect of that decision, the application of subsection (5) shall be stayed until the application is disposed of and, where leave is granted, until the judicial review proceeding has been heard and disposed of and all appeals therefrom have been heard and disposed of or the time normally limited for filing such appeals has elapsed.

R.S.C. 1985, c. 10 (2nd Supp.), s. 6; R.S.C. 1985, c. 28 (4th Supp.), s. 33; 1992, c. 49, s. 68; 1995, c. 15, s. 15; 1999, c. 31, s. 134.

Case Law

Section 77(1)

Nagy v. Canada (Minister of Employment & Immigration) (March 11, 1994), Doc. IMM-1375-93 (Fed. T.D.) — The applicant sought to review a decision holding that there were insufficient humanitarian and compassionate grounds for allowing an application for permanent residence within Canada. The immigration officer did not give reasons for refusing to recommend that the Minister exercise his discretion under section 114(2). The case law has been consistent and clear to the effect that reasons are not required in this context. Section 77 only requires reasons to be given to a person who sponsors a family member's application for permanent residence where that application is refused. The matter, in this case, had nothing to do with Luis Nagy, the applicant's sponsor, since he was not part of the section 114(2) application and therefore no reasons were required.

Lidder v. Canada (Minister of Employment & Immigration) (1992), 136 N.R. 254 (Fed. C.A.) — The respondent promised his dying sister that he would take care of her children upon her death, which occurred in 1982. He submitted an undertaking of assistance (family class) to sponsor his now orphaned nephew. At the time the respondent submitted his undertaking of assistance the nephew was 17 years of age. By the time the nephew received the application for permanent residence from the Canadian High Commission in Delhi, the nephew was already 18 years of age. The respondent was informed that the nephew's application was refused due to the fact that he was 18 years of age when his application was received.

The Court noted that there are four kinds of estoppel available: estoppel by matter of record, estoppel by deed, estoppel by representation and promissory estoppel. The branch of estoppel at issue in this case was estoppel by representation. In order for the doctrine of estoppel by representation to apply there must be the following elements:

1. a representation of fact made with the intention that it be acted upon or that a reasonable person would assume was intended to be acted upon;

2. the representee must act upon the representation; and

3. the representee must have altered his position in reliance upon the representation and thereby suffered a prejudice.

Neither the doctrine of estoppel nor the related doctrine of reasonable or legitimate expectation creates a substantive right. They are part of the rules of procedural fairness which govern administrative bodies. A public authority may be bound by its undertakings as to the procedure it will follow, but in no case can those undertakings cause the public authority to forego the requirements of the law. The effective date of a sponsored application is the date of the filing of the application itself. At that point in time the nephew was over the age of 18 years and could not be sponsored as a member of the family class. Accordingly, the respondent had not sponsored an undertaking by a member of the family class and could not appeal to what was then the Immigration Appeal Board, and thus the Board was without jurisdiction to hear and in this case allow the respondent's appeal. Accordingly, the decision of the Board was quashed. Costs were awarded against the Crown on a solicitor and client basis.

McKay v. Canada (Minister of Employment & Immigration) (1988), 5 Imm. L.R. (2d) 287 (Imm. App. Bd.) — The appellant appealed the refusal to approve the sponsored application of his mother, her daughter and her son. The basis of the refusal was that the mother had no intention to come to Canada as a permanent resident, but was merely applying to facilitate the admission to Canada of her children. At the time of the interview of the mother, she affixed her mark on an application for permanent residence. On the same date, she affixed her mark to a statutory declaration that was inconsistent with the application for permanent residence. There was nothing to indicate that the visa officer had attempted to resolve the apparent contradiction between the two documents before making a decision. Furthermore, the appellant, who was also interviewed by immigration authorities, was not given an opportunity to explain the two documents. Thus, the refusal was held to be not valid in law. The mother was found to have an intention to reside permanently in Canada.

Sashi v. Canada (Minister of Employment & Immigration) (1987), 3 Imm. L.R. (2d) 288 (Fed. T.D.) — The applicant sought to quash a decision of a visa officer in India refusing sponsorship applications for the applicant's mother and his adopted daughter. The visa officer refused to accept the sponsorship of the daughter because, as a result of his inquiries, he concluded that the provisions of the *Hindu Adoptions and Maintenance Act* had not been complied with. It was held that a visa officer has not only a right but a duty to ensure that all immigrants meet the requirements of the Act and Regulation. In this case, that included making certain that the sponsored child had been legally adopted within the meaning of section 2(1) of the Regulation. The officer's decision was not reached improperly or without justification. The officer did reach a conclusion that involved an interpretation of Hindu law, and he ought to have afforded the applicant some opportunity for counter-argument. However, the relief sought in this case, *i.e.*, *certiorari* and *mandamus*, was discretionary, and in all the circumstances the motion was dismissed.

Pangli v. Canada (Minister of Employment & Immigration) (1987), 4 Imm. L.R. (2d) 266, 81 N.R. 216 (Fed. C.A.) — This was an appeal with leave from a decision of the Immigration Appeal Board dismissing the appellant's appeal from the refusal of the Minister to approve the application for landing of the appellant's father, mother, and two brothers. The basis of the refusal was a statutory declaration from the appellant's father indicating an intention to go to Canada to visit for one year. This statutory declaration was contradicted by the application for permanent residence also completed by the appellant's father. The appeal was allowed. In cases where the written record is not decisive but rather is ambiguous, officers charged with making a section 79(1) determination ought to take steps to resolve the conflict and ambiguity. In this case, a further questioning of the appellant's father with a view to affording him the opportunity to state finally and unequivocally what his intention was, was required. Absent any evidence that such a course of action was pursued, the determination, pursuant to section 79(1), could not be allowed to stand. The Court did not comment on whether a person could hold primary and secondary intentions with respect to coming to Canada.

Canada (Minister of Employment & Immigration) v. Singh (P.) (1987), 2 Imm. L.R. (2d) 44 (Fed. C.A.) — This was an appeal to the Federal Court of Appeal from a decision of the

Immigration Appeal Board allowing the respondent Pal Singh's appeal from the refusal by an immigration officer to approve the application for landing made by the wife and children of the respondent.

The Immigration Appeal Board, from whose decision this appeal was taken, had held that the letter of refusal had not properly informed the respondent of the reasons for such refusal. The Board considered the refusal letter by itself and in complete isolation from the evidence contained in the record and, therefore, erred in law in concluding that the refusal letter was not adequate.

The reasons were formulated in the language of the regulation but were readily intelligible and sufficient for the immediate purpose of allowing the sponsor to determine whether to appeal. Further, the reasons were adequate enough to allow the sponsor, soon after receiving them, to appeal the immigration officer's decision promptly. The Board, at the conclusion of the hearing, remained unconvinced that Pal Singh was married to the woman who claimed to be his wife and that her offspring were his own children. This is the same basis upon which the letter of refusal had been issued. Further, the Board's decision did not say in what respect the letter of refusal was defective; and, further, in assessing the validity of the immigration officer's decision, the Board was entitled to consider an inter-departmental memorandum, which the officer had prepared and which more fully expounded his reasons for refusal.

The appeal was allowed, the decision of the Immigration Appeal Board was set aside and the decision of the immigration officer refusing the application was held to have been made in accordance with the law.

Reyes de Jesus v. Canada (Minister of Employment & Immigration) (1987), 1 Imm. L.R. (2d) 217 (Imm. App. Bd.) — This was an appeal from the refusal of a sponsored application for landing. The appellant was seeking to sponsor his mother. The application was refused on the basis that the mother had not satisfied the immigration officer that she complied with the definition of "immigrant" given in section 2(1) of the *Immigration Act*. This decision was based upon previous statutory declarations, which the mother had filed when she was seeking visitor's visas to come to Canada. These declarations denied an intention to reside permanently in Canada. This was found to be unfair because the declarations from the previous applications, upon which the officer relied, were not raised with the mother when she was interviewed. The Board found that it was the interviewing officer's duty to consider the mother's intention at the time of the interview and to allow her to explain the previous declarations. The Board also suggested that it would be sufficient if the mother's intention to reside permanently in Canada was formulated after the interview, which resulted in her application being rejected, but before the hearing of the sponsor's appeal.

Vadsaria v. Canada (Secretary of State for External Affairs) (1986), 7 F.T.R. 299 (Fed. T.D.) — The initial application of Mumtaz Vadsaria to sponsor her mother and her sisters was refused because the evidence submitted to prove the relationship was found to be false. The applicant appealed to the Immigration Appeal Board, which found that, in fact, one of the sponsorees, Dhaulat Bhimani, was the mother of the applicant. This decision was binding upon the respondents, and there was, therefore, no longer any determination to be made or any proof to be required of that relationship. The respondent, however, was still free to consider whether there was evidence that the persons included as sisters in the application were proven to be such. The actions of the respondents in withholding such a finding, until acceptable proof was put forward, was in accordance with the Act and regulations and not subject of an order in the nature of *mandamus* as set out in section 18 of the *Federal Court Act*.

Mundi v. Canada (Minister of Employment & Immigration) (1985), 63 N.R. 310 (Fed. C.A.) — This appeal arose from the refusal of a visa officer to approve the application of the appellant's father, Ajmer Singh Mundi, for the landing of himself, his wife, his son,

Balwinder, and two daughters. The application had been sponsored by the appellant who was at all material times a Canadian citizen. Ajmer Singh Mundi forwarded a false school leaving certificate for the purpose of establishing the date of birth of Balwinder Singh and to prove that Balwinder was under 21 years of age at the time of the application. The failure to satisfy the visa officer, with respect to Balwinder's age by means of this false school leaving certificate, did not affect the admissibility of Ajmer Singh, his wife and daughters because the false certificate, respecting Balwinder's age, was not relevant to the admissibility of the other family members. Section 9(3) was not a basis for refusing Ajmer Singh and the other family members because the false certificate was relevant only to Balwinder's admissibility as a dependant and had no bearing on whether the admission of the applicant and the rest of the family was contrary to the Act or regulations. Further, section 79(1) did not allow the visa officer to refuse the application of the entire family simply because Balwinder was not a dependant and, therefore, not entitled to a visa. The application could only be refused in total if Ajmer Singh, who made the application, did not meet the requirements of the Act or Regulations.

Owens v. Canada (Minister of Manpower & Immigration) (March 27, 1984), Doc. A-615-83 (Fed. C.A.) — The sponsoree filed an application for permanent residence on February 22, 1981. At that time the sponsoree was not free to marry the sponsor because his divorce was not final. The sponsoree signed the application on May 19, 1981, at which time he swore before an official of the Government of Canada that the contents of his application were true. On this date the sponsoree was free to marry.

The application was refused. The respondent had taken the view that the relevant date was February 22, 1981, the date of the filing of the application. The Immigration Appeal Board agreed with the respondent; however, the Federal Court of Appeal allowed the appeal and set aside the Board's decision because it decided that the relevant date was May 19, 1981, the date the sponsoree swore to the truth of the facts contained in the application.

Grewal v. Canada (Minister of Employment & Immigration) (January 18, 1984), Doc. V82-6005 (Imm. App. Bd.) — This was a sponsorship appeal from the refusal to accept the application for permanent residence of the father of the sponsor and his accompanying dependant. It was possible to establish the relationship of the father, the mother and one brother of the sponsor. It was not possible to establish the relationship of another young man and woman who were alleged to be a brother and a sister of this sponsor. A majority of the Board was of the opinion that entry should be denied only to those not proven eligible and that the father, the mother and brother whose relationship to the sponsor was established should be permitted to come to Canada. The minority would have disallowed the application of all parties because other alleged dependants were inadmissible under the regulations.

Canada (Minister of Employment & Immigration) v. Bechan (May 18, 1983), Doc. A812-82 (Fed. C.A.) — Bechan sponsored an application for landing by a member of the family class. The application was refused on the basis that the applicant for landing was a person described in section 19(1)(h). The Federal Court of Appeal upheld the Immigration Appeal Board's decision allowing the appeal on the basis that section 19(1)(h) referred only to immigrants at a point of entry. The applicant had made her application for landing at Port of Spain, Trinidad and, accordingly, the basis for the rejection of her application was invalid. Therefore, the Minister's appeal from the Immigration Appeal Board's decision was dismissed. The Court noted that the sponsor is entitled to be accurately informed of the grounds for the rejection of the application for permanent residence so that proper preparation of the appeal permitted by this Act could be effected.

Bala v. Canada (Minister of Employment & Immigration) (January 11, 1983), Doc. T81-9204 (Imm. App. Bd.) — The sponsor appealed the refusal of the Minister to approve the application for permanent residence of his parents, his brother and his sister. The basis of the refusal was the lack of proper or satisfactory evidence with respect to the age of the brother and sister. The Board received and accepted the evidence of a professor of radiology at the Faculty of Medicine at the University of Toronto when he gave evidence of the age of these two children and accepted and concluded that they were under the age of 21 years at the time the application for permanent residence was filed. Accordingly, the sponsor's appeal was allowed.

Tse v. Canada (Minister of Employment & Immigration) (1983), 45 N.R. 252 (Fed. C.A.) — The Court made reference to the law of Hong Kong which legitimized the status of a concubine lawfully taken before October 7, 1971; the three children whom the appellant wished to sponsor were thus designated issue of a marriage for purposes of the Act and regulations. The Court first determined the domicile of the appellant, because legitimacy must be determined in accordance with the law of that province. The law of Ontario at the time of the sponsorship application had eliminated the concept of illegitimacy and made every child legitimate as of the date of its birth.

O'Grady v. Whyte (1982), 42 N.R. 608 (Fed. C.A.) — There is no duty on immigration officials to make a decision on a sponsorship application when an application for landing has not been made.

Mauger v. Canada (Minister of Employment & Immigration) (1979), 109 D.L.R. (3d) 246 (Fed. T.D.) — The Court reaffirmed its view that a spouse had a right to withdraw a sponsorship application and disapproved of the proposition that public policy should forbid the withdrawal of sponsorship applications.

Canada (Minister of Manpower & Immigration) v. Tsiafakis, [1977] 2 F.C. 216 (Fed. C.A.) — The right to sponsor is not a preliminary question. A person who seeks to sponsor someone for admission to Canada has a right to make an application in the prescribed form and to have his right to sponsor determined on the basis of that application. Accordingly, an immigration officer has a duty to supply the prescribed form to an applicant and, on his failure to do so, *mandamus* will issue.

Section 77(3)

Kaloti v. Canada (Minister of Citizenship & Immigration) (1998), 153 F.T.R. 289 (Fed. T.D.) — The applicant moved against the decision of the Appeal Division dismissing his appeal on the grounds that it was *res judicata*. On August 26, 1990, the applicant filed an undertaking of assistance to sponsor the application of his fiancée. On May 28, 1993, a visa officer refused this application pursuant to subsection 4(3) of the Regulations, on the ground that the marriage was not *bona fide*. The applicant appealed to the Appeal Division which confirmed the decision of the visa officer and dismissed the appeal for lack of jurisdiction because the applicant's spouse was not a member of the family class under subsection 4(3) of the Regulations. In 1996, the applicant re-sponsored a new application for permanent residence for his wife which was denied by the visa officer, that decision lead to the Appeal Division's second decision which is the one under attack.

Paragraph 4(3) of the Regulations cannot be a "forward-looking test". The test is whether or not the spouse in question "entered into the marriage primarily for the purpose of gaining admission to Canada . . . and not with the intention of residing permanently with the other spouse". Clearly both criteria apply to the intention of the spouse at the time of the marriage, thus the matter became *res judicata* and the Appeal Division could not hear it a second time.

Res judicata has an application in public law, otherwise applicants could reapply with the same application and abuse the process of administrative tribunals. The doctrine would not prevent an applicant from launching a second application based on changed circumstances provided, of course, that the change of circumstances was relevant to the matter to be decided.

Chow v. Canada (Minister of Citizenship & Immigration) (1998), 45 Imm. L.R. (2d) 170, 153 F.T.R. 236 (Fed. T.D.) — This was an appeal from a decision by the Immigration Appeal Division that it did not have jurisdiction to hear the applicant's appeal because there had been no refusal of an application for landing by a member of the applicant's family class. The family class includes parents of a sponsor but not siblings unless the sibling is an orphan who is under 19 years of age and is unmarried. A parent who is sponsored may bring accompany dependants and these may include the sponsor siblings. The applicant's father applied to do so in this case. He sought to add his son and his daughter to his and his wife's application, an application sponsored by the applicant. The son was not granted a visa. The applicant appealed to the Immigration Appeal Division. The Appeal Division does not have jurisdiction to hear the appeal because the son is not a member of the applicant's family class. The procedure that should be followed is to challenge the non-inclusion of the son in the landing application in a judicial review application to the Federal Court, not an appeal to the Immigration Appeal Division.

Sandhu v. Canada (Minister of Citizenship & Immigration) (1998), 45 Imm. L.R. (2d) 90, 150 F.T.R. 310 (Fed. T.D.) — The applicant sought to review a decision of a visa officer that the applicant's father and three of his brothers who had been included in the father's sponsored application for landing were not dependant sons and therefore, would have to be deleted from the application if it was to be further processed.

In March 1992, the applicant had filled an undertaking of assistance sponsoring his father, mother, three brothers and a sister. The applicant's father filed a family class application and this application was refused in June 1993. On appeal, the Appeal Division of the IRB reversed the refusal, and consideration of the family class application was resumed. On this application, the applicant objected to the "piece meal" manner of dealing with the father's family class application, which had stretched over a period of five years. It would have been preferable if the visa officer had considered all aspects of the family class application, so that the applicant and his family members would have had all the information before them on which to make an informed decision as to the appropriate course of action. In the absence of such information the applicant had appealed the original rejection of his sponsorship only later to find out, after incurring significant expense and after significant delay, that his three brothers would not be able to join him in Canada in any event. There was, however, no obligation in law for the visa officer to behave in this way. Where a decision of a visa officer denying an application for landing, on the basis that the sponsor does not meet the requirements of the Immigration Regulations respecting sponsors, is overturned by the Appeal Division, the only issue that is *res judicata* is the conformity of the sponsor. Whether the persons covered by the family class application meet the requirements of the *Immigration Act* and related regulations remains open for assessment.

Dosanjh v. Canada (Minister of Citizenship & Immigration) (1997), 41 Imm. L.R. (2d) 204 (Imm. & Ref. Bd. (App. Div.)) — The Minister moved by way of a preliminary motion to dismiss the appeal for lack of jurisdiction. In October 1994, the appellant filed an undertaking of assistance to sponsor her father, her mother and her brother as permanent residents. In March 1995, the principal applicant filed his application for permanent residence naming his wife and son as his dependants. The principal applicant received a letter in November 1995, indicating that a visa officer had determined that the applicant's brother was not a dependant son. Neither the appellant, nor the principal applicant heard anything further from the visa office with the result that the appellant filed a notice of appeal in January 1996.

The decision of the visa officer to cease processing is not an implied or constructive refusal of the application. Further, the Appeal Division does not have jurisdiction to compel the visa office to continue processing. What is required is an order in the nature *mandamus* which is within the exclusive jurisdiction of the Federal Court. Accordingly, the Minister's motion was allowed and the appeal dismissed for lack of jurisdiction.

Canada (Minister of Citizenship & Immigration) v. Gill (1997), 137 F.T.R. 237 (Fed. T.D.); affirmed (1999), 240 N.R. 194 (Fed. C.A.) — The respondent and her husband executed an undertaking of assistance as the sponsors for landing of the husband's adopted daughter. An application for permanent residence was submitted on behalf of the daughter and shortly thereafter the respondent's husband withdrew his sponsorship resulting in the refusal of the application. The respondent appealed that refusal to the Appeal Division of IRB.

There is no provision in the *Immigration Act* and regulations that directly contemplates joint sponsorship, nor is there any provision negativing such a possibility. The applicant Minister's inland processing policy manuals specifically contemplates the possibility of joint sponsors. Accordingly, the Court concluded that the decision of the Appeal Division that the respondent was a joint sponsor and therefore entitled to appeal was upheld and the application for judicial review dismissed.

Dimacali-Victoria v. Canada (Minister of Citizenship & Immigration) (August 29, 1997), Doc. IMM- 3323-96 (Fed. T.D.) — The applicant sought to review a decision of the Immigration Appeal Division wherein the Appeal Division dismissed an appeal made pursuant to section 77(3)(b).

The determination of the IAD under paragraph 77(3)(b) is wholly a matter of judgment and discretion and the law gives, to persons such as the applicant, no right to any particular outcome. The IAD was found to have made no reviewable error. It exercised its discretion in accordance with well established legal principles, that is to say, in a *bona fide* manner uninfluenced by irrelevant considerations and not arbitrarily or illegally. Accordingly, the application in this case was dismissed.

Canada (Minister of Citizenship & Immigration) v. Subala (1997), 134 F.T.R. 298 (Fed. T.D.) — The Minister sought to review a decision of the Appeal Division of the IRB, which allowed an appeal from a decision of a visa officer refusing an application for landing based on family class. The respondent sponsored an application for landing by a person who was not, when the visa officers decision was made, an adopted son of the respondent. Due to the fact that a condition precedent for the granting of landing was absent, the visa officer was obliged to refuse the application as it was not made under section 77(1), *i.e.*, not made by a member of a family class. Because the applicant for landing was not a member of the family class, the appeal did not come within section 77 of the *Immigration Act* and the Appeal Division did not have jurisdiction to consider it.

The judicial review application was allowed and the decision of the Appeal Division was set aside.

Khan v. Canada (Minister of Citizenship & Immigration) (1997), 43 Imm. L.R. (2d) 101 (Imm. & Ref. Bd. (App. Div.)) — The appellant appeals the refusal of her sponsored application for landing of her husband on the grounds that their marriage was a "marriage of convenience".

This appeal raised a preliminary matter of *res judicata*. The appellant had attempted to sponsor her husband in 1991. The application had been refused in 1992 and an appeal from that refusal had been dismissed in 1994. The issue in the previous proceeding was the appellant's and her husband's intention at the time the marriage was entered into. In dismissing the appeal in 1994, the Appeal Division upheld the visa officer's decision that the applicant had entered into the marriage for the purpose of gaining admission into Canada as a member of the family class and not with the intention of residing permanently with the appellant. Thus, the issue of the appellant's and the applicant's intention at the time of the marriage was determined in the previous proceeding.

The Court found that the principal of *res judicata* applied and dismissed the appellant's appeal.

Kirpal v. Canada (Minister of Citizenship & Immigration) (1996), 35 Imm. L.R. (2d) 229, [1997] 1 F.C. 352, 121 F.T.R. 229 (Fed. T.D.) — The applicant's father, mother and brother arrived in Canada in 1987. They entered as visitors and their status expired in 1988. In November 1990, the applicant gave an undertaking of assistance and the three applicants applied to be exempted from subsection 9(1) of the Act. Eventually, the three were exempted from subsection 9(1) and subsequent to that determination the applicant's father was found to be medically inadmissible.

Subsection 77(1) clearly contemplates the refusal of an application for landing that is formulated in Canada with respect to persons who fit the concept of "member of the family class". Accordingly, the Appeal Division made no reviewable error in concluding that it had jurisdiction under subsection 77(3) of the Act to entertain the appeal.

On the question of whether there were compassionate or humanitarian considerations that warrant the granting of special relief the tribunal identified a range of such considerations. Against those it weighed the countervailing considerations, mainly the legal impediment arising from the applicant's father's failing health. The tribunal was found to have erred in engaging in this weighing process. In addition, the tribunal failed to consider whether or not compassionate or humanitarian considerations could be found to apply with respect to the applicant's mother and brother, whether or not the granting of special relief in favour of the father could be found to be warranted.

Parmar v. Canada (Minister of Citizenship & Immigration) (1996), 38 Imm. L.R. (2d) 316 (Imm. & Ref. Bd. (App. Div.)) — This was a preliminary motion by the applicant, the Minister of Citizenship and Immigration, to have the respondent Tarsem Singh Parmar's appeal dismissed for lack of jurisdiction. The respondent, Parmar, had filed an undertaking of assistance seeking to bring his father, mother and three sisters to Canada. Two of his three sisters were refused on the basis that they were not enrolled and in full time attendance at a educational institution since attaining the age of 19 years and therefore were not dependant daughters within the meaning of the immigration regulations. Medical instructions were issued for the father, mother and one sister who were found to be members of the family class.

An application for permanent residence can be split and the ineligibility of an alleged accompanying dependant of a member of the family class is not a bar to the admission of the member of the family class and other admissible accompanying dependants. The visa officer has a positive duty to issue visas to the applicants who are both eligible and admissible. When the splitting of such an application has occurred and the members of the family class have been issued visas there is no right of appeal to the Appeal Division in respect of the ineligible applicants who are claimed to be accompanying dependants as there has been no refusal of an application for landing by a member of the family class.

Muia v. Canada (Minister of Citizenship & Immigration) (1996), 113 F.T.R. 234 (Fed. T.D.) — On July 25, 1991, the applicant sought permanent resident status by way of an application sponsored by his wife. On November 19, 1991, the applicant requested that the Governor-in-Counsel facilitate his admission by exempting him from subsection 9(1) of the Act. An immigration officer allowed that request. On December 16, 1994, while the applicant's application was in process, the applicant was convicted of conspiracy to traffic and was sentenced to seven years in prison.

An inquiry was convoked and it was determined that the applicant was described in paragraphs 19(1)(c) of the Act and the applicant was ordered deported.

The Minister never gave a decsion with respect to the application for permanent residence and thus the sponsor had no opportunity to appeal the refusal of the application.

The Court dismissed the motion to quash the deportation order, but did issue an order in the nature of *mandamus* requiring the Minister to give a decision with respect to the application for permanent residence.

Pathak v. Canada (Secretary of State) (1995), 93 F.T.R. 74 (Fed. T.D.) — This was an application for judicial review of a decision of the Appeal Division of the IRB by which it determined that it did not have jurisdiction to hear the applicant's appeal pursuant to section 77(3).

The applicant was a permanent resident of Canada. The applicant's spouse was a citizen of India. The applicant requested an exemption on humanitarian and compassionate grounds. The application was refused. The applicant then appealed the refusal.

The Appeal Division did not err in dismissing the applicant's appeal for lack of jurisdiction. The only right of review of the decision made by the senior Immigration Officer that there were insufficient humanitarian and compassionate grounds to warrant processing from within Canada, was an application for leave and for judicial review filed with the Federal Court. Recent changes in the definition of landing did not give the Appeal Division jurisdiction to hear the matter.

Litt v. Canada (Minister of Citizenship & Immigration) (1995), 26 Imm. L.R. (2d) 153 (Fed. T.D.) — A visa officer refused admission to the applicant's father because two medical officers had formed the opinion that the father was suffering from quadriparesis, upper and lower motor neuron type. This decision was appealed to the Immigration and Refugee Board which found that the refusal was valid in law. The medical notification stated "should family support fail, he would place considerable demands on social services".

The evidence was that three family members were committed to supporting the father. There was not sufficient evidence to lead the medical officer to speculate that family support might fail. The speculation about the potential failure of family support was not based on the evidence. Further, there was an insufficient linkage between the evidence of the applicant's father's medical condition and the issue of whether the applicant's father might reasonably be expected to cause excessive demands on health or social services. The issue before the visa officer and the Appeal Division was the question of excessive demands on health or social services. It was not the father's medical condition. A medical condition itself is not necessarily evidence of a reasonable expectation of excessive demand on health or social services. This is not to say that there could not be a medical condition that, obviously, would lead to such a conclusion, but rather that such a conclusion was not obvious in this case. The decision of the visa officer was quashed.

Canada (Solicitor General) v. Bisla (1994), 88 F.T.R. 312 — The applicant Minister, sought judicial review of a decision of the Appeal Division. The respondent was a citizen of India who had obtained permanent residence in Canada and then married the sponsored applicant. The visa officer refused to approve the application on the grounds that the marriage was one of convenience. The husband, and the sponsored applicant's cousin, expressed their own opinion regarding the sponsored applicant's intention of residing with her husband. The Appeal Board accepted their opinions without examining the actual intention of the wife. It was the sponsored applicant's responsibility to prove that she had the intention of residing permanently with her husband. It was not sufficient to find what her husband, or her cousin, believed was her intention.

Finally, the Court noted that answers given on the issue of the entering into a marriage, primarily for the purpose of gaining admission to Canada, could also be relevant to the assessment of the intention of residing permanently with the sponsoring spouse.

Atwal v. Canada (Secretary of State) (1994), 25 Imm. L.R. (2d) 80, 82 F.T.R. 73 — The applicant sought to review a decision of the Appeal Division of the Immigration and Refugee Board affirming the refusal of the application for landing sponsored by the applicant for his father, mother and three brothers.

The applicant received his Canadian visa in 1985 at which time he swore that he had a brother, Parbhjit Singh. When the applicant undertook to sponsor his parents he made no reference to this alleged brother, Parbhjit Singh. The applicant testified that Parbhjit Singh is not his brother and that he had included him in his family at the request of a third party with the hope that when the applicant sponsored his parents and brothers that Parbhjit Singh would be included as an accompanying dependant and obtain a visa to Canada.

The Appeal Division rejected the evidence of the applicant and his witnesses on this point. One item of evidence that the applicant filed was a sworn statement of his father which described who his children were and by implication that Parbhjit Singh was not one of his children. This document was directly relevant to the issue of the identity of the applicant's family members which was the issue in this case. The Tribunal's failure to refer to this specific document, which was directly relevant to the central issue being addressed by the Tribunal, led to a conclusion that the Tribunal had erred in law or based its decision on an erroneous finding of fact that it made without regard for all the material before it.

Accordingly, the application was allowed and the matter remitted to the Appeal Division to be heard again by a differently constituted panel.

Canada (Solicitor General) v. Kainth (1994), 26 Imm. L.R. (2d) 226, 81 F.T.R. 318n, 170 N.R. 367 (Fed. C.A.) — The Appeal Division allowed the appeal of the respondent and overturned a refusal by an immigration officer of the sponsored application for landing of the respondent's spouse. The Board decided that, although the refusal was legal and moreover that the spouse had been deported a few years previously, there were sufficient humanitarian or compassionate grounds to grant the spouse permanent residence. This decision was upheld by the Trial Division on a judicial review application. However, the Trial Division judge certified a serious question of general importance. The Solicitor General then appealed to the Court of Appeal.

Section 69.4(2) is broad enough to permit the Appeal Division to decide that it has jurisdiction to permit the respondent's spouse to be landed, notwithstanding the fact that the spouse did not have the Minister's consent as required by section 55(1) and notwithstanding the provisions of section 19(1)(i).

Accordingly, the appeal was dismissed.

Canada (Minister of Employment & Immigration) v. Hundal (1994), 167 N.R. 75 (Fed. C.A.) — This appeal by the Minister from a decision of the Appeal Division did not succeed. The Appeal Division had to decide whether the respondent had validly adopted Simrit Kaur Hundal in a 1983 adoption ceremony which had been conducted in India pursuant to section 11(vi) of the *Hindu Adoption and Maintenance Act*, 1956.

A visa officer in 1984 had no objection to the validity of the adoption. However, unusual circumstances prevented the mother and daughter from being united and when the matter was reconsidered by a visa officer in 1988 he came to a different conclusion.

The Court disagreed with the opinion of the Appeal Division that the first officer's decision in 1983 precluded a different decision by an officer in 1988. The officer in 1988 was entitled to view the matter in light of the facts as they appeared to him at that time. Notwithstanding this error by the Board, the appeal of the Minister was dismissed.

Rattan v. Canada (Minister of Employment & Immigration) (1994), 73 F.T.R. 195 — The applicant sought an order quashing a decision dismissing an appeal pursuant to section 77(3). An immigration officer had refused to approve the sponsored application of the applicant's husband on the basis that the marriage was one of convenience.

An appeal under section 77 is not a judicial review where only the correctness of the immigration officer's decision, on the basis of the material before him or her, is under consideration. The Appeal Division's role is to determine if the sponsoree is in fact a member of the class of persons excluded by section 4(3) of the regulations. The Appeal Division's role is not merely to determine whether the immigration officer's decision was correctly taken. For the purpose of determining the issue before it, the sponsor's evidence and the immigration officer's decision must be reviewed by the Board in coming to its decision. If the sponsor can satisfy the panel that the immigration officer's conclusions were incorrect, the appeal is allowed.

There was evidence sufficient to support both the immigration officer's conclusions and the Appeal Division's decision that the husband lacked an intention to reside permanently with the applicant. Accordingly, the application was dismissed.

Grewal v. Canada (Minister of Employment & Immigration) (1993), 62 F.T.R. 308 — The applicant arrived in Canada in July of 1990 and made a claim for refugee status. Prior to a determination of that claim he married a permanent resident, who sought to sponsor his application. The officer who interviewed both the applicant and his spouse concluded that the marriage was for immigration purposes and recommended that the application for landing be denied.

Where a statutory appeal lies judicial review will not proceed. The right of appeal conferred by section 77 belongs to the sponsor, in this instance the applicant's wife, and not the applicant. There is no authority which would allow a court to conclude that a right of appeal belonging to one individual operates as a bar to a right of judicial review belonging to another. The Court ruled, therefore, that it did have jurisdiction to hear the applicant's application for judicial review.

Deol v. Canada (Minister of Employment & Immigration) (1992), 18 Imm. L.R. (2d) 1 (Fed. C.A.) — This appeal was directed against the decision of the Appeal Division of the Immigration and Refugee Board in which the Board dismissed an appeal from an immigration officer's refusal of an application for landing. The refusal was of a sponsored application of the appellant's widowed mother and her two dependant daughters on the ground that one of the daughters was suffering from mental retardation. There is now considerable authority as to the Board's role *vis-a-vis* the opinions of medical officers. It may not question the medical diagnosis, but when requested, it should enquire into the reasonableness of their conclusion as to the probable demands on government services. The Board did not enquire into the reasonableness of the medical officers' conclusion, but rather assumed, from the sole fact of agreement as to the existence of mental retardation, that the conclusion was reasonable. The mere invocation of mental retardation leads to no particular conclusion. Mental retardation is a condition covering a wide range of possibilities from the total inability to function to near normality. The concept cannot be used as a stereotype because it is far from an unequivocal notion. It is not the fact alone of mental retardation that is relevant, but the degree and the probable consequences of that degree of retardation for excessive demands on government services.

The Board had failed to make that assessment in this case and its decision was set aside. It was noted that the two medical officers had entered the sponsored dependant's intended occupation as "new worker". The tests of admissibility must be relevant to the purpose for which admission is sought. The medical officers may well have imposed a higher standard of medical admissibility because they failed to realize that the daughter in question would enter as a sponsored dependant.

Kaur v. Canada (Minister of Employment & Immigration) (1990), 12 Imm. L.R. (2d) 1 (Fed. C.A.) — Satnam Singh made an application for permanent residence which was sponsored by the appellant, a landed immigrant, who had married him in India. The application was refused and the sponsor's appeal was dismissed by the Immigration Appeal Board. Satnam Singh had been deported from Canada and the consent of the Minister required for his admission into the country had been refused. Requirement of the Minister's written consent set out in section 57(1) of the *Immigration Act* cannot be overcome and replaced by a favourable decision of the Immigration Appeal Board based on its so-called "equitable jurisdiction". The Court further noted that in the context of this case no evidence had been adduced which would have warranted the granting of equitable relief in any event. The Court distinguished the case of the *M.E.I. v. Narwal* (1990), 10 Imm. L.R. (2d) 183, on the basis that in that case the good faith of the spouses had never been in doubt.

Kahlon v. Canada (Minister of Employment & Immigration) (1989), 7 Imm. L.R. (2d) 91, 97 N.R. 349 (Fed. C.A.) — This was an appeal by a sponsoring Canadian citizen from the dismissal by the Immigration Appeal Board of his appeal against a visa officer's refusal of the application for landing of his father, mother, brother and two sisters. Each applicant completed an individual application for landing. The Board found that the father and mother were not married and that none of the brothers and sisters had been proved to be children of the mother. This decision was given prior to May 1, 1985, when the definitions of son and daughter, in the *Immigration Regulations*, were changed. Prior to May 1, 1985, the children of a sponsored parent had to be legitimate in order to be eligible for admission as dependants of that parent.

The Board's decision, however, was given on December 16, 1985. The decision on an appeal from this type of refusal, is a hearing *de novo* in a broad sense. The Court's duty was to consider, when it decided the appeal, whether the brothers and sisters were, in fact, eligible to be sponsored by the appellant as dependants of his father. The Board was obliged to apply the law as it stood when it made its decision. At that time, the dependants were eligible to be sponsored. Accordingly, the appeal was allowed, the decision of the Board set aside and the matter was remitted to the Board for reconsideration on a basis not inconsistent with the Federal Court's reasons.

Brar v. Canada (Minister of Employment & Immigration) (1988), 5 Imm. L.R. (2d) 264 (Fed. C.A.) — The Immigration Appeal Board does not have jurisdiction to award costs in the absence of a specific statutory provision to that affect.

Dubey v. Canada (Minister of Employment & Immigration) (1987), 17 F.T.R. 319 (Fed. T.D.) — The Court was requested to quash a refusal, by the respondents, of an application for a visitor's visa on the grounds that the proposed visitor was required in Canada as a witness on behalf of the applicant at an Immigration Appeal Board hearing. The applicant at the hearing was attempting to prove that his marriage to the proposed visitor was *bona fide*. The sponsor in this case had, in fact, married another lady in February 1983 and divorced her in December 1984. In February 1985, less than 2 months after his divorce was final, the sponsor submitted the sponsorship in question. The sponsoree, when she was questioned about the sponsor, indicated that she knew nothing about him. She did not know his level of education, what he did for a living, and did not know the names of his family members.

Further, the immigration officer, who refused the visitor's visa application, noted that in India where marriages are arranged the prospective partners are well briefed about each other and, thus, are very knowledgeable about the person with whom they have been paired. The officer was found to have been exercising his best judgment and was aware of all the facts when he opted to refuse the application. The Court was not satisfied that no other means existed whereby the evidence of the sponsoree could be reviewed. Further, the Court pointed out that the applicant was seeking an unusual benefit, namely, the admission to Canada of someone whose previous applications for admission to Canada had been refused. No denial of natural justice was found on the facts of this case. There was no evidence that the sponsoree was refused entry because she would testify on behalf of the applicant. The application was dismissed.

Swinton v. Canada (Minister of Employment & Immigration) (1987), 4 Imm. L.R. (2d) 274 (Imm. App. Bd.) — Mr. Swinton sponsored the application for permanent residence of his father. His father's sworn affidavit indicated that while he intended to travel to Canada to be reunited with his son, he was not selling any of his property because he did not know how long he intended to live in Canada. The appeal from the refusal was allowed. The law does not require people to have an intention to abandon their homeland forever and never return to it, or to come to Canada never to leave it again. Further, in order to make out an intention to establish permanent residence in Canada, it is not necessary to forswear forever the formulation of a later intention to leave Canada to take up permanent residence, whether in an immigrant's native land or elsewhere.

Stuart v. Canada (Minister of Employment & Immigration) (1987), 31 Admin. L.R. 161, 5 Imm. L.R. (2d) 97, [1988] 3 F.C. 157, 96 N.R. 32 (Fed. C.A.) — This application was made to obtain *certiorari* to quash the respondent's decision not to grant a visitor's visa to the applicant's spouse to enter Canada for the purpose of testifying as a witness at the applicant's appeal hearing before the Immigration Appeal Board. The applicant had sought to sponsor his spouse for entry as a member of the family class, but the respondent claimed that the marriage was entered into only for the purposes of gaining admission to Canada. It was determined that the applicant would be denied a fair hearing if he was prevented from calling his wife as a witness. Her son, who was 5 years old, was not granted permission to enter Canada. *Certiorari* was granted on condition that the applicant's spouse remain in custody for the purpose of ensuring her immediate return to Guyana after any attendance before the Immigration Appeal Board. The basis for admission was section 19(3) of the Act.

Rajpaul v. Canada (Minister of Employment & Immigration) (1987), 24 Admin. L.R. 153 (Fed. T.D.); varied 31 Admin. L.R. 191, 96 N.R. 32, 5 Imm. L.R. (2d) 97, [1988] 3 F.C. 157 (Fed. C.A.) — The applicant sought *certiorari* quashing the respondent's decision not to grant a visitor's visa to Sumintra Ramdas to enter Canada for the purpose of testifying as a witness. The applicant had applied to sponsor Ramdas, whom he alleged to be his wife. The application was refused on the basis that the marriage had been entered into primarily for the purpose of gaining admission into Canada as a family class immigrant and not with the intention of residing permanently with the other spouse as contemplated by the Regulation. *Certiorari* was granted.

The outcome of the applicant's appeal to the Immigration Appeal Board, obviously, would depend upon the Board's assessment of the spouse's credibility on the issue of her primary purpose in entering into the marriage. The applicant had a substantive right to a fair hearing and could not be denied the opportunity to present this crucial evidence and testimony to the Board. It was a condition of the discretionary remedy that the spouse remain in detention pending the giving of evidence at the respondent's option. This latter condition was agreed to during the argument by counsel for the applicant.

The Court noted that in this case there was no previous conduct in Canada by the sponsoree that would justify the Court withholding *certiorari* by refusing to exercise its discretion.

Canada (Minister of Employment & Immigration) v. Courtney (1986), [1987] 2 F.C. 22 (Fed. C.A.) — The respondent's mother came to Canada on August 22, 1982, as a visitor. Prior to the expiration of her mother's visitor's status, the respondent and her mother attended at a Canada Immigration Centre and requested consideration for the mother as an applicant for permanent residence from within Canada. This request was refused on the basis that insufficient humanitarian and compassionate grounds existed. The immigration officer, at the time of the interview, received the mother's completed application for landing and the undertaking of assistance given by the respondent. The Notice of Appeal from the refusal was filed with the Immigration Appeal Board. The Board allowed the appeal, concluding that a basis had been established to warrant the granting of relief on compassionate or humanitarian grounds pursuant to section 79(2)(b) of the Act. The Minister appealed successfully. Until an exemption has been granted by the Governor in Council under section 115(2), no application for landing exists that "could be granted." Thus, the Immigration Appeal Board cannot acquire jurisdiction under section 79(2)(b).

Kaushal v. Canada (Minister of Employment & Immigration) (1987), 2 Imm. L.R. (2d) 118 (Imm. App. Bd.) — This was an appeal from the refusal of a sponsored application for landing. The application was filed on November 5, 1980. It took over 4 years for the application to be processed. By the time the application was processed, one of the sponsoree's was over 23 years of age. Thus, the visa officer did not err in concluding that the sponsoree fell outside the definition of dependant as set out in section 2(1) of the regulation. There could be estoppel in this case to prevent the Commission from asserting this proposition because the visa officer was charged with the statutory duty that he was obliged to fill. He was required to apply the Act and regulation when carrying out an assessment required by section 9(2) of the Act. The administrative abuse reflected in the long delay in processing the application was not an abuse over which the Immigration Appeal Board had any jurisdiction. The Board held that section 79(2)(b) of the Act was irrelevant because the sponsoree was not a member of the family class, and, therefore no amount of humanitarian or compassionate consideration could avail the sponsor in the appeal.

Bailon v. Canada (Minister of Employment & Immigration) (June 16, 1986), Doc. A-783-85 (Fed. C.A.) — The appellant sponsored an application for landing by her mother and her half-brother, the latter being just under 21 years of age. Because of his age, the half-brother could only have been admitted as a dependant of his mother, who was a member of the family class. The application for landing by the appellant's mother, the only member of the family class to apply, was not refused. Section 79 of the *Immigration Act* gives a sponsor a right of appeal from the refusal of an application by a member of the family class, not from the refusal to include an alleged dependant of such member. The Board rightly declined jurisdiction to hear the appeal.

Vadsaria v. Canada (Secretary of State for External Affairs) (1986), 7 F.T.R. 299 (Fed. T.D.) — For digest, see section 77, subheading *Subsection (1), supra.*

Mohamed v. Canada (Minister of Employment & Immigration), [1986] 3 F.C. 90 (Fed. C.A.) — This was an appeal from a decision of the Immigration Appeal Board dismissing an appeal from a refusal to approve a sponsored application for landing made by the appellant's father, mother, brother and sister. The ground for that refusal was that the appellant's mother was medically inadmissible. By the time of the appeal before the Immigration Appeal Board, the mother was no longer suffering from the medical condition that made her inadmissible. The first issue was whether her condition, at the time of the hearing of the appeal, was relevant. Mr. Justice Hugessen and Mr. Justice McQuaid concluded that the medical condition at the time the visa officer refused the application was relevant. The Chief Justice concluded that the relevant medical condition was that which the mother was in at the time of her appeal before the Immigration Appeal Board. The majority were of the view that the fact of the improvement in the mother's medical condition was relevant to whether special relief should be granted on the appeal pursuant to section 79(2)(b). The Court was unanimous, however, in quashing the Immigration Appeal Board's decision on other grounds.

Lavi v. Canada (Minister of Employment & Immigration) (April 24, 1985), Doc. T83-9929 (Imm. App. Bd.) — The Minister contended that the conviction rendered against the husband of the appellant made the husband inadmissible by reason of section 19(2)(a)(i) of the *Immigration Act*. The refusal letter referred to the equivalent Canadian offences as being either section 233(1) or (4) of the *Criminal Code*. The Board asserted in its decision that the reference in the refusal to those subsections did not restrict the Board to make a determination of whether either of those two provisions was the correct equivalent Canadian offence. The Board asserted that in making its determination it may, if necessary, explore various other provisions of the Canadian law.

Kalair v. Canada (Minister of Employment & Immigration) (1984), 10 Admin. L.R. 107 (Fed. C.A.) — The applicant signed an application to sponsor the landing in Canada of his adopted daughter. The application was refused because the daughter had not established that she was the legally adopted daughter of the applicant. The Immigration Appeal Board dismissed the applicant's appeal. This decision was set aside because the Board based its decision upon evidence which had been adduced before in two earlier cases as to the existence and effect of certain aspects of the law of India bearing upon whether there had been a legal adoption in the eyes of that law. The Court held that the Board had deprived the applicant of the right to challenge the accuracy of that evidence and had, therefore, erred in relying upon it.

Toor v. Canada (Minister of Employment & Immigration) (1983), 144 D.L.R. (3d) 554 (Fed. C.A.) — A Canadian citizen applied to sponsor his wife and three children for admission. A visa officer refused to allow the wife and children to proceed to Canada and the sponsor appealed. The Immigration Appeal Board dismissed this appeal, holding that the wife did not meet the requirements of the Act and regulations because she had no intention of taking up residence in Canada when she filed her application for permanent residence. The Federal Court of Appeal set aside the finding as not being supportable on the evidence. Because the sponsor husband was a Canadian citizen, the wife's ineligibility had no bearing upon whether the children met the requirements of the Act or the Regulation.

Tappin v. Canada (Minister of Employment & Immigration) (March 11, 1983), Doc. T-9084-82 (Fed. T.D.) — This was a motion for a writ of *mandamus* ordering the respondents to accept Gladwin Tappin's application for permanent residence to determine whether it would be contrary to the *Immigration Act* and regulations to grant him landing, determine whether he required special permission to apply for landing from within Canada, to notify Gladwin Tappin whether his application had been accepted or rejected and to notify Arlene Tappin, in writing, whether her application to sponsor Gladwin Tappin as a member of the family class had been accepted or rejected. The applicant had already been advised that there were insufficient humanitarian grounds to make an exception to the Act and regulation to warrant dealing with the application for permanent residence from within Canada. It was held that special permission to apply from within Canada had been denied. Once there was a proper refusal to deal with the application for landing made within Canada, there was no application for landing to be dealt with by the respondents and in its absence, the application to sponsor was a nullity. The decision refusing to accept an application for landing from within Canada need not, where sponsorship by a Canadian citizen is involved, be so framed as to permit a right of appeal to the Immigration Appeal Board under section 79(2) of the Act.

Tsang v. Canada (Minister of Employment & Immigration) (April 1, 1981), Doc. T80-9437 (Imm. App. Bd.) — The appellant sponsored the application for permanent residence of her father. The father's application was refused on the grounds that he did not satisfy the medical requirements for immigrants and that his admission would cause excessive demands on health or social services. The appellant sought an order from the Immigration Appeal Board directing the Minister to produce the medical information upon which the decision was based. The Board found that the sponsoree, having signed a medical release in his application for permanent residence, authorized the release of medical information by Health and Welfare Canada to the Minister of Employment and Immigration and, thus, found that the Minister was entitled to the medical information, which was in fact in the possession of Health and Welfare Canada. The Board concluded that it had jurisdiction to order production prior to the hearing of the appeal of the medical information sought by the appellant. The order for production was not made in this case because it was premature as no notice of the application for an order to produce had been given to the doctors from Health and Welfare Canada from whom production was sought.

Section 77(3.01)

Lam v. Canada (Minister of Citizenship & Immigration) (1997), 45 Imm. L.R. (2d) 179 (Fed. T.D.) — This is an application to review a decision wherein the Minister's delegate formed the opinion that the applicant constituted a danger to the public pursuant to section 77(3.1)(b). The applicant was sponsored from within Canada by his wife, a Canadian citizen. The applicant has two Canadian born children. His application disclosed two offences in Hong Kong. The first conviction in February 1974 was for membership in a triad's society and the second conviction in 1988 was for blackmail. The applicant's application for landing was refused on the ground that he was inadmissible as a result of these convictions. The applicant's wife filed an appeal. Prior to the appeal being filed, the applicant had been ordered deported and an adjudicator had determined that the conviction for blackmail was equivalent to extortion and also that there were reasonable grounds to believe that the applicant was a member of a criminal organization because of his conviction in 1974.

In June 1997, the Minister's delegate issued an opinion that the applicant constituted a danger to the public in Canada. This decision followed a recommendation set out in a ministerial opinion report. The report quotes facts that were never in issue, ignores others and does not mention that the Hong Kong file relating to this offence was not available because it had been destroyed.

There must be support for a finding that an individual constitutes a present or future danger. It is the height of fantasy to assume that the Minister's delegate in normal circumstances goes beyond the opinion report when making a decision. There can be no other reason for the preparation of the opinion report, other than to limit the degree to which the Minister's delegate will find it necessary to review the material detail.

The Court found that in the absence of reason, the decision on its face must be characterized as perverse and was accordingly set aside.

Tsang v. Canada (Minister of Citizenship & Immigration) (1997), 37 Imm. L.R. (2d) 1, 211 N.R. 131, 125 F.T.R. 319 (note) (Fed. C.A.) — In November, 1991, Lannie Tsang submitted an undertaking to sponsor her husband. The husband filed an application in January, 1993, based on his wife's sponsorship. This application was refused because the applicant, Peter

Tsang, was a member of an inadmissable class described in paragraph 19(1)(c). Lannie Tsang appealed this refusal to the Appeal Division of the IRB pursuant to subsection 77(3).

Bill C-44 came into force on July 10, 1995. Lannie Tsang's appeal had not yet been heard. The appeal was heard on July 25, 1995, and continued on August 10, 1995, when the appeal concluded and the decision was reserved. On September 8, 1995, the applicant Peter Tsang was certified a danger to the public. The decision of the Appeal Division was still under reserve at that time.

The Court of Appeal held that it was open to the Minister to issue a public danger opinion and extinguish the right of the sponsor in circumstances where the appeal had been launched before 1995 and had already been heard but not yet disposed of at the time the opinion was given.

Section 77(4)

Darius v. Canada (Minister of Employment & Immigration) (1990), 12 Imm. L.R. (2d) 127 (Fed. C.A.) — On June 7, 1984, the Board allowed an appeal by the Minister against the decision of an adjudicator. On April 29, 1988, the Board varied its decision rendered on June 7, 1984 pursuant to a request by the respondent Darius that the June 7, 1984 decision was based on an error of law. The Minister appealed the Board's decision to vary its June 7, 1984 order. This appeal was allowed. The Board was held not to have the power to rescind its decisions when the decision was made in full compliance with all the requirements of natural justice. The mere fact that the decision was wrong in law did not give the Board the right to correct it and this was held to be so even though the effect of the decision was to deprive the respondent of the right to claim refugee status. The proper means to correct the error was an appeal of the Board's decision which had not taken place in this case.

Section 77(5)

King v. Canada (Minister of Citizenship & Immigration) (1996), 115 F.T.R. 306 (Fed. T.D.) — The visa officer refused the applicant's application for landing for medical reasons. The Appeal Division of the Immigration and Refugee Board allowed an appeal from that decision in law, but not in equity. The Board found that the evidence did not support the conclusion of the medical notification.

When a decision of a visa officer denying an application for landing for medical reasons is overturned by the Appeal Division on the basis of an error in the medical assessment, the only issue that is *res judicata* is the medical decision found to be erroneous. Therefore, a visa officer can subsequently request further medical information and an applicant is required to establish that his or her admission into Canada would not be contrary to section 19.

Mangat v. Canada (Secretary of State) (February 25, 1985), Doc. T-153-85 (Fed. T.D.) — The applicant gave an undertaking of assistance to the application for permanent residence of certain of his relatives. The relatives were refused for medical reasons. The Immigration Appeal Board allowed the applicant's appeal because the medical reports, upon which rejection of the family application had been based, had expired. Subsequent to the successful appeal, a new decision was taken that again rejected the applications for permanent residence of the applicant's family. Counsel for the applicant contended that the Board's decision on the first appeal meant that the medical problem, identified in the expired certificates, could no longer be taken into account by the visa officer even if confirmed by new unexpired certificates. This argument was rejected. The Board was held to have taken no "decision" that the medical problem was to be ignored, but, rather, it was concluded that the Board had decided that the condition of rejection had not, as a matter of law, been properly proved, and, thus, consideration of new and proper medical evidence was not precluded. *Mandamus* was granted directing a visa officer to reconsider issuing a visitor's visa. The previous application for a visitor's visa had been rejected on the basis that the applicant had not satisfied relevant health requirements. The Court noted that the circumstances, relevant to medical opinions given under section 19(1)(a) of the Act, are different depending on the purpose and duration for which admission is sought. Here, the only medical opinions that the visa officer could have had available were those prepared in relation to the family's application for admission for permanent residence. Thus, the visa officer's decision to refuse to issue a visa was quashed and *mandamus* was ordered against the respondents requiring that they direct a visa officer to reconsider the question of issuing a visitor's visa to the applicant's family.

78. [Repealed 1992, c. 49, s. 69.]

Notice and Hearing

79. Notice of appeal — A person who proposes to appeal to the Appeal Division shall give notice of the appeal in such manner and within such time as is prescribed by the rules of the Appeal Division.

R.S.C. 1985, c. 28 (4th Supp.), s. 33.

80. (1) Hearings in public — Subject to subsections (2) and (3), an appeal to the Appeal Division shall be conducted in public.

(2) Confidentiality — Where the Appeal Division is satisfied that there is a serious possibility that the life, liberty or security of any person would be endangered by reason of the appeal being conducted in public, the Appeal Division may, on application therefor, take such measures and make such order as it considers necessary to ensure the confidentiality of the appeal.

(3) Idem — Where the Appeal Division considers it appropriate to do so, the Appeal Division may take such measures and make such order as it considers necessary to ensure the confidentiality of any hearing held in respect of any application referred to in subsection (2).

R.S.C. 1985, c. 28 (4th Supp.), s. 33; 1992, c. 49, s. 70.

Adjudication Division

80.1 (1) Sole and exclusive jurisdiction — Subject to section 40.2, an adjudicator has sole and exclusive jurisdiction to hear and determine all questions of law and fact, including questions of jurisdiction, that may arise in the course of proceedings that are required by this Act to be held before an adjudicator.

(2) Powers — An adjudicator has all the powers and authority of a commissioner appointed under Part I of the *Inquiries Act* and, without restricting the generality of the foregoing, may, for the purposes of any proceedings that are required by this Act to be held before an adjudicator,

(a) issue a summons to any person requiring the person to appear at the time and place set out in the summons to testify with respect to all matters within that person's knowledge relative to the subject-matter of the proceedings and to bring and

produce any document, book or paper in the person's possession or under the person's control relative to the subject-matter of the proceedings;

(b) administer oaths and examine any person under oath;

(c) issue commissions or requests to take evidence in Canada; and

(d) do all other things necessary to provide for the full and proper conduct of the proceedings.

(3) Sittings — Adjudicators shall sit at the times and at the places in Canada that are considered necessary by the Chairperson for the proper conduct of their business.

(4) Informal proceedings — An adjudicator shall deal with all proceedings as informally and expeditiously as the circumstances and considerations of fairness permit.

(5) Rules of evidence — An adjudicator is not bound by any legal or technical rules of evidence and, in any proceedings, may receive and base a decision on evidence adduced in the proceedings and considered credible or trustworthy in the circumstances of the case.

1992, c. 49, s. 70.

Case Law

Section 80.1(1)

Watt v. Liebelt (1998), [1999] 2 F.C. 455, (sub nom. *Watt v. Canada (Minister of Citizenship & Immigration))* 169 D.L.R. (4th) 336, 236 N.R. 302, (sub nom. *Watt v. Canada (Minister of Citizenship & Immigration))* [1999] 2 C.N.L.R. 326 (Fed. C.A.) — The issue on this appeal involved a question of whether it would be contrary to an existing aboriginal right guaranteed in the constitution for an aboriginal person who is a foreign national, and neither a Canadian citizen nor registered under the *Indian Act*, to be ordered to depart from Canada for a crime committed here. The appellant was born in the state of Washington and was a U.S. citizen and a member of the Colville Federated Tribe. He did not have Canadian citizenship and was not registered as an Indian under the *Indian Act* of Canada.

The appellant was convicted in British Columbia of cultivating marijuana and as a result of that conviction was brought to inquiry and ordered deported.

At the hearing before the adjudicator, the appellant raised the argument that by virtue of his aboriginal rights he cannot be ordered to leave Canada. The adjudicator determined that she had no jurisdiction to determine whether the appellant was "an aboriginal person of Canada", a determination critical to any finding that the guarantee of section 35 of the *Constitution Act 1982*, would guarantee the rights which the appellant was asserting. The appellant sought judicial review of this order in the Federal Court Trial Division. The judge dismissed the application on the basis that whether or not such aboriginal rights had existed or whether the appellant was entitled to rely on them, any such rights must have been extinguished by sections 4 and 5 of the *Immigration Act*.

The Court ruled that the motions judge erred in finding extinguishment of the rights as claimed. There was neither adequate evidence of the existence and definition of the right nor of a government intention to relinquish it. The sovereign nature of Canada is not a legal barrier per se to the existence of the aboriginal rights claimed by the appellant. The adjudicator, having declined to receive evidence in light of her view of her inability to determine the issues the appellant was raising, created a position where there was not a sufficient record for the Court to be in a position to make the determinations that the appeal required.

The Court ruled that the adjudicator did have the necessary powers to decide this matter. The Court noted the practical problems of requiring an adjudicator to resolve this kind of an issue and noted in its judgement section 18.3 of the *Federal Court Act* as a solution to the problem.

Ashoornia v. Canada (Minister of Employment & Immigration) (1994), 28 Imm. L.R. (2d) 94 (Fed. T.D.) — This was an application for judicial review of a credible basis hearing. The applicant was a citizen of Iran. She was arrested and detained on her arrival in Canada. When arrested she was in possession of false documents. Prior to the credible basis hearing, the applicant attended at least two detention reviews. At the detention reviews the adjudicator continued the applicant's detention. He concluded that she should be detained because she had lied to enter Canada and had no friends or relatives in Canada and therefore no reason to remain here. The adjudicator's decision at the detention review was based in large measure on the assessment of the applicant's credibility. The adjudicator, who had twice attended the detention reviews, also acted as the adjudicator at the credible basis hearing.

In the detention reviews the adjudicator had canvassed exactly the same evidence as he subsequently heard at the credible basis inquiry and had concluded that the applicant was not credible. In such a situation, a reasonable apprehension of bias was created by the adjudicator's presence at the credible basis hearing and the application for judicial review was allowed.

Editor's Note: Although the refugee determination provisions have been changed, the principle in this case may be of broader import.

Khakh v. Canada (Minister of Employment & Immigration) (1993), [1994] 1 F.C. 548, 23 Imm. L.R. (2d) 38, 70 F.T.R. 26 — The applicant sought to overturn a decision of a credible basis panel holding a hearing under refugee provisions no longer in effect. The applicant alleged a reasonable apprehension of bias. The respondent argued that in failing to raise an objection on this basis before the credible basis panel, the applicant waived his rights to subsequently raise the issue. A reasonable apprehension of bias should be raised at the first opportunity. There is no waiver unless the party entitled to make the objection is fully aware of the nature of the disqualification and has adequate opportunity to make the objection. The Court will imply waiver where a party or its representative knows of the facts that give rise to an apprehension of bias and, notwithstanding, does not object. The party or its representative must be fully cognizant of the right to take objection. In this case, the adjudicator had, after the applicant requested an interpreter, refused the interpreter after testing the applicant in English. As the hearings progressed the adjudicator noticed that the applicant's English was deteriorating and this was taken to mean that the adjudicator had formed the view that the applicant was not doing his best in English. The failure of the unrepresented applicant to object to the adjudicator's jurisdiction on the basis of reasonable apprehension of bias, after this comment was made, was not taken to be a waiver of his rights to object before the Federal Court.

Asante v. Canada (Minister of Employment & Immigration) (1993), 64 F.T.R. 10 — The applicant was a citizen of Ghana. She came to Canada on October 12, 1989, having obtained a visitor's visa to Canada. Her visitor's visa was valid for one month and this visa was later extended to January 11, 1990. When the applicant could not go to the United States to study she claimed refugee status, but subsequently had her visitor's visa extended to July 11, 1990. On May 29, 1990, an immigration officer made a report pursuant to paragraph 27(2)(e) of the *Immigration Act*. A direction for inquiry was issued on July 4, 1990. At the conclusion of the inquiry the adjudicator issued a departure notice to the applicant. Later, a first-level panel concluded that there was no credible basis for the applicant's claim for Convention refugee status.

At the time the section 27 report was made and at the time the direction for inquiry was issued, the applicant was in Canada on a validly subsisting visitor's visa. There was no authority under the Act to make a report or to issue a direction for inquiry. Therefore, the adjudicator had no jurisdiction to proceed with the inquiry and issue a departure notice. Accordingly, the departure notice issued in this case was set aside.

Boakye v. Canada (Minister of Employment & Immigration) (1993), 151 N.R. 184 (Fed. C.A.) — During the course of the applicant's credible-basis hearing, discrepancies and contradictions appeared in her evidence. An attempt was made to claim that these discrepancies were based on faulty interpretation. The applicant's solicitor, who was fluent in the languages in issue, was called as a witness. He testified that the translation was competent and that he would have intervened had it been otherwise. Secondly, he testified that, in meeting with his client to review the transcript, she had not complained about the translation. The evidence of the solicitor as to the competence of the translation did not relate to anything that could be the subject of the solicitor/client privilege. It was evidence as to facts which he had observed in circumstances that were in no way confidential. Accepting that what was said at the review of the evidence between the applicant and her solicitor was the subject of privilege, the applicant was represented by another lawyer when the privileged evidence was given. That lawyer did not assert any claim of privilege at the time the evidence was received and accordingly, the Court declined to quash the credible basis determination.

Editor's Note: Although decided under the old refugee determination system, the principles in this case may have a broader implication.

Arthur v. Canada (Minister of Employment & Immigration) (1992), 18 Imm. L.R. (2d) 22, 98 D.L.R. (4th) 254, 147 N.R. 288 (Fed. C.A.) — The applicant was a refugee claimant who had been detained prior to her credible-basis hearing under the legislation previously in effect. The same adjudicator who detained her was one of the two members of the credible-basis tribunal. The applicant's counsel objected to the adjudicator's participation because the adjudicator had made, at the bail hearing, a negative decision about the applicant's credibility. The mere fact of a second hearing before the same adjudicator, without more, does not give rise to a reasonable apprehension of bias. The presence of other factors indicating a predisposition by the adjudicator as to the issue to be decided may, however, give rise to such a reasonable apprehension. One consideration of major significance will be the relationship of the issues in the two hearings. A second consideration will be the finality of the second decision. If both decisions are interlocutory, it may be of little significance that the matter in issue is the same, but where the second decision is a final one, the similarity in issues may become more important. There was no predisposition by the adjudicator on the applicant's general credibility in this case and the application was dismissed.

Armadale Communications Ltd. v. Canada (Adjudicator appointed under Immigration Act), 14 Imm. L.R. (2d) 13, [1991] 3 F.C. 242, 127 N.R. 342, 83 D.L.R. (4th) 440 (Fed. C.A.) — An adjudicator presiding in an immigration inquiry has the practical capability to decide Charter issues. There is nothing in the *Immigration Act* to indicate any intention to preclude him or her from having and exercising the power to find a legislative provision inconsistent with the Charter. Accordingly, the Federal Court of Appeal under section 28 has jurisdiction to review those decisions.

Editor's Note: See, however, section 40.2

Singh (M.J.) v. Canada (Minister of Employment & Immigration) (1991), 14 Imm. L.R. (2d) 126, 46 F.T.R. 184, [1992] 1 F.C. 332 — The applicant was the subject of an Immigration inquiry. At the outset of the hearing, counsel for the applicant indicated that she intended to raise a preliminary jurisdictional argument under section 52 of the *Constitution Act*. The adjudicator indicated that the tribunal would proceed with the Immigration inquiry and then deal with the constitutional issues. The applicant then commenced this proceeding. The action of the adjudicator in deciding to proceed this way is not subject to review under section 18 of the *Federal Court Act*. It is essentially a procedural decision and one entirely within the competence of the adjudicator. Second, the Court observed that constitutional issues cannot be decided in a factual vacuum. In doubtful cases, there is a practical advantage for an adjudicator to be in a position to make a determination on the merits of the case at the same time that the constitutional validity of a provision is considered for the simple reason that a favourable adjudication on the merits may obviate the necessity of a long and protracted constitutional proceeding. The application for *certiorari* and *mandamus* was dismissed.

Bissoondial v. Canada (Minister of Employment & Immigration) (1991), 14 Imm. L.R. (2d) 119, 47 F.T.R. 316 — The applicant had claimed to be a Convention refugee and a credible basis hearing was being conducted. The applicant raised substantive constitutional questions and wanted them dealt with prior to the evidence of the credible basis for the refugee claim being heard. The adjudicator decided that the tribunal would hear evidence on the inquiry, the credible basis hearing and the constitutional issues. Counsel for the applicant objected and wanted the constitutional issues decided prior to the credible basis hearing. The action of the adjudicator in making this decision is not subject to review. The decision is essentially procedural in nature and entirely within the competence of the adjudicator. The adjudicator and Refugee Board member conducting the credible basis hearing are not a court of competent jurisdiction; they cannot grant a general declaration declaring provisions of the *Immigration Act* unconstitutional. They can, however, respect the provisions of section 52(1) of the *Constitution Act* when considering and applying any enactment that is within their jurisdictional competence. The tribunal is limited in applying constitutional arguments to the facts of the particular matter before it within its statutory jurisdiction. Accordingly, the application for judicial review was dismissed.

Akthar v. Canada (Minister of Employment & Immigration), 14 Imm. L.R. (2d) 39, 50 Admin. L.R. 153, [1991] 3 F.C. 32, 129 N.R. 71 (Fed. C.A.) — In this case, the applicant argued that the length of time between the original formulation of his refugee claim and the holding of the credible basis hearing was unreasonably lengthy and therefore offended section 7 of the *Charter of Rights*. The first stage tribunal did not hear the applicant's claim until just over 2 1/2 years after his arrival. Any claim in a non-criminal case to Charter relief based on delay requires evidence or at the very least some inference from the surrounding circumstances that the claimant has in fact suffered prejudice or unfairness because of the delay. The delay in this case did not give rise to a Charter remedy and the application was dismissed.

Editor's Note: The refugee determination process has been changed, but the principle may still be applicable.

Blanusa v. Canada (Minister of Employment & Immigration) (1989), 27 F.T.R. 107 (Fed. T.D.) — The applicant argued that, because there were grounds under the *Extradition Act* and the Extradition Treaty with the United States upon which he might resist extradition under those instruments, proceedings under the *Immigration Act* to deport him ought to be prohibited. It was contended that to proceed with the deportation hearing would automatically violate section 7 of the Charter because the applicant would not be able to raise in the deportation proceedings objections to his removal which were, by their nature, only available in the extradition proceedings. Extradition and immigration proceedings are separate processes. The applicant was being proceeded against under the *Immigration Act* because he violated the laws of Canada by staying in this country for over two years. He was being proceeded against under the *Extradition Act* and Treaty because he had allegedly committed kidnappings and murders in the United States. There was no basis for thinking that the deportation hearing was illegal or unconstitutional and accordingly the application was dismissed.

Mohammad v. Canada (Minister of Employment & Immigration), [1989] 2 F.C. 363, 55 D.L.R. (4th) 321, 21 F.T.R. 240 (note) (Fed. C.A.) — It is not a pre-condition to the operation of section 19(1)(c) that the Governor-in-Council shall have considered the question of rehabilitation and be dissatisfied that the person concerned has brought himself within the exception. The report mandated by section 27(1) requires the authorizing immigration officer to possess information that the person concerned has been convicted of the kind of criminal act specified in section 19(1)(c) and to have knowledge that the person concerned has not satisfied the Governor in Council as to his rehabilitation.

The policy directives, whether made pursuant to regulatory authority or general administrative capacity, are no more than directions and are unenforceable by members of the public. The procedural formalities which are required in respect to an immigration officer when initiating a section 27(1) report are minimal, first, because this is a purely administrative decision and, secondly, because the officer when issuing the section 27(1) report is merely the initiator of the inquiry process. An immigration officer before issuing a section 27(1) report is, therefore, not required to give the person concerned an opportunity to answer allegations contained in that report. On the facts, the immigration officer who issued the section 27(1) report had sufficient knowledge and information upon which to base the report; further, the applicant was given full particulars of the allegations against him.

The Court of Appeal adopted the motion's judge's findings that there was nothing irregular in the fact that the high profile nature of the case placed pressure on the respondent's representatives to proceed with dispatch.

The requirement of institutional independence is included in the rules of natural justice as well as enshrined in the Charter.

The test for institutional independence is whether a reasonable and right minded individual, having informed himself of the scheme whereby adjudicators are appointed under the *Immigration Act* and of the basis upon which they perform their duties, would be likely to conclude that an adjudicator appointed under and acting pursuant to that scheme, more likely than not, would decide fairly the inquiries under the *Immigration Act* over which he presided. While the case-presenting officers and adjudicators are both civil servants under the direction of the same Minister, they operate in separate and distinct divisions of the Commission. Case-presenting officers have no supervisory role *vis-à-vis* adjudicators. They do not report to a common superior and it is only at the apex of the organization chart that their respective hierarchies merge. As far as legal direction is concerned, adjudicators can and do seek advice on difficult legal issues from lawyers on the staff of the Adjudication Directorate, who have no connection or association with the Enforcement Branch. On the subject of monitoring, there is evidence that monitoring practice focuses primarily on how hearings are conducted; with respect to security of tenure, adjudicators, like other civil servants, have the protection afforded pursuant to section 31 of the *Public Service Employment Act*. Additionally, they have the protection of a three stage grievance procedure. The fact that adjudicators are members of the same bargaining unit as case-presenting officers is a neutral circumstance which does not give rise to any apprehension one way or the other. The practice of appointing adjudicators to other positions on an acting basis does not give rise to reasonable apprehension of a lack of independence. The Court relied on the uncontradicted evidence of an adjudicator to the effect that the decisions made by him were made independently and without direction from anyone else.

Finally, it was pointed out that the assignment of cases is rationally based; complex cases are usually assigned to the more experienced adjudicators. There was nothing to suggest that particular cases were assigned to particular adjudicators, let alone any evidence to suggest that the adjudicator chosen to conduct his inquiry was chosen on any basis other than the rational basis referred to previously. The Court concluded for these reasons that reasonable persons, reasonably informed, would view adjudicators appointed under the *Immigration Act* as being independent, keeping in mind the fact that they are for the most part laypersons in the hierarchy of *quasi*-judicial tribunals; and bearing in mind that their decisions are subject to judicial review by the Court; and that they have all taken an oath of office to "faithfully and honestly fulfill their duties" devolving upon them. Accordingly, the appellant's appeal was dismissed.

Southam Inc. v. Canada (Minister of Employment & Immigration) (1987), 3 Imm. L.R. (2d) 226 (Fed. T.D.) — The adjudicators were prohibited from conducting detention review hearings in the absence of the applicants unless the applicants' right-of-access was outweighed or limited in any given case by counter-balancing rights or interests. Further, if any objections to the public's access were raised, the applicants were to be given an opportunity to present submissions on the point.

Satiacum v. Canada (Minister of Employment & Immigration) (1985), 64 N.R. 358 (Fed. C.A.) — The circumstances that the adjudicator and the case presenting officer were both public servants employed in the same department of government, without more, was not such as to give rise to a reasonable apprehension of bias. An informed person viewing the matter realistically and practically would not conclude that it was more likely than not that the adjudicator would not decide fairly.

Grewal v. Canada (Minister of Employment & Immigration) (October 1, 1984), Doc. A-836-84 (Fed. C.A.) — An inquiry was held to determine whether the applicant was a person who had entered Canada as a visitor and remained in Canada after ceasing to be a visitor. The Court concluded that once a person has been made the subject of an inquiry to determine his right to stay in Canada, the mere fact that after the start of the inquiry he leaves the country for a time does not deprive the adjudicator of his jurisdiction to continue and complete the inquiry.

Singh v. Canada (Minister of Employment & Immigration) (September 21, 1984), Doc. A-258-84 (Fed. C.A.) — The section 20 report convoking the inquiry alleged that the applicant was described in section 19(1)(h) of the *Immigration Act*. In the course of the inquiry, the applicant testified that he intended to remain permanently in Canada. He was, therefore, a person described in section 19(2)(d) because of his failure to obtain an immigrant visa before appearing at a port-of-entry contrary to section 9(1) of the Act. The exclusion order was based on sections 19(2)(d) and 9(1). The exclusion order was set aside because the subject of the inquiry must be advised of the allegations against him at the outset of the inquiry and if those allegations are changed, altered or substituted during the course of the inquiry, he must then be advised of the revised allegations and given an opportunity to meet them. This finding was supported by the provisions of sections 29 and 31 of the regulations and the requirement of procedural fairness.

Cambouras v. Canada (Minister of Employment & Immigration) (1984), 68 N.R. 158 (Fed. C.A.) — The applicant had been ordered deported at an earlier proceeding and entered Canada without a Minister's permit. At his inquiry, after the latter entry, he sought to establish that he was a permanent resident of Canada. The Federal Court approved the adjudicator's refusal to hear this evidence concluding that the applicant was in fact asking the adjudicator to revise the previous deportation order which was beyond the adjudicator's jurisdiction.

Mavour v. Canada (Minister of Employment & Immigration), [1984] 2 F.C. 122 (Fed. C.A.) — The applicant was arrested on March 15, 1983. An inquiry was caused to be held on March 22, 1983. On that day the inquiry was adjourned to March 30, 1983. The applicant was detained throughout this period, not only in respect of the immigration proceedings but also in respect of outstanding criminal charges. On March 30, 1983, the inquiry was not resumed because there was no case presenting officer available. The inquiry was resumed on April 6, 1983. The adjudicator did not lose jurisdiction by her failure to resume the inquiry on March 30, 1983, the date to which it had been adjourned. Further, the adjudicator's "offer" to release the applicant from detention that was to expire on April 12, 1983, at 4:00 p.m. was, in effect, a decision to release the applicant subject to the condition, among others, that the necessary security or cash deposit be made before a certain time. This was a condition which was within the authority of the adjudicator to impose under section 104(3) of the Act.

Kaur v. Canada (Minister of Employment & Immigration) (1984), 58 N.R. 221 (Fed. C.A.) — The applicant sought admission to Canada as an immigrant. Following a report made pursuant to section 20(1) of the *Immigration Act*, she was made the subject of an inquiry. That inquiry adjourned after the applicant claimed to be a Convention refugee. During the adjournment the applicant left the country for the United States, was refused permission to enter that country and immediately came back to Canada where she reapplied to be admitted as an immigrant. The inquiry, which had been adjourned, culminated in an exclusion order. The adjudicator who presided over the inquiry did not lose jurisdiction when the applicant left Canada for the United States. Once a person seeking admission to Canada has been made the subject of an inquiry in order to determine her admissibility, the mere fact that she, after the start of the inquiry either left Canada or manifested an intention no longer to seek admission, does not deprive the adjudicator of his jurisdiction to continue the inquiry.

Brenner v. Canada (Minister of Employment & Immigration), [1983] 1 F.C. 172 (Fed. T.D.) — The adjudicator determined that the applicant was a person described in section 27(2)(a) because the applicant was inadmissible as a member of a class described in section 19(2)(a)(ii). The applicant applied to the adjudicator for a grant of entry under section 19(3). The adjudicator decided that she had no jurisdiction to entertain the application. A writ of *mandamus* compelling the adjudicator to consider the application under section 19(3) was refused on the ground that her decision brought the person within section 32(6) and, therefore, the adjudicator had no discretion to grant entry to such a person under 19(3).

Allen v. Canada (Minister of Employment & Immigration) (1980), [1981] 1 F.C. 761 (Fed. C.A.) — It is sufficient for an adjudicator to state at the opening of an inquiry that he has been advised that an inquiry is to be held concerning the applicant. No written direction or particular document for the initiation of the inquiry is required.

Grewal v. Canada (Minister of Employment & Immigration) (1980), [1981] 1 F.C. 12, 112 D.L.R. (3d) 30, 37 N.R. 535 (Fed. C.A.) — An adjudicator cannot legally make an exclusion order against an applicant on the ground that he was a person described in section 19(1)(i) unless he determines that the person seeking to come to Canada is "at the time he makes his decision, a member of the inadmissible class" described in section 19(1)(i).

Caccamo v. Canada (Minister of Manpower & Immigration) (1977), [1978] 1 F.C. 366, 75 D.L.R. (3d) 720, 16 N.R. 405 (Fed. C.A.) — The statement of the Director of Information of the Department of Manpower and Immigration reported in a major newspaper as to the reason why the department had instituted deportation proceedings is not sufficient to give rise to a reasonable apprehension of bias in the inquiry which occurred as a result of that decision.

Douglas v. Canada (Minister of Manpower & Immigration), [1972] F.C. 1050 (Fed. C.A.) — Under the *Immigration Act*, R.S.C. 1970, it was held that where the Minister is proceeding in respect of a conviction for an offence that is under appeal, prohibition will not issue to stop the inquiry. The proper procedure is to put the accused before the officer conducting the inquiry and, if necessary, proceed by way of appeal from his decision.

Section 80.1(2)

Goyal v. Canada (Minister of Employment & Immigration) (1992), 9 C.R.R. (2d) 188 (Fed. C.A.) — In the context of the *Immigration Act* and regulations, fairness required that the party bearing the onus of proof should have a right of reply and the failure to provide such an opportunity constituted reviewable error.

Dee v. Canada (Minister of Employment & Immigration) (1991), 14 Imm. L.R. (2d) 1, 135 N.R. 247, 83 D.L.R. (4th) 371 (Fed. C.A.) — The applicant sought to quash a deportation order on the ground that the adjudicator denied him natural justice when he refused to allow the applicant to call two immigration officers as witnesses. There was no merit in this submission. The adjudicator's refusal to call these two officers was based on his opinion that the facts the applicant's counsel intended to prove through these witnesses were irrelevant. The adjudicator was correct in so deciding and accordingly there was no denial of natural justice in his refusal to permit the applicant to call these two officers as witnesses.

Reference re Immigration Act (1991), (sub nom. *Immigration Act, Re)* 137 N.R. 64 (Fed. C.A.) — An application for directions under Rule 1501 will be dismissed unless the following conditions are fulfilled:

1. the issue referred to in the reference under section 28(4) of the *Federal Court Act* is one for which the solution can put an end to the dispute that is before the tribunal;

2. the issue is one that has been raised in the course of the action before the tribunal that makes the reference;

3. the issue results from facts that have been proved or admitted before the tribunal; and

4. the issue is referred to the Court by order from the tribunal which order in addition to formulating the issue shall relate the observations of fact that give rise to the reference.

In this particular case the conditions were not met and the reference purportedly made under section 28(4) of the *Federal Court Act* and Rule 1501 was vacated.

Prassad v. Canada (Minister of Employment & Immigration), [1989] 1 S.C.R. 560, [1989] 3 W.W.R. 289, 36 Admin. L.R. 72, 7 Imm. L.R. (2d) 253, 93 N.R. 81, 57 D.L.R. (4th) 663 (S.C.C.) — The appellant had previously been deported from Canada. The appellant re-entered Canada without having obtained the written consent of the Minister and then became subject to a report. At the outset of the inquiry, the appellant applied to the Minister of Employment and Immigration for a Minister's Permit authorizing her to remain in Canada and to the Governor-in-Council for an exemption from the regulations pursuant to section 114(2). Counsel requested an adjournment of the inquiry to permit the appellant's application to be considered. The adjudicator refused, made a deportation order and that decision was the subject of a section 28 application which was dismissed by the Federal Court of Appeal. The Supreme Court of Canada dismissed this appeal holding that an adjudicator acting pursuant to section 27(3) is neither bound to accede to a request for an adjournment nor is bound to refuse it. The adjudicator had discretion in this type of case. The adjudicator must be cognizant that a "full and proper inquiry be held" and must ensure that statutory duty to hold an inquiry is fulfilled. The adjudicator might consider the number of adjournments already granted, the length of time for which the adjournment is sought and whether or not the purpose of the adjournment could have been affected prior to the commencement of the inquiry.

Mohammad v. Canada (Minister of Employment & Immigration) (1988), [1989] 2 F.C. 363, 55 D.L.R. (4th) 321, 21 F.T.R. 240 (note) (Fed. C.A.) — The applicant sought to stay the proceedings of an inquiry pending his appeal to the Federal Court of Appeal of a judgment of the Trial Division dismissing his application for *certiorari* and prohibition. Assuming that the applicant had a serious case to argue on appeal, there was no irreparable injury in allowing the inquiry to start. If the applicant was ultimately successful in the Court of Appeal, the final judgment of that Court would be quite capable of giving him adequate remedy. Holding the inquiry and pursuing it through all of its stages up to but not including the possible issuance of a removal order will not deprive the applicant of any legal right or have the practical effect of placing him in a position that the final judgment cannot cure.

Noble v. Canada (Minister of Employment & Immigration) (February 13, 1985), Doc. A-1162-84 (Fed. C.A.) — The absence of a verbatim transcript of the inquiry did not invalidate the deportation order herein. A partial extract from the minutes of the inquiry was available. Furthermore, the adjudicator swore a statutory declaration confirming the accuracy of the partial transcript insofar as it reported his determination of the case. The existence of the partial transcript together with the adjudicator's statutory declaration operated so as to impose on the applicant an obligation to satisfy the Court, perhaps by way of affidavit evidence from the counsel at the inquiry, that there were procedural irregularities sufficiently serious that entitled the Court to set aside the deportation order. No such material was filed on this application and, accordingly, the application was dismissed.

Kosley v. Canada (Minister of Employment & Immigration), [1985] 1 F.C. 797 (Fed. C.A.) — There is no specific requirement in the Act or regulations that the proceedings at an inquiry be transcribed. As a matter of practice, they usually are.

Kravets v. Canada (Minister of Employment & Immigration), [1985] 1 F.C. 434 (Fed. T.D.) — This application raised issues dealing with the impact of section 15 of the Canadian *Charter of Rights and Freedoms* on section 19 of the *Immigration Act*. The applicant sought various orders for *mandamus* and *certiorari* concerning decisions or actions of the Minister and her officers and concerning an impending inquiry by an adjudicator. The respondent Minister sought an adjournment to prepare for the application. The adjournment was granted. The Court ruled that section 24(1) of the Charter empowered it to issue an order in the nature of prohibition preventing an adjudicator, in the future, from making a removal order or issuing a departure notice until the present application had been disposed of by the Trial Division. The Court noted that section 24(1) of the Charter applied to "anyone whose rights ... have been infringed or denied." The Court decided that this language was broad enough to cover the present situation, which, at this stage in the proceedings, involved only an allegation of a past denial of Charter rights and an allegation of an apprehended denial of Charter rights in a future inquiry.

Bowen v. Canada (Minister of Employment & Immigration), [1984] 2 F.C. 507 (Fed. C.A.) — The applicant initially refused to testify at the inquiry on the advice of her counsel but later retreated from this position also on the advice of her counsel. The Commission, however, presented its case without the applicant's testimony. Section 11(c) of the *Charter of Rights* was held to be inapplicable to the applicant because it could not be said that the applicant was being compelled to be a witness at her inquiry when the counsel representing her conceded her compellability as a witness. It was further held that section 11(c) of the Charter had no application to the testimony to be given by the applicant because the applicant could not be said to be "a person charged with an offence". The Court observed section 24 of the Charter did not apply because it was a condition precedent to the operation of that section that a person's rights or freedoms as guaranteed by the Charter be infringed or denied. The Court having decided that the applicant's rights or freedoms as guaranteed by the Charter had not been infringed or denied, was of the view that the conditions precedent to the operation of section 24 had not been met.

Green v. Canada (Minister of Employment & Immigration), [1984] 1 F.C. 441 (Fed. C.A.) — The *Jiminez-Perez* case does not require an adjudicator who receives an application under section 115(2) during the course of an inquiry to adjourn the inquiry immediately pending decision on that application by the Governor-in-Council. The adjudicator is required to proceed with the inquiry as expeditiously as possible in the circumstances of each case. The power of an adjudicator to adjourn is restricted to adjournments "for the purpose of ensuring a full and proper inquiry." The Court also noted that the decision in the *Tam* case was based on unusual facts.

Schaaf v. Canada (Minister of Employment & Immigration), [1984] 3 W.W.R. 1, 52 N.R. 54 (Fed. C.A.) — An admission of fact offered by counsel and confirmed by the subject of the inquiry is evidence upon which an adjudicator is entitled to act. Errors in law which could not and did not have any effect upon the outcome of the inquiry are not a basis for relief under section 28 of the *Federal Court Act*. The adjudicator erred in law when he did not, after deciding to hear testimony, give an opportunity to the subject of the inquiry or his counsel to present evidence and make submissions. This failure was caused by the conduct of the applicant and his counsel who indicated that the allegation in question was not contested. Accordingly, the errors could not have affected the ultimate decision at the inquiry and, therefore, the section 28 application was dismissed.

Ioannidis v. Canada (Minister of Employment & Immigration), [1983] 1 F.C. 369 (Fed. C.A.) — A deportation order was made on the ground that the applicant was a person described in section 27(2)(d) of the *Immigration Act*. The Court noted that it was wrong for the adjudicator to rule that in view of the applicant's refusal to answer the questions of the case presenting officer, the applicant would not be allowed to testify on his own behalf. This did not vitiate either the inquiry or the deportation order because counsel did not at any time during the inquiry seek to have his client testify and it could not be inferred from the record that the applicant would have testified had it not been for the ruling made by the adjudicator. Further, the Court could find nothing in the Canadian *Charter of Rights* preventing an adjudicator presiding over an inquiry under the *Immigration Act* from drawing legitimate inferences from the fact that the subject of the inquiry had refused to testify.

R. v. Wooten (1983), 9 C.C.C. (3d) 513 (B.C. S.C.) — This was an appeal by the Crown from an acquittal of the respondent of an offence under section 95(g) of the *Immigration Act*. The respondent was arrested and detained on the grounds that he was in Canada without the permission of the Minister and that he had falsely represented material facts to enable him to remain in the country. During the inquiry, the case presenting officer sought to call the respondent as a witness. The respondent's counsel objected. The adjudicator ruled against the respondent on this question. The respondent was sworn as a witness but refused to answer any questions. The respondent was charged under section 95(g) and acquitted on the basis that section 95(g) was inoperative as it offended sections 7 and 11(c) of the *Charter of Rights*. The respondent was held not to be a person "charged with an offence" and, therefore, not subject to the protection of section 11(c) of the Charter. The Court adopted previous decisions which had characterized immigration inquiries as civil proceedings. Section 7 of the Charter was not applicable because the inquiry was a civil proceeding and there was, therefore, nothing fundamentally unjust in compelling the person who was the subject of the immigration inquiry to testify.

Webb v. Canada (Minister of Manpower & Immigration) (1981), [1982] 1 F.C. 687, 125 D.L.R. (3d) 510, 39 N.R. 495 (Fed. C.A.) — The Court left open the question of whether *R. v. Cole*, [1980] 6 W.W.R. 552 (Man. Co. Ct.) was rightly decided. The Court did point out, however, that where the applicant does not refuse to testify, the principles enunciated in section 2(d) of the *Bill of Rights* do not avail.

R. v. Forrester (1982), 2 C.C.C. (3d) 467 (Ont. C.A.) — The appellant answered a number of questions at an inquiry before refusing to answer a question on the grounds that her answer might tend to incriminate her and declining an offer of the protection of the *Canada Evidence Act*, R.S.C. 1970, c. E-10. The Ontario Court of Appeal upheld her conviction under section 95 and adopted the reasons of the Federal Court in *Chana v. Canada (Minister of Manpower & Immigration)*, [1977] 2 F.C. 496 (Fed. T.D.).

Tam v. Canada (Minister of Employment & Immigration) (1982), 46 N.R. 1 (Fed. C.A.) — An inquiry was adjourned for the applicant to seek consideration from the Minister under section 115(2) [s. 114(2)] of the Act. On June 15, 1982, when the inquiry resumed, the applicant had received no final decision, although the Minister had undertaken to give one after consulting his local officials. The adjudicator refused a further adjournment and ordered the applicant deported. The deportation order was quashed because fairness required that the inquiry not proceed until the applicant had received the Minister's answer. The deportation order was also set aside, per Heald J., because the adjudicator erred in refusing to allow the applicant's counsel to make submissions with respect to the section 115(2) application.

Cheung v. Canada (Minister of Employment & Immigration) (1981), 36 N.R. 563 (Fed. C.A.) — An adjudicator's refusal to issue a summons permitting an alien to cross-examine the author of a statutory declaration containing admissions allegedly made by the alien is an error in law; the adjudicator's findings, based upon the untested statutory declarations, could not stand.

Anderson v. Canada (Minister of Employment & Immigration) (1980), [1981] 2 F.C. 30, 113 D.L.R. (3d) 243, 36 N.R. 423 (Fed. C.A.) — Where an adjudicator finds an applicant to be a member of an inadmissible class other than the inadmissible class specified in the section 27 report, and bases his departure notice on that finding, the departure notice will be set aside.

R. v. Cole, [1980] 6 W.W.R. 552, 4 Man. R. (2d) 363, 17 C.R. (3d) 145, 54 C.C.C. (2d) 324, 115 D.L.R. (3d) 382 (Man. Co. Ct.), leave to appeal refused [1981] 1 W.W.R. 596 (Man. C.A.) — A person who fails to answer questions put to him at an immigration inquiry may not be prosecuted for an offence contrary to section 95(g) due to the protection in section 2(d) of the Canadian Bill of Rights with respect to the right of a person not to "incriminate" himself.

Akpanson v. Canada (Minister of Employment & Immigration) (1979), [1980] 1 F.C. 732 (Fed. T.D.) — An adjudicator has the power to compel an immigration officer to attend and testify where the immigration officer has changed the petition or student status to visitor status in circumstances where the reason for the change is not otherwise apparent. Where an adjudicator refuses to receive the evidence of such an immigration officer, an order to issue a writ of *mandamus* may be obtained.

Chana v. Canada (Minister of Manpower & Immigration), [1977] 2 F.C. 496, 74 D.L.R. (3d) 491 (Fed. T.D.) — Under the old Act, an alien was held to be compellable to give evidence at a special inquiry. The Court was of the view that the alien's rights under section 2(d) of the *Canadian Bill of Rights* were not violated due to the fact that the alien was allowed to have counsel and was fully safeguarded against incriminating himself by virtue of the protections contained in the *Canada Evidence Act*, R.S.C. 1970, c. E-10.

Ramjit v. Canada (Minister of Manpower & Immigration) (1975), [1976] 1 F.C. 184 (Fed. C.A.) — Where the record of the proceedings does not contain the direction, and where nothing in the record of the proceedings shows that the person who issued the direction that was read at the inquiry was the Deputy Minister, or a person acting for the Deputy Minister, the deportation order will be set aside.

Canada (Minister of Manpower & Immigration) v. Brooks (1973), [1974] S.C.R. 850, 36 D.L.R. (3d) 522 (S.C.C.) — Duplicity in a direction for inquiry is not a ground for annulling the deportation order made at such inquiry. All that is required is that the subject of the inquiry be made aware of the allegations made against him under the relevant provisions of the *Immigration Act* and that he is given an opportunity to meet them.

R. v. Wolfe, [1965] 1 C.C.C. 343 (B.C. S.C.) — Under the *Immigration Act*, R.S.C. 1952, a witness was held to have the right to object to self-incriminating questions and to claim the protection of section 5 of the *Canada Evidence Act*, R.S.C. 1970, c. E-10, in respect of those questions. The Court ruled that the alien who was the subject of the proceedings was required to answer truthfully all questions put to him by the inquiry officer.

Section 80.1(5)

Cambouras v. Canada (Minister of Employment & Immigration) (1984), 68 N.R. 158 (Fed. C.A.) — For digest, see section 80.1(1), *supra*.

Ioannidis v. Canada (Minister of Employment & Immigration), [1983] 1 F.C. 369 (Fed. C.A.) — For digest, see section 80.1(2), *supra*.

Cheung v. Canada (Minister of Employment & Immigration) (1981), 36 N.R. 563 (Fed. C.A.) — The applicant's right to cross-examine any witness presented by the case presenting officer cannot lightly be interfered with by an adjudicator. Only when there are proper grounds can an adjudicator refuse to allow the person concerned to present evidence and cross-examine. Where the right to cross-examine is interfered with improperly, a deportation order will be set aside.

Canada (Attorney General) v. Jolly, [1975] F.C. 216, 54 D.L.R. (3d) 277, 7 N.R. 271 (Fed. C.A.) — The requirement that evidence be credible and trustworthy is met if the evidence is admitted but accorded little or no weight because the contents of the documents were not proved in accordance with the rules of evidence in a civil action. It would be wrong, however, in law for the document to be rejected because it had not been proven in accordance with the rules of evidence in a civil action, as this standard is not imported in the statutory rules of evidence in immigration matters.

Security

81. (1) Definition of "Review Committee" — In this section and sections 81.1, 81.2 and 82, "Review Committee" has the same meaning as in the *Canadian Security Intelligence Service Act*.

(2) Report to Review Committee — Where the Minister and the Solicitor General are of the opinion, based on security or criminal intelligence reports received and considered by them, that a person who has made or is deemed by subsection 73(3) to have made an appeal pursuant to paragraph 70(1)(*b*) or 70(3)(*b*) or a member of the family class whose application for landing is the subject of an appeal under subsection 77(3) made by a person who has sponsored the application for landing is a person described,

(a) in the case of a permanent resident, in paragraph 19(1)(*c*.2), subparagraph 19(1)(*d*)(ii), paragraph 19(1)(*e*), (*f*), (*g*), (*k*) or (*l*) or 27(1)(*a*.1), subparagraph 27(1)(*a*.3)(ii) or paragraph 27(1)(*g*) or (*h*), or

(b) in any other case, in paragraph 19(1)(*c*.2), (*d*), (*e*), (*f*), (*g*), (*j*), (*k*) or (*l*),

they may make a report to the Review Committee.

(3) **Notice to appellant** — Within ten days after a report referred to in subsection (2) is made, the Minister and the Solicitor General of Canada shall cause a notice to be sent informing the person who made the appeal of the report and stating that following an investigation in relation thereto, the appeal may be dismissed.

(4) **Application of the Canadian Security Intelligence Service Act** — Where a report is made to the Review Committee pursuant to subsection (2), the Review Committee shall investigate the grounds on which it is based and for that purpose subsections 39(2) and (3) and sections 43, 44 and 48 to 51 of the *Canadian Security Intelligence Service Act* apply, with such modifications as the circumstances require, to the investigation as if the investigation were conducted in relation to a complaint made pursuant to section 42 of that Act, except that

(a) a reference in any of those provisions to "deputy head" shall be read as a reference to the Minister and the Solicitor General of Canada; and

(b) paragraph 50(*a*) of that Act does not apply with respect to the person concerning whom the report is made.

(4.1) **Investigation to cease** — If the Review Committee is of the opinion that it cannot perfom its duties described in subsections (4) and (5) to (8), it must cease its investigation and give notice to the Minister and the person referred to in subsection (2).

(5) **Statement to be sent to person affected** — The Review Committee shall, as soon as practicable after a report is made to it pursuant to subsection (2), send to the person who made the appeal referred to in that subsection a statement summarizing such information available to it as will enable the person to be as fully informed as possible of the circumstances giving rise to the report.

(6) **Effect of report** — Notwithstanding anything in this Act, where a report concerning any person is made to the Review Committee pursuant to subsection (2), the hearing of an appeal concerning the person made or deemed by subsection 73(3) to have been made pursuant to paragraph 70(1)(*b*) or 70(3)(*b*) or made pursuant to section 77 shall not be commenced or, if commenced, shall be adjourned until the Review Committee has, pursuant to subsection (7), made a report to the Governor in Council with respect to that person and the Governor in Council has made a decision in relation thereto.

(7) **Report to Governor in Council** — The Review Committee shall, on completion of an investigation in relation to a report made to it pursuant to subsection (2), make a report to the Governor in Council containing its conclusion whether or not a certificate should be issued under subsection 82(1) and the grounds on which that conclusion is based.

(8) **Report to appellant** — The Review Committee shall, at the same time as or after a report is made pursuant to subsection (7), provide the person who made the appeal referred to in subsection (2) with a report containing the conclusion referred to in subsection (7).

R.S.C. 1985, c. 30 (3rd Supp.), s. 9; 1992, c. 49, s. 71; 1997, c. 22, s. 7.

81.1 (1) **Appointment of a judge** — After consultation by the Prime Minister of Canada with the Leader of the Opposition in the House of Commons and the leader in the House of Commons of each party having at least twelve members in that House, the Governor in Council may appoint a retired judge of a superior court for a term of three to five years to perform the duties of the Review Committee described in subsection 81(4) and (5) to (8).

(2) **Tenure and reappointment** — The appointed person holds office during good behaviour and may be removed by the Governor in Council at any time for cause. The person is eligible to be re-appointed.

(3) **Remuneration and expenses** — The appointed person shall be paid, for each day that the person performs duties under this Act, such remuneration as is fixed by the Governor in Council and is entitled to be paid reasonable travel and living expenses incurred in the course of their duties under this Act while absent from their ordinary place of residence.

1997, c. 22, s. 8.

81.2 (1) **Referral** — The Minister may refer to the person appointed under subsection 81.1(1) any case that the Review Committee has ceased to investigate under subsection 81(4.1) and, in that case, the Minister must make a report described in subsection 81(2) to the appointed person and send the notice described in subsection 81(3).

(2) **Application of subsections 81(4) and (5) to (8)** — Subsections 81(4) and (5) to (8) apply to the appointed person as if that person were the Review Committee.

1997, c. 22, s. 8.

81.3 **Annual reports** — The person appointed under subsection 81.1(1) must, not later than September 30 in each fiscal year, submit to the Solicitor General of Canada a report of the activities of the person during the preceding fiscal year and the Solicitor General of Canada must cause the report to be laid before each House of Parliament on any of the first fifteen days on which that House is sitting after the day the Solicitor General of Canada receives it.

1997, c. 22, s. 8.

82. (1) **Security certificates** — Where, after considering a report made under subsection 81(7) by the Review Committee or the person appointed under subsection 81.1(1), the Governor in Council is satisfied that the person with respect to whom the report was made is a person referred to in paragraph 81(2)(a) or (b), as the case may be, the Governor in Council may direct the Minister to issue a certificate to that effect.

(2) **Effect of certificate** — Notwithstanding anything in this Act, the Appeal Division shall dismiss any appeal made or deemed by subsection 73(3) to have been made pursuant to paragraph 70(1)(*b*) or 70(3)(*b*) or made pursuant to section 77 if a certificate referred to in subsection (1), signed by the Minister, is filed with the Appeal Division.

(3) **Evidence** — A certificate issued under subsection (1) is, in any prosecution or other proceeding under or arising out of this Act, conclusive proof of the matters stated therein and shall be received by the Appeal Division without proof of the signature or official character of the person appearing to have signed the certificate unless called into question by the Minister.

R.S.C. 1985, c. 28 (4th Supp.), s. 33; 1997, c. 22, s. 9.

Case Law

Section 82(1)

Ukponmwan v. Canada (Minister of Citizenship & Immigration) (1998), 151 F.T.R. 317 (Fed. T.D.) — On August 10, 1998, the applicant applied for leave to review a decision of an immigration enforcement officer directing the applicant to report for removal on August 13, 1998. This decision gave effect to a deportation order dated January 29, 1996, that became executory when the applicant's claim for refugee status was denied and leave to review that decision was refused.

The applicant's grounds for his application were that he would likely be subject to detention and torture by the Nigerian authorities on return, both because he is a member of a particular tribe and a member of a resistance group. Since it would undermine the jurisdiction of the Court over this application if the applicant were removed to Nigeria prior to its disposition the Court held that it had jurisdiction to stay a removal until the application had been determined.

Secondly, the Court found that it had jurisdiction to review the validity of the directions for the applicant's removal to Nigeria.

Section 82(3)

Chiarelli v. Canada (Minister of Employment & Immigration), [1992] 1 S.C.R. 711, 16 Imm. L.R. (2d) 1 — This appeal calls into question the constitutionality of the statutory scheme pursuant to which a permanent resident can be deported from Canada if he is found to have been convicted of an offence for which a term of imprisonment of 5 years or more may be imposed. A further attack was brought against the interaction of that scheme with the investigations conducted by the Security Intelligence Review Committee (SIRC) into the activities of persons reasonably believed to be involved in certain types of criminal or subversive activity.

The respondent was convicted of a number of criminal offences and in January 1986, a report was written pursuant to section 27 of the *Immigration Act* identifying the respondent as a permanent resident described in 27(1)(d)(ii). As a result of this report an inquiry was directed pursuant to section 27(3). A deportation order was made against the respondent pursuant to section 32(2). The respondent appealed to the Immigration Appeal Board. That appeal was adjourned after the Solicitor General and the Minister of Employment and Immigration made a joint report to the SIRC. The report indicated that in the opinion of the Ministers the respondent was a person described in section 19(1)(d)(ii). The SIRC conducted the required investigation and reported to the Governor-in-Council pursuant to section 81(7). The Governor-in-Council adopted the conclusion of the SIRC and directed the appellant Minister to issue a certificate under section 82(1) with respect to the respondent's appeal. This certificate was issued, with the result that the respondent could not assert compassionate grounds as a reason for allowing the appeal.

The SIRC conducted its investigation and hearing first by reading a document entitled "Statement of Circumstances" as well as two summaries of information. The first day's hearing was held *in camera* and the respondent was excluded from the hearing and provided only with a summary of the evidence. The respondent was permitted to attend the second day of the hearing. The respondent declined, objected to the fairness and constitutionality of the proceeding before the SIRC, submitted no evidence at the hearing, and chose not to cross-examine two RCMP witnesses who had testified on the first day. Counsel did make submissions to the SIRC.

Section 27(1) requires an immigration officer in possession of information that a permanent resident falls into one of its enumerated classes to forward a report to the Deputy Minister. An inquiry is then held by an adjudicator in cases where the Deputy Minister considers one is warranted. Section 32(2) provides that where an adjudicator decides that a person who is the subject of an inquiry does fall within one of the classes in section 27(1), the adjudicator shall, except in the case of a Convention refugee, make a deportation order. All persons who fall within section 27(1)(d)(ii) have deliberately violated an essential condition under which they were permitted to remain in Canada. In such a situation there is no breach of fundamental justice in giving practical effect to the termination of their right to remain in Canada. In the case of a permanent resident, deportation is the only way in which to accomplish this. There is nothing inherently unjust about a mandatory order. The fact of the deliberate violation of the condition imposed by section 27(1)(d)(ii) is sufficient to justify a deportation order. Accordingly, sections 27(1)(d)(ii) and 32(2) are not contrary to section 7 of the *Charter of Rights*.

The deportation authorized by sections 27(1)(d)(ii) and 32(2) is not cruel and unusual punishment as described in section 12 of the *Charter of Rights*.

Section 6 of the *Charter* specifically provides for differential treatment of citizens and permanent residents. Accordingly, sections 27(1)(d)(ii) and 32(2) do not violate section 15 of the Charter. Permanent residents are given mobility rights in section 6(2). Only citizens are accorded the right to enter, remain in and leave Canada in section 6(1). There is no discrimination contrary to section 15 in a deportation scheme that applies to permanent residents but not citizens.

The effect of the security certificate in this case is to direct the Immigration Appeal Board to dismiss any appeal based on the existence of compassionate or humanitarian considerations. The permanent resident's right of appeal after a certificate has been issued is restricted to questions of law, fact or mixed law and fact.

The *Immigration Act*, S.C. 1910, c. 27, did not provide any specific grounds of appeal. A person ordered deported could only resort to the Minister, who had authority to overturn a deportation order on unspecified grounds. The *Immigration Act*, R.S.C. 1952, c. 325, provided for an Immigration Appeal Board; however, appeals against deportation orders remained under the control of the Minister. The Board heard only those appeals directed to it by the Minister, and the Minister retained the power to confirm or quash the Appeal Board's decision or substitute his decision as he deemed just and proper. The 1966 *White Paper on Immigration* recommended that a reconstituted Immigration Appeal Board have authority to deal conclusively with appeals against deportation orders except in security cases. The *Immigration Appeal Board Act*, 1967 for the first time conferred upon the Board the power to stay or quash a deportation order made against a permanent resident on the basis of all the circumstances of the case. This new power was subject to the discretion of the Minister and the Solicitor General, who could certify their opinion based on security or criminal intelligence reports that it would be contrary to the national interest to permit such relief. This reserves to the Crown the right similar to the prerogative right which existed at common law, to determine that the continued presence in Canada of an alien, subject to a deportation order, was not conducive to the public good. The *Immigration Appeal Board Act* was repealed by the *Immigration Act*, 1976. However, this new Act did not change the nature of the decision that could be made by the Board having regard to all the circumstances of the case. That decision remained as it had been under the 1967 Act, an exercise of discretion based on compassionate grounds. Section 83 of the *Immigration Act*, 1976 limited the availability of relief based on all the circumstances of the case. Such an appeal had to be dismissed if the Minister and Solicitor General certified their opinion that it would be contrary to the national interest to permit such an appeal. In 1984 the SIRC was established by the *Canadian Security Intelligence Service Act*, S.C. 1984, c. 21. The Review Committee was assigned various functions under several Acts, including the *Immigration Act*, 1976. Sections 83 and 82.1 of the *Immigration Act*, 1976 were repealed and amended versions were substituted. The decision to direct the issuance of a security certificate, however, remained with the Governor-in-Council. Thus, there has never been a universally available right of appeal from a deportation order on humanitarian or compassionate grounds or "having regard to all the circumstances of the case." Such an appeal has historically been a purely discretionary matter. The right of appeal required to comply with the principles of fundamental justice is a true appeal which enables the decision of first instance to be questioned on factual and legal grounds. The absence of an appeal on wider grounds does not violate section 7.

The procedure followed by the Security Intelligence Review Committee in this case recognized competing individual and state interests and attempted to find a reasonable balance between them. It was not necessary that the respondent be given details of the criminal intelligence investigation techniques or police sources used to acquire the information upon which the two Ministers relied in issuing the certificate. The respondent was given an opportunity to respond by calling his own witnesses or by requesting that he be allowed to cross-examine the RCMP officers who testified *in camera*. Such a procedure was sufficient to meet the requirements of the principles of fundamental justice.

Applications and Appeals to the Federal Court

82.1 (1) Judicial review by Federal Court — An application for judicial review under the *Federal Court Act* with respect to any decision or order made, or any matter arising, under this Act or the rules or regulations thereunder may be commenced only with leave of a judge of the Federal Court — Trial Division.

(2) Exception — Subsection (1) does not apply with respect to a decision of a visa officer on an application under section 9, 10, or 77 or to any other matter arising thereunder with respect to an application to a visa officer.

(3) Application for leave — An application under this section for leave to commence an application for judicial review shall be filed with the Federal Court — Trial Division and served within fifteen days after the day on which the applicant is notified of the decision or order or becomes aware of the other matter.

(4) Consideration of application for leave — Unless a judge of the Federal Court — Trial Division directs otherwise, an application under this section for leave to commence an application for judicial review shall be disposed of without personal appearance.

(5) Extension — A judge of the Federal Court — Trial Division may, for special reasons, allow an extended time for filing and serving an application under this section for leave to commence an application for judicial review.

(6) Day and place of review — Subject to subsection (7), where leave to commence an application for judicial review is granted, the application for judicial review shall be deemed to have been commenced and the judge granting leave shall fix the day and place for the hearing of the application for judicial review.

(7) Fixing day for review — In fixing a day pursuant to subsection (6), the judge shall set the matter down for a day that is no sooner than thirty days, and no later than

ninety days, after the day on which leave to commence the application for judicial review was granted, unless the parties agree that the matter may be set down on an earlier day.

(8) Review in summary way — Any application for leave to commence an application for judicial review, and any application for judicial review, under this section shall be determined without delay and in a summary way.

(9) Right of minister — The Minister may, in accordance with subsection (1), make an application for leave to commence an application for judicial review with respect to any decision of the Refugee Division whether or not the Minister presented evidence, questioned witnesses, made representations or otherwise took part in the proceedings before the Refugee Division.

(10) Information obtained in confidence — With respect to any application for judicial review of a decision by a visa officer to refuse to issue a visa to a person on the grounds that the person is a person described in any of paragraphs 19(1)(*c*.1) to (*g*), (*k*) and (*l*),

> **(a) the Minister may make an application to the Federal Court — Trial Division, *in camera*, and in the absence of the person and any counsel representing the person, for the non-disclosure to the person of information obtained in confidence from the government or an institution of a foreign state or from an international organization of states or an institution thereof;**
>
> **(b) the Court shall, *in camera*, and in the absence of the person and any counsel representing the person,**
>
> > **(i) examine the information, and**
> >
> > **(ii) provide counsel representing the Minister with a reasonable opportunity to be heard as to whether the information should not be disclosed to the person on the grounds that the disclosure would be injurious to national security or to the safety of persons;**
>
> **(c) the information shall be returned to counsel representing the Minister and shall not be considered by the Court in making its determination on the judicial review if, in the opinion of the Court, the disclosure of the information to the person would not be injurious to national security or to the safety of persons; and**
>
> **(d) if the Court determines that the information should not be disclosed to the person on the grounds that the disclosure would be injurious to national security or to the safety of persons, the information shall not be disclosed but may be considered by the Court in making its determination.**

R.S.C. 1985, c. 28 (4th Supp.), s. 19; 1990, c. 8, s. 53; 1992, c. 49, s. 73.

Case Law

Chow v. Canada (Minister of Citizenship & Immigration) (1998), 45 Imm. L.R. (2d) 170, 153 F.T.R. 236 (Fed. T.D.) — This was an appeal from a decision by the Immigration Appeal Division that it did not have jurisdiction to hear the applicant's appeal because there had been no refusal of an application for landing by a member of the applicant's family class. The family class includes parents of a sponsor but not siblings unless the sibling is an orphan who is under 19 years of age and is unmarried. A parent who is sponsored may bring accompany dependants and these may include the sponsor siblings. The applicant's father applied to do so in this case. He sought to add his son and his daughter to his and his wife's application, an application sponsored by the applicant. The son was not granted a visa. The applicant appealed to the Immigration Appeal Division. The Appeal Division does not have jurisdiction to hear the appeal because the son is not a member of the applicant's family class. The procedure that should be followed is to challenge the non-inclusion of the son in the landing application in a judicial review application to the Federal Court, not an appeal to the Immigration Appeal Division.

Rajadurai v. Canada (Minister of Citizenship & Immigration) (March 30, 1999), Doc. IMM-4014-98, IMM-4402-98 (Fed. T.D.) — The applicants were sisters in Sri Lanka who applied as assisted family class applicants. The submissions made on their behalf included the representation that even if they had not obtained sufficient points they should be granted landing on humanitarian and compassionate grounds. The decision by the visa officer to refuse to issue a visa was based on the fact that the Minister's delegate denied admission on humanitarian and compassionate grounds. Accordingly, leave to proceed was required. The French text of subsection 82.1(2) is clearer than the English in conveying the idea that it is decisions that the visa officer makes on his or her own, rather than those he or she makes as a conduit for another, that are exempt from the leave requirements as set out in subsection 82.1(1).

Tei v. Canada (Minister of Citizenship & Immigration) (1998), 48 Imm. L.R. (2d) 120, 161 F.T.R. 51 (Fed. T.D.) — The applicant submitted an application for permanent residence under the investor category and included his wife. The applicant's wife had a conviction for making a false statement for the purpose of obtaining a certificate of identity and had been sentenced to a fine of $1,500 Hong Kong dollars. The applicant submitted an application for rehabilitation, and the applicant and his wife were interviewed in June 1997 for the purpose of determining whether the visa officer would recommend to the program manager that the wife was rehabilitated. The result of the interview was a negative recommendation and on July 16, 1997, the program manager concurred with this recommendation.

The applicant's Notice of Motion challenged the visa officer's decision refusing the applicant's application for permanent residence, when in fact, the applicant was really challenging the Minister's decision refusing to grant rehabilitation. The Minister is the decision-maker. The visa officer's role is that of advisor in that he made a recommendation and submitted the application along with supporting documents. If the visa officer drew unreasonable conclusions or relied on erroneous facts or indeed failed to take into account relevant facts, then these defects or errors would be germane in a review of the decision itself which was made by the Minister's delegate. By challenging the visa officer's recommendation, the applicant is also putting into play the validity of the Minister's decision. The applicant should have sought judicial review of the Minister's determination. The Court noted that leave of the Court would have been required to review this decision and that leave had not been obtained.

Accordingly, the application for judicial review was dismissed.

Ching v. Canada (Minister of Citizenship & Immigration) (1997), 137 F.T.R. 313 (Fed. T.D.) — The applicant applied to the Minister to authorize his admission to Canada as a visitor or in the alternative to authorize his admission on a Minister's permit. Decisions of the type under review in this application do not fall within the exception set out in subsection 82.1(2) and accordingly leave is required.

Sajjan v. Canada (Minister of Citizenship & Immigration) (1997), (sub nom. *Canada (Minister of Citizenship & Immigration) v. Sajjan)* 216 N.R. 150, 39 Imm. L.R. (2d) 56 (Fed. C.A.) — A decision of the Immigration Appeal Division respecting a decision of a visa officer may only be judicially reviewed with leave of a judge of the Federal Court.

Chan v. Canada (Minister of Citizenship & Immigration), 34 Imm. L.R. (2d) 259, [1996] 3 F.C. 349, 43 Admin. L.R. (2d) 314, 37 C.R.R. (2d) 112, 136 D.L.R. (4th) 433, 114 F.T.R.

247 (Fed. T.D.) — This was an application for judicial review of a decision of a visa officer. The decision denied the applicant's application for permanent residence on the basis that the applicant was inadmissable pursuant to paragraph 19(1)(c.2) of the *Immigration Act*.

During the course of the application the respondent advised the Court that it intended to bring an application pursuant to section 82.1(10). Section 82.1(10) does not contravene section 7 of the *Charter of Rights and Freedoms*. The evidence withheld pursuant to section 82.1(10) is carefully reviewed by a judge of the Federal Court, who must consider whether the information could be revealed. The applicant does not get a summary of the confidential evidence as in the case of a certificate filed under section 40.1, however, the applicant is informed of the reason why he or she has been denied admission to Canada. In this case, the applicant was told that the officer had reason to believe that she was member of the Sun Yee On triad. There was nothing to prevent the applicant from seeking judicial review of the decision and providing affidavit evidence to show that she was not a member of the triad. When disclosure of information could be injurious to national security the applicant's rights must be balanced against the state's legitimate interests.

In this case, the applicant had been issued a visa prior to the visa officer becoming concerned about her triad membership. The applicant argued that when making the decision to revoke the visa, the visa officer was *functus officio*. This doctrine applies to administrative bodies, however, the principle is more flexible and less formalistic when applied to administrative decision-making, as opposed to judicial decision-making. Administrative decision-making can be re-opened in the interest of justice where the enabling statute contemplates a reconsideration of a decision. The *Immigration Act* is silent on the question of whether a visa officer may review decisions already made. The Court noted that if an applicant was wrongly denied a visa, there would be nothing to stop a visa officer from reconsidering that decision once new information was provided. Applying the same logic the Court concluded that a visa officer, upon receiving information that the applicant was a member of an inadmissable class, had jurisdiction to reconsider the earlier decision granting in the visa.

Aguiar v. Canada (Minister of Citizenship & Immigration) (1995), 106 F.T.R. 304 — The applicant sought an extension of time within which to serve an application for leave and for judicial review. When seeking an exceptional extension beyond the prescribed time limit, a salient consideration in moving the Court to grant such extension is "whether or not there is a good case on the merits".

In support of this motion for extended time the applicant's solicitor filed an affidavit. This practise was criticized. In this regard the Court relied upon *Lex Tex Canada Ltd. v. Duratex Inc.*, [1979] 2 F.C. 722 (Fed. T.D.) at p. 723. On the record in this case there was no means of determining what the applicant's case was or how good it might be on the merits and, accordingly, the application was dismissed.

Ayala-Barriere v. Canada (Minister of Citizenship & Immigration) (1995), 31 Imm. L.R. (2d) 99, 101 F.T.R. 310 — This is an example of a situation where the Court awarded costs against the Minister. The senior immigration officer made an honest mistake with respect to whether the applicants had been recognized by the UNHCR as refugees in Guatemala. More could have been done, and should have been done, to clarify the situation, if there was any ambiguity in the letter which the officer misunderstood.

This was a clear case, however, involving a situation where the Minister had made an error and therefore, that the applicant's case was not frivolous, or without merit. The respondent, however, decided to proceed with the judicial review application even though it knew that an error had been committed, and even though it was aware of the true nature of the applicant's status in Guatemala. In those circumstances the Court decided that it would be appropriate to award costs.

Dhaliwal v. Canada (Minister of Citizenship & Immigration) (June 6, 1995), Doc. IMM-7381-93 (Fed. T.D.) — The respondent successfully moved to dismiss this application for judicial review on the basis that it sought to quash a response from the visa officer which was not, in fact, a decision. The visa officer made a decision on September 22, 1993. The matter referred to in the motion for judicial review was simply a courtesy response from the visa officer affirming the May 20 decision. There was no new evidence or new issues introduced by counsel in his request for reconsideration. Counsel cannot extend the date of decision by writing a letter with the intention of provoking a reply. Due to the fact that there was no decision on September 22 to review, the application for judicial review was dismissed.

Langner v. Canada (Minister of Employment & Immigration) (1994), 98 F.T.R. 188, (sub nom. *Langner v. Ministre de l'Emploi & de l'Immigration)* 184 N.R. 230, 97 F.T.R. 118 (note) (C.A.), affirmed (1995), 29 C.R.R. (2d) 184, leave to appeal to S.C.C. refused (1995), 30 C.R.R. (2d) 188 (note), 193 N.R. 400 (note) (S.C.C.) — There are four applicants — two parents and two children. The parents sought to set aside a decision refusing an exemption under section 114(2) of the *Immigration Act*. The children sought a declaration that they were entitled to remain in Canada and that no removal order should be made against their parents. Further, there was a claim by the children to have the definition of "sponsor" in the *Immigration Regulations* declared inoperative. The plaintiff, Ewa Langner, in the action for a declaration, was appointed guardian of her children.

At the Trial Division all applications were refused.

With respect to the motion to quash the decision under section 114(2) there was no doubt that the parents, having been granted leave, had the necessary standing to challenge this decision. The parents, in their challenge, did not assert that they had personally been denied their Charter rights. Accordingly, they could not base their action on section 24(1) of the *Charter*. A person seeking a remedy under section 24(1) must personally have been a victim of an infringement of his or her Charter rights and such person may not base his or her application on an infringement of the rights of third parties.

The Langner children were not affected by the decision refusing to recognize the humanitarian and compassionate reasons asserted by their parents, and accordingly, they had no standing as plaintiffs in respect of the remedy of quashing the decision under section 114(2).

Both parents and children maintained a joint application to have the definition of a "sponsor" declared inoperative. It should be noted that the children are Canadian citizens. The Langner parents could not maintain an action or a declaration with respect to the definition of a "sponsor" because they were not capable of sponsoring an application for landing. Due to the fact that the parents were not given permission to make an application for landing, the children could not ever be in a position where there was anything for them to sponsor and, therefore, the children had no standing to attack the definition of "sponsor" in the *Immigration Regulations*.

The Court also set out the three part test for public interest standing. Those criteria are:

1. There must be a serious issue as to the Act's validity;
2. The applicants must be directly affected by the Act or have a genuine interest in its validity; and,
3. There must be no other reasonable and effective way to bring the Act's validity before the Court.

The children were found not to have met the test on the facts of this case, and therefore, could not have public interest standing for purposes of their request for a declaration.

The Court of Appeal upheld the decision of the trial judge and held that the removal of the parents would not offend the obligations contracted by Canada when it ratified the *Convention on the Rights of the Child*. The Court referred specifically to Articles 9 and 10 of the Convention in that regard. It was further observed that the effect of allowing the appeal would be to create a situation in which one would need only to have a child on Canadian soil in order to avoid the effect of Canadian immigration laws — a situation which the Court was not prepared to countenance.

Finally, the Court of Appeal noted that the appellant parents' decision to take their children to Poland with them, or to leave them with family members was a private decision and one which did not involve the Government of Canada. There was, therefore, no government action which could bring the *Charter* into play.

Engel v. Canada (Secretary of State) (1994), 83 F.T.R. 64, 26 Imm. L.R. (2d) 221 — This was an application for a stay of a deportation order. The Court noted that the tests of irreparable harm and balance of convenience are intertwined and rely on a decision of the Federal Court of Appeal in *Turbo Resources Ltd. v. Petro Canada Inc.*, 24 C.P.R. (3d) 1 (Fed. C.A.). The Court found that they are not two separate elements of the test for a stay but rather two components of a single element and, depending upon the facts before the Court, and perhaps on the nature of the issue in dispute, more weight might be given to balance of convenience on the facts of one case and more weight to irreparable harm on the facts of another. In order to determine balance of convenience one must look not simply to the convenience of the parties but to the convenience of the public or the public interest as well.

On the facts of this case, the Court found that there would be no irreparable harm and declined to order a stay.

Yamani v. Canada (Solicitor General) (1994), 27 Imm. L.R. (2d) 116, 80 F.T.R. 307 (Fed. T.D.) — The applicant applied for injunctive relief, pursuant to section 18.2 of the *Federal Court Act*. The injunction was granted and the Court had to consider, among other issues, whether the balance of convenience favoured the granting of the stay. The public interest in the maintenance of processes must be considered even where the stay is considered an exemption from the general public requirement in question and not one involving a suspension of that requirement generally.

The Court referred to *RJR-MacDonald Inc. v. Canada (Attorney General)* (1994), 164 N.R. 1 (S.C.C.) at pages 38–39. It noted that in the case of a public authority the onus of demonstrating irreparable harm is less than that of a private applicant. The test will nearly always be satisfied upon proof that the authority is charged with the duty of promoting or protecting the public interest and upon some indication that the impugned legislation, regulation or activity was undertaken pursuant to that responsibility. Once these requirements have been met the Court should, in most cases, assume that irreparable harm to the public interest would result from restraint of that action.

In this case deciding that the balance of convenience favoured granting a stay, the Court noted that important as the public interest is in maintaining the statutory processes, the case had not been pursued by the Crown as a matter of great urgency. Further, the grant of the stay preserved the status quo as far as the applicant was concerned and did not interfere significantly with the exercise of their lawful responsibilities by the authorities. This case, if a stay was granted, would not result in a "cascade of stays and exemptions".

The Court granted a stay but only to the extent of ordering that no removal or deportation order be issued against the applicant pending the final determination of the various applications for judicial review now scheduled to be heard by the Court. This interfered as little as possible with the inquiry process as established under the *Immigration Act*.

Sholev v. Canada (Minister of Employment & Immigration) (1994), 78 F.T.R. 188 (Fed. T.D.) — The applicant was a refused refugee claimant who learned of the refusal of his claim on April 11, 1994. The applicant, on May 10, filed an application for leave and for judicial review, including an application for an extension of time to commence the proceedings. The applicant applied for a stay of the removal order on the basis that the removal order was automatically stayed by virtue of section 49(1)(c)(i). A stay of execution of a removal order becomes effective by operation of section 49(1)(c)(i) once the applicant files in the Federal Court an application for leave and for judicial review, even if the application is filed beyond the fifteen-day period ordinarily provided by section 82.1(2), whenever the application includes or is accompanied by an application for an extension of time to commence proceedings. The stay was effective from May 10, 1994. From that day the matter was before the Court, subject to the applicant meeting all further requirements to perfect the application. If those further steps are not taken, the application will be dismissed and thus disposed of by the Court.

Parliament, by enacting section 82.1(5), recognized that there may be special cases which warrant proceedings for leave and judicial review to commence, even though the applicant had not met the time ordinarily limited for filing. It would be inconsistent to construe section 49(1)(c)(i) as not providing for a stay of execution of a removal order pending determination of whether special reasons for an extension exist. Otherwise, the most deserving cases initiated by late filing would not have the benefit of the statutory stay.

Singh (G.) v. Canada (Minister of Employment & Immigration) (1993), 69 F.T.R. 142 (Fed. T.D.) — The applicants sought to set aside a decision that they were not Convention refugees. This case discusses how findings on the evidence can be successfully challenged in the Trial Division.

The Court commented that section 18.1(4)(d) of the *Federal Court Act* sets out disjunctive conditions under which a decision will be set aside. For purposes of paragraph (c) of that section, the Court noted that findings of fact which are unsupported by adequate evidence are errors in law — the so-called "no evidence rule". Section 18.1(4)(d) allows the Court to set aside a decision which is made "without regard for the material before it". This grants a broader right of review than the traditional "no evidence" test. It compels the setting aside of tribunal decisions where they are unreasonable. The phrase "perverse or capricious manner or without regard for the material before it" is accurately discussed in J.A. Kavanagh, *A Guide to Judicial Review* (1978) at 57–58.

The findings of fact can be divided into two classifications: findings of primary facts and inferences of fact which are drawn from the primary facts. Courts are reluctant to interfere with findings of primary facts made by tribunals. In areas where a tribunal has a particular expertise in drawing inferences, courts are inclined to treat those inferences with deference. If, however, the inference is of a type which is based on common experience, then the Court is in equally as good a position as the tribunal to draw the inference and in that case deference is not shown.

In this particular case, the inferences of fact drawn by the Board did not stand up upon a review of the evidence and the decision refusing refugee status was set aside.

Garcia v. Canada (Minister of Employment & Immigration) (1993), 65 F.T.R. 177 (Fed. T.D.) — The applicant sought to stay an order removing him from Canada pending the disposition of an application for leave and for judicial review of a decision of an immigration officer denying him an exemption, on humanitarian and compassionate grounds, from the visa requirements of section 9(1) of the *Immigration Act* as provided under section 114(2) of the Act.

This case is an example of one where the Court found irreparable harm would result from removal from Canada due to the precarious state of the applicant's mind. The applicant had submitted psychiatric evidence of his fragile psychological condition for which he had been under treatment in Canada for a number of years since his arrival. This fragile condition extended to serious suicidal intentions if faced with deportation to his country of origin. The Court noted that the only inconvenience to the respondent in this matter on the question of where the balance of convenience lay was the minimal delay in removing the applicant from Canada, should his application for leave not be granted.

Hernandez v. Canada (Minister of Employment & Immigration) (1993), 154 N.R. 231 (Fed. C.A.) — The "unreasonable delay" argument should not be perceived by counsel as a fertile basis for setting aside decisions in refugee hearings. It is closer to legal reality for one to presuppose that rarely, if ever, will the argument be successfully invoked.

Edumadze v. Canada (Minister of Employment & Immigration) (1993), 59 F.T.R. 269 (Fed. T.D.) — This is an example of a case where an adjudicator's decision to proceed in the absence of counsel was not quashed. The Court noted that if every refugee claimant was entitled to judicial review because of the non-availability of counsel, the system would be in chaos. In this case five adjournments were granted, two of which were peremptory, before the decision was made to proceed in the absence of counsel.

Rubilar v. Canada (Minister of Employment & Immigration) (August 17, 1992), Doc. 92-T-487 (Fed. T.D.) — The applicant sought an extension of time within which to file affidavits in support of an application for leave to commence proceedings for judicial review. The applicant requested a 30-day extension within which to file affidavits due to the fact that the applicant's counsel was having difficulty in contacting the applicant prior to the time for filing. This request for an extension of time was not forwarded to the Court by registry staff. Accordingly, no decision was made before the time for filing had passed. The respondent argued that the applicant's leave application should be dismissed due to an absence of supporting material or in the absence of an order extending the time. Where there is a possibility that an applicant will be prejudiced as a result of internal Court procedures, an extension of time will be granted. Accordingly, the applicant was directed to file supporting affidavit material within five days of the Court's order extending the time and the respondent Minister was given 30 days after the date of filing to respond to the application for leave.

Membreno-Garcia v. Canada (Minister of Employment & Immigration), [1992] 3 F.C. 306, 7 Admin. L.R. (2d) 38, 17 Imm. L.R. (2d) 291, 93 D.L.R. (4th) 620, 55 F.T.R. 104 (Fed. C.A.) — The applicant had applied for refugee status but a first-level tribunal found that there was no credible basis to the applicant's claim. The applicant applied for leave to commence an application for judicial review, which leave was granted. The applicant then sought a stay of the deportation order pending the outcome of the appeal.

In the present case, the deportation order flowed from and was underpinned by the decision finding no credible basis to the applicant's claim. If that decision was invalid then the deportation order was invalid. In such circumstances, a challenge has in fact been made to the validity of the deportation order.

In *Lodge v. Canada (Minister of Employment & Immigration)*, [1979] 1 F.C. 775 (Fed. C.A.), the Court stated the principle to be applied in deciding whether a permanent injunction should be granted to restrain a Minister of the Crown from performing his statutory duty. In *Toth v. Canada (Minister of Employment & Immigration)* (1988), 6 Imm. L.R. (2d) 123 (Fed. C.A.), the Court held that it had jurisdiction to grant a stay in cases such as this one. Since that time, the Trial Division's jurisdiction has been made clear by the addition of section 18.2 of the *Federal Court Act*.

The only requirement under section 18.2 is that the judge consider the interim order "appropriate". It may be that in the absence of at least an indirect attack on the deportation order the Court would not consider a stay appropriate.

In determining when a stay order is "appropriate" the Court referred to the criteria set out in *Toth*. Given that leave had been granted, the applicant clearly had an arguable case. On the basis of the applicant's affidavit evidence it would be hard to reach any other conclusion than that the applicant would suffer irreparable harm if he was returned to El Salvador. Insofar as the balance of convenience is concerned, the test set out in *Metropolitan Stores (MTS) Ltd. v. Manitoba Food & Commercial Workers, Local 832,* [1987] 1 S.C.R. 110 (S.C.C.), is not relevant. In that case, the validity of one section of the statute was under attack and thus an interlocutory injunction order in favour of one litigant impliedly would lead to similar orders respecting all individuals covered by the allegedly unconstitutional section in question. The section itself would in fact be rendered inoperative pending the determination of its validity. In the present case the legislative provisions of the statute were not challenged. One decision by an adjudicative body operating under the statute with respect to one specific individual was being challenged. An injunction or a stay order in such a case will not suspend the operation of any part of the legislation. Thus, the public interest considerations expressed in *Metropolitan Stores Ltd.* are not in issue.

When considering the balance of convenience in these types of cases the extent to which the granting of the stay might become a practice which thwarts the efficient operation of the immigration legislation is a valid consideration. The present procedures were put in place because a practice had grown up in which cases totally devoid of merit were initiated in Court for the sole purpose of buying the applicants further time in Canada. There is a public interest in having a system which operates in an efficient, expeditious and fair manner and which, to the greatest extent possible, does not lend itself to abusive practices. This is the public interest which must be weighed against the potential harm to the applicant if a stay is not granted.

The situation here in this case is quite different from that which exists, for example, when applicants seek humanitarian and compassionate reviews on the eve of the execution of a deportation order and then argue that a stay should be granted because of the uncompleted nature of that review. Such a case is the type of situation in which there is a potential for creating a practice which undermines the orderly operation of the legislation.

Another significant factor in considering the balance of convenience test is the degree of delay which is incurred, if any, in prosecuting the applicant's appeal. Similarly, when the applicant knows of the decision which underlies the challenge to the deportation order and does not seek leave to commence a section 18 proceeding until the very last moment, there is reason to assume that the seeking of leave and the subsequent request for the staying of the deportation order are primarily time-buying manoeuvres.

In the present case, the balance of convenience was said to lie with the applicant and the stay was granted.

Editor's Note: Although the refugee procedures have changed, the principle stated herein may still be useful.

Khan v. Canada (Minister of Employment & Immigration) (1992), 53 F.T.R. 158 (Fed. T.D.) — An earlier inquiry concerning the applicant's continuing presence in Canada was quashed by decision of the Court (*Khan v. Canada (Minister of Employment & Immigration*) (1989), 9 Imm. l.R. (2d) 107 (Fed. T.D.). The preliminary question was whether the application for a stay was properly before the Court in light of the decision in *Ontario Khalsa Darbar Inc. v. Canada (Minister of Employment & Immigration)* (1991), 15 Imm. L.R. (2d)

179 (Fed. T.D.), which held that leave is required to bring an application for a stay in immigration proceedings pursuant to 82.1 of the *Immigration Act*. Previously, *Toth v. Canada (Minister of Employment & Immigration)* (1988), 6 Imm. L.R. (2d) 123; 86 N.R. 302 (Fed. C.A.) acknowledged the inherent jurisdiction of the Court to deal with an application for a stay in appropriate circumstances without the necessity of leave being applied for. Section 18.2 of the *Federal Court Act*, in force since February 1, 1992, provided authority for the issuance of interim orders in relation to the matters before the Court and was sufficient to give jurisdiction to consider an application for a stay which in this case was interrelated with an application for leave to seek judicial review.

In this case there was no evidence of irreparable harm and the application for a stay was dismissed. The inquiry in question might result in a departure notice and, further, even if a deportation order were issued, removal would only occur after a pre-removal review. This review could result in a decision that there were humanitarian or compassionate considerations which justified permanent residence. Accordingly, the concerns of the applicant about the outcome of the inquiry were speculative and as such not evidence of irreparable harm.

Hosein v. Canada (Minister of Employment & Immigration) (1992), 4 Admin. L.R. (2d) 162, 17 Imm. L.R. (2d) 125, 53 F.T.R. 86 (Fed. T.D.) — This was an application for an order staying an inquiry until the applicant's application for leave to commence judicial review proceedings was determined, and if leave be granted until those proceedings were finally disposed of by the Court. This application was accompanied by an application for leave pursuant to 82.1. The orders in question were sought in respect of a decision by a first-level tribunal to the effect that it would not hear evidence and argument in relation to section 7 of the *Charter*. The tribunal then proceeded to find the applicant did not have a credible basis for his claim to being a Convention refugee. The tribunal adjourned and then scheduled a resumption of its hearing. The application for leave to seek judicial review was not considered when this application for a stay was heard.

The Court's jurisdiction to order a stay of proceedings was not limited by section 18.2 of the *Federal Court Act* by the necessity to apply for leave to seek judicial review. In an appropriate case, particularly one where the issue raised in an application for leave is arguable but would be moot or the jurisdiction of the Court would be rendered nugatory by failure to grant a stay, a stay may be ordered within the discretion of the Court.

The Court was not persuaded that a stay of proceedings was required at the time the application was heard. Further steps in the process of consideration of the applicant's situation were required before he would be excluded from Canada. The leave for judicial review now sought by the application could proceed in the ordinary course. If the leave application was not completed before steps were taken to remove the applicant, the applicant could apply for leave to stay implementation of those procedures at that time. The test for intervention is set out in the *Toth* case (*Toth v. Canada (Minister of Employment & Immigration)* (1988), 6 Imm. L.R. (2d) 123, 86 N.R. 302 (Fed. C.A.)).

It was determined that it was inappropriate at this stage to stay proceedings of the tribunal and the application was dismissed.

Canada (Minister of Employment & Immigration) v. Conception (December 12, 1991), Doc. A-1042-91 (Fed. C.A.) — An application governed by section 82.1 can only seek leave to commence a proceeding. It cannot also seek interlocutory relief which might be sought if leave were granted.

Ontario Khalsa Darbar Inc. v. Canada (Minister of Employment & Immigration) (1991), 15 Imm. L.R. (2d) 179, 48 F.T.R. 109 (Fed. T.D.) — This case was begun as an action with a Statement of Claim. The plaintiffs requested a date for the hearing of an application for an interlocutory injunction on an urgent basis. The plaintiffs had not sought nor obtained leave to commence these proceedings. Leave is required for this application pursuant to section 82.1(1) of the *Immigration Act*. The Court declined to appoint a special date for the hearing of the application for the injunction. The application for the injunction was not dismissed but the Court ordered that no materials be filed in respect of the application for the injunction until leave was sought and obtained.

Sayed v. Canada (Minister of Employment & Immigration) (April 29, 1991), Doc. 90-T-825 (Fed. T.D.) — Counsel applied to the Court to re-consider its pronouncement that leave to appeal be denied. This application was pursuant to rule 337 of the *Federal Court Rules*. This application was successful and the order denying leave was varied to allow the application to proceed.

Aguiar v. Canada (Minister of Employment & Immigration) (1991), 13 Imm. L.R. (2d) 280 (Fed. T.D.) — Applications for leave to proceed are generally to be in writing. Leave to make representations orally is rarely given. The usual reason, when permission is given, is on grounds of urgency, however, urgency is not the only ground. In this case, the husband and wife were both interviewed by the same immigration officer. A joint decision was rendered refusing their application for consideration on humanitarian and compassionate grounds. The husband applied for and obtained leave to commence proceedings. The wife's grounds in her application for leave are almost identical to the husband's. In these circumstances, leave was granted to argue the application orally.

Mahabir v. Canada (Minister of Employment & Immigration) (1991), 137 N.R. 377, [1992] 1 F.C. 133, 85 D.L.R. (4th) 110, 15 Imm. L.R. (2d) 303 (Fed. C.A.) — A member of the Convention Refugee Determination Division and an adjudicator determined that there was no credible or trustworthy evidence of the applicant's claim to Convention refugee status. The applicant then commenced a section 28 application without the leave required by section 82.1(1) of the *Immigration Act*. This application was quashed. Having chosen to seek a Charter remedy by a proceeding authorized by the *Immigration Act* rather than suing for a declaration of those rights, the applicant was bound by the condition precedent that he obtain leave to proceed. Section 24 of the Charter and section 52 of the *Constitution Act* do not of themselves give jurisdiction to a court. Section 24 gives a remedial power and section 52.1 gives a declaratory power to be exercised in disposing of matters properly before the Court. A decision or order, whether it concerns the Constitution or not, is made under the *Immigration Act* when it is made by a tribunal that derives its authority to make decisions or orders from the Act. Finally, the decision that the credible basis provisions of the *Immigration Act* were not rendered inoperative by the Charter was not a final decision. A constitutional question is not necesarily a substantive question before a given tribunal. The constitutional question here went to the right of the tribunal to conduct its proceedings and not to any substantive right of the applicant. All that the decision here finally decided was that the proceeding would continue. Since the decision of the tribunal as to the constitutional question was not a final decision, it was not reviewable under section 28 of the *Federal Court Act*.

Gill v. Canada (Minister of Employment & Immigration) (1991), 15 Imm. L.R. (2d) 75, (sub nom. *Gill (H.K.) v. Canada (Minister of Employment & Immigration))* 49 F.T.R. 291 (T.D.) — The applicant originally applied in 1980 to sponsor her parents together with her brother and sister for landing in Canada. This application was denied because there was difficulty in documenting the relationship. She reapplied in 1984 to sponsor just her parents. In April 1987, after she had initiated court action, visas were issued to her parents to allow them to enter Canada so that blood tests could be done. The tests were carried out and the parental relationship established. The applicant's parents have remained in Canada ever since; however, the slowness with which their application for permanent residence was being processed caused the applicant to commence these *mandamus* proceedings. The Court held that leave to commence the application was required. The application could not be characterized as one to a visa officer simply because information is being sought abroad or because an application by the applicant's brother for landed status is related to the parents' application. The Court noted that the brother's application was not part of the proceedings with respect to which *mandamus* was sought.

Coliseum v. Canada (Minister of Employment & Immigration) (1991), 13 Imm. L.R. (2d) 24 (Fed. T.D.) — It is inappropriate, when considering whether or not to grant leave, to deal with the merits of the application, save to the extent necessary to deal with the application for leave. The requirement for leave to be granted was added to the Act to avoid a multiplicity of section 18 applications of a frivolous nature. Leave should not be granted lightly; on the other hand, if there is even a scintilla of evidence indicating that there might be some serious issue to deal with at the hearing of the section 18 motion, leave should be granted.

Bains v. Canada (Minister of Employment & Immigration) (1990), 47 Admin. L.R. 317, 109 N.R. 239 (Fed. C.A.) — The only question to be considered in disposing of an application for leave under section 82.1(1) or 82.3(1) is whether or not a fairly arguable case is disclosed for the relief proposed to be sought if leave is granted. Further, the need for material not immediately available has to be established by the applicant and the mere stated intention to rely on such material does not, without an application and an order to that end, operate to extend the time provided by the *Federal Court Immigration Rules* for the applicant to file an affidavit and/or representations in support of the leave application. The requirement for leave is, in reality, the other side of the coin of the traditional jurisdiction to summarily terminate proceedings that disclose no reasonably arguable case. The requirement for leave does not deny refugee claimants access to the Court. The right to apply for leave is, itself, a right of access to the court and the requirement that leave be obtained before an appeal or application for judicial review may proceed does not impair the right guaranteed by refugee claimants under either sections 7 or 15 of the Charter.

Saleh v. Canada (Minister of Employment & Immigration) (September 22, 1989), Doc. 89-T-667 (Fed. T.D.) — On application for leave, one should grant such a request unless it is plain and obvious that the applicant would have no reasonable chance of succeeding on the section 18 application. The Court applied the same test as set out in rule 419(a) of the Federal Court rules dealing with a motion to strike.

Brar v. Canada (Solicitor General) (1989), 30 F.T.R. 284 (Fed. T.D.) — The Court determined that section 82.1 applied to this action and that accordingly leave to bring the motion and initiate the action was required. The Court determined that the test for leave was whether the application raises a serious issue to be heard. Where no serious issue with no possibility of success in a hearing or in an action was found, leave was to be denied.

Arulampalan v. Canada (Minister of Employment & Immigration) (1989), 8 Imm. L.R. (2d) 172, 30 F.T.R. 239 (Fed. T.D.) — The requirement under section 83.1 that an applicant for section 18 of the *Federal Court Act* relief obtain leave of the Court first does not violate section 15 of the Charter.

82.2 No appeal from decision of Federal Court — trial division on application for leave — No appeal lies to the Federal Court of Appeal from a judgment of the Federal Court — Trial Division on an application under section 82.1 for leave to commence an application for judicial review under the *Federal Court Act*.

R.S.C. 1985, c. 28 (4th Supp.), s. 19; 1990, c. 8, s. 54; 1992, c. 49, s. 73.

Case Law

Forde v. Canada (Minister of Citizenship & Immigration) (1997), 210 N.R. 194 (Fed. C.A.) — The Minister appealed against a decision of the Trial Division in which a judge ordered that "a stay currently exists in this case and the respondent's application [for reconsideration] is dismissed with costs in the cause".

In December 1994, a deportation order was made against the respondent. He appealed to the Appeal Division of the IRB, but before the appeal was heard, a delegate of the Minister decided the respondent was a danger to the public in Canada. In February 1996, the respondent applied for leave to judicially review that opinion but at no time did he file an application for leave to review the deportation order.

In March 1996, the Trial Division issued a stay of the deportation order "until such time as the application for judicial review is finally disposed of". This order was clearly ancillary to the leave application then pending and was authorized by section 18.2 of the *Federal Court Act*. In August 1996, the Trial Division dismissed the application for leave, thus terminating any judicial review proceeding. The original stay, granted in March 1996, thus came to an end, however, the Trial Division, in September 1996, granted a "continuation" of the already terminated stay and when the Minister applied for reconsideration of this order and a declaration that the stay no longer existed, the learned judge of the Trial Division made the order which is now a subject of this appeal.

The Trial Division has a carefully defined judicial review jurisdiction in respect of "any decision or order made or any matter arising under the [Immigration] Act". The decision of the Minister pursuant to subsection 70(5) is such a decision. During the course of disposing of an application for leave to seek judicial review of such a decision, the Court is authorized by section 18.2 to make ancillary orders, such as a stay. Once the leave application was disposed of there was no longer a leave or review proceeding to which a stay could be ancillary under section 18.2. Section 50(1)(b) of the *Federal Court Act* was never intended to give a general mandate to the Trial Division to stop deportations which are no longer under attack in the Court.

This appeal was properly brought without a question having been certified as the putative stay was no longer related to any application for leave proceeding under subsection 82.1(1) and thus an appeal was not barred by section 82.2.

Muttiah v. Canada (Secretary of State (January 31, 1995), Doc. IMM-787-94 (Fed. T.D.) — The applicant was a citizen of Sri Lanka and sought to overturn a negative determination by a panel of the CRDD. The panel's primary finding was that the applicant did not have a well-founded fear of persecution at the hands of the LTTE in the North of Sri Lanka. In addition, the panel went on to consider whether Colombo was an internal flight alternative (IFA) for the applicant. With respect to this question the applicant had produced a psychiatric report which the panel failed to address in its reasons.

It was reasonably open to the panel to conclude that there was no serious possibility that the applicant would face persecution at the hands of the Sri Lankan authorities in the North.

The Court declined to certify for appeal, a question related to the manner in which the panel should have dealt with the psychiatric report. Questions for certification, in addition to raising broad issues of public importance, must be capable of being dispositive of an appeal. The question with respect to the psychiatric report related to a portion of the decision which could not be dispositive of the appeal and, accordingly, the Court declined to certify the question.

Reza v. Canada (1994), 18 O.R. (3d) 640 (note) (S.C.C.) — This was an appeal from a decision of the Ontario Court of Appeal setting aside an order made by a motions judge staying the respondent's application for a declaration that certain provisions of the *Immigration Act* infringed the *Charter of Rights*. The issue on appeal was whether there was any basis for the Court of Appeal's interference with the motions judge.

The respondent came to Canada from Iran and claimed refugee status. It was found that there was no credible basis for referring his claim to the Immigration and Refugee Board and a deportation order was issued. Leave to commence a judicial review application was refused. The respondent's case was reviewed on humanitarian and compassionate grounds a number of times. After the last refusal the respondent unsuccessfully sought leave to commence an application for judicial review. The respondent subsequently brought an application in Ontario for a declaration that certain sections of the *Immigration Act* infringed his Charter rights. The respondent also brought a motion at the same time for an interlocutory injunction restraining the Minister from removing him. The appellant Minister took the position before the Ontario Court (General Division) that the Court should decline to exercise its jurisdiction on the ground that it was more appropriate for a constitutional challenge to sections of the *Immigration Act* to be heard in the Federal Court.

In March, 1992 a motions judge granted the Minister's motion and stayed the respondent's application for declaratory and injunctive relief. The deportation order, however, was stayed by Galligan J.A. pending disposition of the respondent Reza's appeal to the Ontario Court of Appeal. In October, 1992 the Court of Appeal allowed the respondent Reza's appeal and ordered that the decision of the motions judge be set aside.

The Supreme Court of Canada allowed the Minister's appeal and was generally in agreement with the dissenting decision in the Court of Appeal of Ontario. The Supreme Court of Canada agreed that there was no basis for interfering with the motions court judge's decision to stay the proceedings. The Ontario Court and the Federal Court had concurrent jurisdiction to hear the respondent's application. Pursuant to section 106 of the *Courts of Justice Act*, R.S.O. 1990, c. C.43, any judge of the General Division has a discretion to stay proceedings. The motions court judge properly exercised his discretion on the basis that Parliament had created a comprehensive scheme of review of immigration matters and the Federal Court was an effective and appropriate forum. The Court was of the view that this was the correct approach. The motions court judge took into account all relevant considerations in exercising his discretion to grant a stay and there was no basis for an appellate court to interfere with his decision. The appeal was allowed and the decision of the motions judge restored.

Rafique v. Canada (Minister of Employment & Immigration) (October 29, 1992), Doc. 92-T-991 (Fed. T.D.); quashed (1993), 154 N.R. 233 (Fed. C.A.) — The decision to extend or not the time for filing affidavits and representations in support of an application for leave to commence proceedings for judicial review is an integral aspect of the jurisdiction to consider the application for leave. No appeal to the Court of Appeal lies in relation to that decision and, accordingly, there is no authority in the Court to extend the time for filing a notice of appeal in respect of a decision refusing an extension of time for the filing of documents.

Editor's Note: Although the refugee provisions have changed and section 82.2 has been changed, the principle here may be of some importance.

Duggal v. Canada (Minister of Employment & Immigration) (1992), 18 Imm. L.R. (2d) 20 (Fed. C.A.) — The Court of Appeal has no power to stay the execution of a removal order where it is deprived of jurisdiction by section 82.2(1) of the *Immigration Act* to entertain an appeal from a decision of the Trial Division. The power to stay can only be implied from the Court's power to hear an appeal. If such jurisdiction is denied, then the power to stay is absent. Not even the allegation that its Charter right is being violated can give the Court of Appeal a statutory jurisdiction to hear an appeal where Parliament has seen fit to withhold it.

82.3 [Repealed 1992, c. 49, s. 73.]

83. (1) Certification necessary to appeal — A judgment of the Federal Court — Trial Division on an application for judicial review with respect to any decision or order made, or any matter arising, under this Act or the rules or regulations thereunder may be appealed to the Federal Court of Appeal only if the Federal Court — Trial Division has at the time of rendering judgment certified that a serious question of general importance is involved and has stated that question.

(2) Commencement of appeal — Where a judgment of the Federal Court — Trial Division is appealed to the Federal Court of Appeal pursuant to subsection (1), the appeal shall be commenced by filing a notice of appeal within fifteen days after the pronouncement of the judgment.

(3) Extension — A judge of the Federal Court — Trial Division may, for special reasons, extend the time referred to in subsection (2) for filing a notice of appeal.

(4) Refusal not subject to appeal — For greater certainty, a refusal of the Federal Court — Trial Division to certify that a serious question of general importance is involved in any matter is not subject to appeal.

R.S.C. 1985, c. 28 (4th Supp.), s. 19; 1992, c. 49, s. 73.

Case Law

Section 83(1)

Romachkine v. Canada (Minister of Citizenship & Immigration) (1999), 235 N.R. 263 (Fed. C.A.) — The appellant's application for permanent residence was refused. The appellant filed an application for judicial review supported by the affidavit of a person employed as a paralegal in the law firm of the appellant's previous legal counsel. The respondent filed a motion to strike the supporting affidavit and dismiss the application for judicial review. The motions judge granted the respondent's motion, struck the affidavit and dismissed the application for judicial review. No question was certified by the motions judge.

The impugned decision was clearly "a judgement of the Federal Court — Trial Division on an application for judicial review with respect to a decision or order made under the Immigration Act", within the meaning of subsection 83(1). There being no question certified, there can be no appeal.

This case is distinguishable from *Moldeveanu v. Canada (Minister of Citizenship & Immigration)* (August 27, 1997), Doc. A-413-97 (Fed. T.D.), where the Court accepted jurisdiction on the basis that the respondent had only sought the striking out of the supporting affidavit and there had been no order dismissing the application. In such a case, there was no judgement on the application and subsection 83(1) did not therefore apply.

Pushpanathan v. Canada (Minister of Employment & Immigration) (1998), 226 N.R. 201, (sub nom. *Pushpanathan v. Canada (Minister of Citizenship & Immigration))* 160 D.L.R. (4th) 193, (sub nom. *Pushpanathan v. Canada (Minister of Citizenship & Immigration))* [1998] 1 S.C.R. 982, 43 Imm. L.R. (2d) 117, 11 Admin. L.R. (3d) 1 (S.C.C.); amended (sub nom. *Pushpanathan v. Canada (Minister of Citizenship & Immigration))* [1998] 1 S.C.R. 1222, 11 Admin. L.R. (3d) 130 (S.C.C.) — This appeal raised two questions, firstly, the standard of judicial review over decisions of the IRB and secondly, the meaning of the exclusion from refugee status set out in Article 1F(c) of the *United Nations Convention Relating to the Status of Refugees*. The appellant left Sri Lanka in 1983 and spent time in India and France before arriving in Canada via Italy in March 1985. He claimed Convention refugee status. The claim was never adjudicated on because the appellant was granted permanent resident status in May 1987 under an administrative program. In December 1987, the appellant was arrested and charged with conspiracy to traffic in heroin. The appellant was convicted and sentenced to eight years in prison.

In September 1991, the appellant, then on parole, renewed his claim to Convention refugee status. In June 1992, a conditional deportation order was issued against the appellant. Deportation was conditional upon a determination that the claimant was not a Convention refugee and accordingly the appellant's claim was referred to the CRDD. The Board decided that the appellant was not a Convention refugee. The Federal Court Trial Division and the Federal Court of Appeal refused to reverse that decision on an application for judicial review.

A correctness standard applies to the determinations of law by the IRB.

Conspiracy to traffic in a narcotic is not a violation of Article 1F(c) of the *United Nations Convention Relating to the Status of Refugees*.

Even though international trafficking in drugs is an extremely serious problem that the United Nations has taken extraordinary measures to eradicate, in the absence of clear indications that the international community recognizes drug trafficking as a sufficiently serious and sustained violation of fundamental human rights as to amount to persecution, either through a specific designation as an act contrary to the purposes and principles of the United Nations, or through international instruments which otherwise indicate that trafficking is a serious violation of fundamental human rights, individuals should not be deprived of the essential protections contained in the Convention for having committed those acts.

Yuen v. Canada (Minister of Citizenship & Immigration) (1998), 227 N.R. 74, 47 Imm. L.R. (2d) 65 (Fed. C.A.) — The normal meaning of the language of section 83 covers judicial review of a decision of a visa officer, because that is a "decision...made...under this Act...". Accordingly, the Court did not have jurisdiction to entertain this appeal, because the Trial Division judge who heard the matter declined to certify a question, accordingly the appeal was dismissed for want of jurisdiction.

Brar v. Canada (Minister of Citizenship & Immigration) (1997), 139 F.T.R. 79, 41 Imm. L.R. (2d) 194 (Fed. T.D.) — Pursuant to section 83(1) of the *Immigration Act*, the question can only be certified at the time of rendering judgment. Section 83(1) precludes certification after the judgment has been pronounced in written form.

Accordingly, this application for reconsideration under Rules 324, 327 and 1733 of the *Federal Court Rules* and Rule 18 of the *Immigration Rules* was dismissed.

Su v. Canada (Minister of Citizenship & Immigration) (1997), 225 N.R. 34, 144 F.T.R. 320 (note) (Fed. C.A.) — This matter came on as a show cause proceeding to determine whether the appellant's appeal should be dismissed for want of jurisdiction. The Trial Division judge had refused to award costs and had refused to certify the question of costs so that an appeal might be taken. The appellant contended that a refusal of costs is not a judgment within the meaning of section 83(1) and therefore not subject to the requirement of a certified question. This argument was dismissed by the Court. The refusal of costs is an integral part of judgment disposing of an application for judicial review and is clearly within the limitations of subsection 83(1). No question having been certified, the Court had no jurisdiction to entertain the appeal.

Canada (Minister of Citizenship & Immigration) v. Adam (1997), 137 F.T.R. 68 (Fed. T.D.); reconsideration granted (December 3, 1997), Doc. IMM-3380-96 (Fed. T.D.) — This was an application for reconsideration of an order sending a matter back for redetermination in accordance with the Court's reasons. The order was based upon a point not taken by counsel, namely the applicability of the exception in paragraph 19(1)(l).

Where a case is decided on a point that was not taken by counsel, the merits of the application are not open for reconsideration, rather counsel will be permitted an opportunity to submit a question for certification following a review of the reasons.

Moldevenau v. Canada (Minister of Citizenship & Immigration) (August 27, 1997), Doc. A-413-97 (Fed. C.A.) — The appellant sought to appeal from an order striking out an affidavit filed in support of an application for judicial review of a decision of a visa officer. The affidavit was struck out by a judge of the Trial Division on the basis that it did not meet the requirement that such an affidavit be based upon personal knowledge and belief. The order of the Trial Division had the effect of leaving the originating notice of motion in limbo, incapable of being disposed of by the Court. This was not the sort of order that was contemplated by subsection 83(1). Accordingly, the requirements that a question be certified and stated pursuant to the subsection as a precondition to launching the appeal are inapplicable. Accordingly, the appeal was quashed.

Richards v. Canada (Minister of Citizenship & Immigration) (1996), 36 Imm. L.R. (2d) 105 (Fed. T.D.) — This decision raised the same issues as those in *Williams* (IMM-3320-95). The Court decided to defer a final decision until the appeal process in the *Williams* case was exhausted. The Court declined to issue an order disposing of the application and certify this decision so that it could be joined with *Williams*, due to the fact that there were no issues in this case which were additional to those already before the Court in *Williams*.

Samoylenko v. Canada (Minister of Citizenship & Immigration) (1996), 116 F.T.R. 144 (Fed. T.D.) — This decision related to four separate applications for judicial review of a decision of a post claim determination officer to the effect that the applicants were not members of the Post Determination Refugee Claimants in Canada class.

The decision of an immigration official not to recommend an individual as being eligible for the PDRCC class takes no right away. Thus, the Court will not intervene unless the officer can be shown to have exercised his or her discretion pursuant to improper purposes, irrelevant considerations, with bad faith, or in a patently unreasonable manner. Thus, the standard of review of such decisions is high.

With respect to certification of questions for appeal, the general principle is that decisions of the Trial Division on applications for judicial review of decisions or orders under the *Immigration Act* are not subject to appeal. The certification process is an exception to that general rule. The certification process should not be used simply to circumvent the general rule. Rather, its use should be restricted to circumstances where a specific question that is both serious and of general importance, and that will be determinative of the appeal, is identified. In this case, the applicants recommended for certification, questions covering a whole range of issues pleaded before the trial division. In essence, counsel was seeking to circumvent the general rule established in subsection 83(1).

Accordingly, the application was dismissed and no question was certified for appeal.

Chu v. Canada (Minister of Citizenship & Immigration) (1996), 116 F.T.R. 68 (Fed. T.D.) — Subsection 83(1) requires that only "serious questions of general importance" be certified. Similar language in the *Ontario Rules of Civil Procedure* has been interpreted to mean that the section contemplates issues of broad significance or general application that are felt to warrant resolution by a higher level of judicial authority. The Federal Court of Appeal has added as well the requirement that an issue in order to be certified must also be determinative of the appeal.

Huynh v. R. (1996), 34 Imm. L.R. (2d) 199, [1996] 2 F.C. 976, 36 C.R.R. (2d) 93, 134 D.L.R. (4th) 612, 197 N.R. 62, 112 F.T.R. 240 (note) (Fed. C.A.), leave to appeal to S.C.C refused (1996), 38 C.R.R. (2d) 376 (note), 39 C.R.R. (2d) 376 (note), 138 D.L.R. (4th) vii (note), 206 N.R. 238 (note) (S.C.C.) — This was an appeal from a judgment of the Trial Division which had answered in the negative, two questions of law which had been stated for a preliminary determination pursuant to Rule 474. As was customary in proceedings under that rule the parties had agreed to a statement of facts as the basis for the decision and the appeal.

The two questions asked were as follows:

1. Does section 83 of the *Immigration Act* contravene section 7 of the *Charter of Rights*?

2. Does section 83 of the *Immigration Act* contravene section 15 of the *Charter of Rights*?

With respect to the second question the Court answered it in the negative. Of necessity the *Immigration Act* deals differently with citizens and non-citizens. Accordingly, citizenship is not a relevant personal characteristic and there was no discrimination contrary to section 15.

With respect to the first question the Court noted that the provision of a right of appeal is not a requirement of fundamental justice. The attachment of conditions to a right of appeal will only run afoul of section 7 if it can be shown:

a. That the result of the appeal may, by itself, place the appellant's section 7 rights in jeopardy; and,

b. That such conditions are contrary to the principles of fundamental justice.

The appellant had a full hearing of his refugee claim before the credible basis tribunal, a hearing that complied with the requirements of fundamental justice. If the appellant's rights to life, liberty and security of the person are in jeopardy, such jeopardy is brought about by the decision of the credible basis tribunal and not by the judgement of the Court. The judge of the Trial Division sitting in judicial review of that decision, tested for its compliance with the requirements of fundamental justice, and while he refused to intervene he cannot, in any sense, be said to have confirmed it. The power of a judge of the Trial Division sitting in judicial review is confined to setting aside the decision and sending the matter back for a new hearing, or, as in fact happened in this case, declining to intervene. An appeal of that judgement cannot possibly have any adverse impact upon the appellant's rights to life, liberty and security of the person. Accordingly, the appellant had failed to demonstrate that section 83 of the *Immigration Act* had put his right to life, liberty or security of the person in jeopardy.

Section 83(1) subjects the right of appeal to the issuance of a certificate by the Trial Division judge "at the time of rendering judgement". This section, coupled with Rule 18, can create difficulties for an appellant where the judge's reasons for disposing of the judicial review application turn on a question which was not argued fully or at all at the hearing. It can and does happen that judges will decide a case on a point that was not taken by counsel. In such a situation the provisions of Rule 1733 could appropriately be invoked. Further, if the Court has any uncertainty at all as to whether its grounds for decision may raise a new question which was not foreseeable by counsel, it can issue its formal order a reasonable period of time after its reasons to give counsel sufficient opportunity to respond. On the facts of this case the appellant failed to make out any case that the reasons for dismissing his application raised some new question of general importance which he could not have foreseen. Accordingly, the appellant failed to convince the Court that he had suffered any actual deprivation of his right to know the case he had to meet.

Section 83 did not make the trial judge the sole arbiter of whether or not his own decisions should be the subject of appellate review. The inquiry which section 83 mandates is "does this case raise a serious issue of general importance". This is an issue which judges of the Trial Division will have no difficulty in answering in the affirmative in appropriate cases. The duty imposed by section 83 on a judge of the Trial Division is remarkably similar to that imposed on the Court of Appeal in the United Kingdom as a precondition to obtaining leave to appeal to the House of Lords in criminal matters. Accordingly, section 83 does not allow a judge to sit in appeal of himself or herself and does not therefore contravene section 7 of the *Charter of Rights*.

Malouf v. Canada (Minister of Citizenship & Immigration) (1995), 190 N.R. 230, 104 F.T.R. 320 (note) (Fed. C.A.) — The Court of Appeal declined to answer two questions that had been certified by a judge of the Trial Division on the basis that the questions did not bear on the reasons for which the judge had allowed the application for judicial review and that therefore the Court of Appeal's answers to those questions could not affect the outcome of the judicial review proceeding.

Balaga v. Canada (Minister of Citizenship & Immigration) (1995), 187 N.R. 315 (Fed. C.A.) — An application was made to the Trial Division by a group called the Defence for Children International — Canada to intervene in an application for judicial review. The application to intervene was dismissed. An appeal from that order is subject to the provisions of section 83(1) of the *Immigration Act*, and is not governed by section 27 of the *Federal Court Act*. Accordingly, the appeal in this case was quashed for want of jurisdiction due to the fact that section 83 had not been complied with prior to the appeal being taken.

Gyamfuah v. Canada (Minister of Employment & Immigration) (1994), 25 Imm. L.R. (2d) 89, 80 F.T.R. 58 — The applicant moved for reconsideration of the Court's decision with a view to obtaining certification of a question for appeal after the release of the Court's decision. In order to be certified pursuant to section 83(1) a question must be one which, in the opinion of the motions Judge, transcends the interests of the immediate parties to the litigation and contemplates issues of broad significance or general application. Such a question will be identified by counsel when they read the Board's decision, when they prepare an application for leave and for judicial review, or, during oral argument. It is inconceivable that a serious question of general importance could remain invisible until after a decision is made on a judicial review application.

Osei v. Canada (Secretary of State) (July 14, 1994), Doc. IMM-4839-93 (Fed. T.D.) — In this decision the Court discussed the proper test be applied in a situation where there have been changes in the country which the applicants left prior to the hearing of the claim.

The Court described the unsettled state of the jurisprudence to the date of its decision and noted that there are differing views in the Court as to the proper test to be applied. One test applies the criteria set down by Professor Hathaway in his book, *The Law of Refugee Status* (1991), pages 200–203.

The Court noted that a different view also exists in the jurisprudence. That view holds that the only evidence required is evidence of the change in circumstances. The tribunal's task was to reach a conclusion relating to the future, that a change had occurred, and by reason of that change the particular applicant's claim of persecution was no longer well founded because there was no objective basis for it.

Finally, the Court noted that with respect to the certification of decisions for appeal that there was a disturbing trend indicating that these appeals were not being pursued. The Court noted that when a trial Judge certifies a question, he or she expects that the question will be placed before the Court of Appeal. Often times a second request for certification is refused because the Judge knows that the question in issue has already been certified. Further, the Court noted that stays pending a decision on the certified question are not being sought or granted. In this case the Court refused to dispose of the case before a decision on the issue of the proper test was rendered by the Court of Appeal. The Court had previously noted that this issue was or had been already certified for consideration by the Court of Appeal.

Kayumba v. Canada (Solicitor General) (1994), 24 Imm. L.R. (2d) 201, 76 F.T.R. 238 — The Court dismissed an application for a stay of execution of a deportation order. After rendering its decision, the Court was asked to certify a question pursuant to section 83(1). The Court ruled that section 83(1) did not give the Court jurisdiction to certify a question of general importance in connection with an application for a stay of execution of a deportation order.

Sereno v. Canada (Solicitor General) (1993), 75 F.T.R. 71 — The Court has no jurisdiction to certify a matter in connection with an application for a stay related to an application for leave made pursuant to section 82.1.

Section 83(2)

Dasent v. Canada (Minister of Citizenship & Immigration) (1995), 28 Imm. L.R. (2d) 28, 92 F.T.R. 103 (Fed. T.D.) — The respondent moved to extend the time for filing a notice of appeal. The order that was being appealed was signed by the Judge on December 8, 1994, but not entered in the registry until December 13, 1994. The order in question was pronounced upon the date on which the judge signed it, namely December 8, 1994.

The notice of appeal must be filed within 15 days after the pronouncement of the judgment which includes the order. The time in this case expired on December 23, 1994. The respondent attempted to file the notice of appeal on December 28, 1994.

In arriving at the decision to extend the time the Court considered, firstly, special circumstances. In this case the Court found that the respondent's counsel was probably misled by the date stamp on the judgment. The Court then considered whether there was prejudice to the applicant in extending the time, whether the respondent had an intention to appeal within the 15 days, whether the delay in requesting an extension was undue, and finally whether the interests of justice mandated the granting of an extension.

Section 83(3)

Dasent v. Canada (Minister of Citizenship & Immigration) (1995), 28 Imm. L.R. (2d) 28, 92 F.T.R. 103 — For Digest, see section 83(2), supra.

84. (1) Rules — Subject to the approval of the Governor in Council, the Chief Justice of the Federal Court may make rules governing the practice and procedure in relation to

> **(a) applications under section 82.1 for leave to commence an application for judicial review,**
>
> **(b) applications for judicial review under the *Federal Court Act* with respect to any decision or order made, or any matter arising, under this Act or the rules or regulations thereunder, and**
>
> **(c) appeals referred to in section 83,**

and those rules shall be binding notwithstanding any rule or practice that would otherwise be applicable.

(2) Inconsistencies — In the event of an inconsistency between any of the provisions of sections 82.1 to 83 of this Act and any provision of the *Federal Court Act*, the provisions of this Act prevail to the extent of the inconsistency.

R.S.C. 1985, c. 28 (4th Supp.), s. 19; 1992, c. 49, s. 73.

84.1 [Repealed 1992, c. 49, s. 73.]

84.2 [Repealed 1992, c. 49, s. 73.]

PART V — OBLIGATIONS OF TRANSPORTATION COMPANIES

85. (1) General liability for removal — Subject to subsection (2), a transportation company that has brought a person to Canada may be required by the Minister to convey that person, or cause that person to be conveyed,

(a) to the country from which that person came to Canada or to such other country as the Minister may approve at the request of the company, in the case of a person who is allowed to leave Canada pursuant to subsection 20(1) or 23(4), (4.01) or (4.2) or who is required to leave Canada by reason of the making of a rejection order;

(b) to the United States, in the case of a person who is required to leave Canada by reason of the making of a direction to return to that country pursuant to subsection 20(2) or 23(5); or

(c) to such country as is determined pursuant to subsection 52(2) or (3), in the case of a person who is required to leave Canada by reason of the making of a removal order.

(2) Liability where U.S.A. refuses to allow return — Where a person referred to in subsection (1) has come to Canada through the United States and that country refuses to allow that person to return or to be returned to it, the transportation company that brought the person to the United States shall convey him or cause him to be conveyed

(a) in the case of a person referred to in paragraph (1)(*a*) or (*b*), to the country from which the person came to the United States or to such other country as may be approved by the Minister at the request of the transportation company; and

(b) in the case of a person referred to in paragraph (1)(*c*), to such country other than the United States as is determined pursuant to subsection 52(2) or (3).

(3) Removal costs of persons not admitted — A transportation company is liable to pay all removal costs of any person whom it is required to convey or cause to be conveyed pursuant to this section if the person has not been granted admission and at the time of arrival in Canada was not in possession of a valid and subsisting visa.

(4) Reimbursement for removal costs of persons admitted — A transportation company is entitled to be reimbursed by Her Majesty for the removal costs that it incurs in conveying or causing to be conveyed pursuant to this section any person

who has been granted admission or who at the time of arrival in Canada was in possession of a valid and subsisting visa.

(5) Application — This section does not apply in relation to persons who enter Canada as or to become members of a crew.

R.S.C. 1985, c. 28 (4th Supp.), s. 20; 1992, c. 49, s. 74; 1995, c. 15, s. 16.

Case Law

Section 85(2)

Chan v. McFarlane, [1962] O.R. 798 (Ont. C.A.) — The word "through" the United States in the *Immigration Act*, R.S.C. 1952, implied continuous transit through that country in the course of a journey to Canada from elsewhere; it did not include a situation where the respondent resided in the United States for 10 years before coming to Canada. The Court held that the respondent had come to Canada from the United States and not through the United States.

86. Liability for removal of members of crew — Where a person enters Canada as or to become a member of a crew of a vehicle and ceases to be a visitor pursuant to subsection 26(1), the transportation company that operates that vehicle may be required by the Minister to convey that person, or cause that person to be conveyed, to the country from which that person came to Canada, or to such other country as the Minister may approve at the request of the company, and the company is liable to pay all removal costs in respect of that person.

R.S.C. 1985, c. 28 (4th Supp.), s. 21; 1992, c. 49, s. 75.

87. (1) Transportation of persons ordered removed — Where, pursuant to section 85 or 86, a transportation company is required to convey a person, or cause a person to be conveyed, from Canada, it shall be notified of that requirement and be given an opportunity to convey that person, or to cause that person to be conveyed, on one of its own vehicles or otherwise.

(2) Idem, by other company — Where a transportation company referred to in subsection (1), after having been notified, is not prompt in furnishing transportation, the Minister may direct that arrangements be made for the removal from Canada, by another transportation company and at the expense of Her Majesty, of the person to be conveyed from Canada.

(3) Reimbursement of costs — The transportation company referred to in subsection (1) is liable, on demand, to reimburse Her Majesty for all removal costs incurred under subsection (2) in respect of the person conveyed from Canada.

1992, c. 49, s. 76.

88. (1) Duties of transportation companies — Every transportation company that is required to convey any person who is ordered removed from Canada, is rejected from Canada or is allowed or required to leave Canada shall

> **(a) detain and guard safely the person concerned until that person can be placed on board the vehicle on which he is to be conveyed; and**
>
> **(b) accept on board such vehicle, guard safely and convey the person in accordance with the removal or rejection order or other order or direction.**

(2) **No charge for transportation** — A transportation company referred to in subsection (1) shall, subject to any agreement between the company and the person being conveyed respecting return fares, refrain from, directly or indirectly, making any charge or taking any remuneration or security in respect thereof.

89. (1) **Duty to present passengers for examination** — A transportation company bringing persons to Canada shall, on the arrival of each one of its vehicles in Canada, present each passenger seeking to come into Canada to an immigration officer for examination at such place as may be designated by a senior immigration officer and shall not allow any person to leave the vehicle

(a) at any place other than that designated by a senior immigration officer; or

(b) until permission has been granted by a senior immigration officer.

(2) **Required facilities** — The Minister may, in writing, require any transportation company to provide, equip and maintain free of charge to Her Majesty adequate areas, offices, laboratories and other facilities, including buildings, accommodation, equipment, furnishings and fixtures, for the proper interviewing, examination and detention of persons brought to Canada or to be removed from Canada via the vehicles, bridges, tunnels or airports of the company.

(3) **Powers of minister** — The Minister may

(a) cause to be made such improvements as the Minister considers desirable to any facility provided pursuant to subsection (2);

(b) post, on or about the facility, any signs that the Minister considers appropriate for its operation or safe use; and

(c) continue to use the facility for as long as the Minister requires it for the purposes mentioned in subsection (2).

(4) **Construction and repairs** — Where a facility pursuant to subsection (2) is not adequate for the purposes mentioned in that subsection, the Minister may require the transportation company to carry out any construction or repairs in order to render the facility adequate for those purposes, and if the transportation company fails to do so, the Minister may have the construction or repairs carried out and the transportation company shall be liable for all reasonable costs incurred by the Minister, which costs may be recovered by Her Majesty in right of Canada.

(5) **Notice** — A requirement under subsection (4) shall be communicated by the personal delivery of a notice to the transportation company or by sending the notice to the transportation company, and the notice may specify the period within which or the manner in which the construction or repairs are to be carried out.

(6) **Arbitration** — Subject to subsection (7) and to any regulations made under paragraph 114(1)(*q*.11), a dispute over the adequacy of a facility may be resolved by arbitration in accordance with the *Commercial Arbitration Act*.

(7) **Canada Labour Code** — Any facility that fails to meet the applicable requirements of Part II of the *Canada Labour Code* shall be deemed not to be adequate for the purposes mentioned in subsection (2).

1992, c. 49, s. 77.

89.1 (1) Duty to check travel documents — Every transportation company shall ensure that the persons it brings to Canada are in possession of all visas, passports and travel documents required by this Act or the regulations unless the visas, passports and travel documents are being held by the company in accordance with any regulations made under paragraph 114(1)(*q*.1).

(2) Application — Subsection (1) applies from the time the transportation company embarks the persons at the final embarkation point before arrival in Canada until they are presented to an immigration officer for examination in accordance with subsection 89(1).

R.S.C. 1985, c. 28 (4th Supp.), s. 22; 1992, c. 49, s. 78.

Case Law

R. v. Deutsche Lufthansa AG (1994), 25 Imm. L.R. (2d) 85 (Ont. C.A.) — Lufthansa was convicted of three charges under section 89.1. The facts were that an Iranian family of three was flown by Lufthansa from Germany to Canada. The family was using forged documents, purchased together with airline tickets from smugglers in Bombay, India. On arrival in Toronto, Canadian Immigration officers boarded the aircraft to carry out a discretionary and random pre-disembarkation screening. The officers walked up and down the aisles asking passengers to display their documents. The family displayed no documents and claimed refugee status.

The Summary Conviction Appeal judge held that Convention refugees require no travel documents. The Appeal judge found as a fact that one of the three people on the plane had been found to be a Convention refugee and, therefore, the Appeal judge set aside the convictions and acquitted Lufthansa on all three charges. The Summary Conviction Appeal judge reasoned that because a Convention refugee could not be prosecuted for, amongst other matters, not having travel documents, the carrier which had brought the refugee to Canada should not be prosecuted under section 89.1. This conclusion was found to be an error. Section 89.1 imposes an obligation on the carrier to ensure that a passenger has the appropriate travel documents. There is no more practical way of a carrier carrying out this obligation than physically checking the documents in the hands of the passenger. Whether the documents ultimately prove adequate or whether the passenger ultimately needs any documents at all are matters which are irrelevant to compliance with section 89.1.

Section 95.1(2) provides immunity for Convention refugees. That is a matter which concerns the passenger and Canada Immigration. It does not concern the carrier nor does it extend immunity to any carrier.

Lufthansa could not be convicted in this case because it had not presented the passengers to Immigration. The presentation of the passengers by the carrier to Canadian Immigration is an element of the offence under section 89.1. What happened here is that pursuant to section 90(1) immigration officers boarded and inspected the aircraft as well as the persons on it. Presentation by the airline never occurred and therefore these prosecutions were premature.

Accordingly, the acquittals of the airline by the Summary Conviction Appeal judge were confirmed, although on a different basis.

R. v. Koninklijke Luchtvaart Maatschappij N.V. (1993), 22 Imm. L.R. (2d) 63 (Ont. Gen. Div.) — Three passengers were originally scheduled to fly from Damascus to Chicago. They missed their connecting flight in Amsterdam and were rerouted to Chicago via Toronto. All three passengers sought entry to Canada for the purpose of travelling onward to the United States. All three were granted entry pursuant to section 19(3) of the *Immigration Act*.

The prosecution of KLM for an offence contrary to section 89.1 failed because the prosecution failed to prove that the passengers did not possess the documents required by the *Immigration Act* and regulations.

In fact, all three were lawfully admitted to Canada on such documents as they did possess. Accordingly, KLM's appeal from its conviction was allowed.

90. (1) **Rights of immigration officers — Immigration officers may**

(a) board and inspect any vehicle bringing persons to Canada;

(b) examine any person carried by that vehicle;

(c) examine any record or document respecting any such person and seize and remove any such record or document for the purpose of obtaining copies thereof or extracts therefrom; and

(d) hold that vehicle until the inspection and examination are completed.

(2) **Order to detain on board vehicle — An immigration officer may order the master of a vehicle to detain and guard safely on board the vehicle any person who arrived in Canada on that vehicle and who**

(a) is not seeking admission to Canada;

(b) has been allowed to leave Canada pursuant to subsection 20(1) or 23(4), (4.01) or (4.2); or

(c) is required to leave Canada by reason of the making of a rejection order.

1992, c. 49, s. 79; 1995, c. 15, s. 17.

90.1 [Ceased to have effect July 1, 1989. See R.S.C. 1985, c. 29 (4th Supp.), s. 8(2).]

[Editor's Note: Section 90.1 was enacted by R.S.C. 1985 (4th Supp.), c. 29, s. 8(1) and became effective October 3, 1988. Section 90.1 was subsequently amended by R.S.C. 1985 (4th Supp.), c. 28, s. 35, effective January 1, 1989. By virtue of R.S.C. 1985 (4th Supp.), c. 29, s. 8(2), section 90.1 ceased to be in force July 1, 1989.]

91. (1) **Medical treatment — Where a medical officer is of the opinion that a person seeking to come into Canada is or may be, either pending his admission or pending his leaving Canada where admission has not been granted, suffering from sickness or mental or physical disability or has been in contact with a contagious or infectious disease, a senior immigration officer or a medical officer may direct that the person**

(a) be afforded medical treatment or held for observation and diagnosis on board the vehicle by which he was brought to Canada or at an immigrant station; or

(b) be taken to a suitable hospital or other place for treatment, observation and diagnosis.

(2) **Costs of medical treatment, etc. — Any costs of treatment, medical attention and maintenance incurred with respect to a person described in subsection (1) may be recovered from the transportation company that brought the person to Canada unless that person is in possession of a valid and subsisting visa and the transportation company establishes to the satisfaction of the Deputy Minister that that person's condition is not a result of any negligence of the transportation company.**

(3) **Costs of attendant accompanying sick person** — A senior immigration officer or a medical officer may, where he considers it advisable for the proper care of a person referred to in subsection (1), authorize that a member of the person's family or other suitable attendant be kept with the person during the period of medical attention and treatment, including, where applicable, the person's journey to the port of entry from which the person will leave Canada, and the costs thereof may be recovered from the transportation company that brought the person referred to in subsection (1) to Canada where costs of treatment, medical attention and maintenance may be recovered from the transportation company pursuant to subsection (2).

(4) **Medical and hospital costs for crew members** — Where a person who is a member of the crew of a vehicle receives medical treatment or is hospitalized in Canada, the transportation company of whose vehicle that person is a member of the crew shall pay all costs incurred for the medical treatment or hospitalization as well as all costs incurred with respect to the departure from Canada of that person.

91.1 (1) **Administration fees — preliminary assessment** — The Minister may, in accordance with the regulations, make a preliminary assessment of an administration fee against a transportation company in respect of any member of a class of persons prescribed for the purposes of this section

(a) who is brought to Canada by the company and who is the subject of a report pursuant to paragraph 20(1)(*a*) or a report pursuant to paragraph 27(2)(*f*) for having eluded examination; or

(b) who enters Canada as or to become a member of the crew of a vehicle operated by the company and who is the subject of a report pursuant to paragraph 27(2)(*e*) as a member of a crew who has ceased to be a visitor pursuant to paragraph 26(1)(*c*.1).

(2) **Notice and written submissions** — Notice of a preliminary assessment under subsection (1) shall be given to a transportation company in accordance with any regulations and, within thirty days after the notice is given, the company may file written submissions with the Minister regarding the assessment.

(3) **Final assessment and notice** — After considering any submissions filed under subsection (2), the Minister may confirm, vary or rescind the preliminary assessment and the company shall, in accordance with any regulations, be given notice of the final assessment.

(4) **Deemed final assessment** — Where notice is given pursuant to subsection (2) and no written submission is filed within the period referred to in that subsection, the preliminary assessment shall be deemed to be a final assessment, and the transportation company shall be liable under the assessment on the day that immediately follows the expiration of that period.

(5) **Liability** — Where notice of final assessment is given to a transportation company pursuant to subsection (3), the transportation company shall be liable under the assessment on the day the notice of final assessment is sent to the company.

1992, c. 49, s. 80.

92. (1) General security — **The Deputy Minister may issue a direction to any transportation company requiring it to deposit with Her Majesty in right of Canada such sum of money, in Canadian currency, or such other prescribed security as the Deputy Minister deems necessary as a guarantee that the company will pay all amounts for which it may become liable under this Act after the direction is issued.**

(2) Special purpose security — **Where a vehicle owned or operated by a transportation company that has not deposited the required sum of money or other security pursuant to a direction issued under subsection (1) comes into Canada, the Deputy Minister may issue a direction to the master of the vehicle or to the transportation company requiring the master or company to deposit with Her Majesty in right of Canada such sum of money, in Canadian currency, or such other prescribed security as the Deputy Minister deems necessary as a guarantee that the company will pay all amounts for which it may become liable under this Act in respect of that vehicle after the direction is issued.**

(3) Additional security — **Where the Deputy Minister is of the opinion that any security deposited pursuant to a direction under subsection (1) or (2) does not provide a sufficient guarantee that the transportation company will pay the amounts, the Deputy Minister may issue a direction to the master or the company that deposited the security requiring the master or company to deposit with Her Majesty in right of Canada such sum of money, in Canadian currency, as the Deputy Minister deems necessary as additional security.**

(4) Failure to comply with directions — **Where a master or transportation company fails to comply with a direction under subsection (1), (2) or (3), the Minister may direct an immigration officer**

> **(a) to detain any vehicle of the transportation company for a period of not more than forty-eight hours; or**
>
> **(b) to seize and hold any vehicle of the company, including any vehicle detained pursuant to paragraph (*a*).**

(5) Failure to pay amounts — **Where a transportation company becomes liable to pay any amount under this Act and the required sum of money or prescribed security has not been deposited in respect of the transportation company pursuant to a direction under subsection (1), (2) or (3), the Minister may direct that an immigration officer**

> **(a) detain any vehicle of the company for a period of not more than forty-eight hours; or**
>
> **(b) seize and hold any vehicle of the company, including any vehicle detained pursuant to paragraph (*a*).**

(5.1) Detention of vehicles — **A transportation company shall comply with the orders of an immigration officer given pursuant to a direction to detain a vehicle of the company under subsection (4) or (5).**

(6) Notice of seizure — **A person who seizes a vehicle pursuant to a direction under subsection (4) or (5) shall take such measures as are reasonable in the circumstances to give notice of the seizure to any person who the person seizing the vehicle believes on reasonable grounds is entitled to make an application under section 93.1 in respect of the vehicle.**

(7) **Return or sale of seized vehicle** — Where a vehicle of a transportation company is seized pursuant to a direction under subsection (4) or (5), the Minister may

(a) return the vehicle to the master of the vehicle or to the company on receipt of

(i) an amount equal to the value of the vehicle at the time of its seizure, as determined by the Minister, or any lesser amount acceptable to the Minister, or

(ii) an amount equal to the expense of holding the vehicle and either compliance with the direction to deposit security or receipt of the amount that the company is liable to pay, as the case may be; or

(b) on the expiration of thirty days after the seizure, have the vehicle sold by public auction.

(7.1) **Liable for costs** — Where a vehicle of a transportation company is detained pursuant to a direction under subsection (4) or (5), the transportation company shall be liable for all costs that relate to the detention of the vehicle.

(8) **Notice of sale** — Notice of a sale under subsection (7) setting out the time and place thereof and a general description of the vehicle to be sold shall be published a reasonable time before the vehicle is sold at least once in one or more newspapers of general circulation in the area where the sale is to be held.

(9) **Application of proceeds of sale** — Any surplus remaining from a sale under subsection (7) after deduction of the sum or other security required to be deposited or the fine or amount, as the case may be, and the expenses incurred in holding and selling the vehicle shall be paid to the transportation company.

(10) **Surrender of security** — Any sum or prescribed security deposited pursuant to a direction under subsection (1), (2) or (3) may be returned or cancelled on a direction from the Deputy Minister that the sum or security is no longer required.

R.S.C. 1985, c. 28 (4th Supp.), s. 23; 1992, c. 49, s. 81.

92.1 (1) **Certificates** — Where a master or transportation company does not deposit the required sum of money or other security in accordance with a direction under subsection 92(1), (2) or (3), the Minister may, on the expiration of thirty days after the date of the direction, certify that it has not been deposited.

(2) **Judgments** — On production to the Federal Court, a certificate under subsection (1) shall be registered in that Court and, when registered, the certificate has the same effect, and all proceedings may be taken to enforce it, as if it were a judgment obtained in that Court for a debt of the amount specified in the certificate.

(3) **Costs** — The fees for registering the certificate are recoverable in the same way as if they had been certified and the certificate had been registered under this section.

1992, c. 49, s. 82.

93. **Deduction from security in certain cases** — The Minister, on giving written notice to a transportation company, may direct that any amount for which the transportation company is liable pursuant to subsection 85(3), section 86, subsection 87(3) or section 91, or any administration fee finally assessed against the transportation company pursuant to section 91.1, be deducted from any sum of money deposited as a

guarantee in respect of the company pursuant to a direction under subsection 92(1), (2) or (3), or be realized from any prescribed security so deposited.

R.S.C. 1985, c. 28 (4th Supp.), ss. 23, 35; 1992, c. 49, s. 82.

93.1 (1) **Claiming interest** — Where a vehicle has been seized pursuant to a direction under subsection 92(4) or (5), any person, other than the master of the vehicle or the transportation company, who claims an interest in the vehicle as owner, mortgagee, lien-holder or holder of any like interest may, within sixty days after the seizure, apply by notice in writing to a judge for an order under subsection (5).

(2) **Day of hearing** — The judge to whom an application is made under subsection (1) shall fix a day for a hearing of the application not less than thirty days after the day of filing of the application.

(3) **Notice** — A person making an application under subsection (1) shall serve a notice of the application and of the hearing on the Minister not later than fifteen days after a day for the hearing of the application is fixed pursuant to subsection (2).

(4) **Service of notice** — The service of a notice under subsection (3) is sufficient if it is sent by registered mail addressed to the Minister.

(5) **Order that interest not affected** — Where, on the hearing of an application made under subsection (1), it is made to appear to the satisfaction of the judge that the applicant acquired the interest in respect of which the applicant is applying in good faith prior to the seizure, the applicant is entitled to an order declaring that the applicant's interest is not affected by the seizure and declaring the nature and extent of the applicant's interest.

(6) **Appeal** — A person who makes an application under subsection (1) or the Minister may appeal to the court of appeal from an order made under subsection (5) and the appeal shall be asserted, heard and decided according to the ordinary procedure governing appeals to the court of appeal from orders or judgments of a judge.

(7) **Return of vehicle** — The Minister shall, on application made to the Minister by a person who has obtained a final order under this section,

(a) direct that the vehicle to which the interest of the person relates be returned to the person; or

(b) direct that an amount equal to the value of the interest of the person, as declared in the order, be paid to the person.

(8) **Limit on amount paid** — The total amount paid under paragraph (7)(*b*) in respect of a vehicle shall, where the vehicle was sold or otherwise disposed of under this Act, not exceed the proceeds of the sale or disposition, if any, less any costs incurred by Her Majesty in respect of the vehicle, and, where there are no proceeds of a disposition of a vehicle under this Act, no payment shall be made pursuant to paragraph (7)(*b*) in respect of the vehicle.

(9) **Definitions** — In this section,

"court of appeal" means, in the province in which an order under this section is made, the court of appeal for that province as defined in the definition "court of appeal" in section 2 of the *Criminal Code*;

"judge" means

(a) in the Province of Quebec, a judge of the Superior Court for the district in which the vehicle, in respect of which an application for an order under this section is made, was seized,

(a.1) in the Province of Ontario, a judge of the Superior Court of Justice,

(b) [Repealed 1992, c. 51, s. 52.]

(c) in the Provinces of Nova Scotia, British Columbia, Prince Edward Island and Newfoundland, a judge of the Supreme Court thereof,

(d) in the Provinces of New Brunswick, Manitoba, Alberta and Saskatchewan, a judge of the Court of Queen's Bench thereof, and

(e) in the Yukon Territory and the Northwest Territories, a judge of the Supreme Court of the territory, and in Nunavut, a judge of the Nunavut Court of Justice.

R.S.C. 1985, c. 28 (4th Supp.), s. 23; 1990, c. 16, s. 12; 1990, c. 17, ss. 23, 47; 1992, c. 51, s. 52; 1993, c. 28, s. 78 (Sched. III, item 71) [Repealed 1999, c. 3, (Sched., item 15).]; 1998, c. 30, s. 14(i); 1999, c. 3, s. 67.

PART VI — ENFORCEMENT

Offences and Punishment

94. (1) Specific offences respecting immigration — Every person is guilty of an offence who

(a) comes into Canada at any place other than a port of entry and fails to appear before an immigration officer for examination as required by subsection 12(1);

(b) comes into Canada or remains in Canada by use of a false or improperly obtained passport, visa or other document pertaining to the admission of that person or by reason of any fraudulent or improper means or misrepresentation of any material fact;

(c) [Repealed 1992, c. 49, s. 83.]

(d) escapes or attempts to escape from lawful custody or detention under this Act;

(e) knowingly fails to comply with any term or condition subject to which that person was released from detention pursuant to paragraph 23(3)(*b*) or subsection 103(3), (3.1), (5) or (7);

(f) eludes examination or inquiry under this Act or, having received a summons under this Act, fails, without valid excuse, to attend an inquiry or a hearing or, where required by any such summons, to produce any document, book or paper that the person has or controls relative to the subject-matter of the inquiry or hearing;

(g) refuses to be sworn or to affirm or declare, as the case may be, or to answer a question put to the person at the examination, inquiry or hearing under this Act;

(h) knowingly makes any false or misleading statement at any examination, inquiry or hearing under this Act or in connection with the admission of any person or the application for admission by any person;

(h.1) provides information to a senior immigration officer for the purposes of subsection 23(4.1), 27(5) or 45(5) knowing that information to be false or misleading;

(i) knowingly makes a false promise of employment or any false representation by reason of which a person is induced to seek admission or is assisted in any attempt to seek admission or by reason of which that person's admission is procured;

(j) for the purpose of encouraging, inducing, deterring or preventing immigration into Canada, publishes, disseminates or causes or procures the publication or dissemination of any false or misleading information or representations as to the opportunities for employment in Canada or other false or misleading information or representations, knowing that the information or representations are false or misleading;

(k) remains in Canada without the written authority of an immigration officer after having ceased to be a visitor;

(l) knowingly contravenes any existing term or condition subject to which that person was granted admission or contravenes any term or condition added or as varied pursuant to subsection 17(2);

(m) knowingly induces, aids or abets or attempts to induce, aid or abet any person to contravene any provision of this Act or the regulations; or

(n) imports or exports, by mail or otherwise, in order to contravene this Act or the regulations, a visa, passport or other travel document, any document or thing that may serve to establish the identity of a person or any document or thing purporting to be any of those document or things.

(1.1) Proof of offence — Proof that a person imported or exported a forged document or a document or thing referred to in paragraph (1)(*n*) that is blank, incomplete, altered or not genuine is, in the absence of evidence to the contrary, proof that the person intends to contravene this Act or the regulations.

(2) Punishment — Every person who is guilty of an offence under subsection (1) is liable

(a) on conviction on indictment, to a fine not exceeding five thousand dollars or to imprisonment for a term not exceeding two years or to both; or

(b) on summary conviction, to a fine not exceeding one thousand dollars or to imprisonment for a term not exceeding six months or to both.

R.S.C. 1985, c. 28 (4th Supp.), s. 24; 1992, c. 49, s. 83; 1995, c. 15, s. 18.

Case Law

Section 94(1)(b)

R. v. Mossavat (1995), 29 Imm. L.R. (2d) 41 (Ont. Gen. Div.), affirmed (1995), 30 Imm. L.R. (2d) 201, 85 O.A.C. 1 (Ont. C.A.) — Two families from Iran consisting of 8 individuals paid a smuggler to assist them to leave Iran and become refugees elsewhere. They left Iran and arrived in Ecuador. In Ecuador they met a person who, for a significant sum of money, obtained false passports. This person also obtained airline tickets for passage to Toronto by New York City. The appellant, a Canadian citizen, travelled on the flight from Ecuador to Toronto and disposed of the envelope containing the passport and airline tickets after the plane landed in Toronto. The appellant was prosecuted under section 94(1)(b) of the *Immigration Act*. The phrase "to come into Canada" describes a process which must begin outside Canada and end inside Canada. Precisely where that process begins and just how many stages it has will depend upon the facts of the individual case. The trial judge concluded on the facts before him that the process was under way in Ecuador. The Appeal Court adopted that conclusion and dismissed the appeals.

R. v. Dirie (1994), 27 Imm. L.R. (2d) 265 (Ont. Prov. Div.) — The accused was travelling on a Canadian passport. He was travelling with a person named Abdiazzis Ali Sahal, who presented himself to Canada Immigration and made a refugee claim. The accused, Dirie, had provided Mr. Sahal with a Canadian passport so that he could board the aircraft and make the journey to Canada. Once a person presents a passport or travel documents to a transportation company with a view to travelling to Canada, his entry into Canada has commenced and thus the passport has been used to "come into Canada" within the meaning of section 94(1)(b).

The fact that a refugee claimant cannot be charged under section 94(1)(b) by reason of the provisions of section 95.1 does not mean that there is no longer a provision which has been contravened. There has been a deferral of prosecution, or exemption from prosecution, but that is all. The immunity does not extend to anyone charged with aiding and abetting any person to contravene the section.

R. v. Grospe (1988), 6 W.C.B. (2d) 44 — Section 95(b) creates a single offence that can be committed in a number of different ways, rather than a number of separate and distinct offences. The fact that the accused could have been charged with committing the offence under section 95(b) of the Act in a different way, did not mean that the present offence was not proven. In this case, the accused had made materially false statements on an application for permanent residence. The accused had argued that the Crown should have charged her with misrepresentation of a material fact rather than entering Canada by use of an improperly obtained visa. The accused was convicted.

R. v. Ferreira, (Orally) (July 7, 1986) (Ont. Prov. Ct.) — The accused was charged with entering Canada by improper means, and those means were specified as a fraudulent United States visitor's visa contained in his Portuguese passport. Despite the fact that an American visa is not a condition precedent for entering Canada and that tendering a fraudulent American visa would not, therefore, be misrepresenting a material fact, it was still held that to offer knowingly a passport containing an apparently unexpired but forged American visa constituted an attempt to come into Canada by improper means. The Court found that the accused knew that the American visa was fraudulent, and a conviction was registered.

Section 94(1)(g)

Bowen v. Canada (Minister of Employment & Immigration), [1984] 2 F.C. 507 (Fed. C.A.) — The applicant initially refused to testify at the inquiry on the advice of her counsel but later retreated from this position also on the advice of her counsel. The Commission, however, presented its case without the applicant's testimony. Section 11(c) of the *Charter of Rights* was held to be inapplicable to the applicant because it could not be said that the applicant was being compelled to be a witness at her inquiry when the counsel, representing her, conceded her compellability as a witness. It was further held that section 11(c) of the Charter had no application to the testimony to be given by the applicant because the applicant could not be said to be "a person charged within an offence." The Court observed that section 24 of the Charter did not apply because it was a condition precedent to the operation of that section that a person's rights or freedoms as guaranteed by the Charter not be infringed or denied. The Court having decided that the applicant's rights or freedoms, as guaranteed by the Charter had not been infringed or denied, was of the view that the conditions precedent to the operation of section 24 had not been met.

R. v. Wooten (1983), 9 C.C.C. (3d) 513 (B.C. S.C.) — This was an appeal by the Crown from an acquittal of the respondent of an offence under section 95(g) of the *Immigration Act*. The respondent was arrested and detained on the grounds that he was in Canada without the permission of the Minister and that he had falsely represented a material fact to enable him to remain in the country. During the inquiry, the case presenting officer sought to call the respondent as a witness. The respondent's counsel objected. The adjudicator ruled against the respondent on this question. The respondent was sworn as a witness but refused to answer any questions. The respondent was charged under section 95(g) and acquitted on the basis that section 95(g) was inoperative as it offended sections 7 and 11(c) of the *Charter of Rights*. The respondent was held not to be a person "charged with an offence" and, therefore, not subject to the protection of section 11(c) of the Charter. The Court adopted previous decisions which had characterized an immigration inquiry as a civil proceeding and there was, therefore, nothing fundamentally unjust in compelling the person who was the subject of the immigration inquiry to testify.

Sondhi, Re (August 17, 1983) (Ont. Prov. Ct.) — Section 11(c) of the *Canadian Charter of Rights and Freedoms, Constitution Act*, 1982, Pt. I, does not apply to an applicant testifying before an inquiry because the applicant is not "charged" with an offence in that proceeding.

R. v. Forrester (1982), 2 C.C.C. (3d) 467 (Ont. C.A.) — The appellant answered a number of questions at an inquiry before refusing to answer a question on the grounds that her answer might tend to incriminate her and declining an offer of the protection of the *Canada Evidence Act*, R.S.C. 1970, c. E-10. The Ontario Court of Appeal upheld her conviction under section 95 and adopted the reasons of the Federal Court in *Chana* (summarized below).

Webb v. Canada (Minister of Manpower & Immigration), [1982] 1 F.C. 687 (Fed. C.A.) — Where the applicant does not refuse to testify, the principles enunciated in section 2(d) of the *Canadian Bill of Rights*, R.S.C. 1970, App. III, do not avail. The Court left open the correctness of the decision in *Cole*.

R. v. Cole, [1980] 6 W.W.R. 552 (Man. Co. Ct.), leave to appeal denied [1981] 1 W.W.R. 596 (Man. C.A.) — A person who fails to answer questions put to him at an immigration inquiry may not be prosecuted for an offence under section 95(g) owing to the protection in section 2(d) of the *Canadian Bill of Rights*, R.S.C. 1970, App. III, with respect to self-incrimination.

Chana v. Canada (Minister of Manpower & Immigration), [1977] 2 F.C. 496 (Fed. T.D.) — An alien was a compellable witness at a special inquiry under the old Act. The alien's rights under section 2(d) of the *Canadian Bill of Rights*, R.S.C. 1970, App. III, were not violated because the alien was entitled to retain counsel and was fully safeguarded against incriminating himself by virtue of the *Canada Evidence Act*, R.S.C. 1970, c. E-10.

Section 94(1)(k)

R. v. Malhotra, [1981] 2 W.W.R. 560 (Man. Prov. Ct.) — There was some evidence that the accused engaged in employment. Section 26(1)(b) of the Act operated to strip the accused of his status as a visitor. Therefore, there was a *prima facie* case against the accused under this section.

R. v. Malhotra (No. 1), [1981] 2 W.W.R. 563 (Man. Prov. Ct.) — Section 95(k) creates an offence of absolute liability.

Section 94(1)(m)

R. v. Jupiter (1983), 35 C.R. (3d) 286 (Ont. Co. Ct.) — Court noted that while it is common to speak of aiding and abetting, the two concepts are not the same and either activity constitutes a sufficient basis for liability under this section. Abetting is defined as instigating, promoting or procuring a crime to be committed, while aiding means assisting or helping without necessarily encouraging or instigating the act. While the appellant was motivated by the highest principles of family concern, the Court noted that as a general proposition if a person aids another, knowing that the other intends to commit an offence, he aids in that offence even if his motive is something else. Accordingly, the appeal in this case was dismissed and the conviction affirmed.

94.1 Organizing entry into Canada — Every person who knowingly organizes, induces, aids or abets or attempts to organize, induce, aid or abet the coming into Canada of a person who is not in possession of a valid and subsisting visa, passport or travel document where one is required by this Act or the regulations is guilty of an offence and liable

(a) on conviction on indictment, to a fine not exceeding one hundred thousand dollars or to imprisonment for a term not exceeding five years, or to both; or

(b) on summary conviction, to a fine not exceeding ten thousand dollars or to imprisonment for a term not exceeding one year, or to both.

R.S.C. 1985, c. 29 (4th Supp.), s. 9; 1992, c. 49, s. 84.

Case Law

R. v. Chen (December 18, 1998), Bentley Prov. J. (Ont. Prov. Div.) — The defendants were facing 33 charges under sections 94.1 and 94.2 of the Immigration Act. The defendants had argued at the conclusion of their preliminary hearing, that sections 94.1 and 94.2, cannot extend to any actions of an accused person in relation to a person who has cleared the port-of-entry.

The Court found that the objects of section 94.1 and 94.2 are consistent with an interpretation that is not restrictive in the manner contemplated by the defence. The activities of individuals who assist people to illegally come into Canada include those who are involved in such operations regardless of whether it occurs before entry or after entry. Failure to adopt such an interpretation would defeat the intention and purpose of the legislation.

Abetting is defined as instigating, promoting or procuring a crime. Aiding, means assisting or helping, induce is defined as influencing an act, and organize means to initiate or make arrangements for, to enlist (a person or a group).

94.2 Idem — Every person who knowingly organizes, induces, aids or abets or attempts to organize, induce, aid or abet the coming into Canada of a group of ten or more persons who are not in possession of valid and subsisting visas, passports or travel documents where such visas, passports or travel documents are required by this Act or the regulations is guilty of an offence and is liable on conviction on indictment to a fine not exceeding five hundred thousand dollars or to imprisonment for a term not exceeding ten years, or to both.

R.S.C. 1985, c. 29 (4th Supp.), s. 9.

Case Law

R. v. Chen (December 18, 1998), Bentley Prov. J. (Ont. Prov. Div.) — The defendants were facing 33 charges under sections 94.1 and 94.2 of the Immigration Act. The defendants had argued at the conclusion of their preliminary hearing, that sections 94.1 and 94.2, cannot extend to any actions of an accused person in relation to a person who has cleared the port-of-entry.

The Court found that the objects of section 94.1 and 94.2 are consistent with an interpretation that is not restrictive in the manner contemplated by the defence. The activities of individuals who assist people to illegally come into Canada include those who are involved in such operations regardless of whether it occurs before entry or after entry. Failure to adopt such an interpretation would defeat the intention and purpose of the legislation.

Abetting is defined as instigating, promoting or procuring a crime. Aiding, means assisting or helping, induce is defined as influencing an act, and organize means to initiate or make arrangements for, to enlist (a person or a group).

94.3 No proceedings without consent — No proceedings for an offence under section 94.1 or section 94.2 shall be instituted except by or with the personal consent in writing of the Attorney General of Canada or Deputy Attorney General of Canada.

R.S.C. 1985, c. 29 (4th Supp.), s. 9.

94.4 Disembarking persons at sea — Every person who, being the master or a member of a crew of a vehicle used for transportation by sea, disembarks or allows the disembarkation of, or attempts to disembark or attempts to allow the disembarkation of, a person or group of persons at sea for the purpose of inducing, aiding or abetting that person or group of persons to come into Canada in contravention of this Act or the regulations is guilty of an offence and is liable on conviction on indictment to a fine not exceeding five hundred thousand dollars or to imprisonment for a term not exceeding ten years, or to both.

R.S.C. 1985, c. 29 (4th Supp.), s. 9.

94.5 Counselling false statements — Every person who knowingly counsels, induces, aids or abets, or who knowingly attempts to counsel, induce, aid or abet, any other person to make any false or misleading statement in connection with a claim by that other person to be a Convention refugee is guilty of an offence and liable

(a) on conviction on indictment, to a fine not exceeding ten thousand dollars or to imprisonment for a term not exceeding five years, or to both; or

(b) on summary conviction, to a fine not exceeding two thousand dollars or to imprisonment for a term not exceeding six months, or to both.

R.S.C. 1985, c. 29 (4th Supp.), s. 9.

94.6 (1) Offences relating to approved businesses or funds — Every person is guilty of an offence who

(a) knowingly submits any false or misleading information to the Minister in relation to an application for the approval of a business or fund or in a report required in relation to an approved business or fund;

(b) knowingly makes any false or misleading representation about an approved business or fund or falsely represents that a business or fund is approved;

(c) manages or controls an approved business or fund and fails to comply with any term or condition governing the approval; or

(d) fails to do anything that the person is required to do under paragraph 102.001(2)(*b*) or section 102.003.

(2) Punishment — Every person who is guilty of an offence under subsection (1) is liable

(a) on conviction on indictment,

(i) for the first offence, to a fine not exceeding one hundred thousand dollars or to imprisonment for a term not exceeding two years, or to both, or

(ii) for a subsequent offence, to a fine not exceeding five hundred thousand dollars or to imprisonment for a term not exceeding five years, or to both; or

(b) on summary conviction,

(i) for a first offence, to a fine not exceeding fifty thousand dollars, or

(ii) for a subsequent offence, to a fine not exceeding one hundred thousand dollars or to imprisonment for a term not exceeding two years, or to both.

1992, c. 49, s. 85.

95. Offence where return is without Minister's consent — Every person against whom a removal order is made who is removed from or leaves Canada and comes into Canada contrary to subsection 55(1) or (2) is guilty of an offence and liable

(a) on conviction on indictment, to imprisonment for a term not exceeding two years; or

(b) on summary conviction, to a fine not exceeding one thousand dollars or to imprisonment for a term not exceeding six months or to both.

Case Law

R. v. Jones (February 19, 1997), Doc. CA C25992 (Ont. C.A.) — This was a crown appeal against sentence. The respondent, an American citizen, was convicted under section 55(1) and 95 of the *Immigration Act*, for entering Canada without a Minister's Permit after having been deported.

The trial judge erred in principle in imposing a sentence at the lower range of available sentences. The respondent had an extensive criminal record including 8 immigration offences over a period of 8 years for the same or similar offences as the one before the Court. The sentence was varied and increased to 15 months.

R. v. Maunder (1983), 46 Nfld. & P.E.I.R. 361, 135 A.P.R. 361 (Nfld. C.A.) — The appellant appealed a sentence of one year imposed under section 96. The appeal was dismissed because the appellant had disregarded other deportation orders and following his removal from Canada pursuant to such orders, had returned to Canada without the consent of the Minister and engaged in criminal activity.

R. v. Singh (1982), 63 C.C.C. (2d) 156 (Man. Co. Ct.) — The onus is upon the accused to demonstrate that he had lawful authority to enter Canada. The required ministerial consent was an excuse contemplated by section 730 of the Code, the proof of which rested upon the accused. An inference of the existence of ministerial consent did not arise from the admission of the accused to Canada as a visitor because the official who admitted the accused did not have the authority of the Minister to give the required consent. Although this offence is one of strict liability, the accused failed to prove that he used due diligence to avoid committing the offence.

95.1. (1) Deferral — No person who claims to be a Convention refugee and has notified an immigration officer of the claim shall, pending disposition of the claim, be charged with or convicted of

(a) an offence under paragraph 94(1)(*a*), (*b*), (*k*) or (*l*),

(b) an offence under paragraph 94(1)(*f*), (*g*) or (*h*) in relation to an examination of that person under this Act,

(c) an offence under section 95 or 98 in relation to the coming into Canada of that person or an examination of that person under this Act, or

(d) an offence under section 57, paragraph 340(*c*) or any of sections 354, 366, 368, 374 or 403 of the *Criminal Code* in relation to the coming into Canada of the person,

if that person came to Canada directly from the country that the person left, or outside of which the person remains, by reason of fear of persecution.

(2) Exemptions — No person who is determined by the Refugee Division to be a Convention refugee shall be charged with or convicted of

(a) an offence under paragraph 94(1)(*a*), (*b*), (*k*) or (*l*),

(b) an offence under paragraph 94(1)(*f*), (*g*) or (*h*) in relation to an examination of that person under this Act,

(c) an offence under section 95 or 98 in relation to the coming into Canada of that person or an examination of that person under this Act, or

(d) an offence under section 57, paragraph 340(*c*) or any of sections 354, 366, 368, 374 or 403 of the *Criminal Code* in relation to the coming into Canada of the person,

if that person came to Canada directly from the country that the person left, or outside of which the person remains, by reason of fear of persecution.

(3) Exceptions — Subsections (1) and (2) do not apply to any person who fails to notify an immigration officer of a claim to be a Convention refugee before the day that is

(a) three months after the expiry of the period during which the person is authorized to remain in Canada, in the case of a person who came into Canada as a visitor or under the authority of a permit; or

(b) three months after the person last came into Canada, in any other case.

R.S.C. 1985, c. 28 (4th Supp.), s. 25; 1992, c. 49, s. 86.

96. (1) Unauthorized employment of visitors and others — Every person who knowingly engages in any employment any person, other than a Canadian citizen or permanent resident, who is not authorized under this Act to engage in that employment is guilty of an offence and is liable

(a) on conviction on indictment, to a fine not exceeding five thousand dollars or to imprisonment for a term not exceeding two years or to both; or

(b) on summary conviction, to a fine not exceeding one thousand dollars or to imprisonment for a term not exceeding six months or to both.

(2) **Deemed knowledge** — For the purposes of subsection (1), a person knowingly engages in any employment a person who is not authorized to engage in that employment where, by the exercise of reasonable diligence, he would have known that the person was not so authorized.

(3) **Identifiable special social insurance number cards** — The Minister may by order direct the Canada Employment Insurance Commission continued by the *Department of Human Resources Development Act* to issue to persons, other than Canadian citizens or permanent residents, Social Insurance Number Cards whereby the holders of such cards are identified as persons who may be required by or under this Act to obtain authorization to engage or continue in employment in Canada.

1996, c. 11, s. 62.

97. (1) **Offences respecting immigration officers and adjudicators** — Every person is guilty of an offence who

(a) being an immigration officer or an adjudicator, wilfully makes or issues any false document or statement in respect of any matter relating to his duties under this Act or accepts, agrees to accept or induces or assists any other person to accept any bribe or other benefit in respect of any matter relating to his duties under this Act or otherwise wilfully fails to perform his duties under this Act;

(b) being an immigration officer or an adjudicator, contravenes any provision of this Act or the regulations or knowingly induces, aids or abets or attempts to induce, aid or abet any other person to do so;

(c) gives, offers or promises to give any bribe or consideration of any kind to, or makes any agreement or arrangement with, an immigration officer or an adjudicator to induce him in any way not to perform his duties under this Act;

(d) not being an immigration officer or an adjudicator, personates or holds himself out to be an immigration officer or an adjudicator, or takes or uses any name, title, uniform or description or otherwise acts in any manner that may reasonably lead any person to believe that he is an immigration officer or an adjudicator; or

(e) obstructs or impedes an immigration officer or an adjudicator in the performance of his duties under this Act.

(2) **Punishment** — Every person who is guilty of an offence under subsection (1) is liable

(a) on conviction on indictment, to a fine not exceeding ten thousand dollars or to imprisonment for a term not exceeding five years or to both; or

(b) on summary conviction, to a fine not exceeding one thousand dollars or to imprisonment for a term not exceeding six months or to both.

Case Law

Section 97(2)

R. v. MacInnis (1991), 95 Nfld. & P.E.I.R. 332, 301 A.P.R. 332 (Nfld. T.D.) — The accused, a former Immigration officer, pleaded guilty to 11 counts of breach of section 97(1)(a) of the

Immigration Act. The accused had accepted a benefit, namely sexual intercourse, from two young women in respect of matters relating to his duties under the *Immigration Act*, namely assessing and granting applications for temporary entry to Canada. The remaining nine counts in the indictment related to the issuance of Canadian visas by the accused as a result of his wilfully failing to perform his duties by properly assessing these persons.

In cases of this nature, a breach of trust is the major factor. The accused, as an Immigration officer, was in a position of trust being placed there by the Department of Immigration. Society generally must have confidence that those persons occupying positions of public trust are worthy of the trust that is placed in them. Such persons must act in the utmost good faith and when they do not, not only must they be deterred but a sentence must be imposed so that others similarly situated will also be deterred.

The two counts of accepting sexual intercourse as a benefit resulted in a six-month sentence on each count concurrent. The other nine counts resulted in a sentence of three months consecutive to the six-month sentence. Thus the total length of imprisonment was nine months.

97.01 [Repealed 1992, c. 49, s. 87.]

97.1 (1) Offence relating to transportation companies — general — Every person who contravenes subsection 88(1), 89(1), 90(2) or 92(5.1), or any provision of the regulations designated pursuant to paragraph 114(1)(*q*.12) for the purposes of this subsection, is guilty of an offence and liable on summary conviction

(a) for a first offence, to a fine not exceeding ten thousand dollars; or

(b) for a subsequent offence, to a fine not exceeding fifty thousand dollars or to imprisonment for a term not exceeding six months, or to both.

(2) Failure to check travel documents — Every person who contravenes section 89.1 is guilty of an offence and liable

(a) on conviction on indictment,

(i) for a first offence, to a fine not exceeding twenty-five thousand dollars, or

(ii) for a subsequent offence, to a fine not exceeding one hundred thousand dollars or to imprisonment for a term not exceeding three years, or to both; or

(b) on summary conviction,

(i) for a first offence, to a fine not exceeding ten thousand dollars, or

(ii) for a subsequent offence, to a fine not exceeding fifty thousand dollars or to imprisonment for a term not exceeding six months, or to both.

(3) Failure to comply with designated regulations — Every person who contravenes any provision of the regulations designated pursuant to paragraph 114(1)(*q*.12) for the purposes of this subsection is guilty of an offence and liable on summary conviction

(a) for a first offence, to a fine not exceeding five thousand dollars; or

(b) for a subsequent offence, to a fine not exceeding ten thousand dollars or to imprisonment for a term not exceeding six months, or to both.

(4) Due diligence defence — No person shall be found guilty of an offence under this section if it is established that the person exercised all due diligence to prevent its commission.

R.S.C. 1985, c. 28 (4th Supp.), s. 35; R.S.C. 1985, c. 29 (4th Supp.), s. 10; 1992, c. 49, s. 87.

98. General punishment — Every person who knowingly contravenes any provision of this Act or the regulations or any order or direction lawfully made or given thereunder for which no punishment is elsewhere provided in this Act is guilty of an offence and liable on summary conviction to a fine not exceeding five thousand dollars or to imprisonment for a term not exceeding one year, or to both.

1992, c. 49, s. 87.

Case Law

R. v. Gravelle (1988), 5 W.C.B. (2d) 365 — Section 12(1) of the *Immigration Act* provides that every person seeking to come into Canada should appear before an immigration officer at the port-of-entry. The accused, who was a status Indian, had crossed an international boundary by going under a closed gate at customs.

The Court held that the combination of section 12(1) and section 99 of the *Immigration Act*, created an offence of strict liability rather than absolute liability. On the particular facts of this case, the accused was acquitted.

99. (1) Officers, etc., of corporations — Where a corporation commits an offence under this Act, any officer, director or agent of the corporation who directed, authorized, assented to, acquiesced in or participated in the commission of the offence is a party to and guilty of the offence and is liable on conviction to the punishment provided for the offence whether or not the corporation is prosecuted or convicted.

(2) Offences by employees or agents — In any prosecution for an offence under this Act, it is sufficient proof of the offence to establish that it was committed by an employee or agent of the accused, whether or not the employee or agent is identified or prosecuted for the offence, unless the accused establishes that the offence was committed without his knowledge or consent and that the accused exercised all due diligence to prevent its commission.

100. Offences outside Canada — Any act or omission that would by reason of this Act or the regulations be punishable as an offence if committed in Canada is, if committed outside Canada, an offence under this Act or the regulations and may be tried and punished in Canada.

101. (1) Venue — Any proceedings in respect of an offence under this Act may be instituted, tried and determined at the place in Canada where the offence was committed or at the place in Canada where the person charged with the offence is or has an office or place of business at the time of the institution of such proceedings.

(2) Where commission outside Canada — Any proceedings in respect of an offence under this Act that is committed outside Canada may be instituted, tried and determined at any place in Canada.

102. (1) Enforcement of bonds — Where pursuant to any provision of this Act, other than section 92, a bond is required to be posted, the bond may be enforced in accordance with its terms in the Federal Court for the face value of the bond, which face value shall be deemed to be liquidated damages.

(2) Disposition of fines — All fines and forfeitures imposed or recovered under this Act belong to Her Majesty and form part of the Consolidated Revenue Fund.

Case Law

Section 102(1)

Canada (A.G.) v. Khimani (1985), 50 O.R. (2d) 476 (Ont. Div. Ct.) — The Attorney General of Canada claimed $2,000 plus interest owing under a performance bond given by the defendant under section 18(1) of the Act. The defendant entered into the performance bond on June 10, 1982 with the result that one, Yasmin Jetha, was permitted to enter Canada as a visitor. The bond guaranteed that the visitor would leave by August 9, 1982, but the visitor left September 22, 1982. The defendant admitted to being aware on August 9, 1982, that the failure of Yasmin Jetha to leave Canada was a breach of the bond. The trial judge refused to give judgment in favour of the plaintiff, Attorney General of Canada, and purported to exercise an equitable jurisdiction set out in section 78(3) of the Courts of *Justice Act*, S.O. 1984, c. 11. This decision was overturned, it being held that, whatever sympathy the Court may have had for the defendant (respondent), the finding that the terms and conditions of the bond had been breached meant that the Court must enforce payment of the bond.

Examination of Approved Business and Funds

102.001 (1) Minister may conduct examination — The Minister may conduct an examination of any business or fund approved by the Minister in order to ensure that it is being operated, managed and promoted in accordance with this Act and the regulations.

(2) Powers of examination — In conducting an examination, the Minister may

(a) inquire into the affairs of the business or fund, or of any person who manages, operates or promotes it, and examine

(i) any books, papers, documents, correspondence, electronic data, communications, negotiations, transactions, loans, borrowings or payments that relate to the business or fund,

(ii) any property or other assets that are at any time held or controlled by or on behalf of the business or fund,

(iii) any liabilities, debts, undertakings or obligations that exist, and any financial or other conditions that prevail, at any time, in relation to the business or fund, and

(iv) any relationship that exists at any time between the business or fund and any person by reason of investments, commissions promised, secured or paid, interests held or acquired, the lending or borrowing of money, stock or other property, the transfer, negotiation or holding of stock, interlocking directorates, common control, undue influence or control or any other relationship;

(b) require the business or fund, or any person who operates, manages, promotes or audits it, to provide information and explanations, to the extent that they are reasonably able to do so, in respect of the business or fund or of any entity in which it has an investment;

(c) subject to section 102.002, at any reasonable time, enter and inspect any building, receptacle or place in which the Minister believes on reasonable grounds there is any thing referred to in paragraph *(a)*; and

(d) seize any thing that the Minister believes on reasonable grounds will afford evidence in respect of the commission of an offence under this Act.

(3) **Inspection and copying of things seized** — Any thing seized under paragraph (2)*(d)* shall be made available for inspection or copying by the person from whom it was seized at a mutually convenient time and place if the person asks to inspect or copy it.

1992, c. 49, s. 88.

102.002 (1) **Warrant required to enter dwelling-place** — The Minister may not enter a dwelling-place for any of the purposes of section 102.001 except with the consent of the occupant or under the authority of a warrant.

(2) **Authority to issue warrant** — A justice of the peace who is satisfied by information on oath in the form set out as Form 1 in Part XXVIII of the *Criminal Code*, modified according to the circumstances,

(a) that the conditions for entry described in paragraph 102.001(2)*(c)* exist in relation to a dwelling-place,

(b) that entry to the dwelling-place is necessary for the conduct of an examination under section 102.001, and

(c) that entry to the dwelling-place has been refused or there are reasonable grounds to believe that entry will be refused,

may at any time issue a warrant under the justice's hand authorizing the Minister to enter the dwelling-place, subject to any conditions that may be specified in the warrant.

1992, c. 49, s. 88.

102.003 **Records** — Every person who operates, manages or promotes an approved business or fund shall ensure that all records that relate to transactions involving the business or fund are kept in Canada, including the original of all books, papers, documents and correspondence and copies of all electronic data and communications that relate to those transactions.

1992, c. 49, s. 88.

Seizure and Forfeiture

102.01 (1) **Seizure of vehicle** — An immigration officer or a peace officer may, where the officer believes on reasonable grounds that a vehicle was used in any manner in connection with the commission of an offence under section 94.1, 94.2 or 94.4, seize the vehicle as forfeit.

(2) **Seizure of evidence** — An immigration officer or a peace officer may, where the officer believes on reasonable grounds that an offence has been committed under

section 94.1, 94.2 or 94.4, seize any thing that the officer believes on reasonable grounds will afford evidence in respect of the contravention.

(3) Notice of seizure of vehicle — An immigration officer or a peace officer who seizes a vehicle under subsection (1) shall take such measures as are reasonable in the circumstances to give notice of the seizure to any person who the officer believes on reasonable grounds is entitled to make an application under section 102.2 in respect of the vehicle.

R.S.C. 1985, c. 29 (4th Supp.), s. 11; 1992, c. 49, s. 89.

102.02 (1) Information for search warrant — A justice of the peace who is satisfied by information on oath in the form set out as Form 1 in Part XXVIII of the *Criminal Code*, modified according to the circumstances, that there are reasonable grounds to believe that there may be found in a building, receptacle or place

(a) any vehicle that was used in any manner in connection with an offence under section 94.1, 94.2 or 94.4, or

(b) any thing that there are reasonable grounds to believe will afford evidence in respect of the commission of an offence under section 94.1, 94.2, 94.4 or 94.6,

may at any time issue a warrant under the justice's hand authorizing an immigration officer or peace officer to search the building, receptacle or place for any such vehicle or thing and to seize the vehicle or thing.

(2) Execution in another territorial jurisdiction — A justice of the peace may, where a building, receptacle or place referred to in subsection (1) is in a territorial division other than the one in which the justice of the peace has jurisdiction, issue a warrant in a form similar to the form referred to in subsection (1), modified according to the circumstances, and the warrant may be executed in the other territorial division after it has been endorsed, in the manner set out in Form 28 of Part XXVIII of the *Criminal Code*, by a justice of the peace having jurisdiction in that territorial division.

(3) Seizure of things not specified — An immigration officer or a peace officer who executes a warrant issued under subsection (1) may seize, in addition to any vehicle or thing mentioned in the warrant,

(a) any vehicle that the officer believes on reasonable grounds was used in any manner in connection with the commission of an offence under section 94.1, 94.2 or 94.4; or

(b) any thing that the officer believes on reasonable grounds will afford evidence in respect of the commission of an offence under section 94.1, 94.2, 94.4 or 94.6.

(4) Form of search warrant — A warrant issued under subsection (1) may be in the form set out as Form 5 in Part XXVIII of the *Criminal Code*, modified according to the circumstances.

(5) Where warrant not necessary — An immigration officer or a peace officer may exercise any of the powers referred to in subsection (1) without a warrant if the conditions for obtaining the warrant exist but by reason of exigent circumstances it would not be practical to obtain the warrant.

(6) Exigent circumstances — For the purposes of subsection (5), "exigent circumstances" means circumstances in which the delay necessary to obtain a warrant under

subsection (1) would result in danger to human life or safety or the loss or destruction of any thing liable to seizure.

R.S.C. 1985, c. 29 (4th Supp.), s. 11; 1992, c. 49, s. 90.

102.03 Powers of entry — For the purpose of exercising the authority under section 102.02, an immigration officer or a peace officer may, with such assistance as the officer deems necessary, break open any door, window, lock, fastener, floor, wall, ceiling, compartment, plumbing fixture, box, container or any other thing.

R.S.C. 1985, c. 29 (4th Supp.), s. 11.

102.04 Limitation for seizures — No seizure may be made under section 102.01 or 102.02 more than six years after the contravention or use in respect of which the seizure is made.

R.S.C. 1985, c. 29 (4th Supp.), s. 11.

102.05 (1) Custody of things seized — Any thing that is seized under section 102.01 or 102.02 shall forthwith be placed in the custody of a senior immigration officer.

(2) Report where evidence seized — Where an immigration officer or a peace officer seizes any thing as evidence under section 102.01 or 102.02, the officer shall forthwith report the circumstances of the seizure to the Deputy Minister.

(3) Return of evidence — Any thing that is seized under section 102.01 or 102.02 as evidence alone shall be returned forthwith on completion of all proceedings in which the thing seized may be required.

R.S.C. 1985, c. 29 (4th Supp.), s. 11.

102.06 (1) Copies of records, books, or documents — Where any record, book or document is examined or seized under this Act, the Minister, or the officer by whom the record, book or document is examined or seized, may make or cause to be made one or more copies thereof, and a copy of any such record, book or document purporting to be certified by the Minister or a person authorized by the Minister is admissible in evidence and has the same probative force as the original record, book or document would have if it had been proved in the ordinary way.

(2) Detention of records seized — No records, books or documents that have been seized as evidence under this Act shall be detained for a period of more than three months after the time of seizure, unless, before the expiration of that period,

(a) the person from whom they were seized agrees to their further detention for a specified period of time;

(b) a justice of the peace is satisfied on application that, having regard to the circumstances, their further detention for a specified period of time is warranted and the justice so orders; or

(c) judicial proceedings are instituted in which the things seized may be required.

R.S.C. 1985, c. 29 (4th Supp.), s. 11.

102.07 Return of vehicle seized — A senior immigration officer may, subject to this or any other Act of Parliament, return any vehicle that has been seized under sec-

tion 102.01 or 102.02 to the person from whom it was seized or to any person authorized by the person from whom it was seized on receipt of

(a) an amount of money of a value equal to

(i) the value of the vehicle at the time of the seizure, as determined by the Minister, or

(ii) such lesser amount as the Minister may direct; or

(b) where the Minister so authorizes, security satisfactory to the Minister.

R.S.C. 1985, c. 29 (4th Supp.), s. 11.

102.08 **Vehicles no longer forfeit** — Vehicles in respect of which money or security is received under section 102.07 shall cease to be forfeit from the time the money or security is received and the money or security shall be held as forfeit in lieu thereof.

R.S.C. 1985, c. 29 (4th Supp.), s. 11.

102.09 **Forfeitures accrue automatically from time of contravention** — Subject to the reviews and appeals established by this Act, any vehicle seized as forfeit under section 102.01 is forfeit from the time of the commission of an offence under section 94.1, 94.2 or 94.4 in respect of which the vehicle was seized and no act or proceeding subsequent to the commission of the offence is necessary to effect the forfeiture of the vehicle.

R.S.C. 1985, c. 29 (4th Supp.), s. 11; 1992, c. 49, s. 91.

102.1 **Review of forfeiture** — The forfeiture of any vehicle seized under section 102.01 or any money or security held as forfeit in lieu thereof is final and not subject to review or to being restrained, prohibited, removed, set aside or otherwise dealt with except to the extent and in the manner provided by section 102.12.

R.S.C. 1985, c. 29 (4th Supp.), s. 11.

102.11 **Report to Deputy Minister** — Where a vehicle has been seized under section 102.01 or 102.02, the officer who seized the vehicle shall forthwith report the circumstances of the seizure to the Deputy Minister.

R.S.C. 1985, c. 29 (4th Supp.), s. 11.

102.12 (1) **Request for Minister's decision** — Any person

(a) from whom a vehicle is seized under section 102.01 or 102.02,

(b) who owns a vehicle that is seized under section 102.01 or 102.02, or

(c) from whom money or security is received pursuant to section 102.07 in respect of a vehicle seized under section 102.01 or 102.02,

may, within thirty days after the day of the seizure, request a decision of the Minister under section 102.14 by giving notice in writing to the Minister.

(2) **Burden of proof** — The burden of proof that notice was given under subsection (1) lies on the person claiming to have given the notice.

R.S.C. 1985, c. 29 (4th Supp.), s. 11.

102.13 (1) **Notice of reasons for seizure** — Where a decision of the Minister under section 102.14 is requested pursuant to section 102.12, the Deputy Minister shall

forthwith serve on the person who requested the decision written notice of the reasons for the seizure in respect of which the decision is requested.

(2) Evidence — The person on whom a notice is served under subsection (1) may, within thirty days after the notice is served, furnish such evidence in the matter as the person desires to furnish.

(3) Idem — Evidence may be given pursuant to subsection (2) by affidavit made before any justice of the peace, commissioner for taking oaths or notary public.

R.S.C. 1985, c. 29 (4th Supp.), s. 11.

102.14 (1) Decision of the Minister — After the expiration of the thirty days referred to in subsection 102.13(2), the Minister shall, as soon as is reasonably possible, decide, in respect of the vehicle that was seized, whether the vehicle was used in connection with the commission of an offence under section 94.1, 94.2 or 94.4.

(2) Notice of decision — The Minister shall, forthwith on making a decision under subsection (1), serve on the person who requested the decision written notice thereof.

(3) Judicial review — The decision of the Minister under subsection (1) is not subject to review or to being restrained, prohibited, removed, set aside or otherwise dealt with except to the extent and in the manner provided by subsection 102.17(1).

R.S.C. 1985, c. 29 (4th Supp.), s. 11; 1992, c. 49, s. 92.

102.15 Where there is no offence committed — Subject to this or any other Act of Parliament, where the Minister decides, pursuant to section 102.14, that there has been no offence committed under section 94.1, 94.2 or 94.4 in respect of a vehicle or that the vehicle was not used in the manner described therein, the Minister shall forthwith authorize the removal from custody of the vehicle or the return of any money or security taken in respect thereof.

R.S.C. 1985, c. 29 (4th Supp.), s. 11; 1992, c. 49, s. 93.

102.16 (1) Where there is contravention — Where the Minister decides, pursuant to section 102.14, that the vehicle referred to in that section was used in the manner described therein, the Minister may, subject to such terms and conditions as the Minister may determine,

(a) return the vehicle on receipt of an amount of money of a value equal to

(i) the value of the vehicle at the time of the seizure, as determined by the Minister, or

(ii) such lesser amount as the Minister may direct; or

(b) remit any portion of any money or security taken, and where the Minister considers that insufficient money or security was taken or where no money or security was received, demand such amount of money as the Minister considers sufficient, not exceeding an amount determined under subsection (2).

(2) Amount demanded in respect of a vehicle under paragraph (1)(b) — The amount of money that the Minister may demand under paragraph (1)(*b*) in respect of a vehicle shall not exceed an amount equal to the value of the vehicle at the time of the seizure, as determined by the Minister.

R.S.C. 1985, c. 29 (4th Supp.), s. 11.

102.17 (1) Federal Court — A person who requests a decision of the Minister under section 102.14 may, within ninety days after being notified of the decision, appeal the decision by way of an action to the Federal Court — Trial Division in which that person is the plaintiff and the Minister is the defendant.

(2) Ordinary action — The *Federal Court Act* and the *Federal Court Rules* applicable to ordinary actions apply in respect of actions instituted under subsection (1), except as varied by special rules made in respect of such actions.

R.S.C. 1985, c. 29 (4th Supp.), s. 11.

102.18 Restoration of vehicle or thing pending — Where an appeal is taken by the Minister from any judgment that orders the Minister to give or return any thing that has been seized under section 102.01 or 102.02 to any person, the execution of the judgment shall not be suspended if the person to whom the vehicle or thing is ordered given or returned gives such security to the Minister as the court that rendered the judgment, or a judge thereof, considers sufficient to ensure delivery of the vehicle or thing or the full value thereof to the Minister if the judgment so appealed is reversed.

R.S.C. 1985, c. 29 (4th Supp.), s. 11.

102.19 Service of notices — The service of the Deputy Minister's notice under section 102.13 or the notice of the Minister's decision under section 102.14 is sufficient if it is sent by registered mail addressed to the person on whom it is to be served at the person's latest known address.

R.S.C. 1985, c. 29 (4th Supp.), s. 11.

102.2 (1) Claiming interest — Where a vehicle is seized as forfeit under this Act, any person, other than the person in whose possession the vehicle was when seized, who claims an interest therein as owner, mortgagee, lien-holder or holder of any like interest may, within sixty days after the seizure, apply by notice in writing to a judge for an order under subsection (5).

(2) Day of hearing — The judge to whom an application is made under subsection (1) shall fix a day for a hearing of the application not less than thirty days after the day of filing of the application.

(3) Notice — A person making an application under subsection (1) shall serve a notice of the application and of the hearing on the Minister not later than fifteen days after a day for the hearing of the application is fixed pursuant to subsection (2).

(4) Service of notice — The service of a notice under subsection (3) is sufficient if the notice is sent by registered mail addressed to the Minister.

(5) Order that interest not affected — Where, on the hearing of an application made under subsection (1), it is made to appear to the satisfaction of the judge

> **(a) that the applicant acquired the interest in respect of which the applicant is applying in good faith prior to the contravention in respect of which the seizure was made,**
>
> **(b) that the applicant is innocent of any complicity in the contravention that resulted in the seizure and of any collusion in relation to that contravention, and**

(c) that the applicant exercised all reasonable care with respect to the person permitted to obtain possession of the vehicle to satisfy the applicant that the vehicle was not likely to be used in connection with the commission of an unlawful act or, in the case of a mortgagee or lien-holder, that the applicant exercised such care with respect to the mortgagor or lien-giver,

the applicant is entitled to an order declaring that the applicant's interest is not affected by the seizure and declaring the nature and extent of the applicant's interest at the time of the contravention.

(6) **Appeal** — A person who makes an application under subsection (1) or the Minister may appeal to the court of appeal from an order made under subsection (5) and the appeal shall be asserted, heard and decided according to the ordinary procedure governing appeals to the court of appeal from orders or judgments of a judge.

(7) **Return of vehicle** — The Minister shall, on application made to the Minister by a person who has obtained a final order under this section,

(a) direct that the vehicle to which the interest of the person relates be returned to the person; or

(b) direct that an amount equal to the value of the interest of the person, as declared in the order, be paid to the person.

(8) **Limit on amount paid** — The total amount paid under paragraph (7)(*b*) in respect of a vehicle shall, where the vehicle was sold or otherwise disposed of under this Act, not exceed the proceeds of the sale or disposition, if any, less any costs incurred by Her Majesty in respect of the vehicle, and, where there are no proceeds of a disposition of a vehicle under this Act, no payment shall be made pursuant to paragraph (7)(*b*) in respect of the vehicle.

(9) **Definitions** — In this section,

"court of appeal" means, in the province in which an order under this section is made, the court of appeal for that province as defined in the definition "court of appeal" in section 2 of the *Criminal Code*;

"judge" means

(a) in the Province of Quebec, a judge of the Superior Court for the district in which the vehicle, in respect of which an application for an order under this section is made, was seized,

(a.1) in the Province of Ontario, a judge of the Superior Court of Justice,

(b) [Repealed 1992, c. 51, s. 53.]

(c) in the Provinces of Nova Scotia, British Columbia, Prince Edward Island and Newfoundland, a judge of the Supreme Court thereof,

(d) in the Provinces of New Brunswick, Manitoba, Alberta and Saskatchewan, a judge of the Court of Queen's Bench thereof, and

(e) in the Yukon Territory and the Northwest Territories, a judge of the Supreme Court of the territory, and in Nunavut, a judge of the Nunavut Court of Justice.

R.S.C. 1985, c. 29 (4th Supp.), s. 11; 1990, c. 16, s. 13; 1990, c. 17, ss. 24, 47; 1992, c. 51, s. 53; 1993, c. 28, s. 78 (Sched. III, item 72) [Repealed 1999, c. 3, (Sched., item 15).]; 1998, c. 30, s. 14(i); 1999, c. 3, s. 68.

102.21 Disposal — A vehicle the forfeiture of which is final under this Act shall be disposed of in such manner as the Minister may direct or be sold by public auction or public tender or by the Minister of Public Works and Government Services pursuant to the *Surplus Crown Assets Act*, subject to such regulations as may be prescribed.

R.S.C. 1985, c. 29 (4th Supp.), s. 11; 1996, c. 16, s. 60.

Arrest and Detention

103. (1) Warrant for arrest — The Deputy Minister or a senior immigration officer may issue a warrant for the arrest and detention of any person where

(a) an examination or inquiry is to be held, a decision is to be made pursuant to subsection 27(4) or a removal order or conditional removal order has been made with respect to the person; and

(b) in the opinion of the Deputy Minister or that officer, there are reasonable grounds to believe that the person poses a danger to the public or would not appear for the examination, inquiry or proceeding in relation to the decision or for removal from Canada.

(2) Arrest without warrant — Every peace officer in Canada, whether appointed under the laws of Canada or of any province or municipality thereof, and every immigration officer may, without the issue of a warrant, and order or a direction for arrest or detention, arrest and detain or arrest and make an order to detain

(a) for an inquiry, or for a determination by a senior immigration officer under subsection 27(4), any person who on reasonable grounds is suspected of being a person referred to in paragraph 27(2)(*b*), (*e*), (*f*), (*g*) or (*h*), or

(b) for removal from Canada, any person against whom a removal order has been made that is to be executed,

where, in the opinion of the officer, there are reasonable grounds to believe that the person poses a danger to the public or would not appear for the inquiry or the determination or for removal from Canada.

(3) Detention and release from detention by adjudicator — Where an inquiry is to be held or is to be continued with respect to a person or a removal order or conditional removal order has been made against a person, an adjudicator may make an order for

(a) the release from detention of the person, subject to such terms and conditions as the adjudicator deems appropriate in the circumstances, including the payment of a security deposit or the posting of a performance bond;

(b) the detention of the person where, in the opinion of the adjudicator, the person is likely to pose a danger to the public or is not likely to appear for the inquiry or its continuation or for removal from Canada; or

(c) the imposition of such terms and conditions as the adjudicator deems appropriate in the circumstances, including the payment of a security deposit or the posting of a performance bond.

(3.1) Detention and release from detention by senior immigration officer — Where an exclusion order, a departure order or a conditional departure order

has been made by a senior immigration officer against a person, a senior immigration officer may make an order

(a) for the release from detention of the person, subject to such terms and conditions as the senior immigration officer deems appropriate in the circumstances, including the payment of a security deposit or the posting of a performance bond;

(b) for the detention of the person where, in the opinion of the senior immigration officer, the person is likely to pose a danger to the public or is not likely to appear for removal from Canada; or

(c) imposing on the person such terms and conditions as the senior immigration officer deems appropriate in the circumstances, including the payment of a security deposit or the posting of a performance bond.

(4) **Notification of detention for examination or inquiry** — Where any person is detained for an examination or inquiry pursuant to this section, the person who detains or orders the detention of that person shall forthwith notify a senior immigration officer of the detention and the reasons therefor.

(5) **Release from detention by senior immigration officer** — A senior immigration officer may, within forty-eight hours from the time when a person is placed in detention pursuant to this Act, order that the person be released from detention subject to such terms and conditions as the officer deems appropriate in the circumstances, including the payment of a security deposit or the posting of a performance bond.

(6) **Review of decision for detention** — Where any person is detained pursuant to this Act for an examination, inquiry or removal and the examination, inquiry or removal does not take place within forty-eight hours after that person is first placed in detention, or where a decision has not been made pursuant to subsection 27(4) within that period, that person shall be brought before an adjudicator forthwith and the reasons for the continued detention shall be reviewed, and thereafter that person shall be brought before an adjudicator at least once during the seven days immediately following the expiration of the forty-eight hour period and thereafter at least once during each thirty day period following each previous review, at which times the reasons for continued detention shall be reviewed.

(7) **Release from detention by adjudicator** — Where an adjudicator who conducts a review pursuant to subsection (6) is satisfied that the person in detention is not likely to pose a danger to the public and is likely to appear for an examination, inquiry or removal, the adjudicator shall order that the person be released from detention subject to such terms and conditions as the adjudicator deems appropriate in the circumstances, including the payment of a security deposit or the posting of a performance bond.

(8) **Retaking into custody** — Where an adjudicator has ordered that a person be released from detention pursuant to paragraph (3)(*a*) or subsection (7), that adjudicator or any other adjudicator may at any time thereafter order that the person be retaken into custody and held in detention if the adjudicator becomes satisfied that the person is likely to pose a danger to the public or is not likely to appear for an examination, inquiry or removal.

(9) Review is in public — Subject to subsections (10) and (11) and to any rules of the place where a person is detained, a review under subsection (6) of the reasons for the person's continued detention shall be conducted in public.

(10) Confidentiality — An adjudicator who is satisfied that there is a serious possibility that the life, liberty or security of any person would be endangered by reason of a review of the reasons for a person's continued detention being held in public may, on application therefor, take such measures and make such order as the adjudicator considers necessary to ensure the confidentiality of the review.

(11) Idem — An adjudicator who considers it appropriate to do so may take such measures and make such order as the adjudicator considers necessary to ensure the confidentiality of any hearing held in respect of any application referred to in subsection (10).

R.S.C. 1985, c. 28 (4th Supp.), s. 27; 1992, c. 49, s. 94; 1995, c. 15, s. 19.

Case Law

Section 103(1)

Bhatti v. Canada (Minister of Citizenship & Immigration) (1996), 33 Imm. L.R. (2d) 277, 112 F.T.R. 274 (Fed. T.D.); affirmed (1996), 199 N.R. 154, 117 F.T.R. 30 (note) (Fed. C.A.) — The applicant sought to set aside a decision of an adjudicator, ordering the continued detention of the applicant.

The applicant, a citizen of India, arrived in Canada and claimed refugee status. Refugee status was granted in September 1991. In March 1993, pursuant to section 69.2(2), the Minister requested leave to apply to the refugee division to reconsider and vacate its determination. The Minister alleged that the applicant had failed to reveal that he was an active member of the Khalistan Commando force, a Sikh terrorist organization. In April 1994, a panel of the Refugee division vacated the determination that the applicant was a refugee. An application for judicial review was filed by the applicant and this application was dismissed in February 1995.

In February 1995, the applicant left Canada for the United States and returned to Canada in February 1996. Subsequent to his return, the applicant made a new refugee claim and on February 9, 1996 the applicant was arrested under a warrant issued pursuant to section 103(1) of the Act. On February 13, 1996 the applicant was released. On February 20, 1996 a senior immigration officer advised the applicant that his new refugee claim would not be referred to as senior immigration officer for a decision on eligibility, because the applicant was still subject to a deportation order which had not been lawfully executed. Further, on February 20, 1996 a new warrant was issued for the applicant's arrest and the applicant was in fact arrested on the evening of February 20, 1996. On February 23, 1996, an adjudicator decided that the applicant's detention should continue. A further detention review was conducted on March 4, with the same result.

The Minister retains at all times full discretion as to the timing and mode of execution of her removal orders. In this instance, the Minister chose to execute the order without prior notice and resorted to the arrest of the applicant for the purpose of insuring that the applicant would be placed on a departing flight out of Canada. The ongoing detention of the applicant was not envisioned at the time of his arrest on February 20, 1996. It only became necessary as a result of a stay granted by the Court so that it could hear this application. In the absence of some new element the Minister could not simply proceed to re-arrest a person who had been released by an adjudicator in the hope of obtaining an order for his or her continued detention from a different adjudicator. That is not what took place here. The arrest of the applicant was made for the sole purpose of effecting removal from Canada. There is no basis for the suggestion that the Minister proceeded as she did to overcome the earlier decision of the adjudicator releasing the applicant.

The arrest of the applicant on February 20, 1996 was lawful and the adjudicators properly assumed jurisdiction to conduct reviews of his continued detention since that time. Accordingly, the application was dismissed.

Bhatti v. Canada (Minister of Citizenship & Immigration) (1996), 199 N.R. 154, 117 F.T.R. 30 (note) (Fed. C.A.) — An appellant who, after being arrested under a warrant issued under subsection 103(1), had been released by an adjudicator pursuant to subsection 103(7), could legally be re-arrested for removal under subsection 103(1) or 103(2) without any need for his being retaken into custody, under subsection 103(8).

Sahin v. Canada (Minister of Citizenship & Immigration) (1994), 85 F.T.R. 99, 24 C.R.R. (2d) 276, [1995] 1 F.C. 214 — This was an application to review a decision of an adjudicator ordering the applicant to remain in detention. The applicant made a refugee claim immediately upon his arrival in Canada and a conditional departure order was made against him. The applicant had remained in detention since his arrival on July 28, 1993, and his detention was reviewed at least every 30 days. The applicant was determined to be a Convention refugee on February 16, 1994, and the Minister filed an application for leave to review that decision. Leave was granted.

Under section 103(1) a person subject to a conditional removal order may be detained where the Deputy Minister or a senior immigration officer are of the opinion that there are reasonable grounds to believe that the person poses a danger to the public or would not appear for examination.

Section 103 provides for continuing reviews at least once each 30 day period. Nothing in this section provides for a maximum period of time for detention, or for any consideration of the total length of time an individual may have been in detention.

Section 7 Charter considerations are relevant to the exercise of discretion by an Adjudicator under section 103. Indefinite detention may constitute a deprivation of liberty that is not in accordance with the principles of fundamental justice. A lengthy detention, for practical purposes, approaches what might be reasonably termed indefinite. When applying Charter principles an adjudicator should consider:

1. The reasons for the detention, *i.e.*, is the applicant considered a danger to the public or is there a concern that he or she would not appear for removal. A stronger case for continuing a long detention would likely present itself when the individual was considered a danger to the public.

2. The length of time in detention and the length of time detention will likely continue. If an individual has been held in detention for some period, and a further lengthy detention is anticipated, these facts would tend to favour release.

3. Has the applicant or the respondent caused any delay or has either not been as diligent as reasonably possible. Unexplained delay, and even unexplained lack of diligence, count against the offending party.

4. The availability, effectiveness and appropriateness of alternatives to detention such as outright release, bail bond, periodic reporting, confinement to a particular location or geographic area, the requirement to report changes of address or telephone numbers.

The decision of the adjudicator was set aside because he did not take into account the considerations required by section 7 of the Charter.

Douglas, Re (1981), 5 W.C.B. 354 (Ont. H.C.) — A detention order issued under section 104(1) signed by an immigration officer in a space designated "authorized officer and title" is valid on its face.

Section 103(2)

Bhatti v. Canada (Minister of Citizenship & Immigration) (1996), 199 N.R. 154, 117 F.T.R. 30 (note) (Fed. C.A.) — An appellant who, after being arrested under a warrant issued under subsection 103(1), had been released by an adjudicator pursuant to subsection 103(7), could legally be re-arrested for removal under subsection 103(1) or 103(2) without any need for his being retaken into custody, under subsection 103(8).

Rios v. Canada (Minister of Employment & Immigration), [1990] 3 F.C. 632, 11 Imm. L.R. (2d) 122, 115 N.R. 394 (Fed. C.A.) — This case raises the question of what is meant by the word "elude" in section 27(2) of the *Immigration Act.* The majority concluded that the word "elude" has the connotation either of artifice or surreptitiousness or of the intention to repudiate the obligation or escape the effect of the law in a general way. In the context of this case it would mean, not being present at a particular inquiry, and having the intention of not complying with the obligation of the law. Failure to attend at an examination raises a *prima facie* case under section 27(2)(f) such that an immigration officer could believe that the person in question eluded examination or inquiry and appropriate enforcement action taken. The person concerned would be able, however, to have his or her case subsequently adjudicated upon in relation to his or her real intentions and this did not happen in this case. This will not render administration of the Act difficult. Accordingly the majority ruled that the section 28 application to set aside the deportation order issued against the applicant should succeed. The minority agreed that a person does not elude an inquiry within the meaning of section 27(2)(f) if that person has reasonable grounds for believing that he has good cause for not appearing at the inquiry.

Khan v. Canada (Minister of Employment & Immigration) (1989), 9 Imm. L.R. (2d) 107, 30 F.T.R. 161, [1990] 1 F.C. 30 (Fed. T.D.) — The applicant entered Canada as a foreign domestic and obtained employment with an employer other than the one specified in the employment authorization. In fact, she misrepresented her true employer to the immigration authorities. The question was whether the immigration officers were justified in arresting the appellant instead of writing and forwarding a report of the matter to the Deputy Minister. The reason for arresting the applicant without warrant disappeared upon the making of a phone call to her sister. The applicant was 8 months pregnant and, therefore, not a danger to the public. One of the officers deposed in his affidavit that, having ascertained her true place of employment and residence, he decided that it would not be necessary to detain her until the inquiry. If the applicant was held in detention pursuant to section 103, such detention endured for only about 2 hours. In effect, there is a "dis-arrest" provision which resides in section 103(5) of the Act. If this takes place, the applicant is no longer held in detention pursuant to section 28. This has the effect of requiring the officers to comply with the provisions of section 27(2) and forward a written report to the Deputy Ministry setting out the details of the case. In the result, the inquiry which had been instituted pursuant to section 28 was quashed.

R. v. Kwok (1986), 18 O.A.C. 38 (Ont. C.A.) — Although decided on the admittedly unique situation existing at a port-of-entry, this decision may have some application by analogy in the type of situation envisioned by this section. The appellant arrived at Pearson International Airport aboard a flight originating in London. He was examined by a senior immigration officer and detained pending an immigration inquiry. The immigration officer who interviewed the appellant had doubts as to the *bona fides* of the appellant as a genuine visitor and wrote a report pursuant to section 20 of the Act for the benefit of the acting senior immigration officer. A person is not detained within the meaning of section 10 of the *Charter of Rights and Freedoms* until the restriction on his freedom has gone beyond that required for the processing of his application for entry. The fact that some questioning preceded the advice required by section 10 did not by itself offend the section. The obligation to inform a person of his rights under section 10(b) of the Charter is an obligation to inform, without delay, but that does not mean immediately. Further, the admission into evidence of a conversation preceding the section 10 warning did not bring the administration of justice into disrepute.

Section 103(3)

Omoruyi v. Canada (Secretary of State) (May 17, 1995), Doc. IMM-4311-94 (Fed. T.D.) — The applicant was detained in custody by an adjudicator. Pursuant to the *Immigration Act*, reviews of that detention were conducted from time to time. The applicant sought to review one of the orders requiring his continued detention and accordingly applied for leave to commence a judicial review application in respect of that decision. While a judicial review application was pending pursuant to the *Act* adjudicators continued to review the applicant's detention and one of them ordered the applicant's release with the result that at the time the application for judicial review was heard the applicant was no longer in custody.

The applicant continued his judicial review application notwithstanding the fact of his release and the Court declined to hear the application ruling that the issue was moot. The Court noted that it had a discretion to address a moot issue but declined to do so in this case.

Canada (Minister of Citizenship & Immigration) v. Salinas-Mendoza, [1995] 1 F.C. 251 (T.D.) — An order of an adjudicator releasing the respondent from custody was quashed because the adjudicator abdicated her role in some essential aspects in the face of a decision by a judge of the Provincial Court of British Columbia to release the respondent on bail, pending the hearing of a sexual assault charge.

The standard for release under section 103 of the *Immigration Act* is essentially the same as that under the bail provisions of the *Criminal Code*. Where terms are incorporated into the *Criminal Code* bail order, and where those terms are considered appropriate for the protection of the public interest, it is essential that the same terms be incorporated into the adjudicator's decision releasing the applicant so that if the *Criminal Code* bail ceases to be effective, appropriate safeguards will still be in place until the applicant's right to remain in Canada is determined.

Ashoornia v. Canada (Minister of Employment & Immigration) (1994), 28 Imm. L.R. (2d) 94 (Fed. T.D.) — This was an application for judicial review of a credible basis hearing. The applicant was a citizen of Iran. She was arrested and detained on her arrival in Canada. When arrested she was in possession of false documents. Prior to the credible basis hearing, the applicant attended at least two detention reviews. At the detention reviews the adjudicator continued the applicant's detention. He concluded that she should be detained because she had lied to enter Canada and had no friends or relatives in Canada and therefore no reason to remain here. The adjudicator's decision at the detention review was based in a large measure on the assessment of the applicant's credibility. The adjudicator, who had twice attended the detention reviews, also acted as the adjudicator at the credible basis hearing.

In the detention reviews the adjudicator had canvassed exactly the same evidence as he subsequently heard at the credible basis inquiry and had concluded that the applicant was not credible. In such a situation, a reasonable apprehension of bias was created by the adjudicator's presence at the credible basis hearing and the application for judicial review was allowed.

Editor's Note: Although the refugee determination provisions have been changed, the principle in this case may be of broader import.

Pursley v. Canada (Minister of Employment & Immigration) (1989), 8 Imm. L.R. (2d) 211, 29 F.T.R. 204 (Fed. C.A.) — The applicant entered Canada on April 22, 1989 and was arrested pursuant to section 103 of the *Immigration Act*. An adjudicator refused to release the applicant pending his inquiry. If the detaining authority or the adjudicator refused the legal duty to hold a bail hearing or give proper consideration to an application for bail, the trial division would entertain an application to compel the performance of those duties.

In this particular case, the adjudicator having refused to grant bail after a hearing, the trial division had no further jurisdiction and the application to quash the adjudicator's decision was dismissed.

Webb v. Lower Mainland Regional Correctional Centre (1988), 4 W.C.B. (2d) 175 (B.C. C.A.) — Section 104 of the *Immigration Act* does not contravene the provision in section 9 of the *Charter of Rights* against arbitrary detention. The legislation requires reasons for the opinion that the accused should be detained and provides for regular reviews of that decision.

Mavour v. Canada (Minister of Employment & Immigration), [1984] 2 F.C. 122 (Fed. C.A.) — The applicant was arrested on March 15, 1983. An inquiry was caused to be held on March 22, 1983. On that day the inquiry was adjourned to March 30, 1983. The applicant was detained throughout this period, not only in respect of the immigration proceedings but also in respect of outstanding criminal charges. On March 30, 1983, the inquiry was not resumed because there was no case presenting officer available. The inquiry was resumed on April 6, 1983. The adjudicator did not lose jurisdiction by her failure to resume the inquiry on March 30, 1983, the date to which it had been adjourned. Further, the adjudicator's "offer" to release the applicant from detention that was to expire on April 12, 1983, at 4:00 p.m. was, in effect, a decision to release the applicant subject to the condition, among others, that the necessary security or cash deposit be made before a certain time. This was a condition which was within the authority of the adjudicator to impose under section 104(3) of the Act.

Section 103(5)

Khan v. Canada (Minister of Employment & Immigration) (1989), 9 Imm. L.R. (2d) 107, 30 F.T.R. 161, [1990] 1 F.C. 30 (Fed. T.D.) — For digest, see section 103, subheading *Subsection (2), supra.*

Section 103(6)

Chaudhry v. Canada (Minister of Citizenship & Immigration), [1999] 3 F.C. 3 (Fed. T.D.); affirmed (September 7, 1999), Doc. A-175-99 (Fed. C.A.) — This is an application to review a decision of an adjudicator who held that he had no jurisdiction to unilaterally order a detention review under section 103(6), in the absence of a request by a senior immigration officer. Since no such request had been made with respect to the applicant, the adjudicator stated that he was unable to review the reasons for the continuation of the applicant's detention. The applicant sought an order requiring the adjudicator to conduct such a review.

The applicant had been convicted of two counts of trafficking narcotics and had been sentenced to 14 years imprisonment. Subsequent to the convictions an inquiry was held and the applicant was ordered deported. On April 19, 1995, a warrant for his arrest and detention was issued under subsection 103(1). On the day that the warrant was issued an order was also made under subsection 105(1), directing the person in charge of the institution where the applicant was incarcerated to detain him until the expiration of his sentence or until the expiration of his sentence as reduced by operation law. The purpose of this later order was to ensure that the person who had been ordered deported and was the subject of a warrant of arrest did not go free after serving a sentence but rather was delivered up to an immigration officer.

The Court found that an order made under subsection 105(1) detained the applicant within the meaning of section 103(6). Subsection 103(6) provides important procedural protections when the examination, inquiry, or removal of a person cannot take place promptly. Thus if the proceeding or the removal does not incur within 48 hours, the person is entitled to a detention review "forthwith" and if it is delayed further, within the next 7 days and every 30 days thereafter. Such provisions are an appropriate check on the exercise of a most unusual power, namely the power of administrative officials to detain, without hearing, a person who has not been charged with, or convicted of a criminal offence, or who would otherwise be at liberty.

The Court granted a declaratory order that a person against whom a subsection 105(1) order had been issued was detained pursuant to the Immigration Act, within the meaning of subsection 103(6), and that the review provisions of that section applied to orders made under subsection 105(1).

McIntosh v. Canada (Minister of Citizenship & Immigration) (1995), 30 Imm. L.R. (2d) 314 (Fed. T.D.) — The applicant challenged the decision of an adjudicator continuing his detention. The adjudicator, in conducting his review, incorporated the previous decision of another adjudicator. This was not an error. If, as the adjudicator perceived the matter before him, there were no new circumstances, and he simply had to decide the question of continuing detention based upon information that previously was considered, it was in order for the adjudicator to incorporate the previous decision into his own. If, however, that decision did not adhere to the requirements of procedural fairness, then the decision under review is similarly tainted.

In this case, at the time of the previous decision the applicant's father attended at the detention centre where his son was being held, for the purpose of giving evidence. The father was denied access to the detention centre and on this basis the detention order was set aside. It was not for the Court to speculate as to the effect of the father's evidence on the decision to detain. The adjudicator had an obligation to admit the evidence when it was available. In failing to do so a basic rule of procedural fairness was breached.

Reza v. Canada, [1994] 2 S.C.R. 394, 24 Imm. L.R. (2d) 117, 22 Admin. L.R. (2d) 79, 116 D.L.R. (4th) 61 (S.C.C.) — This was an appeal from a decision of the Ontario Court of Appeal setting aside an order made by a motions judge staying the respondent's application for a declaration that certain provisions of the *Immigration Act* infringed the *Charter of Rights*. The issue on appeal was whether there was any basis for the Court of Appeal's interference with the motion judge.

The respondent came to Canada from Iran and claimed refugee status. It was found that there was no credible basis for referring his claim to the Immigration and Refugee Board and a deportation order was issued. Leave to commence a judicial review application was refused. The respondent's case was reviewed on humanitarian and compassionate grounds a number of times. After the last refusal the respondent unsuccessfully sought leave to commence an application for judicial review. The respondent subsequently brought an application in Ontario for a declaration that certain sections of the *Immigration Act* infringed his Charter rights. The respondent also brought a motion at the same time for an interlocutory injunction restraining the Minister from removing him. The appellant Minister took the position before the Ontario Court (General Division) that the Court should decline to exercise its jurisdiction on the ground that it was more appropriate for a Constitutional challenge to sections of the *Immigration Act* to be heard in the Federal Court.

In March 1992 a motions judge granted the Minister's motion and stayed the respondent's application for declaratory and injunctive relief. The deportation order, however, was stayed by Galligan J.A. pending disposition of the respondent Reza's appeal to the Ontario Court of Appeal. In October 1992 the Court of Appeal allowed the respondent Reza's appeal and ordered that the decision of the motions judge be set aside.

The Supreme Court of Canada allowed the Minister's appeal and was generally in agreement with the dissenting decision in the Court of Appeal of Ontario. The Supreme Court of Canada agreed that there was no basis for interfering with the motions court judge's decision to stay the proceedings. The Ontario Court and the Federal Court had concurrent jurisdiction to hear the respondent's application. Pursuant to section 106 of the *Courts of Justice Act*, R.S.O. 1990, c. C.43, any judge of the General Division has a discretion to stay proceedings. The motions court judge properly exercised his discretion on the basis that Parliament had created a comprehensive scheme of review of immigration matters and the Federal Court was an effective and appropriate forum. The Court was of the view that this was the correct approach. The motions court judge took into account all relevant considerations in exercising his discretion to grant a stay and there was no basis for an appellate court to interfere with his decision. The appeal was allowed and the decision of the motions judge restored.

Bembenek v. Canada (Minister of Employment & Immigration) (1991), 15 Imm. L.R. (2d) 229, 69 C.C.C. (3d) 34 (Ont. Gen. Div.) — *Habeas corpus* is a two-step procedure. The first step, the granting of the writ of *habeas corpus ad subjiciendum*, brings the prisoner before the court. The task of the court on the return of that writ is to determine whether or not the prisoner is detained according to regular process of law. Usually the two *habeas corpus* steps are heard together.

In immigration matters, the Ontario court almost always declines to grant *habeas corpus* because the Federal Court is ordinarily a better forum in which to challenge immigration proceedings. It is only in unusual cases that the court enters upon the consideration of the availability of *habeas corpus* in immigration matters.

In order to prove that the immigration proceedings are a disguised form of extradition, the applicant has to establish that the Canadian immigration officials when they sought deportation acted in bad faith without a legitimate Canadian immigration objective.

Before the judgment of the Supreme Court of Canada in *R. v. Gamble* (1988), 45 C.C.C. (3d) 204, it was firmly established that the applicant had to be in some form of detention before the writ was available and that a person who was on bail at the time of the application cannot avail himself of the writ. The *Gamble* case, however, implied that *habeas corpus* is now available whenever any liberty interest protected by section 7 of the Charter is infringed.

The applicant in this case was in custody on the extradition proceedings. Although those proceedings were separate from the immigration proceedings they both involved the fact that the applicant was an escaped convict subject to a life sentence for murder. Further, the surety in the immigration matter rendered the applicant back into custody and in that sense the applicant was deprived of her liberty on the immigration matter. Even if the applicant were still free on the immigration release order she would still be subject to potential retaking under section 103(8), and a Minister's appeal or application to review the release order represented a very strong potential threat to the liberty of the applicant in the immigration proceedings. The potential for retaking and the appeal or review of the release order standing alone might not have represented a sufficient deprivation of liberty to justify an application for *habeas corpus*, but they did not stand alone in this case. The applicant was physically in custody on a matter flowing in part from the same factual substratum as the proceeding challenged in this application. Because her surety had withdrawn, the immigration proceedings represented a significant additional hurdle to the applicant's liberty. All of these facts taken together represented a deprivation of the applicant's liberty interest secured by section 7.

The Court of Appeal has stated unequivocally in *Peiroo v. Canada (Minister of Employment & Immigration)* (1989), 69 O.R. (2d) 253 at 261–262 that this Court in immigration proceedings should ordinarily exercise its discretion to refuse to hear *habeas corpus* applications because there are more appropriate and effective alternative remedies under the *Immigration Act*.

In this case, however, there was a multiplicity of pending and potential proceedings. A significant delay would have resulted had the Court declined to exercise its jurisdiction. Whatever the merits of the applicant's argument, a final determination on the merits would have been delayed greatly had the Court declined its jurisdiction. Given the urgent need for final determination on the merits, the Court concluded that it would have brought the administration of justice into disrepute and produced even more delay and more multiplicity of proceedings had the Court declined its jurisdiction.

The real mischief of disguised extradition is the case where extradition fails because the evidence of foreign crime is too weak for extradition and deportation is sought to achieve indirectly what could not be achieved directly through extradition. Disguised extradition is typically established when the evidence is not strong enough for extradition and the authorities of both countries collude and use deportation to achieve the removal of the person concerned to the requesting state. The applicant had not established in this case that the case for extradition was so weak that the authorities decided to launch immigration proceedings for the improper purpose of a groundless extradition.

In asserting that the immigration proceedings were nevertheless a disguised form of extradition the applicant was forced to bear a heavy burden of showing bad faith. The applicant was required to show the immigration proceedings were a sham. It is a legitimate Canadian immigration objective to deport convicted criminals in order to prevent Canada from becoming a haven for such persons. Thus, deportation is a legitimate process open to the government to achieve this policy objective. If there is a good faith basis to seek deportation then it takes very strong evidence to show that there is some disguised reason for immigration officials doing what it is ordinarily their duty to do.

In testing the question of bad faith it is necessary to decide first whether there is an apparently legitimate reason for immigration officials seeking deportation, and secondly what would be gained from deportation rather than extradition.

The mere presence in Canada of an escaped American convict under life sentence for murder provides an obviously legitimate reason for deportation. There was no evidence that anyone gained speed by seeking deportation instead of extradition. An examination of the evidence did not establish that the Canadian immigration proceedings were a sham and a disguised form of extradition with no legitimate Canadian immigration purpose, nor did it establish that the respondent Minister's officials were acting in bad faith. Accordingly, the application for *habeas corpus* was dismissed.

Vega v. Canada (Minister of Employment & Immigration) (1990), 11 Imm. L.R. (2d) 160 (Ont. H.C.) — The applicant was granted visitor's status upon his admission to Canada. He received no extensions of his status and remained in Canada after the expiry of that status. Ultimately, the applicant was arrested by police when he went to report the loss of his passport and other vital documents. The applicant was denied release pending his inquiry and applied for *habeas corpus*. The Court accepted that it had jurisdiction to issue writ of *habeas corpus* and to order the release of the applicant in the appropriate circumstances. The Court denied the relief on the basis that a person who could show reasonable and probable grounds for complaining about his detention under the *Habeas Corpus Act* could also proceed under section 82.1 of the *Immigration Act*.

Noor v. Canada (Minister of Employment & Immigration) (1990), 70 D.L.R. (4th) 248 (Que. C.A.) — This case deals with the Quebec Court of Appeal's description of the availability of the remedy of *habeas corpus* in the province of Quebec with respect to immigration proceedings. The Supreme Court has jurisdiction to deal with an application for *habeas corpus* and *certiorari* in aid, even if the Federal Court had jurisdiction under section 82.1 of the *Immigration Act* to review the decision of the adjudicator and the member of the Refugee Division with respect to the issue of a credible basis for claiming refugee status. A provincial Supreme Court has the authority to issue *certiorari* in aid of *habeas corpus* to review the validity of a detention authorized by a federal board. *Certiorari* in aid of *habeas corpus* is prudent to ensure the widest possible scope for review. *Habeas corpus* is available to challenge an unlawful deprivation of liberty. Further, the continuation of an initially valid deprivation of liberty can be challenged by way of *habeas corpus*, if it becomes unlawful. *Habeas corpus* is not now and never has been a static, narrow, formalistic remedy. Its scope has grown to achieve the protection of individuals against erosion of their right to be free from wrongful restraints upon their liberty. Expelling a person from Canada illegally and against his will is a deprivation of liberty. In the context of this case, the Supreme Court had jurisdiction to hear the application, to examine not only the detention order, but also the validity of the order first made by the adjudicator with respect to the credible basis for the refugee claim, as this decision was in fact the reason for the expulsion order although the review goes only to the exercise of jurisdiction and not the correctness of the decision.

The Court reviewed the record and concluded that the first level panel had satisfied the obligation to permit the refugee claimant to present evidence and cross-examine witnesses and make representations and the application for *habeas corpus* was dismissed.

Peiroo v. Canada (Minister of Employment & Immigration) (1989), 69 O.R. (2d) 253, 38 Admin. L.R. 247, 8 Imm. L.R. (2d) 89, 60 D.L.R. (4th) 574, 34 O.A.C. 43 (Ont. C.A.) — The applicant for *habeas corpus* failed to show that the available review and appeal process established by Parliament under the *Immigration Act* was inappropriate or less advantageous than the *habeas corpus* jurisdiction of the Supreme Court. Accordingly, the Court dismissed the *habeas corpus* application noting that the relief sought was clearly within the purview of the statutory review and appeal process set out by the *Immigration Act*.

Both jurisprudence and logic suggest that review of immigration matters should be left with the Federal Court of Canada which has review and appeal jurisdiction with respect to many aspects of immigration law and which has geographical jurisdiction throughout Canada.

Webb v. Lower Mainland Regional Correctional Centre (1988), 4 W.C.B. (2d) 175 (B.C. C.A.) — Section 104 of the *Immigration Act* does not contravene the provision in section 9 of the *Charter of Rights* against arbitrary detention. The legislation requires reasons for the opinion that the accused should be detained and provides for regular reviews of that decision.

R. v. Cushnie (1988), 4 W.C.B. (2d) 377 (Que. S.C.) — The accused applied to the Quebec Superior Court for *habeas corpus* with *certiorari* in aid. The accused had received a sentence of imprisonment for a conviction in Canada and had now served that sentence. He was being detained pursuant to a deportation order made shortly after his conviction. The accused had not yet been deported because the immigration authorities had been unsuccessful in obtaining a birth certificate showing that he had been born in the United States, to which country he was to be deported. The American authorities had been aware of the accused's presence in Canada for a significant period of time, but had not made any attempt to extradite him on outstanding American charges. The Court was entitled to review the orders of an adjudicator under the *Immigration Act* pursuant to the *certiorari* proceedings to determine if there had been an error in continually renewing the detention order.

The accused's prior convictions in the United States were insufficient to justify a conclusion that the accused was a danger to the public. Further, there was no evidence upon which it could be concluded that the accused would seek to avoid removal from Canada. The continued incarceration of the accused constituted cruel and unusual treatment in violation of section 12 of the *Charter of Rights*. Accordingly, the accused was ordered released. Appeal to the Quebec Court of Appeal was dismissed (1989), 54 D.L.R. (4th) 420.

Southam Inc. v. Canada (Minister of Employment & Immigration), [1987] 3 F.C. 329, 3 Imm. L.R. (2d) 226, 13 F.T.R. 138, 33 C.R.R. 376 (Fed. T.D.) — The adjudicators were prohibited from conducting detention review hearings in the absence of the applicants unless the applicants' right-of-access was outweighed or limited in any given case by counter-balancing rights or interests. Further, if any objections to the public's access were raised, the applicants were to be given an opportunity to present submissions on the point.

Chan v. R. (1985), 54 Nfld. & P.E.I.R. 348 (P.E.I. S.C.) — The applicant was apprehended as being a person referred to in section 27(2) and was detained by an order issued pursuant to section 104(2) pending inquiry. The inquiry was held, the applicant claimed refugee status, the refugee claim was refused and the applicant appealed to the Immigration Appeal Board. He then brought this application in *habeas corpus* to inquire into the legality of his detention. Weekly reviews of the applicant's detention were held pursuant to section 104(6). Due to section 18 of the *Federal Court Act*, the Supreme Court had no jurisdiction in *certiorari* as it applied to any person reportedly exercising jurisdiction under the *Immigration Act*. The only jurisdiction in the Supreme Court was to review the legality of the applicant's detention through the medium of *habeas corpus*. Without *certiorari* in aid of *habeas corpus*, the Court was only able to examine the warrant of committal and to find if the warrant was regular on its face. The warrant of committal issued under section 104 of the *Immigration Act* was regular on its face and, therefore, the application in *habeas corpus* to inquire into the legality of the applicant's detention was refused.

Mavour v. Canada (Minister of Employment & Immigration), [1984] 2 F.C. 122 (Fed. C.A.) — For digest, see section 103, subheading *Subsection (3), supra*.

Bauer v. R. (February 28, 1984), Doc. T-125-84 (Fed. T.D.) — There is no enforceable duty under the *Immigration Act*, the Common Law or the *Canadian Charter of Rights and Freedoms* to provide a reporter, when requested at a detention review hearing, unless the refusal is so tainted with unfairness as to require intervention by judicial review.

Bauer v. R., supra — There is no mandatory duty on an adjudicator to permit the attendance of persons other than the applicant at detention review proceedings. The Court did not say that a detainee had no right at all to call evidence or witnesses.

Bauer v. R., supra — There is no procedure in the *Immigration Act* or regulations requiring the production of summaries prepared by immigration officials at detention review proceedings.

Brannson v. Canada (Minister of Employment & Immigration) (1980), 5 W.C.B. 408 (Ont. H.C.) — Failure to comply with section 104(6) constitutes a breach of the statutory duty; it did not, however, result in any loss of jurisdiction.

R. v. Rojas (1978), 20 O.R. (2d) 590 (Ont. C.A.) — Imprisonment was held to be justified since the objective of deportation was not sufficiently unlikely or illusory to require the Provincial Court to release the applicant. The applicant had entered the country illegally and the authorities had made *bona fide* efforts to effect his deportation; therefore, his detention had not ceased to be lawful.

Pereira v. Canada (Minister of Manpower & Immigration) (1976), 14 O.R. (2d) 355 (Ont. C.A.) — The Ontario Court of Appeal held that the jurisdiction of Provincial Superior Courts to review decisions of federal tribunals by way of *certiorari* and other extraordinary remedies was removed to the Federal Court by sections 18 and 28 of the *Federal Court Act*, R.S.C. 1970 (2nd Supp.), c. 10. Those sections did not involve applications for *habeas corpus* with respect to federal tribunals and such applications, therefore, remained within the jurisdiction of the Provincial Superior Courts.

Paterson, Ex parte (1971), 3 C.C.C. (2d) 181, 18 D.L.R. (3d) 84 (B.C. S.C.) — On an application for a writ of *habeas corpus* without *certiorari* in aid to release an applicant who was in custody, the Court cannot go behind the deportation order.

Rebrin v. Bird, [1961] S.C.R. 376, 35 C.R. 412, 130 C.C.C. 55, 27 D.L.R. (2d) 622 (S.C.C.) — Under the *Immigration Act*, R.S.C. 1952, it was held that the deportation order was not defective for failure to specify the place to which the applicant was to be deported, provided the order was in prescribed form and there was statutory authority for the form and supporting regulations.

Section 103(7)

Salilar v. Canada (Minister of Citizenship & Immigration), [1995] 3 F.C. 150, 97 F.T.R. 110, 31 Imm. L.R. (2d) 299 — The issue here concerned the validity of the decision of an adjudicator who, after reviewing the circumstances of the applicant's continuing detention, declined to order his release.

The applicant claims to be a citizen of Liberia. As a stowaway aboard a merchant ship from India, he was removed from the vessel on its arrival in Halifax in 1992. He then made a claim to refugee status which was refused. While in Canada, the applicant was convicted of a number of crimes — possession of a dangerous weapon, two counts of theft, uttering a threat, mischief, failing to appear and two counts of assault. On the day scheduled for his release from jail after he completed serving his sentence in respect of his last set of convictions, an adjudicator made the first determination that the applicant should be detained pursuant to Section 103 of the *Immigration Act*. That decision was reviewed on a number of occasions and the applicant's detention was continued after each such review.

It is important that adjudicators consider only relevant factors in dealing with the decision that they must make in this situation. Each review must be a hearing *de novo*, that is, in the sense that the concern at the time of the review, is whether there are reasons to satisfy the adjudicator that the person in detention is not likely to pose a danger to the public and is likely to appear for examination, inquiry, and removal. It is not sufficient that the adjudicator proceed by accepting the decisions of previous adjudicators and considering primarily what may have happened since the last previous decision.

The adjudicator should start with the premise that detention is an extraordinary restraint and that while section 103(7) would appear to put significant onus on the person in detention, there must also be an onus upon the Minister and his officials to demonstrate each time that there are reasons which warrant detention of the person in question.

The mere fact that the applicant was convicted of the offences described in this case does not in itself result in a determination that he is likely to pose a danger to the public or even that he may pose a danger to the public. Conviction for a criminal offence and sentencing for it do not lead to the conclusion when a sentence is served, there is a continuing likelihood of danger to the public warranting continuing detention. The probability of such a danger has to be determined from the circumstances of each case.

The likelihood of early action by Immigration officials to remove the applicant is only one factor and perhaps a minor factor in the ultimate assessment of the likelihood of the applicant's appearance for removal if released from detention. Other factors to be considered are referred to by way of example by Rothstein J. in *Sahin v. Canada (Minister of Citizenship & Immigration)* (1994), 85 F.T.R. 99, 24 C.R.R. (2d) 276, [1995] 1 F.C. 214, 30 Imm. L.R. (2d) 33, affirmed (1995), 184 N.R. 354, 97 F.T.R. 80 (note), 31 C.R.R. (2d) 374 (Fed. C.A.).

The Court set aside the decision continuing the applicant's detention to be effective when the continuing detention of the applicant is further reviewed in accordance with Section 103(7) on or before July 10, 1995.

Section 103(8)

Singh v. Canada (Minister of Employment & Immigration) (October 29, 1987), Doc. No. A-749-86 (Fed. C.A.) — The adjudicator ordered the release of the applicant who had made a refugee claim at an inquiry. The adjudicator also ordered the Commission to take the applicant back into custody if he was found not to be a convention refugee. Section 104(8) was found not to justify this type of order. That subsection contemplates a retaking into custody at a later point in time only after the circumstances have changed to the point where the retaking into custody has been justified.

103.1 (1) Detention — Where, with respect to a person seeking to come into Canada,

(a) the person is unable to satisfy an immigration officer with respect to that person's identity, or

(b) in the opinion of the Deputy Minister or a person designated by the Deputy Minister, there is reason to suspect that the person may be a member of an inadmissible class described in paragraph 19(1)(*e*), (*f*), (*g*), (*j*), (*k*), or (*l*),

an immigration officer shall detain the person and forthwith report the detention to a senior immigration officer who may continue or order the continuation of the detention for a period not exceeding seven days from the time the person was first detained under this Act.

(2) Additional period of detention — Where, with respect to a person detained under subsection (1), the Minister certifies in writing

(a) that

(i) the person's identity has not been established, or

(ii) the Minister has reason to suspect that the person may be a member of an inadmissible class described in paragraph 19(1)(*e*), (*f*), (*g*), (*j*), (*k*) or (*l*), and

(b) that an additional period of detention is required to investigate the matter referred to in subparagraph (*a*)(i) or (ii),

the person shall be brought before an adjudicator forthwith and at least once during every seven day period thereafter, at which times the adjudicator shall review the reasons for the person's continued detention.

(3) **Minister may amend certificate** — Where the Minister has issued a certificate under subsection (2), the Minister may amend the certificate to which the detention relates to include any matter referred to in subparagraph (2)(*a*)(i) or (ii), following which the person shall be brought before an adjudicator forthwith and at least once during every seven day period thereafter, at which times the adjudicator shall review the reasons for the person's continued detention.

(4) **Review every seven days** — Where a person is detained under subsection (1) and the Minister has not issued a certificate under subsection (2), the person shall be brought before an adjudicator forthwith after the expiration of the period during which the person is being detained and that person shall be brought before an adjudicator at least once during every seven day period thereafter, at which times the reasons for continued detention shall be reviewed.

(5) **Continued detention if efforts being made** — Where an adjudicator who conducts a review under subsection (2) or (3) is satisfied that reasonable efforts are being made by the Minister to investigate the matter referred to in subparagraph (2)(*a*)(i) or (ii), the adjudicator shall continue the person's detention.

(6) **Review in camera** — Every review under subsection (2) or (3) of the detention of a person suspected of being a member of an inadmissible class described in paragraph 19(1)(*e*), (*f*), (*g*), (*j*), (*k*) or (*l*) shall be conducted *in camera*.

(7) **Review is ex parte** — Where

(a) the Minister is of the opinion that any evidence or information to be presented by or on behalf of the Minister at any review under subsection (2) or (3) of the detention of a person referred to in subsection (6) should not be disclosed on the grounds that its disclosure would be injurious to national security or to the safety of persons, and

(b) a request therefor is made by the Minister,

the adjudicator shall order that the review or any part thereof be conducted in the absence of the person and any counsel representing the person.

(8) **Application to have order quashed** — Any person excluded by an order under subsection (7) from the whole or any part of the review under subsection (2) or (3) may apply to the Chief Justice of the Federal Court or to a judge of that Court designated by the Chief Justice for the purposes of this subsection to have the order quashed and sections 37 and 38 of the *Canada Evidence Act* shall apply, with such modifications as the circumstances may require, to such applications.

(9) **Application of order** — Unless quashed, an order under subsection (7) shall, with respect to the person to whom the order relates, apply to every review under subsection (2) or (3), or part thereof, at which the Minister is of the opinion that any evidence or information to be presented by or on behalf of the Minister at the review, or part thereof, should not be disclosed on the grounds that its disclosure would be injurious to national security or to the safety of persons.

(10) **Appropriate order** — Where the adjudicator who conducts a review under subsection (2) or (3) does not continue a person's detention under subsection (5), the adjudicator shall make the appropriate order under subsection 103(3).

(11) **Idem** — An adjudicator who conducts a review under subsection (4) shall make the appropriate order under subsection 103(3).

(12) **Idem** — Where, with respect to a person under detention under this section, the Minister is of the opinion

(a) that the person's identity has been established, and

(b) that the person is not a person described in paragraph 19(1)(*e*), (*f*), (*g*), (*j*), (*k*) or (*l*),

a senior immigration officer shall forthwith bring the person before an adjudicator who shall make the appropriate order under subsection 103(3).

(13) **Application notwithstanding section 23 or 103** — This section applies notwithstanding section 23 or 103.

(14) **Right to counsel** — Every person detained under this section shall be informed that the person has the right to retain and instruct counsel and shall be given a reasonable opportunity to obtain such counsel.

R.S.C. 1985, c. 29 (4th Supp.); 1992, c. 1, s. 77; 1992, c. 49, s. 95.

104. **Failure to comply** — Where a person fails to comply with any of the terms or conditions imposed under paragraph 103(3)(*c*) or with any of the terms or conditions subject to which he is released from detention under any provision of this Act

(a) any security deposit that may have been made either pursuant to paragraph 103(3)(*c*) or as a condition of the person's release may be declared forfeited by the Minister, or

(b) the terms of any performance bond that may have been posted may be enforced

and, where the person has been released from detention, he may be retaken into custody forthwith and held in detention.

105. (1) **Where person in institution** — Notwithstanding the *Corrections and Conditional Release Act*, the *Prisons and Reformatories Act* or any Act of a provincial legislature, where a warrant has been issued or an order has been made pursuant to subsection 103(1) or (3) with respect to any person who is incarcerated in any place of confinement pursuant to the order of any court or other body, the Deputy Minister may issue an order to the person in charge of the place directing that

(a) the person continue to be detained until the expiration of the sentence to which the person is subject or until the expiration of the sentence or term of confinement as reduced by the operation of any statute or other law or by an act of clemency; and

(b) the person be delivered, at the expiration of the sentence or term of confinement referred to in paragraph (*a*), to an immigration officer to be taken into custody.

(2) **Temporary absences** — **Nothing in subsection (1) shall limit the authority of any person, pursuant to any Act referred to in that subsection, to grant an escorted temporary absence pursuant to any of those Acts.**

1994, c. 26, s. 35; 1995, c. 15, s. 20.

106. **Authority to execute warrants and orders** — **Any warrant issued or order made under paragraph 12(3)(*b*), subsection 20(1), paragraph 23(3)(*a*), subsection 40.1(2), 90(2), 103(1), (2), (3) or (8) or 103.1(1) or section 105 is, notwithstanding any other law, sufficient authority to the person to whom it is addressed or who may receive and execute it to arrest and detain the person with respect to whom the warrant or order was issued or made.**

R.S.C. 1985, c. 29 (4th Supp.), s. 13; 1992, c. 49, s. 96.

107. **Place of detention** — **Where a person is detained pursuant to this Act, that person shall be detained at an immigrant station or other place satisfactory to the Deputy Minister.**

Injunctions

107.1 (1) **Injunctions relating to approved businesses or funds** — **Where, on application by the Minister to the Federal Court — Trial Division, it appears likely to the Court that a person who has obtained the approval of the Minister for a business or fund has done or failed to do anything, or is about to do anything, in contravention of any term or condition governing the approval, the Court may issue an injunction ordering any person named in the application**

(a) to refrain from doing anything that it appears to the Court may be in contravention of any term or condition governing the approval; or

(b) to do anything that it appears to the Court may ensure compliance with any term or condition governing the approval.

(2) **Notice** — **No injunction shall issue under subsection (1) unless forty-eight hours notice is given to each person named in the application or the urgency of the situation is such that service of notice would not be consistent with the purposes of this Act.**

1992, c. 49, s. 97.

PART VII — GENERAL

Consultations and Agreements with Provinces

108. (1) **Consultations with provinces** — **The Minister shall consult with the provinces respecting the measures to be undertaken to facilitate the adaptation of permanent residents to Canadian society and the pattern of immigrant settlement in Canada in relation to regional demographic requirements.**

(2) **Federal-provincial agreements** — **The Minister, with the approval of the Governor in Council, may enter into an agreement with any province or group of provinces for the purpose of facilitating the formulation, coordination and implementation of immigration policies and programs.**

International Agreements

108.1 International agreements — The Minister, with the approval of the Governor in Council, may enter into agreements with other countries for the purpose of facilitating the coordination and implementation of immigration policies and programs including, without restricting the generality of the foregoing, agreements for sharing the responsibility for examining refugee claims and for sharing information concerning persons who travel between countries that are parties to such agreements.

1992, c. 49, s. 98.

Immigration Officers

109. (1) Appointment of immigration officers — Immigration officers shall be appointed or employed under the *Public Service Employment Act.*

(2) Designation of immigration officers — Notwithstanding subsection (1), the Minister may designate any person or class of persons as immigration officers for the purposes of this Act and that person or class of persons shall have such of the powers, duties and functions of an immigration officer as are specified by the Minister.

110. (1) Authority of immigration officers — An immigration officer has the authority and powers of a peace officer to enforce any provision of this Act, the regulations or any warrant, order or direction made under this Act or the regulations respecting the arrest, detention or removal from Canada of any person.

(2) Identification and seizure of documents — An immigration officer may

(a) require the following persons to comply with the regulations providing for their identification, namely,

(i) persons who seek admission,

(ii) persons who make an application pursuant to subsection 9(1), section 10, subsection 10.2(1) or section 16,

(iii) persons who are arrested pursuant to section 103,

(iv) persons against whom a removal order or conditional removal order has been made, and

(v) persons who claim to be Convention refugees;

(a.1) search persons seeking to come into Canada who the immigration officer believes on reasonable grounds have not revealed their identity or who have hidden on or about their person documents that are relevant to their admissibility and may search any vehicle that conveyed the persons to Canada and their luggage and personal effects;

(a.2) search persons seeking to come into Canada who the immigration officer believes on reasonable grounds have committed, or who are in possession of documents that may be used in the commission of, an offence under section 94.1, 94.2

or 94.4 may search any vehicle that conveyed the persons to Canada and their luggage and personal effects;

(a.3) examine at a port of entry or any other place in Canada, for the purposes of this Act or the regulations, any visa, passport or other travel document, any document or thing that may serve to establish the identity of a person or any document or thing purporting to be any of those documents or things that is imported into or about to be imported into or exported from Canada.

(b) seize and hold at a port of entry or any other place in Canada any thing or document if the immigration officer believes on reasonable grounds that that action is required to facilitate the carrying out of any provision of this Act or the regulations; and

(c) for the purposes of this Act and the regulations, seize and hold any thing or document if the immigration officer believes on reasonable grounds that it has been fraudulently or improperly obtained or used or that action is necessary to prevent its fraudulent or improper use.

(2.01) Interpretation — Notwithstanding subsection 42(2) of the *Canada Post Corporation Act*, a thing or document that is detained under the *Customs Act* and seized by an immigration officer under paragraph (2)(*b*) or (*c*) is not in the course of post for the purposes of the first-named Act.

(2.1) Fingerprints to be destroyed — Subject to section 6 of the *Privacy Act*, any fingerprints that were taken pursuant to regulations made pursuant to paragraph 114(1)(*o*) of a person who is subsequently determined under this Act to be a Convention Refugee shall be destroyed when the person becomes a Canadian citizen.

(3) Temporary assistants — An immigration officer may, in cases of emergency, employ such temporary assistants as the officer deems necessary to enable him to carry out his duties under this Act and the regulations and those temporary assistants shall, during their employment, have the authority and powers referred to in subsection (1), but no such employment shall continue for a period exceeding forty-eight hours unless approved by the Minister.

R.S.C. 1985, c. 28 (4th Supp.), s. 28; 1992, c. 49, s. 99; 1995, c. 15, s. 21.

Case Law

Section 110(1)

R. v. Roye (April 2, 1984), Doc. T-8647-82 (Fed. T.D.) — In this case the Minister successfully maintained an action against the defendant for assaulting two immigration officers acting within the scope of their authority and judgment was obtained in the amount of $7,089 plus costs.

Section 110(2)

Gassmann v. Canada (Minister of Employment & Immigration) (1990), 11 Imm. L.R. (2d) 149, 36 F.T.R. 105 (Fed. T.D.) — *Mandamus* will compel the Minister to return a passport which the department turned over to a foreign government (the Federal Republic of Germany). The applicant entered Canada as a visitor and in the course of applying for an extension his passport was taken by the immigration authorities. The passport was not returned to the applicant but an interview was scheduled and ultimately the applicant was advised that the German government had cancelled or confiscated his passport. The Minister justified what was done under section 110(2)(c) of the *Immigration Act*. There was no evidence to suggest that the passport had been improperly obtained or used, or that action was necessary to prevent its fraudulent or improper use. Further, the Minister's officials did not tell the applicant what they had done with his passport, namely, returned it to the government of the Federal Republic of Germany and did not allow him to make representations to them prior to taking the action that they contemplated. Accordingly, an order was issued directing the Minister to return the passport to the applicant.

Nunes v. Canada (Minister of Employment & Immigration), [1986] 3 F.C. 112 (Fed. C.A.) — The search and seizure of documents under the *Immigration Act* can be made as part of the examination of persons seeking admission to Canada. This search and seizure was not contrary to the *Charter of Rights*. Thus, the two letters were admissible at an inquiry directed to whether the applicant was a true visitor to Canada. The adjudicator's decision, based on such letters, was upheld; the decision in *Mahtab v. Canada (Comm. de l'emploi & l'immigration)*, [1986] 3 F.C. 101 (Fed. T.D.) was expressly overruled.

110.1 (1) Authority for personal searches — The search of a person under section 110 must be authorized by a senior immigration officer.

(2) Reasonable grounds for searches — Where a senior immigration officer considers that there are reasonable grounds for the search of a person under section 110, the senior immigration officer shall authorize the search.

(3) Searches by same sex — No person shall be searched under section 110 by a person who is not of the same sex, and if there is no immigration officer of the same sex at the place at which the search is to take place, an immigration officer may authorize any suitable person of the same sex to perform the search.

1992, c. 49, s. 100.

111. Oaths and evidence — Every immigration officer has the authority to administer oaths and to take and receive evidence under oath on any matter arising out of this Act.

112. [Repealed 1992, c. 49, s. 101.]

Peace Officers

113. Duties of peace officers to execute orders — Every peace officer and every person in immediate charge or control of an immigrant station shall, when so directed by the Deputy Minister, an adjudicator, a senior immigration officer or an immigration officer, receive and execute any written warrant or order issued or made under this Act or the regulations for the arrest, detention or removal from Canada of any person.

Regulations

114. (1) Regulations — The Governor in Council may make regulations

(a) prescribing classes of immigrants and providing for the establishment, and the application to such classes, of selection standards based on such factors as family relationships, education, language, skill, occupational or business experience and

other personal attributes and attainments, together with demographic considerations and labour market conditions in Canada, for the purpose of determining whether or not and the degree to which an immigrant will be able to become successfully established in Canada;

(a.1) specify classes of immigrants for the purposes of subsection 6(8) in respect of which the immigrant and any or all dependants shall be assessed;

(a.2) defining, for the purposes of this Act, what constitutes becoming successfully established in Canada;

(a.3) specifying, with respect to any prescribed class of immigrants, at what stage of assessing applications for visas all or part of the selection standards provided for under paragraph (*a*) shall be applied;

(a.4) prescribing a class of persons who may be granted landing on the basis of their business experience, accumulated net worth and intention to make investments in Canada that meet prescribed standards;

(a.5) authorizing the Minister to approve businesses and funds and requiring persons in the class prescribed pursuant to paragraph (*a*.4)

> **(i) to invest in businesses or funds approved by the Minister as fostering the development of a strong and viable economy and regional prosperity in Canada, and**
>
> **(ii) to satisfy any selection standards established pursuant to paragraph (*a*);**

(a.6) respecting the approval of businesses and funds under any regulations made under paragraph (*a*.5), including regulations

> **(i) prescribing terms and conditions governing their approval, including terms and conditions requiring provincial approval, and terms and conditions under which approval may be suspended, revoked or amended,**
>
> **(ii) authorizing the Minister to impose additional terms and conditions in relation to any approval, and**
>
> **(iii) authorizing the Minister to require any person who manages or controls an approved business or fund to submit periodic reports regarding compliance with the terms and conditions governing the approval;**

(b) prescribing classes of immigrants in respect of which the number of immigrants who may be issued visas or granted landing in any calendar year shall be subject to a numerical limitation;

(b.1) specifying, with respect to any class of immigrants, that accompanying dependants shall not be included for the purposes of any number referred to in subsection 7(10);

(c) prescribing, for the purposes of subsection 6(2), classes of persons whose applications for landing may be sponsored by Canadian citizens and permanent residents;

(d) for the purposes of subsection 6(3),

> **(i) designating classes of persons and admission requirements in respect of any such class and specifying, with respect to any such class, at what stage of assessing applications for admission all or part of the admission requirements shall be applied, and**

(ii) prescribing admission requirements for Convention refugees and specifying at what stage of assessing applications for admission all or part of the admission requirements shall be applied and whether the number of Convention refugees who may be issued a visa or be admitted into Canada in any calendar year shall be subject to a numerical limitation;

(d.1) respecting the sponsoring of persons for the purposes of subsection 6(4);

(e) prescribing, for the purposes of subsection 6(5), classes of immigrants and landing requirements in respect of immigrants and their dependants and specifying, with respect to any such class, at what stage of assessing applications for landing all or part of the landing requirements shall be applied;

(f) respecting the method of selecting immigrants, including regulations specifying, with respect to any prescribed class of immigrants, whether immigrants of that class, or immigrants of that class and any or all of their dependants, as the case may be, shall be selected

(i) on the basis of when their applications were made and duly completed in accordance with the regulations,

(ii) on a comparative basis, in relation to applications received during any specific period, to determine who will be best able to become successfully established in Canada, or

(iii) on any other basis;

(f.1) specifying, with respect to any prescribed class of immigrants the selection of which is on a comparative basis in relation to applications received during any specified period, whether the application of immigrants who are not issued visas may be reconsidered on a comparative basis in relation to applications received during another period, or on any other basis;

(f.2) authorizing, with respect to any prescribed class of immigrants, visa officers not to assess applications for visas where the Minister considers it necessary for the purpose of complying with the immigration plan currently in force;

(f.3) authorizing, with respect to Convention refugees and classes of persons prescribed for the purposes of subsection 6(3), immigration officers not to assess applications for visas or applications for admission where the Minister considers it necessary for the purposes of the immigration plan currently in force;

(f.4) authorizing, with respect to any prescribed class of immigrants, immigration officers not to assess applications for visas or applications for landing under subsection 6(5) where the Minister considers it necessary for the purpose of complying with the immigration plan currently in force;

(f.5) prescribing a date for the purposes of subsection 7(1);

(g) prescribing universities, colleges and other institutions not described in paragraph 10(*a*) for the taking of any academic, professional or vocational training course at which persons, other than Canadian citizens and permanent residents, may not be authorized to come into Canada and prescribing courses at any such university, college or other institution for the taking of which authorization may not be obtained under section 10;

Proposed Addition — 114(1)(g.1)

(g.1) prescribing the period of validity of visas;

1992, c. 49, s. 102. [Not in force at date of publication.]

(h) prescribing the circumstances in which a returning resident permit shall be issued to a permanent resident who makes an application pursuant to subsection 25(1);

Proposed Amendment — 114(1)(h)

(h) prescribing the maximum duration of student and employment authorizations;

Proposed Addition — 114(1)(h.1)– (h.3)

(h.1) prescribing the terms and conditions under which a document referred to in section 10.3 or subsection 70.1(1) may be issued, the maximum duration of any such document, which duration shall not be less than three years, and the circumstances in which the production of that document may be required;

(h.2) prescribing the maximum duration of grants of entry and of their extensions;

(h.3) prescribing criteria respecting the extension of the period during which visitors may remain in Canada pursuant to paragraph 17(2)(*c*);

1992, c. 49, s. 102. [Not in force at date of publication.]

(i) specifying the documentation that may be required in respect of any class of visitors;

(j) prohibiting persons or classes of persons, other than Canadian citizens and permanent residents, from engaging or continuing in employment in Canada without authorization, prescribing the types of terms and conditions that may be imposed in connection with such an authorization and exempting any person or class of persons from the requirement to obtain such an authorization;

(j.1) prohibiting persons or classes of persons, other than Canadian citizens and permanent residents, from attending any university or college, or taking any academic, professional or vocational training course, in Canada without authorization, prescribing the types of terms and conditions that may be imposed in connection with such an authorization and exempting any person or class of persons from the requirement to obtain such an authorization;

(j.2) prescribing classes of employment and specifying whether the number of employment authorizations, not including extensions, to be issued in respect of any such class in any calendar year will be subject to a numerical limitation;

(j.3) authorizing, with respect to any prescribed class of employment, immigration officers not to assess applications for employment authorizations where the Minister considers it necessary for the purpose of complying with the immigration plan currently in force;

(j.4) designating classes of persons for the purposes of subsection 12(1) who may be examined in a manner approved by the Minister instead of appearing before an immigration officer at a port of entry;

(k) requiring any person to deposit security with the Minister to guarantee the performance by that person of any obligation assumed by that person with respect to the admission of any other person;

(l) [Repealed 1992, c. 49, s. 102.]

(m) prescribing the factors to be considered in determining whether, for medical reasons, any person is or is likely to be a danger to public health or to public safety;

Proposed Addition — 114(1)(m.1), (m.2)

(m.1) prescribing social services for the purposes of subparagraph 19(1)(*a*)(ii);

(m.2) prescribing classes of immigrants that shall be exempted from the application of subparagraph 19(1)(*a*)(ii);

1992, c. 49, s. 102. [Not in force at date of publication.]

(m.3) requiring or authorizing the interview of persons by visa officers for the purpose of assessing visa applications and applications for student and employment authorizations and respecting the places where such interviews may be conducted;

(n) requiring or authorizing the examination of persons outside Canada for the purpose of determining whether those persons shall be allowed to come into Canada or may be granted admission;

(o) requiring persons referred to in paragraph 110(2)(*a*) to provide photographs of themselves or to be fingerprinted or photographed or both;

(p) prescribing the costs and expenses to be included in determining removal costs;

(p.1) respecting the payment of fees for services provided in the administration of this Act and prescribing the amount of those fees;

(p.2) prescribing classes of persons who are or are not members of a crew;

(q) requiring transportation companies to ensure, in prescribed circumstances, that immigrants and visitors being carried to Canada by them are in possession of valid visas where required;

(q.1) with respect to transportation companies bringing persons into Canada,

> **(i) requiring or authorizing those companies to hold the visas, passports or travel documents of those persons in order to ensure that the visas, passports or travel documents are available for examination by an immigration officer at the port of entry,**
>
> **(ii) providing for the disposition by those companies, on the arrival of those persons in Canada, of any visas, passports or travel documents held by those companies, and**
>
> **(iii) requiring those companies to furnish such documentary evidence for examination by an immigration officer at the port of entry as is necessary to establish the identity and itinerary for travel to Canada of those persons;**

(q.11) for determining the adequacy of any area, office, laboratory or other facility for the purposes mentioned in subsection 89(2);

(q.12) designating, for the purposes of subsection 97.1(1) or (3), provisions of any regulation made under paragraph (*q*), (*q*.1), (*t*), (*cc*), (*dd*), (*ee*), (*ff*), (*gg*) or (*hh*);

(q.2) [Repealed 1992, c. 49, s. 102.]

(q.3) establishing a tariff of administration fees to be assessed pursuant to section 91.1 for the purpose of recovering any costs of administering this Act, other than removal costs, and prescribing criteria for the purpose of assessing those fees;

(q.4) prescribing procedures for giving notice to transportation companies of assessments pursuant to section 91.1 and directions under section 93;

(r) prescribing costs for the purposes of section 55.1;

(s) prescribing, for the purpose of sharing responsibility for the examination of persons who claim to be Convention refugees, countries that comply with Article 33 of the Convention;

(s.1) prescribing, for the purposes of subsection 69.1(10.1), countries that respect human rights;

(s.2) specifying periods during which a certificate of departure referred to in section 32.02 may be issued;

(t) prohibiting transportation companies from knowingly carrying to Canada persons, other than Canadian citizens or permanent residents, who are, in the opinion of the Minister, members of any of the classes described in subsection 19(1);

(u) authorizing the Minister to make loans for any of the purposes referred to in subsection 119(1) and prescribing the rate of interest, if any, to be charged on those loans and the manner in which the terms of repayment of those loans shall be determined;

(u.1) prescribing the maximum amount of outstanding advances to the Minister under subsection 119(1);

(v) requiring any person, other than a person who is a member of the bar of any province, to make an application for and obtain a licence from such authority as is prescribed before the person may appear before an adjudicator, the Refugee Division or the Appeal Division as counsel for any fee, reward or other form of remuneration whatever;

(w) authorizing the issuance of visas to prescribed officials and representatives of foreign governments, states and international organizations and the suites and families of those persons and prescribing the classes of persons by whom those visas may be issued;

(x) establishing the procedures to be followed at examinations;

(y) prescribing the manner in which immigration officers shall carry out their duties and exercise their powers, whether in Canada or elsewhere;

(z) prescribing the manner in which an application may be made under section 15 or 16 and the information to be provided therewith;

(aa) requiring any person or class of persons, other than a Canadian citizen, to be in possession of a valid and subsisting passport or other travel document;

(bb) providing for the return or other disposition of any travel or other document that has been seized and held pursuant to paragraph 110(2)(*b*) or (*c*);

(cc) requiring a transportation company to collect and give to an immigration officer any written report required to be made to an immigration officer by any person leaving Canada;

(dd) specifying the manifests, bills of health or other records or documents concerning persons carried by vehicles to or from Canada that shall be maintained and carried on vehicles;

(ee) requiring the identification, supervision and detention of persons to be carried in transit through Canada;

(ff) specifying the obligations and duties of transportation companies and members of crews to safeguard persons on board vehicles, to report the escape of persons in their custody and to take such precautions as may be required to prevent those persons from unlawfully coming into Canada and, in the case of persons in their custody who are required under this Act to leave Canada, from failing to leave Canada;

(gg) requiring the master of a vehicle to make a written report to an immigration officer in respect of any person who has secreted himself in or on a vehicle coming to Canada and to hold that person in custody on the vehicle;

(hh) requiring the owner or master of a vehicle to maintain and provide an immigration officer with lists and other information concerning the members of the crew of the vehicle and their discharge, transfer, desertion or hospitalization in Canada and to notify an immigration officer of any such discharge, transfer, desertion or hospitalization in Canada;

(ii) providing for the disposition of property carried by persons who die in Canada while at an immigrant station or other place in the custody or under the supervision of an immigration officer;

(ii.1) defining any term or expression that by this Act is to be defined by the regulations;

(ii.2) prescribing the classes of immigrants in respect of which landing shall be granted subject to terms and conditions, and prescribing those terms and conditions;

(ii.3) prescribing the terms and conditions that may be imposed by an immigration officer including, where such terms and conditions are for the purpose of providing adequate health or social services or for fostering a strong and viable economy and regional prosperity in Canada, terms and conditions concerning place of residence and occupation;

(ii.4) specifying, with respect to any province that has entered into an agreement pursuant to section 108 whereby the province has sole responsibility for the selection of immigrants of certain classes of immigrants, the terms and conditions prescribed under paragraph (*ii*.3) that may not be imposed in respect of immigrants of those classes of immigrants who intend to reside in the province;

(ii.5) specifying what constitutes a duly completed application for the purposes of this Act and the regulations;

(ii.6) prescribing the circumstances under which an immigration officer shall approve an application to vary or cancel any term or condition imposed pursuant to subsection 14(5);

Proposed Addition — 114(1)(ii.7)

(ii.7) prescribing for the purposes of paragraph 25.1(*a*) the circumstances under which a person shall be deemed not to cease to be a permanent resident; and

1992, c. 49, s. 102. [Not in force at date of publication.]

(jj) prescribing any matter required or authorized by this Act to be prescribed.

(2) **Exemption from regulations** — The Governor in Council may, by regulation, authorize the Minister to exempt any person from any regulation made under subsection (1) or otherwise facilitate the admission of any person where the Minister is satis-

fied that the person should be exempted from that regulation or that the person's admission should be facilitated owing to the existence of compassionate or humanitarian considerations.

(3) **Consent of province** — The Minister may exercise the powers referred to in subsection (2) in respect of a person who intends to reside in a province that has entered into an agreement pursuant to section 108 whereby the province has sole responsibility for the selection of such persons, only if the province has given its consent.

(4) **Regulations do not apply** — Where a province has entered into an agreement pursuant to section 108 whereby the province has sole responsibility for the selection of certain prescribed classes of immigrants,

> (a) the selections standards established under paragraph (1)(*a*) and all regulations made pursuant to paragraphs (1)(*b*.1) and (*f*), and
>
> (b) the landing requirements prescribed under paragraph (1)(*e*), other than the landing requirements relating to membership in inadmissible classes described in section 19,

shall not apply in respect of any immigrant of any such class who intends to reside in that province.

(5) **Idem** — Where a province has entered into an agreement pursuant to section 108 whereby the province has sole responsibility for the selection of immigrants of the class of immigrants prescribed under paragraph (1)(*a*.4),

> (a) regulations made pursuant to subparagraph (1)(*a*.5)(i) shall not apply in relation to immigrants to the extent that they intend to invest in a business or fund in that province; and
>
> (b) regulations made pursuant to subparagraph (1)(*a*.5)(ii) shall not apply in relation to immigrants who intend to reside in that province.

(6) **Regulations must be consistent with agreements** — Regulations made pursuant to paragraphs (1)(*a*.4) and (*f*) must be consistent with all agreements entered into with provinces pursuant to section 108.

(7) **Renewal** — A country may be prescribed as a country under paragraph (1)(s) for a maximum period of two years, but any such prescription may be renewed.

(8) **Factors** — The Governor in Council shall take the following factors into account when determining whether to prescribe a country under paragraph (1)(*s*) or to renew any prescription made under that paragraph:

> (a) whether the country is a party to the Convention;
>
> (b) the country's policies and practices with respect to Convention refugee claims;
>
> (c) the country's record with respect to human rights; and
>
> (d) whether the country is a party to an agreement with Canada concerning the sharing of responsibility for examining refugee claims, notwithstanding that this factor is not a requirement for a country to be prescribed.

(9) **Monitoring** — After prescribing a country under paragraph (1)(*s*), the Governor in Council shall monitor that country in relation to the factors described in subsection (8).

(10) Retroactive application of regulations — A regulation made under any of paragraphs (1)(*a*) to (*f*.4) and (*j*.2) and (*j*.3) may, if it so provides, in relation to any prescribed class of immigrants or prescribed class of employment specified in the regulation, or in relation to any application for the approval of a business or fund, be retroactive and apply in respect of

(a) all applications for landing, for an employment authorization or for the approval of a business or fund, as the case may be, pending on the day on which the regulation comes into force;

(b) any pending application for landing, for an employment authorization or for the approval of a business or fund, as the case may be, made after a date specified in the regulation that is before the day on which the regulation comes into force; or

(c) any pending application for landing, for an employment authorization or for the approval of a business or fund, as the case may be, that, on the day on which the regulation comes into force, had been assessed to the extent specified in the regulation.

(11) Idem — Where the Minister is authorized by regulations made under paragraph (1)(*a*) to award units of assessment in respect of factors that an immigration officer must take into consideration in deciding whether a visa may be issued to an immigrant, any change that is brought about by a regulation made under that paragraph to the number of units of assessment that may be awarded by the Minister shall, if the regulation so provides, apply retroactively in respect of

(a) all applications for landing pending on the day on which the regulation comes into force;

(b) any pending application for landing made after a date specified in the regulation that is before the day on which the regulation comes into force; or

(c) any pending application for landing that, on the day on which the regulation comes into force, had been assessed to the extent specified in the regulation.

(12) Idem — For greater certainty, where a regulation referred to in subsection (10) or (11) is expressed to apply retroactively, the regulation applies in respect of applications made before the coming into force of that subsection as well as in respect of applications made after the coming into force of that subsection.

R.S.C. 1985, c. 28 (4th Supp.), s. 29; R.S.C. 1985, c. 29 (4th Supp.), s. 14; 1990, c. 38, s. 1; 1990, c. 49, s. 102; 1994, c. 26, s. 36.

Case Law

Section 114(1)(a)

Singh (A.) v. R. (1996), 37 Imm. L.R. (2d) 140, (sub nom. *Singh v. Canada (Minister of Citizenship & Immigration)*) 123 F.T.R. 241 (Fed. T.D.); affirmed (1998), (sub nom. *Singh v. Canada (Minister of Citizenship & Immigration)*) 234 N.R. 71 (Fed. C.A.) — The plaintiff had been the subject of an inquiry in which it had been found that he had obtained permanent resident status by reason of a material representation, namely that he had failed to disclose the birth of a son. The plaintiff was ordered deported at the immigration inquiry and appealed that order to the appeal division of the IRB. The appeal was founded on paragraph 70(3)(b) of the Act and was dismissed. The question of the vires of regulations 6(1)(a), 9(1)(a) and 10(1)(a) was not raised before the appeal division and was not raised in the application for leave. The question of the vires of those regulations was raised at the argument of the judicial review application. The Court refused to consider the matter because the issue of the regulations had not been raised before the appeal division.

The plaintiff then commenced this action for a declaration. If a party to litigation could have raised an issue before a competent tribunal, that party fails to raise the issue at the peril of being estopped on the basis of *res judicata* when purporting to raise that same issue in subsequent litigation in which the same adversary is engaged. In the action for declaration, the parties were the same as in the proceeding before the appeal division. Accordingly, on the ground of *res judicata*, summary judgement was pronounced dismissing the plaintiff's claim with costs.

The Court went on to conclude that the impugned regulations were enacted for the clear purpose of administration of the *Immigration Act*. The regulations were authorized by the Act at various junctures and in section 114. Accordingly, it was found that the regulations were *intra vires*. [Affirmed (Nov. 6, 1998), Doc. A-1014-96 (Fed. C.A.).]

D'Souza v. Canada (Minister of Employment & Immigration) (1990), 12 Imm. L.R. (2d) 268, [1991] 1 F.C. 505, 39 F.T.R. 1 (Fed. T.D.) — Ms. D'Souza applied for permanent residence as an independent immigrant. Her application was submitted under cover of a letter sent by her prospective employer and noted her occupation as executive secretary. The applicant was advised by letter that a barrier to acceptance of her application was the fact that there was only a limited demand in Canada for persons in her occupation. Accordingly, the applicant was advised to obtain a confirmation of her offer of employment by the local CEC. In the meantime, her application was refused.

There is no requirement arising by implication in the Act or regulations that the visa officer must consult on his own initiative the National Employment Service. The applicant must demonstrate to the satisfaction of the visa officer that the criteria for admission have been met. So long as the procedures developed and followed by the Commission to fulfil its responsibilities in relation to immigration matters are not inconsistent with the requirements of the Act and regulations, there can be no objection in law to them. The Minister must have discretion to develop administrative procedures to meet his or her statutory and regulatory responsibilities. The Court should intervene to limit that discretion only where it is clear that the procedures are inconsistent with or otherwise beyond the authority of the Minister under the Act and regulations.

The decision to withhold the grant of a visa until confirmation of employment had been communicated from the National Employment Service to the visa officer was not an improper delegation of authority. The regulations, in particular item 5 of schedule 1, provide for the visa officer assessing an application for permanent residence having reference to arranged employment and to consider that criterion for admission based on information provided by the National Employment Service. If this determination of particular aspects of employment is considered to be delegation, then it is delegation made by the regulations and it is authorized. It is not a delegation made by the visa officer.

The assessment criteria established by schedule 1 to the regulations are not inconsistent with the Act and regulations. The requirement that a local CEC office validate arranged employment falls clearly within section 114(1)(a) as a matter within "labour market conditions in Canada for the purpose of determining whether or not an immigrant will be able to become successfully established in Canada". In the detail of factors to be considered by the National Employment Service in considering matters within item 5 of schedule 1, the Service must be careful to consider only those matters which can be justified as being clearly within the factors set out in the schedule. Section 20(3) of the regulations is much more precise than item 5 of schedule 1. While it may be a worthwhile objective of the Employment Service to insist upon the training of Canadians, such a requirement is not clearly within the factors to be considered in relation to item 5 of schedule 1. It is not appropriate to insist that the prospective employer of an applicant/immigrant first be expected to train persons already in Canada before authorization is given to arranged employment nor is it appropriate to insist in practice upon any standard minimum period for a prospective employer to seek unsuccessfully an employee through the CEC services. The employment officer must be prepared to look at whatever evidence the prospective employer may have of the efforts to hire Canadian citizens or permanent residents. The visa officer fulfilled his duties in this case and accordingly the applications for *certiorari* and *mandamus* were dismissed.

Section 114(1)(d)

Jafari v. Canada (Minister of Employment & Immigration), 30 Imm. L.R. (2d) 139, [1995] 2 F.C. 595, 125 D.L.R. (4th) 141, 180 N.R. 330, 95 F.T.R. 159 (note) (Fed. C.A.) — This was an appeal from a decision of the Trial Division which declared section 3(2)(f) of the *Refugee Claimants Designated Class Regulations ultra vires* of the Governor in Council.

The respondent was a citizen of Iran who arrived in Canada on November 16, 1986 and immediately claimed refugee status. His claim had not been dealt with when the *Refugee Claimants Designated Class Regulations* were brought into effect on December 27, 1989. To be eligible for the backlog, a claimant was required to have been in Canada on January 1, 1989 and to have signified before that date an intention to make a refugee claim.

Section 3(2)(f) provided that the class did not include a person who left Canada after the coming into force of the regulations, and remained outside of Canada for more than 7 days. In July 1990 the claimant attempted to cross into the United States surreptitiously. He was apprehended and it was necessary for him to spend 12 days in the United States before he was returned to Canada. On October 4, 1991 he was advised that he was not entitled to be dealt with under the backlog as he had absented himself from Canada for more than 7 days.

The practical effect of the backlog regulations was that those who fell within the designated class could, where found to have a credible basis for their claim, apply for landing.

It is not for a Court to determine the wisdom of delegated legislation or to assess its validity on the basis of the Court's policy preferences. The essential question is: does the statutory grant of authority permit this particular delegated legislation? In looking at the statutory source of authority, one must seek all possible indicia as to the purpose and scope of permitted delegated legislation. Any limitations, express or implied, must be taken into account. One must then look to the regulation to see whether it conforms and where it is argued that the regulation was not made for the purposes authorized by the statute, one must try to identify one or more of those purposes for which the regulation was adopted. A broad discretionary power, including a regulation making power, may not be used for a completely irrelevant purpose. The relevant powers are in sections 114(d) and (e) of the *Immigration Act*. These powers are to be exercised for the purposes of section 6(2) of the *Immigration Act*.

Section 6(2) authorizes the Governor in Council to designate classes of persons other than those already found to be Convention refugees, for purposes of admission. It requires that those classes include persons whose admission would be in accordance with Canada's humanitarian tradition with respect to the displaced and the persecuted. This does not mean that every regulation must facilitate the admission of more refugee claimants. This section combined with section 114(1)(e) authorizes regulations which classify such persons in some way and which may exempt some of those classes from some of the requirements of some of the regulations.

Section 6(2) and sections 114(d) and (e) authorize systems of classification of refugee claimants and the provision of preferential treatment for some or all of those classified. The backlog regulations might have excluded, from the backlog, anyone who had not remained in Canada constantly since making his or her claim. The regulations, whatever they may be, must, of course, be seen as in some way, related to the purpose of the Act, but this does not mean that a Court can review them to see if they are necessary, wise or effective in practice.

There was evidence on behalf of the appellant as to the purpose of the regulations. While some of the reasons were not compelling, and in some way may have been misconceived, the Court cannot say that they were completely unrelated to the purposes of the statute. Accordingly, section 3(2)(f) of the regulations is not *ultra vires* the Governor in Council.

Section 114(1)(e)

Mitra v. Canada (Minister of Citizenship & Immigration) (1996), 36 Imm. L.R. (2d) 213, 124 F.T.R. 98 (Fed. T.D.) — This is an application to set aside the decision of an immigration officer directing that an immigration inquiry be held regarding the applicant. In 1991, the applicant applied for a visa pursuant to the Foreign Domestic Workers programme. In order to meet the requirements to enter Canada, she made misrepresentations concerning her age, marital status and whether she had children. The applicant was admitted and subsequently lived and worked in Canada as a domestic worker. Canadian immigration authorities have in effect a policy not instituting removal proceedings against persons who have come to Canada under the Foreign Domestic Workers programme and who have made misrepresentations concerning their marital status and whether they have children.

After the applicant was made aware of this policy she advised the manager of the immigration centre in Prince George that she had made misrepresentations. At an interview regarding her misrepresentations the applicant executed a statutory declaration concerning the details. The applicant was advised that if she obtained a divorce from her husband she would be landed.

After receiving approval from the legal services society of British Columbia, the applicant retained a family law lawyer to initiate divorce proceedings against her husband in the Philippines. A letter was sent from the lawyer to immigration Canada stating that divorce proceedings had been commenced.

In January 1994, the applicant contacted the West Coast Domestic Workers Association, a publicly funded organization whose goal is to help domestic workers for the purpose of obtaining some assistance in their immigration matters. Counsel was assigned to the applicant and this counsel wrote to the manager of the immigration centre in Prince George and made representations on the applicant's behalf. Four days later the manager of the immigration centre directed that an inquiry be commenced.

At the inquiry, counsel conceded that misrepresentations had been made but took issue with the propriety of the proceeding. In December 1994, an adjudicator ruled that she did not have jurisdiction to review the procedure that resulted in the direction for inquiry being made. The adjudicator then issued a departure order against the applicant.

The application to quash the departure order was allowed. The evidence was clear that the respondent had in place a policy where by individuals in similar situations to the applicant would not be removed. There is no question that the respondent is at liberty to implement such a policy. Having done so, however, it was incumbent on the respondent to apply that policy to all concerned in an even handed and consistent manner. A public authority is required to exercise its discretionary power fairly and impartially. The applicant was making every possible effort to comply with the requirements of the policy by obtaining the necessary divorce. The applicant was not provided with advance notice that the direction for inquiry was to issue, nor has the respondent provided any reasonable explanation as to why that decision was made.

The Court found that there had been a breach of the duty of fairness and allowed the application.

Jafari v. Canada (Minister of Employment & Immigration), 30 Imm. L.R. (2d) 139, [1995] 2 F.C. 595, 125 D.L.R. (4th) 141, 180 N.R. 330, 95 F.T.R. 159 (note) (Fed. C.A.) — For digest, see section 114(1)(d), supra.

Dawkins v. Canada (Minister of Employment & Immigration), [1992] 1 F.C. 639, 45 F.T.R. 198 (Fed. T.D.) — The applicant sought an order quashing the decision of an Immigration officer that there were insufficient humanitarian and compassionate grounds for the exercise of discretion under section 114(2). It is not appropriate for a reviewing Court to interfere with the exercise of a statutorily granted discretion unless it is clear that this discretion was exercised unreasonably, in bad faith or was based on irrelevant considerations. The Court should not, in effect, substitute its own conclusion on an issue for that of the administrator vested with the discretion. The respondent Minister did not fetter the discretion of Immigration officers by preventing them from considering those in the refugee backlog as eligible for the same treatment as those in the illegal *de facto* resident policy on the ground that they had previously come to the attention of the respondent. It cannot seriously be disputed that general standards are necessary for the effective exercise of discretion in section 114(2) cases. This is necessary to ensure a certain level of consistency from one decision to another and to avoid a patchwork of arbitrary and haphazard decisions. Uniformity in decision making must be balanced against a need to consider individual cases on their own merits. There is a fundamental difference between humanitarian and compassionate considerations referred to in section 114(2) and public policy also referred to in section 114(2). Public policy has no objective content and must be defined by those having the authority to define public policy. Immigration officers do not have the right and obligation to define their own public policy. With respect to the humanitarian and compassionate considerations, the guidelines are not to be regarded as exhaustive and definitive but rather the officers are expected to use their best judgment. In the context of this case, the officer was found not to have fettered her discretion or to have acted unfairly or unreasonably and accordingly the application was dismissed.

Virk v. Canada (Minister of Employment & Immigration) (1991), 46 F.T.R. 145 (Fed. T.D.) — This was an application to quash an Immigration officer's refusal to find sufficient public policy grounds or humanitarian and compassionate considerations to justify relief under section 114(2) of the Act. When dealing with a matter of public policy, it is completely within the mandate of an Immigration officer to seek the advice of a supervisory authority. The spousal relationship and its effect on a section 114(2) application is a public policy issue. The guidelines state that no additional hardship need be established in cases of a genuine marriage. The guidelines also say that there is no obligation to deal favourably with spouses who are inadmissible under section 19 of the *Immigration Act*. In this case, the officer's decision to refuse relief under section 114(2) was upheld.

Johal v. Canada (Minister of Employment & Immigration) (1987), 4 Imm. L.R. (2d) 105, 15 F.T.R. 164 (Fed. T.D.) — The applicant had arrived in Canada in 1980 and was a valid visitor until May 14, 1981. The applicant then resided illegally in Canada until February 7, 1987, when he attended at a Canada Immigration Centre to apply for permanent resident status under the *de facto* illegal residents programme. The guidelines for this programme attempt to determine whether an illegal immigrant has economically and socially established himself in Canada. On February 16, 1987, the applicant was interviewed by an immigration officer, who then recommended to his manager that the application be favourably considered. The manager reviewed the officer's recommendation and concluded that the applicant did not meet the requirements of the programme. His decision was overturned by the Court because the guidelines for this programme were not followed nor were they applied fairly. The manager was required to do more than merely make a few telephone calls and meet with the officer in question before failing to accept the officer's recommendation. Further, the applicant was entitled to an opportunity to reply to some of the discrepancies which were affecting the manager's decision. Also, the applicant is required to establish that he has adapted himself socially to Canada. The manager had no information in this regard which would justify overturning the interviewing officer's recommendation. The Court pointed out that the shortage of personnel to handle these types of applications was no excuse for the application not being handled properly and fairly. Accordingly, the Court ordered the quashing of the decision of the respondent to refuse the applicant's application under the *de facto* illegal residents programme. Further, the Court directed the Minister to assess and determine the application under that programme in accordance with the guidelines set forth. Further, the Court ordered that the ongoing inquiry, in respect of the applicant, be prohibited from continuing.

De Gala v. Canada (Minister of Employment & Immigration) (1987), 8 F.T.R. 179 (Fed. T.D.) — The applicant was a 50-year-old single person from the Phillipines who came to Canada to work as a domestic for her niece. The applicant received negative initial and final assessments in interviews under the Foreign Domestic programme. Although the applicant was not a "new entrant" within the meaning of the Foreign Domestic guidelines, it was held that the "new entrant" portion of the guidelines applied to all domestics. The "guidelines or policy" as expressed in the Immigration Manual for the Foreign Domestic programme are significant and must be followed in order for procedural fairness to occur in a particular case. The applicant was not asked to contact a Canada Employment Centre for counselling and determination of training and skill upgrading needs. The evidence indicated that the interviewing officer was neither flexible nor lenient in either of the assessment interviews as required by the guidelines. The applicant had a grade 6 education as well as training as a seamstress, and this was held to be sufficient for someone seeking employment as a domestic.

The applicant was denied the use of her relative as an interpreter at the initial assessment and, in fact, no interpreter was provided. The Court observed that a person who is to be interviewed can and should be allowed to be accompanied during the interview. The Court observed, however, that the officer conducting the interview should have set conditions to prevent interference with the interview process. Failure to have a friend present who spoke English, as well as the failure to have an interpreter at the initial interview, and the conduct of the initial interview in English, undermined the assertion that the applicant was not sufficiently conversant in the English language to be able to establish herself in Canada. Accordingly, the applicant was found to have been treated in an unfair manner and the decision whereby she was found not to have demonstrated evidence of her ability to become self-sufficient in Canada was set aside.

Aboc v. Canada (Minister of Employment & Immigration) (1986), 7 F.T.R. 236 (Fed. T.D.) — The applicant arrived at Toronto International Airport in July 1982. She was interviewed in the usual way and ultimately was given an employment authorization, which the respondent at all times considered to be an authorization under the Foreign Domestic programme. There was no evidence of even a verbal explanation of the programme being given to the applicant at the time she entered Canada. The initial negative assessment was not communicated to the applicant. Subsequent assessments that questioned the genuineness of her degree in the Philippines were not communicated to the applicant. Due to the fact that no one had informed the applicant of what was expected of her, an order in the nature of *certiorari* setting aside the refusal to grant the applicant access to status in Canada under the Foreign Domestic programme was issued. Further, an order was made that the applicant be allowed to continue in Canada and to return to the situation the applicant was in at the port-of-entry when she first came here. This order directed that the applicant be treated as any other fresh applicant in the Foreign Domestic programme in accordance with the existing provisions of the Statute and Regulations.

Williams v. Canada (Minister of Employment & Immigration), [1985] 2 F.C. 153 (Fed. T.D.) — The applicant was born in Jamaica. She was unmarried and had 5 children, all of whom lived in Jamaica. The applicant arrived in Canada in September 1979 for a 3-week visit and remained in Canada ever since. The applicant was informed by a lawyer in late 1983 that the long-term illegal migrants' programme did not apply to her because she had not been "underground" for 5 years. On May 29, 1984, the applicant was apprehended and a deportation order was made June 8, 1984. Judicial review of this order was dismissed in November 1984. The applicant's removal in December 1984 was deferred in order that the applicant's case could be reviewed to determine whether she then qualified under the long-term illegal migrants' programme. The applicant did not qualify under the programme. During the period when the applicant's case was being considered, the long-term illegal migrants' programme was modified in such a way that the applicant would have been eligible for the programme but for the fact of her apprehension. The application to restrain the applicant's removal was dismissed. Where a person has been lawfully ordered deported, and the procedure that he or she wishes to invoke is a purely discretionary one in the hope that he or she might be granted a Minister's permit to stay in Canada, any requirement of fairness in the exercise of the Minister's discretion is minimal. Such a case does not involve a benefit to which the applicant is legally entitled nor denial of any rights legally vested in the applicant. There was no denial of fairness because the applicant did not, albeit for different reasons, come within the old or new guidelines of the long-term illegal migrants' programme.

Section 114(2)

On January 28, 1993, the Governor-in-counsel granted the Minister this authority in Regulation 2.1 of the *Immigration Act Regulations*. This Regulation gives the Minister the power to grant exemptions from any regulation on the basis of humanitarian and compassionate grounds. We have accordingly transferred the cases summarized under this subsection to Immigration Regulation 2.1, because the principles annunciated under those cases may still be important.

Orders

115. Powers of Minister — The Minister may, by order,

(a) establish such forms as the Minister deems necessary for the purposes of the administration of this Act, other than forms relating to claims, appeals and applications before the Refugee Division or the Appeal Division; and

(b) designate ports of entry and immigrant stations for the purposes of this Act.

R.S.C. 1985, c. 28 (4th Supp.), s. 30.

Evidence

116. (1) Proof of documents — Every document purporting to be a removal order, conditional removal order, rejection order, warrant, order, summons, direction or other document signed by the Minister, the Minister of Health, the Deputy Minister, an adjudicator, an immigration officer, a master or other person authorized or required by or under this Act to make the document is, in any prosecution or other proceeding under or arising out of this Act, evidence of the facts contained therein without proof of the signature or the official character of the person appearing to have signed the document, unless called into question by the Minister or any person acting for the Minister or for Her Majesty.

(2) Forms established by Minister — Every form purporting to be a form established by the Minister shall be deemed to be a form established by the Minister under this Act, unless called into question by the Minister or any person acting for the Minister or for Her Majesty.

(3) Certificates respecting international agreements — A document purporting to be a certificate issued by or under the authority of the Minister of Foreign Affairs stating

(a) that any convention, treaty or other international agreement was or was not in force and that Canada was or was not a party thereto, or

(b) that Canada agreed or did not agree to accept and apply the provisions of any convention, treaty or other international agreement in an armed conflict in which Canada was involved,

is admissible in evidence in any proceeding under this Act without proof of the signature or authority of the person appearing to have issued it, and is proof of the facts so stated.

R.S.C. 1985, c. 30 (3rd Supp.), s. 10; R.S.C. 1985, c. 28 (4th Supp.), s. 31; 1992, c. 49, s. 103; 1995, c. 5, s. 25; 1996, c. 8, s. 32.

Case Law

Douglas, Re (1981), 5 W.C.B. 354 (Ont. H.C.) — A detention order was signed by an immigration officer in a space designated "authorized officer and title." Section 118 had the effect of making this a valid detention order without proof of the signature or of the official character of the apparent signatory.

Jakubowski v. Canada (Minister of Employment & Immigration), [1980] 2 F.C. 448 (Fed. C.A.) — A memorandum purporting to be signed by a senior immigration officer, reciting that the officer had been informed that the applicant was not a Convention refugee and requiring the inquiry to resume, was evidence of the facts it contained unless called into question by the Minister or by a person acting for him or for Her Majesty.

Ramjit v. Canada (Minister of Manpower & Immigration) (1975), [1976] 1 F.C. 184 (Fed. C.A.) — The document read at the inquiry and referred to as a direction was not marked as an exhibit to the transcript. The Court held that there was nothing in the record of the proceedings to show, therefore, that the person who issued the direction was authorized to do so. The document was in fact marked as Exhibit "A", although the Exhibit "A" before the Federal Court did not correspond to what was described in the transcript and read at the proceedings.

117. Reports privileged — No security or criminal intelligence report, information or evidence referred to in subsection 39(2), section 40.1 or subsection 81(2) may be required to be produced in evidence before a court, person or body with jurisdiction to compel the production of information.

R.S.C. 1985, c. 29 (4th Supp.), s. 15; 1992, c. 49, s. 104.

Recovery of Payments, Costs and Fines

118. (1) Assignment of undertakings to provinces — Where any person or organization gives an undertaking to the Minister to assist any immigrant in becoming successfully established in Canada, that undertaking may by notice in writing be assigned by the Minister to Her Majesty in right of any province.

(2) Recovery for breach of undertaking — Any payments of a prescribed nature made directly or indirectly to an immigrant that result from a breach of an undertaking referred to in subsection (1) may be recovered from the person or organization that gave the undertaking in any court of competent jurisdiction as a debt due to Her Majesty in right of Canada or in right of any province to which the undertaking is assigned.

(3) Debt due to Crown — All costs incurred by Her Majesty for which any person is liable under this Act and all fines, court costs and administration fees imposed on or finally assessed against any person under this Act may be recovered as a debt due to Her Majesty.

(4) Charge on property — All costs incurred by Her Majesty in right of Canada or in right of any province for which any person or organization is liable under this Act and all fines, court costs and administration fees imposed on or finally assessed against any person or organization under this Act shall, until they are paid, be a charge on the property of the person or organization and may be enforced or collected by the seizure and sale of such property or a portion thereof under the warrant or order of a superior, county or district court.

1992, c. 49, s. 105.

Case Law

Section 118(2)

Bilson v. Kokotow (1978), 23 O.R. (2d) 720 (Ont. C.A.) — An undertaking to the Government of Canada to provide for the accommodation, care and maintenance of a prospective immigrant does not create any contractual right enforceable by the immigrant.

Loans to Immigrants

119. (1) Loans to immigrants — The Minister of Finance may, from time to time, advance to the Minister out of the Consolidated Revenue Fund such sums as the Minister may require to enable the Minister to make loans to such classes of immigrants and such other classes of persons as may be prescribed for the purpose of

(a) paying the costs of establishing that they and their families may be granted admission;

(b) paying the costs of obtaining transportation to Canada and transportation from the port of arrival to the place of destination in Canada for them and their families; and

(c) paying the reasonable living expenses of those persons and their families and such other expenses as are prescribed in order to assist those persons in establishing themselves successfully in Canada.

(2) **Repayment to Receiver General** — The Minister shall pay to the Receiver General all moneys the Minister receives by way of repayments of loans made under subsection (1) and all payments of interest thereon.

(3) **Limitation** — The total amount of outstanding advances to the Minister under subsection (1) shall not at any time exceed the amount prescribed under paragraph 114(1)(*u*.1).

(4) **Report to Parliament** — The Minister shall, within six months following the commencement of each fiscal year or, if Parliament is not then sitting, within the first fifteen days next thereafter that either house of Parliament is sitting, cause to be laid before Parliament a report setting out the total number and amount of loans made under subsection (1) during the preceding fiscal year.

R.S.C. 1985, c. 46 (2nd Supp.), s. 1; R.S.C. 1985, c. 1 (4th Supp.), s. 27; 1990, c. 38, s. 2; 1992, c. 49, s. 106.

Assistance on Leaving Canada

120. **Assistance in certain cases** — The Minister may direct that the costs of transportation from Canada and any related expenses be paid out of moneys appropriated by Parliament in the case of persons

(a) whose costs of transportation are not, under this Act, payable by a transportation company;

(b) who should, in the opinion of the Minister, be assisted in leaving Canada in order to avoid separation of a family or for other good cause; and

(c) who are, in the opinion of the Minister, unable to defray, without hardship, their own costs of transportation.

Delegation

121. (1) **Delegation of authority** — Subject to subsection (1.1), the Minister or the Deputy Minister, as the case may be, may authorize such persons employed in the public service of Canada as the Minister or Deputy Minister deems proper to exercise any of the powers and perform any of the duties and functions that may be or are required to be exercised or performed by the Minister or Deputy Minister, as the case may be, under this Act or the regulations.

(1.1) **Exception** — The Minister or the Deputy Minister, as the case may be, may not authorize the exercising of the powers or the performing of the duties and functions referred to in subsection 9(5), paragraphs 19(1)(*c*.2), (*f*), (*k*) and (*l*), subsections 39(2),

40(1) and 40.1(1), subparagraph 46.01(1)(*e*)(ii), paragraph 53(1)(*b*) and subsections 81(2) and 82(1).

(2) Idem — Any power exercised or duty or function performed under subsection (1) by any person authorized to exercise or perform it shall be deemed to have been exercised or performed by the Minister or Deputy Minister, as the case may be.

R.S.C. 1985, c. 28 (4th Supp.), s. 32; R.S.C. 1985, c. 29 (4th Supp.), s. 16; 1992, c. 1, s. 78; 1992, c. 49, s. 107; 1995, c. 15, s. 22.

Case Law

Keram v. Canada (Minister of Employment & Immigration) (1986), 72 N.R. 250 (Fed. C.A.) — The appellant, who was the subject of a removal order, had been denied Ministerial consent to return to Canada by an immigration official in New Delhi, India. This appeal from the decision of the Immigration Appeal Board was dismissed. Section 123 of the *Immigration Act* permits the Minister to delegate not only the power to consent but, also, the power to withhold consent.

Beeston v. Canada (Minister of Employment & Immigration) (1982), 132 D.L.R. (3d) 766, 41 N.R. 260 (Fed. C.A.) — The applicant applied for adjournment so that his request for a Minister's permit could be dealt with directly by the Minister of Employment and Immigration. The adjournment was refused because the manager of the immigration centre in Vancouver had already refused, on behalf of the Minister, the request for issuance of a Minister's permit. Because this authority had been delegated pursuant to the provisions of section 123 of the Act, it was held that the adjudicator was correct in refusing the request for an adjournment.

Transitional

122. Deemed date of landing — Where a person has been granted landing pursuant to an application made under subsection 124(1) of the *Immigration Act, 1976*, chapter 52 of the Statutes of Canada, 1976-77, that person shall, for the purpose of the *Citizenship Act*, be deemed to have been granted landing on the earlier of the day on which he came into Canada under the authority of the permit referred to in that subsection, or, where he is and has been in Canada under the authority of such a permit for a continuous period of time in excess of twelve months, the first day of that continuous period of time.

123. Deportation, effect of former act — Where a person acquired Canadian domicile in accordance with the *Immigration Act*, chapter I-2 of the Revised Statutes of Canada, 1970, and did not lose Canadian domicile before April 10, 1978, a deportation order may not be made against that person on the basis of any activity, carried on by him before that date, for which a deportation order could not have been made against him under that Act.

SCHEDULE

(Subsection 2(1))

Sections E and F of Article 1 of the United Nations Convention Relating to the Status of Refugees

E. This Convention shall not apply to a person who is recognized by the competent authorities of the country in which he has taken residence as having the rights and obligations which are attached to the possession of the nationality of that country.

F. The provisions of this Convention shall not apply to any person with respect to whom there are serious reasons for considering that:

(a) he has committed a crime against peace, a war crime, or a crime against humanity, as defined in the international instruments drawn up to make provision in respect of such crimes;

(b) he has committed a serious non-political crime outside the country of refuge prior to his admission to that country as a refugee;

(c) he has been guilty of acts contrary to the purposes and principles of the United Nations.

R.S.C. 1985, c. 28 (4th Supp.), s. 34.

Case Law

Brzezinski v. Canada (Minister of Citizenship & Immigration), 45 Imm. L.R. (2d) 262, [1998] 4 F.C. 525, 148 F.T.R. 296 (Fed. T.D.) — The applicants claimed Convention refugee status and they were determined by the tribunal to be excluded from the definition by reason of the fact that they had committed serious non-political crimes outside the country of refuge.

The evidence was that the applicants, who described themselves as gypsy's, supported themselves by stealing, both prior to seeking refuge in Canada and subsequently. Their stealing was by way of shoplifting.

The extent of theft and shoplifting in Canada may be a serious social problem. The acts of stealing acknowledged by the applicants are crimes. They are serious matters. They are not, however, serious crimes within the meaning of Article 1(F)(b), which is part of the laws of Canada through its incorporation in the Immigration Act. On the evidence in this case it appears that the applicants were charged with summary conviction offences in Canada. Their sentences ranged between fines and one 14-day period of detention. The sanction against the applicants repeated conduct, should they succeed in establishing their well-founded fear of persecution in Poland, must be found in Canada's Criminal and Immigration laws. The response however cannot be Article 1(F)(b).

Chan v. Canada (Minister of Citizenship & Immigration) (1999), 49 Imm. L.R. (2d) 11 (Fed. T.D.) — The applicant sought to review a decision of the CRDD, dismissing his claim for refugee status on the ground that he was excluded by virtue of Article 1, Section (F)(b). The Court noted that the decision of the Supreme Court of Canada in *Pushpanathan v. Canada (Minister of Citizenship & Immigration)*, [1998] 1 S.C.R. 982, held that drug trafficking offences were not included in Article 1(F)(c).

The Court concluded that the panel was correct in its determination that in the circumstances of this case the applicant was excluded by reason of Article 1(F)(b). The panel rightfully took into account that while the appellants conviction was for the unlawful use of a communications facility, that conviction arose out of an offence involving serious drug trafficking in which the applicant and at least one other person were involved. Accordingly, the application of judicial review was dismissed.

Shahpari v. Canada (Minister of Citizenship & Immigration) (1998), 44 Imm. L.R. (2d) 139, 146 F.T.R. 102 (Fed. T.D.) — The applicants sought to review the question of whether section E of Article I of the *Geneva Convention* applied to them. The applicants were citizens of Iran. In 1984 they moved to France and after seven years of temporary residence in France were issued a "Carte de Resident" which was valid for 10 years. After residing in France until 1994, the applicants came to Canada and within one month made a refugee application.

The burden of proving that section E applies rests with the party asserting it, in this case the respondent. It did not assist the applicant in this case that she allowed her visa to expire. The evidence allowed the panel to conclude that the visa could be renewed. Applicants should remember that actions they themselves take, which are intended to result in their not being able to return to a country which has already granted them refugee status, may well evidence an absence of the subjective fear of persecution in their original country. Further, if applicants are entitled to renounce the protection they receive from one country and claim protection from another, it gives them a right to emigrate to another country without complying with the usual requirements, solely by reason of their unilateral renunciation of the protection that they have been afforded by the country they are leaving.

Bamlaku v. Canada (Minister of Citizenship & Immigration) (1998), 142 F.T.R. 140 (Fed. T.D.) — The applicant sought to review a negative decision of the CRDD, which was based on the applicant's being excluded from protection pursuant to section F(a) of Article 1 of the Convention. The applicant joined the Marine Transportation Authority in Ethiopia where he was assigned to security duties at a strategic facility comprised of a port and oil refinery. The applicant informed on some or all of the individuals he investigated to security forces of the government notwithstanding his opposition to the government. He also secretly joined the Ethiopian People's Revolutionary Party. The applicant then informed against persons who were enemies of the Ethiopian People's Revolutionary Party and turned them over to the security forces of the Ethiopian government. The result was that these persons were arrested, detained and probably tortured. The applicant expressed no remorse at this result. He acknowledged that his motivation was mixed — partly they were enemies of the Ethiopian People's Revolutionary Party and partly he feared they represented threats of terrorist activity against the oil refinery in respect of which he was employed. The applicant testified that any such terrorist activity would have resulted in significant civilian casualties.

The CRDD made no reviewable error. The applicant in informing on the persons in question was not motivated by humanitarian considerations alone. The applicant was also motivated by the fact that such persons were enemies of the Ethiopian People's Revolutionary Party. The tribunal had reasons for considering that the applicant was a person within the scope of Section F and was accordingly its decision was not reviewable.

Pushpanathan v. Canada (Minister of Employment & Immigration) (1998), 226 N.R. 201, (sub nom. *Pushpanathan v. Canada (Minister of Citizenship & Immigration))* 160 D.L.R. (4th) 193, (sub nom. *Pushpanathan v. Canada (Minister of Citizenship & Immigration))* [1998] 1 S.C.R. 982, 43 Imm. L.R. (2d) 117, 11 Admin. L.R. (3d) 1 (S.C.C.); amended (sub nom. *Pushpanathan v. Canada (Minister of Citizenship & Immigration))* [1998] 1 S.C.R. 1222, 11 Admin. L.R. (3d) 130 (S.C.C.) — This appeal raised two questions, firstly, the standard of judicial review over decisions of the IRB and secondly, the meaning of the exclusion from refugee status set out in Article 1F(c) of the *United Nations Convention Relating to the Status of Refugees*. The appellant left Sri Lanka in 1983 and spent time in India and France before arriving in Canada via Italy in March 1985. He claimed Convention refugee status. The claim was never adjudicated on because the appellant was granted permanent resident status in May 1987 under an administrative program. In December 1987, the appellant was arrested and charged with conspiracy to traffic in heroin. The appellant was convicted and sentenced to eight years in prison.

In September 1991, the appellant, then on parole, renewed his claim to Convention refugee status. In June 1992, a conditional deportation order was issued against the appellant. Deportation was conditional upon a determination that the claimant was not a Convention refugee and accordingly the appellant's claim was referred to the CRDD. The Board decided that the appellant was not a Convention refugee. The Federal Court Trial Division and the Federal Court of Appeal refused to reverse that decision on an application for judicial review.

A correctness standard applies to the determinations of law by the IRB.

Conspiracy to traffic in a narcotic is not a violation of Article 1F(c) of the *United Nations Convention Relating to the Status of Refugees.*

Even though international trafficking in drugs is an extremely serious problem that the United Nations has taken extraordinary measures to eradicate, in the absence of clear indications that the international community recognizes drug trafficking as a sufficiently serious and sustained violation of fundamental human rights as to amount to persecution, either through a specific designation as an act contrary to the purposes and principles of the United Nations, or through international instruments which otherwise indicate that trafficking is a serious violation of fundamental human rights, individuals should not be deprived of the essential protections contained in the Convention for having committed those acts.

Ledezma v. Canada (Minister of Citizenship & Immigration) (November 5, 1997), Doc. IMM-3785-96 (Fed. T.D.) — The applicants sought to review a negative decision with respect to their claim for refugee status.

The Board rejected the refugee claim because of a lack of credible and trustworthy evidence from the principal applicant with respect to his persecution for his political beliefs. In addition, the Board concluded that the applicant was excluded under Article 1(F)(a) of the UN convention for being an accomplice to crimes against humanity.

The Court elected to review the exclusion order to ensure that it was error free, even though the decision about the exclusion would not be dispositive of the judicial review application. Exclusion by Canada under Article 1(F)(a) of the Convention is a serious matter which could affect the applicant for the rest of his life and accordingly, even though the Board's decision would stand on the basis of its credibility findings, the Court agreed to undertake a review of the exclusion order.

Suliman v. Canada (Minister of Citizenship & Immigration) (1997), 133 F.T.R. 178 (Fed. T.D.) — The applicants sought to review a negative decision of a panel of the CRDD. The Board found that the male applicant was excluded under Article 1(F)(a) of the Convention, on the basis that he committed crimes against humanity. The decision of the panel was set aside. The Board did not expressly consider whether the crimes committed by the police constituted crimes against humanity. Crimes against humanity must generally be committed in a wide spread systematic fashion. This requirement does not mean that a crime against humanity cannot be committed against one person, but in order to elevate a domestic crime such as murder or assault to the realm of international law an additional element will have to be found. This element is that the person who has been victimized is a member of a group which has been targeted systematically and in a widespread manner for one of the crimes of murder, extermination, enslavement, deportation or other inhuman acts. The Board should have considered whether the victims of police abuse in this case were "...members of a group which have been targeted systematically and in a widespread manner for one of the crimes mentioned..."

Hamdan v. Canada (Minister of Citizenship & Immigration) (1997), 38 Imm. L.R. (2d) 20 (Fed. T.D.) — This was an application to review a negative decision of the CRDD. The applicant, a citizen of Iraq, claimed refugee status in February 1995. Before coming to Canada the applicant had resided in the Philippines since May 1986. From 1986 until 1992 he had legal status in the Philippines as a student. After the expiry of his student visa, he stayed in the Philippines illegally for approximately one year. He tried to come to Canada with false travel documents, but was turned back in Hong Kong. He returned to the Philippines and subsequently filed a refugee claim with the United Nations High Commissioner for Refugees. His claim was accepted. The fact that the applicant has a well founded fear of persecution in Iraq was confirmed by the board and was not at issue in this application. The board determined that the applicant was not a convention refugee on the basis of the exclusion in Article 1(E) of the convention.

Article 1(E) is incorporated into Canadian law under section 2 of the *Immigration Act* under the definition of convention refugee. The primary source for understanding the meaning and application of Article 1(E) must the text of the article itself. It is clear that the article is intended to operate where a person has been recognized "as having the rights and obligations which are attached to the possession of the nationality" of the country in which he has taken residence. With respect to the criteria in *Shamlou v. Canada* (1995), 103 F.T.R. 241, the Court observed that the relevant criteria would change depending on the rights which normally accrue to citizens in the country which is being scrutinized. The Court did not comment on whether all the criteria set out in the *Shamlou* case must be satisfied for exclusion under Article 1(E). In this case, the Court found it to be critical that the applicant had neither the right to work nor the right to receive social services in the Philippines.

Accordingly, the Court concluded that the board had applied the wrong test in determining that the applicant had the rights and obligations attaching to nationality of the Philippines. The decision of the board was set aside and the matter remitted back for rehearing by a freshly constituted panel.

Wassiq v. Canada (Minister of Citizenship & Immigration) (1996), 33 Imm. L.R. (2d) 238, 112 F.T.R. 143 (Fed. T.D.) — The applicants applied to review a negative decision of the IRB. The applicants were citizens of Afghanistan. In 1981, they successfully applied as Convention refugees in Germany. In 1991, they left Germany and came to Canada and sought refugee status here.

A panel of the IRB had decided that the applicants had a wellfounded fear of persecution in respect of Afghanistan, but that Canada had assumed responsibility for them and that Germany was obliged to allow them to return. Therefore, the Board found that the convention did not apply to the applicants by virtue of Section E of Article 1.

Refugee claims were never meant to allow a claimant to seek out better protection than that from which he or she already benefitted. If by reason of their absence from Germany and sojourn in Canada, the applicants were in effect entitled to renounce the protection they received from Germany and claim protection from Canada such a result would be anomalous. In substance, it would give a person who had Convention refugee status in one country the right to emigrate to another country without complying with the usual requirements.

Whether Canada or Germany should be responsible for the applicants should ideally be determined as between the governments of Canada and Germany. A decision of a panel of the IRB that Germany should have responsibility for the applicants, which is in effect the decision in this case, is not binding on Germany. The real issue is whether Germany recognizes that the applicants may return.

On the evidence before it, the panel could not have arrived at such a conclusion and therefore could not have found that section E of Article 1 was applicable to the applicants. Accordingly, the application for judicial review was allowed and the matter remitted back to a differently constituted panel.

Kanesharan v. Canada (Minister of Citizenship & Immigration) (1996), 35 Imm. L.R. (2d) 185, 120 F.T.R. 67 (Fed. T.D.) — The applicant a Sri Lankan Tamil fled Sri Lanka and went to the United Kingdom in 1990. In 1991, the applicant unsuccessfully applied for convention refugee status in the U.K. The applicant was however given permission to remain in the U.K. until September 1993. This right to remain included the right to make trips from and to the United Kingdom during that period. This right was extended to May 1997. The applicant eventually made his way to Canada where he made a claim which was the subject of this application.

A panel of the IRB decided that Article 1(E) of the 1951 U.N. convention applied to the applicant. Thus, the issue before the Federal Court was whether, with respect to the United Kingdom, the applicant had the rights and obligations which are normally attached to persons possessing U.K. nationality.

The Court noted that in the United Kingdom, the home office reserved the right to remove persons similarly situated to the applicant to their country of nationality should the prevailing circumstances change significantly in a positive manner. Further, the Court noted it was only in 1997, when the applicant's extended right to remain in the U.K. had concluded that the applicant would be considered by the home office to be eligible for indefinite leave to remain in that country.

Accordingly, the Court found that article 1(e) of the U.N. convention did not apply to the applicant, quashed the decision of the IRB and remitted the matter back for reconsideration.

Bazargan v. Canada (Ministre de l'Emploi & de l'Immigration) (1996), 205 N.R. 282, 119 F.T.R. 240 (note) (Fed. C.A.) — The respondent joined the Iranian national police in 1960 and pursued his career there until 1980. Between 1960 and 1977, he climbed the ranks of the military hierarchy and became a colonel. From 1974 to 1977, he worked in Tehran as the officer in charge of liaison between the police forces and SAVAK. SAVAK, from which the respondent had received some of his training, was an internal security agency under the Shah's personal authority. During that period, the respondent was in charge of the network for exchanging classified information between the police forces and SAVAK. The respondent was appointed to that position because of his knowledge of intelligence, espionage and counterespionage. In 1977, the respondent, became a chief of the police forces in a province in southwestern Iran and held that position until the fall of the monarchist regime in 1979.

A panel of the IRB had determined that the respondent was a refugee within the meaning of subsection 2(1) but that he was excluded from convention protection due to article 1(F). This decision was overturned by the motions judge on a judicial review application. A court of appeal allowed the appeal and reinstated the decision of the panel of the IRB.

The Court has expressly refused to make formal membership in an organization a condition for the exclusion to apply. Membership in an organization that committed atrocities helps to determine whether the condition of personal and knowing participation has been met. It is important not to turn what is actually a factual presumption into a legal condition.

The Minister does not have to prove the respondent's guilt. The minister has to show that there is serious reason for considering that the respondent is guilty, the burden of proof resting on a minister is "less than a balance of probabilities".

In this appeal the inferences and the conclusions of the panel were based on the evidence and were reasonable. The IRB is a specialized tribunal and it has complete jurisdiction to draw the inferences that can reasonably be drawn.

Sumaida v. Canada (Minister of Citizenship & Immigration) (1995), 35 Imm. L.R. (2d) 315, 116 F.T.R. 1 (Fed. T.D.) — The applicant applied for judicial review of a negative decision of a panel of the IRB. The applicant was a citizen of Iraq. As a student in England he voluntarily served Iraq by reporting to the Iraqi secret police the names of members of a group opposed to the government in Iraq. The group in question was an organization supported by the Shia community in Iraq. It was aligned with the government of Iran and its political and military aims were the overthrow of the Iraq government and the establishment of an Iranian style theocracy in Iraq.

On the question of whether the applicant was excluded pursuant to section F of article 1 of the United Nations convention, the Court noted that the appropriate definition of crimes against humanity speaks of crimes or acts committed against "any civilian population". The board did not address the meaning "civilian" and thus did not consider whether in the murky world of terrorism it would be possible for the members of the sect involved to be considered non-civilians. Accordingly, the decision of the board was set aside.

Pushpanathan v. Canada (Minister of Citizenship & Immigration) (1995), 191 N.R. 247 (Fed. C.A.) — The appellant left Sri Lanka in May 1983 and spent nearly two years in India. He then proceeded to Canada by way of France and Italy arriving here on March 21, 1985 where upon he made a claim for Convention refugee status. In December, 1987 the appellant was among 8 individuals arrested on charges of conspiracy to traffic in heroin. He received an 8 year sentence and was released on parole. A panel of the IRB determined that the appellant was excluded from entitlement to claim the status of a Convention refugee due to paragraph F(c) of Article 1 of the *International Convention on the Status of Refugees.*

The Court of Appeal upheld the decision of the Trial Division and concluded that paragraph F(c) of Article 1 can apply to acts committed by a refugee claimant after his arrival in Canada. It was also held that the paragraph can apply to persons otherwise within his terms, even with respect to acts not committed in the name of, or on behalf of a state. Article 1 of the Convention is dedicated to defining which individuals may have the right, in international law, to be recognized as refugees. The exceptions, found in paragraph F, deny refugee status to certain individuals who might otherwise be within the global definition. Finally, the Court concluded that trafficking in narcotics was an act contrary to the purposes and principles of the United Nations. The Court pointed out that the United Nations adopted a Convention against the illicit traffic in narcotics in 1988 and that this Convention was ratified by Canada in 1988. This Convention called upon Canada and other signatory states to establish criminal offenses domestically to prevent, among other things, trafficking in narcotics. In Canada, such a measure was the *Narcotic Control Act*, which is the law under which the appellant was convicted. Accordingly, trafficking in narcotics is contrary to the purposes and principles of the United Nations and the appellant was properly excluded from the refugee process. Accordingly, the appeal was dismissed.

Atef v. Canada (Minister of Citizenship & Immigration), [1995] 3 F.C. 86, 96 F.T.R. 217, 32 Imm. L.R. (2d) 106 — This was an application to review a negative decision of a panel of the CRDD which had concluded that the applicant was a person to whom section F(c) of Article 1 of the *United Nations Convention Relating to the Status of Refugees* applied.

The applicant, a citizen of Iran, was convicted in Canada of possession of heroin for the purpose of trafficking.

It was not necessary for the panel to determine whether the applicant was a Convention refugee within the meaning of the definition. There is no requirement for the Board to determine this question when applying Article 1F(c) of the Convention. The panel could have conducted an inclusion analysis, but there was no error in not so doing.

The applicant raised arguments suggesting that his rights under sections 7 and 12 of the Charter had been infringed. The panel correctly determined that these arguments were premature. The panel was dealing with the question of whether the applicant was entitled to claim refugee status and not with the execution of the deportation order. The exclusion of an individual from claiming such status does not, by itself, imply or lead to any positive act which may affect the life, liberty or security of the person. This type of reasoning also lead to a conclusion that the applicant's arguments with respect to section 12 of the Charter were also premature.

Finally, the applicant contended that the definition of Convention refugee, which incorporated Article 1F(c) of the Convention, violated the applicant's right to fundamental justice under section 7 of the Charter on account of vagueness. It was argued that Article 1F(c) provided no substantive notice to society in the sense that society was given no notice of what actions are contrary to the principles and purposes of the United Nations. Further it was argued that Article 1F(c) did not provide meaningful boundaries of conduct or delineate areas of risk because the general public is unaware of the initiatives taken by the United Nations to curb drug trafficking.

The doctrine of vagueness is founded on the principles of fair notice to citizens and the limitation of enforcement discretion. Fair notice comprises two aspects:

1. A formal aspect, namely, an acquaintance with the actual text of the statute; and,

2. A substantive aspect, namely, an understanding that certain conduct is the subject of legal restrictions.

The limitation of enforcement discretion relates to the fact that a law must not be so imprecise that the power to decide becomes fused with the power to prosecute. The various factors to be considered in determining whether a law is vague are:

A. The need for flexibility and the interpretative role of the Courts;

B. The impossibility of achieving absolute certainty, a standard of intelligibility being more appropriate; and,

C. The possibility that many varying judicial interpretations of a given disposition may exist and perhaps co-exist.

Applying those factors the Court concluded that Article 1F(c) was not unconstitutionally vague.

Arica v. Canada (Minister of Employment & Immigration) (1995), 182 N.R. 392 (Fed. C.A.) — The appellant was denied refugee status because there were serious reasons for considering that he had been involved in acts constituting crimes against humanity.

Under section 69.1(5) there is no obligation on the Minister to give notice to claimants of the former's intention to participate in the hearing. The purpose of the notice, which is directed solely at the Board, is to empower the Minister to question a claimant and other witnesses and to make representations, otherwise the Minister's participation is limited to the presentation of evidence.

Further, the Board was not required to balance the nature of the crimes committed by the appellant against the fate that awaits him should he be returned to Peru. This was the finding of the Court in *Gonzalez v. Canada (Minister of Employment & Immigration)* (1994), 24

Imm. L.R. (2d) 229. Section 7 of the Charter, which was not argued in the *Gonzalez* case, does not alter the extant law. A decision in which it was found that the appellant was not entitled to claim refugee status does not, by itself, imply or lead to any positive act which may affect the life, liberty or security of the person.

Kabirian v. Canada (Solicitor General) (1995), 93 F.T.R. 222 (Fed. T.D.) — The panel of the CRDD concluded that there was a reasonable possibility that the applicant would be persecuted if he were to return to Iran. Despite this conclusion the tribunal found that the applicant was excluded from the definition of Convention refugee under section F(c) of Article 1 of the Convention.

The applicant deserted the Iranian Army and took refuge in Canada in 1985. In October, 1986 he was convicted of trafficking 26 grams of heroin and sentenced to 3 years in prison. In view of the unresolved ambiguity concerning the intention of the signatories to the Convention with respect to the scope of section F(c), the subsequent conventions and protocols of the United Nations concerning the struggle against drug trafficking should be considered when interpreting the words "...contrary to the purposes and principles of the United Nations".

Section F(c) of Article 1 of the Convention is applicable to someone convicted of heroin trafficking in Canada, even in the absence of proof of an international aspect to his crime. The activities of the United Nations in the struggle against illegal drug trafficking are conducted both internationally and nationally. Further, a trafficker constitutes an indispensable link in the chain of distribution of drugs.

The panel did not err in concluding that section F(c) of Article 1 of the Convention applied to the applicant.

Srour v. Canada (Solicitor General) (1995), 91 F.T.R. 24 — The applicant, a citizen of Lebanon, was denied refugee status on the basis that he was a person covered by section F(a) of Article 1 of the U.N. Convention. The Court reviewed the principles that govern this exclusion and reaffirmed that it was unnecessary to analyze the validity of the applicant's fear of persecution if the exclusion applied.

After reviewing the principles the Court applied them in this case and concluded that the applicant was rightly excluded from the definition.

Kroon v. Canada (Minister of Employment & Immigration) (1995), 89 F.T.R. 236 — The applicant, his wife and children sought to set aside a negative decision of the CRDD. The panel concluded that although the claimants may subjectively fear persecution in Estonia, what they suffered or might suffer is discrimination at most. Their claims that they face a reasonable chance of persecution were held to be not well founded. The purpose of Article 1E of the U.N. Convention is to support regular immigration laws of countries in the international community. If a person faces threat of persecution in his own country but is living in another country, with or without refugee status, and there faces no threat of persecution, but rather enjoys the same basic rights as nationals of the second country, then the function of Article 1E is to exclude such a person as a potential refugee claimant in Canada. The panel did not err by considering the basic rights which the applicant was apparently entitled to under the Constitution and laws of Estonia, and comparing those with the rights acknowledged for Estonian nationals. The tribunal's assessments of the rights to which the male applicant would be entitled were he to return and register in Estonia as a foreign national cannot be said to be in error. In light of the special role and expertise of the CRDD the Court should defer to the tribunal's assessment on issues of this sort which fall within its particular specialized capacities, unless the tribunal's finding is found to be patently unreasonable.

Malouf v. Canada (Minister of Citizenship & Immigration) (1994), 26 Imm. L.R. (2d) 20, 86 F.T.R. 124, [1995] 1 F.C. 537 — The applicant sought to overturn an unfavourable decision of the CRDD. The applicant, who was a citizen of Lebanon, left there in 1977 and obtained permanent resident status in the United States. The applicant pleaded guilty to possession of cocaine for the purpose of trafficking and fled to Canada before his sentencing.

The panel excluded the applicant from the refugee process by applying the exclusion in section F(b) of Article 1 of the Convention. That section excluded the applicant from the protection of the Geneva Convention on the basis that he had committed a serious, non-political crime outside of Canada and prior to his admission to Canada. Once the panel concluded that the exclusion clause might apply to the applicant, it should have, through the Refugee Hearing Officer, given notice to the Minister and provided an opportunity for the Minister to make representations. Then, whether or not the Minister intervened, it would have been open to the panel to conclude that the exclusion clause applied to the applicant.

For purposes of section F(b) the country of refuge was Canada, notwithstanding the fact that there was more than one country of refuge. There were serious reasons for considering that the applicant had committed a serious non-political crime outside of Canada, prior to his admission to Canada as a refugee claimant, that is, in the United States.

The CRDD erred in failing to consider the applicant's Convention refugee claim as against Lebanon and in failing to balance the risk to the applicant that would flow from his return to Lebanon by reason of the exclusion clause against the seriousness of the non-political crime here at issue. Once that balancing was conducted, the panel would have been in a position to determine whether the serious non-political crimes were of such a nature as to warrant the application of the exclusion clause, and the imposition on the applicant of the risk that would flow from his return to Lebanon. No balancing would be required had the panel concluded that the applicant was not, in fact, a refugee from Lebanon.

Gil v. Canada (Minister of Employment & Immigration) (1994), 25 Imm. L.R. (2d) 209, 174 N.R. 292, 119 D.L.R. (4th) 497, [1995] 1 F.C. 508 (C.A.) — This case raises the question of what is meant by the phrase a "serious non-political crime" in section F of Article 1 of the Convention.

The appellant is an Iranian citizen, the son of a wealthy family which had been an active supporter of the Shah's regime. The family experienced considerable difficulties after the coming into power of the government that overthrew the Shah. The appellant joined an underground student group and, in due course, became associated with a larger militant group of anti-government activists. In the years 1980 and 1981 the appellant personally took part in five or six incidents of bombing and arson. Those attacks were directed against wealthy supporters of the regime. These incidents lead to the injury and death of innocent bystanders. The appellant was arrested and interrogated by the authorities but never confessed to his activities and he was ultimately released by the authorities, without being charged, and eventually fled to Canada.

A panel of the CRDD found that the appellant had a well-founded fear of persecution but that he was excluded by the provision in section 1F(b) of the Convention.

A panel of the CRDD concluded that the appellant's crimes were non-political. Accordingly, the appeal raised the question of what was meant by political crime. The characterization of crimes as political is found in both extradition and refugee law. The Court noted that there was a need for even greater caution characterizing the crime as political for the purposes of applying section 1F(b) than for the purpose of denying extradition. The Court developed an incidence test as a means of resolving whether a crime is political. The appellant met the first branch of the test because Iran, in the years in question, was a turbulent society in which a number of armed groups were in conflict with the regime and the appellant's testimony that he was a member of one such group was accepted as credible. The appellant's claim failed the second branch of the test. There was no objective rational connection between injuring the commercial interests of certain wealthy supporters and any realistic goal of forcing the regime itself to fall or change. Further, the means used by the appellant excluded his crimes from any claim to be political in nature. The attacks were not carried out against armed adversaries and were bound to injure innocent bystanders. The use of deadly force against unarmed civilian commercial targets in circumstances where serious injury or death to innocent bystanders was inevitable rendered the violence used wholly disproportionate to any legitimate political objective.

Randhawa v. Canada (Minister of Employment & Immigration) (1994), 93 F.T.R. 151 — The applicant was found to have a well-founded fear for a Convention reason but was excluded as an accomplice in the commission of crimes against humanity. The applicant was a member of the Punjab State Police Force. He testified that he was aware that that organization regularly tortured and murdered suspects in the course of its investigation. The applicant testified about 3 instances where he refused to abuse prisoners with whom he was involved. Ultimately, he was asked to resign by reason of irreconcilable differences of opinion with the police.

There was no evidence before the Board about why the applicant did not resign until he was asked. He was not questioned about this issue, thus to draw an inference from the fact that he did not resign earlier, and to make a finding of a shared common purpose based on that inference, was an error. The preponderance of evidence was to the effect that the applicant shared no common purpose with the police force, notwithstanding the fact that he knew about its activities.

The finding that the applicant was an accomplice was a perverse finding because it was not supported by the evidence. Accordingly, the application was allowed and the matter was directed to be redetermined, without a hearing, in accordance with the reasons of the Court.

Thamotharampillai v. Canada (Minister of Employment & Immigration), [1994] 3 F.C. 99, 77 F.T.R. 114 — This was an application for judicial review of a negative decision of the CRDD. The applicant was found, by the relevant minister of the Government of Canada in February of 1985, to be a Convention refugee. On the 30th day of August, 1990 he was convicted of conspiracy to traffic in a narcotic and sentenced to three years. The CRDD found the applicant to have a well-founded fear of persecution. It found the applicant not to have an internal flight alternative. Despite these findings, it found the applicant not to be a Convention refugee as he was a person to whom the Convention did not apply because, in the terms of Article 1F(c) of the Convention, he was a person with respect to whom there were serious reasons for considering that he had been guilty of acts contrary to the purposes and principles of the United Nations. The crime committed by the applicant was one with international implications. Heroin was not a locally-produced narcotic. The crime in question was a crime against which the United Nations has initiated, coordinated and undertaken a range of international initiatives. It was a crime within Canada that potentially had fearful social, cultural and humanitarian, to say nothing of its economic, repercussions. Accordingly, the CRDD was correct in concluding that Article 1F(c) of the Convention excluded the applicant from Convention refugee status.

Gonzalez v. Canada (Minister of Employment & Immigration), [1994] 3 F.C. 646, 24 Imm. L.R. (2d) 229, 170 N.R. 302, 115 D.L.R. (4th) 403 (Fed. C.A.) — This was an appeal from a decision of the Refugee Division, which found the appellant excluded from the definition of Convention refugee by reason of section F(a) of Article 1 of the *United Nations Convention Relating to the Status of Refugees* because the Board found that there was serious reason to believe that the appellant had committed a crime against humanity. The Board proceeded directly to that finding and made no finding on the merits of the refugee claim. The appellant had admitted to killing civilians on two occasions when his military unit in Nicaragua encountered armed counter-revolutionaries. The Court noted that as a practical matter it would have been better had the Refugee Division dealt with the merits of the claim as well as the applicability of the exclusion. The Court noted that if the claim was well-founded but for the application of the exclusion and if it were found on appeal that the exclusion had been wrongly applied to the appellant, then the Court could have made the necessary declaration without requiring the Refugee Division to deal with the matter again. The Court found that, on the particular facts and circumstances of this case, the appellant was a soldier engaged in an action against an armed enemy and that his actual participation in the killing of innocent civilians fell short of a crime against humanity. The Court indicated that it did not wish to be understood as saying that the killing of civilians by a soldier while engaged in an action against an armed enemy could never amount to a war crime or a crime against humanity, each case will depend on its own individual facts and circumstances.

Equizabal v. Canada (Minister of Employment & Immigration), 24 Imm. L.R. (2d) 277, [1994] 3 F.C. 514, 170 N.R. 329 (Fed. C.A.) — The appellant was denied refugee status on the basis that he was included in Article 1(F) of the Convention and therefore excluded from the definition of refugee. The specific finding of the CRDD was that the appellant had committed crimes against humanity by torturing civilians. The appellant sought and obtained leave to apply for judicial review, which application was dismissed. The Trial Division judge certified a serious question of general importance.

The appellant was a citizen of Guatemala who was forcibly recruited by the Guatemalan military. He described in his evidence before the CRDD four military missions which involved the torture of civilians. A crime against humanity is not only a domestic offence, but is rather an offence with the additional component of barbarous cruelty. On the uncontradicted evidence of the appellant, it is obvious that he was guilty of barbarous cruelty in the four incidents he described in his evidence.

The defence of obedience to the orders of a superior based on compulsion was also considered. The first matter to be assessed was whether the orders in issue were manifestly unlawful. A manifestly unlawful order must be one that offends the conscience of every reasonable right-thinking person. It must be an order which is obviously and flagrantly wrong. The Court had no difficulty in concluding that the orders here in issue were manifestly unlawful. The appellant and two other soldiers were ordered on one occasion to beat four persons and torture them over a period of three hours. Torturing the truth out of someone is manifestly unlawful, by any standard.

On the question of compulsion, the issue was whether the appellant faced an imminent, real and inevitable threat to his life. Stern punishment or demotion would not be sufficient. The appellant's evidence summarized two reasons why, notwithstanding his understanding that the penalty for desertion was only twelve months in jail, he would be killed: firstly, he knew of three other deserters who were apprehended and never heard from again; secondly, he believed he would be killed by his lieutenant because of his knowledge of relatives of persons whom the lieutenant had tortured personally. The first reason was dismissed as it was pure speculation without any credible evidence to support it. The second reason was not supported by the record. The record established that before the third mission, the appellant advised his lieutenant that he would no longer participate in such torture. As a result he was never forced to torture anyone again. He was thereafter, on two occasions, assigned to act as a guard while others did the torturing. There was, therefore, no evidence that the appellant was facing an imminent, real and inevitable threat to his life.

Accordingly, the appeal was dismissed and the decision that the appellant had committed a crime against humanity, as that expression appears in Article 1F of the *Convention relating to the status of refugees*, was upheld.

Cardenas v. Canada (Minister of Employment & Immigration) (1994), 74 F.T.R. 214 — The applicant was unsuccessful in his claim for refugee status because he was found to have been an accomplice to crimes against humanity. The applicant was from Chile and had an association with the political faction, the Manuel Rodriguez Patriotic Front. In quashing the Board's decision, the Court noted that the Board had made little effort to link the applicant to specific criminal activities. Rather, it chose to refer only in general terms to shootings and bombings. The Board should have endeavoured to carefully detail the criminal acts which it considered the applicant to have committed.

The Board's decision was quashed on this and other grounds.

Sivakumar v. Canada (Minister of Employment & Immigration) (1993), 163 N.R. 197, [1994] 1 F.C. 433 (Fed. C.A.), leave to appeal to S.C.C. refused (1996), 175 N.R. 324 (note) (S.C.C.) — The appellant was found to have a well-founded fear of persecution at the hands of the Sri Lankan government on the basis of his political opinion. The Refugee Division decided to exclude the appellant on the basis of section 1(F)(a) of Article 1 of the *United Nations Convention Relating to the Status of Refugees* as someone who had committed crimes against humanity.

It is possible to be liable for war crimes as an accomplice even though one has not personally committed the acts amounting to the crime. The starting point for complicity in an international crime is "personal and knowing participation". Mere by-standers or on-lookers are not accomplices. A person who aids in or encourages the commission of a crime, or a person who willingly stands guard while it is being committed, is usually responsible, although each case will depend upon its own facts. Further, those involved in planning or conspiring to commit a crime, even thought not personally present at the scene, might also be accomplices, depending on the facts of the case. Additionally, a commander may be responsible for international crimes committed by those under his command, but only if there is knowledge or reason to know about the crimes. There can also be complicity through association. Individuals may be rendered responsible for the acts of others because of their close association with the principal actors. An individual's complicity in international crimes committed by his or her organization is stronger if the individual member in questions holds a position of importance within the organization. The closer one is to being a leader rather than an ordinary member, the more likely it is that an inference will be drawn that one knew of the crime and shared the organization's purpose in committing that crime. Remaining in an organization in a leadership position with knowledge that the organization was responsible for crimes against humanity may constitute complicity. An important factor in this type of association is whether the individual protested against the crime or tried to stop its commission or attempted to withdraw from the organization.

Association with a person or organization responsible for international crimes may constitute complicity if there is personal and knowing participation or toleration of the crimes. Mere membership in a group responsible for international crimes is not enough unless the purpose of the organization is the commission of international crimes.

Crimes against humanity are defined in Article 6 of the Charter of the International Military Tribunal. Crimes against humanity must generally be committed in a wide-spread, systematic fashion. Further, historically a crime against humanity was generally committed against a country's own nationals.

The Court of Appeal on the facts of this case concluded that the appellant was properly excluded in the factual context of this case and dismissed his appeal.

Moreno v. Canada (Minister of Employment & Immigration) (1993), 21 Imm. L.R. (2d) 221, [1994] 1 F.C. 298, 159 N.R. 210, 107 D.L.R. (4th) 424 (Fed. C.A.) — The appellants appealed the rejection of their refugee claims because of the applicability of the exclusion clause appended to the definition of a Convention refugee. The application of the exclusion clause was premised on the Board's finding that there were serious reasons for considering that Mr. Moreno had committed crimes against humanity during the four months he served in the Salvadoran army.

In early January, 1988 the appellant, having just completed grade nine, was forcibly recruited into the army. He was sixteen years old. He spent four months in military service immersed in the army's training program. During this period he was assigned to general guard duty. On one occasion he was required to stand watch outside of a prisoner's cell — a cell to which the appellant had not been given a key — while the prisoner was interrogated, tortured and eventually killed. Later, the appellant participated in five armed confrontations with guerrilla forces over a 20-day period. As part of their training the recruits pledged their willingness to kill all guerrillas, as well as civilians believed to be guerrilla supporters. Immediately following the military campaign against the guerilla forces the appellant was granted a three-day leave. He returned home, deserted the army and fled El Salvador.

The exclusion clause does not depend on whether a claimant has been charged or convicted. The Minister's burden is merely to meet the standard of proof embraced by the term "serious reasons for considering". The standard of proof is only relevant to questions of fact. Whether the act of killing civilians can be classified as a crime against humanity is a question of law. It is also a question of law whether the appellant's acts or omissions as a guard constituted a crime against humanity. Further, it is a question of law whether membership in a military organization, such as the Salvadoran army, constitutes sufficient complicity to warrant application of the exclusion clause.

Mere membership in an organization involved in international offences is not sufficient basis on which to invoke the exclusion clause. An exception to this rule arises where the organization is one whose very existence is premised on achieving political or social ends by any means deemed necessary. Membership in a secret police force may be deemed sufficient grounds for invoking the exclusion clause. Membership in a military organization involved in armed conflict with guerrilla forces comes within the ambit of the general rule and not the exception.

With respect to a guard, mere presence at the scene of a crime (torture) is not sufficient to invoke the exclusion clause. The act, however, of keeping watch with a view to preventing the intended victim from escaping may well attract criminal liability. The Court applied the criteria in *R. v. Dunlop*, [1979] 2 S.C.R. 881 (S.C.C.) to determine this aspect of the appeal and concluded that the appellant's acts or omissions would not have been sufficient to attract criminal liability as a matter of law. Criminal liability, however, was not the only issue to be determined. The Court had to decide whether the appellant's conduct satisfied the criteria set out in *Ramirez*, "personal and knowing participation in persecutory acts". A person forcibly conscripted into the military, and who on one occasion witnessed the torture of a prisoner while on assigned guard duty, cannot be considered at law to have committed a crime against humanity because *mens rea* remains an essential element of the crime. Complicity rests on the existence of a shared common purpose as between principal and accomplice. In this case the appellant disassociated himself from the actual perpetrators by deserting the army within a relatively short period after his forcible enlistment. The closer a person is involved in the decision-making process and the less he or she does to thwart the commission of inhumane acts, the more likely criminal responsibility will attach. Sixteen year-old foot soldiers should not be accorded the same legal treatment as those who commanded the war.

The Court noted that it would have been preferable for the Board to make a determination with respect to the appellant's refugee claim notwithstanding its decision to apply the exclusion clause.

Finally, the Court considered whether the female appellant's claim, which was dependent upon that of her husband, should fail as a result of the application of the exclusion clause. Normally, if there is a likelihood that the principal claimant will be exposed to persecution, then it is as likely that those who are dependent on that claimant will also be persecuted on the basis of that relationship. Thus, even where the exclusion clause applies to one claimant, it cannot be said that those persons dependent on that claimant will therefore no longer be subject to persecution.

Accordingly, the appeal was allowed and the matter referred to a differently constituted panel for consideration on the basis that section F of Article 1 of the Convention had no application to the claims of these appellants.

Nehru, Re (1993), 21 Imm. L.R. (2d) 53 (Imm. & Ref. Bd. (Ref. Div.)) — The issue before the Refugee Division was whether the claimant was described in Schedule F referred to in the definition of a Convention refugee. The Minister's representative referred to the fact that the claimant had been convicted of trafficking in a narcotic and sentenced to four months' imprisonment and that trafficking in narcotics was contrary to the purposes and principles of the United Nations.

The panel was of the opinion that countering world drug trafficking was the purpose of the United Nations. The panel was prepared to find that persons who committed acts that are contrary to this initiative do not deserve international protection by countries who are signatories to the 1951 Convention and the 1967 Protocol.

In this case, however, the panel viewed the claimant's involvement in the illicit drug trafficking as marginal. It noted that the length of sentence (four months) did not persuade it of the seriousness of the offence committed by the claimant. Further, the Court that convicted the claimant recommended that monies possessed by the police at the time of his arrest be returned to him. Thus, the panel concluded that the claimant should not be excluded from protection and that he was not a person described in Schedule F of the definition.

Ramirez v. Canada (Minister of Employment & Immigration) (1992), 85 D.L.R. (4th) 173, 135 O.R. 390 (Fed. C.A.) — The Refugee Division determined that the appellant was not a Convention refugee even though he had a well-founded fear of persecution by reason of his political opinion. The appellant was found to be excluded from the definition by virtue of Section F of Article One of the *United Nations Convention Relating to the Status of Refugees*. The appellant had engaged in criminal acts which were either war crimes or crimes against humanity.

The Court determined that the phrase "serious reasons for considering" appearing in Section F of Article One established a lower standard of proof than the balance of probabilities. The Court saw no great difference between the phrases "serious reasons for considering" and "reasonable grounds to believe" appearing in sections 19(1)(j) and 27(1)(g) and (h).

There was no issue as to which party bore the onus. The government must establish that it has reasonable grounds for excluding claimants and accordingly bore the burden of establishing serious reasons for considering that the claimant was excluded by Section F of Article One. Finally, the Court concluded that accomplices as well as principal actors are included in the exclusion. In order to be an accomplice the individual must be shown to be a personal and knowing participant in the crimes against peace, war crimes or crimes against humanity which are referred to in Section F. The appellant was by his own evidence an accomplice in acts which were either war crimes or crimes against humanity and accordingly his appeal was dismissed.

TRANSITIONAL PROVISIONS

S.C. 1995, c. 15, ss. 26, 27

108. Plan for 1993 — Notwithstanding subsection 7(1) of the *Immigration Act*, as enacted by this Act, the Minister may table the immigration plan for 1993 at any time during that year.

109. Provisions apply — Subject to sections 110 to 120, every provision of the *Immigration Act* as enacted by this Act shall, on the coming into force of that provision, apply in respect of every application, proceeding or matter under that Act or the regulations made thereunder that is pending or in progress immediately before the coming into force of that provision.

110. Inquiries and hearings — Any inquiry or hearing under any provision of the *Immigration Act* amended or repealed by this Act that was commenced before the coming into force of the amendment or repeal shall continue to a determination as though that provision had not been amended or repealed.

Case Law

Bubla v. Canada (Solicitor General) (1995), 179 N.R. 375 (Fed. C.A.) — The appellant became a permanent resident of Canada on February 24, 1986. On November 24, 1987 the appellant was convicted in Austria for importing heroin and was sentenced to 5 years in prison. On March 3, 1992 an adjudicator ordered the appellant deported because he had been convicted of an offence outside of Canada that constituted an offence that may be punishable under an Act of Parliament and for which a maximum term was 10 years of imprisonment or more. On that same day, March 3, 1992, the appellant filed an appeal of the adjudicator's decision to the Appeal Division of the IRB. Before the appeal was heard several amendments to the *Immigration Act* came into force on February 1, 1993 and section 19(1)(c) was amended. The appellant's appeal was heard on February 2, 1993, one day after the amendments to section 19(1)(c) came into force. The substantive law as amended should apply to determine the validity of the deportation order.

The Appeal Division concluded that section 110 did not apply because "the hearing" before the Appeal Division did not commence until after the law was amended. Therefore, the Appeal Division concluded that the appeal was not excepted from the general provisions of section 109.

When the application for judicial review was heard by the Trial Division that Judge concluded that the law existing prior to the amendments should have been applied. The Trial Division Judge concluded that the "inquiry" commenced before the adjudicator and had not yet been determined because the decision flowing from it was under appeal and the appeal thus fell within section 110. The Trial Division Judge quashed the decision of the Appeal Division on the basis that it wrongly had resorted to section 109.

The Court of Appeal found that the Trial Judge wrongly concluded that section 110 applied to the appeal. The reference to "hearing" in section 110 must be taken to refer to the actual sitting of the Appeal Division at which oral evidence and argument were presented to the Board. This hearing commenced on February 2, 1993, the day after the amendments came into effect. Therefore, the situation before the Court did not fall within the special provisions of section 110. The appeal was launched on March 3, 1992 and was heard commencing February 2, 1993. It was thus a proceeding which was pending on February 1, 1993 when the amendments came into effect. Therefore, section 109 made those amendments applicable to that proceeding.

It is a fundamental principle of law that an appeal body, unless clearly empowered otherwise, is obliged to determine whether the decision of the body appealed from was correct at the time it was made and in the circumstances under which it was made. The authority of the Appeal Division, both before and after the amendments in question, is set out in section 70(1). The Appeal Division may consider the correctness in law of the decision to issue a deportation order, but clearly such a decision involves examining the law as it stood at the time the deportation order was made. The Appeal Division can, pursuant to section 70(1)(b) consider "all the circumstances of the case" to see if the person should be removed from Canada. This obviously may include factors not before the adjudicator on the inquiry. The Appeal Division in the present case never directed its mind to its jurisdiction under section 70(1)(b) because it treated the deportation order as being wrong in law. This latter finding was based not on the correctness of the deportation order at the time it was made but on the law as it existed after February 1, 1993. The jurisdiction of the Appeal Division remains exactly as it was before and that jurisdiction is to determine the correctness in law of a decision already taken by the adjudicator. Such correctness must be measured by the law in force at the time the adjudicator decided unless Parliament has clearly indicated otherwise.

Accordingly, the Court of Appeal agreed with the principle result reached by the Trial Judge, namely that the matter should be referred back to the Appeal Division.

111. Determination by senior immigration officer — Where, immediately before the day this section comes into force, a direction for an inquiry had been made under subsection 23(4) or section 27 of the *Immigration Act* and the inquiry had not commenced as of that day, the matter shall be referred to a senior immigration officer who is authorized to make a determination under paragraph 23(4)(*b*) or subsection 27(4) of the *Immigration Act*, as enacted by this Act.

112. Credible basis and removal orders — Notwithstanding section 110,

(a) every claim to be a Convention refugee made between January 1, 1989 and the day on which this section comes into force, and in respect of which no determination of credible basis had been made as of that day, shall be referred to the Refugee Division; and

(b) any order, including any removal order or conditional deportation order, made as a result of any inquiry or hearing referred to in that section shall be made on the basis of the provisions of the *Immigration Act* in force on the day the order is made.

113. Departure notice deemed to be departure order — A departure notice issued to a person before the day this section comes into force shall be deemed to be a deportation order on the later of the expiration of

(a) ninety days after the day this section comes into force; and

(b) the period specified in the departure notice for the person to leave Canada.

114. Applications for leave — Any application for leave to commence an application for judicial review and any application for leave to appeal made pursuant to section 82.1, 82.3 or 83, as the case may be, of the *Immigration Act*, as those sections read immediately before the coming into force of section 73 of this Act, and in respect of which no decision was made on that date, shall be disposed of by the Federal Court — Trial Division in accordance with sections 82.1 to 84 of that Act, as enacted by section 73 of this Act, and all such applications for leave shall be deemed to be applications for leave to commence an application for judicial review.

115. Idem — Where an application for leave to commence an application for judicial review or an application for leave to appeal was made pursuant to section 82.1, 82.3 or 83, as the case may be, of the *Immigration Act* before the day section 73 of this Act comes into force and leave was granted in respect thereof but the application for judicial review, or the appeal, had not been commenced as of that day, then

(a) if leave was granted within fifteen days before the coming into force of section 73, the application shall be deemed to be an application to commence an application for judicial review made under section 82.1 of the *Immigration Act*, as enacted by section 73 of this Act, for which leave was granted and the Chief Justice of the Federal Court, or a judge of that Court designated by the Chief Justice for the purposes of this section, shall fix the day and place for the hearing of the application for judicial review; and

(b) if leave was granted at any time before those fifteen days, the Chief Justice of the Federal Court, or a judge of that Court designated by the Chief Justice for the purposes of this section, may, on application therefor, if the Chief Justice or the other judge considers there are special reasons for doing so, direct that the application shall be deemed to be an application to commence an application for judicial review made under section 82.1 of the *Immigration Act*, as enacted by section 73 of this Act, for which leave was granted and, where such a direction is made, the Chief Justice, or the other judge, shall fix the day and place for the hearing of the application for judicial review.

116. Appeals, etc. — Any application for judicial review and any appeal that was commenced pursuant to section 82.1, 82.3 or 83, as the case may be, of the *Immigration Act*, as that section read immediately before the coming into force of section 73 of this Act, and that had not been set down for hearing before that date, shall be heard by the Federal Court — Trial Division in accordance with sections 82.1 to 84 of that Act, as enacted by section 73 of this Act, and all such appeals shall be deemed to be applications for judicial review.

117. Idem — Any application for judicial review and any appeal pursuant to section 82.1, 82.3 or 83, as the case may be, of the *Immigration Act*, as that section read immediately before the coming into force of section 73 of this Act, that had been set down for hearing before that date and for which no decision had been rendered before that date, shall be heard by the Federal Court of Appeal as though section 73 of this Act had not come into force.

118. Direction of chief justice — The Chief Justice of the Federal Court may direct that section 114, 115, 116 or 117, as the case may be, shall not apply in respect of any application or appeal if the Chief Justice considers it to be in the interest of the administration of justice to do so, and where the Chief Justice so directs, the Chief Justice shall indicate in the direction how the application or appeal shall be heard and disposed of.

119. **Financial liability** — The financial liability of a person under any provision of the *Immigration Act* amended by this Act that arises from any act or omission done before the coming into force of the amendment to that provision shall be determined as though the amendment were not in force.

120. **Barristers and solicitors** — Any barrister or solicitor designated to represent a person in accordance with subsection 30(2) or (3) of the *Immigration Act*, as that subsection read before the coming into force of section 19 of this Act, may continue to represent those persons, at the Minister's expense, as though the *Immigration Act* had not been amended by this Act.

121. **Persons continue to hold office** — Every person who immediately before the coming into force of section 63.3 of the *Immigration Act*, as enacted by this Act, was appointed or employed under the *Public Service Employment Act* in any capacity in that portion of the Canada Employment and Immigration Commission known as the Adjudication Branch shall continue to hold office in that capacity in the Adjudication Division of the Immigration and Refugee Board.

TRANSITIONAL PROVISIONS

S.C. 1997, c. 22, s. 11

26. **Conditional departure notice or conditional exclusion order becomes deportation order** — A conditional departure notice or a conditional exclusion order issued before February 1, 1993 becomes a deportation order on the latest of

(a) the day on which this section comes into force,

(b) the expiration of the period normally allowed for making an application for judicial review, in accordance with the *Immigration Act*, of a decision of the Refugee Division,

(c) the day on which a decision is made under the *Immigration Act*

(i) refusing to grant leave for judicial review of a decision of the Refugee Division, or

(ii) refusing to grant leave to appeal a decision of the Refugee Division in accordance with the *Immigration Act*, as it read immediately before February 1, 1993,

(d) the expiration of the period normally allowed for taking an appeal, in accordance with the *Immigration Act*, from a decision of the Federal Court — Trial Division in relation to a decision of the Refugee Division, and

(e) the expiration of the period normally allowed for taking an appeal from a decision of the Federal Court of Appeal in relation to a decision of the Refugee Division, the day on which application for leave to appeal from a decision of the Federal Court of Appeal is dismissed by the Supreme Court of Canada or, where

leave to appeal is granted, the day on which the Supreme Court of Canada reaches a decision in the matter.

27. (1) Inquiries — Where a senior immigration officer has caused an inquiry to be held under subsection 23(4.2) of the *Immigration Act* as that provision read on the day immediately before the coming into force of this section with respect to a person described in paragraph 23(4)(*b*) of the *Immigration Act* as that provision read on the day immediately before the coming into force of this section and the adjudicator has not commenced the hearing on or before that day, the case shall be referred to a senior immigration officer who shall take the appropriate action under subsection 23(4) or (4.01) of the *Immigration Act* as enacted by this Act.

(2) Inquiries — Where a senior immigration officer has caused an inquiry to be held under subsection 27(6) of the *Immigration Act* as that provision read on the day immediately before the coming into force of this section with respect to a person described in paragraph 27(4)(*b*) of the *Immigration Act* as enacted by this Act and the adjudicator has not commenced the hearing on or before that day, the case shall be referred to a senior immigration officer who shall take the appropriate action under subsection 27(4) of the *Immigration Act* as enacted by this Act.

TRANSITIONAL PROVISIONS

S.C. 1997, c. 22, s. 11

11. (1) Immigration Act — If, before section 4 of this Act comes into force, a legal proceeding has been commenced with respect to an investigation under subsection 39(5) of the *Immigration Act*, a final decision in that proceeding that the Review Committee must cease its investigation is deemed to be the decision of the Review Committee under subsection 39(5.1) of that Act, as enacted by subsection 4(2) of this Act.

(2) Immigration Act — If, before section 7 of this Act comes into force, a legal proceeding has been commenced with respect to an investigation under subsection 81(4) of the *Immigration Act*, a final decision in that proceeding that the Review Committee must cease its investigation is deemed to be the decision of the Review Committee under subsection 81(4.1) of that Act, as enacted by subsection 7(2) of this Act.

IMMIGRATION REGULATIONS, 1978

Regulations Respecting Admission and Removal From Canada of Persons Who are Not Canadian Citizens

SOR/78-172, as am. SOR/78-316; SOR/78-624; SOR/78-744; SOR/78-745; SOR/78-938; SOR/79-51; SOR/79-167; SOR/79-240; SOR/79-347; SOR/79-392; SOR/79-686; SOR/79-851; SOR/80-21; SOR/80-601; SOR/80-763; SOR/80-779; SOR/81-4; SOR/81-461; SOR/81-612; SOR/81-624; SOR/81-720; SOR/81-822; SOR/81-869; SOR/81-954; SOR/82-593; SOR/82-613; SOR/82-636; SOR/82-702; SOR/82-723; SOR/83-36; SOR/83-339; SOR/83-540; SOR/83-675; SOR/83-696; SOR/83-836; SOR/83-837; SOR/83-902; SOR/84-140; SOR/84-211; SOR/84-215; SOR/84-216; SOR/84-245; SOR/84-809; SOR/84-849; SOR/84-850; SOR/85-131; SOR/85-225; SOR/85-1038; SOR/85-1081; SOR/85-1085; SOR/85-1107; SOR/86-109; SOR/86-196; SOR/86-472; SOR/86-703; SOR/86-769; SOR/86-865; SOR/86-1053; SOR/86-1119; SOR/87-47; SOR/87-115; SOR/87-393; SOR/87-573; SOR/87-585; SOR/87-594; SOR/87-697; SOR/88-37; SOR/88-111; SOR/88-127; SOR/88-143; SOR/88-180; SOR/88-207; SOR/88-286; SOR/88-469; SOR/88-517; SOR/88-537; SOR/88-589; SOR/88-597; SOR/88-653; SOR/89-38; SOR/89-42; SOR/89-80; SOR/89-129; SOR/89-168; SOR/89-245; SOR/89-411; SOR/89-585; SOR/90-202; SOR/90-215; SOR/90-455; SOR/90-456; SOR/90-605; SOR/90-750; SOR/91-156; SOR/91-157; SOR/91-322; SOR/91-323; SOR/91-422; SOR/91-433; SOR/91-497; SOR/92-14; SOR/92-101; SOR/92-133; SOR/92-194; SOR/92-214; SOR/92-234; SOR/92-290; SOR/92-589; SOR/93-15; SOR/93-44; SOR/93-224; SOR/93-225; SOR/93-412; SOR/93-609; SOR/94-22; SOR/94-131; SOR/94-242; SOR/94-318; SOR/94-561; SOR/94-578; SOR/94-635; SOR/94-674; SOR/94-681; SOR/94-773; SOR/95-24; SOR/95-71; SOR/95-121; SOR/95-135; SOR/95-353; SOR/95-393; SOR/95-461; SOR/95-476; SOR/96-146; SOR/96-165; SOR/96-290; SOR/96-321; SOR/97-86; SOR/97-145; SOR/97-146; SOR/97-182; SOR/97-184; SOR/97-209; SOR/97-236; SOR/97-242; SOR/97-243; SOR/97-316; SOR/97-464; SOR/97-574; SOR/98-270; SOR/98-544; SOR/98-591; SOR/99-74; SOR/99-146; SOR/99-254; SOR/99-329.

Short Title

1. These Regulations may be cited as the *Immigration Regulations, 1978*.

Interpretation

2. (1) In these Regulations,

"accompanying dependant", with respect to a person, means a dependant of that person to whom a visa is issued at the time a visa is issued to that person for the purpose of enabling the dependant to accompany or follow that person to Canada and, if the dependant is the spouse of that person, who is at least 16 years of age at the time the visa is issued;

"Act" means the *Immigration Act*;

"active business operations" [Repealed SOR/99-146, s. 1(1).]

"administration fee" means an administration fee that is assessed pursuant to subsection 91.1(1) of the Act and that represents a portion of the total average costs incurred by Her Majesty in respect of persons referred to in paragraphs 91.1(1)(a) and (b) of the Act, including costs related to

(a) examinations,

(b) the first 72 hours of detention of persons under the Act,

(c) inquiries,

(d) investigations respecting deserters, stowaways and persons who elude examination,

(e) fingerprinting and photographing and checks of national and international police and government records,

(f) the use of interpreters, and

(g) hearings before the Board;

"admissibility loan" means a loan made to a person to enable that person to meet the cost of medical services necessary in order to establish that he and his dependants are not members of the class of persons described in paragraph 19(1)(a) of the Act;

"adopted" means a person who is adopted in accordance with the laws of a province or of a country other than Canada or any political subdivision thereof, where the adoption creates a genuine relationship of parent and child, but does not include a person who is adopted for the purpose of gaining admission to Canada or gaining the admission to Canada of any of the person's relatives;

"agent" means, with respect to a fund, the Minister acting as agent on behalf of a fund that has been approved by a province other than Quebec or the Minister acting as mandatary on behalf of a fund that has been approved by the province of Quebec;

"allocation period" means, with respect to the provincial allocation of an investor, the period of five years beginning on the first day of the second month after the month in which the agent receives the investment;

"approved business" [Repealed SOR/99-146, s. 1(1).]

"approved fund" means a fund that is approved by the Minister under section 6.12;

"artificial transaction" [Repealed SOR/99-146, s. 1(1).]

"assistance loan" means a loan made to a person to enable the person to pay their reasonable living expenses, including those of their dependants in Canada, and any expenses that are incurred or are to be incurred by the person and their dependants in Canada for medical care or medical insurance or that are reasonably necessary to enable the person to engage or continue in employment;

"assisted relative" means a relative, other than a member of the family class, who is an immigrant and is an uncle or aunt, a brother or sister, a son or daughter, a nephew or niece or a grandson or granddaughter of a Canadian citizen or permanent resident who is at least 19 years of age and who resides in Canada;

"aunt", with respect to any person, means a sister of the father or mother of that person;

"brother", with respect to any person, means a son of the father or mother of that person;

"Canadian controlled" [Repealed SOR/99-146, s. 1(1).]

"Canadian financial institution" [Repealed SOR/99-146, s. 1(1).]

"case presenting officer" means an immigration officer who represents the Minister at hearings held pursuant to subsection 46(3) of the Act, as amended by S.C. 1988, c. 35, s. 14, or at inquiries;

"Convention refugee seeking resettlement" means a person, other than a person whose case has been rejected in accordance with the Comprehensive Plan of Action adopted by the International Conference on Indo-Chinese Refugees on June 14, 1989, who is a Convention refugee

> **(a) who is outside Canada,**
>
> **(b) who is seeking admission to Canada for the purpose of resettling in Canada, and**
>
> **(c) in respect of whom there is no possibility, within a reasonable period of time, of a durable solution;**

"country of citizenship", in respect of a Convention refugee seeking resettlement, means each country of which the Convention refugee is a citizen;

"daughter" means, with respect to a person, a female

> **(a) who is the issue of that person and who has not been adopted by another person, or**
>
> **(b) who has been adopted by that person before having attained 19 years of age;**

"debt obligation" has the same meaning as in subsection 2(1) of the *Canada Business Corporations Act*;

"dependant", means,

> **(a) with respect to a person who applies for a loan referred to in section 45,**
>
> > **(i) the spouse of that person,**
> >
> > **(ii) any son or daughter of that person or of the spouse of that person, where the son or daughter is less than 19 years of age and unmarried at the time the son's or daughter's application for an immigrant visa is received by an immigration officer, and**
> >
> > **(iii) any son or daughter of a son or daughter referred to in subparagraph (ii), where the son or daughter is less than 19 years of age and unmarried at the time the son's or daughter's application for an immigrant visa is received by an immigration officer,**
>
> **(b) with respect to a person referred to in subsection 6(3), a son or daughter of that person, where the son or daughter is less than 19 years of age and unmarried, or**

(c) with respect to a person other than a person referred to in paragraph (a) or (b),

(i) the spouse of the person,

(ii) any dependent son or dependent daughter of that person or of the spouse of that person, and

(iii) any dependent son or dependent daughter of a son or daughter referred to in subparagraph (ii);

(d) [Revoked SOR/93-412, s. 1.]

"dependent daughter" means a daughter who

(a) is less than 19 years of age and unmarried,

(b) is enrolled and in attendance as a full-time student in an academic, professional or vocational program at a university, college or other educational institution and

(i) has been continuously enrolled and in attendance in such a program since attaining 19 years of age or, if married before 19 years of age, the time of her marriage, and

(ii) is determined by an immigration officer, on the basis of information received by the immigration officer, to be wholly or substantially financially supported by her parents since attaining 19 years of age or, if married before 19 years of age, the time of her marriage, or

(c) is wholly or substantially financially supported by her parents and

(i) is determined by a medical officer to be suffering from a physical or mental disability, and

(ii) is determined by an immigration officer, on the basis of information received by the immigration officer, including information from the medical officer referred to in subparagraph (i), to be incapable of supporting herself by reason of such disability;

"dependent son" means a son who

(a) is less than 19 years of age and unmarried,

(b) is enrolled and in attendance as a full-time student in an academic, professional or vocational program at a university, college or other educational institution and

(i) has been continuously enrolled and in attendance in such a program since attaining 19 years of age or, if married before 19 years of age, the time of his marriage, and

(ii) is determined by an immigration officer, on the basis of information received by the immigration officer, to be wholly or substantially financially supported by his parents since attaining 19 years of age or, if married before 19 years of age, the time of his marriage, or

(c) is wholly or substantially financially supported by his parents and

(i) is determined by a medical officer to be suffering from a physical or mental disability, and

(ii) is determined by an immigration officer, on the basis of information received by the immigration officer, including information from the medical officer referred to in subparagraph (i), to be incapable of supporting himself by reason of such disability;

"designated field of study" means a field of study that has been designated by the Minister, after review of the field of study and after consultation with the governments of the provinces, as being a field of study that, when followed by an immigrant, would not give the immigrant an education profile that would enhance the immigrant's employability;

"designated institution" means a secondary school, college, university, trade school or other institution that has been designated by the Minister, after consultation with the foreign government of the country in which the institution operates or with representatives of Canadian educational authorities, as an institution that does not conform to the educational standards or practices of the jurisdiction in which the institution operates;

"designated occupation" means an occupation in a locality or area in Canada designated by the Minister, after consultation with the relevant provincial authority, as a locality or area in which workers in that occupation are in short supply;

"durable solution", in respect of a Convention refugee seeking resettlement, means

(a) the voluntary repatriation of the Convention refugee to the Convention refugee's country of citizenship or of habitual residence,

(b) the resettlement of the Convention refugee in the Convention refugee's country of citizenship or of habitual residence, in a neighbouring country or in the country of asylum, or

(c) an offer of resettlement by a country other than Canada;

"eligible business" [Repealed SOR/99-146, s. 1(1).]

"eligible business or commercial venture" [Revoked SOR/93-412, s. 1.]

"employment authorization" means a document issued by an immigration officer whereby the person to whom it is issued is authorized to engage or continue in employment in Canada;

"entrepreneur" means an immigrant

(a) who intends and has the ability to establish, purchase or make a substantial investment in a business or commercial venture in Canada that will make a significant contribution to the economy and whereby employment opportunities will be created or continued in Canada for one or more Canadian citizens or permanent residents, other than the entrepreneur and his dependants, and

(b) who intends and has the ability to provide active and on going participation in the management of the business or commercial venture;

"escrow agent" [Repealed SOR/99-146, s. 1(1).]

"father" means

(a) with respect to any person who has not been adopted, the male of whom that person is the issue, and

(b) with respect to any person who has been adopted, the male who has adopted that person;

"fiancée" includes a fiancé;

"final disposition" [Repealed SOR/99-146, s. 1(1).]

"financial statements" [Repealed SOR/99-146, s. 1(1).]

"fund" means a corporation that is controlled by the government of a province and that is authorized to create or continue employment in Canada in order to foster the development of a strong and viable economy;

"fund manager" [Repealed SOR/99-146, s. 1(1).]

"government-administered venture capital fund" [Repealed SOR/99-146, s. 1(1).]

"granddaughter", with respect to any person, means a daughter of a daughter or son of that person;

"grandfather", with respect to any person, means the father of the father or mother of that person;

"grandmother", with respect to any person, means the mother of the mother or father of that person;

"grandson", with respect to any person, means a son of a son or daughter of that person;

"gross Canadian income", for the purposes of section 5, includes business and investment income, but does not include any provincial allowance paid for a program of instruction or training, any payment of a prescribed nature referred to in Schedule VI, any child tax benefit paid under the *Income Tax Act*, any monthly guaranteed income supplement paid under the *Old Age Security Act* or amounts paid under the *Employment Insurance Act* other than special benefits;

"guarantee" [Repealed SOR/99-146, s. 1(1).]

"investment" means, with respect to an investor, a sum of $400,000 that

(a) in the case of an investor other than an investor in a province, is paid by the investor to the agent for allocation to all approved funds in existence as of the date the allocation period begins and that is not refundable, during the allocation period, once a visa has been issued to the investor, and

(b) in the case of an investor in a province, is invested by the investor in accordance with an investment proposal within the meaning of the law of the province and is not refundable for a period of at least five years, as calculated in accordance with the laws of the province;

"investor" means an immigrant who

(a) has successfully operated, controlled or directed a business,

(b) indicates to the Minister, in writing, that they intend to make an investment or have made an investment, and

(c) has a net worth, accumulated by their own endeavours, of at least $800,000;

"investor in a province" means an investor who indicates, in writing, that they intend to make an investment or who has made an investment in a province the government of which has, under subsection 108(2) of the Act, entered into an agreement with the Minister whereby the province has sole responsibility for the selection of immigrant investors;

"irrevocable investment" [Revoked SOR/93-412, s. 1.]

"live-in caregiver" means a person who provides, without supervision, in a private household in Canada in which the person resides, child care, senior home support care or care of the disabled;

"marriage" means the matrimony recognized as a marriage by the laws of the country in which it took place, but does not include any matrimony whereby one party to that matrimony became at any given time the spouse of more than one living person;

"material fact" [Repealed SOR/99-146, s. 1(1).]

"member of the deferred removal orders class" [Revoked SOR/97-182, s. 1.]

"member of the country of asylum class" has the same meaning as in section 1 of the *Humanitarian Designated Classes Regulations;*

"member of the source country class" has the same meaning as in section 1 of the *Humanitarian Designated Classes Regulations;*

"member of the family class", which respect to any sponsor, means

(a) the sponsor's spouse,

(b) the sponsor's dependent son or dependent daughter,

(c) the sponsor's father or mother,

(d) the sponsor's grandfather or grandmother,

(e) the sponsor's brother, sister, nephew, niece, grandson or granddaughter, who is an orphan and is under 19 years of age and unmarried,

(f) the sponsor's fiancée,

(g) any child under 19 years of age whom the sponsor intends to adopt and who is

(i) an orphan,

(ii) an abandoned child whose parents cannot be identified,

(iii) a child born outside of marriage who has been placed with a child welfare authority for adoption,

(iv) a child whose parents are separated and who has been placed with a child welfare authority for adoption, or

(v) a child one of whose parents is deceased and who has been placed with a child welfare authority for adoption, or

(h) one relative regardless of the age or relationship of the relative to the sponsor, where the sponsor does not have a spouse, son, daughter, father, mother, grandfather, grandmother, brother, sister, uncle, aunt, nephew or niece

(i) who is a Canadian citizen,

(ii) who is a permanent resident, or

(iii) whose application for landing the sponsor may otherwise sponsor;

"member of the live-in caregivers in Canada class" means an immigrant who

(a) is in Canada as a live-in caregiver and who

(i) has submitted the immigrant's initial application for an employment authorization as a live-in caregiver to a visa office,

(ii) is in possession of a valid and subsisting employment authorization to work as a live-in caregiver,

(iii) has completed a total of two years of employment in Canada as a live-in caregiver within three years after being admitted to Canada, and

(iv) is not, or whose dependants are not, the subject of an inquiry under the Act or of an appeal or application for judicial review following an inquiry under the Act, or

(b) is in Canada as a foreign domestic under the Foreign Domestic Program and who

(i) is in possession of a valid and subsisting employment authorization to work as a foreign domestic,

(ii) has completed a total of two years of employment in Canada as a foreign domestic within three years after being admitted to Canada, and

(iii) is not, or whose dependants are not, the subject of an inquiry under the Act or of an appeal or application for judicial review following an inquiry under the Act;

Also see Immigration Regulation 11.3.

"member of the post-determination refugee claimants in Canada class" means an immigrant in Canada

(a) who the Refugee Division has determined on or after February 1, 1993 is not a Convention refugee, other than an immigrant

(i) who has withdrawn the immigrant's claim to be a Convention refugee,

(ii) whom the Refugee Division has declared to have abandoned a claim to be a Convention refugee, pursuant to subsection 69.1(6) of the Act,

(iii) whom the Refugee Division has determined does not have a credible basis for the claim, pursuant to subsection 69.1(9.1) of the Act,

(iv) who has left Canada at any time after it was determined that the immigrant is not a Convention refugee,

(v) who, as a result of a determination by the Refugee Division, is considered to be a person referred to in section F of Article 1 of the *United Nations Convention Relating to the Status of Refugees*, set out in the schedule to the Act,

(vi) who is a person described in paragraph 19(1)(c), subparagraph 19(1)(c.1)(i), paragraph 19(1)(e), (f), (g), (j), (k) or (l) or subparagraph 27(1)(a.1)(i) of the Act, or

(vii) who has been the subject of a removal order, has left Canada and has, since the date of execution of the removal order, stayed in the United States or St. Pierre and Miquelon for a period of not more than six months, and

(b) [Revoked SOR/97-182, s. 1.]

(c) who if removed to a country to which the immigrant could be removed would be subjected to an objectively identifiable risk, which risk would apply in every

part of that country and would not be faced generally by other individuals in or from that country,

(i) to the immigrant's life, other than a risk to the immigrant's life that is caused by the inability of that country to provide adequate health or medical care,

(ii) of extreme sanctions against the immigrant, or

(iii) of inhumane treatment of the immigrant;

Also see Immigration Regulation 11.4.

"member of the undocumented Convention refugee in Canada class" means a Convention refugee

(a) who has been determined to be a Convention refugee, where all rights of appeal and judicial review have been exhausted and a period of five years has elapsed since the date of that determination,

(b) who has not been the subject of a decision of the Refugee Division under subsection 69.3(4) of the Act resulting in the cessation or vacation of the member's status as a Convention refugee,

(c) whose country of nationality or, if stateless, whose country of former habitual residence is a country, set out in Schedule XII, that is in turmoil and does not have a central authority that can issue identity documents,

(d) who applied to an immigration officer pursuant to subsection 46.04(1) of the Act for landing as a Convention refugee and was not granted landing, in accordance with subsection 46.04(8) of the Act, for the sole reason of not being in possession of a valid and subsisting passport or travel document or a satisfactory identity document, and

(e) who has paid the applicable fees, in respect of the application referred to in paragraph (d), under the *Immigration Act Fees Regulations* that were in effect at the time the application was made;

"minimum holding period" [Repealed SOR/99-146, s. 1(1).]

"minimum investment" [Repealed SOR/99-146, s. 1(1).]

"mother" means

(a) with respect to any person who has not been adopted, the female of whom that person is the issue, and

(b) with respect to any person who has been adopted, the female who adopted that person;

"National Employment Service" means the employment service referred to in Part VII of the *Unemployment Insurance Act, 1971*;

"National Occupational Classification" means the *National Occupational Classification*, including the *Career Handbook* and all other component publications, published by the Minister of Human Resources Development, as amended from time to time;

"nephew", with respect to any person, means a son of a brother or sister of that person;

"niece", with respect to any person, means a daughter of a sister or brother of that person;

"offering memorandum" [Repealed SOR/99-146, s. 1(1).]

"offering period" [Repealed SOR/99-146, s. 1(1).]

"ordinarily resident" [Repealed SOR/99-146, s. 1(1).]

"orphan" means a person whose father and mother are both deceased;

"payments made or due on account of financial obligations", for the purposes of section 5, includes business and investment expenses that are deductible under the *Income Tax Act*, but does not include payments on a first mortgage loan or hypothecary loan, or payments for rent in respect of a principal residence;

"person concerned" means

> **(a) with respect to an inquiry, the person who is the subject of the inquiry and includes any member of that person's family who may be included in any deportation order or conditional deportation order made against that person or in any departure order or conditional departure order issued to that person, and**
>
> **(b) with respect to a hearing held pursuant to subsection 44(3) of the Act, as amended by S.C. 1988, c. 35, s. 14, the person who is the subject of the hearing;**

"privately administered venture capital fund" [Repealed SOR/99-146, s. 1(1).]

"provincial allocation" means, with respect to an investor in relation to an approved fund, the portion of the investor's investment in the approved fund calculated in accordance with subsection (5);

"provincial nominee" means an immigrant whose admission is considered, pursuant to an agreement under section 109 of the Act between the Minister and the government of the province to which the immigrant intends to proceed, to be of significant benefit to the industrial development of that province;

"recipient" [Revoked SOR/93-412, s. 1.]

"related person" [Repealed SOR/99-146, s. 1(1).]

"retired person" [Revoked SOR/91-433, s. 1.]

"self-employed person" means an immigrant who intends and has the ability to establish or purchase a business in Canada that will create an employment opportunity for himself and will make a significant contribution to the economy or the cultural or artistic life of Canada;

"sister", with respect to any person, means a daughter of the mother or father of that person;

"son" means, with respect to a person, a male

> **(a) who is the issue of that person and who has not been adopted by another person, or**
>
> **(b) who has been adopted by that person before having attained 19 years of age:**

"sponsor" means a person who

> **(a) is a Canadian citizen or permanent resident who is at least 19 years of age, sponsors an application for landing of a member of the family class and satisfies an immigration officer that the person will reside in Canada exclusively and with-**

out interruption beginning on the date of giving an undertaking in respect of the application for landing until the member is granted landing in Canada, and that the person will reside in Canada after that time, or

(b) is a Canadian citizen who is at least 19 years of age, sponsors an application for landing of a member of the family class referred to in subsection 6(3) and satisfies a visa officer that, at the time of giving an undertaking in respect of the application for landing, the person resided exclusively outside Canada and that the person will reside in Canada when the member is granted landing in Canada;

"spouse", with respect to any person, means the party of the opposite sex to whom that person is joined in marriage;

"student authorization" means a document issued by an immigration officer whereby the person to whom it is issued is authorized

(a) to attend a university or college authorized by statute or charter to confer degrees, or

(b) to take an academic, professional or vocational training course at a university, college or other institution not described in paragraph (a);

"transportation loan" means a loan to enable the person to whom it is made to obtain transportation for himself or his dependants or both to the place of final destination in Canada and to pay the reasonable living expenses necessarily incurred during the course of the journey;

"uncle", with respect to any person, means a brother of the father or mother of that person;

"undertaking" means,

(a) for the purposes of sections 5 to 6,

(i) where the Minister has, pursuant to section 108 of the Act, entered into an agreement with the government of the province in which the member of the family class intends to reside, which province is responsible for the determination and application of financial criteria for sponsorship and the administration of sponsorship undertakings, an undertaking in writing that is required by the laws of that province and that is given to that government by a person residing in that province, to assist the member of the family class and the member's dependants in becoming successfully established in Canada for a period of up to 10 years, as determined by an official designated by that government or by the laws of that province, or

(ii) in any other case, an undertaking in writing given to the Minister by a person to provide for the essential needs of the member of the family class and the member's dependants for a period of 10 years and to ensure that the member and the member's dependants are not dependent on any payment of a prescribed nature referred to in Schedule VI, and

(b) for the purposes of section 7.1, an undertaking in writing given to the Minister to make provision for the lodging, care and maintenance of and resettlement assistance for a Convention refugee seeking resettlement, and their accompanying dependants, for a period determined in accordance with paragraph 7.1(2)(a);

"unmarried" [Revoked SOR/92-101, s. 1.]

(2) For the purpose of paragraph 19(2)(c) of the Act, "family" with respect to any visitor includes any accompanying relative who is dependent on that visitor or on whom that visitor is dependent for support.

(3) For the purpose of paragraph 27(1)(f) of the Act, "family" with respect to any person includes those persons who were granted admission as members of the family class or assisted relatives of that person.

(3.1) For the purposes of subsections 29(3) and 69(2) of the Act, as amended by S.C. 1988, c. 35, s. 18, "family", with respect to the person who is the subject of inquiry or proceedings, includes any relative of that person.

(4) For the purposes of subsection 33(1) of the Act, "family" includes any relative who is dependent for support on the member of the family

> **(a) against whom a deportation order or conditional deportation order is or may be made; or**
>
> **(b) to whom a departure order or conditional departure order is or may be issued.**

(5) For the purposes of the definition "provincial allocation" in subsection (1), the provincial allocation shall be calculated as of the first day of the allocation period in accordance with the formula

A + B

where

A **equals $200,000 divided by the number of approved funds that are not suspended; and**

B **equals $200,000 multiplied by the gross domestic product at market prices of the province that has approved the non-suspended fund, divided by the total of the gross domestic products at market prices of all the provinces that have approved a fund that is not suspended.**

(5.1) [Repealed SOR/99-146, s. 1(4).]

(5.2) [Repealed SOR/99-146, s. 1(4).]

(6) For the purpose of subsection (5), the gross domestic product is that for the calendar year before the calendar year that immediately precedes the date of provincial allocation, as set out in the table entitled "Provincial accounts GDP at market prices by province (millions of dollars)" in the *Canadian Economic Observer Historical Statistical Supplement*, published by Statistics Canada.

(6.1) [Repealed SOR/99-146, s. 1(4).]

(6.2) [Repealed SOR/99-146, s. 1(4).]

(7) For the purposes of subparagraph (b)(i) of the definitions "dependent son" and "dependent daughter", where a person has interrupted a program of studies for an aggregate period not exceeding one year, the person shall not be considered thereby to have failed to have continuously pursued a program of studies.

(7.1) [Repealed SOR/97-182, s. 1.]

(7.2) [Repealed SOR/97-182, s. 1.]

(8) [Repealed SOR/99-146, s. 1(5).]

(9) [Repealed SOR/99-146, s. 1(5).]

SOR/79-167, s. 1; SOR/79-851, s. 1; SOR/83-339, s. 1; SOR/83-540, s. 1; SOR/83-837, s. 1; SOR/84-850, s. 1; SOR/85-225, s. 1; SOR/85-1038, s. 1; SOR/85-1081, s. 1; SOR/88-286, s. 1; SOR/88-537, s. 1; SOR/89-38, s. 1; SOR/89-585, s. 1; SOR/90-750, s. 1; SOR/91-433, s. 1; SOR/92-101, s. 1; SOR/92-214, s. 1; SOR/92-290, s. 1; SOR/93-44, s. 1; SOR/93-412, s. 1; SOR/94-681, s. 1; SOR/97-86, s. 1; SOR/97-145, s. 1; SOR/97-182, s. 1; SOR/97-184, s. 1; SOR/97-242, s. 1; SOR/98-544, s. 1; SOR/99-74, s. 1; SOR/99-146, s. 1

Case Law

Section 2(1)

Accompanying dependant

Canada (Minister of Employment & Immigration) v. De Decaro, [1993] 2 F.C. 408, 103 D.L.R. (4th) 564, 155 N.R. 129 (Fed. C.A.) — In October 1988, a visa officer issued an immigrant visa to Ignazio De Decaro. He also issued an immigrant visa to two dependants who were to accompany Mr. De Decaro, namely the respondent and her daughter. Ignazio De Decaro died before coming to Canada. The respondent did come and arrived at Dorval on July 11, 1989 accompanied by her daughter and another child, who was born in the U.S. after Ignazio De Decaro's death and which child had never obtained a visa to Canada.

The respondent then applied for landing for herself and her two children. This was denied on the ground that the respondent's admission contravened section 19(2)(d) of the *Immigration Act* because the respondent did not meet the requirements of section 9(1) of the Act.

The adjudicator found that when the respondent applied for admission to Canada, she held a valid immigrant's visa since her visa had not been revoked by the proper authorities. The adjudicator found that the respondent's husband's death did not automatically invalidate the visa. Further, the adjudicator found that there was no need to refer to section 12 of the regulations because that provision did not enact a condition of admission, consequently its infringement did not mean the respondent could not be admitted.

The Appeal Division of the I.R.B. dismissed the Minister's appeal on the basis that the respondent, before appearing at a port of entry, had duly obtained an immigrant visa which had never been revoked or cancelled by the proper authorities and thus the respondent had the right to be admitted to Canada unless she was inadmissible on some other ground than the lack of a valid visa.

The Minister's appeal to the Court of Appeal was allowed. Pratte J.A. held that the definition of "accompanying dependant" illustrated that the visa issued to a person in this class was of a very special type which was issued solely to enable its holder to accompany or follow another person to Canada. The holder of such a visa who applied for admission without the other person accompanying or preceding him or her into Canada did not therefore meet the requirements of section 9(1) of the Act.

Further, after her husband's death the respondent became inadmissible by virtue of section 12 of the regulations. Her marital status had changed since she obtained her visa and in order to be admitted to Canada she had to establish not only that she was eligible, but also that she met all the conditions for obtaining a visa. The respondent never discharged this burden of proof.

Marceau J.A. agreed that the decision of the Appeal Division should be set aside. He saw no reference in the Act or regulations to visas which become invalid, are revoked or become ineffective. The technique in his view used to cover cases of changes in the immigrant's status between the time the visa is issued and the time he or she arrives at the Canadian border is contained in section 12 of the regulations. In his view, issuing an immigrant visa is not the granting of landing. Such issuance simply means that the visa officer has formed the opinion that the applicant meets the requirements of the Act and regulations for admission to Canada. The visa is evidence of a conclusion by an immigration officer whose function is to determine from outside Canada whether applicants are admissible and that conclusion will usually be accepted by his or her colleague at the port of entry. However, the rule is still that a foreign national arriving in Canada with a view to residing here must satisfy the immigration officer of his admissibility at the port of entry. Section 12 of the regulations imposes on an immigrant a duty to disclose any change in the facts which may have influenced the issuing of the visa and if there has been such a change, it requires the immigrant to meet new requirements. The visa is not void, but the visa in itself does not confer the right of entry. It is the new requirements of section 12 of the regulations that must be met.

In Marceau J.A.'s view the respondent could not establish that she met the requirements of section 12 since she was granted a visa in consideration of her husband's presence. The adjudicator accordingly was wrong to think that she met the conditions of admission set out by the Regulation and the Appeal Division could not confirm the adjudicator's finding on the ground that the Minister had not discharged the burden of proving that the respondent was inadmissible or that her visa had been cancelled, as the Minister was under no burden of proof and cancellation of a visa as a concept does not exist.

Given that the Court intended to allow the appeal, it then had to consider section 73(3). The majority was of the view that the respondent before her husband's death possessed a valid visa. However, after that death it was impossible for the condition attached to the visa to be performed so that the visa ceased to have any validity. Accordingly, section 73(3) conferred no right of appeal to the Appeal Division on the respondent.

Marceau J.A. was of the view that the respondent was in possession of a valid visa and that the matter should be returned to the Appeal Division as it was still under a duty to consider whether on compassionate or humanitarian grounds the respondent should not be removed from Canada.

Adopted

Gill v. Canada (Minister of Citizenship & Immigration) (1998), 48 Imm. L.R. (2d) 163, 229 N.R. 267 (Fed. C.A.) — This was an appeal from a decision of the Trial Division. The appellant, a landed immigrant, adopted a grandson of his deceased brother and then attempted to sponsor the application of his adopted son to Canada. The application was rejected. The appellant, as sponsored, appealed but the Immigration and Refugee Board upheld the rejection. The Board agreed with the immigration officials that there had been no intent to transfer the adopted son from the family of his birth to the appellant. In deciding on the nature and quality of the relationship between the adoptee and his sponsor, the Immigration and Refugee Board is not prohibited from reliance on the sort of material considered in this case which relates to facts posterior to the time of the adoption. The Board has a broad jurisdiction to consider such evidence as may appear to it as credible and trustworthy and necessary for dealing with the subject matter before it. The Board relied on post adoption interviews to find that the law of the foreign country had not been complied with on the basis that the required intent to transfer the child from his birth family to his family of adoption was lacking. This is quite acceptable and warranted. Intent is generally inferred from conduct whether before, during or after the fact. The appeal was dismissed.

Canada (Minister of Citizenship & Immigration) v. Dular (1997), 138 F.T.R. 254, (sub nom. *Dular v. Canada (Minister of Citizenship and Immigration))* 48 C.R.R. (2d) 262, [1998] 2

F.C. 81 (Fed. T.D.); affirmed (October 22, 1998), Décary J.A., Létourneau J.A., Noël J.A. (Fed. C.A.); leave to appeal to S.C.C. refused (September 9 ,1999), Doc. 26992 (S.C.C.) — The respondent is the adoptive parent of Dharmendra Prakash Dular (hereinafter Prakash). Prakash was born on December 12, 1971. He was under the respondent's continuous care since December 18, 1971, but was not officially adopted until December 17, 1990 five days after his 19th birthday. In May or June 1991, the respondent filed an undertaking of assistance. On October 15, 1991, Prakash submitted his application for landing. Prakash sought landing as a member of the family class based on the fact that he was the adopted son of the respondent. Prakash's application for landing was refused. At the time that Prakash filed his application for landing the respondent could sponsor an adopted unmarried son as long as the adoption occurred before the son's 19th birthday. These regulations were amended on March 27, 1992 and February 1, 1993. The Board determined that the relevant provisions relating to the respondent and Prakash were the 1993 amended regulations. Thus, as long as Prakash was adopted before his 19th birthday and was unmarried the respondent could sponsor his application for landing. Prakash, however, was legally adopted 5 days after his 19th birthday.

The Board found that the age 19 restriction in the revised regulations violated the equality rights provided under section 15 of the Charter. The Board found that this violation was not saved by section 1 of the Charter.

The Trial Division judge agreed with the Board that discrimination based on adoptive parentage is an analogous ground of discrimination under section 15 of the Charter and therefore that the 19 year age restriction violated section 15 of the Charter.

The Trial Division judge found that the Board properly outlined the text to be implied for purposes of a section 1 analysis. The Trial Division judge found, however, that the panel of the Appeal Division erred in its application of the first branch of the test to the facts of this case. Accordingly, it referred the matter back to a differently constituted panel for a rehearing and reconsideration in accordance with these reasons.

Pabo v. Canada (Minister of Citizenship & Immigration) (1996), 34 Imm. L.R. (2d) 53 (Imm. & Ref. Bd. (App. Div.)) — The appellant adopted her niece and nephew from the Philippines. She then sponsored them to Canada as her dependent children. The visa officer refused their applications on the basis that they were not adopted within the meaning of that term in section 2(1) of the *Immigration Regulations.*

Once the legal validity of an adoption has been established, the appeal division is required to determine from the facts of the case whether the adoption created a parent and child relationship.

The Appeal Division found that the adoptions did not in this case create such a relationship and took into account the following:

1. The communications between the appellant and the adopted children did not persuade the appeal division that the relationships are more than what one would expect between an aunt and her niece and nephew.

2. The appellant's financial contribution to her family did not significantly change subsequent to the adoptions.

3. The appellant's testimony did not provide further evidence of a parent and child relationship.

4. At the interview, the applicants' fathers told the visa officers that the adoptions took place mainly for economic reasons. Both fathers indicated that because the appellant had a good job, she would be better able to support the children than they would.

5. When the applicants were interviewed and asked why they wanted to go to Canada, they replied that it was for the purpose of continuing their studies and so that they could send money back to their parents. No importance was given to the relationship between the applicants and the appellant. Finally, the appeal division noted that the adoptions produced no negative reaction or sense of loss from either the applicants or their natural parents.

The Appeal Division concluded that the refusal by the visa officer was valid in law and dismissed the appeal.

Borno v. Canada (Ministre de la Citoyenneté & de l' Immigration) (1996), 118 F.T.R. 104 (Fed. T.D.) — The applicant was adopted in accordance with the laws of Haiti and sponsored by her adoptive mother, with the result that the applicant arrived in Canada as a permanent resident in 1986. The applicant became a Canadian citizen in 1992 and in 1993 attempted to sponsor her natural mother's application for permanent residence. This application was rejected by a visa officer on the ground that the natural mother was not the applicant's mother for the purposes of the immigration regulations. The applicant unsuccessfully appealed to the appeal division of the IRB and then sought judicial review of that decision on the basis that the adoption of the applicant had not been approved by the Province of Quebec as required by the laws of that province and that therefore the adoption was not valid.

The definition of "adopted" in subsection 2(1) of the regulations is unambiguous. A person adopted in accordance with the laws of a country other than Canada is adopted for purposes of the regulation. There is no further requirement under the *Immigration Act*. Accordingly, the application for judicial review was dismissed.

Guzman v. Canada (Minister of Citizenship & Immigration) (1995), 33 Imm. L.R. (2d) 28 (Imm. & Ref. Bd. (App. Div.)) — The appellant was appealing the refusal of the sponsored application for her adopted son. The application was refused because no genuine parental relationship was found to exist. The appellant was the natural grandmother of the applicant and her mother by adoption.

Some factors that assist in assessing a relationship of parent and child are (a) the motivation of the adopting parent; (b) to a lesser extent the motivation and conditions of the natural parent(s); (c) the authority and suasion of the adopting parent(s) over the adopted child; (d) supplanting of the authority of the natural parent(s) by that of the adoptive parent(s); (e) relationship of the adopted child with the natural parent(s) after adoption; (f) treatment of the adopted child versus natural children by the adopting parent; (g) the relationship between the adopted child and the adopting parent before the adoption; (h) changes flowing from a new status of the adopted child such as records, entitlements, etc. and including documentary acknowledgment that the child is the son or daughter of the adoptive parent(s) and finally; (i) arrangements and actions taken by the adopting parent(s) as it relates to caring, providing and planning for the adopted child. The appeal division noted that the list is not exhaustive.

In this particular case the appeal division, after considering these factors, came to the conclusion that the applicant was the adopted daughter of the appellant within the meaning of the word adopted as contained in section 2(1) of the *Immigration Regulations*.

Canada (Minister of Employment & Immigration) v. Sidhu (1993), 152 N.R. 225 (Fed. C.A.) — The respondent and his wife purported to adopt the daughter of the respondent's sister in India. An application for permanent residence was made to Canadian authorities on behalf of the child. In view of the fact that the sponsor had already two living daughters at the time of the adoption, the visa officer refused to issue the visa on the ground that the adoption was invalid by virtue of section 11 of the *Hindu Adoptions and Maintenance Act,*

1956 of India. The Appeal Division had declined to give effect to section 11(2) of the Indian statute because it was discriminatory and invalid as contrary to public order in Canada.

It is undoubtedly correct law to refuse a Canadian statute which would in effect discriminate on the basis of religion. The Appeal Division, however, has no jurisdiction under the *Immigration Act* to grant a foreign adoptive status which was not valid under foreign law on the grounds that the cause of the invalidity is contrary to Canadian public policy. It's jurisdiction is limited by the *Immigration Act*, which in turn in subject to the *Constitution Act, 1867*. Parliament has not purported to legislate independently on the subject matter of adoption for immigration purposes. On that very point, it defers to foreign legislation.

The visa officer and the Appeal Division essentially had to decide a question of fact. They had before them the relevant foreign legislation and the evidence which rebutted the presumption of validity of the deed of adoption possessed by the respondents. They had the power and duty to determine the status in India of the child, but only for purposes of landing in Canada. The appeal, however, was allowed on other grounds and referred back to the Appeal Division for re-hearing.

Singh (A.) v. Canada (Minister of Employment & Immigration), [1990] 3 F.C. 37, 11 Imm. L.R. (2d) 1, 116 N.R. 176 (Fed. C.A.), leave to appeal to S.C.C. refused (1991), 13 Imm. L.R. (2d) 46 (note), 131 N.R. 319 (note) (sub nom. *Brar v. Canada (Minister of Employment & Immigration)*) (S.C.C.) — The appellant sought to sponsor, for admission to Canada as a permanent resident, a person whom the appellant claimed as his son by virtue of an adoption in India under the provision of the applicable Indian legislation, the *Hindu Adoptions and Maintenance Act 1956*. There was a registered deed of adoption produced, bearing a date substantially after the time of the alleged adoption. Section 16 of the *Hindu Adoptions and Maintenance Act 1956* provides that a registered deed of adoption creates a presumption that the adoption is in compliance with the law. The Court noted that the terms "son" and "adopted" are defined in the *Immigration Regulations*. The question for the visa officer and the Immigration Appeal Board, in this case, was whether there had been, prior to the child's thirteenth birthday, an adoption in accordance with the laws of India which created a relationship of parent and child so as to make the adoptee the sponsor's "son". This is an issue of Canadian law. The inquiry is directed more to historical fact than to present status and the determination whether the *Hindu Adoptions and Maintenance Act 1956* has been complied with is only a part of the responsibility which Canadian legislation gives to the visa officer and the Board. Presumptions imposed by Indian law in Indian courts are of no assistance in determining if a person qualifies as an adopted son for the very special purposes of the *Immigration Act* and regulations. Further, the Court noted that the presumption in section 16 was directed towards "the court" and concluded that it was procedural in nature and therefore not intended to bind Canadian courts — courts over which the Parliament of India has no jurisdiction.

Editor's Note: The definitions of "adopted," "daughter," and "son" have since been changed, but the principles in this case may still be applicable.

Sashi v. Canada (Minister of Employment & Immigration) (1987), 3 Imm. L.R. (2d) 288 (Fed. T.D.) — The applicant sought to quash a decision of a visa officer in India refusing sponsorship applications for the applicant's mother and his adopted daughter. The visa officer refused to accept the sponsorship of the daughter because, as a result of his inquiries, he concluded that the provisions of the *Hindu Adoptions and Maintenance Act* had not been complied with. It was held that a visa officer has not only a right but a duty to ensure that all immigrants meet the requirements of the Act and regulations. In this case, that included making certain that the sponsored child had been legally adopted within the meaning of section 2(1) of the regulation. The officer's decision was not reached improperly or without justification. The officer did reach a conclusion that involved an interpretation of Hindu law, and he ought to have afforded the applicant some opportunity for counter-argument. However, the relief sought in this case, *i.e.*, *certiorari* and *mandamus*, was discretionary, and in all the circumstances the motion was dismissed.

Case presenting officer

Orelien v. Canada (Minister of Employment & Immigration) (1991), [1992] 1 F.C. 592, 15 Imm. L.R. (2d) 1, 135 N.R. 50 (Fed. C.A.) — The power and duty of a case presenting officer to cross-examine claimants does not impair any right accorded a refugee claimant by section 7 of the Charter or paragraph 2(e) of the *Bill of Rights*. The power to cross-examine cannot be isolated from other mandated attributes of the screening process, namely, an oral hearing, the right to counsel, a reasonable opportunity to present evidence, to cross-examine witnesses, to make representations, and finally the requirement that the tribunal give reasons for its decision if it is adverse.

Satiacum v. Canada (Minister of Employment & Immigration) (1985), 64 N.R. 358 (Fed. C.A.) — The circumstance that the adjudicator and the case presenting officer were both public servants employed in the same department of government, without more, was not such as to give rise to a reasonable apprehension of bias. An informed person viewing the matter realistically and practically would not conclude that it was more likely than not that the adjudicator would not decide fairly.

Daughter

See summaries under subheading *Son/Daughter, infra.*

Dependant

Moore v. Canada (Minister of Employment & Immigration) (December 6, 1978), Doc. 78-3016 (Imm. App. Bd.) — For the purposes of the Act and regulations, "dependant" is a term of art and includes a spouse whether or not that spouse is actually dependent for support upon the prospective immigrant.

Dependant daughter/Dependant son

Patel v. Canada (Minister of Citizenship & Immigration) (April 21, 1999), Doc. IMM-2678-98 (Fed. T.D.) — The issue here was whether the visa officer erred in determining that private institutes in India are not other educational institutions for the purpose of the definition of dependant son as set out in the Immigration Regulations.

There is nothing in the phrase "other educational institution" which requires the institution to be under the control management or supervision of any government authority. Accordingly, private institutions fall within the meaning of these words.

Patel v. Canada (Minister of Citizenship & Immigration) (1998), 155 F.T.R. (Fed. T.D.) — This was an application to review a decision of a visa officer to delete the applicant's son from an application for permanent residence. The applicant and his family were interviewed by a visa officer who determined that the son was not a genuine dependant. Later on, the applicant, through his immigration consultant, requested that the decision of this officer be reconsidered. The officer had been transferred to a different section of the Canadian High Commission in New Delhi, and a new officer took over the file. This new officer reviewed the file including the interview notes of the first officer and school documents provided by the applicant and then determined that the applicant had not been in attendance as a full-time student and was therefore not a dependant son within the meaning of the Regulations.

Although the Court recognized that a portion of the second officer's decision was based on the documentary record, it could not determine the extent to which the second officer had relied on the interview notes of the first officer. The fact of the reliance on those notes tainted the decision because it meant that the officer who heard the applicant (the first officer) did not decide the matter. Therefore the decision of the visa officer was set aside. The Court went on to indicate that it did not read the term "in attendance" in the Immigration Regulation definition of dependant son as including a qualitative aspect. The Court was of the view that if the documentary record states that the son or daughter is enrolled and is in full-time attendance then, in the Court's view, that should suffice.

Tewg v. Canada (Minister of Citizenship & Immigration) (1998), 42 Imm. L.R. (2d) 307, 141 F.T.R. 135 (Fed. T.D.) — This was an application to review a decision of a visa officer refusing an application for permanent residence. The applicant was included as an accompanying dependant in his mother's application. Although over the age of 19, the applicant was included as a dependant son. The mother was advised during the course of processing that a visa could not be issued to the applicant because he did not have a valid passport. Due to the fact that the applicant could not obtain a passport until the completion of his compulsory service, the mother and the other members of the family immigrated to Canada. The applicant reapplied for permanent residence after completing his military service. This application was refused.

The visa officer considered whether favourable consideration could be given to the applicant under the policy relating to "last remaining family members". The visa officer proceeded on the basis that the applicant could not receive favourable consideration under this policy because his relatives had proceeded to Canada without him and therefore he could not demonstrate emotional dependency and secondly, because compulsory military service precluded the applicant from being financially or emotionally dependent on his relatives.

The fact that the applicant's relatives left without him was an irrelevant consideration. The visa officer was under a duty to consider all of the applicant's particular circumstances and make an assessment of emotional dependency. The visa officer also had a duty to consider all the financial circumstances of the applicant and make a determination as to his financial dependency. The visa officer could not assume that two years of compulsory military service precluded any possibility of financial or emotional dependence. The decision of the visa officer was set aside.

Canada (Minister of Citizenship & Immigration) v. Dular (1997), 138 F.T.R. 254, (sub nom. *Dular v. Canada (Minister of Citizenship and Immigration)*) 48 C.R.R. (2d) 262, [1998] 2 F.C. 81 (Fed. T.D.); affirmed (October 22, 1998), Décary J.A., Létourneau J.A., Noël J.A. (Fed. C.A.); leave to appeal to S.C.C. refused (September 9, 1999), Doc. 26922 (S.C.C.) — The respondent is the adoptive parent of Dharmendra Prakash Dular (hereinafter Prakash). Prakash was born on December 12, 1971. He was under the respondent's continuous care since September 18, 1971, but was not officially adopted until December 17, 1990 five days after his 19th birthday. In May or June 1991, the respondent filed an undertaking of assistance. On October 15, 1991, Prakash submitted his application for landing. Prakash sought landing as a member of the family class based on the fact that he was the adopted son of the respondent. Prakash's application for landing was refused. At the time that Prakash filed his application for landing the respondent could sponsor an adopted unmarried son as long as the adoption occurred before the son's 19th birthday. These regulations were amended on March 27, 1992 and February 1, 1993. The Board determined that the relevant provisions relating to the respondent and Prakash were the 1993 amended regulations. Thus, as long as Prakash was adopted before his 19th birthday and was unmarried the respondent could sponsor his application for landing. Prakash, however, was legally adopted 5 days after his 19th birthday.

The Board found that the age 19 restriction in the revised regulations violated the equality rights provided under section 15 of the Charter. The Board found that this violation was not saved by section 1 of the Charter.

The Trial Division judge agreed with the Board that discrimination based on adoptive parentage is an analogous ground of discrimination under section 15 of the Charter and therefore that the 19 year age restriction violated section 15 of the Charter.

The Trial Division judge found that the Board properly outlined the text to be implied for purposes of a section 1 analysis. The Trial Division judge found ,however, that the panel of the Appeal Division erred in its application of the first branch of the test to the facts of this case. Accordingly, it referred the matter back to a differently constituted panel for a rehearing and reconsideration in accordance with these reasons.

Malkana v. Canada (Minister of Citizenship & Immigration) (1996), 37 Imm. L.R. (2d) 288, 125 F.T.R. 71 (Fed. T.D.) — This was an application to review a decision of a visa officer which determined that the applicant did not meet the definition of "dependent son" set out in section 2(1) of the *Immigration Regulations.*

The applicant is a citizen of India, and the son of Mohinder Singh. The applicant's father was sponsored for immigration to Canada by the applicant's brother. In his father's application for landing, the applicant and his mother were included as dependants. The family was interviewed in March 1995 and the applicant was questioned about his education program.

The visa officer's decision letter reflected a conclusion either that the applicant did not regularly attend classes in courses for which he was registered or if he was in attendance the "quality" of his attendance was not such as to constitute "attendance" within the terminology of the definition. This finding flowed from the questioning of the applicant during the family interview. The applicant was unable to demonstrate knowledge related to his diploma course in computers and to his political science and history studies.

The visa officer was careful to express to the applicant and his family members her concern with regard to the applicants "attendance". The visa officer provided the applicant and his family with an opportunity to respond to her concern.

The Court rejected the submission that the visa officer was required to give the applicant and his family advanced notice of the line of questioning to be pursued at the interview. The Court concluded that the decision of the visa officer was one that was reasonably open to her and accordingly the application for judicial review was dismissed.

Khaira v. Canada (Minister of Citizenship & Immigration) (1996), 35 Imm. L.R. (2d) 257, 122 F.T.R. 63 (Fed. T.D.) — The applicant sought to review a decision of a visa officer which determined that the applicant did not meet the definition of "dependent son" set out in the immigration regulations. As a result, the applicant was deleted from the sponsored application of his father for landing in Canada.

The concept of "continuously enrolled and in attendance in an academic, professional or vocational program...." has some flexibility by reason that the continuous enrollment and attendance may be interrupted for an aggregate period not exceeding one year. The test of enrollment and in attendance as a full time student must be met both at the time the application for an immigrant visa is received and at the time the visitor visa is issued.

It is not essential to fall within the definition that an individual be in full time attendance. The essential elements are that the individual be enrolled and that he/she be in attendance and that his or her enrollment and attendance be as a full-time student. The concept of a full-time student is not synonymous with the concept of a student who is in full time attendance. The concept of a full-time student goes to the nature of the students enrollment and is to be contrasted with that of a part-time student. Actual attendance at the courses for which he or she has enrolled is another matter.

An applicant has to establish that he or she was "in attendance" at the program for which he or she was enrolled. The concept of attendance has both a quantitative and qualitative element. In this case, the visa officer was concerned on the quantitative component because the applicant had only attended some 77% of his classes. Further, the applicant fell short on the qualitative component, in that his responses to the visa officer's questions regarding what was going on in class were found to be entirely inadequate. Thus, the conclusion of this visa officer that the applicant while enrolled continuously and on a full time basis in an appropriate educational institution, was not "in attendance" at that institution, was reasonably open to him.

Canada (Minister of Citizenship & Immigration) v. Jimenez (1995), 36 Imm. L.R. (2d) 300, 102 F.T.R. 283 (Fed. T.D.) — This was an application by the Minister to set aside a decision of the Appeal Division determining that the respondent's appeal should be allowed.

The respondent came to Canada under the Foreign Domestic programme and did not have any dependants accompanying her. The respondent was granted landing on November 22, 1991. On December 17, 1992, the respondent signed undertakings in support of her daughter and her son. Applications for permanent residence were submitted by the daughter and son on April 26, 1993. At the time these applications were filed, the daughter was 24 and the son was 22. Both children indicated that they had submitted similar applications in August, 1990. The respondent's daughter had received the form letter dated August 7, 1990 indicating that the respondent had applied for permanent residence in Canada and that the dependants of the respondent including unmarried children under the age of 21 must also meet the requirements of the *Immigration Act* and regulations.

On June 18, 1993, the children were interviewed and it was determined that both were over the age of 19, were not enrolled full-time in any educational program, and did not meet the definition of dependant daughter or dependant son. Prior to March 1, 1992, the *Immigration Regulations* provided that a son or daughter had to be an issue of the person, unmarried, and not adopted by another person, in order to be included as a member of the Family Class. There was no age restriction. After March 1, 1992, the Immigration Regulations defined a dependant son or dependant daughter, as among other things, under 19 years of age.

By letter dated August 26, 1993, the respondent was informed that, notwithstanding the sponsorship of the applications of her children, their applications were refused because they did not meet the requirements of the *Immigration Regulations*. The respondent appealed to the Appeal Division and by a decision dated January 11, 1995, the Appeal Division allowed the appeal, concluding that the respondent's children had made applications for permanent residence in August, 1990 and that the visa applications had never been refused.

The Court concluded that the applications for permanent residence filed in August, 1990 were entitled to be processed under the pre-1992 definitions of son or daughter. There is no doubt that the applicant had every right to refuse the applications for permanent residence from the respondent's children but decided, in its wisdom, to do nothing. Accordingly, the Minister's application for judicial review was dismissed.

Canada (Minister of Citizenship & Immigration) v. Nikolova (1995), 31 Imm. L.R. (2d) 104, 102 F.T.R. 72 (Fed. T.D.) — The Minister applied for judicial review of a decision of the Appeal Division. The Appeal Division held that the respondent's son was a dependant son and a member of the Family Class as provided for in the Immigration Regulations. The respondent submitted a sponsored application for permanent residence for her son who was living in, and a citizen of Bulgaria. The respondent's son was 18 years of age when the respondent first submitted a sponsored application. When the respondent's son reached his 19th birthday on March 4, 1992, he joined the Bulgarian military service by conscription. On June 10, 1992, the son received an immigrant visa but this visa expired in August 1992 when the son was still 19 years of age. Because of his military service, the son was unable to come to Canada at that time. On September 15, 1992, the respondent received a letter from the Canadian Embassy explaining that she could sponsor her son once he had completed his military service. Accordingly, the respondent completed an undertaking on behalf of her son on May 31, 1993. The son completed his military service in September 1993 and then immediately enrolled in post-graduate studies in Bulgaria. At that time, he was 20 years of age. The application for permanent residence submitted by the son was received on October 12, 1993 at which time the son was 20 years of age. This application was refused by a visa officer because the son was determined not to be a dependant son nor a member of the Family Class within the regulations.

The application of the Minister was successful. There was no estoppel by representation or conduct. This principle cannot be invoked to preclude the execution of a statutory duty nor to confer a statutorily defined status on a person who does not fall within the statutory definition. The principle of legitimate expectations cannot arise unless there has been a regular practice over an extended period of time which a person could reasonably expect to continue. Furthermore, this principle only applies to procedural rather than substantive matters. No substantive rights are created by the doctrine of estoppel by representation or conduct.

The transcript of the appeal reveals that the Board member refused to receive submissions regarding the respondent's ability to fulfil her undertaking of assistance. This had been one of the reasons upon which the sponsored application had been refused, and accordingly, it was procedurally unfair for the Board member to refuse to receive submissions on this issue.

Kaur v. Canada (Minister of Citizenship & Immigration) (1995), 96 F.T.R. 150 (Fed. T.D.) — In order to qualify as a dependent daughter under paragraph (c) of the definition, three criteria must be met:

1. The daughter must be wholly or substantially financially supported by her parents; and,

2. determined by a medical officer to be suffering from a physical or mental disability; and,

3. determined by an Immigration Officer to be incapable of supporting herself by reason of that disability.

Canada (Minister of Employment & Immigration) v. Brar (1993), 152 N.R. 157 (Fed. C.A.) — The respondent sponsored the application of her father, her mother and brother. Her brother was born on April 15, 1964. The father's (the principle applicant) application for permanent residence was received by the visa office on April 15, 1985. The determination of the brother's age was governed by section 25(9) of the *Interpretation Act*. The fact that the last day on which the brother was less than 21 years was a Sunday, a day on which the visa office was not opened, was of no assistance in determining the brother's age. The brother could not be said to be less than 21 years of age on the date when the application of the father was received by the visa office.

Editor's Note: Notwithstanding amendments to the definition of "dependent son", and "dependent daughter", the principle enunciated in this case may still be applicable.

Entrepreneur

Yazdanian v. Canada (Minister of Citizenship & Immigration) (March 26, 1999), Doc. IMM-4894-97 (Fed. T.D.) — The applicant sought to review the decision of a visa officer rejecting his application for permanent residence. The applicant applied under the entrepreneur class. He had been running his own business in Iran for over 30 years and currently operated a poultry feed business and a farm. His estimated net worth was in excess of $4 million dollars. The visa officer concluded that she was not satisfied that the applicant had the ability to establish a business in Canada. During cross-examination the visa officer stated that she and her colleagues considered the term active as "day-to-day operational activity as opposed to someone sitting outside the country just investing money or popping by once a month". Requiring day-to-day operational activity is too high a burden. Active and ongoing participation in the management of a business simply means being in a position to continually cause action or change in the operation of a business. The entrepreneur need not be present for the day-to-day running of the operation.

The visa officer was also concerned about the applicant's lack of "western" business experience. Experience in the "west" may be a factor to take into account in assessing an application from a non-western background, due to the fact that working in business conditions are different. The Court pointed out however, that too much emphasis on western business experience would deny applications from successful business people who have excelled in business in other cultures. The decision of the visa officer was set aside.

Kong v. Canada (Minister of Citizenship & Immigration) (1999), 159 F.T.R. 315 (Fed. T.D.) — This was an application to set aside the decision of a visa officer refusing the applicant's application for permanent residence as an entrepreneur. The decision of the visa officer was set aside in this case. The applicant indicated on his application that he intended to purchase or make a substantial investment in a business. The visa officer's rejection letter indicated that the officer was not satisfied that the applicant had acquired the knowledge and ability to establish and provide ongoing participation in the management of the business. The officer sited the applicant's lack of preparation, lack of effort and progress in learning one of Canada's two official languages, and lack of knowledge of the Canadian business environment. The officer did not determine whether the applicant had the ability or intent to purchase or make a substantial investment in a business when this was the option the applicant indicated on his application for permanent residence.

Bakhshaee v. Canada (Minister of Citizenship & Immigration) (1998), 45 Imm. L.R. (2d) 196, 154 F.T.R. 158 (Fed. T.D.) — The applicant sought to review the decision of a visa officer which found that the applicant did not meet the definition of an entrepreneur.

It is not fairness, but the regulations, that impose a duty on a visa officer to determine whether the conditions of the definition are met. Under Part A of the definition of entrepreneur an applicant has the option of seeking admission on the basis of his intention and ability "to establish, purchase *or* make a substantial investment in a business or commercial venture in Canada". An applicant may well decide to base his application and submit evidence with regard to only one of these three options. In such a case a visa officer need not examine the other options. In the case at bar, the applicant limited himself to allegations and evidence pertaining to the establishment of a business. The visa officer cannot be faulted for not having examined the other options with respect to which there was simply no evidence.

Shih-Chin v. Canada (Minister of Citizenship & Immigration) (1998), 45 Imm. L.R. (2d) 289, (sub nom. *Chou v. Canada (Minister of Citizenship & Immigration))* 148 F.T.R. 245 (Fed. T.D.) — The applicant sought to review the decision of a visa officer refusing the applicant's application for permanent residence in the entrepreneur category. Because a company in one year (1994) does not show a profit, does not make that company an unprofitable company. This is especially true when the company made significant profits in the years 1992 and 1993.

Where a visa officer will not accept the valuation which the applicant has placed upon share holdings in a particular company, the officer can ask for a financial statement or some other document to allow the applicant to demonstrate such value. If the value of shares is a concern for the visa officer, she should ask for evidence establishing the value as stated.

The visa officer questioned the applicant's ability to provide active and ongoing participation in the management of a business, on the basis that he was a minority shareholder in the companies he was involved in and that as a result had no control. Being a minority shareholder does not indicate a lack of ability to provide active and ongoing participation in the management of a business.

Finally, the visa officer failed in her duty of fairness to the applicant by not asking him to explain what the visa officer found to be contradictions as to his work history.

The application for judicial review in this case was successful and the decision of the visa officer set aside.

Yeung v. Canada (Minister of Citizenship & Immigration) (1998), 150 F.T.R. 78 (Fed. T.D.) — The applicant sought to review the decision of a visa officer refusing his application as an entrepreneur. The visa officer concluded that the applicant's net worth was not entirely accumulated by his own endeavour and on this basis it was argued that the visa officer had imported additional requirements into the definition of an entrepreneur.

A visa officer can consider an applicant's business history, i.e., his success or failure in assessing his ability to establish a business in Canada and to participate in the management of such a business. Ability is one of the relevant criteria in the definition of an entrepreneur. A visa officer is entitled to consider self-generated net worth not from the perspective of accumulated wealth, but rather as to whether the applicant had the ability to establish and manage a business in Canada that would have a significant economic benefit and that was what the visa officer had done in this case. Accordingly, the application for judicial review was dismissed.

So v. Canada (Minister of Citizenship & Immigration) (1998), 139 F.T.R. 157, 42 Imm. L.R. (2d) 33 (Fed. T.D.) — The applicant sought to review a negative decision of a visa officer with respect to his application for permanent residence as an entrepreneur. The applicant worked as an assistant bank account supervisor and later as a supervisor for the credit department. Under his position the applicant had responsibility for approving credit facilities to customers and for supervising the day to day operations of the credit department which was composed of 17 people. The visa officer concluded that the applicant did not have the necessary experience to run a business in Canada and therefore, he concluded that he did not meet the definition of an entrepreneur.

There is nothing in the regulations which specifically requires that an applicant under the entrepreneur category have the prior experience of running or managing a business. The sole question to be determined in this application was whether or not the applicant had the ability to provide active participation in the management of the business. The applicant supervised the staff of 17 people in his bank branch and was in charge of the day to day operations of the bank. He had the authority to approve credit facilities and in such a capacity had to deal with business people and assess the viability of their businesses.

The regulations do not require an entrepreneur to launch a new business venture by himself. The visa officer imported additional requirements into the criteria. Accordingly, the matter was referred back to another visa officer for redetermination.

Ping-Nam v. Canada (Minister of Citizenship & Immigration) (1997), 38 Imm. L.R. (2d) 211 (Fed. T.D.) — This was an application for judicial review of a decision of a visa officer refusing the applicant's application for a permanent visa in the entrepreneur category.

The applicant was a stateless person who resided in Hong Kong. From 1970 to 1996, the applicant operated a stall at the local poultry wholesalers market. Since 1992, the applicant had employed one full-time worker. The business involved the purchasing of poultry from local farmers, the grading of the poultry, the transportation of the poultry to market, and the reselling of the poultry. The business had virtually no assets and since 1992, profits from the business were $5,000 per year. The applicant's net worth was approximately $1.7 million Canadian.

The visa officer refused the application on the basis that the applicant who enjoyed several advantages in Hong Kong, such as the ability to communicate in Cantonese, several years of business experience, good contacts and low overhead had been unable to generate more than $5,000 Canadian in profits and only employed one full-time worker. The visa officer did not believe that the applicant had the ability to establish a business that would make a significant contribution to the Canadian economy.

The visa officer was entitled to look at the applicant's business history as a factor when considering whether the applicant met the definition of entrepreneur.

The Court found no reviewable error and dismissed the application for judicial review.

Tam v. Canada (Minister of Citizenship & Immigration) (1997), 38 Imm. L.R. (2d) 116, 130 F.T.R. 237 (Fed. T.D.) — The applicant sought to review a decision of a visa officer refusing the applicant's application for permanent residence under the entrepreneur category.

Nowhere in the definition of "entrepreneur" is it indicated that an applicant must have been responsible for the "overall management and performance" of a business, nor is it correct to say the applicant must intend to be responsible for "overall management" of his or her proposed business in Canada.

Mak v. Canada (Minister of Citizenship & Immigration) (1997), 38 Imm. L.R. (2d) 15 (Fed. T.D.) — This is an application to review a decision of a visa officer refusing the applicant's application for permanent residence as an entrepreneur. The applicant had been employed since 1980 with a company in Hong Kong involved in the production and distribution of liquors, wines and cognacs. Since 1987, the applicant had worked as one of four sales managers. The applicant managed a department having annual sales of $26,445,000 Cdn. and the applicant was responsible for sales to dealers and wholesalers in Hong Kong. The applicant was responsible for all aspects of operations within his department, including staffing, budgeting, forecasting, market analysis, promotion and customer relations. The applicant reported to the general sales manager who in turn reported to the chairman of the company. In May 1996, the applicant reported a net worth of $850,000, and in addition his wife had savings of approximately $140,000.

The application was refused on the basis that the applicant would be unable to manage a business in Canada that would be successful. The decision of the visa officer was set aside. When assessing the application of a potential entrepreneur the duty of fairness requires a visa officer to assess the applicant not only on the applicant's ability to establish a business, but also the ability to purchase or make a substantial investment in a business or commercial venture. Since this was not done by the visa officer in this case, the decision was set aside and the matter referred back to another officer for redetermination.

Hui v. Canada (Minister of Citizenship & Immigration) (January 9, 1997), Doc. IMM-2502-95 (Fed. T.D.) — The applicant was a citizen of the Peoples Republic of China. The other applicants are his wife and two children. The applicant worked as a production co-ordinator from 1979 to 1985. In 1985 he opened a vegetarian restaurant in Hong Kong. In 1991, he was instrumental in establishing a vegetarian restaurant in Vancouver with his wife and two other partners. In 1994, the applicant applied for permanent residence under the entrepreneur category. This application arose out of a rejection of that application.

The visa officer interviewed the applicant and reviewed his application for permanent residence. She concluded that he did not meet the definition of an entrepreneur as his business in Hong Kong had shown losses or very low profits since it was established. She considered profitability to be one of the factors reflecting on the applicants ability to manage a business. The applicant did have a net worth of $2 million, however, these funds were derived not from the profits of his businesses but rather from family money acquired by way of inheritance. Thus, his net worth was not an indication of his ability to manage businesses. Finally, the visa officer considered the applicant's business interest in Canada to be more of an investment business as the applicant had not taken an active part in the management of the Vancouver restaurant.

The application for judicial review was dismissed.

Chiu v. Canada (Minister of Citizenship & Immigration) (1996), 35 Imm. L.R. (2d) 281, 121 F.T.R. 39 (Fed. T.D.) — This was an application to review a decision of a visa officer refusing the applicant's application for permanent residence. The applicant, a citizen of Hong Kong, has a wife and three children. After graduating with a bachelor of arts degree in Hong Kong in 1982, the applicant established an import-export business and in 1985 set up a travel company. That business involved both travel and trading which focused on Vietnam. In 1990, the applicant formed a third company located in Vietnam which was engaged in importing computer parts and assembling, installing and repairing personal computers. The applicant had been successful in these ventures and had amassed savings and assets of over $1.5 million.

The applicant had applied for permanent residence as an entrepreneur. His stated intention was to open a trading and travel business in Vancouver similar to the one he operated in Hong Kong. He also proposed to import computer parts from Asia and the United States to assemble the computers in Canada and sell them here and through his company in Vietnam. At the immigration interview, the officer questioned the applicant to satisfy herself that he met the definition of an entrepreneur. The officer deposed that she read the definition to the applicant and on several occasions during the interview asked him how his background enabled him to meet the definition and how his proposed businesses would significantly benefit Canada. The officer deposed that the applicant was vague at the interview about his proposed businesses and their viability.

The officer concluded that the applicant had done little if any research into the feasibility of establishing his proposed businesses and on that basis made a negative decision with respect to permanent residence.

The application for judicial review was dismissed. The officer asked the applicant to demonstrate a basic understanding of the markets in which he intended to do business. The applicant was unable to do so. This line of questioning was entirely within the officer's jurisdiction as she was charged with determining whether the applicant could establish a commercial venture which would employ people and contribute significantly to the Canadian ecomony. The fact that other immigration officers follow-up the implementation of an applicants business plan does not relieve the initial interviewing officer from the need to be satisfied that a viable venture is planned. It is for the interviewing officer to establish that an applicant meets requirements of the definition.

Chan v. Canada (Minister of Employment & Immigration) (1994), 24 Imm. L.R. (2d) 305, 79 F.T.R. 263 (Fed. T.D.) — The issue in this judicial review was whether the words "that will make a significant contribution to the Canadian economy", contained in the definition of an entrepreneur, are *ultra vires*.

Section 3 of the *Immigration Act* sets forth the objectives of Canada's immigration policy. Paragraph (h) recognizes the need to foster the development of a strong and viable economy and the prosperity of all regions in Canada. Therefore, the regulations made by the Governor in Council and their administration must be considered having regard to Canada's immigration policy. When Parliament authorized the Governor in Council to make regulations respecting selection standards based on personal attributes and attainments, it intended that the Governor in Council have the discretion to more fully describe the personal attributes and attainments having regard to Canada's immigration policy objectives and in particular to Canada's domestic interests, including the need to foster the development of a strong and viable economy. Therefore, the words "that will make a significant contribution to the economy" are not *ultra vires* the *Immigration Act*.

With respect to entrepreneurs, the scheme of the *Immigration Act* and regulations was that a prospective immigrant was expected to represent to a visa officer the immigrant's intention and ability to establish, purchase or invest in a business or a commercial venture in Canada. When the immigrant lands, the immigration officer at the port of entry attaches conditions to the immigrant's visa so that the representations made to the visa officer survive the landing and the immigrant can be required to fulfil them.

The assessment of whether an applicant has fulfilled the terms and conditions must concern itself with the two-year period following the applicant's landing. Whether a business will make a significant contribution to the Canadian economy or create or continue employment for Canadian citizens or permanent residents is not something that lends itself to a momentary assessment. The notion of a significant contribution to the economy with the continuation of employment are on-going circumstances and require more long-term assessment. The immigration officer must be permitted the scope to reasonably satisfy himself or herself that the business or commercial venture has and will make a significant contribution and that employment opportunities will be created in a meaningful way.

Finally, there may be many reasons for bankruptcy and bankruptcy alone would not preclude the applicant from having met the conditions attached to his landing, but these are circumstances for objective assessment by an immigration officer.

Muliadi v. Canada (Minister of Employment & Immigration) (1986), 18 Admin. L.R. 243 (Fed. C.A.) — The appellant was a resident of Indonesia. He applied to come to Canada on the basis that he fell within the entrepreneurial category as an immigrant. His application was refused and that refusal was upheld by the Trial Division. The Court of Appeal overruled the Trial Division because the officer responsible for the disposing of the application failed to inform the appellant of the negative assessment of the appellant's business by the Province of Ontario, and to give the appellant a fair opportunity of correcting or contradicting that assessment before making the decision required by the statute. Further, the wording of the refusal and the conduct of the officer at the interview of the appellant suggested that the decision to refuse the appellant's application was, in fact, being made by the Government of Ontario official with whom the visa officer consulted about the viability of the proposal, rather than by the visa officer himself. The uncontradicted evidence indicated that the visa officer had stated that he was sympathetic to the appellant's application but had to deny the application because the Ontario Government had refused it. Finally, the appeal was allowed because the visa officer, in his letter, indicated that he had paid particular attention to whether employment opportunities for "a significant number of Canadians would be created." The language of the definition of an entrepreneur did not impose such a requirement; therefore, the visa officer exceeded his jurisdiction and, for that reason as well, his decision could not stand.

Editor's Note: Some of the relevant regulations, including the definition of "entrepreneur", have been amended since this case arose. The Court's analysis of the propriety of the visa officer's decision may be more important than the result of the application.

Investor

He v. Canada (Minister of Citizenship & Immigration) (January 20, 1999), Doc. IMM-1377-98 (Fed. T.D.) — The applicant filed for permanent residence under the investor category. The applicant was asked to bring to the interview audited financial statements and corresponding profit tax assessment. The applicant brought to the interview 34 monthly financial statements, corresponding monthly tax receipts from municipal government authorities based on those financial statements, and an audit report prepared by a Chinese accountant. The visa officer refused to accept the financial statements, because they were unreliable and unverified. The reasons given by the visa officer not to give any weight to the 34 monthly financial statements and the tax receipts because they were not certified by an accounting firm acceptable to the visa officer is a serious error. Unless the visa officer has some evidence that the audit by the Chinese accounting firm should not be accepted, the audit should be accepted and some weight, as the visa officer deems appropriate in using her discretion reasonably, should be given to those documents.

Koo v. Canada (Minister of Citizenship & Immigration) (1998), 43 Imm. L.R. (2d) 251, 149 F.T.R. 268 (Fed. T.D.) — The applicant sought to review a decision of a visa officer refusing the applicant's application as an investor. A visa officer must assess the qualifications of an applicant to determine whether the applicant's responsibilities amount to operating, directing or controlling a business and not whether the responsibilities amount to operating, directing or controlling the entire business with which the applicant is employed. The visa officer erred by requiring that the applicant own the company as a whole and failed to assess whether his responsibilities were consistent with operating, directing or controlling a business.

Tsai v. Canada (Minister of Citizenship & Immigration) (1997), 136 F.T.R. 36, 42 Imm. L.R. (2d) 114 (Fed. T.D.) — The applicant sought to review a decision of Gregory Chubak refusing the applicant's application for permanent residence in the investor category.

The applicant had significant business experience, a senior manager's position and a significant equity position in his company. The application was refused because the applicant shared control of the company with two other persons on a management committee.

The decision of the visa officer was set aside.

The officer had imported a requirement into the investor definition, namely that the applicant have unfettered operational control, and had thus fallen into error. There is no requirement for an applicant in the investor category to have sole or final decision-making power in a company. The matter was sent back to a different visa officer to be reconsidered.

Kwok v. Canada (Minister of Citizenship & Immigration) (1997), 43 Imm. L.R. (2d) 64, 138 F.T.R. 221 (Fed. T.D.) — The applicant applied for an immigrant visa in the investor category. One of the requirements is that the immigrant have a net worth, accumulated by the immigrant's own endeavours, of at least $500,000. In making this calculation, the visa officer disregarded the value of assets held in the applicant's spouse's name and only took into account 50% of the value of the assets held in joint tenancy by the applicant and his spouse. The evidence before the visa officer was insufficient to justify treating all of the assets of the applicant and his spouse, or even a full value of their joint assets, as assets accumulated by the applicant's own endeavours that should be included in the calculation of his own net worth. If the value of the assets of spouses were to be aggregated in the calculation of the net worth of an investor class applicant then this could have been made clear in the Regulations.

The Court also noted that with respect to the notion of operating a business, title was an irrelevant consideration as was ownership of shares. Salary is a relevant consideration as are performance bonuses or profit sharing. The reporting relationship is relevant to control, but as with title, is much less relevant to the question of operation.

Cheng v. Canada (Secretary of State) (1994), 25 Imm. L.R. (2d) 162, 83 F.T.R. 259 (Fed. T.D.) — The applicant was denied an immigrant visa under the Investor Program. The applicant applied for permanent residence in Canada at the High Commission in Hong Kong. After the applicant and his wife were interviewed, they were refused on the grounds that the officer was not satisfied that the applicant had successfully operated, controlled or directed a business within the meaning of the Regulations.

The applicant worked for the Tai Sang Industrial Company Ltd., one of the largest toy manufacturers in Hong Kong, as a Sales Manager. He worked there since 1982 and was responsible for all aspects of sales from the Hong Kong region, and for sales in mainland China since 1992. He was a supervisor of 14 sales people.

The applicant relied on section 5.49 of Chapter IS-5 of the guidelines in the immigration manual, which stated that the investor category was not limited to owners, presidents or vice-presidents, but was intended to extend to persons who have held a post of significant responsibility, such as a manager of a particular division or section of a larger company.

The officer's decision was contrary to the manual. While the guidelines in the manual are not legislative in nature, they ought to be followed by an immigration officer in making a decision so that some consistency is achieved within the department. Further, the guidelines offer some perspective on the policy of the Immigration Department with respect to the Investor Program. An inflexible application of the guidelines is not required. However, if the policy of the department is to apply the criteria to middle managers and the like, where their experience and the facts of the given case warrant such an application, then such a policy ought to be followed.

The officer did not follow the policy expressed in the manual in this case. That in itself was not an error worthy of referring the matter back for redetermination. However, the officer's reasoning imported additional requirements into the criteria for qualifying for the Investor Program, namely, the operation, or responsibility for the operation of the company as a whole. If the officer found that the applicant was responsible for the operation of an integral profit-generating part of the business, then the applicant ought to have met the criteria absent some other factor.

The strict reading of the definition of "investor" is not consistent with policies of Immigration Canada as set out in the regulations or as expressed in the guidelines. It is not intended that the applicant operate a wholly-owned business or a wholly-owned undertaking. Accordingly, the officer's decision was set aside.

Chen v. Canada (Minister of Employment & Immigration) (1993), 20 Imm. L.R. (2d) 290, 65 F.T.R. 73 (Fed. T.D.) — The applicant submitted an application for landing pursuant to the Investor class category and was refused by a visa officer.

The applicant was a graduate in civil engineering. Since graduation, he worked fulltime in the Soil and Water Conservation Bureau of the Department of Agriculture of Taiwan Province. In 1977, the applicant purchased land in Taiwan for $500,000 Cdn. for use as a commercial orchard. The applicant personally performed sloping and contouring of the land and designed and built an irrigation system for it. The land is now used to grow oranges and olive trees. The applicant hired a manager to deal with farm operations. The farm produces approximately $60,000 Cdn. per year profit, and the applicant owned the farm at the time of this application. The officer concluded that the applicant had no experience in operating, controlling or directing a commercial business and relied upon the fact that the applicant had hired a manager to be responsible for the operation of the farm.

The decision of the officer that the applicant did not operate the farm could not be criticized. However, the evidence did not disclose that the visa officer had properly directed herself to the question of whether the applicant controlled the farm or whether he directed it. There was nothing in the material to indicate that the officer had addressed anything other than whether the applicant had experience in operating the farm.

The definition of Investor in the *Immigration Regulations* requires only that the applicant demonstrate that he has successfully either operated, controlled or directed a business or commercial undertaking. The words in context are disjunctive. It is therefore incumbent on a visa officer to assess each aspect separately to determine whether an applicant falls under at least one of the criteria. The visa officer concluded from the fact the applicant was not involved in the operation of the farm that he also did not control or direct it. In coming to this conclusion she failed to give a distinct meaning to each of the words. The fact that the applicant owned the farm and earned the profits and would presumably be responsible for the losses at least *prima facie* suggested that he must have had some involvement in controlling or directing it. This was a matter for the visa officer to determine by addressing the issues of control and direction distinctly and specifically. The failure of the officer to consider each criteria separately and make an assessment in respect of each constituted an error in law.

The Court went on to note that when the visa officer became concerned that the applicant might not qualify in the Investor class, she should have questioned him specifically on each of the criteria separately. To simply express to the applicant a concern in a general way and then expect a meaningful response is not consistent with the requirement of procedural fairness. The visa officer is not required to conduct a seminar with each applicant as to the requirements of the *Immigration Act* or regulations or indeed to phrase questions always using specific words or formulas. However, where the requirements to be met under the Act or Regulations are fairly straightforward and the visa officer has a concern that an applicant might not qualify, it does not place too great a burden on the visa officer to address each requirement specifically and illicit answers such that a clear assessment can be made.

The decision of the visa officer was set aside and the matter was returned for redetermination in accordance with the reasons of the Court. The redetermination could be made by the same visa officer or by a different one at a location convenient to the applicant.

Member of the family class

Canada (Minister of Citizenship & Immigration) v. Dular (1997), 138 F.T.R. 254, (sub nom. *Dular v. Canada (Minister of Citizenship and Immigration))* 48 C.R.R. (2d) 262, [1998] 2 F.C. 81 (Fed. T.D.); affirmed (October 22, 1998), Décary J.A., Létourneau J.A., Noël J.A. (Fed. C.A.); leave to appeal to S.C.C. refused (September 9, 1999), Doc. 26922 (S.C.C.) — The respondent is the adoptive parent of Dharmendra Prakash Dular (hereinafter Prakash). Prakash was born on December 12, 1971. He was under the respondent's continuous care since December 18, 1971, but was not officially adopted until December 17, 1990 five days after his 19th birthday. In May or June 1991, the respondent filed an undertaking of assistance. On October 15, 1991, Prakash submitted his application for landing. Prakash sought landing as a member of the family class based on the fact that he was the adopted son of the respondent. Prakash's application for landing was refused. At the time that Prakash filed his application for landing the respondent could sponsor an adopted unmarried son as long as the adoption occurred before the son's 19th birthday. These regulations were amended on March 27, 1992 and February 1, 1993. The Board determined that the relevant provisions relating to the respondent and Prakash were the 1993 amended regulations. Thus, as long as Prakash was adopted before his 19th birthday and was unmarried the respondent could sponsor his application for landing. Prakash, however, was legally adopted 5 days after his 19th birthday.

The Board found that the age 19 restriction in the revised regulations violated the equality rights provided under section 15 of the Charter. The Board found that this violation was not saved by section 1 of the Charter.

The Trial Division judge agreed with the Board that discrimination based on adoptive parentage is an analogous ground of discrimination under section 15 of the Charter and therefore that the 19 year age restriction violated section 15 of the Charter.

The Trial Division judge found that the Board properly outlined the text to be implied for purposes of a section 1 analysis. The Trial Division judge found, however, that the panel of the Appeal Division erred in its application of the first branch of the test to the facts of this case. Accordingly, it referred the matter back to a differently constituted panel for a rehearing and reconsideration in accordance with these reasons.

Hunt v. Canada (Minister of Citizenship & Immigration) (1997), 134 F.T.R. 301 (Fed. T.D.) — The applicant sought to review a decision of the Appeal Division of the IRB dismissing the applicant's appeal from a visa officer's refusal of applications for permanent residence of her two sons, which applications were sponsored by the applicant.

The applicant was a citizen of the Philippines and a permanent resident of Canada. She had come to Canada in 1992 under the sponsorship of her fiancee. At the time she applied to come to Canada she had three unmarried children living at home with her. The applicant advised the visa officer that only one of the three children would accompany her to Canada. The applicant was advised that the two unmarried children who would not then be accompanying would have to be examined nonetheless. When the applicant arrived in Canada her record of landing was endorsed with a notation that two of her unmarried children had submitted applications for landing. In January 1994, the two sons who had remained behind submitted new applications for admission to Canada for permanent residence. On their application forms, they indicated that they were supposed to go with their mother but due to financial constraints were not able to. In the interval the *Immigration Regulations* were changed restricting the family class to children less than 19 years of age and unmarried, whereas at the time the applicant had applied to come to Canada family, class included children regardless of age, so long as they were still unmarried. The visa officer refused the applications and the Appeal Division dismissed the applicant's appeal.

The doctrine of legitimate expectation cannot create a substantive right, only a procedural one. The right sought here is relief from a change in the law, that is to say, a change in the *Immigration Regulations*. Such relief would be substantive and not procedural. Therefore the application for judicial review was dismissed.

Lidder v. Canada (Minister of Employment & Immigration) (1992), 136 N.R. 254 (Fed. C.A.) — The respondent promised his dying sister that he would take care of her children upon her death, which occurred in 1982. He submitted an undertaking of assistance (family class) to sponsor his now orphaned nephew. At the time the respondent submitted his undertaking of assistance the nephew was 17 years of age. By the time the nephew received the application for permanent residence from the Canadian High Commission in Delhi, the nephew was already 18 years of age. The respondent was informed that the nephew's application was refused due to the fact that he was 18 years of age when his application was received.

The Court noted that there are four kinds of estoppel available: estoppel by matter of record, estoppel by deed, estoppel by representation and promissory estoppel. The branch of estoppel at issue in this case was estoppel by representation. In order for the doctrine of estoppel by representation to apply there must be the following elements:

1. a representation of fact made with the intention that it be acted upon or that a reasonable person would assume was intended to be acted upon;

2. the representee must act upon the representation; and

3. the representee must have altered his position in reliance upon the representation and thereby suffered a prejudice.

Neither the doctrine of estoppel nor the related doctrine of reasonable or legitimate expectation creates a substantive right. They are part of the rules of procedural fairness which govern administrative bodies. A public authority may be bound by its undertakings as to the procedure it will follow, but in no case can those undertakings cause the public authority to forego the requirements of the law. The effective date of a sponsored application is the date of the filing of the application itself. At that point in time the nephew was over the age of 18 years and could not be sponsored as a member of the family class. Accordingly, the respondent had not sponsored an undertaking by a member of the family class and could not appeal to what was then the Immigration Appeal Board, and thus the Board was without jurisdiction to hear, and in this case allow, the respondent's appeal. Accordingly, the decision of the Board was quashed. Costs were awarded against the Crown on a solicitor and client basis.

Canada (Minister of Employment & Immigration) v. Narwal (1990), 10 Imm. L.R. (2d) 183, 26 R.F.L. (3d) 95 (Fed. C.A.) — The respondent landed in Canada in 1983 as a fiancée and was married. A year later, the respondent was divorced. The respondent then married her former husband's brother in England. During the period of her visit to England, a child, who was later born in Canada, was conceived. The husband returned to India after the marriage in England and filed an application for permanent residence which was sponsored by the respondent. During an interview, the applicant denied that his brother had in any way been related to the respondent. The respondent maintained regular correspondence with her new husband and visited him in India. The new husband's application for permanent residence was refused but the refusal was overturned by the Immigration Appeal Board. They decided that the validity of the marriage was governed by the law of India and that there was a custom permitting a woman to marry the brother of her former husband. The decision of the Board was based on humanitarian and compassionate grounds and the appeal was allowed on that basis. The Court observed that the Board erred in deciding that the substantial validity of the marriage was to be determined by the law of India, because there was on the facts a reasonable probability that the family would live in Canada with their Canadian born child.

The Court held that the respondent was validly married by the law of Canada and that the Board had jurisdiction to grant relief on humanitarian and compassionate grounds. The Minister's appeal was dismissed.

This case departs from the traditional view that the law governing capacity to marry is that of the domicile of both parties at the time of the marriage.

Canada (Minister of Employment & Immigration) v. Taggar, [1989] 3 F.C. 576, 8 Imm. L.R. (2d) 175, 60 D.L.R. (4th) 431, 99 N.R. 321 (Fed. C.A.) — The Minister appealed from a decision of the Immigration Appeal Board allowing an appeal by the respondent from the refusal of a visa officer to grant an immigrant visa to Ranjit Taggar, an Indian citizen whom the respondent had sponsored as her husband. The respondent had married Ranjit Taggar a few months after her previous marriage to his brother had ended in divorce. Under the *Hindu Marriage Act, 1955*, a marriage is null and void if one of the parties was "the wife of the brother ... of the other" unless "the custom or usage governing each of them permits of a marriage between the two." As Ranjit Taggar had no evidence of such custom, the visa officer rejected his application for a visa. Ranjit Taggar submitted a new application and this time accompanied it with a copy of a judgment of an Indian Court in an action for a declaration that he had brought against the respondent. That judgment declared the respondent and Ranjit Taggar to be legally married. The visa officer refused to issue a visa taking the view that the judgment did not establish the validity of the marriage. Customs must be clearly proved to exist and the onus of establishing them rests upon those who rely on their existence. A custom that is not established is therefore deemed not to exist. The declaratory judgment produced by the respondent's husband was a judgment "in personam" which the respondent agrees bound only the two parties to the action. The existence of a custom was not an issue in that case. The judgment, therefore, did not prove the custom, therefore, the marriage was invalid and, therefore, the Board had no jurisdiction to hear the appeal because the respondent was not married to the person whom she was seeking to sponsor and, therefore, Ranjit Taggar's application for permanent residence was not an application by a member of the family class.

Darkwah v. Canada (Minister of Employment & Immigration (1987), 4 Imm. L.R. (2d) 223 (Imm. App. Bd.) — This appeal from a refusal to approve the sponsored applications for landing in Canada by the sponsors, for the sisters, was allowed. The applicants submitted their own birth certificates, their brother's (sponsor) proof of birth and their parents' death certificates. The visa officer found the death certificates acceptable. He was not satisfied about the validity of the birth certificates. The birth certificates were issued prior to the sponsorship undertaking and, thus, should not have been considered self-serving. No effort was made by the visa officer to prove the birth certificates invalid or unacceptable by requesting relevant information from the competent authorities in Ghana. Failing that, the visa officer should have accepted the documents on their face value. The appeal was allowed.

Sashi v. Canada (Minister of Employment & Immigration) (1987), 3 Imm. L.R. (2d) 288 (Fed. T.D.) — For digest, see section 2.01, subheading *Subsection (1), Adopted, supra.*

Rattan v. Canada (Minister of Employment & Immigration) (1987), 1 Imm. L.R. (2d) 317 (Imm. App. Bd.) — This appeal was from the refusal of a sponsored application for landing of the appellant's spouse. The sponsor was a Canadian citizen, and the only child of the marriage was Canadian born. The spouse of the appellant (the father) had left Canada voluntarily after being advised he must make his sponsored application from outside Canada. The basis for the refusal was that the marriage was not permitted by the *Hindu Marriage Act, 1955* because the appellant had been previously married to the sponsoree's uncle. The Board noted that while capacity to marry is presumed to be governed by the prenuptial domicile of the parties, an exception exists where it can be inferred that at the time of the marriage the parties intended to establish their home in a certain country (Canada) and did, in fact, establish it there within a reasonable time. In such a situation, the issue is whether the marriage is valid according to the laws of Canada, which it was. Accordingly, the refusal was found to be invalid and the appeal was allowed.

Mahida v. Canada (Minister of Employment & Immigration) (1987), 11 F.T.R. 150 (Fed. T.D.) — On May 10, 1984, the applicant executed an undertaking of assistance to sponsor her father and her two brothers. A copy of the undertaking was received in New Delhi on May 24, 1984. Necessary application forms were sent on June 27, 1984. These forms were either not received or not returned. Subsequently, in March 1985 and April 1985, further application forms were forwarded to the proposed immigrants. Finally, on May 10, 1985 the forms were completed and returned to New Delhi. A brother reached the age of 21 years on February 10, 1985 and was considered to be no longer eligible for an immigrant visa as an accompanying family member. Had it not been for the failure of the proposed immigrants to receive, or their failure to return, the application forms, the application with respect to the son would have been treated in the same manner as the others, and an immigrant visa would ostensibly have been issued to him. It was held that the effective date to determine the inadmissibility of the son was the date of the undertaking of assistance and not the date when the immigration applications were duly completed. It was noted that the delays were beyond the control of both the immigration services and the proposed immigrants. There was no active or passive conduct by either of the parties for delay to impede the processing of the application.

Member of the live-in caregiver in Canada class

Mitra v. Canada (Minister of Citizenship & Immigration) (1996), 36 Imm. L.R. (2d) 213, 124 F.T.R. 98 (Fed. T.D.) — This is an application to set aside the decision of an immigration officer directing that an immigration inquiry be held regarding the applicant. In 1991, the applicant applied for a visa pursuant to the Foreign Domestic Workers programme. In order to meet the requirements to enter Canada, she made misrepresentations concerning her age, marital status and whether she had children. The applicant was admitted and subsequently lived and worked in Canada as a domestic worker. Canadian immigration authorities have in effect a policy of not instituting removal proceedings against persons who have come to Canada under the Foreign Domestic Workers programme and who have made misrepresentations concerning their marital status and whether they have children.

After the applicant was made aware of this policy she advised the manager of the immigration centre in Prince George that she had made misrepresentations. At an interview regarding her misrepresentations, the applicant executed a statutory declaration concerning the details. The applicant was advised that if she obtained a divorce from her husband she would be landed.

After receiving approval from the legal services society of British Columbia, the applicant retained a family law lawyer to initiate divorce proceedings against her husband in the Philippines. A letter was sent from the lawyer to Immigration Canada stating that divorce proceedings had been commenced.

In January 1994, the applicant contacted the West Coast Domestic Workers Association, a publicly funded organization whose goal is to help domestic workers for the purpose of obtaining some assistance in their immigration matters. Counsel was assigned to the applicant and this counsel wrote to the manager of the immigration centre in Prince George and made representations on the applicant's behalf. Four days later the manager of the immigration centre directed that an inquiry be commenced.

At the inquiry, counsel conceded that misrepresentations had been made but took issue with the propriety of the proceeding. In December 1994, an adjudicator ruled that she did not have jurisdiction to review the procedure that resulted in the direction for inquiry being made. The adjudicator then issued a departure order against the applicant.

The application to quash the departure order was allowed. The evidence was clear that the respondent had in place a policy where by individuals in similar situations to the applicant would not be removed. There is no question that the respondent is at liberty to implement such a policy. Having done so, however, it was incumbent on the respondent to apply that policy to all concerned in an even handed and consistent manner. A public authority is required to exercise its discretionary power fairly and impartially. The applicant was making every possible effort to comply with the requirements of the policy by obtaining the necessary divorce. The applicant was not provided with advance notice that the direction for inquiry was to issue, nor has the respondent provided any reasonable explanation as to why that decision was made.

The Court found that there had been a breach of the duty of fairness and allowed the application.

Caletena v. Canada (Solicitor General) (1994), 23 Imm. L.R. (2d) 177, 74 F.T.R. 78 (Fed. T.D.) — The applicant was admitted to Canada on May 5, 1989 as a member of the "Live-in Caregivers in Canada" class. Since that time she had been employed as a nanny on both a full-time and part-time basis, as a chambermaid by the Convention Inn in Edmonton and as a part-time receptionist. On May 14, 1993 her application for permanent residence was accepted subject to medical examinations. On September 27, 1993 she was informed that two of her infant children failed to pass their medical examinations. Accordingly, her application for permanent residence was refused, a voluntary departure notice was issued and her temporary employment authorization was terminated effective November 1, 1993.

Applicants under the Live-in Caregivers Programme are not attempting to gain entry or remain in Canada by failing to comply with our laws. The programme is designed to assist workers who are invited to enter Canada on employment authorizations. There is the implication, at least, that those administering the program will encourage and assist people, such as the applicant, to upgrade their skills and seek permanent residence. In the present case, the applicant did all that was expected of her as a foreign domestic worker. She was gainfully employed and by all accounts a highly satisfactory employee.

The applicant wished to contest the medical evidence but had not been afforded an opportunity to know what it was or to make answer to it prior to the respondent's decision of September 27, 1993. Accordingly, in view of the unique nature of the foreign domestic programme, the applicant was permitted to remain in Canada and continue her employment until such time as the leave application for judicial review was perfected.

Turingan v. Canada (Minister of Employment & Immigration) (1993), 72 F.T.R. 316 (Fed. T.D.) — The applicant came to Canada from the Philippines and worked as a live-in caregiver. During most of the period she resided with her respective employers. In July, 1992, however, she began to experience sharp stomach pain associated with a previously diagnosed peptic ulcer. She found that she could relieve the pain on a diet of rice, vegetables, fish and meat while her employer's family preferred pasta dishes. Embarrassed at the prospect of imposing her diet on her employer's family, she began to have supper and stay over at her friend's apartment, returning to work the next day. The applicant's application for permanent residence was refused on the basis that she did not meet the requirements of the Live-in Caregiver Programme because she had not worked as a live-in caregiver the required 24 months. It was conceded by counsel for the Minister that there had been a mistake in the calculation of the length of time and both parties were in agreement that the application should be allowed.

The Court noted, however, that the primary purpose of the Live-in Caregiver Programme was to encourage people to come to Canada to fill a void which exists in our labour market. In consideration for their commitment to work in the domestic field, the Program's participants are virtually guaranteed permanent residence status provided that they work the required twenty-four-month period. The immigration officer, therefore, had limited discretion to refuse permanent residence status once it had been determined that the participant had worked the required twenty-four months.

The applicant had provided a credible explanation about her living arrangements during the period of her stomach illness. The Court questioned the merits of the Department taking a harsh stance in this type of application. If the Department, however, intended to adopt a strict interpretation of the programme requirements, the basic principles of fairness required that the Department inform the applicant of its conclusions and afford her an opportunity to correct her breach before compelling her to leave the country.

The purpose of the Live-in Caregiver programme is to facilitate the attainment of permanent residence status. It is therefore incumbent on the Department to adopt a flexible and constructive approach in its dealings with the programme's participants. The Department's role is not to deny permanent residence on merely technical grounds, but rather to work with, and assist the participants in reaching their goal of permanent residence status.

Member of the Post Determination Refugee Claimants in Canada Class

Dervishi v. Canada (Minister of Citizenship & Immigration) (1999), 236 N.R. 375 (Fed. C.A.) — This was an appeal from a motions judge who had held that evidence relied on by the Post-Claims Determination Officer following receipt of the respondent's submission was not novel or significant and therefore did not have to be disclosed. The Court declined to revisit its decision in *Mancia v. Canada (Minister of Citizenship & Immigration)* (1998), 226 N.R. 134 (Fed. C.A.). The Court noted that needless litigation over whether post-submission evidence is novel or significant could be avoided if officers either abstained from using such evidence or supplied it to claimants and gave them an opportunity to respond to it before making a PDRCC decision.

Mancia v. Canada (Minister of Citizenship & Immigration), 45 Imm. L.R. (2d) 131, [1998] 3 F.C. 461, 226 N.R. 134, 161 D.L.R. (4th) 488 (Fed. C.A.) — The appellant came to Canada in April 1992, and claimed to be a Convention refugee. In May 1993, a panel of the CRDD determined that the appellant was not a Convention refugee. In August 1995, the appellant was advised by letter, that he was eligible to be considered as a member of the PDRCC class. The August 1995 letter, invited the appellant to make such submissions as he thought relevant to the nature and extent of any risk he would face and to file them before September 15, 1995. The appellant filed his submissions on September 11, 1995 and in February 1996 a post claims determination officer informed the appellant that he was not a member of the PDRCC class. The decision record in the case indicated that the officer had considered, amongst other documents, three articles published after September 11, 1995, i.e., after the date of the appellant's written submissions. All the documents were in the public domain and available at any public library.

The Court of Appeal determined that the reasons of the trial judge were irreproachable and were in accord with the general principles applicable to the duty of fairness.

The objective in any given case is to ensure that at the end of the process an applicant has been treated fairly considering the circumstances of the case, the nature of the proceedings, the rules under which the decision-maker is acting, and the subject matter which is being dealt with. The principle applicable with respect to disclosure of evidence, not within the knowledge of the person, is that each party to a hearing is entitled to be informed of and to make representations with respect to evidence which effects the disposition of the case. An applicant is deemed to know from his past experience with the refugee process what type of evidence of general country conditions the immigration officer will be relying on and where to find that evidence. Consequently, fairness does not dictate that he/she be informed of what is available to him or her in documentation centres. Secondly, where the immigration officer intends to rely on evidence which is not normally found, or was not available at the time the applicant filed his submissions, in documentation centres, fairness dictates that the applicant be informed of any novel and significant information which evidences a change in the general country conditions that may affect the disposition of the case.

To reach a correct conclusion regard must be had to (a) the nature of the proceeding and the rules under which the decision-maker is acting; (b) the context of the proceeding; and (c) the nature of the documents at issue in such proceedings. The Court considered each of these criteria and applied it in this case and dismissed the appeal. With respect to documents relied upon from public sources in relation to general country conditions which were available and accessible at documentation centres at the time submissions were made, fairness does not require the post claims determination officer to disclose them in advance of determining the matter. Secondly, with respect to the documents relied upon from public sources in relation to general country conditions which become available after the filing of an applicant's submissions, fairness requires disclosure by the post claims determination officer where the documents are novel and significant and where they evidence changes in the general country conditions that may effect the decision.

Whether or not the failure to disclose a document passes the fairness test is essentially a question of fact. Provided that the motions judge has not proceeded on some wrong or improper principle his finding will rarely be disturbed by the Court of Appeal.

Razavi v. Canada (Minister of Citizenship & Immigration) (1998), 43 Imm. L.R. (2d) 28, 144 F.T.R. 36 (Fed. T.D.) — The applicant was an unsuccessful refugee claimant and was deemed by Regulation 11.4(2) to have made an application for landing as a member of the Post Determination Refugee Claimants Class in Canada (PDRCC). The applicant failed to make written submissions in support of that application within a time period described by the regulations. Approximately 1 1/2 months following the expiry of the legislative time limit a lawyer requested an extension of time to permit the applicant to make submissions.

A Post Claims Determination Officer has no jurisdiction to consider a request for an extension of the time limit in subsections 11.4(3), (4), and (5) in the absence of an express legislative provision permitting him to do so. The dictates of fundamental justice enshrined in section 7 of the Charter do not require the PCDO to entertain the applicant's request to extend the time limit prescribed in the regulations prior to making his administrative decision on the deemed application.

Eftekhari v. Canada (Minister of Citizenship & Culture) (1998), 143 F.T.R. 157 (Fed. T.D.) — The applicants sought to review a decision of a Post Claim Determination Officer who determined that there was insufficient evidence that the applicants would face an objective risk to their lives if they were removed to Pakistan.

The applicants were all born in Iran and therefore could be removed to Iran under paragraph 52(2)(a) of the *Immigration Act*. There was no risk assessment conducted in respect of Iran. In failing to conduct such an assessment the PCD officer fell into reviewable error.

Hsit v. Canada (Minister of Citizenship & Immigration) (December 9, 1997), Doc. IMM-296-97 (Fed. T.D.) — This was an application to review a decision of a Post Claimant Determination Review officer which determined that the applicant was not at risk if returned to Myanmar. The applicant was found not to be a convention refugee and then became eligible for a risk assessment.

The officer noted in his decision that the CRDD has concluded that the applicant was not credible due to the delay in the making of the refugee claim and noted that the applicant had not provided any new information to address the panel's concerns. The record prepared by the respondent and delivered to the Court on this application contained written submissions made by the applicant through her solicitor. These submissions in part attempted to explain the delay. These submissions therefore constituted new evidence which was germane to the issue of credibility and which was clearly overlooked or ignored by the officer who had stated the applicant had not provided any new information to address the panel's concerns with respect to credibility. Accordingly, the decision of the officer was set aside and the matter referred for redetermination.

Sokhan v. Canada (Minister of Citizenship & Immigration) (July 7, 1997), Doc. IMM-3067-96 (Fed. T.D.) — This was an application to set aside the decision of a Post Claim Determination Officer wherein the applicant was determined not to be a member of the PDRCC class.

The applicant, a citizen of Iran, made a Convention refugee claim which was denied. Following this decision an immigration officer undertook to review the applicant's circumstances to determine whether he was a member of the PDRCC. The question before the officer was whether the applicant would be subjected to an objectively identifiable risk of extreme sanctions or inhuman treatment, which would apply in every part of Iran, and which risk would not be faced generally by other individuals from that country.

Post determination review officer's decisions do not confer on the individual a right but rather a special status or privilege. Accordingly, the standard for successful judicial review is very high. The Court will only intervene if the officer exercises his or her discretion pursuant to improper purposes, irrelevant considerations, with bad faith or in a patently unreasonable manner. In the circumstances of this case, the Court declined to intervene.

Sinnappu v. Canada (Minister of Citizenship & Immigration), 42 C.R.R. (2d) 143, 126 F.T.R. 29, [1997] 2 F.C. 791 (Fed. T.D.) — The applicants, who were unsuccessful refugee claimants, challenged the constitutional validity of removal orders requiring their deportation to Sri Lanka. The Board concluded that one of the male applicants had good grounds for fearing persecution in the North of Sri Lanka. However, the Board further found on the basis of the documentary and oral evidence that this applicant had an internal flight alternative in Colombo. The applicants challenged the denial of their refugee claims and their applications for leave were dismissed in September 1993. In April 1995, after a review of their circumstances by the respondent the applicants were informed that they were not members of the PDRCC. A copy of the risk analysis decision was included with that notification. The applicants had not received the PDRCC kit and had no knowledge that such a review was being conducted. Further, the applicants did not receive a letter dated in April 1995 advising them that they were not members of the PDRCC. In December 1995, the applicants were directed to report for removal to Colombo in January 1996. In December 1995, the applicants filed an application for leave, challenging the decision of the Minister to remove them to Sri Lanka. In January 1996, the removal orders were stayed pending a decision of the application for leave and judicial review. In October 1996, the applicants made an application for humanitarian and compassionate consideration. At the hearing of this application no decision had been made on that application. In November 1996, leave to apply for judicial review was granted.

The first question for the Court was whether the removal orders infringed section 7 or 12 of the *Charter of Rights*. A threshold question to be determined in the first stage of a section 7 analysis is whether the deportation of the applicants to a country engaged in armed conflict constitutes a deprivation of their right to life, liberty or security of the person. The Court did not answer that question because it was of the view the legislative scheme prescribed in the Act and regulations for risk assessment following the unsuccessful refugee claim did not violate the principles of fundamental justice.

Notwithstanding the fact that the legislative scheme was constitutionally valid, the evidence disclosed that the element of risk with respect to the applicants was not properly evaluated in their application for membership in the PDRCC class. The applicants instituted the present proceedings rather than taking steps to challenge the PDRCC class decision. The Court accordingly directed the Minister not to remove the applicants to Sri Lanka until her officials had made a decision on the outstanding application for humanitarian or compassionate relief, which application was based at least in part on the risks allegedly facing the applicants on their return.

The Court also determined that the legislative scheme leading to the removal orders in question did not violate section 7 of the *Charter of Rights*.

De Leon v. Canada (Minister of Citizenship & Immigration) (1996), 124 F.T.R. 273 (Fed. T.D.) — The Post Determination Refugee Claimants in Canada Class (PDRCC) was created by regulations enacted pursuant to the regulation making power set out in paragraph 114(1)(e) of the Act. That subparagraph in turn relies upon section 6(5) of the Act, which deals with landing in Canada on public policy or humanitarian and compassionate grounds. These regulations offer applicants an exemption from Canadian immigration law which requires an individual seeking permanent landing in Canada to do so from outside Canada. A negative decision by a Post Claims Determination Officer does not deprive an applicant of a previously acquired right. The Court should not set aside discretionary decisions by such officers unless their discretion has been shown to have been exercised pursuant to improper purposes, irrelevant considerations with bad faith or in a patently unreasonable manner.

Dervishi v. Canada (Minister of Citizenship & Immigration) (1996), 36 Imm. L.R. (2d) 63, 122 F.T.R. 52 (Fed. T.D.); reversed (1999), 236 N.R. 375 (Fed. C.A.) — This was an application to review a decision of a Post Claim Determination Officer wherein the officer determined that the applicant was not a member of the post-determination refugee claimants in Canada class (PDRCC class). The applicant made submissions to the officer on January 14, 1995 with respect to his PDRCC review. In those submissions reliance was placed on country reports on human rights practices for 1993. The officer's decision was dated September 6, 1995. Between the date the applicant's submissions were made, and the date of the decision, country reports on human rights practices for 1994 was published. The officer relied on the later version and not the version relied on by the applicant.

Reliance on publicly available documentation regarding country conditions does not amount to a reliance on extrinsic evidence, and therefore a breach of the duty of fairness owed in matters such as this, does not occur. However, where the officer relies on documentation published after the applicant has made his or her submissions and which was therefore obviously not available for consideration when those submissions were made, such documentation does amount to extrinsic evidence and the applicant should therefore be given an opportunity to respond to any portions of that documentation upon which the officer intends to rely when making his or her decision.

Garcia v. Canada (Minister of Citizenship & Immigration) (1996), 36 Imm. L.R. (2d) 114, 122 F.T.R. 37 (Fed. T.D.) — This was an application to review a decision of a Post-claim Determination Officer, wherein the officer determined that the applicant was not a member of Post-determination Refugee Claimants in Canada class (PDRCC class). The duty of fairness owed to the applicant on the facts of this matter was no higher than that described in *Shah v. Canada (Minister of Employment & Immigration)* (1994), 170 N.R. 238 (Fed. C.A.). Decisions of the type under review in this application are "discretionary". The type of decision under review is equivalent to a "humanitarian and compassionate" decision in terms of the duty of fairness owed.

Samoylenko v. Canada (Minister of Citizenship & Immigration) (1996), 116 F.T.R. 144 (Fed. T.D.) — This decision related to four separate applications for judicial review of a decision of a post claim determination officer to the effect that the applicants were not members of the Post Determination Refugee Claimants in Canada class.

The decision of an immigration official not to recommend an individual as being eligible for the PDRCC class takes no right away. Thus, the Court will not intervene unless the officer can be shown to have exercised his or her discretion pursuant to improper purposes, irrelevant consideration, with bad faith, or in a patently unreasonable manner. Thus, the standard of review of such decisions is high.

With respect to certifications of questions for appeal, the general principle is the decisions of the trial division on applications for judicial review of decisions or orders under the *Immigration Act* are not subject to appeal. The certification process is an exception to that general rule. The certification process should not be used simply to circumvent the general rule. Rather, its use should be restricted to circumstances where a specific question that is both serious and of general importance, and that will be determinative of the appeal, is identified. In this case, the applicants recommended for certification questions covering a whole range of issues pleaded before the trial division. In essence, counsel was seeking to circumvent the general rule established in subsection 83(1).

Accordingly, the application was dismissed and no question was certified for appeal.

Quintanilla v. Canada (Minister of Citizenship & Immigration) (1996), 105 F.T.R. 315 (Fed. T.D.) — This was an application for an order setting aside a decision of a Post Claim Determination Officer (PCDO) wherein the applicants were determined not to be members of the Post Determination Refugee Claimants in Canada class (PDRCC). The question before the PCDO was whether these particular applicants would be subjected to an objectively identifiable risk of extreme sanctions, or of inhuman treatment, which would apply in every part of their country, which risk would not be faced generally by other individuals in or from their country. The fact that a panel of the Refugee Division positively decided the claims of the applicant's brother and sister does not have any bearing on the applicant's claim and cannot be used to suggest that they would now be at risk if they were returned to their home country (Guatemala).

A determination by a PCDO is not a second refugee hearing, but rather is a statutory review designed to provide a final risk assessment after a refugee claim has been conducted. In this particular case there was nothing to indicate that the officer had erred in his application of the PDRCC class definition and, accordingly, the application was dismissed.

Moskvitchev v. Canada (Minister of Citizenship & Immigration) (1995), 95 D.T.C. 152 (Eng.) (Fed. T.D.) — This was an application to review a decision of a post claim determination officer to the effect that the applicants were not members of the Post Determination Refugee Claimants in Canada Class (PDRCC).

The Court noted that the discretion to determine whether a person is a member of this class or not, is subject to judicial review if the officer exercises, his or her discretion pursuant to improper purposes, irrelevant considerations, with bad faith, or in a patently unreasonable manner.

It was also noted that the officer filed an affidavit to outline, in some detail, the documents that he had taken into consideration before making his decision. This practise was not recommended as it was not necessary. There is a presumption that a tribunal has considered all the documents filed before it. The mere fact that a decision-maker fails to recite all the evidence when rendering his or her decision does not necessarily imply that he or she ignored any evidence, if a review of the reasons suggests that he did consider the totality of the evidence.

Baranchook v. Canada (Minister of Citizenship & Immigration) (1995), 105 F.T.R. 46 (Fed. T.D.) — The applicant sought to review a decision of the Post Claim Determination Unit (PCDU) that he was not a member of the Post Determination Refugee Claimant in Canada

Class (PDRCC). In upholding the officer's decision the Court noted that the PDRCC process is not a "broader" screening method than that for Convention Refugee determination. The PDRCC "net" can only catch those refugees who have fallen through the Convention Refugee "net". The PDRCC process requires that an individual qualify for Convention Refugee determination and fail (for instance because he could not establish a link between his fear of persecution and the grounds enumerated in the definition of Convention Refugee) in order to qualify for PDRCC consideration.

Gharib v. Canada (Minister of Citizenship & Immigration) (1995), 30 Imm. L.R. (2d) 291, 99 F.T.R. 208 (Fed. T.D.) — The applicant applied to review a decision determining that he was not a member of the Post Determination Refugee Claimant's Class (PDRCC). The applicant was found not to be a Convention refugee. Following this decision an immigration officer undertook to review the applicant's circumstances to determine whether the applicant was a member of the PDRCC. It was determined that the applicant was not a member of that class.

Section 6(5) of the *Immigration Act* permits an exemption to the visa requirement in subsection 9(1) by allowing an immigrant, and all dependants, to be granted landing for reasons of public policy, or compassionate and humanitarian considerations. To qualify, an immigrant must be a member of a class prescribed by regulations under paragraph 114(1)(e). The Governor in Council has prescribed a class of immigrants defined in s. 2(1) of the *Immigration Regulations* as the PDRCC class.

The decision of an immigration official not to recommend an individual as being eligible for the PDRCC class takes no right away. Being qualified as a member of the class offers an individual special and further consideration under the immigration laws and regulations. Thus, the Court will not intervene in discretionary decisions of this type unless such a discretion can be shown to have been exercised pursuant to improper purposes, irrelevant considerations, bad faith, or in a patently unreasonable way.

In this case the application was allowed because the officer relied on extrinsic evidence not disclosed to the applicant. This constituted a breach of the duty of fairness and resulted in the matter being returned to a different officer for a new determination.

Bochnakov v. Canada (Minister of Citizenship & Immigration) (1995), 26 Imm. L.R. (2d) 242, 91 F.T.R. 93 (Fed. T.D.) — The applicants entered Canada as Convention refugee claimants from the United States. Their claims were denied. By reason of the denial of the applicants' Convention refugee claims they became subject to application of the PDRCC Regulations. The PDRCC regulations are intended to clarify the review process applicable to persons who are found not to be Convention refugees, but who would be subject to an objective identifiable risk if they were removed. The applicants' application to be included in the PDRCC class was denied and the applicants applied for leave and judicial review of that decision.

The PDRCC Regulations do not entitle the applicants to remain in Canada until the completion of the leave and judicial review proceedings. An otherwise eligible individual loses his eligibility for membership in the PDRCC class, and for landing, only if he or she voluntarily leaves Canada. Such eligibility is not affected if the person leaves pursuant to a removal order.

Self-Employed person

Du v. Canada (Minister of Citizenship &Immigration) (1998), 44 Imm. L.R. (2d) 102, 146 F.T.R. 37 (Fed. T.D.) — The applicant sought to review a decision of a visa officer refusing the applicant's application for immigration to Canada as a self-employed person. The applicant applied for immigration as a medical acupuncturist. The tests applied to cases where the applicant is accomplished in a cultural field are not easily adaptable to cases where the applicant wishes to start a business in Canada. Where the contribution to be made is artistic or cultural, past business experience, even in the cultural or artistic field, may be of little importance. However, where the contribution is to the Canadian economy and there is, therefore, greater emphasis on the commercial nature of the business, past business experience, may be quite important. When dealing with the establishment of a business, a visa officer might well be interested in matters such as the applicant's experience as an employer, manager or in obtaining financing.

The applicant must satisfy the requirement that the business she will establish in Canada will make a significant contribution to the economy. There is no suggestion in material put before the visa officer that an acupuncture business would make a significant contribution to the Canadian economy. The only evidence was a letter from the Sheppard Rehabilitation Centre which stated that they would like to implement Chinese acupuncture therapy at their clinic. Their letter did not even assert that the applicant would establish or purchase such a business there.

Liu v. Canada (Minister of Citizenship & Immigration) (1998), 44 Imm. L.R. (2d) 93 (Fed. T.D.) — The applicant sought to review a decision of the visa officer refusing her application for permanent residence as a self-employed person. The applicant failed to present an effective business plan. The visa officer's notes of her interview with the applicant disclosed that the applicant's plans for becoming self-employed in Canada were vague in the extreme. Nothing was provided from the Chinese Canadian community to indicate the contribution that the applicant could make to the Canadian cultural scene as an actress and as a dance and drama teacher. Nothing of significance was provided from those in the PRC who are familiar with the applicant's talents that spoke to her experience and accomplishments as a teacher or as a model. Accordingly, the application for judicial review was dismissed.

Stephen v. Canada (Minister of Citizenship & Immigration) (1997), 135 F.T.R. 312, 40 Imm. L.R. (2d) 149 (Fed. T.D.) — The applicant sought to review the refusal of his independent application. The applicant applied to be considered in the self-employed and entrepreneur categories. The visa officer concluded that the applicant had never been self-employed nor had he run a business, and on this basis the visa officer held that the applicant did not have the ability to establish a business that would make a significant contribution to the economy. The applicant intended to establish a photo laboratory. The visa officer concluded that the applicant could not make a significant contribution to the economy or to artistic and cultural life through the sale of his photographs. The officer noted that the applicant had not won a photographic award since 1976 and did not sell his photographs to a significant degree.

It is clear that the visa officer interpreted the regulations as reserving the self-employed category for "extraordinary individuals". The standard required that a person applying under the self-employed category be experienced and established as a self-employed person and/or be internationally recognized in their artistic or cultural field. While international recognition and establishment as a self-employed person have been recognized to be relevant factors, they are not necessary conditions for consideration under the self-employed category. The application for judicial review was allowed.

Margarosyan v. Canada (Minister of Citizenship & Immigration) (1996), 37 Imm. L.R. (2d) 53, 123 F.T.R. 196 (Fed. T.D.) — The applicant sought to review a decision of a visa officer refusing her application for permanent residence in the self-employed category. The applicant had received extensive training as a classical ballet dancer. At the time of her application for permission to come to Canada she was teaching classical ballet at Istanbul University in Turkey and was the principal dancer in a national ballet group. Her application was refused because she did not have an intention to establish her own school or dance company upon her arrival in Canada. The applicant first intended to work for existing schools or companies and perhaps later on start her own business.

The Court found that there was nothing in the material before the visa officer to suggest that the applicant's intention to start her own business was speculative. It was true, that the time when the applicant would establish her own business was undetermined, but there was nothing in the definition which required an intent to establish a business immediately upon arrival in Canada or within any finite period following arrival.

The applicant's qualifications and experience as a dancer and as a teacher of classical ballet were not in question. The applicant had placed before the visa officer, evidence of the continuing need for persons with training such as hers, as well as evidence that there existed in Canada many opportunities for teaching professionals with applicant's level of expertise. The level of business experience required to operate a ballet school in Canada would be substantially easier to acquire than the artistic and teaching skills possessed by the applicant.

Accordingly, the decision of the visa officer was set aside and the matter referred back for reconsideration by a different officer.

Grube v. Canada (Minister of Citizenship & Immigration) (1996), 34 Imm. L.R. (2d) 219, 118 F.T.R. 163 (Fed. T.D.) — This was an application to set aside a decision of the visa officer to the effect that the applicants did not have sufficient units of assessment to be admitted to Canada as self-employed persons and permanent residents.

Section 11.1 of the regulations implicitly requires that an interview be held where an applicant is applying as a self-employed person. Thus, the visa officer erred in determining that each of these applicants did not qualify for permanent residence based on their plans to be self-employed persons, without granting them an interview.

Further the visa officer placed undue emphasis on a lack of past business experience. Such experience may well be a factor to be favourably considered when determining whether an applicant is likely to become successfully established as a self-employed person in Canada, but it is not the sole criterion to be considered, and it must be considered in light of the occupation sought to be undertaken. Past business experience may be of greater significance in relation to certain occupations than it is to others. Similarly, while an international reputation may be an asset of assistance in indicating that an applicant is likely to become successfully established in Canada, there is no requirement that an applicant possess such a reputation to be admitted to Canada as a self-employed music teacher.

Ho v. Canada (Minister of Employment & Immigration) (1989), 8 Imm. L.R. (2d) 38, 27 F.T.R. 241 (Fed. T.D.); affirmed (1990), 11 Imm. L.R. (2d) 12 (Fed. C.A.) — Applications for permanent residence under the self-employed provisions involve a two-stage assessment process. The first phase of the assessment involves a paper-screening process in which immigration officials evaluate documents submitted by the applicant and decide if the application process should be continued. If the applicant passes this phase, he is interviewed by a visa officer. One of the most significant factors in any assessment is the applicant's possibility of supporting himself in Canada. Points are therefore awarded for both occupational demand in the paper-screening step and in the final assessment for experience in the occupation for which the candidate is qualified and prepared to follow in Canada. Where an applicant is not awarded any units of assessment for experience, an immigrant visa cannot be issued unless the visa officer believes that there are good reasons why the number of points do not reflect the chances of the applicant to become successfully established in Canada and those reasons have been approved by a senior officer. A candidate for self-employment must be someone who intends and who has the ability to establish or purchase a business in Canada that will create an employment opportunity for himself and will make a significant contribution to the economy or the cultural or the artistic life of Canada. In addition, the visa officer will award 30 points of assessment to an applicant seeking to be self-employed if, in the visa officer's opinion, the applicant will be able to become successfully established in his business in Canada.

The purpose of the *Immigration Act* is to permit immigration, not prevent it, and it is the corresponding obligation of immigration officers to provide a thorough and fair assessment in compliance with the terms and spirit of the legislation. In this case, the visa officer interpreted the regulations in such a narrow fashion as to render meeting qualifications virtually impossible and, as a result, treated the applicant unfairly. The applicant was an accomplished musician who was able to teach and, on the question of whether the applicant could be self-employed as a teacher, his only apparent failure was in the lack of actual experience. Undue emphasis was placed on the lack of experience as a result of which there was a fundamental breach of the duty of fairness. Accordingly, the application was allowed and the visa officer's decision set aside.

Yang v. Canada (Minister of Employment & Immigration) (1989), 36 Admin. L.R. 235, 8 Imm. L.R. (2d) 48, 27 F.T.R. 74 (Fed. T.D.) — This is an application for an order by way of *certiorari* quashing the decision of the respondent refusing the applicant's request for permanent residence in Canada.

Applications for permanent residence under the self-employed provisions involve a two-stage assessment process. The first phase is a paper-screening process in which immigration officials evaluate documents submitted by the applicant and decide if the application process should be continued. If the applicant passes this phase, he is invited to an interview. One of the most significant factors in any assessment is the applicant's possibility of supporting himself in Canada. Points are therefore awarded for occupational demand in the paper-screening step and for experience in the final assessment. Where an applicant is not awarded any units of assessment for experience, an immigrant visa cannot be issued unless the visa officer believes there are good reasons why the number of points do not reflect the chances of the applicant to become successfully established in Canada and those reasons have been approved by a senior immigration officer. A candidate for self-employment is also subject to the definition of a self-employed person and must be someone who intends to and has the ability to establish or purchase a business in Canada that will create an employment opportunity for himself and will make a significant contribution to the economy or the artistic or cultural life of Canada. In addition, the visa officer will award 30 units of assessment to an applicant seeking to be self-employed if it is his opinion that the applicant will be able to become successfully established in his business in Canada.

The purpose of the *Immigration Act* is to permit immigration, not prevent it, and it is the corresponding obligation of immigration officers to provide a thorough and fair assessment in compliance with the terms and spirit of the legislation.

The applicant was from the People's Republic of China and had been residing in the United States since 1986. In 1987, she applied for permanent residence and stated that she was planning to pursue the profession of a self-employed music teacher. The applicant received training in China in both Oriental and Occidental music. She arrived in the United States on a student visa and was awarded a scholarship and completed a Master's degree in music. The applicant performed extensively in China and participated in one vocal competition in the United States.

The applicant was interviewed and, at the conclusion of the interview, the applicant learned that a decision could not be made until the officer consulted her colleagues and reviewed the requested documents. The applicant hand-delivered the requested documents on November 17, 1987. The applicant received a letter of refusal dated November 16, 1987.

The written refusal concentrated on the visa officer's opinion that the applicant's business would be unsuccessful and that the applicant would not make a significant contribution to the economy or cultural or artistic life of Canada. The visa officer's notes, taken during the interview, however, dealt exclusively with the applicant's experience. The visa officer's notes indicated that the refusal was also based on a lack of self-employed experience in the applicant's intended occupation of self-employed music teacher. The Court noted that the applicant was an accomplished musician and had experience as a teacher and concluded that the visa officer had placed an undue emphasis on the applicant's lack of experience as a self-employed teacher and that the interpretation taken by the visa officer made it almost impossible for the applicant to succeed. This interpretation was found to be a fundamental breach of the duty of fairness.

Further, no questions were posed dealing with the possibilities of the applicant's contributions to cultural, economic or artistic life. The officer, at least partially, based her refusal on these criteria and yet did not, at the time of the interview, give any indication of a negative assessment on this basis nor provide the applicant with an opportunity to reply to those criteria.

Finally, the Court noted that the decision made by the officer predated the receipt of the requested documentary information. The decision of the visa officer was set aside and the respondent was directed to carry out an assessment of the applicant in accordance with the *Immigration Act* and Regulations in a manner consistent with the interpretation placed upon them in the Court's reasons.

Son/Daughter

Canada (Minister of Citizenship & Immigration) v. Dular (1997), 138 F.T.R. 254, (sub nom. *Dular v. Canada (Minister of Citizenship and Immigration))* 48 C.R.R. (2d) 262, [1998] 2 F.C. 81 (Fed. T.D.); affirmed (October 22, 1998), Décary J.A., Létourneau J.A., Noël J.A. (Fed. C.A.); leave to appeal to S.C.C. refused (September 9, 1999), Doc. 26922 (S.C.C.) — The respondent is the adoptive parent of Dharmendra Prakash Dular (hereinafter Prakash). Prakash was born on December 12, 1971. He was under the respondent's continuous care since December 18, 1971, but was not officially adopted until December 17, 1990 five days after his 19th birthday. In May or June 1991, the respondent filed an undertaking of assistance. On October 15, 1991, Prakash submitted his application for landing. Prakash sought landing as a member of the family class based on the fact that he was the adopted son of the respondent. Prakash's application for landing was refused. At the time that Prakash filed his application for landing the respondent could sponsor an adopted unmarried son as long as the adoption occurred before the son's 19th birthday. These regulations were amended on March 27, 1992 and February 1, 1993. The Board determined that the relevant provisions relating to the respondent and Prakash were the 1993 amended regulations. Thus, as long as Prakash was adopted before his 19th birthday and was unmarried the respondent could sponsor his application for landing. Prakash, however, was legally adopted 5 days after his 19th birthday.

The Board found that the age 19 restriction in the revised regulations violated the equality rights provided under section 15 of the Charter. The Board found that this violation was not saved by section 1 of the Charter.

The Trial Division judge agreed with the Board that discrimination based on adoptive parentage is an analogous ground of discrimination under section 15 of the Charter and therefore that the 19 year age restriction violated section 15 of the Charter.

The Trial Division judge found that the Board properly outlined the text to be implied for purposes of a section 1 analysis. The Trial Division judge found, however, that the panel of the Appeal Division erred in its application of the first branch of the test to the facts of this case. Accordingly, it referred the matter back to a differently constituted panel for a rehearing and reconsideration in accordance with these reasons.

Singh v. Canada (Minister of Employment & Immigration), [1990] 3 F.C. 37, 11 Imm. L.R. (2d) 1, 116 N.R. 176 (Fed. C.A.), leave to appeal to S.C.C. refused (1991), 13 Imm. L.R. (2d) 46 (note), 131 N.R. 319 (note) (sub nom. *Brar v. Canada (Minister of Employment & Immigration)*) (S.C.C.) — For digest, see section 2, subheading adopted, *supra*.

Sashi v. Canada (Minister of Employment & Immigration) (1987), 3 Imm. L.R. (2d) 288 (Fed. T.D.) — For digest, see section 2.01, subheading *Subsection (1), Adopted, supra.*

Tse v. Canada (Minister of Employment & Immigration) (1983), 45 N.R. 252 (Fed. C.A.) — The Court made reference to the law of Hong Kong which legitimized the status of a concubine lawfully taken before October 7, 1971; the 3 children whom the appellant wished to sponsor were thus designated issue of a marriage for purpose of the Act and regulations. The Court first determined the domicile of the appellant, because legitimacy must be determined in accordance with the law of that province. The law of Ontario at the time of the sponsorship application had eliminated the concept of illegitimacy and made every child legitimate as of the date of its birth.

Sponsor

Athwal v. Canada (Minister of Citizenship & Immigration) (1998), 43 Imm. L.R. (2d) 46 (Imm. & Ref. Bd. (App. Div.)) — The applicant appealed from the refusal of the sponsored applications of his wife, son and daughter. The issue in this appeal was the meaning of the word “sponsor” under subsection 2(1) of the regulation. The Appeal Division noted that the problematic aspect of the definition is the meaning of “resides in Canada”.

The Appeal Division concluded that for a person who is absent from Canada to continue to reside in Canada within the definition of sponsor, he or she must maintain much more of a connection with Canada than simply not having the intention to abandon Canada as a permanent resident. The Appeal Division noted 12 factors which could be considered in determining whether the appellant remained a resident for the purposes of sponsorship. These include: (1) whether the appellant maintained a residence in Canada; (2) whether a spouse and/or children resided in Canada; (3) whether the appellant maintained his personal and family assets in Canada; (4) whether the appellant paid Canadian income tax on his global income; (5) whether the appellant maintained investments in Canada; (6) whether the appellant visits Canada whenever he can; and (7) whether the appellant maintains such things as bank accounts, health insurance, club memberships in Canada. On the totality of the evidence the Appeal Division found the refusal valid and dismissed the appeal.

Transitional Provisions

2.01 If an immigrant, before April 1, 1999, has applied for an immigrant visa as an investor and has signed any document referred to in clause 1(v)(iii)(A) of Schedule X, as that Schedule read immediately before that date, or, in the case of an investor in a province, has either applied for a selection certificate under section 3.1 of *An Act re-*

***specting immigration to Québec*, R.S.Q., c. I-0.2, or applied for an immigrant visa as an investor, and signed an investment agreement in accordance with the law of the province, the relevant provisions of these Regulations respecting an applicant for an immigrant visa as investor, an approved business, an investor, an investor in a province, a fund manager, an eligible business, an approved fund, a fund, an escrow agent, a privately administered venture capital fund continue to apply as they read immediately before April 1, 1999 to all persons governed by their application before that date.**

SOR/93-412, s. 2; SOR/94-674, s. 1; SOR/99-146, s. 2

2.02 Section 6 shall apply as it read immediately before April 1, 1997 in respect of the issuance of an immigrant visa to a member of the family class if a sponsor provides the Minister with an undertaking in respect of that member, in form IMM 1344 in the version of that form as it read immediately before April 1, 1997, not later than the close of business on April 18, 1997.

SOR/97-145, s. 2

2.03 (1) For the purpose of an assessment by a visa officer under section 8, in respect of an application for a visa that was made under section 9 of the Act before May 1, 1997 and was still pending on that date, the applicable factors set out in Schedule I, as that Schedule read immediately before May 1, 1997, shall apply.

(2) If an application for a visa referred to in subsection (1) is refused, the visa officer shall reassess the applicant in accordance with the applicable factors set out in Schedule I, as that Schedule read on May 1, 1997.

SOR/97-242, s. 2

2.04 For the purposes of these Regulations, a person who, before May 1, 1997, was a member of the deferred removal orders class may submit an application for landing as a member of that class not later than 120 days after becoming a member of that class and, for that purpose, subsections 2(7.1) and (7.2), paragraph 11.2(c), sections 11.401 and 11.42, paragraph 19(4)(s), subsection 19.1(3), paragraph 20(5)(a) and section 23.2 continue to apply as they read immediately before May 1, 1997.

SOR/97-182, s. 3

Case Law

Mitov v. Canada (Minister of Citizenship & Immigration) (1996), 33 Imm. L.R. (2d) 70, 107 F.T.R. 228 (Fed. T.D.) — This was an application to review a decision that the applicant was not eligible for the Deferred Removal Orders Class (DROC) as defined in the *Immigration Regulations*.

The applicant arrived in Canada in March 1990 and sought Convention refugee status. His claim was denied in January 1992. There was nothing in the supporting affidavits before the Court to indicate that the applicant or his counsel received notice of the negative decision. In April, 1995 the applicant was involved in a motor vehicle accident. The applicant remained at the scene and called the police who discovered that there was an outstanding immigration warrant for the arrest of the applicant. At the applicant's detention review hearing the adjudicator received a letter asking the applicant to report for removal in April 1993. The adjudicator released the applicant on the basis that there was insufficient evidence to support the allegation that the applicant had been properly advised of the removal arrangements.

In May 1995 the applicant made a DROC application which was refused on the basis that the applicant had hindered and delayed his own removal by not attending for removal in April 1993. The immigration officer who made the decision was asked to reconsider and was referred to the fact that the adjudicator who released the applicant had concluded that there was insufficient evidence of communication of removal arrangements. The applicant was advised that the DROC decision would be reviewed only if the immigration office which had issued the warrant admitted that the warrant was issued in error and that the adjudicator's decision would not be considered.

The application for judicial review succeeded. The jurisdiction of an immigration officer is limited in arriving at a DROC decision. The officer is, however, acting in an administrative capacity and must comply with the duty of fairness. Fairness includes the obligation to consider all of the evidence, including the evidence put forward that the warrant was not valid and was effectively set aside by the adjudicator. The immigration authorities failed to put cogent evidence before the adjudicator or the Court that the applicant was actually informed that he was the subject of removal. The officer fettered her decision by refusing to read or consider evidence that substantiated the applicant's position. Accordingly, the application was allowed and the matter referred back to a different immigration officer for reconsideration.

Ministerial Exemptions

2.1 The Minister is hereby authorized to exempt any person from any regulation made under subsection 114(1) of the Act or otherwise facilitate the admission to Canada of any person where the Minister is satisfied that the person should be exempted from that regulation or that the person's admission should be facilitated owing to the existence of compassionate or humanitarian considerations.

SOR/93-44, s. 2

Case Law

Baker v. Canada (Minister of Citizenship & Immigration) (1999), 174 D.L.R. (4th) 193 (S.C.C.) — The appellant entered Canada as a visitor in 1981, and had remained ever since. She was not a permanent resident but had worked illegally for 11 years. She had 4 children all of whom were born in Canada. The appellant was ordered deported in 1992, after it was determined that she had worked illegally in Canada and had overstayed her visitor's visa.

In 1993, the appellant applied for an exemption from the requirement to apply for permanent residence outside Canada, based upon humanitarian and compassionate considerations. In April 1994, it was determined that there were insufficient humanitarian and compassionate grounds to warrant processing the appellant's application from within Canada. The letter advising her of this decision contained no reasons for the decision. The appellant's counsel was provided with the notes made by the immigration officer who interviewed Ms. Baker. These notes were used by the immigration officer who made the decision. Following the refusal of her application, the appellant was served with a direction to report to Pearson Airport for removal. Her deportation was stayed pending the result of this appeal.

At the Trial Division, the application for judicial review was dismissed. The Court held that the immigration officer who made the decision was not required to provide reasons. In the absence of evidence to the contrary, he acted in good faith and made a decision based on correct principles. The trial judge certified an appeal under the following terms: "Given that the *Immigration Act* does not expressly incorporate the language of Canada's international obligations, with respect to the international Convention on the Rights of the Child, must federal immigration authorities treat the best interests of the Canadian child as the primary consideration in assessing an application under section 114(2) of the *Immigration Act*?"

The Federal Court of Appeal held that the appeal was limited to the question that had been certified and as well, rejected a challenge to the constitutionality of section 83(1). The Court noted that a treaty cannot have legal effect in Canada unless implemented through domestic legislation and that the Convention had not been adopted in either federal or provincial legislation. The Court held that legislation should be interpreted to avoid conflicts with Canada's international obligations, but otherwise declined to apply the Convention.

The Supreme Court of Canada declined to consider the various *Charter* issues raised by the parties because the issues involved in the case could be resolved under principles of administrative law and statutory interpretation.

The certification of a question of general importance is the trigger by which an appeal is justified. The object of the appeal was still the judgement itself, not the certified question. Once a question has been certified, all aspects of the appeal may be considered by the Court of Appeal. The Court reviewed the criteria that should be used in determining what procedural rights the duty of fairness requires in a given set of circumstances. The Court emphasized that underlying all of these factors was the notion that the purpose of the participatory rights contained within the duty of procedural fairness was to ensure that administrative decisions are made using a fair and open procedure appropriate to the decision being made and to its statutory, institutional and social context and to provide those affected by the decision with an opportunity to put forward their views and evidence fully and have them considered by the decision-maker.

One important consideration relevant to determining what is required by the common law duty of procedural fairness is, the more that the process provided for the function of the tribunal, the nature of the decision-making body and the determinations that must be made to reach a decision resemble judicial decision-making, the more likely it is that procedural protections closer to the trial model will be required. A second factor is the nature of the statutory scheme and the terms of the statute pursuant to which the body operates. The third factor is the importance of the decision to the individual or individuals affected. The more important the decision the more stringent the procedural protections that will be mandated. In addition, the legitimate expectations of the person challenging the decision may also determine what procedures the duty of fairness requires. If a claimant has a legitimate expectation that a certain procedure will be followed, this procedure will be required by the duty of fairness. Similarly, if a claimant has a legitimate expectation that a certain result will be reached, fairness may require more extensive procedural rights than would otherwise be accorded. The doctrine of legitimate expectations cannot lead to substantive rights outside the procedural domain. Lastly, the analysis of what procedures the duty of fairness requires also takes into account and respects the choices of procedure made by the agency itself, particularly when the statute leaves to the decision-maker the ability to choose its own procedures or when the agency has an expertise in determining what procedures are appropriate. This list is held not to be exhaustive.

An oral hearing is not a general requirement for humanitarian and compassionate decisions. The appellant had the opportunity to put forward in written form, through her lawyer, information about her situation, her children, and their emotional dependence on her as well as documentation in support of her application provided by a social worker and a psychiatrist.

In certain circumstances, the duty of procedural fairness will require the provision of a written explanation for a decision. The circumstances in this case constituted one of the situations where reasons were necessary because of the profound importance of a humanitarian and compassionate decision to those affected. It would be unfair for a person subject to a decision such as this one, which is so critical to their future, not to be told why the result was reached. The reasons requirement was fulfilled in this case because the appellant was provided with the notes of the officer. Because there was no other record of the reasons for making the decision, the notes of the reviewing officer were taken by inference to be the reasons for the decision. Accepting documents such as these notes is part of the flexibility that is necessary when courts evaluate the requirements of the duty of fairness with a recognition of the day-to-day realities of administrative agencies.

Procedural fairness also requires that decisions be made free from a reasonable apprehension of bias. The duty to act in a manner that does not give rise to a reasonable apprehension of bias applies to all immigration officers who play a significant role in the making of any decision, whether they are subordinate reviewing officers or the ones who make the final decision. The Court concluded, in this matter that a well-informed member of the community would perceive bias when reading the reviewing officer's comment. The note did not disclose the existence of an open mind or a weighing of particular circumstances free from stereotype.

The Court found that the appropriate standard of review of a humanitarian and compassionate decision was reasonableness. The Court then examined whether the decision in this case and the immigration officer's interpretation of the scope of the discretion conferred upon him was unreasonable. An unreasonable decision is one that is not supported by any reason that can stand up to a somewhat probing examination. A Court reviewing a conclusion on the reasonableness standard must determine whether any reasons support it. The defect, if there is one, could be in the evidentiary foundation itself or in the logical process by which conclusions are sought from that foundation. The Court concluded that the approach taken in regard to the children's interest indicated that this decision was unreasonable. The officer was dismissive of the interest of the children and this was an unreasonable exercise of the discretion conferred by the section, notwithstanding the important deference that should be given to the decision of the officer. Deference requires a respectful attention to the reasons offered, or which could be offered, in support of a decision.

Section 114(2) and regulation 2.1 require that a decision-maker exercise the power based upon "compassionate or humanitarian consideration". These words and their meaning must be central in determining whether an individual humanitarian and compassionate decision is a reasonable exercise of the power conferred by Parliament. Determining whether the approach taken by the officer was within the boundaries set out by the words of the statute and the values of administrative law required a contextual approach. A reasonable exercise of the power conferred by the section requires close attention to the interests and needs of children. Children's rights and attention to their interests are central humanitarian and compassionate values in Canadian society. Indication of children's interests are important considerations governing the manner in which humanitarian and compassionate powers should be exercised. One of the objectives of the Act in section 3(c) is the facilitation of the reunion in Canada of Canadian citizens and permanent residents with their close relatives from abroad. This section is consistent with a large and liberal interpretation of the values underlying the *Immigration Act* and its purposes. Parliament places a high value on keeping citizens and permanent residents together with their close relatives who are already in Canada. The obligation to take seriously and place important weight on keeping children in contact with both parents is suggested by the objective articulated in section 3(c).

The ratification by Canada of the Convention on the Rights of the Child and the recognition of the importance of children's rights and the best interests of children in other international instruments ratified by Canada, is a further indication of the importance of children's interests when making a humanitarian and compassionate decision. The Convention has not been implemented by Parliament, and, therefore, its provisions have no direct application within Canadian law. Nevertheless, the values reflected in international human rights law may help inform the contextual approach to statutory interpretation in judicial review. Finally, the guidelines issued by the Minister further emphasize that an important factor in a humanitarian and compassionate decision is the connection between family members.

The reasons for this decision did not indicate that it was made in a manner which was alive, attentive, or sensitive to the interests of the Canadian born children of the appellant and did not consider them as an important factor in making the decision. For this reason, the decision was unreasonable and must be overturned.

Lorenzana v. Canada (Minister of Citizenship and Immigration) (May 14, 1999), Doc. IMM-3256-98 (Fed. T.D.) — The applicant was an unsuccessful refugee claimant. A Post-Claim Determination Officer found the applicant not to be a member of the post-determination refugee claimants in Canada class. The applicant sought to challenge the refusal of his request for permanent residence on humanitarian and compassionate grounds. The applicant's main reason for wishing to apply for permanent residence was his fear of returning to Guatemala. The applicant's reasons for fearing return to Guatemala were the same as those presented in his refugee claim. The applicant did not have any new information to present concerning in his fear. The officer was not required to conduct an independent risk assessment in the absence of either additional evidence or a submission that on his return the applicant would be subjected to unduly harsh sanction.

Charles v. Canada (Minister of Citizenship & Immigration) (1999), 241 N.R. 398 (Fed. C.A.) — The requirements of fairness are very limited in the processing of requests for special ministerial exemptions from the law under section 114(2) of the Immigration Act, based on humanitarian and compassionate grounds. Accordingly, it is not a breach of the duty of fairness for an immigration officer to deny counsel the right to pose questions to the applicant or to suggest responses to him or her. The Court expressly made no comment on counsel's right to make representations as that was not an issue raised by this case.

Lukic v. Canada (Minister of Citizenship & Immigration) (March 10, 1999), Doc. IMM-1515-98 (Fed. T.D.) — This was an application to review a decision of an immigration officer refusing an application under subsection 114(2). The applicant was 78 years old and born in Croatia, where her siblings still live. Her husband was dead. Counsel for the applicant had maintained that the officer had fettered her discretion by treating the fact that the applicant and her daughter were not financially self-sufficient as determinative of her claim to be granted permanent residence status on humanitarian and compassionate grounds. A decision-maker unlawfully fetters her discretion only when she treats one factor as decisive regardless of the presence or strength of countervailing considerations. On the facts of this case, the notes of the officer indicate that she had considered factors militating in favour of granting the application but found them insufficiently compelling when weighed against the factors that the applicant's daughter had insufficient financial means to sponsor her mother, and that the applicant was unlikely ever to be self supporting if permitted to remain in Canada.

The application for judicial review was dismissed.

Cojocar v. Canada (Minister of Citizenship & Immigration) (January 21, 1999), Doc. IMM-2499-97 (Fed. T.D.) — This was an application to review a decision of an immigration officer refusing humanitarian and compassionate relief. The applicant, a citizen of Romania claimed refugee status. The refugee division dismissed his claim and the applicant subsequently applied for landing on compassionate and humanitarian grounds. The applicant was interviewed by an immigration officer to whom he reiterated his fear of returning to his native country. The officer requested an opinion from a Post-Claims Determination Officer (PCDO) assessing the risk to which the applicant was likely to be exposed.

The PCDO concluded that the applicant would not be at risk if returned home. The report of this officer was not disclosed to the applicant. The PCDO's information came from the documentation centre. It was agreed that documents containing "general country conditions" are exempt from disclosure. The phrase "general country conditions" is intended to distinguish matters that are of general knowledge from those on which the applicant is likely to be particularly well-informed and therefore should be heard, because, for example, they concern the claimant personally or the claimant's activities. The failure to disclose the report in this case was not a breach of the minimal content of the duty of fairness. The report contained information that was readily available to the public including the applicant and his counsel and it was reasonable for them to anticipate that the PCDO would consult it. Accordingly, the report was not extrinsic evidence.

Redman v. Canada (Minister of Citizenship & Immigration) (1998), 157 F.T.R. 120 (Fed. T.D.) — In this judicial review of a negative humanitarian and compassionate decision the issue involved extrinsic evidence. The immigration officer received an anonymous letter that was prejudicial to the applicants and was not disclosed to them. The immigration officer filed an affidavit saying that she did not consider the letter as relevant to the assessment of the applicant's application. In the immigration context anonymous prejudicial letters are particularly nasty. Fairness requires that when such potentially damaging information is received it must be disclosed so that an applicant may be satisfied before a decision is made that it will be disregarded or that he/she has had an opportunity to respond to it.

Maharatnam v. Canada (Minister of Citizenship & Immigration) (1998), 46 Imm. L.R. (2d) 62, 149 F.T.R. 307 (Fed. T.D.) — This was an application to review and set aside a decision of an immigration officer who determined that the applicant was not entitled to favourable consideration under subsection 114(2) of the Immigration Act.

In examining whether humanitarian and compassionate circumstances exist, immigration officers must examine whether there exists a special situation in the person's home country and whether undo hardship would likely result from removal. In most cases, such persons will have indicated an intention to claim refugee status. The onus is on the applicant to satisfy the officer about a particular situation that exists in their country and that their personal circumstances in relation to that situation make them worthy of positive discretion. Counsel for the applicant addressed this issue in this case and therefore the officer was called upon to conduct what is known as a "risk assessment".

In this case, the Court was not satisfied that the officer conducted a risk assessment as required and accordingly set aside the officer's decision.

Nijjar v. Canada (Minister of Citizenship & Immigration) (1997), 139 F.T.R. 308, 42 Imm. L.R. (2d) 54 (Fed. T.D.) — The applicants sought to review a decision that they did not come within the definition of "dependant" pursuant to subsection 2(1) of the regulations. They also sought to review a decision that they ought not to be given favourable humanitarian and compassionate consideration. This latter request must be submitted to a visa officer for consideration. The decision of the immigration program officer in this case was accordingly set aside and the matter remitted back to the immigration program officer who was instructed to refer the application to a visa officer for consideration of the humanitarian and compassionate request.

Karakulak v. Canada (Minister of Citizenship & Immigration) (1996), 119 F.T.R. 288 (Fed. T.D.) — This was an application to review a decision of the area manager to the effect that there were insufficient humanitarian and compassionate grounds to exempt the applicants from the requirements of the Act.

In October 1993, the applicants made an application for landing from within Canada on humanitarian and compassionate grounds. In January 1994, an immigration officer recommended to the area manager that the applicants not be processed for landing on those grounds. The area manager accepted this recommendation and concluded that there were insufficient humanitarian and compassionate grounds in this case.

One ground upon which review was sought, was on the basis that following a request for release of documents under the *Privacy Act*, the applicants discovered that extrinsic evidence or third party evidence was considered by the area manager and that this extrinsic evidence had not been disclosed to them.

The failure to disclose extrinsic evidence is only a breach of the principles of natural justice, if the extrinsic evidence is subsequently relied on by the immigration officer making the impugned decision. There was nothing in the recommending officers notes or in the immigration officer's decision implicity or explicitly which suggested that the extrinsic evidence had been a factor in the decision.

Accordingly, the application was dismissed.

Lee v. Canada (Minister of Citizenship & Immigration) (July 29, 1996), Doc. IMM-1511-95 (Fed. T.D.) — This was an application for judicial review of a decision determining that there were insufficient humanitarian and compassionate considerations to warrant having the applicant's application for permanent residence processed from within Canada. The officer in giving her decision referred to the absence of "compelling" humanitarian and compassionate considerations.

It is not helpful to add descriptive words to statutory language. The officer's notes, however, in this case, indicated that the correct test was used during her assessment of the applicant's file and accordingly the application was dismissed.

Duale v. Canada (Minister of Citizenship & Immigration) (1996), 34 Imm. L.R. (2d) 8, 115 F.T.R. 239 (Fed. T.D.) — An immigration officer's determination that insufficient humanitarian and compassionate grounds existed to warrant the processing of an application for permanent residence from within Canada was set aside, because the officer wrote "I don't believe that they [the applicants] are at any greater risk in Somalia than anyone else in the general population". This comment was taken to mean that the officer had imposed a requirement on the applicants that they be at a "greater risk" than anyone else in the country. This requirement was inconsistent with the intent and purpose of immigration policy in Canada and accordingly the decision was set aside and the matter remitted for reconsideration.

Nadarajah v. Canada (Minister of Citizenship & Immigration) (1996), 33 Imm. L.R. (2d) 234, 112 F.T.R. 296 (Fed. T.D.); affirmed (1999), 237 N.R. 15 (Fed. C.A.) — Information on country conditions that was not in the applicants' immigration files, but was considered in a PDRCC risk assessment, does not constitute extrinsic evidence. The country conditions information was within the ambit of the subject matter the applicants knew would be considered on the section 114(2) review. There was no indication that this information was not available to the applicants had they taken steps to obtain it. Accordingly, there was no need for the applicants to be given notice of this information and an opportunity to respond to it. The Court noted that the result might have been different if the information on country conditions had been information to which the applicants could not have had access and if such information was material to the decision that was being made.

Wekpe v. Canada (Minister of Citizenship & Immigration) (1996), 33 Imm. L.R. (2d) 274 (Fed. T.D.) — The officer denied an application for humanitarian and compassionate relief on the basis that public policy considerations and humanitarian and compassionate considerations were not intended to overcome a criminal inadmissibility.

The factors to be considered in an H&C application are all the factors before the officer, including any criminal conviction. The officer did not weigh all the factors but instead considered herself bound by the fact that the applicant was criminally inadmissible.

Accordingly, the officer's decision was set aside.

Al-Joubeh v. Canada (Minister of Citizenship & Immigration) (1996), 33 Imm. L.R. (2d) 77, 109 F.T.R. 235 (Fed. T.D.) — The applicant, a Lebanese national, came to Canada and claimed refugee status, unsuccessfully. The applicant was also assessed to determine if he could be admitted to Canada as a member of the Post Determination Refugee Claimants in Canada class (PDRCC). It was decided that he could not. For purposes of that assessment it was determined that the applicant would not be at risk if he was returned to Lebanon. Parallel to the PDRCC assessment the applicant applied under section 114(2) of the *Immigration Act*. An internal immigration memorandum required a visa officer, where the 114(2) application was related solely or primarily to the question of whether the applicant would be at risk if returned to his or her native country, to seek an opinion from the post claims review section which meant that the officer dealing with the section 114 review relied upon the opinion of the officer who rejected the applicant's PDRCC application. The immigration officers's reliance on the memorandum was reasonable. The memorandum was a reasonable guideline for processing 114(2) claims in these circumstances.

During the course of consulting with the post claims review section the visa officer brought to the section's attention new information which resulted in an updated assessment by the section. The officer fell into error in not providing the applicant with an opportunity to respond to this updated assessment before relying on it. For that reason alone the decision of the visa officer was set aside.

Dasent v. Canada (Minister of Citizenship & Immigration) (1996), 193 N.R. 303, 107 F.T.R. 80 (note), 39 Admin. L.R. (2d) 62 (Fed. C.A.); appeal to S.C.C. refused (October 3, 1996), Doc. 25219 (S.C.C.) — A Trial Division judge certified two questions for consideration by the Court of Appeal. The first one dealt with whether, in a judicial review of a humanitarian and compassionate decision that was based in part on an earlier humanitarian and compassionate decision, from which judicial review was not sought, procedural errors in the earlier process may be the subject of that review.

Procedural errors alleged to have been committed in making a particular recommendation must be challenged on judicial review of that recommendation within the time permitted by the statute, or within an extended time granted by the Court. Once that time has elapsed an immigration officer considering a new application for humanitarian and compassionate considerations, is entitled to take note of the evidence, conclusions, and recommendations in the first application. The officer cannot, however, be bound to make the same decision. A new application requires a new decision by the officer, having regard to events which may have occurred since the first recommendation. On judicial review of the later decision it is not open to an applicant to challenge the validity or procedures of the decision on the first application.

The second question was whether information in a case file obtained from a spouse in a separate spousal interview, at which the applicant was not present, constituted extrinsic evidence not brought forward by an applicant to which the applicant must be afforded an opportunity to respond.

The Court did not consider that the statements by a spouse are extrinsic evidence. The onus was on the applicant to satisfy the immigration officer that humanitarian and compassionate grounds existed. Her spouse was there to support her claim that there was a *bona fide* marriage, and his statements cannot be seen to be extrinsic evidence not brought forward by her. If the applicant and her spouse did not, in separate interviews, tell the same story this was a factor which the immigration officer could legitimately take into account.

Accordingly, the Court allowed the appeal and set aside the decision of the Trial Division judge.

Silva v. Canada (Minister of Citizenship & Immigration) (1995), 95 F.T.R. 62 — The applicant, a citizen of Brazil, arrived in Canada in 1988 and made a refugee claim which was processed through the backlog clearance program. The claim was found to lack a credible basis, however the applicant married a Canadian citizen and requested consideration on a humanitarian and compassionate basis in December 1992. This request was approved in principle at about the same time as the applicant's husband wrote to Immigration to advise that the marriage had failed. The applicant passed medical and security checks and was called in to Immigration so that the removal order outstanding against the applicant as the result of her failed refugee claim could be executed. The applicant appeared at Immigration without her husband and explained that her marriage had failed.

The withdrawal of sponsorship was effective in this case because the removal order was still outstanding and its execution was a condition precedent to landing. The Court referred to the Court of Appeal decision in *Sivacilar v. Canada (Minister of Employment & Immigration)* (1984), 57 N.R. 57 (Fed. C.A.) and distinguished it on the basis that in that case the right to remain in Canada had been acquired and nothing remained to be done in the granting of landing. Accordingly, the application for judicial review was dismissed.

Carson v. Canada (Minister of Citizenship & Immigration) (1995), 95 F.T.R. 137 (Fed. T.D.) — The applicant sought to review a decision refusing the applicant an exemption pursuant to section 114(2) of the *Immigration Act* from the requirements of section 9(1) of the *Immigration Act*. Tonya Carson is a Canadian citizen who had married the applicant, William Carson. A fundamental issue in the case involved a *bona fides* of the marriage. The Court rules that Mrs. Carson had no standing in the judicial review application. She was a Canadian citizen who did not require any exemption from the *Immigration Act* or regulations. Further, whether she had standing or not had no impact on the ultimate issue in the matter.

The Court observed that an applicant in this type of case did not have a case to meet, rather the applicant was trying to persuade the decision maker that he or she should be provided with exceptional treatment and be exempted from the general requirements of the law. Accordingly, no hearing need be held and no reasons be provided. In order to succeed in an attack on a humanitarian and compassionate decision the applicant must persuade the Court that the decision maker erred in law, proceeded on some wrong or improper principle, or acted in bad faith.

On the evidence the Court was satisfied that no error was committed by the decision maker with respect to his consideration of the *bona fides* of the marriage. Further, the Court was satisfied that the decision maker had not ignored counsel's submissions, thus, the Court concluded that no error of law was committed by the immigration officer.

Tse v. Canada (Minister of Citizenship & Immigration) (April 27, 1995), Doc. IMM-1191-94 (Fed. T.D.) — The decision refusing humanitarian and compassionate relief was set aside. The officer determined that the marriage of the applicant and his wife was not *bona fide*. In doing so the officer relied on interview notes arising from a prior application by the applicant for such exemption. In reaching her decision the officer made that "boiler plate" statement that she considered all the evidence. The officer made no reference to the fact that since the marriage the applicant's wife had become pregnant and they were expecting their first child. Even if the applicant's marriage had not been *bona fide* a year earlier when the first humanitarian and compassionate decision was made, the reviewing officer on the second application has to address her mind to whether or not changed circumstances existed which now demonstrated that the marriage had become genuine. A "boiler plate" reference to having reviewed all the evidence is not sufficient.

Black v. Canada (Minister of Citizenship & Immigration) (1995), 28 Imm. L.R. (2d) 81, 93 F.T.R. 57 — The applicant applied to quash a decision refusing her an exemption from the visa requirements of section 9(1) of the *Immigration Act*. The applicant arrived in Canada on July 10, 1987 in possession of a valid visitor's visa. She began work almost immediately and continued to work essentially as a housekeeper. She has a husband and three children in Jamaica whom she supports by virtue of her work in Canada. The Immigration Officer who made the decision did not specifically respond to the check list that was part of the earlier *Illegal de Facto* Residents Policy.

Effective February 1, 1993 the "public policy" base for exemption from the visa requirements of section 9(1) was repealed. No obligation fell on Immigration Officers to consider and apply all of the criteria that existed prior to February 1, 1993 for *Illegal de Facto* Residents cases. Such cases were now to be dealt with as humanitarian and compassionate consideration cases. Accordingly, the application was dismissed.

Charran v. Canada (Minister of Citizenship & Immigration) (1995), 89 F.T.R. 113 — The applicant claimed refugee status which was denied. The Federal Court declined to review the negative determination. The applicant then applied under section 114(2) for permission to apply for permanent resident status from within Canada. The basis of the applicant's request involved his second child who had sustained brain damage and paralysis in one arm at birth. Several operations over a two year period were required and these operations were not available in Guyana. The applicant argued that the removal from Canada threatened the child's physical and emotional well being. The section 114 decision does not directly effect the legal status of the child who is a Canadian citizen and had, therefore, the right to remain in Canada. Whether or not the Canadian born son leaves Canada with his parents is a parental decision, therefore the decision to deny relief under section 114(2) did not violate the child's section 7 rights. Further, the applicant's claim to relief cannot be based on the infringement of the rights of a third party. The applicant's Charter rights have not personally been infringed by the discretionary decision not to allow him to apply for permanent residence from within Canada. Separation of the family unit does not result from the decision at issue. The decision whether to take the child to Guyana or leave him in Canada is a parental decision and does not engage the protection of the Charter. Canada's international obligations to the protection of the family and the protection of the child are not enforceable under Canadian law unless those obligations are specifically adopted as part of domestic law. The officer's decision denying relief was upheld.

Marques v. Canada (Minister of Citizenship & Immigration) (1995), 27 Imm. L.R. (2d) 209 (Fed. T.D.) — The applicant applied unsuccessfully for humanitarian and compassionate consideration. The applicant was the father of a Canadian citizen child who had cerebral palsy and had to remain in Canada for treatment. One officer prepared the case history and recommended that the request for humanitarian and compassionate consideration be refused. The decision maker, however, was a second officer. This officer made notes on the file to the effect that he had reviewed the case and, in his opinion, it did not merit consideration under section 114(2). There was, however, no indication as to what the decision maker, in fact, did in the performance of his duties. There was no affidavit filed in these proceedings from the officer who actually made the decision. There was, thus, no indication that the officer had taken into account the interest of the Canadian citizen child. It was clear that the first officer, who made the negative recommendation, had taken the child's interest into consideration, but there was no such indication from the second officer, who was the one who actually made the decision. In those circumstances the decision denying relief under section 114(2) was quashed.

Sorkhabi v. Canada (Secretary of State) (1994), 26 Imm. L.R. (2d) 287, 89 F.T.R. 224 — This case provides an example of a situation where a visa officer, considering an application under section 114(2), relied on extrinsic evidence not brought forward by the applicant and failed to give the applicant a chance to respond to such evidence. The negative decision of the immigration officer was set aside and the matter referred back for redetermination.

Chan v. Canada (Minister of Citizenship & Immigration) (1994), 87 F.T.R. 62 — There is no obligation to provide formal reasons for a negative decision under section 114(2). The notes of the immigration officer, who initially reviews the application, are relevant in assessing whether there has been an ignoring of relevant evidence or a taking into account of irrelevant considerations. These notes should not be elevated to the status of formal reasons, however. There was no indication in the notes as to the applicant's present relationship with her family, or her reconciliation with family members. The notes leave the impression that the applicant is still estranged from her family. The length of time the applicant has been in Canada, her immediate family's presence here, and her reintegration into that family, are not referred to in the recommendation section of the notes. Accordingly, the Court concluded that the recommending officer based his decision on a misunderstanding of the evidence, and the decision of the officer was set aside.

Williams v. Canada (Minister of Citizenship & Immigration) (1994), 84 F.T.R. 194 — This was an application to review a decision that insufficient humanitarian and compassionate grounds existed to warrant processing the applicant's request for landing from within Canada. To succeed in attacking a section 114(2) decision the applicant must show that the decision maker erred in law, proceeded on some wrong or improper principle, or acted in bad faith.

The applicant was given a full opportunity to state his case. He was represented by a solicitor, and written submissions with attached exhibits were made and considered. The case history notes prepared by the immigration officer disclosed that the officer did consider the claimant's attributes as well as his criminal record. It noted his extraordinary business sense, his extensive family support system and his philanthropic nature.

The application was dismissed.

Agbonkpolor v. Canada (Minister of Employment & Immigration) (1994), 25 Imm. L.R. (2d) 280, 85 F.T.R. 39 — The applicant married a Canadian and sought special relief on humanitarian and compassionate grounds under section 114(2). The Court noted that the reference to public policy had been deleted from section 114(2). It is also noted that the spousal policy set out in the employment and immigration examination and enforcement manual at 9.06 was an aspect of public policy considerations. Accordingly, since February 1993, spousal policy is just one of many factors that the Minister must consider in making a humanitarian and compassionate grounds determination. Accordingly, Minister's officials were not bound to decide this 114(2) application by applying for the spousal policy guidelines set out in the manual.

Spousal policy considerations were only one aspect of the humanitarian and compassionate determination decision.

Hinson v. Canada (Minister of Citizenship & Immigration) (1994), 26 Imm. L.R. (2d) 40, 85 F.T.R. 44 — The applicant, a Jehovah's Witness and a citizen of Ghana, was denied convention refugee status. He thereafter applied for permanent residence status relying on section 114(2) of the Act, for a request to be exempted from section 9(1). On April 21, 1993 an immigration consultant retained by the applicant, received a telephone call from a representative of the Immigration office, informing the consultant that the 114(2) application was successful. A few months later the applicant received a letter, signed by the Assistant Manager, informing him that the application under section 114(2) had been unsuccessful.

The discrepancy between the telephone call and the subsequent letter gave rise to the question of whether the telephone call was a decision. The Court said that, given the repercussions for any applicant of a section 114(2) determination, it could not find that a telephone call could be accepted as a final determination of the application. The telephone call was, accordingly, not a decision and was therefore not subject to judicial review.

Drame v. Canada (Minister of Employment & Immigration) (1994), 82 F.T.R. 177 (Fed. T.D.) — This was an application to review a decision of an immigration officer refusing an exemption pursuant to section 114(2).

The applicant arrived in Canada from Guinea and claimed refugee status. She married and applied for a section 114(2) exemption. The applicant's refugee claim was found to have had a credible basis but the applicant withdrew the claim after her marriage. The Court noted that in trying to determine whether a marriage was one of substance and entered into in good faith and not merely for immigration purposes, that officers should ask themselves when considering the facts, what would a reasonable person do in such a situation. The immigration officer's notes made no reference to the fact that the applicant was pregnant at the time of her interview, nor was there any note in the file to reflect the fact that the applicant gave birth shortly after the interview. The Court noted that the father of the child was the applicant's husband.

The Court concluded that the immigration officer did not consider the applicant's application as a reasonable person would have done and that the officer, by ignoring these facts, did not exercise her discretion in good faith. Accordingly, the decision of the officer was set aside.

Pagal v. Canada (Minister of Citizenship & Immigration) (1994), 82 F.T.R. 106 — The applicant came to Canada under the Foreign Domestic Workers programme. She met and married a Canadian citizen and a child was born. Subsequently, the marriage broke down. The applicant was granted custody rights. The immigration officer's decision that insufficient humanitarian and compassionate grounds existed to permit the applicant to remain in Canada, was quashed. The immigration officer did not consider the effect on the child of losing *de facto* contact with his father. The officer had merely considered whether the father's visitation rights could be amended should the mother leave Canada for the Philippines and take the child with her.

Chaudhry v. Canada (Minister of Employment & Immigration) (1994), 25 Imm. L.R. (2d) 139, 83 F.T.R. 81, [1995] 1 F.C. 104 — The applicants applied to quash a decision of the CRDD whereby the applicants' motion for a rehearing of their Convention refugee claim was dismissed.

The applicants were citizens of Pakistan who sought to be recognized as Convention refugees by reason of a well-founded fear of persecution based on their religion and membership in a particular social group. They were determined not to be Convention refugees and sought to re-open their claims to present evidence not available at the time of the CRDD decision to the effect that a change in country conditions had occurred since the decision in their case. Specifically, they sought to adduce evidence showing an increase in incidents of persecution against members of their religion.

The CRDD found that it had the jurisdiction to address the issue of whether or not it had the jurisdiction to re-open a claim. It then concluded that it could not re-open a matter where the sole purpose of the re-opening would be the hearing of new facts.

The Court found that the CRDD did not err in law in finding that, notwithstanding the Charter, it could not re-open the hearing solely for the purpose of hearing new evidence of changed country conditions.

The mechanism for dealing with post-proceeding evidence is section 114(2) of the *Immigration Act.* That section, and the Minister's practise in connection with that section, ensures that claimants have a meaningful opportunity to have new evidence of changed country conditions heard by an authoritative body. In this regard the Court noted that the discretionary decisions of post-claim determination officers are subject to judicial review by the Federal Court if such discretion is exercised pursuant to improper purposes, based on irrelevant considerations, made with bad faith, or otherwise are patently unreasonable. Accordingly, the application for judicial review in this case was dismissed.

Shah v. Canada (Minister of Employment & Immigration) (1994), 81 F.T.R. 320n, 170 N.R. 238 (Fed. C.A.) — The decision under appeal is that of an immigration officer charged with making a recommendation to the Governor in Council as to the exercise of the latter's discretion to grant an exemption to the applicant from the requirements of section 9(1) of the *Immigration Act* on humanitarian or compassionate grounds. The content of the duty of fairness in this type of situation is minimal. The decision itself is wholly a matter of judgment and discretion and the law gives the applicant no right to any particular outcome. In this respect the decision differs from many others where the law establishes criteria which, if met, give rise to certain rights. In a case such as this the applicant must persuade the decision maker that he or she should be given exceptional treatment and exempted from the general requirements of the law. No hearing need be held and no reasons need be given. The officer is not required to put before the applicant any tentative conclusions that he or she may be drawing from the material, nor even any apparent contradictions that are of concern. If the decision maker is going to rely on extrinsic evidence, not brought forward by the applicant, he or she must give the applicant a chance to respond to such evidence. In the case of perceived contradictions the failure to draw them specifically to the applicant's attention may go to the weight that should later be attached to them but does not affect the fairness of the decision.

The appeal in this case was dismissed.

Osei-Boadu v. Canada (Minister of Employment & Immigration) (May 20, 1994), Doc. No. 93-T-59 (Fed. T.D.) — This was an application for judicial review of a decision of an immigration officer determining that there were insufficient humanitarian and compassionate grounds to warrant processing the applicant's request for landing from within Canada. The applicant and his wife were citizens of Ghana. They arrived in Canada in October 1987 and claimed refugee status. They were assessed in July 1991 to determine whether there were sufficient humanitarian and compassionate grounds. Written submissions were filed, along with letters in support of the humanitarian and compassionate application. On July 30, 1991 the applicant and his wife were advised that there were insufficient grounds and that they would be given an oral hearing before the CRDD to determine if there was a credible basis for their refugee claim. The applicant complained that he was not given any reasons for dissolving his claim. The failure to give reasons is not a basis for concluding that the decision was reached by an unfair process. Unless there is an express duty to give reasons for a decision, reasons need not be given. The application was dismissed.

Eliyathamby v. Canada (Minister of Employment & Immigration) (1994), 76 F.T.R. 156 — The applicant sought to review a negative CRDD decision. The applicant was a Tamil and as such faced persecution in the Jaffna area of Sri Lanka. The stated ground of review was that the Board had misconstrued significant aspects of the evidence. One piece of evidence was a letter from the United Nations High Commissioner for Refugees, dated July 9, 1992, to the Chair of the Immigration and Refugee Board. The letter dealt with the mandated return of persons from Sri Lanka as well as the question of an internal flight alternative. The Court could not conclude that the Board had applied an improper test or otherwise misconstrued the evidence and therefore dismissed the application. However, the Court noted that the UNHCR letter applied not only to the refugee question, but also was relevant to the assessment of whether humanitarian and compassionate grounds existed. The letter stated that individuals moving from an unsafe area in the north could not normally be expected to return in safety and dignity to the south and therefore should be allowed to stay in Convention countries for humanitarian reasons. The Court noted that it assumed that this letter would be taken into account when humanitarian and compassionate assessment was made of the applicant's case.

Nagy v. Canada (Minister of Employment & Immigration) (March 11, 1994), Doc. IMM-1375-93 (Fed. T.D.) — The applicant sought to review a decision holding that there were insufficient humanitarian and compassionate grounds for allowing an application for permanent residence within Canada. The immigration officer did not give reasons for refusing to recommend that the Minister exercise his discretion under section 114(2). The case law has been consistent and clear to the effect that reasons are not required in this context. Section 77 only requires reasons to be given to a person who sponsors a family member's application for permanent residence where that application is refused. The matter, in this case, had nothing to do with Luis Nagy, the applicant's sponsor, since he was not part of the section 114(2) application and therefore no reasons were required.

Ivanov v. Canada (Minister of Employment & Immigration) (1993), 21 Imm. L.R. (2d) 250, 68 F.T.R. 63 — The applicant sought to set aside a negative decision on a humanitarian and compassionate request pursuant to section 114(2). No reasons were given for the negative humanitarian decision. Submissions had been forwarded to the respondent's representative outlining the applicant's long term common-law relationship and the intention of the common-law partner to sponsor the applicant as soon as the partner obtained landing.

The immigration file contained information about the applicant's long term common-law relationship and about his intent to marry. The Commission's own directives indicate that this is *prima facie* grounds warranting a favourable consideration. If the immigration officer had doubts about the marriage, the rules of natural justice and fairness dictated that the applicant should be allowed the opportunity to respond to those concerns. No interview was held in the present case and no opportunity to respond to those concerns was given to the applicant.

Accordingly, the negative decision was set aside and the matter referred back for reconsideration.

Muse v. Canada (Solicitor General) (1993), 68 F.T.R. 144, 22 Imm. L.R. (2d) 276 — The applicant, a citizen of Somalia, unsuccessfully claimed refugee status. The applicant then submitted a request to the Minister of Employment of Immigration and to the Governor General in Council, requesting permission to be admitted to Canada as a permanent resident pursuant to section 114(2) of the Act. The request was denied, in part because the applicant could not demonstrate that he was at any greater risk than anyone else in the general population of Somalia under the prevailing conditions in that country in December 1992. The respondent's officials, in requiring the applicant to be at greater risk than anyone else in the population, fettered their own discretion by imposing a rigid requirement which was inconsistent with the intent of the *Immigration Act* and ministerial policy. The decision was quashed and the respondent directed to properly reconsider the applicant's request for section 114(2) relief.

Ramoutar v. Canada (Minister of Employment & Immigration), 21 Imm. L.R. (2d) 203, 65 F.T.R. 32, [1993] 3 F.C. 370 (Fed. T.D.) — This application was for judicial review to quash a decision not to refer the applicant's case to the Governor in Council for an exemption, from the requirements of section 9(1) of the *Immigration Act*, on humanitarian and compassionate grounds.

The applicant had married a Canadian citizen. An Immigration officer, after reviewing the case, felt there was a reasonable doubt about the *bona fides* of the marriage and declined to refer the matter to the Governor in Council.

In assessing the *bona fides* of the applicant's marriage to a Canadian citizen on the basis of requiring proof of such *bona fides* beyond a reasonable doubt, the respondent erred in law. Proceedings under section 114(2) of the *Immigration Act* are civil in nature and therefore the appropriate standard of proof is proof on a balance of probabilities — the standard applicable in civil proceedings.

Maraj v. Canada (Minister of Employment & Immigration) (1993), 19 Imm. L.R. (2d) 90 (Fed. T.D.) — This was an application for leave to commence a proceeding under section 18.1 of the *Federal Court Act* to quash a decision of an immigration officer finding insufficient humanitarian and compassionate grounds to permit an application for landing from within Canada.

A portion of this decision deals with the method by which the Governor in Council functions in the Canadian constitutional system of government.

Ferrerya v. Canada (Minister of Employment & Immigration) (1992), 56 F.T.R. 270 (Fed. T.D.) — The applicant arrived in Canada as a visitor. He asserted a claim for Convention refugee status and that claim was found to have no credible basis. The applicant did not report to Immigration authorities and remained in Canada illegally. He finally resurfaced, making an application for landed immigrant status on the basis that he had a Canadian wife. The applicant was exempted from subsection 9(1) of the *Immigration Act*. An Order in Council exempting an individual from the visa requirements of subsection 9(1) does not confer a right to permanent residence. The exemption's effect is to allow the making of an application for landing despite the fact that the applicant is already within Canada. In this case there was no final determination of the applicant's application made on the merits prior to the subsection 9(1) waiver being given. Therefore the waiver did not accord to the applicant any right to permanent residence in Canada.

Dick v. Canada (Minister of Employment & Immigration) (1992), 17 Imm. L.R. (2d) 25, 52 F.T.R. 318 (Fed. T.D.) — The applicant sought orders in the nature of *certiorari* and *mandamus*. *Certiorari* to quash a decision determining that there was insufficient humanitarian and compassionate grounds upon which to accept an application for permanent residence. The motion for relief in the nature of *mandamus* was to compel the respondent Minister to provide the applicant with a full and fair interview in accordance with the law and in accordance with the duty of fairness.

There was a disagreement as to what occurred at the impugned interview. The applicant in her affidavit set out her recollection of what took place, the immigration officer in his affidavit set out his version. There was no cross-examination on the affidavits, which made it difficult for the Court to determine the question of credibility.

The onus was on the applicant to satisfy the Court that there was reversible error warranting judicial interference. This was not an appeal or a retrial matter. The Court, in the absence of error in the legal sense, could not substitute its opinion for the discretion exercised by the Immigration officer in coming to the decision he did.

The evidence failed to make out that there was a likelihood of bias on the part of the officer and the case was dismissed.

Said v. Canada (Minister of Employment & Immigration) (1992), 91 D.L.R. (4th) 400 (Fed. T.D.) — The applicant made a claim for refugee status which was found to have no credible basis. The immigration manual provides that such persons are to have their claims reviewed to see if humanitarian and compassionate grounds exist for permitting them to remain in Canada, but does not provide that the person concerned is entitled to notice or to make any submissions before such interview takes place. Although section 114(2) does not vest any rights in an applicant, it creates a duty of fairness in the Minister when exercising the power contained in that subsection. At a minimum the applicant must have some opportunity to state his case. The Governor in Council is not required to give any reasons for its decision to grant or refuse discretionary relief.

Editor's Note: Although the subsection has been amended, the principles enunciated in this case may still be useful.

Ha v. Canada (Minister of Employment & Immigration) (1992), 8 Admin. L.R. (2d) 59, 56 F.T.R. 74 (Fed. T.D.) — An immigration officer rejected the applicant's request for landing on humanitarian and compassionate grounds. An order was also sought prohibiting the commencement of the credible basis hearing until such time as a new humanitarian and compassionate interview was conducted. The applicant was a refugee claimant from Hong Kong. He was in the refugee backlog and received a notice to attend an interview to determine whether sufficient humanitarian and compassionate grounds existed to grant landing. Counsel for the applicant was unable to attend this interview due to short notice. He did write a four-page letter in which he requested that the interview be rescheduled. The immigration officer who conducted the interview declined to reschedule and concluded that no sufficient humanitarian and compassionate grounds existed to justify landing the applicant.

There is no obligation under subsection 114(2) to conduct an interview or hearing. There is no authority for the submission that the claimant is entitled to be represented by counsel once an interview is offered. The right to counsel is dealt with in section 30 of the Act and in sections 27 to 39 of the regulations. These provisions refer to the right to counsel at an inquiry. There is no corresponding statutory right to counsel during a subsection 114(2) interview.

Given that an interview is offered there is a duty to act fairly. The concept of what constitutes procedural fairness in purely administrative proceedings varies depending on the type and nature of the proceedings, the nature of the rights involved, possible burdens of the process and the possibility of harm if an adverse decision is reached. The applicant has no legal right to remain in Canada until such time as he is found to be a Convention refugee. The determination of whether humanitarian and compassionate grounds exist is discretionary and can be made without personal appearance. It is a decision that involves no complex legal issues. A negative determination does not lead to removal, but rather the claim then proceeds to the next stage in the process, an oral hearing into the merits, at which time there is a right to legal representation. The duty of fairness dictates that the *audi alteram partem* principle be adhered to and in many instances this will require the services of a qualified interpreter.

The Court concluded that there was no procedural unfairness and dismissed the application.

Editor's Note: The refugee provisions have changed but the principles enunciated in the case may be useful.

Pollard v. Canada (Minister of Employment & Immigration) (1991), 48 F.T.R. 153 (Fed. T.D.) — This case illustrates the difference between strict judicial review and an appeal *per se*. Although the Immigration officer's decision could not be legitimately quashed on *certiorari*, the Court commented that it was unfortunate in the extreme that there was no genuine appeal to the Court. In this case, the applicant sought to quash a decision of an Immigration official at the Toronto Backlog Clearance Centre wherein that official determined that there were insufficient humanitarian and compassionate grounds upon which to accept the applicant's application for permanent residence.

The Court commented that the disgraceful problem with the application of the guidelines is that they make it possible to arrive at the conclusion that the decision-maker wished to formulate all along. The Court found, with genuine sorrow, that there was no basis in terms of judicial review for quashing the officer's decision.

Cheema v. Canada (Minister of Employment & Immigration) (1991), 15 Imm. L.R. (2d) 117, (sub nom. *Cheema v. Ministre de l'emploi et de l'Immigration)* 44 F.T.R. 154 (Fed. T.D.) — The applicant, a citizen of India, made a refugee claim and was denied refugee status. This occurred in 1986. The applicant applied for redetermination of his claim under the procedure that was then applicable, and his motion for redetermination was dismissed and a removal order was made against him. The applicant did not appear for execution of the order. In 1990, the applicant was arrested and ultimately in February 1991 returned to India. Prior to his return, the applicant attempted to make an application under section 114(2) but was informed by a representative of the Immigration Commission that no such application was possible. This decision was held to contravene section 7 of the Charter. The applicant was entitled to present his humanitarian grounds to the Minister even though his refugee claim had been dismissed. The Court noted that this decision did not necessarily include the right of the applicant to return to the country, noting that the hearing, at least for the moment, need not necessarily be held in the party's physical presence but could be held by way of telephone communication. Accordingly, the Court directed both parties to conduct a hearing in this manner and made an order under section 24 of the Charter to this effect.

Vaca v. Canada (Minister of Employment & Immigration) (1991), 15 Imm. L.R. (2d) 315, 50 F.T.R. 10 (Fed. T.D.) — The applicant and his wife arrived from Ecuador and claimed refugee status, although the record was silent about the date that the claim was first made. The applicant attended for a humanitarian and compassionate interview. That interview could not take place because the Minister could not locate the applicant's file. In allowing the application the Court noted that the immigration officer indicated that she had read the applicant's affidavit, fully explained to the applicant the purpose of a humanitarian and compassionate review, explained how usually a person seeking to land in Canada must apply from outside the country but if they establish special circumstances it could be recommended that a person be landed from within Canada, asked the applicant the factors he wished considered and considered those factors, listened to representations from counsel and then, after listening to all the oral representations, read the written representations and made a decision within 30 minutes. The Court felt that a 30-minute hearing covering all the material filed and hearing representations was not doing justice to the applicant, notwithstanding an offer to allow further written submissions that day. The Court commented on the myriad of letters and affidavits of support from family, friends and neighbours, the English language certificate, the doctor's and priest's support, the purchase of the home, the participation in a business all of which might go to the establishment of a case on humanitarian and compassionate grounds. An order in the nature of *certiorari* was granted, quashing the decision of the Immigration officer and directing the respondent to properly review the applicant's request for consideration under subsection 114(2). The Court also directed that a different Immigration officer review the material from the one who made the original decision.

Parihar v. Canada (Minister of Employment & Immigration) (1991), 16 Imm. L.R. (2d) 144, 50 F.T.R. 236 (Fed. T.D.) — The applicants brought a motion to quash a decision of an immigration officer which determined that there were insufficient humanitarian and compassionate grounds to allow the applicant to apply for landed immigrant status from within Canada. The applicant, Balvir, married the applicant, Mohinder, on November 3, 1990. Mohinder is a permanent resident. The officer noted that information provided in the marriage questionnaire was materially different from the information given at the interview, causing the officer to believe that the marriage was entered into for the purpose of obtaining permanent resident status.

The Court commented twice that it would be preferable if the humanitarian and compassionate interviews were tape recorded to avoid the situation where the Court is presented with conflicting affidavits about what occurred at the interview. The subsequently prepared affidavit of the Immigration officer is not part of the record. The Court noted that it was troubling to see affidavits prepared a considerable time after the event by officers who must interview a great number of people over the course of several months. So far as memory was concerned, the Court stated that it would have expected that the individuals being interviewed would have a clearer memory of what occurred because it was an experience unique to them. It was in this context that the Court noted it would be much fairer for all concerned if the interviews were taped.

In this particular case, the Court concluded that the applicants' memories of the events were likely sharper than the officers, although the Court took care not to suggest that it was casting any doubts on the officer's attempt to accurately reconstruct what occurred, and quashed the decision that there were not sufficient humanitarian and compassionate grounds.

Vidal v. Canada (Minister of Employment & Immigration) (1991), 13 Imm. L.R. (2d) 123 (Fed. T.D.). See also *Dadwah v. Canada (Minister of Employment & Immigration)* (1991), 13 Imm. L.R. (2d) 123 (Fed. T.D.) — The Court set out certain basic propositions which are self-evident and which must be kept in mind in dealing with section 114(2) applications. They are as follows:

1. In section 114(2), Parliament authorized the Governor in Council to make exceptions to the rules found in the Act and Regulations. There is therefore nothing inconsistent with the Act in the Governor in Council creating such exceptions by regulation.

2. The exceptions so made are for the benefit of those in whose favour they are made and do not detract from the normal application of the general rules to all others.

3. The discretion conferred under section 114(2) is conferred on the Governor in Council, not on the immigration officer who conducts the interview. The latter reports to the Minister with a recommendation. By the normal processes of Cabinet Government, the Minister of Employment and Immigration in turn would review the report and recommendation and, if in agreement, make a recommendation to the Governor in Council for the exercise of his discretion.

4. There is nothing in law to prevent the Minister or the Governor in Council from exercising discretion in favour of an applicant where special submissions are made on behalf of the applicant directly to the Minister or Governor in Council either in the absence of any recommendation from an Immigration Officer or despite a negative decision of the immigration officer.

5. There are two grounds for favourable action under section 114(2); public policy and compassionate or humanitarian considerations. These two grounds are quite different. Humanitarian and compassionate considerations have some kind of objective meaning intended by Parliament which must not be artificially narrowed through the fettering of the discretion of immigration officers in applying those words. Subject to certain very broad limitations the content of "public policy" must be defined by those having the authority to fix public policy and the political responsibility for its content.

6. The Court should not interfere with the exercise of discretion by an officer or body authorized by statute to exercise that discretion unless it is clear that the discretion has been exercised in bad faith or on grounds unrelated to the purposes for which the discretion is granted.

Guidelines for the exercise of discretion on humanitarian and compassionate considerations are permissible so long as these guidelines are intended to be statements of general policy or rough "rules of thumb" and not an exhaustive definition binding on immigration officers.

An applicant cannot complain if an immigration officer fails or refuses to follow the Minister's guidelines nor can he complain if an immigration officer applies any factor in lieu of those in the guidelines as long as this is done in good faith and the factor is not wholly irrelevant to any conceivable view of humanitarian and compassionate considerations. Further, it is for the officer to decide if he is convinced of the truth of the applicant's assertions unless perhaps he makes findings of fact which are clearly without regard to the material before him. It is not for the Court to sit in appeal on his findings of fact or his weighing of the various factors. The guidelines issued after the *Yhap* decision appear to be statements of general policy and similar in tone to that of chapter 9 of the manual which was viewed with approval by Jerome A.C.J. in the *Yhap* case. These guidelines treat separately the humanitarian and compassionate grounds in the public policy situation.

In the *Dadwah* case, the officer's recommendation was set aside because the officer stated that the rather unusual circumstances suffered by the Dadwahs in Trinidad were not sufficient grounds for a favourable decision because they did not come within the guidelines. It was open to the officer to reject these allegations on the basis of credibility and this Court could not review such a finding if made in good faith. The officer could have rejected this aspect of the applicant's case on the grounds that in her view it did not involve a situation where humanitarian and compassionate considerations were relevant if she honestly reached that conclusion but the officer was not entitled to reject the case simply because it was not covered by the guidelines. Accordingly, the officer's decision was set aside. With respect to the *Vidal* matter, that decision was upheld because no similar error was made.

Editor's Note: The subsection has been amended but the principles enunciated here may still be useful.

Orantes v. Canada (Minister of Employment & Immigration) (1990), 34 F.T.R. 184 — The Court criticized very strongly the fact that the application for leave was not filed by the Student Legal Aid Clinic because of the onset of Christmas holidays but nevertheless extended the time for filing a notice seeking leave to appeal. The applicant sought orders in the nature of *certiorari* and *mandamus* in regard to the respondent's having invoked section 19(1)(b) of the Act and their not having invoked section 114(1) of the Act in his favour. The denial of permanent residence was based on the fact that the applicant and his dependants had been in receipt of social assistance since 1986 and that neither his Canadian citizen son nor permanent resident son were in a financial position to sponsor him or his dependents. Section 114(2), it was noted, provides that the Cabinet may by regulation exempt any person from any regulation made under section 114(1). Cabinet cannot repeal, suspend or override or exempt anyone from any provision of the *Immigration Act* itself, just the regulations. Without parliamentary authority, the Governor in Council has no authority to exempt anyone from the law. If parliamentary democracy is to survive in Canada, Parliament must make choices about which foreigners, if any, may be legally admitted for permanent residence and not become helpless in the face of asserted entries by aliens no matter how sympathetic their cases. It takes a certain degree of intellectual toughness to support the principles of democracy in the face of various individuals who seek migration into Canada against the will of the democratically elected representatives of the people. If the Charter is interpreted in such a manner as to obviate the will of Parliament in a matter such as this, it is the sort of frustration which would ultimately destroy national government by amputating the lawful means of governance. Whether it is even appropriate to require genuine refugees to be able to support themselves in this applicant's circumstances is a question of policy which cannot be resolved by a Court since the requirement does not violate the Constitution. Accordingly, the application for leave to appeal was dismissed.

Yhap v. Canada (Minister of Employment & Immigration) (1990), 9 Imm. L.R. (2d) 243 (Fed. T.D.) — The applicant indicated an intention to claim refugee status in Canada prior to January 1, 1989 and was included in the backlog clearance program established by the Minister. The Minister refused to consider the applicant under the operations memorandum dealing with Chinese nationals who had temporary status in Canada. That policy was not intended to replace provisions which have been made for refugees whether recent arrivals or members of the backlog from the People's Republic of China but rather was intended to act as a supplemental protection for other individuals from that country. Regardless of what promises and what guarantees have been made by the Minister, the applicant is entitled, by virtue of section 114(2) to a review as to whether humanitarian and compassionate grounds exist sufficient to warrant landing in Canada. This law must be applied evenly to all persons. The discretion confirmed by section 114(2) is not to be exercised by the Minister and her officials subject to inflexible and self-imposed limitations, although an expression of flexible general policy, such as that contained in chapter 9 of the immigration manual would be entirely lawful. The policy directives and guidelines pertaining to the humanitarian and compassionate review portion of the backlog clearance program were set out in a document entitled "Refugee Claimants Backlog Procedures". These guidelines limit their application to particular classes of persons, mainly "members of official delegations, athletic teams or cultural groups", and persons in "family dependency situations" described more specifically in the guidelines. Officers have not been questioning applicants on humanitarian and compassionate issues which fall outside the designated criteria. These policy guidelines constituted a fetter on the statutory power of the Governor in Council to both exempt persons from the requirement of section 9(1) of the Act and to authorize the landing of persons for humanitarian and compassionate reasons pursuant to section 114(2). The applicant is entitled to a full and fair review to determine the existence of humanitarian or compassionate considerations. The right to this review was confirmed by the Supreme Court of Canada in the *Canada (Minister of Employment & Immigration) v. Jiminez-Perez*, [1984] 2 S.C.R. 565 (S.C.C.) and this consideration is to take place independently of the consideration of the basic merits of any other application advanced by the applicant. Even in the case where it is evident that all other claims and applications advanced by the applicant are doomed to failure, the applicant's right to consideration on humanitarian and compassionate grounds may not be unduly restricted. The factor that may properly be taken into account in exercising a discretion may become an unlawful fetter upon discretion if it is elevated to the status of a general rule that results in the pursuit of consistency at the expense of the merits of individual cases.

The discretion afforded an immigration officer by section 114(2) is wide. The officer is asked to consider reasons of public policy as well as the existence of compassionate or humanitarian considerations. Neither the section of the *Immigration Act* which sets out definitions of terms nor the regulations describe in any greater detail how this section is to be applied nor what interpretation the officer is to give to the rather broad terms contained in this section. Chapter 9 of the immigration manual assists an officer in assessing situations and the humanitarian and compassionate issues raised by them which include problems with spouses, family dependencies, difficulties with return to the country of origin, illegal *de facto* residents, and situations involving marriage breakdowns. By comparison, the guidelines contained in "Refugee Claimants Backlog Procedure" are rigid and inflexible. These criteria are limited and refer only to a carefully selected segment of the backlog population. Applicants who are not members of official delegations, athletic teams or cultural groups and who are not close family members of Canadian residents are excluded from the review subject to these criteria. Chapter 9, on the other hand, constitutes a general policy or rough "rules of thumb" which are appropriate and lawful structuring of the discretion conferred by section 114(2). These guidelines might have acted as a model for the drafting of guidelines to be used in conjunction with a humanitarian and compassionate review of refugee claimants in the backlog. Accordingly, the decision of the immigration officer at the backlog clearance centre with respect to the respondent was quashed and an order in the nature of *mandamus* was issued compelling the Minister to provide the applicant with a full and fair interview of his humanitarian and compassionate claim.

Kaur v. Canada (Minister of Employment & Immigration) (1987), 5 Imm. L.R. (2d) 148 (Fed. T.D.) — The applicants were married to each other pursuant to an arranged marriage as is the custom of their religion. The marriage took place in Canada and a request pursuant to section 115(2) was made to permit the application for permanent residence to proceed from within Canada. This request was denied by the respondent. The letter from the department indicated that the marriage was entered into for "immigration purposes." This opinion was based on the fact that the information provided by the applicants, with respect to their marriage, was contradictory and inconsistent. This decision was set aside because the department did not provide the applicants with any information about the inconsistencies, nor did it indicate whether the inconsistencies were the sole reason for its decision. Finally, there was no opportunity granted to the applicants to comment on these inconsistencies.

Sobrie v. Canada (Minister of Employment & Immigration) (1987), 3 Imm. L.R. (2d) 81 (Fed. T.D.) — Immediately following his arrival in Canada from Africa, the applicant claimed status as a Convention refugee. At each stage his application was denied. Ultimately, the applicant became the subject of an exclusion order. Notwithstanding the extensive file that the respondent had on the applicant, the applicant must be given an opportunity to illustrate to the Minister the existence of humanitarian and compassionate grounds under section 115(2). The immigration officials had assumed, quite logically, that their extensive file provided all the information that could possibly be relevant to that determination. However, the applicant had to be given an opportunity to provide information to support his claim, something that had not occurred to date. This did not mean that the applicant was entitled to a full oral hearing; however, it followed that for the Minister to act fairly in considering an application under this section, he must be able to direct his mind to what the applicant felt were the humanitarian and compassionate circumstances of his case. An order was issued compelling the respondent to review his decision that no humanitarian or compassionate grounds existed and to consider written submissions made by the applicant on this issue. Prohibition to restrain the respondent from removing the applicant from Canada until his claim had been dealt with was refused because prohibition did not lie to restrain the Minister from carrying out his statutory duty pending a discretionary decision on a collateral submission.

Downes v. Canada (Minister of Employment & Immigration) (1986), 4 F.T.R. 215 (Fed. T.D.) — The applicant was a citizen of Barbados who came to Canada in 1980 and decided to stay. While in Canada, he fathered a child, who was born April 4, 1985. He obtained custody of his infant son from a Provincial Court. The applicant had four other children living with their two natural mothers in Barbados, support for whom he contributed. After his arrest, the inquiry was held in abeyance pending the termination of this Notice of Motion. Two requests were made by the applicant for an officer-in-charge of the hearing in Canada, based on humanitarian and compassionate grounds. Both requests were denied without the benefit of a personal interview.

The contention that the relationship between the parent father and his infant son was a "liberty interest" within the meaning of section 7 of the Charter was rejected. Normal connotation of the words "liberty" and "security of the person" was held to be suggestive of physical well-being in the context of freedom from arbitrary arrest, detention, imprisonment and unlawful restriction or restraint of the person. Emotional stress was held not to be the sort of deprivation of security of the person that was contemplated by section 7 of the *Charter of Rights*. There was no evidence that the child's security of the person would be prejudicially affected if he was forced to accompany his father to Barbados. There was, further, no evidence of any real or likely threat to the physical integrity or well-being of the infant applicant if the father returned to Barbados and the infant remained in Canada. The only stress flowed from the normal and natural filial concerns or anxieties that would arise on enforced separation from the father parent.

The right to freedom of association was held not to extend to embrace the filial association of parent and child in its ordinary everyday meaning, and, thus, there was no denial of the applicant's right to freedom of association under the Charter.

Finally, with respect to the principles of fundamental justice, it was held that Canada had the right to enact immigration laws and to implement immigration policy that may dictate the extent to which persons can enter or be permitted to remain in Canada. The decision to refuse an in-person officer-in-charge interview was purely administrative. Finally, the request was considered on its merits, and insufficient compassionate and humanitarian grounds were found to exist.

The Minister's response to the first request for an officer-in-charge interview set out to a reasonable and sufficient degree the nature of the case the applicant had to meet. Thus, the Court concluded that the manner in which the requests were dealt with exemplified fairness, and, ultimately, the Court was satisfied that the applicant was treated fairly in the circumstances. Accordingly, the applications were dismissed.

Ochnio v. Canada (Minister of Employment & Immigration) (September 23, 1985), Doc. T-1919-85 (Fed. T.D.) — The applicant sought an order quashing a refusal of an employment authorization. The applicant, Jan Ochnio, a medical research physician, was lawfully admitted to Canada as a visitor on a scholarship to undertake a year of post doctoral studies in his specialty, cancer research, at the University of British Columbia.

In January 1985, while in Canada, the applicants made inquiries about applying for permanent residence. Special assessment interviews were arranged and conducted on July 17, 1985 and August 6, 1985. The applicants were seeking an exemption from section 9(1) of the *Immigration Act* pursuant to section 115(2) of the Act, the requirement that they have an immigrant visa before appearing at a port-of-entry. The immigration officers who conducted the interviews in July and August recommended that an application for landing should be processed from within Canada and that the applicants should be exempt from section 9(1) of the Act.

After the August 6, 1985, interview, counsel for applicants was advised that he could expect a decision within two weeks. On their behalf, counsel requested an employment authorization and was advised that this could not be issued until a decision had been made to grant the exemption. Counsel was finally informed that the officers' decision to recommend positively an exemption had been forwarded to the regional office but had not been accepted at that level. The regional office indicated that it would reconsider the case should the applicants be able to obtain a letter from the British Columbia College of Physicians and Surgeons stating that there was a need for the applicants' services in British Columbia. The decision to refuse to issue an employment authorizations was quashed. Operations memorandum IS 2.51 clearly indicated that the authority to make recommendations of this type was to be kept at the examining officers' level unless the officers' decision was negative, in which case the officers were to have recourse to the advice of a manager or supervisor. In this case, because the officers had decided to positively recommend an exemption from section 9(1), it was their duty to forward this recommendation to the Governor in Council and they were in error in seeking the concurrence of the regional office in their positive recommendation.

This type of decision by immigration officers was held to be an administrative function; the officers were bound to follow the policy of the government and had a duty to act fairly and conform to regulations and policy. The Court indicated that it could perceive an abuse of policy in this area if superiors, not working in the field, could override the decision of the interviewing officers, particularly in circumstances where they could reject the decision without specifying reasons or offering any explanations.

Jiminez-Perez v. Canada (Minister of Employment & Immigration), [1984] 2 S.C.R. 565, [1985] 1 W.W.R. 577, 9 Admin. L.R. 280, 14 D.L.R. (4th) 609 (S.C.C.) — The Minister of Employment and Immigration through his officers is under a duty to consider applications for exemption on compassionate or humanitarian grounds from the requirement of section 9 of the *Immigration Act* and to advise the applicants of the results of their application. The application for landing from within Canada should be considered and adjudicated upon if and when the exemption sought from section 9(1) is granted. That application would be subject to whatever rights of appeal are granted by the *Immigration Act*.

Kee v. Canada (Minister of Employment & Immigration) (March 9, 1984), Doc. T-2776-83 (Fed. T.D.) — The applicant sought an order prohibiting the respondent from proceeding with the execution of a deportation order, pending the determination of the applicant's criminal conviction appeal and the application pursuant to section 115(2) of the *Immigration Act* for special consideration. Prohibition will not issue directing the Minister of Employment and Immigration to disobey a valid deportation order which he is under a statutory duty to carry out solely on the grounds that the applicant has not exhausted every legal remedy available to him.

Singh v. Canada (Minister of Employment & Immigration) (November 18, 1984), Doc. T-2287-83 (Fed. T.D.) — The fact that an application is pending before the Governor in Council requesting discretionary relief under this section of the *Immigration Act* creates no legal grounds for ordering a Minister not to carry out a lawful deportation order.

Persad v. Canada (Minister of Employment & Immigration) (October 18, 1983), Doc. A-140-83 (Fed. C.A.) — In view of the provisions of sections 50, 51 and 52 of the *Immigration Act*, the Court was not prepared to import into the provisions of section 115(2) a power to suspend a deportation order pending a decision by the Governor in Council on the appellant's application under section 115(2).

3. [Revoked SOR/93-44, s. 3.]

Members of the Family Class

4. (1) Subject to subsections (2) and (3), the family class is hereby prescribed as a class of immigrants for the purposes of subsection 6(1) of the Act.

(2) The family class does not include a spouse or son or daughter referred to in

(a) subparagraph 6(5)(a)(i) or (ii) in respect of whom a visa officer did not make a determination under paragraph 6(1)(a);

(b) subparagraph 9(2)(a)(i) or (ii) in respect of whom a visa officer did not make a determination under paragraph 9(1)(a); or

(c) subparagraph 10(4)(a)(i) or (ii) in respect of whom a visa officer did not make a determination under paragraph 10(1)(a) or (1.1)(b).

(3) The family class does not include a spouse who entered into the marriage primarily for the purpose of gaining admission to Canada as a member of the family class and not with the intention of residing permanently with the other spouse.

(3.1) The family class does not include a spouse who is less than 16 years of age.

(4) The family class does not include a person who is adopted, or is intended to be adopted, otherwise than in accordance with the provisions of the *Convention on Protection of Children and Co-operation in respect of Intercountry Adoption* that was signed at The Hague on May 29, 1993 and that came into force on May 1, 1995, where the province of intended destination and the country of origin have implemented that Convention.

SOR/82-702, s. 1; SOR/83-675, s. 1; SOR/84-140, s. 1; SOR/85-225, s. 2; SOR/88-286, s. 2; SOR/88-537, s. 2; SOR/91-422, s. 1; SOR/92-101, s. 2; SOR/93-44, s. 4; SOR/97-146, s. 1; SOR/98-544, s. 2

Case Law

Section 4(3)

Carson v. Canada (Minister of Citizenship & Immigration) (1995), 95 F.T.R. 137 (Fed. T.D.) — The applicant sought to review a decision refusing the applicant an exemption pursuant to section 114(2) of the *Immigration Act* from the requirements of section 9(1) of the *Immigration Act*. Tonya Carson is a Canadian citizen who had married the applicant, William Carson. A fundamental issue in the case involved the *bona fides* of the marriage. The Court ruled that Mrs. Carson had no standing in the judicial review application. She was a Canadian citizen who did not require any exemption from the *Immigration Act* or regulations. Further, whether she had standing or not had no impact on the ultimate issue in the matter.

The Court observed that an applicant in this type of case did not have a case to meet, rather the applicant was trying to persuade the decision-maker that he or she should be provided with exceptional treatment and be exempted from the general requirements of the law. Accordingly, no hearing need be held and no reasons be provided. In order to succeed in an attack on a humanitarian and compassionate decision the applicant must persuade the Court that the decision maker erred in law, proceeded on some wrong or improper principle, or acted in bad faith.

On the evidence the Court was satisfied that no error was committed by the decision maker with respect to his consideration of the *bona fides* of the marriage. Further, the Court was satisfied that the decision-maker had not ignored counsel's submissions, thus, the Court concluded that no error of law was committed by the immigration officer.

Tse v. Canada (Minister of Citizenship & Immigration) (April 27, 1995), Doc. IMM-1191-94 (Fed. T.D.) — The decision refusing humanitarian and compassionate relief was set aside. The officer determined that the marriage of the applicant and his wife was not *bona fide*. In doing so, the officer relied on interview notes arising from a prior application by the applicant for such exemption. In reaching her decision, the officer made that "boiler plate" statement that she considered all the evidence. The officer made no reference to the fact that since the marriage the applicant's wife had become pregnant and they were expecting their first child. Even if the applicant's marriage had not been *bona fide* a year earlier when the first humanitarian and compassionate decision was made, the reviewing officer on the second application has to address her mind to whether or not changed circumstances existed which now demonstrated that the marriage had become genuine. A "boiler plate" reference to having reviewed all the evidence is not sufficient.

Drame v. Canada (Minister of Employment & Immigration) (1994), 82 F.T.R. 177 (Fed. T.D.) — This was an application to review a decision of an immigration officer refusing an exemption pursuant to section 114(2).

The applicant arrived in Canada from Guinea and claimed Refugee status. She married and applied for a 114(2) exemption. The applicant's refugee claim was found to have had a credible basis but the applicant withdrew the claim after her marriage. The Court noted that in trying to determine whether a marriage was one of substance and entered into in good faith and not merely for immigration purpose, the officers should ask themselves when considering the facts, what would a reasonable person do in such a situation. The immigration officer's notes made no reference to the fact that the applicant was pregnant at the time of her interview, nor was there any note in the file to reflect the fact that the applicant gave birth shortly after the interview. The Court noted that the father of the child was the applicant's husband.

The Court concluded that the immigration officer did not consider the applicant's application as a reasonable person would have done and that the officer, by ignoring these facts, did not exercise her discretion in good faith. Accordingly, the decision of the officer was set aside.

Ellis v. Canada (Minister of Employment & Immigration) (1994), 27 Imm. L.R. (2d) 124 (Fed. T.D.) — This was an application to review a decision determining that there were insufficient grounds to warrant processing an application for permanent residence from within Canada. An applicant had married a Canadian and it was determined by an immigration officer after interviewing the applicant and her spouse, that the marriage was one of convenience. The Court reiterated that discrepancies in the answers given by the applicant and her spouse at the marriage interviews need not be disclosed prior to a decision being made.

The immigration officer was informed after the marriage interview by a co-worker that the applicant and her spouse had been overheard talking about the fact that they had no wedding photographs and how they could obtain some. This type of negative information, if it was going to be relied upon by the officer, would have to be disclosed to the applicant and her spouse so that they would have an opportunity to explain it.

Notwithstanding the lack of disclosure the application was dismissed because the officer had already reached her decision prior to receiving this negative information.

Adebiyi v. Canada (Minister of Employment & Immigration) (1994), 73 F.T.R. 230 (Fed. T.D.) — This was an application to review a decision determining that there were insufficient humanitarian and compassionate grounds to warrant processing the applicant's application for permanent residence from within Canada. The applicant, a national of Nigeria, claimed refugee status and then married a permanent resident of Canada. His claim to refugee status was denied. Both the applicant and his wife were questioned separately to determine if their marriage was *bona fide*.

The applicant had every reason to be aware that his credibility was suspect in light of the decision of the Refugee Division in his case and that the timing of his marriage might well be considered suspect. Neither of these issues were addressed in the written representations received in support of the humanitarian and compassionate application. The marriage interview process is conducted separately for the very purpose of avoiding collusion between the claimant and his witness as to the circumstance of the marriage. Procedural fairness does not require that the respondent disclose the discrepancies arising out of the separate interview of the applicant and his spouse, nor does it require the provision of an opportunity to respond to those discrepancies. The Court preferred the reasoning of Noel J. in *Grewal v. Canada (Minister of Employment & Immigration)* (1993), 62 F.T.R. 308 (Fed. T.D.) to the decision of Rothstein J. in *Ramoutar v. Canada (Minister of Employment & Immigration)*, [1993] 3 F.C. 370, 21 Imm. L.R. (2d) 203, 65 F.T.R. 32 (Fed. T.D.).

Singh (R.) v. Canada (Minister of Employment & Immigration) (October 8, 1993), Doc. T-2011-92 (Fed. T.D.) — Ramesh Singh arrived in Canada and claimed refugee status. The claim was refused. He subsequently married a permanent resident of Canada. The waiver of the visa requirement included in section 9(1) was refused because the marriage was viewed as one of convenience.

Procedural fairness does not require that an applicant be given an opportunity to respond to discrepancies arising from spousal interviews. The interview process is conducted separately for the very purpose of avoiding collusion between the claimant and his witnesses as to the circumstances of the alleged *bona fide* marriage and for the purpose of elucidating the truth.

The interview process, in this case, was not subject to criticism and the application for judicial review was refused.

Ramoutar v. Canada (Mininster of Employment & Immigration), 21 Imm. L.R. (2d) 203, 65 F.T.R. 32, [1993] 3 F.C. 370 (Fed. T.D.) — This application was for judicial review to quash a decision not to refer the applicant's case to the Governor in Council for an exemption, from the requirements of section 9(1) of the *Immigration Act*, on humanitarian and compassionate grounds.

The applicant had married a Canadian citizen. An Immigration officer, after reviewing the case, felt there was a reasonable doubt about the *bona fides* of the marriage and declined to refer the matter to the Governor in Council.

In assessing the *bona fides* of the applicant's marriage to a Canadian citizen on the basis of requiring proof of such *bona fides* beyond a reasonable doubt, the respondent erred in law. Proceedings under section 114(2) of the *Immigration Act* are civil in nature and therefore the appropriate standard of proof is proof on a balance of probabilities — the standard applicable in civil proceedings.

Canada (Minister of Employment & Immigration) v. Narwal (1990), 10 Imm. L.R. (2d) 183, 26 R.F.L. (3d) 95 (Fed. C.A.) — The respondent landed in Canada in 1983 as a fiancée and was married. A year later, the respondent was divorced. The respondent then married her former husband's brother in England. During the period of her visit to England, a child, who was later born in Canada, was conceived. The husband returned to India after the marriage in England and filed an application for permanent residence which was sponsored by the respondent. During an interview, the applicant denied that his brother had in any way been related to the respondent. The respondent maintained regular correspondence with her new husband and visited him in India. The new husband's application for permanent residence was refused but the refusal was overturned by the Immigration Appeal Board. They decided that the validity of the marriage was governed by the law of India and that there was a custom permitting a woman to marry the brother of her former husband. The decision of the Board was based on humanitarian and compassionate grounds and the appeal was allowed on that basis. The Court observed that the Board erred in deciding that the substantial validity of the marriage was to be determined by the law of India, because there was on the facts a reasonable probability that the family would live in Canada with their Canadian born child.

The Court held that the respondent was validly married by the law of Canada and that the Board had jurisdiction to grant relief on humanitarian and compassionate grounds. The Minister's appeal was dismissed.

This case departs from the traditional view that the law governing capacity to marry is that of the domicile of both parties at the time of the marriage.

Canada (Minister of Employment & Immigration) v. Taggar, [1989] 3 F.C. 576, 8 Imm. L.R. (2d) 175, 60 D.L.R. (4th) 431, 99 N.R. 321 (Fed. C.A.) — The Minister appealed from a decision of the Immigration Appeal Board allowing an appeal by the respondent from the refusal of a visa officer to grant an immigrant visa to Ranjit Taggar, an Indian citizen whom the respondent had sponsored as her husband. The respondent had married Ranjit Taggar a few months after her previous marriage to his brother had ended in divorce. Under the *Hindu Marriage Act, 1955*, a marriage is null and void if one of the parties was "the wife of the brother ... of the other" unless "the custom or usage governing each of them permits of a marriage between the two." As Ranjit Taggar had no evidence of such custom, the visa officer rejected his application for a visa. Ranjit Taggar submitted a new application and this time accompanied it with a copy of a judgment of an Indian Court in an action for a declaration that he had brought against the respondent. That judgment declared the respondent and Ranjit Taggar to be legally married. The visa officer refused to issue a visa taking the view that the judgment did not establish the validity of the marriage. Customs must be clearly proved to exist and the onus of establishing them rests upon those who rely on their existence. A custom that is not established is therefore deemed not to exist. The declaratory judgment produced by the respondent's husband was a judgment "in personam" which the respondent agrees bound only the two parties to the action. The existence of a custom was not an issue in that case. The judgment, therefore, did not prove the custom, therefore, the marriage was invalid and, therefore, the Board had no jurisdiction to hear the appeal because the respondent was not married to the person whom she was seeking to sponsor and, therefore, Ranjit Taggar's application for permanent residence was not an application by a member of the family class.

Kaur v. Canada (Minister of Employment & Immigration) (1987), 5 Imm. L.R. (2d) 148 (Fed. T.D.) — The applicants were married to each other pursuant to an arranged marriage, as is the custom of their religion. The marriage took place in Canada and a request pursuant to section 115(2) was made to permit the application for permanent residence to proceed from within Canada. This request was denied by the respondent. The letter from the Department indicated that the marriage was entered into for "immigration purposes." This opinion was based on the fact that the information provided by the applicants, with respect to their marriage, was contradictory and inconsistent. This decision was set aside because the Department did not provide the applicants with any information about the inconsistencies, nor did it indicate whether the inconsistencies were the sole reason for its decision. Finally, there was no opportunity granted to the applicants to comment on these inconsistencies.

Ahn v. Canada (Minister of Employment & Immigration) (1987), 2 Imm. L.R. (2d) 23 (Imm. App. Bd.) — This was an appeal from the refusal of a sponsored application for landing. The appellant had emigrated from South Korea in 1975. He returned there in 1984 and married the applicant, whom the appellant had known, at least to some extent, before he emigrated. The marriage was arranged by the appellant's brother and solemnized in Korea. The sponsored application was refused because, in the opinion of the immigration officer, the sponsoree had entered into the marriage primarily for the purpose of gaining admission to Canada as a member of the family class, and not with the intention of residing permanently with her spouse. Refusal was held to be invalid. Section 4(3) of the regulation sets out a double test: if the sponsoree's or applicant's intention falls outside the terms of either test, he or she is a spouse for the purposes of the definition of the family class. The Board noted that the motive behind an intention and the intention itself are not the same thing. Further, it was observed that even if it could be said that the sponsoree's intention was primarily to obtain admission to Canada for her younger son, that was not the exclusionary intention set out in section 4(3) of the regulation. Accordingly, the appeal was allowed.

Horbas v. Canada (Minister of Employment & Immigration), [1985] 2 F.C. 359 (Fed. T.D.) — This was an application to quash a decision rejecting Imelda Horbas as a spouse described in section 4(3) of the regulation and for an order in the nature of *mandamus* requiring the respondents to process her application fairly and in accordance with the law. The application was dismissed. Section 4(3) was held to be not inconsistent with the *Charter of Rights and Freedoms* and in any event justified under section 1 of the Charter. Counsel for the respondents invoked section 1 and filed in support a study conducted by the Employment and Immigration Commission prior to the adoption of section 4(3) of the regulation. An officer disqualifying a spouse under section 4(3) must apply a twofold test. First, a marriage must be entered into primarily for the purpose of gaining admission into Canada, and, second, there must be no intention on the part of the prospective immigrant of residing permanently with the sponsoring spouse. Section 7 of the Charter was held not to enshrine a constitutional guarantee of the right of any Canadian to choose anyone in the world as a marital partner and bring such person to Canada to live with them. Section 4(3) of the regulation did not violate section 15 of the Charter; it did not discriminate against persons whose cultures practised arranged marriages because in order to be disqualified under section 4(3) there must be no intention on the part of the prospective immigrant to permanently reside with the other spouse. On the question of whether the subsection was erroneously applied, it was noted that this issue could better be dealt with on an appeal to the Immigration Appeal Board, which was available to the Canadian sponsor, Joseph Horbas, because he was a Canadian citizen. On the application of section 2(d) of the Charter, the "freedom of association" clause, the Court seemed to say that the right to cohabit was not part of the constitutionally guaranteed freedom of association.

Sahota v. Canada (Minister of Employment & Immigration) (1985), 21 Admin. L.R. 95 (Fed. T.D.) — Section 4(3) of the *Immigration Regulations* speaks from the day on which it was enacted, namely April 1, 1984. It does not apply to applications submitted prior to that date.

Sponsorship of Members of the Family Class

5. (1) For the purposes of paragraph (2)(i) and subsections (3) to (5), "spouse" includes a person of the opposite sex who is cohabiting with the sponsor in a conjugal relationship at the time the sponsor gives an undertaking, having cohabited with the sponsor for a continuous period of at least one year.

(2) Subject to subsections (6) and (7) and section 5.1, a person who is a Canadian citizen or permanent resident and who meets the following requirements is authorized to sponsor the application for landing of any member of the family class:

(a) the person is a sponsor within the meaning of paragraph (a) or (b) of the definition "sponsor" in subsection 2(1);

(b) the person gives an undertaking;

(c) in the case of a permanent resident, the person is not subject to a removal order or a conditional removal order, other than a removal order that is of no effect because the person has, after the date of the order, been granted lawful permission to establish permanent residence in Canada;

(d) the person is not confined in any penitentiary, jail, reformatory or prison;

(e) the person is not a bankrupt within the meaning of section 2 of the *Bankruptcy and Insolvency Act*;

(f) subject to subsection (5) and except where the member of the family class to be sponsored is a member referred to in subsection 6(3), for the 12-month period preceding the date of giving the undertaking, the person's gross Canadian income less all payments made or due on account of financial obligations is equal to or greater than the applicable amount of the Low Income Cut-off (LICO) referred to in Schedule IV, which amount shall be determined in accordance with subsection (3);

(g) at the date of giving the undertaking, the person is not in default in respect of any obligations that the person has assumed under any other undertaking given or co-signed with respect to any other person and the other person's dependants or in respect of a loan made under section 45;

(h) where the member of the family class to be sponsored is at least 19 years of age, or is less than 19 years of age and is the person's spouse or fiancée, the person has entered into a written agreement with the member to the effect that

(i) the person undertakes to provide for the essential needs of the member and the member's accompanying dependants for a period of 10 years,

(ii) the person declares that their financial obligations do not prevent them from honouring their agreement with the member and their undertaking to the Minister in respect of the member's application for landing, and

(iii) the member undertakes to make every reasonable effort to provide for the member's essential needs and those of the member's accompanying dependants; and

(i) if the person's spouse has co-signed the undertaking referred to in paragraph (b), the spouse has also entered into the agreement referred to in paragraph (h).

(3) For the purposes of determining the applicable amount of Low Income Cut-off (LICO) for a person referred to in paragraph (2)(f),

(a) the size of the person's family unit is that of a family unit comprising the person, the person's dependants, the member of the family class to be sponsored by the person and all dependants of the member, whether those dependants are accompanying dependants or not, and all other persons and their dependants in respect of whom

(i) the person has given or co-signed an undertaking that is still in effect, and

(ii) the person's spouse, where the person's spouse has co-signed the undertaking referred to in paragraph (2)(b), has given or co-signed another undertaking that is still in effect; and

(b) the size of the area of residence is the size of the area where the person resides.

(4) The spouse of a sponsor, within the meaning of paragraph (a) of the definition "sponsor" in subsection 2(1), may co-sign the undertaking given by the sponsor such that the sponsor and the sponsor's spouse are jointly and severally liable for the obligations contained in the undertaking, if the spouse meets the requirements set out in that paragraph, other than the requirement to sponsor an application for landing of a member of the family class, and meets the requirements set out in paragraphs (2)(c) to (e) and (g).

(5) Where the spouse of a sponsor has co-signed an undertaking in accordance with subsection (4), the gross Canadian income and the payments made or due on account of financial obligations of the spouse for the 12-month period preceding the date of the undertaking are included in the gross Canadian income and the payments made or due on account of financial obligations of the sponsor that are referred to in paragraph (2)(f), respectively.

(6) Where charges have been laid against a person who is a permanent resident and who has given or co-signed an undertaking in respect of the application for landing of a member of the family class alleging that the person has committed one of the following offences, an immigration officer shall not make a determination respecting the authorization to sponsor that application for landing until the courts have made a final determination in respect of the charges:

(a) an indictable offence, or an offence, other than an offence designated as a contravention under the *Contraventions Act*, for which the offender may be prosecuted by indictment or for which the offender is punishable on summary conviction, that may be punishable by way of indictment under any Act of Parliament by a maximum term of imprisonment of less than 10 years; or

(b) an offence under any Act of Parliament, other than an offence designated as a contravention under the *Contraventions Act*, for which a term of imprisonment of five years or more may be imposed.

(7) Where an immigration officer has reasonable grounds to believe that a person who is a permanent resident and who has given or co-signed an undertaking in respect of the application for landing of a member of the family class is the subject of a report referred to in subsection 27(1) of the Act, the immigration officer shall not make a determination respecting the authorization to sponsor that application until it has been finally determined whether the person is authorized to remain in Canada.

SOR/97-145, s. 3.

5.1 Paragraphs 5(2)(e) to (i) do not apply in the case of an undertaking in respect of a member of the family class who intends to reside in the Province of Quebec.

SOR/97-145, s. 3.

Application for a Visa by a Member of the Family Class

6. (1) Subject to subsections (1.1), (3.1), (3.2), (4), (5) and (6), where a member of the family class makes an application for an immigrant visa, a visa officer may issue an immigrant visa to the member and the member's accompanying dependants if

(a) he and his dependants, whether accompanying dependants or not, are not members of any inadmissible class and otherwise meet the requirements of the Act and these Regulations;

(b) the sponsor and, if the sponsor's spouse has co-signed the undertaking referred to in paragraph 5(2)(b), the sponsor's spouse meet the applicable requirements set out in section 5, subject to section 5.1 in the case of an undertaking in respect of a member of the family class who intends to reside in the Province of Quebec;

(b.1) where a visa officer has received information indicating that the sponsor is no longer able to fulfil the undertaking, the visa officer, after recalculating or having an immigration officer recalculate the amount of the sponsor's gross Canadian income less financial obligations, as described in paragraph 5(2)(f), for the 12-month period preceding the date on which the sponsored member of the family class and the member's dependants meet the requirements of the Act and these Regulations referred to in paragraph (a), has determined that that amount is equal to or greater than the amount of the Low Income Cut-off (LICO) referred to in paragraph 5(2)(f) for the 12-month period preceding that date, or has accepted the determination of an immigration officer to that effect;

(c) subject to paragraph (c.1), in the case of any of the following members of the family class who is a child or orphan, the child welfare authority of the province in which the child or orphan is to reside has stated in writing that it has no objection to the proposed arrangements for the reception and care of the child or orphan, namely,

(i) a child described in paragraph (b) of the definition "member of the family class" in subsection 2(1) who has been adopted outside Canada by the sponsor while the sponsor was residing in Canada,

(ii) an orphan described in paragraph (e) of the definition "member of the family class" in subsection 2(1), or

(iii) a child described in paragraph (g) of the definition "member of the family class" in subsection 2(1);

(c.1) in the case of a child described in paragraph (b) of the definition "member of the family class" in subsection 2(1) adopted outside Canada by the sponsor while the sponsor was residing in Canada or in the case of a child described in paragraph (g) of that definition, the province of intended destination and the country of origin have implemented the *Convention on Protection of Children and Co-operation in respect of Intercountry Adoption* that was signed at The Hague on May 29, 1993 and that came into force on May 1, 1995, and the central authorities of that province and of that country have approved the adoption;

(d) in the case of a fianceé,

(i) the sponsor and the fianceé intend to reside together permanently after being married and have not become engaged primarily for the purpose of the fianceé gaining admission to Canada as a member of the family class,

(ii) there are no legal impediments to the proposed marriage of the sponsor and the fianceé under the laws of the province in which they intend to reside, and

(iii) the sponsor and the fianceé have agreed to marry each other within ninety days after the admission of the fianceé; and

(e) in the case of a person described in paragraph (b) of the definition "member of the family class" in subsection 2(1), or a dependant of a member of the family class, who has been adopted, the person or dependant was adopted before having attained 19 years of age and was not adopted for the purpose of gaining admission to Canada of the person or dependant, or gaining the admission to Canada of any of the person's or dependant's relatives.

(1.01) Paragraph (1)(e) is retroactive and applies in respect of all applications for landing made by members of the family class pending on April 15, 1994.

(1.1) Where a visa officer does not issue an immigrant visa as an accompanying dependant to a son or daughter of a member of the family class referred to in subsection (1), or of the spouse of that member of the family class, the visa officer shall not issue an immigrant visa as an accompanying dependant to a son or daughter of that son or daughter.

(2) [Revoked SOR/97-145, s. 4.]

(3) Paragraph (1)(b.1) does not apply where the sponsored member of the family class is a person who

(a) is the sponsor's spouse and does not have any dependent sons or dependent daughters;

(b) is the sponsor's spouse and has dependent sons or dependent daughters, each of whom, at the time the sponsor gives the undertaking referred to in paragraph 5(2)(b),

(i) is less than 19 years of age and unmarried, and

(ii) does not have children; or

(c) is the sponsor's dependent son or dependent daughter and, at the time the sponsor gives the undertaking referred to in paragraph 5(2)(b),

(i) is less than 19 years of age and unmarried, and

(ii) does not have children.

(3.1) Paragraph (1)(b.1) does not apply in the case of an undertaking in respect of a member of the family class who intends to reside in the Province of Quebec.

(3.2) Subject to subsection (3.3), a visa officer shall not issue an immigrant visa to a member of the family class who intends to reside in the Province of Quebec, unless the Minister responsible for the administration of the laws of that Province in respect of immigration is of the opinion that the sponsor of the member will be able to fulfil the undertaking referred to in paragraph 5(2)(b).

(3.3) Subsection (3.2) does not apply to a person referred to in paragraph (3)(a), (b) or (c).

(3.4) Where charges have been laid against a person who is a permanent resident and who has given or co-signed an undertaking in respect of the application for landing of a

member of the family class alleging that the person has committed one of the following offences, a visa officer shall not make a determination respecting the member's application for an immigrant visa until the courts have made a final determination in respect of the charges:

(a) an indictable offence, or an offence, other than an offence designated as a contravention under the *Contraventions Act*, for which the offender may be prosecuted by indictment or for which the offender is punishable on summary conviction, that may be punishable by way of indictment under any Act of Parliament by a maximum term of imprisonment of less than 10 years; or

(b) an offence under any Act of Parliament, other than an offence designated as a contravention under the *Contraventions Act*, for which a term of imprisonment of five years or more may be imposed.

(3.5) Where a visa officer has reasonable grounds to believe that a person who is a permanent resident and who has given or co-signed an undertaking in respect of the application for landing of a member of the family class is the subject of a report referred to in subsection 27(1) of the Act, the visa officer shall not make a determination respecting the member's application for an immigrant visa until it has been finally determined whether the person is authorized to remain in Canada.

(4) [Revoked SOR/92-101, s. 3.]

(5) For the purposes of subsection (1), a visa officer

(a) is not required to determine whether a dependant is a member of an inadmissible class if the dependant is

(i) the spouse of the applicant, where, on the basis of written evidence, an immigration officer is satisfied that the spouse is separated from and no longer cohabiting with the applicant or,

(ii) a son or daughter of the applicant, or of the spouse of that applicant, where an immigration officer is satisfied that custody or guardianship of the son or daughter has been legally vested in

(A) the spouse of the applicant, referred to in subparagraph (i), or

(B) a former spouse of the applicant, and

(iii) [Revoked SOR/92-101, s. 3.]

(iv) [Revoked SOR/92-101, s. 3.]

(b) shall not issue an immigrant visa to a dependant referred to in paragraph (a) as an accompanying dependant.

(6) A visa officer shall not issue an immigrant visa to a dependent son or dependent daughter referred to in paragraph (b) of the definition "member of the family class" in subsection 2(1) or a dependent son or dependent daughter of a member of the family class unless

(a) at the time the application for an immigrant visa is received by an immigration officer, the son or daughter meets the criteria respecting age, and marital or student status set out in the definitions "dependent son" and "dependent daughter" in subsection 2(1); and

(b) at the time the visa is issued, the son or daughter meets the criteria respecting marital or student status set out in those definitions.

SOR/79-167, s. 2; SOR/82-702, s. 2; SOR/83-675, s. 2; SOR/84-140, s. 2; SOR/84-850, s. 2; SOR/85-225, ss. 4, 5; SOR/88-286, s. 3; SOR/91-157, s. 1; SOR/92-101, s. 3; SOR/93-44, s. 5; SOR/94-242, s. 1; SOR/97-145, s. 4; SOR/97-146, s. 2.

Case Law

Section 6(1)(a)

Parmar v. Canada (Minister of Citizenship & Immigration) (1996), 38 Imm. L.R. (2d) 316 (Imm. & Ref. Bd. (App. Div.)) — This was a preliminary motion by the applicant, the Minister of Citizenship and Immigration, to have the respondent Tarsem Singh Parmar's appeal dismissed for lack of jurisdiction. The respondent, Parmar, had filed an undertaking of assistance seeking to bring his father, mother and 3 sisters to Canada. Two of his 3 sisters were refused on the basis that they were not enrolled and in full time attendance at an educational institution since attaining the age of 19 years and therefore were not dependent daughters within the meaning of the immigration regulations. Medical instructions were issued for the father, mother and one sister who were found to be members of the family class.

An application for permanent residence can be split and the ineligibility of an alleged accompanying dependent of a member of the family class is not a bar to the admission of the member of the family class and other admissible accompanying dependants. The visa officer has a positive duty to issue visas to the applicants who are both eligible and admissible. When the splitting of such an application has occurred and the members of the family class have been issued visas there is no right of appeal to the Appeal Division in respect of the ineligible applicants who are claimed to be accompanying dependents as there has been no refusal of an application for landing by a member of the family class.

Canada (Minister of Citizenship & Immigration) v. Nikolova (1995), 31 Imm. L.R. (2d) 104, 102 F.T.R. 72 (Fed. T.D.) — The Minister applied for judicial review of a decision of the Appeal Division. The Appeal Division held that the respondent's son was a dependant son and a member of the Family Class as provided for in the *Immigration Regulations*. The respondent submitted a sponsored application for permanent residence for her son who was living in, and a citizen of Bulgaria. The respondent's son was 18 years of age when the respondent first submitted a sponsored application. When the respondent's son reached his 19th birthday on March 4, 1992, he joined the Bulgarian military service by conscription. On June 10, 1992, the son received an immigrant visa but this visa expired in August 1992 when the son was still 19 years of age. Because of his military service, the son was unable to come to Canada at that time. On September 15, 1992, the respondent received a letter from the Canadian Embassy explaining that she could sponsor her son once he had completed his military service. Accordingly, the respondent completed an undertaking on behalf of her son on May 31, 1993. The son completed his military service in September 1993 and then immediately enrolled in post-graduate studies in Bulgaria. At that time, he was 20 years of age. The application for permanent residence submitted by the son was received on October 12, 1993 at which time the son was 20 years of age. This application was refused by a visa officer because the son was determined not to be a dependant son nor a member of the Family Class within the regulations.

The application of the Minister was successful. There was no estoppel by representation or conduct. This principle cannot be invoked to preclude the execution of a statutory duty nor to confer a statutorily defined status on a person who does not fall within the statutory definition. The principle of legitimate expectations cannot arise unless there has been a regular practice over an extended period of time which a person could reasonably expect to continue. Furthermore, this principle only applies to procedural rather than substantive matters. No substantive rights are created by the doctrine of estoppel by representation or conduct.

The transcript of the appeal reveals that the Board member refused to receive submissions regarding the respondent's ability to fulfil her undertaking of assistance. This had been one of the reasons upon which the sponsored application had been refused, and accordingly, it was procedurally unfair for the Board member to refuse to receive submissions on this issue.

Anthony v. Canada (Minister of Employment & Immigration) (December 16, 1985), Doc. T-84-9706 (Imm. App. Bd.) — The appellant, a citizen of Jamaica, was granted landing at Toronto International Airport on August 8, 1981 in order to marry her sponsor, Frank Anthony. The application for permanent residence, completed on January 27, 1981, was false in that the appellant listed only 2 of her 4 children and wrote, in her own handwriting, "I have no other children." The appellant's misrepresentations diverted the visa officer from carrying out his duties under the Act and regulation, which required that he determine whether *all* the appellant's dependants met the requirements of the Act and regulation before he could issue an immigrant visa to her. The Board dismissed the appellant's appeal, ruling that a deportation order, made under section 27(1)(e) of the Act, was valid.

Grewal v. Canada (Minister of Employment & Immigration) (January 18, 1984), Doc. V82-6005 (Imm. App. Bd.) — This was a sponsorship appeal from the refusal to accept the application for permanent residence of the father of the sponsor and his accompanying dependant. It was possible to establish the relationship of the father, the mother and one brother of the sponsor. It was not possible to establish the relationship of another young man and woman who were alleged to be a brother and a sister of this sponsor. A majority was of the opinion that entry should be denied only to those not proven eligible and that the father, the mother and brother whose relationship to the sponsor was established should be permitted to come to Canada. The minority would have disallowed the application of all parties because other alleged dependants were inadmissible under the regulation.

Bala v. Canada (Minister of Employment & Immigration) (January 11, 1983), Doc. T81-9204 (Imm. App. Bd.) — The sponsor appealed the refusal of the Minister to approve the application for permanent residence of his parents, his brother and his sister. The basis of the refusal was the lack of proper or satisfactory evidence with respect to the age of the brother and sister. The Board received and accepted the evidence of a professor of radiology at the Faculty of Medicine at the University of Toronto when he gave evidence of the age of these 2 children and accepted and concluded that they were under the age of 21 years at the time the application for permanent residence was filed. Accordingly, the sponsor's appeal was allowed.

Section 6(1)(b)

Khakoo v. Canada (Minister of Citizenship & Immigration) (1995), 103 F.T.R. 284 (Fed. T.D.) — The applicants arrived in Canada on November 6, 1990 and entered as "visitors." In March 1991 they made a claim for refugee status which was ultimately rejected. Their application for admission was sponsored in 1994 by a daughter of the female applicant who is a Canadian citizen. The visa office in Detroit denied the application on the basis that the applicant had been receiving welfare benefits for four years and that there was a long-term and continuing lack of support from the sponsor.

It was not disputed that the applicant's sponsor had a right of appeal to the Appeal Division of the IRB. However, the applicants had no such right and therefore the Court held that the applicants could bring an application for judicial review to quash the visa officer's decision.

The visa officer was acting under subsection 6(1) of the regulations. Within the terms of paragraph 6(1)(b), the applicants were sponsored, the sponsor had given an undertaking and there was no evidence that the sponsor was in default under any other undertakings given by her and there was the express opinion of another immigration officer that the sponsor would be able to fulfil this undertaking. In these circumstances, the applicants fell within the exception contained within section 19(1)(b) of the *Immigration Act*, and accordingly, the refusal of the application was an error in law and the refusal was quashed.

Johl v. Canada (Minister of Employment & Immigration) (1987), 1 Imm. L.R. (2d) 111 (Imm. App. Bd.) — This is an appeal from the refusal of a sponsored application for permanent residence. The appellant sponsored applications for his father, mother, sister and brother. The applicants were refused because the principal applicant was unable or unwilling to support himself, his wife and children without adequate settlement arrangements having been made by the sponsor. Whether a sponsor has an income at least equal to the low income cut-off per year for the number of his dependants, plus the number of his sponsorees, is but one factor that an immigration officer should consider in deciding whether the sponsor will be able to fulfill his undertaking. Other matters to be considered are the stability of the sponsor's employment and prospects for advancement; the willingness of the sponsor, his spouse and close relatives to do everything possible for the sponsorees; prospects of future employment of the sponsorees; the likelihood of the sponsorees establishing themselves quickly and easily; the ownership of a house and other assets; the sponsor's opportunity to get other work in case of lay-off; and, finally, whether the sponsor's skills are in a declining or expanding trade. The Board also stated that immigration officers are failing in their statutory duty if they do not give the sponsors or applicants, as the case may be, reasons for refusal couched in such a degree of particularity that they will know why there have been refusals and what cases must be met on appeal.

Section 6(1)(d)

Kaur v. Canada (Minister of Employment & Immigration) (May 8, 1985), Doc. T-2490-84 (Fed. T.D.) — The applicant wanted to bring her financé to Canada so that they could be married. Apart from attempting to sponsor her fiancé, the applicant went to India and went through a form of marriage in that country with her fiancé. The initial application of the fiancé for permanent residence was turned down and one of the factors in the rejection was related to the opinion that the Indian marriage was invalid. The sponsor appealed to the Immigration Appeal Board, which observed that the marriage was to be presumed valid until ruled otherwise by a Court of competent jurisdiction. The respondent persisted in raising the question of validity of the Indian marriage and refusing to process the initial application for permanent residence. *Certiorari* was granted quashing this decision and the respondent was directed to process the application in accordance with the existing law and regulations, which the Court understood would result in the admission of the fiancé for a sufficient period for the marriage to take place. The validity of the Indian marriage was irrelevant to the determination of the application because the applicant was attempting to bring over a husband-to-be for the purpose of marriage in Canada.

Gabriel v. Canada (Minister of Employment & Immigration) (1984), 60 N.R. 108 (Fed. C.A.) — The appellant was landed on condition that she marry within 90 days. This condition could not be obeyed as a result of circumstances beyond the appellant's control. Even though a condition is impossible to fulfill, so long as the person concerned knew of that condition and continued to remain in Canada in breach of that condition, such a person has knowingly contravened a condition attached to the grant of landing. Even if the word "contravene" requires a positive act, the omission to do something which a person is required to do, is the commission of a positive act. It is an act of failure to do something required to be done and, accordingly, satisfies the definition of the term "contravenes".

Owens v. Canada (Minister of Manpower & Immigration) (March 27, 1984), Doc. A-615-83 (Fed. C.A.) — The sponsoree filed an application for permanent residence on February 22, 1981. At that time the sponsoree was not free to marry the sponsor because his divorce was not final. The sponsoree signed the application on May 19, 1981 at which time he swore before an official of the Government of Canada that the contents of his application were true. On this date the sponsoree was free to marry.

The application was refused. The respondent had taken the view that the relevant date was February 22, 1981, the date of the filing of the application. The Immigration Appeal Board agreed with the respondent; however, the Federal Court of Appeal allowed the appeal and set aside the Board's decision because it decided that the relevant date was May 19, 1981, the date the sponsoree swore to the truth of the facts contained in the application.

6.1 (1) Subject to subsection (3) and section 5.1, for the purposes of subsection 6(2) of the Act, a Canadian citizen or permanent resident who is authorized to sponsor the application for landing of a member of the family class pursuant to section 5 shall do so in writing in the form fixed by the Minister.

(2) Where a sponsor sponsors an application for landing of a member of the family class described in paragraph (h) of the definition "member of the family class" in subsection 2(1) and that member is unable to meet the requirements of the Act and these Regulations or dies, the sponsor may sponsor the application for landing of another member of the family class described in that paragraph.

(3) A person who is adopted outside Canada and whose adoption is subsequently revoked by a foreign authority may only sponsor an application for landing made by a member of the family class if an immigration officer is satisfied that the revocation of the adoption was not obtained for the purpose of sponsoring an application for landing made by that member.

SOR/93-44, s. 6; SOR/97-145, s. 5.

Case Law

Section 6.1(1)

Porter v. Canada (Mininster of Employment & Immigration) (April 14, 1988), Doc. A-353-87 (Fed. C.A.) — The visa officer's refusal of an application for permanent residence that, in fact, is based on an administrative delay of the Minister's own creation is invalid in law. The Government's duty is to facilitate family class applications, not to frustrate them.

Sashi v. Canada (Minister of Employment & Immigration) (1987), 3 Imm. L.R. (2d) 288 (Fed. T.D.) — The applicant sought to quash a decision of a visa officer in India refusing sponsorship applications for the applicant's mother and his adopted daughter. The visa officer refused to accept the sponsorship of the daughter because, as a result of his inquiries, he concluded that the provisions of the *Hindu Adoptions and Maintenance Act* had not been complied with. It was held that a visa officer has not only a right but a duty to ensure that all immigrants meet the requirements of the Act and regulations. In this case, that included making certain that the sponsored child had been legally adopted within the meaning of section 2(1) of the regulation. The officer's decision was not reached improperly or without justification. The officer did reach a conclusion that involved an interpretation of Hindu law, and he ought to have afforded the applicant some opportunity for counter-argument. However, the relief sought in this case, *i.e.*, *certiorari* and *mandamus*, was discretionary, and in all the circumstances the motion was dismissed.

Rattan v. Canada (Minister of Employment & Immigration) (1987), 1 Imm. L.R. (2d) 317 (Imm. App. Bd.) — This appeal was from the refusal of a sponsored application for landing of the appellant's spouse. The sponsor was a Canadian citizen, and the only child of the marriage was Canadian born. The spouse of the appellant (the father) had left Canada voluntarily after being advised he must make his sponsored application from outside Canada. The basis for the refusal was that the marriage was not permitted by the *Hindu Marriage Act, 1955* because the appellant had been previously married to the sponsoree's uncle. The Board noted that while capacity to marry is presumed to be governed by the prenuptial domicile of the parties, an exception exists where it can be inferred that at the time of the marriage the parties intended to establish their home in a certain country (Canada) and did, in fact, establish it there within a reasonable time. In such a situation, the issue is whether the marriage is valid according to the laws of Canada, which it was. Accordingly, the refusal was found to be invalid and the appeal was allowed.

Johl v. Canada (Minister of Employment & Immigration) (1987), 1 Imm. L.R. (2d) 111 (Imm. App. Bd.) — This is an appeal from the refusal of the sponsored application for permanent residence. The appellant sponsored applications for his father, mother, sister and brother. The applicants were refused because the principle applicant was unable or unwilling to support himself, his wife and children without adequate settlement arrangements having been made by the sponsor. Whether a sponsor has an income at least equal to the low income cut-off per year for the number of his dependants, plus the number of his sponsorees, is but one factor that an immigration officer should consider in deciding whether the sponsor will be able to fulfill his undertaking. Other matters to be considered are the stability of the sponsor's employment and prospects for advancement; the willingness of the sponsor, his spouse and close relatives to do everything possible for the sponsorees; prospects of future employment of the sponsorees; the likelihood of the sponsorees establishing themselves quickly and easily; the ownership of a house and other assets; the sponsor's opportunity to get other work in case of lay-off; and, finally, whether the sponsor's skills are in a declining or expanding trade. The Board also stated that immigration officers are failing in their statutory duty if they do not give the sponsors or applicants, as the case may be, reasons for refusal couched in such a degree of particularity that they will know why there have been refusals and what cases must be met on appeal.

Canada (Information Commissioner) v. Canada (Minister of Employment & Immigration), [1986] 3 F.C. 63 (Fed. T.D.) — This was an application under the Access to Information Act, section 42(1)(a), for a review of the refusal by the Canada Employment and Immigration Commission to disclose the immigration file relating to the sponsorship by one, D.F., of his wife, P.F. The request was denied because the applicant sought personal information about another person. A complaint was lodged with the Information Commissioner, who recommended release of the information. The respondent Minister released five pages but refused to disclose a further 200 pages of documents. Pursuant to section 42(1)(a), that refusal was reviewed. The respondent was ordered to disclose the records in issue to the Information Commissioner. The purpose of the *Access to Information Act* was to codify the right to access to information held by the Government. It was not to codify the Government's right to refuse to release such information. Exemptions from the right to disclose are exceptional and must be confined to those exemptions specifically set out in the statute.

Wong v. Canada (Minister of Employment & Immigration) (1986), 64 N.R. 309 (Fed. C.A.) — Chong Wong delivered an undertaking respecting his father, mother and brother to come to Canada from the People's Republic of China on October 29, 1981. Prior to November 5, 1981, Chong delivered application forms for admission to Canada partially completed, as required by the guidelines for dealing with persons emigrating from the People's Republic of China. On December 27, 1981, Biu, the accompanying dependant of the father of Chong, turned 21.

The trial judge had held that the application had not been made prior to November 5, 1981 because the forms had not been completed by that time. This was overruled on the basis that the application was deemed to have been submitted when whatever it was that was done by the applicant had the effect of initiating the process leading to the issuance or refusal of the visa.

Singla v. Canada (Minister of Employment & Immigration) (1986), 1 F.T.R. 264 (Fed. T.D.) — The applicant applied to sponsor his mother and his 2 brothers. The respondent Minister denied the application because there was not sufficient evidence to prove that Mrs. Singla, the mother of the applicant, was also the mother of the 2 dependent sons. New evidence was later found by the applicant. He did not wish to make a new application because his 2 brothers were over the age of 21 by this time. His hope was to have the original application opened to consider this new evidence (blood tests). The Court ruled that the respondent Minister had a duty to consider the new evidence and to reopen the original application. A new application was held not to suffice because the brothers would, at the time of that application, be over the age of 21. The Court noted that the applicant had pressed his case with all due diligence. Further, the new evidence (blood tests) was not known to the applicant at the time of the original application. Thus, an order of *certiorari* issued, quashing the refusal to consider further the original application for landing. *Mandamus* issued requiring the respondent to reconsider such application on the basis of the new information submitted by the applicant.

Mundi v. Canada (Minister of Employment & Immigration) (1985), 63 N.R. 310 (Fed. C.A.) — This appeal arose from the refusal of a visa officer to approve the application of the appellant's father, Ajmer Singh Mundi, for the landing of himself, his wife, his son, Balwinder, and 2 daughters. The application had been sponsored by the appellant, who was at all material times a Canadian citizen. Ajmer Singh Mundi forwarded a false school leaving certificate for the purpose of establishing the date of birth of Balwinder Singh and to prove that Balwinder was under 21 years of age at the time of the application. The failure to satisfy the visa officer, with respect to Balwinder's age by means of this false school leaving certificate, did not affect the admissibility of Ajmer Singh, his wife and daughters because the false certificate, respecting Balwinder's age, was not relevant to the admissibility of the other family members. Section 9(3) was not a basis for refusing Ajmer Singh and the other family members because the false certificate was relevant only to Balwinder's admissibility as a dependant and had no bearing on whether the admission of the applicant and the rest of the family was contrary to the Act or regulations. Further, section 79(1) did not allow the visa officer to refuse the application of the entire family simply because Balwinder was not a dependant and, therefore, not entitled to a visa. The application could only be refused in total if Ajmer Singh, who made the application, did not meet the requirements of the Act or regulations.

Editor's Note: This case may have a much broader import than family class applications.

Vashi v. Canada (Minister of Employment & Immigration) (October 15, 1985), Doc. T-1459-85 (Fed. T.D.) — The applicant married her husband on May 2, 1983. She submitted an undertaking on June 9, 1983 at the Canada Immigration Centre in Toronto. The husband submitted an application to the Canadian High Commission in New Delhi on July 19, 1983. At the date of this proceeding, no decision had been taken with respect to the application for permanent residence. The Court ordered that, due to the unexplained delays in this case, a decision be taken by December 31, 1985, subject to the respondents being able to show a need for an extension at that time.

Kaur v. Canada (Minister of Employment & Immigration) (May 8, 1985), Doc. T-2490-84 (Fed. T.D.) — The applicant wanted to bring her fiancé to Canada so that they could be married. Apart from attempting to sponsor her fiancé, the applicant went to India and went through a form of marriage in that country with her fiancé. The initial application of the fiancé for permanent residence was turned down and one of the factors in the rejection was related to the opinion that the Indian marriage was invalid. The sponsor appealed to the Immigration Appeal Board, which observed that the marriage was to be presumed valid until ruled otherwise by a Court of competent jurisdiction. The respondent persisted in raising the question of the validity of the Indian marriage and refusing to process the initial application for permanent residence. *Certiorari* was granted quashing this decision and the respondent was directed to process the application in accordance with the existing law and regulations, which the Court understood would result in the admission of the fiancé for a sufficient period for the marriage to take place. The validity of the Indian marriage was irrelevant to the determination of the application because the applicant was attempting to bring over a husband-to-be for the purpose of marriage in Canada.

Toor v. Canada (Minister of Employment & Immigration) (1983), 144 D.L.R. (3d) 554 (Fed. C.A.) — A Canadian citizen applied to sponsor his wife and three children for admission. A visa officer refused to allow the wife and children to proceed to Canada and the sponsor appealed. The Immigration Appeal Board dismissed this appeal, holding that the wife did not meet the requirements of the Act and regulations because she had no intention of taking up residence in Canada when she filed her application for permanent residence. The Federal Court of Appeal set aside this finding as not being supportable on the evidence. Because the sponsor's husband was a Canadian citizen, the wife's ineligibility had no bearing upon whether the children met the requirements of the Act or the regulations.

Reece v. Canada (Minister of Employment & Immigration) (1981), [1982] 2 F.C. 743 (Fed. T.D.) — The petitioner applied for the issue of a writ of *mandamus*, ordering the Minister to render a decision on her pending application for permanent residence, and for a writ of prohibition, preventing the holding of an inquiry. The application for *mandamus* was dismissed because there was no requirement for consideration of an application not made from abroad. Accordingly, the application for prohibition also failed.

O'Grady v. Whyte (1982), 42 N.R. 608 (Fed. C.A.) — The respondent attempted to sponsor his putative daughter who was living in Jamaica. The daughter came to Canada and while in Canada a sponsorship application was turned over to immigration officials in Hamilton. The respondent was advised that the application could not be processed because the daughter did not fall within the definition of the term as it appears in the Immigration Regulation, section 2(1). *Mandamus* was issued to compel the immigration officials to dispose of the application. On appeal this order was set aside because no application for permanent residence on behalf of the daughter had been made in Jamaica, nor had an Order in Council been issued under section 115(2) of this Act exempting her from the requirement of section 9(1). The Court held that there was no duty upon an immigration official to make a decision on a sponsorship application because the underlying requirement of a landing application had not been met.

Lawrence v. Canada (Minister of Employment & Immigration), [1980] 1 F.C. 779 (Fed. T.D.) — Where the sponsoree had no immigrant visa but was present in Canada, the department was required to give the sponsor a decision on her application. Given that the sponsoree was obligated under a departure notice to leave Canada not later than April 1, 1980, the decision should be made prior to the date. The Court upheld the right of the department to refuse the application on the ground that the sponsoree did not meet the requirements of the *Immigration Act* or Regulation because he had not applied for a visa at a visa office outside Canada. The Court also referred to the anomalous result that occurs where the department refuses to make a decision on the sponsorship application, namely the Immigration Appeal Board lacks jurisdiction to entertain an appeal at that stage by the sponsor.

Gill v. Canada (Minister of Employment & Immigration), [1979] 2 F.C. 782 (Fed. C.A.) — A son is entitled to sponsor his natural father for admission to Canada.

Tsiafakis v. Canada (Minister of Manpower & Immigration), [1977] 2 F.C. 216 (Fed. C.A.) — Even though an immigration officer is satisfied that a sponsor cannot make an application on behalf of a prospective sponsored relative, he must supply the prescribed form to the sponsor and, should he fail to do so, *mandamus* will issue.

Investors

6.11 The investor class is hereby prescribed as a class of persons who may be granted landing on the basis of their business experience, accumulated net worth and intention to make investments in Canada that meet the standards set out in these Regulations.
SOR/93-412, s. 3

Approval of Funds

6.12 The Minister is authorized to approve a fund if

(a) the fund has been approved by a province;

(b) the province provides documentation to the Minister stating that, in the event of the default of the fund to transfer the provincial allocation to the agent in accordance with paragraph 6.13(g), the province will be liable to transfer to the agent an amount equal to the provincial allocation in order to repay the investor under paragraph 6.13(h);

(c) the fund to be approved will be the only non-suspended approved fund in the province; and

(d) the fund has entered into an agreement with the Minister designating the Minister as agent for the purpose of

(i) receiving the provincial allocation and keeping it until the beginning of the allocation period unless the provincial allocation is repaid under paragraph 6.13(b),

(ii) transferring the provincial allocation to the approved fund at the beginning of the allocation period in accordance with paragraph 6.13(d), unless the approved fund is suspended under subsection 6.14(1),

(iii) preparing and delivering to the investor a debt obligation and notifying the investor of the date of receipt of the investment at the beginning of the allocation period in accordance with paragraph 6.13(e),

(iv) receiving the provincial allocation transferred by an approved fund at the end of the allocation period in accordance with paragraph 6.13(g),

(v) in the event of default by the fund to transfer the provincial allocation under paragraph 6.13(g), receiving the provincial allocation from the province in accordance with paragraph 6.13(h), and

(vi) repaying the provincial allocation to the investor in accordance with paragraph 6.13(i).

SOR/93-412, s. 3; SOR/94-674, s. 2; SOR/96-321, s. 1; SOR/97-243, s. 1; SOR/97-574, s. 1(a); SOR/98-591, s. 1(a); SOR/99-146, s. 3

6.13 An approval of a fund under section 6.12, whether or not the fund has been suspended, is subject to the following terms and conditions:

(a) the approved fund shall receive the provincial allocation through the agent;

(b) the approved fund shall, through the agent, repay the provincial allocation to the investor within 90 days after the date of the receipt by the agent of the request for repayment by the investor, as long as the request for repayment has been received before a visa has been issued to the investor;

(c) the approved fund shall repay the provincial allocation to the agent within 30 days after the agent informs the fund that the investor has chosen to withdraw before the issuance of a visa;

(d) on the first day of the allocation period, an approved fund that is not suspended shall receive, through the agent, the provincial allocation;

(e) on the first day of the allocation period, an approved fund that receives the provincial allocation shall issue to the investor, throught the agent, a debt obligation that is in an amount equal to the provincial allocation, that is due and payable 30 days after the expiry of the allocation period and that cannot be transferred but can be pledged as security, and shall notify the investor through the agent of the date of receipt of the investment;

(f) during the allocation period, the approved fund shall use the provincial allocation for the purpose of creating or continuing employmnet in Canada to foster the development of a strong and viable economy;

(g) at the end of the allocation period, the approved fund shall transfer the provincial allocation to the agent for repayment in accordance with paragraph (i);

(h) in the event of default by the approved fund to transfer the provincail allocation to the agent under paragraph (g), the province shall transfer an amount equal to the provincial allocation to the agent for repayment in accordance with paragraph (i); and

(i) 30 days after the expiry of the allocation period, the agent shall repay the provincial allocation to the investor thereby extinguishing the debt obligation in respect of that provincial allocation.

SOR/93-412, s. 3; SOR/94-674, s. 3; SOR/96-321, s. 2; SOR/97-243, s. 1; SOR/97-296, s. 1; SOR/97-574, s. 1(b); SOR/98-591, s. 1(b); SOR/99-146, s. 3

Suspension of Approval of Funds

6.14 (1) The Minister shall suspend the approval of a fund if

(a) the province that approved the fund has withdrawn its approval;

(b) the fund no longer qualifies as a fund as that term is defined in subsection 2(1);

(c) the documentation provided by the province to the Minister in accordance with paragraph 6.12(b) is no longer valid and no valid documentation has been provided by the province to replace it;

(d) the agreement between the fund and the Minister referred to in paragraph 6.12(b) is no longer valid; or

(e) the fund is not in compliance with the terms and conditions set out in section 6.13.

(2) If the Minister suspends an approval under subsection (1), the Minister is authorized to impose additional terms and conditions on the fund repecting the lifting of the suspension.

(3) If the Minister has imposed additional terms and conditions under subsection (2) and the fund has complied with those additional terms and conditions, the Minister shall lift the suspension of the approval.

SOR/93-412, s. 3; SOR/94-674, s. 4; SOR/96-321, s. 3; SOR/97-243, s. 1; SOR/97-574, s. 1(c); SOR/98-591, s. 1(c); SOR/99-146, s. 3

Revocation of Approval of Funds

6.15 The Minister shall revoke the approval of a fund if

(a) the approved fund has repaid the provincial allocation to all its investors;

(b) the approval of the fund has been suspended; and

(c) if applicable, the approved fund did not comply with the additional terms and conditions imposed under subsection 6.14(2).

SOR/93-412, s. 3; SOR/99-146, s. 3

Additional Terms and Conditions

6.16 The Minister is authorized to impose terms and conditions in relation to any approval of a fund in addition to those set out in sections 6.12 and 6.13.

SOR/93-412, s. 3; SOR/99-146, s. 3

Periodic Reports

6.17 The Minister is authorized to require each approved fund to submit, until all investors have been repaid in accordance with paragraph 6.13(i), the following periodic reports demonstrating compliance with paragraph 6.13(f);

(a) a quarterly report on the use of provincial allocations, including

(i) the name of the recipients of the portion of the provincial allocations invested,

(ii) a description and the terms of the security received for that investment,

(iii) the date on which the portion of the provincial allocations is invested,

(iv) the date on which the portion of the provincial allocations invested is recovered by the approved fund,

(v) a brief description of the use of the portion of the provincial allocations invested,

(vi) the number of person years of employment created by the portion of the provincial allocations invested, and

(vii) the code for each recipient of the investment as set out in the *Canadian Standard Industrial Classification for Companies and Enterprises, 1980*; and

(b) annual audited financial statements for the approved fund, submitted within 180 days after the end of each financial year.

SOR/93-412, s. 3; SOR/99-146, s. 3

6.18 [Repealed SOR/99-146, s. 3.]

6.19 [Repealed SOR/99-146, s. 3.]

Admission Requirements for Convention Refugees Seeking Resettlement

7. (1) Where a person seeks admission to Canada as a Convention refugee seeking resettlement, the person and their accompanying dependants, if any, are subject to the following admission requirements:

(a) a visa officer is satisfied that the person is a Convention refugee seeking resettlement;

(b) a visa officer determines that

(i) a group or corporation is sponsoring the application for admission of the person and the accompanying dependants in accordance with section 7.1,

(ii) financial or other assistance is available in Canada for the person and the accompanying dependants, or

(iii) the person has sufficient financial resources to provide for the lodging, care and maintenance, and for the resettlement in Canada, of the person and the accompanying dependants;

(c) where the person and the accompanying dependants intend to reside in a place in Canada other than the Province of Quebec, a visa officer determines that the person and the accompanying dependants will be able to become successfully established in Canada, taking into consideration

(i) the ability of the person and the accompanying dependants to communicate in one of the official languages of Canada,

(ii) the age of the person,

(iii) the level of education, the work experience and the skills of the person and the accompanying dependants,

(iv) the number and ages of the accompanying dependants, and

(v) the personal suitability of the person and their accompanying dependants, including their adaptability, motivation, initiative, resourcefulness and other similar qualities; and

(d) where the person and the accompanying dependants intend to reside in the Province of Quebec, the person and the accompanying dependants will, in the opinion of the appropriate minister of that Province, based on regulations made under *An Act respecting Immigration to Québec*, R.S.Q., c. I-O.2, as amended from time to time, be able to become successfully established in that Province.

(2) Subject to subsection (4), where a person referred to in subsection (1) and their accompanying dependants meet the applicable admission requirements and any other requirements of the Act and these Regulations, the visa officer may issue an immigrant visa to that person and the accompanying dependants.

(3) Where a visa officer does not issue an immigrant visa as an accompanying dependant to a son or daughter of a person referred to in subsection (1), or to a son or daughter of the spouse of that person, the visa officer shall not issue an immigrant visa as an accompanying dependant to a son or daughter of that son or daughter.

(4) A visa officer shall not issue an immigrant visa to an accompanying dependant of a person referred to in subsection (1) unless

> **(a) at the time the application for admission is received by a visa officer, the accompanying dependant, except if the dependant is the person's spouse, meets the criteria set out in paragraph (a), (b), (c) of the definition "dependent son" or "dependent daughter" in subsection 2(1), as the case may be; and**
>
> **(b) at the time the visa is issued, the accompanying dependant, except if the dependant is the person's spouse, meets the criteria referred to in paragraph (a), except for the one respecting age set out in paragraph (a) of the definition "dependent son" or "dependent daughter" in subsection 2(1), as the case may be.**

(5) Subsections (1) to (4) are retroactive and apply to all applications for landing made by Convention refugees seeking resettlement that are pending on the day those subsections come into force.

SOR/88-286, s. 4; SOR/91-157, s. 2; SOR/92-101, s. 4; SOR/92-133, s. 1; SOR/97-184, s. 2; SOR/98-270, s. 2.

Sponsorship

7.1 (1) Subject to subsections (2) and (3), an application for admission of a Convention refugee seeking resettlement, and the Convention refugee's accompanying dependants, may be sponsored by

> **(a) a group that consists of not fewer than five individuals, each of whom is a Canadian citizen or permanent resident, has attained at least 19 years of age and resides in the expected community of settlement; or**
>
> **(b) a corporation that has representatives in the expected community of settlement.**

(2) Subject to subsection (3), the conditions under which a group or corporation referred to in subsection (1) may sponsor an application for admission of a Convention refugee seeking resettlement and the Convention refugee's accompanying dependants are the following:

> **(a) in the case of a group, the group has given a joint undertaking signed by each member of the group to the Minister, in the form fixed by the Minister, for a period of not less than one year and not more than two years, as determined by an immigration officer based on the recommendation of a visa officer who has taken into consideration the factors referred to in paragraph 7(1)(c);**
>
> **(b) in the case of a corporation, the corporation**
>
> > **(i) has entered into a sponsorship agreement with the Minister under which the corporation agrees to make provision for the lodging, care and mainte-**

nance of and resettlement assistance for the Convention refugee seeking resettlement and the Convention refugee's accompanying dependants, and

(ii) has given the Minister an undertaking in the form and for the period referred to in paragraph (a) in respect of the Convention refugee and the Convention refugee's accompanying dependants;

(c) neither the members of the group nor the corporation is in default in respect of any other undertaking; and

(d) the immigration officer is satisfied, based on documentation provided by the group or corporation, that the group or corporation

(i) has made or will make adequate arrangements in the expected community of settlement for the reception of the Convention refugee and the Convention refugee's accompanying dependants, and

(ii) has sufficient financial resources and expertise to fulfil the undertaking referred to in paragraph (a) or subparagraph (b)(ii), as the case may be.

(3) If a Convention refugee seeking resettlement and the Convention refugee's accompanying dependants intend to reside in the Province of Quebec, the group or corporation referred to in subsection (1) must meet the requirements for sponsorship of regulations made under *An Act respecting immigration to Québec*, R.S.Q., c. I-0.2, as amended from time to time.

(4) Subsections (1), (2) and (3) are retroactive and apply in respect of all applications for landing made by Convention refugees seeking resettlement that are pending on May 1, 1998.

SOR/97-184, s. 2; SOR/98-270, s. 3

Prescribed Class of Immigrants for the Purposes of Subsection 6(8) of the Act

7.2 (1) For the purposes of subsection 6(8) of the Act, the Convention refugees seeking resettlement class is prescribed as a class of immigrants, the members and all accompanying dependants of which are to be assessed.

(2) Subsection (1) is retroactive and applies in respect of all applications for landing made by Convention refugees seeking resettlement that are pending on the day that subsection comes into force.

SOR/97-184, s. 2.

Selection Criteria

8. (1) Subject to section 11.1, for the purpose of determining whether an immigrant and the immigrant's dependants, other than a member of the family class, a Convention refugee seeking resettlement or an immigrant who intends to reside in the Province of Quebec, will be able to become successfully established in Canada, a visa officer shall assess that immigrant or, at the option of the immigrant, the spouse of that immigrant

(a) in the case of an immigrant, other than an immigrant described in paragraph (b) or (c), on the basis of each of the factors listed in Column I of Schedule I;

(b) in the case of an immigrant who intends to be a self-employed person in Canada, on the basis of each of the factors listed in Column I of Schedule I, other than the factor set out in item 5 thereof;

(c) in the case of an entrepreneur, an investor or a provincial nominee, on the basis of each of the factors listed in column I of Schedule I, other than the factors set out in items 4 and 5 thereof;

(d) [Revoked SOR/85-1038, s. 3.]

(e) [Revoked SOR/91-433, s. 3.]

(2) A visa officer shall award to an immigrant who is assessed on the basis of factors listed in Column I of Schedule I the appropriate number of units of assessment for each factor in accordance with the criteria set out in Column II thereof opposite that factor, but he shall not award for any factor more units of assessment than the maximum number set out in Column III thereof opposite that factor.

(3) [Revoked SOR/85-1038, s. 3.]

(4) Where a visa officer assesses an immigrant who intends to be a self-employed person in Canada, he shall, in addition to any other units of assessment awarded to that immigrant, award 30 units of assessment to the immigrant if, in the opinion of the visa officer, the immigrant will be able to become successfully established in his occupation or business in Canada.

SOR/79-347, s. 1; SOR/79-686, s. 1; SOR/79-851, s. 2; SOR/85-1038, s. 3; SOR/91-157, s. 3; SOR/91-433, s. 3; SOR/92-133, s. 2.

Case Law

Section 8(1)

Dogra v. Canada (Minister of Citizenship & Immigration) (April 23, 1999), Doc. IMM-3413-98 (Fed. T.D.) — The applicant, a citizen of India, sought to review the refusal of her application of permanent residence as a school and guidance counsellor. At the applicant's interview, the officer raised with the applicant the relevance to Canada of her experience as a guidance counsellor in India, and suggested that with education cutbacks and the laying off of teachers, the applicant might find it difficult to find employment in Canada in her intended occupation. In his letter of decision, the officer noted that the applicant would not know how to provide personal guidance to Canadian students who for the most part came from an entirely different background than the applicant.

One of contemporary Canada's defining characteristics is its multicultural nature. Our major cities in particular have a vibrant ethnic diversity and richness and relative harmoniousness that are the envy of many. For a visa officer to reject an application for permanent residence as a school guidance counsellor because students in Canada "for the most part come from an entirely different background than yourself" seem to the Court to be quite at odds with the reality of today's Canada. The Court noted that the officer seemed quite impervious to the possibility that many boards of education might well regard the applicant's national origin and experience as a valuable asset in assisting children.

Even though the CCDO and the NOC were designed for the purpose of evaluating the market readiness of the applicants, the Court inclined to the view that it was not normally appropriate for visa officer's to engage in the exercise of assessing the Canadian relevance of an applicant's education, training and experience when they are consistent with the terms of the statutory criteria.

Wang v. Canada (Minister of Citizenship & Immigration) (1999), 49 Imm. L.R. (2d) 70 (Fed. T.D.) — This was an application to review the decision of a visa officer refusing the applicant's application. The applicant was a citizen of the People's Republic of China. He obtained a secondary school diploma in 1975, worked in restaurants, and in 1984 received a certificate on the successful completion of a one-year vocational program at a cooking school. He stated that after graduating, he was employed until 1990 as a senior chef in a hotel. The applicant entered the United States in 1990 and made a refugee claim which was rejected. He has since remained there without status. He has been employed at the same Chinese restaurant in New York since 1991 where he has been head chef since 1993. The applicant was interviewed in Detroit. The visa officer awarded 10 units of assessment under the education factor. The visa officer relied on a document issued by the Canadian Embassy in Beijing and stated that the applicant's secondary school diploma did not qualify him for university entrance because he had not written the national examination. It was procedurally unfair for the visa officer to rely on this document because it was not disclosed to the applicant for comment.

When the visa officer was questioning the applicant about his experience as a senior grade chef in China, she told him that she had a document that made it clear that this position was only available in China to a person who had worked for 5 years as a middle grade chef. It was a breach of the duty of fairness for the visa officer not to show to the applicant the document on which she was relying so that he might comment on the accuracy of the translation or such other matters as seemed appropriate to him. It is important for visa officers not forget that ensuring that qualified applicants are issued with visas is just as important as screening out those who do not satisfy the statutory selection criteria. The propriety of the visa officers' questions is thus subject to judicial scrutiny to ensure that they are reasonably calculated to elicit relevant information from people who may have not proficiency in either of Canada's official languages, or who are the product of other cultures, for ordinary citizens' encounters with public officials are intimidating experiences and not occasions for telling one's story in a forthcoming and open manner. The application for judicial review was allowed.

Azim v. Canada (Minister of Citizenship & Immigration) (1999), 49 Imm. L.R. (2d) 127 (Fed. T.D.) — The applicant sought an order quashing a decision of a visa officer refusing the applicant's application for landing. The National Occupational Classification (NOC) is a catalogue of occupations in Canada prepared by Human Resources Canada. It sets out a description of, and the requirement to be met, in order to engage in the occupations that are described.

Chapter 2112 describes the occupation of chemist and states that a bachelor's degree in chemistry is a minimum qualification. The applicant's B.Sc. degree was obtained after 2 years of study, not 3, and the visa officer did not consider this to be a bachelor's degree as described in the NOC. He considered that a bachelor's degree for NOC purposes required 3 years of full-time study. The text of the criteria to be addressed under the education factor in Schedule 1 refers to a first level university degree that requires at least 3 years of full-time study. This suggests that not all first level university degrees require 3 years of full-time study. The Court noted the difference in terminology between that used with respect to the education factor in Schedule 1 of the Regulations and that used in the National Occupations Classification, and that the NOC did not define a first level university degree as one requiring 3 years of full-time study.

Accordingly, the Court found that the applicant had a bachelor's degree for purposes of the NOC and set aside the decision of the visa officer.

Goel v. Canada (Minister of Citizenship & Immigration) (December 18, 1998), Doc. IMM-129-98 (Fed. C.A.) — The applicant sought to review a decision of a visa officer denying her permanent resident status. On April 16, 1997, the Canadian Consulate General Area Processing Centre in Buffalo first received the applicant's application for permanent residence. The visa officer found that the application was incomplete. Consequently, it was returned to the applicant with a direction that the application form be properly completed. The direction contained the following statement "all processing of your application is stopped and will not resume until you have complied with the above instructions . . . ." The clear and specific wording of the letter sent to the applicant indicated that the processing of the application had actually begun as of April 1997, and thus the applicant was entitled to an assessment under the CCDO and was not caught by the May 1, 1997 cut-off date for reference to that publication.

Olajuwon v. Canada (Minister of Citizenship & Immigration) (1998), 47 Imm. L.R. (2d) 249, 150 F.T.R. 158 (Fed. T.D.) — This was an application to set aside a decision of a visa officer refusing the applicant's application for permanent residence. The applicant requested that he be assessed in one of two alternate occupations which he indicated he would seek to pursue if admitted to Canada.

The letter of rejection referred to an assessment of the applicant in relation to only one of those two occupations. The visa officer in her affidavit swore that she had assessed the applicant in relation to the occupation not referred to in the letter of rejection.

The decision of the visa officer was set aside. A visa officer has a duty to assess an applicant for permanent residence in the occupations for which he requests assessment and the results of that assessment are to be set out in any letter rejecting the application.

Mahrez v. Canada (Minister of Citizenship and Immigration) (1998), 46 Imm. L.R. (2d) 132, (Fed. T.D.) — The applicant sought to review a decision of an immigration officer refusing the applicant's application for permanent residence as an independent applicant. The applicant filed his application in France. An immigration officer did a preliminary examination of the application and specified that the interview should focus on the level of the applicant's knowledge of the languages, his experience as a manufacturer's agent, and contained a note to the effect that if the applicant did not have the points required for a manufacturers agent that the applicant should be assessed as an accountant. The immigration officer who actually interviewed the applicant assessed him as a manufacturer's agent but not as an accountant.

The application for judicial review was dismissed. The applicant never indicated either in writing or orally that if he failed to qualify as a manufacturer's agent, he wanted to be assessed as an accountant or that he was also ready and prepared to work as an accountant. Item 4 of Schedule 1 provides that units of assessment shall be awarded on the basis of the occupation that the applicant is qualified for and is prepared to follow in Canada.

Hossain v. Canada (Minister of Citizenship & Immigration) (April 17, 1998), Doc. IMM-2016-97 (Fed. T.D.) — This was an application to review a decision by the visa officer denying the applicant's application for permanent residence. The applicant stated that his intended occupation was as a sales promotion administrator. At the applicant's interview with the visa officer she advised him that she was unable to award him any points for experience in that category. She further advised him that she was prepared to qualify him for the position of shoe store manager because he had related experience for four years in a shoe store in New York, however, under this category, it would not be possible to award any points for demand.

The Court did not accept the applicant's submission that there was a duty on the visa officer to assist an applicant or to request supplementary information for that applicant. The onus is upon the applicant rather, to supply the visa officer with all relevant information which may assist in the discharge of the visa officer's duties. It is, however, the duty of a visa officer before disposing of an application to advise the applicant, where a negative assessment is contemplated, of that fact and then provide to the applicant a fair and reasonable opportunity of answering whatever it is that is against him.

In this particular case, the visa officer complied with the duty imposed upon her by the relevant jurisprudence and the application was dismissed.

Tekotev v. Canada (Minister of Citizenship & Immigration) (February 27, 1998), Doc. IMM-1275-97 (Fed. T.D.) — The applicant sought to overturn a refusal of his application for permanent residence. A visa officer determined that the applicant could speak, read and write English with difficulty and awarded him "0" units of assessment on that account. As a result the applicant was awarded 68 units. The visa officer instructed her personal assistant to perform reading and writing tests on the applicant. As to the reading test the personal assistant recorded errors made by the applicant. These were provided to the visa officer who made notes of the errors and in particular the words with which the applicant was unfamiliar. As to the writing test the visa officer reviewed the applicant's written replies to the questions asked by the assistant and noted numerous errors in the reply.

The visa officer did not delegate her duty to assess the applicant's ability with the English language to her assistant. The visa officer reviewed the results of the applicant's reading test with the applicant. Even if there was an improper delegation when the personal assistant performed the test and recorded the error, that error was corrected by the visa officer reviewing the reading test directly with the applicant. This review is sufficient to constitute an assessment by the visa officer of the applicant's ability to read English. Accordingly, the application for judicial review was dismissed.

Valentinov v. Canada (Minister of Citizenship & Immigration) (1998), 143 F.T.R. 46 (Fed. T.D.) — The applicants sought to review a decision of a visa officer refusing the applicants' application for permanent residence. Immediately prior to their interview, the applicants were interviewed by the visa officer's administrative assistant, who administered two tests in order to determine the level at which the applicants read, wrote and comprehended English. The visa officer incorporated into her affidavit a brief text in English that the applicant was requested to read and the visa officer attested that she reviewed her assistant's comments about how well the applicant was able to read English. The visa officer rejected the application awarding the applicants 69 units of assessment. The Court found an unauthorized delegation of the visa officer's duty to assess the applicant's ability to read English. Accordingly, the decision of the visa officer was set aside.

Huang v. Canada (Minister of Citizenship & Immigration) (1998), 41 Imm. L.R. (2d) 247 (Fed. T.D.) — This was an application to review a decision of a visa officer refusing the applicant's application for permanent residence. Based on her translation of a document which had been provided by the applicant, the visa officer concluded that the applicant had improperly obtained her Grade 2 Chinese chef certificate. This was a serious allegation which should have been put to the applicant by the visa officer; however, the visa officer was not in possession of this information until after the applicant's interview was completed. The visa officer breached the principles of procedural fairness by a) relying on a document without the applicant having been given an opportunity to review and comment on it; and b) by failing to put such a serious allegation of impropriety to the applicant so that he could respond.

Ahmed v. Canada (Minister of Citizenship & Immigration) (January 16, 1998), Doc. IMM-2600-96 (Fed. T.D.) — The applicant sought to review the decision of a visa officer refusing his application for permanent residence under the independant immigrant category. The provision of self assessment guide booklets to candidates for admission to Canada is for the purpose of providing information only. By providing these guide booklets, the government does not create a legitimate expectation that the visa officer will be bound in any way by the candiate's own assessment of his or her chances of success. The visa officer is bound only by the terms of the Act and regulations regardless of whether such terms are accurately reflected in the guide booklet. Accordingly, the application for judicial review was dismissed.

Nakamine v. Canada (Minister of Citizenship & Immigration) (1998), 41 Imm. L.R. (2d) 255 (Fed. T.D.) — This is an application to review a refusal of an application for permanent residence under the independent category as a chef cook. The applicant was a citizen of Japan, and was awarded "0" units of assessment for his experience. The applicant had no formal training as a chef, but this occupation in Japan is learned on the job. Due to the fact that the applicant intended to work as a cook in a Japanese restaurant in Canada, formal training ought not to have been an essential factor. The applicant had more than two years of experience working in various restaurants in Japan and Canada and accordingly was entitled to more than "0" units of assessment for experience, at least as a cook, if not as a chef.

Parmar v. Canada (Minister of Citizenship & Immigration) (1997), 139 F.T.R. 203 (Fed. T.D.) — The applicant was seeking to quash a decision refusing his application for a permanent residence. The applicant applied as an assisted relative having received a family business job offer from his brother-in-law, who ran a convenience store in Bobcaygeon, Ontario. The job in question was designated as assistant manager retail. At the paper screening of the residency application the applicant was awarded seven points for SVP. These figures were generated by a computerized information processing system or "CAIPS".

The applicant submitted that under IS 1:18 of the immigration manual the family job program is to be viewed as a means of reunifying families as much as supplying workers to employers unable to find suitable employees in Canada, and the family reunification aspects of the program are to be accorded equal, if not more, significance than are job market considerations. Immigration manual guidelines do not fetter the discretion of a visa officer. Policy directives whether made pursuant to regulatory authority or general administrative capacity are no more than directions and are unenforceable by members of the public. The guidelines are non-binding and not exhaustive; they are guidance for the exercise of discretion.

Regulation 11(1) requires the officer to consider whether the applicant is able to carry out the proposed job notwithstanding an alleged lack of experience. This regulation applies only where the applicant has not been awarded any points for experience. On the facts of this case, the applicant had received four points for experience and as a consequence the visa officer made no error in not relying on subsection 11(1)(b) in arriving at her decision.

The visa officer must consider the applicant's whole work experience and the occupations inherent in it and must provide the applicant with an opportunity to submit evidence of his/her qualifications. Where there is no evidence presented of alternative or inherent occupations, the officer does not err in failing to consider occupations other than those which the applicant has requested. In this case, there was no evidence that the officer failed to consider the applicant's whole work experience or to give him an opportunity to submit evidence of his qualifications. The decision that the applicant was not qualified for any other occupation inherent from his work experience that would enable an applicant to succeed was not made capriciously, perversely, or without regard to the material before the officer.

The application for judicial review was dismissed.

Khattab v. Canada (Minister of Citizenship & Immigration) (1997), 135 F.T.R. 239, 40 Imm. L.R. (2d) 311 (Fed. T.D.) — The applicant applied for permanent residence as an independent immigrant and indicated that he would seek employment as a manufacturer's representative. He was called in for an interview and later informed that he had not been assessed enough points to qualify. That determination, however, assessed the applicant's suitability as an appliance salesman, and not the category which the applicant indicated on his application form. The visa officer did not indicate to the applicant her concern that he was not suited to consideration as a manufacturer's representative and that she would be evaluating him as an appliance salesman. This constituted reviewable error, accordingly, the decision of the visa officer was set aside.

Su v. Canada (Minister of Citizenship & Immigration) (1997), 136 F.T.R. 52, 42 Imm. L.R. (2d) 110 (Fed. T.D.); quashed (1997), 225 N.R. 34, 144 F.T.R. 320 (note) (Fed. C.A.) — This was an application to set aside the refusal by a visa officer of the applicant's application for permanent residence. A preliminary assessment of the applicant's application resulted in 73 points. An interview was required so that the applicant's level of experience could be assessed. The applicant could not attend at the interview, because the applicant could not obtain a U.S. visa. Due to the fact that the applicant failed to attend the interview his application was refused. The analyst who did the initial screening recommended that the applicant attend an interview. The record supports the conclusion that the visa officer who finally denied the application so decided because it was apparent that the applicant did not attend the interview. There is no indication that the visa officer considered the total circumstances and merits of the application. Subsection 9(2) of the *Immigration Act* requires the visa officer to assess the application on its merits. The visa officer failed to exercise any independent judgement in this matter and thereby fettered the exercise of her discretion. The application was allowed and the decision of the visa officer set aside.

Samolenko v. Canada (Minister of Citizenship & Immigration) (July 28, 1997), Doc. IMM-4141-96 (Fed. T.D.) — The applicant sought to review a negative decision by a visa officer with respect to her application for permanent residence under the independent category. The applicant listed her occupation as a computer graphics specialist, in addition, the applicant alleged that she sent a supplementary application to the visa officer prior to the refusal that was the subject matter of this proceeding. That supplementary application was said to have contained an additional occupational category, namely that of an arts supervisor. The respondent disputed receipt of the supplementary application. The applicant was not assessed as an arts supervisor.

A visa officer has a duty to assess an application with reference to each occupation represented by the applicant as one for which he or she is qualified and prepared to pursue in Canada. Further, there is the clear responsibility on the part of a visa officer to assess alternative occupations inherent in the applicant's work experience.

There was no evidence to establish that the supplementary application was in fact before the visa officer. The copy of the supplementary application submitted by the applicant as part of its application for judicial review did not contain any evidence to suggest receipt of it by the respondent. The respondent specifically denied that any supplementary application was received by the embassy. The only evidence submitted by the applicant was an affidavit of a solicitor who practised in association with counsel for the applicant. This solicitor's affidavit deposed that the source of his information and belief was the applicant's solicitor, who could not reasonably be expected to have personal knowledge of the matter.

Accordingly, the applicant had failed to prove that the supplementary application was before the visa officer and the application for judicial review was therefore dismissed.

Mohammad v. Canada (Minister of Citizenship & Immigration) (1997), 131 F.T.R. 52 (Fed. T.D.) — The applicant applied for permanent residence as an independent applicant. The applicant described his intended occupation as mechanic. He provided documents setting out his experience as a washing machine mechanic and technician, as well as his experience in the repair and maintenance of laundry machines generally. The visa officer concluded that the applicant did not have the required experience as a laundry machine mechanic, however, the officer decided to assess the applicant in the occupation of mechanical engineering technician.

At no time was the applicant advised that he was disqualified under his intended occupation as a laundry machine mechanic. It is not sufficient for the officer to disclose his decision in reasons for excluding the applicant from his intended occupation in his affidavit. The failure to advise the applicant that he was disqualified and the failure to provide him an opportunity to submit information on the alternative occupation constituted together a reviewable error. Accordingly the application was allowed.

Azarpajooh v. Canada (Minister of Citizenship & Immigration) (1997), 128 F.T.R. 203 (Fed. T.D.) — This was an application to review a decision of a visa officer refusing the applicant's application for permanent residence as an independent applicant. The applicant was found to lack the requisite number of points to obtain a visa based on such factors as occupational demand in the assessed occupation of "manager, engineering" and experience in the alternate occupation of "civil engineer".

The visa officer assessed the applicant under the specific occupation "managers, engineering" because the applicant had always been employed in a managerial capacity. The applicant had the requisite total number of points for the occupation of "manager, engineering" based on such factors as experience and education. However, the applicant was required to receive a minimum number of points under the factor of occupational demand, and since the applicant received no points in this category his application was refused. The visa officer assessed the applicant under the alternative occupation "civil engineer". The visa officer determined that although the applicant had experience as "manager, engineering" his experience as a "civil engineer" was very limited. The visa officer did not provide a point tally or breakdown for the alternate occupation of "civil engineer".

The visa officer failed to provide procedural fairness. The visa officer had the duty to clearly inform the applicant that he was only being fully considered under the category of "manager, engineering" which was an occupation which the applicant had not specified in his original application. The visa officer has a duty to reveal to the applicant what was in her mind so that the applicant could, if he desired, dispute the visa officers finding and disabuse her of assumptions.

Furthermore, there were some suggestions in the visa officers notes that the applicant was involved in design work. The visa officer failed to break down the applicant's duties in his previous employment and award units of assessment for experience for his design work, particularly at his current position at the consulting firm. In her letter to the applicant the visa officer did not acknowledge any possibility that the applicant had performed design work. Accordingly, failure to award any points for experience as a "civil engineer" was found to be unreasonable.

Mozumder v. Canada (Minister of Citizenship & Immigration) (March 21, 1997), Doc. IMM-2766-95 (Fed. T.D.) — The applicant sought to review a decision of a visa officer refusing the applicant's application for permanent residence. A visa officer is under no statutory or common law duty to advise an applicant that his or her spouse can be assessed for landing. It is the applicant's responsibility to designate who will be assessed. Subsection 8(1) of the *Immigration Regulations* makes it mandatory for the visa officer to assess only one or the other. The option contemplated by subsection 1 must be exercised by the immigrant who is the principle applicant, prior to the visa officer's undertaking the assessment rather than after such an assessment has been conducted.

Mou v. Canada (Minister of Citizenship & Immigration) (1997), 125 F.T.R. 203 (Fed. T.D.) — The applicant sought to review the decision of a visa officer refusing his application for permanent residence as an independent applicant. The visa officer in Buffalo, New York attributed 68 units of assessment, 2 short of the required minimum of 70.

The applicant's intended occupation in Canada was that of a linguist. He held the equivalent of a master of arts degree from the Department of Chinese Language and Literature of Shanghai Teachers University. The applicant was at the time of this application a doctoral student and teaching assistant at the University of British Columbia.

The applicant received 5 out of a maximum of 10 units for personal suitability, because the visa officer was of the view that the "marketability" of the applicant's qualifications as a linguist in ancient Chinese language and literature was uncertain in Canada. The consideration of the "marketability" of the applicant's intended occupation under the personal suitability factor constituted double counting. The applicant was assessed less units under both personal suitability and occupational demand for the same reason. In addition the visa officer incorrectly awarded the 15 units under the educational factor because of her characterization of the applicant's master of arts degree as a first level university degree. After the applicant successfully completed a comprehensive exam, the University of British Columbia had recognized his master of arts degree and accepted him in its doctorate program. The visa officer was aware of this fact and should have awarded the applicant 16 units for his second level university degree. The decision of the visa officer was set aside and the matter remitted for reconsideration.

The Court noted that there was no provision in the legislation or regulations upon which to determine the lock-in date for the reconsidered application. The applicant's material in this case was first received on April 12, 1995 with a payment of $2,950 for processing and landing fees. On April 19, 1995 a consular official returned the money order and requested payment of an additional $100, the payment of the higher amount of $3,050 was received on April 26, 1995. If the applicant's application had been deemed to be received on April 12, 1995, he would have received 2 units for the age factor. The applicant was assessed no units under this heading, presumably because his application was deemed to be received on April 26th, four days after his 49th birthday. Further, on April 12, 1995 when the applicant's material was received his son was under 19 years of age. Pursuant to paragraph 3(3)(a) of the fees regulations the processing fee for a dependent son under 19 years of age is $100. The son's 19th birthday was on April 16, 1995. The consular official requested the payment of $3,050 on April 19, 1995 when the son was no longer 19 years of age, in doing so the son's fee may have been set at $100 on the basis of the material having been received on April 12th when he was under the age of 19. In this circumstance, no right of landing fee was payable for the son, in this case the application was assigned of file number as early as the consular letter of April 19, 1995 requesting the additional funds. On April 19, 1995 the applicant was not yet 49 years old and was still eligible for 2 units. Further, the funds that had been received by the consular official on April 12, 1995 was sufficient to cover the processing and landing fees of both the applicant and his spouse. In requesting the additional $100 on April 19, 1995, the consular official was either locking-in the date of April 12, 1995 or erroneously requesting insufficient additional funds. Because of these exceptional and unusual circumstances the Court concluded that the rights of the applicant should be assessed as of April 12, 1995 when the application forms together with sufficient fees for both the applicant and his spouse were received.

The Court noted that the applicant's son was not a party to the proceeding, but that it would be unfortunate if the proper exercise of discretion could not assure that the son's rights were not prejudicially affected by the errors of both the applicant and the respondent in the calculation of the son's fees. Finally, the Court noted the necessity for a clear lock-in date in these types of applications, one that would be within the control of the applicant and not subjected to arbitrary determination.

John v. Canada (Minister of Citizenship & Immigration) (1997), 36 Imm. L.R. (2d) 192 (Fed. T.D.) — The applicant sought to review a decision of a visa officer that he did not qualify for permanent residence as an independent applicant.

The visa officer perused the educational documents provided by the applicant. The officer referred the question of the significance to be given to Trinidadian educational documents to the High Commission in Trinidad. While the officer is undoubtedly able to seek advice on such an issue from qualified and informed colleagues, procedural fairness made it mandatory for him to give the applicant an opportunity to rebut the assessment made on the basis of the advice received from those colleagues. At the very least the officer should have given the applicant an opportunity to make written submissions on the matter before a decision was made.

Accordingly, the decision of the visa officer was set aside.

Cai v. Canada (Minister of Citizenship & Immigration) (January 17, 1997), Doc. IMM-883-96 (Fed. T.D.) — This was an application to review a decision of a visa officer refusing the applicant's application for permanent residence. The visa officer assessed the applicant an administrative clerk and denied the application on the basis that the applicant had achieved zero units of assessment. The applicant had originally applied for consideration under the occupation of executive secretary. The visa officer refused to assess her under that occupation on the ground that the applicant did not have the standard training requirements required to be considered in this occupation.

The onus is on the applicant to fully satisfy the visa officer of the existence of all the positive ingredients in his or her application. In making his or her assessment, the visa officer is not only called upon to compare the applicant's experience and qualifications with those set out in schedule I of the regulations, but is also obliged to consider the applicant under every occupation he or she designates in his or her application. This visa officer is also vested with the clear responsibility to assess alternate occupations inherent in the applicant's work experience. If however, the visa officer ascertains that an applicant does not meet the criteria for the occupation under which he or she seeks to be assessed it is not unreasonable for the visa officer to hold that the applicant cannot be further assessed in that occupational category.

The applicant was given some opportunity to explain the duties she had performed and her various positions. The visa officer also noted that there was nothing in the supporting documentation supplied by the applicant to indicate that the tasks she had performed in her various positions were commensurate with those performed by secretaries or executive secretaries in Canada.

The application for judicial review was denied.

He v. Canada (Minister of Citizenship & Immigration) (1997), 36 Imm. L.R. (2d) 244 (Fed. T.D.) — The applicant applied for permanent residence and was assessed according to the CCDO occupation as a chef/cook. The CCDO provides that the specific vocational preparation for such an occupation as 7. In accordance with schedule 1 of the regulations, this translates into an equivalent of 15 units of assessment out of a possible 18.

Specific vocational preparation includes training in the following forms; 1) university, or college training; 2) vocational training; 3) apprenticeship; 4) in plant training; 5) on the job training; and 6) experience in other jobs. In determining whether the applicant had reached level 7 of vocational preparation, the visa officer was required to consider all 6 forms of training; in this case the visa officer had only considered one of those forms.

Accordingly, the Court decided that the visa officer had misinterpreted the provisions which she applied and set aside her decision.

Editors Note: the CCDO has been replaced by the NOC, however, the principle in this case may still be of some assistance.

Hussain v. Canada (Minister of Citizenship & Immigration) (1997), 36 Imm. L.R. (2d) 232 (Fed. T.D.) — This is an application to review a decision of a visa officer refusing the applicant's application for permanent residence. The applicant received 67 units, 3 less than the 70 required by the schedule. The applicant challenged the assessment only in respect of the personal suitability factor.

The visa officer did not err in taking into account a lack of knowledge of Canada in the assessment of personal suitability. Further, the visa officer did not double count with respect to the assessment of language ability under the personal suitability factor. The unambiguous words of the regulation as well as the relevant jurisprudence indicate that the category of personal suitability is intended to be somewhat of a basket clause encompassing a general concern with the applicant's ability to successfully survive economically in this country. The assessment of language ability in that context does not amount to double counting.

Dhesi v. Canada (Minister of Citizenship & Immigration) (January 8, 1997), Doc. IMM-3008-95 (Fed. T.D.) — This was an application to review a decision of a visa officer who refused the applicant's application for permanent residence on the ground that the applicant was not a "dependent son". The visa officer found that the applicant had not been attending school continuously. The applicant's answers about his schooling were contradictory and tended to suggest that the applicant was confused. Further there was a contradiction between the applicant's oral answers and the documents which he submitted. There was a duty of fairness upon the visa officer to clarify the matter.

The decision of the visa officer was set aside and the matter referred back for reconsideration.

Amir v. Canada (Minister of Citizenship & Immigration) (1996), 125 F.T.R. 158 (Fed. T.D.) — The applicant sought to review a decision of the Canadian Consulate in Buffalo refusing his application for permanent residence.

The applicant, a citizen of Pakistan, had been working first as a cook, then a chef in the United States. While in school the applicant studied English. In 1973 to 1983 he was employed as a seaman by the Kuwait Shipping Company where English was spoken by the employees. The applicant had visited over 100 cities on all continents during that employment.

The visa officer, under the factor language, awarded the applicant three units for reading, three units for writing and zero units for speaking English. Given the fact that the applicant had been living and working in the United States for 6 1/2 years and dealing with restaurant customers in the English language and that the interview was carried out in English, the assessment of zero for speaking English was patently unreasonable.

Under factor 9, personal suitability, the visa officer assessed only two units out of a maximum of ten. The fact that the applicant intended to visit his wife and his children back in Pakistan once a year was not a relevant factor to be used against him in the context of personal suitability. Secondly, the visa officer's observation that the applicant had not taken steps to "elevate his level of education" was inappropriate. Personal suitability is an economic factor which allows a visa officer to form an opinion as to whether the applicant will succeed in his field in this country. The officer was required to bear in mind in this case that the applicant was going to attempt to succeed in Canada as a short order cook and not a university professor.

The decision of the visa officer was set aside.

Malkana v. Canada (Minister of Citizenship & Immigration) (1996), 37 Imm. L.R. (2d) 288, 125 F.T.R. 71 (Fed. T.D.) — This was an application to review a decision of a visa officer which determined that the applicant did not meet the definition of "dependent son" set out in section 2(1) of the *Immigration Regulations*.

The applicant is a citizen of India, and the son of Mohinder Singh. The applicant's father was sponsored for immigration to Canada by the applicant's brother. In his father's application for landing, the applicant and his mother were included as dependents. The family was interviewed in March 1995 and the applicant was questioned about his education program.

The visa officer's decision letter reflected a conclusion either that the applicant did not regularly attend classes in courses for which he was registered or if he was in attendance the "quality" of his attendance was not such as to constitute "attendance" within the terminology of the definition. This finding flowed from the questioning of the applicant during the family interview. The applicant was unable to demonstrate knowledge related to his diploma course in computers and to his political science and history studies.

The visa officer was careful to express to the applicant and his family members her concern with regard to the applicants "attendance". The visa officer provided the applicant and his family with an opportunity to respond to her concern.

The Court rejected the submission that the visa officer was required to give the applicant and his family advanced notice of the line of questioning to be pursued at the interview. The Court concluded that the decision of the visa officer was one that was reasonably opened to her and accordingly the application for judicial review was dismissed.

Issaeva v. Canada (Minister of Citizenship & Immigration) (1996), 37 Imm. L.R. (2d) 91, 124 F.T.R. 178 (Fed. T.D.) — The applicant is a citizen of the Russian Federation. She submitted an application for permanent residence under the independent category and listed her intended occupation as a general economist.

With her application she filed her economics degree and her workbook indicating that she was employed as the Leading Economic Researcher at the Moscow Institute of National Economy and latterly as the Economy and Finance Deputy Director of a business. In addition, the applicant filed a letter from a Canadian export and import firm, S.D.P. Industries International, which deals in markets of the former USSR. The letter indicated that the applicant had provided recommendations on matters relating to organizational structures of industrial enterprises, marketing policies, operating efficiency, productive methods and future consumption. The letter also stated that S.D.P. Industries was prepared to offer the applicant a job in Canada as soon as she obtained her permanent visa. The applicant attended an interview at the Canadian Embassy in June 1995. In September 1995, the visa officer wrote the applicant refusing her application. The letter indicates that the applicant was assessed as a "manager administration" and alternatively as a "financial manager". In the assessment for "manager administration" the applicant obtained 75 units of assessment.

However, the visa officer's decision states that this was an occupation which was not open to prospective independent immigrants. No mention was made of the occupation of general economist which was the occupation which was a basis of the applicant's application.

The applicant was not assessed in accordance with the *Immigration Act* and regulations. An assessment is not an informal or preliminary determination by a visa officer. The terms "assess" or "assessment" mean a process of applying to the prospective immigrant the factors listed in column 1 of schedule 1 of the regulations. This was not done with respect to the applicants stated occupation of general economists.

The Court noted that the visa officer selected the occupational classification in which to assess the applicant. The applicant obtained more than the minimum number of units required for an immigrant visa, however, the applicant was still denied a visa because the occupation chosen according to the visa officer was not open to prospective independent immigrants. It seems unfair for a visa officer to refuse to assess a prospective immigrant in her claimed occupation, to select another occupation, conclude that the immigrant obtained the minimum number of units, and then decide that obtaining those units was of no assistance as the occupation chosen by the visa officer was one not open to prospective immigrants.

A prospective immigrant should be assessed in accordance with the Act and regulations under his or her claimed occupation. This does not preclude a visa officer from also assessing a prospective immigrant under alternative occupations if the facts and circumstances warrant. Assessing on the basis of a prospective immigrant's claimed occupation, however, is a minimum requirement.

The decision of the visa officer was set aside.

Ting v. Canada (Minister of Citizenship & Immigration) (1996), 36 Imm. L.R. (2d) 197, 122 F.T.R. 238 (Fed. T.D.) — This application sought to review a decision of a visa officer refusing the application for permanent residence on the ground that she awarded only 68 units of assessment when a minimum of 70 were required. The applicant was a young woman, 32 years of age. She held a bachelors degree in arts and a masters degree in arts from Chinese universities and a masters degree in arts from Laval University in Quebec City. She was an interpreter and a tour guide in China and a teacher of French in Beijing from 1986 to 1993. The applicant intended to work as an interpreter in Vancouver.

The visa officer in Buffalo awarded only 4 units out of 10 for personal suitability. The officer determined that the applicant was not strongly suited to successfully establish herself in the occupation of an interpreter in Vancouver, because of her limited communication skills and experience in the English language. During the interview the applicant required frequent repetition and simplification to understand English. The visa officer failed to properly apply the criteria of adaptability. Adaptability is a forward looking element. It was common ground that Vancouver harboured a very large and prosperous Chinese community. The applicant was a university trained scholar with 3 university degrees and proficient in 3 languages. Her career as an interpreter, a tour guide and a teacher of French, plus the fact that she has been able to adapt herself at a French university in the Province of Quebec, showed a high degree of adaptability.

Further the visa officer failed to exercise her discretion under subsection 11(3) of the regulations. A proper exercise of that discretion would have resulted in the awarding of two more units so as to grant a visa to an otherwise highly qualified applicant.

The decision of the visa officer was set aside.

Chiu v. Canada (Minister of Citizenship & Immigration) (1996), 35 Imm. L.R. (2d) 281, 121 F.T.R. 39 (Fed. T.D.) — This was an application to review a decision of a visa officer refusing the applicant's application for permanent residence. The applicant, a citizen of Hong Kong, has a wife and three children. After graduating with a bachelor of arts degree in Hong Kong in 1982, the applicant established an import-export business and in 1985 set up a travel company. That business involved both travel and trading which focused on Vietnam. In 1990, the applicant formed a third company located in Vietnam which was engaged in importing computer parts and assembling, installing and repairing personal computers. The applicant had been successful in these ventures and had amassed savings and assets of over $1.5 million.

The applicant had applied for permanent residence and entrepreneur. His stated intention was to open a trading and travel business in Vancouver similar to the one he operates in Hong Kong. He also proposed to import computer parts from Asia and the United States to assemble the computers in Canada and sell them here and through his company in Vietnam. At the immigration interview, the officer questioned the applicant to satisfy herself that he met the definition of an entrepreneur. The officer deposed that she read the definition to the applicant and on several occasions during the interview asked him how his background enabled him to meet the definition and how his proposed businesses would significantly benefit Canada. The officer deposed that the applicant was vague at the interview about his proposed businesses and their viability.

The officer concluded that the applicant had done little if any research into the feasibility of establishing his proposed businesses and on that basis made a negative decision with respect to permanent residence.

The application for judicial review was dismissed. The officer asked the applicant to demonstrate a basic understanding of the markets in which he intended to do business. The applicant was unable to do so. This line of questioning was entirely within the officer's jurisdiction as she was charged with determining whether the applicant could establish a commercial venture which would employ people and contribute significantly to the Canadian ecomony. The fact that other immigration officers follow-up the implementation of an applicants business plan does not relieve the initial interviewing officer from the need to be satisfied that a viable venture is planned. It is for the interviewing officer to establish that an applicant meets requirements of the definition.

Tam v. Canada (Minister of Citizenship & Immigration) (1996), 35 Imm. L.R. (2d) 207 (Fed. T.D.) — This was an application to set aside a decision denying the applicant's application for permanent residence. The applicant was a 29 year citizen of Hong Kong, who was employed as an administrative officer at a rug company which employed 25 people, and had an international clientele. The applicant travelled to Japan routinely on company business. Following an initial paper screening the applicant was invited for an interview. During the interview the officer questioned the applicant about his education, qualifications, occupation, experience, motivation and knowledge of Canada.

In assessing the applicant's personal suitability, the visa officer considered the resourcefulness, initiative, adaptability and motivation of the applicant as evidenced by his work history and travel. The applicant was awarded five units out of a possible ten. The visa officer took a negative view of the fact that the applicant had only worked for one company since leaving school.

The fact that the applicant had only worked in one job during his employment history, did not support the view that the applicant had very little initiative, adaptability or motivation. In addition, the officer owed a duty of fairness which required that the officer advise the applicant of his concerns, about the fact that the applicant had worked at only one job in his employment history and provide the applicant with an opportunity to respond before any decision was made.

Accordingly, the application was allowed, the decision of the visa officer set aside, and the matter remitted back for redetermination.

Paik v. Canada (Minister of Citizenship & Immigration) (1996), 35 Imm. L.R. (2d) 52 (Fed. T.D.) — This was an application to set aside a decision of a visa officer refusing the applicant's application for permanent residence.

In August 1994, the applicant had applied for permanent residence and provided a reference from an assistant professor of aeronautics. This letter referred to the applicant as being employed as a computer systems analyst for the solid mechanics group at the California Institute of Technology. The visa officer could not understand how the applicant could be so employed when he had not been enrolled as a student for several terms and, accordingly, contacted Cal-Tech, and as well the professor who provided the letter of reference. Subsequent to receiving information from both the institution and the professor, the visa officer refused the application.

The refusal was set aside. The visa officer's decision to award the applicant zero units of assessment for work experience was based on information provided to her by the person who signed the applicant's letter of reference. There was a conflict between the information provided and what was stated in the letter of reference. The officer had a duty to advise the applicant of the contradiction and give him an opportunity to explain it before she made a decision.

Stefan v. Canada (Minister of Citizenship & Immigration) (1995), 35 Imm. L.R. (2d) 21 (Fed. T.D.) — This was an application for judicial review of a negative decision of a visa officer. The officer awarded the applicant five out of ten points for personal suitability. The overall assessment fell one point short of the 70 points required for a successful visa application. The officer based his conclusion about the applicant's personal suitability on the following factors:

1. the applicant, although a civil engineer, had not taken any computer courses to train her to pursue her profession in Canada;
2. that her learning pace during her English studies were slow; and
3. she had no special knowledge of Canada.

Personal suitability allows an officer to consider an applicant's adaptability, motivation, initiative and resourcefulness in the context of that applicant's prospects for successful establishment in Canada.

The applicant was given the maximum points for her educational achievements. Although her education was considered a second time when the officer assessed her personal suitability, education during this portion of the assessment was considered from a different perspective. The question was whether the applicant had the training necessary to use her professional qualifications as a civil engineer. The Court found no fault with this approach.

With respect to language, the applicant was given points for her language ability, but the officer then looked at her language training again and concluded from her slow learning pace that she was not very adaptable. The Court found no fault with this type of analysis. What must be seen in an analysis under personal suitability is an assessment focused on the four factors and not on the skill level already recorded in other parts of the assessment.

The Court did not consider knowledge of Canada to be an extraneous factor. It was reasonable to infer that someone who wanted to bring her family to Canada, but had not taken the trouble to learn something about Canada, lacked the initiative and resourcefulness necessary for successful establishment in the country.

Accordingly, the judicial review application was dismissed.

Grube v. Canada (Minister of Citizenship & Immigration) (1996), 34 Imm. L.R. (2d) 219, 118 F.T.R. 163 (Fed. T.D.) — This was an application to set aside a decision of the visa officer to the effect that the applicants did not have sufficient units of assessment to be admitted to Canada as self-employed persons and permanent residents.

Section 11.1 of the regulations implicitly requires that an interview be held where an applicant is applying as a self-employed person. Thus, the visa officer erred in determining that each of these applicants did not qualify for permanent residence based on their plans to be self-employed persons, without granting them an interview.

Further the visa officer placed undue emphasis on a lack of past business experience. Such experience may well be a factor to be favourably considered when determining whether an applicant is likely to become successfully established as a self-employed person in Canada, but it is not the sole criterion to be considered, and it must be considered in light of the occupation sought to be undertaken. Past business experience may be of greater significance in relation to certain occupations than it is to others. Similarly, while an international reputation may be an asset of assistance in indicating that an applicant is likely to become successfully established in Canada, there is no requirement that an applicant possess such a reputation to be admitted to Canada as a self-employed music teacher.

Bridgemohan v. Canada (Minister of Citizenship & Immigration) (1996), 36 Imm. L.R. (2d) 91, 109 F.T.R. 32 (Fed. T.D.) — The applicant sought an order quashing a decision of a visa officer not to grant him a permanent visa. The applicant's counsel wrote to the relevant visa officer in support of the applicant's application and requested a recommendation to the Minister to overcome a deportation order which had previously been issued to the applicant's wife. In such circumstances it was unfair to reject the application on the ground of the wife's inadmissibility. It is a practice in many visa offices not to process a subsection 55(1) request for ministerial consent until the visa application has been assessed. If the application would not, in any event, be successful, little is to be gained by processing the subsection 55(1) request. The applicant's educational background was crucial to the application and a review of the file and the visa officer's affidavit lead the Court to the conclusion that the assessment in this respect was not properly done. It is a failure of natural justice to reject an application because a subsection 55(1) consent had not been obtained when a request for such a consent had been made at the time the application was filed. The decision of the visa officer was quashed.

The Court distinguished an earlier decision in respect of the applicant's brother in which a request for Ministerial consent had not been made.

Lin v. Canada (Minister of Citizenship & Immigration) (1996), 33 Imm. L.R. (2d) 8, 107 F.T.R. 225 (Fed. T.D.) — This was an application to review a decision of a visa officer rejecting the applicant's application for permanent residence as an independent immigrant under the assisted relative class. The visa officer imported the notion of English language ability into the concept of specific vocational preparation. A visa officer should not take into account the language capability of an applicant when assessing the award of units with respect to another category listed in schedule 1 to the regulations. The decision of the visa officer was set aside and the matter was remitted to a different visa officer for reconsideration.

Maharaj v. Canada (Minister of Citizenship & Immigration) (1995), 103 F.T.R. 205 (Fed. T.D.) — The applicant submitted an application for permanent residence in March 1993. The application was accompanied by a cheque intended to pay certain government fees, however, the cheque was made payable to the wrong party and was returned to the applicant. The applicant resubmitted his application and paid the processing fee in November 1993. In August 1993 section 17 of the regulations was changed and this resulted in a situation where the lock in date for the applicant became critical. If the lock-in date was March 1993 the applicant would receive 8 more units for education than if the lock-in date was November 1993.

The application could not be processed until the required fee was paid. Accordingly, the lock in date for the applicant was November 1993.

Bridgemohan v. Canada (Minister of Citizenship & Immigration) (1995), 31 Imm. L.R. (2d) 110, 103 F.T.R. 62 (Fed. T.D.) — A visa officer refused the applicant permission to come to Canada as a permanent resident. The applicant was a citizen of Trinidad and Tobago who had entered Canada in 1988 and made an unsuccessful refugee claim. The applicant was deported in December 1992. One of the bases for refusing the applicant's application for a permanent visa was that the applicant, having been deported, required the Minister's consent under section 55 of the Act, and that failing such consent the applicant was inadmissible as described in paragraph 19(1)(i) of the *Immigration Act.*

There is no basis for the proposition that an applicant should not have to pursue the Minister's consent until the applicant is aware of whether or not but for the lack of consent, his application for landing would otherwise be approved. There is no basis in law for an assumption that the visa officer would, in the course of his or her consideration of the application, seek the Minister's consent on the applicant's behalf.

Accordingly, the visa officer's refusal of the application on this basis was upheld.

Dragone v. Canada (Minister of Citizenship & Immigration) (1995), 31 Imm. L.R. (2d) 97 (Fed. T.D.) — An immigration officer concluded that the applicant did not obtain sufficient units of assessment. The officer assessed the applicant's language abilities. With respect to personal suitability the officer again referred to the applicant's lack of ability in English. The officer had no discretion to take language into account in his assessment of personal suitability. Accordingly, the officer's decision was set aside and the case remitted to a different immigration officer for review and reconsideration.

Prelipcean v. Canada (Minister of Citizenship & Immigration) (May 11, 1995), Doc. IMM-4425-93 (Fed. T.D.) — The applicant first applied to come to Canada as a Convention Refugee in February, 1992. This application was refused. The first interview focused entirely on whether the applicant qualified as a Convention refugee. The applicant, at the time of her interview, had submitted an application for permanent residence but the contents of that application were not addressed at the first interview because once it was determined that the applicant was not a Convention refugee, questions about her potential employment in Canada were not relevant. The applicant did not apply to judicially review this decision.

Following the first decision the applicant retained counsel and thereafter applied as an independent applicant in September 1992. The applicant stated that her intended occupation was civil draftswoman. The applicant was interviewed in October 1992 and resubmitted the application form for permanent residence that she had filed at the time of her first application. The occupation of civil draftswoman had been removed as a designated occupation in August 1992. Thus, at the time a second application was refused, there was no occupational demand units available to the applicant. At the time of the first interview in connection with the Convention refugee application, 10 points were available for this occupation.

The first and second applications were not, in reality, one application. The first application was for Convention refugee status. Once that status was denied no question of employment was relevant. At the time of the second interview the question of the applicant's occupation was discussed in detail. It's unfortunate that at that time no points were available to the applicant in regard to her occupation.

There was no failure of procedural fairness in the fact that the visa officer considered that these were, in fact, two separate applications for permanent residence. Accordingly, the application for judicial review was dismissed.

Nicolae v. Canada (Secretary of State) (1995), 29 Imm. L.R. (2d) 148, 90 F.T.R. 280 (Fed. T.D.) — This was an application to quash the decision of a visa officer refusing the applicant's request for permanent residence.

The Court outlined a number of duties of visa officers appraising immigrant applications. An adopted summary of those duties was set out in *Saggu v. Canada (Minister of Citizenship & Immigration)* (1994), 87 F.T.R. 137 (Fed. T.D.), specifically:

> 1. A visa officer has a duty to consider fully the submissions and information provided by an applicant. The applicant must be given an opportunity to provide information in support of his current experience in each included occupation.
>
> 2. The visa officer has a duty to assess an application with reference to the occupation represented by the applicant as the one for which he or she is qualified and prepared to pursue in Canada. This duty extends to each such occupation. There is a clear responsibility on the part of a visa officer to assess alternate occupations inherent in the applicant's work experience. The visa officer must consider an applicant's aptitudes, previous work experience, and whether or not this constitutes experience in the intended occupations.
>
> 3. The onus is on the applicant to establish that he or she meets the selection criteria established by the regulations and that admission to Canada would not be contrary to the Act or regulations.
>
> 4. Where a visa officer has an impression of a deficiency in the proof being offered there may be a duty to give the applicant some opportunity to disabuse the officer of that crucial impression.
>
> 5. A visa officer must not improperly fetter his or her discretion.
>
> 6. A visa officer should exercise the section 11(3) discretion to grant landing only if it appears that the total units awarded do not reflect the particular applicant's chances of successful establishment. If there is no information upon which a visa officer may draw that conclusion, the opportunity to exercise the section 11(3) discretion does not arise.

In this case there was an error of law in the allocation of points in the occupational category, as well as a failure to grant the applicant an opportunity to disabuse the visa officer's concerns as to his experience in the field of electrical engineering. Accordingly, the decision of the visa officer was quashed.

Ling v. Canada (Minister of Employment & Immigration) (1994), 26 Imm. L.R. (2d) 205 (Fed. T.D.) — The applicant applied for permanent residence in the entrepreneur category. She intended to establish a business for the sale and rental of musical instruments, and the teaching of music lessons. The applicant operated a similar business in Hong Kong, which had only shown a profit in one year of operation. The applicant was denied a permanent visa. The analysis of the visa officer was based entirely on her assessment of the viability of the business of the applicant in Hong Kong. The visa officer was entitled to consider as a factor in her analysis, the success of a similar business operated by the applicant, however, the visa officer failed to consider other matters, such as the specific proposal of the applicant for the establishment of a business and the market analysis which had been conducted with respect to that business and therefore, the officer failed to address significant factors in her interview of the applicant and in her decision to refuse the application. Accordingly, the refusal was quashed.

Western Opportunities Ltd. v. R. (September 16, 1993), Doc. T-3131-92 (Fed. T.D.) — This was an application by the defendants to strike the plaintiff's statement of claim on the grounds that it did not disclose a reasonable cause of action. Two doctors residing in Hong Kong, who apparently qualified under the immigrant investor program and who had invested with the plaintiff company, were refused visas without even being granted an interview.

The reasons given for the refusal was that doctors would be unable to demonstrate that they controlled or directed a financially successful business or commercial undertaking. It was further alleged that the agents or servants of the Minister applied invalid or arbitrary tests inconsistent with the policy of the Immigration Department. The Court declined to strike out the statement of claim. It was not plain and obvious that this action as pleaded revealed no cause of action. Breach of statute does not automatically give rise to tort liability. The acts constituting breach of a statutory duty by the Minister may, however, constitute actionable negligence. The named defendants were, however, struck as party defendants so that the only defendant remaining was Her Majesty the Queen. Pursuant to section 17 of the *Federal Court Act*, the Court had no jurisdiction to entertain this claim against the named defendants.

Nanji v. Canada (Minister of Employment & Immigration) (1993), 21 Imm. L.R. (2d) 60, 66 F.T.R. 158 (Fed. T.D.) — The applicant applied for permanent residence in Canada as an Assisted Relative. The applicant indicated that he wished to be considered as the principal applicant and he signed the Immigration Application. His wife accompanied him to the interview and Mrs. Nanji was asked some questions about her intended occupation as a secretary. The facts disclosed that Mr. Nanji was the only applicant and there was no implied application by the applicant's wife.

The word immigrant means a person who seeks landing. In this case the only person who sought landing was the applicant.

Pursuant to section 8 of the regulations, the visa officer is required to assess the immigrant or, at the option of the immigrant, the spouse of that immigrant. It is the responsibility of the applicant to designate who will be assessed. A visa officer is not required to assess both the applicant and his spouse. Section 8 makes it mandatory for the visa officer to assess only one or the other.

This application to quash the visa officer's decision to refuse the application without assessing the applicant's wife and her intended occupation was dismissed.

Yang v. Canada (Minister of Employment & Immigration) (1992), 56 F.T.R. 155, 17 Imm. L.R. (2d) 229 (Fed. T.D.) — The decision refusing the applicant's application for permanent residence was quashed. The applicant submitted an application for permanent residence in Hong Kong. The applicant was interviewed and refused on the basis that she failed to accumulate sufficient credits under the selection criteria. The applicant was awarded 9 units for education. This determination was based on the policy of the Ministry that units of assessment are awarded in the educational factor only for education received to the end of secondary school. The applicant's position was that she should have been awarded 12 units of assessment for education. In Taiwan, secondary school education is completed within a nine year period following which the student proceeds to college. Accordingly, the tenth, eleventh and twelfth year of schooling are completed at a college rather than a high school. The Ontario Ministry of Education had provided the applicant with a letter indicating that it considers the 5 year diploma from the National Tai Chung Institute of Commerce to have an educational attainment comparable to someone with an Ontario Secondary School Diploma.

Further, in the affidavit of Ms. Yang she deposed that at the interview she was never asked any questions pertaining to her educational background.

The visa officer had a duty to consider the applicant's submission that she was entitled to the maximum number of units of assessment in the education category. The failure to do so left a doubt as to whether a proper assessment of the applicant had taken place. Accordingly, an order in the nature of *certiorari* was granted and a new assessment by a different visa officer was ordered.

Yeung v. Canada (Minister of Employment & Immigration) (1992), 17 Imm. L.R. (2d) 191, 53 F.T.R. 205 (Fed. T.D.) — Mr. Yeung was a citizen of Hong Kong. He was employed as a production manager. He filed an application for permanent residence on December 12, 1989 together with the prescribed processing fee. The application form had a notation that the applicant's sister in Canada was willing to assist. At the time the application was received the occupation factor for production managers was one point. On January 30, 1991 the occupation demand for this occupation was set at 0. Mr. Yeung's application was reviewed in February 1991 and refused because the occupational demand on that date was 0.

The assessment date or lock-in date for determining the number of points to be awarded is the date of the original application and payment of the processing fee. This is true whether the independent applicant has a relative willing to assist or not.

Choi v. Canada (Minister of Employment & Immigration) (1991), 15 Imm. L.R. (2d) 265, [1992] 1 F.C. 763 (Fed. C.A.) — The appellant attended at the Canadian Commission in Hong Kong and enquired about how to apply for permanent residence. He was provided with a pre-application questionnaire ("PAQ") but was not told that he could make a formal application until the applicant completed a PAQ and filed it with the Commission on October 16, 1987. On October 28, 1987 the appellant received the PAQ back with information that he had received a positive assessment. The appellant completed the Application for Permanent Residence ("IMM8") and paid the required processing fee. The appellant did this on November 6, 1987.

At the time of the assessment of his PAQ the occupational demand for his skills was 10 units. Effective November 2, 1987 the demand was reduced to one unit. The appellant received 65 units including the one unit of assessment for occupational demand against a requirement of 70 units for issuance of a visa. Had the appellant received the 10 units of assessment that were in effect in October 1987 he would have obtained 74 units and qualified for Permanent Residence. An Application for an Immigrant Visa is made when it duly initiates the process leading to the issue or refusal of the visa and not only when that processing is committed to a particular official authorized to dispose of the application. Any other date, except the date of the application, would be purely arbitrary as a lock-in date for the occupational demand factor, depending solely on the vagaries of the administrative process. The application date is the only date within the control of the applicant and is consequently the only date that can be established without arbitrariness.

It was an irresistible conclusion from the evidence that departmental policy was to withhold from applicants the information that they could proceed either by way of a PAQ or directly and immediately by a formal application. If applicants knew enough to request an application form they were given one. If they did not they were dealt with cursorily by being given a PAQ, which had the effect of enormously reducing the administrative burden on the visa officers.

When the Canadian government, through its agents, undertakes to supply information to immigration applicants as to how to become immigrants it assumes a duty to provide this information accurately. This does not imply that Canadian authorities must provide a detailed exegesis of Canadian immigration law but it does mean that immigration authorities have an obligation to provide basic information and to make available the appropriate forms.

The exigencies of fairness therefore require that the time of the appellant's application be deemed to be the date on which he returned the completed PAQ to the Hong Kong office with the consequence that the units of assessment for occupational demand in his case should be deemed to be 10 units.

The appeal was allowed with costs, the decision of the visa officer set aside and the matter returned to a visa officer for reconsideration on the basis that the occupational demand factor for the appellant should be deemed to be 10 units of assessment.

Mohammad v. Canada (Minister of Employment & Immigration) (1991), 48 F.T.R. 96, 14 Imm. L.R. (2d) 104 (Fed. T.D.) — This was an application for *certiorari* to quash the decision of a visa officer denying the applicant's request for permanent resident status and *mandamus* to compel the respondent to process the application in accordance with the *Immigration Act* and the regulations. The applicant, a resident of Pakistan, submitted an application on November 28, 1988 requesting permanent resident status in Canada as an assisted relative. This application was forwarded by his Toronto solicitor to the Canadian High Commission in Islamabad, Pakistan. The applicant's occupation was identified as sales representative/ food products. An applicant for permanent residence must obtain an aggregate of 70 units. One of the criteria to be considered is occupational demand. A list of occupational categories and their corresponding units of assessment is maintained by the Canada Employment and Immigration Commission. This list is periodically updated and the units of assessment are increased or decreased to reflect labour market demand. On November 28, 1988, there were 10 units of assessment available for occupational demand in the category in which the applicant had requested assessment, however, the application was stamped received by the Canadian High Commission on January 16, 1989 by which time the units of assessment for occupational demand had been decreased to 1. According to departmental policy, units of assessment lock in as of the date that the application is received by the appropriate visa officer. This provision of the policy guidelines did not offend the duty of fairness. When applications are submitted by mail or courier, if there is some lengthy delay for receipt by the proper office, the onus rests with the applicant to satisfy the Court that the unreasonable delay should not be attributed to him. This onus was not met in this case and the application was dismissed.

Gaffney v. Canada (Minister of Employment & Immigration) (1991), 12 Imm. L.R. (2d) 185, 121 N.R. 256, 40 F.T.R. 79 (note) (Fed. C.A.) — This was an appeal from a decision of the Trial Division refusing to quash the rejection of the appellant's application for landing as an independent immigrant by a visa officer in San Francisco. The visa officer considered that his duty to assess alternative occupations was limited to a category and did not extend to occupations in other categories which an immigrant was both qualified and willing to follow. The only evidence as to what transpired at the interview was set out in the appellant's affidavit. When the appellant's counsel was apprised of the refusal letter, he wrote the Consulate General pointing out that the appellant's work experience met other definitions in the *Canadian Classification and Dictionary of Occupations* (CCDO). The visa officer replied to the effect that in the interview the appellant's entire work experience had been canvassed and that these occupations had been considered. That letter was exhibited to the appellant's affidavit in support of his motion to quash. The appellant did not, of course, depose to the truth of the contents. The visa officer's notes were exhibited to the affidavit of another Immigration officer who could not depose to the truth of the notes. The visa officer has a duty to assess an application with reference to the occupation represented by the applicant (or his or her spouse) as the one for which he or she is qualified and prepared to pursue in Canada.

That duty extends to each such occupation. The appellant in his affidavit alleged that the visa officer had failed to assess him in a number of occupations for which he was qualified and was prepared to pursue. There was no evidence to the contrary and the appeal was allowed and the Trial Division was directed to re-hear the application for *certiorari* and *mandamus.*

Editor's Note: On May 1, 1997, the CCDO was replaced by the NOC. The principle in this case, however, may be of interest.

Uy v. Canada (Minister of Employment & Immigration) (1991), [1991] 2 F.C. 201, 12 Imm. L.R. (2d) 172, 121 N.R. 248, 40 F.T.R. 80 (note) (Fed. C.A.) — This is an appeal from the Trial Division which refused *certiorari* quashing the refusal by a visa officer of the appellant's independent application. The appellant had been a qualified medical doctor in the Philippines and was a resident in pediatrics in the United States when he applied for admission to Canada as a medical technologist. The visa officer refused to assess him in respect of that occupation because he did not believe that the appellant would pursue the occupation in Canada. In doing so, the visa officer erred in law. There was no suggestion in this case that the visa officer had assessed the appellant for the occupation of medical technologist. The visa officer awarded him 70 or more units and then invoked section 11(3) of the regulations by reason of his conclusion as to the appellant's intentions. Section 6 of the Act requires a visa officer to assess any immigrant who applies for landing in the manner prescribed by the Act and regulations. Section 8(1) of the regulations imposes in mandatory terms a duty to assess and nothing in either the Act or regulations permits a visa officer to refuse to assess in respect of the occupation or alternative occupations which the immigrant states he or she intends to pursue in Canada. The general discretion given a visa officer by section 9(1) of the regulations must be subordinated to the particular discretion given by section 11(3) where, notwithstanding the award of at least 70 units, the visa officer is of the opinion that those units do not reflect the chances of the particular immigrant becoming successfully established in Canada. The reasons for that opinion must be committed to writing and submitted to and approved by a senior immigration officer. Accordingly, the appeal was allowed.

D'Souza v. Canada (Minister of Employment & Immigration) (1990), 12 Imm. L.R. (2d) 268, 39 F.T.R. 1 (Fed. T.D.) — Ms. D'Souza applied for permanent residence as an independent immigrant. Her application was submitted under cover of a letter sent by her prospective employer and noted her occupation as executive secretary. The applicant was advised by letter that a barrier to acceptance of her application was the fact that there was only a limited demand in Canada for persons in her occupation. Accordingly, the applicant was advised to obtain a confirmation of her offer of employment by the local CEC. In the meantime, her application was refused.

There is no requirement arising by implication in the Act or Regulations that the visa officer must consult on his own initiative the National Employment Service. The applicant must demonstrate to the satisfaction of the visa officer who has been entrusted to decide that the criteria for admission have been met. So long as the procedures developed and followed by the Commission to fulfil its responsibilities in relation to immigration matters are not inconsistent with the requirements of the Act and regulations, there can be no objection in law to them. The Minister must have discretion to develop administrative procedures to meet his or her statutory and regulatory responsibilities. The Court should intervene to limit that discretion only where it is clear that the procedures are inconsistent with or otherwise beyond the authority of the Minister under the Act and regulations.

The decision to withhold the grant of a visa until confirmation of employment had been communicated from the National Employment Service to the visa officer was not an improper delegation of authority. The regulations, in particular item 5 of schedule 1, provide for the visa officer assessing an application for permanent residence in part by having referenced to arranged employment and to consider that criterion for admission based on information provided by the National Employment Service. If this determination of particular aspects of employment is considered to be delegation, then it is delegation made by the regulations and it is authorized. It is not a delegation made by the visa officer.

The assessment criteria established by schedule 1 to the regulations are not inconsistent with the Act and regulations. The requirement that a local CEC office validate arranged employment falls clearly within section 114(1)(a) as a matter within "labour market conditions in Canada for the purpose of determining whether or not an immigrant will be able to become successfully established in Canada." In the detail of factors to be considered by the National Employment Service in considering matters within item 5 of schedule 1, the Service must be careful to consider only those matters which can be justified as being clearly within the factors set out in the schedule. Section 20(3) of the regulations is much more precise than item 5 of schedule 1. While it may be a worthwhile objective of the Employment Service to insist upon the training of Canadians, such a requirement is not clearly within the factors to be considered in relation to item 5 of schedule 1. It is not appropriate to insist that the prospective employer of an applicant/immigrant first be expected to train persons already in Canada before authorization is given to arranged employment nor is it appropriate to insist in practice upon any standard minimum period for a prospective employer to seek unsuccessfully an employee through the CEC services. The employment officer must be prepared to look at whatever evidence this prospective employer may have of his efforts to hire Canadian citizens or permanent residents. The visa officer fulfilled his duties in this case and accordingly the applications for *certiorari* and *mandamus* were dismissed.

Yu v. Canada (Minister of Employment & Immigration) (1990), 11 Imm. L.R. (2d) 176, 36 F.T.R. 296 (Fed. T.D.) — *Certiorari* was sought to quash a decision refusing the applicant's request for permanent residence status in Canada. The applicant applied pursuant to the independent provisions of the Immigration Regulations under section 8 and schedule 1 of those regulations. In her application, she indicated that her intended occupation was as a librarian. In accordance with the Act, the applicant was required to establish that she met the selection criteria established by the regulations for determining whether she would be able to become successfully established in Canada and that her admission to Canada would not be contrary to the Act or regulations.

The visa officer, under section 8(1)(a) of the regulations, was required to assess the applicant on the basis of each of the factors in schedule 1, three of which related to the applicant's intended occupation in Canada. Factor 2, specific vocational preparation, was assessed in relation to the amount of formal training specified in the CCDO. Factor 3, experience, was assessed by years in the intended occupation. Factor 4, occupational demand, was assessed in relation to occupational opportunities in Canada. If the applicant is not deemed qualified for the occupation, then, regardless of the occupational demand, no units of assessment were to be awarded under factor 4 or under factor 3.

Schedule 1 required that the applicant's experience as a librarian could not be assessed favourably if she were unqualified by training for the occupation of librarian in Canada. There were no grounds for arguing unfairness merely because the visa officer did not stress all of the concerns he may have had at the interview arising directly from the Act and regulations. The Act and regulations pertinent to admission are available to the applicants whose task is to establish to the satisfaction of the visa officer that they meet the criteria set out and that their admission to Canada would not be contrary to the Act. This is to be distinguished from a situation where the decision refusing the application is made by reference to information other than the regulations provided for in assessing the applicant. The CCDO relied upon in this case is specifically incorporated by reference in schedule 1, factor 2 and thus is part of the regulations. Where it is concluded that the applicant lacks the specific vocational preparation expected in Canada, years of experience in the occupation elsewhere cannot count towards the units required for assessment in meeting the criteria for admission. In this case the visa officer's decision was upheld and the motion to quash dismissed.

Editor's Note: On May 1, 1997, the CCDO was replaced by the NOC. The principle in this case, however, may be of interest.

Fong v. Canada (Minister of Employment & Immigration) (1990), 11 Imm. L.R. (2d) 205, 35 F.T.R. 305, [1990] 3 F.C. 705 (Fed. T.D.) — The application for permanent residence by the applicant began with an undertaking by his sister who was a Canadian citizen and living in Canada. A confirmation of offer of employment for the applicant was also obtained and forwarded to the visa officer. The applicant was interviewed but the visa officer had no notes of that interview and did not record in the computer the results of the interview. The basis of the refusal was that the applicant did not meet the job requirement by reason of his lack of experience, his lack of management in production line experience, his poor knowledge of English and limited education and funds. The applicant failed on points. The visa officer's decision was overturned. There was no cogent evidence that the visa officer went beyond the intended job description of production line manager and the CCDO definition thereof and directed a specific line of questioning about the applicant's actual work experience in the garment industry broken down into its constituent elements, for the purpose of making an appropriate assessment with respect to the applicant's adaptability or transferability to the intended occupation. Further, the visa officer committed a breach of the duty of fairness by his failure to afford the applicant an adequate opportunity to answer the specific case against him on the issue of related experience *vis-à-vis* the job offer of production line manager. The visa officer could have done this and should have done this once it became apparent that the application was likely to fail on that score. In this case the visa officer had simply asked the applicant if there was any other information relevant to the case that had not been covered, which the applicant might wish to add for the officer's consideration. This was held to be not sufficient. Finally, the Court noted that the visa officer owed a duty to the applicant to tell him by appropriate questions of his immediate impression regarding the deficiency of proof of intended and related employment and the likely consequences thereof in order to give the applicant some opportunity of disabusing the visa officer of that crucial impression. Accordingly, the visa officer's decision was set aside and the Respondent Minister was directed to consider the application of the applicant according to the relevant provisions of the *Immigration Act* and Regulations.

Editor's Note: On May 1, 1997, the CCDO was replaced by the NOC. The principle in this case, however, may be of interest.

Li v. Canada (Minister of Employment & Immigration) (1990), 9 Imm. L.R. (2d) 263 (Fed. T.D.) — The applicant requested permanent residence in Canada as an independent applicant pursuant to section 6(1) of the *Immigration Act*. Such applications involve a two-stage process during which it is the visa officer's duty to apply criteria set forth in the legislation and award points based on the ability of the applicant to become successfully established in Canada.

The first phase of the assessment is a paper-screening process in which immigration officials evaluate documents submitted by applicants and decide if the application process should be continued. If the applicant passes this phase, he is invited to an interview with a visa officer. During the interview, the officer assesses the employment experience of the applicant and awards points for other factors based on information presented at that time.

One of the most significant factors in any assessment is the applicant's possibility of employment in Canada. Points are awarded both for occupational demand in the screening step and for experience in the final assessment. This process requires reference to the Canadian Classification and Dictionary of Occupations (CCDO). Assessment of any one intended occupation begins with the matching of the applicant's work routine with the specific occupation from the CCDO.

There is a clear responsibility on the part of a visa officer to assess alternate occupations inherent in the applicant's work experience. Where his work experience suggests that the occupation may be appropriate, the visa officer must assess the applicant in the designated occupation regardless of which alternate occupations the officer has seen fit to consider.

The applicant's present occupation in the Philippines was that of a proprietor of two businesses. The applicant spends approximately 90 per cent of his time dealing with the wholesale distribution of office machines and considered that the best designation in the CCDO was that of "Commercial Traveller". Further, in a letter to the Canadian Consulate General, the applicant asserted that he had the necessary qualifications as a "Sales Representative, Office Machines", a subclassification of Commercial Traveller. The officer formed the impression that the applicant sold only hand calculators on a retail basis. The officer concluded that the applicant lacked product and plant experience and stated that he was "unable to assess your application in that category." The decision was set aside and the visa officer was required to evaluate the applicant's work experience in the category the applicant originally requested. The respondent Minister was directed to carry out the required assessment through a different visa officer.

Editor's Note: On May 1, 1997, the CCDO was replaced by the NOC. The principle in this case, however, may be of interest.

Ho v. Canada (Minister of Employment & Immigration) (1990), 11 Imm. L.R. (2d) 12 (Fed. C.A.) — The visa officer initially awarded the respondent 8 points for experience and changed that to "nil" because the officer spoke to someone at CEIC. The discretion of a visa officer to grant an immigrant visa is to be exercised according to law, *i.e.*, the *Immigration Act* and regulations. A visa officer cannot properly take account of general directives not having the force of law nor instructions from head office particular to the case at hand. Those improperly fetter him in the exercise of the discretion that Parliament, not the Canada Employment and Immigration Commission, has entrusted to him.

Fung v. Canada (Minister of Employment & Immigration) (1989), 8 Imm. L.R. (2d) 236, 27 F.T.R. 182 (Fed. T.D.) — The applicant applied for permanent residence in Canada pursuant to the assisted relative provisions in the immigration regulations. Such applications involve a two-stage assessment process during which it is the visa officer's duty to apply criteria set forth in the legislation and to award points based on the ability of the applicant to become successfully established in Canada.

The first phase of the assessment is a paper-screening process. If the applicant passes this phase, he or she is invited to an interview with a visa officer. Points are awarded both for occupational demand in the paper-screening step and for experience in the final assessment.

The applicant identified his employment as a tally clerk and a checker. His intended occupation in Canada was listed as a production clerk. After consultation with her superiors, the visa officer indicated to the applicant that he required more experience in order to qualify as a production clerk in Canada. The visa officer had a duty to make an assessment of the applicant's work experience sufficient to evaluate it with respect to that applicant's intended occupation. The finding that the applicant lacked experience as a production clerk indicated to the Court that the applicant's experience had been explored at the interview. This section 18 application, the Court observed, was not an appellant review. To succeed, the applicant was required to do more than persuade the Court that it might have reached a different conclusion than the visa officer. Accordingly, the application was dismissed.

Editor's Note: On May 1, 1997, the CCDO was replaced by the NOC. The principle in this case, however, may be interest.

Ho v. Canada (Minister of Employment & Immigration) (1989), 8 Imm. L.R. (2d) 38, 27 F.T.R. 241 (Fed. T.D.); affirmed (1990), 11 Imm. L.R. (2d) 12 (Fed. C.A.) — Applications for permanent residence under the self-employed provisions involve a two-stage assessment process. The first phase of the assessment involves a paper-screening process in which immigration officials evaluate documents submitted by the applicant and decide if the application process should be continued. If the applicant passes this phase, he is interviewed by a visa officer. One of the most significant factors in any assessment is the applicant's possibility of supporting himself in Canada. Points are therefore awarded for both occupational demand in the paper-screening step and in the final assessment for experience in the occupation for which the candidate is qualified and prepared to follow in Canada. Where an applicant is not awarded any units of assessment for experience, an immigrant visa cannot be issued unless the visa officer believes that there are good reasons why the number of points do not reflect the chances of the applicant to become successfully established in Canada and those reasons have been approved by a senior officer. A candidate for self-employment must be someone who intends and who has the ability to establish or purchase a business in Canada that will create an employment opportunity for himself and will make a significant contribution to the economy or the cultural or the artistic life of Canada. In addition, the visa officer will award 30 points of assessment to an applicant seeking to be self-employed if, in the visa officer's opinion, the applicant will be able to become successfully established in his business in Canada.

The purpose of the *Immigration Act* is to permit immigration, not prevent it, and it is the corresponding obligation of immigration officers to provide a thorough and fair assessment in compliance with the terms and spirit of the legislation. In this case, the visa officer interpreted the regulations in such a narrow fashion as to render meeting qualifications virtually impossible and, as a result, treated the applicant unfairly. The applicant was an accomplished musician who was able to teach and, on the question of whether the applicant could be self-employed as a teacher, his only apparent failure was in the lack of actual experience. Undue emphasis was placed on the lack of experience as a result of which there was a fundamental breach of the duty of fairness. Accordingly, the application was allowed and the visa officer's decision set aside.

Yang v. Canada (Minister of Employment & Immigration) (1989), 36 Admin. L.R. 235, 8 Imm. L.R. (2d) 48, 27 F.T.R. 74 (Fed. T.D.) — This is an application for an order by way of *certiorari* quashing the decision of the respondent refusing the applicant's request for permanent residence in Canada.

Applications for permanent residence under the self-employed provisions involve a two-stage assessment process. The first phase is a paper-screening process in which immigration officials evaluate documents submitted by the applicant and decide if the application process should be continued. If the applicant passes this phase, he is invited to an interview. One of the most significant factors in any assessment is the applicant's possibility of supporting himself in Canada. Points are therefore awarded for occupational demand in the paper-screening step and for experience in the final assessment. Where an applicant is not awarded any units of assessment for experience, an immigrant visa cannot be issued unless the visa officer believes there are good reasons why the number of points do not reflect the chances of the applicant to become successfully established in Canada and those reasons have been approved by a senior immigration officer. A candidate for self-employment is also subject to the definition of a self-employed person and must be someone who intends and has the ability to establish or purchase a business in Canada that will create an employment opportunity for himself and will make a significant contribution to the economy or the artistic or cultural life of Canada. In addition, the visa officer will award 30 units of assessment to an applicant seeking to be self-employed if it is his opinion that the applicant will be able to become successfully established in his business in Canada.

The purpose of the *Immigration Act* is to permit immigration, not prevent it, and it is the corresponding obligation of immigration officers to provide a thorough and fair assessment in compliance with the terms and spirit of the legislation.

The applicant is from the People's Republic of China and had been residing in the United States since 1986. In 1987, she applied for permanent residence and states that she was planning to pursue the profession of a self-employed music teacher. The applicant received training in China in both Oriental and Occidental music. She arrived in the United States on a student visa and was awarded a scholarship and completed a master's degree in music. The applicant performed extensively in China and participated in one vocal competition in the United States.

The applicant was interviewed and, at the conclusion of the interview, the applicant learned that a decision could not be made until the officer consulted her colleagues and reviewed the requested documents. The applicant hand-delivered the requested documents on November 17, 1987. The applicant received a letter of refusal dated November 16, 1987.

The written refusal concentrated on the visa officer's opinion that the applicant's business would be unsuccessful and that the applicant would not make a significant contribution to the economy or cultural or artistic life of Canada. The visa officer's notes, taken during the interview, however, deal exclusively with the applicant's experience. The visa officer's notes indicate that the refusal was also based on a lack of self-employed experience in the applicant's intended occupation of self-employed music teacher. The Court noted that the applicant was an accomplished musician and had experience as a teacher and concluded that the visa officer had placed an undue emphasis on the applicant's lack of experience as a self-employed teacher and that the interpretation taken by the visa officer made it almost impossible for the applicant to succeed. This interpretation was found to be a fundamental breach of the duty of fairness.

Further, no questions were posed dealing with the possibilities of the applicant's contributions to cultural, economic or artistic life. The officer, at least partially, based her refusal on these criteria and yet did not, at the time of the interview, give any indication of a negative assessment on this basis nor provide the applicant with an opportunity to reply to those criteria.

Finally, the Court noted that the decision made by the officer pre-dated the receipt of the requested documentary information. The decision of the visa officer was set aside and the respondent was directed to carry out an assessment of the applicant in accordance with the *Immigration Act and Regulations* in a manner consistent with the interpretation placed upon them in the Court's reasons.

Hajariwala v. Canada (Minister of Employment & Immigration) (1988), 6 Imm. L.R. (2d) 222, 34 Admin. L.R. 206, 23 F.T.R. 241, [1989] 2 F.C. 79 (Fed. T.D.) — The Court observed that those seeking landing in Canada must satisfy an immigration officer that they meet the selection standards set out in the regulations. It is the responsibility of the applicant to produce all relevant information which may assist in his application. The extent to which immigration officers may wish to offer assistance, counselling or advice may be a matter of individual preference or even a matter of departmental policy from time to time but it is not an obligation that is imposed upon the officers by the Act or the regulations.

Section 18 reviews are not appellate reviews. To succeed, the applicant must do more than establish the possibility that the Court would have reached a different conclusion than the visa officer in the assessment. There must be either an error of law apparent on the face of the record or a breach of the duty of fairness appropriate to this essentially administrative assessment. The regulations permit the applicant to be assessed in "an occupation". The factors listed in column 1 of schedule 1 require that the experience of the applicant be assessed with regard to his intended occupation. There is no reason why the actual experience and time spent in each of the various responsibilities in an occupation cannot be broken down to award units of assessment for experience in intended occupations. As a matter of fairness, the record should show that the applicant was given the opportunity to provide information in support of his current experience in each included occupation. The record must clearly indicate reasons which support the visa officer's assignment of a specific experience rating to the intended occupations or reasons which support the refusal to do so. In this case, the officer did not believe that the various responsibilities which the applicant carried out in his business in India should be broken down into separate components for the purposes of awarding units of assessment for experience in his alternative intended occupation of material purchasing or garment sales representative. Accordingly, the officer refused to issue a visa and in so doing erred in law. The officer's decision was set aside.

Muliadi v. Canada (Minister of Employment & Immigration (1986), 18 Admin. L.R. 243 (Fed. C.A.) — The appellant was a resident of Indonesia. He applied to come to Canada on the basis that he fell within the entrepreneurial category as an immigrant. His application was refused and that refusal was upheld by the Trial Division. The Court of Appeal overruled the Trial Division because the officer responsible for the disposing of the application failed to inform the appellant of the negative assessment of the appellant's business by the Province of Ontario, and to give the appellant a fair opportunity of correcting or contradicting that assessment before making the decision required by the statute. Further, the wording of the refusal and the conduct of the officer at the interview of the appellant suggested that the decision to refuse the appellant's application was, in fact, being made by the Government of Ontario official, with whom the visa officer consulted about the viability of the proposal, rather than by the visa officer himself. The uncontradicted evidence indicated that the visa officer had stated that he was sympathetic to the appellant's application but had to deny the application because the Ontario Government had refused it. Finally, the appeal was allowed because the visa officer, in his letter, indicated that he had paid particular attention to whether employment opportunities for "a significant number of Canadians would be created." The language of the definition of an entrepreneur did not impose such a requirement; therefore, the visa officer exceeded his jurisdiction and, for that reason as well, his decision could not stand.

Editor's Note: Some of the relevant regulations have been amended since this case arose. The Court's analysis of the propriety of the visa officer's decision may be more important than the result of the application.

Section 8(4)

Lam v. Canada (Minister of Employment & Immigration) (1991), 15 Imm. L.R. (2d) 275, 49 F.T.R. 200 (Fed. T.D.) — The applicant applied for permanent residence as a self-employed person. The visa officer rejected the application without ever affording the applicant an interview. The visa officer determined that the applicant could not have met the minimum requirement of 70 units of assessment to qualify as a self-employed person even if he had been accorded the maximum 10 units of assessment for personal suitability after an interview. Because the officer determined that the applicant did not meet the definition of a self-employed person, he did not give the applicant the 30 units of assessment for self-employment described in Regulation 8(4).

Schedule 1 of the regulations in Factor 9 describes, under the criteria for personal suitability, the units of assessment awarded on the basis of an interview with the person to reflect the personal suitability of the person and his dependents to become successfully established in Canada. Schedule 1, Factor 9, was taken to mean that the officer doing the assessment must award up to 10 units depending on his finding as to personal suitability. Where the maximum 10 units are awarded, the interviewing officer must have been satisfied that the prospective immigrant has the personal suitability to become successfully established in Canada.

By not having granted the applicant an interview the officer was not in a position to determine whether he would have allowed the 30 units of assessment in section 8(4) of the regulations. Further, section 11(3) of the regulations permits a visa officer to issue a visa even if the applicant is not awarded the necessary units of assessment. If the applicant has all the qualities mentioned in Factor 9 of Schedule 1, a visa officer cannot form a valid opinion under section 11(3) without an interview. The visa officer has no discretion not to grant the interview mentioned in Factor 9. It is incumbent upon a visa officer to follow the procedure set out in statute. The officer has no discretion in deciding whether or not to grant an interview pursuant to Factor 9 under column 1 of Schedule 1 of the regulations. The decision of the officer in this case was quashed. The Minister was directed to reconsider the applicant's application and another visa officer was to effect this reconsideration.

Editor's Note: See, however, sections 8(1) and 11.1 of the Immigration Regulations.

Ho v. Canada (Minister of Employment & Immigration) (1989), 8 Imm. L.R. (2d) 38, 27 F.T.R. 241 (Fed. T.D.); affirmed (1990), 11 Imm. L.R. (2d) 12 (Fed. C.A.) — For digest, see section 8, subheading *Subsection 1, supra.*

Yang v. Canada (Minister of Employment & Immigration) (1989), 36 Admin. L.R. 235, 8 Imm. L.R. (2d) 48, 27 F.T.R. 74 (Fed. T.D.) — For digest, see section 8, subheading *Subsection 1, supra.*

9. (1) Subject to subsection (1.01) and section 11, where an immigrant other than a member of the family class, an assisted relative or a Convention refugee seeking resettlement makes an application for a visa, a visa officer may issue an immigrant visa to him and his accompanying dependants if

(a) he and his dependants, whether accompanying dependants or not, are not members of any inadmissible class and otherwise meet the requirements of the Act and these Regulations;

(b) where the immigrant and the immigrant's accompanying dependants intend to reside in a place in Canada other than the Province of Quebec, on the basis of the assessment of the immigrant or the spouse of that immigrant in accordance with section 8, and

(i) in the case of an immigrant other than an entrepreneur, an investor or a provincial nominee, he is awarded at least 70 units of assessment,

(ii) in the case of an entrepreneur or a provincial nominee, he is awarded at least 25 units of assessment, and

(iii) in the case of an investor other than an investor in a province, the investor has made an investment and is awarded at least 25 units of assessment; and

(iv) [Repealed SOR/99-146, s. 4.]

(c) where the immigrant and the immigrant's accompanying dependants intend to reside in the Province of Quebec,

(i) the Minister of Cultural Communities and Immigration of that Province is of the opinion, based on regulations made under *An Act respecting the Ministère des Communautés culturelles et de l'Immigration* (R.S.Q., 1977, c. M-23.1), as amended from time to time, that the immigrant and the immigrant's accompanying dependants will be able to become successfully established in that Province, and

(ii) in the case of an investor in a province, the investor has made an investment.

(1.01) Where a visa officer does not issue an immigrant visa as an accompanying dependant to a son or daughter of an immigrant referred to in subsection (1), or of the spouse of that immigrant, the visa officer shall not issue an immigrant visa as an accompanying dependant to a son or daughter of that son or daughter.

(1.02) A visa officer shall not issue an immigrant visa to an investor in a province or to that investor's accompanying dependants if the visa officer is informed that the Minister has engaged in consultations with the province in respect of the interpretation or implementation of the agreement entered into between the province and the Minister in respect of the selection of immigrant investors and the consultations have not been successfully completed.

(2) For the purposes of subsection (1), a visa officer

(a) is not required to determine whether a dependant is a member of an inadmissible class if the dependant is

(i) the spouse of the applicant, where, on the basis of written evidence, an immigration officer is satisfied that the spouse is separated from and no longer cohabiting with the applicant, or

(ii) a son or daughter of the applicant, or of the spouse of that applicant, where an immigration officer is satisfied that custody or guardianship of the son or daughter has been legally vested in

(A) the spouse of the applicant, referred to in subparagraph (i), or

(B) a former spouse of the applicant; and

(iii) [Revoked SOR/92-101, s. 5.]

(iv) [Revoked SOR/92-101, s. 5.]

(b) shall not issue an immigrant visa to a dependant referred to in paragraph (a) as an accompanying dependant.

(3) [Revoked SOR/89-585, s. 2.]

SOR/79-851, s. 3; SOR/83-675, s. 3; SOR/85-1038, s. 4, SOR/88-286, s. 5; SOR/89-585, s. 2; SOR/90-750, s. 2; SOR/91-157, s. 4; SOR/91-322, s. 1; SOR/91-433, s. 4; SOR/92-101, s. 5; SOR/93-412, s. 4; SOR/99-146, s. 4

Case Law

Section 9(1)

Singh (G.) v. Canada (Minister of Citizenship & Immigration) (1995), 106 F.T.R. 66 (Fed. T.D.) — The applicant, a citizen of India, applied for permanent residence as an assisted relative. His application was received by the Canadian Consulate General in Buffalo in February, 1990. The applicant entered Canada in 1981 as a visitor, however he was discovered working illegally at a car wash. He then made a claim for Convention refugee status which he later withdrew on his return to India. He entered Canada again in 1987 and has been living here since that time. In 1991 he made a second claim for Convention refugee status which he also subsequently abandoned. The applicant worked legally as a machinist at a company in Mississauga from 1988 until the company went bankrupt in 1990. He has not been employed since then.

The applicant was interviewed in connection with his independent application in June 1992. The officer's decision was not made until May 1994, and was not communicated to the applicant until October 1994. During the 28 month period between the interview and communication of the decision, the applicant's solicitor sent 12 letters to the respondent requesting information about the status of the applicant's file. The respondent replied twice with form letters indicating that the matter was proceeding normally.

In her decision, the officer informed the applicant that he had received the necessary 70 points but that she had a discretion pursuant to section 11(3) of the Regulations to refuse to issue a visa. The officer stated that although Mr. Singh had been in Canada for a substantial amount of time he had not acquired reasonable language skills, had not sought substantial employment opportunities and therefore, did not appear to demonstrate motivation, initiative, adaptability and the resourcefulness required to successfully establish himself in Canada. The officer informed Mr. Singh that he came within the inadmissable class of persons described in subsection 19(2)(d) of the Act.

Fairness requires that an applicant receive a timely decision. What that means will vary with the circumstances in each case. A two and a half year delay between an interview and notification is unacceptable where there are no special circumstances which account for the delay. In exercising her discretion the officer was directing her attention to the applicant's ability to establish himself in Canada. This is a forward looking exercise. To accord offers of employment, which are bona fide, little weight because they are not certified by a CEIC is to apply an irrelevant consideration to the decision. The offers demonstrated that once landed the applicant had good employment prospects. The fact that he could not accept the offers prior to landing was irrelevant. Further, the officer's interview notes indicated that certified job offers were not discussed. It was simply agreed that the applicant would send letters of employment to the officer within 60 days of the interview. The applicant did this and in the circumstances it was incumbent on the officer to notify the applicant if the documents he provided were insufficient to fulfil her requirements.

The officer's notes disclose no factual basis for her conclusion that the applicant's failure to secure a job was caused by lack of motivation. The applicant was not interviewed about his job search efforts. Therefore the conclusion about the applicant's motivation was not well founded. The applicant had worked as a machinist for 2 years and had secured offers of employment with poor English skills. It was therefore clear that he could be employed with minimal spoken English. There may be cases in which language skills will impact on an applicant's ability to make a living, but on the facts of this case language did not appear to be an obstacle to the applicant's employment.

The officer's decision was set aside and the matter referred back for redetermination by a different visa officer.

Nicolae v. Canada (Secretary of State) (1995), 29 Imm. L.R. (2d) 148, 90 F.T.R. 280 (Fed. T.D.) — This was an application to quash the decision of a visa officer refusing the applicant's request for permanent residence.

The Court outlined a number of duties of visa officers appraising immigrant applications. An adopted summary of those duties was set out in *Saggu v. Canada (Minister of Citizenship & Immigration)* (1994), 87 F.T.R. 137 (Fed. T.D.), specifically:

1. A visa officer has a duty to consider fully the submissions and information provided by an applicant. The applicant must be given an opportunity to provide information in support of his current experience in each included occupation.

2. The visa officer has a duty to assess an application with reference to the occupation represented by the applicant as the one for which he or she is qualified and prepared to pursue in Canada. This duty extends to each such occupation. There is a clear responsibility on the part of a visa officer to assess alternate occupations inherent in the applicant's work experience. The visa officer must consider an applicant's aptitudes, previous work experience, and whether or not this constitutes experience in the intended occupations.

3. The onus is on the applicant to establish that he or she meets the selection criteria established by the regulations and that admission to Canada would not be contrary to the Act or Regulations.

4. Where a visa officer has an impression of a deficiency in the proof being offered there may be a duty to give the applicant some opportunity to disabuse the officer of that crucial impression.

5. A visa officer must not improperly fetter his or her discretion.

6. A visa officer should exercise the section 11(3) discretion to grant landing only if it appears that the total units awarded do not reflect the particular applicant's chances of successful establishment. If there is no information upon which a visa officer may draw that conclusion, the opportunity to exercise the section 11(3) discretion does not arise.

In this case there was an error of law in the allocation of points in the occupational category, as well as a failure to grant the applicant an opportunity to disabuse the visa officers concerns as to his experience in the field of electrical engineering. Accordingly, the decision of the visa officer was quashed.

Yang v. Canada (Minister of Employment & Immigration) (1992), 56 F.T.R. 155, 17 Imm. L.R. (2d) 229 (Fed. T.D.) — The decision refusing the applicant's application for permanent residence was quashed. The applicant submitted an application for permanent residence in Hong Kong. The applicant was interviewed and refused on the basis that she had failed to accumulate sufficient credits under the selection criteria. The applicant was awarded 9 units for education. This determination was based on the policy of the Ministry that units of assessment are awarded in the educational factor only for education received to the end of secondary school. The applicant's position was that she should have been awarded 12 units of assessment for education. In Taiwan, secondary school education is completed within a nine year period following which the student proceeds to college. Accordingly, the tenth, eleventh and twelfth year of schooling are completed at a college rather than a high school. The Ontario Ministry of Education had provided the applicant with a letter indicating that it considers the 5 year diploma from the National Tai Chung Institute of Commerce to have an educational attainment comparable to someone with an Ontario Secondary School Diploma. Further, in the affidavit of Ms. Yang she deposed that at the interview she was never asked any questions pertaining to her educational background.

The visa officer had a duty to consider the applicant's submission that she was entitled to the maximum number of units of assessment in the education category. The failure to do so left a doubt as to whether a proper assessment of the applicant had taken place. Accordingly, an order in the nature of *certiorari* was granted and a new assessment by a different visa officer was ordered.

Editor's Note: The regulations concerning education assessment have changed, but the principles outlined in this case may still be important.

Choi v. Canada (Minister of Employment & Immigration) (1991), 15 Imm. L.R. (2d) 265, [1992] 1 F.C. 763 (Fed. C.A.) — The appellant attended at the Canadian Commission in Hong Kong and enquired about how to apply for permanent residence. He was provided with a pre-application questionnaire ("PAQ") but was not told that he could make a formal application until the applicant completed a PAQ and filed it with the Commission on October 16, 1987. On October 28, 1987 the appellant received the PAQ back with information that he had received a positive assessment. The appellant completed the Application for Permanent Residence ("IMM8") and paid the required processing fee. The appellant did this on November 6, 1987.

At the time of the assessment of his PAQ the occupational demand for his skills was 10 units. Effective November 2, 1987 the demand was reduced to one unit. The appellant received 65 units including the one unit of assessment for occupational demand against a requirement of 70 units for issuance of a visa. Had the appellant received the 10 units of assessment that were in effect in October 1987 he would have obtained 74 units and qualified for Permanent Residence. An Application for an Immigrant Visa is made when it duly initiates the process leading to the issue or refusal of the visa and not only when that processing is committed to a particular official authorized to dispose of the application. Any other date, except the date of the application, would be purely arbitrary as a lock-in date for the occupational demand factor, depending solely on the vagaries of the administrative process. The application date is the only date within the control of the applicant and is consequently the only date that can be established without arbitrariness.

It was an irresistible conclusion from the evidence that departmental policy was to withhold from applicants the information that they could proceed either by way of a PAQ or directly and immediately by a formal application. If applicants knew enough to request an application form they were given one. If they did not they were dealt with cursorily by being given a PAQ, which had the effect of enormously reducing the administrative burden on the visa officers.

When the Canadian government, through its agents, undertakes to supply information to immigration applicants as to how to become immigrants it assumes a duty to provide this information accurately. This does not imply that Canadian authorities must provide a detailed exegesis of Canadian immigration law but it does mean that immigration authorities have an obligation to provide basic information and to make available the appropriate forms.

The exigencies of fairness therefore require that the time of the appellant's application be deemed to be the date on which he returned the completed PAQ to the Hong Kong office with the consequence that the units of assessment for occupational demand in his case should be deemed to be 10 units.

The appeal was allowed with costs, the decision of the visa officer set aside and the matter returned to a visa officer for reconsideration on the basis that the occupational demand factor for the appellant should be deemed to be 10 units of assessment.

Lam v. Canada (Minister of Employment & Immigration) (1991), 15 Imm. L.R. (2d) 275, 49 F.T.R. 200 (Fed. T.D.) — The applicant applied for permanent residence as a self-employed person. The visa officer rejected the application without ever affording the applicant an interview. The visa officer determined that the applicant could not have met the minimum requirement of 70 units of assessment to qualify as a self-employed person even if he had been accorded the maximum 10 units of assessment for personal suitability after an interview. Because the officer determined that the applicant did not meet the definition of a self-employed person, he did not give the applicant the 30 units of assessment for self-employment described in Regulation 8(4).

Schedule 1 of the regulations in Factor 9 describes, under the criteria for personal suitability, the units of assessment awarded on the basis of an interview with the person to reflect the personal suitability of the person and his dependents to become successfully established in Canada. Schedule 1, Factor 9, was taken to mean that the officer doing the assessment must award up to 10 units depending on his finding as to personal suitability. Where the maximum 10 units are awarded, the interviewing officer must have been satisfied that the prospective immigrant has the personal suitability to become successfully established in Canada.

By not having granted the applicant an interview the officer was not in a position to determine whether he would have allowed the 30 units of assessment in section 8(4) of the regulations. Further, section 11(3) of the regulations permits a visa officer to issue a visa even if the applicant is not awarded the necessary units of assessment. If the applicant has all the qualities mentioned in Factor 9 of Schedule 1, a visa officer cannot form a valid opinion under section 11(3) without an interview. The visa officer has no discretion not to grant the interview mentioned in Factor 9. It is incumbent upon a visa officer to follow the procedure set out in statute. The officer has no discretion in deciding whether or not to grant an interview pursuant to Factor 9 under column 1 of Schedule 1 of the regulations. The decision of the officer in this case was quashed. The Minister was directed to reconsider the applicant's application and another visa officer was to effect this reconsideration.

Editor's Note: See, however, sections 8(1) and 11.1 of the Immigration Regulations.

Gaffney v. Canada (Minister of Employment & Immigration) (1991), 12 Imm. L.R. (2d) 185, 121 N.R. 256, 40 F.T.R. 79 (note) (Fed. C.A.) — This was an appeal from a decision of the Trial Division refusing to quash the rejection of the appellant's application for landing as an independent immigrant by a visa officer in San Francisco. The visa officer considered that his duty to assess alternative occupations was limited to a category and did not extend to occupations in other categories which an immigrant was both qualified and willing to follow. The only evidence as to what transpired at the interview was set out in the appellant's affidavit. When the appellant's counsel was apprised of the refusal letter, he wrote the Consulate General pointing out that the appellant's work experience met other definitions in the *Canadian Classification and Dictionary of Occupations* (CCDO). The visa officer replied to the effect that in the interview the appellant's entire work experience had been canvassed and that these occupations had been considered. That letter was exhibited to the appellant's affidavit in support of his motion to quash. The appellant did not, of course, depose to the truth of the contents. The visa officer's notes were exhibited to the affidavit of another Immigration officer who could not depose to the truth of the notes. The visa officer has a duty to assess an applicant with reference to the occupation represented by the applicant (or his or her spouse) as the one for which he or she is qualified and prepared to pursue in Canada. That duty extends to each such occupation. The appellant in his affidavit alleged that the visa officer had failed to assess him in a number of occupations for which he was qualified and was prepared to pursue. There was no evidence to the contrary and the appeal was allowed and the Trial Division was directed to re-hear the application for *certiorari* and *mandamus*.

Editor's Note: On May 1, 1997, the CCDO was replaced by the NOC. The principle in this case, however, may be of interest.

Fong v. Canada (Minister of Employment & Immigration), 11 Imm. L.R. (2d) 205, 35 F.T.R. 305, [1990] 3 F.C. 705 (Fed. T.D.) — The application for permanent residence by the applicant began with an undertaking by his sister who was a Canadian citizen and living in Canada. A confirmation of offer of employment for the applicant was also obtained and forwarded to the visa officer. The applicant was interviewed but the visa officer had no notes of that interview and did not record in the computer the results of the interview. The basis of the refusal was that the applicant did not meet the job requirement by reason of his lack of experience, his lack of management in production line experience, his poor knowledge of English and limited education and funds. The applicant failed on points. The visa officer's decision was overturned. There was no cogent evidence that the visa officer went beyond the intended job description of production line manager and the CCDO definition thereof and directed a specific line of questioning about the applicant's actual work experience in the garment industry broken down into its constituent elements, for the purpose of making an appropriate assessment with respect to the applicant's adaptability or transferability to the intended occupation. Further, the visa officer committed a breach of the duty of fairness by his failure to afford the applicant an adequate opportunity to answer the specific case against him on the issue of related experience *vis-à-vis* the job offer of production line manager. The visa officer could have done this and should have done this once it became apparent that the application was likely to fail on that score. In this case the visa officer had simply asked the applicant if there was any other information relevant to the case that had not been covered, which the applicant might wish to add for the officer's consideration. This was held to be not sufficient. Finally, the Court noted that the visa officer owed a duty to the applicant to tell him by appropriate questions of his immediate impression regarding the deficiency of proof of intended and related employment and the likely consequences thereof in order to give the applicant some opportunity of disabusing the visa officer of that crucial impression. Accordingly, the visa officer's decision was set aside and the respondent Minister was directed to consider the application of the applicant according to the relevant provisions of the *Immigration Act* and Regulations.

Editor's Note: On May 1, 1997, the CCDO was replaced by the NOC. The principle in this case, however, may be of interest.

Muliadi v. Canada (Minister of Employment & Immigration) (1986), 18 Admin. L.R. 243 (Fed. C.A.) — The appellant was a resident of Indonesia. He applied to come to Canada on the basis that he fell within the entrepreneurial category as an immigrant. His application was refused and the refusal was upheld by the Trial Division. The Court of Appeal overruled the Trial Division because the officer responsible for the disposing of the application failed to inform the appellant of the negative assessment of the appellant's business by the Province of Ontario, and to give the appellant a fair opportunity of correcting or contradicting that assessment before making the decision required by the statute. Further, the wording of the refusal and the conduct of the officer at the interview of the appellant suggested that the decision to refuse the appellant's application was, in fact, being made by the Government of Ontario official with whom the visa officer consulted about the viability of the proposal, rather than by the visa officer himself. The uncontradicted evidence indicated that the visa officer had stated that he was sympathetic to the appellant's application but had to deny the application because the Ontario Government had refused it. Finally, the appeal was allowed because the visa officer, in his letter, indicated that he had paid particular attention to whether employment opportunities for "a significant number of Canadians would be created." The language of the definition of an entrepreneur did not impose such a requirement; therefore, the visa officer exceeded his jurisdiction and, for that reason as well, his decision could not stand.

Editor's Note: Some of the relevant regulations have been amended since this case arose. The Court's analysis of the propriety of the visa officer's decision may be more important than the result of the application.

Section 9(2)

Yuen v. Canada (Minister of Citizenship & Immigration) (1997), 140 F.T.R. 81 (Fed. T.D.); quashed (1998), 47 Imm. L.R. (2d) 65, 227 N.R. 74 (Fed. C.A.) — The applicant sought to review the refusal of her application for permanent residence in the entrepreneur category. The visa officer found that the applicant was qualified; however, he refused her application, in part, because her husband was criminally inadmissible. The officer found that the applicant's husband was her dependant and that she was not separated from him.

It is necessary to consider the context in which the term separated is used in the *Immigration Act*. Where visa officers are required to determine whether parties are separated, this will necessitate the consideration of the specific circumstances of each case including, where appropriate, customs in countries and cultures other than Canada. It is necessary to be cautious not to blindly attribute customs and assumptions applicable in Canada when assessing separations in foreign cultures.

The scheme of section 9 of the regulations is to treat an applicant for an immigrant visa and all his/her dependants whether accompanying or not as a family group. If any dependent is inadmissible the applicant is also inadmissible.

Under section 9(2)(a), if the visa officer is satisfied the spouse is separated from and no longer cohabiting with the applicant, no determination of inadmissibility of a separated spouse is required. The object is to ensure as far as possible that a family is not disunited by reason of the granting of an immigrant visa to an applicant. Where spouses are no longer united in marriage granting an immigrant visa to an applicant will have no disuniting effect on the family. If the visa officer is not satisfied that the spouse is separated, he or she must proceed under paragraph 9(1)(a).

The Court then reviewed the circumstances of this case and concluded that the applicant was not separated from her husband and that her husband was criminally inadmissible and that the refusal of her application was correct in law.

10. (1) Subject to subsections (1.1) and (1.2) and section 11, where an assisted relative makes an application for an immigrant visa, a visa officer may issue an immigrant visa to the assisted relative and accompanying dependants of the assisted relative if

(a) he and his dependants, whether accompanying dependants or not, are not members of any inadmissible class and otherwise meet the requirements of the Act and these Regulations;

(b) in the case of an assisted relative who intends to reside in a place other than the Province of Quebec, on the basis of an assessment made in accordance with section 8, the assisted relative is awarded at least 65 units of assessment; and

(b.1) [Revoked SOR/91-157, s. 5.]

(c) in the case of an assisted relative who intends to reside in the Province of Quebec, the Minister of Cultural Communities and Immigration of that Province is of the opinion based on these Regulations or regulations made under *An Act respecting the Ministère des Communautés culturelles et de l'Immigration* (R.S.Q., 1977, c. M-23.1), as amended from time to time, that the assisted relative will be able to become successfully established in that Province;

(d) [Revoked SOR/93-44, s. 7.]

(1.1) Subject to subsection (1.2) and section 11, a visa officer may issue an immigrant visa to an assisted relative and accompanying dependants of the assisted relative if

(a) the assisted relative

(i) signified to a visa officer at the time an application for an immigrant visa was made that an undertaking would be submitted on the assisted relative's behalf, where the assisted relative has made the application for an immigrant visa before February 1, 1993,

(ii) was notified in writing by a visa officer after an application for an immigrant visa was made but before February 1, 1993 that the application would be assessed or re-assessed on receipt of an undertaking submitted on the assisted relative's behalf, where the assisted relative has made the application for an immigrant visa before February 1, 1993, or

(iii) is a person on whose behalf an undertaking has been submitted before February 1, 1993, and submits an application for an immigrant visa before February 1, 1994;

(b) the assisted relative and the assisted relative's dependants, whether accompanying dependants or not, are not members of any inadmissible class and otherwise meet the requirements of the Act and these Regulations;

(c) a Canadian citizen or permanent resident who is at least 19 years of age and who resides in Canada has submitted an undertaking on the assisted relative's behalf

(i) in the case of an assisted relative referred to in subparagraph (a)(i) or (ii), before January 31, 1994, or

(ii) in the case of an assisted relative referred to in subparagraph (a)(iii), before February 1, 1993;

(d) in the case of an assisted relative who intends to reside in a place in Canada other than the Province of Quebec,

(i) on the basis of an assessment in accordance with section 8, the assisted relative is awarded

(A) where the assisted relative is a brother, sister, son or daughter of the person who has given the undertaking referred to in paragraph (c), at least 55 units of assessment, and

(B) in any other case, at least 60 units of assessment, and

(ii) the person who has given the undertaking referred to in paragraph (c)

(A) is not in default in respect of any obligations assumed by the person under any other undertaking given by the person with respect to any member of the family class or an assisted relative, and

(B) will, in the opinion of an immigration officer, be able to fulfil the undertaking; and

(e) in the case of an assisted relative who intends to reside in the Province of Quebec,

(i) the Minister of Cultural Communities and Immigration of that Province is of the opinion based on these Regulations or regulations made under *An Act respecting the Ministère des Communautés culturelles et de l'Immigration* (R.S.Q., 1977, c. M-23.1), as amended from time to time, that the assisted relative will be able to become successfully established in that Province, and

(ii) the person who has given an undertaking referred to in paragraph (c) will, in the opinion of the Minister of Cultural Communities and Immigration of that Province, be able to fulfil that undertaking.

(1.2) Where a visa officer does not issue an immigrant visa to a son or daughter, as an accompanying dependant, of an assisted relative referred to in subsection (1) or (1.1), or of the spouse of that assisted relative, the visa officer shall not issue an immigrant visa to a son or daughter of that son or daughter as an accompanying dependant.

(2) [Revoked SOR/93-44, s. 7.]

(3) [Revoked SOR/91-157, s. 5.]

(4) For the purposes of subsection (1), a visa officer

(a) is not required to determine whether a dependant is a member of an inadmissible class if the dependant is

(i) the spouse of the applicant, where, on the basis of written evidence, an immigration officer is satisfied that the spouse is separated from and no longer cohabiting with the applicant, or

(ii) a son or daughter of the applicant, or of the spouse of that applicant, where the immigration officer is satisfied that custody or guardianship of the son or daughter has been legally vested in

(A) the spouse of the applicant, referred to in subparagraph (i), or

(B) a former spouse of the applicant, and

(iii) [Revoked SOR/92-101, s. 6.]

(iv) [Revoked SOR/92-101, s. 6.]

(b) shall not issue an immigrant visa to a dependant referred to in paragraph (a) as an accompanying dependant.

SOR/79-167, s. 3; SOR/83-675, s. 4; SOR/85-1038, s. 5; SOR/88-286, s. 6; SOR/91-157, s. 5; SOR/92-101, s. 6; SOR/93-44, s. 7.

Case Law

Section 10(1)

Lin v. Canada (Minister of Citizenship & Immigration) (1996), 33 Imm. L.R. (2d) 8, 107 F.T.R. 225 (Fed. T.D.) — This was an application to review a decision of a visa officer rejecting the applicant's application for permanent residence as an independent immigrant under the assisted relative class. The visa officer imported the notion of English language ability into the concept of specific vocational preparation. A visa officer should not take into account the language capability of an applicant when assessing the award of units with respect to another category listed in schedule 1 to the regulations. The decision of the visa officer was set aside and the matter was remitted to a different visa officer for reconsideration.

11. (1) Subject to subsections (3) and (5), a visa officer shall not issue an immigrant visa pursuant to subsection 9(1) or 10(1) or (1.1) to an immigrant who is assessed on the basis of factors listed in column I of Schedule I and is not awarded any units of assessment for the factor set out in item 3 thereof unless the immigrant

(a) has arranged employment in Canada and has a written statement from the proposed employer verifying that he is willing to employ an inexperienced person in the position in which the person is to be employed, and the visa officer is satisfied that the person can perform the work required without experience; or

(b) is qualified for and is prepared to engage in employment in a designated occupation.

(2) Subject to subsections (3) and (4), a visa officer shall not issue an immigrant visa pursuant to section 9 or 10 to an immigrant other than an entrepreneur, an investor, a provincial nominee or a self-employed person unless

(a) the units of assessment awarded to that immigrant include at least one unit of assessment for the factor set out in item 4 of column I of Schedule I;

(b) the immigrant has arranged employment in Canada; or

(c) the immigrant is prepared to engage in employment in a designated occupation.

(3) A visa officer may

(a) issue an immigrant visa to an immigrant who is not awarded the number of units of assessment required by section 9 or 10 or who does not meet the requirements of subsection (1) or (2), or

(b) refuse to issue an immigrant visa to an immigrant who is awarded the number of units of assessment required by section 9 or 10,

if, in his opinion, there are good reasons why the number of units of assessment awarded do not reflect the chances of the particular immigrant and his dependants of becoming successfully established in Canada and those reasons have been submitted in writing to, and approved by, a senior immigration officer.

(4) [Revoked SOR/91-157, s. 6.]

(5) A visa officer shall not issue an immigrant visa to an accompanying dependant of an immigrant referred to in subsection 9(1) or an assisted relative referred to in subsection 10(1) or (1.1) unless

(a) at the time the application for an immigrant visa is received by an immigration officer, the dependant or relative meets the criteria respecting age, and marital or student status set out in the definitions "dependent son" and "dependent daughter" in subsection 2(1); and

(b) at the time the visa is issued, the dependant or relative meets the criteria respecting marital or student status set out in those definitions.

SOR/79-167, s. 4; SOR/79-851, s. 4; SOR/81-461, s. 1; SOR/85-1038, s. 6; SOR/91-157, s. 6; SOR/91-433, s. 5; SOR/92-101, s. 7; SOR/93-44, s. 8.

Case Law

Section 11(1)

Nakamine v. Canada (Minister of Citizenship & Immigration) (1998), 41 Imm. L.R. (2d) 255 (Fed. T.D.) — This is an application to review a refusal of an application for permanent residence under the independent category as a chef/cook. The applicant was a citizen of Japan, and was awarded "0" units of assessment for his experience. The applicant had no formal training as a chef, but this occupation in Japan is learned on the job. Due to the fact that the applicant intended to work as a cook in a Japanese restaurant in Canada, formal training ought not to have been an essential factor. The applicant had more than two years of experience working in various restaurants in Japan and Canada and, accordingly, was entitled to more than "0" units of assessment for experience, at least as a cook, if not as a chef.

Paik v. Canada (Minister of Citizenship & Immigration) (1996), 35 Imm. L.R. (2d) 52 (Fed. T.D.) — This was an application to set aside a decision of a visa officer refusing the applicant's application for permanent residence.

In August 1994, the applicant had applied for permanent residence and provided a reference from an assistant professor of aeronautics. This letter referred to the applicant as being employed as a computer systems analyst for the solid mechanics group at the California Institute of Technology. The visa officer could not understand how the applicant could be so employed when he had not been enrolled as a student for several terms and, accordingly, contacted Cal-Tech and the professor who provided the letter of reference. Subsequent to receiving information from both the institution and the professor, the visa officer refused the application.

The refusal was set aside. The visa officer's decision to award the applicant zero units of assessment for work experience was based on information provided to her by the person who signed the applicant's letter of reference. There was a conflict between the information provided and what was stated in the letter of reference. The officer had a duty to advise the applicant of the contradiction and give him an opportunity to explain it before she made a decision.

Haughton v. Canada (Minister of Citizenship & Immigration) (1996), 34 Imm. L.R. (2d) 284, 111 F.T.R. 226 (Fed. T.D.) — The applicant applied at the Canadian Consulate in Buffalo for permanent residence under the category of independent skilled worker. The applicant sought to be classified and assessed as an executive secretary. The skills mentioned by the visa officer in the refusal letter were not in the CCDO definition of an executive secretary. Rather, these appear to be requirements that the visa officer considered, based solely on his own ideas of those skills, which are required to be a successful executive secretary in a contemporary Canadian office environment.

The visa officer is bound by the CCDO definition. While it may be that there is a problem with outdated definitions provided in the CCDO, a visa officer is none the less not permitted to substitute his/her own criteria for a given occupation.

Having found that the visa officer erred in considering criteria in addition to the CCDO, it was then necessary for the Court to determine if this error affected the visa officer's overall assessment. In one interview, the visa officer reclassified the applicant from an executive secretary to a stenographer and in the process lowered her units, exclusive of personal suitability, from 63 to 48. A visa officer, when considering personal suitability, is required to consider economic establishment as it relates to the factors of adaptability, motivation and initiative. When economic considerations are at stake, it is reasonable to assume that the occupation in which one is classified is relevant to such an assessment. Therefore, the Court was not satisfied that the visa officer would have, but for the error in applying the CCDO, made the same personal suitabilities assessment. Accordingly the application for judicial review was allowed and the matter remitted for redetermination by a different visa officer, in a manner not inconsistent with the court's reasons.

Editor's Note: On May 1, 1997, the CCDO was replaced by the NOC. The principle in this case, however, may be of interest.

Gaffney v. Canada (Minister of Employment & Immigration) (1991), 12 Imm. L.R. (2d) 185, 121 N.R. 256, 40 F.T.R. 79 (note) (Fed. C.A.) — This was an appeal from a decision of the Trial Division refusing to quash the rejection of the appellant's application for landing as an independent immigrant by a visa officer in San Francisco. The visa officer considered that his duty to assess alternative occupations was limited to a category and did not extend to occupations in other categories which an immigrant was both qualified and willing to follow. The only evidence as to what transpired at the interview was set out in the appellant's affivadit. When the appellant's counsel was apprised of the refusal letter, he wrote the Consulate General pointing out that the appellant's work experience met other definitions in the *Canadian Classification and Dictionary of Occupations* (CCDO). The visa officer replied to the effect that in the interview the appellant's entire work experience had been canvassed and that these occupations had been considered. That letter was exhibited to the appellant's affidavit in support of his motion to quash. The appellant did not, of course, depose to the truth of the contents. The visa officer's notes were exhibited to the affidavit of another Immigration officer who could not depose to the truth of the notes. The visa officer has a duty to assess an applicant with reference to the occupation represented by the applicant (or his or her spouse) as the one for which he or she is qualified and prepared to pursue in Canada. That duty extends to each such occupation. The appellant in his affidavit alleged that the visa officer had failed to assess him in a number of occupations for which he was qualified and was prepared to pursue. There was no evidence to the contrary and the appeal was allowed and the Trial Division was directed to re-hear the application for *certiorari* and *mandamus*.

Editor's Note: On May 1, 1997, the CCDO was replaced by the NOC. The principle in this case, however, may be of interest.

Fong v. Canada (Minister of Employment & Immigration) (1990), 11 Imm. L.R. (2d) 205, 35 F.T.R. 305, [1990] 3 F.C. 705 (Fed. T.D.) — The application for permanent residence by the applicant began with an undertaking by his sister who was a Canadian citizen and living in Canada. A confirmation of offer of employment for the applicant was also obtained and forwarded to the visa officer. The applicant was interviewed but the visa officer had no notes of that interview and did not record in the computer the results of the interview. The basis of the refusal was that the applicant did not meet the job requirement by reason of his lack of experience, his lack of management in production line experience, his poor knowledge of English and limited education and funds. The applicant failed on points.

The visa officer's decision was overturned. There was no cogent evidence that the visa officer went beyond the intended job description of production line manager and the CCDO definition thereof and directed a specific line of questioning about the applicant's actual work experience in the garment industry broken down into its constituent elements, for the purpose of making an appropriate assessment with respect to the applicant's adaptability or transferability to the intended occupation. Further, the visa officer committed a breach of the duty of fairness by his failure to afford the applicant an adequate opportunity to answer the specific case against him on the issue of related experience *vis-à-vis* the job offer of production line manager. The visa officer could have done this and should have done this once it became apparent that the application was likely to fail on that score. In this case the visa officer had simply asked the applicant if there was any other information relevant to the case that had not been covered, which the applicant might wish to add for the officer's consideration. This was held to be not sufficient. Finally, the Court noted that the visa officer owed a duty to the applicant to tell him by appropriate questions of his immediate impression regarding the deficiency of proof of intended and related employment and the likely consequences thereof in order to give the applicant some opportunity of disabusing the visa officer of that crucial impression. Accordingly, the visa officer's decision was set aside and the Respondent Minister was directed to consider the application of the applicant according to the relevant provisions of the *Immigration Act and Regulations.*

Editor's Note: On May 1, 1997, the CCDO was replaced by the NOC. The principle in this case, however, may be of interest.

Section 11(3)

Lau v. Canada (Minister of Citizenship & Immigration) (January 21, 1999), Doc. IMM-6349-98 (Fed. T.D.) — This was an application to judicially review a visa officer's decision denying the applicant permanent residence. The applicant had already been before the Court twice and both times he was successful and the visa officer's decisions were overturned. In this case, a visa officer had denied the application for a third time and the applicant was judicially reviewing that decision.

The applicant on a previous assessment was assessed at 71 points, yet the visa officer in China had exercised discretion under section 11(3) of the Regulations and refused the application. When a visa officer exercises his or her discretion he or she must do so on the basis of the facts as they stand at the time of the exercise of that discretion.

At the time of his original application, the applicant had received a job offer from each of his two brothers in Canada. However, when these offers were assessed, the one brother no longer owned a restaurant, and as an employee, was not in a position to extend an offer of employment. Similarly, the second brother was not financially able to extend an offer of employment since, based on audited financial statements, his restaurant was not generating sufficient profits.

The visa officer considered these facts and determined that the job offers at the time he exercised his discretion were not viable. The visa officer correctly employed the current timeframe in determining whether or not to exercise discretion.

Lam v. Canada (Minister of Citizenship & Immigration) (1998), 152 F.T.R. 316 (Fed. T.D.) — A visa officer may inquire further if he or she considers that a further inquiry into an application is warranted. A visa officer cannot be wilfully blind in assessing an application and must act in good faith. However, there is no general obligation on a visa officer to make further inquiries when an application is ambiguous. The onus is on an applicant to file a clear application together with such supporting documentation as he or she considers advisable. The onus does not shift to the visa officer and there is no entitlement to a personal interview if the application is ambiguous or supporting material is not included.

Where an applicant has reason to believe that he or she may be successfully established in Canada irrespective of the units of assessment determination, he or she should apply for a determination under subsection 11(3) setting forth relevant reasons. Otherwise, while the visa officer may do so on his or her own volition, there is no obligation on the visa officer to exercise a discretion under subsection 11(3).

Akhtar v. Canada (Minister of Citizenship & Immigration) (1998), 147 F.T.R. 142 (Fed. T.D.) — The applicant sought to review a decision of a visa officer in which the officer exercised negative discretion notwithstanding the fact that the applicant was awarded 79 units of assessment.

It is not a precondition to exercise a negative discretion that the applicant be awarded "0" units for personal suitability.

Khan v. Canada (Minister of Citizenship & Immigration) (1997), 128 F.T.R. 126 (Fed. T.D.) — The applicant sought to review a decision of a visa officer refusing her application as an independent applicant. The applicant relied in part on the assistant relative category in making her application.

Subsection 11(3) of the regulations gives the visa officer a particular discretion to issue a visa notwithstanding an award of less than 65 units. The inclusion of this discretion is clearly for the purpose for covering situations where the selection criteria failed to properly assess what they are designed to assess, namely the ability of the applicant to become successfully established in Canada. In considering the scope of regulation 11(3) it is proper to look at the factors set out in the selection criteria to determine what they are designed to assess. While the discretion conferred under section 11(3) is a broad one it is not unrestricted. The visa officer clearly discounted the applicant's *bona fide* job offer to the point where he considered that it was not available. This was not a question of assigning weight to the job offer but amounted to completely ignoring a relevant consideration.

Accordingly, the officer did not exercise his discretion under subsection 11(3) according to law and as a result his decision was set aside.

Mao v. Canada (Minister of Citizenship & Immigration) (January 16, 1997), Doc. IMM-844-96 (Fed. T.D.) — This was an application to review a decision of a visa officer refusing the applicant's independent application for permanent residence. The visa officer informed the applicant at the interview that while the applicant had sufficient points to pass, she was going to recommend that negative discretion be exercised and that the application be refused. This recommendation was to be based upon the officer's belief that the applicant could not successfully establish and be employed in his intended occupation in Canada.

The visa officer acted in accordance with the requirements of the *Immigration Act* and the regulations by first submitting her reasons for recommending the negative exercise of discretion to a senior immigration officer for approval. The reasons cited by the visa officer, namely the applicant's deficient English language skills and his limited funds, were relevant considerations which accurately reflect his chances of becoming successfully established economically in Canada. Provided that the reasons invoked by the visa officer for exercising negative discretion are relevant to the applicant's chance of becoming successfully established economically and not to some other measure of success, he or she may properly base his or her decision on any number of factors including those found in schedule I of the regulations.

Channa v. Canada (Minister of Citizenship & Immigration) (1996), 124 F.T.R. 290 (Fed. T.D.) — The applicant sought to review a decision of a visa officer refusing his application for permanent residence. The applicant scored 59 points, at the pre-interview stage, and was not granted an interview.

In the absence of a specific statutory provision reasons are not required when an interview is denied. Further, where the statute only requires reasons when positive discretion is exercised under section 11(3) of the regulations, the Court is not prepared to conclude that reasons are also required when that discretion is not exercised.

Counsel for the applicant acknowledged that before the hearing he received more than one telephone call from the respondent's counsel pointing out that arguments in the memorandum of argument were without merit. The applicant abandoned those arguments when the judicial review application was heard, but substituted for them new arguments which came as a total surprise to the respondent's counsel. Counsel is not entitled to proceed without notice and whether he was asked or not, counsel ought to have advised the respondent's counsel that he was abandoning the applicant's memorandum of argument and planning to present new arguments. There were no special reasons under rule 16 which would justify a costs award against the applicant. It was the solicitors conduct which brought the case forward without notice. Accordingly, the Court ordered that counsel for the applicant personally pay to the respondent $100 in court costs.

Hoballahi v. Canada (Minister of Citizenship & Immigration) (1996), 37 Imm. L.R. (2d) 98, 124 F.T.R. 164 (Fed. T.D.) — The applicant challenged a decision of a visa officer refusing a permanent visa on the basis that the applicant would not be able to establish himself successfully in Canada due to his inability to speak well in English or French. Although the applicant had been awarded more than the required number of units of assessment, the visa officer exercised, in a negative fashion, his discretion under paragraph 11(3)(b). The applicant's academic qualifications and work experience were informally assessed by the Canadian Counsel of Professional Engineers (CCPE). There was nothing to suggest that in making that assessment the CCPE consider the purported language skills of the applicant. In the reasons for refusal, the visa officer commented negatively on the applicant's wife having "no work skills" to assist in the support of the family. The officer made no mention of the assistance to be provided to the applicant by his relatives in Canada. That evidence was relevant and ought to have been addressed by the visa officer in his reasons, particularly, given his emphasis on the inability of the applicant's wife to assist in their establishment in Canada.

Under paragraph 11(3)(b), a visa officer may not exercise his discretion alone; rather his written reasons for refusing to issue the visa must be submitted to a senior immigration officer for approval. In order to satisfy the requirements of regulation 11(3)(b) the visa officer must outline in his reasons, in a fair and accurate manner, all relevant information to ensure that the senior immigration officer may properly exercise his discretion. In this case, erroneous and incomplete information was contained in the reasons submitted by the visa officer and accordingly the senior immigration officer could not be said to have exercised his discretion on a proper factual foundation.

The decision of the visa officer was set aside.

Ting v. Canada (Minister of Citizenship & Immigration) (1996), 36 Imm. L.R. (2d) 197, 122 F.T.R. 238 (Fed. T.D.) — The applicant sought to review a decision of a visa officer refusing the application for permanent residence on the ground that she awarded only 68 units of assessment when a minimum of 70 were required.

The applicant was a young woman, 32 years of age. She held a bachelors degree in arts and a masters degree in arts from Chinese universities and a masters degree in arts from Laval University in Quebec City. She was an interpreter and a tour guide in China and a teacher of French in Beijing from 1986 to 1993. The applicant intended to work as an interpreter in Vancouver.

The visa officer in Buffalo awarded only 4 units out of 10 for personal suitability. The officer determined that the applicant was not strongly suited to successfully establish herself in the occupation of an interpreter in Vancouver, because of her limited communication skills and experience in the English language. During the interview the applicant required frequent repetition and simplification to understand English.

The visa officer failed to properly apply the criteria of adaptability. Adaptability is a forward looking element. It was common ground that Vancouver harboured a very large and prosperous Chinese community. The applicant was a university trained scholar with 3 university degrees and proficient in 3 languages. Her career as an interpreter, a tour guide and a teacher of French, plus the fact that she has been able to adapt herself at a French university in the

Province of Quebec, showed a high degree of adaptability. Further the visa officer failed to exercise her discretion under subsection 11(3) of the regulations. A proper exercise of that discretion would have resulted in the awarding of two more units so as to grant a visa to an otherwise highly qualified applicant.

The decision of the visa officer was set aside.

Bekele v. Canada (Minister of Citizenship & Immigration) (1996), 34 Imm. L.R. (2d) 256 (Fed. T.D.) — This is an application to review a decision of a visa officer. The officer reviewed the factors listed in column 1, schedule 1 of the Immigration Regulations and concluded that the applicant received 70 units of assessment, however, the officer used paragraph 19(1)(b) of the *Immigration Act* to refuse the applicant admission. That paragraph provides that an applicant is inadmissable if the officer has reasonable grounds to believe that the applicant will be unable to support him or herself without social assistance. The officer's affidavit disclosed that she relied on the guidelines in the immigration manual which suggested that an applicant needed funds in the amount of $7,238 to be self supporting in Canada during his first 6 months. The applicant was approximately $2,200 below the suggested guideline and accordingly, the officer found him inadmissable. The officer's decision was not unreasonable. The officer considered only economic factors in exercising her discretion in a negative manner. These factors included the applicant's lack of funds, his debt, his lack of family, and the absence of a job offer. Accordingly, the application for judicial review was refused.

Singh (G.) v. Canada (Minister of Citizenship & Immigration) (1995), 106 F.T.R. 66 (Fed. T.D.) — The applicant, a citizen of India, applied for permanent residence as an assisted relative. His application was received by the Canadian Consulate General in Buffalo in February 1990. The applicant entered Canada in 1981 as a visitor, however he was discovered working illegally at a car wash. He then made a claim for Convention refugee status which he later withdrew on his return to India. He entered Canada again in 1987 and has been living here since that time. In 1991 he made a second claim for Convention refugee status which he also subsequently abandoned. The applicant worked legally as a machinist at a company in Mississauga from 1988 until the company went bankrupt in 1990. He has not been employed since then.

The applicant was interviewed in connection with his independent application in June 1992. The officer's decision was not made until May 1994, and was not communicated to the applicant until October 1994. During the 28 month period between the interview and communication of the decision, the applicant's solicitor sent 12 letters to the respondent requesting information about the status of the applicant's file. The respondent replied twice with form letters indicating that the matter was proceeding normally.

In her decision, the officer informed the applicant that he had received the necessary 70 points but that she had a discretion pursuant to section 11(3) of the regulations to refuse to issue a visa. The officer stated that although Mr. Singh had been in Canada for a substantial amount of time he had not acquired reasonable language skills, had not sought substantial employment opportunities and therefore, did not appear to demonstrate motivation, initiative, adaptability and the resourcefulness required to successfully establish himself in Canada. The officer informed Mr. Singh that he came within the inadmissable class of persons described in subsection 19(2)(d) of the Act.

Fairness requires that an applicant receive a timely decision. What that means will vary with the circumstances in each case. A two and a half year delay between an interview and notification is unacceptable where there are no special circumstances which account for the delay. In exercising her discretion the officer was directing her attention to the applicant's ability to establish himself in Canada. This is a forward looking exercise. To accord offers of employment, which are *bona fide*, little weight because they are not certified by a CEIC is to apply an irrelevant consideration to the decision. The offers demonstrated that once landed the applicant had good employment prospects. The fact that he could not accept the offers prior to landing was irrelevant. Further, the officer's interview notes indicated that certified job offers were not discussed. It was simply agreed that the applicant would send letters of employment to the officer within 60 days of the interview. The applicant did this and in the circumstances it was incumbent on the officer to notify the applicant if the documents he provided were insufficient to fulfil her requirements.

The officer's notes disclose no factual basis for her conclusion that the applicant's failure to secure a job was caused by lack of motivation. The applicant was not interviewed about his job search efforts. Therefore the conclusion about the applicant's motivation was not well founded. The applicant had worked as a machinist for two years and had secured offers of employment with poor English skills. It was therefore clear that he could be employed with minimal spoken English. There may be cases in which language skills will impact on an applicant's ability to make a living, but on the facts of this case language did not appear to be an obstacle to the applicant's employment.

The officer's decision was set aside and the matter referred back for redetermination by a different visa officer.

Savin v. Canada (Minister of Citizenship & Immigration) (1995), 102 F.T.R. 67 (Fed. T.D.) — This is an application to review a decision of a visa officer exercising negative discretion pursuant to subsection 11(3) of the *Immigration Regulations*. The officer awarded the applicant 70 points but concluded that the applicant lacked motivation and resourcefulness to establish herself in her chosen occupation in Canada and refused the applicant's independent application.

Given that the selection criteria have an economic emphasis, a visa officer's discretion should be exercised in the same economic spirit. A visa officer properly exercises the discretion conferred by this subsection if the officer has good reasons for believing that the applicant would have difficulty in making a living in Canada.

The visa officer's decision in this case sought to mesh personal suitability and low occupational demand. In both of these categories, the applicant had received a below average score albeit not zero. A visa officer must be given some discretion to determine that for a combination of reasons, an applicant would not become economically self-sufficient in Canada.

A visa officer is not obliged to inform each applicant of his or her negative impressions as they arise, particularly when the negative impression concerns some aspect of the applicant which is not amenable to change such as personal suitability or language ability.

Accordingly, the application for judicial review was dismissed.

Dumbrava v. Canada (Minister of Citizenship & Immigration) (1995), 31 Imm. L.R. (2d) 76, 101 F.T.R. 230 (Fed. T.D.) — The applicant submitted an application for permanent residence. After an interview the application was refused and this refusal was communicated to the applicant. The applicant's solicitor then wrote to the visa officer stating that her decision was wrong in law and requesting that it be reviewed. The officer responded to the solicitor's letter and elaborated on her reasons for having refused the application the first time. This second letter constituted a decision and the relevant time period started to run from the date of that letter. However, the decision-making power of a visa officer is statutory and, as such, the power to reconsider must be found in the statute. Slips and obvious errors can be corrected after a decision has been rendered, however, due to the fact that the statute does not provide a visa officer with the power to reconsider, the visa officer does not have jurisdiction to again decide the matter as was done in this case. Accordingly, the application to review the second decision of the visa officer was dismissed.

Shum v. Canada (Minister of Citizenship & Immigration) (1995), 30 Imm. L.R. (2d) 233, 100 F.T.R. 39 (Fed. T.D.) — The applicant sought judicial review of the decision of a visa officer refusing the applicant permanent residence in Canada because he did not meet the requirements under the independent category. The applicant agreed that he did not have the requisite 60 points to obtain an interview. However, the applicant requested the exercise of positive discretion pursuant to Regulation 11(3).

An interview is not required before a person is entitled to ask for discretion to be exercised. The lack of an interview will be generally harmful to the person's chances of success but there is no reason why the prospective immigrant should not be entitled to obtain a determination from a visa officer under subsection 11(3). If a person cannot meet the requirements of section 9, section 11 is applicable and subsection 11(3) specifically enables a visa officer to issue an immigrant visa to an immigrant who is not awarded the number of units of assessment required by section 9. There is nothing in subsection 11(3) requiring an interview before discretion can be exercised.

So v. Canada (Minister of Employment & Immigration) (1995), 28 Imm. L.R. (2d) 153, 93 F.T.R. 153 (Fed. T.D.) — The applicant sought an order setting aside the decision of an immigration officer refusing immigrant visas to the applicant and his family. The applicant scored a total of 69 points on his assessment, whereas 70 were required to issue a visa.

The decision of the officer was set aside. A public official exercising a discretionary power vested in him by statute is required to do so in good faith. Whether this requirement has been met is a question to be decided on the basis of the relevant circumstances. The officer did not show good faith in this case. He disregarded pertinent and relevant facts, such as the applicant's 20 years of experience as a chef, and was influenced by factors which should not have played a roll in his decision making at all, such as the applicants having remained in Canada after his status had expired. His conclusion that the applicant only had a 40% chance of becoming established in Canada was perverse in light of the fact that the applicant had saved a substantial amount of money and had secured gainful employment as a head chef.

Notwithstanding the fact that the respondent was willing to consent to the application, the Court ordered costs in the amount of $7,500 in part because the officer's superiors were made aware of the errors committed by the officer in rendering his decision but took no action to rectify it.

Chen v. Canada (Minister of Employment & Immigration), [1995] 1 S.C.R. 725, 27 Imm. L.R. (2d) 1, 179 N.R. 70, 123 D.L.R. (4th) 536 (S.C.C.) — The appellant, a citizen of the People's Republic of China, worked in Canada from 1983 to 1985 as a microbiology technologist. He then moved to the United States and worked at the University of Illinois under a temporary visa. He applied for landed immigrant status in 1987 in New York. He was interviewed and assessed a sufficient number of points to qualify for a permanent visa. Fifteen months elapsed due to a delay in obtaining background and security clearances. In December, 1988, the appellant sent a Christmas card to the visa officer who interviewed him. The note inside the Christmas card thanked her for her efforts and in addition the appellant enclosed the sum of $500.00. This conduct was brought to the attention of the visa officer's supervisor. The applicant was then re-interviewed and ultimately, pursuant to section 11(3) of the regulations, the visa officer purported to exercise the discretion contained under that section to refuse the applicant a permanent visa.

At the Trial Division level the decision of the visa officer was set aside. The trial division judge found that it was inconceivable that section 11(3) was intended to give a Visa Officer an unlimited mandate to decide whether a particular immigrant is generally suitable or not as a future member of Canadian society. Specifically, section 11(3) does not allow a visa officer to ignore the number of units of assessment awarded an applicant and determine for non-economic reasons that an immigrant does not have a chance at becoming successfully established in Canada.

The Minister appealed and the Court of Appeal overruled the trial judge. There was, however, in the Court of Appeal, a dissenting judgment. That judgment did not condone the actions of the respondent, but determined that section 11(3) was not intended to vest visa officers with a broad residual discretion when deciding whether to grant or deny visas. The dissenting Justice in the Court of Appeal expressed agreement with the trial division judge and concluded that when deciding a person's ability to successfully establish himself in Canada, the determination criteria must be restricted to matters relating to their ability to make a living. The dissenting justice was of the view that a determination under section 11(3) cannot and should not be influenced by conduct which suggests moral turpitude.

The appellant appealed to the Supreme Court of Canada, which allowed the appeal. The Court indicated that it shared the view of the trial division judge and the dissenting judge in the Court of Appeal and would, for the reasons expressed by them, allow the appeal.

Lam v. Canada (Minister of Employment & Immigration) (1991), 15 Imm. L.R. (2d) 275, 49 F.T.R. 200 (Fed. T.D.) — The applicant applied for permanent residence as a self-employed person. The visa officer rejected the application without ever affording the applicant an interview. The visa officer determined that the applicant could not have met the minimum requirement of 70 units of assessment to qualify as a self-employed person even if he had been accorded the maximum 10 units of assessment for personal suitability after an interview. Because the officer determined that the applicant did not meet the definition of a self-employed person, he did not give the applicant the 30 units of assessment for self-employment described in Regulation 8(4).

Schedule 1 of the regulations in Factor 9 describes, under the criteria for personal suitability, the units of assessment awarded on the basis of an interview with the person to reflect the personal suitability of the person and his dependents to become successfully established in Canada. Schedule 1, Factor 9, was taken to mean that the officer doing the assessment must award up to 10 units depending on his finding as to personal suitability. Where the maximum 10 units are awarded, the interviewing officer must have been satisfied that the prospective immigrant has the personal suitability to become successfully established in Canada.

By not having granted the applicant an interview the officer was not in a position to determine whether he would have allowed the 30 units of assessment in section 8(4) of the regulations. Further, section 11(3) of the regulations permits a visa officer to issue a visa even if the applicant is not awarded the necessary units of assessment. If the applicant has all the qualities mentioned in Factor 9 of Schedule 1, a visa officer cannot form a valid opinion under section 11(3) without an interview. The visa officer has no discretion not to grant the interview mentioned in Factor 9. It is incumbent upon a visa officer to follow the procedure set out in statute. The officer has no discretion in deciding whether or not to grant an interview pursuant to Factor 9 under column 1 of Schedule 1 of the regulations. The decision of the officer in this case was quashed. The Minister was directed to reconsider the applicant's application and another visa officer was to effect this reconsideration.

Editor's Note: See, however, sections 8(1) and 11.1 of the Immigration Regulations.

Gaffney v. Canada (Minister of Employment & Immigration) (1991), 12 Imm. L.R. (2d) 185, 121 N.R. 256, 40 F.T.R. 79 (note) (Fed. C.A.) — This was an appeal from a decision of the trial division refusing to quash the rejection of the appellant's application for landing as an independent immigrant by a visa officer in San Francisco. The visa officer considered that his duty to assess alternative occupations was limited to a category and did not extend to occupations in other categories which an immigrant was both qualified and willing to follow. The only evidence as to what transpired at the interview was set out in the appellant's affidavit. When the appellant's counsel was apprised of the refusal letter, he wrote the Consulate General pointing out that the appellant's work experience met other definitions in the *Canadian Classification and Dictionary of Occupations* (CCDO). The visa officer replied to the effect that in the interview the appellant's entire work experience had been canvassed and that these occupations had been considered. That letter was exhibited to the appellant's affidavit in support of his motion to quash. The appellant did not, of course, depose to the truth of the contents. The visa officer's notes were exhibited to the affidavit of another immigration officer who could not depose to the truth of the notes. The visa officer has a duty to assess an applicant with reference to the occupation represented by the applicant (or his or her spouse) as the one for which he or she is qualified and prepared to pursue in Canada. That duty extends to each such occupation. The appellant in his affidavit alleged that the visa officer had failed to assess him in a number of occupations for which he was qualified and was prepared to pursue. There was no evidence to the contrary and the appeal was allowed and the trial division was directed to re-hear the application for *certiorari* and *mandamus*.

Uy v. Canada (Minister of Employment & Immigration), [1991] 2 F.C. 201, 12 Imm. L.R. (2d) 172, 121 N.R. 248, 40 F.T.R. 80 (note) (Fed. C.A.) — This is an appeal from the Trial Division which refused *certiorari* quashing the refusal by a visa officer of the appellant's independent application. The appellant had been a qualified medical doctor in the Philippines and was a resident in pediatrics in the United States when he applied for admission to Canada as a medical technologist. The visa officer refused to assess him in respect of that occupation because he did not believe that the appellant would pursue the occupation in Canada. In doing so, the visa officer erred in law. There was no suggestion in this case that the visa officer had assessed the appellant for the occupation of medical technologist. The visa officer awarded him 70 or more units and then invoked section 11(3) of the regulations by reason of his conclusion as to the appellant's intentions. Section 6 of the Act requires a visa officer to assess any immigrant who applies for landing in the manner prescribed by the Act and regulations. Section 8(1) of the regulations imposes in mandatory terms a duty to assess and nothing in either the Act or regulations permits a visa officer to refuse to assess in respect of the occupation or alternative occupations which the immigrant states he or she intends to pursue in Canada. The general discretion given a visa officer by section 9(1) of the regulations must be subordinated to the particular discretion given by section 11(3) where, notwithstanding the award of at least 70 units, the visa officer is of the opinion that those units do not reflect the chances of the particular immigrant becoming successfully established in Canada. The reasons for that opinion must be committed to writing and submitted to and approved by a senior immigration officer. Accordingly, the appeal was allowed.

Wang v. Canada (Minister of Employment & Immigration) (1991), 12 Imm. L.R. (2d) 178, 121 N.R. 243, 40 F.T.R. 239 (note) (Fed. C.A.) — This was an appeal from a decision of the trial division refusing *certiorari* to quash the decision of a visa officer rejecting the appellant's independent application. The refusal letter is the decision which is the subject of the application for prerogative relief and is properly to be considered by the Court. It is evidence of the decision made by the visa officer and the reasons he made it but it is not conclusive evidence of whether he arrived at his decision in a manner required by law. In this case, whether the visa officer really did consider the evidence of the appellant's experience or whether he dealt with the application as he did to avoid a refusal under section 11(3) of the regulations, would require the concurrence of a senior immigration officer. Any presumption that the proceedings were fairly conducted and in accordance with the law is rebuttable by extraneous evidence, in this case the appellant's deposition. Second, in this case as in many others, an immigration officer, not the visa officer who made the decision, made an affidavit attaching as an exhibit a memorandum made by the visa officer who made the decision refusing the applicant's application. The trial judge, before whom this matter had originally been argued, ordered that the memorandum be struck from the record. The Court, on the appeal by the applicant from the trial division's refusal of the motion for *certiorari*, confirmed that there was no justification for deviating from evidentiary norms in these applications. There is no justice in according one witness to the proceeding an opportunity to present evidence in a manner that precludes it being tested by cross-examination. Given that visa officers inhabit premises in which may be found other functionaries before whom affidavits may be sworn, there is no practical reason why the visa officer's version of the truth cannot with equal convenience be produced in an affidavit. A disappointed applicant, who wishes to cross-examine a visa officer, will be exercising this right at some considerable expense and this provided some guarantee that the right of cross-examination would not be exercised in a frivolous manner. In this particular case the appeal was allowed.

Zeng v. Canada (Minister of Employment & Immigration) (1989), 27 F.T.R. 56 (Fed. T.D.) — Sections 9 and 11(3) of the regulations empower the visa officer to refuse even those applicants who have achieved the necessary number of points. Three things follow from this:

1. The first is that Parliament has recognized the ability to successfully establish oneself in Canada as a consideration that may outweigh other factors, including the acquisition of the required number of points in every category.

2. If the officer enjoys a discretion to refuse those who have amassed a high number of points, it follows even more strongly that he has the discretion to refuse applicants whose point total is below the required minimum.

3. Where the officer acts within this discretion, his decision is beyond the reach of a motion or *certiorari* whether or not the Court would have reached the same result as the officer.

11.1 For the purpose of determining whether an immigrant and the immigrant's dependants will be able to become successfully established in Canada, a visa officer is not required to conduct an interview unless, based on a review of the visa application and the documents submitted in support thereof,

(a) the immigrant is an immigrant described in paragraph 8(1)(a) and is awarded, for the factors set out in column I of items 1 to 8 of Schedule I, including, where required by these Regulations, at least one unit of assessment for each of the factors set out in column I of items 3 and 4 of that Schedule,

(i) at least 60 units of assessment, where the immigrant is not an assisted relative,

(ii) at least 55 units of assessment, where the immigrant is an assisted relative referred to in paragraph 10(1)(b),

(iii) at least 45 units of assessment, where the immigrant is an assisted relative referred to in clause 10(1.1)(d)(i)(A), and

(iv) at least 50 units of assessment, where the immigrant is an assisted relative referred to in clause 10(1.1)(d)(i)(B); or

(b) the immigrant is an entrepreneur, an investor, a provincial nominee or a self-employed person.

SOR/92-133, s. 3; SOR/93-44, s. 9.

Case Law

Cui v. Canada (Minister of Citizenship & Immigration) (November 25, 1998), Doc. IMM-1269-98 (Fed. T.D.) — The Court observed that it would be preferable if interviews of applicants for permanent resident status be tape-recorded so as to minimize the possibility for contradictory descriptions, such as those set out in the respective affidavits in this case.

Su v. Canada (Minister of Citizenship & Immigration) (1998), 152 F.T.R. 136 (Fed. T.D.) — The applicant had applied for permanent resident status and was residing in Canada while the application was being processed in the United States. The applicant was requested to attend for an interview but was unable to do so, because he could not gain admission to the United States. The Canadian consulate refused to issue the applicant a minister's permit and refused to intervene with Chinese authorities to facilitate the applicant's application for a passport extension. Finally, a visa officer sent the applicant a letter advising that his application had been denied.

There is no legal obligation upon the Canadian consulate to assist applicants in obtaining the proper authorization from a foreign jurisdiction to enable them to attend an interview. The applicant submitted his application in Buffalo. The procedure to have a file transferred was outlined by the visa officer. It is not the concern of the immigration authorities that the applicant is out of status and has chosen to continue to reside in Canada without any status, and that the Chinese consulate has chosen not to renew his passport. The Canadian Government has no control over the actions of foreign governments. Accordingly, the application for judicial review was dismissed.

Channa v. Canada (Minister of Citizenship & Immigration) (1996), 124 F.T.R. 290 (Fed. T.D.) — The applicant sought to review a decision of a visa officer refusing his application for permanent residence. The applicant scored 59 points, at the pre-interview stage, and was not granted an interview.

In the absence of a specific statutory provision reasons are not required when an interview is denied. Further, where the statute only requires reasons when positive discretion is exercised under section 11(3) of the regulations, the Court is not prepared to conclude that reasons are also required when that discretion is not exercised.

Counsel for the applicant acknowledged that before the hearing he received more than one telephone call from the respondent's counsel pointing out that arguments in the memorandum of argument were without merit. The applicant abandoned those arguments when the judicial review application was heard, but substituted for them new arguments which came as a total surprise to the respondent's counsel. Counsel is not entitled to proceed without notice and whether he was asked or not, counsel ought to have advised the respondent's counsel that he was abandoning the applicant's memorandum of argument and planning to present new arguments. There were no special reasons under rule 16 which would justify a costs award against the applicant. It was the solicitors conduct which brought the case forward without notice. Accordingly, the Court ordered that counsel for the applicant personally pay to the respondent $100 in court costs.

Chiu v. Canada (Minister of Citizenship & Immigration) (1996), 35 Imm. L.R. (2d) 281, 121 F.T.R. 39 (Fed. T.D.) — This was an application to review a decision of a visa officer refusing the applicant's application for permanent residence. The applicant, a citizen of Hong Kong, has a wife and three children. After graduating with a bachelor of arts degree in Hong

Kong in 1982, the applicant established an import-export business and in 1985 set up a travel company. That business involved both travel and trading which focused on Vietnam. In 1990, the applicant formed a third company located in Vietnam which was engaged in importing computer parts and assembling, installing and repairing personal computers. The applicant had been successful in these ventures and had amassed savings and assets of over $1.5 million.

The applicant had applied for permanent residence as an entrepreneur. His stated intention was to open a trading and travel business in Vancouver similar to the one he operates in Hong Kong. He also proposed to import computer parts from Asia and the United States to assemble the computers in Canada and sell them here and through his company in Vietnam. At the immigration interview, the officer questioned the applicant to satisfy herself that he met the definition of an entrepreneur. The officer deposed that she read the definition to the applicant and on several occasions during the interview asked him how his background enabled him to meet the definition and how his proposed businesses would significantly benefit Canada. The officer deposed that the applicant was vague at the interview about his proposed businesses and their viability.

The officer concluded that the applicant had done little, if any, research into the feasibility of establishing his proposed businesses and, on that basis, made a negative decision with respect to permanent residence.

The application for judicial review was dismissed. The officer asked the applicant to demonstrate a basic understanding of the markets in which he intended to do business. The applicant was unable to do so. This line of questioning was entirely with in the officer's jurisdiction as she was charged with determining whether the applicant could establish a commercial venture which would employ people and contribute significantly to the Canadian ecomony. The fact that other immigration officers follow-up the implementation of an applicant's business plan does not relieve the initial interviewing officer from the need to be satisfied that a viable venture is planned. It is for the interviewing officer to establish that an applicant meets the requirements of the definition.

Bhajan v. Canada (Minister of Citizenship & Immigration) (1996), 34 Imm. L.R. (2d) 189, 110 F.T.R. 42 (Fed. T.D.) — This was an application to review a decision of a visa officer closing the applicant's file when the applicant failed to appear for an interview.

The respondent's policy of closing files in these circumstances was unfair. The policy precludes the consideration of exceptional circumstances, such as, an applicant's non attendance due to the fact that the applicant required surgery. Further, the policy was not disclosed to applicants before they choose the location for their interview and for that reason as well, the policy was unfair.

Absent a statutory discretion, it would not be contrary to law to put a policy in place which precludes the exercise of discretion as long as the policy meets the minimal requirements of fairness, which exists in a wholly administrative context, where there are no rights at issue. This type of situation is to be distinguished from that in which there is a statutory discretion which cannot be fettered.

Baluyut v. Canada (Minister of Employment & Immigration), [1992] 3 F.C. 420, 56 F.T.R. 186 (Fed. T.D.) — The applicant sought to quash a decision by a visa officer refusing to interview her in support of her application for permanent residence without the personal appearance of her spouse at the interview. The applicant is a citizen of the Philippines who had been living by herself in the United States and working there as a registered nurse. Her husband and their two children lived in the Philippines. The applicant applied as a principal applicant for permanent residence in Canada and listed her husband and children as her dependants. The applicant was notified to attend a personal interview to determine her admissibility. She was required to bring her spouse to the interview. The applicant advised the Canadian Consulate in Los Angeles that her husband would be unable to attend the interview. She had an application for an H-1 visa pending and, thus, her husband would have difficulty obtaining a visa to the United States. Through her counsel she suggested that her husband be interviewed at the Canadian Embassy in Manila. Eventually this suggestion was rejected and the applicant was informed that both she and her husband would be required to attend in Los Angeles on the date scheduled for the interview. The applicant attended by herself at the Canadian Consulate. The officer assigned to deal with her case refused to proceed with the interview. The applicant explained why her husband could not attend and the visa officer spoke to a Vice Consul about what decision she should make and then carried out the Vice Consul's instructions.

The decision of the visa officer was set aside. The Court found that the visa officer had failed to exercise her own discretion and had thereby committed jurisdictional error. The Court found, on the facts, that the visa officer had simply carried out the instructions of her superior with respect to the conduct of the interviews and had not made the decision herself. In so doing the visa officer had committed jurisdictional error and her decision to refuse the interview was quashed. *Mandamus* was directed to the respondent Minister's officials at the Consulate in Los Angeles directing them to interview the applicant and to then transfer the file to Manila so that the spouse and dependants could be interviewed.

Lam v. Canada (Minister of Employment & Immigration) (1991), 15 Imm. L.R. (2d) 275, 49 F.T.R. 200 (Fed. T.D.) — The applicant applied for permanent residence as a self-employed person. The visa officer rejected the application without ever affording the applicant an interview. The visa officer determined that the applicant could not have met the minimum requirement of 70 units of assessment to qualify as a self-employed person even if he had been accorded the maximum 10 units of assessment for personal suitability after an interview. Because the officer determined that the applicant did not meet the definition of a self-employed person, he did not give the applicant the 30 units of assessment for self-employment described in Regulation 8(4).

Schedule 1 of the regulations in Factor 9 describes, under the criteria for personal suitability, the units of assessment awarded on the basis of an interview with the person to reflect the personal suitability of the person and his dependents to become successfully established in Canada. Schedule 1, Factor 9, was taken to mean that the officer doing the assessment must award up to 10 units depending on his finding as to personal suitability. Where the maximum 10 units are awarded, the interviewing officer must have been satisfied that the prospective immigrant has the personal suitability to become successfully established in Canada.

By not having granted the applicant an interview the officer was not in a position to determine whether he would have allowed the 30 units of assessment in section 8(4) of the regulations. Further, section 11(3) of the regulations permits a visa officer to issue a visa even if the applicant is not awarded the necessary units of assessment. If the applicant has all the qualities mentioned in Factor 9 of Schedule 1, a visa officer cannot form a valid opinion under section 11(3) without an interview. The visa officer has no discretion not to grant the interview mentioned in Factor 9. It is incumbent upon a visa officer to follow the procedure set out in statute. The officer has no discretion in deciding whether or not to grant an interview pursuant to Factor 9 under column 1 of Schedule 1 of the regulations. The decision of the officer in this case was quashed. The Minister was directed to reconsider the applicant's application and another visa officer was to effect this reconsideration.

Prescribed Classes of Immigrants for the Purposes of Subsections 6(5) and (8) of the Act

11.2 The following classes are prescribed as classes of immigrants for the purposes of subsections 6(5) and (8) of the Act:

(a) the live-in caregivers in Canada class;

(b) the post-determination refugee claimants in Canada class; and

(c) [Revoked SOR/97-182, s. 4].

(d) the undocumented Convention refugee in Canada class.

SOR/93-44 s. 10; SOR/94-681, s. 2; SOR/97-86, s. 2; SOR/97-182, s. 4.

11.3 A member of the live-in caregivers in Canada class and the member's dependants, if any, are subject to the following landing requirements:

(a) the member must not have been admitted to Canada as a live-in caregiver by reason of any misrepresentation of the education, training or experience requirements referred to in paragraph 20(1.1)(a) or (b), whether the misrepresentation was made by the member or by another person;

(b) the member must not be, and no dependant of the member is, a person described in section 19 of the Act, as determined by an immigration officer pursuant to subsection 6(8) of the Act;

(c) the member must have submitted an application for landing to an immigration officer; and

(d) where the member or a dependant of the member was the subject of an inquiry under the Act, a conditional removal order or removal order must not have been made against the member or dependant or, if such an order was made, it must have been quashed.

(e) [Revoked SOR/93-412, s. 5.]

SOR/93-44 s. 10; SOR/93-412, s. 5; SOR/94-242, s. 2.

Case Law

Ling v. Canada (Minister of Citizenship & Immigration) (1997), 134 F.T.R. 317 (Fed. T.D.) — The applicant sought to review a decision of an immigration officer deciding that the applicant was not a member of the live-in caregivers in Canada class for permanent residence. The reason for the refusal was the 1976 conviction of the applicant's dependant husband for assault occasioning bodily harm. This conviction rendered the husband inadmissible and by reason of paragraph 11.3(b) of the Immigration Regulations and subsection 6(8) of the *Immigration Act*, the applicant was rendered ineligible by reason of her husband's inadmissibility.

There was no duty on the immigration officer to suspend consideration of the application for permanent residence and refer the matter of the husband's criminal conviction to the Governor in Council to enable the Governor in Council to become satisfied that the husband had rehabilitated himself. Over the period from September 1993, when the application was filed until April 1995, when it was dismissed, it was open to the applicant or her husband to take steps to satisfy the Governor in Council that the husband had rehabilitated himself. It would impose on an immigration officer a requirement not envisaged by the *Immigration Act* or regulations to hold an application for permanent resident status in abeyance and take steps to assist an applicant or her dependant to satisfy the Governor in Council of rehabilitation of the dependant. The onus is on the applicant to prove his or her application and adduce all relevant evidence that may insist in doing so. Accordingly, the application was dismissed.

Caletena v. Canada (Solicitor General) (1994), 23 Imm. L.R. (2d) 177, 74 F.T.R. 78 (Fed. T.D.) — The applicant was admitted to Canada on May 5, 1989 as a member of the "Live-in Caregivers in Canada" class. Since that time she had been employed as a nanny on both a full-time and part-time basis, as a chambermaid by the Convention Inn in Edmonton and as a part-time receptionist. On May 14, 1993 her application for permanent residence was accepted subject to medical examinations. On September 27, 1993 she was informed that two of her infant children failed to pass their medical examinations. Accordingly, her application for permanent residence was refused and a voluntary departure notice was issued and her temporary employment authorization was terminated effective November 1, 1993.

Applicants under the Live-in Caregivers Programme are not attempting to gain entry or remain in Canada by failing to comply with our laws. The programme is designed to assist workers who are invited to enter Canada on employment authorizations. There is the implication, at least, that those administering the programme will encourage and assist people, such as the applicant, to upgrade their skills and seek permanent residence. In the present case, the applicant did all that was expected of her as a foreign domestic worker. She was gainfully employed and by all accounts a highly satisfactory employee.

The applicant wished to contest the medical evidence but had not been afforded an opportunity to know what it was or to make answer to it prior to the respondent's decision of September 27, 1993. Accordingly, in view of the unique nature of the foreign domestic program, the applicant was permitted to remain in Canada and continue her employment until such time as the leave application for judicial review was perfected.

Turingan v. Canada (Minister of Employment & Immigration) (1993), 72 F.T.R. 316 (Fed. T.D.) — The applicant came to Canada from the Philippines and worked as a live-in caregiver. During most of the period she resided with her respective employers. In July, 1992, however, she began to experience sharp stomach pain associated with a previously diagnosed peptic ulcer. She found that she could relieve the pain on a diet of rice, vegetables, fish and meat while her employer's family preferred pasta dishes. Embarrassed at the prospect of imposing her diet on her employer's family, she began to have supper and stay over at her friend's apartment, returning to work the next day. The applicant's application for permanent residence was refused on the basis that she did not meet the requirements of the Live-in Caregiver Programme because she had not worked as a live-in caregiver the required twenty-four months. It was conceded by counsel for the Minister that there had been a mistake in the calculation of the length of time and both parties were in agreement that the application should be allowed.

The Court noted, however, that the primary purpose of the Live-in Caregiver Programme was to encourage people to come to Canada to fill a void which exists in our labour market. In consideration for their commitment to work in the domestic field, the programme's participants are virtually guaranteed permanent residence status provided that they work the required twenty-four-month period. The immigration officer, therefore, had limited discretion to refuse permanent residence status once it had been determined that the participant had worked the required 24 months.

The applicant had provided a credible explanation about her living arrangements during the period of her stomach illness. The Court questioned the merits of the Department taking a harsh stance in this type of application. If the Department, however, intended to adopt a strict interpretation of the programme requirements, the basic principles of fairness required that the Department inform the applicant of its conclusions and afford her an opportunity to correct her breach before compelling her to leave the country.

The purpose of the Live-in Caregiver Programme is to facilitate the attainment of permanent residence status. It is therefore incumbent on the Department to adopt a flexible and constructive approach in its dealings with the programme's participants. The Department's role is not to deny permanent residence on merely technical grounds, but rather to work with and assist the participants in reaching their goal of permanent residence status.

11.4 (1) A member of the post-determination refugee claimants in Canada class and the member's dependants, if any, are subject to the following landing requirements:

(a) the member must not be, and no dependant of the member is, a person described in any of paragraphs 19(1)(c) to (g) and (j) to (l) and (2)(a) or subparagraph 19(2)(a.1)(i) of the Act, as determined by an immigration officer pursuant to subsection 6(8) of the Act;

(b) the member must not have been, and no dependant of the member has been, convicted of an offence referred to in paragraph 27(2)(d) of the Act for which a term of imprisonment of more than six months has been imposed or a maximum term of imprisonment of five years or more may be imposed;

(c) the member must have been in Canada on the day on which the member became a member of the post-determination refugee claimants in Canada class and must have remained in Canada since that day; and

(d) the member must be in possession of a valid and subsisting passport or travel document or satisfactory identity documents.

(2) For the purposes of subsection 6(5) of the Act, a person whom the Refugee Division

(a) during the period beginning on February 1, 1993 and ending on April 30, 1997, has determined is not a Convention Refugee is deemed to have submitted an application for landing as a member of the post-determination refugee claimants in Canada class to an immigration officer on the day that the determination is made; and

(b) on or after May 1, 1997, has determined is not a Convention Refugee and who intends to apply for landing as a member of the post-determination refugee claimants in Canada class shall submit an application for a determination of whether the person is a member of that class to an immigration officer not later than 15 days after the day the person is notified of the determination by the Refugee Division.

(3) A person, other than a person referred to in any of subparagraphs (a)(i) to (vii) of the definition "member of the post-determination refugee claimants in Canada class" in subsection 2(1), may make written submissions to an immigration officer respecting any of the matters referred to in paragraph (c) of that definition. The submissions must be received by an immigration officer before

(a) in the case of a person referred to in paragraph (2)(a) whose application for landing is still pending, the later of June 1, 1997 and the day the immigration officer makes a determination respecting that application; and

(b) in the case of a person who submits an application for a determination referred to in paragraph (2)(b), the later of the end of a period of 30 days after the

day the person submits the application and the day the immigration officer makes the determination.

(4) The immigration officer shall take into account

(a) all submissions made by a person in accordance with paragraph (3)(a) before making a determination respecting the person's application for landing and shall not make that determination before June 1, 1997; and

(b) all submissions made by a person in accordance with paragraph (3)(b) before determining whether the person is a member of the post-determination refugee claimants in Canada class and shall not make that determination before the end of the 30 day period referred to in that paragraph.

(5) Notwithstanding subsection (4), an immigration officer may make a determination respecting an application for landing before the date referred to in paragraph (4)(a) or make a determination referred to in paragraph (2)(b) before the end of the 30 day period referred to in paragraph (4)(b), if the person making the application for landing or the person making the application for the determination is a person referred to in any of subparagraphs (a)(i) to (vii) of the definition "member of the post-determination refugee claimants in Canada class" in subsection 2(1).

(6) If the immigration officer determines that a person who has submitted an application for a determination referred to in paragraph (2)(b) is a member of the post-determination refugee claimants in Canada class, the person may submit an application for landing as a member of that class. The application for landing must be submitted to an immigration officer not later than 180 days after the day the person is notified of the determination by the immigration officer.

SOR/93-44 s. 10; SOR/93-412, s. 6; SOR/97-182, s. 5.

Case Law

Section 11.4(2)

Adam v. Canada (Minister of Citizenship & Immigration) (1998), 60 C.C.R. (2d) 354, 16 F.T.R. 42 (Fed. T.D.) — A Post Claim Determination Officer has no discretion inherent or otherwise to extend the time limits for a PDRCC application.

The applicant in this case had also suggested that sections 11.4(2)(b) and 11.4(3)(b) were in violation of section 7 of the *Charter of Rights*. The applicant was found not to have exhausted his legislative avenues of recourse by making a humanitarian and compassionate application prior to making this argument and therefore was found not to be able to establish a *Charter* breach.

Finally, the applicant complained about the inadequacy of her counsel. The age of the applicant, her particular vulnerability without parental guidance and her reliance on friends, relatives and her lawyer for advice made the applicant an unusual and particularly sympathetic case. However, this was not that type of "extraordinary case that would necessitate overturning the decision to the inadequacy of counsel."

11.401 [Revoked SOR/97-182, s. 6].

11.402 (1) Subject to subsection (3), a member of the undocumented Convention refugee in Canada class and the member's dependants, if any, are subject to the following landing requirements:

(a) the member has made an application to an immigration officer for landing as a member of the undocumented Convention refugee in Canada class;

(b) the member has made a solemn declaration in writing, attesting to the truthfulness, to the best of the member's knowledge and belief, of the information contained in the member's application for landing referred to in paragraph (a) and confirming that the member's identity and the identities of the dependants included in that application correspond to the identities of the persons described in the information that the member provided to the Refugee Division pursuant to subsection 14(1) of the *Convention Refugee Determination Division Rules*, or, where the identities do not correspond, identifying and explaining any changes or discrepancies between the application for landing and that information;

(c) the member has not been the subject of a decision of the Refugee Division under subsection 69.3(4) of the Act resulting in the cessation or vacation of the member's status as a Convention refugee;

(d) the member's country of nationality or, if stateless, the member's country of former habitual residence is, on the date of the application for landing referred to in paragraph (a), a country that is set out in Schedule XII;

(e) the dependants included in the member's application for landing referred to in paragraph (a) are dependants who were included in the member's application for landing as a Convention refugee made under subsection 46.04(1) of the Act, and

(i) the member and those dependants have been residing in Canada since the date of the application under that provision of the Act, or

(ii) where the member has been determined to be a Convention refugee before January 31, 1997, those dependants have been residing in Canada since November 16, 1996; and

(f) neither the member nor any of the member's dependants belongs to a class referred to in any of paragraphs 19(1)(c.1) to (g) and (j) to (l) of the Act or has been convicted of an offence under an Act of Parliament for which a term of imprisonment of more than six months has been imposed or for which a term of imprisonment of five years or more may be imposed.

(2) A son or daughter of the member referred to in subsection (1) who, at the date of the member's application for landing as a Convention refugee under subsection 46.04(1) of the Act, was less than nineteen years of age and unmarried shall continue to be considered a dependant son or dependant daughter, as the case may be, for the purposes of subsection (1), unless the son or daughter marries after that date.

(3) A member of the undocumented Convention refugee in Canada class shall not be considered to have failed to meet the requirements of subsection (1) for the sole reason that the member's dependants do not meet the requirements of paragraph (1)(e) or (f).

SOR/97-86, s. 3.

Case Law

Ponnampalam v. Canada (Minister of Citizenship & Immigration) (1996), 34 Imm. L.R. (2d) 166, 117 F.T.R. 294 (Fed. T.D.) — There is no provision in the *Immigration Act* or regulations that confers jurisdiction on an immigration officer to extend the time provided for an application for landing by a member of the Deferred Removal Orders Class (DROC).

The inability to apply for landing under the DROC regulations is not the same as deportation. Deportation of a failed refugee claimant is a separate procedure. The process leading to a deportation order or the execution of that order may engage section 7 of the Charter, but not the DROC decision standing alone.

Mumin v. Canada (Minister of Citizenship & Immigration) (1996), 35 Imm. L.R. (2d) 217 (Fed. T.D.) — This was an application to set aside a decision determining that the applicant was not eligible for consideration under the Deferred Removal Orders Class. The applicant obtained an application for landing kit from an office of the Canada Immigration Centre. This kit did not contain a single green sheet of paper explaining that the minimum period of legal employment was no longer an eligibility criteria. The applicant followed the instructions in the kit with the result that he applied more than a 120 days after becoming eligible with the result that his application was refused.

The decision of the immigration officer refusing the application was set aside. A public authority abuses its discretionary power when it exercises it in a manner which causes an injustice to the individual while at the same time providing no benefit to the public. The courts are entitled under circumstances such as these, to weigh the harm to the applicant against the public interest. There was nothing to be gained and no benefit to the public to be served by compelling the applicant to bear the consequences of the erroneous and incomplete information given to him by the respondent and upon which he honestly relied to his detriment.

The application was allowed, the decision of the immigration office set aside, and the application referred back for reconsideration.

11.41 (1) Where an immigration officer has reasonable grounds to believe that a member of a prescribed class of immigrants referred to in paragraph 11.2(a), (b) or (d), or a dependant of that member, has committed an offence referred to in paragraph 19(1)(c) or (2)(a), subparagraph 19(2)(b)(i) or paragraph 27(1)(d) of the Act, the immigration officer is not required to make a determination respecting the member's application for landing

> **(a) for a period of up to one year after the application for landing has been submitted to the immigration officer, so that charges may be laid against the member or the dependant of the member; or**
>
> **(b) where charges are laid against the member or the dependant of the member, until the courts have made a final determination in respect of the charges.**

(2) Subsection (1) does not apply to a member of the post-determination refugee claimants in Canada class or the undocumented Convention refugee in Canada class or to a dependant of such a member where an immigration officer has reasonable grounds to believe that the member or dependant has committed an offence referred to in subparagraph 19(2)(b)(i) of the Act.

SOR/93-412, s. 7; SOR/94-681, s. 4; SOR/97-86, s. 4.

11.411 Where an immigration officer has reasonable grounds to believe that there is an application under subsection 69.2(1) or (2) of the Act pending in respect of a member of the undocumented Convention refugee in Canada class for the cessation or vacation of the member's status as a Convention refugee, the immigration officer is not required to

make a determination respecting the member's application for landing until a decision has been rendered on the pending application.

SOR/97-86, s. 5.

11.42 [Revoked SOR/97-182, s. 7.]

Prescribed Date for the Purposes of Subsection 7(1) of the Act

11.5 The Minister shall cause the immigration plan for the next calendar year to be laid before each House of Parliament not later than November 1 of each calendar year.

SOR/93-44, s. 10; SOR/94-561, s. 1.

Examination of Immigrants at Ports of Entry

12. An immigrant who has been issued a visa and who appears before an immigration officer at a port of entry for examination pursuant to subsection 12(1) of the Act is required

(a) if his marital status has changed since the visa was issued to him, or

(b) if any other facts relevant to the issuance of the visa have changed since the visa was issued to him or were not disclosed at the time of issue thereof,

to establish that at the time of the examination

(c) the immigrant and the immigrant's dependants, whether accompanying dependants or not, where a visa was issued to the immigrant pursuant to subsection 6(1), section 9 or subsection 10(1) or (1.1) or 11(3) or (4), or

(d) the immigrant and the immigrant's accompanying dependants, in any other case,

meet the requirements of the Act, these Regulations and the *Humanitarian Designated Classes Regulations*, including the requirements for the issuance of the visa.

SOR/83-540, s. 2; SOR/93-44, s. 1; SOR/97-14, s. 4.

Case Law

McLeod v. Canada (Minister of Employment & Immigration) (1998), 46 Imm. L.R. (2d) 295, (sub nom. *McLeod v. Canada (Minister of Citizenship & Immigration))* [1999] 1 F.C. 257, 234 N.R. 89 (Fed. C.A.) — The two appellants and their mother obtained immigrant visas in 1992 while in Jamaica. The mother was the principal applicant and the appellants applied as accompanying dependants. These visas were to expire on December 21, 1992. On November 23, 1992, the mother died. On December 3, 1992, they proceeded to Canada and informed immigration officers of their mother's death. They were denied admission and an inquiry was held on April 8, 1993. They were issued exclusion orders based on paragraph 19(2)(d) of the Act and section 12 of the Regulations. They appealed to the Appeal Division. The Appeal Division held that the appellants were in possession of valid visas and that the Appeal Division therefore had jurisdiction to entertain the appeal. The exclusion orders were quashed on the basis of compassion or humanitarian consideration. The Minister launched an application for judicial review and Noel J., on the consent of both parties, allowed the application and set the Appeal Division decision aside. By agreement he certified this question: "when does a validly issued immigrant visa cease to be valid?"

The Court concluded that there was no adequate basis for deducing from the language of the Act a sanction of invalidity based on a change of circumstances after the issue of a visa. Such a change of circumstances may be a ground for refusal of admission under section 12 of the Regulations, but not on the basis of the invalidity of the visa.

Canada (Minister of Employment & Immigration) v. De Decaro, [1993] 2 F.C. 408, 103 D.L.R. (4th) 564, 155 N.R. 129 (Fed. C.A.) — In October 1988 a visa officer issued an immigrant visa to Ignazio De Decaro. He also issued an immigrant visa to two dependants who were to accompany Mr. De Decaro, namely the respondent and her daughter. Ignazio De Decaro died before coming to Canada. The respondent did come and arrived at Dorval on July 11, 1989 accompanied by her daughter and another child, who was born in the U.S. after Ignazio De Decaro's death and which child had never obtained a visa to Canada.

The respondent then applied for landing for herself and her two children. This was denied on the ground that the respondent's admission contravened section 19(2)(d) of the *Immigration Act* because the respondent did not meet the requirements of section 9(1) of the Act.

The adjudicator found that when the respondent applied for admission to Canada, she held a valid immigrant's visa since her visa had not been revoked by the proper authorities. The adjudicator found that the respondent's husband's death did not automatically invalidate the visa. Further, the adjudicator found that there was no need to refer to section 12 of the regulations because that provision did not enact a condition of admission, and consequently, its infringement did not mean the respondent could not be admitted.

The Appeal Division of the I.R.B. dismissed the Minister's appeal on the basis that the respondent, before appearing at a port of entry, had duly obtained an immigrant visa which had never been revoked or cancelled by the proper authorities and thus the respondent had the right to be admitted to Canada unless she was inadmissible on some other ground than the lack of a valid visa.

The Minister's appeal to the Court of Appeal was allowed. Pratte J.A. held that the definition of "accompanying dependant" illustrated that the visa issued to a person in this class was of a very special type which was issued solely to enable its holder to accompany or follow another person to Canada. The holder of such a visa who applied for admission without the other person accompanying or preceding him or her into Canada did not therefore meet the requirements of section 9(1) of the Act.

Further, after her husband's death the respondent became inadmissible by virtue of section 12 of the regulations. Her marital status had changed since she obtained her visa and in order to be admitted to Canada she had to establish not only that she was eligible, but also that she met all the conditions for obtaining a visa. The respondent never discharged this burden of proof.

Marceau J.A. agreed that the decision of the Appeal Division should be set aside. He saw no reference in the Act or regulations to visas which become invalid, are revoked or become ineffective. The technique in his view used to cover cases of changes in the immigrant's status between the time the visa is issued and the time he or she arrives at the Canadian border is contained in section 12 of the regulations. In his view, issuing an immigrant visa is not the granting of landing. Such issuance simply means that the visa officer has formed the opinion that the applicant meets the requirements of the Act and regulations for admission to Canada. The visa is evidence of a conclusion by an immigration officer whose function is to determine from outside Canada whether applicants are admissible and that conclusion will usually be accepted by his or her colleague at the port of entry. However, the rule is still that a foreign national arriving in Canada with a view to residing here must satisfy the immigration officer of his admissibility at the port of entry. Section 12 of the regulations imposes on an immigrant a duty to disclose any change in the facts which may have influenced the issuing of the visa and if there has been such a change, it requires the immigrant to meet new requirements. The visa is not void, but the visa in itself does not confer the right of entry. It is the new requirements of section 12 of the regulations that must be met.

In Marceau J.A.'s view the respondent could not establish that she met the requirements of section 12 since she was granted a visa in consideration of her husband's presence. The adjudicator accordingly was wrong to think that she met the conditions of admission set out by the Regulation and the Appeal Division could not confirm the adjudicator's finding on the ground that the Minister had not discharged the burden of proving that the respondent was inadmissible or that her visa had been cancelled, as the Minister was under no burden of proof and cancellation of a visa as a concept does not exist.

Given that the Court intended to allow the appeal, it then had to consider section 73(3). The majority was of the view that the respondent, before her husband's death, possessed a valid visa. However, after that death it was impossible for the condition attached to the visa to be performed so the visa ceased to have any validity. Accordingly, section 73(3) conferred no right of appeal to the Appeal Division on the respondent.

Marceau J.A. was of the view that the respondent was in possession of a valid visa and that the matter should be returned to the Appeal Division as it was still under a duty to consider whether on compassionate or humanitarian grounds the respondent should not be removed from Canada.

Members of a Crew

12.1 (1) The following classes of persons are not members of a crew:

(a) members of a crew who have deserted;

(b) members of a crew whom an immigration officer believes on reasonable grounds have deserted;

(c) members of a crew who are hospitalized and who fail to return to the vehicle or to leave Canada within 72 hours after leaving the hospital or within such longer period as may be specified by an immigration officer; and

(d) members of a crew who have been discharged or are otherwise unable or unwilling to perform the duties of a member of a crew and who fail to leave Canada within 72 hours after the discharge or inability or unwillingness to perform those duties or within such longer period as may be specified by an immigration officer.

(2) The following classes of persons who are conveyed on a vehicle are not members of a crew:

(a) persons whose fare is waived in exchange for work to be performed during the voyage;

(b) persons who are on board the vehicle for a purpose other than that of performing duties that relate to the operation of the vehicle and who are not normally on board the vehicle but who, pursuant to a service contract with a transportation company, perform maintenance or repairs while the vehicle is in Canada or during the voyage; and

(c) any other person who is on board the vehicle for a purpose other than that of performing duties that relate to the operation of the vehicle or the provision of services to passengers or members of the crew.

SOR/93-44, s. 12.

Alternate Manners of Examination

12.2 For the purposes of subsection 12(1) of the Act, the following classes of persons may be examined in a manner approved by the Minister instead of appearing before an immigration officer at a port of entry:

(a) members of a crew of a ship that transports oil or liquid natural gas and that docks at a production installation or artificial island to which the *Canadian Laws Offshore Application Act* applies, for the purpose of loading oil or liquid natural gas;

(b) persons who leave Canada and proceed directly to a production installation or artificial island to which the *Canadian Laws Offshore Application Act* applies, and return directly to Canada from the production installation or artificial island without entering the territorial waters of a foreign state;

(c) members of a crew of a ship of foreign registry, other than members of a crew referred to in paragraph (a);

(d) members of a crew of a ship of Canadian registry.

(e) Canadian citizens or permanent residents who are seeking to come into Canada at remote locations after being outside Canada for no longer than 72 hours, where no immigration officer is assigned or where there is no means by which the persons may report for examination;

(f) United States citizens or permanent residents who seek to come into Canada at remote locations, where no immigration officer is assigned or where there are no means by which the persons may report for examination;

(g) citizens or permanent residents of Canada or the United States who seek to come into Canada at places other than a port of entry, where no immigration officer is assigned but where the persons have access to an immigration or customs office by means of a telephone or other means of telecommunication; and

(h) persons who are seeking to come into Canada at a port of entry where facilities are in place for automatic screening of persons seeking to come into Canada.

SOR/93-44, s. 12; SOR/94-242, s. 3.

Visitors' Visas

13. (1) A visitor who is a person referred to in Schedule II is not required to make an application for and obtain a visa before he appears at a port of entry.

(2) A visa officer may issue a visitor's visa to any person who meets the requirements of the Act and these Regulations if that person establishes to the satisfaction of the visa officer that he will be able

(a) to return to the country from which he seeks to come to Canada; or

(b) to go from Canada to some other country.

(3) A diplomatic or consular officer of Canada may, while he is outside Canada, issue a visa to any person who in Canada may be granted privileges or immunities in accordance with the law of Canada as a representative or official of a foreign government or international organization.

(4) Every visitor who is required to obtain a visa, student authorization or employment authorization before he appears at a port of entry shall be in possession of a valid visa, student authorization or employment authorization, as the case may be, when he appears at a port of entry.

SOR/79-51, s. 1; SOR/80-21, s. 1; SOR/80-779, s. 1.

Case Law

Section 13(1)

Okadia v. Canada (Minister of Employment & Immigration) (1983), 5 D.L.R. (4th) 187, 55 N.R. 116 (Fed. C.A.) — Section 13(1) of the *Immigration Regulations* and Schedule II to that regulation are not discriminatory and do not infringe the Canadian *Charter of Rights*.

Section 13(2)

Kenig v. Canada (Minister of Citizenship & Immigration) (1998), 158 F.T.R. 249 (Fed. T.D.) — The applicant sought to review the decision of a visa officer refusing the applicant a visa permitting her to come to Canada as a visitor.

While an applicant's ties to her home country are a factor to be considered, the visa officer, in this case, regarded those ties as the sole factor to be taken into account to the exclusion of substantial evidence as to the temporary nature of the applicant's proposed visit. This amounted to a fettering of the discretion of the visa officer and constituted reviewable error.

The visa officer attested, in his affidavit, that he read and reviewed supporting documentation submitted by the applicant and her representative in support of earlier applications for a visitor's visa. That supporting documentation appears not to have been made a part of the tribunal record filed in this matter. In light of the fact that the visa officer attested that he read and reviewed that documentation it should have constituted part of the record.

De La Cruz v. Canada (Minister of Employment & Immigration) (1988), 26 F.T.R. 285, 7 Imm. L.R. (2d) 75 (Fed. T.D.) — The applicants were citizens of the Philippines. They applied for permanent residence in Canada at the Canadian Consulate General in San Francisco. The applicants were scheduled to be interviewed in San Francisco; however, their applications for tourist visas to the United States were refused by the United States Embassy in Manila. They, therefore, decided to apply at the Consulate in Toronto for a United States visa.

The application for visitors' visas made at the Canadian Embassy in Manila was refused. This decision was upheld. The duty of the visa officer is to accord proper consideration to any application. The officer is not required to issue a visitor's visa unless convinced that the applicant fulfils the legislative requirements. Once the visa officer turns his mind to the issue and disposes of the application for visitors' visas, there remains no duty to be performed that is enforceable by *mandamus*.

To succeed on an application for *certiorari*, the applicants must do more than establish the possibility that the Court might have reached a different conclusion than the visa officer. There must be either an error of law apparent on the face of the record or a breach of the duty of fairness appropriate to this essentially administrative decision. It is not improper for the visa officer to refuse the visitors' visas on the basis of an outstanding application for permanent residence. It is the intent of the applicant that is properly the focus of the visa officer's examination. No policy dictates refusal simply because the applicants intend to apply for United States visas. Further, the officer had not based his decision solely on the refusal of United States officials to grant the applicants' request for visas to the United States. Accordingly, the decision of the visa officer was upheld.

Kahlon v. Canada (Minister of Employment & Immigration), [1986] 3 F.C. 386 (Fed. C.A.), reversing [1985] 2 F.C. 124 (Fed. T.D.) — The applicant sponsored his relatives' family class application for permanent residence. The application was denied and the applicant appealed to the Immigration Appeal Board. The visa officer refused to issue visitors' visas to the relatives who were required as witnesses at his appeal. The visas were refused on the basis that the applicants were not *bona fide* visitors because their intention was to testify at the applicant's appeal. An order of *mandamus* was issued requiring the Minister to grant the relatives visitors' visas to allow them to testify at the appeal. This order was reversed on appeal. *Mandamus* will issue to require performance of a duty; it cannot, however, dictate the result to be reached. *Certiorari* might have been available to quash the refusal of the visitors' visas and to refer the matter back for reconsideration but the respondent had not sought this type of order.

Passports and Travel Documents

14. (1) Subject to subsection (2), every immigrant shall be in possession of

(a) a valid and subsisting passport issued to that immigrant by the country of which he is a citizen or national, other than a diplomatic, official or other similar passport;

(b) a valid and subsisting travel document issued to that immigrant by the country of which he is a citizen or national;

(c) a valid and subsisting identity or travel document

(i) that was issued to that immigrant by a country, and

(ii) that is of the type issued to non-national residents of the country of issue, refugees or stateless persons who are unable to obtain a passport or other travel document from their country of citizenship or nationality, or who have no country of citizenship or nationality; or

(d) a valid and subsisting identify or travel document issued to that immigrant and specified in item 1 of Schedule VII.

(2) Subsection (1) does not apply to a person who is a Convention refugee seeking resettlement, a member of the country of asylum class or a member of the source country class and who is in possession of a valid and subsisting immigrant visa where, in the opinion of the visa officer who issued the immigrant visa, it would, in practice, be impossible for that person to obtain a passport or an identity or travel document.

(3) Subject to subsection (4), every visitor shall be in possession of

(a) a valid and subsisting passport valid for travel to Canada, issued to that visitor by the country of which he is a citizen or national and recognized by the country of issue as giving that visitor the right to enter the country of issue;

(b) a valid and subsisting travel document issued to that visitor by the country of which he is a citizen or national and recognized by the country of issue as giving that visitor the right to enter the country of issue;

(c) a valid and subsisting identity or travel document that

(i) was issued to that visitor by a country,

(ii) is recognized by the country of issue as giving that visitor the right to enter the country of issue, and

(iii) is of the type issued to non-national residents of the country of issue, refugees or stateless persons who are unable to obtain a passport or other travel document from their country of citizenship or nationality, or who have no country of citizenship or nationality; or

(d) a valid and subsisting identity or travel document issued to that visitor and specified in item 2 of Schedule VII.

(4) Subsection (3) does not apply to

(a) a visitor who is a citizen of the United States;

(b) a visitor seeking entry from the United States or St. Pierre and Miquelon who has been lawfully admitted to the United States for permanent residence;

(c) a visitor seeking entry from Greenland who is a resident of Greenland;

(d) a visitor seeking entry from St. Pierre and Miquelon who is a citizen of France and a resident of St. Pierre and Miquelon;

(e) a member of the armed forces of a country that is a designated state for the purposes of the *Visiting Forces Act* who is seeking entry in order to carry out his official duties, other than a person who has been designated as a civilian component of that visiting force; or

(f) a visitor who is seeking entry as or in order to become a member of the crew of a vehicle and who is in possession of a seaman's identity document issued to him pursuant to International Labour Organization conventions, or an airline flight crew licence or crew member certificate issued to him in accordance with International Civil Aviation Organization specifications.

(5) A passport, identity or travel document specified in item 3 of Schedule VII is not a valid and subsisting passport, identity or travel document for the purposes of subsections (1) and (3).

(6) Every visitor seeking entry may be required to produce sufficient documentary evidence to establish to the satisfaction of an immigration officer that he will be able to return to the country from which he seeks entry or to go from Canada to some other country.

SOR/78-745, s. 1; SOR/80-21, s. 2; SOR/83-339, s. 2; SOR/84-809, s. 1; SOR/89-38, s. 2; SOR/94-242, s. 4; SOR/97-184, s. 5.

Student Authorizations

14.1 Subject to sections 14.2 and 14.3, no person, other than a Canadian citizen or a permanent resident, shall attend any university or college or take any academic, professional or vocational training course in Canada unless that person possesses a valid and subsisting student authorization.

SOR/89-38, s. 3; SOR/90-202, s. 1.

14.2 Section 14.1 does not apply to a person who seeks to come into Canada for the purpose of attending a university or college, or taking an academic, professional or vocational training course or a person in Canada who is attending or seeks to attend a university or college or is taking or seeks to take an academic, professional or vocational training course if

(a) the person is the dependant of any diplomatic or consular officer, representative or official, properly accredited, of a country other than Canada or of the United Nations or any of its agencies or of any intergovernmental organization of which Canada is a member who is coming into or is in Canada to carry out official duties or any member of the staff of that officer, representative or official, or

(b) the sole course taken or to be taken is a French or English language training course that is three months or less in duration.

SOR/89-38, s. 3; SOR/92-101, s. 8.

14.3 (1) There shall be exempt from the requirement to obtain a student authorization, for any of the purposes referred to in section 14.1, any person

(a) who was in Canada on January 1, 1989 or had, prior to that date, been directed to return to the United States pursuant to subsection 23(5) of the Act to await the availability of an adjudicator to preside at an inquiry to be held on or after that date; and

(b) whose intention to make a claim to be a Convention refugee was signified by the person before January 1, 1989 to

(i) an immigration officer, who recorded that intention before that date, or a person acting on an immigration officer's behalf, who an immigration officer is satisfied recorded that intention before that date, or

(ii) an adjudicator in the course of an inquiry respecting the person's status in Canada.

(2) No exemption under subsection (1) applies to a person who

(a) has been determined to be a Convention refugee under the Act as it read before January 1, 1989;

(b) is the subject of a removal order or a departure order and has not been removed from, or has not otherwise left, Canada;

(c) has failed to appear for

(i) completion, pursuant to paragraph 12(3)(a) of the Act, of an examination,

(ii) an inquiry respecting that person's status in Canada, or for the continuation of such an inquiry, where the person was given an appointment therefor, or

(iii) an examination under oath with respect to the person's claim to be a Convention refugee, or for the continuation of such an examination, where the person was given an appointment therefor; or

(d) is described in paragraph 19(1)(c), (e), (f), (g) or (j) or 27(2)(c) of the Act.

(3) There shall be exempt from the requirement to obtain a student authorization, for any of the purposes referred to in section 14.1, any person who is a dependant of a person exempt under subsection (1).

SOR/90-202, s. 2; SOR/92-14, s. 1; SOR/93-44, s. 29; SOR/94-22, s. 1.

15. (1) Every application for a student authorization shall be accompanied by

(a) a letter from a university, college or other institution referred to in paragraph 10(a) or (b) of the Act accepting the applicant to attend or to take any specified course at the university, college or other institution;

(b) sufficient documentation to enable an immigration officer to satisfy himself that the applicant has sufficient financial resources available to him, without engaging in employment in Canada,

(i) to pay his tuition fees,

(ii) to maintain himself and any dependants who will come into Canada during the period for which he seeks a student authorization, and

(iii) to pay the transportation costs to and from Canada for himself and any dependants referred to in subparagraph (ii); and

(c) the consent in writing of the government of the province in which the applicant wishes to study where such consent is required by that government pursuant to an agreement entered into by the Minister with that government pursuant to section 108 of the Act.

(1.01) Paragraphs (1)(a) and (b) do not apply in respect of an application to attend a primary or secondary school that is submitted by a dependant of a holder of a student authorization or employment authorization.

(1.1) Subparagraph 15(1)(b)(ii) does not apply in respect of an application submitted by

(a) a person whose claim to Convention refugee status has been referred to the Refugee Division pursuant to subsection 48.02(2) or 48.03(5) of the Act, as amended by S.C. 1988, c. 35, s. 14; or

(b) a dependant of a person referred to in paragraph (a).

(2) A person who seeks to come into Canada for a purpose referred to in paragraph 10(a) or (b) of the Act is not required to obtain a student authorization before that person appears at a port of entry if that person is a dependant of

(a) [Revoked SOR/89-38, s. 4.]

(b) a member of the armed forces of a country that is a designated state for the purposes of the *Visiting Forces Act* who is coming to or is in Canada in order to carry out his official duties, including a person who has been designated as a civilian component of that visiting force;

(c) a clergyman or member of a religious order coming to or in Canada for the temporary carrying out of his religious duties;

(d) an employee of a foreign news company coming to or in Canada for the purpose of reporting on Canadian events;

(e) a person coming to or in Canada to engage in athletic or other sport activities or events as a player, manager, coach, trainer or administrative employee for a Canadian-based team, group or organization or a person engaged as a referee, umpire or other similar official with respect to any athletic or other sport activity or event in Canada;

(f) a person in possession of a valid and subsisting student authorization;

(g) a person in possession of a valid and subsisting employment authorization; or

(h) a representative of a foreign government sent by that government to take up duties with a federal or provincial agency pursuant to an exchange agreement with Canada.

(3) A person who seeks to come into Canada for a purpose referred to in paragraph 10(a) or (b) of the Act is not required to obtain a student authorization before that person appears at a port of entry if that person is

(a) a national of the United States;

(b) a person who has been lawfully admitted to the United States for permanent residence;

(c) a resident of Greenland;

(d) a resident of St. Pierre and Miquelon; or

(e) a person whose application for a student authorization has been approved in writing by a visa officer but to whom the authorization has not been issued.

SOR/78-938, s. 1; SOR/79-240, s. 2; SOR/83-339, s. 3; SOR/88-111, s. 1; SOR/89-38, s. 4; SOR/92-101, s. 9; SOR/93-44, s. 13; SOR/93-412, s. 9.

Case Law

Totrova v. Canada (Minister of Citizenship & Immigration) (1998), 47 Imm. L.R. (2d) 123 (Fed. T.D.) — The applicant sought to review a decision of a visa officer refusing her application for a student visa. The applicant was a 30-year-old professional interpreter and translator. She was divorced and had sole custody of her 10-year-old child who was to accompany her to Canada. The applicant intended to come to Canada to pursue a 2-year MBA course at the University of Toronto. She applied for a student visa at the Canadian Embassy in Moscow and this was turned down by a visa officer who was of the view that because the applicant had been sentimentally involved with Canadians in the recent past and because her child was accompanying her, he was of the opinion that her ties to her home country were too weak and that she would not return to Russia. The applicant reapplied for a student visa. This was turned down on the basis that the visa officer was not satisfied that she was entering Canada for a temporary purpose. The visa officer was satisfied that the applicant had adequate financial arrangements in place to support the applicant and her son for the duration of their stay in Canada. The officer was also concerned over the vague nature of the applicant's future plans.

These two key considerations that is, insufficient ties to Russia, and a vague nature of the applicant's future plans, were totally inconsistent with the undisputed evidence that the applicant still had her parents, her son's father and a boyfriend in Russia. The applicant also confirmed to the visa officer that she would not seek to stay permanently in Canada because of the apparent possibility of increased employment opportunities in Russia. Given the clear and stated purpose in her application for a student visa of embarking upon a 2-year course of study at the University of Toronto which is clearly a temporary purpose, and given the fact that the applicant never expressed the intention of remaining in Canada after her studies, save for the possibility of obtaining 1 or 2 years' employment experience should that become possible, the visa officer's decision was based on erroneous findings of fact made without regard for that evidence.

Mittal (Litigation Guardian of) v. Canada (Minister of Citizenship & Immigration) (1998), 147 F.T.R. 285 (Fed. T.D.) — The applicant sought to review a visa officer's refusal to issue student authorizations to the applicants. Guidelines for the use of officers in assessing applications for student visas were in existence at the time this case arose. Guidelines serve as general policy or rough rules of thumb to structure the discretion conferred upon visa officers. Guidelines should not fetter the visa officer's exercise of discretion by crystallizing into binding and conclusive rules. The applicant and his brother were citizens of India and lived in New Delhi with their parents. In March 1997, they applied for temporary entry into Canada as students for the 1997-1998 academic year. The visa officer decided that the applicants did not have sufficient funds for their tuition fees, maintenance and transportation costs.

The applicant's material concerning the financing of their 1-year academic stay was straightforward. Letters of acceptance, courses in grades 5 and 8 from their private school in Toronto established partial payment of $7,500 tuition fee for each student. A Canadian chartered bank confirmed that it held $10,000 in mutual fund investments for each child. The applicant's uncle and aunt who reside in Scarborough, Ontario undertook to provide all material support during their stay. The same chartered bank confirmed that it employed the uncle as an accountant manager at an annual salary of $43,000. The uncle deposed that the applicants also had term deposits with the chartered bank. The visa officer received other information concerning the business and land investments of the applicants' father.

The family's net worth was not relevant to an assessment of the applicants' ability to meet the criteria of paragraph 15(1)(b) of the *Immigration Regulations*. The applicants had sufficient financial resources for the 1-year period for which the student authorizations were sought.

The visa officer also found that there were no credible reasons for the applicants to be studying in Canada. It is in the nature of student visas that they are issued for limited periods of time. The question of *bona fides* is not so much whether the applicant is a prospective immigrant but whether the applicant is a prospective illegal immigrant.

16. (1) A person in Canada may make an application for the purpose of obtaining a student authorization

(a) if that person is

(i) a person referred to in subsection 15(2),

(ii) a person in possession of a valid and subsisting student authorization,

(iii) a person in possession of a permit issued by the Minister under section 37 of the Act or a dependant of that person,

(iv) a person whose claim to Convention refugee status has been referred to the Refugee Division but the claim has not been finally determined,

(v) a dependant of a person referred to in subparagraph (iv), or

(vi) a person referred to in paragraph 15(3)(e);

(b) where the taking of the course for the purpose of which he makes an application for a student authorization would only be incidental and secondary to the main purpose of his presence in Canada; or

(c) if that person has been authorized to remain in Canada as a visitor pursuant to subsection 27(2.1) of the Act and was in possession of a valid and subsisting student authorization at the time the person ceased to be a visitor.

(2) [Revoked SOR/80-601, s. 1.]

SOR/79-240, s. 3; SOR/80-21, s. 3; SOR/80-601, s. 1; SOR/89-38, s. 5; SOR/93-44, s. 14; SOR/93-412, s. 10.

Case Law

Section 16(1)

Kouchaki v. Canada (Minister of Employment & Immigration) (November 29, 1984), Doc. T-3070-83 (Fed. T.D.) — The applicant is the plaintiff in a civil action seeking a declaration that the reason for the refusal of the extension of his student visa was unlawful and that the plaintiff was entitled to remain in Canada to study, effective September 30, 1983. The plaintiff also sought the quashing of the departure notice issued at the conclusion of the inquiry herein. Where the validity of the deportation order is not in question prohibition will not lie to permit the applicant to exhaust all legal remedies. However, if the Minister wishes to refuse extensions, this must be done fairly which implies the giving of a reason for the refusal. Because the action questions the validity of the decision to refuse to renew a student visa and raises substantial issues, justice required that the applicant be permitted to remain in Canada until trial.

Kouchaki v. Canada (Minister of Employment & Immigration); Shamsvandi v. Canada (Minister of Employment & Immigration) (April 6, 1984), Doc. T-3070-83, T-3096-83 (Fed. T.D.) — Both of these cases were applications for an interlocutory interim order prohibiting the defendent from proceeding with an inquiry. The plaintiffs entered Canada in 1981 and were authorized to study. Various extensions of this authorization were granted. On September 30, 1983 a further extension was refused and a direction for inquiry was issued and separate inquiries commenced in November 1983. In the main actions the plaintiffs are attacking the validity of the defendants' refusal to extend their authorizations to study. Pending final disposition of these actions, the interlocutory interim order was sought prohibiting the conduct of the inquiry.

An individual permitted to enter Canada to pursue a course of study should, normally, have his student authorization extended to enable him to complete those studies. Where it is alleged that the individual is conducting himself in a manner which is inconsistent with his student status the respondent minister is under a duty to act in accordance with the provisions of this Act. Further, the Court does not have a general power to suspend the performance of a statutory duty in cases where the performance of the statutory duty might have an adverse affect on some right which the applicant has sought to assert in another forum. Section 51 of the *Immigration Act* specifies the cases in which the execution of a removal order may be stayed. By implication this section excludes any other stay of execution, including one in the exercise of judicial discretion.

The Court should not issue an order directing the respondent not to proceed with an inquiry which he is under a statutory duty to hold solely because the applicants have not exhausted legal remedies available to them.

17. (1) A student authorization may not be obtained by any person for the purpose of taking any academic, professional or vocational training course unless that course

(a) is of at least six months duration and at the rate of at least twenty-four hours of instruction per week;

(b) is given at any institution described in paragraph 10(a) of the Act or any other publicly-funded institution;

(c) is recommended by a minister of the Government of Canada, other than the Minister of Employment and Immigration, or by a minister of the government of any province or by any agency of the Government of Canada or the government of any province;

(d) is incidental and secondary to the main purpose of that person's presence in Canada; or

(e) involves upgrading of skills or language training and is given at an institution that operates under a provincial or federal licence.

(2) No visitor may be granted entry for the purpose of taking any academic, professional or vocational training course at any university, college or other institution listed in Schedule III.

SOR/80-21, s. 4; SOR/89-38, s. 6.

Employment Authorizations

18. (1) Subject to subsections 19(1) to (2.2), no person, other than a Canadian citizen or permanent resident, shall engage or continue in employment in Canada without a valid and subsisting employment authorization.

(2) No person who is in possession of a valid and subsisting employment authorization shall continue in employment in Canada unless he complies with each of the terms and conditions specified in the authorization.

SOR/89-80, s. 1.

19. (1) Subsection 18(1) does not apply to a person who seeks to come into Canada for the purpose of engaging in employment or a person in Canada who seeks to engage or continue in employment

(a) as a properly accredited diplomat, consular officer, representative or official

(i) of a country, other than Canada,

(ii) of the United Nations or any of its agencies, or

(iii) of any intergovernmental organization in which Canada participates, or

as a member of the suite of any such diplomat, consular officer, representative or official;

(b) as a member of the armed forces of a country that is a designated state for the purposes of the *Visiting Forces Act*, including a person who has been designated as a civilian component of that visiting force pursuant to paragraph 4(c) of that Act;

(c) as a clergyman, a member of a religious order or a lay person to assist a congregation or a group in the achievement of its spiritual goals where the duties to be performed by that person will consist mainly of preaching of doctrine, presiding at liturgical functions or spiritual counselling;

(d) as a performing artist, a member of a group of performing artists or a member of the staff of the performing artists or the group, where the artist or the group and the staff that accompanies the artist or the group, as the case may be, number not less than 15;

(e) as a member of the crew of a vehicle of foreign ownership or foreign registry engaged predominantly in the international transportation of goods or passengers;

(e.1) as a civil aviation inspector of a recognized national aeronautical authority, conducting inspections of flight operation procedures or cabin safety of a commercial air carrier operating international flights;

(f) as an employee of a foreign news company for the purpose of reporting on Canadian events;

(g) as a representative of a business carrying on activities outside Canada or of a foreign government for the purpose of purchasing Canadian goods or services for that business or foreign government, including a person coming to or in Canada for the purpose of

> **(i) inspecting, during or after manufacturing, the quality of the goods purchased, or**
>
> **(ii) acquiring training or familiarization with the goods or services purchased,**

where that representative will not be actively engaged in production of goods or services in Canada;

(h) as a representative of a business carrying on activities outside Canada or of a foreign government coming to or in Canada for a period of less than 90 days for the purpose of selling goods or services for that business or foreign government, where that representative will not be engaged in making sales to the general public;

(i) as a permanent employee of a corporation, union or other organization carrying on business or operating outside Canada who is coming to or in Canada for a period of less than 90 days for the purpose of consulting with other employees or members of that corporation, union or other organization, or inspecting a Canadian branch office or headquarters on behalf of that corporation, union or other organization;

(j) for the purpose of rendering emergency medical or other services for the preservation of life or property;

(j.1) as an accredited representative or an adviser participating in an aviation accident or incident investigation conducted under the authority of the Canadian Transportation Accident Investigation and Safety Board;

(k) as a member of a non-Canadian-based team to engage or assist in sport activities or events or as an individual participant to engage in sport activities or events other than as a referee, umpire or similar official;

(l) as a judge, referee or similar official in an international sporting event organized by an international amateur sporting association and hosted by a Canadian organization;

(m) as a judge at an animal show competition;

(n) as an external examiner of a degree-qualifying thesis or project;

(o) as a guest speaker for the sole purpose of making a speech or delivering a paper at a dinner, graduation, convention or similar function;

(p) as an expert witness for the sole purpose of testifying in proceedings before a regulatory board or tribunal or a court;

(q) as a permanently employed personal servant coming into or in Canada for a period of less than 90 days for the purpose of performing his regular duties with his employer during the latter's sojourn in Canada;

(r) as an officer of a foreign government sent by his government to take up duties with a federal or provincial agency pursuant to an exchange agreement with Canada;

(s) as a medical elective or clinical clerk at a Canadian medical teaching institution, where that person will merely be observing clinical or medical procedures;

(t) as a trainee with a Canadian parent or subsidiary corporation, where that trainee will not be actively engaged in the production of goods or services;

(u) as an executive of the organizing committee of a convention or meeting or as a member of the administrative support staff of such a committee who is permanently employed by the organization holding the convention or meeting;

(v) as a person who pursuant to paragraphs 1 to 3 under the heading "Canada" in Annex 1502.1 of the Agreement as defined in section 2 of the *Canada-United States Free Trade Agreement Implementation Act* is exempted from the requirement to obtain an employment authorization;

(w) as a person who, pursuant to paragraphs 1 to 5 under Annex 1603.A of the Agreement, as defined in subsection 2(1) of the *North American Free Trade Agreement Implementation Act*, is exempted from the requirement to obtain an employment authorization;

(x) as a person who holds a student authorization and who, during the period that the person is a full-time student at the local campus of a university or college, is employed on that campus; or

(y) as a person who, pursuant to paragraphs 1 to 5 of Annex K-03, Section I of the Agreement, as defined in subsection 2(1) of the *Canada-Chile Free Trade Agreement Implementation Act*, is exempted from the requirement to obtain an employment authorization.

(1.1) The operation of paragraph (1)(v) is suspended during the period in which paragraph (1)(w) is in force.

(2) Notwithstanding subsection (1), no person described in that subsection may engage or continue in employment in Canada in any secondary employment without an employment authorization.

(2.1) There shall be exempt from the requirement to obtain an employment authorization, for any of the purposes referred to in subsection 18(1), any person who seeks to engage or continue in employment in Canada in an occupation other than an occupation in which the protection of public health is essential and who is a person, or a dependant of a person, exempt under subsection 14.3(1).

(2.2) There shall be exempt from the requirement to obtain an employment authorization, for any of the purposes referred to in subsection 18(1), any person, or a dependant of a person,

(a) who is exempt under subsection 14.3(1);

(b) who seeks to engage or continue in employment in Canada in an occupation in which the protection of public health is essential; and

(c) who has undergone a medical examination and is in possession of a valid and subsisting certificate of medical assessment signed by a medical officer and stating that in the opinion of the medical officer the person is not suffering from any disease, disorder, disability or other health impairment that may endanger public health.

(3) A person who seeks to come into Canada for a purpose referred to in paragraph 10(c) of the Act, other than a person referred to in subsection (1), may apply for an employment authorization at a port of entry if

(a) that person is

(i) a national of the United States,

(ii) a person who has been lawfully admitted to the United States for permanent residence,

(iii) a resident of St. Pierre and Miquelon or Greenland,

(iv) a person referred to in paragraph 4(d), (f), (g) or (h) or 20(5)(b) or (d),

(v) a person whose application for an employment authorization has been approved in writing by a visa officer but to whom the authorization has not been issued, or

(vi) a person referred to in paragraph 20(5)(e), other than a person who is seeking to come into Canada for the purpose of establishing a business in Canada; and

(b) except in the case of a person described in paragraph 20(5)(b), (d) or (e), the person possesses sufficient documentation to enable an immigration officer to form an opinion for the purposes of paragraph 20(1)(a).

(4) A person in Canada may make an application for the purpose of obtaining an employment authorization if he is

(a) a person referred to in paragraph (1)(a), (b), (c), (f) or (r) or a dependant of that person;

(b) a person who is in possession of a valid and subsisting student authorization or a dependant of that person;

(c) a person who is in possession of a valid and subsisting employment authorization or a dependant of that person;

(d) a person engaged in sport activities or events as a player, manager, coach, trainer or administrative employee of a Canadian based team, group or organization or a dependant of that person or a person engaged as a referee, umpire or other similar official with respect to any sport activity or event in Canada;

(e) the holder of a permit referred to in section 37 of the Act or a dependant of that person;

(f) a person required in Canada to carry out emergency repairs to industrial equipment in order to prevent disruption of employment;

(g) a person who is a member of the crew of a ship of foreign ownership or foreign registry that is operated in Canadian waters;

(h) a person under contract to fulfill a single or continuous guest engagement in the performing arts, except where the engagement is merely incidental to a commercial activity that does not limit itself to artistic presentation or constitutes employment in a permanent position in a Canadian organization;

(i) a person who has applied for an exemption pursuant to section 2.1 and who has been referred by an immigration officer for a determination of whether the person is a member of an inadmissible class, where the application for exemption has not been refused;

(j) a person who has been determined to be a Convention refugee

(i) under these Regulations, or

(ii) under section 71.1 of the Act, as amended by S.C. 1988, c. 35, s. 18, by the Refugee Division;

(k) a person who, in the opinion of an immigration officer, could not otherwise subsist without public assistance and who

(i) has made a claim referred to in subsection 43(1) of the Act that he is a Canadian citizen, which claim has not been finally determined,

(ii) has been made a claim to be a Convention refugee that has been referred to the Refugee Division before February 1, 1993, pursuant to subsection 46.02(2) or 46.03(1) of the Act as that subsection read before February 1, 1993, which claim has not been finally determined,

(iii) is a person with respect to whom the execution of a removal order has been stayed by the Board,

(iv) is a person against whom a removal order has been made that cannot be executed,

(v) is a person referred to in paragraph 52(1)(b) of the Act with respect to whom the Minister has stayed the execution of a removal order or a person whose presence is required in Canada in any criminal proceedings,

(vi) is a person awaiting the determination of an appeal under the Act commenced with respect to a removal order or a conditional removal order made against that person, or

(vii) is a person who is a visitor, entered Canada on or before August 31, 1990, has not left Canada for more than seven consecutive days since that date and is awaiting the determination of the person's application made pursuant to section 5 of the *Self-Exiled Persons Designated Class Regulations*;

(l) a person who has been authorized to remain in Canada as a visitor pursuant to subsection 27(2.1) of the Act and was in possession of a valid and subsisting employment authorization at the time the person ceased to be a visitor;

(m) a person referred to in subparagraph (3)(a)(v);

(n) a member of the post-determination refugee claimants in Canada class or a dependant of the member, where the dependant was in Canada on the day on which that member became a member of the post-determination refugee claimants in Canada class;

(o) a member of the live-in caregivers in Canada class or a dependant of the member, where the dependant was in Canada on the day on which that member became a member of the live-in caregivers in Canada class;

(p) a person who is a visitor, and

(i) who is a citizen of a country that, on January 1, 1994, was a NAFTA country, as defined in subsection 2(1) of the *North American Free Trade Agreement Implementation Act*,

(ii) who is submitting an application for the purpose of working as a trader or investor, intra-company transferee, or professional, as described in Section B, C or D, as applicable of Annex 1603 of the Agreement, as defined in

subsection 2(1) of the *North American Free Trade Agreement Implementation Act*, and

(iii) whose country of citizenship, described in subparagraph (i), grants, to Canadian citizens who submit an application within that country for the purpose referred to in subparagraph (ii), treatment equivalent to that accorded by Canada to citizens of that country who submit an application within Canada for that purpose, including treatment in respect of multiple entries based on a single application;

(q) a person who has made a claim to be a Convention refugee that has been referred to the Refugee Division pursuant to section 46.02 of the Act but that has not been finally determined, and who

(i) could not otherwise subsist without public assistance,

(ii) has undergone, and whose dependants in Canada have undergone, a medical examination by a medical officer, the results of which have been submitted by the medical officer to an immigration officer,

(iii) has been photographed and fingerprinted pursuant to paragraph 44(e), and

(iv) has submitted to the Board the form referred to in subrule 14(2) of the *Convention Refugee Determination Division Rules*; or

(r) a person who, following a determination by the Refugee Division that the person is not a Convention refugee, applies for leave to commence an application for judicial review under the *Federal Court Act* or for judicial review, and who

(i) could not otherwise subsist without public assistance,

(ii) has undergone, and whose dependants in Canada have undergone, a medical examination by a medical officer, the results of which have been submitted by the medical officer to an immigration officer, and

(iii) has been photographed and fingerprinted pursuant to paragraph 44(e).

(s) [Revoked SOR/97-182, s. 8.]

(5) [Revoked SOR/84-849, s. 1.]

SOR/78-624, s. 1; SOR/78-734, s. 1; SOR/78-938, s. 2; SOR/80-21, ss. 5, 6; SOR/80-601, s. 2; SOR/83-339, s. 4; SOR/84-849, s. 1; SOR/85-131, s. 1; SOR/86-109, s. 1; SOR/86-703, s. 1; SOR/89-38, s. 7; SOR/89-42, s. 1; SOR/89-80, s. 2; SOR/89-168, s. 1; SOR/90-202, s. 3; SOR/91-497, s. 1; SOR/92-14, s. 2; SOR/92-101, s. 10; SOR/93-44, s. 15; SOR/93-225, s. 1; SOR/93-412, s. 11; SOR/93-609, s. 1; SOR/94-22, s. 2; SOR/94-131, s. 1; SOR/94-681, s. 6; SOR/94-773, s. 1; SOR/95-24, s. 1; SOR/95-353, s. 5; SOR/97-182, s. 8; SOR/97-316, s. 1; SOR/99-254, s. 1.

Case Law

Section 19(2)

Canada (Minister of Employment & Immigration) v. O'Brien (1993), 22 Imm. L.R. (2d) 28, 161 N.R. 141 (Fed. C.A.) — The respondent, an American citizen, was authorized by an employment authorization to work as a treasurer of the Detroit/Windsor Tunnel Company. During a strike by employees of the Canadian subsidiary — the Detroit/Windsor Subway Company — the respondent, along with several Canadian supervisors, engaged in collecting tolls and inspecting vehicles for hazardous materials. On appeal it was held that these extra duties forced upon the respondent by the strike did not constitute secondary employment because they were duties normally expected to be done by management employees in an extraordinary situation.

In the context of this case the Court referred to the Canadian Classification and Dictionary of Occupations ("CCDO") as an internal document of the Department that was not useful in this proceeding because it was vague, imprecise, did not easily fit all categories of occupations in the actual world of employment and was unsatisfactory as an arbitrary definition of occupations.

Section 19(4)

Sharoni v. Canada (Minister of Employment & Immigration) (November 30, 1988), Doc. T-1002-88 (Fed. T.D.) — This application for an order of *mandamus* directing the respondent Minister to issue a work authorization pursuant to sections 20(5)(a) and 19(4)(k)(v) of the regulation was dismissed.

Mr. Sharoni arrived at a Toronto immigration office on May 17, 1988. He indicated that he had been in Canada illegally since 1985 and intended to pursue a claim for refugee status. On May 20, 1988, the applicant returned to the immigration office and asked for a work permit. He indicated that he had been charged with a criminal offence and was released on a recognizance. It was his submission that he had thereby become a person whose presence was required in a criminal proceeding. Section 19(4)(k)(v) of the regulation did not benefit the applicant because it was confined to those whose presence was required as a witness in criminal proceedings.

Piperno v. Canada (Minister of Employment & Immigration) (February 3, 1984), Doc. T-101-84 (Fed. T.D.) — The following decision illustrates how the Court will analyze applications for *mandamus* directed to an immigration officer to compel the issuance of an employment authorization. The regulations have changed since this decision was granted; thus, the reasoning process may be more important than the resolution of the application.

The applicant claimed refugee status in Canada. His claim had been denied and there was an application before the Immigration Appeal Board for redetermination of the claim. The applicant had obtained two offers of part-time employment. He made two applications for an employment authorization and both were refused. *Mandamus* was denied because the immigration officer had a discretion with respect to issuing the employment authorization. There was no evidence of bad faith, and, thus, the officer in refusing could not be said to have breached his duty to act fairly towards the applicant. There was no evidence that regulatory provisions enacted for the applicant's protection had not been observed. Finally, the discretion could not be said to have been exercised on a wrong principle because the officer gave no reasons in refusing the authorization. The fact that no reasons were given could not be attacked because the Act did not require the officer to give reasons for refusing the authorization.

19.1 (1) An employment authorization issued to a person referred to in paragraph 19(4)(q) is subject to terms and conditions respecting

(a) the types of employment in which the person may engage;

(b) prohibitions against attending any university, college or other institution and against taking any academic, professional or vocational training course at any university, college or other institution; and

(c) evidence of compliance with the terms or conditions that the employment authorization is subject to.

(2) An employment authorization issued to a person referred to in paragraph 19(4)(r) is subject to terms and conditions respecting

(a) the types of employment in which the person may engage;

(b) the identity and location of the employer with which the person may engage or continue in employment;

(c) prohibitions against attending any university, college or other institution and against taking any academic, professional or vocational training course at any university, college or other institution; and

(d) evidence of compliance with the terms or conditions that the employment authorization is subject to.

(3) [Revoked SOR/97-182, s. 9.]

SOR/94-131, s. 2; SOR/94-681, s. 7; SOR/97-182, s. 9.

19.2 (1) Subject to subsection (2), an employment authorization issued to a person referred to in paragraph 19(4)(q) is valid for the lesser of the period beginning on the day on which

(a) the employment authorization is issued and ending on the day on which, following a Refugee Division determination that the person is not a Convention refugee, an immigration officer determines that the person is not a member of the post-determination refugee claimants in Canada class;

(b) the employment authorization is issued and ending on the day on which the Refugee Division determines that the person has abandoned the claim; and

(c) the person's claim to be a Convention refugee was referred to the Refugee Division pursuant to section 46.02 of the Act and ending nine months after that date.

(2) An immigration officer may extend the period of validity referred to in paragraph (1)(c) where the Minister or the Refugee Division is responsible for any significant delay in the hearing or determination of the claim.

(3) An employment authorization issued to a person referred to in paragraph 19(4)(r) is valid until the day on which

(a) the Federal Court — Trial Division denies the application for leave to commence an application for judicial review; or

(b) following a final judicial determination that the person is not a Convention refugee, an immigration officer determines that the person is not a member of the post-determination refugee claimants in Canada class.

SOR/94-131, s. 2.

20. (1) An immigration officer shall not issue an employment authorization to a person if,

(a) in his opinion, employment of the person in Canada will adversely affect employment opportunities for Canadian citizens or permanent residents in Canada; or

(b) the issue of the employment authorization will affect

(i) the settlement of any labour dispute that is in progress at the place or intended place of employment, or

(ii) the employment of any person who is involved in such a dispute.

(1.01) Paragraph (1)(b) does not apply where all or substantially all of the workers involved in a labour dispute are not Canadian citizens or permanent residents and the hiring of workers to replace the workers involved in the labour dispute is not prohibited by Canadian law applicable in the province where the workers involved in the labour dispute are employed.

(1.1) An immigration officer shall not issue an employment authorization to any person who seeks admission to Canada as a live-in caregiver unless the person

(a) has successfully completed a course of study that is equivalent to successful completion of Canadian secondary school;

(b) has the following training or experience, in a field or occupation related to the employment for which the employment authorization is sought, namely,

(i) successful completion of six months of full-time training in a classroom setting, as part of the course of study referred to in paragraph (a) or otherwise, or

(ii) completion of one year of full-time paid employment, including at least six months of continuous employment with one employer, in that field or occupation within the three years immediately prior to the day on which the person submits an application for an employment authorization to a visa office; and

(c) has the ability to speak, read and understand English or French at a level sufficient to communicate effectively in an unsupervised setting.

(1.11) Paragraphs (1.1)(a) and (b) are retroactive and apply in respect of all applications for employment authorizations made by persons seeking admission to Canada as a live-in caregiver pending on April 15, 1994.

(1.2) An immigration officer shall not issue an employment authorization to a person referred to in paragraph 19(4)(q) or (r) if the medical examination of the person or any of the person's dependants in Canada is incomplete.

(2) An immigration officer shall not issue an employment authorization to any person who has previously engaged in employment in Canada without proper authorization or has contravened the terms or conditions of a previous employment authorization unless the immigration officer is satisfied that

(a) a period of one year has elapsed since the previous engagement or contravention ceased;

(b) the previous engagement or contravention was unintentional or was excusable for any other reason;

(c) in the case of a person described in paragraph 19(4)(i), (j) or (k), that person could not subsist without public assistance if he did not have an employment authorization; or

(d) in the case of a person referred to in paragraph 19(4)(e)

(i) whose country of last permanent residence before he came to Canada is in a state of war or experiencing serious disruption of public order,

(ii) whose place of last permanent residence before he came to Canada has recently experienced a serious natural disaster, or

(iii) who was, immediately before coming to Canada, a member of a class designated pursuant to paragraph 114(1)(d) of the Act,

that person could not otherwise subsist without public assistance.

(3) In order to form an opinion for the purposes of paragraph (1)(a), an immigration officer shall consider

(a) whether the prospective employer has made reasonable efforts to hire or train Canadian citizens or permanent residents for the employment with respect to which an employment authorization is sought;

(b) the qualifications and experience of the applicant for the employment for which the employment authorization is sought; and

(c) whether the wages and working conditions offered are sufficient to attract and retain in employment Canadian citizens or permanent residents.

(4) Where an immigration officer considers the questions set out in paragraphs (3)(a) and (c), he shall take into consideration the opinion of an officer of the office of the National Employment Service serving the area in which the person seeking an employment authorization wishes to engage in employment.

(5) Notwithstanding paragraph (1)(a) and subsections (3) and (4), an immigration officer may issue an employment authorization to

(a) a person described in paragraph 19(4)(f), (h), (i), (j), (k), (n), (o), (q) or (r);

(b) a person coming to or in Canada to engage in employment pursuant to

(i) an international agreement between Canada and one or more foreign countries or an arrangement entered into with one or more foreign countries by the Government of Canada or by or on behalf of one of the provinces, other than an arrangement concerning seasonal workers, or

(ii) an agreement entered into with a province or group of provinces by the Minister pursuant to subsection 108(2) of the Act;

(c) a person in possession of a valid and subsisting student authorization in respect of whom paragraph (1)(a) should not, in the opinion of the immigration officer, be applied for the reason that that person has become temporarily destitute through circumstances totally beyond the control of that person and of any person on whom that person is dependent for the financial resources referred to in paragraph 15(1)(b);

(d) a person whose employment is related to a research, educational or training program approved by the Minister;

(e) a person in respect of whom paragraph (1)(a) should not, in the opinion of the immigration officer, be applied for the reason that

(i) his employment will create or maintain significant employment, benefits or opportunities for Canadian citizens or permanent residents,

(ii) he is to be employed by a Canadian religious or charitable organization without remuneration, or

(iii) his employment would result in reciprocal employment of Canadian citizens in other countries; or

(f) a person described in paragraph 19(4)(e) and in respect of whom paragraph (1)(a) should not, in the opinion of an immigration officer, be applied for humanitarian or compassionate reasons arising from

(i) a state of war or other event causing serious disruption of public order in that person's country of last permanent residence before he came to Canada,

(ii) a recent serious natural disaster at that person's place of last permanent residence before he came to Canada, or

(iii) the fact that the person was, immediately before coming to Canada, a member of a class designated pursuant to paragraph 114(1)(d) of the Act.

SOR/78-624, s. 2; SOR/78-744, s. 2; SOR/79-240, s. 4; SOR/79-392, s. 1; SOR/80-21, s. 7; SOR/81-612, s. 1; SOR/83-339, s. 5; SOR/84-849, s. 2; SOR/86-703, ss. 2, 3; SOR/89-168, s. 2; SOR/92-214, s. 2; SOR/93-412, s. 12; SOR/93-609, s. 2; SOR/94-131, s. 3; SOR/94-242, s. 5; SOR/94-681, s. 8; SOR/95-135, s. 1; SOR/97-182, s. 10; SOR/97-184, s. 6.

Case Law

Section 20(2)

Piperno v. Canada (Minister of Employment & Immigration) (February 3, 1984), Doc. T-101-84 (Fed. T.D.) — The following decision illustrates how the Court will analyze applications for *mandamus* directed to an immigration officer to compel the issuance of an employment authorization. The regulations have changed since this decision was granted; thus, the reasoning process may be more important than the resolution of the application.

The applicant claimed refugee status in Canada. His claim had been denied and there was an application before the Immigration Appeal Board for redetermination of the claim. The applicant had obtained two offers of part-time employment. He made two applications for an employment authorization and both were refused. *Mandamus* was denied because the immigration officer had a discretion with respect to issuing the employment authorization. There was no evidence of bad faith, and, thus, the officer in refusing could not be said to have breached his duty to act fairly towards the applicant. There was no evidence that regulatory provisions enacted for the applicant's protection had not been observed. Finally, the discretion could not be said to have been exercised on a wrong principle because the officer gave no reasons in refusing the authorization. The fact that no reasons were given could not be attacked because the Act did not require the officer to give reasons for refusing the authorization.

Section 20(4)

Singh (G.) v. Canada (Minister of Citizenship & Immigration) (1995), 106 F.T.R. 66 (Fed. T.D.) — The applicant, a citizen of India, applied for permanent residence as an assisted relative. His application was received by the Canadian Consulate General in Buffalo in February, 1990. The applicant entered Canada in 1981 as a visitor, however he was discovered working illegally at a car wash. He then made a claim for Convention refugee status which he later withdrew on his return to India. He entered Canada again in 1987 and has been living here since that time. In 1991 he made a second claim for Convention refugee status which he also subsequently abandoned. The applicant worked legally as a machinist at a company in Mississauga from 1988 until the company went bankrupt in 1990. He has not been employed since then.

The applicant was interviewed in connection with his independent application in June 1992. The officer's decision was not made until May 1994, and was not communicated to the applicant until October 1994. During the 28 month period between the interview and communication of the decision, the applicant's solicitor sent 12 letters to the respondent requesting information about the status of the applicant's file. The respondent replied twice with form letters indicating that the matter was proceeding normally.

In her decision, the officer informed the applicant that he had received the necessary 70 points but that she had a discretion pursuant to section 11(3) of the regulations to refuse to issue a visa. The officer stated that although Mr. Singh had been in Canada for a substantial amount of time he had not acquired reasonable language skills, had not sought substantial employment opportunities and therefore, did not appear to demonstrate motivation, initiative, adaptability and the resourcefulness required to successfully establish himself in Canada. The officer informed Mr. Singh that he came within the inadmissable class of persons described in subsection 19(2)(d) of the Act.

Fairness requires that an applicant receive a timely decision. What that means will vary with the circumstances in each case. A two and a half year delay between an interview and notification is unacceptable where there are no special circumstances which account for the delay. In exercising her discretion the officer was directing her attention to the applicant's ability to establish himself in Canada. This is a forward looking exercise. To accord offers of employment, which are *bona fide*, little weight because they are not certified by a CEIC is to apply an irrelevant consideration to the decision. The offers demonstrated that once landed the applicant had good employment prospects. The fact that he could not accept the offers prior to landing was irrelevant. Further, the officer's interview notes indicated that certified job offers were not discussed. It was simply agreed that the applicant would send letters of employment to the officer within 60 days of the interview. The applicant did this and in the circumstances it was incumbent on the officer to notify the applicant if the documents he provided were insufficient to fulfil her requirements.

The officer's notes disclose no factual basis for her conclusion that the applicant's failure to secure a job was caused by lack of motivation. The applicant was not interviewed about his job search efforts. Therefore the conclusion about the applicant's motivation was not well founded. The applicant had worked as a machinist for two years and had secured offers of employment with poor English skills. It was therefore clear that he could be employed with minimal spoken English. There may be cases in which language skills will impact on an applicant's ability to make a living, but on the facts of this case language did not appear to be an obstacle to the applicant's employment.

The officer's decision was set aside and the matter referred back for redetermination by a different visa officer.

Section 20(5)

Sharoni v. Canada (Minister of Employment & Immigration) (November 30, 1988), Doc. T-1002-88 (Fed. T.D.) — This application for an order of *mandamus* directing the respondent Minister to issue a work authorization pursuant to sections 20(5)(a) and 19(4)(k)(v) of the regulation was dismissed.

Mr. Sharoni arrived at a Toronto immigration office on May 17, 1988. He indicated that he had been in Canada illegally since 1985 and intended to pursue a claim for refugee status. On May 20, 1988, the applicant returned to the immigration office and asked for a work permit. He indicated that he had been charged with a criminal offence and was released on a recognizance. It was his submission that he had thereby become a person whose presence was required in a criminal proceeding. Section 19(4)(k)(v) of the regulation did not benefit the applicant because it was confined to those whose presence was required as a witness in criminal proceedings.

Medical Examinations

21. (1) Subject to subsections (2) and (3), the following classes of visitors shall undergo a medical examination by a medical officer:

(a) persons seeking to engage or continue in employment in Canada in an occupation in which protection of public health is essential; and

(b) persons who

(i) are seeking entry or extension of their visitor's status for an aggregate period in excess of six consecutive months, including an actual or proposed period of absence from Canada of less than 14 days, and

(ii) have resided or sojourned, at any time during the one year period immediately preceding the date of seeking entry, for six consecutive months, in an area that in the opinion of the Minister of National Health and Welfare has a higher incidence of serious communicable disease than Canada.

(2) Subsection (1) does not apply to

(a) a person described in paragraph 19(1)(a) who is coming to or is in Canada to carry out his official duties unless that person seeks to engage or continue in secondary employment in Canada;

(b) a dependant of a person described in paragraph 19(1)(a) unless that dependant seeks to engage or continue in employment in Canada; or

(c) a member of the armed forces of a country that is a designated state for the purposes of the *Visiting Forces Act* coming to or in Canada in order to carry out his official duties, other than a person who has been designated as a civilian component of that visiting force, unless that member seeks to engage or continue in secondary employment in Canada.

(d) [Revoked SOR/87-594, s. 1.]

(e) [Revoked SOR/87-594, s. 1.]

(3) Every person who has undergone an examination pursuant to subsection (1) is not required to undergo a further examination unless that person has resided or sojourned since the examination outside Canada for a period in excess of six consecutive months.

(4) Every person of a class referred to in subsection (1) who is seeking entry shall, when he appears at a port of entry, be in possession of a valid certificate of medical assessment stating that the person is not a member of a class described in paragraph 19(1)(a) of the Act.

SOR/79-240, s. 5; SOR/82-593, s. 1; SOR/83-339, s. 6; SOR/85-1107, s. 1; SOR/86-865, s. 1; SOR/87-594, s. 1

22. For the purpose of determining whether any person is or is likely to be a danger to public health or to public safety or whether the admission of any person would cause or might reasonably be expected to cause excessive demands on health or social services, the following factors shall be considered by a medical officer in relation to the nature,

severity or probable duration of any disease, disorder, disability or other health impairment from which the person is suffering, namely,

(a) any reports made by a medical practitioner with respect to the person;

(b) the degree to which the disease, disorder, disability or other impairment may be communicated to other persons;

(c) whether medical surveillance is required for reasons of public health;

(d) whether sudden incapacity or unpredictable or unusual behaviour may create a danger to public safety;

(e) whether the supply of health or social services that the person may require in Canada is limited to such an extent that

(i) the use of such services by the person might reasonably be expected to prevent or delay provision of those services to Canadian citizens or permanent residents, or

(ii) the use of such services may not be available or accessible to the person;

(f) whether medical care or hospitalization is required;

(g) whether potential employability or productivity is affected; and

(h) whether prompt and effective medical treatment can be provided.

SOR/78-316, s. 2.

Case Law

Cui v. Canada (Minister of Citizenship & Immigration) (November 25, 1998), Doc. IMM-1269-98 (Fed. T.D.) — The Court observed that it would be preferable if interviews of applicants for permanent resident status be tape-recorded so as to minimize the possibility for contradictory descriptions, such as those set out in the respective affidavits in this case.

Hussain v. Canada (Minister of Citizenship & Immigration) (1998), 45 Imm. L.R. (2d) 13, 159 F.T.R. 203 (Fed. T.D.) — This was an application to quash the decision of a visa officer who refused the applicant's application for permanent residence. On his application form the applicant had identified executive secretary as his intended occupation. The applicant also had a letter from his superior setting out the duties he performed as an executive secretary. The visa officer attached no weight to the fact that the applicant reported to the general manager of purchasing because "based on [his] local knowledge" this was more indicative of the applicant's years of service than it was of his degree of responsibility. The visa officer's "local knowledge" constituted an extraneous factor. The applicant was unaware that the visa officer was relying in part on this local knowledge. Fairness required that the visa officer disclose this to the applicant so that he would have an opportunity to respond to it.

The principle objectives of the administration of immigration control are first, to facilitate the entry into Canada of persons who meet the requirements under the Immigration Act and Regulations and second, to ensure that those who do not are excluded. Both objectives are of equal importance and neither is likely to be achieved if visa officers do not adopt a procedure for determining visa applications that is calculated to produce accurate and thoughtful decisions. Officers should not be burdened by procedural duties imposed by the Court that prevent them from processing applications in an expeditious and cost effective manner.

The visa officer's practice of asking an applicant at the close of an interview whether he or she wishes to add anything is not sufficient to satisfy the duty to make reasonable inquiries imposed by the duty of fairness. This practice fails to advise an applicant of the concerns that a visa officer may have in such a way as to provide the applicant with a reasonable opportunity to disabuse the visa officer of his or her particular concerns.

Su v. Canada (Minister of Citizenship & Immigration) (1998), 152 F.T.R. 136 (Fed. T.D.) — The applicant had applied for permanent resident status and was residing in Canada while the application was being processed in the United States. The applicant was requested to attend for an interview but was unable to do so, because he could not gain admission to the United States. The Canadian consulate refused to issue the applicant a minister's permit and refused to intervene with Chinese authorities to facilitate the applicant's application for a passport extension. Finally a visa officer sent the applicant a letter advising that his application had been denied.

There is no legal obligation upon the Canadian consulate to assist applicants in obtaining the proper authorization from a foreign jurisdiction to enable them to attend an interview. The applicant submitted his application in Buffalo. The procedure to have a file transferred was outlined by the visa officer. It is not the concern of the immigration authorities that the applicant is out of status and has chosen to continue to reside in Canada without any status and that the Chinese consulate has chosen not to renew his passport. The Canadian Government has no control over the actions of foreign governments. Accordingly, the application for judicial review was dismissed.

Ludwig v. Canada (Minister of Citizenship & Immigration) (1996), 33 Imm. L.R. (2d) 213, 111 F.T.R. 271 (Fed. T.D.) — This was an application to judicially review a negative decision of a visa officer which determined that the applicant was medically inadmissible.

Medical officers must be careful not to apply the Medical Officers Handbook too rigidly. They must be flexible enough to look beyond the guidelines in the handbook and to decide the admissibility of each applicant on the basis of that person's individual circumstances. If medical officers determine that they are bound by the handbook and cannot diverge from its guidelines, that would be a fetter on their discretion. If medical officers recognize that they may be flexible in their application of the guidelines in the handbook and determine the admissibility of each person on the basis of individual circumstances, then they will not have fettered their discretion. The handbook reflects common medical knowledge in practice, and as such, it is similar to a medical journal or textbook.

The Court concluded that the medical officer in this case did not fetter his discretion in applying the guidelines set out in the Medical Officers Handbook.

Ajanee v. Canada (Minister of Citizenship & Immigration) (1996), 33 Imm. L.R. (2d) 165, 110 F.T.R. 172 (Fed. T.D.) — This was an application to review a decision of a visa officer, determining that the applicant was medically inadmissible.

A visa officer has no authority to review the diagnostic assessment of medical officers. It is the medical officers who must reach the opinion that admission of the person concerned "would cause or might reasonably be expected to cause excessive demands on health or social services". The reasonableness of that opinion maybe an issue for the visa officer. Where on the evidence before him or her a question arises whether the opinion is reasonable, the visa officer may elect to seek further medical advice. Where no serious question arises on the record before him or her, the visa officer may act on the basis of the opinion as it is presented to him or her.

In this case, the Court found that the visa officer acted on the basis of the opinion of the medical officers in circumstances where no question of the reasonableness of that opinion arose. The only medical information available to the visa officer at the time of his decision was the advice included in the form of the Medical Notification from the medical officers.

If the medical officers determination turns out to be unreasonable, then the decision of the visa officer based on that unreasonable opinion may be set aside. A reviewing court is competent to review the evidence to determine whether the medical officers opinion is reasonable in the circumstances of the case. A medical opinion will be considered unreasonable because of incoherence or inconsistency, absence of supporting evidence, failure to consider cogent evidence or failure to consider the factors set out in section 22 of the regulations.

Sabater v. Canada (Minister of Citizenship & Immigration) (1995), 31 Imm. L.R. (2d) 59, 102 F.T.R. 268 (Fed. T.D.) — The applicants sought to overturn the refusal of their application for permanent residence by a visa officer. The visa officer determined that the 14-year-old female applicant was medically inadmissible.

One of the examining medical officers was of the opinion that the 14-year-old applicant was suffering from mental retardation. The opinion, however, gave no indication of the level or degree of retardation, and, as a result, it was difficult to determine the basis upon which it could be said that the applicant's admission would cause excessive demands on social services. One of the assessments relied upon by the medical officer had referred to the mental illness as "mild mental deficiency or retardation." The Court did not wish to say that a person suffering from mild mental retardation could not be found to cause excessive demands on social services. However, it would be reasonable for there to be a higher onus of proof on the medical officer to demonstrate excessive demand in such a situation.

The medical officers referred to an article prepared by the Assistant Director, Immigration, Overseas Health Services, where the effects of severe and moderate retardation were costed out. There was no costing out in the article, however, of mild mental retardation.

Accordingly, this was found to be an error making the medical officer's opinion unreasonable. The medical officers, in forming their opinion, are entitled to consider relevant factors not provided for under section 22 of the regulations. The Court further observed that services provided by schools to the handicapped may be considered as social services. The application was allowed.

Ismaili v. Canada (Minister of Citizenship & Immigration) (1995), 29 Imm. L.R. (2d) 1, 100 F.T.R. 139 (Fed. T.D.) — The applicant sought review of a decision of a visa officer denying the applicant's application for permanent residence on the ground that the applicant's minor son was inadmissible pursuant to subparagraph 19(1)(a)(ii). On judicial review applications of this type, the work of the court would be made much simpler if the respondent would regularly make available the medical officers' record.

Section 22 of the regulations is enacted pursuant to subsection 114(1)(m). The wording of that subsection requires that section 22 of the regulations should be read as only prescribing the factors to be considered on the health and safety issue. Section 22 is not applicable to determine whether the admission of any person would cause or might reasonably be expected to cause demands on health or social services.

Gao v. Canada (Minister of Employment & Immigration) (1993), 18 Imm. L.R. (2d) 306 (Fed. T.D.) — This was an application for judicial review to quash a decision of an immigration officer which found the applicant inadmissible under 19(1)(a)(ii) of the *Immigration Act* on the ground that his young son suffered from a disability.

The applicant entered Canada as a visiting scholar and was issued student and employment authorizations in 1984. He returned to China in 1985 and was allegedly persecuted for his participation in pro-democracy activities. In December 1985 he returned to Canada on a student visa to complete his studies. In early 1986 his wife and son arrived in Canada on visitors' visas. The son had been assessed in Shanghai and found healthy and assessed M1. In the fall of 1987 the son began attending a special school because of developmental delay and was required to undergo a second medical assessment. The son was diagnosed "mental retardation". The prognosis was "guarded".

In January 1988, an opinion signed by two concurring medical officers classified the applicant's son as M7 (medically inadmissible). In July 1988, the applicant claimed Convention refugee status and fell under the "backlog" rules. In February 1990, he was called to a preliminary interview and a third medical assessment was ordered. This report made no mention of mental retardation. In May 1990, Health and Welfare Canada requested extensive specific information with respect to the son's mental development. The son was then referred to the Glendale Lodge Society where an intensive medical, psychological, hearing and speech profile was carried out. The ensuing report was forwarded to Health and Welfare Canada in September 1990. In December 1991, the applicant was informed that his son was still medically inadmissible. The respondent Minister submitted affidavit evidence which established that the Glendale report was reviewed on December 12, 1990. The son was assessed at M5 (also inadmissible). The evidence was that Immigration was notified of this assessment in November 1991. The applicant was not made aware of the December 1990 assessment of the Glendale report or of its communication to Immigration in November 1991 nor did he receive the second medical notification arising from that assessment.

The governing principle arising from the jurisprudence is that the reviewing Court is not competent to make findings of fact related to medical diagnosis but is competent to review the evidence to determine whether the medical officers' opinion is reasonable in the circumstances of the case. The reasonableness of the opinion is to be assessed, not only when it was given, but also at the time when it was relied upon by the immigration officer since it is that decision which is being reviewed. The grounds of reasonableness include incoherence or inconsistency, absence of supporting evidence, failure to consider cogent evidence, or failure to consider the factors stipulated in section 22 of the regulations.

The medical opinion of 1988 was unreasonable at the time it was relied upon in December 1991. Health and Welfare's assessment of the Glendale report led to an M5 assessment which was inconsistent with the M7 assessment in 1988. The contradictory information should have alerted the officer to the need for further investigation. He or she should have called for an updated examination of the son and a full second medical opinion that would take into account all of the factors in section 22 of the regulations.

Further, the last information the applicant had was the hopeful Glendale assessment. The applicant was not given an opportunity to respond to the negative assessment of that report by Health and Welfare Canada and this was held to be unfair.

Bola v. Canada (Minister of Employment & Immigration) (1990), 11 Imm. L.R. (2d) 14, 107 N.R. 311 (Fed. C.A.) — The majority agreed that the Court of Appeal should refrain from intervening to contradict an honest assessment by the Immigration and Refugee Board of the sufficiency of a medical certificate on the basis of which the visa officer abroad had formed an opinion so long as the assessment was not tainted by any misconception of the law or any patently erroneous understanding of the medical officer's expressed statement of opinion.

The Court of Appeal is sitting in appeal and its role is not to re-do what the Board did as if it was, itself, a second Immigration and Refugee Board. In this particular case, the majority thought that the Board's reasons were clear and accurate as to the law and that the analysis of the medical certificate was carefully made and accordingly the appeal was dismissed.

Canada (Minister of Employment & Immigration) v. Jiwanpuri (1990), 10 Imm. L.R. (2d) 241, 109 N.R. 293 (Fed. C.A.) — The visa officer refused to grant the applications for landing which the respondent had sponsored on behalf of her father and her sister. The respondent disputed the refusal and the Immigration and Refugee Board allowed the appeal, a decision from which the Minister appealed to the Court. Members of the Board do not have the expertise required to question the correctness of the medical diagnosis reached by the medical officers. Even with the help of medical witnesses, it is not a function of the Board to do so. The Board is not expected to make a choice between the written opinion of the medical officers and that of other doctors as to the diagnosis of a medical condition of an applicant for landing. The Act has made membership in the inadmissible class in section 19(1)(a) the immediate consequence of the expressed opinion of two medical officers, without providing for a different result, if other doctors could be found who would be of a different opinion. In this case, the Board was therefore wrong in finding that, in the case of the father, the diagnosis of mental retardation was erroneous and incorrect; however, it is within the province of the Board to inquire into the reasonableness of the opinion, although that reasonableness is to be assessed at the time when the visa officer made his decision since it is that decision which is being appealed. The reasonableness of the opinion is not to be assessed strictly on the basis of the facts as they appear to the visa officers or the medical officers and is open to the appellant to show that those facts were wrongly seen or interpreted or that they were insufficient to lead to the conclusion drawn. The decision of the Board, taken as a whole in this case, was to the effect that the opinion of the medical officers was unreasonable. The factors which medical officers must take into account are set out in section 22 of the regulations. The medical officers, in arriving at their opinion, applied only one relevant factor as set out in section 22. They also applied a number of factors which are not set out in the regulations. Accordingly, the Board was justified in concluding that their opinion was not reasonable.

Sall v. Canada (Minister of Employment & Immigration) (1989), 9 Imm. L.R. (2d) 179, 29 F.T.R. 176 (Fed. T.D.) — The applicants were refused permanent residence status on medical grounds. In upholding this decision, the Court relied on *Mohamed v. Canada (Minister of Employment & Immigration)*, [1986] 3 F.C. 90 (Fed. C.A.) which observed that it was open to the applicant to show that the medical officer's opinion was unreasonable. The Court further observed that evidence which simply tended to show that the person was no longer suffering from the medical condition which formed the basis of the medical officer's opinion was not sufficient. The decision of *Stefanska v. Canada (Minister of Employment & Immigration)* (1988), 6 Imm. L.R. (2d) 66 (Fed. T.D.) observed that the decision must be made by a duly constituted authority acting without abuse of power, in good faith and with objectivity. The Court observed that the diagnosis stated in the medical notification was accurate and fully supported the opinion of the physicians who signed it that these were questions of fact and not of law. Where the entries in the medical notification were so inconsistent with each other that they made the document as a whole incoherent, then, of course, such a medical notification would not constitute the opinion of a medical officer.

Badwal v. Canada (Minister of Employment & Immigration) (1989), 9 Imm. L.R. (2d) 85, 64 D.L.R. (4th) 561 (Fed. C.A.) — The appellant's father was refused a visa for admission to Canada for health reasons. The Immigration Appeal Board upheld the visa officer's decision and dismissed the appeal. The Federal Court of Appeal allowed the appeal because of the wording of the medical narrative. Certainty in prognosis is not required. The Act requires an expression of probabilities. The use of the word "may" does not automatically mean that the narrative is insufficient where the medical narrative makes excessive demands on the health or social system contingent upon deterioration of the appellant's current state. The corollary must be that, in the absence of deterioration, there will be no excessive demands. Parliament requires a judgment of probability based upon an appreciation of the applicant's present condition. Where the narrative does not address the probability of deterioration, the opinion that the sponsored father's presence in Canada will make excessive demands on the health or social system is self-contradictory.

Pattar v. Canada (Minister of Employment & Immigration) (1988), 8 Imm. L.R. (2d) 79, 98 N.R. 98 (Fed. C.A.) — It is open to the Board to determine whether a particular medical certificate contains on its face the clear expression of the medical opinion required to give effect to the inadmissibility in section 19(1)(a) of the Act. In doing so, the Board must look to the whole document and the mere reading of the word "possible" in the description of the prognosis in the narrative of the profile does not lead determinatively to a conclusion of insufficiency.

Canada (Minister of Employment & Immigration) v. Sihota (1989), 8 Imm. L.R. (2d) 1 (Fed. C.A.) — This was an appeal by the Minister of Employment and Immigration from a decision of the Immigration Appeal Board that allowed the respondent's appeal against the refusal of the sponsored application of her father for landing in Canada. The Board erred by finding confusion in the medical notification where none existed. Fairly read, the medical notification clearly supported the visa officer's conclusion and no other. The other ailments disclosed in the notification were not susceptible to the description expressed in the narrative of the medical notification as a "condition which is likely to endanger public health." "Pulmonary tuberculosis possibly active" is amenable to that description. Section 22 of the *Immigration Regulations* requires only that the medical notification address specifically and clearly those diseases which alone or in combination are relevant to the opinion under section 19(1)(a) of the Act.

Lee v. Canada (Minister of Employment & Immigration) (1986), 4 F.T.R. 86 (Fed. T.D.) — Early in 1984, the applicant, Sing Lee, of Hong Kong, made an application for permanent residence in Canada for himself and for four of his children, one of whom was the applicant, Hon Man Lee. Hon Man Lee was a congenital deaf mute and he was rejected on medical grounds. This decision was quashed because both medical officers had failed to consider medical reports, which had been provided by the applicant, prior to certifying that the applicant, Hon Man Lee, was medically inadmissible. This failure to consider these reports was a breach of the duty of fairness, which the respondents owed the applicant.

Interviews

22.1 (1) An immigration officer may require that an applicant for landing who is in Canada, or an applicant for an immigrant visa, and dependants of the applicant, if any, be interviewed for the purpose of assessing the application.

(2) An immigration officer may require that an applicant for a visitor visa, student authorization or employment authorization and accompanying dependants of the applicant, if any, be interviewed for the purpose of assessing the application.

(3) An interview referred to in subsection (1) or (2) shall be conducted

(a) where the application is submitted to a visa office, in that visa office or at any appropriate location specified by a visa officer; or

(b) where the application is submitted in Canada, at the location where the application is submitted or at any other appropriate location specified by an immigration officer.

SOR/93-44, s. 16.

Case Law

Baluyut v. Canada (Minister of Employment & Immigration), [1992] 3 F.C. 420, 56 F.T.R. 186 (Fed. T.D.) — The applicant sought to quash a decision by a visa officer refusing to interview her in support of her application for permanent residence without the personal appearance of her spouse at the interview. The applicant is a citizen of the Philippines who had been living by herself in the United States and working there as a registered nurse. Her husband and their two children lived in the Philippines. The applicant applied as a principal applicant for permanent residence in Canada and listed her husband and children as her dependants. The applicant was notified to attend a personal interview to determine her admissibility. She was required to bring her spouse to the interview. The applicant advised the Canadian Consulate in Los Angeles that her husband would be unable to attend the interview. She had an application for an H-1 visa pending and thus her husband would have difficulty obtaining a visa to the United States. Through her counsel she suggested that her husband be interviewed at the Canadian Embassy in Manila. Eventually this suggestion was rejected and the applicant was informed that both she and her husband would be required to attend in Los Angeles on the date scheduled for the interview. The applicant attended by herself at the Canadian Consulate. The officer assigned to deal with her case refused to proceed with the interview. The applicant explained why her husband could not attend and the visa officer spoke to a Vice Consul about what decision she should make and then carried out the Vice Consul's instructions.

The decision of the visa officer was set aside. The Court found, on the facts, that the visa officer had simply carried out the instructions of her superior with respect to the conduct of the interviews and had not made the decision herself. In so doing, the visa officer had committed jurisdictional error and her decision to refuse the interview was quashed. *Mandamus* was directed to the respondent Minister's officials at the Consulate in Los Angeles directing them to interview the applicant and to then transfer the file to Manila so that the spouse and dependants could be interviewed.

Lam v. Canada (Minister of Employment & Immigration) (1991), 15 Imm. L.R. (2d) 275, 49 F.T.R. 200 (Fed. T.D.) — The applicant applied for permanent residence as a self-employed person. The visa officer rejected the application without ever affording the applicant an interview. The visa officer determined that the applicant could not have met the minimum requirement of 70 units of assessment to qualify as a self-employed person even if he had been accorded the maximum 10 units of assessment for personal suitability after an interview. Because the officer determined that the applicant did not meet the definition of a self-employed person, he did not give the applicant the 30 units of assessment for self-employment described in Regulation 8(4).

Schedule 1 of the regulations in Factor 9 describes, under the criteria for personal suitability, the units of assessment awarded on the basis of an interview with the person to reflect the personal suitability of the person and his dependents to become successfully established in Canada. Schedule 1, Factor 9, was taken to mean that the officer doing the assessment must award up to 10 units depending on his finding as to personal suitability. Where the maximum 10 units are awarded, the interviewing officer must have been satisfied that the prospective immigrant has the personal suitability to become successfully established in Canada.

By not having granted the applicant an interview the officer was not in a position to determine whether he would have allowed the 30 units of assessment in section 8(4) of the regulations. Further, section 11(3) of the regulations permits a visa officer to issue a visa even if the applicant is not awarded the necessary units of assessment. If the applicant has all the qualities mentioned in Factor 9 of Schedule 1, a visa officer cannot form a valid opinion under section 11(3) without an interview. The visa officer has no discretion not to grant the interview mentioned in Factor 9. It is incumbent upon a visa officer to follow the procedure set out in statute. The officer has no discretion in deciding whether or not to grant an interview pursuant to Factor 9 under column 1 of Schedule 1 of the regulations. The decision of the officer in this case was quashed. The Minister was directed to reconsider the applicant's application and another visa officer was to effect this reconsideration.

Editor's Note: See, however, sections 8(1) and 11.1 of the Immigration Regulations.

Terms and Conditions of Admission

23. (1) Subject to section 23.1, where an immigration officer, senior immigration officer or adjudicator may impose conditions under the Act in respect of an immigrant, the only terms and conditions that may be imposed are the following:

(a) the times and places at which the immigrant shall report for medical examination, surveillance or treatment;

(b) in the case of an investor other than an investor in a province, that, although the investor may pledge the debt obligation as security at any time, they cannot transfer the debt obligation until the day following the last day of the allocation period;

(b.1) in the case of an investor in a province, that, although the investor may pledge the security received for the investment at any time, they cannot transfer the security until the day following the last day of the period referred to in paragraph (b) of the definition "investment" in subsection 2(1).

(c) the times and places at which the immigrant shall furnish evidence of compliance with the terms or conditions imposed.

(2) [Revoked SOR/93-412, s. 13.]

(3) Where an immigration officer, senior immigration officer or adjudicator may impose conditions under the Act in respect of a visitor, the only terms and conditions that may be imposed are the following:

(a) a prohibition against engaging in employment in Canada;

(b) a prohibition against attending any university, college or other institution and against taking any academic, professional or vocational training course at any university, college or other institution;

(c) attendance at a university, college or other institution specified by the immigration officer, senior immigration officer or adjudicator;

(d) the type of employment in which the visitor may engage;

(e) the employer with which the visitor may engage or continue in employment;

(f) the location in which the visitor may engage or continue in employment;

(g) the period during which the visitor may engage or continue in employment;

(h) the period during which the visitor may remain in Canada;

(i) the area within which the visitor may travel in Canada;

(j) where the visitor is granted entry to become a member of a crew of a vehicle, the period within which the visitor shall join the vehicle;

(k) the times and places at which the visitor shall report for medical examination, surveillance or treatment or for any other purpose;

(l) the times and places at which the visitor shall furnish evidence of compliance with the terms or conditions imposed; and

(m) a prohibition against attending any university, college or other institution listed in Schedule III and against taking any academic, professional or vocational training course at any university, college or other institution listed in that Schedule.

SOR/79-851, s. 5; SOR/80-601, s. 3; SOR/83-837, s. 3; SOR/84-849, s. 3; SOR/85-1038, s. 7; SOR/89-38, s. 8; SOR/89-585, s. 3; SOR/90-750, s. 3; SOR/93-44, s. 17; SOR/93-412, s. 13; SOR/99-146, s. 5

23.1 (1) Entrepreneurs and their dependants are prescribed as a class of immigrants in respect of which landing shall be granted subject to the condition that, within a period of not more than two years after the date of an entrepreneur's landing, the entrepreneur

(a) establishes, purchases or makes a substantial investment in a business or commercial venture in Canada so as to make a significant contribution to the economy and whereby employment opportunities in Canada are created or continued for one or more Canadian citizens or permanent residents, other than the entrepreneur and the entrepreneur's dependants;

(b) participates actively and on an on-going basis in the management of the business or commercial venture referred to in paragraph (a);

(c) furnishes, at the times and places specified by an immigration officer, evidence of efforts to comply with the terms and conditions imposed pursuant to paragraphs (a) and (b); and

(d) furnishes, at the time and place specified by an immigration officer, evidence of compliance with the terms and conditions imposed pursuant to paragraphs (a) and (b).

(2) Fiancées of sponsors and dependants of fiancées are prescribed as a class of immigrants in respect of which landing shall be granted subject to the condition that

(a) within a period of 90 days after the date of a fiancée's landing, the fiancée marries the sponsor; and

(b) the fiancée furnishes, at the times and places specified by an immigration officer, evidence of compliance with the terms and conditions imposed.

(3) The terms and conditions set out in subsections (1) and (2) are in addition to the terms and conditions that may be imposed pursuant to subsection 23(1).

SOR/93-44, s. 17

Case Law

Section 23.1(2)

Gabriel v. Canada (Minister of Employment & Immigration) (1984), 60 N.R. 108 (Fed. C.A.) — The appellant was landed on condition that she marry within 90 days. This condition could not be obeyed as a result of circumstances beyond the appellant's control. Even though a condition is impossible to fulfill, so long as the person concerned knew of that condition and continued to remain in Canada in breach of that condition, such a person has knowingly contravened a condition attached to the grant of landing. Even if the word "contravene" requires a positive act, the omission to do something which a person is required to do, is the commission of a positive act. It is an act of failure to do something required to be done and, accordingly, satisfies the definition of the term "contravenes".

23.2 [Revoked SOR/97-182, s. 11.]

24. (1) Every application made to an immigration officer by a person pursuant to section 15 or 16 of the Act shall be in a form established by the Minister by order pursuant to paragraph 115(a) of the Act, and shall, where applicable, be accompanied by

(a) the documentation referred to in subsection 15(1);

(b) the consent in writing of the government of the province in which the applicant is hospitalized or institutionalized where such consent is required by that government pursuant to an agreement entered into by the Minister with that government pursuant to subsection 108(2) of the Act or is required by or pursuant to legislation of that province;

(c) any other documentation or information that the applicant considers relevant; and

(d) on request, any other documentation or information that an immigration officer considers necessary for the purpose of assessing the application.

(2) Where an application has been made pursuant to section 15 or 16 of the Act, an immigration officer may request that the applicant appear for an interview.

(2.1) [Revoked SOR/89-38, s. 9.]

(3) [Revoked SOR/94-242, s. 6.]

SOR/79-240, s. 6; SOR/88-111, s. 2; SOR/89-38, s. 9; SOR/89-129, s. 1; SOR/94-242, s. 6

Duration of Visitor Status

24.1 For the purposes of subsection 26(2) of the Act, the prescribed period is six months.

SOR/93-412, s. 14

Deposits and Bonds

25. (1) Where the Deputy Minister issues a direction to a transportation company pursuant to subsection 92(1) or (2) of the Act requiring it to deposit a security other than a sum of money in Canadian currency, the Deputy Minister may require that any security deposited be

(a) an irrevocable stand-by letter of credit in favour of the Government of Canada, the form and substance of which have been fixed by the Deputy Minister and that has been issued or confirmed by a bank as defined in section 2 of the *Bank Act*; or

(b) an irrevocable line of credit with a bank as defined in section 2 of the *Bank Act*

(i) that designates the Crown as its agent for the purposes of drawing against the line of credit to realize any amount or administration fee referred to in section 93 of the Act, and

(ii) that is accompanied by an undertaking to the Government of Canada, the form and substance of which has been fixed by the Deputy Minister and in which the transportation company undertakes

(A) not to revoke the line of credit, and

(B) not to revoke the designation of the Crown as agent.

(2) Where a senior immigration officer requires any person or group or organization of visitors to make a deposit or post a performance bond pursuant to any provision of the Act, he shall provide to that person or group or organization of visitors a receipt or other documentary record specifying the circumstances in which the deposit may be forfeited or the bond enforced.

SOR/89-38, s. 10; SOR/93-44, s. 18

Returning Resident Permits

26. (1) When a permanent resident intends to leave Canada for any period of time or is outside Canada, he may make an application, orally or in writing, to an immigration officer for a returning resident permit.

(2) Subject to subsection (3), an immigration officer shall issue a returning resident permit to a permanent resident who has made an application therefor where the permanent resident

(a) has provided the immigration officer with two clearly identifiable photographs of himself;

(b) has appeared for an interview if requested by the immigration officer; and

(c) intends to leave or left Canada

(i) for the purpose of carrying out his duties as a representative or employee of a corporation or business organization established in Canada or as a representative or employee of the Government of Canada or of a province or a municipality in Canada,

(ii) for the purpose of upgrading his professional, academic or vocational qualifications,

(iii) for the purpose of accompanying a member of his family who is a Canadian citizen or has been issued a returning resident permit, or

(iv) in any circumstances not referred to in subparagraphs (i) to (iii) that the immigration officer deems appropriate.

(3) An immigration officer shall not issue a returning resident permit where the immigration officer and a senior immigration officer believe on reasonable grounds that the person applying therefor has ceased or will cease to be a permanent resident under subsection 24(1) of the Act.

(4) An immigration officer may, pursuant to subsection (2), issue a returning resident permit

(a) valid for a period not exceeding twelve months; or

(b) with the approval of a senior immigration officer, valid for a period not exceeding twenty-four months.

SOR/86-865, s. 2

Case Law

El-Amin v. Canada (Minister of Citizenship & Immigration) (1997), 38 Imm. L.R. (2d) 45, 127 F.T.R. 283 (Fed. T.D.) — This was an application to review a decision of an immigration officer refusing to issue a returning resident permit (RRP) to the applicant.

The applicant, a citizen of Lebanon but born in Kuwait, arrived in Canada in 1990, and obtained permanent residency in 1992. The applicant subsequently travelled to Lebanon, married and upon returning to Canada took training in AutoCAD design. The applicant immediately obtained employment after this training but was laid off after 7 months. Subsequent to losing his job, the applicant was unable to find permanent employment in Canada. In 1993, the applicant travelled to Kuwait where he had previously worked and in January 1994, secured employment in that country. In May 1994, the applicant returned to Canada in order to accompany his wife whom he sponsored. At the end of May both the applicant and his wife returned to Kuwait. The applicant returned to Canada in September 1994 leaving again in October. The applicant returned to Canada in November 1995 and upon his return was admitted as a permanent resident. The applicant's intention at this point was to keep his employment in Kuwait for 2 additional years, after which time he would come to Canada since he had no permanent status in Kuwait and was not permitted to own property there. On his last visit to Canada the applicant purchased a condominium.

The visa officer refused the applicant's application because the reason for his absence was to be employed by a non-Canadian company. The immigration officer did not exercise her discretion properly when determining whether to grant the RRP, because she required the applicant to meet the sole criterion set out in section 26(2)(c)(i). In doing so the visa officer fettered her discretion and accordingly her decision was set aside.

Certificates of Departure

27. (1) Subject to subsection (2), a certificate of departure referred to in section 32.02 of the Act that verifies that a person in respect of whom a departure order has been issued has left Canada may be issued not later than 30 days

> **(a) where the departure order is stayed, after the day on which the stay is no longer in effect;**
>
> **(b) where the Minister has declared a moratorium in respect of the removal of all nationals of the country of which the person is a national, after the end of the moratorium; or**
>
> **(c) in any other case, after the day on which the departure order becomes effective.**

(2) In the case of a person who claims to be a Convention refugee but who has been determined by the Refugee Division not to be a Convention refugee, a certificate of departure referred to in subsection (1) may be issued not later than 30 days after the latest of

> **(a) if the person does not submit an application for a determination referred to in paragraph 11.4(2)(b) within the period referred to in that paragraph, the day on which the person is notified by the Refugee Division of its determination;**
>
> **(b) the day on which the person is notified that an immigration officer has determined that the person is not a member of the post-determination refugee claimants in Canada class;**

(c) if the person is a member of the post-determination refugee claimants in Canada class but an immigration officer has determined that the person shall not be granted landing, the day on which the person is notified of that determination; and

(d) where the departure order is stayed, the day on which the stay ceases to have effect.

SOR/88-180, s. 1; SOR/89-38, s. 11; SOR/93-44, s. 19; SOR/97-182, s. 12

27.1 A conditional removal order or a copy thereof shall be considered to have been served on a person who claims to be a Convention refugee if it is sent by ordinary mail to the person at that person's last known address.

SOR/93-412, s. 15

28.-39.5 [Revoked SOR/93-44, s. 19.]

Applications for Landing

40. An application for landing pursuant to subsection 46.04(1) of the Act shall be filed with an immigration officer

(a) in the case of a person determined to be a Convention refugee during the period beginning on February 1, 1993 and ending on October 1, 1995, within 180 days after October 1, 1995;

(b) in the case of a person determined to be a Convention refugee after October 1, 1995, within 180 days after the person has been determined to be a Convention refugee; and

(c) in the case of a person determined to be a Convention refugee before February 1, 1993 and whose case was appealed to a higher court by the Minister and not finally determined as of that date,

(i) where the final determination of Convention refugee status has been made on or before October 1, 1995, within 180 days after October 1, 1995, and

(ii) where the final determination of Convention refugee status is made after October 1, 1995, within 180 days after the date on which the final determination is made;

(d) [Repealed SOR/99-74, s. 2.]

SOR/80-601, s. 4; SOR/89-38, s. 19; SOR/95-461, s. 1; SOR/97-86, s. 6; SOR/99-74, s. 2

Refusal of Sponsored Applications

41. (1) Where an immigration officer refuses to approve an application for landing that has been made by a member of the family class and has been sponsored, the immigration officer shall,

(a) where the refusal to approve the application is made on the grounds referred to in paragraph 79(1)(a) of the Act, provide to the sponsor, or

(b) where the refusal to approve the application is made on the grounds referred to in paragraph 79(1)(b) of the Act, provide to the member of the family class

a summary of the information on which his reason for refusal is based.

(1.1) Notwithstanding subsection (1), where the refusal to approve an application is made pursuant to paragraph 79(1)(b) of the Act on the grounds that the member of the family class is a person described in any of paragraphs 19(1)(d) to (g) of the Act, the immigration officer shall inform the member of the family class of those grounds only.

(2) Where an application for landing made by a member of the family class has been refused pursuant to subsection 77(1) of the Act, an immigration officer shall inform the sponsor in writing that, if he is a Canadian citizen or permanent resident, he has a right of appeal to the Appeal Division pursuant to subsection 77(3) of the Act.

SOR/84-809, s. 2; SOR/86-472, s. 1; SOR/89-38, s. 20; SOR/90-202, s. 6

Removal Costs

42. The costs and expenses incurred by Her Majesty to be included in determining removal costs that may be assessed against a transportation company are the following:

(a) expenses incurred within or outside Canada with respect to the transportation of the person who is removed from Canada;

(b) accommodation costs incurred during the removal of the person from Canada; and

(c) accommodation and travel expenses incurred by an escort provided for the person who is removed from Canada.

SOR/93-44, s. 20

42.1 The prescribed costs for the purposes of section 55.1 of the Act for a person who has been removed to a destination set out in column I of an item of Schedule VIII are the costs set out in column II of that item.

SOR/93-44, s. 20

Administration Fees — Preliminary Assessments

42.2 (1) Subject to subsection (2), a preliminary assessment of an administration fee may be made against a transportation company, pursuant to section 91.1 of the Act, in respect of any member of the following classes of persons:

(a) persons who are members of an inadmissible class described in paragraph 19(2)(d) of the Act because the persons were presented to an immigration officer without a valid and subsisting visa, passport or travel document required by the Act or these Regulations;

(b) persons that the transportation company may not carry to Canada, pursuant to subsection 50(2);

(c) persons who are exempt, pursuant to subsection 14(4), from the requirement to possess a valid and subsisting passport or travel document but who fail to produce sufficient documentary evidence pursuant to subsection 14(6);

(d) persons who have eluded examination under the Act; and

(e) persons who remain in Canada after they have ceased to be visitors by reason of paragraph 26(1)(c.1) of the Act.

(2) The classes of persons referred to in subsection (1) shall not include persons who are

(a) granted entry pursuant to subsection 19(3) or 23(2) of the Act or allowed by a senior immigration officer to come into Canada pursuant to section 22 of the Act;

(b) issued a permit by the Minister pursuant to paragraph 37(1)(a) of the Act before the opening of an inquiry;

(c) allowed to leave Canada forthwith pursuant to paragraph 20(1)(b), subsection 23(4) or paragraph 23(4.2)(b) of the Act and who leave Canada; or

(d) the subject of an exclusion order made by a senior immigration officer pursuant to subsection 23(4) of the Act and who leave Canada.

SOR/93-44, s. 20

42.3 (1) Subject to subsections (2) and (3), where the Minister makes a preliminary assessment of an administration fee against a transportation company in respect of persons set out in column I of an item of Schedule IX, the Minister shall assess against the transportation company the administration fee set out in column II of that item.

(2) Where a memorandum of understanding between the transportation company and the Minister, in accordance with subsection (4), is in effect for the purpose of improving the performance of the transportation company with respect to its duty under section 89.1 of the Act and the transportation company demonstrates that it is complying with the memorandum of understanding, the Minister shall assess against the transportation company, in respect of persons set out in column I of an item of Schedule IX, the administration fee set out in column III of that item.

(3) Where a memorandum of understanding referred to in subsection (2) contains contravention rate performance standards for the purpose of reducing the administration fee referred to in subsection (1) and the transportation company demonstrates that it is complying with the provisions referred to in subsection (4), the Minister shall assess against the transportation company, in respect of persons set out in column I of an item of Schedule IX, the portion of the administration fee specified in one or more of paragraphs (a) to (c), as set out in the memorandum of understanding:

(a) where the transportation company is the subject of a number of assessments under subsection 91.1(1) of the Act that is equal to or less than the number fixed in the memorandum, for the period specified in the memorandum for the purpose of reducing the administration fee by one half, the Minister shall assess against the transportation company the administration fee set out in column IV of that item, in respect of each assessment of an administration fee that is made in the immediately following period specified in the memorandum;

(b) where the transportation company is the subject of a number of assessments under subsection 91.1(1) of the Act that is equal to or less than the number fixed in the memorandum, for the period specified in the memorandum for the purpose of reducing the administration fee by three-quarters, the Minister shall assess against the transportation company the administration fee set out in column V of that item, in respect of each assessment of an administration fee that is made in the immediately following period specified in the memorandum; and

(c) where the transportation company is the subject of a number of assessments under subsection 91.1(1) of the Act that is equal to or less than the number fixed in the memorandum for the period specified in the memorandum, for the purpose of reducing the administration fee to zero, the Minister shall assess against the

transportation company the administration fee set out in column VI of that item, in respect of each assessment of an administration fee that is made in the immediately following period specified in the memorandum.

(4) A memorandum of understanding referred to in subsection (2) shall include provisions respecting

(a) document screening;

(b) the use of technological aids;

(c) the training of personnel in document screening;

(d) fraud prevention;

(e) gate checks;

(f) information exchange;

(g) performance standards in respect of document screening, contravention rates and interdiction rates;

(h) compliance monitoring of the provisions of the memorandum of understanding;

(i) hiring practices related to members of a crew;

(j) the holding of documents under section 50.1;

(k) the provision of advance passenger manifest or crew list information; and

(l) stowaways.

(5) Subsections (2) and (3) do not apply in respect of an administration fee assessed in respect of persons referred to in paragraph 42.2(1)(e).

SOR/93-44, s. 20

Notices

42.4 A senior immigration officer shall

(a) where a removal order or conditional removal order is made against a person, so inform the transportation company that is or may be required, pursuant to section 85 of the Act, to convey the person or cause the person to be conveyed from Canada; and

(b) where a removal order is made against a person or where a conditional removal order made against a person becomes effective, serve on the transportation company a notice requiring it, pursuant to section 85 of the Act, to convey the person or cause the person to be conveyed from Canada and specifying whether the transportation company is liable to pay removal costs pursuant to section 86 of the Act.

SOR/93-44, s. 20

42.5 (1) A notice of a preliminary assessment referred to in section 91.1 of the Act shall be served personally or by registered mail on a representative of the transportation company.

(2) The person who serves a notice of a preliminary assessment shall complete and sign an affidavit of service or a certificate of service that certifies that the notice was served on the transportation company.

(3) Service of a notice of a preliminary assessment by registered mail shall be considered to have been served on the seventh day after the day on which the notice was mailed.

SOR/93-44, s. 20

Photographs and Fingerprints

43. All immigrants and visitors shall provide with their applications for a visa the number of clearly identifiable photographs of themselves that may reasonably be required by an immigration officer.

SOR/81-624, s. 1; SOR/93-44, s. 21

44. An immigration officer may require the following persons to be photographed and fingerprinted:

(a) persons who seek admission;

(b) persons who make an application pursuant to subsection 9(1), section 10, subsection 10.2(1) or section 16 of the Act;

(c) persons who are arrested pursuant to section 103 of the Act;

(d) persons against whom a removal order or conditional removal order has been made; or

(e) persons who claim to be Convention refugees pursuant to subsection 44(1) of the Act.

SOR/89-38, s. 21; SOR/93-44, s. 21

Loans

45. (1) The Minister may make transportation loans to immigrants and to persons who are

(a) Canadian citizens or permanent residents residing in Canada who have made an application to the Minister for financial assistance to obtain, for dependants who are seeking landing, transportation to Canada and transportation from their port of arrival to their place of destination in Canada;

(b) seeking landing and are in possession of a permit; or

(c) Convention refugees or members of a class of persons designated pursuant to paragraph 114(1)(d) of the Act who are in Canada, are seeking landing and have made an application to the Minister for financial assistance to obtain, for dependants who are seeking landing, transportation to Canada and transportation from their port of arrival to their place of destination in Canada.

(2) The Minister may make assistance loans to permanent residents, Convention refugees and persons who are lawfully in Canada and seeking landing.

(2.1) In order to assist immigrants in establishing themselves successfully in Canada, the Minister may make loans, for the purpose of paying the fees set out in the *Immigra-*

tion Act Fees Regulations **for the conferral of a right of landing on an immigrant, to an immigrant and to persons who are**

(a) Canadian citizens or permanent residents residing in Canada who have made an application to the Minister for financial assistance for an immigrant who is seeking landing, in order to pay the fees for the conferral of a right of landing;

(b) seeking landing and are in possession of a permit; or

(c) Convention refugees or members of a class of immigrants prescribed pursuant to paragraph 114(1)(e) of the Act who are in Canada, are seeking landing and have made an application to the Minister for financial assistance for another immigrant who is seeking landing, in order to pay the fees for the conferral of a right of landing on that immigrant.

(3) The Minister may make an admissibility loan

(a) to immigrants who are

(i) Convention refugees seeking resettlement, or

(ii) members of a class of persons designated pursuant to paragraph 114(1)(d) of the Act; and

(b) to persons who are

(i) permanent residents residing in Canada who are Convention refugees or were, immediately before coming to Canada, members of a class of persons designated pursuant to paragraph 114(1)(d) of the Act and who have made an application to the Minister for financial assistance to establish that their dependants who are seeking landing may be granted admission, or

(ii) Convention refugees or were, immediately before coming to Canada, members of a class of persons designated pursuant to paragraph 114(1)(d) of the Act who are in Canada, are seeking landing and have made an application to the Minister for financial assistance to establish that their dependants who are seeking landing may be granted admission.

(4) The maximum amount of outstanding advances to the Minister under subsection 119(1) of the Act is one hundred and ten million dollars.

SOR/83-540, s. 4; SOR/90-456, s. 1; SOR/95-121, s. 1; SOR/97-184, s. 7

46. (1) Where a loan is made to a person pursuant to section 45, it shall, subject to section 47, be repaid in full by consecutive monthly instalments commencing

(a) in the case of a loan referred to in subsection 45(1) or (3), 30 days after the day on which the person for whose benefit the loan is made arrives in Canada;

(b) in the case of a loan referred to in subsection 45(2), 30 days after the day on which the proceeds of the loan are paid to or for the benefit of that person; and

(c) in the case of a loan referred to in subsection 45(2.1), on the earlier of 30 days after the day on which the immigrant for whose benefit the loan is made arrives in Canada and 30 days after the day on which the proceeds of the loan are paid to or for the benefit of that immigrant.

(2) A loan made to a person pursuant to section 45 is, subject to section 47, repayable

(a) where the amount of the loan is not more than $1,200, during a period of 12 months,

(b) where the amount of the loan is more than $1,200 but not more than $2,400, during a period of 24 months,

(c) where the amount of the loan is more than $2,400 but not more than $3,600, during a period of 36 months,

(d) where the amount of the loan is more than $3,600 but not more than $4,800, during a period of 48 months, or

(e) where the amount of the loan is more than $4,800, during a period of 60 months,

commencing on the day on which the first monthly instalment is payable.

(3) Where the employer of a person to whom a loan is made pursuant to section 45 is willing to institute repayment of the loan by means of a payroll deduction scheme, the Minister may require repayment by such means.

SOR/83-540, s. 5; SOR/83-836, s. 1; SOR/95-121, s. 2

47. (1) Where a loan is made to a person pursuant to section 45 and that person satisfies an immigration officer that by reason of his income, assets and liabilities he cannot reasonably repay the loan in accordance with the requirements of section 46, the immigration officer may, subject to subsection (2), defer commencement of repayment of the loan, defer payments, vary the amount of payments or extend the repayment period.

(2) An immigration officer shall not grant a deferral, variation or extension under subsection (1) the effect of which would be to extend a repayment period referred to in subsection 46(2) beyond

(a) an additional 24 months in the case of a loan made to a Convention refugee or a member of a class of persons designated pursuant to paragraph 114(1)(d) of the Act; or

(b) an additional six months in the case of a loan made to any other person.

SOR/83-836, s. 2; SOR/97-184, s. 8

48. (1) Where a loan is made pursuant to section 45 to a person, other than a Convention Refugee, a member of a class of persons designated pursuant to paragraph 114(1)(d) of the Act or a member of a class of immigrants prescribed pursuant to paragraph 114(1)(e) of the Act who is selected by a visa officer under section 6 of the Act, the loan shall bear interest at a rate equal to the rate that is established by the Minister of Finance for loans made by that Minister to Crown corporations and that is in effect on the first day of January in the year in which the loan is approved and the interest shall be accrued beginning

(a) 30 days after the day on which the person for whose benefit the loan is made arrives in Canada, in the case of a loan referred to in subsection 45(1) or (3);

(b) 30 days after the day on which the proceeds of the loan are paid to or for the benefit of that immigrant, in the case of a loan referred to in subsection 45(2); or

(c) on the earlier of 30 days after the day on which the person for whose benefit the loan is made arrives in Canada and 30 days after the day on which the proceeds of the loan are paid to or for the benefit of that immigrant, in the case of a loan referred to in subsection 45(2.1).

(1.1) Where a loan is made pursuant to section 45 to a person, who is a Convention Refugee, a member of a class of persons designated pursuant to paragraph 114(1)(d) of

the Act or a member of a class of immigrants prescribed pursuant to paragraph 114(1)(e) of the Act, and where that person is selected by a visa officer under section 6 of the Act, the loan shall bear interest at a rate equal to the rate that is established by the Minister of Finance for loans made by that Minister to Crown corporations and that is in effect on the first day of January in the year in which the loan becomes interest bearing and that loan shall bear interest beginning on

(a) the first day of the thirteenth month after that person's landing in Canada, where the amount of the loan is not more than $1,200;

(b) the first day of the twenty-fifth month after that person's landing in Canada, where the amount of the loan is more than $1,200 but not more than $2,400; or

(c) the first day of the thirty-seventh month after that person's landing in Canada, where the amount of the loan is more than $2,400.

(2) Where a loan is made pursuant to section 45 to any person who has previously obtained a loan under that section that has not been repaid, the loan shall bear interest at a rate equal to the rate of interest payable on the loan that was previously obtained.

SOR/79-240, s. 7; SOR/83-836, s. 3; SOR/95-121, s. 3

Return or other Disposition of Seized Documents

49. (1) Subject to subsection (2), where an immigration officer has seized and holds any travel or other document pursuant to paragraph 110(2)(b) of the Act, the immigration officer may return the document to the person from whom it was seized

(a) immediately, where the person is granted admission or allowed to come into Canada; or

(b) at the time the person is removed from Canada or allowed to leave Canada.

(2) Where an immigration officer has seized and holds any travel or other document pursuant to paragraph 110(2)(b) or (c) of the Act, the immigration officer

(a) may retain or destroy the document if the immigration officer has reasonable grounds to believe that the document is fraudulent or was improperly issued, obtained or used and the rightful holder or issuing authority was a party to the fraud or improper issuance, obtention or use;

(b) may retain or destroy the document if the immigration officer has reasonable grounds to believe that the document has been fraudulently or improperly obtained or used or may be fraudulently or improperly used; or

(c) in any other case, may

(i) return the document to the rightful holder or to the issuing authority if the rightful holder is known, or

(ii) retain or destroy the document or return the document to the issuing authority if the rightful holder is not known.

SOR/93-412, s. 16

Case Law

Section 49(2)

Gassmann v. Canada (Minister of Employment & Immigration) (1990), 11 Imm. L.R. (2d) 149, 36 F.T.R. 105 (Fed. T.D.) — *Mandamus* will compel the Minister to return a passport which the department turned over to a foreign government (the Federal Republic of Germany). The applicant entered Canada as a visitor and in the course of applying for an extension his passport was taken by the immigration authorities. The passport was not returned to the applicant but an interview was scheduled and ultimately the applicant was advised that the German government had cancelled or confiscated his passport. The Minister justified what was done under section 110(2)(c) of the *Immigration Act*. There was no evidence to suggest that the passport had been improperly obtained or used, or that action was necessary to prevent its fraudulent or improper use. Further, the Minister's officials did not tell the applicant what they had done with his passport, namely, returned it to the government of the Federal Republic of Germany and did not allow him to make representations to them prior to taking the action that they contemplated. Accordingly, an order was issued directing the Minister to return the passport to the applicant.

Obligations of Transportation Companies

50. (1) [Revoked SOR/89-38, s. 22.]

(2) When the Minister informs a transportation company that a named person, who is not a Canadian citizen or a permanent resident, is, in his opinion, a member of any of the classes described in subsection 19(1) of the Act, the transportation company shall not carry that person to Canada.

SOR/89-38, s. 22

50.1 (1) A transportation company bringing persons into Canada may hold the visa, passport or other travel document of any passenger carried or to be carried by it in order to ensure that the visa, passport or travel document is available for examination by an immigration officer at the port of entry if the transportation company issues to the passenger a receipt therefor in a form established by the Minister.

(2) On the arrival in Canada of a passenger whose visa, passport or travel document is held by a transportation company, the transportation company shall, at the time it presents the passenger for examination in accordance with subsection 89(1) of the Act, give the visa, passport or travel document and a copy of the receipt issued therefor to an immigration officer at the port of entry.

(3) Where evidence is necessary to establish the identity or itinerary for travel to Canada of a passenger brought by a transportation company to Canada, the transportation company shall, at the request of an immigration officer, furnish to the immigration officer at the port of entry not later than 72 hours after the arrival of the passenger, unless an extension of no more than seven days is granted by an immigration officer, any of the following documents as requested, where the transportation company has access to the documents or information to be specified in the documents:

(a) a copy of the passenger's ticket voucher;

(b) a document specifying the passenger's travel itinerary, including the passenger's country of embarkation and dates of travel; and

(c) a document specifying the type of travel or identity document carried by the passenger, the country of issue and number of the document and the name of the person to whom the document was issued.

SOR/89-411, s. 1; SOR/93-44, s. 22

51. Where a person who is held in custody under the Act by a transportation company or by a member of a crew escapes from custody, the transportation company or member of the crew shall notify an immigration officer forthwith of the escape and, where requested to do so by an immigration officer, shall provide forthwith a written report that sets out the details of the escape.

SOR/93-44, s. 23

52. Where a person has stowed away in or on a vehicle coming to Canada,

(a) the transportation company shall notify an immigration officer of the presence of the stowaway as soon as the vehicle enters Canadian territory and, where requested to do so by an immigration officer, shall provide forthwith a written report that sets out the details of the case; and

(b) the master shall hold that stowaway in custody on the vehicle until that stowaway can be presented to an immigration officer for examination.

SOR/93-44, s. 23

53. (1) Where a ship of foreign registry, other than a pleasure yacht as defined in section 2 of the *Canada Shipping Act*, arrives in Canada, the master shall provide an immigration officer forthwith with an accurate and complete list of the members of the crew.

(2) Before the departure of a ship referred to in subsection (1) from its final port of call in Canada, the master shall provide an immigration officer with copies of the list of the members of the crew that were endorsed by an immigration officer at the port of entry, which copies of the list shall include all changes to the list that occurred while the ship was in Canada.

(3) The master of a ship of Canadian registry, other than a pleasure yacht as defined in section 2 of the *Canada Shipping Act*, shall, only where requested to do so by an immigration officer, provide an immigration officer forthwith with an accurate and complete list of the members of the crew.

(4) The master of a ship referred to in subsection (3) shall, on each arrival of the ship in Canada, notify an immigration officer of the presence of any members of the crew who are not Canadian citizens or permanent residents.

SOR/93-44, s. 23

54. (1) The master of a vehicle shall notify an immigration officer forthwith and, where requested by an immigration officer to do so, shall provide forthwith a written report that sets out the details, where any member of the crew, other than a Canadian citizen or permanent resident,

(a) deserts;

(b) is hospitalized;

(c) fails to rejoin the vehicle at the time fixed by the master when the member of the crew left the vehicle; or

(d) has ceased for any other reason to perform the person's duties as a member of the crew.

(2) The master of a vehicle shall notify an immigration officer forthwith and, where requested by an immigration officer to do so, shall provide forthwith a written report

that sets out the details, where any person is granted entry as or to become a member of the crew but fails to join the vehicle at the time expected by the master.

SOR/93-44, s. 23

Offences Relating to Obligations of Transportation Companies

54.1 Contravention of any of the following provisions, designated for the purposes of subsection 97.1(1) of the Act, constitutes an offence:

(a) carrying a person, in contravention of subsection 50(2);

(b) failure to give a visa, passport or travel document to an immigration officer, in contravention of subsection 50.1(2);

(c) failure to furnish documents to an immigration officer, in contravention of subsection 50.1(3);

(d) failure to notify an immigration officer of an escape, in contravention of section 51;

(e) failure to notify an immigration officer of the presence of a stowaway, in contravention of paragraph 52(a);

(f) failure to hold a stowaway in custody, in contravention of paragraph 52(b);

(g) failure to provide an accurate and complete list of members of the crew, in contravention of subsection 53(1), (2) or (3);

(h) failure to notify an immigration officer of the presence of any members of the crew who are not Canadian citizens or permanent residents, in contravention of subsection 53(4);

(i) failure to notify an immigration officer that a member of the crew has deserted, in contravention of paragraph 54(1)(a);

(j) failure to notify an immigration officer that a member of the crew is hospitalized or has ceased to perform the person's duties as a member of a crew, in contravention of paragraph 54(1)(b) or (d);

(k) failure to notify an immigration officer that a member of the crew has failed to rejoin the vehicle, in contravention of paragraph 54(1)(c); and

(l) failure to notify an immigration officer that a person granted entry into Canada as or to become a member of the crew has failed to join the vehicle, in contravention of subsection 54(2).

SOR/93-44, s. 23

54.2 Contravention of section 51, paragraph 52(a), 54(1)(a), (b), (c) or (d) or subsection 54(2) for failure to provide a written report, designated for the purposes of subsection 97.1(3) of the Act, constitutes an offence.

SOR/93-44, s. 23

Property of Deceased Persons

55. Where a person, other than a Canadian citizen or permanent resident, dies in Canada at an immigrant station or at some other place while he is under the control and supervision of an immigration officer, a senior immigration officer shall

(a) prepare a written report accounting for all moneys and personal property belonging to the person at that station or place,

and, unless otherwise directed by the Minister,

(b) where a relative of the person is known by the senior immigration officer to be in Canada, deliver the moneys and personal property and a copy of the written report referred to in paragraph (a) to the relative and obtain a receipt therefor, or

(c) in any case not referred to in paragraph (b), deliver the moneys and personal property and a copy of the written report referred to in paragraph (a) to the consular authorities in Canada of the country of which that person was a citizen or resident and obtain a receipt therefor.

Payments of Prescribed Nature

56. For the purposes of subsection 118(2) of the Act, payments that result from a breach of an undertaking and that are made directly or indirectly to an immigrant under an item described in column I of Schedule VI are payments that may be recovered from the person or organization that gave the undertaking as a debt due to Her Majesty in right of Canada or in right of any province to which the undertaking is assigned.

SOR/81-954, s. 1; SOR/99-329, s. 1

SCHEDULE I

(ss. 3, 7, 8 and 11)

Column I Factors	Column II Criteria	Column III Max. Units
1. Education	(1) Subject to subsections (2) to (4), units of assessment shall be awarded as follows: (a) where a diploma from a secondary school has not been completed, zero units; (b) where a diploma from a secondary school has been completed, the greater number of the following applicable units: (i) in the case of a diploma that does not lead to entrance to university in the country of study and does not include trade or occupational certification in the country of study, five units, (ii) in the case of a diploma that may lead to entrance to university in the country of study, ten units, and (iii) in the case of a diploma that includes trade or occupational certificate in the country of study, ten units;	16

Column I Factors	Column II Criteria	Column III Max. Units
	(c) where a diploma or apprenticeship certificate that requires at least one year of full-time classroom study has been completed at a college, trade school or other post-secondary institution, the greater number of the following applicable units: **(i) in the case of a diploma or apprenticeship certificate program that requires completion of a secondary school diploma referred to in subparagraph (b)(i) or (iii) as a condition of admission, ten units, and** **(ii) in the case of a diploma or apprenticeship certificate program that requires completion of a secondary school diploma referred to in subparagraph (b)(ii) as a condition of admission, thirteen units;** **(d) where a first-level university degree that requires at least three years of full-time study has been completed, fifteen units; and** **(e) where a second- or third- level university degree has been completed, sixteen units.** **(2) Units of assessment shall only be awarded for a diploma, degree or apprenticeship certificate referred to in any of paragraphs (1)(b) to (e) that has been completed at an institution other than a designated institution and in a field of study other than a designated field of study.** **(3) Only a single diploma, degree or apprenticeship certificate shall be taken into consideration when determining the units of assessment to be awarded in accordance with the applicable paragraph of subsection (1).** **(4) The units of assessment set out in paragraph (1)(b) to (e) shall not be awarded cumulatively, and the number of units of assessment set out in the applicable paragraph that awards the greatest number of units shall be awarded.**	
2. Education and Training	**(1) To be measured by the amount of formal education and professional, vocational, apprenticeship, in-plant or on-the-job training specified in the *National Occupational Classification* as being necessary to acquire the information, techniques and skills required for the occupation in which the applicant is assessed under item 4. Units of assessment shall be awarded as follows:** **(a) when no formal education or training is required, one unit;** **(b) when some secondary school education, on-the-job training or experience is required, two units;** **(c) when a secondary school diploma is required, five units;** **(d) when the completion of course work, training, workshops or experience related to the occupation, ordinarily on the completion of secondary school, is required, seven units;**	**18**

Column I Factors	Column II Criteria	Column III Max. Units
	(e) when a certificate or diploma of a college or technical school is required or when the completion of an apprenticeship program, a specialized training program or a vocational school training program is required, fifteen units; (f) when a university degree at the bachelor's level is required, seventeen units; and (g) when a university degree at the master's or doctoral level or a professional degree that requires additional education beyond the bachelor's level is required, eighteen units. (2) When more than one Education/Training Indicator is identified in the *National Occupational Classification* for a given occupation, the lowest of the ratings shall be used to assess the Education and Training Factor.	
3. Experience	Units of assessment shall be awarded for experience in the occupation in which the applicant is assessed under item 4 or, in the case of an entrepreneur, for experience in the occupation for which the entrepreneur is qualified and that the entrepreneur is prepared to follow in Canada, as follows: (a) when the number of units awarded under item 2 is one or two, two units for the first year of experience; (b) when the number of units awarded under item 2 is five to seven, two units for each year of experience not exceeding two years; (c) when the number of units awarded under item 2 is 15, two units for each year of experience not exceeding three years; and (d) when the number of units awarded under item 2 is 17 or 18, two units for each year of experience not exceeding four years.	8
4. Occupational Factor	(1) Units of assessment shall be awarded on the basis of employment opportunities in Canada in the occupation (a) for which the applicant meets the employment requirements for Canada as set out in the *National Occupational Classification*; (b) in which the applicant has performed a substantial number of the main duties as set out in the *National Occupational Classification*, including the essential ones; and (c) that the applicant is prepared to follow in Canada. (2) The employment opportunities shall be determined by taking into account labour market activity on both an area and a national basis, following consultation with the Department of Human Resources Development, provincial governments and any other relevant organizations and institutions.	10
	Ten units shall be awarded if, in the opinion of the visa officer,	10

Column I Factors	Column II Criteria	Column III Max. Units
5. Arranged Employment or Designated Occupation	(a) the person has arranged employment in Canada that, based on the information provided by the National Employment Service, offers reasonable prospects of continuity and wages and working conditions sufficient to attract and retain in employment Canadian citizens or permanent residents, (b) based on information provided by the National Employment Service, employment of the person in Canada will not adversely affect employment opportunities for Canadian citizens or permanent residents in Canada, and (c) the person will likely be able to meet all federal, provincial and other applicable licensing and regulatory requirements related to the employment, or if, in the opinion of the visa officer, (d) the person is qualified for and is prepared to engage in employment in a designated occupation, (e) based on information provided by the National Employment Service, employment in the designated occupation offers reasonable prospects of continuity and wages and working conditions sufficient to attract and retain in employment Canadian citizens or permanent residents, and (f) the person will likely be able to meet all federal, provincial and other applicable licensing or regulatory requirements related to employment in the designated occupation.	
6. Demographic Factor	Units of assessment shall be awarded as determined by the Minister after consultation with the provinces and such other persons, organizations and institutions as he deems appropriate concerning regional demographic needs, labour market considerations and the ability of the national infrastructure to accommodate population growth.	10
7. Age	Ten units of assessment shall be awarded with respect to a person who is at least 21 years of age and not more than 44 years of age. Where a person is more than 44 years or less than 21 of age, two units shall be subtracted from the maximum of ten units for each year by which the person exceeds 44 or is less than 21 years of age.	10
8. Knowledge of English and French Languages	(1) For the first official language, whether English or French, as stated by the person, credits shall be awarded according to the level of proficiency in each of the following abilities, namely, speaking, reading and writing, as follows: (a) for an ability to speak, read or write fluently three credits shall be awarded for each ability; (b) for an ability to speak, read or write well but not fluently, two credits shall be awarded for each ability; and (c) for an ability to speak, read or write with difficulty, no credits shall be awarded for that ability.	15

Column I Factors	Column II Criteria	Column III Max. Units
	(2) For the second official language, whether English or French, as stated by the person, credits shall be awarded according to the level of proficiency in each of the following abilities, namely, speaking, reading and writing, as follows:	
	(a) for an ability to speak, read or write fluently, two credits shall be awarded for each ability;	
	(b) for an ability to speak, read or write well but not fluently, one credit shall be awarded for each ability; and	
	(c) for an ability to speak, read or write with difficulty, no credits shall be awarded for that ability.	
	(3) Units of assessment shall be awarded on the basis of the total number of credits awarded under subsections (1) and (2) as follows:	
	(a) for zero credits or one credit, zero units;	
	(b) for two to five credits, two units; and	
	(c) for six or more credits, one unit for each credit.	
9. Personal Suitability	**Units of assessment shall be awarded on the basis of an interview with the person to reflect the personal suitability of the person and his dependants to become successfully established in Canada based on the person's adaptablility, motivation, initiative, resourcefulness and other similar qualities.**	**10**
10.	**[Revoked SOR/85-1038, s. 8.]**	

SOR/79-197, s. 5; SOR/85-1038, s. 8; SOR/93-44, ss. 24, 25; SOR/93-412, ss. 17, 18; SOR/97-184, s. 9; SOR/97-242, ss. 3-5

Case Law

Factor 1

Lo v. Canada (Minister of Citizenship & Immigration) (1997), 38 Imm. L.R. (2d) 235, 133 F.T.R. 156 (Fed. T.D.) — The applicant sought to review a decision of the visa officer, rejecting the applicant's application for permanent residence.

The applicant was married and in his early 40's, and he and his spouse had two sons, the older of whom was a Canadian citizen. The applicant's parents, three sisters, and one brother, all lived in Canada and were either Canadian citizens or landed immigrants. The applicant had lived and studied in Canada for some seven years. He attended four post-secondary educational institutions, but received no certificate or diploma from any of them. He also undertook post-secondary courses in Hong Kong and received certificates evidencing successful completion. At the time of this application the applicant had worked for his employer for over nine years in his chosen field of property management.

The applicant sought to meet the requirements for immigration in the assisted relative category. He was awarded 62 units of assessment as opposed to the 65 units required for successful acceptance. The number of units required had been reduced from 70 due to the fact that the applicant was applying as an assisted relative. If the applicant had been awarded the maximum units of assessment available for either education or personal suitability, he would have earned sufficient units of assessment to qualify as an assisted relative.

In her affidavit the officer indicated that she had concerns regarding the pattern of the applicant's educational pursuits with specific focus on the fact that he did not pursue any course of education in Canada to the point of achieving a certificate or degree. The applicant's pattern of educational pursuits influenced the visa officer both in respect of her assessment for education and personal suitability.

The fact that the applicant did not pursue any course of education to the point of a certificate or degree in relation to the education factor was entirely appropriate. However, with respect to the personal suitability factor, nowhere in the material is it evident that the applicant was notified of the visa officer's concern that the applicant's pattern of educational pursuits in Canada might evidence a lack of initiative and/or motivation. There was no evidence in the record that the applicant was given an opportunity to respond to such a concern.

The failure to give any credit for post-secondary education experience that has not led to a certificate or degree under the education factor, and reliance on the same consideration to discount the applicant's assessment in respect of the personal suitability factor amounted to "double counting" of a consideration, notwithstanding the visa officer's evidence to the contrary.

The conscious decision of an individual to pursue a broad and varied education without regard to the formalities of obtaining a certificate or degree does not necessarily indicate a lack of motivation or initiative. Traditionally, the pursuit of a degree rather than, or in addition to, an education has been the norm. It is arguable that those who fly in the face of traditional courses of action in the conscious pursuit of knowledge in its broadest form are to be commended rather than penalized. The Court did not conclude that the applicant was pursuing knowledge for its own sake, but merely commented that on the material before the Court, there was no information as to why the applicant attended a range of institutions in Canada without receiving a certificate or degree from any of them.

Yang v. Canada (Minister of Employment & Immigration) (1992), 56 F.T.R. 155, 17 Imm. L.R. (2d) 229 (Fed. T.D.) — The decision refusing the applicant's application for permanent residence was quashed. The applicant submitted an application for permanent residence in Hong Kong. The applicant was interviewed and refused on the basis that she had failed to accumulate sufficient credits under the selection criteria. The applicant was awarded 9 units for education. This determination was based on the policy of the Ministry that units of assessment are awarded in the educational factor only for education received to the end of secondary school. The applicant's position was that she should have been awarded 12 units of assessment for education. In Taiwan, secondary school education is completed within a nine year period following which the student proceeds to college. Accordingly, the tenth, eleventh and twelfth year of schooling are completed at a college rather than a high school. The Ontario Ministry of Education had provided the applicant with a letter indicating that it considers the 5 year diploma from the National Tai Chung Institute of Commerce to have an educational attainment comparable to someone with an Ontario Secondary School Diploma. Further, in the affidavit of Ms. Yang she deposed that at the interview she was never asked any questions pertaining to her educational background.

The visa officer had a duty to consider the applicant's submission that she was entitled to the maximum number of units of assessment in the education category. The failure to do so left a doubt as to whether a proper assessment of the applicant had taken place. Accordingly, an order in the nature of *certiorari* was granted and a new assessment by a different visa officer was ordered.

Editor's Note: The regulations concerning education assessment have changed, but the principles outlined in this case may still be important.

Factor 2

He v. Canada (Minister of Citizenship & Immigration) (1997), 36 Imm. L.R. (2d) 244 (Fed. T.D.) — The applicant applied for permanent residence and was assessed according to the CCDO occupation as a chef/cook. The CCDO provides that the specific vocational preparation for such an occupation is 7. In accordance with schedule 1 of the regulations, this translates into an equivalent of 15 units of assessment out of a possible 18.

Specific vocational preparation includes training in the following forms: 1) university, or college training; 2) vocational training; 3) apprenticeship; 4) in plant training; 5) on the job training; and 6) experience in other jobs. In determining whether the applicant had reached level 7 of vocational preparation, the visa officer was required to consider all 6 forms of training, in this case the visa officer had only considered one of those forms.

Accordingly, the Court decided that the visa officer had misinterpreted the provisions which she applied and set aside her decision.

Editor's Note: The CCDO has been replaced by the NOC, however, the principle in this case may still be of some assistance.

Factor 3

Nakamine v. Canada (Minister of Citizenship & Immigration) (1998), 41 Imm. L.R. (2d) 255 (Fed. T.D.) — This is an application to review a refusal of an application for permanent residence under the independent category as a chef/cook. The applicant was a citizen of Japan, and was awarded "0" units of assessment for his experience. The applicant had no formal training as a chef, but this occupation in Japan is learned on the job. Due to the fact that the applicant intended to work as a cook in a Japanese restaurant in Canada, formal training ought not to have been an essential factor. The applicant had more than two years of experience working in various restaurants in Japan and Canada and accordingly was entitled to more than "0" units of assessment for experience, at least as a cook, if not as a chef.

Yu v. Canada (Minister of Employment & Immigration) (1990), 11 Imm. L.R. (2d) 176, 36 F.T.R. 296 (Fed. T.D.) — *Certiorari* was sought to quash a decision refusing the applicant's request for permanent residence status in Canada. The applicant applied pursuant to the independent provisions of the *Immigration Regulations* under section 8 and schedule 1 of those regulations. In her application, she indicated that her intended occupation was as a librarian. In accordance with the Act, the applicant was required to establish that she met the selection criteria established by the regulations for determining whether she would be able to become successfully established in Canada and that her admission to Canada would not be contrary to the Act or regulations.

The visa officer, under section 8(1)(a) of the regulations, was required to assess the applicant on the basis of each of the factors in schedule 1, three of which related to the applicant's intended occupation in Canada. Factor 2, specific vocational preparation, was assessed in relation to the amount of formal training specified in the CCDO. Factor 3, experience, was assessed by years in the intended occupation. Factor 4, occupational demand, was assessed in relation to occupational opportunities in Canada. If the applicant is not deemed qualified for the occupation, then, regardless of the occupational demand, no units of assessment were to be awarded under factor 4 or under factor 3.

Schedule 1 required that the applicant's experience as a librarian could not be assessed favourably if she were unqualified by training for the occupation of librarian in Canada. There were no grounds for arguing unfairness merely because the visa officer did not stress all of the concerns he may have had at the interview arising directly from the Act and regulations. The Act and regulations pertinent to admission are available to the applicants whose task is to establish to the satisfaction of the visa officer that they meet the criteria set out and that their admission to Canada would not be contrary to the Act. This is to be distinguished from a situation where the decision refusing the application is made by reference to information other than the regulations provided for in assessing the applicant. The CCDO relied upon in this case is specifically incorporated by reference in schedule 1, factor 2 and thus is part of the regulations. Where it is concluded that the applicant lacks the specific vocational preparation expected in Canada, years of experience in the occupation elsewhere cannot count towards the units required for assessment in meeting the criteria for admission. In this case the visa officer's decision was upheld and the motion to quash dismissed.

Hajariwala v. Canada (Minister of Employment & Immigration) (1988), 6 Imm. L.R. (2d) 222, 34 Admin. L.R. 206, 23 F.T.R. 241, [1989] 2 F.C. 79 (Fed. T.D.) — The Court observed that those seeking landing in Canada must satisfy an immigration officer that they meet the selection standards set out in the regulations. It is the responsibility of the applicant to produce all relevant information which may assist in his application. The extent to which immigration officers may wish to offer assistance, counselling or advice may be a matter of individual preference or even a matter of departmental policy from time to time but it is not an obligation that is imposed upon the officers by the Act or the regulations.

Section 18 reviews are not appellate reviews. To succeed, the applicant must do more than establish the possibility that the Court would have reached a different conclusion than the visa officer in the assessment. There must be either an error of law apparent on the face of the record or a breach of the duty of fairness appropriate to this essentially administrative assessment. The regulations permit the applicant to be assessed in "an occupation". The factors listed in column 1 of schedule 1 require that the experience of the applicant be assessed with regard to his intended occupation. There is no reason why the actual experience and time spent in each of the various responsibilities in an occupation cannot be broken down to award units of assessment for experience in intended occupations. As a matter of fairness, the record should show that the applicant was given the opportunity to provide information in support of his current experience in each included occupation. The record must clearly indicate reasons which support the visa officer's assignment of a specific experience rating to the intended occupations or reasons which support the refusal to do so. In this case, the officer did not believe that the various responsibilities which the applicant carried out in his business in India should be broken down into separate components for the purposes of awarding units of assessment for experience in his alternative intended occupation of material purchasing or garment sales representative. Accordingly, the officer refused to issue a visa and in so doing erred in law. The officer's decision was set aside.

Factor 4

Azim v. Canada (Minister of Citizenship & Immigration) (1999), 49 Imm. L.R. (2d) 127 (Fed. T.D.) — The applicant sought an ordered quashing a decision of a visa officer refusing the applicant's application for landing. The National Occupational Classification (NOC) is a catalogue of occupations in Canada prepared by Human Resources Canada. It sets out a description of, and the requirement to be met in order to engage in, the occupations that are described.

Chapter 2112 describes the occupation of chemist and states that a bachelor's degree in chemistry is a minimum qualification. The applicant's B.Sc. degree was obtained after 2 years of study, not 3, and the visa officer did not consider this to be a bachelor's degree as described in the NOC. He considered that a bachelor's degree for NOC purposes required 3 years of full-time study. The text of the criteria to be addressed under the education factor in Schedule 1 refers to a first level university degree that requires at least 3 years of full-time study. This suggests that not all first level university degrees require 3 years of full-time study. The Court noted the difference in terminology between that used with respect to the education factor in Schedule 1 of the Regulations and that used in the National Occupations Classification, and that the NOC did not define a first level university degree as one requiring 3 years of full-time study.

Accordingly, the Court found that the applicant had a bachelor's degree for purposes of the NOC and set aside the decision of the visa officer.

Khattab v. Canada (Minister of Citizenship & Immigration) (1997), 135 F.T.R. 239, 40 Imm. L.R. (2d) 311 (Fed. T.D.) — The applicant applied for permanent residence as an independent immigrant and indicated that he would seek employment as a manufacturer's representative. He was called in for an interview and later informed that he had not been assessed enough points to qualify. That determination, however, assessed the applicant's suitability as an appliance salesman, and not the category which the applicant indicated on his application form. The visa officer did not indicate to the applicant her concern that he was not suited to consideration as a manufacturer's representative and that she would be evaluating him as an appliance salesman. This constituted reviewable error. Accordingly, the decision of the visa officer was set aside.

Samolenko v. Canada (Minister of Citizenship & Immigration) (July 28, 1997), Doc. IMM-4141-96 (Fed. T.D.) — The applicant sought to review a negative decision by a visa officer with respect to her application for permanent residence under the independent category. The applicant listed her occupation as a computer graphics specialist. In addition, the applicant alleged that she sent a supplementary application to the visa officer prior to the refusal that was the subject matter of this proceeding. That supplementary application was said to have contained an additional occupational category, namely, that of an arts supervisor. The respondent disputed receipt of the supplementary application. The applicant was not assessed as an arts supervisor.

A visa officer has a duty to assess an application with reference to each occupation represented by the applicant as one for which he or she is qualified and prepared to pursue in Canada. Further, there is the clear responsibility on the part of a visa officer to assess alternative occupations inherent in the applicant's work experience.

There was no evidence to establish that the supplementary application was in fact before the visa officer. The copy of the supplementary application submitted by the applicant as part of her application for judicial review did not contain any evidence to suggest receipt of it by the respondent. The respondent specifically denied that any supplementary application was received by the embassy. The only evidence submitted by the applicant was an affidavit of a solicitor who practised in association with counsel for the applicant. This solicitor's affidavit deposed that the source of his information and belief was the applicant's solicitor, who could not reasonably be expected to have personal knowledge of the matter.

Accordingly, the applicant had failed to prove that the supplementary application was before the visa officer and the application for judicial review was therefore dismissed.

Mohammad v. Canada (Minister of Citizenship & Immigration) (1997), 131 F.T.R. 52 (Fed. T.D.) — The applicant applied for permanent residence as an independent applicant. The applicant described his intended occupation as mechanic. He provided documents setting out his experience as a washing machine mechanic and technician, as well as his experience in the repair and maintenance of laundry machines generally. The visa officer concluded that the applicant did not have the required experience as a laundry machine mechanic, however, the officer decided to assess the applicant in the occupation of mechanical engineering technician.

At no time was the applicant advised that he was disqualified under his intended occupation as a laundry machine mechanic. It is not sufficient for the officer to disclose his decision in reasons for excluding the applicant from his intended occupation in his affidavit. The failure to advise the applicant that he was disqualified and the failure to provide him an opportunity to submit information on the alternative occupation constituted together a reviewable error. Accordingly the application was allowed.

Azarpajooh v. Canada (Minister of Citizenship & Immigration) (1997), 128 F.T.R. 203 (Fed. T.D.) — This was an application to review a decision of a visa officer refusing the applicant's application for permanent residence as an independent applicant. The applicant was found to lack the requisite number of points to obtain a visa based on such factors as occupational demand in the assessed occupation of "manager, engineering" and experience in the alternate occupation of "civil engineer".

The visa officer assessed the applicant under the specific occupation "managers, engineering" because the applicant had always been employed in a managerial capacity. The applicant had the requisite total number of points for the occupation of "manager, engineering" based on such factors as experience and education. However, the applicant was required to receive a minimum number of points under the factor of occupational demand and, since the applicant received no points in this category, his application was refused. The visa officer assessed the applicant under the alternate occupation "civil engineer". The visa officer determined that although the applicant had experience as "manager, engineering" his experience as a "civil engineer" was very limited. The visa officer did not provide a point tally or breakdown for the alternate occupation of "civil engineer".

The visa officer failed to provide procedural fairness. The visa officer had the duty to clearly inform the applicant that he was only being fully considered under the category of "manager, engineering" which was an occupation which the applicant had not specified in his original application. The visa officer has a duty to reveal to the applicant what was in her mind so that the applicant could, if he desired, dispute the visa officer's finding and disabuse her of assumptions.

Furthermore, there were some suggestions in the visa officer's notes that the applicant was involved in design work. The visa officer failed to break down the applicant's duties in his previous employment and award units of assessment for experience for his design work, particularly at his current position at the consulting firm. In her letter to the applicant, the visa officer did not acknowledge any possibility that the applicant had performed design work. Accordingly, failure to award any points for experience as a "civil engineer" was found to be unreasonable.

Mou v. Canada (Minister of Citizenship & Immigration) (1997), 125 F.T.R. 203 (Fed. T.D.) — The applicant sought to review the decision of a visa officer refusing his application for permanent residence as an independent applicant. The visa officer in Buffalo, New York attributed 68 units of assessment, 2 short of the required minimum of 70.

The applicant's intended occupation in Canada was that of a linguist. He held the equivalent of a Master of Arts degree from the Department of Chinese Language and Literature of Shanghai Teachers University. The applicant was at the time of this application a doctoral student and teaching assistant at the University of British Columbia.

The applicant received 5 out of a maximum of 10 units for personal suitability, because the visa officer was of the view that the "marketability" of the applicant's qualifications as a linguist in ancient Chinese language and literature was uncertain in Canada. The consideration of the "marketability" of the applicant's intended occupation under the personal suitability factor constituted double counting. The applicant was assessed less units under both personal suitability and occupational demand for the same reason. In addition, the visa officer incorrectly awarded the 15 units under the educational factor because of her characterization of the applicant's Master of Arts degree as a first level university degree. After the applicant successfully completed a comprehensive exam, the University of British Columbia had recognized his master of arts degree and accepted him into its doctorate program. The visa officer was aware of this fact and should have awarded the applicant 16 units for his second level university degree. The decision of the visa officer was set aside and the matter remitted for reconsideration.

The Court noted that there was no provision in the legislation or regulations upon which to determine the lock-in date for the reconsidered application. The applicant's material in this case was first received on April 12, 1995 with a payment of $2,950 for processing and landing fees. On April 19, 1995 a consular official returned the money order and requested payment of an additional $100. The payment of the higher amount of $3,050 was received on April 26, 1995. If the applicant's application had been deemed to be received on April 12, 1995, he would have received 2 units for the age factor. The applicant was assessed no units under this heading, presumably because his application was deemed to be received on April 26th, four days after his 49th birthday. Further, on April 12, 1995, when the applicant's material was received, his son was under 19 years of age. Pursuant to paragraph 3(3)(a) of the fees regulations, the processing fee for a dependent son under 19 years of age is $100. The son's 19th birthday was on April 16, 1995. The consular official requested the payment of $3,050 on April 19, 1995 when the son was no longer 19 years of age. In doing so, the son's fee may have been set at $100 on the basis of the material having been received on April 12, 1995 when he was under the age of 19. In this circumstance, no right of landing fee was payable for the son. In this case, the application was assigned a file number as early as the consular letter of April 19, 1995 requesting the additional funds. On April 19, 1995 the applicant was not yet 49 years old and was still eligible for 2 units. Further, the funds that had been received by the consular official on April 12, 1995 were sufficient to cover the processing and landing fees of both the applicant and his spouse. In requesting the additional $100 on April 19, 1995, the consular official was either locking-in the date of April 12, 1995 or erroneously requesting insufficient additional funds. Because of these exceptional and unusual circumstances, the Court concluded that the rights of the applicant should be assessed as of April 12, 1995 when the application forms together with sufficient fees for both the applicant and his spouse were received.

The Court noted that the applicant's son was not a party to the proceeding, but that it would be unfortunate if the proper exercise of discretion could not assure that the son's rights were not prejudicially affected by the errors of both the applicant and the respondent in the calculation of the son's fees. Finally, the Court noted the necessity for a clear lock-in date in these types of applications, one that would be within the control of the applicant and not subjected to arbitrary determination.

Cai v. Canada (Minister of Citizenship & Immigration) (January 17, 1997), Doc. IMM-883-96 (Fed T.D.) — This was an application to review a decision of a visa officer refusing the applicant's application for permanent residence. The visa officer assessed the applicant as an administrative clerk and denied the application on the basis that the applicant had achieved zero units of assessment. The applicant had originally applied for consideration under the occupation of executive secretary. The visa officer refused to assess her under that occupation on the ground that the applicant did not have the standard training requirements required to be considered in this occupation.

The onus is on the applicant to fully satisfy the visa officer of the existence of all the positive ingredients in his or her application. In making his or her assessment, the visa officer is not only called upon to compare the applicant's experience and qualifications with those set out in schedule I of the regulations, but is also obliged to consider the applicant under every occupation he or she designates in his or her application. The visa officer is also vested with the clear responsibility to assess alternate occupations inherent in the applicant's work experience. If however, the visa officer ascertains that an applicant does not meet the criteria for the occupation under which he or she seeks to be assessed it is not unreasonable for the visa officer to hold that the applicant cannot be further assessed in that occupational category.

The applicant was given some opportunity to explain the duties she had performed and her various positions. The visa officer also noted that there was nothing in the supporting documentation supplied by the applicant to indicate that the tasks she had performed in her various positions were commensurate with those performed by secretaries or executive secretaries in Canada.

The application for judicial review was denied.

Haughton v. Canada (Minister of Citizenship & Immigration) (1996), 34 Imm. L.R. (2d) 284, 111 F.T.R. 226 (Fed. T.D.) — The applicant applied at the Canadian Consulate in Buffalo for permanent residence under the category of independent skilled worker. The applicant sought to be classified and assessed as an executive secretary. The skills mentioned by the visa officer in the refusal letter were not in the CCDO definition of an executive secretary. Rather, these appear to be requirements that the visa officer considered, based solely on his own ideas of those skills which are required to be a successful executive secretary in a contemporary Canadian office environment.

The visa officer is bound by the CCDO definition. While it may be that there is a problem with outdated definitions provided in the CCDO, a visa officer is none the less not permitted to substitute his/her own criteria for a given occupation.

Having found that the visa officer erred in considering criteria in addition to the CCDO, it was then necessary for the Court to determine if this error effected the visa officer's overall assessment. In one interview, the visa officer reclassified the applicant from an executive secretary to a stenographer and in the process lowered her units exclusive of personal suitability from 63 to 48. When considering personal suitability a visa officer is required to consider economic establishment as it relates to the factors of adaptability, motivation and initiative. When economic considerations are at stake, it is reasonable to assume that the occupation in which one is classified is relevant to such an assessment. Therefore, the Court was not satisfied that the visa officer would have, but for the error in applying the CCDO, made the same personal suitabilities assessment. Accordingly, the application for judicial review was allowed and the matter remitted for redetermination by a different visa officer, in a manner not inconsistent with the court's reasons.

Yeung v. Canada (Minister of Employment & Immigration) (1992), 17 Imm. L.R. (2d) 191, 53 F.T.R. 205 (Fed. T.D.) — Mr. Yeung was a citizen of Hong Kong. He was employed as a production manager. He filed an application for permanent residence on December 12, 1989 together with the prescribed processing fee. The application form had a notation that the applicant's sister in Canada was willing to assist. At the time the application was received the occupation factor for production managers was 1 point. On January 30, 1991, the occupation demand for this occupation was set at 0. Mr. Yeung's application was reviewed in February 1991 and refused because the occupational demand on that date was 0.

The assessment date or lock-in date for determining the number of points to be awarded is the date of the original application and payment of the processing fee. This is true whether the independent applicant has a relative willing to assist or not.

Choi v. Canada (Minister of Employment & Immigration) (1991), 15 Imm. L.R. (2d) 265, [1992] 1 F.C. 763 (Fed. C.A.) — The appellant attended at the Canadian Commission in Hong Kong and enquired about how to apply for permanent residence. He was provided with a pre-application questionnaire ("PAQ") but was not told that he could make a formal application until the applicant completed a PAQ and filed it with the Commission on October 16, 1987. On October 28, 1987 the appellant received the PAQ back with information that he had received a positive assessment. The appellant completed the Application for Permanent Residence ("IMM8") and paid the required processing fee. The appellant did this on November 6, 1987.

At the time of the assessment of his PAQ, the occupational demand for his skills was 10 units. Effective November 2, 1987, the demand was reduced to 1 unit. The appellant received 65 units including the one unit of assessment for occupational demand against a requirement of 70 units for issuance of a visa. Had the appellant received the 10 units of assessment that were in effect in October 1987 he would have obtained 74 units and qualified for Permanent Residence. An Application for an Immigrant Visa is made when it duly initiates the process leading to the issue or refusal of the visa and not only when that processing is committed to a particular official authorized to dispose of the application. Any other date, except the date of the application, would be purely arbitrary as a lock-in date for the occupational demand factor, depending solely on the vagaries of the administrative process. The application date is the only date within the control of the applicant and is consequently the only date that can be established without arbitrariness.

It was an irresistible conclusion from the evidence that departmental policy was to withhold from applicants the information that they could proceed either by way of a PAQ or directly and immediately by a formal application. If applicants knew enough to request an application form they were given one. If they did not they were dealt with cursorily by being given a PAQ, which had the effect of enormously reducing the administrative burden on the visa officers.

When the Canadian government, through its agents, undertakes to supply information to immigration applicants as to how to become immigrants, it assumes a duty to provide this information accurately. This does not imply that Canadian authorities must provide a detailed exegesis of Canadian immigration law but it does mean that immigration authorities have an obligation to provide basic information and to make available the appropriate forms.

The exigencies of fairness therefore require that the time of the appellant's application be deemed to be the date on which he returned the completed PAQ to the Hong Kong office with the consequence that the units of assessment for occupational demand in his case should be deemed to be 10 units.

The appeal was allowed with costs, the decision of the visa officer set aside and the matter returned to a visa officer for reconsideration on the basis that the occupational demand factor for the appellant should be deemed to be 10 units of assessment.

Mohammad v. Canada (Minister of Employment & Immigration) (1991), 48 F.T.R. 96, 14 Imm. L.R. (2d) 104 (Fed. T.D.) — This was an application for *certiorari* to quash the decision of a visa officer denying the applicant's request for permanent resident status and *mandamus* to compel the respondent to process the application in accordance with the *Immigration Act* and the regulations. The applicant, a resident of Pakistan, submitted an application on November 28, 1988, requesting permanent resident status in Canada as an assisted relative. This application was forwarded by his Toronto solicitor to the Canadian High Commission in Islamabad, Pakistan. The applicant's occupation was identified as sales representative/food products. An applicant for permanent residence must obtain an aggregate of 70 units. One of the criteria to be considered is occupational demand. A list of occupational categories and their corresponding units of assessment is maintained by the Canada Employment and Immigration Commission. This list is periodically updated and the units of assessment are increased or decreased to reflect labour market demand. On November 28, 1988, there were 10 units of assessment available for occupational demand in the category in which the applicant had requested assessment, however, the application was stamped received by the Canadian High Commission on January 16, 1989 by which time the units of assessment for occupational demand had been decreased to 1. According to departmental policy, units of assessment lock in as of the date that the application is received by the appropriate visa officer. This provision of the policy guidelines did not offend the duty of fairness. When applications are submitted by mail or courier, if there is some lengthy delay for receipt by the proper office, the onus rests with the applicant to satisfy the Court that the unreasonable delay should not be attributed to him. This onus was not met in this case and the application was dismissed.

Gaffney v. Canada (Minister of Employment & Immigration) (1991), 12 Imm. L.R. (2d) 185, 121 N.R. 256, 40 F.T.R. 79 (note) (Fed. C.A.) — This was an appeal from a decision of the Trial Division refusing to quash the rejection of the appellant's application for landing as an independent immigrant by a visa officer in San Francisco. The visa officer considered that his duty to assess alternative occupations was limited to a category and did not extend to occupations in other categories which an immigrant was both qualified and willing to follow. The only evidence as to what transpired at the interview was set out in the appellant's affidavit. When the appellant's counsel was apprised of the refusal letter, he wrote the Consulate General pointing out that the appellant's work experience met other definitions in the *Canadian Classification and Dictionary of Occupations* (CCDO). The visa officer replied to the effect that in the interview the appellant's entire work experience had been canvassed and that these occupations had been considered. That letter was exhibited to the appellant's affidavit in support of his motion to quash. The appellant did not, of course, depose to the truth of the contents. The visa officer's notes were exhibited to the affidavit of another Immigration officer who could not depose to the truth of the notes. The visa officer has a duty to assess an application with reference to the occupation represented by the applicant (or his or her spouse) as the one for which he or she is qualified and prepared to pursue in Canada. That duty extends to each such occupation. The appellant in his affidavit alleged that the visa officer had failed to assess him in a number of occupations for which he was qualified and was prepared to pursue. There was no evidence to the contrary and the appeal was allowed and the Trial Division was directed to re-hear the application for *certiorari* and *mandamus*.

Editor's Note: On May 1, 1997, the CCDO was replaced by the NOC. The principle in this case, however, may be of interest.

Yu v. Canada (Minister of Employment & Immigration) (1990), 11 Imm. L.R. (2d) 176, 36 F.T.R. 296 (Fed. T.D.) — *Certiorari* was sought to quash a decision refusing the applicant's request for permanent residence status in Canada. The applicant applied pursuant to the independent provisions of the *Immigration Regulations* under section 8 and schedule 1 of those regulations. In her application, she indicated that her intended occupation was as a librarian. In accordance with the Act, the applicant was required to establish that she met the selection criteria established by the Regulations for determining whether she would be able to become successfully established in Canada and that her admission to Canada would not be contrary to the Act or Regulations.

The visa officer, under section 8(1)(a) of the regulations, was required to assess the applicant on the basis of each of the factors in schedule 1, three of which related to the applicant's intended occupation in Canada. Factor 2, specific vocational preparation, was assessed in relation to the amount of formal training specified in the CCDO. Factor 3, experience, was assessed by years in the intended occupation. Factor 4, occupational demand, was assessed in relation to occupational opportunities in Canada. If the applicant is not deemed qualified for the occupation, then, regardless of the occupational demand, no units of assessment were to be awarded under factor 4 or under factor 3.

Schedule 1 required that the applicant's experience as a librarian could not be assessed favourably if she were unqualified by training for the occupation of librarian in Canada. There were no grounds for arguing unfairness merely because the visa officer did not stress all of the concerns he may have had at the interview arising directly from the Act and regulations. The Act and regulations pertinent to admission are available to the applicants whose task is to establish to the satisfaction of the visa officer that they meet the criteria set out and that their admission to Canada would not be contrary to the Act. This is to be distinguished from a situation where the decision refusing the application is made by reference to information other than the regulations provided for in assessing the applicant. The CCDO relied upon in this case is specifically incorporated by reference in schedule 1, factor 2 and thus is part of the regulations. Where it is concluded that the applicant lacks the specific vocational preparation expected in Canada, years of experience in the occupation elsewhere cannot count towards the units required for assessment in meeting the criteria for admission. In this case the visa officer's decision was upheld and the motion to quash dismissed.

Li v. Canada (Minister of Employment & Immigration) (1990), 9 Imm. L.R. (2d) 263 (Fed. T.D.) — The applicant requested permanent residence in Canada as an independent applicant pursuant to section 6(1) of the *Immigration Act.* Such applications involve a two-stage process during which it is the visa officer's duty to apply criteria set forth in the legislation and award points based on the ability of the applicant to become successfully established in Canada.

The first phase of the assessment is a paper-screening process in which immigration officials evaluate documents submitted by applicants and decide if the application process should be continued. If the applicant passes this phase, he or she is invited to an interview with a visa officer. During the interview, the officer assesses the employment experience of the applicant and awards points for other factors based on information presented at that time.

One of the most significant factors in any assessment is the applicant's possibility of employment in Canada. Points are awarded both for occupational demand in the screening step and for experience in the final assessment. This process requires reference to the Canadian Classification and Dictionary of Occupations (CCDO). Assessment of any one intended occupation begins with the matching of the applicant's work routine with the specific occupation from the CCDO.

There is a clear responsibility on the part of a visa officer to assess alternate occupations inherent in the applicant's work experience. Where his work experience suggests that the occupation may be appropriate, the visa officer must assess the applicant in the designated occupation regardless of which alternate occupations the officer has seen fit to consider.

The applicant's present occupation in the Philippines was that of a proprietor of two businesses. The applicant spends approximately 90 per cent of his time dealing with the wholesale distribution of office machines and considered that the best designation in the CCDO was that of "Commercial Traveller". Further, in a letter to the Canadian Consulate General, the applicant asserted that he had the necessary qualifications as a "Sales Representative, Office Machines", a subclassification of Commercial Traveller. The officer formed the impression that the applicant sold only hand calculators on a retail basis. The officer concluded that the applicant lacked product and plant experience and stated that he was "unable to assess your application in that category." The decision was set aside and the visa officer was required to evaluate the applicant's work experience in the category the applicant originally requested. The respondent Minister was directed to carry out the required assessment through a different visa officer.

Factor 5

D'Souza v. Canada (Minister of Employment & Immigration) (1990), 12 Imm. L.R. (2d) 268, 39 F.T.R. 1 (Fed. T.D.) — Ms. D'Souza applied for permanent residence as an independent immigrant. Her application was submitted under cover of a letter sent by her prospective employer and noted her occupation as executive secretary. The applicant was advised by letter that a barrier to acceptance of her application was the fact that there was only a limited demand in Canada for persons in her occupation. Accordingly, the applicant was advised to obtain a confirmation of her offer of employment by the local CEC. In the meantime, her application was refused.

There is no requirement arising by implication in the Act or regulations that the visa officer must consult on his own initiative the National Employment Service. The applicant must demonstrate to the satisfaction of the visa officer who has been entrusted to decide that the criteria for admission have been met. So long as the procedures developed and followed by the Commission to fulfil its responsibilities in relation to immigration matters are not inconsistent with the requirements of the Act and regulations, there can be no objection in law to them. The Minister must have discretion to develop administrative procedures to meet his or her statutory and regulatory responsibilities. The Court should intervene to limit that discretion only where it is clear that the procedures are inconsistent with or otherwise beyond the authority of the Minister under the Act and regulations.

The decision to withhold the grant of a visa until confirmation of employment had been communicated from the National Employment Service to the visa officer was not an improper delegation of authority. The regulations, in particular item 5 of schedule 1, provide for the visa officer assessing an application for permanent residence in part by having referenced to arranged employment and to consider that criterion for admission based on information provided by the National Employment Service. If this determination of particular aspects of employment is considered to be delegation, then it is delegation made by the Regulations and it is authorized. It is not a delegation made by the visa officer.

The assessment criteria established by schedule 1 to the regulations are not inconsistent with the Act and regulations. The requirement that a local CEC office validate arranged employment falls clearly within section 114(1)(a) as a matter within "labour market conditions in Canada for the purpose of determining whether or not an immigrant will be able to become successfully established in Canada." In the detail of factors to be considered by the National Employment Service in considering matters within item 5 of schedule 1, the Service must be careful to consider only those matters which can be justified as being clearly within the factors set out in the schedule. Section 20(3) of the regulations is much more precise than item 5 of schedule 1. While it may be a worthwhile objective of the Employment Service to insist upon the training of Canadians, such a requirement is not clearly within the factors to be considered in relation to item 5 of schedule 1. It is not appropriate to insist that the prospective employer of an applicant/immigrant first be expected to train persons already in Canada before authorization is given to arranged employment nor is it appropriate to insist in practice upon any standard minimum period for a prospective employer to seek unsuccessfully an employee through the CEC services. The employment officer must be prepared to look at whatever evidence this prospective employer may have of his efforts to hire Canadian citizens or permanent residents. The visa officer fulfilled his duties in this case and accordingly the applications for *certiorari* and *mandamus* were dismissed.

Singh (G.) v. Canada (Minister of Citizenship & Immigration) (1995), 106 F.T.R. 66 (Fed. T.D.) — The applicant, a citizen of India, applied for permanent residence as an assisted relative. His application was received by the Canadian Consulate General in Buffalo in February 1990. The applicant entered Canada in 1981 as a visitor, however he was discovered working illegally at a car wash. He then made a claim for Convention refugee status which he later withdrew on his return to India. He entered Canada again in 1987 and has been living here since that time. In 1991 he made a second claim for Convention refugee status which he also subsequently abandoned. The applicant worked legally as a machinist at a company in Mississauga from 1988 until the company went bankrupt in 1990. He has not been employed since then.

The applicant was interviewed in connection with his independent application in June 1992. The officer's decision was not made until May 1994, and was not communicated to the applicant until October 1994. During the 28 month period between the interview and communication of the decision, the applicant's solicitor sent 12 letters to the respondent requesting information about the status of the applicant's file. The respondent replied twice with form letters indicating that the matter was proceeding normally.

In her decision, the officer informed the applicant that he had received the necessary 70 points but that she had a discretion pursuant to section 11(3) of the regulations to refuse to issue a visa. The officer stated that although Mr. Singh had been in Canada for a substantial amount of time he had not acquired reasonable language skills, had not sought substantial employment opportunities and therefore, did not appear to demonstrate motivation, initiative, adaptability and the resourcefulness required to successfully establish himself in Canada. The officer informed Mr. Singh that he came within the inadmissable class of persons described in subsection 19(2)(d) of the Act.

Fairness requires that an applicant receive a timely decision. What that means will vary with the circumstances in each case. A two and a half year delay between an interview and notification is unacceptable where there are no special circumstances which account for the delay. In exercising her discretion the officer was directing her attention to the applicant's ability to establish himself in Canada. This is a forward looking exercise. To accord offers of employment, which are bona fide, little weight because they are not certified by a CEIC is to apply an irrelevant consideration to the decision. The offers demonstrated that once landed the applicant had good employment prospects. The fact that he could not accept the offers prior to landing was irrelevant. Further, the officer's interview notes indicated that certified job offers were not discussed. It was simply agreed that the applicant would send letters of employment to the officer within 60 days of the interview. The applicant did this and in the circumstances it was incumbent on the officer to notify the applicant if the documents he provided were insufficient to fulfil her requirements.

The officer's notes disclose no factual basis for her conclusion that the applicant's failure to secure a job was caused by lack of motivation. The applicant was not interviewed about his job search efforts. Therefore, the conclusion about the applicant's motivation was not well founded. The applicant had worked as a machinist for two years and had secured offers of employment with poor English skills. It was therefore clear that he could be employed with minimal spoken English. There may be cases in which language skills will impact on an applicant's ability to make a living, but on the facts of this case language did not appear to be an obstacle to the applicant's employment.

The officer's decision was set aside and the matter referred back for redetermination by a different visa officer.

Factor 8

Lin v. Canada (Minister of Citizenship & Immigration) (1996), 33 Imm. L.R. (2d) 8, 107 F.T.R. 225 (Fed. T.D.) — This was an application to review a decision of a visa officer rejecting the applicant's application for permanent residence as an independent immigrant under the assisted relative class. The visa officer imported the notion of English language ability into the concept of specific vocational preparation. A visa officer should not take into account the language capability of an applicant when assessing the award of units with respect to another category listed in schedule 1 to the regulations. The decision of the visa officer was set aside and the matter was remitted to a different visa officer for reconsideration.

Factor 9

Wen v. Canada (Minister of Citizenship & Immigration) (March 10, 1999), Doc. IMM-1556-98 (Fed. T.D.) — The applicant sought to review a decision of a visa officer. The decision of the visa officer was set aside. The officer was unable to explain her below average assessment of the applicant's personal suitability. The officer could not point to any factors justifying her low assessment. In order to justify a below average assessment of personal suitability, a visa officer should be able to at least indicate some specific areas of concern which prompt the low mark and not simply recite a standard list of relevant factors.

Barua v. Canada (Minister of Citizenship and Immigration) (1998), 47 Imm. L.R. (2d) 283, 157 F.T.R. 65 (Fed. T.D.) — This was an application to review the refusal of the applicant's independent application. As a matter of principle a visa officer may have regard, in the category of personal suitability, to an aspect of something that has already been assessed, provided that this aspect can be related to the applicant's motivation, adaptability, resourcefulness, initiatives and other similar qualities that will enable the applicant to become economically established in Canada. The fact that an applicant has no family support in Canada because there are no relatives here, does not have a personal suitability aspect.

The visa officer erred in law when he included under the assessment of the applicant's personal suitability to become successfully established in Canada, the fact that the applicant had no family support in Canada. In this case, the visa officer awarded the applicant a total of 6 out of a possible 10 units of assessment for personal suitability. The Court found it inconceivable that the visa officer would have awarded two more units of assessment for personal suitability, which the applicant needed to become entitled to a visa, if the visa officer had omitted the applicant's lack of relatives in Canada from the several factors that he considered when assessing personal suitability and the Court accordingly dismissed the application.

B'Ghiel v. Canada (Minister of Citizenship & Immigration) (1998), 45 Imm. L.R. (2d) 198, 152 F.T.R. 103 (Fed. T.D.) — This was an application to set aside a decision of a visa officer. In the officer's assessment of the factor "personal suitability", the officer referred to the fact that the applicant did not have relatives or close friends established in Canada to assist him. Having or not having relatives or close friends in Canada cannot be described as a personal "quality" similar to those which are listed in factor 9. There are other provisions in the Act and Regulations where the existence of relatives in Canada may be taken into account. Secondly, the officer mentioned the applicant's failure to demonstrate that he would be able to obtain employment in his field. This also constituted an example of double counting. Factor 4 deals with employment opportunities in Canada.

The visa officer's letter to the applicant explaining her decision contains a number of considerations which were properly taken into account. It is impossible for the Court to know what weight the officer gave to each of those considerations and what weight was attached to the factors which were improperly considered. Accordingly, the application was allowed and the decision of the visa officer set aside.

Lo v. Canada (Minister of Citizenship & Immigration) (1997), 38 Imm. L.R. (2d) 235, 133 F.T.R. 156 (Fed. T.D.) — The applicant sought to review a decision of the visa officer, rejecting the applicant's application for permanent residence.

The applicant was married and in his early 40's, and he and his spouse had two sons, the older of whom was a Canadian citizen. The applicant's parents, three sisters, and one brother, all lived in Canada and were either Canadian citizens or landed immigrants. The applicant had lived and studied in Canada for some seven years. He attended four post-secondary educational institutions, but received no certificate or diploma from any of them. He also undertook post-secondary courses in Hong Kong and received certificates evidencing successful completion. At the time of this application the applicant had worked for his employer for over nine years in his chosen field of property management.

The applicant sought to meet the requirements for immigration in the assisted relative category. He was awarded 62 units of assessment as opposed to the 65 units required for successful acceptance. The number of units required had been reduced from 70 due to the fact that the applicant was applying as an assisted relative. If the applicant had been awarded the maximum units of assessment available for either education or personal suitability, he would have earned sufficient units of assessment to qualify as an assisted relative.

In her affidavit the officer indicated that she had concerns regarding the pattern of the applicant's educational pursuits with specific focus on the fact that he did not pursue any course of education in Canada to the point of achieving a certificate or degree. The applicant's pattern of educational pursuits influenced the visa officer both in respect of her assessment for education and personal suitability.

The fact that the applicant did not pursue any course of education to the point of a certificate or degree in relation to the education factor was entirely appropriate. However, with respect to the personal suitability factor, nowhere in the material is it evident that the applicant was notified of the visa officer's concern that the applicant's pattern of educational pursuits in Canada might evidence a lack of initiative and/or motivation. There was no evidence in the record that the applicant was given an opportunity to respond to such a concern.

The failure to give any credit for post-secondary education experience that has not led to a certificate or degree under the education factor, and reliance on the same consideration to discount the applicant's assessment in respect of the personal suitability factor amounted to "double counting" of a consideration, notwithstanding the visa officer's evidence to the contrary.

The conscious decision of an individual to pursue a broad and varied education without regard to the formalities of obtaining a certificate or degree does not necessarily indicate a lack of motivation or initiative. Traditionally, the pursuit of a degree rather than, or in addition to, an education has been the norm. It is arguable that those who fly in the face of traditional courses of action in the conscious pursuit of knowledge in its broadest form are to be commended rather than penalized. The Court did not conclude that the applicant was pursuing knowledge for its own sake, but merely commented that on the material before the Court there was no information as to why the applicant attended a range of institutions in Canada without receiving a certificate or degree from any of them.

Mou v. Canada (Minister of Citizenship & Immigration) (1997), 125 F.T.R. 203 (Fed. T.D.) — The applicant sought to review the decision of a visa officer refusing his application for permanent residence as an independent applicant. The visa officer in Buffalo, New York attributed 68 units of assessment, 2 short of the required minimum of 70.

The applicant's intended occupation in Canada was that of a linguist. He held the equivalent of a Master of Arts degree from the Department of Chinese Language and Literature of Shanghai Teachers University. The applicant was at the time of this application a doctoral student and teaching assistant at the University of British Colombia.

The applicant received 5 out of a maximum of 10 units for personal suitability, because the visa officer was of the view that the "marketability" of the applicant's qualifications as a linguist in ancient Chinese language and literature was uncertain in Canada. The consideration of the "marketability" of the applicant's intended occupation under the personal suitability factor constituted double counting. The applicant was assessed less units under both personal suitability and occupational demand for the same reason. In addition the visa officer incorrectly awarded the 15 units under the educational factor because of her characterization of the applicant's Master of Arts degree as a first level university degree. After the applicant successfully completed a comprehensive exam, the University of British Colombia had recognized his Master of Arts degree and accepted him in its doctorate program. The visa officer was aware of this fact and should have awarded the applicant 16 units for his second level university degree. The decision of the visa officer was set aside and the matter remitted for reconsideration.

The Court noted that there was no provision in the legislation or regulations upon which to determine the lock-in date for the reconsidered application. The applicant's material in this case was first received on April 12, 1995 with a payment of $2,950 for processing and landing fees. On April 19, 1995 a consular official returned the money order and requested payment of an additional $100. The payment of the higher amount of $3,050 was received on April 26, 1995. If the applicant's application had been deemed to be received on April 12, 1995, he would have received 2 units for the age factor. The applicant was assessed no units under this heading, presumably because his application was deemed to be received on April 26th, four days after his 49th birthday. Further, on April 12, 1995, when the applicant's material was received, his son was under 19 years of age. Pursuant to paragraph 3(3)(a) of the fees regulations the processing fee for a dependent son under 19 years of age is $100. The son's 19th birthday was on April 16, 1995. The consular official requested the payment of $3,050 on April 19, 1995 when the son was no longer 19 years of age. In doing so, the son's fee may have been set at $100 on the basis of the material having been received on April 12, 1995 when he was under the age of 19. In this circumstance, no right of landing fee was payable for the son. In this case the application was assigned a file number as early as the consular letter of April 19, 1995 requesting the additional funds. On April 19, 1995 the applicant was not yet 49 years old and was still eligible for 2 units. Further, the funds that had been received by the consular official on April 12, 1995 was sufficient to cover the processing and landing fees of both the applicant and his spouse. In requesting the additional $100 on April 19, 1995, the consular official was either locking-in the date of April 12, 1995 or erroneously requesting insufficient additional funds. Because of these exceptional and unusual circumstances the Court concluded that the rights of the applicant should be assessed as of April 12, 1995 when the application forms together with sufficient fees for both the applicant and his spouse were received.

The Court noted that the applicant's son was not a party to the proceeding, but that it would be unfortunate if the proper exercise of discretion could not assure that the son's rights were not prejudicially affected by the errors of both the applicant and the respondent in the calculation of the son's fees. Finally, the Court noted the necessity for a clear lock-in date in these types of applications, one that would be within the control of the applicant and not subjected to arbitrary determination.

Hussain v. Canada (Minister of Citizenship & Immigration) (1997), 36 Imm. L.R. (2d) 232 (Fed. T.D.) — This is an application to review a decision of a visa officer refusing the applicant's application for permanent residence. The applicant received 67 units, 3 less than the 70 required by the schedule. The applicant challenged the assessment only in respect of the personal suitability factor.

The visa officer did not err in taking into account a lack of knowledge of Canada in the assessment of personal suitability. Further, the visa officer did not double count with respect to the assessment of language ability under the personal suitability factor. The unambiguous words of the regulation, as well as the relevant jurisprudence, indicate that the category of personal suitability is intended to be somewhat of a basket clause encompassing a general concern with the applicant's ability to successfully survive economically in this country. The assessment of language ability in that context does not amount to double counting.

Amir v. Canada (Minister of Citizenship & Immigration) (1996), 125 F.T.R. 158 (Fed. T.D.) — The applicant sought to review a decision of the Canadian Consulate in Buffalo refusing his application for permanent residence.

The applicant, a citizen of Pakistan, had been working first as a cook, then a chef in the United States. While in school the applicant studied English. In 1973 to 1983 he was employed as a seaman by the Kuwait Shipping Company where English was spoken by the employees. The applicant had visited over 100 cities on all continents during that employment.

The visa officer, under the language factor, awarded the applicant three units for reading, three units for writing and zero units for speaking English. Given the fact that the applicant had been living and working in the United States for 6 1/2 years and dealing with restaurant customers in the English language and that the interview was carried out in English, the assessment of zero for speaking English was patently unreasonable.

Under factor 9, personal suitability, the visa officer assessed only two units out of a maximum of ten. The fact that the applicant intended to visit his wife and his children back in Pakistan once a year was not a relevant factor to be used against him in the context of personal suitability. Secondly, the visa officer's observation that the applicant had not taken steps to "elevate his level of education" was inappropriate. Personal suitability is an economic factor which allows a visa officer to form an opinion as to whether the applicant will succeed in his field in this country. The officer was required to bear in mind in this case that the applicant was going to attempt to succeed in Canada as a short order cook and not a university professor.

The decision of the visa officer was set aside.

Ting v. Canada (Minister of Citizenship & Immigration) (1996), 36 Imm. L.R. (2d) 197, 122 F.T.R. 238 (Fed. T.D.) — The applicant sought to review a decision of a visa officer refusing the application for permanent residence on the ground that she awarded only 68 units of assessment when a minimum of 70 were required.

The applicant was a young woman, 32 years of age. She held a Bachelors degree in arts and a Masters degree in arts from Chinese universities and a Masters degree in arts from Laval University in Quebec City. She was an interpreter and a tour guide in China and a teacher of French in Beijing from 1986 to 1993. The applicant intended to work as an interpreter in Vancouver.

The visa officer in Buffalo awarded only 4 units out of 10 for personal suitability. The officer determined that the applicant was not strongly suited to successfully establish herself in the occupation of an interpreter in Vancouver because of her limited communication skills and experience in the English language. During the interview, the applicant required frequent repetition and simplification to understand English.

The visa officer failed to properly apply the criteria of adaptability. Adaptability is a forward-looking element. It was common ground that Vancouver harboured a very large and prosperous Chinese community. The applicant was a university trained scholar with 3 university degrees and proficient in 3 languages. Her career as an interpreter, a tour guide and a teacher of French, plus the fact that she has been able to adapt herself at a French university in the Province of Quebec, showed a high degree of adaptability. Further, the visa officer failed to exercise her discretion under subsection 11(3) of the Regulations. A proper exercise of that discretion would have resulted in the awarding of two more units so as to grant a visa to an otherwise highly qualified applicant.

The decision of the visa officer was set aside.

Tam v. Canada (Minister of Citizenship & Immigration) (1996), 35 Imm. L.R. (2d) 207 (Fed. T.D.) — This was an application to set aside a decision denying the applicant's application for permanent residence. The applicant was a 29 year citizen of Hong Kong, who was employed as an administrative officer at a rug company which employed 25 people, and had an international clientele. The applicant travelled to Japan routinely on company business. Following an initial paper screening the applicant was invited for an interview. During the interview the officer questioned the applicant about his education, qualifications, occupation, experience, motivation and knowledge of Canada.

In assessing the applicant's personal suitability, the visa officer considered the resourcefulness, initiative, adaptability and motivation of the applicant as evidenced by his work history and travel. The applicant was awarded five units out of a possible ten. The visa officer took a negative view of the fact that the applicant had only worked for one company since leaving school.

The fact that the applicant had only worked in one job during his employment history, did not support the view that the applicant had very little initiative, adaptability or motivation. In addition, the officer owed a duty of fairness which required that the officer advise the applicant of his concerns about the fact that the applicant had worked at only one job in his employment history, and provide the applicant with an opportunity to respond before any decision was made.

Accordingly, the application was allowed, the decision of the visa officer set aside, and the matter remitted back for redetermination.

Chatrova v. Canada (Minister of Citizenship & Immigration) (1996), 34 Imm. L.R. (2d) 59, 111 F.T.R. 308 (Fed. T.D.) — The applicant sought an order quashing a decision of a visa officer refusing her independent application for permanent residence. The decision of the visa officer was overturned because the applicant's language skills were not properly evaluated.

The visa officer in the refusal letter noted that the applicant's English was good but not "flawless". An applicant is not required to have flawless English in order to be awarded three points. The visa officer has to assess whether the applicant's English is "fluent". The officer's notes in this regard indicated that the assessment was proper and the Court did not place to much emphasis on the wording of the visas officer's letter.

The applicant had claimed fluency in the three areas of reading, writing and speaking. The visa officer accepted the applicant's self assessment insofar as reading was concerned and awarded her three points. The applicant was awarded two points for her verbal skills because the officer determined the applicant's English was good but not fluent. The visa officer however, assumed that the applicant's writing ability was comparable to her speaking ability, and not to her reading ability. No test was done nor was the applicant asked to demonstrate her writing ability. This was a significant error. In the circumstances of this case, the applicant was entitled to be alerted to the fact that her self assessment was being questioned before any burden can be said to fall upon her to provide further evidence. It was part of the circumstances of this case that the visa officer had awarded the applicant 68 units of assessment and refused her application because she did not meet the 70 unit requirement.

The visa officer also considered that the applicant's deficiency in the area of language ability was a reason for not awarding her more points under factor 9 (personal suitability). Taking the applicant's language skills into account in this manner resulted in the language skills being "double-counted".

A further issue arose with respect to whether a visa officer can go outside the CCDO definition in assessing the applicant's experience. Visa officers are instructed to assess potential immigrants, in accordance with factors described in Schedule I to the *Immigration Regulations*. Some of the 9 factors are inter-related. This is particularly true for factor 4 (occupational demand); factor 3 (experience); and factor 2 (specific vocational of preparation). The number of points a potential immigrant is given under factor 4 depends upon the occupation that the applicant is qualified for and is prepared to follow in Canada. There is no description of what constitutes an occupation. Factor 3 (experience) and factor 2 (specific vocational of preparation) are connected to factor 4. The number of points to be awarded with respect to experience relates to experience in the occupation in which the applicant is assessed under factor 4. The number of points awarded for specific vocational preparation are measured by the amount of training specified in the CCDO as necessary for average performance in the occupation. In addition, factor 2 (specific vocational preparation) and factor 3 (experience) are inter-related. The number of points awarded for experience is directly related to the SVP factor. A potential immigrant who lacks formal education in the relevant occupation can still obtain points by having had experience in that occupation. The degree in formal education required for each occupation is specifically linked to the occupation listing and description in the CCDO.

The applicant's lack of computer skills was counted under both the experience factor and the personal suitability factor. Thus, it was double counted. An applicant should not be faulted as lacking in adaptability, motivation, initiative and resourcefulness for not having acquired skills in English language computer software, when that skill is not part of the CCDO occupation description. To fault an applicant for lacking knowledge of English language computer software, when the government published occupation description makes no reference to such a skill is not reasonable.

Stefan v. Canada (Minister of Citizenship & Immigration) (1995), 35 Imm. L.R. (2d) 21 (Fed. T.D.) — This was an application for judicial review of a negative decision of a visa officer. The officer awarded the applicant five out of ten points for personal suitability. The overall assessment fell one point short of the 70 points required for a successful visa application. The officer based his conclusion about the applicant's personal suitability on the following factors:

1. the applicant, although a civil engineer, had not taken any computer courses to train her to pursue her profession in Canada;
2. that her learning pace during her English studies were slow; and
3. she had no special knowledge of Canada.

Personal suitability allows an officer to consider an applicant's adaptability, motivation, initiative and resourcefulness in the context of that applicant's prospects for successful establishment in Canada.

The applicant was given the maximum points for her educational achievements. Although her education was considered a second time when the officer assessed her personal suitability, education during this portion of the assessment was considered from a different perspective. The question was whether the applicant had the training necessary to use her professional qualifications as a civil engineer. The Court found no fault with this approach.

With respect to language, the applicant was given points for her language ability, but the officer then looked at her language training again and concluded from her slow learning pace that she was not very adaptable. The Court found no fault with this type of analysis. What must be seen in an analysis under personal suitability is an assessment focused on the four factors and not on the skill level already recorded in other parts of the assessment.

The Court did not consider knowledge of Canada to be an extraneous factor. It was reasonable to infer that someone who wanted to bring her family to Canada, but had not taken the trouble to learn something about Canada, lacked the initiative and resourcefulness necessary for successful establishment in the country.

Accordingly, the judicial review application was dismissed.

Dragone v. Canada (Minister of Citizenship & Immigration) (1995), 31 Imm. L.R. (2d) 97 (Fed. T.D.) — An immigration officer concluded that the applicant did not obtain sufficient units of assessment. The officer assessed the applicant's language abilities. With respect to personal suitability, the officer again referred to the applicant's lack of ability in English. The officer had no discretion to take language into account in his assessment of personal suitability. Accordingly, the officer's decision was set aside and the case remitted to a different immigration officer for review and reconsideration.

Ho v. Canada (Minister of Employment & Immigration) (1994), 88 F.T.R. 146 (Fed. T.D.) — The applicant commenced an originating application to set aside a decision of a visa officer. The applicant filed the affidavit of her sister in support of her originating notice of application. Those paragraphs of the sister's affidavit, which were based on information and belief, were struck out as offensive to Rule 1603.

The visa officer made an assessment of the applicant's personal suitability as required by item 9 of Schedule I. Personal suitability is meant to encompass factors not already specifically assessed in the other Schedule I items. The visa officer in this case considered the applicant's language deficiency in assessing personal suitability. Knowledge of English and French is specifically assessed at item 8 of Schedule I. It was therefore, not open to the visa officer to consider language in assessing the applicant pursuant to item 9.

The decision of the visa officer was quashed.

Lam v. Canada (Minister of Employment & Immigration) (1991), 15 Imm. L.R. (2d) 275, 49 F.T.R. 200 (Fed. T.D.) — The applicant applied for permanent residence as a self-employed person. The visa officer rejected the application without ever affording the applicant an interview. The visa officer determined that the applicant could not have met the minimum requirement of 70 units of assessment to qualify as a self-employed person even if he had been accorded the maximum 10 units of assessment for personal suitability after an interview. Because the officer determined that the applicant did not meet the definition of a self-employed person he did not give the applicant the 30 units of assessment for self-employment described in Regulation 8(4).

Schedule 1 of the regulations in Factor 9 describes, under the criteria for personal suitability, the units of assessment awarded on the basis of an interview with the person to reflect the personal suitability of the person and his dependents to become successfully established in Canada. Schedule 1, Factor 9, was taken to mean that the officer doing the assessment must award up to 10 units depending on his finding as to personal suitability. Where the maximum

10 units are awarded, the interviewing officer must have been satisfied that the prospective immigrant has the personal suitability to become successfully established in Canada.

By not having granted the applicant an interview, the officer was not in a position to determine whether he would have allowed the 30 units of assessment in section 8(4) of the regulations. Further, section 11(3) of the regulations permits a visa officer to issue a visa even if the applicant is not awarded the necessary units of assessment. If the applicant has all the qualities mentioned in Factor 9 of Schedule 1, a visa officer cannot form a valid opinion under section 11(3) without an interview. The visa officer has no discretion not to grant the interview mentioned in Factor 9. It is incumbent upon a visa officer to follow the procedure set out in statute. The officer has no discretion in deciding whether to grant an interview pursuant to Factor 9 under column 1 of Schedule 1 of the regulations. The decision of the officer in this case was quashed. The Minister was directed to reconsider the applicant's application and another visa officer was to effect this reconsideration.

Editor's Note: See, however, sections 8(1) and 11.1 of the Immigration Regulations.

SCHEDULE II

(s. 13)

1. Citizens of Andorra, Antigua and Barbuda, Australia, Austria, Bahamas, Barbados, Belgium, Botswana, Brunei, Costa Rica, Cyprus, Denmark, Dominica, Finland, France, Federal Republic of Germany, Greece, Grenada, Hungary, Iceland, Ireland, Italy, Japan, Kiribati, Liechtenstein, Luxembourg, Malaysia, Malta, Mexico, Monaco, Namibia, Nauru, Netherlands, New Zealand, Norway, Papua New Guinea, Portugal, Republic of Korea, St. Kitts and Nevis, St. Lucia, St. Vincent, San Marino, Saudi Arabia, Singapore, Slovenia, Solomon Islands, Spain, Swaziland, Sweden, Switzerland, Tuvalu, Vanuatu, Western Samoa and Zimbabwe.

SOR/97-464, s. 1

2. British Citizens and British Overseas Citizens who are re-admissible to the United Kingdom.

3. Citizens of British dependent territories who derive their citizenship through birth, descent, naturalization or registration in one of the British dependent territories of Anguilla, Bermuda, British Virgin Islands, Cayman Islands, Falkland Islands, Gibraltar, Montserrat, Pitcairn, St. Helena or the Turks and Caicos Islands.

4. Persons holding passports or travel documents issued by the Holy See.

5. Nationals of the United States and persons lawfully admitted to the United States for permanent residence.

6. Persons who seek entry to become members of a crew of a vehicle that is in Canada and members of a crew who seek entry, other than citizens of a foreign country with which the Government of Canada has entered into an agreement whereby such persons or members of a crew are required to obtain visas.

6.1. Persons who are in transit through Canada on a flight that stops in Canada solely for the purpose of refuelling and who

(a) are in possession of a valid visa to enter the United States on a flight bound for the United States; or

(b) have been lawfully admitted to the United States and are on a flight originating in the United States.

8. Members of the armed forces of a country that is a designated state for the purposes of the *Visiting Forces Act* who are seeking entry in order to carry out their official duties, other than persons who have been designated as civilian components of that force.

9. Persons coming to Canada from the United States for an interview with a United States consular officer concerning a United States immigrant visa where they are in possession of evidence satisfactory to an immigration officer that they will be granted re-entry to the United States.

10. [Revoked SOR/83-902, s. 6.]

11. Persons in possession of valid and subsisting student authorizations or employment authorizations seeking to return as visitors to Canada from the United States or St. Pierre and Miquelon where the authorizations were issued prior to the departure of those persons from Canada.

12. Persons holding passports containing a valid and subsisting "Diplomatic Acceptance", "Consular Acceptance" or "Official Acceptance" stamp issued by the Chief of Protocal for the Department of External Affairs on behalf of the Government of Canada.

13. Persons visiting Canada who, during that visit, also visit the United States or St. Pierre and Miquelon and return to Canada therefrom as visitors within the period authorized on their initial entry or any extension thereto.

14. Persons holding valid and subsisting diplomatic passports issued to them by a country with which Canada has entered into an agreement whereby each country is to exempt holders of such passports from the requirement to obtain visas.

15. Persons holding valid and subsisting official, special or service passports issued to them by a country with which Canada has entered into an agreement whereby each country is to exempt from the requirement to obtain visas those holders of such passports who are seeking entry in order to carry out their official duties.

16. Citizens of Israel who are in possession of valid and subsisting national Israeli passports.

17. Persons holding a valid and subsisting Special Administrative Region passport issued by the Government of the Hong Kong Special Administrative Region of the People's Republic of China.

18. Persons holding a valid and subsisting British National (Overseas) Passport issued to them by the Government of the United Kingdom as a person born, naturalized or registered in Hong Kong.

19. Persons who are in possession of valid documentation establishing that they are civil aviation inspectors of a recognized national aeronautical authority, who are seeking entry for the purpose of conducting inspections of flight operation procedures or cabin safety of a commercial air carrier operating international flights.

20. Persons who are in possession of valid documentation establishing that they are seeking entry as accredited representatives or as advisers in order to participate in an aviation accident or incident investigation conducted under the authority of the Canadian Transportation Accident Investigation and Safety Board.

SOR/78-745, s. 2; SOR/80-21, s. 8; SOR/80-763, s. 1; SOR/81-4, s. 1; SOR/81-624, s. 2; SOR/81-720, ss. 1, 2; SOR/81-822, s. 1; SOR/81-869, ss. 1, 2; SOR/82-613, s. 1; SOR/82-636, s. 1; SOR/83-339, ss. 7, 8; SOR/83-696, s. 1; SOR/83-902, ss. 1-6; SOR/84-211, s. 1; SOR/84-215, s. 1; SOR/84-216, s. 1; SOR/84-245, s. 1; SOR/84-809, s. 3; SOR/85-1085, ss. 1, 2; SOR/86-196, s. 1; SOR/86-769, ss. 1, 2; SOR/86-865, s. 3; SOR/86-1119, s. 1; SOR/87-47, s. 1; SOR/87-115, ss. 1, 2; SOR/87-393, s. 1; SOR/87-573, s. 1; SOR/87-585, s. 1; SOR/87-697, s. 1; SOR/88-33, s. 1; SOR/88-37, s. 1; SOR/88-143, s. 1; SOR/88-469, s. 1; SOR/88-597, s. 1; SOR/88-653, s. 1; SOR/90-215, s. 1; SOR/90-455, s. 1; SOR/90-605, s. 1; SOR/91-323, s. 1; SOR/92-234, s. 1; SOR/93-15, s. 1; SOR/93-44, s. 26; SOR/93-244, ss. 1, 2; SOR/94-242, s. 7; SOR/94-318, ss. 1, 2; SOR/94-635, s. 1; SOR1/95-71, s. 1; SOR/95-393, ss. 1, 2; SOR/96-146, s. 1; SOR/96-290, s. 1; SOR/97-209, s. 1; SOR/97-236, ss. 1, 2; SOR/97-464, s. 1; SOR/99-254, s. 2

SCHEDULE III

(Subsection 17(2) and paragraph 23(3)(m))

1. [Revoked SOR/86-865, s. 4.]

2. General Welding School, 61 Jarvis Street, Toronto, Ontario

3. [Revoked SOR/83-540, s. 6.]

4. Radvis University, Charlottetown, Prince Edward Island

5. The Way College of Biblical Research, London, Ontario.

SOR/82-723, s. 1; SOR/83-36, s. 1; SOR/83-540, s. 6; SOR/86-865, s. 4; SOR/93-412, s. 19

SCHEDULE IV

(Paragraph 5(2)(f))

1. The Low Income Cut-off (LICO) is the applicable figure from the document entitled *Low Income Cut-offs (LICOs)* published annually by Statistics Canada under the authority of the *Statistics Act*.

SOR/79-167, s. 6; SOR/97-145, s. 6

SCHEDULE V

[Repealed SOR/93-44, s. 27.]

SCHEDULE VI

(s. 56)

Column 1	
Payments of Prescribed Nature	
Item	
1.	**as assistance under the *Adjustment Assistance Program* or under the *Resettlement Assistance Program***
2.	**(a) as income assistance or social services under subsection 2(1) of the *Guaranteed Available Income For Need Act* (R.S.B.C. 1979, c. 158)**
	(b) as a child care subsidy under paragraph 4(a) of the *BC Benefits (Child Care) Act* (R.S.B.C., 1996, c. 26)
	(c) as income assistance or benefits under section 3 of the *BC Benefits (Income Assistance) Act* (R.S.B.C., 1996, c. 27)
	(d) as hardship assistance under section 4 of the *BC Benefits (Income Assistance) Act* (R.S.B.C., 1996, c. 27)
	(e) as a youth allowance or benefit under section 4 of the *BC Benefits (Youth Works) Act* (R.S.B.C., 1996, c. 28)
	(f) as a disability allowance or benefits under section 2 of the *Disability Benefits Program Act* (R.S.B.C., 1996, c. 97)
3.	**as "assistance", "municipal assistance" or "social allowance" under the *Social Allowances Act* (R.S.M. 1970, ch. S-160)**
4.	**as "assistance" under the *Social Welfare Act* (R.S.N.B. 1973, ch. 6-11)**
5.	**as social assistance under the *Social Assistance Act* (R.S.N. 1970, ch. 353)**
6.	**(i) as assistance under the *Social Assistance Act* (S.N.S. 1970, ch. 16), or**
	(ii) as benefits under the *Family Benefits Act* (S.N.S. 1977, ch. 8)
7.	**as "assistance" under the *Welfare Assistance Act* (R.S.P.E.I. 1974, ch. W-4)**
8.	**as "assistance" under the *Saskatchewan Assistance Act* (R.S.S. 1978, ch. S-8)**
9.	**(a) as a "handicap benefit" under the *Assured Income for the Severely Handicapped Act* (R.S.A. 1980, c. A-48);**
	(b) as "social assistance" under the *Social Development Act* (R.S.A. 1980, c. S-16); or
	(c) as "student financial assistance" under the *Students Finance Act* (R.S.A. 1980, c. S-24).
10.	**(a) as assistance under the *General Welfare Assistance Act* (R.S.O., 1990, c. G.6); or**
	(b) as benefits under the *Family Benefits Act* (R.S.O., 1990, c. F.2)

Column 1

Payments of Prescribed Nature

Item

(c) as "basic financial assistance" under section 5 of the *Ontario Works Act, 1997*, (S.O. 1997, c. 25, Sch. A)

(d) as "income support" under section 3 of the *Ontario Disability Support Program Act, 1997*, (S.O. 1997, c. 25, Sch. B)

SOR/81-954, s. 2; SOR/83-540, s. 7; SOR/94-578, s. 1; SOR/96-165, s. 1; SOR/99-329, ss. 2–4

SCHEDULE VII

(Section 14)

1. (1) A travel document issued by the International Committee of the Red Cross, Geneva, Switzerland, to enable and facilitate emigration.

(2) A passport or travel document issued by the Palestinian Authority.

(3) An exit visa issued by the Government of the Union of Soviet Socialist Republics to former citizens of that country compelled to relinquish their nationality in order to emigrate therefrom.

(4) A British National (Overseas) Passport issued by the Government of the United Kingdom to persons born, naturalized or registered in Hong Kong.

(5) A passport issued by the Government of the Hong Kong Special Administrative Region of the People's Republic of China.

2. (1) A laissez-passer issued by the United Nations.

(2) A passport or travel document issued by the Palestinian Authority.

(3) A document issued by the Organization of American States entitled "Official Travel Document".

(4) A passport issued by the Government of the United Kingdom to a British Overseas Citizen.

(5) A British National (Overseas) Passport issued by the Government of the United Kingdom to persons born, naturalized or registered in Hong Kong.

(6) A passport issued by the Government of the Hong Kong Special Administrative Region of the People's Republic of China.

3. (1) Any passport, identity or travel document purporting to be issued by Bophuthatswana, Ciskei, Transkei, or Venda.

(2) Any passport, identity or travel document purporting to be issued by the All Palestine Government.

(3) Any passport issued by the Government of the United Kingdom entitled 'British Visitor's Passport'.

SOR/84-809, s. 4; SOR/86-196, s. 2; SOR/86-1053, s. 1; SOR/90-605, s. 2; SOR/95-476, s. 1

SCHEDULE VIII

(Section 42.1)

Item	Column I Destination	Column II Costs
1.	United States or St. Pierre and Miquelon	$ 750
2.	Any other destination	1,500

SOR/93-44, s. 28

SCHEDULE IX

(Section 42.3)

		Administration Fees				
Item	Column I Persons	Column II	Column III	Column IV	Column V	Column VI
1.	Members of a crew who have deserted	$3,200	N/A	N/A	N/A	N/A
2.	Any other persons	3,200	2,400	1,600	800	0

SOR/93-44, s. 28; SOR/94-242, s. 8

SCHEDULE X

[Repealed SOR/99-146, s. 6.]

SCHEDULE XI

[Repealed SOR/99-146, s. 6.]

SCHEDULE XII — LIST OF COUNTRIES

(Subsection 2(1) and paragraph 11.402(1)(d))

Item	Country
1.	Afghanistan
2.	Somalia

SOR/97-86, s. 7; SOR/99-74, s. 4

[Editor's Note: Items 1 and 2 of Schedule XII cease to be in force on January 31, 2001, per SOR/99-74, s. 4.]

HUMANITARIAN DESIGNATED CLASSES REGULATIONS

SOR/97-183, as am. SOR/98-271; SOR/98-596.

Interpretation

1. The definitions in this section apply in these Regulations.

"accompanying dependant", with respect to a person, means a dependant of that person to whom a visa is issued at the time a visa is issued to that person for the purpose of enabling the dependant to accompany or follow that person to Canada.

"Act" means the *Immigration Act*.

"country of citizenship" means, in respect of an immigrant, each country of which the immigrant is a citizen.

"daughter" has the same meaning as in subsection 2(1) of the *Immigration Regulations, 1978*.

"dependant", in respect of a member of the country of asylum class or a member of the source country class, means

> **(a) the member's spouse;**
>
> **(b) a dependent son or dependent daughter of the member or of the member's spouse; or**
>
> **(c) a dependent son or dependent daughter of a son or daughter referred to in paragraph (b).**

"dependent daughter" has the same meaning as in subsection 2(1) of the *Immigration Regulations, 1978*.

"dependent son" has the same meaning as in subsection 2(1) of the *Immigration Regulations, 1978*.

"durable solution" means, in respect of a member of the country of asylum class and a member of the source country class,

> **(a) the voluntary repatriation of a member to the member's country of citizenship or of habitual residence;**
>
> **(b) the resettlement of a member in the member's country of citizenship or of habitual residence, in a neighbouring country or in the country of asylum; or**
>
> **(c) an offer of resettlement by a country other than Canada.**

"member of the country of asylum class" means an immigrant, other than a person whose case has been rejected in accordance with the Comprehensive Plan of Action adopted by the International Conference on Indo-Chinese Refugees on June 14, 1989,

> **(a) who has left the immigrant's country of citizenship or of habitual residence;**

(b) who has been and continues to be seriously and personally affected by civil or armed conflict or a massive violation of human rights in the immigrants's country of citizenship or of habitual residence;

(c) in respect of whom there is no possibility, within a reasonable period, of a durable solution;

(d) in respect of whom a determination has been made under paragraph 4(1)(b); and

(e) who is outside Canada and is seeking admission to Canada for the purpose of resettling in Canada.

"member of the source country class" means an immigrant

(a) who is residing in the immigrant's country of citizenship or of habitual residence, where the immigrant's country of citizenship or of habitual residence is a source country set out in the schedule;

(b) who

(i) is being seriously and personally affected by civil or armed conflict in the immigrant's country of citizenship or of habitual residence,

(ii) as a direct result of acts committed outside Canada that in Canada would be considered a legitimate expression of free thought or a legitimate exercise of civil rights pertaining to dissent or to trade union activity,

(A) is being or has been detained or imprisoned in that country with or without charge, or

(B) is being or has been subjected to some other recurring form of penal control, or

(iii) by reason of a well-founded fear of persecution for reasons of race, religion, nationality, political opinion or membership in a particular social group is unable or, by reason of such fear, unwilling to avail himself of the protection of the immigrant's country of citizenship or of habitual residence;

(c) in respect of whom there is no possibility, within a reasonable period, of a durable solution;

(d) in respect of whom a determination has been made under paragraph 4(1)(b); and

(e) who is seeking admission to Canada for the purpose of resettling in Canada.

"son" has the same meaning as in subsection 2(1) of the *Immigration Regulations, 1978.*

"source country" means a country

(a) where persons are in a refugee-like situation as a result of civil or armed conflict or because their fundamental human rights are not respected;

(b) where an immigration officer works or makes routine working visits and is able to process visa applications without endangering their own safety, the safety of applicants or the safety of Canadian embassy staff;

(c) where circumstances warrant humanitarian intervention by the Department of Citizenship and Immigration to implement overall Canadian government humanitarian strategies, which intervention is in keeping with the work of the United Nations High Commissioner for Refugees; and

(d) that has been designated by the Minister as a source country, after consultation with the Department of Foreign Affairs and International Trade and non-governmental organizations concerned with the sponsoring of immigrants who are in a refugee-like situation.

"spouse" has the same meaning as in subsection 2(1) of the *Immigration Regulations, 1978*.

"undertaking" means an undertaking in writing given to the Minister to make provision for the lodging, care and maintenance of and resettlement assistance for a member of the country of asylum class or a member of the source country class, and the member's accompanying dependants, for a period determined in accordance with paragraph 5(2)(a).

SOR/98-271, s. 1

Designated Classes

2. The following classes of persons are designated as classes of persons for the purposes of subsection 6(3) of the Act:

(a) the country of asylum class; and

(b) the source country class.

Exemption — Immigration Regulations, 1978

3. Members of the country of asylum class and members of the source country class are exempt from the application of sections 7 to 9.1 of the *Immigration Regulations, 1978*.

Admission Requirements

4. (1) Where a person seeks admission to Canada as a member of the country of asylum class or a member of the source country class, the person and their accompanying dependants, if any, are subject to the following admission requirements:

(a) a visa officer is satisfied that the person is a member of the country of asylum class or a member of the source country class, as the case may be;

(b) a visa officer determines that

(i) a group or corporation is sponsoring the application for admission of the person and the accompanying dependants in accordance with section 5,

(ii) financial or other assistance is available in Canada for the person and the accompanying dependants, or

(iii) the person has sufficient financial resources to provide for the lodging, care and maintenance, and for the resettlement in Canada, of the person and the accompanying dependants;

(c) where the person and the accompanying dependants intend to reside in a place in Canada other than the Province of Quebec, a visa officer determines that the

person and the accompanying dependants will be able to become successfully established in Canada, taking into consideration

(i) the ability of the person and the accompanying dependants to communicate in one of the official languages of Canada,

(ii) the age of the person,

(iii) the level of education, the work experience and the skills of the person and the accompanying dependants,

(iv) the number and ages of the accompanying dependants, and

(v) the personal suitability of the person and the accompanying dependants, including their adaptability, motivation, initiative, resourcefulness and other similar qualities; and

(d) where the person and the accompanying dependants intend to reside in the Province of Quebec, the person and the accompanying dependants will, in the opinion of the appropriate minister of that Province, based on regulations made under *An Act respecting Immigration to Québec*, R.S.Q., c. I-O.2, as amended from time to time, be able to become successfully established in that Province.

(2) Subject to subsection (4), where a person referred to in subsection (1) and their accompanying dependants meet the applicable admission requirements and any other requirements of the Act, these Regulations and the *Immigration Regulations, 1978*, the visa officer may issue an immigrant visa to that person and the accompanying dependants.

(3) Where a visa officer does not issue an immigrant visa as an accompanying dependant to a son or daughter of a person referred to in subsection (1), or to a son or daughter of the spouse of that person, the visa officer shall not issue an immigrant visa as an accompanying dependant to a son or daughter of that son or daughter.

(4) A visa officer shall not issue an immigrant visa to an accompanying dependant of a person referred to in subsection (1) unless

(a) at the time the application for admission is received by a visa officer, the accompanying dependant, except if the dependant is the person's spouse, meets the criteria set out in paragraph (*a*), (*b*) or (*c*) of the definition "dependent son" or "dependent daughter" in subsection 2(1) of the *Immigration Regulations, 1978*, as the case may be; and

(b) at the time the visa is issued, the accompanying dependant, except if the dependant is the person's spouse, meets the criteria referred to in paragraph (*a*), except for the one respecting age set out in paragraph (*a*) of the definition "dependent son" or "dependent daughter" in subsection 2(1) of the *Immigration Regulations, 1978*, as the case may be.

SOR/98-271, s. 2

Sponsorship

5. (1) Subject to subsections (2) and (3), an application for admission of a member of the country of asylum class or a member of the source country class, and the member's accompanying dependants, may be sponsored by

(a) a group that consists of not fewer than five individuals, each of whom is a Canadian citizen or permanent resident, has attained at least 19 years of age and resides in the expected community of settlement; or

(b) a corporation that has representatives in the expected community of settlement.

(2) Subject to subsection (3), the conditions under which a group or corporation referred to in subsection (1) may sponsor an application for the admission of a member of the country of asylum class or a member of the source country class, and the member's accompanying dependants, are the following:

(a) in the case of a group, the group has given a joint undertaking signed by each member of the group to the Minister, in the form fixed by the Minister, for a period of not less than one year and not more than two years, as determined by an immigration officer based on the recommendation of a visa officer who has taken into consideration the factors referred to in paragraph 4(1)(*c*);

(b) in the case of a corporation, the corporation

(i) has entered into a sponsorship agreement with the Minister under which the corporation agrees to make provision for the lodging, care and maintenance of and resettlement assistance for the member of the country of asylum class or the member of the source country class, as the case may be, and the member's accompanying dependants, and

(ii) has given the Minister an undertaking in the form and for the period referred to in paragraph (a) in respect of the member and the member's accompanying dependants;

(c) neither the members of the group nor the corporation is in default in respect of any other undertaking; and

(d) the immigration officer is satisfied, based on documentation provided by the group or corporation, that the group or corporation

(i) has made or will make adequate arrangements in the expected community of settlement for the reception of the member and the member's accompanying dependants, and

(ii) has sufficient financial resources and expertise to fulfil the undertaking referred to in paragraph (a) or subparagraph (b)(ii), as the case may be.

(3) If a member of the country of asylum class or a member of the source country class and their accompanying dependants intend to reside in the Province of Quebec, the group or corporation referred to in subsection (1) must meet the sponsorship requirements of regulations made under *An Act respecting immigraiton to Québec*, R.S.Q., c. I-0.2, as amended from time to time.

(4) Subsections (1), (2) and (3) are retroactive and apply in respect of all applications for landing made by members of the country of asylum class and members of the source country class that are pending on May 1, 1998.

SOR/98-271, s. 3

Prescribed Classes of Immigrants for the Purposes of Subsection 6(8) of the Act

6. For the purposes of subsection 6(8) of the Act, the country of asylum class and the source country class are prescribed as classes of immigrants, the members and accompanying dependants of which are to be assessed.

Regulations Cease to Have Effect

7. ***These Regulations cease to have effect on December 31, 1999.***

SOR/98-271, s. 4; SOR/98-596, s. 1

Repeal

8. The Indochinese Designated Class Regulations are repealed.

9. The Self-Exiled Persons Designated Class Regulations are repealed.

10. The Political Prisoners and Oppressed Persons Designated Class Regulations are repealed.

11. The Indochinese Designated Class (Transitional) Regulations are repealed.

Coming Into Force

12. These Regulations come into force on May 1, 1997.

SCHEDULE

(Section 1)

Source Countries

Bosnia-Herzegovina

Colombia

Croatia

Democratic Republic of the Congo

El Salvador

Guatemala

Sudan

SOR/98-271, s. 5; SOR/98-596, s. 2

REFUGEE CLAIMANTS DESIGNATED CLASS REGULATIONS

Regulations Respecting the Designation of a Refugee Claimants Designated Class and Certain Exemptions that Apply to that Class

SOR/90-40, as am. SOR/92-13; SOR/92-722; SOR/94-21.

Short Title

1. These Regulations may be cited as the *Refugee Claimants Designated Class Regulations*.

Interpretation

2. In these Regulations,

"Act" means the *Immigration Act;*

"dependant" in respect of a member of the Refugee Claimants Designated Class, means a dependant as defined in paragraph (*a*) of the definition "dependant" in subsection 2(1) of the *Immigration Regulations, 1978* who is in Canada on the day an application for landing is made by that member;

"Refugee Claimants Designated Class" means a class of persons designated pursuant to section 3.

Designation of Class

3. (1) Subject to subsection (2), the Refugee Claimants Designated Class is hereby designated for the purpose of subsection 6(2) of the Act as a class the admission of members of which would be in accordance with Canada's humanitarian tradition with respect to the displaced and the persecuted, and shall consist of those persons who

(a) were in Canada on January 1, 1989 or had been directed back, prior to that date, to the United States, pursuant to subsection 23(5) of the Act, to await the availability of an adjudicator for an inquiry scheduled to be held on or after that date;

(b) signified, before January 1, 1989, an intention to make a claim to be a Convention refugee

(i) to an immigration officer, who recorded that intention before that date, or to a person acting on behalf of an immigration officer, who an immigration officer is satisfied recorded that intention before that date, or

(ii) to an adjudicator prior to the conclusion of an inquiry respecting those persons' status in Canada; and

(c) have been determined to have a credible basis for their claim to be a Convention refugee pursuant to

(i) subsection 46.01(6) or (7) of the Act, or

(ii) subsection 43(1) of an *Act to Amend the Immigration Act and to Amend other Acts in consequence thereof*, R.S., c. 28 (4th Supp.).

(2) The Refugee Claimants Designated Class shall not include a person who

(a) has been determined to be a Convention refugee under the Act as it read before January 1, 1989;

(b) is the subject of a removal order or a departure notice and has not been removed from or otherwise left Canada;

(c) has made an application for landing pursuant to these Regulations or the *Refugee Claims Backlog Regulations*, as it read before its revocation by Order in Council P.C. 1989-467 on March 23, 1989, which application has been refused;

(d) has failed to appear for

(i) an examination that was adjourned pursuant to subsection 12(3) of the Act,

(ii) an inquiry respecting that person's status in Canada or for the continuation of such an inquiry for which the person was given an appointment, or

(iii) an examination under oath with respect to a claim to be a Convention refugee or for the continuation of such an examination for which the person was given an appointment;

(e) is described in any of paragraphs 19(1)(*c*) to (*g*), (*j*) or 27(2)(*c*) of the Act;

(f) left Canada after the coming into force of these Regulations and remained outside Canada for more than seven days;

(g) is determined by the Refugee Division not to be a Convention refugee; or

(h) has not, on or before December 11, 1992, provided to an immigration officer sufficient current information in respect of that person's whereabouts in Canada for a hearing to be initiated for the purpose of making the determination referred to in paragraph (1)(*c*).

SOR/92-722, s. 1.

Case Law

Section 3(2)(d)

Khan v. Canada (Secretary of State) (1995), 94 F.T.R. 78 (Fed. T.D.) — The applicant claimed refugee status on his arrival in Canada in October 1986. On December 1, 1986 he appeared for an inquiry and it was adjourned. The applicant received a notice requiring him to attend an examination under oath on February 17, 1987. The applicant did not attend but telephoned immigration authorities two days later and asked for, and received, a new examination date.

A person in the applicant's circumstances cannot be said to have "failed to appear" for the purposes of section 3(2)(d)(iii) of the *Backlog Regulations*.

Accordingly, the applicant ought to have been processed under the *Backlog Regulations* and the referral to the Board in this case was improper.

The decision denying the applicant's claim for refugee status was set aside.

Section 3(2)(f)

Jafari v. Canada (Minister of Employment & Immigration), 180 N.R. 330, 125 D.L.R. (4th) 141, [1995] 2 F.C. 595, 30 Imm. L.R. (2d) 139, 95 F.T.R. 159 (note) (Fed. C.A.) — This was an appeal from a decision of the Trial Division which declared section 3(2)(f) of the Refugee Claimants Designated Class Regulations *ultra vires* of the Governor in Council.

The respondent was a citizen of Iran who arrived in Canada on November 16, 1986 and immediately claimed refugee status. His claim had not been dealt with when the Refugee Claimants Designated Class Regulations were brought into effect on December 27, 1989. To be eligible for the backlog, a claimant was required to have been in Canada on January 1, 1989 and to have signified before that date an intention to make a refugee claim.

Section 3(2)(f) provided that the class did not include a person who left Canada after the coming into force of the regulations, and remained outside of Canada for more than 7 days. In July, 1990, the claimant attempted to cross into the United States surreptitiously. He was apprehended and it was necessary for him to spend 12 days in the United States before he was returned to Canada. On October 4, 1991, he was advised that he was not entitled to be dealt with under the backlog as he had absented himself from Canada for more than 7 days.

The practical effect of the backlog regulations was that those who fell within the designated class could, where found to have a credible basis for their claim, apply for landing.

It is not for a Court to determine the wisdom of delegated legislation or to assess its validity on the basis of the Court's policy preferences. The essential question is: does the statutory grant of authority permit this particular delegated legislation? In looking at the statutory source of authority, one must seek all possible indicia as to the purpose and scope of permitted delegated legislation. Any limitations, express or implied, must be taken into account. One must then look to the regulation to see whether it conforms and where it is argued that the regulation was not made for the purposes authorized by the statute, one must try to identify one or more of those purposes for which the regulation was adopted. A broad discretionary power, including a regulation making power, may not be used for a completely irrelevant purpose. The relevant powers are in sections 114(d) and (e) of the Immigration Act. These powers are to be exercised for the purposes of section 6(2) of the Immigration Act.

Section 6(2) authorizes the Governor in Council to designate classes of persons other than those already found to be Convention refugees, for purposes of admission. It requires that those classes include persons whose admission would be in accordance with Canada's humanitarian tradition with respect to the displaced and the persecuted. This does not mean that every regulation must facilitate the admission of more refugee claimants. This section combined with section 114(1)(e) authorizes regulations which classify such persons in some way and which may exempt some of those classes from some of the requirements.

Section 6(2) and sections 114(d) and (e) authorize systems of classification of refugee claimants and the provision of preferential treatment for some or all of those classified. The backlog regulations might have excluded, from the backlog, anyone who had not remained in Canada constantly since making his or her claim. The regulations, whatever they may be, must, of course, be seen as in some way related to the purpose of the Act, but this does not mean that a Court can review them to see if they are necessary, wise or effective in practice.

There was evidence on behalf of the appellant as to the purpose of the regulations. While some of the reasons were not compelling, and in some way may have been misconceived, the Court cannot say that they were completely unrelated to the purposes of the statute. Accordingly, section 3(2)(f) of the regulations is not *ultra vires* the Governor in Council.

Application for Landing

4. A member of the Refugee Claimants Designated Class may make an application for landing to an immigration officer.

Exemption

5. For the purpose of an application for landing made pursuant to section 4, a member of the Refugee Claimants Designated Class and the dependants of that member are exempt from the requirements of subsection 9(1) of the Act and sections 4 to 11 and subsection 14(1) of the *Immigration Regulations, 1978*.

Implementation

6. (1) Subject to subsections (2) to (4), where a member of the Refugee Claimants Designated Class makes an application for landing, an immigration officer may grant landing to the member and the member's dependants if the member and the dependants meet the requirements of the Act and of the *Immigration Regulations, 1978* except those from which they are exempt under section 5.

(2) An immigration officer may refuse to grant landing to a member of the Refugee Claimants Designated Class and the member's dependants if the member or any of the member's dependants refuses to be photographed or fingerprinted under subsection 44(2) of the *Immigration Regulations, 1978*.

(3) Where an immigration officer is of the opinion that the information provided to that officer by a member of the Refugee Claimants Designated Class or a dependant of the member in respect of the member's application for landing or the dependant's application is insufficient or where the officer has reasonable grounds to doubt the accuracy of the information, that officer may request additional information or verification of the information before granting or refusing landing.

(4) An immigration officer who grants landing may subject the landing to the term or condition that the person report for medical observation or treatment at a time and place specified by the officer.

Case Law

Kaisersingh v. Canada (Minister of Citizenship & Immigration) (1995), 89 F.T.R. 276 — Section 6(2) of the *Immigration Act* refers to the Governor in Council's authority to designate classes of persons who may be admitted to Canada in accordance with Canada's humanitarian tradition with respect to the displaced and the persecuted. The backlog class was defined as persons who were:

1. in Canada on January 1, 1989; and,
2. who had not had their refugee claims finally determined; and,
3. who had been found to have a credible basis for their claims.

This class was further defined by excluding individuals described in sections 19(1)(c) to (g), (j) or 27(2)(c). Persons within the class obtained the benefit of section 4 of the *Backlog Regulations* and were entitled to apply for landing. Section 6 of the *Backlog Regulations* provided that on such an application an immigration officer may grant landing to members of the class if they met the requirements of the Act and Regulations, except for the requirement of section 9(1) of the Act. In determining whether a person meets the requirements of the *Immigration Act*, an officer is entitled to take into account section 19(1)(b) and refuse landing to persons who are unable to support themselves. Such an exclusion includes persons who fail to report income with the Ontario Housing Authority and thereby demonstrate an unwillingness to support themselves.

Yhap v. Canada (Minister of Employment & Immigration) (1990), 9 Imm. L.R. (2d) 243 (Fed. T.D.) — The applicant indicated an intention to claim refugee status in Canada prior to January 1, 1989 and was included in the backlog clearance program established by the Minister. The Minister refused to consider the applicant under the operation's memorandum dealing with Chinese nationals who had temporary status in Canada. That policy was not intended to replace provisions which have been made for refugees, whether recent arrivals or members of the backlog from the People's Republic of China, but rather was intended to act as a supplemental protection for other individuals from that country. Regardless of what promises and what guarantees have been made by the Minister, the applicant is entitled, by virtue of section 114(2) to a review as to whether humanitarian and compassionate grounds exist sufficient to warrant landing in Canada. This law must be applied evenly to all persons. The discretion conferred by section 114(2) is not to be exercised by the Minister and her officials subject to inflexible and self-imposed limitations, although an expression of flexible general policy, such as that contained in chapter 9 of the immigration manual, would be entirely lawful. The policy directives and guidelines pertaining to the humanitarian and compassionate review portion of the backlog clearance program were set out in a document entitled "Refugee Claimants Backlog Procedures". These guidelines limit their application to particular classes of persons, mainly "members of official delegations, athletic teams or cultural groups", and persons in "family dependency situations" described more specifically in the guidelines. Officers have not been questioning applicants on humanitarian and compassionate issues which fall outside the designated criteria. These policy guidelines constituted a fetter on the statutory power of the Governor in Council to both exempt persons from the requirement of section 9(1) of the Act and to authorize the landing of persons for humanitarian and compassionate reasons pursuant to section 114(2). The applicant is entitled to a full and fair review to determine the existence of humanitarian or compassionate considerations. The right to this review was confirmed by the Supreme Court of Canada in *Jiminez-Perez v. Canada (Minister of Employment & Immigration)* (1984), [1984] 2 S.C.R. 565 (S.C.C.) and this consideration is to take place independently of the consideration of the basic merits of any other application advanced by the applicant. Even in the case where it is evident that all other claims and applications advanced by the applicant are doomed to failure, the applicant's right to consideration on humanitarian and compassionate grounds may not be unduly restricted. A factor that may properly be taken into account in exercising a discretion may become an unlawful fetter upon discretion if it is elevated to the status of a general rule that results in the pursuit of consistency at the expense of the merits of individual cases.

The discretion afforded an immigration officer by section 114(2) is wide. The officer is asked to consider reasons of public policy as well as the existence of compassionate or humanitarian considerations. Neither the section of the *Immigration Act* which sets out definitions of terms nor the regulations describe in any greater detail how this section is to be applied nor what interpretation the officer is to give to the rather broad terms contained in this section. Chapter 9 of the immigration manual assists an officer in assessing situations and the humanitarian and compassionate issues raised by them which include problems with spouses, family dependencies, difficulties with return to the country of origin, illegal *de facto* residents, and situations involving marriage breakdowns. By comparison, the guidelines contained in "Refugee Claimants Backlog Procedures" are rigid and inflexible. These criteria are limited and refer only to a carefully selected segment of the backlog population. Applicants who are not members of official delegations, athletic teams or cultural groups and who are not close family members of Canadian residents are excluded from the review subject to these criteria. Chapter 9, on the other hand, constitutes a general policy or rough "rules of thumb" which are appropriate and lawful structuring of the discretion conferred by section 114(2). These guidelines might have acted as a model for the drafting of guidelines to be used in conjunction with a humanitarian and compassionate review of refugee claimants in the backlog. Accordingly, the decision of the immigration officer at the backlog clearance centre with respect to the respondent was quashed and an order in the nature of *mandamus* was issued compelling the Minister to provide the applicant with a full and fair interview of his humanitarian and compassionate claim.

7. [Revoked SOR/94-21, s. 1.]

IMMIGRATION ACT FEES REGULATIONS

SOR/97-22, as am. SOR/97-202; SOR/98-592; SOR/99-228.

Interpretation

1. The definitions in section 2 of the *Immigration Act* and subsection 2(1) of the *Immigration Regulations, 1978* apply in these Regulations.

General

2. In addition to any other requirement of the Act or the regulations made under the Act, an application is not a duly completed application until the prescribed fees in relation to it are paid.

Case Law

Section 2

Xiao v. Canada (Minister of Citizenship & Immigration) (1998), 44 Imm. L.R. (2d) 121, 149 F.T.R. 147 (Fed. T.D.) — This was an application to review a decision of a visa officer who rejected the applicant's application at the paper-screening stage. The applicant was a chef by trade. He submitted his application on April 30, 1997, and included supporting material and a bank draft for $3,150.00 Cdn. The material was returned with a note advising that the correct fee was $3,250.00 Cdn. The applicant resubmitted the application on May 30, 1997 and included the original bank draft and an additional money order for $100.00. A visa officer rejected the application in November 1997, on the basis that the applicant did not have sufficient units of assessment. At issue was whether the visa officer should have applied the CCDO criteria instead of the NOC criteria due to the fact that the application was originally reviewed prior to May 1, 1997.

Application fees for permanent residency are twofold: a) the cost recovery fee or application processing fee; and b) the right of landing fee. An applicant for landing is required to pay the processing fee at the time of the application. The right of landing fee must be paid sometime before the issuance of the visa. In this case, the applicant submitted both fees at the time of the application. However, his remittance was $100.00 short of the total required. In refusing the application, the visa officer referred to the fact that it was established and well known that applications submitted without the exact fee would not be processed.

Although the Minister may issue guidelines and other non-binding instruments as a matter of administrative practice, it was clear that this rule was mandatory in nature and much more than a mere guideline. The Minister's authority to make such requirements is derived exclusively from the relevant legislation. There was no authority in the Immigration Act, the Immigration Act Regulations, or the Immigration Act Fees Regulations for such a requirement. It was no answer to state that nothing in the Act or Regulations prohibited the Minister from behaving in this fashion. The Minister's authority must be found in explicit and positive language in a relevant statute or regulation. Here the Immigration Act Fees Regulations are silent on whether applications may be returned for overpayments.

Accordingly, the decision of the visa officer was set aside.

3. The fees set out in column III of an item of the schedule are to be paid for services or rights, provided or conferred under the Act, set out in column I of that item by the persons set out in column II of that item at the time set out in column IV of that item.

Remission

4. Remission is hereby granted of the fee set out in item 19 of the schedule where a right of landing is not conferred by or on behalf of Her Majesty on an immigrant, so that the fee is refunded, by the Minister, to the person who paid it.

Repeal

5. The Immigration Act Fees Regulations are repealed.

Coming Into Force

6. These regulations come into force on January 2, 1997.

SCHEDULE [1] — FEES

Number in brackets added editorially by Carswell

(Section 3)

Fee for Applications for Ministerial Exemption and for Landing in Canada

Item	Column I Service or right	Column II Person	Column III Fee ($)	Column IV Time
1.	**Processing a duly completed application under section 2.1 of the *Immigration Regulations, 1978* and under subsection 5(2) of the Act**	**(1) Subject to subsection (2), the following applicants must pay the fee:** **(a) an applicant who is 19 years of age or older or who is married regardless of their age; and** **(b) the applicant in respect of each dependant who** **(i) is 19 years of age or older, or** **(ii) is married regardless of their age.**	**500**	**At the time of application**
		(2) The following applicants must pay the fee: **(a) an applicant who is less than 19 years of age; and**	**100**	**At the time of application**

Column I Item Service or right	Column II Person	Column III Fee ($)	Column IV Time
	(b) the applicant in respect of each dependant who is less than 19 years of age.		

Fee for Processing Applications for Landing

Column I Item Service or right	Column II Person	Column III Fee ($)	Column IV Time
2. Processing a duly completed application for landing	**(1) Subject to subsections (2) and (3), where a member of the family class submits an application in respect of the member and their dependants, if any, the following applicants must pay the fee:** **(a) an applicant who is 19 years of age or older or who is married or a fiancée referred to in subsection 23.1(2) of the *Immigration Regulations, 1978* regardless of their age; and** **(b) the applicant in respect of each dependant who** **(i) is 19 years of age or older, or** **(ii) is married regardless of their age.**	**500**	**At the time of application**
	(2) Subject to subsection (3), the following applicants must pay the fee: **(a) an applicant who is less than 19 years of age; and** **(b) the applicant in respect of each dependant who is less than 19 years of age.**	**100**	**At the time of application**
	(3) Unless the member or dependant has already paid the applicable fee, the sponsor who submits an undertaking in support of the application must pay the fee.		**At the time of the undertaking**
	(4) Subject to subsection (5), where an entrepreneur, investor or self-employed person submits an application in respect of themselves and their dependants, if any, the following applicants must pay the fee: **(a) the applicant; and**	**1,000**	**At the time of application**
	(b) the applicant in respect of each dependant who **(i) is 19 years of age or older, or** **(ii) is married regardless of their age.**	**500**	**At the time of application**

Column I Item Service or right	Column II Person	Column III Fee ($)	Column IV Time
	(5) The applicant in respect of each dependant who is less than 19 years of age must pay the fee.	**100**	**At the time of application**
	(6) Subject to subsections (7) and (8), where a person, other than a person referred to in any of subsections (1) to (5), submits an application in respect of themselves and their dependants, if any, the following applicants must pay the fee: **(a) the applicant; and** **(b) the applicant in respect of each dependant who** **(i) is 19 years of age or older, or** **(ii) is married regardless of their age.**	**500**	**At the time of application**
	(7) Subject to subsection (8), the applicant in respect of each dependant who is less than 19 years of age must pay the fee.	**100**	**At the time of application**
	(8) The following applicants need not pay the fee: **(a) a person whom a visa officer has determined to be a convention refugee seeking resettlement;** **(b) a member of a class of persons designated by the Governor in Council pursuant to subsection 6(3) and paragraph 114(1)(d) of the Act, other than the Refugee Claimants Designated Class as defined in section 2 of the *Refugee Claimants Designated Class Regulations*; and** **(c) a member of the undocumented Convention refugee in Canada class and their dependants, when the member applies for landing under paragraph 11.402(1)(a) of the *Immigration Regulations, 1978*.**		

Fee for Processing Applications for a Status Document

Item	Column I Service or right	Column II Person	Column III Fee ($)	Column IV Time
3.	Processing a duly completed application for a visitor visa to come into Canada once (where the applicant is the person, the person in respect of each dependant or a dependant); a duly completed application made by a person authorized pursuant to section 16 of the Act to apply to extend the period during which the person is authorized to remain in Canada; or a duly completed application for a returning resident permit	(1) Subject to subsection (2) or (3), the following persons must pay the fee: (a) the applicant; and (b) the applicant in respect of each dependant. (2) In the case of an application for a visitor visa to come into Canada once, the following persons need not pay the fee: (a) a properly accredited diplomat, consular officer, representative or official of a country, other than Canada, of the United Nations or any of its agencies, or of any intergovernmental organization in which Canada participates, or a member of the suite of any such person, and their dependants;	Where the fee is for a visitor visa to come into Canada once, $75 for each applicant and dependant to a maximum of $400 for an applicant and their dependants who apply at the same place and at the same time, or $75 for each applicant or dependant in all other cases	At the time of application

Column I		Column II	Column III	Column IV
Item	Service or right	Person	Fee ($)	Time
		(b) a member of the armed forces of a country that is a designated state for the purposes of the *Visiting Forces Act*, including a person who has been designated as a civilian component of that visiting force pursuant to paragraph 4(c) of that Act, and their dependants;		
		(c) a clergyman, a member of a religious order or a lay person who is to assist a congregation or a group in the achievement of its spiritual goals, where the duties to be performed by the person are to consist mainly of preaching doctrine, presiding at liturgical functions or spiritual counselling, and their dependants;		
		(d) persons seeking to come into Canada, other than members of a group of performing artists and their staff, who apply at the same time and at the same place, for a student authorization or an employment authorization;		
		(e) the following persons attending meetings in Canada:		
		(i) participants attending meetings hosted by organizations of the United Nations or by the Government of Canada,		
		(ii) representatives of the Organization of American States (OAS) or participants attending meetings hosted by the OAS, and		
		(iii) representatives of the Caribbean Development Bank;		

Column I		Column II	Column III	Column IV
Item	Service or right	Person	Fee ($)	Time
		(f) persons travelling by transportation company vehicles to destinations other than Canada, who transit through or stop over in Canada for vehicle refuelling, or for the continuation of their journey with another transportation company vehicle, where the duration of their stay does not exceed 48 hours; and (g) the following persons entering Canada in connection with the Pan-American Games when held in Canada, namely, (i) all competitors, coaches, judges, team officials, medical staff and members of national and international sports organizing bodies participating in those Games, and (ii) performers participating in the Festival of the Americas associated with those Games. (3) In the case of an application made by a person authorized pursuant to section 16 of the Act to apply to extend the period during which the person is authorized to remain in Canada, the following persons need not pay the fee: (a) a person who, at the same time, applies for an employment authorization or a student authorization; (b) a person in Canada who has made a claim to be a Convention refugee that has not yet been decided by the Refugee Division;		

Column I		Column II	Column III	Column IV
Item	Service or right	Person	Fee ($)	Time
		(c) a person whom the Refugee Division has determined to be a Convention refugee; (d) a person whom a visa officer has determined to be a Convention refugee seeking resettlement; (e) a person described in paragraph 3(2)(a), (b) or (c); (f) an officer of a foreign government sent by that government to take up duties with a federal or provincial agency pursuant to an exchange agreement with Canada; (g) a dependant of (i) a person described in paragraph 5(2)(d), (e), (f) or (g), (ii) a participant in a program sponsored by the Canadian International Development Agency, or (iii) a recipient of a Government of Canada scholarship or fellowship; and (h) a citizen of a country with which Canada has entered into an agreement whereby neither country is to charge for the processing of a duly completed application for extension of status.		
4.	Processing a duly completed application for a visitor visa to come into Canada more than once	The following persons, other than a person referred to in any of paragraphs 3(2)(a) to (f), must pay the fee:	$150 for each applicant and dependant to a maximum of $400 for an applicant and their dependants that apply at the same place and at the same time	At the time of application
		(a) the applicant; and		

Column I Item Service or right	Column II Person	Column III Fee ($)	Column IV Time
	(b) the applicant in respect of each dependant.		

Fee for Processing Applications for an Employment Authorization

Column I Item Service or right	Column II Person	Column III Fee ($)	Column IV Time
5. Processing a duly completed application for an employment authorization	(1) Subject to subsection (2), the applicant must pay the fee. (2) The following persons need not pay the fee: (a) a person in Canada who has made a claim to be a Convention refugee that has not yet been decided by the Refugee Division and any dependant of the person; (b) a person whom the Refugee Division has determined to be a Convention refugee and any dependant of the person; (c) a person whom a visa officer has determined to be a Convention refugee seeking resettlement and any dependant of the person; (d) a person in possession of a valid and subsisting student authorization in respect of whom paragraph 20(1)(a) of the *Immigration Regulations, 1978* should not be applied for the reason that the person has become temporarily destitute through circumstances totally beyond their control, and any person on whom that person is dependent for the financial resources referred to in paragraph 15(1)(b) of those regulations;	150	At the time of application

Column I Item Service or right	Column II Person	Column III Fee ($)	Column IV Time
	(e) a person whose employment is related to a research, educational or training program that is on a list entitled "Research, Educational or Training Programs Rendering Participants Eligible for Cost Recovery Fee Exemption", published by the Department of Citizenship and Immigration; **(f) a person in respect of whom paragraph 20(1)(a) of the *Immigration Regulations, 1978* should not be applied for the reason that the person is to be employed by a Canadian religious or charitable organization without remuneration;** **(g) a person described in paragraph 19(4)(e) of the *Immigration Regulations, 1978* and in respect of whom paragraph 20(1)(a) of those Regulations should not be applied for humanitarian or compassionate reasons arising from** **(i) a state of war or other event causing serious disruption of public order in their country of last permanent residence before the person came to Canada,** **(ii) a recent serious natural disaster at their place of last permanent residence before the person came to Canada, or** **(iii) the fact that the person was, immediately before their coming to Canada, a member of a class designated by the Governor in Council pursuant to paragraph 114(1)(d) of the Act;** **(h) a dependant of a person referred to in paragraph 3(2)(a) or (b) where the dependant is referred to in subparagraph 20(5)(e)(iii) of the *Immigration Regulations, 1978*;**		

Column I Item Service or right	Column II Person	Column III Fee ($)	Column IV Time
	(i) a dependant of an officer of a foreign government sent by that government to take up duties with a federal or provincial agency pursuant to an exchange agreement with Canada where the dependant is referred to in subparagraph 20(5)(e)(iii) of the *Immigration Regulations, 1978;*		
	(j) a person in or coming into Canada pursuant to an agreement between Canada and a foreign country or an arrangement entered into with a foreign country by the Government of Canada or by or on behalf of one of the provinces providing for reciprocal employment opportunities of an artistic, cultural or educational nature;		
	(k) a participant in an international student or young workers reciprocal employment program;		
	(l) a citizen of a country with which Canada has entered into an agreement whereby neither country is to charge for the processing of an application for authorization to engage or continue in employment; and		
	(m) an officer of the United States Immigration and Naturalization Service or of the United States Customs carrying out pre-inspection duties, an American member of the International Joint Commission, a United States grain inspector or any other United States Government official in possession of an official United States Government passport and assigned to a temporary posting in Canada, and their dependants.		

Item	Column I Service or right	Column II Person	Column III Fee ($)	Column IV Time
6.	**Processing a duly completed application for employment authorizations by a group of fewer than 15 persons, which group consists of one or more performing artists and their staff applying at the same time and at the same place for the authorizations**	**A person on behalf of the group**	**450**	**At the time of application**

Fee for Processing Applications for Student Authorization

Item	Column I Service or right	Column II Person	Column III Fee ($)	Column IV Time
7.	**Processing a duly completed application for a student authorization**	**(1) Subject to subsection (2), the fee must be paid by the applicant.** **(2) The following persons need not pay the fee:** **(a) a person described in paragraph 5(2)(a), (b), (c) or (m);** **(b) a member of a class of persons designated by the Governor in Council pursuant to subsection 6(3) and paragraph 114(1)(d) of the Act, and their dependants;** **(c) a person described in paragraph 3(2)(a) and their dependants;** **(d) a person described in paragraph 3(2)(b) and their dependants;** **(e) a dependant, studying at the secondary school level or lower, of a person described in paragraph 3(2)(c);** **(f) a student who is seeking renewal of their student authorization and who has become temporarily destitute through circumstances totally beyond their control or the control of any person on whom the student is dependent for financial resources; and**	**125**	**At the time of application**

Item	Column I Service or right	Column II Person	Column III Fee ($)	Column IV Time
		(g) a person in or coming into Canada, under an agreement between Canada and a foreign country or an arrangement entered into with a foreign country by the Government of Canada that provides for reciprocity of student exchange programs.		

Fee for Service with Respect to Minor Contraventions of the Act

Item	Column I Service or right	Column II Person	Column III Fee ($)	Column IV Time
8.	Processing a duly completed application to the Deputy Minister to authorize a person who has been reported to have ceased to be a visitor by reason of any of paragraphs 26(1)(a) to (c) of the Act to remain in Canada as a visitor pursuant to subsection 27(2.1) of the Act; a duly completed application to the Minister by a person described in paragraph 19(2)(a.1) of the Act on the ground that the person has been rehabilitated; a duly completed application for a Minister's permit or an extension of a Minister's permit; or a duly completed application for entry made under subsection 19(3) of the Act	(1) Subject to subsections (2) to (4), the fee must be paid by the applicant.	200	At the time of application
		(2) In the case of a person referred to in paragraph 3(2)(a) or (b) who has been reported to have ceased to be a visitor by reason of any of paragraphs 26(1)(a) to (c) of the Act, that person need not pay the fee.		

Item	Column I Service or right	Column II Person	Column III Fee ($)	Column IV Time
		(3) In the case of an application for a Minister's permit or an extension of a Minister's permit, the following persons need not pay the fee; **(a) a person described in any of paragraphs 3(3)(a) to (h), 5(2)(a) to (m) or 7(2)(a) to (g); and** **(b) a person described in item 1 or 2 of this schedule who is not described in subsection 19(1) or any of paragraphs 19(2)(a) to (c) of the Act, pending completion of the application.** **(4) In the case of an application for entry made under subsection 19(3) of the Act, a person to whom any of paragraphs 3(2)(a) to (f) apply and who has been granted entry solely on the grounds that the person is not in possession of a visitor visa need not pay the fee.**		

Fee for Processing Request in Respect of Criminal Rehabilitation — Paragraph 19(1)(c.1) of the Act

Item	Column I Service or right	Column II Person	Column III Fee ($)	Column IV Time
9.	**Processing a duly completed application to the Minister by a person described in paragraph 19(1)(c.1) of the Act on the ground that the person has been rehabilitated**	**The applicant must pay the fee.**	**1,000**	**At the time of application**

Fee for Processing Requests for Authorization to Come into Canada

Item	Column I Service or right	Column II Person	Column III Fee ($)	Column IV Time
10.	**Processing a duly completed application for the written consent of the Minister to come into Canada pursuant to section 55 of the Act**	**The applicant must pay the fee.**	**400**	**At the time of application**

Fee for the Replacement or Certification of an Immigration Document

Item	Column I Service or right	Column II Person	Column III Fee ($)	Column IV Time
11.	Processing a duly completed application to have a record of landing certified or a duly completed application for the replacement of any document issued by the Department of Citizenship and Immigration	(1) Subject to subsection (2), the fee must be paid by the applicant.	30	At the time of application
		(2) In the case of an application to have a record of landing certified, the following applicants need not pay the fee: (a) a federal, provincial or municipal government agency; and (b) a person in receipt of provincial welfare payments or of assistance under the Adjustment Assistance Program.		

12. [Repealed SOR/98-592, s. 1.]
13. [Repealed SOR/98-592, s. 1.]

General Fees for Services

Item	Column I Service or right	Column II Person	Column III Fee ($)	Column IV Time
14.	Appearing before an immigration officer after business hours to undergo a secondary examination	(1) An applicant who requests that an examination take place after business hours must pay the fee.	$100 for the first four hours and $30 for each additional hour or part of an hour	At the time of appearing
		(2) A transportation company, where one of the company's vehicles that is carrying a person who is to appear before the immigration officer arrives unscheduled at a port of entry after business hours, must pay the fee.		

Item	Column I Service or right	Column II Person	Column III Fee ($)	Column IV Time
15.	Processing a duly completed application for transfer of the applicant's immigration file from one immigration point of service to another and transferring the file, or a duly completed application for immigration statistical data that have not been published by the Department of Citizenship and Immigration and access to the Department's database to respond to each application	(1) Subject to subsection (2), the fee must be paid by the applicant. (2) The following applicants need not pay the fee: (a) an employee of the Department of Citizenship and Immigration; and (b) an employee of the Data Development Division of the Department of Human Resources Development.	Where the fee is for the transfer of an immigration file, $100; and where the fee is for statistical data, $100 for the first 10 minutes or less for access to the Department's database and $30 for each additional minute or less	At the time of application

Fee for Reviewing an Offer of Employment in a Family Business Application

Item	Column I Service or right	Column II Person	Column III Fee ($)	Column IV Time
16.	Review of an offer of employment made to an applicant in respect of a family business	The person submitting the offer of employment to the applicant must pay the fee.	400	At the time of the family business application

Fee for Processing Applications for Alternate Manners of Examination

Item	Column I Service or right	Column II Person	Column III Fee ($)	Column IV Time
17.	Processing a duly completed application made by a member of a class referred to in section 12.2 of the *Immigration Regulations, 1978* for an alternate manner of examination	The applicant, on their own behalf and in respect of each dependant, must pay the fee.	30 for each applicant and dependant	At the time of application

Fee for Processing a Recommendation to Confer the Right of Landing Pursuant to Subsection 38(1) of the Act

Item	Column I Service or right	Column II Person	Column III Fee ($)	Column IV Time
18.	**Processing a recommendation to the Governor in Council pursuant to subsection 38(1) of the Act for the conferral of the right of landing on a person who has resided continuously in Canada for at least five years under the authority of a permit**	**The person on whom the right of landing may be conferred must pay the fee.**	**275**	**At the time the person is notified that an immigration officer has decided to process the recommendation**

Right of Landing Fee

Item	Column I Service or right	Column II Person	Column III Fee ($)	Column IV Time
19.	**Conferral of the right of landing by or on behalf of Her Majesty on any immigrant who is at least 19 years of age at the time of the undertaking, application, notice, reconsideration or issuance**	**(1) Subject to subsections (2) to (5), the fee must be paid by the immigrant.**	**975**	**Before the issuance of the immigrant visa**
		(2) The sponsor must pay the fee where the immigrant or dependant of the immigrant, other than a member of a class of persons designated under paragraph 114(1)(d) of the Act, is sponsored.		**Before the issuance of the immigrant visa**
		(3) The immigrant must pay the fee where the immigrant or dependant, other than a member of a class of persons designated under paragraph 114(1)(d) of the Act, is not sponsored:		
		(a) where a person determined by the Refugee Division to be a Convention refugee makes an application;		**Before landing is granted**
		(b) where a person is a member of a class of immigrants prescribed under paragraph 114(1)(e) of the Act;		**Before landing is granted**

Column I Item Service or right	Column II Person	Column III Fee ($)	Column IV Time
	(c) where a person has applied for an exemption from the requirements of subsection 9(1) of the Act, pursuant to section 2.1 of the *Immigration Regulations, 1978*, and the application for exemption has not been refused; and		**Before landing is granted**
	(d) where it has been recommended by the Minister to the Governor in Council to authorize the landing of the immigrant pursuant to subsection 38(1) of the Act.		**Before landing is granted**
	(4) An immigrant who is a member of a class of persons designated under paragraph 114(1)(d) of the Act must pay the fee.		**Before the issuance of the immigrant visa**

(5) [Revoked SOR/97-202, s. 1.]

SOR/97-202, s. 1; SOR/98-592, s. 1; SOR/99-228, s. 1

Immigration Appeal Division Rules

Rules Governing the Activities of, and The Practice and Procedure in, the Appeal Division of the Immigration and Refugee Board

SOR/93-46, as am. SOR/97-363.

Short Title

1. These rules may be cited as the *Immigration Appeal Division Rules*.

Interpretation

2. In these Rules,

"Act" means the *Immigration Act*;

"Adjudication Division registry" means an office established by the Board pursuant to rule 3 of the *Adjudication Division Rules*;

"Assistant Deputy Chairman" means an Assistant Deputy Chairperson (Immigration Appeal Division);

"counsel" means a person who represents a party in any proceeding before the Appeal Division;

"notice to appear" means a notice to appear referred to in rule 14;

"presiding member" means the member designated pursuant to rule 5;

"registrar" means a person designated pursuant to rule 4;

"registry" means an office established by the Board pursuant to rule 3.

SOR/97-363, s. 1.

Registry and Registrar

3. The Board shall establish one or more offices for the activities of the Appeal Division, each of which is to be known as a registry.

4. The Board shall designate a person to be registrar at each registry.

Presiding Member

5. An Assistant Deputy Chairperson may designate a member to act as presiding member in respect of a hearing of an appeal, application or motion brought before the Appeal Division.

SOR/97-363, s. 2.

Appeals from Removal Orders or Conditional Removal Orders

6. (1) Subject to subrule (2), a person who, following an inquiry or a determination in respect of a removal order or conditional removal order, is appealing that order pursuant to section 70 of the Act shall

(a) where the order was made by an adjudicator,

(i) serve a notice of appeal on the adjudicator at the conclusion of the inquiry, or

(ii) file a notice of appeal, together with a copy of the order, at the Adjudication Division registry within 30 days after the day on which the order was served on the person; or

(b) where the order was made by a senior immigration officer, serve a notice of appeal, together with a copy of the order, on a senior immigration officer within 30 days after the day on which the order was served on the person.

(2) The time limit for filing a notice of appeal of a conditional removal order by a person described in paragraph 70(2)(*a*) of the Act is 30 days after the person receives notice that the conditional removal order has been confirmed under paragraph 46.07(3)(*a*) of the Act.

(3) Where a notice of appeal has been filed or where a senior immigration officer has been served with a notice of appeal pursuant to subrule (1), the registrar of the Adjudication Division or the senior immigration officer, as the case may be, shall file the notice of appeal within 10 days at a registry.

(4) For the purposes of subrule (3), service of a notice of appeal on an adjudicator pursuant to subrule (1) constitutes a filing of the notice of appeal at the Adjudication Division registry.

SOR/97-363, s. 3.

7. (1) Within 45 days after a notice of appeal has been served or filed pursuant to paragraph 6(1)(a), the registrar of the Adjudication Division shall

(a) serve the parties with a certified true copy of a record that consists of

(i) a certified true copy of the order and the notice of confirmation referred to in subrule 6(2), if any,

(ii) a transcript of the proceedings at the inquiry, but not including a transcript of any proceedings before an adjudicator relating to the detention of a party,

(iii) a certified true copy of all documentary evidence filed at the inquiry,

(iv) any written reasons given by the adjudicator for the decision, and

(v) a table of contents; and

(b) file a certified true copy of the record referred to in paragraph *(a)* at the registry.

(2) Within 45 days after a notice of appeal has been served on a senior immigration officer pursuant to paragraph 6(1)(b), a senior immigration officer shall

(a) serve the appellant with a certified true copy of a record that consists of

(i) a certified true copy of the order and the notice of confirmation referred to in subrule 6(2), if any,

(ii) a copy of any report and direction or any statement of arrest in respect of the appellant,

(iii) any reasons given by the senior immigration officer for the decision,

(iv) any other relevant information, and

(v) a table of contents; and

(b) file a certified true copy of the record referred to in paragraph (a) at the registry.

SOR/97-363, s. 4.

Appeals by the Minister

8. Where the Minister appeals a decision pursuant to section 71 of the Act, the notice of appeal shall

(a) be served on the respondent within 30 days after the decision is made;

(b) be filed at the Adjudication Division registry within five days after the service of the notice; and

(c) set out concisely every ground of appeal on which the Minister relies.

SOR/97-363, s. 5.

9. (1) Within 45 days after a notice of appeal has been filed pursuant to paragraph 8*(b)*, the registrar of the Adjudication Division shall serve the parties with a certified true copy of a record that consists of

(a) the decision rendered by the adjudicator;

(b) a transcript of the proceedings at the inquiry, but not including a transcript of any proceedings before an adjudicator relating to the detention of a party;

(c) a certified true copy of all documentary evidence filed at the inquiry;

(d) any written reasons given by the adjudicator for the decision; and

(e) a table of contents.

(2) The registrar of the Adjudication Division shall file a certified true copy of the record referred to in subrule (1) at the registry.

SOR/97-363, s. 6.

Appeals by Sponsors

10. (1) A sponsor who is appealing a refusal to approve an application for landing pursuant to subsection 77(3) of the Act shall file at the registry a notice of appeal and, wherever practicable, a copy of the notice of refusal within 30 days after the day on

which the sponsor has been informed in writing by the Minister of the reasons for the refusal.

(2) Where a notice of appeal has been filed pursuant to subrule (1), the registrar shall forthwith serve the Minister with a certified true copy thereof.

SOR/97-363, s. 6.

11. (1) Within 180 days after a copy of the notice of appeal has been served pursuant to subrule 10(2), an immigration officer shall serve the appellant with a certified true copy of the record described in subrule (2) and file a certified true copy thereof at the registry.

(2) The record shall consist of

(a) a certified true copy of the application for landing;

(b) a certified true copy of the application by the sponsor in support of the application for landing;

(c) certified true copies of all other documents filed by the sponsor and the person being sponsored in support of the application for landing;

(d) a statutory declaration by the immigration officer or visa officer stating all evidence relating to the application for landing and the sponsorship thereof considered by the officer, together with a statement of the reasons for refusing to approve the application for landing;

(e) a certified true copy of the notice of refusal to approve the application for landing provided to the sponsor;

(f) a certified true copy of the notice of refusal to approve the application for landing provided to the person being sponsored; and

(g) a table of contents.

SOR/97-363, s. 6.

Designated Representatives

11.1 Where counsel for a party, other than the Minister, believes that the party is under 18 years of age or is unable to appreciate the nature of the proceeding, counsel shall so advise the Appeal Division forthwith in writing and the Appeal Division shall designate a representative if it concludes that the party is under 18 years of age or is unable to appreciate the nature of the proceeding.

SOR/97-363, s. 6.

Change of Venue

12. (1) A party may apply in accordance with rule 26 to the Appeal Division at the registry where the appeal is pending to have a conference or hearing held at a place other than that set out in the notice to appear.

(2) The Appeal Division, in determining whether to grant a change of venue, may take into consideration, where applicable,

(a) whether it will adversely affect the proper operation of the Appeal Division;

(b) whether it will provide for a full and proper hearing;

(c) whether it will dispose expeditiously of the appeal or application at issue; and

(d) any other relevant facts.

SOR/97-363, s. 6.

Postponements and Adjournments

13. (1) Before the commencement of a hearing, a party may apply in accordance with rule 26 to the Appeal Division to have the hearing postponed.

(2) Before the resumption of a hearing, a party may apply in accordance with rule 26 to the Appeal Division to have the hearing adjourned.

(3) A party whose application for a postponement or adjournment was denied may reapply orally at the commencement or resumption of the hearing.

(4) The Appeal Division, in determining whether a hearing shall be postponed or adjourned, may take into consideration, where applicable,

(a) whether the postponement or adjournment would unreasonably impede the proceeding;

(b) the efforts made by the parties to proceed expeditiously;

(c) the nature and complexity of the issues relevant to the proceeding;

(d) the nature of the evidence to be presented, and the likelihood of causing an injustice to any party by proceeding in the absence of that evidence;

(e) counsel's knowledge of, and experience with, similar proceedings;

(f) the amount of time already afforded the parties for preparation of the case;

(g) the efforts made by the parties to be present at the hearing;

(h) the efforts made by the parties to make an application for a postponement or adjournment of the hearing at the earliest opportunity;

(i) the number of, and reasons for, any previous postponements or adjournments granted;

(j) whether the hearing was set peremptorily; and

(k) any other relevant facts.

Case Law

Gargano v. Canada (Minister of Citizenship & Immigration) (1994), 25 Imm. L.R. (2d) 292, 85 F.T.R. 49 (Fed. T.D.) — The applicant was a permanent resident of Canada who was ordered deported as a result of his criminal record. He appealed this decision and appeared before the Appeal Division without counsel on two occasions. The Board decided to proceed on the second occasion even though counsel was not present, and dismissed the applicant's appeal.

The contents of the rules of natural justice are not fixed and vary according to the seriousness of the consequences of the decision to be made. The consequences of a negative decision in a case such as this are very serious and the maximum safeguards should apply.

Absent specific rules laid down by statute or regulation, administrative tribunals control their own proceedings and adjournment of their proceedings is very much in their discretion, subject to the proviso that they comply with the rules of natural justice.

The criteria for determining whether a panel of the Appeal Division has properly exercised its discretion to disallow counsel are as follows:

1. the seriousness of the charge and of the potential penalty;
2. whether any points of law are likely to arise;
3. the capacity of a particular person to present his or her own case;
4. procedural difficulties;
5. the need for reasonable speed in making the adjudication.

A right to counsel is no more absolute than the right of a tribunal to determine its own process. In the event there is a conflict between the two, in order that the right to counsel may predominate, regard must be had to surrounding circumstances to determine if an applicant has suffered any prejudice. Proceeding without counsel is not prejudicial *per se*. Regard must be had to the circumstances of each case.

In this case the potential outcome of the matter — the removal of the applicant from Canada — is very serious. The applicant could be returned to a country where he does not speak the language, and where he has no surviving family. The fact that the Board's hearing in this case was set down peremptorily is not determinative. The applicant's previous adjournment was at a hearing for which he did not have adequate notice. The right to a fair hearing takes precedence over the need for a quick and speedy hearing.

In this case, the panel, in failing to provide an adjournment in order that he might retain counsel, denied the applicant a fair hearing and breached the rules of natural justice. The denial of a fair hearing always renders a decision invalid, whether or not it may appear to a reviewing court that the hearing would have resulted in a different decision.

Notice to Appear

14. (1) Where a conference or hearing is to be held before the Appeal Division, the Appeal Division shall, in a notice to appear, set out

(a) the date, time and place set for the conference or hearing;

(b) the purpose of the conference or hearing;

(c) the right of any party to be represented by counsel at the party's own expense; and

(d) in the case of an appeal by a person against whom a removal order or conditional removal order has been made, that, if the appellant fails to communicate with the Appeal Division or fails to inform the Appeal Division of the person's most recent address, the Appeal Division may declare the appeal to be abandoned.

(2) Subject to subrules (2.1) and (4), the registrar shall serve the notice to appear referred to in subrule (1) on every party at least 20 days before the date set for the conference or hearing.

(2.1) Subrule (2) does not apply in respect of a conference or hearing that has been postponed or adjourned.

(3) The parties to the proceeding may consent to the conference or hearing being held before the date referred to in subrule (1).

(4) A notice to appear given orally by telephone is valid notice for the purposes of subrule (1), if the parties are served with a written notice to appear at least eight days before the date set for the conference or hearing.

SOR/97-363, s. 7.

Official Languages

15. At least 15 days before the date set for a conference or hearing, as the case may be, a party, other than the Minister, shall notify the Appeal Division, in writing, of the official language in which the party chooses the conference or hearing to be conducted.

Interpreter

16. (1) The Appeal Division shall provide an interpreter to assist a party or a party's witness where the party advises the Appeal Division in writing, at least 15 days before the date set for a conference or hearing, as the case may be, that the party or witness does not understand or speak the language in which the proceeding is to be conducted, or is hearing impaired.

(2) The interpreter shall take an oath or make a solemn affirmation to interpret accurately any statements made, and to translate accurately any documents that the Appeal Division may require to be translated, in the course of the conference or hearing.

Case Law

Yu v. Canada (Minister of Employment & Immigration) (1994), 75 F.T.R. 241 (Fed. T.D.) — The applicant complained about the quality of the interpretation of her testimony and filed in support an affidavit commenting on the accuracy of the translation. The Court could not give effect to the general statements about the quality of interpretation due to the fact that the affidavit lacked sufficient specific examples. However, the decision was set aside because the one example of inaccuracy that was referred to formed the basis for the finding that the applicant's testimony was exaggerated. The Court could not be certain that the Board would have concluded that the fear of persecution was exaggerated had there been a proper interpretation of this evidence. Accordingly, the decision of the Refugee Division was quashed.

Varaich v. Canada (Minister of Employment & Immigration) (1994), 75 F.T.R. 143 (Fed. T.D.) — A tribunal is under a clear duty to make an inquiry into an interpreter's competence once an objection is made. Being the master of his or her proceeding, the adjudicator may call a witness if it is necessary to determine the competence of the interpreter and ensure a fair hearing, but this is not obligatory. The adjudicator did not rely on the interpreter's reputation, but asked the applicant directly what she did not understand. Further, the adjudicator engaged in a relatively lengthy questioning of the interpreter as to his qualifications before concluding that he was competent. Therefore, the applicant did not establish that her right to an interpreter was infringed.

Conferences

17. (1) Where the holding of a conference is necessary for a full and proper hearing and to dispose of an appeal, application or motion expeditiously, the Appeal Division shall direct the parties, by a notice to appear, to attend a conference, to be held before or during a hearing, on any matter related to the appeal, application or motion.

(2) At a conference, the participants shall

(a) provide each other with the number of witnesses they intend to call, the reasons for which each witness will be called, and a copy of any document, report or other material that the participants intend to produce at the hearing; and

(b) attempt to agree on means of simplifying the hearing and, as far as possible, define any pertinent issues, agree on certain facts and receive documents.

(3) An agreement concluded at a conference shall be in writing and signed by the participants or given orally at the hearing and shall govern the hearing to the extent that it is appropriate in order to provide for a full and proper hearing and to dispose of the appeal, application or motion expeditiously.

(4) Forthwith after a conference, a member or, where a member is not present at the conference, a party, shall file at the registry any written agreement concluded and the original of any documents that have been received during the conference.

SOR/97-363, s. 8.

Disclosure

18. (1) Any party shall, in any proceeding, serve on the other party and file at the registry, at least 20 days before the date set for the hearing, a statement of the number of witnesses they intend to call, the reasons for which each witness will be called, and a copy of any document, report or other material that the party intends to produce at the hearing, unless it was produced at a conference held in accordance with rule 17.

(2) A party who intends to reply by way of documentary evidence at a hearing to the documentary evidence referred to in subrule (1) shall, at least 10 days before the date set for the hearing, serve on the other party and file at the registry a copy of the reply.

SOR/97-363, s. 10.

19. A party who intends to call an expert witness at a hearing shall, at least 20 days before the date set for the hearing, serve on the other party and file at the registry a report signed by the expert witness setting out the name, address and qualifications of the expert witness and a brief summary of the substance of the proposed testimony of the expert witness.

SOR/97-363, s. 10.

Applications for Confidentiality

20. (1) An application made pursuant to subsection 80(2) of the Act shall be made to the Appeal Division by motion in accordance with subrules 27(2) to (7).

(2) A person may apply by way of motion in accordance with subrules 27(2) to (7) to be made a party for the purposes of intervening in a motion referred to in subrule (1).

SOR/97-363, s. 11.

Witnesses

21. A party who calls a witness shall pay the witness the applicable fees and allowances set out in the *Federal Court Rules*.

22. (1) The Appeal Division may, at the request of a party or of its own motion, exclude witnesses from a hearing until they are called to testify.

(2) No person may communicate to a witness who has been excluded pursuant to subrule (1) any evidence or testimony that is given during the course of a hearing until after the witness has testified.

23. (1) A party who requests the Appeal Division to issue a summons shall do so in writing and shall file the request at the registry.

(2) Where a person avoids service of a summons or fails to comply with a summons, the party who requested the issuance of the summons may make a written request, together with an affidavit setting out the relevant facts, to the Appeal Division for the issuance of a warrant and shall file the documents at the registry.

(3) A party who requests the issuance of a warrant pursuant to subrule (2) shall provide information to establish that

(a) the person named in the summons

(i) avoided service of the summons, or

(ii) was served with the summons and was paid or offered a reasonable amount of attendance money but failed to comply with the requirements of the summons; and

(b) the appearance of the person named in the summons is necessary to ensure a full and proper hearing.

(4) A warrant issued by the Appeal Division that directs a peace officer to cause the person named in the warrant to be apprehended anywhere in Canada shall indicate the measures to be taken by the peace officer in respect of the detention or release of the person.

(5) The measures referred to in subrule (4) are

(a) detaining the person in custody and forthwith bringing the person before the Appeal Division; or

(b) releasing the person on a recognizance, with or without sureties, conditional on the person's appearance at the date, time and place specified, to give or produce evidence at a hearing before the Appeal Division.

SOR/97-363, s. 12.

Party in Custody

24. Where a party is detained, the Appeal Division may order the person who detains the party to bring the latter in custody to a conference or hearing held in respect of the party.

Hearings

25. The Appeal Division shall permit evidence to be adduced at a hearing by means of such telephone or other communication facilities, including videoconference facilities, as permit all persons participating in the hearing to communicate effectively with each

other, and in such manner as would provide for a full and proper hearing and to dispose of the appeal, application or motion expeditiously, including

(a) the filing of affidavits and other documentary evidence;

(b) the presentation of written or oral arguments or both;

(c) the calling, questioning and cross-examination of witnesses; and

(d) the testimony of any party.

SOR/97-363, s. 13.

Case Law

Canada (Minister of Citizenship & Immigration) v. Dhaliwal-Williams (1997), 131 F.T.R. 19 (Fed. T.D.) — At the commencement of the hearing before the IAD the respondent's counsel advised the panel that he intended to call the respondent and a number of witnesses. After the respondent was examined by her own counsel and cross-examined by the appeals officer, the IAD advised the parties that it would only need to hear from one further witness. This witness then gave brief testimony and the panel adjourned for a short recess. When proceedings resumed the presiding member advised the parties that the panel had to come to a decision and had decided to allow the appeal.

The evidenced showed that the appeals officer representing the applicant intended to make submissions and that the IAD was alive to fact that the appeals officer intended to make representations.

The failure to permit the appeals officer to make representations was procedurally unfair and accordingly, the decision of the IAD was quashed and the matter sent back for rehearing by a differently constituted panel.

Kusi v. Canada (Minister of Employment & Immigration) (1993), 19 Imm. L.R. (2d) 281, 65 F.T.R. 58 (Fed. T.D.) — An adjudicator and member of the Immigration and Refugee Board were conducting a credible basis hearing into the claim of a Convention refugee claimant, pursuant to provisions of the *Immigration Act* in effect on August 19, 1992.

The tribunal accepted as evidence notes taken by an immigration officer, which recorded answers given to him at the port of entry by the applicant. The applicant contested the accuracy of the notes and asked that the officer be produced for cross-examination, a request which was denied by the tribunal.

The decision by the tribunal that there was no credible basis to the applicant's claim was set aside and the matter was remitted back for determination in accordance with the law. Specifically, the Court found that given the importance of the interest, namely the applicant's claim to be a Convention refugee, and given the fact that the applicant contested the accuracy of the notes which were relied upon by the tribunal, the rules of natural justice and of fundamental justice required that the cross-examination, which was sought, be allowed. The Court relied on the jurisprudence in *Canada (Minister of Employment & Immigration) v. Leal* (1991), 129 N.R. 383 (Fed. C.A.) and *Cheung v. Canada (Minister of Employment & Immigration)* (1981), 122 D.L.R. (3d) 41 (Fed. C.A.).

Editor's Note: *Although occurring in the context of a repealed refugee hearing procedure, the principle in this case may have a broader application.*

Applications

26. (1) Subject to subrule (2), an application referred to in rule 12, 13, 38 or 40 shall be

(a) made by a party in writing, specifying the grounds on which the application is made and the facts on which it is based;

(b) filed at the registry; and

(c) served on the other party.

(2) A party may make an application referred to in subrule (1) orally at a hearing where no injustice is likely to be caused to any party.

(3) The Appeal Division may determine an application referred to in subrule (1) after all parties have been given a reasonable opportunity to make representations.

SOR/97-363, s. 14.

Motions

27. (1) Every application that is not provided for in these Rules shall be made by a party to the Appeal Division by motion, unless, where the application is made during a hearing, the members decide that, in the interests of justice, the application should be dealt with in some other manner.

(2) The motion shall consist of

(a) a notice specifying the grounds on which the motion is made;

(b) an affidavit setting out the facts on which the motion is based; and

(c) a concise statement of the law and of the arguments that are relied on by the applicant.

(3) The motion shall be

(a) served on the other party to the proceeding; and

(b) filed, together with proof of service, at the registry within five days after the date of service.

(4) Evidence on the merits of a motion shall be introduced by affidavit, unless the Appeal Division decides that, in the interests of justice, the evidence should be introduced in some other manner.

(5) The other party may, within seven days after being served with a motion, file at the registry a reply stating concisely the law and arguments relied on by the party, accompanied by an affidavit setting out the facts on which the reply is based.

(6) The applicant may, within seven days after being served with a reply, file a response thereto at the registry.

(7) A copy of the reply and affidavit filed pursuant to subrule (5) and of the response filed pursuant to subrule (6) shall be served on the other party within seven days after the date of service of the motion or reply, as the case may be.

(8) The Appeal Division may dispose of a motion without a hearing where no injustice is likely to be caused.

SOR/97-363, s. 15.

Case Law

Barone v. Canada (Minister of Citizenship & Immigration) (1996), 38 Imm. L.R. (2d) 93 (Imm. & Ref. Bd. (Appeal Division)) — This was a motion brought pursuant to rule 27 of the *Immigration Appeal Division Rules* to re-open an appeal. The applicant, a permanent resident, had been ordered deported because he had been convicted of an offence for a which a term of imprisonment of more than 6 months had been imposed. While the applicant's appeal was pending, the Minister certified the applicant pursuant to section 70(5) and the Appeal Division accordingly held that it lost jurisdiction over the applicant and that the applicant had therefore lost his right of appeal.

The basis of the application to re-open was the decision of the Federal Court Trial Division in *Williams v. Canada (Minister of Citizenship & Immigration)* (1996), 35 Imm. L.R. (2d) 286, 121 F.T.R. 226, [1997] 1 F.C. 457 (Fed. T.D.).

The Appeal Division found that there was no basis for ordering the re-opening of the appeal because the scope of the Appeal Division's jurisdiction to re-open does not extend to revisiting determinations on legal issues. The jurisdiction to reopen is limited to revisiting determinations made in the exercise of the Appeal Division's statutory discretion in light of new evidence.

The Appeal Division may have the power to revisit its own determinations with respect to jurisdiction if the criteria in *Chandler v. Assn. of Architects (Alberta)*, [1989] 2 S.C.R. 848 (S.C.C.), are met.

Notice of Constitutional Question

27.1 (1) Where a party serves a notice of constitutional question pursuant to section 57 of the *Federal Court Act*, the party shall also serve on the other party and file at the registry the notice, together with proof of service, at least 10 days before the date set for the hearing before the Appeal Division.

(2) A notice referred to in subrule (1) shall be in Form 2.1, "Notice of Constitutional Question", set out in the *Federal Court Rules* or in any other form that sets out

(a) the name of the appellant;

(b) the Appeal Division file number;

(c) the date, time and place of the hearing;

(d) the specific provisions of law the validity, applicability or effect of which will be questioned;

(e) the material facts relied on; and

(f) the legal basis of the constitutional challenge.

SOR/97-363, s. 16.

Orders

28. A registrar shall sign and seal all orders of the Appeal Division and shall forthwith serve all parties with certified true copies of all such orders.

29. A request made pursuant to subsection 69.4(5) of the Act for written reasons for the disposition of an appeal shall be made to the Appeal Division, in writing, and filed at the registry.

Withdrawal

30. (1) A party may withdraw an appeal, application or motion either orally during a hearing or by notice in writing filed at the registry.

(2) The registrar shall forthwith notify in writing the other party of any withdrawal referred to in subrule (1).

SOR/97-363, s. 17.

Counsel of Record

30.1 (1) Counsel is deemed to be the counsel of record for a party, other than the Minister, where counsel takes a step in a proceeding by agreeing to a date set for a hearing, or by otherwise representing himself or herself as the party's counsel after a hearing date has been set.

(2) The counsel of record for a party ceases to be counsel of record when the party notifies the Appeal Division, pursuant to rule 36, that the counsel no longer represents the party.

(3) The counsel of record for a party may apply to the Appeal Division for an order to be removed as counsel of record, together with an affidavit setting out the grounds for the application, and shall serve a copy of the application and the affidavit on the party.

SOR/97-363, s. 18.

Reinstatement

31. (1) A party who has withdrawn an appeal, application or motion may, by motion made pursuant to subrules 27(2) to (7), apply to the Appeal Division for reinstatement of the appeal, application or motion.

(2) A motion made by a party other than the Minister for reinstatement of an appeal, application or motion shall, where the party is not represented by counsel, include the party's address and telephone number.

(3) The Appeal Division shall grant a motion for reinstatement of an appeal, application or motion where there are sufficient reasons why the appeal, application or motion should be reinstated and it is in the interests of justice to do so.

SOR/97-363, s. 19.

Reopening

32. (1) Where the Appeal Division has declared an appeal to be abandoned by a party, the party may, by motion made pursuant to subrules 27(2) to (7), apply to the Appeal Division for the appeal to be reopened.

(2) A motion made by a party other than the Minister to reopen an appeal shall, where the party is not represented by counsel, include the party's address and telephone number.

(3) The Appeal Division shall grant a motion to reopen an appeal where there are sufficient reasons why the appeal should be reopened and it is in the interests of justice to do so.

SOR/97-363, s. 20.

Stay of Execution of a Removal Order or Conditional Removal Order

33. (1) Where the Appeal Division disposes of an appeal in accordance with paragraph 73(1)(*c*) or (*d*) of the Act, a party may apply in writing to the Appeal Division to take one of the measures referred to in paragraphs 74(3)(*a*) and (*b*) of the Act.

(2) An application made pursuant to subrule (1) shall

(a) state the grounds thereof;

(b) be accompanied by

(i) an affidavit setting out the facts on which the application is based, and

(ii) a concise statement of the law and arguments that are relied on by the applicant;

(c) be served on the other party; and

(d) be filed at the registry, together with two copies thereof, within five days after the date of service on the other party.

(3) Where the Appeal Division reviews a case of its own motion pursuant to subsection 74(2) of the Act, the registrar shall notify the parties of the review 30 days before the date fixed for the review.

Return to Canada for Hearing of Appeal

34. (1) Where a person described in section 75 of the Act informs the Appeal Division in writing of the person's desire to appear in person before the Appeal Division at the hearing of the appeal, the registrar shall forthwith so notify the Minister.

(2) The Minister may, within five days after being notified, file a written submission respecting the return to Canada of the person referred to in subrule (1).

(3) The Appeal Division shall notify the person referred to in subrule (1) of any submission made by the Minister and shall afford the person a reasonable opportunity to respond in writing, unless the Appeal Division decides that no further submission of the person is required and that the person shall be allowed to return to Canada.

Service and Filing

35. (1) Subject to subrule (5), service of any document in the course of a proceeding under these Rules shall be effected by personal service, by prepaid regular mail, by any mail service whereby the sender is provided with an acknowledgement of receipt, by courier or by the telephone transmission of a facsimile of the document in accordance with subrule (3).

(2) A copy of any document served on a party pursuant to subrule (1) shall also be served on that party's counsel, if any.

(3) A document that is served by telephone transmission of a facsimile shall include a cover page setting out

(a) the sender's name, address and telephone number;

(b) the name of the addressee;

(c) the total number of pages transmitted, including the cover page;

(d) the telephone number from which the document is transmitted; and

(e) the name and telephone number of a person to contact in the event of transmission problems.

(4) Service by prepaid regular mail shall be considered to be effected on the date that is seven days after the date of mailing.

(4.1) Where a party, other than the Minister, has not notified the Appeal Division of the party's address or changes thereto as required by rule 36, the Appeal Division may direct that service of any notice required to be given under these Rules be dispensed with if reasonable efforts have been made by the Appeal Division to locate the party.

(5) Where service cannot be effected in accordance with subrule (1), the Chairperson may direct that service be effected by such means as will, to the extent possible, provide a party with the document and as will not likely cause injustice to any party.

(6) [Revoked SOR/97-363, s. 21.]

SOR/97-363, s. 21.

36. A party, other than the Minister, shall notify the Appeal Division forthwith in writing of the party's address, of the name, address for service, telephone number and facsimile number, if any, of the party's counsel and of any changes in that information, including the fact that the party is no longer represented by counsel.

SOR/97-363, s. 22.

37. (1) A document shall be filed at the registry by serving it on an employee of the registry at which the file relating to the appeal is held.

(2) The filing of a telephone transmission of a facsimile is deemed to be effected on the date on which it is received by the registrar, as stamped on the facsimile by an employee of the registry.

(3) All documents submitted in the course of any proceeding under these Rules in a language other than English or French shall be accompanied by a translation in English or French that is certified to be correct, unless the Appeal Division decides that a translation is not necessary to provide for a full and proper hearing.

SOR/97-363, s. 23.

Time Limits

38. The Appeal Division may, on its own motion or on application made by a party in accordance with rule 26 either before or after a time limit set out in these Rules has expired, shorten or extend the time limit in order to provide for a full and proper hearing.

SOR/97-363, s. 24.

General

39. These Rules are not exhaustive and, where any matter that is not provided for in these Rules arises in the course of any proceeding, the Appeal Division may take whatever measures are necessary to provide for a full and proper hearing and to dispose of the matter expeditiously.

40. Where a party does not comply with a requirement of these Rules, the Appeal Division, on its own motion or on application made by the party in accordance with rule 26, may permit the party to remedy the non-compliance or may waive the requirement, if no injustice is likely to be caused to any party and the proceeding will not be unreasonably impeded.

SOR/97-363, s. 25.

CONVENTION REFUGEE DETERMINATION DIVISION RULES

Rules Governing the Activities of, and the Practice and Procedure in, the Convention Refugee Determination Division of the Immigration and Refugee Board

SOR/93-45

Short Title

1. These Rules may be cited as the *Convention Refugee Determination Division Rules*.

Interpretation

2. In these Rules,

"Act" means the *Immigration Act*;

"Assistant Deputy Chairperson" means an Assistant Deputy Chairperson (Convention Refugee Determination Division);

"coordinating member" means a member designated by the Governor in Council pursuant to subsection 59(3) of the Act;

"counsel" means a person authorized pursuant to subsection 69(1) of the Act to represent a party in any proceeding before the Refugee Division;

"member" means a member of the Refugee Division;

"notice to appear" means a notice to appear referred to in rule 15;

"party" means the person concerned or, where the Minister takes part in a proceeding or makes an application, the Minister;

"person concerned" means a person whose claim is referred to the Refugee Division pursuant to section 46.02 or subsection 46.03(1) of the Act, or a person who is the subject of an application made under section 69.2 of the Act;

"presiding member" means the member designated pursuant to rule 5;

"refugee hearing officer" means a person referred to in section 68.1 of the Act;

"registrar" means a person designated pursuant to rule 4;

"registry" means an office established by the Board pursuant to rule 3.

Registry and Registrar

3. The Board shall establish one or more offices for the activities of the Refugee Division, each of which is to be known as a registry.

4. The Board shall designate a person to be registrar at each registry.

Presiding Member

5. An Assistant Deputy Chairperson or coordinating member may designate a member to act as presiding member in respect of a hearing into a claim or an application that, by the Act, must be brought before the Refugee Division.

Referral to the Refugee Division

6. (1) A senior immigration officer shall refer a claim to the Refugee Division pursuant to section 46.02 or subsection 46.03(1) of the Act, by:

(a) forwarding to the Refugee Division

(i) the determination of eligibility of the claim of the person concerned that is made by the senior immigration officer, and

(ii) a copy of any identification and travel documents of the person concerned that are in the possession of the senior immigration officer;

(b) forwarding to the Refugee Division the following information, in writing, namely,

(i) the section of the Act pursuant to which the claim is being referred,

(ii) the name, sex and date of birth of the person concerned,

(iii) if available, the address and telephone number in Canada of the person concerned,

(iv) the name of the counsel, if any, of the person concerned,

(v) the country or countries in which the person concerned fears persecution,

(vi) the official language chosen by the person concerned for communication with the Refugee Division,

(vii) where applicable, the language or dialect of the interpreter required by the person concerned during any proceeding,

(viii) where applicable, the place of detention of the person concerned,

(ix) an indication of whether or not any information had been requested by the Minister pursuant to subsection 69.1(2) of the Act,

(x) the Canada Employment and Immigration Commission Client I.D. Number relating to the claim,

(xi) where applicable, the names of the family members of the person concerned whose claims have been referred to the Refugee Division and the Canada Employment and Immigration Commission Client I.D. Number relating to those family members,

(xii) the date on which, and the method by which, the senior immigration officer serves the person concerned with the information form in accordance with paragraph (*c*),

(xiii) the date of the referral of the claim by the senior immigration officer to the Refugee Division, and

(xiv) the name of the senior immigration officer; and

(c) serving the person concerned with the form that sets out the information to be provided to the Refugee Division pursuant to subrule 14(1).

(2) The senior immigration officer shall forward the documents and information referred to in paragraphs (1)(*a*) and (*b*) to the registry designated by the Refugee Division.

Cessation and Vacation Applications

7. (1) An application for leave made by the Minister pursuant to subsection 69.2(3) of the Act shall

(a) be made by way of notice in writing addressed to the Chairperson and filed at the registry from which the notice of decision in respect of the determination that a person is a Convention refugee was issued;

(b) specify the grounds on which the application is made; and

(c) include an affidavit that sets out the facts on which the application is based.

(2) The registrar shall serve a copy of the Chairperson's decision on the Minister.

(3) Where the Minister obtains leave to make an application pursuant to subsection 69.2(2) of the Act or where the Minister makes an application pursuant to subsection 69.2(1) of the Act, the application shall

(a) be made by way of notice in writing addressed to the Refugee Division and filed at the registry from which the leave was granted or the notice of decision in respect of the determination that a person is a Convention refugee was issued, as the case may be;

(b) specify the grounds on which the application is made; and

(c) include an affidavit setting out the facts on which the application is based.

(4) Where the Minister makes an application referred to in subrule (3), the Minister shall serve on the person concerned a copy of that application and, where applicable, a copy of the decision referred to in subrule (2).

(5) When the requirements of subrules (3) and (4) have been met, the Refugee Division shall serve on the parties a notice to appear.

Participation of the Minister

8. (1) Subject to subrule (2), where the Minister intends to participate at any hearing into a claim pursuant to section 69.1 of the Act, the Minister may, at any time, give notice in writing of the Minister's intention to participate.

(2) The period referred to in subsection 69.1(7.1) of the Act after which a member may determine that a person concerned is a Convention refugee without a hearing is

(a) where the Minister has requested information pursuant to subsection 69.1(2) of the Act, the 15-day period immediately after the day on which the Minister is served with the form that contains the information referred to in subrule 14(1); and

(b) where the Minister has not requested information pursuant to subsection 69.1(2) of the Act, the 28-day period immediately after the day on which the claim

is referred to the Refugee Division by a senior immigration officer pursuant to rule 6.

(3) The Minister shall serve the notice referred to in subrule (1) on the person concerned and shall file the notice at the registry.

Case Law

Section 8(2)(b)

*Canada (Secretary of State) v. Mostameh, (*sub nom. *Canada (Secrétaire d'Etat) v. Mostameh)* — The Minister brought this application. The respondent's case was referred to the Refugee Division on February 17, 1993, and the request for information by the Minister was not made until March 18, 1993.

The Refugee Division may determine that a person is a Convention refugee without holding a hearing if the Minister does not notify the Division within the period specified by the rules that he intends to participate in the hearing. Section 8(2)(b) provides that a member may determine that a person is a Convention refugee without a hearing where the Minister has not requested information under section 69.1(2) during the 28 day period immediately after the day on which the claim is referred to the Refugee Division. In this case the Refugee Division was entitled to confer refugee status on the claimant on April 21, 1993, a date within the 28 day deadline specified in section 8(2)(b). The deadlines in this case are specified by law and it must be assumed that the Minister was aware of it.

There is a significant difference between the nature of the Minister's rights and those of the claimant. The claimant has an established right to participate pursuant to the guarantees made by section 7 of the *Charter of Rights*. The Minister, on the other hand, cannot argue that the right to life, liberty or security of the person has been infringed if the deadlines are strictly enforced. If the Minister intends to intervene he has a duty to notify the Division within the specified deadline, and if through his negligence he fails to do so, his right to participate is lost.

9. (1) Where the Minister informs the Refugee Division pursuant to subparagraph 69.1(5)(*a*)(ii) of the Act that the Minister is of the opinion that matters involving section E or F of Article 1 of the Convention or subsection 2(2) of the Act are raised by the claim, the Minister shall specify the grounds and the parts of section E or F or of subsection 2(2) that in the opinion of the Minister are relevant to the claim and shall set out briefly the law and facts on which the Minister relies.

(2) Where, before the commencement of a hearing, the refugee hearing officer of the Refugee Division is of the opinion that a claim before the Refugee Division might involve Section E or F of Article 1 of the Convention or subsection 2(2) of the Act, the refugee hearing officer shall forthwith notify the Minister and provide the Minister with such information as is necessary.

(3) Where, during a hearing, the refugee hearing officer or a member is of the opinion that a claim before the Refugee Division might involve section E or F of Article 1 of the Convention or subsection 2(2) of the Act, the refugee hearing officer or the member shall so inform the presiding member and, if the presiding member so directs, the refugee hearing officer shall forthwith notify the Minister and provide the Minister with such information as is necessary.

(4) The refugee hearing officer shall serve the person concerned forthwith with a copy of all written information that the refugee hearing officer provides to the Minister pursuant to subrules (2) and (3).

Joinder

10. (1) An Assistant Deputy Chairperson or coordinating member may order that two or more claims or applications be processed jointly where the Assistant Deputy Chairperson or coordinating member believes that no injustice is thereby likely to be caused to any party.

(2) Subject to subsection (3), claims or applications of legal or *de facto* spouse, dependant children, father, mother, brothers or sisters of the person concerned shall be processed jointly.

(3) On application by a party, or on the members' own motion at the time of the hearing, the members may order that the claims or applications be heard separately, where the members believe that hearing the claims or applications jointly is likely to cause an injustice to any party.

Designated Representatives

11. Where counsel of the person concerned believes that the person concerned is under 18 years of age or is unable to appreciate the nature of the proceeding, counsel shall so advise the Refugee Division forthwith in writing so that the Refugee Division may decide whether to designate a representative pursuant to subsection 69(4) of the Act.

Change of Venue

12. (1) A party may apply in accordance with rule 27 to the Refugee Division to have a preliminary conference, conference or hearing held at a place other than that set out in the notice to appear.

(2) An application made under subrule (1) shall be accompanied by a statement of facts to support the application.

(3) The Refugee Division shall grant an application made under subrule (1) if it is satisfied that doing so will not adversely affect the proper operation of the Refugee Division, will provide for a full and proper hearing and will dispose expeditiously of the claim or application at issue.

(4) Where an application made under subrule (1) is granted, the file relating to the claim or application shall be transferred to the registry of the place where the conference or hearing is to be held.

Postponements and Adjournments

13. (1) Before the commencement of a hearing, a party may apply in accordance with rule 27 to the Refugee Division to have the hearing postponed.

(2) Before the resumption of a hearing, a party may apply in accordance with rule 27 to the Refugee Division to have the hearing adjourned.

(3) A party whose application for a postponement or adjournment was denied may reapply orally at the commencement or resumption of the hearing.

(4) The Refugee Division, in determining whether a hearing shall be postponed, or in determining pursuant to subsection 69(6) of the Act whether an adjournment of a hearing would unreasonably impede the proceedings, may take into consideration, where applicable,

(a) the efforts made by the parties to proceed expeditiously;

(b) the nature and complexity of the issues relevant to the proceeding;

(c) the nature of the evidence to be presented, and the likelihood of causing an injustice to any party by proceeding in the absence of the evidence;

(d) counsel's knowledge of, and experience with, similar proceedings;

(e) the amount of time already afforded the parties for preparation of the case;

(f) the efforts made by the parties to be present at the hearing;

(g) the efforts made by the parties to make an application for a postponement or adjournment of the hearing at the earliest opportunity;

(h) the number of, and reasons for, any previous postponements or adjournments granted;

(i) whether the hearing was set peremptorily; and

(j) any other relevant facts.

Case Law

Gargano v. Canada (Minister of Citizenship & Immigration) (1994), 25 Imm. L.R. (2d) 292, 85 F.T.R. 49 (Fed. T.D.) — The applicant was a permanent resident of Canada who was ordered deported as a result of his criminal record. He appealed this decision and appeared before the Appeal Division without counsel on two occasions. The Board decided to proceed on the second occasion even though counsel was not present, and dismissed the applicant's appeal.

The contents of the rules of natural justice are not fixed and vary according to the seriousness of the consequences of the decision to be made. The consequences of a negative decision in a case such as this are very serious and the maximum safeguards should apply.

Absent specific rules laid down by statute or regulation, administrative tribunals control their own proceedings and adjournment of their proceedings is very much in their discretion, subject to the proviso that they comply with the rules of natural justice.

The criteria for determining whether a panel of the Appeal Division has properly exercised its discretion to disallow counsel are as follows:

1. the seriousness of the charge and of the potential penalty;
2. whether any points of law are likely to arise;
3. the capacity of a particular person to present his or her own case;
4. procedural difficulties;
5. the need for reasonable speed in making the adjudication.

A right to counsel is no more absolute than the right of a tribunal to determine its own process. In the event there is a conflict between the two, in order that the right to counsel may predominate, regard must be had to surrounding circumstances to determine if an applicant has suffered any prejudice. Proceeding without counsel is not prejudicial *per se*. Regard must be had to the circumstances of each case.

In this case the potential outcome of the matter — the removal of the applicant from Canada — is very serious. The applicant could be returned to a country where he does not speak the language, and where he has no surviving family. The fact that the Board's hearing in this case was set down peremptorily is not determinative. The applicant's previous adjournment was at a hearing for which he did not have adequate notice. The right to a fair hearing takes precedence over the need for a quick and speedy hearing.

In this case, the panel, in failing to provide an adjournment in order that he might retain counsel, denied a fair hearing and breached the rules of natural justice. The denial of a fair hearing always renders a decision invalid, whether or not it may appear to a reviewing court that the hearing would have resulted in a different decision.

Information Respecting Claim

14. (1) A person concerned shall provide the Refugee Division with information respecting the claim, including

(a) the name, sex, marital status, date and place of birth, nationality or, where applicable, nationalities at birth, current nationality or, where applicable, nationalities, ethnic group or tribe and religion of the person concerned, and the country or, where applicable, countries in which the person concerned fears persecution;

(b) the country or, where applicable, countries of residence of the person concerned in the last ten years and the status, if any, of the person concerned in each of those countries;

(c) the name, date of birth, nationality or, where applicable, nationalities and whereabouts of the spouse, children, parents and brothers and sisters, if any, of the person concerned;

(d) those identity and travel documents that were not given by the person concerned to a senior immigration officer;

(e) where applicable, a statement to the effect that the person concerned has destroyed or disposed of identity documents that were in the person's possession, and the list of documents destroyed or disposed of and the reasons for the destruction or disposal;

(f) a detailed statement of the formal education or professional training and work history of the person concerned;

(g) where applicable, a statement to the effect that the person concerned has applied for a Canadian visa and the result of the application;

(h) a detailed statement of the route taken by the person concerned to Canada from the country or, where applicable, countries in which the person concerned fears persecution, including arrival and departure dates and method of transportation along that route;

(i) the date and place in Canada at which the person concerned first stated to a Canadian official the intention to claim Convention refugee status in Canada;

(j) the date, duration and purpose of any previous trips to Canada made by the person concerned;

(k) where applicable, a statement to the effect that the person concerned, since the date referred to in paragraph (i), has been in the country or countries in which the person concerned fears persecution;

(l) the type, document number, source of issue, date of issue and date of expiration of all documents used by the person concerned to travel to Canada, that were required to leave the country or countries in which the person concerned fears persecution, or were applied for by the person concerned after arrival in Canada for the purpose of travelling outside Canada, and, where applicable, an indication of any such documents that were not genuine or that were not issued in the name of the person concerned;

(m) where applicable, a statement to the effect that military or other service is compulsory in the country or countries in which the person concerned fears persecution, and details of the service, including draft age, length of service required and duration of actual service, dates of service, and whether the service was voluntary or due to conscription, and, where the person concerned did not serve or complete the service, the reasons why;

(n) where applicable, a statement to the effect that the person concerned is sought by the authorities in any country and the reasons therefor;

(o) the date and nature of any crime or offence committed by the person concerned;

(p) the date, place and disposition of any claim for Convention refugee status filed by the person concerned, or by any member of the family of the person concerned, in Canada, in another country or with the United Nations High Commissioner for Refugees;

(q) a statement of the grounds on which the claim of the person concerned is based;

(r) a statement of the facts on which the claim is based;

(s) the address and telephone number of the person concerned in Canada;

(t) the name, address and telephone number of counsel, if any, for the person concerned;

(u) where applicable, a statement to the effect that the person concerned requires an interpreter for the purpose of participating in proceedings before the Refugee Division and the language or dialect required for interpretation;

(v) the official language chosen by the person concerned for communication with the Refugee Division;

(w) a signed declaration by the person concerned that the information provided in accordance with this rule is true and correct to the best knowledge and belief of the person concerned;

(x) where the person concerned

(i) understands the language in which the information and documents referred to in this subrule are filed, a signed declaration by the person concerned that the person concerned fully understands the contents of the information and documentation, and

(ii) does not understand the language in which the information and documents referred to in this subrule are filed, a declaration of an interpreter stating that the information and documentation have been translated to the person; and

(y) any other relevant document.

(2) The information referred to in subsection (1) shall be

(a) provided on the form that was served on the person pursuant to paragraph 6(1)(*c*) or on a similar form; and

(b) filed

(i) in three copies, one being the original,

(ii) at the registry designated by the Refugee Division, and

(iii) within 28 days after the day on which the form is served on the person concerned pursuant to paragraph 6(1)(*c*), or within 35 days after that day where the information is filed by prepaid regular mail.

(3) In the case of a stateless person concerned, a reference in subrule (1) to the person's nationality shall be read as a reference to the person's country of former habitual residence.

Case Law

Section 14(1)

Barrera v. Canada (Minister of Employment & Immigration) (November 10, 1993), Doc. A-1552-92 (Fed. T.D.) — The applicant sought to challenge a negative decision of the CRDD on the basis that the Board did not have the right to refer to the personal information form (PIF) in its decision, as that document had not been entered in evidence. Although the PIF was not entered in evidence as an exhibit, the members of the Board, the hearing officer, and counsel for the applicant referred to it during the hearing. Several contradictions between the testimony and the PIF were noted by the Board and the hearing officer, and were pointed out to the applicant during the hearing. The applicant was often unable to explain the contradictions. Counsel for the claimant made no objection to the fact that the PIF was not entered as an exhibit. The failure of the Board to enter the PIF as an exhibit was merely an omission that goes only to form. It does not constitute an error of law requiring the intervention of the Court. In its decision the Court sought to distinguish *Aquino v. Canada (Minister of Employment & Immigration)* (1992), 144 N.R. 315 (Fed. C.A.)

Aquino v. Canada (Minister of Employment & Immigration) (1992), 144 N.R. 315 (Fed. C.A.) — The appellant claimed to be a Convention refugee. The Convention Refugee Determination Division (CRDD) dismissed the appellant's claim and made adverse findings as to the appellant's credibility.

The appellant objected to the quality of the interpretation the interpreter provided during the hearing. The transcript indicated that the appellant had appeared to answer some questions without waiting for translation and the panel member interrupted the interpreter on several occasions to correct the translation. Further, the appellant's counsel did not object to the interpretation during the hearing. Accordingly, this objection to the quality of the interpretation was not a ground upon which the appeal could succeed.

The PIF form was not identified on the record nor entered as an exhibit, although it was clearly on the table at the hearing and referred to in some of the questions. It was the perceived inconsistencies between the PIF and the appellant's testimony which formed a basis for the finding that the appellant was not credible. These inconsistencies were not put to the appellant at the hearing.

The PIF is a document required to be filed by every Convention refugee claimant. It is among the material an adjudicator is required to file with the registry of the CRDD when a claim is referred there. It is not a document which may be judicially noticed or which any legislative provision deems to be evidence in a proceeding before the Division. Accordingly, the PIF cannot in the present circumstances be found to be "evidence adduced in the proceedings" within section 68(3). Thus, the CRDD erred in law in basing findings of credibility on perceived discrepancies between the PIF, which was not in evidence, and the appellant's *viva voce* evidence. The decision of the CRDD was set aside and the matter remitted for rehearing by a differently constituted panel.

Notice to Appear

15. Where the Refugee Division directs a party to appear before it, the Refugee Division shall serve on that party a notice that sets out

> **(a) the date, time and place at which the party is to appear;**
>
> **(b) the reason for which the party is to appear;**
>
> **(c) the right of any party to be represented by counsel at the party's own expense;**
>
> **(d) in the case of a claim referred to the Refugee Division, that where a person concerned fails to appear at the date, time and place specified, the Refugee Division may declare the claim to have been abandoned; and**
>
> **(e) in the case of an application made pursuant to section 69.2 of the Act, that where the Minister fails to appear at the date, time and place specified, the Refugee Division may declare the application to have been abandoned.**

Official Languages

16. Where the person concerned wishes to have a conference or hearing conducted in the official language other than the language chosen by the person concerned pursuant to paragraph 14(1)(*v*), the person concerned shall so notify the Refugee Division, in writing, at least 15 days before the date set for the conference or hearing, as the case may be.

Interpreter

17. (1) The Refugee Division shall provide an interpreter to assist a party or witness where the party or witness advises the Refugee Division in writing at least 15 days before the date set for a conference or hearing, as the case may be, that the party or witness does not understand or speak the language in which the conference or hearing is to be conducted, or is hearing impaired.

(2) The interpreter shall take an oath or make a solemn affirmation to interpret accurately any statements made, and to translate accurately any documents that the Refugee Division may require to be translated, in the course of the conference or hearing.

Case Law

Xhelilaj v. Canada (Minister of Citizenship & Immigration) (1997), 39 Imm. L.R. (2d) 47, 132 F.T.R. 161 (Fed. T.D.) — This was an application to review a negative decision of the CRDD. Throughout the hearing there were complaints by the applicants and their counsel about the quality of interpretation. The first two interpreters were not speaking the same dialect as the applicants. The third interpreter on the third day appeared to have a better comprehension of the evidence of the applicants.

Section 14 of the *Charter of Rights* stipulates that a party to, or a witness in any proceeding who does not understand or speak the language has the right to the assistance of an interpreter. The quality of the interpretation must meet at least these five criteria: continuity, precision, impartiality, competency and contemporaneousness. The interpretation of testimony should be as good as — no better and no worse than — the testimony that the applicant would give if the source language were the language of the court.

A perusal of the transcript at the hearing coupled with the fact that three different interpreters had to be called in and the fact that the Board had to carry out audits of the work of two of the interpreters, indicate that the quality of the translation did not meet the standards required. Accordingly, the application for judicial review was allowed.

Yu v. Canada (Minister of Employment & Immigration) (1994), 75 F.T.R. 241 (Fed. T.D.) — The applicant complained about the quality of the interpretation of her testimony and filed in support an affidavit commenting on the accuracy of the translation. The Court could not give effect to the general statements about the quality of interpretation due to the fact that the affidavit lacked sufficient specific examples. However, the decision was set aside because the one example of inaccuracy that was referred to formed the basis for the finding that the applicant's testimony was exaggerated. The Court could not be certain that the Board would have concluded that the fear of persecution was exaggerated had there been a proper interpretation of this evidence. Accordingly, the decision of the Refugee Division was quashed.

Varaich v. Canada (Minister of Employment & Immigration) (1994), 75 F.T.R. 143 (Fed. T.D.) — A tribunal is under a clear duty to make an inquiry into an interpreter's competence once an objection is made. Being the master of his or her proceeding, the adjudicator may call a witness if it is necessary to determine the competence of the interpreter and ensure a fair hearing, but this is not obligatory. The adjudicator did not rely on the interpreter's reputation, but asked the applicant directly what she did not understand. Further, the adjudicator engaged in a relatively lengthy questioning of the interpreter as to his qualifications before concluding that he was competent. Therefore, the applicant did not establish that her right to an interpreter was infringed.

Preliminary Conference

18. (1) The Refugee Division may, by a notice to appear, direct the parties to attend, and participate in, a preliminary conference with a refugee hearing officer on any matter concerning a claim, in order to provide for a full and proper hearing and to dispose expeditiously of the claim.

(2) During the preliminary conference, the refugee hearing officer shall,

(a) ascertain that the information form referred to in rule 14 has been properly completed and signed by the person concerned;

(b) review the information and documents provided by the person concerned, in order to

(i) ascertain whether there is any missing information or discrepancy,

(ii) ascertain the basis for the claim of the person concerned, and

(iii) define, and, where possible, arrive at a consensus with the person concerned regarding issues that relate to the claim;

(c) where possible, identify the evidence that the person concerned intends to produce at the hearing; and

(d) where necessary, discuss any other matter with the person concerned that could assist in expediting the claim.

(3) After the preliminary conference, the refugee hearing officer shall make a report, and

(a) where the Minister has given notice of the Minister's intention to participate at a hearing within the periods referred to in subrule 8(2) or where the refugee hearing officer is of the opinion that the person cannot be determined to be a Convention refugee without a hearing, shall notify the registrar so that a date for a hearing may be fixed; or

(b) where the Minister has not given notice of the Minister's intention to participate at a hearing within the periods referred to in subrule 8(2), and where the refugee hearing officer is of the opinion that the person could be determined to be a Convention refugee without a hearing, shall forward the file to a member so that the member may decide, in accordance with subsection 69.1(7.1) of the Act and rule 19, whether the person concerned is a Convention refugee, without a hearing into the matter.

Determination of Claim Without a Hearing

19. (1) Where a member receives a file pursuant to paragraph 18(3)(*b*), the member, before determining that the person concerned is a Convention refugee without a hearing into the matter, shall verify that

(a) the Minister has not given notice of the Minister's intention to participate at the hearing within the periods referred to in subrule 8(2); and

(b) the information with respect to the claim that is provided by the person concerned is sufficient to enable the member to determine that the person concerned is a Convention refugee, without a hearing into the matter.

(2) Where, after verification of the matters in subrule (1), a member determines that the person concerned is a Convention refugee, the member shall forthwith render the member's decision and shall send the file to the registrar.

(3) Where a member decides that the person concerned cannot be determined to be a Convention refugee without a hearing into the matter, the member shall send the file to the registrar so that a date for a hearing may be fixed.

Conferences

20. (1) The Refugee Division may direct the parties, by a notice to appear, to attend a conference, that is to be held before or during a hearing, with one or more members or a refugee hearing officer on any matter related to a claim or application, in order to provide for a full and proper hearing and to dispose of the claim or application expeditiously.

(2) At the conference, the participants, unless they have done so at a preliminary conference held pursuant to rule 18, shall

> **(a) exchange the names and addresses of witnesses that they intend to call, copies of any document that they intend to produce and of any statement of the facts, information and opinions of which they are in possession and that they intend to produce as evidence at the hearing; and**
>
> **(b) attempt to agree on means of simplifying the hearing and, as far as possible, define any pertinent issues, agree upon certain facts and receive documents.**

(3) Any agreement concluded at a conference shall be in writing and signed by the participants or given orally at the hearing and shall govern the hearing to the extent that the Refugee Division considers appropriate in order to provide for a full and proper hearing and to dispose of the claim or application expeditiously.

(4) Forthwith after a conference, a member or the refugee hearing officer, as the case may be, shall file at the registry any written agreement concluded and the original of any documents that have been received during the conference.

Disclosure

21. A party or a refugee hearing officer who intends to call an expert witness at a hearing shall, at least 20 days before the date set for the hearing, serve on every party and file at the registry a report signed by the expert witness, setting out the name, address and qualifications of the expert witness and a brief summary of the substance of the proposed testimony of the expert witness.

Applications for Public Hearings and Confidentiality

22. (1) A person who makes an application pursuant to subsection 69(2) of the Act shall do so in writing to the Refugee Division and shall file it at the registry.

(2) The Refugee Division shall notify the parties forthwith of the application referred to in subrule (1).

(3) An application that is made pursuant to subsection 69(3) of the Act in response to an application referred to in subrule (1) shall be made to the Refugee Division in writing and filed at the registry.

(4) Subject to any measure taken or any order made pursuant to subsection 69(3.1) of the Act, the Refugee Division shall notify the person referred to in subrule (1) and every party forthwith of the application referred to in subrule (3).

Witnesses

23. (1) A party who calls a witness shall pay the witness the applicable fees and allowances set out in the *Federal Court Rules*.

(2) The Board shall pay witnesses called by the refugee hearing officer the applicable fees and allowances set out in the *Federal Court Rules*.

24. (1) The Refugee Division may, at the request of a party or of its own motion, exclude witnesses from a hearing until they are called to testify.

(2) No person may communicate to a witness who has been excluded pursuant to subrule (1) any evidence or testimony that is given during the course of a hearing until after the witness has testified.

25. (1) A party or refugee hearing officer who makes an application to summon a witness shall do so in writing and shall file it at the registry.

(2) Where a person fails to comply with a summons, the party who applied for the issuance of the summons may make an application in writing, accompanied by an affidavit setting out the facts on which the application is based, to the Refugee Division for a warrant and shall file the application at the registry.

(3) An application made under subrule (2) shall contain information to establish that

(a) the person named in the summons was served with the summons and was paid or offered a reasonable amount of attendance money but failed to comply with the requirements of the summons; and

(b) the appearance of the person named in the summons is necessary to ensure a full and proper hearing.

(4) A warrant issued on an application made under subrule (2) that directs a peace officer to cause the person named therein to be apprehended anywhere in Canada shall indicate the measures to be taken by the peace officer in respect of the detention or release of the person.

(5) The measures referred to in subrule (4) may include

(a) detaining the person in custody and forthwith bringing the person before the Refugee Division; and

(b) releasing the person on a recognizance, with or without sureties, conditional on the person's appearance at the date, time and place specified, to give or produce evidence at a hearing before the Refugee Division.

Person Concerned in Custody

26. Where a person concerned is detained, the Refugee Division may order the person who detains the person concerned to bring the latter in custody to a conference or hearing held in respect of the person concerned.

Applications

27. (1) Subject to subrule (2), an application referred to in rules 12, 13, 38 or 40 shall be

(a) made in writing;

(b) filed at the registry; and

(c) served on every party.

(2) A party or, where applicable, a refugee hearing officer may make any application that is provided for in these Rules orally at a hearing where the members are satisfied that no injustice is likely to be caused to any party thereby.

(3) The Refugee Division may determine an application when it is satisfied that all parties have been given a reasonable opportunity to make representations.

Motions

28. (1) Every application that is not provided for in these Rules shall be made by a party to the Refugee Division by motion, unless, where the application is made during a hearing, the members decide that, in the interests of justice, the application should be dealt with in some other manner.

(2) The motion shall consist of

(a) a notice specifying the ground on which the motion is made;

(b) an affidavit setting out the facts on which the motion is based; and

(c) a concise statement of the law and of the arguments that are relied on by the applicant.

(3) The motion shall be

(a) served on the other party to the proceeding; and

(b) filed in duplicate, together with proof of service thereof, at the registry within five days after the date of service.

(4) Evidence in support of a motion shall be introduced by affidavit, unless the Refugee Division decides that, in the interests of justice, the evidence should be introduced in some other manner.

(5) The other party may, within seven days after being served with a motion, file at the registry a reply stating concisely the law and arguments relied on by the party, accompanied by an affidavit setting out the facts on which the reply is based.

(6) A refugee hearing officer may, within seven days after the day on which the motion was filed, file at the registry a summary of the matters that the refugee hearing officer believes that the Refugee Division should take into consideration when deciding on the motion.

(7) The applicant may, within seven days after being served with a reply referred to in subrule (5) or a summary referred to in subrule (6), file a response thereto at the registry.

(8) A copy of the reply and affidavit filed pursuant to subrule (5), of the summary filed pursuant to subrule (6) and of the response filed pursuant to subrule (7) shall be served

on every party within seven days after the date of service of the motion, reply or summary, as the case may be.

(9) The Refugee Division, on being satisfied that no injustice is likely to be caused, may dispose of a motion without a hearing.

Decisions

29. In the event of a split decision on an interlocutory matter, the presiding member shall have the deciding vote.

30. The registrar shall sign all notices of decisions of the Refugee Division and shall forthwith serve the Minister and the person concerned with a copy of all such notices.

31. A request made to the Refugee Division pursuant to paragraph 69.1(11)(*b*) or 69.3(7)(*b*) of the Act for written reasons for a decision shall be in writing and filed at the registry.

Abandonment

32. (1) Before declaring a claim to have been abandoned pursuant to subsection 69.1(6) of the Act or an application to have been abandoned pursuant to subsection 69.3(2) of the Act, the Refugee Division shall serve on the parties a notice to appear directing them to attend a hearing on the abandonment.

(2) The notice to appear shall also inform the parties that where, at the end of a hearing concerning an abandonment, the Refugee Division does not declare the claim or application to have been abandoned, the Refugee Division will forthwith commence or resume the hearing into the claim or application.

Withdrawal

33. (1) A party may withdraw a claim or application either orally during a hearing or by notice in writing filed at the registry.

(2) The registrar shall forthwith notify in writing the Minister or the person concerned, as the case may be, of any withdrawal of a claim or application.

Reinstatement

34. (1) A party who has withdrawn a claim or application may, by motion made pursuant to subrule 28(2) to (8), apply to the Refugee Division for reinstatement of the claim or application.

(2) The application for reinstatement shall be served on the Minister even where the Minister is not a party.

(3) The Refugee Division may grant the application for reinstatement of a claim or application if it is satisfied that there are sufficient reasons why the claim or application should be reinstated and that it is in the interests of justice to do so.

Service and Filing

35. (1) Subject to subrule (5), service of any document in the course of any proceeding under the Rules shall be effected by personal service, by prepaid regular mail, by any mail service whereby the sender is provided with an acknowledgement of receipt, or by the telephone transmission of a facsimile of the document in accordance with subrule (3).

(2) A copy of any document served on a party pursuant to subrule (1), with the exception of the document referred to in paragraph 6(1)(*c*), shall also be served on that party's counsel, if any.

(3) A document that is served by telephone transmission of a facsimile shall include a cover page setting out

(a) the sender's name, address and telephone number;

(b) the name of the addressee;

(c) the total number of pages transmitted, including the cover page;

(d) the telephone number from which the document is transmitted; and

(e) the name and telephone number of a person to contact in the event of transmission problems.

(4) Service by prepaid regular mail shall be considered to be effected on the date that is seven days after the date of mailing.

(5) Where service cannot be effected in accordance with subrule (1), the Chairperson may direct that service be effected by such means as will, to the extent possible, provide a party with the document and as will not likely cause injustice to any party.

(6) After service of a document has been effected by a party, the party shall file proof of service thereof at the registry.

36. The person concerned shall notify the Refugee Division, in writing.

(a) within 10 days after being served with the information form referred to in rule 14, of the address of the party;

(b) forthwith, of the name and address for service of counsel of the person concerned; and

(c) forthwith, of any changes in the information referred to in paragraphs (*a*) and (*b*).

37. (1) A document shall be filed at the registry by serving it on an employee of the registry at which the file relating to the claim or application is held.

(2) The filing of a telephone transmission of a facsimile shall be considered to be effected on the date on which it is received by the registrar, as stamped on the facsimile.

(3) All documents submitted in the course of any proceeding under these Rules in a language other than English or French shall be accompanied by a translation in English or French that is certified to be correct, unless the Refugee Division decides that a translation is not necessary to provide for a full and proper hearing.

Time Limits

38. The Refugee Division may, on application by a party or a refugee hearing officer made in accordance with rule 27 either before or after a time limit set out in these Rules has expired, shorten or extend the time limit, in order to provide for a full and proper hearing.

General

39. These Rules are not exhaustive and, where any matter that is not provided for in these Rules arises in the course of any proceeding, the Refugee Division may take whatever measures are necessary to provide for a full and proper hearing and to dispose of the matter expeditiously.

Case Law

Kusi v. Canada (Minister of Employment & Immigration) (1993), 19 Imm. L.R. (2d) 281, 65 F.T.R. 58 (Fed. T.D.) — An adjudicator and member of the Immigration and Refugee Board were conducting a credible basis hearing into the claim of a Convention refugee claimant, pursuant to provisions of the *Immigration Act* in effect on August 19, 1992.

The tribunal accepted as evidence notes taken by an immigration officer, which recorded answers given to him at the port of entry by the applicant. The applicant contested the accuracy of the notes and asked that the officer be produced for cross-examination, a request which was denied by the tribunal.

The decision by the tribunal that there was no credible basis to the applicant's claim was set aside and the matter was remitted back for determination in accordance with the law. Specifically, the Court found that given the importance of the interest, namely the applicant's claim to be a Convention refugee, and given the fact that the applicant contested the accuracy of the notes which were relied upon by the tribunal, the rules of natural justice and of fundamental justice required that the cross-examination, which was sought, be allowed. The Court relied on the jurisprudence in *Canada (Minister of Employment & Immigration) v. Leal* (1991), 129 N.R. 383 (Fed. C.A.) and *Cheung v. Canada (Minister of Employment & Immigration)*, [1981] 2 F.C. 764, 122 D.L.R. (3d) 41, 36 N.R. 563 (Fed. C.A.).

Editor's Note: *Although occurring in the context of a repealed refugee hearing procedure, the principle in this case may have a broader application.*

Salinas v. Canada (Minister of Employment & Immigration), [1992] 3 F.C. 247, 6 Admin. L.R. (2d) 154, 93 D.L.R. (4th) 631, 17 Imm. L.R. (2d) 118, 142 N.R. 211, 57 F.T.R. 159 (note) (Fed. C.A.) — This was an appeal from an order of the Trial Division whereby a decision of the Refugee Division to reconvene a hearing into the respondent's claim for refugee status was quashed and the Refugee Division ordered to render a decision on the basis of the evidence before it. The basis of the respondent's claim was her fear of persecution by agents of the state of Panama, which was headed by General Noriega. Some time after the conclusion of the respondent's hearing, but before a decision was rendered, the political situation in Panama changed. The presiding member of the panel notified the respondent that the hearing would be reconvened for the purpose of hearing evidence on these recent changes.

The appeal was allowed. The Refugee Division did not exceed its jurisdiction in reconvening the hearing. Section 68 endows the Refugee Division with powers and duties in relation to any proceedings before it. The distinction has been drawn by Parliament between "proceedings" and a "hearing" before the Refugee Division. The hearing is to be conducted in a manner required by section 69.1. The "hearing" is a step in any proceedings. "Proceedings" is a wider term encompassing the entire matter before the Refugee Division including the hearing itself. The Minister, pursuant to section 69.2(1), is able to initiate proceedings for a determination whether any person who was determined to be a Convention refugee has ceased to be so. The Court found force in the argument that evidence of the change of conditions is better addressed in the same proceedings rather than in new proceedings initiated by the Minister subsequent to the Refugee Division's determination.

The Refugee Division was not *functus officio*. It had yet to make a determination of the claim. Until it did, the proceedings were pending and finality had not been reached. In order to arrive at its decision, the Refugee Division could exercise the power conferred by the statute, provided it did so properly by giving the respondent an opportunity to be heard at the reconvened hearing. An inquiry into any change of conditions in the appellant's homeland comes within the general mandate of the Refugee Division in determining the claim.

In *Lawal v. Canada (Minister of Employment & Immigration)*, [1991] 2 F.C. 404 (Fed. C.A.), the Court ruled that the only way for the Refugee Division, after the end of a hearing but before a decision, to consider new evidence beyond that of which it might take judicial notice was by reopening the hearing. The Court's decision in *Longia v. Canada (Minister of Employment & Immigration)*, [1990] 3 F.C. 288 (Fed. C.A.), applies only where the Refugee Division has already reached a decision.

The appeal was allowed. The order of the Trial Division was set aside and the respondent's claim for refugee status was referred back to the Refugee Division for a continuation of the reconvened hearing.

40. Where a party or a refugee hearing officer does not comply with a requirement of these Rules, the Refugee Division, on application made by the party or refugee hearing officer in accordance with rule 27, may permit the party or refugee hearing officer to remedy the non-compliance or may waive the requirement, where it is satisfied that no injustice is thereby likely to be caused to any party or the proceeding will not be unreasonably impeded.

ADJUDICATION DIVISION RULES

Rules Governing the Activities of, and the Practice and Procedure in, the Adjudication Division of the Immigration and Refugee Board

SOR/93-47

Short Title

1. These Rules may be cited as the *Adjudication Division Rules*.

Interpretation

2. In these Rules,

"Act" means the *Immigration Act*;

"counsel" means a person who represents a party in any proceeding before the Adjudication Division;

"director" means a director of the Adjudication Division;

"held" means, in respect of an inquiry, held, reopened, resumed or continued;

"notice to appear" means a notice to appear referred to in rule 9;

"party" means the person concerned or the Minister;

"person concerned" means a person who is the subject of an inquiry or a person referred to in subrule 28(1);

"registrar" means a person designated pursuant to rule 4;

"registry" means an office established by the Board pursuant to rule 3.

Registry and Registrar

3. The Board shall establish one or more offices for the activities of the Adjudication Division, each of which is to be known as a registry.

4. The Board shall designate a person to be registrar at each registry.

Request for Inquiry

5. (1) Where an inquiry is caused to be held pursuant to the Act, the senior immigration officer shall forward to the Adjudication Division a request for inquiry that contains the following information:

(a) the name, sex, date of birth, civil status and citizenship of the person concerned;

(b) the address and telephone number in Canada of the person concerned;

(c) any report and direction that relate to the person concerned;

(d) a statement as to whether the person concerned claims to be a Convention refugee;

(e) a statement as to whether the person concerned is detained and if so, the place of detention;

(f) where any members of the family who are dependent on the person concerned and who are in Canada are included for the purposes of subsection 33(1) of the Act, the name, sex, date of birth, civil status, citizenship, address and telephone number of those dependent family members;

(g) the official language chosen by the person concerned for communication with the Adjudication Division;

(h) where applicable, the language or dialect of the interpreter required by the person concerned for any proceeding;

(i) the Canada Employment and Immigration Commission Client I.D. Number relating to the person concerned;

(j) where applicable, the names of the family members of the person concerned who have been referred to the Adjudication Division for an inquiry and the file number of the Canada Employment and Immigration Commission relating to those family members;

(k) the date on which the senior immigration officer forwards the request for inquiry; and

(l) the name of the senior immigration officer.

(2) The senior immigration officer shall forward the information referred to in subrule (1) to the registry designated by the Adjudication Division.

Joinder

6. (1) The Adjudication Division may order that two or more inquiries be held jointly where the Adjudication Division believes that no injustice is thereby likely to be caused to any party.

(2) Subject to subsection (3), inquiries in respect of the legal or *de facto* spouse, dependant children, father, mother, brothers or sisters of the person concerned shall be held jointly.

(3) On application by a party or on the adjudicator's own motion at the time of the inquiry, the adjudicator may order that inquiries be held separately, where the adjudicator believes that holding hearings jointly is likely to cause an injustice to any party.

Change of Venue

7. (1) A party may apply in accordance with rule 19 to the Adjudication Division to have a conference or hearing held at a place other than that which has been set.

(2) An application made under subrule (1) shall be accompanied by a statement of facts to support the application.

(3) The Adjudication Division shall grant the application made under subrule (1) if it is satisfied that doing so will not adversely affect the proper operation of the Adjudication Division, will provide for a full and proper hearing and will dispose of the inquiry expeditiously.

(4) Where an application made under subrule (1) is granted, the file relating to the inquiry shall be transferred to the registry of the place where the conference or hearing is to be held.

Postponement and Adjournment

8. (1) Before the commencement of a hearing, a party may apply in accordance with rule 19 to the Adjudication Division to have the hearing postponed.

(2) Before the resumption of a hearing, a party may apply in accordance with rule 19 to the Adjudication Division to have the hearing adjourned.

(3) A party whose application for a postponement or adjournment was denied may reapply orally at the commencement or resumption of the hearing.

(4) The Adjudication Division, in determining whether a hearing shall be postponed or adjourned, may take into consideration, where applicable,

(a) whether the postponement or adjournment would unreasonably impede the proceedings;

(b) the efforts made by the parties to proceed expeditiously;

(c) the nature and complexity of the issues relevant to the proceeding;

(d) the nature of the evidence to be presented, and the likelihood of causing an injustice to any party by proceeding in the absence of that evidence;

(e) counsel's knowledge of, and experience with, similar proceedings;

(f) the amount of time already afforded the parties for preparation of the case;

(g) the efforts made by the parties to be present at the hearing;

(h) the efforts made by the parties to make an application for a postponement or adjournment of the hearing at the earliest opportunity;

(i) the number of, and reasons for, any previous postponements or adjournments;

(j) whether the hearing was set peremptorily; and

(k) any other relevant facts.

Case Law

Section 8(4)

Gargano v. Canada (Minister of Citizenship & Immigration) (1994), 25 Imm. L.R. (2d) 292, 85 F.T.R. 49 (Fed. T.D.) — The applicant was a permanent resident of Canada who was ordered deported as a result of his criminal record. He appealed this decision and appeared before the Appeal Division without counsel on two occasions. The Board decided to proceed on the second occasion even though counsel was not present, and dismissed the applicant's appeal.

The contents of the rules of natural justice are not fixed and vary according to the seriousness of the consequences of the decision to be made. The consequences of a negative decision in a case such as this are very serious and the maximum safeguards should apply.

Absent specific rules laid down by statute or regulation, administrative tribunals control their own proceedings and adjournment of their proceedings is very much in their discretion, subject to the proviso that they comply with the rules of natural justice.

The criteria for determining whether a panel of the Appeal Division has properly exercised its discretion to disallow counsel are as follows:

1. the seriousness of the charge and of the potential penalty;
2. whether any points of law are likely to arise;
3. the capacity of a particular person to present his or her own case;
4. procedural difficulties;
5. the need for reasonable speed in making the adjudication.

A right to counsel is no more absolute than the right of a tribunal to determine its own process. In the event there is a conflict between the two, in order that the right to counsel may predominate, regard must be had to surrounding circumstances to determine if an applicant has suffered any prejudice. Proceeding without counsel is not prejudicial *per se*. Regard must be had to the circumstances of each case.

In this case the potential outcome of the matter — the removal of the applicant from Canada — is very serious. The applicant could be returned to a country where he does not speak the language, and where he has no surviving family. The fact that the Board's hearing in this case was set down peremptorily is not determinative. The applicant's previous adjournment was at a hearing for which he did not have adequate notice. The right to a fair hearing takes precedence over the need for a quick and speedy hearing.

In this case, the panel, in failing to provide an adjournment in order that he might retain counsel, denied a fair hearing and breached the rules of natural justice. The denial of a fair hearing always renders a decision invalid, whether or not it may appear to a reviewing court that the hearing would have resulted in a different decision.

Acquah v. Canada (Minister of Employment & Immigration) (1994), 83 F.T.R. 68, 26 Imm. L.R. (2d) 233 (Fed. T.D.) — The applicant had been represented by counsel throughout the credible basis proceedings. On November 26, 1992 the matter was adjourned to December 21, 1992. In the interim period the applicant, who had previously been paying counsel privately, applied for legal aid. The legal aid was refused and the applicant, on December 21, 1992, when the matter was again set to proceed, was in the process of appealing the legal aid refusal. Counsel did not attend with the applicant on December 21, 1992, but rather sent a letter describing the applicant's circumstances. The case proceeded on December 21, 1992 with the applicant being unrepresented.

The application for judicial review was allowed. When the panel became aware of the applicant's difficulties on December 21, 1992, it retired briefly to consider the matter. Upon returning, rather than face the issue squarely, the panel ignored the issue and proceeded as if the applicant was willing to carry on without counsel. In so doing the panel declined its jurisdiction and its decision was set aside.

The Court also dealt with the fact that the unrepresented applicant had not expressly asked for an adjournment. The court found that the adjournment request was implied by reason of the fact that the applicant had produced legal aid documents and counsel's letter when the hearing commenced.

The Court also referred to Rule 8 of the Law Society of Upper Canada Professional Code of Conduct. This rule dealt with the withdrawal of a lawyer's services. The Court concluded that counsel here had deserted the applicant at a critical stage of the credible basis proceeding leaving the applicant in a position of disadvantage and peril. The Court pointed out that the counsel who failed to appear on December 21, 1992 was apparently in violation of this rule.

It should be noted that counsel for the applicant who argued this application for judicial review, was not the same counsel who failed to appear on December 21, 1992.

Osei v. Canada (Minister of Employment & Immigration) (September 2, 1993), Doc. 92-T-1813 (Fed. T.D.) — The applicant claimed Convention refugee status. Pursuant to the procedures in effect at the time this case arose, a credible basis hearing was required to be held. On August 28, 1992 the credible basis tribunal determined that the applicant did not have a credible basis for his claim. The applicant was directed then to reappear on October 23, 1992 in order that an exclusion order could be made against him. On that date the applicant presented a letter from his counsel indicating that counsel was unavailable. The adjudicator properly exercised his discretion to refuse an adjournment. The proper factors to be considered by an adjudicator are set out in *Siloch v. Canada (Minister of Employment & Immigration)* (1993), 18 Imm. L.R. (2d) 239 (Fed. C.A.)at 241–42. Those factors are:

1. whether the applicant has done everything in his or her power to be represented by counsel;
2. the number of previous adjournments granted;
3. the length of time for which the adjournment is being sought;
4. the effect on the immigration system;
5. whether the adjournment would cause needless delay, impede or paralyse the conduct of the inquiry;
6. the fault or blame to be placed on the applicant for not being ready;
7. whether any previous adjournments were granted on a peremptory basis; and
8. any other relevant factors.

Siloch v. Canada (Minister of Employment & Immigration) (1993), 18 Imm. L.R. (2d) 239, 151 N.R. 76 (Fed. C.A.) — Although decided under a regulation which has been repealed, this case does set out certain general observations about when it is appropriate to grant an adjournment.

In the circumstances of this case, the intention of the applicant to proceed was unquestionable. The applicant had no reason to question the reliability of her counsel and did not know until the moment when he did not show up that an adjournment would be necessary. Furthermore, the adjudicator took into consideration a factor unknown to the applicant, *i.e.* that the applicant's counsel was known to be unreliable. The adjudicator did not inquire into the length of the adjournment being sought nor offer the applicant a short adjournment to enable her to find new counsel. There was no reason on the evidence to believe that a short adjournment would affect the immigration system or needlessly delay, impede or paralyze the conduct of the inquiry. Thus, having regard to all the circumstances, the findings of the adjudicator and the deportation order made were quashed and the matter was referred back to another adjudicator for rehearing and reconsideration.

Calles v. Canada (Minister of Employment & Immigration) (1990), 12 Imm. L.R. (2d) 48 (Fed. C.A.) — The deportation order was set aside. The adjudicator refused an adjournment for the sole reason that the inquiry had already been adjourned a number of times in order to enable the applicant to be represented by counsel. The adjudicator should have taken into consideration all the circumstances of the case which clearly show that the applicant had done everything in his power to be represented by legal counsel and that a short adjournment would enable him to achieve that result.

Pacheco v. Canada (Minister of Employment & Immigration) (1990), 11 Imm. L.R. (2d) 28, 71 D.L.R. (4th) 762, 111 N.R. 373 (Fed. C.A.) — The applicant obtained leave to have a deportation order made against her reviewed by the Court. The applicant entered Canada illegally from the United States with her boyfriend concealed in the back of a transport vehicle. At the time of her inquiry, she was 33 ½ weeks into pregnancy. The deportation order in question was made on October 31, 1989 and the birth of her child was expected in November or early December 1989. The case presenting officer recommended a departure notice. The applicant testified that her boyfriend was the father of the child and that his mother and other family members already resided in Canada. Her evidence was also to the effect that he had sought landing pursuant to a Minister's Permit which was shortly to be issued. The two apparently had agreed to be married after the boyfriend became a permanent resident of Canada. The applicant had testified that she could not say how soon after the child was born that she would be able to leave Canada because she did not know whether the baby would be born healthy. The adjudicator was concerned that issuing a departure notice for her departure on a specified date might not be possible given the uncertainties in the case at October 31, 1989. Counsel for the applicant suggested an adjournment until after the child was born. The adjudicator refused the adjournment and issued a deportation order and asserted on two occasions that the adjudicator felt compelled "to decide the case today" or "to make the decision today." This decision amounted to a failure on the part of the adjudicator to exercise his discretion. Nothing in the Act requires the adjudicator to make the deport/depart decision on any specific day; it was open to the adjudicator to adjourn the inquiry and by declining to consider the request, the adjudicator misdirected himself.

Prassad v. Canada (Minister of Employment & Immigration), [1989] 1 S.C.R. 560, [1989] 3 W.W.R. 289, 36 Admin. L.R. 72, 7 Imm. L.R. (2d) 253, 93 N.R. 81, 57 D.L.R. (4th) 663 (S.C.C.) — The issue was whether the adjudicator of an immigration inquiry must adjourn to enable the person concerned to pursue an application to the Minister under section 37(1) of the *Immigration Act*. In a 4 to 2 decision, the majority of the Court held that the adjudicator is neither bound to accede to a request for an adjournment to enable an application under section 37 to be brought, nor is the adjudicator required to refuse it. The adjudicator must consider such factors as the number of adjournments already granted and the length of time for which an adjournment is sought in exercising discretion to adjourn. The adjudicator also must consider the opportunity available to the subject of the inquiry to apply to the Minister prior to the request for an adjournment. The majority of the Court distinguished the case at bar with *Ramawad v. Minister of Manpower & Immigration* (1977), [1978] 2 S.C.R. 375, 81

D.L.R. (3d) 687, 18 N.R. 69 (S.C.C.), and held that *Ramawad* must be read in the context of its facts and the particular employment visa provisions in effect at the time of that decision.

Martin v. Canada (Minister of Employment & Immigration) (May 9, 1988), Doc. A-249-88 (Fed. C.A.) — While there is no obligation on an adjudicator to adjourn when there has been a request to the Governor in Council under section 115(2), the adjudicator does retain discretion to adjourn. If the adjudicator, in refusing an adjournment, fails to exercise that discretion, a section 28 application will be allowed, the exclusion order set aside, and the matter remitted to the adjudicator to resume the inquiry at the point where the applicant requested an adjournment.

Canada (Minister of Employment & Immigration) v. Widmont (1984), [1984] 2 F.C. 274 (Fed. C.A.) — The respondent legally entered Canada from Poland. She spoke neither French nor English. The immigration officer spoke no Polish and there was no interpreter. The respondent was admitted for 4 days. Unaware of this limitation she stayed for a much longer period and married her husband, a Canadian citizen. The respondent sought to clarify her status with the result that a direction for inquiry was issued in her case. She applied for a Minister's permit during the course of the inquiry. Prohibition was granted by the trial division to prevent the inquiry from concluding before the Minister gave his decision on whether or not to issue a permit. On appeal it was held that the refusal of the adjudicator to adjourn was consistent with earlier decisions of the Federal Court on this question. There is a particularly strong dissent on this question by Mr. Justice MacGuigan and the law of *stare decisis* is described in the judgment of Mr. Justice Urie who concurred in the majority decision. This was important because the majority judgment ruled that previous Courts considered the issue raised by this case and, accordingly, the Court in this case was obliged to follow its previous decisions. Mr. Justice Urie noted that the Federal Court of Appeal should refuse to follow its previous decisions only if it was convinced that the earlier decisions were incorrect.

Han v. Canada (Minister of Employment & Immigration) (1984), 52 N.R. 274 (Fed. C.A.) — The respondent was admitted to Canada conditional upon his marrying within 90 days. The marriage did not take place. Request for cancellation of the condition was refused and an inquiry commenced. During the course of the inquiry the respondent acquired the right to apply for citizenship. The adjudicator refused the respondent's request for an adjournment so his application for citizenship could be processed. The Trial Division quashed this decision of the adjudicator. The Court of Appeal overruled the Trial Division and upheld the adjudicator, ruling that the sole purpose of the inquiry was to ascertain whether or not the respondent was described in section 27(1)(b). The Court ruled that the fact that the respondent might have a right to become a Canadian citizen was not relevant to the inquiry and, therefore, there was no need to adjourn the inquiry pending the outcome of the citizenship application. The Court ruled, as well, that the purpose for which the adjournment was sought had nothing to do with ensuring a full and proper inquiry.

The Court observed that section 72(1)(b) of the Act entrusted to the Immigration Appeal Board and not the adjudicator, the exercise of an equitable jurisdiction to order the respondent not be removed from Canada.

Taubler v. Canada (Minister of Employment & Immigration) (1980), [1981] 1 F.C. 620 (Fed. C.A.) — It was within the mandate of an adjudicator to adjourn the inquiry, after the hearing of evidence and argument, so that the subject matter of the report giving rise to the inquiry could be investigated further.

Samra v. Canada (Minister of Employment & Immigration) (1980), [1981] 1 F.C. 626 (Fed. T.D.) — The Court declined to issue a writ of prohibition and followed what it termed "convincing jurisprudence" in concluding that the application for the writ was premature. The applicant argued that the continuation of an inquiry based on his having overstayed was being carried on with unseemly haste because the question of his remaining in Canada as a sponsored relative was about to be decided by the Immigration Appeal Board. The proper course was to request an adjournment of the inquiry pending the outcome of the Immigration Appeal Board's decision. Refusal of the writ was without prejudice to the applicant's instituting further proceedings should the adjournment be refused.

McCarthy v. Canada (Minister of Employment & Immigration) (1978), [1979] 1 F.C. 121 (Fed. C.A.) — At the conclusion of one day's evidence, an inquiry was adjourned to a date which was not convenient for the applicant's counsel. On the resumed date the inquiry was again adjourned to a date when the adjudicator knew that counsel would be out of the country. The inquiry proceeded on this last adjourned date and a deportation order was made. However, the Federal Court set aside the deportation order and referred the matter back to the immigration authorities for a new inquiry.

Notice to Appear

9. (1) Where the Adjudication Division directs a party to appear before it at a conference or hearing, the Adjudication Division shall, in a notice to appear, set out

(a) the date, time and place set for the conference or hearing;

(b) the name and address in Canada of the person concerned;

(c) the Canada Employment and Immigration Commission Client I.D. Number relating to the person concerned;

(d) the names and addresses of the family members of the person concerned referred to in paragraph 5(1)(*f*);

(e) the purpose of the conference or hearing;

(f) the right of the person concerned and any of any person referred to in paragraph (*d*) to be represented by counsel at their own expense;

(g) the requirement that the person concerned inform the Adjudication Division forthwith, in writing, of any change of address of the person concerned or of counsel of the person concerned; and

(h) that the person concerned could be arrested for failing to appear at the date, time and place set for the conference or hearing.

(2) The Adjudication Division shall serve the parties and any person referred to in paragraph (1)(*d*) with the notice to appear and a copy of any report and direction that relate to the person concerned who is subject of the inquiry.

Official Languages

10. At least 15 days before the date set for a conference or hearing, as the case may be, the person concerned shall notify the Adjudication Division, in writing, of the official language in which the person concerned chooses the conference or hearing to be conducted.

Interpreter

11. (1) The Adjudication Division shall provide an interpreter to assist a party or a party's witness where the party advises the Adjudication Division, in writing, at least

15 days before the date set for a conference or hearing, as the case may be, that the party or witness does not understand or speak the language in which the conference or hearing is to be conducted, or is hearing impaired.

(2) The interpreter shall take an oath or make a solemn affirmation to interpret accurately any statements made, and to translate accurately any documents that the Adjudication Division may require to be translated, in the course of the conference or hearing.

Case Law

Varaich v. Canada (Minister of Employment & Immigration) (1994), 75 F.T.R. 143 (Fed. T.D.) — A tribunal is under a clear duty to make an inquiry into an interpreter's competence once an objection is made. Being the master of his or her proceeding, the adjudicator may call a witness if it is necessary to determine the competence of the interpreter and ensure a fair hearing, but this is not obligatory. The adjudicator did not rely on the interpreter's reputation, but asked the applicant directly what she did not understand. Further, the adjudicator engaged in a relatively lengthy questioning of the interpreter as to his qualifications before concluding that he was competent. Therefore, the applicant did not establish that her right to an interpreter was infringed.

Yu v. Canada (Minister of Employment & Immigration) (1994), 75 F.T.R. 241 (Fed. T.D.) — The applicant complained about the quality of the interpretation of her testimony and filed in support an affidavit commenting on the accuracy of the translation. The Court could not give effect to the general statements about the quality of interpretation due to the fact that the affidavit lacked sufficient specific examples. However, the decision was set aside because the one example of inaccuracy that was referred to formed the basis for the finding that the applicant's testimony was exaggerated. The Court could not be certain that the Board would have concluded that the fear of persecution was exaggerated had there been a proper interpretation of this evidence. Accordingly, the decision of the Refugee Division was quashed.

Xie v. Canada (Minister of Employment & Immigration), [1990] 2 F.C. 336, 2 C.R.R. (2d) 374, 10 Imm. L.R. (2d) 284, (sub nom. *Ming v. Canada (Minister of Employment & Immigration)*) 107 N.R. 296 (Fed. C.A.) — Section 46.01(6) does not make it mandatory for the adjudicator and member of the refugee division to hear evidence regarding subparagraphs (a) and (b) of that section as a precondition to a credible basis decision.

The applicant's counsel raised three objections to the interpretation; the speed at which the interpreter was speaking, her dialect in Chinese and her incorporation of English words. The adjudicator took note only of the first objection. The other two problems were not considered. The objection raised by the applicant's counsel was a serious one.

Ictensev v. Canada (Minister of Employment & Immigration) (1988), 7 Imm. L.R. (2d) 306, 43 C.R.R. 147 (Ont. H.C.) — The applicant arrived in Canada and was denied immigrant status. He was released on a bond and attended at his inquiry on two occasions pursuant to the terms of his release. On the second occasion, he was held in detention following the inquiry. At the inquiry, the applicant was not provided with a satisfactory interpreter. The adjudicator did not adjourn the inquiry but, rather, ordered the applicant's detention, and subsequent reviews of that detention relied on the evidence provided through the services of this unsatisfactory interpreter. The failure to provide an interpreter was not only a violation of the regulations under the *Immigration Act*, but was also contrary to section 14 of the *Charter of Rights*. Therefore, the applicant's original detention was illegal. Reliance upon the evidence given through the services of the unsatisfactory interpreter at subsequent detention reviews tainted those detention orders. Therefore, the initial Charter violation was not cured at these subsequent detention review hearings. An order granting the application for *habeas corpus* was made.

Faiva v. Canada (Minister of Employment & Immigration) (1983), 145 D.L.R. (3d) 755 (Fed. C.A.) — An adjudicator does not have authority to proceed with an inquiry and to receive the evidence of the person concerned without an interpreter unless he is satisfied that the person concerned is able to understand and communicate in the language of the inquiry. The adjudicator was clearly not so satisfied and, thus, had no right to continue the inquiry in question or to relax the normal standard or requirement concerning the ability to understand and communicate in the language of the inquiry. Accordingly, the deportation order was set aside.

Conferences

12. (1) The Adjudication Division may direct the parties, by notice to appear, to attend a conference, that is to be held before or during a hearing, on any matter related to the inquiry, in order to provide for a full and proper hearing and to dispose of the inquiry expeditiously.

(2) At the conference the participants shall

> **(a) exchange the names and addresses of witnesses that they intend to call, copies of any document that they intend to produce and of any statement of the facts, information and opinions of which they are in possession and that they intend to produce as evidence at the hearing; and**
>
> **(b) attempt to agree on means of simplifying the hearing and, as far as possible, define any pertinent issues, agree upon certain facts and receive documents.**

(3) Any agreement concluded at a conference shall be in writing and signed by the participants or given orally at the hearing and shall govern the hearing to the extent that the Adjudication Division considers appropriate in order to provide for a full and proper hearing and to dispose of the inquiry expeditiously.

(4) Forthwith after a conference, the adjudicator shall forward to the registry any written agreement concluded and a true copy of any documents that have been received during the conference.

Disclosure

13. A party who intends to call an expert witness at a hearing shall, at least 20 days before the date set for the hearing, serve on the other party a report signed by the expert witness, setting out the name, address and qualifications of the expert witness and a brief summary of the substance of the proposed testimony of the expert witness.

Case Law

Chu v. Canada (Minister of Employment & Immigration) (May 26, 1994), Doc. IMM-2984-93 (Fed. T.D.) — This was an application to set aside the decision of an adjudicator, which held that the applicant was described in sections 19(1)(a)(ii) and 27(2)(e). Mr. Chu entered Canada as a visitor in 1990 and ultimately received permission to remain in the country and engage in employment. In 1992 he was charged with murder and detained in the Clarke Institute. While in the Institute, his visitor status and employment authorization expired.

Subsequent to expiry of these documents, a medical officer advised the Immigration Commission that the applicant was a member of an inadmissable class and this doctor's opinion was concurred in by another medical officer. An immigration inquiry was subsequently held and the applicant was found described in the two sections referred to above. The applicant was found to be not criminally responsible for the charge of murder in a separate proceeding.

The *Immigration Regulations* set out the procedures to be followed by an adjudicator at an inquiry. There are no specific provisions in the Act or regulations concerning disclosure. In the absence of a statutory mandate, the general rule is that fairness and natural justice require the person affected by a tribunal's decision to know the case to be made against him and to be provided with an opportunity to present his own evidence to substantiate his position. In this case the case presenting officer complied with all requests for disclosure made by the applicant's counsel and disclosed a copy of the medical officer's report upon which the case presenting officer intended to rely.

There was, in the context of this case, adequate disclosure by the respondent and the application for judicial review was therefore refused.

Applications for Confidentiality

14. An application referred to in subsection 29(2) or 103(10) of the Act shall be made to the Adjudication Division by motion in accordance with subrules 20(2) to (7).

Witnesses

15. A party who calls a witness shall pay the witness the applicable fees and allowances set out in the *Federal Court Rules*.

16. (1) The Adjudication Division may, at the request of a party or of its own motion, exclude witnesses from a hearing until they are called to testify.

(2) No person may communicate to a witness who has been excluded pursuant to subrule (1) any evidence or testimony that is given during the course of a hearing until after the witness has testified.

17. (1) A party who makes an application to summon a witness shall do so in writing and shall file it at the registry.

(2) Where a person fails to comply with a summons, the party who applied for issuance of the summons may make an application in writing, accompanied by an affidavit setting out the facts on which the application is based, to the Adjudication Division for a warrant and shall file the application at the registry.

(3) An application made under to subrule (2) shall contain information to establish that

> **(a) the person named in the summons was served with the summons and was paid or offered a reasonable amount of attendance money but failed to comply with the requirements of the summons; and**
>
> **(b) the appearance of the person named in the summons is necessary to ensure a full and proper hearing.**

(4) A warrant issued on an application made under subrule (2) that directs a peace officer to cause the person named therein to be apprehended anywhere in Canada shall

indicate the measures to be taken by the peace officer in respect of the detention or release of the person.

(5) The measures referred to in subrule (4) may include

(a) detaining the person in custody and forthwith bringing the person before the Adjudication Division; and

(b) releasing the person on a recognizance, with or without sureties, conditional on the person's appearance at the date, time and place specified, to give or produce evidence at a hearing before the Adjudication Division.

Person Concerned in Custody

18. Where a person concerned is detained, the Adjudication Division may order the person who detains the person concerned to bring the latter in custody to a conference or hearing held in respect of the person concerned.

Applications

19. (1) Subject to subrule (2), every application that is provided for in these Rules, except an application referred to in rules 14 and 17 and subrule 21(3), shall be

(a) made by a party in writing;

(b) filed at the registry; and

(c) served on the other party.

(2) A party may make an application that is provided for in these Rules orally at a hearing where the adjudicator is satisfied that no injustice is likely to be caused to any party thereby.

(3) The Adjudication Division may determine the application when it is satisfied that all parties have been given a reasonable opportunity to make representations.

Motions

20. (1) Every application that is not provided for in these Rules shall be made by a party to the Adjudication Division by motion, unless, where the application is made during a hearing, the adjudicator decides that, in the interests of justice, the application should be dealt with in some other manner.

(2) The motion shall consist of

(a) a notice specifying the grounds on which the motion is made;

(b) an affidavit setting out the facts on which the motion is based; and

(c) a concise statement of the law and of the arguments that are relied on by the applicant.

(3) The motion shall be

(a) served on the other party to the proceeding; and

(b) filed in duplicate, together with proof of service thereof, at the registry within five days after the date of service.

(4) Evidence in support of a motion shall be introduced by affidavit, unless the Adjudication Division decides that, in the interests of justice, the evidence should be introduced in some other manner.

(5) The other party may, within seven days after being served with a motion, file at the registry a reply stating concisely the law and arguments relied on by the party, accompanied by an affidavit setting out the facts on which the reply is based.

(6) The applicant may, within seven days after being served with a reply, file a response thereto at the registry.

(7) A copy of the reply and affidavit filed pursuant to subrule (5) and of the response filed pursuant to subrule (6) shall be served on the other party within seven days after the date of service of the motion or reply, as the case may be.

(8) The Adjudication Division, on being satisfied that no injustice is likely to be caused, may dispose of a motion without a hearing.

Decisions

21. (1) Where, at the conclusion of an inquiry, the adjudicator decides to make a removal order or conditional removal order against a person concerned, the adjudicator shall

(a) date and sign the order and decision that sets out the basis on which the order was made; and

(b) where the person does not have grounds to appeal the decision to the Appeal Division pursuant to section 70 of the Act, inform the person and the person's counsel by a notice in writing of the person's right to file an application for leave to commence an application under section 18.1 of the *Federal Court Act*.

(2) A copy of the documents referred to in paragraphs (1)(*a*) and (*b*) shall be

(a) where the parties or their counsel, or both, are present when the Adjudicator makes the order, given forthwith to the parties or their counsel or both, as the case may be; and

(b) where the parties or their counsel, or both, are absent when the adjudicator makes the order, served on the parties or their counsel or both, as the case may be.

(3) The adjudicator shall, upon a request in writing of a party that is filed within 10 days after the conclusion of an inquiry, provide written reasons for the adjudicator's decision.

Service and Filing

22. (1) Subject to subrule (5), service of any document in the course of any proceeding under these Rules shall be effected by personal service, by prepaid regular mail, by any mail service whereby the sender is provided with an acknowledgement of receipt, or by the telephone transmission of a facsimile of the document in accordance with subrule (3).

(2) A copy of any document served on a party pursuant to subrule (1) shall also be served on that party's counsel, if any.

(3) A document that is served by telephone transmission of a facsimile shall include a cover page setting out

(a) the sender's name, address and telephone number;

(b) the name of the addressee;

(c) the total number of pages transmitted, including the cover page;

(d) the telephone number from which the document is transmitted; and

(e) the name and telephone number of a person to contact in the event of transmission problems.

(4) Service by prepaid regular mail shall be considered to be effected on the date that is seven days after the date of mailing.

(5) Where service cannot be effected in accordance with subrule (1), the Chairperson may direct that service be effected by such means as will, to the extent possible, provide a party with the document and will not likely cause injustice to any party.

(6) After service of a document has been effected by a party, the party shall file proof of service thereof at the registry.

23. The person concerned and any family members of the person concerned referred to in paragraph 5(1)(*f*) shall notify the Adjudication Division forthwith in writing of their addresses and the name and address for service of their counsel, and any changes thereto.

24. (1) A document shall be filed at the registry by serving it on an employee of the registry at which the file relating to the inquiry or the application referred to in subrule 29(1) is held.

(2) The filing of a telephone transmission of a facsimile shall be considered to be effected on the date on which it is received by the registrar, as stamped on the facsimile.

(3) All documents submitted in the course of any proceeding under these Rules in a language other than English or French shall be accompanied by a translation in English or French that is certified to be correct, unless the Adjudication Division decides that translation is not necessary to provide for a full and proper hearing.

Time Limits

25. The Adjudication Division may, on application by a party made in accordance with rule 19 either before or after a time limit set out in these Rules has expired, shorten or extend the time limit, in order to provide for a full and proper hearing.

General

26. These Rules are not exhaustive and, where any matter that is not provided for in these Rules arises in the course of any proceeding, the Adjudication Division may take

whatever measures are necessary to provide for a full and proper hearing and to dispose of the matter expeditiously.

27. Where a party does not comply with a requirement of these Rules, the Adjudication Division, on application made in accordance with rule 19, may permit the party to remedy the non-compliance or may waive the requirement, where it is satisfied that no injustice is thereby likely to be caused to any party or the proceeding will not be unreasonably impeded.

Review of Reasons for Detention

28. (1) Where, pursuant to subsection 103(6) of the Act, a person concerned must be brought before an adjudicator for a review of the reasons for the continued detention of the person concerned, a senior immigration officer shall forward to the Adjudication Division forthwith the following information:

(a) the date and time before which the hearing to review the reasons for the continued detention must be held;

(b) the name and place of detention of the person concerned;

(c) the Canada Employment and Immigration Commission Client I.D. Number relating to the person concerned;

(d) the official language chosen by the person concerned for the hearing for the purposes of rule 10;

(e) where applicable, the language or dialect of the interpreter required by the person concerned for the purposes of rule 11;

(f) the name, address for service and telephone number of the counsel of the person concerned, if any;

(g) the date and time at which the person concerned was detained;

(h) the purpose of the detention; and

(i) whether the review is being held after 48 hours, seven days or 30 days of detention.

(2) The senior immigration officer shall forward the information referred to in subrule (1) to the registry designated by the Adjudication Division.

29. (1) Where a person concerned referred to in subrule 28(1) wishes to be brought before an adjudicator for a review of the reasons for detention pursuant to subsection 103(6) of the Act, the person concerned shall so apply to the Adjudication Division in accordance with rule 19.

(2) The application referred to in subrule (1) shall be accompanied by information referred to in paragraphs 28(1)(*d*) and (*e*) and a statement that sets out the reasons in support of the application.

30. Rule 7 and the time limits referred to in rules 10 and 11 do not apply in respect of the review of the reasons for detention referred to in rules 28 or 29.

FEDERAL COURT ACT

An Act respecting the Federal Court of Canada

R.S.C. 1985, c. F-7, as am. R.S.C. 1985, c. 41 (1st Supp.), s. 11; R.S.C. 1985, c. 30 (2nd Supp.), s. 61; R.S.C. 1985, c. 16 (3rd Supp.); R.S.C. 1985, c. 51 (4th Supp.); S.C. 1990, c. 8; S.C. 1990, c. 37, s. 34; S.C. 1992, c. 1, s. 68; 1992, c. 26, s. 17; 1992, c. 33, s. 69; 1992, c. 49, ss. 127, 128; 1993, c. 27, s. 214; 1993, c. 34, ss. 68–70; 1996, c. 10, s. 229; 1996, c. 22, s. 1; 1996, c. 23, s. 187(c); 1996, c. 31, ss. 82–84; 1998, c. 26, s. 73; 1999, c. 31, s. 92.

.....

JURISDICTION OF TRIAL DIVISION

.....

18. (1) Extraordinary remedies, federal tribunals — Subject to section 28, the Trial Division has exclusive original jurisdiction

(a) to issue an injunction, writ of *certiorari,* writ of prohibition, writ of *mandamus* or writ of *quo warranto,* or grant declaratory relief, against any federal board, commission or other tribunal; and

(b) to hear and determine any application or other proceeding for relief in the nature of relief contemplated by paragraph (a), including any proceeding brought against the Attorney General of Canada, to obtain relief against a federal board, commission or other tribunal.

(2) Extraordinary remedies, members of Canadian Forces — The Trial Division has exclusive original jurisdiction to hear and determine every application for a writ of *habeas corpus ad subjiciendum,* writ of *certiorari,* writ of prohibition or writ of *mandamus* in relation to any member of the Canadian Forces serving outside Canada.

(3) Remedies to be obtained on application — The remedies provided for in subsections (1) and (2) may be obtained only on an application for judicial review made under section 18.1.

1990, c. 8, s. 4

Case Law

Section 18(1)

Van Nguyen v. R. (1997), (sub nom. *Van Nguyen v. Canada))* 134 F.T.R. 241 (Fed. T.D.) — The defendant moved pursuant to Rule 324 to strike out the plaintiff's action, which was for damages for wrongful detention by immigration authorities, on the basis of want for a reasonable cause of action.

The plaintiff, a permanent resident, came from Hong Kong as a stateless person in 1991. He married a Canadian permanent resident with whom he had 3 children. He subsequently acquired a criminal record and was ordered deported. In January 1996, he was declared a danger to the public in Canada. On completing his jail sentence the plaintiff remained in immigration custody pending his removal. However, the Vietnamese government would not provide travel documents and the plaintiff was released. The plaintiff obeyed the terms of his release, but was nevertheless arrested by immigration authorities and was in custody at the time this motion was heard. The present statement of claim set out briefly and in the clearest language that the claim was one for damages for arbitrary and unlawful arrest and detention. The absence of some new wrongdoing at the time of the plaintiff's re-arrest made it impossible for the Court to say that the plaintiff's action was futile, devoid of merit, and could not possibly succeed.

Due to the fact that the plaintiff was not seeking any form of declaratory relief, the defendant could not gain any comfort from section 18(1) of the *Federal Court Act.*

Chesters v. Canada (Minister of Citizenship & Immigration) (1997), 38 Imm. L.R. (2d) 269, 45 C.R.R. (2d) 233, 134 F.T.R. 151 (Fed. T.D.) — A party may, in an action, seek a declaration that legislation of Parliament is contrary to the *Charter of Rights.* The type of declaration mentioned in section 18 of the *Federal Court Act*, is one which impugns the decision of a board, commission or other tribunal. Such a declaration can only be sought in judicial review proceedings.

Section 18(3)

Nagarajah v. R. (May 23, 1996), Doc. A-42-96 (Fed. C.A.) — The Court of Appeal upheld the motion judge's ruling, striking the appellant's statement of claim as disclosing no reasonable cause of action. The motions judge had done so on the basis that the declaratory and injunctive relief sought must be pursued by way of judicial review, as opposed to an action, pursuant to subsections 18(1) and 18(3) of the *Federal Court Act.*

The Court of Appeal was in agreement with the reasons of the motions judge.

Zelzle v. Canada (Minister of Citizenship & Immigration), [1996] 3 F.C. 20, 34 Imm. L.R. (2d) 24, 110 F.T.R. 161 (Fed. T.D.) — This was an application to review an interlocutory decision of a panel of the CRDD, wherein it was determined that a previous CRDD panel had failed to render a decision, leaving the CRDD open to hear the applicant's refugee claim *de novo.*

The applicant made a claim for refugee status on November 26, 1992. The applicant appeared for a hearing on the 15th of November 1993. At the commencement of the hearing, a positive Notice of Decision was found in the CRDD file. This Notice of Decision was dated May 10, 1993. The decision had apparently been made pursuant to the expedited hearing process. The November 15, 1993 panel adjourned the matter pending an inquiry to the registrar. On May 4, 1994, the applicant received a letter stating that the May 10th decision had been signed and left in the file as a result of an administrative error and, as such, that the case would proceed *de novo*. At the *de novo* hearing on January 9, 1995, the applicant made a motion that the panel did not have jurisdiction. On May 29, 1995, this motion was dismissed.

Once the tribunal has rendered a final decision, that tribunal's jurisdiction ceases and the tribunal becomes *functus officio*. In the case of the administrative tribunals, however, justice may require the reopening of administrative proceedings in order to provide relief which would otherwise be available on appeal. This exception was established to allow an administrative tribunal to re-open proceedings where, if the hearing of an application had not been held according to the rules of natural justice, the administrative tribunal may treat its decision as a nullity and reconsider the matter. This exception has usually been invoked by unsuccessful refugee claimants where, for example, the CRDD failed to consider evidence of changed country conditions. While the principal of *functus officio* favours the finality of proceedings, its application is flexible in the case of administrative tribunals.

In the instant case, the CRDD discharged the function committed to it by its enabling legislation by issuing the May 10, 1993 decision, which decision was valid on its face.

The decision on May 29, 1995 resulted in the panel exceeding its jurisdiction in looking beyond the decision and determining that it was an "administrative error". The panel had no jurisdiction to question a decision validly made in conformity with the Act. Once such a decision was made, the November 15 and May 29th panels were *functus officio*, since the decision in respect of the applicant's refugee status had been made. If the Minister had concerns regarding the legitimacy of the May 10, 1993 decision, the proper method by which to address those concerns would have been by way of an application for judicial review.

18.1 (1) Application for judicial review — An application for judicial review may be made by the Attorney General of Canada or by anyone directly affected by the matter in respect of which relief is sought.

(2) Time limitation — An application for judicial review in respect of a decision or order of a federal board, commission or other tribunal shall be made within thirty days after the time the decision or order was first communicated by the federal board, commission or other tribunal to the office of the Deputy Attorney General of Canada or to the party directly affected thereby, or within such further time as a judge of the Trial Division may, either before or after the expiration of those thirty days, fix or allow.

(3) Powers of Trial Division — On an application for judicial review, the Trial Division may

> **(a) order a federal board, commission or other tribunal to do any act or thing it has unlawfully failed or refused to do or has unreasonably delayed in doing; or**
>
> **(b) declare invalid or unlawful, or quash, set aside or set aside and refer back for determination in accordance with such directions as it considers to be appropriate, prohibit or restrain, a decision, order, act or proceeding of a federal board, commission or other tribunal.**

(4) Grounds of Review — The Trial Division may grant relief under subsection (3) if it is satisfied that the federal board, commission or other tribunal

> **(a) acted without jurisdiction, acted beyond its jurisdiction or refused to exercise its jurisdiction;**
>
> **(b) failed to observe a principle of natural justice, procedural fairness or other procedure that it was required by law to observe;**
>
> **(c) erred in law in making a decision or an order, whether or not the error appears on the face of the record;**
>
> **(d) based its decision or order on an erroneous finding of fact that it made in a perverse or capricious manner or without regard for the material before it;**
>
> **(e) acted, or failed to act, by reason of fraud or perjured evidence; or**
>
> **(f) acted in any other way that was contrary to law.**

(5) **Defect in form or technical irregularity — Where the sole ground for relief established on an application for judicial review is a defect in form or a technical irregularity, the Trial Division may**

> **(a) refuse the relief if it finds that no substantial wrong or miscarriage of justice has occurred; and**
>
> **(b) in the case of a defect in form or a technical irregularity in a decision or order, make an order validating the decision or order, to have effect from such time and on such terms as it considers appropriate.**

1990, c. 8, s. 5

Case Law

Section 18.1(1)

Chen v. Canada (Minister of Citizenship & Immigration) (May 21, 1999), Doc. IMM-1553-98 (Fed. T.D.) — The applicant sought to review a decision of the Counsellor, Operations Manager, of the Canadian High Commission in Singapore. The applicant submitted an application for permanent residence. At the time of this application, the applicant lived in Taiwan. The applicant listed her intended occupation as Supervisor, Organization and Methods Analyst. After paper screening, an interview was scheduled. Based on the information provided in the interview, the visa officer concluded that the applicant had less than 1 year of experience which was the minimum required for assessment of time of this application. In response to the refusal letter, the applicant wrote at length requesting a reversal of the visa officer's decision. Upon receiving no response the applicant contacted a Canadian lawyer who sent a fax to the Regional Program Centre in Singapore asking for a review of the issues raised in the applicant's letters. The Operations Manager reviewed the applicant's correspondences and her lawyer's letter in addition to the entire file and also questioned the visa officer. In the result, the manager concluded that the officer's decision was reasonable and so informed the applicant.

The manager's decision was more than merely a courtesy response. The manager was very thorough in his review and this thoroughness clearly implied that his review was more than a matter of courtesy. The conclusion that the manager reached not to propose that the visa officer's decision be changed constituted a decision which was subject to review pursuant to section 18.1 of the *Federal Court Act*.

On the merits the Court dismissed the application for judicial review.

Henry Global Immigration Services v. Canada (Minister of Citizenship & Immigration) (1998), 158 F.T.R. 110 (Fed. T.D.) — The applicant was advised by a visa officer at the Canadian Consulate General in Hong Kong that all correspondence regarding the applicant's clients would be sent directly to the client's residential addresses. The respondent advised this was being done due to the fact that over the past several months, "we have received a number of serious complaints from your clients . . .". This communication in a letter from the respondent to the applicant constituted a decision for purposes of an application for judicial review.

The Court found that the decision ran the risk of putting the applicant out of business, at least in relation to applicant's for landing from the People's Republic of China and thus the applicant was found to have standing to bring an application for judicial review.

Gonzalez v. Canada (Ministre de la Citoyenneté & de l'Immigration) (1998), 158 F.T.R. 290 (Fed. T.D.) — This was an application to review the decision of a senior immigration officer. The officer informed the applicant by letter that the department could not take further action on her claim since her claim was ineligible under subsection 44(1) of the Immigration Act.

On June 6, 1997, prior to the letter in question being sent, a senior immigration officer had issued a departure order against the applicant which was not contested. The departure order was deemed to be a deportation order on July 17, 1997. The applicant claimed refugee status on July 30, 1997 and received the letter, dated August 15, 1997, which was the subject of this application, informing her that her claim was ineligible.

The application was dismissed on the basis that the letter in question was not a decision which may be reviewed by way of an application for judicial review.

Chan v. Canada (Minister of Citizenship & Immigration) (September 24, 1996), Doc. IMM-559-96 (Fed. T.D.) — The applicant sought to review a decision of a visa officer refusing the applicant's application for permanent residence. This application for judicial review raises an issue of timeliness. The decision was made on October 23, 1995. The applicant's counsel, instead of proceeding to commence a judicial review application, elected to seek reconsideration. There was no evidence of reconsideration by the respondent. The applicant filed its application for judicial review on February 19, 1996, without seeking an extension of time until 3 weeks after the respondent had served its motion to dismiss.

The applicant's attempt to provoke a reconsideration from the respondent could not result in extending the date of the refusal and, accordingly, the application for judicial review was dismissed as being untimely.

Cross v. Canada (Minister of Citizenship & Immigration) (1996), 33 Imm. L.R. (2d) 251, 111 F.T.R. 304 (Fed. T.D.) — This was an application to review a decision of an immigration officer who arrested the applicant at the Vancouver pre-trial detention centre and removed him to the U.S. on the same date. The applicant, an American citizen plead guilty to simple assault in the state of Vermont. Upon his release from the detention centre in that state, the applicant came to Canada. At this time there was a warrant outstanding for the applicant in the state of Vermont. As well, the applicant was a prime suspect in a rape/murder investigation occurring in that state.

The issue of mootness is to be decided in two stages. The first stage requires consideration of whether a live controversy remains. The second stage applies if no live controversy remains. The court must then consider whether to exercise its discretion to hear the appeal, notwithstanding that it is moot. With respect to the second stage, there are three criteria for the exercise of the discretion to hear a matter. One, the existence of an adversarial context; two, the concern for judicial economy; and three, the need for the court to demonstrate a measure of awareness of its proper law-making function.

At the date of the hearing of this motion, the applicant was no longer under arrest by Canadian authorities. He had been freed and then immediately turned over to the U.S. authorities sometime earlier. The applicant's removal from Canada in no way altered his legal standing within Canada. There was therefore no live controversy in this matter. Further, there was no reason to believe that this was a case of a recurring nature. Accordingly, the court declined to hear the matter.

Turanskaya v. Canada (Minister of Citizenship & Immigration) (1995), 111 F.T.R. 314 (T.D.), affirmed (1997), 145 D.L.R. (4th) 259, 125 F.T.R. 240 (note), 210 N.R. 235 (C.A.) — The applicant was found by a panel of the CRDD, to be a stateless person.

The respondent conceded that the board had erred in law in requiring the applicant to demonstrate a well founded fear of persecution in respect of both countries of former habitual residence.

The applicant had asked the Court to refer the matter back to the board, with a direction that it declare the applicant to be a Convention refugee.

There will sometimes be situations in which by giving specific directions, the Court will be able to accomplish indirectly what it is not authorized to do directly. It will be able to compel the board to reach a specific conclusion, thereby, in effect, substituting its decision for that made by the board. Specific directions of this type are within the jurisdiction of the court.

The discretion to give directions should be exercised in the context of the Board's decision. The Court should not go behind that decision on matters unrelated to the error brought forward on judicial review.

But for the error which caused the board to require the applicant to demonstrate a well founded fear in respect of both countries of former habitual residence, the board would have declared the applicant to be a Convention refugee.

Accordingly, the Court issued an order directing the board to declare the applicant to be a Convention refugee.

Sivaraj v. Canada (Minister of Citizenship & Immigration) (1996), 107 F.T.R. 64 (Fed. T.D.); affirmed (May 23, 1996), Doc. A-42-96, A-72-96, A-74-96 (Fed. C.A.) — The respondent was attempting to remove the applicant to Sri Lanka. The applicant applied for a stay of the execution of the removal order and the respondent took the position that the statements of claim, which the applicant had used to commence these proceedings, did not disclose a reasonable cause of action.

The applicants came to Canada from Sri Lanka. They unsuccessfully claimed refugee status with the result that removal orders were issued. The applicants then filed a statement of claim in order to obtain declaratory relief that the removal orders violated sections 7 and 12 of the *Canadian Charter of Rights and Freedoms*, and that they contravened the *Geneva Conventions Act*.

The Minister's decision in determining the country of removal was, in fact, a decision made by a federal board, commission, or other tribunal within the meaning of section 18, and is therefore subject to review under section 18.1.

The applicants should not have proceeded by way of action to obtain declaratory relief under the Charter. The proper procedure was by way of application for judicial review. The Court has often, under the rules of judicial review, examined the constitutionality under the Charter of decisions made by federal boards.

The Court did, however, stay the execution of the removal orders, and to avoid a vacuum being created whereby the applicants would have no proceedings before the Court, the Court exercised its jurisdiction under rules 2 and 303 of the *Federal Court Rules* and presumed the proceedings to have been commenced as applications for judicial review.

Efremov v. Canada (Minister of Citizenship & Immigration) (1995), 90 F.T.R. 259 — The applicant sought to quash a negative decision of a panel of the CRDD. In order to quash a decision it must be shown that the Board made an error which was material to the decision. The cumulative effect of a number of errors can also constitute a material error. A microscopic examination of the reasons for the decision is not appropriate. The word "patently" adds nothing to the applicable test. For a decision to be unreasonable it must be plain and obvious that it is so.

Thillaiyampalam v. Canada (Minister of Citizenship & Immigration) (November 24, 1994), Doc. IMM-429-94 (Fed. T.D.) — This application to set aside a negative determination of a panel of the CRDD was unsuccessful. Although the panel made errors on the face of its reasons, those errors did not "go to the heart of its conclusion that this applicant had, on the particular facts of his situation, a viable internal flight alternative". Accordingly, notwithstanding the errors, the application for judicial review was dismissed.

Soimu v. Canada (Secretary of State) (1994), 83 F.T.R. 285 — In a letter dated February 8, 1994, a visa officer refused the applicant's application for permanent residence. On February 14, 1994, counsel for the applicant wrote to the visa officer requesting that she review her decision. On April 20, 1994, the visa officer replied. The April 20 letter, on the facts of this particular case, constitutes a decision by the visa officer and the applicant had, therefore, 30 days pursuant to section 18.1 of the *Federal Court Act*, to seek judicial review. The originating notice was filed on May 19, 1994, within 30 days. Accordingly, the respondent's motion to strike the applicant's originating notice of motion was dismissed.

The Court pointed out that the procedural difficulty occasioned in these proceedings might have been avoided if the applicant had sought judicial review of the February 8, 1994 decision in a timely manner. This would not have precluded the applicant from seeking a review by the visa officer. Had the April 20 letter not resulted from a true review, but merely been a "courtesy response", the applicant might well have been out of time to seek judicial review of the February 8, 1994 decision.

Rodrigues v. Canada (Secretary of State) (1994), 82 F.T.R. 111 — Pedro Rodrigues came from Brazil to Canada and made a refugee claim in 1987. He was subsequently ordered excluded. His application for judicial review was dismissed. In July, 1992, he married a Canadian citizen. John Rodrigues was born a little over a year later. In the spring of 1994, Immigration Canada advised that there were insufficient humanitarian and compassionate factors to intervene in a decision that Pedro Rodrigues must leave the country.

Pedro Rodrigues then brought the present proceedings under section 18.1 of the *Federal Court Act*. The infant son, John Rodrigues, was held to be a person directly affected under section 18.1 of the *Federal Court Act* and, therefore, an order was issued that he be joined as a party and that the style of cause be amended to reflect the addition of Assis John Rodrigues, a minor through his litigation guardian, Assis Pedro Rodrigues.

Sitsabeshan v. Canada (Secretary of State) (1994), 82 F.T.R. 29 — The applicants sought to review a negative determination of the CRDD. The Court found two findings of fact that were erroneous. It was not for the Court to speculate whether the CRDD would have reached the same conclusion if it had not erred in making those two findings of fact. If the decision of the CRDD might have been different, and in this case the Court was satisfied that it very well might have, then the decision of the CRDD will be set aside.

Singh (R.) v. Canada (Secretary of State) (1994), 27 Imm. L.R. (2d) 176, (sub nom. *Singh v. Canada (Secrétaire d'Etat))* 82 F.T.R. 68 — The applicant claimed refugee status in a false name. He later approached the Immigration Commission and properly identified himself and sought to have the Commission amend his name on the documents that had already been placed in his file. The Commission refused.

The decision refusing to amend documents in the applicant's file did not constitute a decision within the meaning of section 18.1 of the *Federal Court Act* and, therefore, the Court had no jurisdiction to consider an application for judicial review of that decision.

Popov v. Canada (Minister of Employment & Immigration) (1994), 75 F.T.R. 90 — The applicant emigrated to Israel from Russia under the Law of Return. He was entitled to do so because one of his grandparents was Jewish. He suffered discrimination in Israel because he was a new immigrant from Russia and because, while he was Jewish as a matter of racial ancestry, he was a member of the Russian Orthodox Christian church. The applicant applied for refugee status in Canada. The CRDD did not accept his claim, but that decision was rendered before the Supreme Court decision in *Ward v. Canada (Minister of Employment &*

Immigration), (sub nom. *Canada (Attorney General) v. Ward*) [1993] 2 S.C.R. 689 and the Federal Court decision in *Zolfagharkhani v. Canada (Minister of Employment & Immigration)*, [1993] 3 F.C. 540, 20 Imm. L.R. 1, 155 N.R. 311 (C.A.).

The application was dismissed from the Bench due to the fact that notwithstanding the errors complained of, no properly instructed Board could have found the applicant to be a Convention refugee. The authority of the Court on a judicial review application is not the same as on an appeal. Even though one might find errors in a Board's decision, that does not, on a judicial review application, result in a decision to send the matter back for rehearing when the Court is convinced that no real purpose will be served by so doing. One does not quash and send it back just for the sake of having a new hearing. When it is clear from the evidence on the record and from the decision that no different result could be reached, the appropriate course of action is to refuse an order requiring that such be done.

The Court noted that the intertwined nature of "appeals" and "judicial review" was found in a recent paper by Madame Justice Desjardins: *Review of Administrative Action in the Federal Court of Canada: The New Style in a Pluralistic Setting*, Law Society of Upper Canada Special Lectures, 1992, at 404.

Chen v. Canada (Minister of Employment & Immigration) (1994), 76 F.T.R. 235 — The applicant sought to overturn a negative decision of the CRDD. The tribunal accepted the applicant's testimony as trustworthy. In the course of giving its reasons, the tribunal misidentified the principal issue. The respondent urged that, despite this error, the conclusions of the tribunal were reasonable on the basis of the evidence before it and the decision as a whole was supportable.

The tribunal did err by not assessing the very basis claimed by the applicant as the grounds of his fear of persecution. While the evidence before the tribunal may be said to support the conclusion it reached, such an assessment is not for the Court on an application for judicial review. Aside from procedural issues, the Court, on a judicial review application, must be concerned with the decision rendered by the tribunal and the reasons expressed for its conclusion.

Alfred v. Canada (Minister of Employment & Immigration) (1994), 76 F.T.R. 231 — In this application to review a negative decision of the CRDD, the applicant argued that the tribunal erred in misconstruing "persecution" and that the tribunal erred in law by ignoring or misconstruing the evidence before it. The respondent made reference to portions of the transcript of the hearing and to the documentary evidence before the tribunal, which it argued would warrant the conclusion that the findings of the tribunal were reasonable. The Court must review the decision as rendered by the tribunal and not the evidence to which the decision itself makes no reference but which would have warranted the conclusions reached by the tribunal if the tribunal had expressed reasons relying upon such evidence. The simple statement that the tribunal had reached its decision "after careful consideration of all the evidence adduced at the hearing" was not sufficient when the decision made little or no reference to the principal basis of the applicant's claim. The application was allowed in this case and the matter sent back for rehearing before a differently constituted panel of the CRDD.

Section 18.1(2)

Brar v. Canada (Minister of Citizenship & Immigration) (1997), 140 F.T.R. 163 (Fed. T.D.) — The applicant applied for permanent residence. The application was made in a self-employed category and his application was refused in January 1996. Counsel wrote to the visa officer in March 1996 asking for a review. Counsel wrote again in June, enclosing an affidavit from the applicant's cousin. In July 1996, the visa officer faxed a letter to counsel referring counsel to the refusal letter in January 1996. The July letter was a courtesy letter and did not constitute a decision as that phrase is employed in section 18.1 of the *Federal Court Act*.

The *Immigration Act* makes no provision for reconsideration of decisions by a visa officer. There is, however, a clear provision for judicial review of alleged errors. On the concept of *functus officio* and its application to administrative tribunals, the Court adopted the remarks of Sopinka J. in *Chandler v. The Association of Architects*, [1989] 2 S.C.R. 848 at p. 861. The application for judicial review was dismissed.

Section 18.1(3)

Gwala v. Canada (Minister of Citizenship & Immigration) (1999), 242 N.R.173 (Fed. C.A.) — Senior immigration officers do not have the implied jurisdiction to decide questions of law. The Trial Division of the Federal Court has jurisdiction in judicial review proceedings to decide constitutional questions which a senior immigration officer could not entertain.

San Vicente Freitas v. Canada (Minister of Citizenship & Immigration), 49 Imm. L.R. (2d) 33, (sub nom. *Freitas v. Canada (Minister of Citizenship & Immigration))* [1999] 2 F.C. 432 (Fed. T.D.) — These reasons arose out of an application for judicial review of a decision of a panel of the CRDD that they determine the applicant not to be a Convention refugee. The applicant was born in Trinidad, but moved to Venezuela at a very young age. In Venezuela he was a political activist. The applicant came to Canada in 1967 and became a landed immigrant. The applicant was steadily employed in Canada for a period of 10 years and then returned to Venezuela as a visitor in 1981. The applicant found conditions had changed and decided to remain there. After the presidential election in 1983, the applicant ceased any political activities in Venezuela and ultimately in 1986, obtained a false passport and returned to Canada. After being back in Canada, the applicant was convicted of a serious criminal offence and sentenced to 9 years. The applicant claimed refugee status against Venezuela.

The applicant's claim was refused, and he applied for leave to review that decision. Leave was granted. However an application to stay execution of the removal order was refused. The decision of the Supreme Court of Canada in the *Pushpanathan v. Canada (Minister of Citizenship & Immigration)*, [1998] 1 S.C.R. 982, mandated that in this case the interpretation of the panel of Article 1F(c) of the Convention was wrong. Accordingly the decision of the panel was set aside. The execution of the removal order did not render the judicial review proceedings moot.

The Court refused to provide a meaningless remedy in the form of a reference back to the CRDD for redetermination that could only be a determination that the applicant is not a Convention refugee because he is not outside the country of his nationality. Similarly, the Court was not prepared to order the respondent to return the applicant to Canada if the return of the applicant should prove to be unnecessary to an effective redetermination by the CRDD. The Court ordered that if the panel of the CRDD determined that it was necessary for the applicant to appear again to allow it to comply with the order of the Court directing a rehearing, the respondent was ordered forthwith to make best efforts to return the applicant to Canada at the respondent's expense. If the panel, without requiring the return of the applicant, working on the assumption that the applicant was in Canada was able to determine that the applicant was a Convention refugee, then the respondent was ordered forthwith to make best efforts to return the applicant to Canada at the respondent's expense.

Vuong v. Canada (Minister of Citizenship & Immigration) (1998), 47 Imm. L.R. (2d) 129, 153 F.T.R. 207 (Fed. T.D.) — This was an application to review and set aside a decision of the Appeal Division wherein the applicant's appeal was dismissed for lack of jurisdiction. The applicant applied to sponsor his adopted daughter. In support of his application he obtained from the People's Committee of the Socialist Republic of Vietnam in the district where he formally resided and where the adoption took place, a document confirming that Xuan was his adopted daughter. The application for landing was refused on the grounds that there was no proof that Xuan was the legally adopted daughter of the applicant. Prior to the hearing before the Appeal Division, the applicant obtained further confirmation from the People's Court of the Socialist Republic of Vietnam that Xuan was his adopted daughter. Prior to the hearing of the appeal, the Minister had also made inquiries through the Canadian Embassy. The government of Vietnam replied that according to the present law of adoption, all adoptions were required to be approved by the People's Committee and recorded in the household register. Since the adoption of the applicant's daughter was not recorded in the household register, the Vietnamese government advised that it could not confirm that the child had been adopted. The Appeal Division determined that the daughter was not a member of the family class and dismissed the appeal for want of jurisdiction.

At the hearing, the Appeal Division had considered documentary evidence and it heard from four witnesses, one of whom was a former lawyer practicing in Vietnam between 1969 and 1975 in the area of public adoption. This witness made it quite clear that customary adoption was a usual and frequent practice among the Vietnamese people and that there was apparently a lax approach to making changes in the household registers. The panel of the Appeal Division found that the applicant's own attempts to have the register changed were genuine, but were thwarted by the nature of the administrative and bureaucratic processes.

The Court allowed the appeal and noted that it was the law applicable at the time of the adoption that was relevant for the purpose of determining whether there had been a valid adoption. The Court noted the uncontradicted evidence of the Vietnamese lawyer and then referred the matter back to a differently constituted panel of the Appeal Division with directions to find that Xuan was the adopted daughter and a member of the family class pursuant to section 2 of the Immigration Regulations.

Alleti v. Canada (Ministre de la Citoyenneté & de l'Immigration) (1998), 147 F.T.R. 310 (Fed. T.D.) — The scope of the powers conferred on the Court under paragraph 18.1(3)(b) of the *Federal Court Act* do not permit the Court to issue a visa to the applicant. The Court can set aside a visa officer's decision and refer the matter back for re-determination in accordance with certain directions. The Court cannot issue specific and conclusive directions with respect to the decision a visa officer must make, unless the conclusion is simple, obvious and inescapable. The directions that the Court is authorized to make will vary with the circumstances of each case. If facts remain to be established, it is the officer who must determine them. If the Court finds an error in law, all the visa officer can do is to act accordingly when re-determining the matter.

Montenegro v. Canada (Minister of Citizenship & Immigration) (1996), 108 F.T.R. 55 (Fed. T.D.) — This was a successful application for judicial review to set aside a negative decision of the CRDD. The applicant was 12 years old at the time the Court's decision was given. The applicant's mother and father married in 1988. They were ultimately divorced in 1992 after their arrival in Canada from El Salvador. The applicant lives with her mother and two younger brothers, both of whom were born in Canada. The applicant's mother married a Canadian citizen and did not want to return to El Salvador. The applicant's father remains in Canada, his claim for Refugee status having been successful, but has little, or no, continuing relationship with the applicant or her sibling.

The Court felt it was appropriate to refer this matter for review by the Minister to determine whether or not the applicant should remain in Canada on humanitarian and compassionate grounds, or some other grounds in accord with the *Immigration Act*. This review was to take place prior to a reconsideration of the applicant's refugee claim. In the event that there was no favourable administrative decision to permit the applicant to remain in Canada, the Court directed that her claim for refugee status be reconsidered by the CRDD.

Marquez v. Canada (Minister of Citizenship & Immigration) (1996), 32 Imm. L.R. (2d) 286 (Fed. T.D.) — The judge in this case reconsidered two of his own previous decisions and came to the conclusion that pursuant to section 18.1(3) of the *Federal Court Act*, the Court has jurisdiction, when allowing an application for judicial review, to provide directions for the decision maker who has to reconsider the matter, which directions may even be specific in relation to the ultimate outcome of the matter.

On the facts of this case, the Court declined to refer the matter for reconsideration with directions that the tribunal determine the applicant to be a Convention refugee. The record was not so clearly conclusive that the only possible conclusion on reconsideration was that the applicant was a Convention refugee, nor was the sole issue one of law which left the ultimate outcome uncontroverted.

Abdullahi v. Canada (Minister of Citizenship & Immigration) (January 10, 1996), Doc. IMM-1610-95 (Fed. T.D.) — The applicants sought to overturn a negative decision of a panel of the IRB. After determining that there was at least one instance in which there was no evidence to support the Board's conclusion, the Court then had to consider what would be the disposition of the judicial review application.

The Court concluded that once the Board's decision is based on a substantial error, which if it had not been made, might have caused the Board to decide otherwise, the decision of the Board should be quashed and referred back for reconsideration by another panel.

In this case the Court found the errors to be substantial and that the decision of the Board might have been different had it not made those errors and, accordingly, the application was allowed.

Memarpour v. Canada (Minister of Citizenship & Immigration) (1995), 104 F.T.R. 55 — At the opening of the hearing of the applicant's refugee claim, the presiding Board member made a statement which indicated that certain evidence about events in Iran was accepted for purposes of the hearing. The Board then, in rendering its decision, made an adverse credibility finding in respect of those events. This was held to be a failure of natural justice. There is no general duty to confront a witness with issues of credibility. Such a requirement exists if credibility becomes an issue for the Board when it has previously been deleted by the Board as a relevant issue.

Having decided that there was a denial of a fair hearing, the Court then must ask itself whether it is nonsensical and contrary to notions of finality and the effective use of public funds and the Board's resources to require a re-hearing. The Court relied upon *Mobile Oil Canada Ltd. v. Canada-Newfoundland Off Shore Petroleum Board*, [1994] 1 S.C.R. 202 at p. 205. In this case, the Court concluded that even if the applicant were to be believed about the events in Iran which were the subject matter of the application, a panel of the IRB would certainly conclude that the applicant did not have a subjective fear of persecution. In those circumstances, the application was dismissed.

Argueta v. Canada (Minister of Employment & Immigration) (April 13, 1994), Doc. IMM-3579-93 (Fed. T.D.) — The applicant sought judicial review contending that the trier of fact had made three errors of law which warranted the setting aside of the decision. The respondent conceded that the law had been misstated or misapplied in two respects, but suggested that applying the law correctly would support the conclusion of the tribunal and, implicitly, that the same result would follow any reconsideration of the matter. In an application for judicial review, aside from procedural issues, the jurisdiction of the Court is concerned with the decision as it has been rendered, not with a decision that might have been but was not given. The Court may review the evidence before the tribunal only in relation to the decision rendered. It is not for the Court to assess what its decision might be on the evidence before the tribunal nor to speculate on the result if the matter is referred back for reconsideration, the outcome of which will be dependent upon the evidence and argument then before the reconsidering tribunal.

Ali v. Canada (Minister of Employment & Immigration) (1994), 24 Imm. L.R. (2d) 289, 76 F.T.R. 182, [1994] 3 F.C. 73, 27 Admin. L.R. (2d) 110 — Section 18.1(3) of the *Federal Court Act* provides jurisdiction for the Court to issue directions of such specificity that they require the CRDD to declare an applicant to be a Convention refugee.

The Court should only exercise this jurisdiction after asking itself questions of this type:

1. Is the evidence on the record so clearly conclusive that the only possible conclusion is that the claimant is a Convention refugee?

2. Is the sole issue to be decided a pure question of law which will be dispositive of the case?

3. Is the legal issue based on uncontroverted evidence and accepted facts?

4. Is there a factual issue that involves conflicting evidence which is central to the claim?

Xie v. Canada (Minister of Employment & Immigration) (1994), 75 F.T.R. 125 — The Court's jurisdiction on applications for judicial review is found in section 18.1(3) of the *Federal Court Act*. There is nothing in the subsection that indicates that the Court has the jurisdiction to substitute its opinion for that of the tribunal whose decision is under judicial review and make the decision that the tribunal should have made. As such words do not appear in the Act, the Court does not have jurisdiction to substitute its decision for that of the tribunal in a judicial review application.

The Court does have jurisdiction to refer a matter back for redetermination in accordance with such directions as it considers appropriate. The Court should only issue directions to a tribunal in the nature of a directed verdict where the case is straightforward and the decision of the Court on the judicial review would be dispositive of the matter before the tribunal.

Siad v. Canada (Minister of Employment & Immigration) (1993), 21 Imm. L.R. (2d) 6, 64 F.T.R. 271 — This was an application for a judicial review of the decision of the CRDD determining that the applicant was not a Convention refugee.

Two errors of law were cited: (1) the Refugee Division erred by not correctly identifying the social group to which the applicant belonged in deciding that her claim did not come within a group recognized in the definition; and (2) it erred in finding that her fear was not related to being a member of the social group that the Board placed her in.

These errors, if that is what they were, were not errors of law. The Refugee Division addressed the question of whether or not the applicant fell within a particular social group but did not identify that group correctly based on the evidence. Such an error is not an error in law. Similarly, a finding that an applicant's fear is based on a fear of random violence and is not a fear arising from being a member of a social group, may be an error, but it is not an error of law. Further, in this case, these findings of fact could not be characterized as having been made in a perverse or capricious manner or without regard to the material before the tribunal. Accordingly, the judicial review application was dismissed.

Nueda v. Canada (Minister of Employment & Immigration) (1993), 21 Imm. L.R. (2d) 211, 65 F.T.R. 24 — The applicant came to Canada on the Foreign Domestic Programme. She was negatively reviewed in November 1983 and December 1984. She did not leave Canada when her employment authorization expired and a warrant for her arrest was executed in October 1987. The applicant claimed refugee status and obtained a work permit and she was employed from July 1988 to June 24, 1992.

It was found that there were no humanitarian and compassionate considerations in her case and a departure notice was issued requiring her to leave Canada by August 1992.

The Court emphasized that it was its responsibility to review the decision of the officers but that it was not sitting in appeal from that decision. The officers had all of the information before them and it could not be found that they had ignored any of it.

Counsel submitted that where a *prima facie* case of a Charter infringement has been made out, the Court must substantially review the decision and go beyond the common law grounds of judicial review. The Court agreed with this submission. It found, however, in this case that no Charter right of the applicant's had been breached. The Court went on to observe that even where there is a substantive review of a decision, section 18.1(3) of the *Federal Court Act* still governs the Trial Division's power on judicial review. In terms of a humanitarian and compassionate review, the Trial Division can direct that the review be conducted and that certain factors or directions be considered. It is not for the Court to conduct a review, but simply to indicate what is required to make a proper decision.

Section 18.1(4)

Gengeswaran v. Canada (Minister of Citizenship & Immigration) (May 19, 1999), Doc. IMM-4318-98 (Fed. T.D.) — Although there is no obligation on the Board to discuss every piece of evidence, it is required to address those pieces which contradict the Board's finding on key issues. The absence of any analysis of documentary evidence which directly contradicts the Board's finding, permits the Court to infer, from the silence, that the tribunal made an erroneous finding of fact without regard to evidence.

Cepeda-Gutierrez v. Canada (Minister of Citizenship & Immigration) (1998), 157 F.T.R. 35 (Fed. T.D.) — This was an application to set aside a decision of a panel of the CRDD. The applicant relied on section 18.1(4)(d) of the *Federal Court Act*. The applicant was a citizen of Mexico who arrived in Canada and claimed refugee status. The Refugee Division found that while he was a taxi driver in Mexico City he had been the subject of beatings and threats of violence by the federal police. The panel found that the claimant's evidence was credible and held that the claimant had a well-founded fear of persecution in Mexico City; however, they rejected his claim on the basis that he had an internal flight alternative.

Section 18.1(4)(d) of the *Federal Court Act* does not authorize the Court to substitute its view of the facts for that of the Board which has the benefit of not only seeing and hearing the witnesses, but also of the expertise of its members in assessing evidence relating to facts that are within their area of specialized expertise. The efficient allocation of decision-making resources between administrative agencies and the Courts strongly indicates that the role to be played in fact-finding by the Court on an application for judicial review should be nearly residual. Thus, in order to attract judicial intervention, the applicant must satisfy the Court not only that the Board made a palpably erroneous finding of material fact, but also that the finding was made without regard to the evidence. The Court may infer that the administrative agency made the erroneous finding of fact without regard to the evidence from the agency's failure to mention in its reasons some evidence before it that was relevant to the finding and pointed to a different conclusion from that reached by the agency. Just as a Court will only defer to an agency's interpretation of its constituent statute if it provides reasons for its conclusion, so a Court will be reluctant to defer to an agency's factual determinations in the absence of express findings and an analysis of the evidence that shows how the agency reached its results. Reasons given by an administrative agency are not to be read hypercritically, nor are agencies to be required to refer to every piece of evidence that they received that is contrary to their finding and to explain how they dealt with it. A statement by the agency in its reasons for decision that in making its findings it considered all of the evidence before it will often suffice to assure a reviewing Court that the agency directed itself to the totality of the evidence. The more important the evidence that is not mentioned specifically, the more willing a Court will be to infer from the silence that the agency made an erroneous finding of fact without regard to the evidence. When the agency refers in some detail to evidence supporting its finding, but is silent on evidence pointing to the opposite conclusion, it will be easier to infer that the agency overlooked the contradictory evidence when making its finding of fact. The Court was not persuaded that the Board erred when it found that the applicant faced no serious possibility of persecution outside Mexico City and therefore it was unnecessary to consider whether the Board's finding was made without regard to the evidence.

The applicant called a psychologist as a witness to explain why it was not reasonable to require the applicant to return to Mexico. In making its decision the panel did not refer to the psychologist's evidence. This evidence was so important to the applicant's case that it can be inferred from the refugee division's failure to mention it that the finding made by the panel was made without regard to this evidence. This inference was made easier by the fact that the Board's reasons dealt with other items of evidence indicating that return would not be unduly harsh. The inclusion of the "boilerplate" assertion that the Board considered all the evidence was not sufficient to prevent this inference from being drawn. Accordingly, the decision of the panel was set aside and the matter remitted to a differently constituted panel.

Khakh v. Canada (Minister of Citizenship & Immigration) (1996), 116 F.T.R. 310 (T.D.) — The applicant was determined not to be a Convention refugee on the basis that he had fabricated incidents of persecution in order to try to obtain refugee status.

The Court commented on judicial decisions about section 18.l(4)(d) and found authority for the proposition that three conditions precedent must be met to justify judicial intervention: (1) the finding of fact must be truly erroneous; (2) the finding must be made capriciously or without regard to the evidence; and (3) the decision must be based on the erroneous finding. Further, the subsection permits review where there was no evidence to support the finding, or where, on an assessment of the evidence as a whole, the finding was unreasonable.

Further, the Court adopted Webster's Third New International Dictionary defintion of "capricious", which defined the word as "marked or guided by caprice: given to changes of interest or attitude according to whims or passing fancies: not guided by steady judgment, intent, or purpose".

Osaloun v. Canada (Minister of Citizenship & Immigration) (June 12, 1996), Doc. IMM-3649-95 (Fed. T.D.) — The issue in this case was whether a panel of the IRB committed an error of natural justice, and if so, whether the breach should be disregarded.

The denial of a right to a fair hearing will render a decision with respect to a refugee claim invalid, unless it can be demonstrated that the claim would in any case be hopeless.

Singh (A.) v. Canada (Minister of Citizenship & Immigration) (1995), 30 Imm. L.R. (2d) 211, 98 F.T.R. 58 — This was an application to review a decision of the Appeal Division of the IRB upholding a deportation order issued against the applicant.

The applicant, his parents and his three sisters were sponsored to come to Canada as members of the family class. The applicant completed the statutory declaration in which he declared that he had never been married and that he had no children. The applicant received an immigrant visa in July, 1990 and returned for a visit to Guyana in 1992. In fact, the applicant had fathered a son in Guyana in 1990, and on his return there in 1992, he married the son's mother and then sponsored his wife and son for entrance to Canada. An adjudicator determined that the applicant had been granted landing by misrepresentation of a material fact (ie. — non-disclosure of the birth of his son).

At the outset of the proceedings before the Appeal Division, counsel for the applicant advised the Tribunal that the appeal was being taken pursuant to paragraph 70(3)(b) of the *Immigration Act* on the ground that having regard to the existence of compassionate or humanitarian considerations, the applicant should not be removed from Canada.

The Appeal Division dismissed the appeal and this application for judicial review related to that dismissal. In the proceedings before the Trial Division, the applicant submitted that Immigration Regulations 6(1)(a), 9(l)(a), and 10(1)(a) are *ultra vires* the *Immigration Act.*

The Trial Division is not entitled to pronounce itself on a question not faced by the administrative authority whose decision it is reviewing. This principle applies when the vires or regulations passed pursuant to the enabling statute is in issue. Accordingly, due to the fact that counsel before the Appeal Division did not challenge the validity of the regulations in question, that issue could not be raised before the Trial Division and the application for judicial review was dismissed.

Rehman v. Canada (Secretary of State) (1995), 92 F.T.R. 297 — The Court was satisfied that there had been a breach of the duty to act fairly. The Court then noted that there was an added requirement before a new hearing could be ordered. Specifically, the Court was required to address its mind to the question of whether the nature of the applicant's claim to refugee status is such that the claim might be described as hopeless or one where the outcome was inevitable, in which case it would be inappropriate to set aside the decision. The Court could not conclude on the facts of this matter that a differently constituted panel of the CRDD would inevitably conclude that these claims must fail. The Court therefore directed that there be a new hearing before a differently constituted panel of the CRDD.

Indrani v. Canada (Secretary of State) (1994), 89 F.T.R. 31 — The applicant arrived in Canada with false documents and claimed refugee status. The applicant married a Canadian permanent resident who sought an exemption for her pursuant to section 114(2). This request was refused.

Three conditions precedent must be met to justify judicial intervention for an erroneous finding of fact. First, the finding must be truly erroneous; second, the finding must be made capriciously or without regard to the evidence; third, the decision must be based upon the erroneous finding. Even if the Court is convinced that a decision is based on an erroneous finding of fact, it cannot intervene unless it is of the view that the tribunal, in making its finding, acted in a perverse and capricious manner, or without regard to the evidence before it.

A reviewing Court should not interfere with the exercise of discretion by an Immigration Officer who is authorized by statute to exercise the discretion unless it is clear that the discretion has been exercised in bad faith or on grounds unrelated to the purposes for which the discretion is granted. In this particular case, the application was dismissed.

Nguy v. Canada (Minister of Employment & Immigration) (1994), 80 F.T.R. 53 — The applicant was determined not to be a Convention refugee. The applicant challenged a finding of fact by the Board that he was not stateless as he had alleged, but was a citizen of Vietnam. The application was dismissed.

In order for an alleged error of fact to be reviewable, the finding must be truly erroneous or the finding must be made capriciously or without regard to the evidence, and the decision must be based on that erroneous finding. The decision that the applicant was eligible for Vietnamese citizenship was not erroneous or capricious and was not central to the negative determination of the applicant's refugee claim.

Alfred v. Canada (Minister of Employment & Immigration) (1994), 76 F.T.R. 231 — In this application to review a negative decision of the CRDD, the applicant argued that the tribunal erred in misconstruing "persecution" and that the tribunal erred in law by ignoring or misconstruing the evidence before it. The respondent made reference to portions of the transcript of the hearing and to the documentary evidence before the tribunal, which it argued would warrant the conclusion that the findings of the tribunal were reasonable. The Court must review the decision as rendered by the tribunal and not the evidence to which the decision itself makes no reference but which would have warranted the conclusions reached by the tribunal if the tribunal had expressed reasons relying upon such evidence. The simple statement that the tribunal had reached its decision "after careful consideration of all the evidence adduced at the hearing" was not sufficient when the decision made little or no reference to the principal bases of the applicant's claim. The application was allowed in this case and the matter sent back for rehearing before a differently constituted panel of the CRDD.

Bogdanov v. Canada (Minister of Employment & Immigration) (March 31, 1994), Doc. A-1658-92 (Fed. T.D.) — This was an application to set aside a negative determination of the CRDD. The applicants were all citizens of Bulgaria and the sole ground urged by the applicants was that the tribunal erred in its assessment that the cumulative effects of the various incidents of discrimination and harassment, as reported by the claimants, did not amount to persecution. The testimony of the applicants, according to the tribunal, "seemed credible, appeared to be given in good faith and without exaggeration".

The standard for the Court to intervene is set out in section 18.1(4)(c) and (d) of the *Federal Court Act*, R.S.C. 1985, c. F-7. The Court must be satisfied that the tribunal "erred in law in making a decision" or "based its decision ... on an erroneous finding of fact that it made in a perverse or capricious manner or without regard to the material before it". The appellants' argument was essentially that the tribunal reached the wrong conclusion in its assessment of the cumulative effect of the evidence. Even if the Court were inclined to share that view, there was no basis for finding that the tribunal's conclusion was unreasonable in law. Further, the tribunal's conclusion that the incidents of harassment did not individually or cumulatively constitute persecution could not be said to be perverse or capricious or made without regard to the material before the tribunal. The conclusion of the tribunal was one open to it on the evidence adduced. Accordingly, the application was dismissed.

Gholam-Nejad v. Canada (Minister of Employment & Immigration) (1994), 25 Imm. L.R. (2d) 51, 77 F.T.R. 44 — This application to review a negative decision of the CRDD was based on the denial to the applicant of her right to counsel because of the alleged manifest incompetence of her representative at the Refugee Board hearing. Section 18.1(4) of the *Federal Court Act* provides for relief where the CRDD acted or failed to act, or failed to observe a principle of natural justice, procedural fairness or other procedure that it was required by law to observe, or erred in law, or based its decision or order on an erroneous finding of fact made in a perverse or capricious manner. Nothing on the face of that subsection would authorize the intervention of the Court where the issue is the failure on the part of the applicant's representative, rather than on the part of the CRDD itself. This is particularly true where the failure of the representative was not at all apparent to the CRDD and, therefore, the representative's failure could not be identified as a failure of the CRDD to ensure natural justice and fairness. Accordingly, this ground of attack could not succeed and the application was dismissed.

Su v. Canada (Minister of Employment & Immigration) (January 24, 1994), Doc. IMM-1597-93 (Fed. T.D.) — This was an application to review a negative determination with respect to a refugee claim. Counsel for the respondent argued that there was evidence on the record that could have led the Board to conclude that the applicant's involvement in the pro-democracy movement prior to 1989 was not of such a nature that it would likely result in repercussions leading to persecution in the Convention refugee sense.

The Court's responsibility on a judicial review application is to review the decision in question on the basis on which it was given. In this case, the decision was based on a finding that the applicant was not credible, and not on a finding that even if the story the applicant was telling was true, the facts recounted would not lead to a finding of persecution.

The Court found that the decision that the applicant was not credible was based on a significant misunderstanding of the evidence and quashed the decision.

Pal v. Canada (Minister of Employment & Immigration) (1993), 70 F.T.R. 289 — The applicant sought review of a decision denying him Convention refugee status.

The applicant was not granted a recess, when he requested one, in order to review documents which were introduced into evidence and which he had not seen previously. The documents were introduced to contradict evidence which he had given. They were written in English. The applicant was testifying through an interpreter. The Court found that in refusing to allow the applicant and his counsel an opportunity to review the evidence, the applicant was denied the opportunity to answer the case against him and a breach of natural justice occurred.

The Court pointed out that relief under section 18.1(4) of the *Federal Court Act* is discretionary and thus, if no prejudice is caused by an erroneous procedure or decision, an order quashing that decision will not normally be given. If no real purpose will be served by requiring another hearing, one will not be ordered.

The Court was unable to conclude that the breach of natural justice which occurred in the context of this case was minor and could not appreciably affect the final decision. The breach was not cured by subsequent actions and accordingly, the decision of the tribunal was quashed.

Singh (G.) v. Canada (Minister of Employment & Immigration) (1993), 69 F.T.R. 142 — The applicants sought to set aside a decision that they were not Convention refugees. This case discusses how findings on the evidence can be successfully challenged in the Trial Division.

The Court commented that section 18.1(4)(d) of the *Federal Court Act* set out disjunctive conditions under which a decision will be set aside. For purposes of paragraph (c) of that section, the Court noted that findings of fact which are unsupported by adequate evidence are errors in law — the so-called "no evidence rule". Section 18.1(4)(d) allows the Court to set aside a decision which is made "without regard for the material before it". This grants a broader right of review than the traditional "no evidence" test. It compels the setting aside of tribunal decisions where they are unreasonable. The phrase "perverse or capricious manner or without regard for the material before it" is accurately discussed in J.A. Kavanagh, *A Guide to Judicial Review* (1978) at 57–58.

The findings of fact can be divided into two classifications: findings of primary facts and inferences of fact which are drawn from the primary facts. Courts are reluctant to interfere with findings of primary facts made by tribunals. In areas where a tribunal has a particular expertise in drawing inferences, courts are inclined to treat those inferences with deference. If, however, the inference is of a type which is based on common experience, then the Court is in equally as good a position as the tribunal to draw the inference and in that case deference is not shown.

In this particular case, the inferences of fact drawn by the Board did not stand up upon a review of the evidence and the decision refusing refugee status was set aside.

Muhammed v. Canada (Minister of Employment & Immigration) (1993), 67 F.T.R. 152 — The applicant applied to set aside a decision which determined that the applicant was not a Convention refugee. Section 18.1(4)(d) of the *Federal Court Act* provides that in an application for judicial review the Court may grant relief, *inter alia*, where the tribunal based its decision or order on an erroneous finding of fact that it made in a perverse or capricious manner or without regard for the material before it. This is the standard set by the Act and it emphasizes that it is not the role of the Court to substitute its decision for that of the tribunal, especially where the decision is based on an assessment of credibility. The decision of the Court of Appeal in *Giron v. Canada (Minister of Employment & Immigration)* (1992), 143 N.R. 238 (Fed. C.A.) was rendered at a time when the jurisdiction of the Court of Appeal included the authority to make the decision the Immigration and Refugee Board should have made, as well as the jurisdiction to refer the matter back to the Board for reconsideration.

The applicant claimed to be a Sudanese national who had been kidnapped by an insurgent force and compelled to train as a rebel. The applicant claimed that when he escaped from the guerrillas, they returned to his parents' home and shot and killed his father and mother. The Board had difficulty believing that the applicant was a national native of Sudan. Secondly, they found implausibilities in aspects of his story. For example, the assumption that the persons who killed his parents were rebel forces looking for him after he deserted. While the Court might have reached a different conclusion on either of these aspects, the panel's findings could not be said to be unreasonable and, therefore, the findings could not be characterized as perverse or capricious or made without regard to the material before the panel. Therefore, the application was dismissed.

Naikar v. Canada (Minister of Employment & Immigration) (June 17, 1993), 93-A-120 (Fed.T.D.) — This was an application for judicial review to set aside a determination of the Convention Refugee Determination Division of the IRB that the applicant did not meet the Convention refugee test.

The application was dismissed. The Court noted that on a judicial review application, it must sometimes balance seeming errors in the Board's decision with the more substantive findings the Board has made. To determine whether the errors are of such a nature that, if not committed, the Board's conclusions would have been substantially different, the true test is the reading of the transcript in an attempt to establish whether any purported errors are of a nature to vitiate the ultimate conclusion.

Boateng v. Canada (Minister of Employment & Immigration) (1993), 65 F.T.R. 81 — The Refugee Division decided that the applicant was not a Convention refugee. There was evidence that persons returning to Ghana were subject to detention for several months. The panel found that this treatment did not amount to persecution. The Court disagreed with this conclusion but declined to upset the panel's decision because this conclusion had no particular relevance to the applicant's case as there was no evidence that the government of Ghana would have reason to believe that the applicant had sought refugee status in Canada.

18.2 Interim orders — On an application for judicial review, the Trial Division may make such interim orders as it considers appropriate pending the final disposition of the application.

1990, c. 8, s. 5

Case Law

Muncan v. Canada (Minister of Citizenship & Immigration) (1998), 141 F.T.R. 241 (Fed. T.D.) — The applicant applied for a stay of a pending removal order. The applicant was convicted of a number of criminal offences and was ordered deported. The applicant appealed to the Appeal Division of the IRB against the deportation order. The Minister declared the applicant to be a danger to the public and the applicant sought to set aside the danger opinion and to stay the execution of the deportation order pending review of the opinion.

There is no jurisdictional limit to the discretion that the Court is empowered to apply under section 18.2. The whole question of whether the discretion should be exercised relates to the merits of each individual case. Regarding an application for a stay of a removal order, the issue is whether it is fair and just to grant it. In considering the entire context in deciding whether to exercise the discretion provided under section 18.2, the Court found that it was far too technical a perspective to require the deportation order to be challenged on judicial review or to limit the application of the appropriate injunctive test to the circumstances of the deportation order itself.

Solis v. Canada (Minister of Citizenship & Immigration), [1997] 2 F.C. 693, 127 F.T.R. 218 (Fed. T.D.) — The applicant sought to stay the execution of a removal order. The applicant came to Canada as a refugee. In 1990, he and his family were granted landed immigrant status. Since 1992, the applicant has been convicted of a number of criminal offences. On the basis of some of the convictions an inquiry was held and a conditional deportation order issued against the applicant. The applicant filed an appeal to the Appeal Division which was still outstanding at the time of this application. While the appeal was pending, the Minister determined that the applicant constituted a danger to the public in Canada. The applicant sought leave to review this opinion, and that application was pending when this application for a stay was heard. The Appeal Division, notwithstanding the issuance of the Minister's opinion, had not decided that it had no jurisdiction to entertain the applicant's appeal with the result that the appeal before the Appeal Division was still outstanding at the time this application was heard.

The application for a stay pursuant to section 18.2 of the *Federal Court Act* was dismissed on the basis that there already existed a statutory stay pursuant to paragraph 49(1)(b). In reaching this decision the Court declined to follow the decision of the Court of Appeal in *Tsang v. the Minister of Citizenship and Immigration*, February 11, 1997, A-179-96, on the basis that the application of section 49(1)(b) was not before the Court of Appeal in that case.

Forde v. Canada (Minister of Citizenship & Immigration) (1997), 210 N.R. 194 (Fed. C.A.) — The Minister appealed against a decision of the Trial Division in which a judge ordered that "a stay currently exists in this case and the respondent's application [for reconsideration] is dismissed with costs in the cause".

In December 1994, a deportation order was made against the respondent. He appealed to the Appeal Division of the IRB, but before the appeal was heard, a delegate of the Minister decided that the respondent was a danger to the public in Canada. In February 1996, the respondent applied for leave to judicially review that opinion but at no time did he file an application for leave to review the deportation order.

In March 1996, the Trial Division issued a stay of the deportation order "until such time as the application for judicial review is finally disposed of". This order was clearly ancillary to the leave application then pending and was authorized by section 18.2 of the *Federal Court Act*. In August 1996, the Trial Division dismissed the application for leave, thus terminating any judicial review proceeding. The original stay, granted in March 1996, thus came to an end, however, the Trial Division in September 1996, granted a "continuation" of the already terminated stay, and when the Minister applied for reconsideration of this order and a declaration that the stay no longer existed, the learned judge of the Trial Division made the order which is now a subject of this appeal.

The Trial Division has a carefully defined judicial review jurisdiction in respect of "any decision or order made or any matter arising under [the *Immigration] Act*". The decision of the Minister pursuant to subsection 70(5) is such a decision. During the course of disposing of an application for leave to seek judicial review of such a decision, the Court is authorized by section 18.2 to make ancillary orders, such as a stay. Once the leave application was disposed of there was no longer a leave or review proceeding to which a stay could be ancillary under section 18.2. Section 50(1)(b) of the *Federal Court Act* was never intended to give a general mandate to the Trial Division to stop deportations which are no longer under attack in the Court.

This appeal was properly brought without a question having been certified as the putative stay was no longer related to any application for leave, proceeding under subsection 82.1(1), and thus an appeal was not barred by section 82.2.

Huseyinov v. Canada (Minister of Employment & Immigration) (1994), 174 N.R. 233 (Fed. C.A.) — The appellants requested an adjournment in order that counsel may have time to consider the implications of proposed new regulations concerning failed refugee claimants.

The adjournment was refused. No such regulations had been adopted. A press release cannot create accrued rights in the appellants. It is the duty of the Court to apply the law as it is, not as it might be, and to hear appeals at the time for which they are set down.

Yamani v. Canada (Solicitor General) (1994), 27 Imm. L.R. (2d) 116, 80 F.T.R. 307 — The applicant applied for injunctive relief, pursuant to section 18.2 of the *Federal Court Act*. The injunction was granted and the Court had to consider, among other issues, whether the balance of convenience favoured the granting of the stay. The public interest in the maintenance of processes must be considered even where the stay is considered an exemption from the general public requirement in question and not one involving a suspension of that requirement generally.

The Court referred to *RJR-MacDonald Inc. v. Canada (Attorney General)* (1994), 164 N.R. 1 (S.C.C.) at pages 38–39. It noted that in the case of a public authority the onus of demonstrating irreparable harm is less than that of a private applicant. The test will nearly always be satisfied upon proof that the authority is charged with the duty of promoting or protecting the public interest and upon some indication that the impugned legislation, regulation or activity was undertaken pursuant to that responsibility. Once these requirements have been met the Court should, in most cases, assume that irreparable harm to the public interest would result from restraint of that action.

In this case deciding that the balance of convenience favoured granting a stay, the Court noted that important as the public interest is in maintaining the statutory processes, the case had not been pursued by the Crown as a matter of great urgency. Further, the grant of the stay preserved the status quo as far as the applicant was concerned and did not interfere significantly with the exercise of their lawful responsibilities by the authorities. This case, if a stay was granted, would not result in a "cascade of stays and exemptions".

The Court granted a stay but only to the extent of ordering that no removal or deportation order be issued against the applicant pending the final determination of the various applications for judicial review now scheduled to be heard by the Court. This interfered as little as possible with the inquiry process as established under the *Immigration Act*.

18.3 (1) Reference by federal tribunal — A federal board, commission or other tribunal may at any stage of its proceedings refer any question or issue of law, of jurisdiction or of practice and procedure to the Trial Division for hearing and determination.

(2) Reference by Attorney General of Canada — The Attorney General of Canada may, at any stage of the proceedings of a federal board, commission or other tribunal, other than a service tribunal within the meaning of the *National Defence Act*, refer any question or issue of the constitutional validity, applicability or operability of an Act of Parliament or of regulations thereunder, to the Trial Division for hearing and determination.

1990, c. 8, s. 5

18.4 (1) Hearings in a summary way — Subject to subsection (2), an application or reference to the Trial Division under any of sections 18.1 to 18.3 shall be heard and determined without delay and in a summary way.

(2) Exception — The Trial Division may, if it considers it appropriate, direct that an application for judicial review be treated and proceeded with as an action.

1990, c. 8, s. 5

Case Law

Shao v. Canada (Minister of Citizenship & Immigration) (February 3, 1999), Doc. IMM-4178-98 (Fed. T.D.) — The applicant requested an expedited hearing of a permanent residency application. The delay by immigration officials in Hong Kong and the anticipated delay in hearing the matter in the Federal Court had resulted in difficulties and anxieties both on behalf of the applicant and the applicant's niece and family who now live in Canada.

Where there is a serious issue focusing on irreparable harm and the other side will not be prejudiced, the Court will usually make a judge available, provided a timetable convenient to counsel and the Court can be agreed upon. The applicant in this case had at best shown a serious inconvenience. Absent irreparable harm or some other exceptional circumstances, a hearing ought not to be expedited because there is still a backlog of immigration matters to be heard by the Court. To expedite an individual hearing will mean either a cancellation of an already scheduled hearing or the deferment of a matter which is also waiting for a hearing date.

Oduro v. Canada (Minister of Employment & Immigration) (1993), 73 F.T.R. 191 — The applicant sought permission to proceed by way of an action so that the entire document entitled Consistency Project — Final Report on Meetings, dated May 19, 1992, be put before the Court so that Board members could be questioned on their perception of the document. Judicial review is intended to proceed in a summary manner. Proceeding by way of action pursuant to section 18.4(2) is exceptional and not to be resorted to except in the clearest circumstances. The Court referred to a decision of Pinard J. in *Edwards v. Canada (Minister of Agriculture)* (1992), 53 F.T.R. 265 at 267, which allowed an application for an injunction and a declaration to be converted into an action in circumstances where counsel submitted there would be many different issues of fact and law, and that in addition there would be a need for extensive cross-examination on the many affidavits filed by both parties. Further, it was argued that the Court should have the benefit of assessing the demeanour and credibility of witnesses under cross-examination, particularly experts. In this case, the applicant referred to censored evidence. The missing portion of the documents in question were deleted pursuant to the provisions of the *Access to Information Act*. The applicant sought to have the matter treated as an action on the basis of speculation there was further evidence which had been censored which could support the allegation of bias. Such speculation did not constitute a basis upon which the Court could exercise its discretion under section 18.4(2).

18.5 Exception to sections 18 and 18.1 — Notwithstanding sections 18 and 18.1, where provision is expressly made by an Act of Parliament for an appeal as such to the Court, to the Supreme Court of Canada, to the Court Martial Appeal Court, to the Tax Court of Canada, to the Governor in Council or to the Treasury Board from a decision or order of a federal board, commission or other tribunal made by or in the course of proceedings before that board, commission or tribunal, that decision or order is not, to the extent that it may be so appealed, subject to review or to be restrained, prohibited, removed, set aside or otherwise dealt with, except in accordance with that Act.

1990, c. 8, s. 5

. . . . .

PROCEDURE

. . . . .

48. (1) How proceeding against Crown instituted — A proceeding against the Crown shall be instituted by filing in the Registry of the Court the original and two copies of a document that may be in the form set out in the schedule and by payment of the sum of two dollars as a filing fee.

(2) Procedure for filing originating document — The original and two copies of the originating document may be filed as required by subsection (1) by being forwarded, together with a remittance for the filing fee, by registered mail addressed to "The Registry, The Trial Division, The Federal Court of Canada, Ottawa, Canada".

(3) Service of originating document — When the original and two copies of the originating document have been filed and the filing fee has been paid as required by this section, an officer of the Registry of the Court shall, after verifying the accuracy of the copies, forthwith, on behalf of the claimant, serve the originating document on Her Majesty by transmitting the copies to the office of the Deputy Attorney General of Canada.

(4) Certificate — When the copies have been transmitted to the office of the Deputy Attorney General of Canada under subsection (3), a certificate signed by an officer of the Registry respecting the date of filing and the date of transmission of the copies shall be delivered, or forwarded by registered mail, to the claimant or the claimant's counsel or solicitor at the address appearing on the originating document, or at such other address as may have been communicated to the Registry for the purpose.

(5) Certificate to be evidence — A certificate under subsection (4) is evidence of the date of filing and the date of service of the originating document referred to in the certificate.

Case Law

Torres-Samuels (Guardian ad litem of) v. Canada (Minister of Citizenship & Immigration) (1998), 42 Imm. L.R. (2d) 290 (B.C. S.C.); affirmed (1998), 47 Imm. L.R. (2d) 9, 57 B.C.L.R. (3d) 357, [1999] 6 W.W.R. 207, 166 D.L.R. (4th) 611 (B.C. C.A.) — This was a petition brought by two Canadian children of Jose Torres, who was the subject of a deportation order under the *Immigration Act.*

The *parens patriae* jurisdiction of the Court is founded on the obvious necessity that the law should place, somewhere, the care of persons who are not able to care for themselves. The interests of the children are engaged only incidentally in the legal process that is unfolding with respect to their father. The Court questioned the extent to which it could, using its *parens patriae* jurisdiction alone, frustrate an otherwise lawful and constitutional process, the focus of which is the legal status or rights of third parties.

The Court found that the petitioners wanted it, pursuant to its *parens patriae* jurisdiction, to substitute a system of immigration with respect to foreign persons who have children born in Canada whereby it will be the superior courts of the provinces that will decide which of such persons shall be permitted to remain in the country. The Court found that its *parens patriae* jurisdiction did not extend that far.

The *parens patriae* jurisdiction of the Court should not be resorted to in a manner that flies in the face of a legislative scheme unless there is a gap in the scheme. Section 114(2) of the *Immigration Act* permits the Minister to exempt a person from deportation, owing to the existence of compassionate or humanitarian consideration; thus there is provision under the *Immigration Act* for the best interests of the children of prospective deportees to be considered. There is no gap justifying the Court's intervention on behalf of the children. The petitioners also asked for a remedy pursuant to section 24(1) of the Charter. The Court declined to exercise its jurisdiction in favour of the Federal Court.

.....

50. (1) Stay of proceedings — The Court may, in its discretion, stay proceedings in any cause or matter,

> **(a) on the ground that the claim is being proceeded with in another court or jurisdiction; or**
>
> **(b) where for any other reason it is in the interest of justice that the proceedings be stayed.**

(2) Idem — The Court shall, on the application of the Attorney General of Canada, stay proceedings in any cause or matter in respect of a claim against the Crown if it appears that the claimant has an action or proceeding in respect of the same claim pending in any other court against a person who, at the time when the cause of action alleged in the action or proceeding arose, was, in respect thereof, acting so as to engage the liability of the Crown.

(3) Lifting of stay — Any stay ordered under this section may subsequently be lifted in the discretion of the Court.

Case Law

Forde v. Canada (Minister of Citizenship & Immigration) (1997), 210 N.R. 194 (Fed. C.A.) — The Minister appealed against a decision of the Trial Division in which a judge ordered that "a stay currently exists in this case and the respondent's application [for reconsideration] is dismissed with costs in the cause".

In December 1994, a deportation order was made against the respondent. He appealed to the Appeal Division of the IRB, but before the appeal was heard, a delegate of the Minister decided that the respondent was a danger to the public in Canada. In February 1996, the respondent applied for leave to judicially review that opinion but at no time did he file an application for leave to review the deportation order.

In March 1996, the Trial Division issued a stay of the deportation order "until such time as the application for judicial review is finally disposed of". This order was clearly ancillary to the leave application then pending and was authorized by section 18.2 of the *Federal Court Act*. In August 1996, the Trial Division dismissed the application for leave, thus terminating any judicial review proceeding. The original stay, granted in March 1996, thus came to an end, however, the Trial Division in September 1996 granted a "continuation" of the already terminated stay, and when the Minister applied for reconsideration of this order and a declaration that the stay no longer existed, the learned judge of the Trial Division made the order which is now a subject of this appeal.

The Trial Division has a carefully defined judicial review jurisdiction in respect of "any decision or order made or any matter arising under [the *Immigration] Act*." The decision of the Minister pursuant to subsection 70(5) is such a decision. During the course of disposing of an application for leave to seek judicial review of such a decision, the Court is authorized by section 18.2 to make ancillary orders, such as a stay. Once the leave application was disposed of there was no longer a leave or review proceeding to which a stay could be ancillary under section 18.2. Section 50(1)(b) of the *Federal Court Act* was never intended to give a general mandate to the Trial Division to stop deportations which are no longer under attack in the Court.

This appeal was properly brought without a question having been certified as the putative stay was no longer related to any application for leave, proceeding under subsection 82.1(1), and thus an appeal was not barred by section 82.2.

JUDGMENTS OF COURT OF APPEAL

.....

52. Powers of Court of Appeal — The Federal Court of Appeal may

(a) quash proceedings in cases brought before it in which it has no jurisdiction or whenever those proceedings are not taken in good faith;

(b) in the case of an appeal from the Trial Division,

(i) dismiss the appeal or give the judgment and award the process or other proceedings that the Trial Division should have given or awarded,

(ii) in its discretion, order a new trial, if the ends of justice seem to require it, or

(iii) make a declaration as to the conclusions that the Trial Division should have reached on the issues decided by it and refer the matter back for a continuance of the trial on the issues that remain to be determined in the light of that declaration; and

(c) in the case of an appeal other than an appeal from the Trial Division,

(i) dismiss the appeal or give the decision that should have been given, or

(ii) in its discretion, refer the matter back for determination in accordance with such directions as it considers to be appropriate.

(d) [Repealed 1990, c. 8, s. 17.]

1990, c. 8, s. 17

Case Law

Punniamoorthy v. Canada (Minister of Employment & Immigration) (1994), 166 N.R. 49 (Fed. C.A.) — The appellant, a citizen of Sri Lanka, was a Tamil who claimed refugee status on the grounds that he had a well-founded fear of persecution by the LTTE. The appellant testified that the EPRLF started forcibly recruiting young men into the Tamil Army. As a result of his standing in the community and long association with the commander of the EPRLF army camp, the appellant was repeatedly asked by parents to obtain their conscripted sons' releases. As a result of his frequent visits to the EPRLF camp, the appellant believed that members of the LTTE thought that he had become a spy or informer. When the LTTE seized control of Jaffna, the appellant was arrested and released after two days in custody. He subsequently fled the country.

The Board offered no reasons for disregarding the appellant's testimony on two of the three grounds upon which it based its decision. Applying the reasoning in *Hilo v. Canada (Minister of Employment & Immigration)* (1991), 15 Imm. L.R. (2d) 199, 130 N.R. 236 (Fed. C.A.), the decision of the Board was quashed. This portion of the appeal went on consent. The parties disagreed on whether the Court should exercise its discretion under section 52(c)(i) of the *Federal Court Act* and declare the appellant a Convention refugee. This decision reviews all of the relevant cases in the last three years on this question.

In order for the Court to exercise its jurisdiction under section 52(c)(i), the evidence on the record must be "so clearly conclusive" that the "only possible conclusion" is that the claimant is a Convention refugee. If the sole issue to be decided involves a pure question of law, which is ultimately decided in favour of the claimant, the Court has no difficulty in declaring a claimant to be a Convention refugee. If the issue revolves around uncontroverted evidence and accepted facts upon which a legal conclusion must be drawn, the Court may be compelled to declare a claimant a Convention refugee.

The Court will not invoke section 52(c)(i) when the factual matter involves conflicting evidence which is central to the refugee determination or the claimant's credibility. It is not necessary, however, for the Board to make positive findings of credibility before the Court will exercise its jurisdiction under section 52(c)(i). The Court may exercise its discretion and declare a claimant to be a Convention refugee where the inconsistencies in the testimony, although not insignificant, were not central to the claim.

The weight of authority is that it is highly improbable that a claimant will be declared a Convention refugee by the Court if the Board has made an overall negative assessment with respect to credibility. The same holds true when the Board disbelieves aspects of the claimant's case which are central or critical to the making of a refugee determination. In this case, the fact that the Court is dealing with matters of credibility critical to the refugee claim is sufficient for it to be cautious in exercising its discretion under section 52(c)(i). Simply because a tribunal falls into error by failing to give adequate reasons for rejecting testimony does not of itself establish the truth of what was said.

The appeal was allowed on consent, the decision of the Board set aside and the matter remitted for rehearing.

Vakeesan v. Canada (Minister of Employment & Immigration) (April 20, 1993), Doc. A-900-90 (Fed. C.A.) — The Court commented that it would not exercise its jurisdiction under paragraph 52(c) of the *Federal Court Act* because the evidence before the Board was not so clearly conclusive of the issue that the Board ought to declare the appellant a Convention refugee, nor was it clear that such a declaration was the only possible conclusion that the Board could reach. The Court referred to two of its own cases in determining when it would exercise its jurisdiction under paragraph 52(c). Those cases were *Nadarajah v. Canada (Minister of Employment & Immigration)*, [1992] 2 F.C. 394, 17 Imm. L.R. (2d) 1, 142 N.R. 161 (Fed. C.A.) and *Mahathmasseelan v. Canada (Minister of Employment & Immigration)* (1991), 15 Imm. L.R. (2d) 29, 137 N.R. 1 (Fed. C.A.)

.....

General

57. (1) Constitutional questions — Where the constitutional validity, applicability or operability of an Act of Parliament or of the legislature of any province, or of regulations thereunder, is in question before the Court or a federal board, commission or other tribunal, other than a service tribunal within the meaning of the *National Defence Act*, the Act or regulation shall not be adjudged to be invalid, inapplicable or inoperable unless notice has been served on the Attorney General of Canada and the attorney general of each province in accordance with subsection (2).

(2) Time of notice — Except where otherwise ordered by the Court or the federal board, commission or other tribunal, the notice referred to in subsection (1) shall be served at least ten days before the day on which the constitutional question described in that subsection is to be argued.

(3) Notice of appeal or application for judicial review — The Attorney General of Canada and the attorney general of each province are entitled to notice of any appeal or application for judicial review made in respect of the constitutional question described in subsection (1).

(4) Right to be heard — The Attorney General of Canada and the attorney general of each province are entitled to adduce evidence and make submissions to the Court or federal board, commission or other tribunal in respect of the constitutional question described in subsection (1).

(5) Appeal — Where the Attorney General of Canada or the attorney general of a province makes submissions under subsection (4), that attorney general shall be deemed to be a party to the proceedings for the purposes of any appeal in respect of the constitutional question described in subsection (1).

1990, c. 8, s. 19

Case Law

Gervasoni v. Canada (Minister of Citizenship & Immigration) (1995), 101 F.T.R. 150
This case involves a constitutional challenge to subparagraph 46.01(1)(e)(i). Notice to the Attorneys General was given prior to leave having been granted but no returnable date was set forth in the notice. A notice contemplated under Section 57 of the *Federal Court Act* must contain a returnable day, date, time and location. In immigration judicial reviews such particulars are not known until leave has been granted. The proper practice, therefore, is to give notice after leave has been granted with the notice containing the appropriate information.

FEDERAL COURT RULES, 1998

SOR/98-106

. . . . .

PART 10 — ORDERS

. . . . .

Rule 397

397. (1) Motion to reconsider — Within 10 days after the making of an order, or within such other time as the Court may allow, a party may serve and file a notice of motion to request that the Court, as constituted at the time the order was made, reconsider its terms on the ground that

(a) the order does not accord with any reasons given for it; or

(b) a matter that should have been dealt with has been overlooked or accidentally omitted.

(2) Mistakes — Clerical mistakes, errors or omissions in an order may at any time be corrected by the Court.

Case Law

Sivakumar v. Canada (Minister of Citizenship & Immigration) (1998), 150 F.T.R. 299 (Fed. T.D.) — The defendants sought an extension of time with which to serve and file a Notice of Appeal to the Federal Court of Appeal from a disclosure order made by a judge of the Trial Division. The Notice of Appeal was not filed within 10 days of the decision, rather the defendants brought a motion for reconsideration within the 10-day period. This motion was dismissed. The defendants argued that in filing a reconsideration application they evidenced a continuing intention to appeal and that they brought the extension application within a reasonable period of time after the dismissal of the reconsideration application. Rule 337(5) (now Rule 397), provides that the Court can reconsider a judgement on the grounds that it did not accord with the reasons or that some matter was overlooked or accidentally omitted. The grounds for reconsideration are narrow. Generally they involve inadvertent mistakes or omissions that should be rectified by the judge who rendered the original judgement. Very often the mistake or omission is obvious. Except in these narrow and often obvious circumstances a dissatisfied litigant's recourse is an appeal. Reconsideration applications and appeals are not interchangeable forms of relief. Reconsideration deals with inadvertent mistakes or omissions. An appeal involves acceptance of the lower court judgement as is, but disagreement with its conclusion. Litigants must decide which recourse to seek.

Where there is doubt, it is likely that reconsideration is not the appropriate course. In any event, a Notice of Appeal should be filed in a timely manner. The application for an extension of time was dismissed.

. . . . .

PART 11 — COSTS

Awarding of Costs Between Parties

Rule 404

404. (1) Liability of solicitor for costs — Where costs in a proceeding are incurred improperly or without reasonable cause or are wasted by undue delay or other misconduct or default, the Court may make an order against any solicitor whom it considers to be responsible, whether personally or through a servant or agent,

(a) directing the solicitor personally pay the costs of a party to the proceeding; or

(b) disallowing the costs between the solicitor and the solicitor's client.

(2) Show cause by solicitor — No order under subsection (1) shall be made against a solicitor unless the solicitor has been given an opportunity to be heard.

(3) Notice to client — The Court may order that notice of an order against a solicitor made under subsection (1) be given to the solicitor's client in a manner specified by the Court.

Case Law

Hafeez v. Canada (Minister of Citizenship & Immigration) (1998), 45 Imm. L.R. (2d) 195 (Fed. T.D.) — When this matter came on for hearing, counsel for the applicant advised the Court that there was no evidence upon which the application was based. Both the Court and representative of the respondent wasted their time preparing for a hearing when in fact there was no basis for the application proceeding. Furthermore, counsel for the applicant did not appear on the matter but retained another counsel to appear one day before the hearing was scheduled to proceed. Accordingly, the Court order costs of $1,000 in favour of the Crown payable personally by the applicant's counsel of record.

Channa v. Canada (Minister of Citizenship & Immigration) (1996), 124 F.T.R. 290 (Fed. T.D.) — The applicant sought to review a decision of a visa officer refusing his application for permanent residence. The applicant scored 59 points, was at the pre-interview stage, and was not granted an interview.

In the absence of a specific statutory provision, reasons are not required when an interview is denied. Further, where the statute only requires reasons when positive discretion is exercised under section 11(3) of the regulations, the Court is not prepared to conclude that reasons are also required when that discretion is not exercised.

Counsel for the applicant acknowledged that, before the hearing, he received more than one telephone call from the respondent's counsel pointing out that arguments in the memorandum of argument were without merit. The applicant abandoned those arguments when the judicial review application was heard, but substituted for them new arguments which came as a total surprise to the respondent's counsel. Counsel is not entitled to proceed without notice and, whether he was asked or not, counsel ought to have advised the respondent's counsel that he was abandoning the applicant's memorandum of argument and planning to present new arguments. There were no special reasons under rule 16 which would justify a costs award against the applicant. It was the solicitors conduct which brought the case forward without notice. Accordingly, the court ordered that counsel for the applicant personally pay to the respondent $100 in court costs.

FEDERAL COURT IMMIGRATION RULES, 1993

Rules of the Federal Court of Canada Respecting the Practice and Procedure for Applications for Leave, Applications for Judicial Review and Appeals Under the Immigration Act

SOR/93-22, as am. SOR/98-235.

[Editor's note: The amending rules came into force on April 25, 1998. Rule 4 applies to all proceedings including further steps taken in proceedings already commenced. See SOR/98-235, s. 9 and 11.]

SHORT TITLE

1. These Rules may be cited as the *Federal Court Immigration Rules, 1993*.

INTERPRETATION

2. In these Rules,

"Act" means the *Immigration Act*;

"appeal" means an appeal under section 83 of the Act;

"application" means an application to a judge of the Federal Court — Trial Division under subsection 82.1(1) of the Act for leave to commence an application for judicial review of any decision or order made, or any matter arising under the Act, and includes an application for judicial review deemed to have been commenced under subsection 82.1(6) of the Act;

"application for judicial review of a decision of a visa officer" means an application to a judge of the Federal Court — Trial Division referred to in subsection 82.1(2) of the Act;

"Minister" [Revoked SOR/98-235, s. 1.]

"tribunal" means the person or body whose decision, order, act or omission is the subject of an application;

"written reasons" includes a transcript of reasons given orally.

SOR/98-235, s. 1

APPLICATION

3. [Revoked SOR/98-235, s. 2.]

4. (1) Subject to subrule (3), except to the extent that they are inconsistent with the Act or these Rules, Parts 1, 2, 3, 6, 7, 10 and 11 and Rules 383 to 385 of the *Federal Court Rules, 1998* apply to applications and appeals.

(2) Except to the extent that they are inconsistent with the Act, Parts 1, 2, 3, 5, 7, 9, 10 and 11 of the *Federal Court Rules, 1998* apply to applications for judicial review of a decision of a visa officer.

(3) Rule 133 of the *Federal Court Rules, 1998* does not apply to service of an application under Rule 7.

SOR/98-235, s. 2

Case Law

Section 4

Zheng v. Canada (Minister of Citizenship & Immigration) (September 30, 1998), Doc. IMM-2686-98 (Fed. T.D.) — Appearing on your own affidavit, in addition to being in the breach of a principle of the common law, is now contrary to rule 82 which prohibits a solicitor from both deposing to an affidavit and presenting arguments based on that affidavit.

Yazdanian v. Canada (Minister of Citizenship & Immigration) (1998), 150 F.T.R. 297 (Fed. T.D.) — The respondent sought to strike out the affidavit of Soheil Javid and paragraphs of a supplementary affidavit of Shirin Drudian. An affidavit may be struck out where it is abusive or clearly irrelevant, or where a party has obtained leave to admit evidence which turns out to be obviously inadmissible, or where the Court is convinced that the matter of admissibility should be resolved at an early date so that a hearing may proceed in an orderly manner.

The respondent's motion was dismissed. While some of the material in the affidavit may border on conjecture and speculation, there was much more to the affidavit than that. At the stage when this motion was brought, before cross-examination, it was inappropriate to strike out the whole of one affidavit and substantially all of the second affidavit. These were matters that should be determined by the trial judge.

Sivakumar v. Canada (Minister of Citizenship & Immigration) (1998), 150 F.T.R. 299 (Fed. T.D.) — The defendants sought an extension of time with which to serve and file a Notice of Appeal to the Federal Court of Appeal from a disclosure order made by a judge of the Trial Division. The Notice of Appeal was not filed within 10 days of the decision, rather the defendants brought a motion for reconsideration within the 10-day period. This motion was dismissed. The defendants argued that in filing a reconsideration application they evidenced a continuing intention to appeal and that they brought the extension application within a reasonable period of time after the dismissal of the reconsideration application. Rule 337(5) (now Rule 397), provides that the Court can reconsider a judgement on the grounds that it did not accord with the reasons or that some matter was overlooked or accidentally omitted. The grounds for reconsideration are narrow. Generally they involve inadvertent mistakes or omissions that should be rectified by the judge who rendered the original judgement. Very often the mistake or omission is obvious. Except in these narrow and often obvious circumstances a dissatisfied litigant's recourse is an appeal. Reconsideration applications and appeals are not interchangeable forms of relief. Reconsideration deals with inadvertent mistakes or omissions. An appeal involves acceptance of the lower court judgement as is, but disagreement with its conclusion. Litigants must decide which recourse to seek.

Where there is doubt, it is likely that reconsideration is not the appropriate course. In any event, a Notice of Appeal should be filed in a timely manner. The application for an extension of time was dismissed.

International Chartering Services Ltd. v. Canada (Minister of Citizenship & Immigration) (1998), 45 Imm. L.R. (2d) 305, 148 F.T.R. 151 (Fed. T.D.) — A motion to strike out an application for leave and for judicial review can only be successful in those exceptional cases where the application is so clearly improper as to be bereft of any possibility of success.

Vilus c. Canada (Ministre de la Citoyenneté et de l'Immigration) (5 mai 1998), n° IMM-1517-98 (C.F. (1re inst.)) — This was a motion by the applicant for leave to amend his application for leave to commence an application for judicial review. On March 26, 1997, the applicant applied for permanent residence as the spouse of a Canadian citizen. On February 19, 1998, the applicant was advised that his application for a ministerial exemption could not be granted and that a report had been issued against him pursuant to section 27. After this report was issued a departure order was made on March 5, 1998. On March 18, 1998, the applicant submitted a claim for Convention refugee status. On March 27, 1998, the applicant was notified pursuant to section 44(1) of the Act that he was not eligible to have his claim determined because a departure order had been previously made against him. On April 3, 1998, the applicant commenced his application for judicial review of the March 27th decision. Through the instant motion, the applicant sought to have the March 5th decision also set aside by means of this application.

The motion was dismissed. It would be incongruous to allow the applicant to challenge the March 5th decision when he had not previously sought such a remedy. The affidavit filed in support of the motion was silent as to why the March 5th decision had not yet been challenged in a separate application for judicial review.

FORM OF APPLICATION

5. (1) An application shall be in accordance with Form IR-1 as set out in the schedule and shall set out

(a) the full names of the parties;

(b) the date and details of the decision, order or other matter in respect of which relief is sought;

(c) the name of the tribunal and, if the tribunal was composed of more than one person, the name of each person who was on the tribunal;

(d) the tribunal's file number, if any;

(e) the precise relief to be sought on the application for judicial review;

(f) the grounds on which the relief is sought, including a reference to any statutory provision or Rule to be relied on;

(g) the proposed place and language of the hearing of the application for judicial review;

(h) whether or not the applicant has received the written reasons of the tribunal; and

(i) the signature, name, address and telephone number of the individual solicitor filing the application, or where the applicant acts in person, his or her signature, name, address for service in Canada, and telephone number.

(2) Unless the Minister is the applicant, the Minister shall be a respondent in an application.

Extension of Time to File and Serve Application

6. (1) Where an extension of time under subsection 82.1(5) of the Act is required, the applicant shall apply for the extension of time in the application for leave.

(2) A request for an extension of time under subsection 82.1(5) of the Act shall be determined at the same time, and on the same materials, as the application for leave.

Case Law

Section 6

Baig v. Canada (Minister of Citizenship & Immigration) (1997), 136 F.T.R. 78, 41 Imm. L.R. (2d) 237 (Fed. T.D.) — In July 1997, the applicant filed an originating Notice of Motion seeking to set aside a decision of a visa officer which denied his application for permanent residence in Canada. In support of that motion, the applicant, with the assistance of counsel, filed an affidavit in which he swore that he received the refusal in June 1997, notwithstanding that the refusal letter was dated in March 1997. At a conference call in September 1997, the applicant and his counsel disclosed to the Court that the visa officer's letter had been received by the applicant's counsel in April 1997 and that the contents had only been communicated to the applicant in June 1997, due to the fact that the applicant was travelling and unavailable to his counsel. Subsequent to the conference call in September 1997, the applicant filed a request for an extension of time and filed a further affidavit which disclosed that the applicant's counsel had been unable to contact him and for that reason had not brought the refusal letter to his attention.

The application for an extension of time was refused. If applicants and their counsel wish the Court to exercise its discretion in their favour, it is imperative that full and frank disclosure be made. The Court indicated to counsel for the applicant that if this type of behaviour were to recur, the Court would consider ordering costs against counsel personally.

Abdi-Egeh v. Canada (Minister of Citizenship & Immigration) (1995), 29 Imm. L.R. (2d) 254, 99 F.T.R. 279 (Fed. T.D.) — The applicant applied for an order extending the time to perfect her application for leave and for an order requiring the respondent to produce all documents in its possession and control. The applicant, in fact, had made a request under the *Privacy Act* and was waiting for the Minister's response to that request at the time the application for an extension was made. The applicant had received from the respondent, pursuant to Rule 9, an indication that no reasons had been given for the decision under review.

The Court denied the request for production. According to section 82.1(8), applications for leave to commence applications for judicial review are to be determined without delay and in a summary way. It would be contrary to the objective of subsection 82.1(8) to allow the *Privacy Act* procedure to be invoked to frustrate the regime for dealing with applications for leave. For similar reasons, the "gap rule" in the general rules and orders of this Court cannot be resorted to achieve the applicant's objective.

The letter containing the immigration officer's decision contained the following: "... we regret to inform you that you do not meet the eligibility criteria for this program due to the following reason(s): You hindered or delayed your removal from Canada." This sentence identified the "reason" why the applicant failed to qualify under DROC. Despite the view of the applicant and of the respondent, the applicant here did receive "reasons" for the impugned decision. That is not to say that the "reasons" given constitute an explanation of the reasoning of the Immigration officer. Such an explanation is not necessary to constitute "reasons."

The Court granted the extension because both the applicant and the respondent were under the mistaken impression that reasons had not been given.

Mendoza v. Canada (Secretary of State) (1994), 24 Imm. L.R. (2d) 317, 82 F.T.R. 92 (Fed. T.D.) — The applicant sought and obtained an extension of time to file and serve her record on the grounds that Legal Service Society of British Columbia approval had just been obtained and that the Court reporters could not prepare a transcript of the proceedings before the CRDD in time to permit the applicant to meet the deadline for filing and serving a record.

In granting the extension the Court considered first whether the request for an extension had been made in a timely fashion; secondly, the fact that the reason for the extension did not relate exclusively to counsel's work load, but rather at least one factor beyond the control of counsel, namely the preparation of the transcript of the CRDD hearing; and finally, the Court considered whether the leave application had any merit.

Chin v. Canada (Minister of Employment & Immigration) (1993), 22 Imm. L.R. (2d) 136, 69 F.T.R. 77 (Fed. T.D.) — On September 1, 1993, the applicant sought an extension of time for filing the application record. On July 28, 1993, he had filed an application for leave. The application record, according to the rules, was required to be filed before August 27, 1993. The application for an extension of time was filed on August 20, 1993. The reason given for seeking an extension was because counsel was going out of town from August 21 to August 27 and was unable to complete the application record. The application for an extension of time was refused. The time limits set out in the rules are meant to be complied with. If they are too short, then requests should be made to have the rules amended. Extensions are not granted because it is the first time that counsel has asked for one or because the work load which counsel has assumed is too great. In order for an application to be successful, some reason for the delay, which is beyond the control of counsel or the applicant, must be given, for example, illness or some other unexpected or unanticipated event. There was no such unanticipated delay in the present case. Courts are often reluctant to disadvantage individuals because their counsel missed deadlines. In matters of this nature, however, counsel is acting in the shoes of his or her client. Client and counsel are one for such purposes. It is too easy a justification for non-compliance with the rules for counsel to say the delay was not in any way caused by the client, and that if an extension is not granted the client will be prejudiced.

The comments of the Court occurred when counsel, after having been apprised of the Court's refusal to extend the time, filed a motion for reconsideration. Such a motion is filed pursuant to Rule 337(5). The Court declined the motion for reconsideration. There was no oversight on the part of the Court respecting the evidence. Accordingly, the motion for reconsideration was dismissed.

Espinoza v. Canada (Minister of Employment & Immigration) (1992), 142 N.R. 158 (Fed. C.A.) — An order for an extension of the time to comply with Rule 9 does not finally dispose of any matter and issue. Such an order is always open to reconsideration whether made peremptorily or not. The policy of the *Immigration Act* and *Federal Court Immigration Rules* is transparently clear and is one of deciding leave applications expeditiously. The dilatory initiation of Legal Aid applications, delays in providing opinion letters, which counsel know will be required, and the ever slower processing of such applications by Legal Aid cannot be permitted to defeat the policy of the Act and rules. Failure to make a Legal Aid application promptly can be good reason to deny an extension.

Kazi v. Kalusny (1991), 13 Imm. L.R. (2d) 258 (Fed. T.D.) — Counsel sought an extension of the time limits provided by section 9 of the rules. One of the bases for the request was that counsel had occupied himself with a long-standing client who was in a more difficult situation than the applicant. The extension was refused. Counsel had an obligation to delegate the file to someone else or to make sure, in some other manner, that the deadlines which apply to these clients were met. With respect to the main motion for leave to commence a proceeding, it was dismissed. There was no material on the file to support the application for leave.

Bains v. Canada (Minister of Employment & Immigration) (1990), 47 Admin. L.R. 317, 109 N.R. 239 (Fed. C.A.) — The only question to be considered in disposing of an application for leave under section 82.1(1) or 82.3(1) is whether or not a fairly arguable case is disclosed for the relief proposed to be sought if leave is granted. Further, the need for material not immediately available has to be established by the applicant and the mere stated intention to rely on such material does not, without an application and an order to that end, operate to extend the time provided by the *Federal Court Immigration Rules* for the applicant to file an affidavit and/or representations in support of the leave application. The requirement for leave is, in reality, the other side of the coin of the traditional jurisdiction to summarily terminate proceedings that disclose no reasonably arguable case. The requirement for leave does not deny refugee claimants access to the Court. The right to apply for leave is, itself, a right of access to the Court and the requirement that leave be obtained before an appeal or application for judicial review may proceed does not impair the right guaranteed by refugee claimants under either section 7 or 15 of the Charter.

Filing and Service of Application

7. (1) Where an application is required to be served under subsection 82.1(3) of the Act, a certified copy of it shall be served on the respondent.

(2) Proof of service of an application on the other parties shall be filed within 10 days after the application is served.

SOR/98-235, s. 3.

Notice of Appearance

8. (1) A respondent who is served with an application shall serve a notice of appearance in accordance with Form IR-2 as set out in the schedule on the applicant and the tribunal, and file it, together with proof of service, within 10 days after service of the application.

(2) A respondent who has failed to file a notice of appearance in accordance with subrule (1) shall not be entitled to any further notice or service of any further document in the proceeding.

Obtaining Tribunal's Decision and Reasons

9. (1) Where an application sets out that the applicant has not received the written reasons of the tribunal, the Registry shall forthwith send the tribunal a written request in Form IR-3 as set out in the schedule.

(2) Upon receipt of a request under subrule (1) a tribunal shall, without delay,

(a) send a copy of the decision or order, and written reasons therefor, duly certified by an appropriate officer to be correct, to each of the parties, and two copies of the Registry; or

(b) if no reasons were given for the decision or order in respect of which the application is made, or reasons were given but not recorded, send an appropriate written notice to all the parties and the Registry.

(3) A tribunal shall be deemed to have received a request under subrule (1) on the tenth day after it was sent by mail by the Registry.

(4) The applicant shall be deemed to have received the written reasons, or the notice referred to in paragraph 9(2)(*b*), as the case may be, on the tenth day after it was sent by mail by the tribunal.

Case Law

Paul v. Canada (Minister of Employment & Immigration) (1994), 81 F.T.R. 14 (Fed. T.D.) — This was a motion on behalf of the applicant for an order compelling the Appeal Division to provide written reasons for its denial of the applicant's appeal of a deportation order. Section 69.4(5) requires reasons to be given, where they are requested, within ten days of the disposition of the appeal. The applicant did not request written reasons within that period of time, but nevertheless argued that Rule 9 of the *Federal Court Rules* must take precedence over the *Immigration Act*. The application was dismissed.

The true purpose of Rule 9 is to ensure that all parties are provided with reasons when they are available, and notified when they are not available. Neither the *Immigration Act* nor the rules compel the Board to produce written reasons, unless requested to do so by one of the parties within ten days following the communication of the decision. Absent an attack on the vires of section 69.4(5), the Board's refusal to provide written reasons, where none were requested, must be upheld.

PERFECTING APPLICATION FOR LEAVE

10. (1) The applicant shall perfect an application for leave by complying with subrule (2)

(a) where the application sets out that the applicant has received the tribunal's written reasons, within 30 days after filing the application; or

(b) where the application sets out that the applicant has not received the tribunal's written reasons, within 30 days after receiving either the written reasons, or the notice under paragraph 9(2)(*b*), as the case may be.

(2) The applicant shall serve on every respondent who has filed and served a notice of appearance, a record containing the following, on consecutively numbered pages, and in the following order

(a) the application for leave,

(b) the decision or order, if any, in respect of which the application is made,

(c) the written reasons given by the tribunal, or the notice under paragraph 9(2)(*b*), as the case may be,

(d) one or more supporting affidavits verifying the facts relied on by the applicant in support of the application, and

(e) a memorandum of argument which shall set out concise written submissions of the facts and law relied upon by the applicant for the relief proposed should leave be granted,

and file it, together with proof of service.

Case Law

Section 10(1)

Bhui v. Canada (Minister of Citizenship & Immigration) (March 11, 1996), Doc. IMM-3385-95 (Fed. T.D.) — The court had before it a motion by the applicant for an extension of the time limits set out in Rule 10(1) for serving and filing the applicant's record.

In January 1996, the applicant filed his record within the time required by the rules. The record did not include a memorandum of argument. Counsel provided the court with an affidavit indicating that he did not feel it was necessary to include a memorandum of argument in the record, and therefore did not do so.

The respondent took the position that the applicant's record was not complete and not perfected within the time period provided by the rules.

The filing and service of the applicant's record are official in the court file. There cannot, therefore, be in this case an extension of time to perform acts that have already been done.

If the motion were granted allowing the inclusion of the memorandum of argument in the applicant's record, there would be no additional delays in dealing with the application and no evidence to suggest that the respondent would otherwise be prejudiced. There was nothing in the evidence to support the suggestion that counsel for the applicant was seeking to file the applicant's record in successive steps in order to avoid the time limits set out in Rule 10.

Accordingly, the memorandum of argument was permitted to be filed with the court as part of the applicant's record.

Moreno v. Canada (Minister of Citizenship & Immigration) (1996), 33 Imm. L.R. (2d) 84, (sub nom. *Moreno v. Canada (Ministre de la Citoyenneté l'Immigration))* 110 F.T.R. 57 (Fed. T.D.) — This was a motion pursuant to Rule 21(2) of the *Federal Court Immigration Rules* for an extension of the time limit under Rule 10(1) for serving and filing the applicant's record.

The Court expects the time limit set out in the rules to be complied with and an automatic extension is not available merely because it is requested. An applicant must show that there was some justification for the delay throughout the whole period of the delay and that the applicant has an arguable case. The applicant must demonstrate some reason for the delay which was beyond its control or the control of its counsel, for example, illness, or some other unexpected or unanticipated event. This motion failed because there was a lack of an explanation for the extension and, furthermore, there were no arguments advanced to show that the applicants had an arguable case.

Amevenu v. Canada (Solicitor General) (1994), 27 Imm. L.R. (2d) 157, 88 F.T.R. 142 (Fed. T.D.) — The applicant failed to file a record within 30 days after the filing of the leave application. The respondent submitted that the application for judicial review should therefore be dismissed. This argument was not considered. The Court granted leave despite the fact that the application record was not filed on time. The respondent, at the time the leave application was pending, did not raise the argument that the record was filed outside of the time limit. To raise the issue of the time limit over 2 months after leave was granted, and only a week before the judicial review application was to be argued, was unfair and the Court declined to consider the respondent's argument.

Section 10(2)

Parveen v. Canada (Minister of Citizenship & Immigration) (April 29, 1999), Doc. IMM-3587-98 (Fed. T.D.) — This was an application to review and set aside a visa officer's decision denying the applicant a permanent visa. The record that was provided to the Court by the respondent was incomplete. It had been "stripped". Counsel for the respondent advised the Court that this occurred because of a "thin file" policy and the difficulty of retaining the full files for all the individuals applying for immigration to Canada in the various embassies abroad.

The period of time within which a person can file an appeal from a visa officer's decision is limited. The Court could not accept that the administrative burden of retaining the full file for that period of time was unduly onerous. The respondent controls the record that is put before the Court, thus any disputes that arise as a result of diffiency in the record should, in general, be interpreted against the respondent. An incomplete record alone could be grounds, in some circumstances, for setting aside a decision.

Finally, the Court refused to adopt the approach suggested by counsel for the respondent to the effect that visa officer's have no interest in these applications. The Court observed that once a visa officer's decision is challenged that he or she has an interest in justifying his or her decision. This was an entirely natural reaction and at that point the visa officer was not, in the Court's view a disinterested person.

Chen v. Canada (Minister of Citizenship & Immigration) (1999), 240 N.R. 376, 174 D.L.R. (4th) 165 (Fed. C.A.) — This was an appeal from a judgement of the trial division dismissing an application to review a determination of a panel of the CRDD that the appellant was not a Convention refugee. The motions judge did not err in refusing to make the audio tape of the proceedings part of the record, or listen to it, in coming to his decision on the matter before him. Neither the Immigration Act nor the relevant Rules require video tapes to be made part of the record. The witness whose credibility was questioned by the refugee division was seen and heard by that body as the trier of fact. They enjoyed unique advantages in coming to their findings and especially so in making findings upon an assessment of the witnesses' credibility. This principle applies even where a court has asked us to review a decision in the light of an audio-taped record. The advantage of having seen the witness is lost to the reviewing court. A tape recording of a proceeding may be accepted to establish some fundamental unfairness in the conduct of a hearing amounting to a denial of natural justice.

The motions judge was under no obligation to make the audio tape part of the record or to listen to it, so as to allow himself to make an independent assessment of the appellant's credibility.

Ou v. Canada (Minister of Citizenship & Immigration) (1999), 48 Imm. L.R. (2d) 131 (Fed. T.D.) — In December 1996, the applicant arrived in Canada from China. He made a claim to refugee status. In July of 1997, he notified the Board of his address and telephone number in Toronto. On that same date, he was informed that his claim would be referred to the Board for determination and that he would be required to appear in September 1997. On September 18, 1997, the Board sent a notice to appear for conference to the applicant at his address. On September 25, 1997, the applicant personally delivered to the Board's registry a letter indicating that he wished to delay his hearing date in order to retain counsel. On October 7, 1997, a Board employee attempted to telephone the applicant to advise him that it was not sufficient for him to deliver a letter requesting a delay and that he was required to attend in person. The employee was told that there was "no such person at that telephone number". On October 30, 1997, the Board sent the applicant a notice to appear for abandonment of a Convention refugee claim. The applicant immediately retained counsel. On December 1,

1997, the applicant attended the abandonment hearing. The Board decided that the applicant had abandoned his claim. It is with respect to that decision that the applicant sought judicial review.

The applicant filed a supplementary affidavit from his landlord's daughter, who indicated that she had received a telephone call from Canadian immigration offices and at the time did not know the applicant's name and as well that her parent's had a number of tenants in the house at that time.

On an application for judicial review an applicant in an attempt to justify his absence from the Board hearing may tender fresh evidence. The Court noted that a finding of abandonment precludes a consideration of a Convention refugee claim on its merits. The Court set aside the Boards decision that the applicant's claim had been abandoned and ordered a new hearing on that question.

Yau v. Canada (Minister of Citizenship & Immigration) (August 18, 1998), Doc. IMM-1609-98 (Fed. T.D.) — The applicant was seeking to review a decision of a visa officer and brought two motions. The first, requested permission to file an additional affidavit, and the second, for an extension of time within which to file the record including the additional affidavit. When the applicant commenced his application for judicial review, he was of the opinion that he had been turned down as a self-employed person for two reasons mentioned by the visa officer in his letter of rejection. These reasons were that the applicant had no experience as a self-employed person and that the landing of the applicant would result in no significant economic benefit to Canada. However, in his affidavit filed in opposition to the applicant, the visa officer suggested additional reasons, namely that the applicant had not supplied him with up-to-date financial data, that the applicant's financial assets were insufficient for his purposes, that the applicant had not conducted any research into the Canadian market, and that the applicant had no business plan.

Assuming that the visa officer refused the applicant, relying on facts that were not drawn to the applicant's attention, and with respect to which the applicant at the interview was given no opportunity to comment, it was appropriate that the applicant be given an opportunity to supplement the information supplied at the original interview. The proposed affidavit was offered for the purpose of showing that evidence of such a nature was available had the visa officer indicated a need to produce it. The affidavit also explained why a business plan and a proof of net worth were not placed before the visa officer namely because they had been stolen some two days earlier in San Francisco.

The proposed affidavit was admitted not for the purpose of showing that the decision of the visa officer was wrong, but for the purpose of supporting an attack on the process.

Kuchin v. Canada (Minister of Citizenship & Immigration) (August 1, 1995), Doc. IMM-1015-95 (Fed. T.D.) — The applicant sought an extension of time to file a reply. There is no provision for any reply evidence, only reply argument. If reply evidence were to be permitted, it would result in the respondent having to give its final argument before all the evidence was filed.

Awogbade v. Canada (Minister of Citizenship & Immigration) (1995), 29 Imm. L.R. (2d) 281, 94 F.T.R. 184 (Fed. T.D.) — The applicant applied for leave to take judicial review proceedings against a decision of the CRDD. One month after filing the originating motion, the applicant's solicitors sought to extend the time for filing her application record. Additional time was refused by the Court and the applicant brought an application for reconsideration of that order.

In a solicitor/client relationship, there is a strong fiduciary obligation on the solicitor's part to act in a professional, timely manner in order to advance the client's interests. The Ontario

Legal Aid plan merely authorizes the payment of fees for the lawyer's services. A professional ethical lawyer will not leave his or her client in the lurch merely because fees are not secured.

It may be that allowing a client's case to turn to ashes while awaiting spurious authorization from legal aid, is contempt of Court.

There are several valid reasons for which a judge could extend the time to file an applicant's record, but waiting for a legal aid certificate is not one of them.

The absence of an application record is a substantive defect as well as a procedural one, and an order dismissing additional time for the filing of an application is a final one.

It is a species of professional misconduct for a lawyer to prefer the securing of his or her own fees over the client's interests.

The Court noted that the reasons of the CRDD had not been filed with the original request for an extension of time and considered that this failure on the part of the applicant's solicitors, provided it with a reason to relieve the applicant of the prejudice created by the conduct of her solicitors, and accordingly, reconsidered its order and granted to the applicant a short extension to file her application record.

Abdullahi v. Canada (Minister of Employment & Immigration) (1995), 91 F.T.R. 309 (Fed. T.D.) — The applicant sought to review a negative decision of the CRDD. Certain evidence referred to by counsel for the applicant was filed under cover of counsel's own affidavit. This documentary evidence post-dated the date of the hearing. The Court was not satisfied of the relevance of the material on the issue of the well-foundedness of the claim in question. The issue before the Court was the relevance of the material in the context of a judicial review application. The documentary evidence covered by counsel's affidavit post-dating the date of the hearing was clearly not before the CRDD and not relevant to the judicial review application and the Court would not take it into account.

Lieu v. Canada (Minister of Employment & Immigration) (June 2, 1994), Doc. IMM-589-94 (Fed. T.D.) — This application for an extension of time for the filing of a record in support of an application for leave and for judicial review was denied. The applicant's record was due on March 9. The applicant's lawyer required a legal aid certificate and as the next monthly meeting of the Area Committee was on March 15, he filed his opinion with the Area Committee on March 12. The affidavit of the applicant's lawyer did not disclose whether or not the opinion was received in time for inclusion on the Area Committee's March 15 agenda. This seemed unlikely as March 12 was a Saturday. No justification for the last-minute filing of the opinion was offered. It could have been prepared as early as mid-February.

The material further disclosed that as of May 23 the Area Committee had not decided whether to issue a legal aid certificate and the Court was asked to grant an open-ended indefinite extension of time. In addition, the material filed did not sufficiently address the merits of the application so as to demonstrate a good case on the merits. Finally, the Court noted that bald allegations of Charter violations without more would not suffice when the onus was on the applicant to show a good case to justify an extension.

Accordingly, the application for an extension of time was dismissed.

Koulibaly v. Canada (Solicitor General) (1993), 93 F.T.R. 241 (Fed. T.D.) — The Court granted an order permitting the applicant to serve and file the applicant's record outside the time allowed under section 10(2) of the *Immigration Rules* of the Federal Court. In support of the motion, the applicant filed the affidavit of his counsel stating that he had been unable to contact the applicant within the time required. It would have been preferable to file the affidavit of the applicant himself, on this question, stating in the affidavit that the applicant had not been available.

Bains v. Canada (Minister of Employment & Immigration) (1990), 47 Admin. L.R. 317, 109 N.R. 239 (Fed. C.A.) — The only question to be considered in disposing of an application for leave under section 82.1(1) or 82.3(1) is whether or not a fairly arguable case is disclosed for the relief proposed to be sought if leave is granted. Further, the need for material not immediately available has to be established by the applicant and the mere stated intention to rely on such material does not, without an application and an order to that end, operate to extend the time provided by the *Federal Court Immigration Rules* for the applicant to file an affidavit and/or representations in support of the leave application. The requirement for leave is, in reality, the other side of the coin of the traditional jurisdiction to summarily terminate proceedings that disclose no reasonably arguable case. The requirement for leave does not deny refugee claimants access to the court. The right to apply for leave is, itself, a right of access to the court and the requirement that leave be obtained before an appeal or application for judicial review may proceed does not impair the right guaranteed by refugee claimants under either section 7 or 15 of the Charter.

RESPONDENT'S AFFIDAVITS AND MEMORANDUM OF ARGUMENT

11. A respondent who opposes an application

(a) may serve on the other parties one or more affidavits, and

(b) shall serve on the other parties a memorandum of argument which shall set out concise written submissions of the facts and law relied upon by the respondent,

and file them, together with proof of service, within 30 days after service of the documents referred to in subrule 10(2).

AFFIDAVITS

12. (1) Affidavits filed in connection with an application shall be confined to such evidence as the deponent could give if testifying as a witness before the Court.

(2) Unless a judge for special reasons so orders, no cross-examination of a deponent on an affidavit filed in connection with an application is permitted before leave to commence an application for judicial review is granted.

Case Law

Section 12(1)

Samolenko v. Canada (Minister of Citizenship & Immigration) (July 28, 1997), Doc. IMM-4141-96 (Fed. T.D.) — The applicant sought to review a negative decision by a visa officer with respect to her application for permanent residence under the independent category. The applicant listed her occupation as a computer graphics specialist. In addition, the applicant alleged that she sent a supplementary application to the visa officer prior to the refusal that was the subject matter of this proceeding. That supplementary application was said to have contained an additional occupational category, namely that of an arts supervisor. The respondent disputed receipt of the supplementary application. The applicant was not assessed as an arts supervisor.

A visa officer has a duty to assess an application with reference to each occupation represented by the applicant as one for which he or she is qualified and prepared to pursue in Canada. Further, there is the clear responsibility on the part of a visa officer to assess alternative occupations inherent in the applicant's work experience.

There was no evidence to establish that the supplementary application was in fact before the visa officer. The copy of the supplementary application submitted by the applicant as part of its application for judicial review did not contain any evidence to suggest receipt of it by the respondent. The respondent specifically denied that any supplementary application was received by the embassy. The only evidence submitted by the applicant was an affidavit of a solicitor who practised in association with counsel for the applicant. This solicitor's affidavit deposed that the source of his information and belief was the applicant's solicitor, who could not reasonably be expected to have personal knowledge of the matter.

Accordingly, the applicant had failed to prove that the supplementary application was before the visa officer and the application for judicial review was therefore dismissed.

Prajapati v. Canada (Minister of Citizenship & Immigration) (1995), 31 Imm. L.R. (2d) 182, 103 F.T.R. 37 (Fed. T.D.) — This was an application to review a decision of a visa officer rejecting the applicant's application for permanent residence.

The sole affidavit filed in support of the application was that of the solicitor of record. The affidavit attested to the filing of the applicant's application. It further attested to the submissions of the undertaking of assistance and annexed that document and attested to the acknowledgement of receipt of the undertaking of assistance, also annexed. The affidavit attested to the fact that the applicant was invited to a personal interview and a copy of the invitation letter was annexed. It also deposed to the fact that the applicant attended the interview and thereafter informed his solicitor that the visa officer was "fully satisfied with the applicant's answers and congratulated him". The applicant's letter to his solicitor in this regard setting out the applicants report of the interview was also annexed. Finally, the affidavit deposed to the rejection of the applicant's application and an annexed copy of the rejection letter. The paragraph referring to the applicant's report of the interview was numbered 6 in the affidavit.

Hearsay evidence is now admissible on a principle basis, the governing principles being the reliability of the evidence and its necessity. Paragraph 6 was clearly hearsay. Its reliability was brought into question by the divergencies between it and the affidavit of the visa officer filed by the respondent. Accordingly, paragraph 6 was struck out.

Due to the fact that the challenge to the affidavit in support of the applicant's application was, in fact, a challenge to the application itself, because if the affidavit was struck out the application would be without a supporting factual basis, it was appropriate for the respondent to argue this issue at the hearing of the motion itself.

Patel v. Canada (Minister of Citizenship & Immigration) (1995), 31 Imm. L.R. (2d) 24, 103 F.T.R. 21 (Fed. T.D.) — This was an application to set aside a decision of a visa officer refusing an application for permanent residence. The application for judicial review was supported by the affidavit of the applicant's solicitor of record. The solicitor's affidavit provided no basis for reviewing the visa officer's decision. The affidavit presented only sworn statements about the application process and a confirmation of a negative reply. There was no information about the conduct of the interview, nor any grounds for disputing the visa officer's assessment. It is wholly inappropriate for solicitors to submit their own affidavits in support of an application for judicial review. The court considered the application on its merits but accorded the solicitor's affidavit very little weight.

Section 12(2)

Kanes v. Canada (Minister of Employment & Immigration) (1993), 22 Imm. L.R. (2d) 223, 72 F.T.R. 226 (Fed. T.D.) — The applicant brought an interlocutory motion in the course of prosecuting an application for leave seeking permission to cross-examine one Lalita Jeethan on an affidavit she filed on the leave application.

The applicant alleged that there were inaccuracies in the affidavit. The inaccuracies in this case could not be clarified further by cross-examination. The answer, if any, must be found in the documentary evidence attached to the affidavit, namely the applicant's application for permanent residence wherein he answered "No" to the question "Have you ... ever been convicted of or currently charged with any crime or offence..." Further, the deponent, Jeethan, claimed no personal involvement in the handling of the file, therefore, the Court could not appreciate how it would be further enlightened by her cross-examination. On the question of when documents were received by the Commission, this issue would be resolved better, the Court felt, by examining the document.

Finally, the Court noted that a judge dealing with an application for leave is not required to make factual findings, but simply to determine whether a serious issue has been raised. The application for leave process is designed to provide a relatively simple and speedy process for the Court to determine whether there is a serious question that should be dealt with by a normal judicial review process. Judges are not expected to make findings of fact or resolve conflicts in the evidence at that stage.

The Court declined to order costs against the applicant in this case because this was a matter of first impression. It did indicate, however, that it would consider ordering costs where future interlocutory motions were brought on such an insubstantial basis.

REPLY MEMORANDUM

13. Where a respondent serves a memorandum of argument, an applicant may serve a memorandum of argument in reply thereto, and shall file it, together with proof of service, within 10 days after the day of service of the respondent's memorandum of argument.

Case Law

Beci v. Canada (Minister of Citizenship & Immigration) (1997), 130 F.T.R. 267 (Fed. T.D.) — The applicant sought leave to file an affidavit in reply to prove certain allegations contained in the applicant's reply.

There is no provision in the *Federal Court Immigration Rules* for evidence in reply. Where it comes to the applicant's attention after the record has been filed, that certain material was before the tribunal at the hearing which is not mentioned in the record, leave can be given for affidavit evidence to be filed in Reply or alternatively, the time may be extended within which to file an amended record.

In this case, new evidence had come to the attention of the applicant's counsel, which might have altered the decision of the tribunal had it been considered. The fact that such information had been uncovered since the tribunal's decision is irrelevant to a judicial review of that decision. Accordingly, the motion for leave was dismissed.

DISPOSITION OF APPLICATION FOR LEAVE

14. (1) Where

(a) any party has failed to serve and file any document required by these Rules within the time fixed, or

(b) the applicant's reply memorandum has been filed, or the time for filing it has expired,

a judge may, without further notice to the parties, determine the application for leave on the basis of the materials then filed.

(2) Where the judge considers that documents in the possession or control of the tribunal are required for the proper disposition of the application for leave, the judge may, by order, specify the documents to be produced and filed and give such other directions as the judge considers necessary to dispose of the application for leave.

(3) The Registry shall send to the tribunal a copy of an order made under subrule (2) forthwith after it is made.

(4) Upon receipt of an order under subrule (2), the tribunal shall, without delay, send a copy of the materials specified in the order, duly certified by an appropriate officer to be correct, to each of the parties, and two copies to the Registry.

(5) The tribunal shall be deemed to have received a copy of the order on the tenth day after it was sent by mail by the Registry.

Case Law

Karakulak v. Canada (Minister of Employment & Immigration) (1995), 98 F.T.R. 81 (Fed. T.D.) — This was an application for an extension of time to file a reply and it arose because the notes of the immigration officer who made the impugned decision were not available and there were no written reasons for the decision. The notes had been refused pursuant to the provisions of the *Privacy Act.* The Court would not order the missing pages produced, nor would it agree to extend the time to file a reply for an unlimited period. The applicant industriously pursued the pages, and if this had not been the case, the applicant would have been required to proceed without them. Immigration Rule 14 enables a judge to order the production of documents refused by a tribunal claiming *quasi*-judicial privilege, but it does not permit a judge to order the production of documents protected by the *Privacy Act.*

Nguyen v. Canada (Minister of Employment & Immigration) (1993), 66 F.T.R. 75, [1994] 1 F.C. 96, 107 D.L.R. (4th) 186 (Fed. T.D.) — The applicant filed an application for leave to challenge a decision of the CRDD denying the applicant refugee status. The applicant obtained a letter from the official reporter of the Board disclosing that no official transcript of the proceedings had been prepared and questioning the accuracy of the Board's quotations of the evidence. The letter from the official reporter was included in the applicant's record. The respondent Minister took the position that there was no evidence that the portions of the testimony quoted were inaccurate. The applicant filed a reply memorandum to which was attached, under cover of an affidavit of the official reporter, a transcript of the proceedings. The respondent Minister objected to the filing of the transcript in reply.

Federal Court Immigration Rule 13 states that an applicant may file a memorandum of argument in reply, but it does not specifically state that no other material may be filed. Federal Court Immigration Rule 4(1) provides that Part I, and other parts of the F*ederal Court Rules*, apply to immigration applications, except to the extent that they are inconsistent with the *Federal Court Immigration Rules. Federal Court Rules* 5 and 6 are sufficient authority for the granting of leave to the applicant to file a copy of the official transcript under cover of the affidavit of the official reporter. In addition, Federal Court Immigration Rule 14(2) provides authority to direct the filing of the transcript.

15. (1) An order granting an application for leave

(a) shall fix the place and language, and a day that is no sooner than thirty days and no later than ninety days after the date of the order, for the hearing of the application for judicial review;

(b) shall specify the time limit within which the tribunal is to send copies of its record required under Rule 17;

(c) shall specify the time limits within which further materials, if any, including affidavits, transcripts of cross-examinations, and memoranda of argument are to be served and filed;

(d) shall specify the time limits within which cross-examinations, if any, on affidavits are to be completed; and

(e) may specify any other matter that the judge considers necessary or expedient for the hearing of the application for judicial review.

(2) The Registry shall send to the tribunal a copy of an order granting leave forthwith after it is made.

(3) The tribunal shall be deemed to have received a copy of the order on the tenth day after it was sent by mail by the Registry.

16. Where leave is granted, all documents filed in connection with the application for leave shall be retained by the Registry for consideration by the judge hearing the application for judicial review.

Obtaining Tribunal's Record

17. Upon receipt of an order under Rule 15, a tribunal shall, without delay, prepare a record containing the following, on consecutively numbered pages and in the following order:

(a) the decision or order in respect of which the application is made and the written reasons given therefor,

(b) all papers relevant to the matter that are in the possession or control of the tribunal,

(c) any affidavits, or other documents filed during any such hearing, and

(d) a transcript, if any, of any oral testimony given during the hearing, giving rise to the decision or order or other matter that is the subject of the application,

and shall send a copy, duly certified by an appropriate officer to be correct, to each of the parties and two copies to the Registry.

Case Law

Parveen v. Canada (Minister of Citizenship & Immigration) (April 29, 1999), Doc. IMM-3587-98 (Fed. T.D.) — This was an application to review and set aside a visa officer's decision denying the applicant a permanent visa. The record that was provided to the Court by the respondent was incomplete. It had been "stripped". Counsel for the respondent advised the Court that this occurred because of a "thin file" policy and the difficulty of retaining the full files for all the individuals applying for immigration to Canada in the various embassies abroad.

The period of time within which a person can file an appeal from a visa officer's decision is limited. The Court could not accept that the administrative burden of retaining the full file for that period of time was unduly onerous. The respondent controls the record that is put before the Court, thus any disputes that arise as a result of diffiency in the record should, in general, be interpreted against the respondent. An incomplete record alone could be grounds, in some circumstances, for setting aside a decision.

Finally, the Court refused to adopt the approach suggested by counsel for the respondent to the effect that visa officers have no interest in these applications. The Court observed that once a visa officer's decision is challenged he or she has an interest in justifying his or her decision. This was an entirely natural reaction and at that point the visa officer was not, in the Court's view, a disinterested person.

Bertold v. Canada (Minister of Citizenship & Immigration) (1997), 126 F.T.R. 216 (Fed. T.D.) — On December 3, 1996, the court granted leave for the applicant to institute judicial review. The Acting Director General, Case Management Branch, failed or neglected to comply with Federal Court Immigration Rule 17 in accordance with the Court's order that certified copies of the tribunal record be sent before or on December 30, 1996.

Section 82.1(7) requires that a judicial review hearing must be set down for hearing no later than 90 days after leave for judicial review was granted. There is nothing in the *Immigration Act* or the *Federal Court Immigration Rules* which allows this time limit to be extended. Due to the fact that neither the *Immigration Act* nor the *Federal Court Immigration Rules* contemplate such an extension, reference may be had to the *Federal Court Rules*. However, Rule 3(1)(c) applies only to extensions of time prescribed by the Rules and to any order. It is clear that the Court cannot extend the period of time prescribed by statute.

It would be unjust to leave the applicant without recourse and, of course, both parties need to have the opportunity to file further affidavits and to cross-examine in regard to the tribunal's record. It would be unjust to let the tribunal (the Acting Director General Case Management Branch) abort the applicant's right to institute judicial review through the tribunal's own failure, neglect or refusal to obey Immigration Rule 17.

The tribunal was found to have perpetrated an injustice upon the applicant by frustrating the Court's powers and was required to show cause why it ought not to be punished for contempt of Court. The Court ordered that either party may prosecute the contempt application under Rule 355(3).

The Court observed that in the event the judicial review application was commenced on the date previously fixed it would be open to the judge seized of the matter to adjourn the application to a later date for completion.

Sajjan v. Canada (Minister of Citizenship & Immigration) (1997), 125 F.T.R. 198 (Fed. T.D.); reversed (1997), 39 Imm. L.R. (2d) 56, (sub nom. *Canada (Minister of Citizenship & Immigration) v. Sajjan)* 216 N.R. 150 (Fed. C.A.) — The applicant sought judicial review of a decision of the Immigration Appeal Division of the IRB, to the effect that the applicant's adopted son was not a member of the family class and that therefore the panel was without jurisdiction to hear an appeal, under subsection 77(3), of a decision of a visa officer under subsection 77(1).

Leave of a judge of the Federal Court is not required to commence this type of application for judicial review. The Appeal Division is not under an obligation to prepare a record, including a transcript, of the oral hearing before the panel and to provide a copy of that record to the applicant. Such an obligation arises under section 17 of the *Federal Court Immigration Rules*. The obligation under section 17 arises "upon receipt of an order under rule 15....". An order under Rule 15 is an order granting an application for leave. No application for leave is required in these circumstances and, accordingly, in the absence of such an application, no obligation is placed on the Board by Rule 17. In the result, the Board was correct in concluding that it had no obligation in law to provide to the applicant a record of the proceedings before the panel. This creates an anomalous situation under which neither an applicant or the Court has a right to require of the Board a record of its proceedings. The Court observed that an amendment to the *Immigration Act* or the *Federal Court Immigration Rules* may be required.

Vergara v. Canada (Minister of Employment & Immigration) (1994), 25 Imm. L.R. (2d) 197, (sub nom. *Ortiz Vergara v. Canada (Ministre de l'Emploi & l'Immigration))* 84 F.T.R. 34 (Fed. T.D.) — The applicant obtained leave to file an application for judicial review from a decision of a panel of the CRDD. The applicant wanted to enter in evidence on the leave application "the Peru File". This file was entered as an exhibit at the refugee hearing.

The interests of justice do not, however, require that all documents entered at the refugee hearing be reproduced in their entirety for purposes of the judicial review application. A party wishing to use documents on the judicial review application which were part of the Standardized Country File, should draw the Court's attention to the exhibits which it intends to use by attaching them to its submission. It should send a copy to the Court and to the other party before the hearing, thus informing them of the documents to which it intends to refer at the hearing. The opposing party, in turn, can append to its own submission documents taken from the Standardized Country File which it intends to use.

Lemiecha v. Canada (Minister of Employment & Immigration) (1993), 72 F.T.R. 49 (Fed. T.D.) — This was an application to review a decision that there were no humanitarian or compassionate grounds to permit the applicants to remain in Canada. The applicants were a married couple and their two children. They arrived in Canada during the summer and autumn of 1989. They claimed Convention refugee status and these claims were denied in August, 1990. In April, 1991, through a solicitor, they applied for a review on humanitarian and compassionate grounds. A medical update on their nine-year old son was completed in September, 1991, but not forwarded to the Immigration Centre. Without either of the medical reports having been brought to their attention, through no fault of the respondent, the humanitarian and compassionate review resulted in a negative decision. A further review was conducted on the eve of what was to be the applicants' departure for Poland. One of the medical reports that had been prepared with respect to the son was forwarded to the officer conducting that review. The officer, after seeking advice from a Canada Immigration physician, refused humanitarian and compassionate relief, and it was that decision that was the subject of this application.

The application failed. The applicants were aware of their nine-year old son's medical condition and its relevance to a humanitarian and compassionate review. The applicants had many months to supply information regarding medical expertise, services and facilities available in Poland and environmental conditions in that country and their relationship to the son's asthmatic condition. The applicants did not submit this information.

Judicial review of a decision of a federal board, commission or other tribunal should proceed on the basis of the evidence that was before the decision maker. Accordingly, the evidence of the medical experts which was tendered on the judicial review application but not submitted to the officer whose decision was under attack, was not admissible. There was essentially no evidence before the officer whose decision was under attack regarding any link between conditions in Poland, environmental or otherwise, and the nine-year old son's medical difficulties. Accordingly, the application for judicial review was dismissed.

Disposition of Application for Judicial Review

18. (1) A judge shall not render judgment in respect of an application for judicial review without first giving the parties an opportunity to make a request that the judge certify that a serious question of general importance as contemplated by section 83 of the Act is involved.

(2) A party who requests that the judge certify that a serious question of general importance is involved shall specify the precise question.

(3) For the purposes of this Rule, an application for judicial review includes an application for judicial review of a decision of a visa officer.

Appeals

19. [Revoked SOR/98-235, s. 4.]

20. (1) An appeal to the Court of Appeal shall be commenced by filing a notice of appeal in Form IR-4 as set out in the schedule within

(a) 15 days after the pronouncement of the judgment under appeal; or

(b) such further time as may be ordered by a judge of the Federal Court — Trial Division.

(2) A notice of appeal shall be served on all parties and proof of service filed within 15 days after the notice of appeal is filed.

SOR/98-235, s. 4.

Case Law

Dasent v. Canada (Minister of Citizenship & Immigration) (1995), 28 Imm. L.R. (2d) 28, 92 F.T.R. 103 (Fed. T.D.) — The respondent moved to extend the time for filing a notice of appeal. The order that was being appealed was signed by the Judge on December 8, 1994, but not entered in the registry until December 13, 1994. The order in question was pronounced upon the date on which the judge signed it, namely December 8, 1994.

The notice of appeal must be filed within 15 days after the pronouncement of the judgment which includes the order. The time in this case expired on December 23, 1994. The respondent attempted to file the notice of appeal on December 28, 1994.

In arriving at the decision to extend the time the Court considered, firstly, special circumstances. In this case the Court found that the respondent's counsel was probably misled by the date stamp on the judgment. The Court then considered whether there was prejudice to the applicant in extending the time, whether the respondent had an intention to appeal within the 15 days, whether the delay in requesting an extension was undue, and finally whether the interests of justice mandated the granting of an extension.

TIME LIMITS

21. (1) [Revoked SOR/98-235, s. 5.]

(2) No time limit prescribed by these Rules may be varied except by order of a judge or prothonotary.

SOR/98-235, s. 5.

Case Law

Section 21(2)

Abaev v. Canada (Minister of Citizenship & Immigration) (1999), 49 Imm. L.R. (2d) 29 (Fed. T.D.) — The applicant brings a motion for an extension of time to file affidavits and extensions of time for the completion of other steps in this proceeding. This was an application to review a visa officer's decision. Pursuant to Federal Court Rule 318, the tribunal (a visa officer in the Immigration Section of the Canadian Consulate General in New York) was required to "transmit" the material in its possession within 20 days of the request for such being made. Transmit means more than merely depositing in the post without regard to the amount of time it might take to reach the applicant or his counsel. The Rules intend that the applicant have access to the relevant tribunal material before his or her affidavits are required to be filed in order to review that material to see if it is relevant for the purpose of preparing the affidavits. The Rules allow for a 10-day difference between the transmitting of the material and the filing of the affidavits. The action taken in this case did not constitute the transmitting of the material to the applicant within the required time. In addition to allowing the application, the Court awarded costs on the motion fixed in the amount of $1,000.00.

Shaker v. Canada (Minister of Citizenship & Immigration) (September 23, 1998), Doc. IMM-3448-98 (Fed. T.D.) — The applicant filed a motion for an extension of time within which to file her application record. The applicant filed, in support, an affidavit evidencing the delay and exhibiting only the cover page of the application record. There was no evidence of an arguable case and so the motion was refused with leave to reapply. The applicant reapplied and this time supported the application by the very record for which leave to file was sought. This material was filed to show an arguable case. In the ordinary course the Court would have returned the record to the applicant. It may well be that all of the evidence of an arguable case is to be found in certain documents and affidavits in the application record. Those documents and affidavits, however, have an independent existence and duplicates could have been exhibited to affidavits with the appropriate explanations in the motion record. Notwithstanding the Court's reservations about the materials, the Court allowed an extension of time to file the application record.

Mikhail v. Canada (Minister of Citizenship & Immigration) (1998), 46 Imm. L.R. (2d) 93, 150 F.T.R. 318 (Fed. T.D.) — This motion sought an extension of time within which to file a reply. The motion is supported by an affidavit exhibiting the reply sought to be filed. The filing of a reply as an exhibit to an affidavit when the reply cannot be filed without leave is improper.

Canada (Minister of Citizenship & Immigration) v. Singh (S.M.) (1997), 140 F.T.R. 102, 41 Imm. L.R. (2d) 284 (Fed. T.D.) — The respondent sought to have the applicant Minister's application for leave struck out, on the grounds that the applicant failed to file an application record within the time allowed. The applicant sought an extension of time within which to file his record.

The applicant failed to satisfy either branch of the test for a time extension set out in *Beilin v. Canada (Minister of Employment & Immigration)* (1994), 88 F.T.R. 132 at 134. The Court can grant an extension notwithstanding this fact for the purpose of doing justice between the parties.

If there had been some indication in the material that the applicant had an arguable case, then the Court would have considered whether, to do justice between the parties, a time extension ought to be allowed. The absence of such evidence required that the application for an extension be dismissed and the respondent's motion seeking a dismissal of the application for judicial review was allowed.

Avalos v. Canada (Minister of Citizenship & Immigration) (1997), (sub nom. *Avalos v. Canada (Ministre de la Citoyenneté & de l'Immigration))* 136 F.T.R. 125 (Fed. T.D.) — The applicants sought an extension of time for filing their records. An application for an extension of time in order to be successful must be accompanied by material which shows some justification for the delay, throughout the whole period of the delay, and secondly that the applicant has an arguable case. With respect to the explanation as to why it was not possible to comply with the whole of the time limit set out in subsection 10 of the Rules, the Court noted that the reason must be beyond the control of counsel or the applicant for example, illness or some other unexpected or unanticipated event.

The Court was not satisfied that this case involve an unexpected event. The Court noted that less than 5 months before, counsel for the applicants approached the Court in two other cases seeking extensions of time allowed by Rule 10 and sighting difficulty in filing the records on time. The Court noted that neither the applicant nor counsel gave any details by affidavit which would suggest that the case was arguable on the merits and accordingly the motion for an extension of time was dismissed.

The Court noted that it would have considered awarding costs against the solicitor personally had there been a request to that effect.

Iakolev v. Canada (Minister of Citizenship & Immigration) (May 10, 1996), Doc. IMM-2576-95 (Fed. T.D.) — This was an application for an extension of time to perfect an application for judicial review.

The ultimate responsibility to compute time limits under the rules rests with the party and its counsel, regardless of any conversation between a counsel's secretary and a registry officer of the court. Most of the supporting affidavit in this matter referred to what was understood by the applicant's counsel from a conversation with the registry of the court. Such evidence was of no assistance in a motion for an extension of time.

When a deadline is missed what is required is an explanation of the efforts spent throughout the entire period prescribed by the time limit.

On the basis of the affidavit material, the application for an extension was dismissed.

Bhui v. Canada (Minister of Citizenship & Immigration) (March 11, 1996), Doc. IMM-3385-95 (Fed. T.D.) — The Court had before it a motion by the applicant for an extension of the time limits set out in Rule 10(1) for serving and filing the applicant's record.

In January 1996 the applicant filed his record within the time required by the rules. The record did not include a memorandum of argument. Counsel provided the Court with an affidavit indicating that he did not feel it was necessary to include a memorandum of argument in the record, and therefore did not do so.

The respondent took the position that the applicant's record was not complete and not perfected within the time period provided by the rules.

The filing and service of the applicant's record are official in the Court file. There cannot, therefore, be in this case an extension of time to perform acts that have already been done.

If the motion were granted allowing the inclusion of the memorandum of argument in the applicant's record, there would be no additional delays in dealing with the application and no evidence to suggest that the respondent would otherwise be prejudiced. There was nothing in the evidence to support the suggestion that counsel for the applicant was seeking to file the applicant's record in successive steps in order to avoid the time limits set out in Rule 10.

Accordingly, the memorandum of argument was permitted to be filed with the Court as part of the applicant's record.

Moreno v. Canada (Minister of Citizenship & Immigration) (1996), 33 Imm. L.R. (2d) 84, (sub nom. *Moreno v. Canada (Ministre de la Citoyenneté & de l'Immigration))* 110 F.T.R. 57 (Fed. T.D.) — This was a motion pursuant to Rule 21(2) of the *Federal Court Immigration Rules* for an extension of the time limit under Rule 10(1) for serving and filing the applicant's record.

The Court expects the time limit set out in the rules to be complied with and an automatic extension is not available merely because it is requested. An applicant must show that there was some justification for the delay throughout the whole period of the delay and that the applicant has an arguable case. The applicant must demonstrate some reason for the delay which was beyond its control or the control of its counsel, for example, illness, or some other unexpected or unanticipated event. This motion failed because there was a lack of an explanation for the extension and, furthermore, there were no arguments advanced to show that the applicants had an arguable case.

Milon v. Canada (Minister of Citizenship & Immigration) (1995), 100 F.T.R. 1 (Fed. T.D.) — The applicant sought an extension of time within which to serve and file his record. An applicant seeking an extension of time must demonstrate (1) a continuing intention to pursue his appeal, (2) that there is some merit in his application, (3) that no prejudice to the respondents arises as a result of the delay, and (4) that a reasonable explanation for the delay exists.

On an application for judicial review, the issue before the court is whether sufficient information existed in front of the decision maker to justify the decision that was made. It would be an error of law to take into account any evidence arising subsequent to the making of the decision under review.

The material in this application did not at all deal with the merits of the case, and so the application for an extension was refused.

Karakulak v. Canada (Minister of Employment & Immigration) (1995), 98 F.T.R. 81 (Fed. T.D.) — This was an application for an extension of time to file a reply and it arose because the notes of the immigration officer who made the impugned decision were not available and there were no written reasons for the decision. The notes had been refused pursuant to the provisions of the *Privacy Act*. The Court would not order the missing pages produced, nor would it agree to extend the time to file a reply for an unlimited period. The applicant industriously pursued the pages, and if this had not been the case the applicant would have been required to proceed without them. Immigration Rule 14 enables a judge to order the production of documents refused by a tribunal claiming quasi-judicial privilege, but it does not permit a judge to order the production of documents protected by the *Privacy Act*.

Awogbade v. Canada (Minister of Citizenship & Immigration) (1995), 29 Imm. L.R. (2d) 281, 94 F.T.R. 184 (Fed. T.D.) — The applicant applied for leave to take judicial review proceedings against a decision of the CRDD. One month after filing the originating motion the applicant's solicitors sought to extend the time for filing her application record. Additional time was refused by the Court and the applicant brought an application for reconsideration of that order.

In a solicitor/client relationship, there is a strong fiduciary obligation on the solicitor's part to act in a professional, timely manner in order to advance the client's interests. The Ontario Legal Aid plan merely authorizes the payment of fees for the lawyer's services. A professional ethical lawyer will not leave his or her client in the lurch merely because fees are not secured.

It may be that the allowing of a client's case to turn to ashes while awaiting spurious authorization from legal aid, is contempt of Court.

There are several valid reasons for which a judge could extend the time to file an applicant's record, but waiting for a legal aid certificate is not one of them.

The absence of an application record is a substantive defect as well as a procedural one, and an order dismissing additional time for the filing of an application is a final one.

It is a species of professional misconduct for a lawyer to prefer the securing of his or her own fees over the client's interests.

The Court noted that the reasons of the CRDD had not been filed with the original request for an extension of time and considered that this failure on the part of the applicant's solicitors, provided it with a reason to relieve the applicant of the prejudice created by the conduct of her solicitors, and accordingly, reconsidered its order and granted to the applicant a short extension to file her application record.

Valyenegro v. Canada (Secretary of State) (1994), 88 F.T.R. 196 (Fed. T.D.) — This was a motion for an extension of time to file the applicant's records. An application for an extension is an interlocutory application, even if in certain circumstances a resulting order refusing an extension might be final in nature.

The burden of justifying an extension of time is on the applicant. It is not incumbent on the respondent to show there is prejudice, but rather the onus is on the applicant to show that there is prejudice to the applicant and that there is not prejudice to the respondent.

It may be assumed that an applicant would be prejudiced if he or she is denied the right to put forward their case. If, however, the applicant does not have a case, he or she cannot be prejudiced if an extension of time is denied. Here the applicant tendered no evidence of an arguable case. There was, therefore, no evidence of any prejudice to the applicant if the request was refused. Accordingly, the application for an extension of time was dismissed.

Subuncuo v. Canada (Minister of Employment & Immigration) (December 4, 1992), Doc. 92-T-1555 (Fed. T.D.) — The respondent Minister sought an order extending the time within which the respondent would be allowed to file and serve written submissions in response to the applicant's application for leave pursuant to section 82.1. The adjudicator in this case had delayed in forwarding a copy of the transcript of the hearing and this delay was determined not to be justifiable. In requesting an extension of time in such a situation, the respondent is essentially using its own conduct as a ground for delay — something an applicant would not be allowed to do. There are no good reasons why tapes could not be used to avoid the delay which arises as a result of waiting for the preparation of a transcript. In this case, however, the applicant had requested a transcript and not a copy of the tape and, accordingly, an extension of time was granted. The result would have been different had the applicant requested a copy of the tape rather than a transcript.

Espinoza v. Canada (Minister of Employment & Immigration) (1992), 142 N.R. 158 (Fed. C.A.) — An order for an extension of the time to comply with Rule 9 does not finally dispose of any matter in issue. Such an order is always open to reconsideration whether made peremptorily or not. The policy of the *Immigration Act* and *Federal Court Immigration Rules* is transparently clear and is one of deciding leave applications expeditiously. The dilatory initiation of Legal Aid applications, delays in providing opinion letters, which counsel know will be required, and the ever slower processing of such applications by Legal Aid cannot be permitted to defeat the policy of the Act and Rules. Failure to make a Legal Aid application promptly can be good reason to deny an extension.

Metodieva v. Canada (Department of Employment & Immigration) (1991), 132 N.R. 38, (sub nom. *Metodieva v. Ministre de l'emploi et de l'immigration)* (Fed. C.A.) — The Convention Refugee Determination Division dismissed the applicant's claim for refugee status. An initial application for leave to appeal was dismissed in December 1990. In May 1991, the applicant made a subsequent application for a leave to appeal and for an extension of the 15-day deadline imposed by section 82.3(4) of the *Immigration Act*. This application was a request to the Court to disregard the final order made by the Court previously refusing leave to appeal. Once an order has been signed by a judge, it is a final order. Apart from clerical mistakes or errors arising from accidental slips or omissions, a party who is not satisfied with such an order may only challenge the order in a manner prescribed by the *Federal Court Act* or by the Rules of the Court and, in immigration matters, by the *Immigration Act* and the *Federal Court Immigration Rules*. Further, in immigration matters, no appeal lies to the Supreme Court of Canada from a judgment of a Federal Court of Appeal judge on an application for leave to commence proceedings or an application for leave to appeal.

The proceedings defined by the Rules of Court are also available to a dissatisfied party. These proceedings are an application to rehear a motion dismissed in the absence of a party, an application to rescind an order made *ex parte* or, in the absence of a party, an application to reconsider the terms of the pronouncement on the grounds (a) that the pronouncement does not accord with the reasons that were given or (b) that some matter that should have been dealt with has been overlooked or accidentally omitted, an application for a rehearing under Rule 1103(3), or an application setting aside a judgment for a new matter or fraud (Rule 1733). Apart from these cases, the Court does not have jurisdiction to reconsider a final order. In the case at bar, the original order dismissing the application for leave to appeal was based on the fact that the application was unsupported by affidavit or other material. The fact that an application was dismissed for a procedural defect does not in any way change the fact that the order made is final and not subject to reconsideration except in the allowable cases referred to above. The absence of an affidavit is a substantive defect as well as a procedural one. Rule 9(1) of the *Federal Court Immigration Rules* makes the filing of an affidavit an integral part of an application, and an application for leave not supported by an affidavit is not complete and cannot be allowed by the Court. The fact that the applicant is a foreigner in Canada does not confer any privilege to be ignorant of Canadian law or any special status in respect of errors which may be made by one's counsel. Accordingly, the application for leave to appeal was dismissed.

Bains v. Canada (Minister of Employment & Immigration) (1990), 47 Admin. L.R. 317, 109 N.R. 239 (Fed. C.A.) — The only question to be considered in disposing of an application for leave under section 82.1(1) or 82.3(1) is whether or not a fairly arguable case is disclosed for the relief proposed to be sought if leave is granted. Further, the need for material not immediately available has to be established by the applicant and the mere stated intention to rely on such material does not, without an application and an order to that end, operate to extend the time provided by the *Federal Court Immigration Rules* for the applicant to file an affidavit and/or representations in support of the leave application. The requirement for leave is, in reality, the other side of the coin of the traditional jurisdiction to summarily terminate proceedings that disclose no reasonably arguable case. The requirement for leave does not deny refugee claimants access to the Court. The right to apply for leave is, itself, a right of access to the Court and the requirement that leave be obtained before an appeal or application for judicial review may proceed does not impair the right guaranteed by refugee claimants under either section 7 or 15 of the Charter.

COSTS

22. No costs shall be awarded to or payable by any party in respect of an application or an appeal under these Rules unless the Court, for special reasons, so orders.

Case Law

Said v. Canada (Minister of Citizenship & Immigration) (April 30, 1999), Doc. A-149-99 (Fed. C.A.) — The applicant, who came to Canada as a Convention refugee, was found guilty in 1992, on five counts of trafficking in heroin and sentenced to 5 years in jail. A deportation order was issued as a result of the convictions and subsequently the appellant was found to be a danger to the public. While the appellant's appeal to the Court of Appeal was pending, he was informed that a removal order had been signed against him by the Minister and a motion for stay was brought on an urgent basis.

The stay was granted and the Court awarded costs in the amount of $1,000.00. The Court could not understand why the removal order was brought to the appellant's attention only 4 days before its execution. The appellant was in custody and therefore could not flee upon service of the document. The very fact of detention made it more difficult and time consuming for his counsel to prepare the motion for stay and gather the necessary supporting material.

Akinsola v. Canada (Minister of Citizenship & Immigration) (1997), 138 F.T.R. 229 (Fed. T.D.) — The Court determined the counsel for the applicant had acted either in bad faith or incompetently. Counsel's actions wasted the court's time and caused serious inconvenience to opposing counsel. The Court awarded costs against counsel personally in the amount of $200.

Singh (J.) v. Canada (Minister of Citizenship & Immigration) (1996), 35 Imm. L.R. (2d) 303, 121 F.T.R. 184 (Fed. T.D.) — The applicant, an Indian national, had resided in Canada continuously since 1981, pursuant to a series of student authorizations, a minister's permit and two visitor's visas. At the time of this application, the applicant was without status. Since 1981, the applicant had lived with his aunt who had adopted him in accordance with Sikh tradition and culture. After the adoption, the aunt submitted an undertaking of assistance which was approved in June 1992. The applicant then applied for permanent residence as a sponsored member of the family class. The applicant was interviewed by an officer at the Canadian Consulate in Buffalo in January 1993. Although a decision was made to refuse the application approximately 9 months after the interview, this decision was not disclosed to the applicant until April 1996 some two and a half years later.

In the period from April, 1993 to February 1996, the applicant's counsel wrote 10 letters asking for the status of the application, seven were written to the officer's attention. The officer personally responded to the first letter and thereafter two form letters were sent to the applicant, neither of which provided accurate information. In addition, three more letters were sent by the applicant's counsel to the senior immigration officer at the consulate describing the circumstances of the case and the extraordinary delay. The senior immigration officer did not respond to counsel's letters.

Costs were awarded for the following three reasons:

1. The delay, caused by the fact that the officer did not address the file between October 1993 and September 1995.

2. The two form letters which were sent contained inaccurate information.

3. The senior immigration officer did not respond to correspondence from the applicant's counsel.

Marques v. Canada (Minister of Citizenship & Immigration) (1996), 35 Imm. L.R. (2d) 81, (sub nom. *Marques v. Canada (Minister of Citizenship & Immigration) (No.2))* 116 F.T.R. 243 (Fed. T.D.) — The respondent consented to an application to review a section 114(2) decision of an immigration officer. The issue in this matter was a question of costs under Rule 22. The Court found special reasons for an award of costs.

The applicant had first filed an application for a visa exemption invoking section 114(2) in April 1994. This application was refused. However, the refusal was the subject of a successful application for judicial review. Following the successful judicial review application, the file was returned to Mississauga CIC, were no action was taken on the file until the fall of 1995. The immigration officer conducting this second interview, had before her the previous decision and the notes of the review conducted in July 1994, which had been set aside by the Court. Despite the fact that the Court had ordered an entirely new review, the matter was not considered afresh. The immigration officer considered merely whether there had been a change of circumstances since the date of the first section 114(2) decision. The officer therefore did not comply with the order of the Court. Immigration officers have a duty to act in accordance with decisions from the Federal Court, as well as in a courteous and professional manner.

Accordingly, the Court found special reasons to award costs to the applicant.

Barbu v. Canada (Secretary of State) (February 2, 1996), Doc. IMM-4015-94 (Fed. T.D.) — This application was to review a decision of a visa officer. Specifically, the visa officer intended to use the discretion conferred by section 11(3) of the Act to deny an application, and did so without consulting a senior immigration officer and without providing that officer with written reasons.

The only issue in this application was whether the applicant was entitled to costs pursuant to rule 1618 of the *Federal Court Rules*. Rule 1618 provides that no cost shall be payable in respect of an application for judicial review unless the Court for special reason so orders. The Court noted that costs have been awarded in cases where there has been an abuse of process. In very unusual cases, circumstances outside the conduct of the judicial review application could be relevant to costs. A simple fact of an error, without more, does not justify a costs award. Such a conclusion would make rule 1618 meaningless, accordingly, no costs were ordered.

Chan v. Canada (Minister of Employment & Immigration) (1994), 82 F.T.R. 244 (Fed. T.D.) — This was an application for costs by the respondent. Costs can be awarded only in special circumstances.

Special circumstances existed in this case. The respondent, from a very early date in the proceedings, was prepared to consent to an application for judicial review. However, the applicant, believing in the strength of the case, insisted that the matter be fully litigated to establish that certain regulations applicable to his landed immigrant status were *ultra vires*. He was unsuccessful.

The Court did not think that an applicant can force a respondent, who is willing to consent, to continue proceedings thereby expending time and resources, without being accountable, at least to some extent, for the costs incurred.

Canada (Minister of Employment & Immigration) v. Ermeyev (1994), 83 F.T.R. 158 (Fed. T.D.) — Costs were awarded against the Minister because the Court viewed that the respondents had been put through a great deal of unnecessary trouble and expense by the way that the Minister's officials had dealt with the respondents. There was, at worst, a technical error committed by the respondents at the time the events giving rise to these proceedings occurred. Once this mistake was discovered, it should not have strained the imagination of immigration officials to find a simple solution, such as the departure of the entire family temporarily to the United States from which they could return together to Canada. Instead, the entire family was put through a series of removal hearings, appeals and court applications over a 4 year period.

Accordingly, at the discontinuance of the Minister's application in this matter, costs were awarded to the respondents.

FEES

23. A fee of $50 shall be paid to the Registry in order to file an application or a notice of appeal.

COMING INTO FORCE

24. These Rules shall come into force on the day on which sections 73, 114, 115, 116, 117 and 118 of *An Act to amend the Immigration Act and other Acts in consequence thereof*, S.C. 1992, c. 49, come into force.

Case Law

Hassan v. Canada (Minister of Employment & Immigration) (1993), 151 N.R. 215 (Fed. C.A.) — Pursuant to the legislation then in effect, the appellants appealed with leave of a judge of the Federal Court of Appeal against a negative decision of the Refugee Division. After leave was obtained and a package of materials received from the Board pursuant to Rules 1305 and 1306(1), counsel for the appellants moved, pursuant to Rule 324, to vary the appeal book to include the standardized country file relied on by the Refugee Division. The Board showed cause why the standardized country file should not be produced. It was held that the Board had acted properly in not producing the whole of the contents of its standardized country files. Section 68 makes it quite plain that Parliament has extended the concept of judicial notice for the Board well beyond what is normally understood. Published information relating to conditions in countries from which refugee claimants come is precisely the type of "information or opinion" that may be expected within the specialized knowledge of the Board. By making this information publicly available and by referring to the then current index at the outset of the hearing, the Board has adequately complied with the notice requirements of subsection 68(5). To the extent that such material has not been specifically referred to by the Board in its reasons, it need not be produced. A party who asks the Court to act on this material in the same way that the Board might have done must bring this material to the attention of the Court. The most convenient method of doing this is for the party to reproduce copies of the document of which it wishes the Court to take notice and annex it to the memorandum of fact and law. It is not appropriate as a matter of routine to encumber the appeal book with material which is likely to be voluminous and which will in most cases have little or no relevance to the issues raised. The application to vary the appeal book was dismissed.

SCHEDULE

Form IR-1

(Rule 5)

FEDERAL COURT OF CANADA
TRIAL DIVISION

Between:

[Insert full name of party or the Minister]

Applicant(s)

and

[The Minister, or full name of other party, if the Minister is the applicant]

Respondent(s)

Application For Leave and for Judicial Review

TO THE RESPONDENT(S)

AN APPLICATION FOR LEAVE TO COMMENCE AN APPLICATION FOR JUDICIAL REVIEW UNDER S. 82.1 OF THE *IMMIGRATION ACT* has been commenced by the applicant.

THIS APPLICATION FOR LEAVE will be disposed of without personal appearance by the parties, in accordance with subsection 82.1(4) of the *Immigration Act*.

IF YOU WISH TO OPPOSE THIS APPLICATION FOR LEAVE, you or a solicitor authorized to practice in Canada and acting for you must forthwith prepare a Notice of Appearance in Form IR-2 prescribed by the *Federal Court Immigration Rules, 1993*, serve it on the tribunal and the applicant's solicitor or, where the applicant does not have a solicitor, serve it on the applicant, and file it, with proof after service, at the Registry, within 10 days of service of this application for leave.

IF YOU FAIL TO DO SO, the Court may nevertheless dispose of this application for leave and, if leave is granted, the subsequent application for judicial review without further notice to you.

Note: Copies of the relevant Rules of Court, information on the local office of the Court and other necessary information may be obtained from any local office of the Federal Court or the Registry of the Trial Division in Ottawa, telephone: (613) 992-4238.

The applicant seeks leave of the Court to commence an application for judicial review of:

(Set out the date and details of the decision, order or other matter in respect of which judicial review is sought.)

(Set out the name, address and telephone number of the tribunal and, if the tribunal was composed of more than one person, the name of each person who was on the tribunal.)

(Set out the tribunal's file number(s), if applicable.)

(Add the following paragraph where applicable.)

[The applicant further applies to the Court to allow an extension of time under subsection 82.1(5) of the *Immigration Act* on the following grounds:

(Set out the grounds for the request for extension of time to file the application for leave.)]

In the event that leave is granted, the applicant seeks the following relief by way of judicial review:

(Set out the precise relief sought should leave be granted, including any statutory provision or Rule relied on.)

In the event that leave is granted, the application for judicial review is to be based on the following grounds:

(Set out the grounds to be argued, including a reference to any statutory provision or Rule to be relied on.)

The applicant has *(has not)* received written reasons from the tribunal.

In the event that leave is granted, the applicant proposes that the applicant for judicial review be heard at ...., in the *(English or French)* language.

(Signature of Solicitor/Applicant)

Name of Solicitor/Applicant

Address

Telephone Number

TO: *(Name(s) and address(es) of Respondent(s))*

SOR/98-235, s. 6.

Form IR-2

(Rule 8)

FEDERAL COURT OF CANADA
TRIAL DIVISION

Between:

Applicant(s)

and

nbsp;

Respondent(s)

Notice of Appearance

The Respondent(s) *(name(s))* intend(s) to respond to this application.

The tribunal's file number(s), as set out in the application is (are):

(Date)

(Name, address and telephone number of Respondent's solicitor, or Respondent if acting in person)

TO: (*Name and address of Applicant's solicitor, or Applicant if acting in person*)

AND TO: (*Name and address of tribunal*)

Form IR-3

(Rule 9)

Registry No.

FEDERAL COURT OF CANADA
TRIAL DIVISION

Between:

Applicant(s)

and

Respondent(s)

Request to Tribunal

TO: (*Name and Address of tribunal*)

RE: (*Set out complete particulars of the decision, order or other matter as they appear in the application, with tribunal's file number(s), if any.*)

DATE:

In an application filed on ...., 199.........., the applicant set out that he/she had not received written reasons for the above-captioned matter.

Pursuant to Rule 9 of the *Federal Court Immigration Rules, 1993*, you are hereby requested, without delay, to

(*a*) send a copy of the decision or order, and written reasons therefor, duly certified by an appropriate officer to be correct, to each of the parties, and two copies to the Registry; or

(*b*) if no reasons were given for the decision or order in respect of which the application is made, or reasons were given but not recorded, send an appropriate written notice to all the parties and the Registry.

(signature of Registry Officer)

Name of Registry Officer

telephone number

Form IR-4

(Rule 20)

FEDERAL COURT OF CANADA

Registry No.

Between:

(*name*)

Appellant

(*Applicant (Respondent) in the Trial Division*)

and

(*name*)

Respondent

(*Applicant (Respondent) in the Trial Division*)

Notice of Appeal (Under Section 83 of the Immigration Act)

THE APPELLANT (*name*) **APPEALS from the judgment of The Honourable** (*name of judge*) **of the Trial Division, delivered on** (*date*).

PURSUANT TO subsection 83(1) of the *Immigration Act*, **the learned Trial Judge certified that the following serious question(s) of general importance was (were) involved:**

(*Set out question(s) certified by Trial Judge.*)

THE APPELLANT SEEKS THE FOLLOWING RELIEF on the determination of the question(s) under section 52 of the *Federal Court Act*:

(*Set out the relief sought, with reference to the specific provisions in section 52 of the Federal Court Act relied on.*)

THE APPELLANT REQUESTS that this appeal be heard at (*place*).

Dated at ...., this ...., day of ...., 19..........

(*Name, address and telephone number*

of Appellant's solicitor)

TO: (*Name and address of Respondent's solicitor or Respondent if acting in person*)

Canada Evidence Act

An Act respecting Witnesses and Evidence

R.S.C. 1985, c. C-5, as am. R.S.C. 1985, c. 19 (3rd Supp.), ss. 17, 18; 1992, c. 1, s. 142 (Sched. V, items 9(1), 9(2)); 1992, c. 47, s. 66; 1993, c. 28, s. 78 (Sched. III, item 8); 1993, c. 34, s. 15; 1994, c. 44, ss. 85–93; 1995, c. 28, s. 47; 1997, c. 18, ss. 116–118; 1998, c. 9, s. 1; 1999, c. 18, ss. 89–91; 1999, c. 28, ss. 149, 150.

.....

[Sections 37 and 38 reproduced.]

Part I — Application

Disclosure of Government Information

37. (1) Objection to disclosure of information — A minister of the Crown in right of Canada or other person interested may object to the disclosure of information before a court, person or body with jurisdiction to compel the production of information by certifying orally or in writing to the court, person or body that the information should not be disclosed on the grounds of a specified public interest.

(2) Where objection made to superior court — Subject to sections 38 and 39, where an objection to the disclosure of information is made under subsection (1) before a superior court, that court may examine or hear the information and order its disclosure, subject to such restrictions or conditions as it deems appropriate, if it concludes that, in the circumstances of the case, the public interest in disclosure outweighs in importance the specified public interest.

(3) Where objection not made to superior court — Subject to sections 38 and 39, where an objection to the disclosure of information is made under subsection (1) before a court, person or body other than a superior court, the objection may be determined, on application, in accordance with subsection (2) by

(a) the Federal Court-Trial Division, in the case of a person or body vested with power to compel production by or pursuant to an Act of Parliament if the person or body is not a court established under a law of a province; or

(b) the trial division or trial court of the superior court of the province within which the court, person or body exercises its jurisdiction, in any other case.

(4) Limitation period — An application pursuant to subsection (3) shall be made within ten days after the objection is made or within such further or lesser time as the court having jurisdiction to hear the application considers appropriate in the circumstances.

(5) Appeal to Court of Appeal — An appeal lies from a determination under subsection (2) or (3)

> **(a) to the Federal Court of Appeal from a determination of the Federal Court-Trial Division; or**
>
> **(b) to the court of appeal of a province from a determination of a trial division or trial court of a superior court of a province.**

(6) Limitation period for appeal under subsection (5) — An appeal under subsection (5) shall be brought within ten days from the date of the determination appealed from or within such further time as the court having jurisdiction to hear the appeal considers appropriate in the circumstances.

(7) Limitation periods for appeals to Supreme Court of Canada — Notwithstanding any other Act of Parliament,

> **(a) an application for leave to appeal to the Supreme Court of Canada from a judgment made pursuant to subsection (5) shall be made within ten days from the date of the judgment appealed from or within such further time as the court having jurisdiction to grant leave to appeal considers appropriate in the circumstances; and**
>
> **(b) where leave to appeal is granted, the appeal shall be brought in the manner set out in subsection 60(1) of the *Supreme Court Act* but within such time as the court that grants leave specifies.**

Case Law

Moumdjian v. Canada (Security Intelligence Review Committee) (1997), *(*sub nom. *Moumdjian v. Security Intelligence Review Committee))* 221 N.R. 188, *(*sub nom. *Moumdjian v. Security Intelligence Review Committee))* 141 F.T.R. 80 (note), 6 Admin. L.R. (3d) 239 (Fed. C.A.) — This was an appeal from an order of a judge of the trial division, sitting as a judge designated by the chief justice pursuant to section 38(1) of the *Canada Evidence Act.* The issue was whether the designated judge erred in sustaining an objection to the disclosure of information that had been placed before the Security Intelligence Review Committee (SIRC) during the course of an investigation by SIRC pursuant to section 39 of the *Immigration Act.*

In the course of its investigation and in the absence of the appellant and his counsel, SIRC received evidence in the form of oral testimony and documents. The disclosure of this evidence was objected to in the certificate filed pursuant to section 37(1) of the *Canada Evidence Act.* The disclosure of correspondence between SIRC and CSIS containing information supplied to SIRC and miscellaneous documents containing other information supplied to SIRC by CSIS was also objected to. All of this evidence was listed in a schedule attached to the section 37(1) certificate. The appellant was provided with a summary of the evidence that was submitted to SIRC in his absence and also with a summary of the argument that was presented to SIRC.

The Court referred to *Henrie v. Canada*, [1989] 2 F.C. 229 (T.D.) for a description of the competing interests at stake and the proper balancing of these interests where an application for judicial review of a SIRC decision is brought. This decision described the balancing that must occur between the principles of openness in the judicial process and the public interest in not disclosing evidence in certain types of cases.

In order to succeed on the appeal, the appellant must satisfy the Court that the Trial Division judge erred in law in refusing to order disclosure. The function of the Court of Appeal in this instance is limited to reviewing the decision of the designated judge so as to be satisfied that it does not disclose an error of the sort enumerated in subsection 18.1(4) of the *Federal Court Act*. If the decision does not reveal such an error, the matter ends and the Court is not entitled to examine any of the information which the judge found ought not to be disclosed.

38. (1) Objection relating to international relations or national defence or security — Where an objection to the disclosure of information is made under subsection 37(1) on grounds that the disclosure would be injurious to international relations or national defence or security, the objection may be determined, on application, in accordance with subsection 37(2) only by the Chief Justice of the Federal Court, or such other judge of that court as the Chief Justice may designate to hear such applications.

(2) Limitation period — An application under subsection (1) shall be made within ten days after the objection is made or within such further or lesser time as the Chief Justice of the Federal Court, or such other judge of that court as the Chief Justice may designate to hear such applications, considers appropriate.

(3) Appeal to Federal Court of Appeal — An appeal lies from a determination under subsection (1) to the Federal Court of Appeal.

(4) Subsections 37(6) and (7) apply — Subsection 37(6) applies in respect of appeals under subsection (3), and subsection 37(7) applies in respect of appeals from judgments made pursuant to subsection (3), with such modifications as the circumstances require.

(5) Special rules for hearings — An application under subsection (1) or an appeal brought in respect of the application shall

(a) be heard *in camera*; and

(b) on the request of the person objecting to the disclosure of information, be heard and determined in the National Capital Region described in the schedule to the *National Capital Act*.

(6) Ex parte representations — During the hearing of an application under subsection (1) or an appeal brought in respect of the application, the person who made the objection in respect of which the application was made or the appeal was brought shall, on the request of that person, be given the opportunity to make representations *ex parte*.

APPENDIX I — IMMIGRATION TO QUEBEC I-0.2

AN ACT RESPECTING IMMIGRATION TO QUÉBEC

R.S.Q., c. I-0.2, as am. S.Q. 1978, c. 82; 1979, c. 32, ss. 9, 10; 1981, c. 9, ss. 1-8; 1981, c. 23, s. 32; U.K. 1982, c. 11, Sched. B, Part. I, s. 33; 1984, c. 44, s. 21; 1984, c. 47, s. 102; 1985, c. 30, s. 55; 1987, c. 75; 1988, c. 41, ss. 69-71; 1990, c. 4, s. 583; 1991, c. 3; 1992, c. 5; 1993, c. 70, ss. 1, 2, 3(2), 4, 6, 7, 10, 11(1), (3), (4), (5), (7), (10), (11), 12–18 [Ss. 3(1), 5, 8, 9, 11(2), (6), (8), (9) not in force at date of publication.]; 1994, c. 15, ss. 12–29; 1996, c. 21, ss. 48, 49; 1997, c. 43, s. 302; 1998, c. 15.

1. [Repealed 1994, c. 15, s. 13.]

DIVISION I — DEFINITION

2. "Foreign National" — In this act, "foreign national" means a person who is neither a Canadian citizen nor a permanent resident within the meaning of the Immigration Act (Revised Statutes of Canada, 1985, chapter I-2) and the regulations thereunder, who settles temporarily in Québec otherwise than as the representative of a foreign government or as an international civil servant.

1978, c. 82, s. 1; 1981, c. 9, s. 3; 1994, c. 15, s. 15

DIVISION II — SELECTION OF FOREIGN NATIONALS

3. Selection of Foreign Nationals — The selection of foreign nationals wishing to settle permanently or temporarily in Québec is effected within the framework of government policy concerning immigrants and foreign nationals. The selection is intended, in particular,

(a) to contribute to the enrichment of the socio-cultural heritage of Québec, to the stimulation of its economic development and to the pursuit of its demographic objectives;

(b) to facilitate the reuniting, in Québec, of Canadian citizens and permanent residents with their close relatives from abroad;

(c) to enable Québec to assume its share of responsibilities regarding the reception of refugees and other persons in a particularly distressful situation;

(d) to favour the coming, among foreign nationals who apply therefor, of persons who will be able to become successfully established in Québec;

(e) to facilitate the conditions of the stay in Québec of foreign nationals wishing to study, work temporarily or receive medical treatment, having regard to the reasons for their coming and the capacity of Québec to receive them.

1978, c. 82, s. 2; 1988, c. 41, s. 69; 1993, c. 70, s. 1; 1994, c. 15, s. 17

3.01 The Minister, having regard to government policy concerning immigrants and foreign nationals, shall establish an annual immigration plan.

The plan shall set out the number of foreign nationals who may settle in Québec and the distribution of that number by class or within a class. That number and its distribution are estimates within the meaning of section 7 of the Immigration Act (Revised Statutes of Canada, 1985, chapter I-2).

The plan shall also indicate the selection activities that are planned for the year concerned.

The plan shall be tabled in the National Assembly not later than 1 November or, if the Assembly is not sitting on that date, not later than the fifteenth day after resumption.

1998, c. 15, s. 1

3.1 Application for Permanent Residence — A foreign national wishing to settle permanently in Québec must, except for the classes and cases prescribed by regulation, file an application for a selection certificate with the Minister of Relations with the Citizens and Immigration in the manner determined by regulation in accordance with the procedure prescribed under paragraph f of section 3.3.

Process — The Minister shall process the application, having regard to the annual immigration plan and to the order of priorities prescribed by regulation.

Selection certificate — The Minister shall issue a selection certificate to the foreign national who meets the conditions and criteria of selection determined by regulation.

Selection certificate — Notwithstanding the third paragraph, the Minister may, in accordance with the regulations, issue a selection certificate to a foreign national in a particularly distressful situation, in particular, in the case of Convention refugees as defined in the Act respecting immigration to Canada, or in any other case where the Minister considers that the results obtained following the application of the selection criteria do not reflect whether or not the foreign national will be able to become successfully established in Québec. Conversely, the Minister may refuse to issue such a certificate to a foreign national who meets the conditions and criteria of selection if he has reasonable grounds to believe that the foreign national does not intend to settle in Québec or is unlikely to settle successfully in Québec or that the settlement of the foreign national would be contrary to public interest.

1978, c. 82, s. 3; 1992, c. 5, s. 1; 1993, c. 70, s. 2; 1994, c. 15, s. 18; 1996, c. 21, s. 48; 1998, c. 15, s. 2

3.1.1 In the cases determined by regulation, an undertaking to assist a foreign national to settle in Québec is required.

Proposed Amendment — 3.1.1

3.1.1 Selection Criteria — Where determined by regulation, an undertaking to assist the foreign national in settling in Québec shall constitute one of the selection criteria prescribed under paragraph b of section 3.3.

[1993, c. 70, s. 3(1). Not in force at date of publication.]

Application for undertaking — The application for an undertaking shall be filed by a person or group of persons determined by regulation according to the conditions

prescribed thereby. If, in the opinion of the Minister, the person or group of persons meets the conditions prescribed by regulation, the undertaking shall be subscribed to according to the terms determined by regulation. The application for an undertaking and the undertaking shall be made on the forms prescribed by the Minister.

The Minister shall issue a certificate of undertaking to a foreign national in whose respect an undertaking has been made and who is not required to file an application for a selection certificate.

1991, c. 3, s. 1; 1993, c. 70, s. 3; 1998, c. 15, s. 3

3.1.2 Application — A foreign national in Québec who does not hold a selection certificate may make an application to the Minister for a certificate of statutory situation. He shall file his application in accordance with the procedure prescribed under paragraph f of section 3.3.

Certificate of identity — The Minister shall issue a certificate of statutory situation to any foreign national who meets the conditions determined by regulation.

1992, c. 5, s. 2; 1993, c. 70, s. 4; 1998, c. 15, s. 4

Proposed Addition — 3.1.3

3.1.3 Conditions — The Minister may impose conditions prescribed under paragraph f.1.2 of section 3.3 which affect the granting of landing under the Immigration Act (Revised Statutes of Canada, 1985, chapter I-2), to a foreign national who applies for a selection certificate.

Conditions — The Minister may, in the cases determined by regulation or at the request of a permanent resident, modify, lift or cancel the conditions imposed.

[1993, c. 70, s. 5. Not in force at date of publication.]

3.2 Temporary foreign nationals — Excepting the classes of foreign nationals excluded by regulation, every foreign national seeking temporary admission to Québec to work, study or receive medical treatment must hold a certificate of acceptance issued by the Minister. He must file an application in accordance with the procedure prescribed under paragraph f of section 3.3.

Certificate of acceptance — The Minister shall issue a certificate of acceptance to the foreign national who meets the conditions determined by regulation.

Certificate of acceptance — Notwithstanding the second paragraph, the Minister may, in cases provided for by regulation, exempt a foreign national from the application of the conditions contemplated in the second paragraph and issue a certificate of acceptance to him.

1978, c. 82, s. 3; 1979, c. 32, s. 9; 1993, c. 70, s. 6; 1998, c. 15, s. 5

3.2.1 Truthfulness of declarations — Where the Minister so requires, any person must, under penalty of refusal of the application for a selection certificate, a certificate of acceptance or a certificate of statutory selection or of the application for an undertaking, demonstrate to the Minister the truthfulness of the declarations made by the person respecting the application and submit to him, in the manner and time determined by him, any document which the Minister deems to be pertinent.

1991, c. 3, s. 2; 1992, c. 5, s. 3; 1993, c. 70, s. 7; 1998, c. 15, s. 6

3.2.2 **Cancellation of certificate** — **The Minister may cancel a selection certificate, a certificate of acceptance, a certificate of statutory situation, an undertaking or a certificate of undertaking**

(a) where the certificate was delivered or the undertaking accepted on the basis of false or misleading information or documents;

(b) where the certificate was delivered or the undertaking accepted by error;

(c) where the conditions required for the issue of the certificate or the acceptance of the undertaking cease to exist.

Minister's decision — **The decision of the Minister shall take effect immediately. It must give reasons and be submitted in writing to the person concerned.**

1991, c. 3, s. 2; 1992, c. 5, s. 4; 1998, c. 15, s. 7

Division III — Integration of Foreign Nationals

3.2.3 **Integration program** — **The Minister shall establish and maintain, for those persons who settle in Québec, an integration program for the purpose of favouring their introduction to Québec life.**

1991, c. 3, s. 2

3.2.4 **Linguistic integration services** — **The Minister, under the integration program, shall provide and take charge of the implementation of linguistic integration services consisting of services of French language instruction and introduction to Québec life.**

1991, c. 3, s. 2

3.2.5 **Eligibility** — **Immigrants domiciled in Québec who are unable to demonstrate, according to the evaluation procedure prescribed by regulation, a knowledge of French adequate to assuring their harmonious integration with the francophone majority of Québec society and who meet the other conditions established by regulation are admissible for linguistic integration services.**

Extension of services — **The maintaining and extension of the services are conditional upon compliance by the student receiving them with the conditions prescribed by regulation.**

1991, c. 3, s. 2

Proposed Amendment — 3.2.5

3.2.5 **Eligibility** — **Immigrants domiciled in Québec who are unable to demonstrate, according to the evaluation procedure prescribed by regulation, a knowledge of French adequate to assuring their harmonious integration with the francophone majority of Québec society who file an application for that purpose with the Minister on the form prescribed by the latter and who meet the other conditions established by regulation are admissible for linguistic integration services.**

[1993, c. 70, s. 8. Not in force at date of publication.]

3.2.6 **Financial assistance** — **The Minister may allocate financial assistance to a student receiving linguistic integration services.**

The application for assistance must be filed with the Minister on the form prescribed by the latter.

1991, c. 3, s. 2; 1993, c. 70, s. 9; 1998, c. 15, s. 8

3.2.7 **Loan** — **The Minister may, according to the conditions prescribed by regulation, grant a loan to an immigrant in a particularly distressful situation with a view to enabling him to discharge the cost or a part of the cost of his immigration to Québec or to assisting him to discharge the costs of becoming established in Québec.**

1991, c. 3, s. 2; 1993, c. 70, s. 10; 1998, c. 15, s. 9

3.2.8 **Deferment of loan repayment** — **The Minister may defer a loan repayment or reduce the obligations of repayment where the borrower shows that he is unable to repay his loan according to the terms and conditions prescribed by regulation.**

Release from debt — **Where it has been impossible to recover a debt resulting from a loan even though the appropriate recovery measures have been applied to it, the Minister may grant a release from the debt.**

1991, c. 3, s. 2

DIVISION IV — REGULATIONS AND AGREEMENTS

3.3 **Regulations** — **The Government may make regulations**

(a) determining classes of foreign nationals who have filed an application for a selection certificate referred to in section 3.1;

(a.1) determining the cases where and the classes of foreign nationals for which an application for a selection certificate is not required;

(b) determining the conditions of selection applicable to each of such classes of foreign nationals, having regard, in particular, to criteria such as the vocational or professional training and experience of the foreign national, the needs of the labour market in Québec as regards his profession, the age and personal qualities, education, knowledge of languages, and financial capacity of the foreign national, the assistance he may receive from relatives or friends residing in Québec, his place of destination in Québec, and the place of establishment of his enterprise; such conditions and criteria may vary within the same class, in particular by reason of the foreign national's contribution to enriching the socio-cultural or economic heritage of Québec;

(b.1) determining the classes of foreign nationals which may be exempted from one or several of the conditions and criteria of selection prescribed under paragraph b and providing that such exemptions may vary within the same class;

(b.2) determining the classes of foreign nationals in respect of which paragraph b applies to a foreign national's dependants, as defined by regulation, and providing for cases of total or partial exemption of dependants from conditions or criteria of selection; such conditions and criteria may vary according to the family situation of the foreign national and also within the same class;

(b.3) determining, from among the criteria prescribed under paragraph b, those which apply to a preliminary processing for selection intended to identify the applications which will be processed, prescribing the classes of foreign nationals to which the criteria will apply and determining the cases of total or partial exemp-

tion of foreign nationals; the criteria may vary according to the class and also within the same class;

(b.4) prescribing the classes of foreign nationals in respect of which a selection interview must be held, determining the cases of total or partial exemption from this obligation and providing that the obligation may vary within the same class;

(c) determining the cases where an undertaking to assist a foreign national to settle in Québec is required and the cases where an undertaking ceases to have effect;

(c.1) determining the persons or groups of persons who may file an application for an undertaking and the conditions of the filing;

(c.2) determining the conditions which must be met by the person or group of persons who subscribe to such an undertaking and prescribing exemptions to one or several conditions by reason of the family situation or minority of the foreign national for whom the undertaking is subscribed;

(c.3) determining the terms of the undertaking and its duration, which may vary according to the age or circumstances of the foreign national or of his family;

Proposed Addition — 3.3(c.4)

(c.4) determining the cases in which an undertaking to assist a foreign national in settling in Québec constitutes one of the conditions and one of the criteria of selection referred to in paragraph b;

[1993, c. 70. s. 11(2). Not in force at date of publication.]

(d) determining the cases where and the classes of foreign nationals to whom the Minister may issue a selection certificate referred to in the fourth paragraph of section 3.1, and determining the procedure to be followed in a case where the Minister considers that the results obtained following the application of the selection criteria do not reflect whether or not the foreign national will be able to become successfully established in Québec;

(d.1) determining the cases where a certificate of statutory situation referred to in section 3.1.2 is to be issued and determining, according to the status of the foreign national as established under the Immigration Act (Revised Statutes of Canada, 1985, chapter I-2), types of certificates of statutory situation and the conditions applicable to each type;

(e) for the purposes of section 3.2, determining, while having particular regard to labour market conditions in Québec, the conditions that must be met by a foreign national seeking to stay temporarily in Québec to work, determining the conditions that must be met by a foreign national seeking to stay temporarily in Québec to study or receive medical treatment, establishing the cases where the Minister may exempt a foreign national from the application of the conditions referred to in the second paragraph of section 3.2 and issue a certificate of acceptance, and determining the classes of foreign nationals who may be excluded from the application of section 3.2;

(f) determining the procedure that must be followed in order to obtain a selection certificate under section 3.1, a certificate of statutory situation under section 3.1.2 or a certificate of acceptance under section 3.2, or in order to subscribe an undertaking;

(f.1) determining the conditions of validity of a selection certificate or a certificate of acceptance and their duration and providing that the duration of a certificate of acceptance may vary, in the case of a foreign national coming to Québec to study, according to whether he is a minor or of age or according to the program of study or the duration of his studies, in the case of a foreign national coming to Québec to work, according to the duration of his employment, his professional experience or the needs of the labour market in Québec in his profession or, in the case of a foreign national coming to Québec to receive medical treatment, according to the duration of the treatment;

(f.1.1) determining the duration of a certificate of statutory situation and the cases in which it lapses and providing that the duration and cases in which it lapses may vary by reason, in particular, of the type of certificate of statutory situation;

Proposed Addition — 3.3(f.1.2)–(f.1.5)

(f.1.2) for the purposes of section 3.1.3, providing conditions affecting the granting of landing under the Immigration Act to a foreign national who applies for a selection certificate under section 3.1 so as to ensure, in particular, the protection of public health, the meeting of regional or sectorial needs for specialized labour, the regional or sectorial creation of enterprises or the financing of such enterprises, and the socio-economic integration of the foreign national, determining classes of foreign nationals according to which such conditions may vary and providing that such conditions may vary within the same class;

(f.1.3) determining the classes of foreign nationals which may be exempted from one or several conditions prescribed under paragraph f.1.2 and providing that such exemptions may vary within the same class;

(f.1.4) determining the duration of the conditions prescribed under section 3.1.3, determining the classes of foreign nationals according to which the duration may vary and providing that the duration may vary within the same class;

(f.1.5) determining the cases in which the conditions prescribed under section 3.1.3 may be modified, lifted or cancelled;

[1993, c. 70, s. 11(6). Not in force at date of publication.]

(f.2) establishing the fees payable for processing an application for an undertaking, a certificate of statutory situation, a selection certificate or a certificate of acceptance, for issuing any such certificate or for subscribing an undertaking, and determining the cases where total or partial exemption from payment is to be granted; the fees may vary in the case of an undertaking according to the family situation of the foreign national, in the case of a certificate of statutory situation according to the authorization allowing the foreign national to be in Canada, in the case of a selection certificate according to the classes of foreign nationals or to the stages in the processing of an application or, in the case of a certificate of acceptance according to the reason for the temporary admission of the foreign national to Québec;

(g) prescribing an order of priorities for the processing of applications for a selection certificate referred to in section 3.1;

(h) determining, with regard to linguistic integration services, the services offered, the teaching program, the conditions of admissibility to the services, the form and tenor of an application, the conditions of obtaining, maintaining and extending the said services, the appropriate training period and the procedure for evaluating the

knowledge of French; these provisions may vary according to services and classes of immigrants or of students;

Proposed Amendment — 3.3(h)

(h) determining, with regard to linguistic integration services, the services offered, the teaching program, the conditions of admissibility to the services, the conditions of obtaining, maintaining and extending the said services, the appropriate training period and the procedure for evaluating the knowledge of French; these provisions may vary according to services and classes of immigrants or of students;

1993, c. 70, s. 11(8) [Not in force at date of publication.]

(i) determining, with regard to financial assistance for the purposes of linguistic integration services, the classes of allocation, the conditions of admissibility, and the conditions of granting, the form and tenor of an application and the nature and schedule of financial assistance; these provisions may vary according to services and classes of immigrants or of students and, within the same class of immigrants or of students, according to the family and financial situation of the students;

Proposed Amendment — 3.3(i)

(i) determining, with regard to financial assistance for the purposes of linguistic integration services, the classes of allocation, the conditions of admissibility, and the conditions of granting and the nature and schedule of financial assistance; these provisions may vary according to services and classes of immigrants or of students and, within the same class of immigrants or of students, according to the family and financial situation of the students;

1993, c. 70, s. 11(9) [Not in force at date of publication.]

(j) determining, with a view to assisting the reception and settlement of immigrants in a particularly distressful situation, the classes of loans, the conditions of granting and of repayment thereof, and the applicable rate of interest.

1978, c. 82, s. 3; 1979, c. 32, s. 10; 1981, c. 23, s. 32; 1984, c. 47, s. 103; 1987, c. 75, s. 1; 1991, c. 3, s. 3; 1992, c. 5, s. 5; 1993, c. 70, s. 11; 1998, c. 15, ss. 1-7, 9, 10(1)–(7), (9)

3.4 **Regulations — The Minister may, by regulation,**

(a) establish the weighting of selection criteria and the passing score and, where expedient, the cutoff score determined in relation to a selection criterion, applicable to the preliminary stage of selection established under paragraph b.3 of section 3.3 and to the selection established under paragraph b of section 3.3, which weighting and which scores may vary according to the family situation of the foreign national, according to the classes of foreign nationals and within the same class of foreign nationals;

(b) determine that the regulation applies to applications that are being processed, or to applications filed after a particular date that are being processed, or to those that have not yet reached a particular stage on the date of coming into force of the regulation.

Regulation — A regulation made under this section is not subject to the requirement to publish contained in section 8 of the Regulations Act (R.S.Q., chapter R-18.1) and, notwithstanding section 17 of that Act, comes into force on the date of its publication in the *Gazette officielle du Québec*, or at any later date fixed in the regulation.

1993, c. 70, s. 12

4. [Repealed 1994, c. 15, s. 21.]

5. [Repealed 1988, c. 41, s. 70.]

6. Agreements — The Minister may, according to law, make any agreement with the Government of Canada or any body thereof and with any other government or body, in conformity with the interests and rights of Québec, to facilitate the carrying out of this act.

Agreements for exchange of information — He may make any agreement, in the same manner and with the same authorities or with any department or body of the Gouvernement du Québec, for the exchange of information obtained under an Act entrusted to the administration of that Government, department or body, in order to attain the immigration objectives or to discharge the obligations incumbent upon him under this Act.

1991, c. 3, s. 4; 1993, c. 70, s. 13; 1994, c. 15, s. 22

7.–8. [Repealed 1984, c. 44, s. 21.]

9.–12. [Repealed 1994, c. 15, s. 23.]

DIVISION V — INVESTIGATIONS

12.1 Inquiries — The Minister or any person designated by him as an investigator or inspector may make inquiries in order to ensure that this Act and the regulations are being complied with and to prevent, detect or repress contraventions to this Act.

1978, c. 82, s. 5; 1991, c. 3, s. 5; 1992, c. 5, s. 6; 1993, c. 70, s. 14

12.1.1 Powers and immunity — In conducting an investigation, the Minister and investigators are vested with the powers and immunity of commissioners appointed under the Act respecting public inquiry commissions (R.S.Q., chapter C-37), except the power to order imprisonment.

1993, c. 70, s. 15

12.1.2 Information — An inspector may, for the purposes of this Act and the regulations, require any information and any document and examine and make copies of such documents.

1993, c. 70, s. 15

12.1.3 Immunity — No inspector may be prosecuted for acts performed in good faith in the carrying out of his duties.

1993, c. 70, s. 15

12.1.4 Identification — On request, an inspector or investigator shall identify himself and produce the certificate signed by the Minister and attesting his capacity.

1993, c. 70, s. 15

12.2 Copy of documents — Any copy of a book, register or document produced for an investigation and certified by the Minister or an investigator as being a true copy of the original, is admissible as proof and has the same probative force as the original.

1978, c. 82, s. 5; 1991, c. 3, s. 5

Division VI — Penal Provisions

12.3 Offence — Every person is guilty of an offence who communicates information he knows or should have known to be false or misleading to the Minister or to an investigator or inspector in relation to an application

(a) for a selection certificate, a certificate of acceptance, a certificate of statutory situation or an undertaking;

(b) for access to linguistic integration services;

(c) for financial assistance for a student receiving linguistic integration services;

(d) for a loan for an immigrant in a particularly distressful situation.

1978, c. 82, s. 5; 1990, c. 4, s. 583; 1991, c. 3, s. 5; 1992, c. 5, s. 7; 1993, c. 70, s. 16; 1998, c. 15, s. 11

12.4 Every person who contributes to the issue of a selection certificate, a certificate of acceptance, a certificate of undertaking or a certificate of statutory situation to a foreign national or to the subscription of an undertaking in favour of a foreign national in contravention of this Act is guilty of an offence.

1991, c. 3, s. 5; 1992, c. 5, s. 8; 1998, c. 15, s. 12

12.4.1 Offence and penalty — Every person who obstructs an inspector in the carrying out of his duties is guilty of an offence.

1993, c. 70, s. 17

12.5 Fine — A natural person is liable to a fine of $500 to $1 000 in the case of an offence under section 12.3, to a fine of $1 000 to $10 000 in the case of an offence under section 12.4, and to a fine of $250 to $1 000 in the case of an offence under section 12.4.1.

Legal person — Where the offence is committed by a legal person, the fine shall be doubled.

Subsequent offence — In the case of a second or subsequent offence, the fine prescribed for a first offence shall be doubled.

1991, c. 3, s. 5; 1993, c. 70, s. 18

12.6 Parties to offence — Where a legal person is guilty of an offence described by this Act, the administrator, director, official or representative of the legal person who prescribed or authorized the performance of the act or the omission which constitutes

the offence or who consented thereto is party to the offence and liable to the penalty prescribed by law.

1991, c. 3, s. 5

12.7 Prescription — Prescription of penal proceedings begins to run, for an offence contemplated by section 12.3, on the date of examination of the information disclosed to the Minister or investigator and, for an offence contemplated by section 12.4, on the date of examination of the application for the selection certificate, the certificate of acceptance, the undertaking or the certificate of statutory situation.

1991, c. 3, s. 5; 1992, c. 5, s. 9; 1998, c. 15, s. 13

13.–16. [Repealed 1994, c. 15, s. 26.]

DIVISION VII — PROCEEDING BEFORE THE ADMINISTRATIVE TRIBUNAL OF QUÉBEC

17. A decision of the Minister may, within 60 days of notification of the decision, be contested before the Administrative Tribunal of Québec by

(a) any person or group of persons whose application for an undertaking is rejected or whose undertaking is cancelled;

(b) any foreign national whose selection certificate or certificate of acceptance is cancelled.

1982, c. 21, s. 1; U.K., 1982, c. 11, Sched. B, Part I, s. 33; 1991, c. 3, s. 6; 1997, c. 43, s. 302

18.–39. [Repealed 1997, c. 43, s. 302.]

DIVISION VIII — FINAL PROVISION

40. The Minister of Relations with the Citizens and Immigration is responsible for the administration of this Act.

1994, c. 15, s. 29; 1996, c. 21, s. 49

This act was formerly entitled "An Act respecting the Ministère de l'immigration". The title was replaced by section 1 of chapter 9 of the statutes of 1981.

The act was formerly entitled "An Act respecting the Ministère des Communautés culturelles et de l'immigration". The title was replaced by 1994, c. 15, s. 12.

Concordance Table

STATUTES OF QUÉBEC, 1968 Chapter 68 IMMIGRATION DEPARTMENT ACT	**REVISED STATUTES Chapter I-0.2 Immigration To Québec** *An Act respecting the Ministère de l'immigration*	
SECTIONS	**SECTIONS**	**REMARKS**
1–3	1–3	
3a	3.1	
3b	3.2	
3c	3.3	
4–5	4–5	
6		Repealed 1974, c. 64, s. 3
7	6	
8	7	
9	8	
10	9	
11	10	
12	11	
13	12	
13a	12.1	
13b	12.2	
13c	12.3	
14	13	
15	14	
16	15	
17	16	
18		Amendment integrated into c. E-18, s. 4
19		Amendment integrated into c. M-34, s. 1
20		Amendment integrated into c. M-14, s. 2
21		Amendment integrated into c. E-7, s. 1
22–23		Omitted

The Concordance Table indicates all section numbers, whether or not they have been renumbered. Other divisions (i.e. Part, Chapter, Division, Subdivision, Paragraph, etc.), where applicable, are indicated only where they have been renumbered.

The term "Omitted" in the "Remarks" column refers to a section that does not appear in the consolidation because it is without effect, not in force, or of a temporary, transitory, local or private character, or because its object has been accomplished or it is a repealing or replacing section.

APPENDIX II — CHAPTER 16 OF NAFTA

CHAPTER 16 OF THE NORTH AMERICAN FREE TRADE AGREEMENT

Chapter Sixteen — Temporary Entry for Business Persons

Article 1601 — General Principles

Further to Article 102 (Objectives), this Chapter reflects the preferential trading relationship between the Parties, the desirability of facilitating temporary entry on a reciprocal basis and of establishing transparent criteria and procedures for temporary entry, and the need to ensure border security and to protect the domestic labor force and permanent employment in their respective territories.

Article 1602 — General Obligations

1. Each Party shall apply its measures relating to the provisions of this Chapter in accordance with Article 1601 and, in particular, shall apply expeditiously those measures so as to avoid unduly impairing or delaying trade in goods or services or conduct of investment activities under this Agreement.

2. The Parties shall endeavour to develop and adopt common criteria, definitions and interpretations for the implementation of this Chapter.

Article 1603 — Grant of Temporary Entry

1. Each Party shall grant temporary entry to business persons who are otherwise qualified for entry under applicable measures relating to public health and safety and national security, in accordance with this Chapter, including the provisions of Annex 1603.

2. A Party may refuse to issue an immigration document authorizing employment to a business person where the temporary entry of that person might affect adversely:

(a) the settlement of any labour dispute that is in progress at the place or intended place of employment; or

(b) the employment of any person who is involved in such dispute.

3. When a Party refuses pursuant to paragraph 2 to issue an immigration document authorizing employment, it shall:

(a) inform in writing the business person of the reasons for the refusal; and

(b) promptly notify in writing the Party whose business person has been refused entry of the reasons for the refusal.

4. Each Party shall limit any fees for processing applications for temporary entry of business persons to the approximate cost of services rendered.

Article 1604 — Provision of Information

1. Further to Article 1802 (Publication), each Party shall:

(a) provide to the other Parties such materials as will enable them to become acquainted with its measures relating to this Chapter; and

(b) no later than one year after the date of entry into force of this Agreement, prepare, publish and make available in its own territory, and in the territories of the other Parties, explanatory material in a consolidated document regarding the requirements for temporary entry under this Chapter in such a manner as will enable business persons of the other Parties to become acquainted with them.

2. Subject to Annex 1604.2, each Party shall collect and maintain, and make available to the other Parties in accordance with its domestic law, data respecting the granting of temporary entry under this Chapter to business persons of the other Parties who have been issued immigration documentation, including data specific to each occupation, profession or activity.

Article 1605 — Working Group

1. The Parties hereby establish a Temporary Entry Working Group, comprising representatives of each Party, including immigration officials.

2. The Working Group shall meet at least once each year to consider:

(a) the implementation and administration of this Chapter;

(b) the development of measures to further facilitate temporary entry of business persons on a reciprocal basis;

(c) the waiving of labour certification tests or procedures of similar effect for spouses of business persons who have been granted temporary entry for more than one year under Section B, C or D of Annex 1603; and

(d) proposed modifications of or additions to this Chapter.

Article 1606 — Dispute Settlement

1. A Party may not initiate proceedings under Article 2007 (Commission — Good Offices, Conciliation and Mediation) regarding a refusal to grant temporary entry under this Chapter or a particular case arising under Article 1602(1) unless:

(a) the matter involves a pattern of practice; and

(b) the business person has exhausted the available administrative remedies regarding the particular matter.

2. The remedies referred to in paragraph (1)(b) shall be deemed to be exhausted if a final determination in the matter has not been issued by the competent authority within one year of the institution of an administrative proceeding, and the failure to issue a determination is not attributable to delay caused by the business person.

Article 1607 — Relation to Other Chapters

Except for this Chapter, Chapters One (Objectives), Two (General Definitions), Twenty (Institutional Arrangements and Dispute Settlement Procedures) and Twenty-two (Final Provisions) and Articles 1801 (Contacts Points), 1802 (Publication), 1803 (Notification and Provision of Information) and 1804 (Administrative Proceedings), no provision of this Agreement shall impose any obligation on a Party regarding its immigration measures.

Article 1608 — Definitions

For purposes of this Chapter:

business person means a citizen of a Party who is engaged in trade in goods, the provision of services or the conduct of investment activities;

citizen means "citizen" as defined in Annex 1608 for the Parties specified in that Annex;

existing means "existing" as defined in Annex 1608 for the Parties specified in that Annex;

temporary entry means entry into the territory of a Party by a business person of another Party without the intent to establish permanent residence.

Annex 1603 — Temporary Entry for Business Persons

Section A. — Business Visitors

1. Each Party shall grant temporary entry to a business person seeking to engage in a business activity set out in Appendix 1603.A.1, without requiring that person to obtain an employment authorization, provided that the business person otherwise complies with existing immigration measures applicable to temporary entry, on presentation of:

(a) proof of citizenship of a Party;

(b) documentation demonstrating that the business person will be so engaged and describing the purpose of entry; and

(c) evidence demonstrating that the proposed business activity is international in scope and that the business person is not seeking to enter the local labor market.

2. Each party shall provide that a business person may satisfy the requirements of paragraph 1(c) by demonstrating that:

(a) the primary source of remuneration for the proposed business activity is outside the territory of the Party granting temporary entry; and

(b) the business person's principal place of business and the actual place of accrual of profits, at least predominantly, remain outside such territory.

A Party shall normally accept an oral declaration as to the principal place of business and the actual place of accrual of profits. Where the Party requires further proof, it shall normally consider a letter from the employer attesting to these matters as sufficient proof.

3. Each Party shall grant temporary entry to a business person seeking to engage in a business activity other than those set out in Appendix 1603.A.1, without requiring that person to obtain an employment authorization, on a basis no less favourable than that provided under the existing provisions of the measures set out in Appendix 1603.A.3, provided that the business person otherwise complies with existing immigration measures applicable to temporary entry.

4. No Party may:

(a) as a condition for temporary entry under paragraph 1 or 3, require prior approval procedures, petitions, labour certification tests or other procedures of similar effect; or

(b) impose or maintain any numerical restriction relating to temporary entry under paragraph 1 or 3.

5. Notwithstanding paragraph 4, a Party may require a business person seeking temporary entry under this Section to obtain a visa or its equivalent prior to entry. Before imposing a visa requirement, the Party shall consult, on request, with a Party whose business persons would be affected with a view to avoiding the imposition of the requirement. With respect to an existing visa requirement, a Party shall consult, on request, with a Party whose business persons are subject to the requirement with a view to its removal.

Section B. — Traders and Investors

1. Each Party shall grant temporary entry and provide confirming documentation to a business person seeking to:

(a) carry on substantial trade in goods or services principally between the territory of the Party of which the business person is a citizen and the territory of the Party into which entry is sought, or

(b) establish, develop, administer or provide advice or key technical services to the operation of an investment to which the business person or the business person's enterprise has committed, or is in the process of committing, a substantial amount of capital, in a capacity that is supervisory, executive or involves essential skills,

provided that the business person otherwise complies with existing immigration measures applicable to temporary entry.

2. No Party may:

(a) as a condition for temporary entry under paragraph 1, require labor certification tests or other procedures of similar effect; or

(b) impose or maintain any numerical restriction relating to temporary entry under paragraph 1.

3. Notwithstanding paragraph 2, a Party may require a business person seeking temporary entry under this Section to obtain a visa or its equivalent prior to entry.

Section C. — Intra-Company Transferees

1. Each Party shall grant temporary entry and provide confirming documentation to a business person employed by an enterprise who seeks to render services to that enterprise or a subsidiary or affiliate thereof, in a capacity that is managerial, executive or involves specialized knowledge, provided that the business person otherwise complies with existing immigration measures applicable to temporary entry. A Party may require the business person to have been employed continuously by the enterprise for one year within the three-year period immediately preceding the date of the application for admission.

2. No Party may:

> **(a) as a condition for temporary entry under paragraph 1, require labor certification tests or other procedures of similar effect; or**
>
> **(b) impose or maintain any numerical restriction relating to temporary entry under paragraph 1.**

3. Notwithstanding paragraph 2, a Party may require a business person seeking temporary entry under this Section to obtain a visa or its equivalent prior to entry. Before imposing a visa requirement, the Party shall consult with a Party whose business persons would be affected with a view to avoiding the imposition of the requirement. With respect to an existing visa requirement, a Party shall consult, on request, with a Party whose business persons are subject to the requirement with a view to its removal.

Section D. — Professionals

1. Each Party shall grant temporary entry and provide confirming documentation to a business person seeking to engage in a business activity at a professional level in a profession set out in Appendix 1603.D.1, if the business person otherwise complies with existing immigration measures applicable to temporary entry, on presentation of:

> **(a) proof of citizenship of a Party; and**
>
> **(b) documentation demonstrating that the business person will be so engaged and describing the purpose of entry.**

2. No Party may:

> **(a) as a condition for temporary entry under paragraph 1, require prior approval procedures, petitions, labor certification tests or other procedures of similar effect; or**
>
> **(b) impose or maintain any numerical restriction relating to temporary entry under paragraph 1.**

3. Notwithstanding paragraph 2, a Party may require a business person seeking temporary entry under this Section to obtain a visa or its equivalent prior to entry. Before imposing a visa requirement, the Party shall consult with a Party whose business persons would be affected with a view to avoiding the imposition of the requirement. With respect to an existing visa requirement, a Party shall consult, on request, with a party whose business persons are subject to the requirement with a view to its removal.

4. Notwithstanding paragraphs 1 and 2, a Party may establish an annual numerical limit, which shall be set out in Appendix 1603.D.4, regarding temporary entry of business persons of another Party seeking to engage in business activities at a professional level in a profession set out in Appendix 1603.D.1, if the Parties concerned have not

agreed otherwise prior to the date of entry into force of this Agreement for those Parties. In establishing such a limit, the Party shall consult with the other Party concerned.

5. A Party establishing a numerical limit pursuant to paragraph 4, unless the Parties concerned agree otherwise:

(a) shall, for each year after the first year after the date of entry into force of this Agreement, consider increasing the numerical limit set out in Appendix 1603.D.4 by an amount to be established in consultation with the other Party concerned, taking into account the demand for temporary entry under this Section;

(b) shall not apply its procedures established pursuant to paragraph 1 to the temporary entry of a business person subject to the numerical limit, but may require the business person to comply with its other procedures applicable to the temporary entry of professionals; and

(c) may, in consultation with the other Party concerned, grant temporary entry under paragraph 1 to a business person who practices in a profession where accreditation, licensing, and certification requirements are mutually recognized by those Parties.

6. Nothing in paragraph 4 or 5 shall be construed to limit the ability of a business person to seek temporary entry under a Party's applicable immigration measures relating to the entry of professionals other than those adopted or maintained pursuant to paragraph 1.

7. Three years after a Party establishes a numerical limit pursuant to paragraph 4, it shall consult with the other Party concerned with a view to determining a date after which the limit shall cease to apply.

Appendix 1603.A.1 — Business Visitors

Research and Design

- **Technical, scientific and statistical researchers conducting independent research or research for an enterprise located in the territory of another Party.**

Growth, Manufacture and Production

- **Harvester owner supervising a harvesting crew admitted under applicable law.**
- **Purchasing and production management personnel conducting commercial transactions for an enterprise located in the territory of another Party.**

Marketing

- **Market researchers and analysts conducting independent research or analysis or research or analysis for an enterprise located in the territory of another Party.**
- **Trade fair and promotional personnel attending a trade convention.**

Sales

- **Sales representatives and agents taking orders or negotiating contracts for goods or services for an enterprise located in the territory of another Party but not delivering goods or providing services.**
- **Buyers purchasing for an enterprise located in the territory of another Party.**

Distribution

- **Transportation operators transporting goods or passengers to the territory of a Party from the territory of another Party or loading and transporting goods or passengers from the territory of a Party, with no unloading in that territory, to the territory of another Party.**
- **With respect to temporary entry into the territory of the United States, Canadian customs brokers performing brokerage duties relating to the export of goods from the territory of the United States to or through the territory of Canada.**
- **With respect to temporary entry into the territory of Canada, United States customs brokers performing brokerage duties relating to the export of goods from the territory of Canada to or through the territory of the United States.**
- **Customs brokers providing consulting services regarding the facilitation of the import or export of goods.**

After-Sales Service

- **Installers, repair and maintenance personnel, and supervisors, possessing specialized knowledge essential to a seller's contractual obligation, performing services or training workers to perform services, pursuant to a warranty or other service contract incidental to the sale of commercial or industrial equipment or machinery, including computer software, purchased from an enterprise located outside the territory of the Party into which temporary entry is sought, during the life of the warranty or service agreement.**

General Service

- **Professionals engaging in a business activity at a professional level in a profession set out in Appendix 1603.D.1.**
- **Management and supervisory personnel engaging in a commercial transaction for an enterprise located in the territory of another Party.**
- **Financial services personnel (insurers, bankers or investment brokers) engaging in commercial transactions for an enterprise located in the territory of another Party.**
- **Public relations and advertising personnel consulting with business associates, or attending or participating in conventions.**
- **Tourism personnel (tour and travel agents, tour guides or tour operators) attending or participating in conventions or conducting a tour that has begun in the territory of another Party.**
- **Tour bus operators entering the territory of a Party:**
  - **(a) with a group of passengers on a bus tour that has begun in, and will return to, the territory of another Party;**
  - **(b) to meet a group of passengers on a bus tour that will end, and the predominant portion of which will take place, in the territory of another Party; or**
  - **(c) with a group of passengers on a bus tour to be unloaded in the territory of the Party into which temporary entry is sought, and returning with no passengers or reloading with the group for transportation to the territory of another Party.**

- **Translators or interpreters performing services as employees of an enterprise located in the territory of another Party.**

Definitions

For purposes of this Appendix:

territory of another Party means the territory of a Party other than the territory of the Party into which temporary entry is sought;

tour bus operator means a natural person, including relief personnel accompanying or following to join, necessary for the operation of a tour bus for the duration of a trip; and

transportation operator means a natural person, other than a tour bus operator, including relief personnel accompanying or following to join, necessary for the operation of a vehicle for the duration of a trip.

Appendix 1603.A.3 — Existing Immigration Measures

1. In the case of Canada, subsection 19(1) of the *Immigration Regulations, 1978*, SOR/78-172, as amended, made under the *Immigration Act*, R.S.C. 1985, c. 1-2, as amended.

2. In the case of the United States, section 101(a)(15)(B) of the *Immigration and Nationality Act*, 1952, as amended.

3. In the case of Mexico, Chapter III of the *Ley General de Poblacion*, 1974, as amended.

Appendix 1603.D.1 — Professionals

PROFESSION[1]	MINIMUM EDUCATION REQUIREMENTS AND ALTERNATIVE CREDENTIALS
General	
Accountant	Baccalaureate or Licenciatura Degree, or C.P.A., C.A., C.G.A., C.M.A.
Architect	Baccalaureate or Licenciatura Degree; or state/provincial license[2]
Computer Systems Analyst	Baccalaureate or Licenciatura Degree; or Post-Secondary Diploma[3] or Post-Secondary Certificate,[4] and three years experience
Disaster Relief Insurance Claims Adjuster (claims adjuster employed by an insurance company located in the territory of a Party, or an independent claims adjuster)	Baccalaureate or Licenciatura Degree, and successful completion of training in the appropriate areas of insurance adjustment pertaining to disaster relief claims; or three years experience in claims adjustment and successful completion of training in the appropriate areas of insurance adjustment pertaining to disaster relief claims

PROFESSION[1]	MINIMUM EDUCATION REQUIREMENTS AND ALTERNATIVE CREDENTIALS
Economist	Baccalaureate or Licenciatura Degree
Engineer	Baccalaureate or Licenciatura Degree; or state/provincial license
Forester	Baccalaureate or Licenciatura Degree; or state/provincial license
Graphic Designer	Baccalaureate or Licenciatura Degree; or Post-Secondary Diploma or Post-Secondary Certificate, and three years experience
Hotel Manager	Baccalaureate or Licenciatura Degree in hotel/restaurant management; or Post-Secondary Diploma or Post-Secondary Certificate in hotel/restaurant management, and three years experience in hotel/restaurant management
Industrial Designer	Baccalaureate or Licenciatura Degree; or Post-Secondary Diploma or Post-Secondary Certificate, and three years experience
Interior Designer	Baccalaureate or Licenciatura Degree; or Post-Secondary Diploma or Post-Secondary Certificate, and three years experience
Land Surveyor	Baccalaureate or Licenciatura Degree; or state/provincial/federal license
Landscape Architect	Baccalaureate or Licenciatura Degree
Lawyer (including Notary in the Province of Quebec)	LL.B., J.D., LL.L., B.C.L. or Licenciatura Degree (five years); or membership in a state/provincial bar
Librarian	M.L.S. or B.L.S. (for which another Baccalaureate or Licenciatura Degree was a prerequisite)
Management Consultant	Baccalaureate or Licenciatura Degree; or equivalent professional experience as established by statement or professional credential attesting to five years experience as a management consultant, or five years experience in a field of specialty related to the consulting agreement
Mathematician (including Statistician)	Baccalaureate or Licenciatura Degree
Range Manager/Range Conservationalist	Baccalaureate or Licenciatura Degree
Research Assistant (working in a post-secondary educational institution)	Baccalaureate or Licenciatura Degree

PROFESSION[1]	MINIMUM EDUCATION REQUIREMENTS AND ALTERNATIVE CREDENTIALS
Scientific Technician/Technologist[5]	Possession of (a) theoretical knowledge of any of the following disciplines: agricultural sciences, astronomy, biology, chemistry, engineering, forestry, geology, geo-physics, meteorology or physics; and (b) the ability to solve practical problems in any of those disciplines, or the ability to apply principles of any of those disciplines to basic or applied research
Social Worker	Baccalaureate or Licenciatura Degree
Sylviculturist (including Forestry Specialist)	Baccalaureate or Licenciatura Degree
Technical Publications Writer	Baccalaureate or Licenciatura Degree; or Post-Secondary Diploma or Post-Secondary Certificate, and three years experience
Urban Planner (including Geographer)	Baccalaureate or Licenciatura Degree
Vocational Counsellor	Baccalaureate or Licenciatura Degree
Medical/Allied Professional	
Dentist	D.D.S., D.M.D., Doctor en Odontologia or Doctor en Cirugia Dental; or state/provincial license
Dietitian	Baccalaureate or Licenciatura Degree; or state/provincial license
Medical Laboratory Technologist (Canada)/Medical Technologist (Mexico and the United States)[6]	Baccalaureate or Licenciatura Degree; or Post-Secondary Diploma or Post-Secondary Certificate, and three years experience
Nutritionist	Baccalaureate or Licenciatura Degree
Occupational Therapist	Baccalaureate or Licenciatura Degree; or state/provincial license
Pharmacist	Baccalaureate or Licenciatura Degree; or state/provincial license
Physician (teaching and/or research only)	M.D. or Doctor en Medicina; or state/provincial license
Physiotherapist/Physical Therapist	Baccalaureate or Licenciatura Degree; or state/provincial license
Psychologist	State/provincial license; or Licenciatura Degree
Recreational Therapist	Baccalaureate or Licenciatura Degree
Registered Nurse	State/provincial license; or Licenciatura Degree

PROFESSION[1]	MINIMUM EDUCATION REQUIREMENTS AND ALTERNATIVE CREDENTIALS
Veterinarian	D.V.M., D.M.V., or Doctor en Veterinaria; or state/provincial license
Scientist	
Agriculturist (Agronomist)	Baccalaureate or Licenciatura Degree
Animal Breeder	Baccalaureate or Licenciatura Degree
Animal Scientist	Baccalaureate or Licenciatura Degree
Apiculturist	Baccalaureate or Licenciatura Degree
Astronomer	Baccalaureate or Licenciatura Degree
Biochemist	Baccalaureate or Licenciatura Degree
Biologist	Baccalaureate or Licenciatura Degree
Chemist	Baccalaureate or Licenciatura Degree
Dairy Scientist	Baccalaureate or Licenciatura Degree
Entomologist	Baccalaureate or Licenciatura Degree
Epidemiologist	Baccalaureate or Licenciatura Degree
Geneticist	Baccalaureate or Licenciatura Degree
Geologist	Baccalaureate or Licenciatura Degree
Geochemist	Baccalaureate or Licenciatura Degree
Geophysicist (including Oceanographer in Mexico and the United States)	Baccalaureate or Licenciatura Degree
Horticulturist	Baccalaureate or Licenciatura Degree
Meteorologist	Baccalaureate or Licenciatura Degree
Pharmacologist	Baccalaureate or Licenciatura Degree
Physicist (including Oceanographer in Canada)	Baccalaureate or Licenciatura Degree
Plant Breeder	Baccalaureate or Licenciatura Degree
Poultry Scientist	Baccalaureate or Licenciatura Degree
Soil Scientist	Baccalaureate or Licenciatura Degree
Zoologist	Baccalaureate or Licenciatura Degree
Teacher	
College	Baccalaureate or Licenciatura Degree
Seminary	Baccalaureate or Licenciatura Degree
University	Baccalaureate or Licenciatura Degree

Notes:

1 A business person seeking temporary entry under this Appendix may also perform training functions relating to the profession, including conducting seminars.

2 "State/provincial license" and "state/provincial/federal license" mean any document issued by a state, provincial or federal government, as the case may be, or under its authority, but not by a local government, that permits a person to engage in a regulated activity or profession.

3 "Post-Secondary Diploma" means a credential issued, on completion of two or more years of post-secondary education, by an accredited academic institution in Canada or the United States.

4 "Post-Secondary Certificate" means a certificate issued, on completion of two or more years of post-secondary education at an academic institution, by the federal government of Mexico or a state government in Mexico, an academic institution recognized by the federal government or a state government, or an academic institution created by federal or state law.

5 A business person in this category must be seeking temporary entry to work in direct support of professionals in agricultural sciences, astronomy, biology, chemistry, engineering, forestry, geology, geophysics, meterorology or physics.

6 A business person in this category must be seeking temporary entry to perform in a laboratory chemical, biological, hematological, immunologic, microscopic or bacteriological tests and analyses for diagnosis, treatment or prevention of disease.

Appendix 1603.D.4 — United States

1. Beginning on the date of entry into force of this Agreement as between the United States and Mexico, the United States shall annually approve as many as 5,500 initial petitions of business persons of Mexico seeking temporary entry under Section D of Annex 1603 to engage in a business activity at a professional level in a profession set out in Appendix 1603.D.1.

2. For purposes of paragraph 1, the United States shall not take into account:

(a) the renewal of a period of temporary entry;

(b) the entry of a spouse or children accompanying or following to join the principal business person;

(c) an admission under section 101(a)(15)(H)(i)(b) of the *Immigration and Nationality Act*, 1952, as may be amended, including the worldwide numerical limit established by section 214(g)(1)(A) of that Act; or

(d) an admission under any other provision of section 101(a)(15) of that Act relating to the entry of professionals.

3. Paragraphs 4 and 5 of Section D of Annex 1603 shall apply as between the United States and Mexico for no longer than:

(a) the period that such paragraphs or similar provisions may apply as between the United States and any other Party other than Canada or any non-Party; or

(b) 10 years after the date of entry into force of this Agreement as between such Parties,

whichever period is shorter.

Annex 1604.2 — Provision of Information

The obligations under Article 1604(2) shall take effect with respect to Mexico one year after the date of entry into force of this Agreement.

Annex 1608 — Country — Specific Definitions

For purposes of this Chapter:

citizen means, with respect to Mexico, a national or a citizen according to the existing provisions of Articles 30 and 34, respectively, of the Mexican Constitution; and

existing means, as between:

(a) Canada and Mexico, and Mexico and the United States, in effect on the date of entry into force of this Agreement; and

(b) Canada and the United States, in effect on January 1, 1989.

APPENDIX III — CHAPTER K OF THE CANADA-CHILE FREE TRADE AGREEMENT

CANADA–CHILE FREE TRADE AGREEMENT (CCFTA) DECEMBER 5, 1996

Chapter K — Temporary Entry for Business Persons

Article K-01 — General Principles

Further to Article A-02 (Objectives), this Chapter reflects the preferential trading relationship between the Parties, the desirability of facilitating temporary entry on a reciprocal basis and of establishing transparent criteria and procedures for temporary entry, and the need to ensure border security and to protect the domestic labour force and permanent employment in their respective territories.

Article K-02 — General Obligations

Each Party shall apply its measures relating to the provisions of this Chapter in accordance with Article K-01 and, in particular, shall apply expeditiously those measures so as to avoid unduly impairing or delaying trade in goods or services or conduct of investment activities under this Agreement.

Article K-03 — Grant of Temporary Entry

1. Each Party shall grant temporary entry to business persons who are otherwise qualified for entry under applicable measures relating to public health and safety and national security, in accordance with this Chapter, including the provisions of Annex K-03 and Annex K-03.1.

2. A Party may refuse to issue an immigration document authorizing employment to a business person where the temporary entry of that person might affect adversely:

(a) the settlement of any labour dispute that is in progress at the place or intended place of employment; or

(b) the employment of any person who is involved in such dispute.

3. When a Party refuses pursuant to paragraph 2 to issue an immigration document authorizing employment, it shall:

(a) inform in writing the business person of the reasons for the refusal; and

(b) promptly notify the other Party in writing of the reasons for the refusal.

4. Each Party shall limit any fees for processing applications for temporary entry of business persons to the approximate cost of services rendered.

Article K-04 — Provision of Information

1. Further to Article L-02 (Publication), each Party shall:

(a) provide to the other Party such materials as will enable it to become acquainted with its measures relating to this Chapter; and

(b) no later than one year after the date of entry into force of this Agreement, prepare, publish and make available in its own territory, and in the territory of the other Party, explanatory material in a consolidated document regarding the requirements for temporary entry under this Chapter in such a manner as will enable business persons of the other Party to become acquainted with them.

2. Each Party shall collect and maintain, and make available to the other Party in accordance with its domestic law, data respecting the granting of temporary entry under this Chapter to business persons of the other Party who have been issued immigration documentation, including data specific to each occupation, profession or activity.

Article K-05 — Working Group

The Parties hereby establish a Temporary Entry Working Group, comprising representatives of each Party, including immigration officials, to consider the implementation and administration of this Chapter and any measures of mutual interest.

Article K-06 — Dispute Settlement

1. A Party may not initiate proceedings under Article N-07 (Commission — Good Offices, Conciliation and Mediation) regarding a refusal to grant temporary entry under this Chapter or a particular case arising under Article K-02 unless:

(a) the matter involves a pattern of practice; and

(b) the business person has exhausted the available administrative remedies regarding the particular matter.

2. The remedies referred to in paragraph (1)(b) shall be deemed to be exhausted if a final determination in the matter has not been issued by the competent authority within one year of the institution of an administrative proceeding, and the failure to issue a determination is not attributable to delay caused by the business person.

Article K-07 — Relation to Other Chapters

Except for this Chapter, Chapters A (Objectives), B (General Definitions), N (Institutional Arrangements and Dispute Settlement Procedures) and P (Final Provisions) and Articles L-01 (Contacts Points), L-02 (Publication), L-03 (Notification and Provision of Information) and L-04 (Administrative Proceedings), no provision of this Agreement shall impose any obligation on a Party regarding its immigration measures.

Article K-08 — Definitions:

For purposes of this Chapter:

business person means a citizen of a Party who is engaged in trade in goods, the provision of services or the conduct of investment activities; and

temporary entry means entry into the territory of a Party by a business person of the other Party without the intent to establish permanent residence.

ANNEX K-03 — TEMPORARY ENTRY FOR BUSINESS PERSONS

Section I — Business Visitors

1. Each Party shall grant temporary entry to a business person seeking to engage in a business activity set out in Appendix K-03.I.1, without requiring that person to obtain an employment authorization, provided that the business person otherwise complies with existing immigration measures applicable to temporary entry, on presentation of:

(a) proof of citizenship of a Party;

(b) documentation demonstrating that the business person will be so engaged and describing the purpose of entry; and

(c) evidence demonstrating that the proposed business activity is international in scope and the business person is not seeking to enter the local labour market.

2. Each Party shall provide that a business person may satisfy the requirements of paragraph 1(c) by demonstrating that:

(a) the primary source of remuneration for the proposed business activity is outside the territory of the Party granting temporary entry; and

(b) the business person's principal place of business and the actual place of accrual of profits, at least, predominantly, remain outside such territory.

A Party shall normally accept an oral declaration as to the principal place of business and the actual place of accrual of profits. Where the Party requires further proof, it shall normally consider a letter from the employer attesting to these matters as sufficient proof.

3. Each Party shall grant temporary entry to a business person seeking to engage in a business activity other than those set out in Appendix K-03.I.1, without requiring that person to obtain an employment authorization, on a basis no less favourable than that provided under the existing provisions of the measures set out in Appendix K-03.I.3, provided that the business person otherwise complies with existing immigration measures applicable to temporary entry.

4. Neither Party may:

(a) as a condition for temporary entry under paragraph 1 or 3, require prior approval procedures, petitions, labour certification tests or other procedures of similar effect; or

(b) impose or maintain any numerical restriction relating to temporary entry under paragraph 1 or 3.

5. Notwithstanding paragraph 4, a Party may require a business person seeking temporary entry under this Section to obtain a visa or its equivalent prior to entry. Before imposing a visa requirement, the Party shall consult with the other Party with a view to avoiding the imposition of the requirement. With respect to an existing visa requirement, a Party shall consult, on request, with the other Party with a view to its removal.

Section II — Traders and Investors

1. Each Party shall grant temporary entry and provide confirming documentation to a business person seeking to:

(a) carry on substantial trade in goods or services principally between the territory of the Party of which the business person is a citizen and the territory of the other Party into which entry is sought, or

(b) establish, develop, administer or provide advice or key technical services to the operation of an investment to which the business person or the business person's enterprise has committed, or is in the process of committing, a substantial amount of capital,

in a capacity that is supervisory, executive or involves essential skills, provided that the business person otherwise complies with existing immigration measures applicable to temporary entry.

2. Neither Party may:

(a) as a condition for temporary entry under paragraph 1, require labour certification tests or other procedures of similar effect; or

(b) impose or maintain any numerical restriction relating to temporary entry under paragraph 1.

3. Notwithstanding paragraph 2, a Party may require a business person seeking temporary entry under this Section to obtain a visa or its equivalent prior to entry.

Section III — Intra-Company Transferees

1. Each Party shall grant temporary entry and provide confirming documentation to a business person employed by an enterprise who seeks to render services to that enterprise or a subsidiary or affiliate thereof, in a capacity that is managerial, executive or involves specialized knowledge, provided that the business person otherwise complies with existing immigration measures applicable to temporary entry. A Party may require the business person to have been employed continuously by the enterprise for one year within the three-year period immediately preceding the date of the application for admission.

2. Neither Party may:

(a) as a condition for temporary entry under paragraph 1, require labour certification tests or other procedures of similar effect; or

(b) impose or maintain any numerical restriction relating to temporary entry under paragraph 1.

3. Notwithstanding paragraph 2, a Party may require a business person seeking temporary entry under this Section to obtain a visa or its equivalent prior to entry. Before imposing a visa requirement, the Party shall consult with the other Party with a view to avoiding the imposition of the requirement. With respect to an existing visa requirement, a Party shall consult, on request, with the other Party with a view to its removal.

Section IV — Professionals

1. Each Party shall grant temporary entry and provide confirming documentation to a business person seeking to engage in a business activity at a professional level in a pro-

fession set out in Appendix K-03.IV.1, if the business person otherwise complies with existing immigration measures applicable to temporary entry, on presentation of:

(a) proof of citizenship of a Party; and

(b) documentation demonstrating that the business person will be so engaged and describing the purpose of entry.

2. Neither Party may:

(a) as a condition for temporary entry under paragraph 1, require prior approval procedures, petitions, labour certification tests or other procedures of similar effect; or

(b) impose or maintain any numerical restriction relating to temporary entry under paragraph 1.

3. Notwithstanding paragraph 2, a Party may require a business person seeking temporary entry under this Section to obtain a visa or its equivalent prior to entry. Before imposing a visa requirement, the Party shall consult with the other Party with a view to avoiding the imposition of the requirement. With respect to an existing visa requirement, a Party shall consult, on request, with the other Party with a view to its removal.

4. Notwithstanding paragraphs 1 and 2, a Party may establish an annual numerical limit, which shall be set out in Appendix K-03.IV.4, regarding temporary entry of business persons of the other Party seeking to engage in business activities at a professional level in a profession set out in Appendix K-03.IV.1, if the Parties have not agreed otherwise prior to the date of entry into force of this Agreement. In establishing such a limit, the Party shall consult with the other Party.

5. A Party establishing a numerical limit pursuant to paragraph 4, unless the Parties agree otherwise:

(a) shall, for each year after the first year after the date of entry into force of this Agreement, consider increasing the numerical limit set out in Appendix K-03.IV.4 by an amount to be established in consultation with the other Party, taking into account the demand for temporary entry under this Section;

(b) shall not apply its procedures established pursuant to paragraph 1 to the temporary entry of a business person subject to the numerical limit, but may require the business person to comply with its other procedures applicable to the temporary entry of professionals; and

(c) may, in consultation with the other Party, grant temporary entry under paragraph 1 to a business person who practices in a profession where accreditation, licensing, and certification requirements are mutually recognized by the Parties.

6. Nothing in paragraph 4 or 5 shall be construed to limit the ability of a business person to seek temporary entry under a Party's applicable immigration measures relating to the entry of professionals other than those adopted or maintained pursuant to paragraph 1.

7. Three years after a Party establishes a numerical limit pursuant to paragraph 4, it shall consult with the other Party with a view to determining a date after which the limit shall cease to apply.

Annex K-03.1

1. Business persons who enter Chile under any of the categories set out in Annex K-03 shall be deemed to be engaged in activities which are in the country's interest.

2. Business persons who enter Chile under any of the categories set out in Annex K-03 and are issued a temporary visa shall have that temporary visa extended for subsequent periods provided the conditions on which it is based remain in effect, without requiring that person to apply for permanent residence.

3. Business persons who enter Chile may also obtain an identity card for foreigners.

Appendix K-03.I.1 — Business Visitors

Research and Design

- **Technical, scientific and statistical researchers conducting independent research or research for an enterprise located in the territory of the other Party.**

Growth, Manufacture and Production

- **Purchasing and production management personnel conducting commercial transactions for an enterprise located in the territory of the other Party.**

Marketing

- **Market researchers and analysts conducting independent research or analysis or research or analysis for an enterprise located in the territory of the other Party.**
- **Trade fair and promotional personnel attending a trade convention.**

Sales

- **Sales representatives and agents taking orders or negotiating contracts for goods or services for an enterprise located in the territory of the other Party but not delivering goods or providing services.**
- **Buyers purchasing for an enterprise located in the territory of the other Party.**

Distribution

- **Customs brokers providing consulting services regarding the facilitation of the import or export of goods.**

After-sales Service

- **Installers, repair and maintenance personnel, and supervisors, possessing specialized knowledge essential to a seller's contractual obligation, performing services or training workers to perform services, pursuant to a warranty or other service contract incidental to the sale of commercial or industrial equipment or machinery, including computer software, purchased from an enterprise located outside the territory of the Party into which temporary entry is sought, during the life of the warranty or service agreement.**

General Service

- **Professionals engaging in a business activity at a professional level in a profession set out in Appendix K-03.IV.1.**
- **Management and supervisory personnel engaging in a commercial transaction for an enterprise located in the territory of the other Party.**
- **Financial services personnel (insurers, bankers or investment brokers) engaging in commercial transactions for an enterprise located in the territory of the other Party.**
- **Public relations and advertising personnel consulting with business associates, or attending or participating in conventions.**
- **Tourism personnel (tour and travel agents, tour guides or tour operators) attending or participating in conventions or conducting a tour that has begun in the territory of the other Party.**
- **Translators or interpreters performing services as employees of an enterprise located in the territory of the other Party.**

Definitions

For purposes of this Appendix:

territory of the other Party means the territory of the Party other than the territory of the Party into which temporary entry is sought.

Appendix K-03.I.3 — Existing Immigration Measures

1. In the case of Canada, subsection 19(1) of the *Immigration Regulations*, 1978, SOR/78-172, as amended, made under the *Immigration Act* R.S.C. 1985, c. I-2, as amended.

2. In the case of Chile, Title I, paragraph 6 of *Decree Law 1094*, Official Gazette, July 19, 1975, *Immigration Law ("Decreto Ley 1094,* Diario Oficial, julio 19, 1975, *Ley de Extranjería"),* and *Title III of Immigration Regulation ("Decreto Supremo 597 del Ministerio del Interior,* Diario Oficial noviembre 24, 1984, *Reglamento de Extranjería*").

Appendix K-03.IV.1 — Professionals

PROFESSION[1]	MINIMUM EDUCATION REQUIREMENTS AND ALTERNATIVE CREDENTIALS[2]
General	
Accountant	Baccalaureate or Licenciatura Degree; or C.P.A., C.A., C.G.A. or C.M.A.; or Contador auditor or Contador público (University Title)[3]
Architect	Baccalaureate or Licenciatura Degree; or state/provincial licence[4]

PROFESSION[1]	MINIMUM EDUCATION REQUIREMENTS AND ALTERNATIVE CREDENTIALS[2]
Computer Systems Analyst	Baccalaureate or Licenciatura Degree; or Post-Secondary Diploma[5] or Post-Secondary Certificate[6], and three years experience
Disaster Relief Insurance Claims Adjuster (claims adjuster employed by an insurance company located in the territory of a Party, or an independent claims adjuster)	Baccalaureate or Licenciatura Degree, and successful completion of training in the appropriate areas of insurance adjustment pertaining to disaster relief claims; or three years experience in claims adjustment and successful completion of training in the appropriate areas of insurance adjustment pertaining to disaster relief claims
Economist (including Commercial Engineer in Chile)	Baccalaureate or Licenciatura Degree
Engineer	Baccalaureate or Licenciatura Degree; or state/provincial licence
Forester	Baccalaureate or Licenciatura Degree; or state/provincial licence
Graphic Designer	Baccalaureate or Licenciatura Degree; or Post-Secondary Diploma or Post-Secondary Certificate, and three years experience
Hotel Manager	Baccalaureate or Licenciatura Degree in hotel/restaurant management; or Post-Secondary Diploma or Post-Secondary Certificate in hotel/restaurant management, and three years experience in hotel/restaurant management
Industrial Designer	Baccalaureate or Licenciatura Degree; or Post-Secondary Diploma or Post-Secondary Certificate, and three years experience
Interior Designer	Baccalaureate or Licenciatura Degree; or Post-Secondary Diploma or Post-Secondary Certificate, and three years experience
Land Surveyor	Baccalaureate or Licenciatura Degree; or state/provincial/national licence
Landscape Architect	Baccalaureate or Licenciatura Degree
Lawyer (including Notary in the Province of Quebec)	LL.B., J.D., LL.L., B.C.L. or Licenciatura Degree (five years) or Abogado, or membership in a state/provincial bar

PROFESSION[1]	MINIMUM EDUCATION REQUIREMENTS AND ALTERNATIVE CREDENTIALS[2]
Librarian	M.L.S. or B.L.S. or Magister en Bibliotecología (for which another Baccalaureate or Licenciatura Degree was a prerequisite)
Management Consultant	Baccalaureate or Licenciatura Degree; or equivalent professional experience as established by statement or professional credential attesting to five years experience as a management consultant, or five years experience in a field of specialty related to the consulting agreement
Mathematician (including Statistician)	Baccalaureate or Licenciatura Degree
Range Manager/Range Conservationalist	Baccalaureate or Licenciatura Degree
Research Assistant (working in a post-secondary educational institution)	Baccalaureate or Licenciatura Degree
Scientific Technician/Technologist[7]	Possession of (a) theoretical knowledge of any of the following disciplines: agricultural sciences, astronomy, biology, chemistry, engineering, forestry, geology, geophysics, meteorology or physics; and (b) the ability to solve practical problems in any of those disciplines, or the ability to apply principles of any of those disciplines to basic or applied research
Social Worker	Baccalaureate or Licenciatura Degree or Asistente Social/Trabajador social (University Title)
Sylviculturist (including Forestry Specialist)	Baccalaureate or Licenciatura Degree
Technical Publications Writer	Baccalaureate or Licenciatura Degree; or Post-Secondary Diploma or Post-Secondary Certificate, and three years experience
Urban Planner (including Geographer)	Baccalaureate or Licenciatura Degree
Vocational Counsellor	Baccalaureate or Licenciatura Degree
Medical/Allied Professional	
Dentist	D.D.S., D.M.D., Doctor en Odontologia or Doctor en Cirugia Dental or Licenciatura en Odontologia; or state/provincial licence

PROFESSION[1]	**MINIMUM EDUCATION REQUIREMENTS AND ALTERNATIVE CREDENTIALS**[2]
Dietitian	**Baccalaureate or Licenciatura Degree or Dietista Nutricional (University Title); or state/provincial licence**
Medical Laboratory Technologist (Canada)/Medical Technologist (Chile, Mexico and the United States of America)[8]	**Baccalaureate or Licenciatura Degree; or Post-Secondary Diploma or Post-Secondary Certificate, and three years experience**
Nutritionist	**Baccalaureate or Licenciatura Degree or Nutricionista/Dietista Nutricional (University Title)**
Occupational Therapist	**Baccalaureate or Licenciatura Degree or Terapeuta Ocupacional (University Title); or state/provincial licence**
Pharmacist	**Baccalaureate or Licenciatura Degree; or state/provincial licence**
Physician (teaching or research only)	**M.D. or Doctor en Medicina or Médico Cirujano/Médico (University Title); or state/provincial licence**
Physiotherapist/Physical Therapist	**Baccalaureate or Licenciatura Degree or Kinesiólogo/Kinesioterapeuta (University Title); or state/provincial licence**
Psychologist	**State/provincial licence; or Licenciatura Degree**
Recreational Therapist	**Baccalaureate or Licenciatura Degree**
Registered Nurse	**State/provincial licence, or Licenciatura Degree, or Enfermera (University Title)**
Veterinarian	**D.V.M., D.M.V. or Doctor en Veterinaria or Médico Veterinario (University Title); or state/provincial licence**
Scientist	
Agriculturist (including Agronomist)	**Baccalaureate or Licenciatura Degree**
Animal Breeder	**Baccalaureate or Licenciatura Degree**
Animal Scientist	**Baccalaureate or Licenciatura Degree**
Apiculturist	**Baccalaureate or Licenciatura Degree**
Astronomer	**Baccalaureate or Licenciatura Degree**
Biochemist	**Baccalaureate or Licenciatura Degree**
Biologist	**Baccalaureate or Licenciatura Degree**
Chemist	**Baccalaureate or Licenciatura Degree**
Dairy Scientist	**Baccalaureate or Licenciatura Degree**
Entomologist	**Baccalaureate or Licenciatura Degree**
Epidemiologist	**Baccalaureate or Licenciatura Degree**

PROFESSION[1]	MINIMUM EDUCATION REQUIREMENTS AND ALTERNATIVE CREDENTIALS[2]
Geneticist	**Baccalaureate or Licenciatura Degree**
Geologist	**Baccalaureate or Licenciatura Degree or Geólogo (University Title)**
Geochemist	**Baccalaureate or Licenciatura Degree**
Geophysicist (including Oceanographer in Mexico and the United States of America)	**Baccalaureate or Licenciatura Degree**
Horticulturist	**Baccalaureate or Licenciatura Degree**
Meteorologist	**Baccalaureate or Licenciatura Degree**
Pharmacologist	**Baccalaureate or Licenciatura Degree**
Physicist (including Oceanographer in Canada and Chile)	**Baccalaureate or Licenciatura Degree for Physicist; Oceanógrafo (University Title)for Oceanographer**
Plant Breeder	**Baccalaureate or Licenciatura Degree**
Poultry Scientist	**Baccalaureate or Licenciatura Degree**
Soil Scientist	**Baccalaureate or Licenciatura Degree**
Zoologist	**Baccalaureate or Licenciatura Degree**
Teacher	
College	**Baccalaureate or Licenciatura Degree**
Seminary	**Baccalaureate or Licenciatura Degree**
University	**Baccalaureate or Licenciatura Degree**

Notes:

1 **A business person seeking temporary entry under this Appendix may also perform training functions relating to the profession, including conducting seminars.**

2 ***Accountant*:**

C.P.A.: Certified Public Accountant; C.A.: Chartered Accountant; C.G.A.: Certified General Accountant; C.M.A.: Certified Management Accountant

***Dentist*:**

D.D.S.: Doctor of Dental Surgery; D.M.D.: Doctor of Dental Medicine

***Lawyer*:**

LL.B.: Bachelor of Laws; J.D.: Doctor of Jurisprudence (not a doctorate); LL.L: Licence en Droit (Québec universities and University of Ottawa); BCL: Bachelor of Civil Law

***Librarian*:**

M.L.S.: Master of Library Science; B.L.S.: Bachelor of Library Science

***Physician*:**

M.D.: Medical Doctor

Veterinarian:

D.V.M.: Doctor of Veterinary Medicine; D.M.V.: Docteur en Médicine Vétérinaire

3 **"University Title" means any document conferred by universities recognized by the Government of Chile and shall be deemed to be equivalent to the Minimum Education Requirements and Alternative Credentials for that profession. In the case of the profession of Lawyer (Abogado), the title is conferred by the Supreme Court of Chile.**

4 **"State/provincial licence" and "state/provincial/national licence" mean any document issued by a provincial or national government, as the case may be, or under its authority, but not by a local government, that permits a person to engage in a regulated activity or profession.**

5 **"Post-Secondary Diploma" means a credential issued, on completion of two or more years of post-secondary education, by an accredited academic institution in Canada or the United Sates of America.**

6 **"Post-Secondary Certificate" means a certificate issued, on completion of two or more years of post-secondary education at an academic institution:**

— in the case of Mexico, by the federal government or a state government, an academic institution recognized by the federal government or a state government, or an academic institution created by federal or state law; and

— in the case of Chile, by an academic institution recognized by the Government of Chile.

7 **A business person in this category must be seeking temporary entry to work in direct support of professionals in agricultural sciences, astronomy, biology, chemistry, engineering, forestry, geology, geophysics, meteorology or physics.**

8 **A business person in this category must be seeking temporary entry to perform in a laboratory chemical, biological, hematological, immunologic, microscopic or bacteriological tests and analyses for diagnosis, treatment or prevention of disease.**

Notwithstanding Annex K-03.IV.4, for the purposes of this Agreement, neither Party shall establish an annual numerical limit regarding temporary entry of business persons of the other Party seeking to engage in business activities at a professional level set out in Appendix K-03.IV.1.

BIBLIOGRAPHY

(A) — Texts and Treatises

Business

Pacific Rim Investment and Business Immigration (Seminar Materials, Sept. 14, 1989). Vancouver: Continuing Legal Education, 1989.

Issues Affecting Transborder Relocation of Business Persons and the Free Trade Agreement (Seminar Papers, June 26, 1989). Mississauga, Ont.: Insight, 1989.

Business Immigration (Programme Materials, Nov. 19, 1987). Toronto: Insight, 1987.

Citizenship. by Benjamin J. Trister and Nan Berezowski. Toronto: Carswell, 1996.

The Annotated Citizenship Act 1993. by F.N. Marrocco and H.M. Goslett. Toronto: Carswell, 1992.

Deportation

Whence They Came: Deportation from Canada, 1900–1935. by Barbara Roberts. Ottawa: University of Ottawa Press, 1988.

Due Process

Due Process and the Law of Immigration. Toronto: Canadian Civil Liberties Association, 1974.

Economics

Economic and Social Impacts of Immigration: A Research Report. by Neil Swan, et al. Ottawa: Economic Council of Canada, 1991.

New Faces in the Crowd: Economic and Social Impact of Immigration: A Statement. Ottawa: Economic Council of Canada, 1991.

Free Trade

Doing Business in the U.S.A. Under Free Trade: How to Get the Right Work Visa for Business/Professionals and Investors. 1st ed. by Mark A. Ivener (Self-counsel business series). North Vancouver, B.C.: International Self-Counsel Press, 1989.

Recent Changes to Canadian/U.S. Immigration Laws. The Free Trade Agreement & Canadian Selection Criteria (Seminar Proceedings). Toronto: Canadian Bar Assoc., 1989.

General

Appeals Before the Immigration Appeal Division. by Andrew Z. Wlodyka and John D. Gardner. Toronto: Carswell, 1996.

Immigration Inquiries. by L.X. Woo. Toronto: Carswell, 1995.

Work Permits and Visas. by Jacqueline R. Bart and Benjamin J. Trister. Toronto: Carswell, 1995.

Advanced Immigration Law. Toronto: Canadian Bar Association — Ontario Continuing Legal Education, 1990.

Canada's Immigration Program. (Backgrounder). by Margaret Young. Ottawa: Library of Parliament, Research Branch, 1990.

Canadian Immigrants and Criminality. by John T. Samuel and Ronald Fanstino-Santos. Ottawa: John T. Samuel, 1990.

Immigration in the 1990s. Canada Employment and Immigration Advisory Council. Ottawa: Canada Employment and Immigration Advisory Council, 1991.

Immigration Law 101. Canadian Bar Association — Ontario, 1991. Institute of Continuing Legal Education. Toronto: Canadian Bar Association, 1991.

Immigration Law, 1991. Seminar Materials: April 18 and 19, 1991. Course co-ordinators Anthony M.M. Remedios, Andrew Z. Wlodyka; instructors Darrel V. Heald, et al. Continuing Legal Education Society of British Columbia.

Immigration Law Update. Winnipeg: Law Society of Manitoba, 1990.

Migrant Workers in Japan: Dispute Resolution. (Introduction to Pacific Rim Law). by Masahiro Kuwabara. Edmonton: Faculty of Law, University of Alberta, 1991.

None is too Many — Canada and the Jews of Europe 1933–1948. 3rd ed. by Irving Abella and Harold Trooper. Toronto: Lester Publishing, 1991.

Guide to Canada-Hong Kong Business 1991. ed. by J. Arthur McInnis. Hong Kong-Canada Festival Corporation, Hong Kong, 1991.

Canada's Immigration Law. Ottawa: Minister of Supply and Services, 1990.

Immigration Law. [Seminar Materials: Apr. 6/90]. Continuing Legal Education Society of British Columbia. Course co-ordinator, Anthony M.M. Remedios; instructors, Michael T.L. Blaxland ... (et al.). Vancouver: 1990.

Immigration to Canada: Who Is Allowed? What is Required? How To Do It! 9th ed. by Gary L. Segal. (Self-counsel legal series). North Vancouver: International Self-Counsel Press, 1990.

Canada's Immigration and Citizenship Bulletin. ed. by Frank N. Marrocco, Henry M. Goslett and Gary W. Moore. Toronto: Canada Law Book Inc., 1989

Canadian Immigration Law Into the Nineties. Toronto: Canadian Bar Assoc., 1989.

Immigration Law: The "Ins and Outs" of Immigration Law (Seminar Materials, March 4, 1989). Toronto: Canadian Bar Assoc., 1989.

Immigration Law. 4th ed. by Thomas Harding and Sorel Leinburd. Vancouver: People's Law School, 1988.

La primauté du droit: la situation des immigrants et des réfugiés au regard des chartes et des textes internationaux. par Sophie Bourque. [Travaux de la Revue juridique des étudiants de l'Université Laval; R.J.E.L. 88-14]. Québec: Université Laval, Faculté de droit, 1988.

Immigration: The Kit. Toronto: Community Legal Education Ontario, 1987.

Haven's Gate: Canada's Immigration Fiasco. by Victor Malarek. Toronto: MacMillan of Canada, 1987.

Choisir d'investir et de vivre au Québec. Direction des communications avec la collaboration de la Direction des services aux investisseurs du ministère des Communautés culturelles et de l'Immigration. 2e éd. Montréal: La Direction, 1987.

Informations pratiques à l'intention des immigrants (Recherche et texte). par Thérèse Lambert Alain et Andrée Morin. 3e éd. Montréal: Direction des communications, en collaboration avec la Direction de l'adaptation du ministère des Communautés culturelles et de l'immigration, 1987.

A Guide to Canada Immigration Law. Rev. ed. by Cameron I. McCannell and Edward J. Holgate, Saskatoon, Sask.: Public Legal Education Association of Saskatchewan, 1986.

Immigration to Canada: Who is Allowed? What is Required? How to Do It? 6th ed. by Gary L. Segal. Vancouver, B.C.: International Self-Counsel Press, 1986.

Basic Immigration Law. Toronto: Canadian Bar Association — Ontario, 1985.

Immigration Law in Canada. by Julius Grey. Toronto: Butterworths, 1984.

Canadian Immigration Law and Procedure. by Christopher Wydrzysinski. Aurora, Ont.: Canada Law Book, 1983.

Immigration: A Booklet. by Mary Anne Carswell. Saskatoon, Sask.: Public Legal Education Association of Saskatchewan, 1980.

Citizenship, Aliens and Immigration: Being Title 27 from Volume 4 of The Canadian Encyclopaedic Digest (Ontario). 3rd ed. by Janet V. Scott and Robert C. Stonehouse. Toronto: Carswell, 1980.

How to Immigrate into Canada. 2nd ed. by Gary Segal. Vancouver, B.C.: Self Counsel, 1977.

How to Nominate a Relative. Canada. Dept. of Manpower and Immigration, 1975.

How Canada Selects Immigrants. Canada: Dept. of Manpower and Immigration, 1975.

L'immigration. par Jacques Brossard. Montréal: Presses de l'Université de Montréal, 1967.

Immigration Appeal Board

Index to the Decisions Rendered by the Immigration Appeal Board. by Richard T. Kurland. Toronto: Carswell, 1988.

Law Reform Commission of Canada. Report No. 18. Obtaining Reasons Before Applying for Judicial Scrutiny — Immigration Appeal Board. Ottawa: 1982.

Immigration Settlement and Adaptation Program

The Immigrant Settlement and Adaptation Program (ISAP): Information for Voluntary Organizations. Ottawa, Ont.: Employment and Immigration, 1986.

Labour and Employment

Immigration Levels, 1991–95: A Policy Paper Presented to the Minister of Employment and Immigration. Canada Employment and Immigration Advisory Council. Ottawa: The Council, 1990.

Canada/U.S. Immigration and Employee Transfers. Toronto: Insight Educational Services, 1984.

Legislation

Recent Changes to Canadian Immigration Law: The Five Year Plan. Toronto: Law Society of Upper Canada, Dept. of Continuing Legal Education, 1990.

Immigration Law: Statutes, Bills and Regulations as Amended to Nov. 1987. by W.H. Angus. Toronto: Osgoode Hall Law School, York University, 1987–88.

Immigration Act Amendments. [Submission to House of Commons re: Bill C-24, Canadian Bar Association — Toronto]. Toronto: The Association, 1987.

Minutes of Proceedings and Evidence of the Legislative Committee on Bill C-55, an Act to Amend the Immigration Act, 1976. Ottawa: Queen's Printer, 1985.

Canada's New Immigration Act: A Guide and Critical Commentary. Toronto: Law Union of Ontario, 1978.

New Directions: A Look at Canada's Immigration Act and Regulations. Ottawa: Employment and Immigration Commission, 1978.

Multiculturism

Interim Report on Demography and Immigration Levels: The Third Report of the Standing Committee on Labour, Employment and Immigration. Ottawa: The Committee, 1990.

Immigration and Multiculturism. [Seminar material, Feb. 23, 1989 Continuing Legal Education Society of B.C.]. Course co-ordinator: Armand A. Petronio. Instructors: Carol M. Huddart et al. Vancouver: 1989.

Policy

Canadian Immigration Law and Policy — Le Droit et la politique de l'immigration. Ottawa: Canadian Bar Association, 1990.

Humanitarian Immigration and Canadian Immigration Policy. Rev. ed. (Current Issue Review). by Grant Purves. Ottawa: Library of Parliament, Research Branch, 1989.

Perspective on Immigration in Canada. [Canada Employment and Immigration Advisory Council Final Report, presented to the Minister of Employment and Immigration]. Ottawa: The Council, 1988.

Canada and Immigration: Public Policy and Public Concern. 2nd ed. by Freda Hawkins. Kingston, Ont.: McGill-Queen's University Press, 1988.

Les politiques menées par certains États de démocratie libérale à l'endroit des communautés culturelles issues de l'immigration internationale. [Études et documents; No 11]. par Guy Bouthillier. Québec: Ministère des Communautés culturelles et de l'Immigration, Direction de la recherche, 1987.

Double Standard: The Secret History of Canadian Immigration Policy. 1st ed. by Reg. Whitaka. Toronto: Lester & Orpen Dennys, 1987.

Humanitarian Immigration and Canadian Immigration Policy. Rev. ed. by Grant Purves. [Current Issue Review; 80-10E]. Ottawa: Library of Parliament, 1986.

Report of Parliament on the Review of Future Directions for Immigration Levels. Ottawa: Employment and Immigration Canada, 1985.

Illegal Aliens, Unemployment and Immigration Policy. by Sobodan Djajic. [Queen's Discussion Paper; No. 591]. Kingston, Ont.: Institute for Economic Research, Queen's University, 1985.

Immigration Policy in Canada, Past and Present. Canada: Dept. of Manpower and Immigration, 1971.

Practice and Procedure

Immigration Law and Practices. by Lorne Waldman. Toronto: Butterworths, 1992.

Immigration Law and Practice in the United Kingdom. 3rd ed. by Ian A. Macdonald and Nicholas J. Blake. Toronto: Butterworths, 1991.

Immigration Manual: Backlog Clearance Program. Ottawa: Employment and Immigration Canada, 1990.

Immigration Law: The Ethics of Practice. Toronto: Dept. of Education, Law Society of Upper Canada, 1990.

The Second Annual Advanced Immigration Law. [Seminar Material, May 27/88. Ch. Gary L. Segal]. Canadian Bar Association — Ontario, Continuing Legal Education. Toronto: 1988.

Immigration 1987. [Seminar Materials, Dec. 4/87]. Course co-ordinator, Dennis G. McCrea. Continuing Legal Education Society of British Columbia. Vancouver: 1987.

Immigration Law: The Advocates' Manual. by Linda Finnigan. Toronto: Community Legal Education Ontario, 1987.

Immigration. [Programme Materials, Nov. 27/87]. Law Society of Upper Canada. Toronto: 1987.

Immigration. [Seminar Materials, Dec. 4/85]. Continuing Legal Education Society of British Columbia. Vancouver: 1985.

Immigration Law — Procedure for the General Practitioner. Law Society of Upper Canada, Continuing Legal Education. Toronto: 1983.

Immigration Practice and Procedure. [Seminar, March 20/82]. Continuing Legal Education Society of British Columbia. Vancouver: 1982.

Immigration Practice and Procedure. [Seminar, Oct. 1980]. Law Society of Upper Canada, Continuing Legal Education. Toronto: 1980.

Immigration Procedure. by Kit Rigg. Vancouver: Vancouver People's Law School, 1975.

Provinces

Immigration to Alberta: Overview from 1982 to 1986. Alberta Manpower, Settlement Services. Edmonton: Alberta Career Development and Employment, Immigration and Settlement, 1987.

Quebec

Canada-Québec Accord Relating to Immigration and Temporary Admission of Aliens. Ottawa: Employment and Immigration Canada, 1991.

Highlights of the Brief on the Immigration and Integration Policy Statement. Québec: Gouvernment du Québec, Conseil du Statut de la femme, 1991.

Immigration: The Canada-Quebec Accord. (Background paper). by Margaret Young. Ottawa: Library of Parliament, Research Branch, 1991.

Refugees

The 1995 Annotated Refugee Convention. by Pia Zambelli. Toronto: Carswell, 1994.

Refugee Determination Proceedings. by Samuel Berman and Caroline McChesney. Toronto: Carswell, 1994.

Agents of Persecution: A Question of Protection. (Discussion paper: No. 3). by Gay Evans. Toronto: Centre for Refugee Studies, 1991.

Canada's Refugee Status Determination System. Rev. ed. (Background paper). by Margaret Young. Ottawa: Library of Parliament Research Branch, 1991.

Civil War Refugees and the Issue of "Singling Out" in a State of Civil Unrest. by Suzanne J. Egan. Toronto: Centre for Refugee Studies, 1991.

Refugee Claimants and the Law. by John William Pullen. Toronto: Institute of Public Administration of Canada, 1991.

Refugee Claims Based on Refusal to Perform Military Service. (Discussion paper: No. 2). by Maureen Smith-Gordon. Toronto: Centre for Refugee Studies, 1991.

Refugee Policy: Canada and the United States. Toronto, York University: Centre for Refugee Studies. Staten Island: Centre for Migration Studies of New York, 1991.

The Law of Refugee Status. by James C. Hathaway. Toronto: Butterworths, 1991.

Attorney-General of Canada v. Ward. by David Petrasek and Suzanne Egan, principal researchers. North York, Ont.: Centre for Refugee Studies and Centre for Research in Public Law and Public Policy, 1990.

Canada's New Refugee Status. (Backgrounder). by Margaret Young. Ottawa: Library of Parliament, Research Branch, 1990.

Canada's Refugee Status Determination System. Rev. Sept. 1990. (Backgrounder paper, BP-185E). by Margaret Young. Ottawa: Library of Parliament, Research Branch, 1990.

Refugee Claimants and the Law: (Regional Crisis Management). (Case Program in Canadian Public Administration). by John William Pullen. Toronto: Institute of Public Administration of Canada, 1990.

Refugee or Asylum?: A Choice for Canada. ed. by Howard Adelman and C. Michael Lanphier. Toronto: York Lanes Press. York University, 1990.

The Refugee Claimant Handbook: Toronto and Area. rewritten by Michael Bossin, John Burge and Belva Spiel. Toronto: Community Legal Education Ontario, 1989.

Canada's New Refugee Status Determination System. by Margaret Young. Ottawa: Library of Parliament, Research Branch, 1989.

Closing The Doors: The Failure of Refugee Protection. by David Matas with Ilana Simon. Toronto: Summerhill Press, 1989.

Refugee Claims: The Role of Board Members and Hearing Officers. Canadian Bar Association — Ontario, Continuing Legal Education. (Seminar Materials). Toronto: 1989.

Refugees and International Relations. by Gil Loescher and Laila Monahan, eds. Oxford; Toronto: Oxford University Press, 1989.

The Sanctuary Trial. by David Matas, on behalf of the International Commission of Jurists. Winnipeg: Legal Research Institute of the University of Manitoba, 1989.

Seminar on New Refugee Determination Process. Vancouver: Canadian Bar Assoc., 1989.

Human Rights and the Protection of Refugees Under International Law. (Conference Proceedings, Nov. 29, 1987). Montreal: Canadian Human Rights Foundation, 1988.

Bill C-55, Refugee Determination Process. [Submission to House of Commons] Canadian Bar Association — Ontario. Toronto: The Association, 1987.

Profil statistique des revendicateurs de statut de réfugié. par Bertrand Lebel. Montréal: Conseil des communautés culturelles et de l'immigration du Québec, 1987.

Aspects légaux et règlementaires de l'immigration au Québec. [Consultation sur les niveaux d'immigration]. Montréal: Ministère des Communautés culturelles et de l'immigration, Direction des communications, 1987.

So You're in the Refugee Backlog. Interclinic Immigration Working Group. Toronto: Community Legal Education Ontario, 1986.

The Convention Refugee Determination Process in Canada. by Margaret Young. [Current Issue Review; 86-25E]. Ottawa: Library of Parliament, 1986.

Refugee Determination in Canada: A Report to the Hon. Flora MacDonald,, Minister of Employment and Immigration. by Gunther W. Plaut. Ottawa: Employment and Immigration Canada, 1985.

Sponsorship

Sponsoring a Foreign National: Rights and Obligations of Sponsors. Ministère des Communautés culturelles et de l'immigration du Québec, Direction de communications, with the collaboration of the Direction des étudiants, garants, travailleurs. Quebec: Le Ministère, 1987.

Sponsoring Refugees: Facts for Canadian Groups and Organizations. Ottawa: Employment and Immigration, 1986.

How to Sponsor a Dependent. Canada. Dept. of Manpower and Immigration, 1975.

War Criminals

Justice Delayed: Nazi War Criminals in Canada. by David Matas. Toronto: Summerhill Press, 1987.

Women

Immigrant Women in Canada: A Policy Perspective, by Shirley B. Seward and Kathryn McDade. [Background paper; BP 1988-1E]. Ottawa: Canadian Advisory Council on the Status of Women.

(B) — Articles and Essays

Aids

Committee (of CBA — Ont.) Suggests Tests for Immigrants be Compulsory to Detect Those Having AIDS. by Michael Crawford. (1986) 13, No. 5 National (Canadian Bar Association) 23.

Business

Recovering Moneys Lost in Immigrant Investor Funds, by H.A. Christie. Canada's Immigration and Citizenship Bulletin 11:7@1, October 1999.

Business and Borders, by H.M. Goslett. Canada's Immigration and Citizenship Bulletin 11:7@3, October 1999.

Immigrant Investor Program Update, by C.M. Small. Canada's Immigration and Citizenship Bulletin 11:6@3, September 1999.

Canada-British Columbia Business Immigration Pilot Project, by G.W. Moore. Canada's Immigration and Citizenship Bulletin 11:4@3, July 1999.

New Immigrant Investor Program, by G.W. Moore. Canada's Immigration and Citizenship Bulletin 10:9@3 January 1999.

Failure to Deliver-Cross-Border Services, by H.M. Goslett. Canada's Immigration and Citizenship Bulletin 10:2@1, April 1998.

The Scope of Business Visitors Provisions and the Spirit of NAFTA, by C.M. Small Canada's Immigration and Citizenship Bulletin 9:9@1, January 1998 .

Report of the Immigrant Investor Program Advisory Panel — Part 2. by N. Seeman. Canada's Immigration and Citizenship Bulletin. 7:9@3, January 1996.

Report of the Immigrant Investor Program Advisory Panel — Part 1 of 2. by N. Seeman. Canada's Immigration and Citizenship Bulletin. 7:8@1, November 1995.

The True Definition of Investor. by Frank N. Marrocco. Canada's Immigration and Citizenship Bulletin. 6:10@2, February 1995.

Entrepreneurial Terms and Conditions Revisted. by C.R. Singer. Canada's Immigration and Citizenship Bulletin. 6:7@3, 1994.

Investor — A Clarification. by Frank N. Marrocco. Canada's Immigration and Citizenship Bulletin. 6:6@2, 1994.

Business Immigration to Quebec. by H.M. Goslett. Canada's Immigration and Citizenship Bulletin. 6:1@1, 1994.

Foreign Domestic Workers — Crisis? What Crisis? by John W. Petrykanyn. Canada's Immigration and Citizenship Bulletin. 5:2@3, 1993.

Entrepreneurial Terms and Conditions (Part II). by Henry M. Goslett. Canada's Immigration and Citizenship Bulletin. 4:10@1, 1993.

Entrepreneurial Terms and Conditions (Part I). by Henry M. Goslett. Canada's Immigration and Citizenship Bulletin. 4:9@2, 1993.

The Economics of Co-operation. by Frank N. Marrocco. Canada's Immigration and Citizenship Bulletin. 4:9@4, 1993.

Intra-Company Transferees and Joint Ventures: A Need for Reform. by Canada's Immigration and Citizenship Bulletin. 4:8@4, 1992.

Business and Bureaucracy — Oil and Water. by Henry M. Goslett. Canada's Immigration and Citizenship Bulletin. 4: 6@1, 1992.

Ontario Securities Act Application to Business Immigration Program Share Offerings. by Glenn M. Rumbell. Canada's Immigration and Citizenship Bulletin. 2:8@3, 1991.

Recent Changes to the Investor Program — Parts I and II. by Henry M. Goslett. Canada's Immigration and Citizenship Bulletin. 2:1@1; 2:2@2, 1990.

Self-Employed Business Applicants. by Henry M. Goslett. Canada's Immigration and Citizenship Bulletin. 1:6@1, 1990.

Investors: Some Problems. by Frank N. Marrocco. Canada's Immigration and Citizenship Bulletin. 1:2@4, 1990.

Employment Authorizations — Port of Entry Applications. by Gary W. Moore. Canada's Immigration and Citizenship Bulletin. 1:9@2, 1990.

The Immigrant Investor Program: The 50/50 Rule — Parts I and II. by Glenn Rumbell. Canada's Immigration and Citizenship Bulletin. 1:10@3; 2:1@2, 1990.

Offshore Trusts for Immigrants to Canada. by Robert Witterick. Canada's Immigration and Citizenship Bulletin. 2:3@3, 1990.

Immigrant Investor Projects — Marketing in Hong Kong. by Hugh Gillespie. Canada's Immigration and Citizenship Bulletin. 2:6@1, 1990.

Investor Program — Minimum Investment Levels Increase. by Henry M. Goslett. Canada's Immigration and Citizenship Bulletin. 2:7@1, 1990.

Non-Resident Investors in Canadian Partnership and Tax Shelters. by Robert Witterick. Canada's Immigration and Citizenship Bulletin. 2:4@3, 1990.

Conundrum: (Employment Authorizations and Visa Applications). by Anita Sulley. (1989), 7 Immigration Law Reporter (2nd Series) 41.

Business Planning and the New Business Immigration Program (Part 1). by Richard Kurland. (1987) 2 Securities and Corporate Regulation Review 31–32, 33–38.

The Immigration Act: Implications for Business. by Shanon O.N. Grauer. in Current Issues in Canadian Business Law. ed. by R.B. Miner. Toronto: Carswell, 1986. 129–151.

Case Comments

Additional Implications of the Pushpanathan Decision, by F.N. Marrocco. Canada's Immigration and Citizenship Bulletin 11:3@1, May 1999.

Judicial Review of Visa Officers in Light of the Pushpanathan Decision — Part III, by F.N. Marrocco. Canada's Immigration and Citizenship Bulletin 11:2@1, April 1999.

Judicial Review of Visa Officers in Light of the Pushpanathan Decision — Part II, by F.N. Marrocco. Canada's Immigration and Citizenship Bulletin 11:1@1, March 1999.

Judicial Review of Visa Officers in Light of the Pushpanathan Decision, by F.N. Marrocco. Canada's Immigration and Citizenship Bulletin 10:10@1, February 1999.

When a Precedent Is Not a Precedent. by F.N. Marrocco. Canada's Immigration and Citizenship Bulletin. 8:4@4, June 1996.

The True Definition of Investor. by Frank N. Marrocco. Canada's Immigration and Citizenship Bulletin. 6:10@2, February 1995.

Investor — A Clarification. by Frank N. Marrocco. Canada's Immigration and Citizenship Bulletin. 6:6@2, September 1994.

Case Summary of Deutsche Lufthansa AG. by S.B. Bush. Canada's Immigration and Citizenship Bulletin. 6:2@1, 1994.

Immigration — The Supreme Court Decision vs. Singh. by Asher Neudorfer. (1986) 2 Administrative Law Journal 17–20, 21–23.

Ministerial Permits and Due Process — Minister of Manpower and Immigration v. Hardaval. by John Hucker. (1978) 16 Osgoode Hall Law Journal 773–777.

Children

Supreme Court of Canada Elevates Rights and Best Interests of Children, by B.J. Caruso. Canada's Immigration and Citizenship Bulletin 11:5@1, August 1999.

Canada's Most Wanted — The Adoption of Foreign Children, by H.M. Goslett. Canada's Immigration and Citizenship Bulletin 11:3@2, May 1999.

Best Interests of the Child and the Immigration Act, by S. Parmar and J.W. Petrykanyn. Canada's Immigration and Citizenship Bulletin 10:3@3, May 1998.

New Stringent View of "Residence", by J.W. Petrykanyn. Canada's Immigration and Citizenship Bulletin 10:1@2, March 1998.

"Our Missing Children" Program, by F. Piscitelli. Canada's Immigration and Citizenship Bulletin 9:10@3, February 1998.

The Langner Decision & Children's Rights — The World is Watching. by J.W. Petrykanyn and F. Rosenzweig. Canada's Immigration and Citizenship Bulletin. 7:7@1, October 1995.

Children's Rights and the Immigration Act: The Langner Case. by J.W. Petrykanyn and F. Rosenzweig. Canada's Immigration and Citizenship Bulletin. 7:6@1, August 1995.

Adopted Children and the Citizenship Act. by John W. Petrykanyn & S. Ahn. Canada's Immigration and Employment Bulletin. 7:1@3, March 1995.

Adopted Children and Equality Before the Law — The McKenna Decision. by F. Rosenzweig. Canada's Immigration and Citizenship Bulletin. 6:6@3, 1994.

Adoptions: An Immigration Perspective — Parts I and II. by Gary W. Moore. Canada's Immigration and Citizenship Bulletin. 1:1@2; 1:2@2, 1990.

Barriers Hurt Children. (1988) 4, No. 4 Canadian Human Rights Advocate 9–10.

Citizenship

Canadian Citizenship — The New Provisions, by H.M. Goslett. Canada's Immigration and Citizenship Bulletin 10:9@2, January 1999.

Changes for Citizenship Appeals, by B.J. Caruso. Canada's Immigration and Citizenship Bulletin 10:7@1, October 1998.

Who has a Claim to Canadian Citizenship? by N. Seeman. Canada's Immigration and Citizenship Bulletin. 8:1@1, March 1996.

Adopted Children and the Citizenship Act. by John W. Petrykanyn & S. Ahn. Canada's Immigration and Employment Bulletin. 7:1@3, March 1995.

U.S. Citizenship Acquired by Birth Abroad. by L.J. Hulka. Canada's Immigration and Citizenship Bulletin. 6:4@4, 1994.

Revitalization of Citizenship Act and Procedures. by H.M. Goslett. Canada's Immigration and Citizenship Bulletin. 6:3@2, 1994.

Once a Canadian, Always a Canadian? N. Sabourin, E. Stevens. Canada's Immigration and Citizenship Bulletin. 5:8@1, 1993.

Loss of U.S. Citizenship aand U.S. Dual Nationality. by Gary W. Moore. Canada's Immigration and Citizenship Bulletin. 5:8@2, 1993.

Citizenship Mail-in Centre. by N. Sabourin. Canada's Immigration and Citizenship Bulletin. 5:6@1, 1993.

Canadianized — Is That The Requirement? by Henry M. Goslett. Canada's Immigration and Citizenship Bulletin. 5:4@3, 1993.

Systemic Delay — R. v. Sadiq. by Frank N. Marrocco. Canada's Immigration and Citizenship Bulletin. 3:4@3, 1991.

The Administration of Citizenship Law in Canada. by Mario Simard. Canada's Immigration and Citizenship Bulletin. 1:1@3, 1990.

Entitlement to Canadian Citizenship Through Birth. by Mario Simard. Canada's Immigration and Citizenship Bulletin. 1:4@3, 1990.

Citizenship Applications and Residence. by Frank N. Marrocco. Canada's Immigration and Citizenship Bulletin. 2:6@2, 1990.

Dual Citizenship: Acquiring Canadian Citizenship. by Glenn M. Rumbell. Canada's Immigration and Citizenship Bulletin. 2:5@3, 1990.

Constitutional

A Few Bad Apples. by B.J. Caruso. Canada's Immigration and Citizenship Bulletin. 7:6@3, August 1995.

Mobility Rights For New Immigrants and Waiving Fundamental Constitutional Rights. by Frank N. Marrocco. Canada's Immigration and Citizenship Bulletin. 4:6@2, 1992.

The Extraterritorial Application of the Charter to Visa Applicants. by D. Galloway. (1991) 23 Ottawa L. Rev. 335.

"Equality Rights in the Federal Independent Immigrant Selection Criteria." by Walter Yan Tom Chi. (June 1990) 31 Cahiers de droit 477.

"Advocacy, Immigration and the Charter." by Barbara Jackman. (1990) 9 Immigration Law Reporter (2nd Series) 286.

"Charter Issues and the Immigration and Refugee Board." by R.G.L. Fairweather. in: Administrative Tribunals and the Charter. ed. by N.R. Finkelstein and B.M. Rogus. (Toronto: Carswell, 1990), p. 69.

Meech Lake: Immigration and the 1987 Constitutional Resolution. by Gary W. Moore. Canada's Immigration and Citizenship Bulletin. 2:4@2, 1990.

Counsellors

Immigration Counsellors — and What To Do About Them. by David Matas. (1986) 5, No. 45 Ontario Lawyers Weekly 4.

Criminal Law

Canadian Equivalents of Foreign Alcohol-Related Driving Offences. by Gary W. Moore. Canada's Immigration and Citizenship Bulletin. 5:10@3, 1994.

Urgency Status for Applications for Criminal Pardons. by J.W. Petrykanyn. Canada's Immigration and Citizenship Bulletin. 5:7@3, 1993.

The Criminal Records Act. by Frank N. Marrocco. Canada's Immigration and Citizenship Bulletin. 5:2@2, 1993.

Criminal Equivalency Under the Immigration Act. by Peter Rosenthal. (Feb 1992) 34 Crim. L.Q. 183.

Criminal Aliens in Canada — Visitors. by Henry M. Goslett. Canada's Immigration and Citizenship Bulletin. 1:9@1, 1990.

Criminal Inadmissibility. by Henry M. Goslett. Canada's Immigration and Citizenship Bulletin. 1:10@1, 1990.

Criminal Inadmissibility — Sentences. by Henry M. Goslett. Canada's Immigration and Citizenship Bulletin. 1:10@4, 1990.

Deportation Implication of Criminal Sentencing. by Henry M. Goslett. Canada's Immigration and Citizenship Bulletin. 2:4@1, 1990.

The Relationship Between Criminal Law and Immigration Law. by Brent Knazan. (1985) 27 Criminal Law Quarterly 476–495.

Immigration Law and the Marihuana User. by Fred L. Ringham. (1979) 37 University of Toronto Faculty of Law Review 254.

Customs

Importing Motor Vehicles. by F.P. Eliadis. Canada's Immigration and Citizenship Bulletin. 5:10@4, 1994.

Customs: General Information for Immigrants — Part I. by Henry M. Goslett. Canada's Immigration and Citizenship Bulletin. 2:9@3, 1991.

Customs: General Information for Immigrants — Part I. by Henry M. Goslett. Canada's Immigration and Citizenship Bulletin. 2:10@3, 1991.

Deportation

The Tasse Report: Redesigning the Removal Process. by J.W. Petrykanyn. Canada's Immigration and Citizenship Bulletin. 8:2@2, April 1996.

Departure Orders. by John Petrykanyn. Canada's Immigration and Citizenship Bulletin. 5:4@1, 1993.

Deportation in the Depression. by S. Imai. (1981) 7 Queen's Law Journal 66–94.

Immigration Inquiries and Appeals from Orders of Deportation. by J.V. Scott. (1971) Special Lectures of the Law Society of Upper Canada 117–135.

Education

Impact of High Immigration Levels on the Educational System. by Gary W. Moore. Canada's Immigration and Citizenship Bulletin. 3:2@1, 1991.

Family Reunification

Strengthening Family Reunification — The New Proposals, by P. Ahlfeld. Canada's Immigration and Citizenship Bulletin 11:4@1, July 1999.

Dependency and the New Family Class Regulations. by Frank N. Marrocco. Canada's Immigration and Citizenship Bulletin. 3:10@4, 1992.

Fundamental Justice and Family Class Immigration: The Example of Pangli v. Minister of Employment and Immigration. by Philip L. Bryden. (Fall 1991) 14 U.T.L.J. 484.

Defining "family": A Comment on the Family Reunification Provisions of the Immigration Act. by Deborah McIntosh. (1988) 3 Journal of Law and Social Policy 104–115.

The Rights to Leave and to Family Reunification. by Irwin Cotler. (1987) 28 Cahiers de droit 625–674.

Tandem Procession of LRFM (Last Remaining Family Member). by Cecil L. Rotenberg. (1987) 2 Immigration Law Reports (2nd Series) 260–263.

Free Trade

Failure to Deliver Cross-Border Services, by H.M. Goslett. Canada's Immigration and Citizenship Bulletin 10:2@1, April 1998.

The Scope of Business Visitors Provisions and the Spirit of NAFTA, by C.M. Small Canada's Immigration and Citizenship Bulletin 9:9@1, January 1998.

Licensing Requirements for Tradespersons and Professionals. by D.M. Haak. Canada's Immigration and Citizenship Bulletin. 6:8@2, 1994.

Visas for Canadian Professional under NAFTA. by H.J. Chang. Canada's Immigration and Citizenship Bulletin. 6:6@1, 1994.

Agressive American Economic Immigration Strategy. by H.M. Goslett. Canada's Immigration and Citizenship Bulletin. 3:9@1, 1992.

North American Free Trade Agreement: An Immigration Overview. by Gary W. Moore. Canada's Immigration and Citizenship Bulletin. 4:7@1, 1992.

The FTA and Business Visitors. by Henry M. Goslett. Canada's Immigration and Citizenship Bulletin. 1:2@1, 1990.

Traders and Investors Under the FTA. by Henry M. Goslett. Canada's Immigration and Citizenship Bulletin. 1:3@1, 1990.

Immigration and the FTA. by Henry M. Goslett. Canada's Immigration and Citizenship Bulletin. 1:1@1, 1990.

Services and Entry under the FTA: A Direction For Reform. Canada's Immigration and Citizenship Bulletin. 2:2@3, 1990.

The Free Trade Agreement: A New Immigration Law Between the United States and Canada. by Mark A. Ivener. (Jan. 1989) 6 Business & the Law 3–4.

General

Leave no Leave, by P. Ahlfeld. Canada's Immigration and Citizenship Bulletin 11:6@1, September 1999.

Who is Telling the Truth?, by F.N. Marrocco. Canada's Immigration and Citizenship Bulletin 11:5@2, August 1999.

Additional Implications of the Pushpanathan Decision, by F.N. Marrocco. Canada's Immigration and Citizenship Bulletin 11:3@1, May 1999.

Judicial Review of Visa Officers in Light of the Pushpanathan Decision — Part III, by F.N. Marrocco. Canada's Immigration and Citizenship Bulletin 11:2@1, April 1999.

Judicial Review of Visa Officers in Light of the Pushpanathan Decision — Part II, by F.N. Marrocco. Canada's Immigration and Citizenship Bulletin 11:1@1, March 1999.

Judicial Review of Visa Officers in Light of the Pushpanathan Decision, by F.N. Marrocco. Canada's Immigration and Citizenship Bulletin 10:10@1, February 1999.

New Processing Rules for Exotic Dancers, by R. Farquhar and J. Petrykanyn. Canada's Immigration and Citizenship Bulletin 10:8@3, December 1998.

New Spousal Work Permit Pilot Project, by H.M. Goslett. Canada's Immigration and Citizenship Bulletin 10:8@1, December 1998.

New Immigrant Application Processing System, by H.M. Goslett. Canada's Immigration and Citizenship Bulletin 10:7@2, October 1998.

To Reason or Not to Reason: That is the Question, by I.H. Sherman, Q.C. Canada's Immigration and Citizenship Bulletin, 10:6@1, September 1998.

ADR Enters the Immigration Arena, by B.J. Caruso. Canada's Immigration and Citizenship Bulletin 10:5@2, August 1998.

Refusal of Visitor Visas — A Perennial Problem, by H.M. Goslett. Canada's Immigration and Citizenship Bulletin 10:5@1, August 1998.

Canadian Passports, by I.H. Sherman, Q.C. Canada's Immigration and Citizenship Bulletin 10:4@1, July 1998.

Missed Opportunities — The Work Permit Program, by H.M. Goslett. Canada's Immigration and Citizenship Bulletin 10:3@1, May 1998.

New Federal Court Rules, by G.W. Moore. Canada's Immigration and Citizenship Bulletin 10:3@2, May 1998.

Employment Validations for Live-in Caregivers: Like Bicycles for Fish, by J.W. Petrykanyn Canada's Immigration and Citizenship Bulletin 9:9@2, January 1998.

The Metropolis Project. by N. Seeman. Canada's Immigration and Citizenship Bulletin. 8:4@1, June 1996.

Canadian Immigration: What's New? by H.M. Goslett. Canada's Immigration and Citizenship Bulletin. 8:3@1, May 1996.

Rising Costs and Complexity in the Immigration Process. by H.M. Goslett. Canada's Immigration and Citizenship Bulletin. 8:2@1, April 1996.

Canadian Immigration — What's New? by H.M. Goslett. Canada's Immigration and Citizenship Bulletin. 7:7@4, October 1995.

Canpass — The Future Has Arrived. by H.M. Goslett. Canada's Immigration and Citizenship Bulletin. 7:6@1, September 1995.

Temporary Entry Under GATS. by Gary W. Moore. Canada's Immigration and Citizenship Bulletin. 7:3@1, May 1995.

Right of Landing Fee. by Barbara Jo Caruso. Canada's Immigration and Citizenship Bulletin. 7:2@4, 1995.

A Journey Across the Atlantic. by Henry M. Goslett. Canada's Immigration and Citizenship Bulletin. 7:1@1, March 1995.

The Latest on PRDs — What, Why, When & How. by Henry M. Goslett. Canada's Immigration and Citizenship Bulletin. 6:9@2, January 1995.

Licensing Requirements for Tradespersons and Professionals. by D.M. Haak. Canada's Immigration and Citizenship Bulletin. 6:8@2, 1994.

Changes to the Immigration Processing Fees. by Barbara Jo Caruso. Canada's Immigration and Citizenship Bulletin. 6:4@2, 1994.

The Uneasy Landing of Mary Poppins. by J.W. Petrykanyn. Canada's Immigration and Citizenship Bulletin. 6:4@1

Opening and Closing the Nanny Gate. by J.W. Petrykanyn. Canada's Immigration and Citizenship Bulletin. 6:3@1, 1994.

New OHIP Rules for Immigrants and Temporary Residents. by B.J. Caruso. Canada's Immigration and Citizenship Bulletin. 6:3@3, 1994.

Marriage Bona Fides Test. by J.W. Petrykanyn. Canada's Immigration and Citizenship Bulletin. 6:2@3, 1994.

Graduated Licensing in Ontario — How Will it Affect New Immigrants and Visitors. by B.J. Caruso. Canada's Immigration and Citizenship Bulletin. 6:1@3, 1994.

Insufficient Funds — An 11th Hour Stumbling Block for Immigrants. by D.S. Lesperance. Canada's Immigration and Citizenship Bulletin. 5:10@3, 1994.

Canadian High Commission in Hong Kong — Open for Business. by H.M. Goslett. Canada's Immigration and Citizenship Bulletin. 5:9@1, 1994.

Japanese Work Permits for Intra-Company Transfers. by Gary W. Moore, G. Psimoulis. Canada's Immigration and Citizenship Bulletin. 5:9@2, 1994.

Indefinite Leave to Remain Status in the United Kingdom: The Returning Resident's Rule. by Gary W. Moore. Canada's Immigration and Citizenship Bulletin. 5:9@3, 1994.

OPIC Update. by H.M. Goslett. Canada's Immigration and Citizenship Bulletin. 5:8@3, 1993.

Reconfiguration — Immigration Shuffles the Visa Office Deck. by D.S. Lesperance. Canada's Immigration and Citizenship Bulletin. 5:7@2, 1993.

Gone Forever. by Frank N. Marrocco. Canada's Immigration and Citizenship Bulletin. 5:6@4, 1993.

A Waste of Time. by Frank N. Marrocco. Canada's Immigration and Citizenship Bulletin. 5:5@4, 1993.

General Immigration Matters. by Gary G. Moore. Canada's Immigration and Citizenship Bulletin. 5:4@2, 1993.

New Rehabilitation Rules "Beg Your Pardon". by John W. Petrykanyn and G. Psimoulis. Canada's Immigration and Citizenship Bulletin. 5:3@1, 1993.

Immigration Consultations — 1993. by Henry M. Goslett. Canada's Immigration and Citizenship Bulletin. 5:3@2, 1993.

Immigration Statistics. by Henry M. Goslett. Canada's Immigration and Citizenship Bulletin. 5:2@4,1993.

Immigration Medicals: What's New. by H.M. Goslett. Canada's Immigration and Citizenship Bulletin. 4:5@2, 1992.

Changes to Immigration Fees Regulations. by H.M. Goslett. Canada's Immigration and Citizenship Bulletin. 3:3@2, 1991.

Dr. Malthus and Mr. Geldof. by David Patterson. (Sept. 1991) 40 Advocate (Van.) 703.

Migration and Refugees: Regional Challenges and Regional Opportunities. by Guy S. Goodwin-Gill. (1991) Can. Council Int. L. 213.

New Directions in U.S. Immigration: A Review of Significant Provisions to the U.S. Immigration Act of 1990. by James F. Egan. (Nov. 1991) 4 Can-U.S. Trade 65.

Organization of Professional Immigration Consultants. by Gary W. Moore. Canada's Immigration and Citizenship Bulletin. 3:8@3, 1991.

Abandonment of Permanent Residence Status. by Gary W. Moore and Henry M. Goslett. Canada's Immigration and Citizenship Bulletin. 3:1@2, 1991.

Five-Year Plan Immigration Levels. by Gary W. Moore. Canada's Immigration and Citizenship Bulletin. 2:9@1.

Hong Kong: Recent Developments in U.K. Nationality and Immigration Law (Part II). by Leslie Kemp. Canada's Immigration and Citizenship Bulletin. 2:8@2, 1991.

Immigration — Quality of Service. by Henry M. Goslett. Canada's Immigration and Citizenship Bulletin. 2:8@1, 1991.

Representations to Canada Immigration. by Martin Levine. Canada's Immigration and Citizenship Bulletin. 3:1@1, 1991.

The Early British Columbia Supreme Court and the "Chinese Question": Echoes of the Rule of Law. by John P.S. McLaren. (1990) 20 Man. L.J. 107.

"Musings from Mudge Island: Dr. Malthus and Mr. Geldof." by Philip d'A. Collings. (Nov. 1990) 48 Advocate (Van.) 924.

"Canadian Immigration Law and Policy: A Study in Politics, Demographics and Economics." by R.G. Atkey. (1990) 16 Canada-United States Law Journal 59.

Canada's Post-Tiananmen Square Policy. by Karen Crozier. Canada's Immigration and Citizenship Bulletin. 1:5@1, 1990.

Family Business Applications. by Henry M. Goslett. Canada's Immigration and Citizenship Bulletin. 1:4@1, 1990.

Not Everyone is Welcome in the U.S.A. by Henry M. Goslett. Canada's Immigration and Citizenship Bulletin. 1:8@1, 1990.

'Til Immigration Do Us Part — Visitor's Visa. by Henry M. Goslett. Canada's Immigration and Citizenship Bulletin. 2:3@2, 1990.

Conflicts of Interest. by Frank N. Marrocco. Canada's Immigration and Citizenship Bulletin. 1:8@4, 1990.

Ethical Responsibilities of Commission Counsel. by Frank N. Marrocco. Canada's Immigration and Citizenship Bulletin. 1:9@4, 1990.

The Returning Resident Permit: Don't Leave Home Without It. by Timothy Morin. Canada's Immigration and Citizenship Bulletin. 1:6@4, 1990.

Immigration Cost Recovery — A Tax Alternative. by Gary W. Moore. Canada's Immigration and Citizenship Bulletin. 1:10@2, 1990.

Immigration Levels 1990: An Overview and Analysis. by Gary W. Moore. Canada's Immigration and Citizenship Bulletin. 1:8@2, 1990.

Foreign Domestic Workers and Misrepresentations: New Policy, Old Practices? by John Petrykanyn. Canada's Immigration and Citizenship Bulletin. 1:8@3, 1990.

Seizure of Vehicles: An Increase in Deterrence. by John Petrykanyn. Canada's Immigration and Citizenship Bulletin. 1:7@3, 1990.

Public Interest Litigation and the Immigration Act. by Frank N. Marrocco. Canada's Immigration and Citizenship Bulletin. 2:6@4, 1990.

Constitutional Reform and Immigration. in Meech Lake and Canada. ed. by R. Gibbons et al. Edmonton: Academic Printing Publishing Inc., 1988. at 201–211.

Conundrum (Entrepreneur programme). by Cecil L. Rotenberg. (1988) 4 Immigration Law Reporter (2nd Series) 293–299.

Law or Hair Splitting: Ingenuity At the Visa Office. by Cecil L. Rotenberg. (1988) 4 Immigration Law Reporter (2nd Series) 248–249.

Recent Developments in Immigration Law. by Michelle Falardeau-Ramsay. in Recent Developments in Administrative Law. edited by Neil R. Finkelstein and Brian MacLeod Rogers. Toronto: Carswell, 1987 243–258.

Health & Welfare and the Law: Which is to Follow Which? (1987) 2 Immigration Law Reporter (2nd Series) 31–32.

The Processing of An Independent Application: How Many Angels Can Dance on the Head of a Pin? by Cecil L. Rotenberg. (1987) 2 Immigration Law Reporter (2nd Series) 109–110.

Canada 1978–1987 Le réfugié face à l'État: Évolution ou stagnation? par Daniel Paquin. dans Le droit dans tous ses états. sous la direction de R.D. Bureau et P. Mackay. Montréal: Wilson & Lafleur, 1987. 211–224.

Immigration Irregularities Charged in Ontario. by Michael Crawford. (1986) 13, No. 2 National (Canadian Bar Association) 34.

The Travel Provisions in Basket III of the Helsinki Accord: The Madrid Conference and Beyond. by D. Turack. (1986) 3 Canadian Human Rights Yearbook 25–45.

Moving to Canada: A Checklist for Immigrants. by H.A. Sherman and J.D. Sherman. (1985) 118, No. 1 CA Magazine 60–69.

L'immigration: ententes politiques et droit constitutionnel. par Jacques Brossard et Yves de Montigny. (1985) 19 Revue Juridique Thémis 305–323.

The Road to Hong Kong. by Karen Loder. (1984) 8, No. 5 Canadian Lawyer 27–30.

Les résidents permanents du Canada. par S. Pérusse. (1981) 41 Revue du Barreau 469–482.

Immigration Law: Ten Years of Increasing Pessimism. by G.J. Wydrzynski. in Decade of Adjustment; Legal Perspectives on Contemporary Social Issues. edited by J. Menezes. Toronto: Butterworths, 1980. 123–145.

The Settlement of Immigrants in Greater Vancouver. by Mary Ashworth. (1977) 53 Canadian Welfare 9.

Immigration Parole and the Alien Offender. by Ian Kelly. (1977) 3 Queen's Law Journal 450–495.

Immigration: Four Options for Canada. by Bonnie Campbell. (1975) 75 The Labour Gazette: A National Journal of Labour Affairs Devoted to a Better Work Environment 297.

Immigration: A Look at Present Trends. by George Sanderson. (1975) 75 Labour Gazette: A National Journal of Labour Affairs Devoted to a Better Work Environment 31–39.

Immigration, Extradition and Asylum in Canadian Law and Practice. by L.C. Green. in Canadian Perspectives on International Law and Organization. edited by R. St. J. Macdonald et al. Toronto: University of Toronto, 1974. 244–303.

The Right to Leave and Re-enter Canada. by H. Batshaw. (1973) 21 Chitty's Law Journal 164–166.

Immigration Act Inquiries. by S.I. Schwartz. (1971) Isaac Pitblado Lectures on Continuing Legal Education 99–103.

White Paper on Immigration. by J. Marchard. (1967) 19 External Affairs: Monthly Bulletin of the Department of External Affairs 97.

The Canadian Immigration Service Abroad. (1962) 19 External Affairs: Monthly Bulletin of the Department of External Affairs 269.

Genetic Testing

DNA — The Genetic Birth Certificate. by J. Clay. Canada's Immigration and Citizenship Bulletin. 6:5@1, 1994.

DNA Genetic Fingerprinting. by Gary W. Moore. Canada's Immigration and Citizenship Bulletin. 3:2@2, 1992.

Genetic Proof of Familiar Relationships in Immigration Cases: Summary of IS 126 and IS 453. by Jennifer Clay. (Mar. 1992) 15 Imm. L.R. (2d) 193.

Homosexuals

From Subversion to Liberation: Homosexuals and the Immigration Act, 1952–1977. by Philip Girard. (1987) 2 Canadian Journal of Law & Society 1–27.

Human Rights

The Langner Decision & Children's Rights — The World is Watching. by J.W. Petrykanyn and F. Rosenzweig. Canada's Immigration and Citizenship Bulletin. 7:7@1, October 1995.

Children's Rights and the Immigration Act: The Langner Case. by J.W. Petrykanyn and F. Rosenzweig. Canada's Immigration and Citizenship Bulletin. 7:6@1, August 1995.

Racism and Constitution: The Constitutional Fate of British Columbia Anti-Asian Immigration Legislation, 1884–1909. by Bruce Ryder. (Fall 1991) 29 Osgoode Hall L.J. 619.

Human Rights Tribunal. by Frank N. Marrocco. Canada's Immigration and Citizenship Bulletin. 1:1@4, 1990.

Involuntary Sedation of Deportees. by Joyce Chan. Canada's Immigration and Citizenship Bulletin. 2:5@1, 1990.

The New Detention Provisions of the Immigration Act: Can They Withstand a Charter Challenge? by Paula Hurwitz. (1989), 47 University of Toronto Faculty of Law Review 587.

Immigration Told to Admit Disabled Persons. (1989), 5 Canadian Human Rights Advocate 3, No. 1.

Otherness and the Black Woman. by J. Herbert. (1989), 3 Canadian Journal of Women & the Law 269.

Human Rights: Introduction. in Meech Lake and Canada. ed. by R. Gibbons et al. Edmonton: Academic Printing Publishing Inc., 1988. at 153–157.

Les statuts respectifs de citoyen, résident et étranger, à la lumière des chartes des droits. par Henri Brun et Christian Brunelle. (1988) 29 Cahiers de droit 689–731.

La primauté du droit: la situation des immigrants et des réfugiés en droit canadien au regard des chartes et des textes internationaux. par Christian Brunelle. (1987) 28 Cahiers de droit 585–624.

International Humanitarian Law and Coloured Movements of Peoples Across State Boundaries by Florentino P. Feliciano. in International Law: Critical Choices for Canada 1985–2000. (Kingston, Ont.: Queen's Law Journal, 1986) 526–550.

The Jamaican Women Case and the Canadian Human Rights Act: Is Government Subject to the Principle of Equal Opportunity? by Anne Bayefsky. (1980) 18 University of Western Ontario Law Review 461–492.

Immigration, Natural Justice and the Bill of Rights. by John Hucker. (1975) 13 Osgoode Hall Law Journal 649–692.

Investment

Recovering Moneys Lost in Immigrant Investor Funds, by H.A. Christie. Canada's Immigration and Citizenship Bulletin 11:7@1, October 1999.

Immigrant Investor Program Update, by C.M. Small. Canada's Immigration and Citizenship Bulletin 11:6@3, September 1999.

New Immigrant Investor Program, by G.W. Moore. Canada's Immigration and Citizenship Bulletin 10:9@3 January 1999.

The American Immigrant Investor (EB-5) Visa Option, by C.W. Pley. Canada's Immigration and Citizenship Bulletin 9:10@1, February 1998.

The True Definition of Investor. by Frank N. Marrocco. Canada's Immigration and Citizenship Bulletin. 6:10@2, February 1995.

Investor — A Clarification. by Frank N. Marrocco. Canada's Immigration and Citizenship Bulletin. 6:6@2, 1994.

Investing Outside of Canada. by Ian Davidson. Canada's Immigration and Citizenship Bulletin. 3:9@3, 1992.

Ontario's Guidelines for Immigrant Investor Program. by H.M. Goslett. Canada's Immigration and Citizenship Bulletin. 3:10@1, 1992.

Labour and Employment

The Uneasy Landing of Mary Poppins. by J.W. Petrykanyn. Canada's Immigration and Citizenship Bulletin. 6:4@1, 1994.

Opening and Closing the Nanny Gate. by J.W. Petrykanyn. Canada's Immigration and Citizenship Bulletin. 6:3@1, 1994.

U.S. Labour Market Information — Pilot Project. by L.J. Hulka. Canada's Immigration and Citizenship Bulletin. 6:1@2, 1994.

Japanese Work Permits for Intra-Company Transfers. by Gary W. Moore, G. Psimoulis. Canada's Immigration and Citizenship Bulletin. 5:9@2, 1994.

Live-In Caregiver Program. by H.M. Goslett. Canada's Immigration and Citizenship Bulletin. 4:4@1, 1992

Employment Authorizations for Designated Class Applicants. by Gary W. Moore. Canada's Immigration and Citizenship Bulletin. 3:7@3, 1991.

One Way Over the Border: U.S. Employment Prospects May Lure Canadians. by Thomas Schofield. (Aug. 1991) 8 Bus. & L. 57.

"The Right to Work: Policy Alternatives for Spouses With Pending Permanent Residence Status." by F. Pearl Eliadis. (Jan. 1991) 11 Immigration Law Reporter (2nd Series) 269.

"The Genesis and Persistence of the Commonwealth Caribbean Seasonal Agricultural Workers Program in Canada." by Irving André. (Summer 1990) 28 Osgoode Hall Law Journal 243.

"Immigrant Women: The Construction of a Labour Market Economy." by Roxana Ng. (1990) 4 Canadian Journal of Women & the Law 96.

Conundrum: Immigration Selection: Occupational and Experience Factors. by C.L. Rotenberg. [Includes Text of Operations Memorandum and Commentary]. (Feb. 1989) 6 Immigration Law Reporter (2nd Series) 24–31.

Policy Change: Domestics 'Foreign Domestic Movement' [Extracts from the Canadian Employment and Immigration Commission's Statement]. (1988) 4 Immigration Law Reporter (2nd Series) 117–126.

Occupational Assessment in Immigration Policy. by Cecil L. Rotenberg. (1988) 3 Immigration Law Reporter (2nd Series) 238–240.

Planning and Accountability in Employment and Immigration Canada. by G. Lussier. (1985) 28 Canadian Public Administration 134–142.

Executive Entry Made Easy — Immigration Lawyers Learn How. by Paul Truster. (1985) 5 No. 26 Ontario Lawyers Weekly 11.

Affirmative Action: The Canadian Experience — Canada Employment and Immigration Commission: Planning an Affirmative Action Program. (1983) 43 No. 4 British Columbia Human Rights Commissions Newsletter 4.

Employment Visas and the Canadian Labour Force. by William L. Marr. (1977) 3 Canadian Public Policy 518.

Immigration Policy: A Labour-related Issue. by George Sanderson. (1976) 76 Labour Gazette: A National Journal of Labour Affairs Devoted to A Better Work Environment 138–143.

CLC Brief on Immigration. (1975) 20 Canadian Labour 34.

Immigration and Labour Critic or Catalyst? by Gordon B. Millins. (1975) 1 Canadian Public Policy 311.

Treatment of Immigrants: The Sweatshop Legacy Still With Us in 1974. by George Sanderson. (1974) 74 Labour Gazette: A National Journal of Labour Affairs Devoted to a Better Work Environment 400–417.

Labour, Manpower and Government Reorganization. by G.P.A. McDonald. (1967) 10 Canadian Public Administration 471.

Legislation

Danger to the Public: Bill C-44. by H.J. Chang. Canada's Immigration and Citizenship Bulletin. 8:3@2, May 1996.

A Few Bad Apples. by B.J. Caruso. Canada's Immigration and Citizenship Bulletin. 7:6@3, August 1995.

Proposed Immigration Regulation Changes. by Henry M. Goslett. Canada's Immigration and Citizenship Bulletin. 5:5@1, 1993.

Bill C-86 — What's Not New. by Henry M. Goslett. Canada's Immigration and Citizenship Bulletin. 5:1@3, 1993.

Proposals to Amend the Immigration Act. by Gary W. Moore. Canada's Immigration and Citizenship Bulletin. 4:5@1, 1992.

Bill C-86 — Presentation to the Legislative Committee by the Organization of Professional Immigration Consultants "Alternative Recommendations". by Gary W. Moore. Canada's Immigration and Citizenship Bulletin. 4:6@3, 1992.

Spousal Sponsorships: Changes to Canadian Marriage Legislation. by John W. Petrykanyn. Canada's Immigration and Citizenship Bulletin. 3:8@1, 1991.

Hong Kong: Recent Developments in U.K. Nationality and Immigration Law — Part 1. by Leslie Kemp. Canada's Immigration and Citizenship Bulletin. 2:7@2, 1990.

Update — New Immigration Requirements. by Gary W. Moore. Canada's Immigration and Citizenship Bulletin. 2:7@4, 1990.

Conundrums (Brief of the C.B.A.-B.C. Branch, Respecting S. 83ff of Bill C-55, Proposed Amendments to the Immigration Act, with Comments by C.L. Rotenberg). (1987) 2 Immigration Law Reporter (2nd Series) 27–30.

Novel Features of the Immigration Act, 1976. by W. Black. (1978) 56 Canadian Bar Review 561–578.

The New Immigration Law: A Technical Analysis. by J.H. Grey. (1978) 10 Ottawa Law Review 103–113.

New Immigration Legislation. by R. Gathercole. (1977) 1 Canadian Legal Aid Bulletin 30–33.

Note on the New Immigration Act 1977. by Stephen Marcus. (1977) 3 Queen's Law Journal 496–507.

Chronique législative, Canada: abrogation de l'article 34 du règlement sur l'immigration. Interlex. (1972) 2 Revue internationale de droit comparé général et spécial 14.

Medical

Immigration Medical Assessments for In-Canada Applicants. by H.M. Goslett. Canada's Immigration and Citizenship Bulletin. 7:10@1, February 1996.

Changes in Health Insurance Eligibility for Refugee Claimants. by L.F. Mascarenhas, M.D., C.C.F.P. Canada's Immigration and Citizenship Bulletin. 7:4@4, 1995.

Photo Health Card. by L.F. Mascarenhas, M.D., C.C.F.P. Canada's Immigration and Citizenship Bulletin. 7:2@3, 1995.

Immigration Medical Assessments — The Role of the Designated Medical Practitioner in Canada. by L.F. Mascarenhas, M.D., C.C.F.P. Canada's Immigration and Citizenship Bulletin. 6:9@3, 1995.

Recent Amendments to Immigration Medical Requirements and Procedures. by Gary W. Moore. Canada's Immigration and Citizenship Bulletin. 6:5@3, 1994.

New OHIP Rules for Immigrants and Temporary Residents. by Barbara Jo Caruso. Canada's Immigration and Citizenship Bulletin. 6:3@3, 1994.

Medical Inadmissibility: Danger to the Public and Excessive Demand. by H.M. Goslett. Canada's Immigration and Citizenship Bulletin. 5:7@1, 1993.

Multiculturalism

Tolerance and the Benefits of Increased Immigration Levels. by John W. Petrykanyn. Canada's Immigration and Citizenship Bulletin. 3:7@1, 1991.

Policy

The Landing of Persons in Canada under Removal Orders. by John W. Petrykanyn. Canada's Immigration and Employment Bulletin. 7:3@2, May 1995.

Discriminatory Dependency Guidelines. by P. Ahlfeld. Canada's Immigration and Citizenship Bulletin. 6:5@2, 1994.

Five-year Plan Immigration Levels 1991–1995. by Gary W. Moore. Canada's Immigration and Citizenship Bulletin. 2:9@1, 1991.

"Discretion, Policy and Section 19(1)(a) of the Immigration Act." by P. Harris Auerbach. (Fall 1990) 6 Journal of Law & Social Policy 133.

Policy Amendment: Current Chapter 11 of the 1.S. Manual Deleted and Re-engrossed Under I.E. 2 — re: Returning Residents. by Cecil L. Rotenberg. (1988) 4 Immigration Law Reporter (2nd Series) 200–206.

The Development of Immigration Law and Policy: The Hong Kong Experience. by Albert H.Y. Chen. (1987/88) 33 McGill Law Journal 631–675.

Policy: Ochnio Principle Clarified in Ontario. by D. Conn. (1987) 1 Immigration Law Reporter (2nd Series) 263–264.

Policy: The Minister's Response to the Bar re ss-83ff Proposed Bill C-55: Argumentum ad Hominem? by Cecil L. Rotenberg. (1987) 2 Immigration Law Reporter (2nd Series) 111–117.

La politique canadienne d'immigration. par F. Crépeau. (1987) 54 Assurances 595–598.

East Indians and Canada's New Immigration Policy. by John Wood. (1978) 4 Canadian Public Policy 547–567.

"Import" of Foreign Policy to Immigration Equation. by C. Passaris. (1976) 6 International Perspectives: A Journal of Opinion on World Affairs 23–28.

Canada's Immigration Policy: Some Comments. by Peter Gunther. (1975) 1 Canadian Public Policy 580.

Immigration and Population: The Canadian Approach. by Freda Hawkins. (1975) 1 Canadian Public Policy 285.

Democratic Concerns and the Control of Immigration. by Warren E. Kalbach. (1975) 1 Canadian Public Policy 302.

Canadian Immigration Policy Since 1962. by William L. Marr. Canadian Public Policy 196.

Immigration Adoption: A Critical Review of 'Three Years in Canada'. by Anthony H. Richmond. (1975) 1 Canadian Public Policy 317.

In Search of a Rational Immigration Policy. by Spencer Star. (1975) 1 Canadian Public Policy 328.

Practice and Procedure

Practice Note, by F.N. Marrocco. Canada's Immigration and Citizenship Bulletin 11:7@2, October 1999.

New Selection Criteria: The View from the Tower. by H.M. Goslett. Canada's Immigration and Citizenship Bulletin. 7:9@1, January 1996.

The New Era in Immigration Selection. by Henry M. Goslett. Canada's Immigration and Citizenship Bulletin. 7:4@1, June 1995.

Temporary Entry Under GATS. by Gary W. Moore. Canada's Immigration and Citizenship Bulletin. 7:3@1, May 1995.

Right of Landing Fee. by Barbara Jo Caruso. Canada's Immigration and Citizenship Bulletin. 7:2@4, 1995.

Deferred Removal Orders Class Program. by John W. Petrykanyn. Canada's Immigration and Employment Bulletin. 6:10@3, February 1995.

Changes to Immigration Processing Fees. by B.J. Caruso. Canada's Immigration and Citizenship Bulletin. 6:4@2, 1994.

Temporary Entry of Minor Children: Custody Application Procedure. by B.J. Caruso. Canada's Immigration and Citizenship Bulletin. 6:2@2, 1994.

Of Counsel and Adjournments. by Frank N. Marrocco. Canada's Immigration and Citizenship Bulletin. 5:8@4, 1993.

The True Intention of the Rule Against "Duel Intent". by B.J. Caruso. Canada's Immigration and Citizenship Bulletin. 5:6@2, 1993.

Proposed Immigration Regulation Changes. by H.M. Goslett. Canada's Immigration and Citizenship Bulletin. 5:5@1, 1993.

The Point System. by J.W. Petrykanyn. Canada's Immigration and Citizenship Bulletin. 5:5@2, 1993.

Changes to Immigration Processing Fees. by Henry M. Goslett. Canada's Immigration and Citizenship Bulletin. 4:8@3, 1992.

Returning Resident Permits No Longer to be Available. by Frank N. Marrocco. Canada's Immigration and Citizenship Bulletin. 4:5@4, 1992.

Unsuccessful Backlog Claimants: Failure to Depart Canada. by John W. Petrykanyn. Canada's Immigration and Citizenship Bulletin. 4:4@4, 1992.

Common Courtesy, Common Sense. Immigration Application. by Frank N. Marrocco. Canada's Immigration and Citizenship Bulletin. 4:2@1, 1992.

Priority Processing of Immigrant Visas. by Paul Billings. Canada's Immigration and Citizenship Bulletin. 4:2@2, 1992.

Access to Immigration Hearings. by Debra M. McAllister. (Nov. 1991) 1 N.J.C.L. 242.

Retiree Program Revoked. by H.M. Goslett. Canada's Immigration and Citizenship Bulletin. 3:5@3, 1991.

Changes to Immigration Fees Regulations. by Henry M. Goslett. Canada's Immigration and Citizenship Bulletin. 3:3@2, 1991.

Federal Court Practices and the Immigration Act (Part 1 of 4). by Frank N. Marrocco and Joyce Chan. Canada's Immigration and Citizenship Bulletin. 2:10@1, 1991.

Federal Court Practices and the Immigration Act (Part 2 of 4). by Frank N. Marrocco and Joyce Chan. Canada's Immigration and Citizenship Bulletin. 3:1@3, 1991.

Federal Court Practices and the Immigration Act (Part 3 of 4). by Frank N. Marrocco and Joyce Chan. Canada's Immigration and Citizenship Bulletin. 3:2@2, 1991.

Federal Court Practices and the Immigration Act (Part 4 of 4). by Frank N. Marrocco and Joyce Chan. Canada's Immigration and Citizenship Bulletin. 3:3@4, 1991.

Representations to Canada Immigration. by Martin Levine. Canada's Immigration and Citizenship Bulletin. 3:1@1, 1991.

"'Credit basis' in the Federal Court of Appeal." by Graham Steele. (Jan. 1991) 11 Immigration Law Reporter (2nd Series) 276.

Equality Rights in the Federal Independent Immigrant Selection Criteria. by Walter Chi Yah Tom. (1990) 31 Les Caliers de Droit 477.

"Practice and Procedure Before the Convention Refugee Determination Division (of the Immigration and Refugee Board) (October 1989)." by R. Holloway. (June 1990) 3 Canadian Journal of Administrative Law & Practice 341.

The Power of Adjudicators: Masters in Their Own House. by Janet Brooks and Timothy Morin. Canada's Immigration and Citizenship Bulletin. 1:6@3, 1990.

Immigration Practice — Ethical Considerations. by Frank N. Marrocco. Canada's Immigration and Citizenship Bulletin. 1:7@4, 1990.

Practising Law in a Foreign Jurisdiction. by Frank N. Marrocco. Canada's Immigration and Citizenship Bulletin. 2:1@4, 1990.

Immigration Reorganization — Ontario Region. by Gary W. Moore. Canada's Immigration and Citizenship Bulletin. 2:1@2, 1990.

Security Certificates. by Frank N. Marrocco. Canada's Immigration and Citizenship Bulletin. 2:4@3, 1990.

Advocacy in Immigration Law. by Mendel Green and Marshall Drukarsh. in Administrative Tribunals: A Practice Handbook for Legal Counsel. ed. by F.R. Moskoff. (Aurora, Ont.: Canada Law Book, 1989) at 29–43.

Out of Sight, Out of Mind: Lawyers and Immigration. (Unethical Practices of Canadian Immigration Lawyers in Foreign Lands). by Sue S. Hanna (1989) 12 No. 9 Canadian Lawyer 22–24.

De l'appel et de l'évocation. par M.A. Parent. (1973) 19 McGill Law Journal 367–384.

Affaires d'immigration en appel. par M.A. Parent. (1972) 32 Revue du Barreau 194–228.

Un tribunal de l'immigration. par Raoul-P. Barbe. (1968) 1 Canadian Legal Studies 311.

Provinces

Canada - British Columbia Business Immigration Pilot Project, by G.W. Moore. Canada's Immigration and Citizenship Bulletin 11:4@3, July 1999.

Manitoba Provincial Nominee Program, by B.A. Kranc. Canada's Immigration and Citizenship Bulletin, 10:9@1, January 1999.

Agreement for Canada-British Columbia Co-Operation on Immigration, by S. Parmar. Canada's Immigration and Citizenship Bulletin 10:7@3, October 1998.

Federal-provincial Relations in Canadian Immigration. by R.A. Vineberg. (1987) 30 Canadian Public Administration 299–317.

L'expérience québécoise (La liberté de circulation internationale). par Louise Robic, (1987) 28 Cahiers de droit 575–624.

Immigration: A Provincial Concern. by Valerie Matthews Lemieux. (1983) 13 Manitoba Law Journal 111.

L'immigration étrangère au Québec. par Bernard Bonin. (1975) 1 Canadian Public Policy 296.

Immigration et droits des provinces. par Jean Mercier. (1944) 4 Revue du Barreau 149.

Refugees

No Refugee Identity Documents are Completely Unacceptable, by H.M. Goslett. Canada's Immigration and Citizenship Bulletin 10:1@1, March 1998.

Changes to Canada's Refugee Status Determination Process. by John W. Petrykanyn. Canada's Immigration and Employment Bulletin. 7:3@3, May 1995.

Ceased to Exist: The Real Test for a Refugee. by John E. Callaghan. Canada's Immigration and Citizenship Bulletin. 4:1@4, 1992.

Refugee Backlog Clearance and the Vaca Decision. by Gary W. Moore. Canada's Immigration and Citizenship Bulletin. 3:9@2, 1992.

The Exception a Refugee's Final Refugee. by John E. Callaghan. Canada's Immigration and Citizenship Bulletin. 4:3@1, 1992.

The Role of the Lawyer in the Refugee Determination Process. by David Matas. (Jan. 1992) 14 Imm. L.R. (2d) 257.

Refugees and the State in Africa: An Examination of the Refugee Impact in the Host Country. by Kevin Dunn. (Fall 1991) 7 Inter. Insights 69.

"Media Access to Refugee Proceedings in Canada." by Marlys Edwardh and Daniel Brodsky. (1991) 29 Alberta Law Review 701.

"No Place Like Home: Assaulted Migrant Women's Claims to Refugee Status and Landings on Humanitarian and Compassionate Grounds." by Felecite Stairs and Lori Pope. (Fall 1990) 6 Journal of Law & Social Policy 148.

"Canada's New Refugee Determination System." by Edward McWhinney. (1989) 27 Canadian Year Book of International Law 295.

A Well-Founded Fear of Persecution: Probability or Possibility Test. by Joyce Chan and Timothy Morin. Canada's Immigration and Citizenship Bulletin. 1:4@4, 1990.

The Credible Basis Test. by Joyce Chan and Timothy Morin. Canada's Immigration and Citizenship Bulletin. 1:3@3, 1990.

The New Refugee Determination Process: Port of Entry Claimants. by Joyce Chan and Timothy Morin. Canada's Immigration and Citizenship Bulletin. 1:2@3, 1990.

The Refugee Backlog: Getting Out. by Frank N. Marrocco. Canada's Immigration and Citizenship Bulletin. 1:5@4, 1990.

The Refugee Division and the Charter. by Timothy Morin. Canada's Immigration and Citizenship Bulletin. 1:7@1, 1990.

Death of the Refugee Backlog Clearance Process. by Gary W. Moore. Canada's Immigration and Citizenship Bulletin. 2:2@1, 1990.

Refugee Backlog Clearance — the Minister's Response to the Yhap Decision. by Gary W. Moore. Canada's Immigration and Citizenship Bulletin. 2:3@1, 1990.

Refugee Backlog Construction Workers: Voluntary Withdrawal. by John Petrykanyn. Canada's Immigration and Citizenship Bulletin. 1:9@3, 1990.

The Refugee Backlog Clearance Proccess. by Frank N. Marrocco. Canada's Immigration and Citizenship Bulletin. 1:3@4, 1990.

Convention Refugees and the Role of the State. by Timothy Morin. Canada's Immigration and Citizenship Bulletin. 2:5@2, 1990.

Postscript: Selective Concern: An Overview of Refugee Law in Canada. by James C. Hathoway. (1989), 34 McGill Law Journal 354.

Fairness in Refugee Determination. by D. Matas. (1989), 18 Manitoba Law Journal 71.

It's Easy to Stop Phony Refugees. by P. Worthington. (1989), 13 Can. Lawyer 44, No. 2.

Postscript: Selective Concern: An Overview of Refugee Law. by James C. Hathaway. (Mar. 1989) 34 McGill Law Journal 354–357.

Restructuring Canadian Refugee Determination Process: A Look at Bills C-55 and C-84. by Brahm Segal. (1988) 29 Cahiers des droit 733–759.

Selective Concern: An Overview of Refugee Law in Canada. by James C. Hathaway. (1987/88) 33 McGill Law Journal 676–715.

Just What is the Procedure for New Refugee Claim. by Mendel M. Green. (1986) 6 No. 4 Lawyers Weekly 4.

Redetermination of a Claim to be a Convention Refugee: A Review of the Jurisprudence. by Roger Cantin. (1984) 15 Revue générale de droit 609–643.

A Policy Within a Policy: The Identification and Admission of Refugees to Canada. by G.E. Dirks. (1984) 17 Canadian Journal of Political Science 279–307.

Resettlement of Minor Refugees: Some Interdisciplinary Issues. by E.D. Pask and A. Jayne. (1984) 4 Canadian Journal of Family Law 275–292.

The Refugee Process In Canada. by James R. Aldridge. in International Law and the Practice of Law in Canada. Canadian Council on International Law, 10th Annual Conference Proceedings. Ottawa: 1981. 117–135.

Certain Aspects of Determining Refugee Status in Present Canadian Immigration Appeal Board Practice. by G.H. Alexandrowicz. in International Law and the Practice of Law in Canada. Canadian Council on International Law 10th Annual Conference Proceedings. Ottawa: 1981. 136–156.

Refugees and the Immigration Act. by Christopher J. Wydrzynski. (1979) 25 McGill Law Journal 154–192.

Sponsorship

Sponsorship of Parents — New Rules. by Gary W. Moore. Canada's Immigration and Citizenship Bulletin. 1:4@2, 1990.

Immigrants on Welfare: The Sponsorship Undertaking. by C.C. Hoppe. (1976) 4, No. 1 Bulletin of Canadian Welfare Law 29, 42–43.

Students

The Student Dilemma. by Henry M. Goslett. Canada's Immigration and Citizenship Bulletin. 6:7@1, October 1994.

Employment Validation Exemption for Foreign Students. by Gary W. Moore. Canada's Immigration and Citizenship Bulletin. 1:3@2, 1990.

The Status of Foreign Students Under the Immigration Act, 1976. by Julius H. Grey. (1982) 27 McGill Law Journal 556–562.

Tax

Canadian Taxation of Foreign Sourced Income: The Foreign Tax Credit. by Tim S. Wach and Barry D. Horne. Canada's Immigration and Citizenship Bulletin. 3:6@4, 1991.

Planning for the Capital Gains Exemption. by Barry D. Horne and Tim S. Wach. Canada's Immigration and Citizenship Bulletin. 3:2@4, 1991.

Planning for the Departure Tax. by B.D. Horne. Canada's Immigration and Citizenship Bulletin. 3:3@3, 1991.

Tax Planning for Immigrants: Capital Assets. by T.S. Wach. Canada's Immigration and Citizenship Bulletin. 2:10@4, 1991.

"Tax Planning for Departure from Canada." by Steve Suarez. (1991) 39 Canadian Tax Journal 1.

Pre-immigration Tax Planning. by Frank L. Chopin. in Canada/United States Taxation. edited by André Laveau. Éditions Y. Blais, 1987. 1–41.

Tax Implications of Moving From United Kingdom to Canada. by R.J. Horner. (1985) 33 Canadian Tax Journal 36–67.

The U.S. Overhauls Its Immigration Law. by Robert F. Leibenluft. (1987) 2, No. 3 Trade Law Topics 32–33.

U.S. Immigration Service Publishes New Regulations for L-1 Status (for Intra-Company Transferees) (1986/87) 2 Trade Law Topics 64–66.

U.S. Immigration

The American Immigrant Investor (EB-5) Visa Option, by C.W. Pley. Canada's Immigration and Citizenship Bulletin 9:10@1, February 1998.

Marketing Your Law Practice on the World Wide Web. by H.J. Chang. Canada's Immigration and Citizenship Bulletin. 8:4@2, June 1996.

Update on U.S. Immigration Reform. by H.J. Chang. Canada's Immigration and Citizenship Bulletin. 7:10@3, February 1996.

The "B-1" Visitor Visa for Business. by H.J. Chang. Canada's Immigration and Citizenship Bulletin. 7:8@2, November 1995.

U.S. Considers Immigration Reforms. by H.J. Chang. Canada's Immigration and Citizenship Bulletin. 7:7@2, October 1995.

Aliens of Extraordinary Ability: O-1 Visas for Artists and Entertainers. by H.J. Chang. Canada's Immigration and Citizenship Bulletin. 7:6@2, September 1995.

Transmission of U.S. Citizenship to Children Born Abroad. by H.J. Chang. Canada's Immigration and Citizenship Bulletin. 7:4@2, 1995.

H-1 Visas for Canadians. by H.J. Chang. Canada's Immigration and Citizenship Bulletin. 7:2@2, 1995.

Family Based U.S. Immigration. by H.J. Chang. Canada's Immigration and Citizenship Bulletin. 7:2@1, 1995.

U.S. Labour Market Information — Pilot Project. by L.J. Hulka. Canada's Immigration and Citizenship Bulletin. 6:10@2, 1995.

"E" Visas for Treaty Nationals. by H.J. Chang. Canada's Immigration and Citizenship Bulletin. 6:10@1, 1995.

Intra-Company Transfers for Small Companies. by H.J. Chang. Canada's Immigration and Citizenship Bulletin. 6:9@1, 1995

U.S. Permanent Residence for Multi-National Executives and Managers. by H.J. Chang. Canada's Immigration and Citizenship Bulletin. 6:8@1, 1994.

The U.S. "Visa Lottery". by Gary W. Moore. Canada's Immigration and Citizenship Bulletin. 4:5@3, 1992.

U.S. Immigration and Nationality Law: The Immigration Act of 1990 — An Analysis of Significant Issues (Part I of IV). by Lynda S. Zengerle, Eleanor Pelta and Laura Foote Reiff. Canada's Immigration and Citizenship Bulletin. 3:3@1, 1991.

U.S. Immigration and Nationality Law: The Immigration Act of 1990 — An Analysis of Significant Issues (Part II of IV). by Lynda S. Zengerle, Eleanor Pelta and Laura Foote Reiff. Canada's Immigration and Citizenship Bulletin. 3:4@1, 1991.

U.S. Immigration and Nationality Law: The Immigration Act of 1990 — An Analysis of Significant Issues (Part III of IV). by Lynda S. Zengerle, Eleanor Pelta and Laura Foote Reiff. Canada's Immigration and Citizenship Bulletin. 3:5@1, 1991.

U.S. Immigration and Nationality Law: The Immigration Act of 1990 — An Analysis of Significant Issues (Part IV of IV). by Lynda S. Zengerle, Eleanor Pelta and Laura Foote Reiff. Canada's Immigration and Citizenship Bulletin. 3:6@1, 1991.

INDEX

References in this index are to sections of the Immigration Act and the Immigration Regulations. Note that the word "Reg." precedes the section references to the Immigration Regulations. Entries without the "Reg." designation refer to sections of the Immigration Act, unless preceded by a "p." designation, which refers to a specific page of the text.

The Immigration Act Fees Regulations, the Immigration Appeal Division Rules, the Convention Refugee Determination Division Rules and the Adjudication Division Rules are indexed separately directly following this index.

D

F

G

Immigration Act Fees Regulations

Immigration Appeal Division Rules

Convention Refugee Determination Division Rules

Adjudication Division Rules

Federal Court Immigration Rules